Julie A. Jacko (Ed.)

Human-Computer Interaction

HCI Intelligent Multimodal Interaction Environments

12th International Conference, HCI International 2007
Beijing, China, July 22-27, 2007
Proceedings, Part III

Springer

Volume Editor

Julie A. Jacko
Georgia Institute of Technology
and Emory University School of Medicine
901 Atlantic Drive, Suite 4100, Atlanta, GA 30332-0477, USA
E-mail: jacko@hsi.gatech.edu

Library of Congress Control Number: 2007930203

CR Subject Classification (1998): H.5.2, H.5.3, H.3-5, C.2, I.3, D.2, F.3, K.4.2

LNCS Sublibrary: SL 2 – Programming and Software Engineering

ISSN 0302-9743
ISBN-10 3-540-73108-3 Springer Berlin Heidelberg New York
ISBN-13 978-3-540-73108-5 Springer Berlin Heidelberg New York

Springer is a part of Springer Science+Business Media

springer.com

Printed in Germany

Typesetting: Camera-ready by author, data conversion by Scientific Publishing Services, Chennai, India
Printed on acid-free paper SPIN: 12078011 06/3180 5 4 3 2 1 0

Foreword

The 12th International Conference on Human-Computer Interaction, HCI International 2007, was held in Beijing, P.R. China, 22-27 July 2007, jointly with the Symposium on Human Interface (Japan) 2007, the 7th International Conference on Engineering Psychology and Cognitive Ergonomics, the 4th International Conference on Universal Access in Human-Computer Interaction, the 2nd International Conference on Virtual Reality, the 2nd International Conference on Usability and Internationalization, the 2nd International Conference on Online Communities and Social Computing, the 3rd International Conference on Augmented Cognition, and the 1st International Conference on Digital Human Modeling.

A total of 3403 individuals from academia, research institutes, industry and governmental agencies from 76 countries submitted contributions, and 1681 papers, judged to be of high scientific quality, were included in the program. These papers address the latest research and development efforts and highlight the human aspects of design and use of computing systems. The papers accepted for presentation thoroughly cover the entire field of Human-Computer Interaction, addressing major advances in knowledge and effective use of computers in a variety of application areas.

This volume, edited by Julie A. Jacko, contains papers in the thematic area of Human-Computer Interaction, addressing the following major topics:

- Multimodality and Conversational Dialogue
- Adaptive, Intelligent and Emotional User Interfaces
- Gesture and Eye Gaze Recognition
- Interactive TV and Media

The remaining volumes of the HCI International 2007 proceedings are:

- Volume 1, LNCS 4550, Interaction Design and Usability, edited by Julie A. Jacko
- Volume 2, LNCS 4551, Interaction Platforms and Techniques, edited by Julie A. Jacko
- Volume 4, LNCS 4553, HCI Applications and Services, edited by Julie A. Jacko
- Volume 5, LNCS 4554, Coping with Diversity in Universal Access, edited by Constantine Stephanidis
- Volume 6, LNCS 4555, Universal Access to Ambient Interaction, edited by Constantine Stephanidis
- Volume 7, LNCS 4556, Universal Access to Applications and Services, edited by Constantine Stephanidis
- Volume 8, LNCS 4557, Methods, Techniques and Tools in Information Design, edited by Michael J. Smith and Gavriel Salvendy
- Volume 9, LNCS 4558, Interacting in Information Environments, edited by Michael J. Smith and Gavriel Salvendy
- Volume 10, LNCS 4559, HCI and Culture, edited by Nuray Aykin
- Volume 11, LNCS 4560, Global and Local User Interfaces, edited by Nuray Aykin

- Volume 12, LNCS 4561, Digital Human Modeling, edited by Vincent G. Duffy
- Volume 13, LNAI 4562, Engineering Psychology and Cognitive Ergonomics, edited by Don Harris
- Volume 14, LNCS 4563, Virtual Reality, edited by Randall Shumaker
- Volume 15, LNCS 4564, Online Communities and Social Computing, edited by Douglas Schuler
- Volume 16, LNAI 4565, Foundations of Augmented Cognition 3rd Edition, edited by Dylan D. Schmorrow and Leah M. Reeves
- Volume 17, LNCS 4566, Ergonomics and Health Aspects of Work with Computers, edited by Marvin J. Dainoff

I would like to thank the Program Chairs and the members of the Program Boards of all Thematic Areas, listed below, for their contribution to the highest scientific quality and the overall success of the HCI International 2007 Conference.

Ergonomics and Health Aspects of Work with Computers

Program Chair: Marvin J. Dainoff

Arne Aaras, Norway
Pascale Carayon, USA
Barbara G.F. Cohen, USA
Wolfgang Friesdorf, Germany
Martin Helander, Singapore
Ben-Tzion Karsh, USA
Waldemar Karwowski, USA
Peter Kern, Germany
Danuta Koradecka, Poland
Kari Lindstrom, Finland
Holger Luczak, Germany
Aura C. Matias, Philippines
Kyung (Ken) Park, Korea
Michelle Robertson, USA
Steven L. Sauter, USA
Dominique L. Scapin, France
Michael J. Smith, USA
Naomi Swanson, USA
Peter Vink, The Netherlands
John Wilson, UK

Human Interface and the Management of Information

Program Chair: Michael J. Smith

Lajos Balint, Hungary
Gunilla Bradley, Sweden
Hans-Jörg Bullinger, Germany
Alan H.S. Chan, Hong Kong
Klaus-Peter Fähnrich, Germany
Michitaka Hirose, Japan
Yoshinori Horie, Japan
Richard Koubek, USA
Yasufumi Kume, Japan
Mark Lehto, USA
Jiye Mao, P.R. China
Robert Proctor, USA
Youngho Rhee, Korea
Anxo Cereijo Roibás, UK
Francois Sainfort, USA
Katsunori Shimohara, Japan
Tsutomu Tabe, Japan
Alvaro Taveira, USA
Kim-Phuong L. Vu, USA
Tomio Watanabe, Japan
Sakae Yamamoto, Japan
Hidekazu Yoshikawa, Japan

Fiona Nah, USA
Shogo Nishida, Japan
Leszek Pacholski, Poland
Li Zheng, P.R. China
Bernhard Zimolong, Germany

Human-Computer Interaction

Program Chair: Julie A. Jacko

Sebastiano Bagnara, Italy
Jianming Dong, USA
John Eklund, Australia
Xiaowen Fang, USA
Sheue-Ling Hwang, Taiwan
Yong Gu Ji, Korea
Steven J. Landry, USA
Jonathan Lazar, USA
V. Kathlene Leonard, USA
Chang S. Nam, USA
Anthony F. Norcio, USA
Celestine A. Ntuen, USA
P.L. Patrick Rau, P.R. China
Andrew Sears, USA
Holly Vitense, USA
Wenli Zhu, P.R. China

Engineering Psychology and Cognitive Ergonomics

Program Chair: Don Harris

Kenneth R. Boff, USA
Guy Boy, France
Pietro Carlo Cacciabue, Italy
Judy Edworthy, UK
Erik Hollnagel, Sweden
Kenji Itoh, Japan
Peter G.A.M. Jorna, The Netherlands
Kenneth R. Laughery, USA
Nicolas Marmaras, Greece
David Morrison, Australia
Sundaram Narayanan, USA
Eduardo Salas, USA
Dirk Schaefer, France
Axel Schulte, Germany
Neville A. Stanton, UK
Andrew Thatcher, South Africa

Universal Access in Human-Computer Interaction

Program Chair: Constantine Stephanidis

Julio Abascal, Spain
Ray Adams, UK
Elizabeth Andre, Germany
Margherita Antona, Greece
Chieko Asakawa, Japan
Christian Bühler, Germany
Noelle Carbonell, France
Jerzy Charytonowicz, Poland
Pier Luigi Emiliani, Italy
Michael Fairhurst, UK
Gerhard Fischer, USA
Zhengjie Liu, P.R. China
Klaus Miesenberger, Austria
John Mylopoulos, Canada
Michael Pieper, Germany
Angel Puerta, USA
Anthony Savidis, Greece
Andrew Sears, USA
Ben Shneiderman, USA
Christian Stary, Austria
Hirotada Ueda, Japan
Jean Vanderdonckt, Belgium

Jon Gunderson, USA
Andreas Holzinger, Austria
Arthur Karshmer, USA
Simeon Keates, USA
George Kouroupetroglou, Greece
Jonathan Lazar, USA
Seongil Lee, Korea
Gregg Vanderheiden, USA
Gerhard Weber, Germany
Harald Weber, Germany
Toshiki Yamaoka, Japan
Mary Zajicek, UK
Panayiotis Zaphiris, UK

Virtual Reality

Program Chair: Randall Shumaker

Terry Allard, USA
Pat Banerjee, USA
Robert S. Kennedy, USA
Heidi Kroemker, Germany
Ben Lawson, USA
Ming Lin, USA
Bowen Loftin, USA
Holger Luczak, Germany
Annie Luciani, France
Gordon Mair, UK
Ulrich Neumann, USA
Albert "Skip" Rizzo, USA
Lawrence Rosenblum, USA
Dylan Schmorrow, USA
Kay Stanney, USA
Susumu Tachi, Japan
John Wilson, UK
Wei Zhang, P.R. China
Michael Zyda, USA

Usability and Internationalization

Program Chair: Nuray Aykin

Genevieve Bell, USA
Alan Chan, Hong Kong
Apala Lahiri Chavan, India
Jori Clarke, USA
Pierre-Henri Dejean, France
Susan Dray, USA
Paul Fu, USA
Emilie Gould, Canada
Sung H. Han, South Korea
Veikko Ikonen, Finland
Richard Ishida, UK
Esin Kiris, USA
Tobias Komischke, Germany
Masaaki Kurosu, Japan
James R. Lewis, USA
Rungtai Lin, Taiwan
Aaron Marcus, USA
Allen E. Milewski, USA
Patrick O'Sullivan, Ireland
Girish V. Prabhu, India
Kerstin Röse, Germany
Eunice Ratna Sari, Indonesia
Supriya Singh, Australia
Serengul Smith, UK
Denise Spacinsky, USA
Christian Sturm, Mexico
Adi B. Tedjasaputra, Singapore
Myung Hwan Yun, South Korea
Chen Zhao, P.R. China

Online Communities and Social Computing

Program Chair: Douglas Schuler

Chadia Abras, USA
Lecia Barker, USA
Amy Bruckman, USA
Peter van den Besselaar, The Netherlands
Peter Day, UK
Fiorella De Cindio, Italy
John Fung, P.R. China
Michael Gurstein, USA
Tom Horan, USA
Piet Kommers, The Netherlands
Jonathan Lazar, USA
Stefanie Lindstaedt, Austria
Diane Maloney-Krichmar, USA
Isaac Mao, P.R. China
Hideyuki Nakanishi, Japan
A. Ant Ozok, USA
Jennifer Preece, USA
Partha Pratim Sarker, Bangladesh
Gilson Schwartz, Brazil
Sergei Stafeev, Russia
F.F. Tusubira, Uganda
Cheng-Yen Wang, Taiwan

Augmented Cognition

Program Chair: Dylan D. Schmorrow

Kenneth Boff, USA
Joseph Cohn, USA
Blair Dickson, UK
Henry Girolamo, USA
Gerald Edelman, USA
Eric Horvitz, USA
Wilhelm Kincses, Germany
Amy Kruse, USA
Lee Kollmorgen, USA
Dennis McBride, USA
Jeffrey Morrison, USA
Denise Nicholson, USA
Dennis Proffitt, USA
Harry Shum, P.R. China
Kay Stanney, USA
Roy Stripling, USA
Michael Swetnam, USA
Robert Taylor, UK
John Wagner, USA

Digital Human Modeling

Program Chair: Vincent G. Duffy

Norm Badler, USA
Heiner Bubb, Germany
Don Chaffin, USA
Kathryn Cormican, Ireland
Andris Freivalds, USA
Ravindra Goonetilleke, Hong Kong
Anand Gramopadhye, USA
Sung H. Han, South Korea
Pheng Ann Heng, Hong Kong
Dewen Jin, P.R. China
Kang Li, USA
Zhizhong Li, P.R. China
Lizhuang Ma, P.R. China
Timo Maatta, Finland
J. Mark Porter, UK
Jim Potvin, Canada
Jean-Pierre Verriest, France
Zhaoqi Wang, P.R. China
Xiugan Yuan, P.R. China
Shao-Xiang Zhang, P.R. China
Xudong Zhang, USA

In addition to the members of the Program Boards above, I also wish to thank the following volunteer external reviewers: Kelly Hale, David Kobus, Amy Kruse, Cali Fidopiastis and Karl Van Orden from the USA, Mark Neerincx and Marc Grootjen from the Netherlands, Wilhelm Kincses from Germany, Ganesh Bhutkar and Mathura Prasad from India, Frederick Li from the UK, and Dimitris Grammenos, Angeliki Kastrinaki, Iosif Klironomos, Alexandros Mourouzis, and Stavroula Ntoa from Greece.

This conference could not have been possible without the continuous support and advise of the Conference Scientific Advisor, Prof. Gavriel Salvendy, as well as the dedicated work and outstanding efforts of the Communications Chair and Editor of HCI International News, Abbas Moallem, and of the members of the Organizational Board from P.R. China, Patrick Rau (Chair), Bo Chen, Xiaolan Fu, Zhibin Jiang, Congdong Li, Zhenjie Liu, Mowei Shen, Yuanchun Shi, Hui Su, Linyang Sun, Ming Po Tham, Ben Tsiang, Jian Wang, Guangyou Xu, Winnie Wanli Yang, Shuping Yi, Kan Zhang, and Wei Zho.

I would also like to thank for their contribution towards the organization of the HCI International 2007 Conference the members of the Human Computer Interaction Laboratory of ICS-FORTH, and in particular Margherita Antona, Maria Pitsoulaki, George Paparoulis, Maria Bouhli, Stavroula Ntoa and George Margetis.

Constantine Stephanidis
General Chair, HCI International 2007

HCI International 2009

The 13th International Conference on Human-Computer Interaction, HCI International 2009, will be held jointly with the affiliated Conferences in San Diego, California, USA, in the Town and Country Resort & Convention Center, 19-24 July 2009. It will cover a broad spectrum of themes related to Human Computer Interaction, including theoretical issues, methods, tools, processes and case studies in HCI design, as well as novel interaction techniques, interfaces and applications. The proceedings will be published by Springer. For more information, please visit the Conference website: http://www.hcii2009.org/

General Chair
Professor Constantine Stephanidis
ICS-FORTH and University of Crete
Heraklion, Crete, Greece
Email: program@hcii2009.org

Table of Contents

Part I: Multimodality and Conversational Dialogue

Preferences and Patterns of Paralinguistic Voice Input to Interactive Media 3
Sama'a Al Hashimi

"Show and Tell": Using Semantically Processable Prosodic Markers for Spatial Expressions in an HCI System for Consumer Complaints 13
Christina Alexandris

Exploiting Speech-Gesture Correlation in Multimodal Interaction 23
Fang Chen, Eric H.C. Choi, and Ning Wang

Pictogram Retrieval Based on Collective Semantics 31
Heeryon Cho, Toru Ishida, Rieko Inaba, Toshiyuki Takasaki, and Yumiko Mori

Enrich Web Applications with Voice Internet Persona Text-to-Speech for Anyone, Anywhere 40
Min Chu, Yusheng Li, Xin Zou, and Frank Soong

Using Recurrent Fuzzy Neural Networks for Predicting Word Boundaries in a Phoneme Sequence in Persian Language 50
Mohammad Reza Feizi Derakhshi and Mohammad Reza Kangavari

Subjective Measurement of Workload Related to a Multimodal Interaction Task: NASA-TLX *vs.* Workload Profile 60
Dominique Fréard, Eric Jamet, Olivier Le Bohec, Gérard Poulain, and Valérie Botherel

Menu Selection Using Auditory Interface 70
Koichi Hirota, Yosuke Watanabe, and Yasushi Ikei

Analysis of User Interaction with Service Oriented Chatbot Systems 76
Marie-Claire Jenkins, Richard Churchill, Stephen Cox, and Dan Smith

Performance Analysis of Perceptual Speech Quality and Modules Design for Management over IP Network 84
Jinsul Kim, Hyun-Woo Lee, Won Ryu, Seung Ho Han, and Minsoo Hahn

A Tangible User Interface with Multimodal Feedback 94
Laehyun Kim, Hyunchul Cho, Sehyung Park, and Manchul Han

Minimal Parsing Key Concept Based Question Answering System 104
Sunil Kopparapu, Akhlesh Srivastava, and P.V.S. Rao

Customized Message Generation and Speech Synthesis in Response to Characteristic Behavioral Patterns of Children 114
Ho-Joon Lee and Jong C. Park

Multi-word Expression Recognition Integrated with Two-Level Finite State Transducer 124
Keunyong Lee, Ki-Soen Park, and Yong-Seok Lee

Towards Multimodal User Interfaces Composition Based on UsiXML and MBD Principles 134
Sophie Lepreux, Anas Hariri, José Rouillard, Dimitri Tabary, Jean-Claude Tarby, and Christophe Kolski

m-LoCoS UI: A Universal Visible Language for Global Mobile Communication 144
Aaron Marcus

Developing a Conversational Agent Using Ontologies 154
Manish Mehta and Andrea Corradini

Conspeakuous: Contextualising Conversational Systems 165
S. Arun Nair, Amit Anil Nanavati, and Nitendra Rajput

Persuasive Effects of Embodied Conversational Agent Teams 176
Hien Nguyen, Judith Masthoff, and Pete Edwards

Exploration of Possibility of Multithreaded Conversations Using a Voice Communication System 186
Kanayo Ogura, Kazushi Nishimoto, and Kozo Sugiyama

A Toolkit for Multimodal Interface Design: An Empirical Investigation 196
Dimitrios Rigas and Mohammad Alsuraihi

An Input-Parsing Algorithm Supporting Integration of Deictic Gesture in Natural Language Interface 206
Yong Sun, Fang Chen, Yu Shi, and Vera Chung

Multimodal Interfaces for In-Vehicle Applications 216
Roman Vilimek, Thomas Hempel, and Birgit Otto

Character Agents in E-Learning Interface Using Multimodal Real-Time Interaction 225
Hua Wang, Jie Yang, Mark Chignell, and Mitsuru Ishizuka

An Empirical Study on Users' Acceptance of Speech Recognition Errors in Text-messaging 232
Shuang Xu, Santosh Basapur, Mark Ahlenius, and Deborah Matteo

Flexible Multi-modal Interaction Technologies and User Interface Specially Designed for Chinese Car Infotainment System 243
Chen Yang, Nan Chen, Peng-fei Zhang, and Zhen Jiao

A Spoken Dialogue System Based on Keyword Spotting Technology 253
Pengyuan Zhang, Qingwei Zhao, and Yonghong Yan

Part II: Adaptive, Intelligent and Emotional User Interfaces

Dynamic Association Rules Mining to Improve Intermediation Between User Multi-channel Interactions and Interactive e-Services 265
Vincent Chevrin and Olivier Couturier

Emotionally Expressive Avatars for Chatting, Learning and Therapeutic Intervention 275
Marc Fabri, Salima Y. Awad Elzouki, and David Moore

Can Virtual Humans Be More Engaging Than Real Ones? 286
Jonathan Gratch, Ning Wang, Anna Okhmatovskaia, Francois Lamothe, Mathieu Morales, R.J. van der Werf, and Louis-Philippe Morency

Automatic Mobile Content Conversion Using Semantic Image Analysis 298
Eunjung Han, Jonyeol Yang, HwangKyu Yang, and Keechul Jung

History Based User Interest Modeling in WWW Access 308
Shuang Han, Wenguang Chen, and Heng Wang

Development of a Generic Design Framework for Intelligent Adaptive Systems 313
Ming Hou, Michelle S. Gauthier, and Simon Banbury

Three Way Relationship of Human-Robot Interaction................. 321
Jung-Hoon Hwang, Kang-Woo Lee, and Dong-Soo Kwon

MEMORIA: Personal Memento Service Using Intelligent Gadgets 331
Hyeju Jang, Jongho Won, and Changseok Bae

A Location-Adaptive Human-Centered Audio Email Notification Service for Multi-user Environments 340
Ralf Jung and Tim Schwartz

Emotion-Based Textile Indexing Using Neural Networks 349
Na Yeon Kim, Yunhee Shin, and Eun Yi Kim

Decision Theoretic Perspective on Optimizing Intelligent Help 358
Chulwoo Kim and Mark R. Lehto

Human-Aided Cleaning Algorithm for Low-Cost Robot Architecture 366
Seungyong Kim, Kiduck Kim, and Tae-Hyung Kim

The Perception of Artificial Intelligence as "Human" by Computer Users 376
Jurek Kirakowski, Patrick O'Donnell, and Anthony Yiu

Speaker Segmentation for Intelligent Responsive Space 385
Soonil Kwon

Emotion and Sense of Telepresence: The Effects of Screen Viewpoint, Self-transcendence Style, and NPC in a 3D Game Environment 393
Jim Jiunde Lee

Emotional Interaction Through Physical Movement 401
Jong-Hoon Lee, Jin-Yung Park, and Tek-Jin Nam

Towards Affective Sensing 411
Gordon McIntyre and Roland Göcke

Affective User Modeling for Adaptive Intelligent User Interfaces 421
Fatma Nasoz and Christine L. Lisetti

A Multidimensional Classification Model for the Interaction in Reactive Media Rooms 431
Ali A. Nazari Shirehjini

An Adaptive Web Browsing Method for Various Terminals: A Semantic Over-Viewing Method 440
Hisashi Noda, Teruya Ikegami, Yushin Tatsumi, and Shin'ichi Fukuzumi

Evaluation of P2P Information Recommendation Based on Collaborative Filtering 449
Hidehiko Okada and Makoto Inoue

Understanding the Social Relationship Between Humans and Virtual Humans 459
Sung Park and Richard Catrambone

EREC-II in Use – Studies on Usability and Suitability of a Sensor System for Affect Detection and Human Performance Monitoring 465
Christian Peter, Randolf Schultz, Jörg Voskamp, Bodo Urban, Nadine Nowack, Hubert Janik, Karin Kraft, and Roland Göcke

Development of an Adaptive Multi-agent Based Content Collection System for Digital Libraries 475
R. Ponnusamy and T.V. Gopal

Using Content-Based Multimedia Data Retrieval for Multimedia Content Adaptation ... 486
Adriana Reveiu, Marian Dardala, and Felix Furtuna

Coping with Complexity Through Adaptive Interface Design ... 493
Nadine Sarter

Region-Based Model of Tour Planning Applied to Interactive Tour Generation ... 499
Inessa Seifert

A Learning Interface Agent for User Behavior Prediction ... 508
Gabriela Şerban, Adriana Tarţa, and Grigoreta Sofia Moldovan

Sharing Video Browsing Style by Associating Browsing Behavior with Low-Level Features of Videos ... 518
Akio Takashima and Yuzuru Tanaka

Adaptation in Intelligent Tutoring Systems: Development of Tutoring and Domain Models ... 527
Oswaldo Vélez-Langs and Xiomara Argüello

Confidence Measure Based Incremental Adaptation for Online Language Identification ... 535
Shan Zhong, Yingna Chen, Chunyi Zhu, and Jia Liu

Study on Speech Emotion Recognition System in E-Learning ... 544
Aiqin Zhu and Qi Luo

Part III: Gesture and Eye Gaze Recognition

How Do Adults Solve Digital Tangram Problems? Analyzing Cognitive Strategies Through Eye Tracking Approach ... 555
Bahar Baran, Berrin Dogusoy, and Kursat Cagiltay

Gesture Interaction for Electronic Music Performance ... 564
Reinhold Behringer

A New Method for Multi-finger Detection Using a Regular Diffuser ... 573
Li-wei Chan, Yi-fan Chuang, Yi-wei Chia, Yi-ping Hung, and Jane Hsu

Lip Contour Extraction Using Level Set Curve Evolution with Shape Constraint ... 583
Jae Sik Chang, Eun Yi Kim, and Se Hyun Park

Visual Foraging of Highlighted Text: An Eye-Tracking Study ... 589
Ed H. Chi, Michelle Gumbrecht, and Lichan Hong

Effects of a Dual-Task Tracking on Eye Fixation Related Potentials (EFRP) 599
Hiroshi Daimoto, Tsutomu Takahashi, Kiyoshi Fujimoto, Hideaki Takahashi, Masaaki Kurosu, and Akihiro Yagi

Effect of Glance Duration on Perceived Complexity and Segmentation of User Interfaces 605
Yifei Dong, Chen Ling, and Lesheng Hua

Movement-Based Interaction and Event Management in Virtual Environments with Optical Tracking Systems 615
Maxim Foursa and Gerold Wesche

Multiple People Gesture Recognition for Human-Robot Interaction 625
Seok-ju Hong, Nurul Arif Setiawan, and Chil-woo Lee

Position and Pose Computation of a Moving Camera Using Geometric Edge Matching for Visual SLAM 634
HyoJong Jang, GyeYoung Kim, and HyungIl Choi

"Shooting a Bird": Game System Using Facial Feature for the Handicapped People 642
Jinsun Ju, Yunhee Shin, and Eun Yi Kim

Human Pose Estimation Using a Mixture of Gaussians Based Image Modeling 649
Do Joon Jung, Kyung Su Kwon, and Hang Joon Kim

Human Motion Modeling Using Multivision 659
Byoung-Doo Kang, Jae-Seong Eom, Jong-Ho Kim, Chul-Soo Kim, Sang-Ho Ahn, Bum-Joo Shin, and Sang-Kyoon Kim

Real-Time Face Tracking System Using Adaptive Face Detector and Kalman Filter 669
Jong-Ho Kim, Byoung-Doo Kang, Jae-Seong Eom, Chul-Soo Kim, Sang-Ho Ahn, Bum-Joo Shin, and Sang-Kyoon Kim

Kalman Filtering in the Design of Eye-Gaze-Guided Computer Interfaces 679
Oleg V. Komogortsev and Javed I. Khan

Human Shape Tracking for Gait Recognition Using Active Contours with Mean Shift 690
Kyung Su Kwon, Se Hyun Park, Eun Yi Kim, and Hang Joon Kim

Robust Gaze Tracking Method for Stereoscopic Virtual Reality Systems 700
Eui Chul Lee, Kang Ryoung Park, Min Cheol Whang, and Junseok Park

EyeScreen: A Gesture Interface for Manipulating On-Screen Objects 710
Shanqing Li, Jingjun Lv, Yihua Xu, and Yunde Jia

GART: The Gesture and Activity Recognition Toolkit 718
Kent Lyons, Helene Brashear, Tracy Westeyn, Jung Soo Kim, and Thad Starner

Static and Dynamic Hand-Gesture Recognition for Augmented Reality Applications 728
Stefan Reifinger, Frank Wallhoff, Markus Ablassmeier, Tony Poitschke, and Gerhard Rigoll

Multiple People Labeling and Tracking Using Stereo for Human Computer Interaction 738
Nurul Arif Setiawan, Seok-Ju Hong, and Chil-Woo Lee

A Study of Human Vision Inspection for Mura 747
Pei-Chia Wang, Sheue-Ling Hwang, and Chao-Hua Wen

Tracing Users' Behaviors in a Multimodal Instructional Material: An Eye-Tracking Study 755
Esra Yecan, Evren Sumuer, Bahar Baran, and Kursat Cagiltay

A Study on Interactive Artwork as an Aesthetic Object Using Computer Vision System 763
Joonsung Yoon and Jaehwa Kim

Human-Computer Interaction System Based on Nose Tracking 769
Lumin Zhang, Fuqiang Zhou, Weixian Li, and Xiaoke Yang

Evaluating Eye Tracking with ISO 9241 - Part 9 779
Xuan Zhang and I. Scott MacKenzie

Impact of Mental Rotation Strategy on Absolute Direction Judgments: Supplementing Conventional Measures with Eye Movement Data 789
Ronggang Zhou and Kan Zhang

Part IV: Interactive TV and Media

Beyond Mobile TV: Understanding How Mobile Interactive Systems Enable Users to Become Digital Producers 801
Anxo Cereijo Roibás and Riccardo Sala

Media Convergence, an Introduction 811
Sepideh Chakaveh and Manfred Bogen

An Improved H.264 Error Concealment Algorithm with User Feedback Design 815
Xiaoming Chen and Yuk Ying Chung

Classification of a Person Picture and Scenery Picture Using Structured Simplicity 821
Myoung-Bum Chung and Il-Ju Ko

Designing Personalized Media Center with Focus on Ethical Issues of Privacy and Security 829
Alma Leora Culén and Yonggong Ren

Evaluation of VISTO: A New Vector Image Search TOol 836
Tania Di Mascio, Daniele Frigioni, and Laura Tarantino

G-Tunes – Physical Interaction Design of Playing Music 846
Jia Du and Ying Li

nan0sphere: Location-Driven Fiction for Groups of Users 852
Kevin Eustice, V. Ramakrishna, Alison Walker, Matthew Schnaider, Nam Nguyen, and Peter Reiher

How Panoramic Photography Changed Multimedia Presentations in Tourism 862
Nelson Gonçalves

Frame Segmentation Used MLP-Based X-Y Recursive for Mobile Cartoon Content 872
Eunjung Han, Kirak Kim, HwangKyu Yang, and Keechul Jung

Browsing and Sorting Digital Pictures Using Automatic Image Classification and Quality Analysis 882
Otmar Hilliges, Peter Kunath, Alexey Pryakhin, Andreas Butz, and Hans-Peter Kriegel

A Usability Study on Personalized EPG (pEPG) UI of Digital TV 892
Myo Ha Kim, Sang Min Ko, Jae Seung Mun, Yong Gu Ji, and Moon Ryul Jung

Recognizing Cultural Diversity in Digital Television User Interface Design 902
Joonhwan Kim and Sanghee Lee

A Study on User Satisfaction Evaluation About the Recommendation Techniques of a Personalized EPG System on Digital TV 909
Sang Min Ko, Yeon Jung Lee, Myo Ha Kim, Yong Gu Ji, and Soo Won Lee

Usability of Hybridmedia Services – PC and Mobile Applications Compared 918
Jari Laarni, Liisa Lähteenmäki, Johanna Kuosmanen, and Niklas Ravaja

m-YouTube Mobile UI: Video Selection Based on Social Influence 926
Aaron Marcus and Angel Perez

Can Video Support City-Based Communities? 933
Raquel Navarro-Prieto and Nidia Berbegal

Watch, Press, and Catch – Impact of Divided Attention on Requirements of Audiovisual Quality 943
Ulrich Reiter and Satu Jumisko-Pyykkö

Media Service Mediation Supporting Resident's Collaboration in ubiTV 953
Choonsung Shin, Hyoseok Yoon, and Woontack Woo

Implementation of a New H.264 Video Watermarking Algorithm with Usability Test 963
Mohd Afizi Mohd Shukran, Yuk Ying Chung, and Xiaoming Chen

Innovative TV: From an Old Standard to a New Concept of Interactive TV – An Italian Job 971
Rossana Simeoni, Linnea Etzler, Elena Guercio, Monica Perrero, Amon Rapp, Roberto Montanari, and Francesco Tesauri

Evaluating the Effectiveness of Digital Storytelling with Panoramic Images to Facilitate Experience Sharing 981
Zuraidah Sulaiman, Nor Laila Md Noor, Narinderjit Singh, and Suet Peng Yong

User-Centered Design and Evaluation of a Concurrent Voice Communication and Media Sharing Application 990
David J. Wheatley

Customer-Dependent Storytelling Tool with Authoring and Viewing Functions 1000
Sunhee Won, Miyoung Choi, Gyeyoung Kim, and Hyungil Choi

Reliable Partner System Always Providing Users with Companionship Through Video Streaming 1010
Takumi Yamaguchi, Kazunori Shimamura, and Haruya Shiba

Modeling of Places Based on Feature Distribution 1019
Yi Hu, Chang Woo Lee, Jong Yeol Yang, and Bum Joo Shin

Knowledge Transfer in Semi-automatic Image Interpretation 1028
Jun Zhou, Li Cheng, Terry Caelli, and Walter F. Bischof

Author Index 1035

Part I

Multimodality and Conversational Dialogue

Preferences and Patterns of Paralinguistic Voice Input to Interactive Media

Sama'a Al Hashimi

Lansdown Centre for Electronic Arts
Middlesex University
Hertfordshire, England
Samaa.alhashimi@gmail.com

Abstract. This paper investigates the factors that affect users' preferences of non-speech sound input and determine their vocal and behavioral interaction patterns with a non-speech voice-controlled system. It throws light on shyness as a psychological determinant and on vocal endurance as a physiological factor. It hypothesizes that there are certain types of non-speech sounds, such as whistling, that shy users are more prone to resort to as an input. It also hypothesizes that there are some non-speech sounds which are more suitable for interactions that involve prolonged or continuous vocal control. To examine the validity of these hypotheses, it presents and employs a voice-controlled Christmas tree in a preliminary experimental approach to investigate the factors that may affect users' preferences and interaction patterns during non-speech voice control, and by which the developer's choice of non-speech input to a voice-controlled system should be determined.

Keywords: Paralanguage, vocal control, preferences, voice-physical.

1 Introduction

As no other studies appear to exist in the paralinguistic vocal control area addressed by this research, the paper comprises a number of preliminary experiments that explore the preferences and patterns of interaction with non-speech voice-controlled media. In the first section, it presents a general overview of the voice-controlled project that was employed for the experiments. In the second section it discusses the experimental designs, procedures, and results. In the third section it presents the findings and their implications in an attempt to lay the ground for future research on this topic. The eventual aim is for these findings to be used in order to aid the developers of non-speech controlled systems in their input selection process, and in anticipating or avoiding vocal input deviations that may either be considered undesirably awkward or serendipitously "graceful" [6]. In the last section, it discusses the conclusions and suggests directions for future research.

The project that propelled this investigation is *sssSnake*; a two-player voice-physical version of the classic 'Snake'. It consists of a table on top of which a virtual snake is projected and a real coin is placed [1]. The installation consists of four microphones, one on each side of the table. One player utters 'sss' to move the snake

J. Jacko (Ed.): Human-Computer Interaction, Part III, HCII 2007, LNCS 4552, pp. 3–12, 2007.

and chase the coin. The other player utters ‘ahhh’ to move the coin away from the snake. The coin moves away from the microphone if an ‘ahhh’ is detected and the snake moves towards the microphone if an ‘ssss’ is detected. Thus players run round the table to play the game.

This paper refers to applications that involve vocal input and visual output as voice-visual applications. It refers to systems, such as *sssSnake*, that involve a vocal input and a physical output as voice-physical applications. It uses the term vocal paralanguage to refer to a non-verbal form of communication or expression that does not involve words, but may accompany them. This includes voice characteristics (frequency, volume, duration, etc.), emotive vocalizations (laughing, crying, screaming), vocal segregates (ahh, mmm, and other hesitation phenomena), and interjections (oh, wow, yoo). The paper presents projects in which paralinguistic voice is used to physically control inanimate objects in the real world in what it calls *Vocal Telekinesis* [1]. This technique may be used for therapeutic purposes by asthmatic and vocally-disabled users, as a training tool by vocalists and singers, as an aid for motor-impaired users, or to help shy people overcome their shyness.

While user-testing *sssSnake*, shy players seemed to prefer to control the snake using the voiceless 'sss' and outgoing players preferred shouting 'aahh' to move the coin. A noticeably shy player asked: “Can I whistle?”. This question, as well as previous observations, led to the hypothesis that shy users prefer whistling. This prompted the inquiry about the factors that influence users’ preferences and patterns of interaction with a non-speech voice-controlled system, and that developers should, therefore, consider while selecting the form of non-speech sound input to employ.

In addition to shyness, other factors are expected to affect the preferences and patterns of interaction. These may include age, cultural background, social context, and physiological limitations. There are other aspects to bear in mind. The author of this paper, for instance, prefers uttering ‘mmm’ while testing her projects because she noticed that ‘mmm’ is less tiring to generate for a prolonged period than a whistle. This seems to correspond with the following finding by Adam Sporka and Sri Kurniawan during a user study of their Whistling User Interface [5];

> *“The participants indicated that humming or singing was less tiring than whistling. However, from a technical point of view, whistling produces purer sound, and therefore is more precise, especially in melodic mode.”* [5]

The next section presents the voice-controlled Christmas tree that was employed in investigating and hopefully propelling a wave of inquiry into the factors that determine these preferences and interaction patterns. The installation was initially undertaken as an artistic creative project but is expected to be of interest to the human-computer interaction community.

2 Expressmas Tree

2.1 The Concept

Expressmas Tree is an interactive voice-physical installation with real bulbs arranged in a zigzag on a real Christmas tree. Generating a continuous voice stream allows users to sequentially switch the bulbs on from the bottom of the tree to the top (Fig. 1 shows an example). Longer vocalizations switch more bulbs on, thus allowing for new forms of expression resulting in vocal decoration of a Christmas tree.

Expressmas Tree employs a game in which every few seconds, a random bulb starts flashing. The objective is to generate a continuous voice stream and succeed in stopping upon reaching the flashing bulb. This causes all the bulbs of the same color as the flashing bulb to light. The successful targeting of all flashing bulbs within a specified time-limit results in lighting up the whole tree and winning.

Fig. 1. A participant uttering 'aah' to control *Expressmas Tree*

2.2 The Implementation

The main hardware components included 52 MES light bulbs (12 volts, 150 milliamps), 5 microcontrollers (Basic Stamp 2), 52 resistors (1 k), 52 transistors (BC441/2N5320), 5 breadboards, regulated AC adaptor switched to 12 volts, a wireless microphone, a serial cable, a fast personal computer, and a Christmas tree.

The application was programmed in Pbasic and Macromedia Director/Lingo. Two Xtras (external software modules) for Macromedia Director were used: asFFT and Serial Xtra. asFFT [4], which employs the Fast Fourier Transform (FFT) algorithm, was used to analyze vocal input signals. On the other hand, the Serial Xtra is used for serial communication between Macromedia Director and the microcontrollers.

One of the five Basic Stamp chips was used as a 'master' stamp and the other four were used as 'slaves'. Each of the slaves was connected to thirteen bulbs, thus allowing the master to control each slave and hence each bulb separately.

3 Experiments and Results

3.1 First Experimental Design and Setting

The first experiment involved observing, writing field-notes, and analyzing video and voice recordings of players while they interacted with *Expressmas Tree* as a game during its exhibition in the canteen of Middlesex University.

Experimental Procedures. Four female students and seven male students volunteered to participate in this experiment. Their ages ranged from 19 to 28 years. The experiment was conducted in the canteen with one participant at a time while passers-by were watching. Each participant was given a wireless microphone and told the following instruction: "use your voice and target the flashing bulb before the time runs out". This introduction was deliberately couched in vague terms.

The participants' interaction patterns and their preferred non-speech sound were observed and video-recorded. Their voice signals were also recorded in Praat [2], at a sampling rate of 44,100 Hz and saved as a 16 Bit, Mono PCM wave file. Their voice input patterns and characteristics were also analyzed in Praat.

Participants were then given a questionnaire to record their age, gender, nationality, previous use of a voice-controlled application, why they stopped playing, whether playing the game made them feel embarrassed or uncomfortable, and which sound they preferred using and why. Finally they filled in a 13-item version of the Revised Cheek and Buss Shyness Scale (RCBS) (scoring over 49= very shy, between 34 and 49 = somewhat shy, below 34 = not particularly shy) [3]. The aim was to find correlations between shyness levels, gender, and preferences and interaction patterns.

Results. Due to the conventional use of a Christmas tree, passers-by had to be informed that it was an interactive tree. Those who were with friends were more likely to come and explore the installation. The presence of friends encouraged shy people to start playing and outgoing people to continue playing. Some outgoing players seemed to enjoy making noises to cause their friends and passers-by to laugh more than to cause the bulbs to light. Other than the interaction between the player and the tree, the game-play introduced a secondary level of interaction; that between the player and the friends or even the passers-by. Many friends and passers-by were eager to help and guide players by either pointing at the flashing bulb or by yelling "stop!" when the player's voice reaches the targeted bulb. One of the players

Table 1. Profile of participants in experiment 1

Participants	Preferred Vocalization	Shyness Score (0-65) 65=very shy	Shyness Level	Participant Profile: Gender	Age	Given Nationality	Have you used Voice-Controlled applications before?	Did playing the game make you feel embarrassed?	Did playing the game make you feel uncomfortable?
1	Ahh	29	Not partic.	F	27	Greek	Y	N	N
2	mmm	35	Somewhat	F	28	Malaysian	N	N	N
3	ooh	41	Somewhat	M	22	British	N	a bit	a bit
4	ooh	41	Somewhat	M	20	Zimbabw	N	a bit	a bit
5	Ahh	42	Somewhat	M	19	British	N	Y	Y
6	Ahh	30	Not partic.	M	19	cypriot	Y	N	N
7	Ahh	38	Somewhat	M	20	British	N	Y	N
8	mmm	37	Somewhat	F	20	Polish	N	a bit	Y
9	Ahh	21	Not partic.	F	20	British	Y	N	N
10	Ahh	37	Somewhat	M	24	British	N	Y	Y
11	mmm	44	Somewhat	M	22	British	N	N	Y

(participant 6) tried persistently to convince his friends to play the game. When he stopped playing and handed the microphone back to the invigilator, he said that he would have continued playing if his friends joined. Another male player (participant 3) stated "my friends weren't playing so I didn't want to do it again" in the questionnaire. This could indicate embarrassment; especially that participant 3 was rated as "somewhat shy" on the shyness scale (Table 1), and wrote that playing the game made him feel a bit embarrassed and a bit uncomfortable.

Four of the eleven participants wrote that they stopped because they "ran out of breath" (participants 1, 2, 4, and 10). One participant wrote that he stopped because he was "embarrassed" (participant 5). Most of the rest stopped for no particular reason while a few stopped for various other reasons including that they lost. Losing could be a general reason for ceasing to play any game, but running out of breath and embarrassment seem to be particularly associated with stopping to play a voice-controlled game such as *Expressmas Tree*.

The interaction patterns of many participants' consisted of various vocal expressions, including unexpected vocalizations such as 'bababa, mamama, dududu, lulululu', 'eeh', 'zzzz', 'oui, oui, oui', 'ooon, ooon', 'aou, aou', talking to the tree and even barking at it. None of the eleven participants preferred whistling, blowing or uttering 'sss'. Six of them preferred 'ahh', while three preferred 'mmm', and two preferred 'ooh'. Most (Four) of the six who preferred 'ahh' were males while most (two) of the three who preferred 'mmm' were females. All those who preferred 'ooh' were males (Fig. 2 shows a graph).

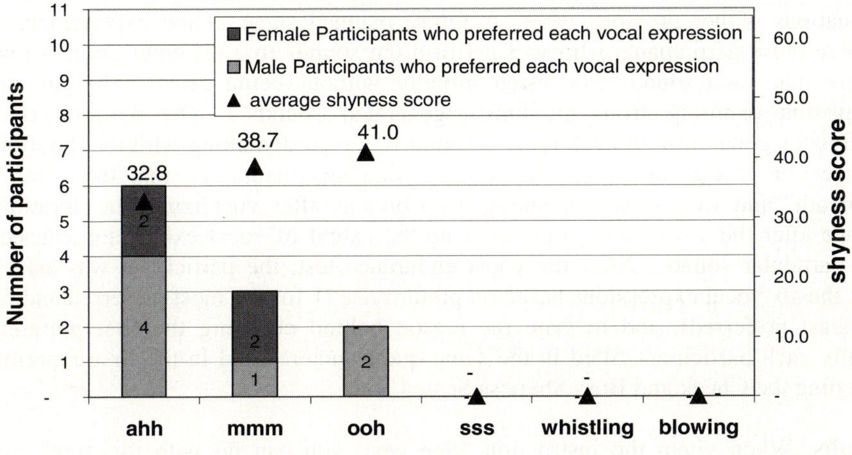

Fig. 2. Correlating the preferences, genders, and shyness levels of participants in experiment 1. Sounds are arranged on the abscissa from the most preferred (left) to the least preferred (right).

3.2 Second Experimental Design and Setting

The second experiment involved observing, writing field-notes, as well as analyzing video-recordings and voice-recordings of players while they interacted with a simplified version of *Expressmas Tree* in a closed room.

Experimental Procedures. Two female students and five male students volunteered to participate in this experiment. Their ages ranged from 19 to 62 years. The simplified version of the game that the participants were presented with was the same tree but without the flashing bulbs which the full version of the game employs. In other words, it only allowed the participant to vocalize and light up the sequence of bulbs consecutively from the bottom of the tree to the top. The experiment was conducted with one participant at a time. Each participant was given a wireless microphone and a note with the following instruction: "See what you can do with this tree". This introduction was deliberately couched in very vague terms. After one minute, the participant was given a note with the instruction: "use your voice and aim to light the highest bulb on the tree". During the first minute of game play, the number of linguistic and paralinguistic interaction attempts were noted. If the player continued to use a linguistic command beyond the first minute, the invigilator gave him/her another note with the instruction: "make non-speech sounds and whenever you want to stop, say 'I am done' ".

The participants' interaction patterns and their mostly used non-speech sounds were carefully observed and video-recorded. Their voice signals were also recorded in Praat [2], at a sampling rate of 44,100 Hz and saved as a 16 Bit, Mono PCM wave file. The duration of each continuous voice stream and silence periods were detected by the asFFT Xtra. Voice input patterns and characteristics were analyzed in Praat.

Each participant underwent a vocal endurance test, in which s/he was asked to try to light up the highest bulb possible by continuousely generating each of the following six vocal expressions: whistling, blowing, 'ahhh', 'mmm', 'ssss', and 'oooh'. These were the six types that were mostly observed by the author during evaluations of her previous work. A future planned stage of the experiement will involve more participants who will perform the sounds in a different order, so as to ensure that each sound gets tested initially without being affected by the vocal exhaustion resulting from previously generated sounds. The duration of the continuous generation of each type of sound was recorded along with the duration of silence after the vocalization. As most participants mentioned that they "ran out of breath" and were observed taking deep breaths after vocalizing, the duration of silence after the vocalization may indicate the extent of vocal exhaustion caused by that particular sound. After the vocal endurance test, the participant was asked to rank the six vocal expressions based on preferrence (1 for the most preferred and 6 for the least preferred), and to state the reason behind choosing the first preference. Finally each participant filled in the same questionnaire used in the first experiment including the Cheek and Buss Shyness Scale [3].

Results. When given the instruction "See what you can do with this tree", some participants didn't vocalize to interact with the tree, despite the fact that they were already wearing the microphones. They thought that they were expected to redecorate it and therefore their initial attempts to interact with it were tactile and involved holding the baubles in an effort to rearrange them. One participant responded: "I can take my snaps with the tree. I can have it in my garden". Another said: "I could light it up. I could put an angel on the top. I could put presents round the bottom". The conventional use of the tree for aesthetic purposes seemed to have overshadowed its interactive application, despite the presence of the microphone and the computer.

Only two participants realized it was interactive; they thought that it involved video tracking and moved backward and forward to interact with it.

When given the instruction "use your voice and aim to light the highest bulb on the tree", four of the participants initially uttered verbal sounds; three uttered "hello" and one 'thought aloud' and varied his vocal characteristics while saying: "perhaps if I speak more loudly or more softly the bulbs will go higher". The three other participants, however, didn't start by interacting verbally; one was too shy to use his voice, and the last two started generating non-speech sounds. One of these two, generated 'mmm' and the other cleared his throat, coughed, and clicked his tongue.

When later given the instruction "use your voice, but without using words, and aim to light the highest bulb on the tree", two of the participants displayed unexpected patterns of interaction. They coughed, cleared their throats, and one of them clicked his tongue and snapped his fingers. They both scored highly on the shyness scale (shyness scores = 40 and 35), and their choice of input might be related to their shyness. One of these two participants persistently explored various forms of input until he discovered a trick to light up all the bulbs on the tree. He held the microphone very close to his mouth and started blowing by exhaling loudly and also by inhaling loudly. Thus, the microphone was continuously detecting the sound input. Unlike most of the other participants who stopped because they "ran out of breath", this participant gracefully utilized his running out of breath as an input. It is not surprising, thereafter, that he was the only participant who preferred blowing as an input. A remarkable observation was that during the vocal endurance test, the pitch and volume of vocalizations seemed to increase as participants lit higher bulbs on the tree. Although *Expressmas Tree* was designed to use voice to cause the bulbs to react, it seems that the bulbs also had an effect on the characteristics of voice such as pitch and volume. This unforeseen two-way voice-visual feedback calls for further research into the effects of the visual output on the vocal input that produced it. Recent focus on investigating the feedback loop that may exist between the vocal input and the audio output seems to have caused the developers to overlook the possible feedback that may occur between the vocal input and the visual output.

The vocal endurance test results revealed that among the six tested vocal expressions, 'ahh', 'ooh', and 'mmm' were, on average, the most prolonged expressions that the participants generated, followed by 'sss', whistling, and blowing, respectively (Fig. 3 shows a graph). These results were based on selecting and finding the duration of the most prolonged attempt per each type of vocal expression. The following equation was formulated to calculate the efficiency of the vocal expression:

$$\text{Vocal expression efficiency} = \text{duration of the prolonged vocalization} - \text{duration of silence after the prolonged vocalization} \qquad (1)$$

This equation is based on postulating that the most efficient and less tiring vocal expression is the one that the participants were able to generate for the longest period and that required the shortest period of rest after its generation. Accordingly, 'ahh', 'ooh', and 'mmm' were more efficient and suitable for an application that requires maintaining what this paper refers to as *vocal flow*: vocal control that involves the generation of a voice stream without disruption in vocal continuity.

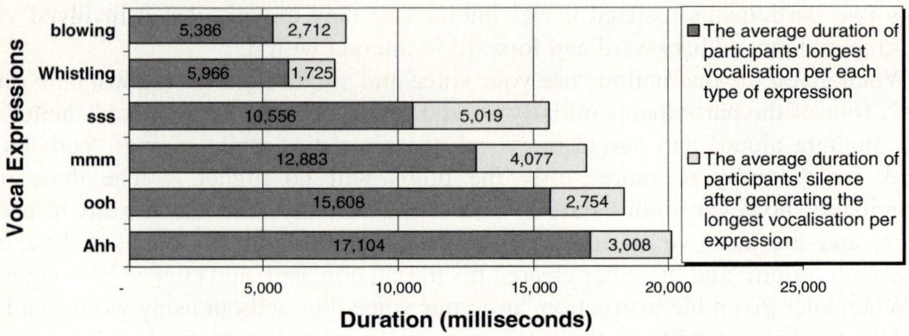

Fig. 3. The average duration of the longest vocal expression by each participant in experiment 2

On the other hand, the results of the preferences test revealed that 'ahh' was also the most preferred in this experiment, followed by 'mmm', whistling, and blowing. None of the participants preferred 'sss' or 'ooh'. The two females who participated in this experiment preferred 'mmm'. This seems to coincide with the results of the first experiment where the majority of participants who preferred 'mmm' where females. It is remarkable to note the vocal preference of one of the participants who was noticeably very outgoing and who evidently had the lowest shyness score. His preference and pattern of interaction, as well as earlier observations of interactions with *sssSnake*, led to the inference that many outgoing people tend to prefer 'ahh' as input. Unlike whistling which is voiceless and involves slightly protruding the lips, 'ahh' is voiced and involves opening the mouth expressively. One of the participants (shyness score = 36) tried to utter 'ahh' but was too embarrassed to continue and he kept laughing before and after every attempt. He stated that he preferred whistling the most and that he stopped because he "was really embarrassed". This participant's

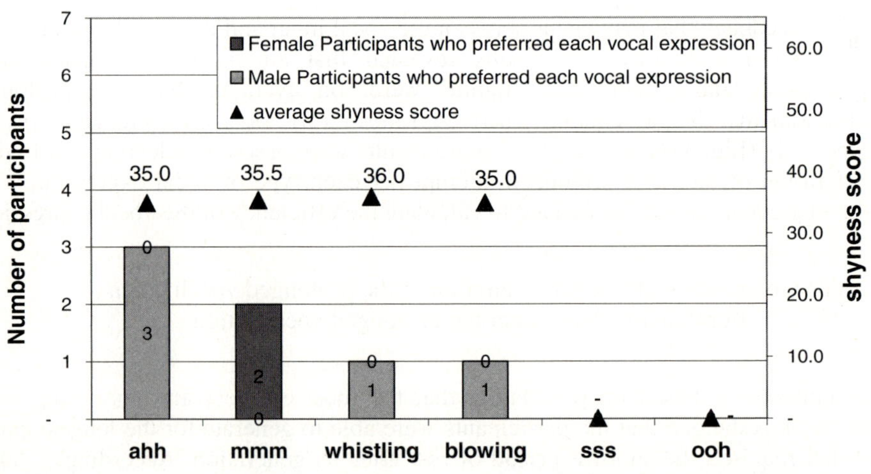

Fig. 4. Correlating the preferences, genders, and shyness levels of participants in experiment 2.Sounds are arranged on the abscissa from the most preferred (left) to the least preferred (right)

preference seems to verify the earlier hypothesis that many shy people tend to prefer whistling to interact with a voice-controlled work. This is also evident in the graphical analysis of the results (Fig. 4 shows an example) in which the participants who preferred whistling had the highest average shyness scores among others. Conversely, participants who preferred the vocal expression 'ahh' had the lowest average shyness scores in both experiments 1 and 2.

Combined results from both experiments revealed that nine of the eighteen participants preferred 'ahh', five preferred 'mmm', two preferred 'ooh', one preferred whistling, one preferred blowing, and no one preferred 'sss'. Most (seven) of the participants who preferred 'ahh' were males, and most (four) of those who preferred 'mmm' were females. One unexpected but reasonable observation from the combined results was that the shyness score of the participants who preferred 'mmm' was higher than the shyness score of those who preferred whistling. A rational explanation for this is that 'mmm' is "less intrusive to make", and that it is "more of an internal sound" as a female participant who preferred 'mmm' wrote in the questionnaire.

4 Conclusions

The paper presented a non-speech voice-controlled Christmas tree and employed it in investigating players' vocal preferences and interaction patterns. The aim was to determine the most preferred vocal expressions and the factors that affect players' preferences. The results revealed that shy players are more likely to prefer whistling or 'mmm'. This is most probably because the former is a voiceless sound and the latter doesn't involve opening the mouth. Outgoing players, on the other hand, are more likely to prefer 'ahh' (and probably similar voiced sounds). It was also evident that many females preferred 'mmm' while many males preferred 'ahh'. The results also revealed that 'ahh', 'ooh', and 'mmm' are easier to generate for a prolonged period than 'sss', which is in turn easier to prolong than whistling and blowing. Accordingly, the vocal expressions 'ahh', 'ooh', and 'mmm' are more suitable than whistling or blowing for interactions that involve prolonged or continuous control. The reason could be that the nature of whistling and blowing mainly involves exhaling but hardly allows any inhaling, thus causing the player to quickly run out of breath. This, however, calls for further research on the relationship between the different structures of the vocal tract (lips, jaw, palate, tongue, teeth etc.) and the ability to generate prolonged vocalizations. In a future planned stage of the experiments, the degree of variation in each participant's vocalizations will also be analyzed as well as the creative vocalizations that a number of participants may generate and that extend beyond the scope of the six vocalizations that this paper explored. It is hoped that the ultimate findings will provide the solid underpinning of tomorrow's non-speech voice-controlled applications and help future developers anticipate the vocal preferences and patterns in this new wave of interaction.

Acknowledgments. I am infinitely grateful to Gordon Davies, for his unstinting mentoring and collaboration throughout every stage of my PhD. I am exceedingly grateful to Stephen Boyd Davis and Magnus Moar for their lavish assistance and supervision. I am indebted to Nic Sandiland for teaching me the necessary technical skills to bring *Expressmas Tree* to fruition.

References

1. Al Hashimi, S., Davies, G.: Vocal Telekinesis; Physical Control of Inanimate Objects with Minimal Paralinguistic Voice Input. In: Proceedings of the 14th ACM International Conference on Multimedia (ACM MM 2006). Santa Barbara, California, USA (2006)
2. Boersma, P., Weenink, D.: Praat; doing phonetics by computer. (Version 4.5.02) [Computer program]. (2006) Retrieved December 1, 2006 from http://www.praat.org/
3. Cheek, J.M.: The Revised Cheek and Buss Shyness Scale (1983) http://www.wellesley.edu/Psychology/Cheek/research.html#13item
4. Schmitt, A.: asFFT Xtra (2003) http://www.as-ci.net/asFFTXtra
5. Sporka, A.J., Kurniawan, S.H., Slavik, P.: Acoustic Control of Mouse Pointer. To appear in Universal Access in Information Society, a Springer-Verlag journal (2005)
6. Wiberg, M.: Graceful Interaction In Intelligent Environments. In: Proceedings of the International Symposium on Intelligent Environments, Cambridge (April 5-7, 2006)

"Show and Tell": Using Semantically Processable Prosodic Markers for Spatial Expressions in an HCI System for Consumer Complaints

Christina Alexandris

Institute for Language and Speech Processing (ILSP)
Artemidos 6 & Epidavrou, GR-15125 Athens, Greece
calex@ilsp.gr

Abstract. The observed relation between prosodic information and the degree of precision and lack of ambiguity is attempted to be integrated in the processing of the user's spoken input in the CitizenShield ("POLIAS") system for consumer complaints for commercial products. The prosodic information contained in the spoken descriptions provided by the consumers is attempted to be preserved with the use of semantically processable markers, classifiable within an Ontological Framework and signalizing prosodic prominence in the speakers spoken input. Semantic processability is related to the reusability and/or extensibility of the present system to multilingual applications or even to other types of monolingual applications.

Keywords: Prosodic prominence, Ontology, Selectional Restrictions, Indexical Interpretation for Emphasis, Deixis, Ambiguity resolution, Spatial Expressions.

1 Introduction

In a Human Computer Interaction (HCI) System involving spoken interaction, prosodic information contained in the users spoken input is often lost. In spoken Greek, prosodic information has shown to contribute both to clarity and to ambiguity resolution and, in contrast, semantics and word order are observed to play a secondary role [2]. The relation between prosodic information and the degree of precision and lack of ambiguity is attempted to be integrated in the processing of the user's spoken input in the CitizenShield ("POLIAS") system for consumer complaints for commercial products (National Project: "Processing of Images, Sound and Language", Meter 3.3 of the National Operational Programme "Information Society", which concerns the Research & Technological Development for the Information Society). The preservation of the prosodic information contained in the spoken descriptions provided by the consumers is attempted to be facilitated with the use of semantically processable markers signalizing prosodic prominence in the speakers spoken input. Semantic processability is related to the reusability and/or extensibility of the present system to multilingual applications or even to other types of monolingual applications. The spoken input is recognized by the system's Speech

J. Jacko (Ed.): Human-Computer Interaction, Part III, HCII 2007, LNCS 4552, pp. 13–22, 2007.

Recognition (ASR) component and is subsequently entered into the templates of the CitizenShield system's automatically generated complaint form.

2 Outline of the CitizenShield Dialog System

The purpose of the CitizenShield dialog system is to handle routine tasks involving food and manufactured products (namely compliants involving quality, product labels, defects and prices), thus allowing the staff of consumer organisations, such as the EKPIZO organisation, to handle more complex cases, such as complaints involving banks and insurance companies. The CitizenShield dialog system involves a hybrid approach to the processing of speaker spoken input in that it involves both keyword recognition and recording of free spoken input. Keyword recognition largely occurs within a yes-no question sequence of a directed dialog (Figure 1). Free spoken input is recorded within a defined period of time, following a question requiring detailed information and/or detailed descriptions (Figure 1). The use of directed dialogs and yes-no questions aims to the highest possible recognition rate of a very broad and varied user group and, additionally, the use of free spoken input processes the detailed information involved in a complex application such as consumer complaints. All spoken input, whether constituting an answer to a yes-no question or constituting an answer to a question triggering a free-input answer, is automatically directed to the respective templates of a complaint form (Figure 2), which are filled in by the spoken utterances, recognized by the system's Automatic Speech Recognition (ASR) component, which is the point of focus in the present paper.

[4.3]: SYSTEM: Does your complaint involve the quality of the product?
[USER: YES/NO/PAUSE/ERROR)] >>>YES

↓

[INTERACTION 5: QUALITY]

↓

[5.1]: SYSTEM: Please answer the following questions with a «yes» or a "no" .
Was there a problem with the products packaging?
[USER: YES/NO/PAUSE/ERROR)]>>>NO

↓

[5.2]: SYSTEM: Please answer the following questions with a «yes» or a "no".
Was the product broken or defective?
[USER: YES/NO/PAUSE/ERROR)] >>>YES

↓

[5.2.1]: SYSTEM: How did you realize this? Please speak freely.
[USER: FREE INPUT/PAUSE/ERROR]>>> FREE INPUT
[TIME-COUNT >Xsec]

↓

[INTERACTION 6]

Fig. 1. A section of a directed dialog combining free input (hybrid approach)

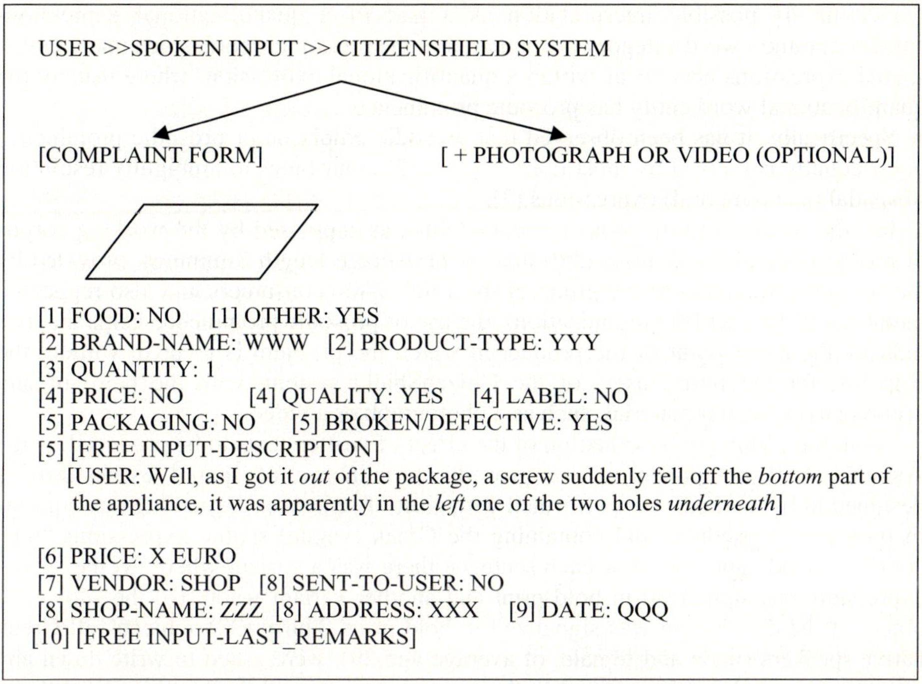

Fig. 2. Example of a section of the data entered in the automatically produced template for consumer complaints in the CitizenShield System (spatial expressions are indicated in italics)

The CitizenShield system offers the user the possibility to provide photographs or videos as an additional input to the system, along with the complaint form. The generation of the template-based complaint forms is also aimed towards the construction of continually updated databases from which statistical and other types of information is retrievable for the use of authorities (for example, the Ministry of Commerce, the Ministry of Health) or other interested parties.

3 Spatial Expressions and Prosodic Prominence

Spatial expressions constitute a common word category encountered in the corpora of user input in the CitizenShield system for consumer complaints, for example, in the description of damages, defects, packaging or product label information. Spatial expressions pose two types of difficulties: They (1) are usually not easily subjected to sublanguage restrictions, in contrast to a significant number of other word-type categories [8], and, (2) Greek spatial expressions, in particular, are often too ambiguous or vague when they are produced outside an in-situ communicative context, where the consumer does not have the possibility to actually "show and tell" his complaints about the product. However, prosodic prominence on the Greek spatial expression has shown to contribute both to the recognition of its "indexical" versus its "vague" interpretation [9], according to previous studies [3], and acts as a default in preventing its possible interpretation as a part of a quantificational expression-another common word category encountered in the present corpora, since many Greek spatial expressions also occur within a quantificational expression, where usually the quantificational word entity has prosodic prominence.

Specifically, it has been observed that prosodic emphasis or prosodic prominence (1) is equally perceived by most users [2] and (2) contributes to ambiguity resolution of spatial (and temporal) expressions [3].

For the speakers filing consumer complaints, as supported by the working corpus of recorded telephone dialogs (580 dialogs of average length 8 minutes, provided by the speakers belonging to the group of the 1500- 2800 consumers and also registered members of the EKPIZO organization), the use of prosodic prominence helps the user indicate the exact point of the product in which the problem is located, without the help (or, for the future users of the CitizenShield system, with the help) of any accompanying visual material, such as a photograph or a video.

An initial ("start-up") evaluation of the effect of written texts to be produced by the system's ASR component where prosodic prominence of spatial expressions is designed to be marked, was performed with a set of sentences expressing descriptions of problematic products and containing the Greek (vague) spatial expressions "on", "next", "round" and "in". For each sentence there was a variant where (a) the spatial expression was signalized in bold print and another variant where (b) the subject or object of the description was signalized in bold print. Thirty (30) subjects, all Greek native speakers (male and female, of average age 29), were asked to write down any spontaneous comments in respect to the given sentences and their variants. 68,3% of the students differentiated a more "exact" interpretation in all (47,3%) or in approximately half (21%) of the sentences where the spatial expressions were signalized in bold print, where 31,5% indicated this differentiation in less than half of the sentences (21%) or in none (10,5%) of the sentences. Of the comments provided, 57,8% focused on a differentiation that may be described as a differentiation between "object of concern" and "point of concern", while 10,5% expressed discourse-oriented criteria such as "indignation/surprise" versus "description/indication of problem". We note that in our results we did not take into account the percentage of the subjects (31,5%) that did not provide any comments or very poor feedback.

The indexical interpretation of the spatial expression, related to prosodic prominence (emphasis), may be differentiated in three types of categories, namely (1) indexical interpretation for emphasizing information, (2), indexical interpretation for ambiguity resolution and (3) indexical interpretation for deixis. An example of indexical interpretation for emphasizing information is the prosodic prominence of the spatial expression "'mesa" ("in" versus "right in" (with prosodic prominence)) to express that the defective button was sunken right in the interior of the appliance, so that it was, in addition, hard to remove. Examples of indexical interpretation for ambiguity resolution are the spatial expressions "'pano" ("on" versus "over" (with prosodic prominence)), "'giro" ("round" versus "around" (with prosodic prominence)) and "'dipla" ("next-to" versus "along" (with prosodic prominence)) for the respective cases in which the more expensive price was inscribed exactly over the older price elements, the case in which the mould in the spoilt product is detectable exactly at the rim of the jar or container (and not around the container, so it was not easily visible) and the case in which the crack in the coffee machines pot was exactly parallel to the band in the packaging so it was rendered invisible. Finally, a commonly occurring example of an indexical interpretation for deixis is the spatial expression "e'do"/"e'ki" ("there"/"here" versus right/exactly here/there" (with prosodic prominence)) in the case in which some pictures may not be clear enough and the deictic effect of the emphasized-indexical elements results to the pointing out of the specific problem or detail detected in the picture/video and not to the picture/video in general. With the use of prosodic prominence, the user is able to enhance his or her demonstration of the problem depicted on the photograph or video or describe it in a more efficient way in the (more common case) in which the complaint is not accompanied by any visual material.

The "indexical" interpretation of a spatial expression receiving prosodic prominence can be expressed with the [+ indexical] feature, whereas, the more "vague" interpretation of the same, unemphasized spatial or temporal expression can be expressed with the [- indexical] feature [3]. Thus, in the framework of the CitizenShield system, to account for prosody-dependent indexical versus vague interpretations for Greek spatial expressions, the prosodic prominence of the marked spatial expression is linked to the semantic feature [+ indexical]. If a spatial expression is not prosodically marked, it is linked by default to the [-indexical] feature. In the CitizenShield system's Speech Recognition (ASR) component, prosodically marked words may be in the form of distinctively highlighted words (for instance, bold print or underlined) in the recognized spoken text. Therefore, the recognized text containing the prosodically prominent spatial expression linked to the [+ indexical] feature is entered into the corresponding template of the system's automatic complaint generation form. The text entered in the complaint form is subjected to the necessary manual (or automatic) editing involving the rephrasing of the marked spatial expression to express its indexical interpretation.

In the case of a possible translation of the complaint forms -or even in a multilingual extension of the system, the indexical markers aid the translator to provide the appropriate transfer of the filed complaint, with the respective semantic equivalency and discourse elements, avoiding any possible discrepancies between Greek and any other language.

4 Integrating Prosodic Information Within an Ontological Framework of Spatial Expressions

Since the proposed above-presented prosodic markers are related to the semantic content of the recognized utterance, they may be categorized as semantic entities within an established ontological framework of spatial expressions, also described in the present study. For instance, in the example of the Greek spatial expression "'mesa" ("in") the more restrictive concepts can be defined with the features [± movement] and [± entering area], corresponding to the interpretations "into", "through", "within" and "inside", according to the combination of features used. The features defining each spatial expression, ranging from the more general to the more restrictive spatial concept, are formalized from standard and formal definitions and examples from dictionaries, a methodology encountered in data mining applications [7]. The prosody-dependent indexical versus vague interpretation of these spatial expressions is accounted for in the form of additional [± indexical] features located at the end-nodes of the spatial ontology. Therefore, the semantics are very restricted at the end-nodes of the ontology, accounting for a semantic prominence imitating the prosodic prominence in spoken texts. The level of the [± indexical] features may also be regarded as a boundary between the Semantic Level and the Prosodic Level.

Specifically, in the present study, we propose that the semantic information conveyed by prosodic prominence can be established in written texts though the use of modifiers. These modifiers are not randomly used, but constitute an indexical ([+indexical]) interpretation, namely the most restrictive interpretation of the spatial expression in question in respect to the hierarchical framework of an ontology. Thus, the modifiers function as additional semantic restrictions or "Selectional Restrictions" [11], [4] within an ontology of spatial expressions.

Selectional Restrictions, already existing in a less formal manner in the taxonomies of the sciences and in the sublanguages of in non-literary and especially, scientific texts, are applied within an ontology-search tree which provides a hierarchical structure to account for the relation between the concepts with the more general ("vague") semantic meaning and the concepts with the more restricted ("indexical") meaning. This mechanism can also account for the relation between spatial expressions with the more general ("vague") semantic meaning and the spatial expressions with the more restricted ("indexical") meaning. Additionally, the hierarchical structure, characterizing an ontology, can provide a context-independent framework for describing the sublanguage-independent word category of spatial expressions.

For example, the spatial expression "'mesa" ("in") (Figure 3) can be defined either with the feature (a) [-movement], the feature (b) [+movement] or with the feature (c) [± movement]. If the spatial expression involves movement, it can be matched with the English spatial expressions "into", "through" and "across" [10]. If the spatial expression does not involve movement, it can be matched with the English spatial expressions "within", "inside" and "indoors" [10]. The corresponding English spatial expressions, in turn, are linked to additional feature structures, as the search is continued further down the ontology. The spatial expression "into" receives the additional feature [+ point] while the spatial expressions "through" and "across", receive the features [+ area], [± horizontal movement] and [+ area], [+ horizontal movement] respectively. The spatial expressions with the [-movement] feature, namely, the expressions, "within", "inside" and "indoors", receive the additional feature [+ building] for "indoors", while the spatial expressions "within" and "inside", receive the features [± object] and [+ object] respectively. The English spatial expression "in" may either signify a specific location and not involve movement, or, in other cases, may involve movement towards a location. All the above-presented spatial expressions can be subject to receive additional restrictions with the feature [+ indexical] as the syntactically realized adverbial modifier "exactly". It should be noted that the English spatial expressions with an indefinite "±" value, namely "in", "through" and "within" also occur as temporal expressions.

To account for prosodically determined indexical versus vague interpretations for the spatial expressions, additional end-nodes with the feature [+ indexical] are added in the respective ontologies, constituting additional Selectional Restrictions. These end-nodes correspond to the terms with the most restrictive semantics to which the adverbial modifier "exactly" ("akri'vos") is added to the spatial expression [1]. With this strategy, the modifier "exactly" imitates the prosodic emphasis on the spatial or temporal expression. Therefore, semantic prominence, in the form of Selectional Restrictions located at the end-nodes of the ontology, is linked to prosodic prominence. The semantics are, therefore so restricted at the end-nodes of the ontologies, that they achieve a semantic prominence imitating the prosodic prominence in spoken texts. The adverbial modifier ("exactly"-"akri'vos") is transformed into a "semantic intensifier". Within the framework of the rather technical nature of descriptive texts, the modifier-intensifier relation contributes to precision and directness aimed towards the end-user of the text and constitutes a prosody-dependent means of disambiguation.

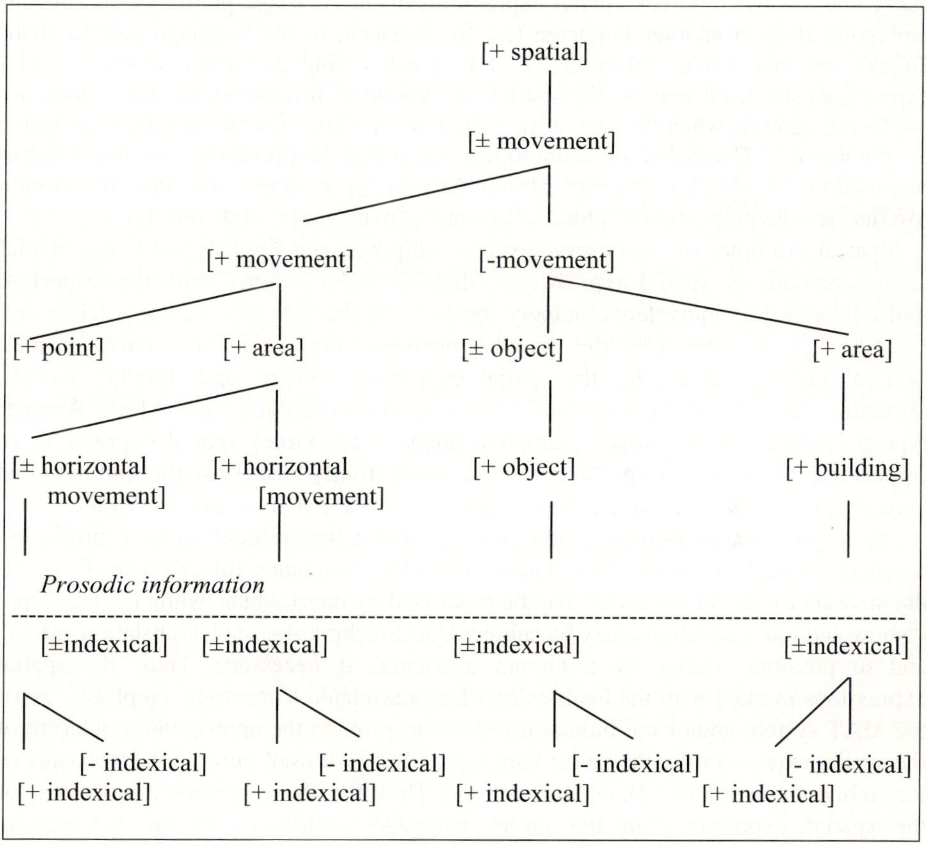

Fig. 3. The Ontology with Selectional Restrictions for the temporal expression "'mesa" ("in")

Therefore, we propose an integration of the use of modifiers acting as Selectional Restrictions for achieving the same effect in written descriptions as it is observed in spoken descriptions, namely directness, clarity, precision and lack of ambiguity.

Specifically, the proposed approach targets to the achievement of the effect of spoken descriptions in a in-situ communicative context with the use of modifiers acting as Selectional Restrictions, located at the end-nodes of the ontologies.

5 Semantically Processable Prosodic Markers Within a Multilingual Extension of the CitizenShield System

The categorization as semantic entities within an ontological framework facilitates the use of the proposed [± indexical] features as prosodic markers to be used in the interlinguas of multilingual HCI systems, such as a possible multilingual extension of the CitizenShield system for consumer complaints. An ontological framework will assist in cases where Greek spatial expressions display a larger polysemy and greater ambiguity than in another language (as, for instance, in the language pair English-Greek) and vice versa. Additionally, it is worth noting that when English spatial expressions are used outside the spatial and temporal framework in which they are produced, namely, when they occur in written texts, they, as well, are often too vague or ambiguous. Examples of ambiguities in spatial expressions are the English prepositions classified as Primary Motion Misfits [6]. Examples of "Primary Motion Misfits" are the prepositions "about", "around", "over", "off" and "through".

Typical examples of the observed relationship between English and Greek spatial expressions are the spatial expressions "'dipla", "'mesa", "'giro" with the respective multiple semantic equivalents, namely 'beside', 'at the side of', 'nearby', 'close by' 'next to' (among others) for the spatial expression "'dipla" and 'in', 'into', 'inside', 'within' (among others) for the spatial expression "'mesa" and, finally, 'round', 'around', 'about' and 'surrounding' for the spatial expression "'giro" [10]. Another typical example of the broader semantic range of the Greek spatial expressions in respect to English is the term "'kato" which, in its strictly locative sense -and not in its quantificational sense, is equivalent to 'down', 'under', 'below' and 'beneath'.

In a possible multilingual extension of the CitizenShield system producing translated complaint forms (from Greek to another language, for example, English), the answers to yes-no questions may be processed by interlinguas, while the free input ("show and tell") questions may be subjected to Machine Assisted Translation (MAT) and to possible editing by a human translator, if necessary. Thus, the spatial expressions marked with the [+indexical] feature, related to prosodic emphasis, assist the MAT system and/or the human translator to provide the appropriate rendering of the spatial expression in the target language, whether it used purely for emphasis (1), for ambiguity resolution (2), or for deixis (3). Thus, the above-presented processing of the spatial expressions in the target language contributes to the Information Management during the Translation Process [5]. The translated text, that may accompany photographs or videos, provides detailed information of the consumer's actual experience. The differences between the phrases containing spatial expressions with prosodic prominence and [+indexical] interpretation and the phrases with the spatial expression without prosodic prominence are described in Figure 4 (prosodic prominence is underlined).

1. Emphasis:
" 'mesa" = "in": ["the defective button was sunken in the appliance"]
" 'mesa" [+indexical] = "right in":
["the defective button was sunken right in (the interior) of the appliance"]

2. Ambiguity resolution:
(a) " 'pano" = "on": ["the more expensive price was inscribed on the older price"]
" 'pano" [+ indexical] ="over":
["the more expensive price was inscribed exactly over the older price"]
(b) " 'giro" = "round": ["the mould was detectable round the rim of the jar"]
" 'giro" [+ indexical] = "around":
["the mould was detectable exactly around the rim of the jar"]
(c) " 'dipla" = "next-to": ["the crack was next to the band in the packaging"]
" 'dipla" [+ indexical] = "along":
["the crack was exactly along (parallel) to the band in the packaging"]

3. Deixis:
"e'do"/"e'ki"= "there"/"here" = ["this picture/ video"]
"e'do"/"e'ki" [+ indexical] = "there"/"here" = ["in this picture/video"]

Fig. 4. Marked multiple readings in the recognized text (ASR Component) for translation processing in a Multilingual Extension of the CitizenShield System

6 Conclusions and Further Research

In the proposed approach, the use of semantically processable markers signalizing prosodic prominence in the speakers spoken input, recognized by the Automatic Speech Recognition (ASR) component of the system and subsequently entered into an automatically generated complaint form, is aimed to the preservation of the prosodic information contained in the spoken descriptions of problematic products provided by the users. Specifically, the prosodic element of emphasis contributing to directness and precision observed in spatial expressions produced in spoken language are transformed into the [+ indexical] semantic feature. The indexical interpretations of spatial expressions in the present application studied are observed to be differentiated into three categories, namely indexical features used purely for emphasis (1), for ambiguity resolution (2), or for deixis (3). The semantic features are expressed in the form of Selectional Restrictions operating within an ontology. Similar approaches may be examined for other word categories constituting crucial word groups in other spoken text types, and possibly in other languages, in an extended multilingual version of the CitizenShield system.

Acknowledgements. We wish to thank Mr. Ilias Koukoyannis and the Staff of the EKPIZO Consumer Organization for their contribution of crucial importance to the development of the CitizenShield System.

References

1. Alexandris, C.: English as an intervening language in texts of Asian industrial products: Linguistic Strategies in technical translation for less-used European languages. In: Proceedings of the Japanese Society for Language Sciences-JSLS 2005, Tokyo, Japan, pp. 91–94 (2005)
2. Alexandris, C., Fotinea, S-E.: Prosodic Emphasis versus Word Order in Greek Instructive Texts. In: Botinis, A. (ed.): Proceedings of ISCA Tutorial and Research Workshop on Experimental Linguistics. Athens, Greece, pp. 65–68 (August 28-30, 2006)
3. Alexandris, C., Fotinea, S.-E., Efthimiou, E.: Emphasis as an Extra-Linguistic Marker for Resolving Spatial and Temporal Ambiguities in Machine Translation for a Speech-to-Speech System involving Greek. In: Proceedings of the 3rd International Conference on Universal Access in Human-Computer Interaction (UAHCI 2005), Las Vegas, Nevada, USA (July 22-27, 2005)
4. Gayral, F., Pernelle, N., Saint-Dizier, P.: On Verb Selectional Restrictions: Advantages and Limitations. In: Christodoulakis, D.N. (ed.) NLP 2000. LNCS (LNAI), vol. 1835, pp. 57–68. Springer, Heidelberg (2000)
5. Hatim, B.: Communication Across Cultures: Translation Theory and Contrastive Text Linguistics, University of Exeter Press (1997)
6. Herskovits, A.: Language, Spatial Cognition and Vision, In: Stock, O. (ed.) Spatial and Temporal Reasoning, Kluwer, Boston (1997)
7. Kontos, J., Malagardi, I., Alexandris, C., Bouligaraki, M.: Greek Verb Semantic Processing for Stock Market Text Mining. In: Christodoulakis, D.N. (ed.) NLP 2000. LNCS (LNAI), vol. 1835, pp. 395–405. Springer, Heidelberg (2000)
8. Reuther, U.: Controlling Language in an Industrial Application. In: Proceedings of the Second International Workshop on Controlled Language Applications (CLAW 98), Pittsburgh, pp. 174–183 (1998)
9. Schilder, F., Habel, C.: From Temporal Expressions to Temporal Information: Semantic tagging of News Messages. In: Proceedings of the ACL-2001, Workshop on Temporal and Spatial Information Processing, Pennsylvania, pp. 1309–1316 (2001)
10. Stavropoulos, D.N. (ed.): Oxford Greek-English Learners Dictionary. Oxford (1988)
11. Wilks, Y., Fass, D.: The Preference Semantics Family. In: Computers Math. Applications, vol. 23(2-5), pp. 205–221. Pergamon Press, Amsterdam (1992)

Exploiting Speech-Gesture Correlation in Multimodal Interaction

Fang Chen[1,2], Eric H.C. Choi[1], and Ning Wang[2]

[1] ATP Research Laboratory, National ICT Australia
Locked Bag 9013, NSW 1435, Sydney, Australia
[2] School of Electrical Engineering and Telecommunications
The University of New South Wales, NSW 2052, Sydney, Australia
{Fang.Chen,Eric.Choi}@nicta.com.au, ningw@student.unsw.edu.au

Abstract. This paper introduces a study about deriving a set of quantitative relationships between speech and co-verbal gestures for improving multimodal input fusion. The initial phase of this study explores the prosodic features of two human communication modalities, speech and gestures, and investigates the nature of their temporal relationships. We have studied a corpus of natural monologues with respect to frequent deictic hand gesture strokes, and their concurrent speech prosody. The prosodic features from the speech signal have been co-analyzed with the visual signal to learn the correlation of the prominent spoken semantic units with the corresponding deictic gesture strokes. Subsequently, the extracted relationships can be used for disambiguating hand movements, correcting speech recognition errors, and improving input fusion for multimodal user interactions with computers.

Keywords: Multimodal user interaction, gesture, speech, prosodic features, lexical features, temporal correlation.

1 Introduction

Advances in human-computer interaction (HCI) research have enabled the development of user interfaces that support the integration of different communication channels between human and computer. Predominately, speech and hand gestures are the two main types of inputs for these multimodal user interfaces. While these interfaces often utilize advanced algorithms for interpreting multimodal inputs, nevertheless, they still need to restrict the task domains to short commands with constrained grammar and limited vocabulary. The removal of these limitations on application domains relies on our better understanding of natural multimodal language and the establishment of predictive theories on the speech-gesture relationships.

Most human hand gestures tend to complement the concurrent speech semantically rather than carrying most of the meaning in a natural spoken utterance [1, 2]. Nevertheless, temporal relationship between these two modalities has been proven to contain useful information for their mutual disambiguation [3]. Recently, researchers

J. Jacko (Ed.): Human-Computer Interaction, Part III, HCII 2007, LNCS 4552, pp. 23–30, 2007.

have shown great interest in the prosody based co-analysis of speech and gestural inputs in multimodal interface systems [1, 4]. In addition to prosody based analysis, co-occurrence analysis of spoken keywords with meaningful gestures can also be found in [5]. However, all these analyses remain largely limited to artificially pre-defined and well-articulated hand gestures. Natural gesticulation where a user is not restricted to any artificially imposed gestures is one of the most attractive means for HCI. However, the inherent ambiguity of natural gestures that do not exhibit one-to-one mapping of gesture style to meaning makes the multimodal co-analysis with speech less tractable [2].

McNeill [2] classified co-verbal hand gestures into four major types by their relationship to the concurrent speech. Deictic gestures, mostly related to pointing, are used to direct attention to a physical reference in the discourse. Iconic gestures convey information about the path, orientation, shape or size of an object in the discourse. Metaphoric gestures are associated with abstract ideas related to subjective notions of an individual and they represent a common metaphor, rather than the object itself. Lastly, gesture beats are rhythmic and serve to mark the speech pace. In this study, our focus will be on the deictic and iconic gestures as they are more frequently found in human-human conversations.

2 Proposed Research

The purpose of this study is to derive a set of quantitative relationships between speech and co-verbal gestures, involving not only just hand movements but also head, body and eye movements. It is anticipated that such knowledge about the speech/gesture relationships can be used in input fusion for better identification of user intentions. The relationships will be studied at two different levels, namely, the prosodic level and the lexical level.

At the prosodic level, we are interested in finding speech prosodic features which are correlated with their concurrent gestures. The set of relationships is expected to be revealed by the temporal alignment of extracted pitch (fundamental frequency of voice excitation) and intensity (signal energy per time unit) values of speech with the motion vectors of the concurrent hand gesture strokes, head, body and eye movements.

At the lexical level, we are interested in finding the lexical patterns which are correlated with the hand gesture phrases (including preparation, stroke and hold), as well as the gesture strokes themselves. It is expected that by using multiple time windows related to a gesture and then looking at the corresponding lexical patterns (e.g. n-gram of the part-of-speech) in those windows, we may be able to utilize these patterns to characterize the specific gesture phrase.

Another task is to work out an automatic gesture classification scheme to be incorporated into the input module of an interface. Since a natural gesture may have some aspects belonging to more than one gesture class (e.g. both deictic and iconic), it is expected that a framework based on probability is needed. Instead of making a hard decision on classification, we will try to assign a gesture phrase into a number of classes with the estimated individual likelihoods.

In addition, it is anticipated that the speech/gesture relationships would be person-dependent to some extent. We are interested in investigating if any of the relationships can be generic enough to be applicable for different users and which other types of relationships have to be specific to individuals. Also we will investigate the influence of a user's cognitive load on the speech/gesture relationships.

3 Current Status

We have just started the initial phase of the study and currently have collected a small set of multimodal corpus for the initial study. We have been looking at some prosodic features in speech that may correlate well with deictic hand gestures. As we are still sourcing the tools for estimating gesture motion vectors from video, we are only able to do a semi-manual analysis. The details of the current status are described in the following sub-sections.

3.1 Data Collection and Experimental Setup

Fifteen volunteers, including 7 females and 8 males, who are 18 to 50 years old, were involved in the data recording part of the experiment. The subjects' nonverbal movements (hand, head and body) and speech were captured from a front camera and a side one. The cameras were placed in such a way so that the head and full upper body could be recorded. The interlocutor was outside the cameras' view in front of the speaker, who was asked to speak on a topic based on his or her own choice for 3 minutes each under 3 different cognitive load conditions. All their speech was recorded with the video camera's internal microphone. All the subjects were required to keep the monologue fluent and natural, and to assume the role of primary speaker.

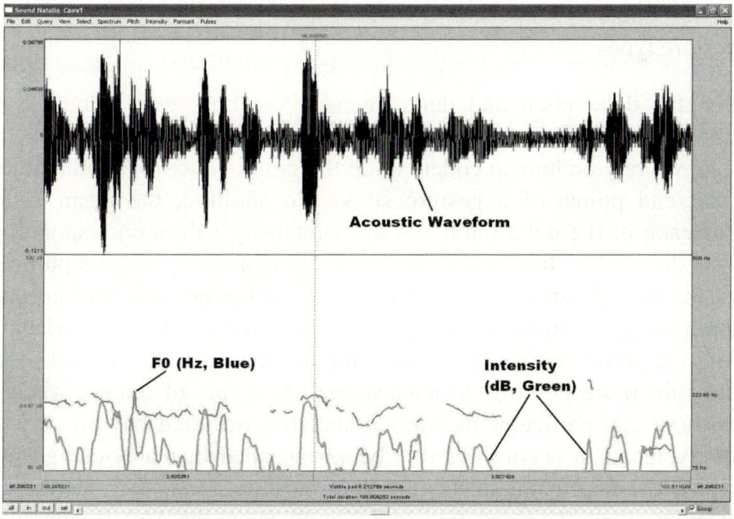

Fig. 1. PRAAT phonetic annotation system

3.2 Audio-Visual Features

In the pilot analysis, the correlation of the deictic hand gesture strokes and the corresponding prosodic cues using delta pitch and delta intensity values of speech is our primary interest. The pitch contour and speech intensity were obtained by employing an autocorrelation method using the PRAAT [6] phonetic annotation system (see Figure 1). A pitch or intensity value is computed every 10ms based on a frame size of 32ms. The delta pitch or delta intensity value is calculated as the difference between the current pitch/intensity value and the corresponding value at the previous time frame. We are interested in using delta values as they reflect more about the time trend and the dynamics of the speech features. These speech prosodic features were then exported to the ANVIL [7] annotation tool for further analysis.

3.3 Prosodic Cues Identification Using ANVIL

Based on the definition of the four major types of hand gestures mentioned in the Introduction, the multimodal data from different subjects were annotated using ANVIL (an example shown in Figure 2). Each data file was annotated by a primary human coder and then verified by another human coder based on a common annotation scheme. The various streams of data and annotation channels include:

- The pitch contour
- The delta pitch contour
- The speech intensity contour
- The speech delta intensity contour
- Spoken word transcription (semantics)
- Head and body postures
- Facial expression
- Eye gaze direction
- Hand gesture types

Basically, the delta pitch and delta intensity contours were added as separated channels through modifying the XML annotation specification file for each data set. At this stage, we rely on human coders to do the gesture classification and to estimate the start and end points of a gesture stroke. In addition, the mean and standard deviation of each of the delta pitch and delta intensity values corresponding to each period of the deictic-like hand movements are computed for analysis purpose. As we realize that the time duration for different deictic stokes are normally not equal, time normalization is applied to the various data channels for a better comparison.

There may be some ambiguity in differentiating between deictic and beat gestures since both of them are pointing to somewhere. As a rule of thumb, when a gesture happens without any particular meaning associated with and having very tiny short and rapid movements, it is considered to be a beat rather than a deictic gesture stroke, no matter how the final hand shapes are very close to each other. Furthermore, it is also regulated based on the semantic annotation by using the ANVIL annotation tool.

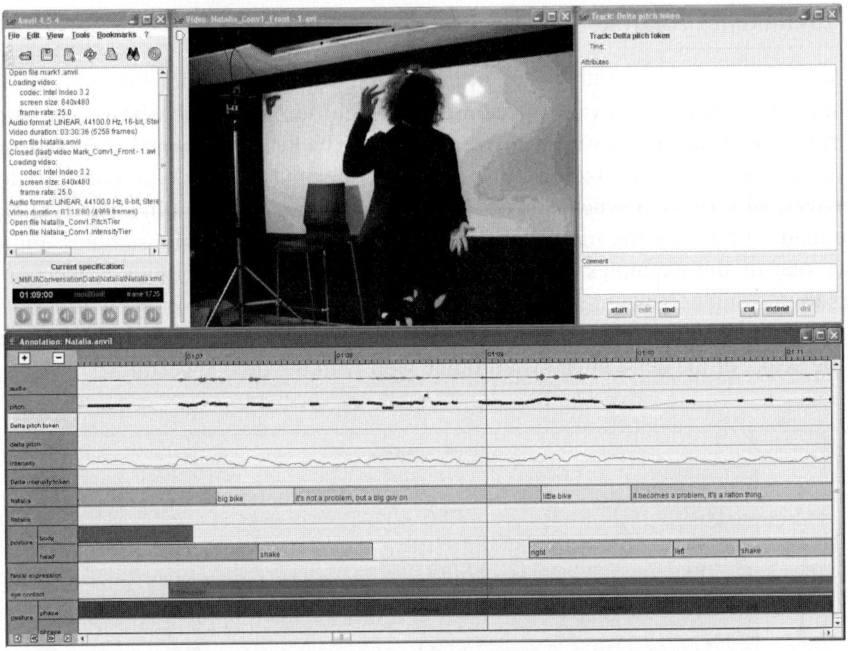

Fig. 2. ANVIL annotation snap shot

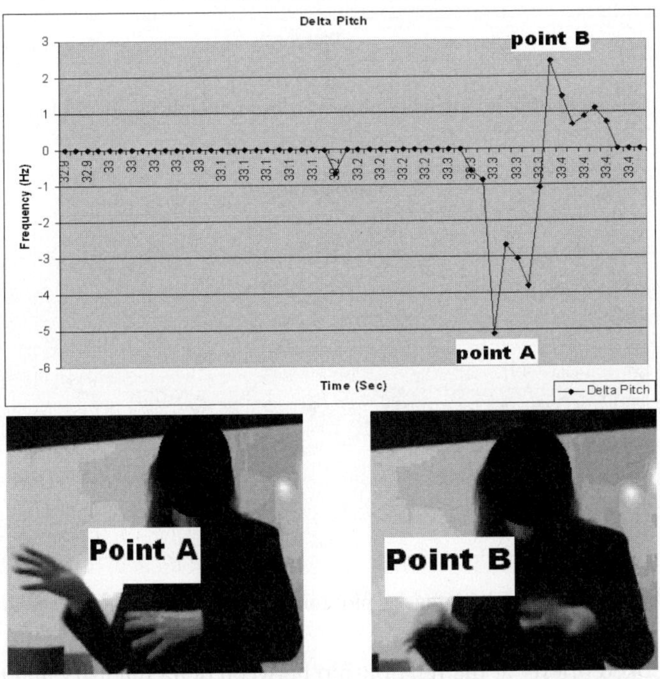

Fig. 3. An example of maximum delta pitch values in synchronization with deictic gesture strokes

3.4 Preliminary Analysis and Results

We started the analysis with the multimodal data collected under the low cognitive load condition. Among 46 valid speech segments chosen particularly based on their co-occurrence with deictic gestures, there are about 65% of the circumstances where the deictic gestures synchronize in time with the peaks of the delta pitch contours. Moreover, 94% of such synchronized delta pitch's average maximum value (2.3 Hz) is more than 10 times of the mean delta pitch value (0.2 Hz) in all the samples. Figure 3 shows one of the examples of the above observed results. In Figure 3, the point **A** refers to one deictic gesture stroke at stationary and the point **B** corresponds to another following deictic gesture within one semantic unit. From the plot, it can be observed that the peaks of the delta pitch synchronize well with the deictic gestures.

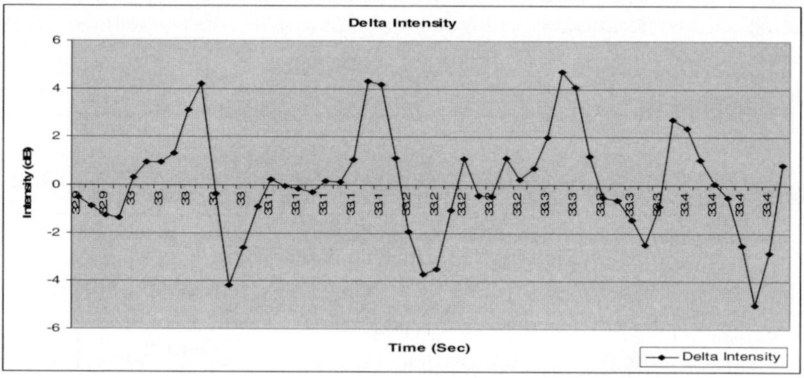

Fig. 4. An example of delta intensity plot for a strong emphasis level of semantic unit

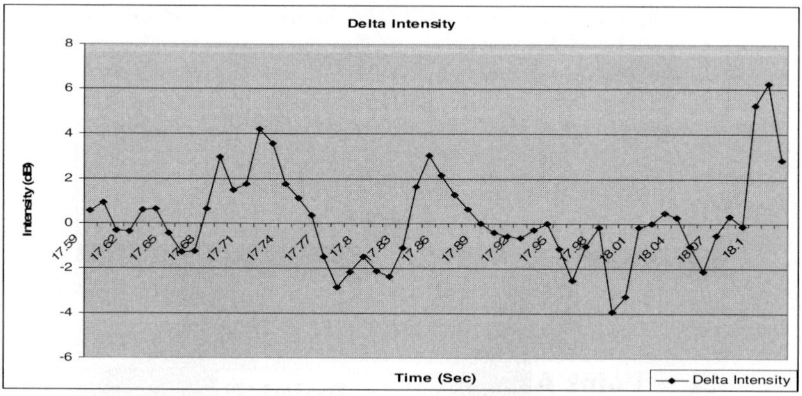

Fig. 5. An example of delta intensity plot for a null emphasis level of semantic unit

We also looked briefly at the relationship between delta intensity and the emphasis level of a semantic unit. Example plots are shown in Figures 4 and 5 respectively. We observed that around 73% of the samples have the delta intensity plots with more peaks and variations at higher emphasis levels. The variation is estimated to be more than 4 dB. It seems that the delta intensity of a speech segment with higher emphasis level tends to have more rhythmic pattern.

Regarding the use of prosodic cue to predict occurrence of a gesture, we found that the deictic gestures are more likely to occur at the interval of [-150ms, 100ms] about the highest peaks of the delta pitch. Among the 46 valid speech segment samples, 78% of the segments have delta pitch values which are greater than 5 Hz and 32% of them have the values greater than 10 Hz. In general, these prosodic cues show us that a deictic-like gesture is likely to occur given a peak in the delta pitch.

Furthermore, the following lexical pattern enables us to have higher confidence in predicting an upcoming deictic-like gesture event which was observed to have 75% likelihood. The cue of the lexical pattern is: verb followed by adverb/pronoun/noun/preposition. For example, as shown in Figure 6, the subject said: "....left it on the taxi". Her intention of doing a hand movement synchronizes with her spoken verb, and the gesture stroke just temporally aligns with the preposition "on". This lexical pattern can potentially be used as a lexical cue to disambiguate different types of gesture between a deictic one and a beat one.

Fig. 6. a) Intention to do a gesture (left); **b**) Transition of the hand movement (middle); **c**) Final gesture stroke (right)

4 Summary

A better understanding of the relationships between speech and gestures is crucial to the technology development of multimodal user interfaces. In this paper, our on-going study on the potential relationships is introduced. At this early stage, we have been only able to get some preliminary results for the investigation on the relationships between speech prosodic features and deictic gestures. Nevertheless these initial results are encouraging and indicate a high likelihood that peaks of the delta pitch values of a speech signal are in synchronization with the corresponding deictic gesture strokes. Much more work is still needed in identifying the relevant prosodic and lexical features for relating natural speech and gestures, and the incorporation of this knowledge into the fusion of different input modalities.

It is expected that the outcomes of the complete study will contribute to the field of HCI in the following aspects:

- A multimodal database for studying natural speech/gesture relationships, involving hand, head, body and eye movements.
- A set of relevant prosodic features for estimating the speech/gesture relationships.
- A set of lexical features for aligning speech and the concurrent hand gestures.
- A set of relevant multimodal features for automatic gesture segmentation and classification.
- A multimodal input fusion module that makes use of the above prosodic and lexical features.

Acknowledgments. The authors would like to express their thanks to Natalie Ruiz and Ronnie Taib for carrying out the data collection, and also thanks to the volunteers for their participation in the experiment.

References

1. Kettebekov, S.: Exploiting Prosodic Structuring of Coverbal Gesticulation. In: Proc. ICMI'04, pp. 105–112. ACM Press, New York (2004)
2. McNeill, D.: Hand and Mind - What Gestures Reveal About Thought. The University of Chicago Press (1992)
3. Oviatt, S.L.: Mutual Disambiguation of Recognition Errors in a Multimodal Architecture. In: Proc. CHI'99, pp. 576–583. ACM Press, New York (1999)
4. Valbonesi, L., Ansari, R., McNeill, D., Quek, F., Duncan, S., McCullough, K.E., Bryll, R.: Multimodal Signal Analysis of Prosody and Hand Motion - Temporal Correlation of Speech and Gestures. In: Proc. EUSIPCO 2002, vol. I, pp. 75–78 (2002)
5. Poddar, I., Sethi, Y., Ozyildiz, E., Sharma, R.: Toward Natural Gesture/Speech HCI - A Case Study of Weather Narration. In: Proc. PUI 1998, pp. 1–6 (1998)
6. Boersma, P., Weenink, D.: Praat - Doing Phonetics by Computer. Available online from http://www.praat.org
7. Kipp, M.: Anvil - A Generic Annotation Tool for Multimodal Dialogue. In: Proc. Eurospeech, pp. 1367–1370. (2001) Also http://www.dfki.de/ kipp/anvil

Pictogram Retrieval Based on Collective Semantics

Heeryon Cho[1], Toru Ishida[1], Rieko Inaba[2], Toshiyuki Takasaki[3], and Yumiko Mori[3]

[1] Department of Social Informatics, Kyoto University, Kyoto 606-8501, Japan
[2] Language Grid Project, National Institute of Information and Communications Technology (NICT), Kyoto 619-0289, Japan
[3] Kyoto R&D Center, NPO Pangaea, Kyoto 600-8411, Japan
cho@ai.soc.i.kyoto-u.ac.jp, ishida@i.kyoto-u.ac.jp, rieko.inaba@nict.go.jp, {toshi,yumi}@pangaean.org

Abstract. To retrieve pictograms having semantically ambiguous interpretations, we propose a semantic relevance measure which uses pictogram interpretation words collected from a web survey. The proposed measure uses ratio and similarity information contained in a set of pictogram interpretation words to (1) retrieve pictograms having implicit meaning but not explicit interpretation word and (2) rank pictograms sharing common interpretation word(s) according to query relevancy which reflects the interpretation ratio.

1 Introduction

In this paper, we propose a method of pictogram retrieval using word query. We have been developing a pictogram communication system which allows children to communicate to one another using pictogram messages [1]. Pictograms used in the system are created by college students majoring in art who are novices at pictogram design. Currently 450 pictograms are registered to the system [2]. The number of pictograms will increase as newly created pictograms are added to the system. Children are already experiencing difficulties in finding needed pictograms from the system. A pictogram retrieval system is needed to support easy retrieval of pictograms.

To address this issue, we propose a pictogram retrieval method in which a human user formulates a word query, and pictograms having interpretations relevant to the query are retrieved. To do this, we utilize pictogram interpretations collected from a web survey. A total of 953 people in the U.S. participated in the survey to describe the meaning of 120 pictograms used in the system. An average of 147 interpretation words or phrases (including duplicate expressions) was collected for each pictogram.

Analysis of the interpretation words showed that (1) one pictogram has multiple interpretations, and (2) multiple pictograms share common interpretation(s). Such semantic ambiguity can influence recall and ranking of the searched result. Firstly, pictograms having implicit meaning but not explicit interpretation word cannot be retrieved using word query. This leads to lowering of recall. Secondly, when the human searcher retrieves several pictograms sharing the same interpretation word using that

J. Jacko (Ed.): Human-Computer Interaction, Part III, HCII 2007, LNCS 4552, pp. 31–39, 2007.

interpretation word as search query, the retrieved pictograms must be ranked according to the query relevancy. This relates to search result ranking.

We address these issues by introducing a semantic relevance measure which uses pictogram interpretation words and frequencies collected from the web survey. Section 2 describes semantic ambiguity in pictogram interpretation with actual interpretations given as examples. Section 3 proposes a semantic relevance measure and its preliminary testing result, and section 4 concludes this paper.

2 Semantic Ambiguity in Pictogram Interpretation

Pictogram is an icon that has clear pictorial similarities with some object [3]. Road signs and Olympic sports symbols are two well known examples of pictograms which have clear meaning [4]. However, pictograms that we deal with in this paper are created by art students who are novices at pictogram design, and their interpretations are not well known. To retrieve pictograms based on pictogram interpretation, we must first investigate how these novice-created pictograms are interpreted. Therefore, we conducted a pictogram survey to respondents in the U.S., and collected interpretations of the pictograms used in the system. Below summarizes the objective, method and data of the pictogram survey.

Objective. An online pictogram survey was conducted to (1) find out how the pictograms are interpreted by humans (residing in the U.S.) and to (2) identify what characteristics, if any, those pictogram interpretations have.

Method. A web survey asking the meaning of 120 pictograms used in the system was conducted to the respondents in the U.S. via the WWW from October 1, 2005 to November 30, 2006.[1] Human respondents were shown a webpage similar to Fig. 1 which contains 10 pictograms per page, and were asked to write the meaning of each pictogram inside the textbox provided below the pictogram. Each time a set of 10 pictograms was shown at random and respondents could choose and answer as many pictogram question sets they liked.

Data. A total of 953 people participated in the web survey. An average of 147 interpretations consisting of words or phrases (duplicate expressions included) was collected for each pictogram. These pictogram interpretations were grouped according to each pictogram. For each group of interpretation words, unique interpretation words were listed, and the occurrence of those unique words were counted to calculate the frequency. An example of unique interpretation words or phrases and their frequencies are shown in Table 1. The word "*singing*" on the top row has a frequency of 84. This means that eighty-four respondents in the U.S. who participated in the survey wrote "*singing*" as the meaning of the pictogram shown in Table 1.

In the next section, we introduce eight specific pictograms and their interpretation words and describe two characteristics in pictogram interpretation.

[1] URL of the pictogram web survey is http://www.pangaean.org/iconsurvey/

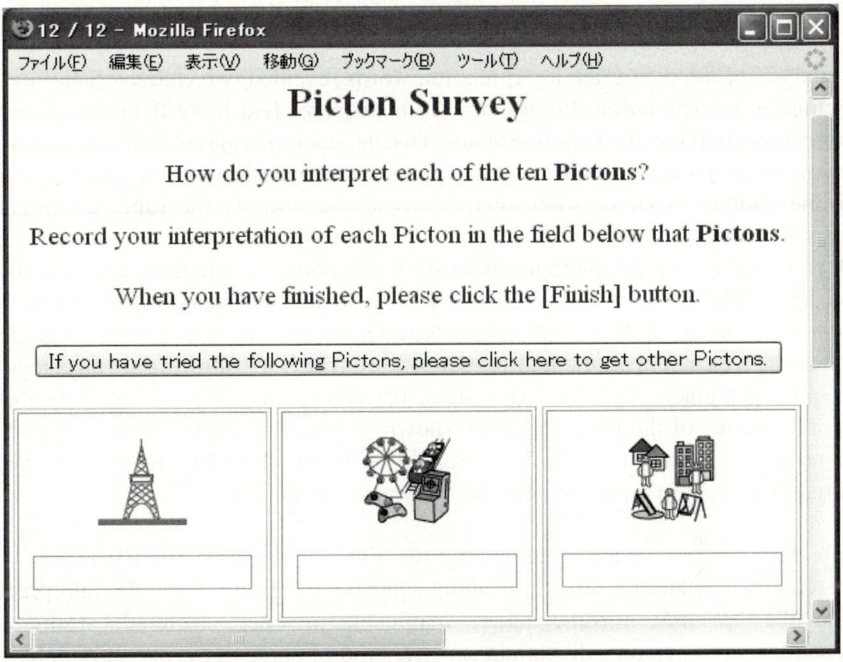

Fig. 1. A screenshot of the pictogram web survey page (3 out of 10 pictograms are shown)

Table 1. Interpretation words or phrases and their frequencies for the pictogram on the left

PICTOGRAM	INTERPRETATIONS	FREQ.
	singing	84
	sing	68
	music	4
	singer	4
	song	2
	a person singing	1
	good singer	1
	happy	1
	happy singing	1
	happy/singing	1
	i like singing	1
	lets sing	1
	man singing	1
	music/singing	1
	musical	1
	siging	1
	sign	1
	sing out loud	1
	sing/singing/song	1
	singing school	1
	sucky singer	1
	talking/singing	1
	TOTAL	179

2.1 Polysemous and Shared Pictogram Interpretation

The analysis of the pictogram interpretation words revealed two characteristics evident in pictogram interpretation. Firstly, all 120 pictograms had more than one pictogram interpretation making them polysemous. That is, each pictogram had more than one meaning to its image. Secondly, some pictograms shared common interpretation(s) with one another. That is, some pictograms shared exactly the same interpretation word(s) with one another.

Here we take up eight pictograms to show the above mentioned characteristics in more detail. For the first characteristic, we will call it *polysemous pictogram interpretation*. For the second, we will call it *shared pictogram interpretation*. To guide our explanation, we categorize the interpretation words into the following seven categories: (i) people, (ii) place, (iii) time, (iv) state, (v) action, (vi) object, and (vii) abstract category. Images of the pictograms are shown in Fig. 2. Interpretations of Fig. 2 pictograms are organized in Table 2. Interpretation words shared by more than one pictogram are marked in *italics* in both the body text and the table.

People. Pictograms containing human figures (Fig. 2 (1), (2), (3), (6), (7), (8)) can have interpretations explaining something about a person or a group of people. Interpretation words like "*friends*, fortune teller, magician, prisoner, criminal, strong man, bodybuilder, tired person" all explain specific kind of person or group of people.

Place. Interpretations may focus on the setting or background of the pictogram rather than the object occupying the center of the setting. Fig. 2 (1), (3), (4), (7) contain human figure(s) or an object like a shopping cart in the center, but rather than focusing on these central objects, words like "church, jail, prison, grocery store, market, gym" all denote specific place or setting related to the central objects.

Time. Concept of time can be perceived through the pictogram and interpreted. Fig. 2 (5), (6) have interpretations like "night, *morning*, dawn, evening, bed time, day and night" which all convey specific moment of the day.

State. States of some objects (including humans) are interpreted and described. Fig. 2 (1), (3), (4), (5), (6), (7), (8) contain interpretations like "*happy*, *talking*, stuck, raining, basket full, *healthy*, sleeping, strong, *hurt*, tired, weak" which all convey some state of the given object.

Action. Words explaining actions of the human figure or some animal are included as interpretations. Fig. 2 (1), (5), (6), (7) include interpretations like "talk, *play*, sleep, *wake up*, exercise" which all signify some form of action.

Object. Physical objects depicted in the pictogram are noticed and indicated. Fig. 2 (4), (5), (7) include interpretations like "food, cart, vegetables, chicken, moon, muscle," and they all point to some physical object(s) depicted in the pictograms.

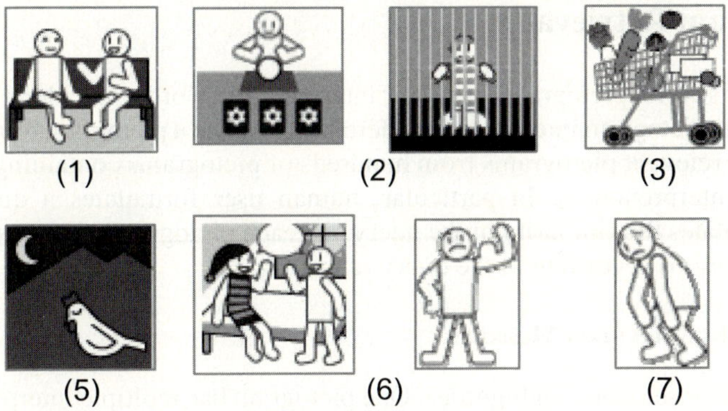

Fig. 2. Pictograms having polysemous interpretations (See Table 2 for interpretations)

Table 2. Polysemous interpretations and shared interpretations (marked in *italics*) found in Fig. 2 pictograms and their interpretation categories

PIC.	INTERPRETATION	CATEGORY
(1)	*friends* / church / *happy*, *talking* / talk, *play*	Person / Place / State / Action
(2)	fortune teller, magician / fortune telling, magic	Person / Abstract
(3)	prisoner, criminal / jail, prison / stuck, raining	Person / Place / State
(4)	grocery store, market / basket full, *healthy* / food, cart, vegetables / shopping	Place / State / Object / Abstract
(5)	night, *morning*, dawn, evening, bed time / sleeping / sleep, *wake up* / chicken, moon	Time / State / Action / Object
(6)	*friends* / *morning*, day and night / *happy*, *talking* / *play*, *wake up*	Person / Time / State / Action
(7)	strong man, bodybuilder / gym / strong, *healthy*, *hurt* / exercise / muscle / strength	Person / Place / State / Action / Object / Abstract
(8)	tired person / tired, weak, *hurt*	Person / State

Abstract. Finally, objects depicted in the pictogram may suggest more abstract concept. Fig. 2 (2), (4), (7) include interpretations like "fortune telling, magic, shopping, strength" which are the result of object-to-concept association. Crystal ball and cards signify fortune telling or magic, shopping cart signifies shopping, and muscle signifies strength.

We showed the two characteristics of pictogram interpretation, *polysemous pictogram interpretation* and *shared pictogram interpretation*, by presenting actual interpretation words exhibiting those characteristics as examples. We believe such varied interpretations are due to differences in how each respondent places his or her focus of attention to each pictogram. As a result, polysemous and shared pictogram interpretations arise, and this in turn, leads to semantic ambiguity in pictogram interpretation. Pictogram retrieval, therefore, must address semantic ambiguity in pictogram interpretation.

3 Pictogram Retrieval

We looked at several pictograms and their interpretation words, and identified semantic ambiguities in pictogram interpretation. Here, we propose a pictogram retrieval method that retrieves relevant pictograms from hundreds of pictograms containing polysemous and shared interpretations. In particular, human user formulates a query, and the method calculates the similarity of the query and each pictogram's interpretation words to rank pictograms according to the query relevancy.

3.1 Semantic Relevance Measure

Pictograms have semantic ambiguities. One pictogram has multiple interpretations, and multiple pictograms share common interpretation(s). Such features of pictogram interpretation may cause two problems during pictogram retrieval using word query. Firstly, when the user inputs a query, pictograms having implicit meaning, but not explicit interpretation words, may fail to show up as relevant search result. This influences recall in pictogram retrieval. Secondly, more than one pictogram relevant to the query may be returned. This influences the ranking of the relevant search result. For the former, it would be beneficial if implicit meaning pictograms are also retrieved. For the latter, it would be beneficial if the retrieved pictograms are ranked according to the query relevancy. To address these two issues, we propose a method of calculating how relevant a pictogram is to a word query. The calculation uses interpretation words and frequencies gathered from the pictogram web survey.

We assume that pictograms each have a list of interpretation words and frequencies as the one given in Table 1. Each unique interpretation word has a frequency. Each word frequency indicates the number of people who answered the pictogram to have that interpretation. The ratio of an interpretation word, which can be calculated by dividing the word frequency by the total word frequency of that pictogram, indicates how much support people give to that interpretation. For example, in the case of pictogram in Table 1, it can be said that more people support "*singing*" (84 out of 179) as the interpretation for the pictogram than "*happy*" (1 out of 179). The higher the ratio of a specific interpretation word of a pictogram, the more that pictogram is accepted by people for that interpretation.

We define *semantic relevance* of a pictogram to be the measure of relevancy between a word query and interpretation words of a pictogram. Let $w_1, w_2, \ldots, w_n$ be interpretation words of pictogram e. Let the ratio of each interpretation word in a pictogram to be $P(w_1|e), P(w_2|e), \ldots, P(w_n|e)$. For example, the ratio of the interpretation word "*singing*" for the pictogram in Table 1 can be calculated as $P(singing|e) = 84/179$. Then the simplest equation that assesses the relevancy of a pictogram e in relation to a query w_i can be defined as follows.

$$P(w_i|e) \tag{1}$$

This equation, however, does not take into account the similarity of interpretation words. For instance, when "*melody*" is given as query, pictograms having similar interpretation word like "*song*", but not "*melody*", fail to be measured as relevant when only the ratio is considered.

PICT	SR	INTERPRETATION WORDS
	0.331	music[109] music notes[3] singing[3] song[3] melody[2] musical[2] a song[1] beats[1] daze[1] flowing music[1] free music[1] jazz[1]
	0.230	singing[84] sing[68] music[4] singer[4] song[2] a person singing[1] good singer[1] happy[1] happy singing[1] happy/singing[1] i like singing[1]
	0.152	singing[38] music[34] sing[18] band[4] choir[4] chior[2] concert[2] a boy singing[1] a child singing[1] american idol[1] arts[1] audition[1]
	0.006	talking[16] praying[15] thinking[13] speaking[8] lonely[5] singing[5] talk[5] pray[3] question[3] reading[3] speaker[3] talking to self[3]

Fig. 3. Semantic relevance (*SR*) calculations for the query "*melody*" (in descending order)

To solve this, we need to define $similarity(w_i,w_j)$ between interpretation words in some way. Using the similarity, we can define the measure of *semantic relevance* $SR(w_i,e)$ as follows.

$$SR(w_i,e)=P(w_j|e)similarity(w_i,w_j) \quad (2)$$

There are several similarity measures. We draw upon the definition of similarity given in [5] which states that similarity between A and B is measured by the ratio between the information needed to state the commonality of A and B and the information needed to fully describe what A and B are. Here, we calculate $similarity(w_i,w_j)$ by figuring out how many pictograms contain certain interpretation words. When there is a pictogram set E_i having an interpretation word w_i, the similarity between interpretation word w_i and w_j can be defined as follows. $|E_i \cap E_j|$ is the number of pictograms having both w_i and w_j as interpretation words. $|E_i \cup E_j|$is the number of pictograms having either w_i or w_j as interpretation words.

$$similarity(w_i,w_j)=|E_i \cap E_j|/|E_i \cup E_j| \quad (3)$$

Based on (2) and (3), the *semantic relevance* or the measure of relevancy to return pictogram e when w_i is input as query can be calculated as follows.

$$SR(w_i,e)=P(w_j|e)|E_i \cap E_j|/|E_i \cup E_j| \quad (4)$$

We implemented a web-based pictogram retrieval system and performed a preliminary testing to see how effective the proposed measure was. Interpretation words and frequencies collected from the web survey were given to the system as data.

Fig. 3 shows a search result using the semantic relevance (*SR*) measure for the query "*melody*." The first column shows retrieved pictograms in descending order of *SR* values. The second column shows the *SR* values. The third column shows interpretation words and frequencies (frequencies are placed inside square brackets). Some interpretation words and frequencies are omitted to save space. Interpretation word matching the word query is written in blue and enclosed in a red square. Notice how the second and the third pictograms from the top are returned as search result although they do not explicitly contain the word "*melody*" as interpretation word.

PICT	SR	INTERPRETATION WORDS
	0.304	cards[90] card game[7] playing cards[6] poker[6] game[5] card[4] games[4] ace[2] aces[2] deck of cards[2] gambling[2]
	0.256	video games[42] games[22] video game[11] game[6] computer[5] computer game[3] computer games[3] vidio games[3]
	0.209	fortune teller[18] magic[8] game[6] fortune telling[5] psychic[5] cards[4] gypsy[4] religion[4] bowling[3] magician[3]
	0.169	colors[62] art[13] paint[7] color[5] painting[5] color chart[2] different colors[2] paint colors[2] game[1]
	0.168	comics[11] super hero[9] entertainment[8] cartoons[6] cartoon[5] superhero[4] learning[3] superman[3] games[2] game[1]
	0.155	winner[49] winning[11] champion[9] first place[8] cheering[5] win[4] event[3] proud[3] award[2] olympics[2] game[1]
	0.093	sports[108] sport equipment[2] active[1] all sports[1] ball games[1] ballgames[1] balls and a bat[1] balls/sports[1] games with balls[1]

Fig. 4. Semantic relevance (*SR*) calculations for the query "*game*" (in descending order)

Since the second and the third pictograms in Fig. 3 both contain musical notes which signify melody, we judge both to be relevant search results. By defining similarity into the *SR* measure, we were able to retrieve pictograms having not only explicit interpretation, but also implicit interpretation.

Fig. 4 shows a search result using the *SR* measure for the query "*game*." With the exception of the last pictogram on the bottom, the six pictograms all contain the word "*game*" as interpretation word albeit with varying frequencies. It is disputable if these pictograms are ranked in the order of relevancy to the query, but the result gives one way of ranking the pictograms sharing a common interpretation word. Since the *SR* measure takes into account the ratio (or the support) of the shared interpretation word, we think the ranking in Fig. 4 partially reflects the degree of pictogram relevancy to the word query (which equals the shared interpretation word). A further study is needed to verify the ranked result and to evaluate the proposed *SR* measure.

One of the things that we found during the preliminary testing is that low *SR* values return mostly irrelevant pictograms, and that these pictogram(s) need to be discarded. For example, the bottom most pictogram in Fig. 3 has an *SR* value of 0.006, and it is not so much relevant to the query "*melody*". Nonetheless it is returned as search result because the pictogram contains the word "*singing*" (with a frequency of 5). Consequently, a positive value is assigned to the pictogram when "*melody*" is thrown as query. Since the value is too low and the pictogram not so relevant, we can discard the pictogram from the search result by setting a threshold.

As for the bottom most pictogram in Fig. 4, the value is 0.093 and the image is somewhat relevant to the query "*game*."

4 Conclusion

Pictograms used in a pictogram communication system are created by novices at pictogram design, and they do not have single, clear semantics. To find out how people interpret these pictograms, we conducted a web survey asking the meaning of 120 pictograms used in the system to respondents in the U.S. via the WWW. Analysis of the survey result showed that these (1) pictograms have polysemous interpretations, and that (2) some pictograms shared common interpretation(s). Such ambiguity in pictogram interpretation influences pictogram retrieval using word query in two ways. Firstly, pictograms having implicit meaning, but not explicit interpretation word, may not be retrieved as relevant search result. This affects pictogram recall. Secondly, pictograms sharing common interpretation are returned as relevant search result, but it would be beneficial if the result could be ranked according to query relevancy.

To retrieve such semantically ambiguous pictograms using word query, we proposed a semantic relevance measure which utilizes interpretation words and frequencies collected from the pictogram survey. The proposed measure takes into account the ratio and similarity of a set of pictogram interpretation words. Preliminary testing of the proposed measure showed that implicit meaning pictograms can be retrieved, and pictograms sharing common interpretation can be ranked according to query relevancy. However, the validity of the ranking needs to be tested. We also found that pictograms with low semantic relevance values are irrelevant and must be discarded.

Acknowledgements. We are grateful to Satoshi Oyama (Department of Social Informatics, Kyoto University), Naomi Yamashita (NTT Communication Science Laboratories), Tomoko Koda (Department of Media Science, Osaka Institute of Technology), Hirofumi Yamaki (Information Technology Center, Nagoya University), and members of Ishida Laboratory at Kyoto University Graduates School of Informatics for valuable discussions and comments. All pictograms presented in this paper are copyrighted material, and their rights are reserved to NPO Pangaea.

References

1. Takasaki, T.: PictNet: Semantic Infrastructure for Pictogram Communication. In: The 3rd International WordNet Conference (GWC-06), pp. 279–284 (2006)
2. Takasaki, T., Mori, Y.: Design and Development of Pictogram Communication System for Children around the World. In: The 1st International Workshop on Intercultural Collaboration (IWIC-07), pp. 144–157 (2007)
3. Marcus, A.: Icons, Symbols, and Signs: Visible Languages to Facilitate Communication. Interactions, 10(3), 37–43 (2003)
4. Abdullah, R., Hubner, R.: Pictograms, Icons and Signs. Thames & Hudson (2006)
5. Lin, D.: An information-theoretic definition of similarity. In: The 15th International Conference on Machine Learning (ICML-98), pp. 296–304 (1998)

Enrich Web Applications with Voice Internet Persona Text-to-Speech for Anyone, Anywhere

Min Chu, Yusheng Li, Xin Zou, and Frank Soong

Micorosoft Research Asia, Beijing, P.R.C., 100080
{minchu,yushli,xinz,frankkps}@microsoft.com

Abstract. To embrace the coming age of rich Internet applications and to enrich applications with voice, we propose a Voice Internet Persona (VIP) service. Unlike current text-to-speech (TTS) applications, in which users need to painstakingly install TTS engines in their own machines and do all customizations by themselves, our VIP service consists of a simple, easy-to-use platform that enables users to voice-empower their content, such as podcasts or voice greeting cards. We offer three user interfaces for users to create and tune new VIPs with built-in tools, share their VIPs via this new platform, and generate expressive speech content with selected VIPs. The goal of this work is to popularize TTS features to additional scenarios such as entertainment and gaming with the easy-to-access VIP platform.

Keywords: Voice Internet Persona, Text-to-Speech, Rich Internet Application.

1 Introduction

The field of text-to-speech (TTS) conversion has seen a great increase in both research community and commercial applications over the past decade. Recent progress in unit-selection speech synthesis [1-3] and Hidden Markov Model (HMM) speech synthesis [4-6] has led to considerably more natural-sounding synthetic speech that is suitable for many applications. However, only a small part of these applications have had TTS features. One of the key barriers for popularizing TTS in various applications is the technical difficulty in installing, maintaining and customizing a TTS engine. In this paper, we propose a TTS service platform, the *Voice Internet Persona* (VIP), which we hope will provide an easy-to-use platform for users to voice-empower their content or applications at any time and anywhere.

Currently, when a user wants to integrate TTS into an application, he has to search the engine providers, pick one from the available choices, buy a copy of the software, and install it on his machines. He or his team has to understand the software. The installing, maintaining and customizing of a TTS engine can be a tedious process. Once a user has made a choice of a TTS engine, he has limited flexibility in choosing voices. It is not easy to demand a new voice unless one wishes to pay for additional development costs. It is virtually impossible for an individual user to have multiple TTS engines with dozens or hundreds voices for use in applications. With the VIP platform, users will not be bothered by technical issues. All their operations would be

J. Jacko (Ed.): Human-Computer Interaction, Part III, HCII 2007, LNCS 4552, pp. 40–49, 2007.

encompassed in the VIP platform, including selecting, employing, creating and managing the VIPs. Users could access the service when they require TTS features. They could browse or search the VIP pool to find the voice they like and use it in their applications, or easily change it to another VIP or use multiple VIPs in the same application. Users could even create their own private voices through a simple interface and built-in tools.

The target users of the VIP service include Web-based service providers such as voice greeting card companies, as well as numerous individual users who regularly or occasionally create voice content such as Podcasts or photo annotations.

This paper is organized as the follows. In Section 2, the design philosophy is introduced. The architecture of the VIP platform is described in Section 3. In Section 4, the TTS technologies and voice-morphing technologies that would be used are introduced. A final discussion is in Section 5.

2 The Design Philosophy

In the VIP platform, multiple TTS engines are installed. Most of them have multiple built-in voices and support some voice-morphing algorithms. These resources are maintained and managed by the service provider. Users will not be involved in technical details such as choosing, installing, and maintaining TTS engines and would not have to worry about how many TTS engines were running and what morphing algorithms would be supported. All user-related operations would be organized around the core object — the VIP.

VIP is an object with many properties, including a greeting sentence, its gender, the age range it represents, the TTS engine it uses, the language it speaks, the base voice it is derived from, the morphing targets it supports, the morphing target that is applied, its parent VIP, its owner and popularity, etc. Each VIP has a unique name, through which users can access it in their applications. Some VIP properties are exposed to users in a VIP *name card* to help identify a particular VIP. New VIPs are easily derived from existing ones by inheriting main properties and overwriting some of them. Within the platform, there is a VIP pool that includes base VIPs to represent all base voices supported by all TTS engines and derived VIPs that are created by applying a morphing target on a base VIP.

The underlying voice-morphing algorithms are rather complicated because different TTS engines support different algorithms and there are many free parameters in each algorithm. Only a small portion of the possible combinations of all free parameters will generate meaningful morphing effects. It's too time-consuming to understand and master these parameters for most users. Instead, a set of morphing targets that is easily understood to users are designed. Each target is attached with several pre-tuned parameter sets, representing the morphing degree or directions. All technical details are hidden from users. What a user would do is pick up a morphing target and select a set of parameters. For example, users can increase or decrease the pitch level and the speech rate, can convert a female voice to a male voice or vice versa, convert a normal voice to a robot-like voice, add a venue effect such as *in the valley* or *under the sea*, or make a Mandarin Chinese voice render Ji'nan or Xi'an dialect. Users will hear a synthetic example immediately after each change in morphing targets or parameters. Currently, four types of morphing targets, as listed in Table 1, are supported in the VIP platform. The technical details on morphing algorithms and parameters are introduced in Section 4.

Table 1. The morphing targets supported in the current VIP platform

Speaking style	Speaker	Accent from local dialect	Venue of speaking
Pitch level	Man-like	Ji'nan accent	Broadcast
Speech rate	Girl-like	Luoyang accent	Concert hall
Sound scared	Child-like	Xi'an accent	In valley
	Hoarse or Reedy	Southern accent	Under sea
	Bass-like		
	Robot-like		
	Foreigner-like		

The goal of the VIP service is to make TTS easily understood and accessible for anyone, anywhere so that more and more users would like to use Web applications with speech content. With this design philosophy, a VIP-centric architecture is designed to allow users to access, customize, and exchange VIPs.

3 Architecture of the VIP Platform

The architecture of the VIP platform is shown in Fig. 1. Users interact with the platform through three interfaces designed for employing, creating and managing VIPs. Only the VIP pool and the morphing target pool are exposed to users. Other resources like TTS engines and their voices are invisible to users and can only be accessed indirectly via VIPs. The architecture allows adding new voices, new languages, and new TTS engines. The three user interfaces are described in Subsection 3.1 to 3.3 below and the underlying technologies in TTS and voice-morphing are introduced in Section 4.

3.1 VIP Employment Interface

The VIP employment interface is simple. Users insert a VIP name tag before the text they want spoken and the tag takes effect until the end of the text unless another tag is encountered. A sample script for creating speech with VIPs is shown in Table 2. After the tagged text is sent to the VIP platform, it is converted to speech with the appointed VIPs and the waveform is delivered back to the users. This is provided along with additional information such as the phonetic transcription of the speech and the phone boundaries aligned to the speech waveforms if they are required. Such information can be used to drive lip-syncing of a talking head or to visualize the speech and script in speech learning applications.

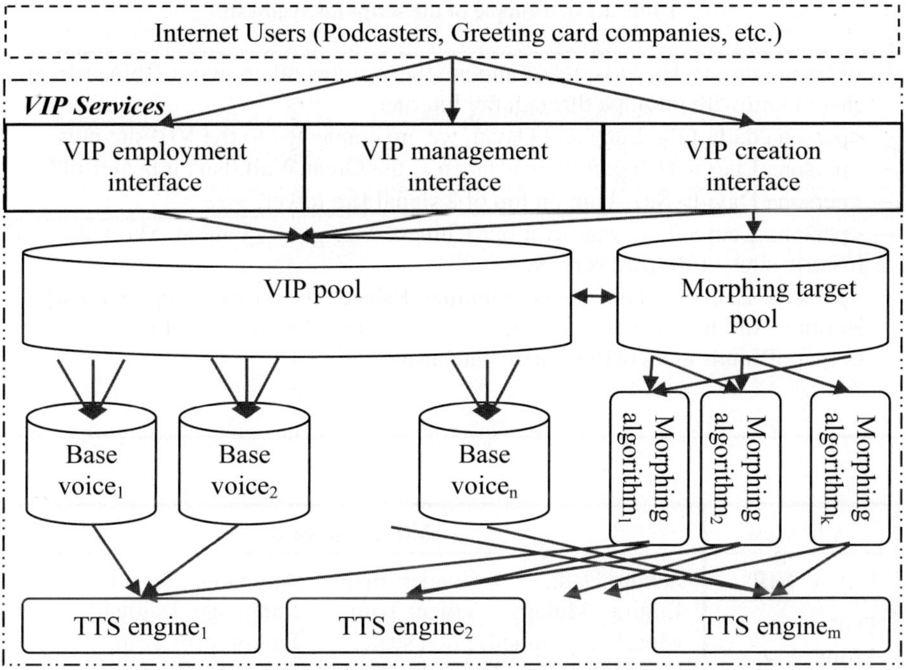

Fig. 1. Architecture of the VIP platform

3.2 VIP Creation Interface

Fig. 2 shows the VIP creation interface. The right window is the VIP view, which consists of a public VIP list and a private list. Users can browse or search the two lists, select a seed VIP and make a clone of one under a new name. The top window shows the name card of the focused VIP. Some properties in the view, such as gender and age range, can be directly modified by the creator. Others have to be overwritten through built-in functions. For example, when the user changes a morphing target, the corresponding field in the name card is adjusted accordingly. The large central window is the morphing view, showing all morphing targets and pre-tuned parameter sets. Users can choose one parameter set in one target as well as clear the morphing setting. After a user finishes the configuration of a new VIP, its name card is sent to the server for storage and the new VIP is shown in his private view.

3.3 VIP Management Interface

After a user creates a new VIP, the new VIP is only accessible to the creator unless the creator decides to share it with others. Through the VIP management interface, users can edit, group, delete, and share their private VIPs. User can also search VIPs by their properties, such as all female VIPs, VIPs for teenage or old men, etc.

Table 2. An example of the script for synthesis

- <persona mom> Hi, kids, let's annotate the pictures taken in our China trip and share them with grandpa through the Internet.
- <persona dad> OK. Lucy and David, we are connected to the VIP site now.
- <persona Lucy> This picture was taken at the Great Wall. Isn't it beautiful?
- <persona David> See, I am on top of a signal fire tower.
- <persona Lucy> This was with our Chinese tour guide, Lanlan. She knows all historic sites in Beijing very well.
- <persona Lanlan> This is the Summer Palace, the largest imperial park in Beijing. And here is the Center Court Area, where Dowager and Emperor used to met officials and conduct their state affairs.

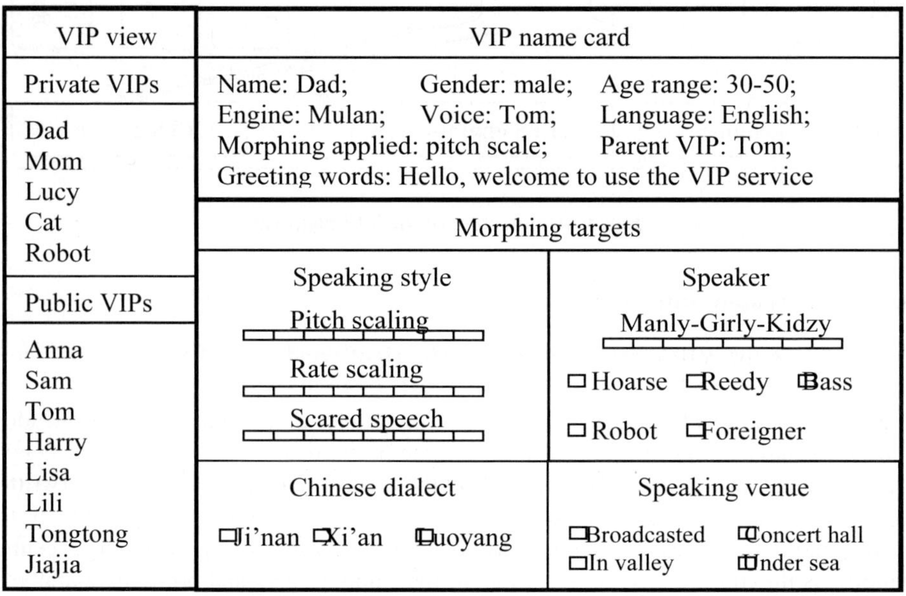

Fig. 2. The interface for creating new VIPs

4 Underlying Component Technologies

4.1 TTS Technologies

There are two TTS engines installed in the current deployment of VIP platform. One is Microsoft Mulan [7], a unit selection based system in which a sequence of waveform segments are selected from a large speech database by optimizing a cost function. These segments are then concatenated one-by-one to form a new utterance.

The other is an HMM-based system [8]. In this system, context dependent phone HMMs have been pre-trained from a speech corpus. In the run-time system, trajectories of spectral parameters and prosodic features are first generated with constraints from statistical models [5] and are then converted to a speech waveform.

4.2 Unit-Selection Based TTS

In a unit-selection based TTS system, naturalness of synthetic speech, to a great extent, depends on the goodness of the cost function as well as the quality of the unit inventory.

Cost Function

Normally, the cost function contains two components, the target cost, which estimates the difference between a database unit and a target unit, and the concatenation cost, which measures the mismatch across the joint boundary of consecutive units. The total cost of a sequence of speech units is the sum of the target costs and the concatenation costs.

In early work [2,9], acoustic measures, such as Mel Frequency Cepstrum Coefficients (MFCC), f_0, power and duration, were used to measure the distance between two units of the same phone type. All units of the same phone are clustered by their acoustic similarity. The target cost for using a database unit in the given context is then defined as the distance of the unit to its cluster center, i.e. the cluster center is believed to represent the target values of acoustic features in the context. With such a definition for target cost, there is a connotative assumption, i.e. for any given text, there always exists a best acoustic realization in speech. However, this is not true in human speech. In [10], it was reported that even under highly restricted condition, i.e., when the same speaker reads the same set of sentences under the same instruction, rather large variations are still observed in phrasing sentences as well as in forming f_0 contours. Therefore, in Mulan, no f_0 and duration targets are predicted for a given text. Instead, contextual features (such as word position within a phrase, syllable position within a word, Part-of-Speech (POS) of a word, etc.) that have been used to predict f_0 and duration targets in conventional studies are used in calculating the target cost directly. The connotative assumption for this cost function is that speech units spoken in similar context are prosodically equivalent to one another in unit selection if we do have a suitable description of the context.

Since, in Mulan, speech units are always joint at phone boundaries, which are the rapid change areas of spectral features, the distances between spectral features at the two sides of the joint boundary is not an optimal measure for the goodness of concatenation. A rather simple concatenation cost is defined in [10]: the continuity for splicing two segments is quantized into four levels: 1) continuous — if two tokens are continuous segments in the unit inventory, the target cost is set to 0; 2) semi-continuous — though two tokens are not continuous in the unit inventory, the discontinuity at their boundary is often not perceptible, like splicing of two voiceless segments (such as /s/+/t/), a small cost is assigned.; 3) weakly discontinuous — discontinuity across the concatenation boundary is often perceptible, yet not very strong, like the splicing between a voiced segment and an unvoiced segment (such as /s/+/ a:/) or vice versa, a moderate cost is used; 4) strongly discontinuous — the discontinuity across the splicing boundary is perceptible and annoying, like the splicing between voiced segments, a large cost is assigned. Type 1 and 2 are preferred in concatenation and the 4th type should be avoided as much as possible.

Unit Inventory

The goal of unit selection is to find a sequence of speech units that minimize the overall cost. High-quality speech will be generated only when the cost of the selected unit sequence is low enough [11]. In other words, only when the unit inventory is large enough so that we always can find a good enough unit sequence for a given text, we will get natural sounding speech. Therefore, creating a high-quality unit inventory is crucial for unit-selection based TTS systems.

The whole process of the collection and annotation of a speech corpus is rather complicated and contains plenty of minutiae that should be handled carefully. In fact, in many stages, human interference such as manually checking or labeling is necessary. Creating a high-quality TTS voice is not an easy task even for a professional team. That is why most state-of-the-art unit selection systems can provide only a few voices. In [12], a uniform paradigm for creating multi-lingual TTS voice databases with focuses on technologies that reduce the complexity and manual work load of the task has been proposed. With such a platform, adding new voices to Mulan becomes relatively easier. Many voices have been created from carefully designed and collected speech corpus (>10 hour of speech) as well as from some available audio resources such as audio books in the public domain. Besides, several personalized voices are built from small, office recording speech corpus, each consisting of about 300 carefully designed sentences read by our colleagues. The large foot-print voices sound rather natural in most situations, while the small ones sound acceptable only in specific domains.

The advantage of unit selection based approach is that all voices can reproduce the main characteristics of the original speakers, in both timber and speaking style. The disadvantages of such systems are that sentences containing unseen context will have discontinuity problem sometime and these systems have less flexibility in changing speakers, speaking styles or emotions. The discontinuity problem becomes more severe when the unit inventory is small.

4.3 HMM Based TTS

To achieve more flexibility in TTS systems, the HMM-based approach has been proposed [1-3]. In such a system, speech waveforms are represented by a source-filter model. Both excitation parameters and spectral parameters are modeled by context dependent HMMs. The training process is similar to that in speech recognition. The main difference lies in the description of context. In speech recognition, normally only the phones immediately before and after the current phone are considered. However, in speech synthesis, all context features that have been used in unit selection systems can be used. Besides, a set of state duration models are trained to capture the temporal structure of speech. To handle the data scarcity problem, a decision tree based clustering method is applied to tie context dependent HMMs. During synthesis, a given text is first converted to a sequence of context-dependent units in the same way as it is done in a unit-selection system. Then, a sentence HMM is constructed by concatenating context-dependent unit models. Then, a sequence of speech parameters, including both spectral parameters and prosodic parameters, are generated by maximizing the output probability for the sentence HMM. Finally, these parameters are converted to a speech waveform through a source-filter synthesis model. In [3], mel-cepstral coefficients are used to represent speech spectrum. In our system [8], Line Spectrum Pair (LSP) coefficients are used.

The requirement for designing, collecting and labeling of speech corpus for training a HMM-based voice is almost the same as that for a unit-selection voice, except that the HMM voice can be trained from a relative small corpus and still maintains reasonably good quality. Therefore, all speech corpus used by the unit-selection system are used to train HMM voices.

Speech generated with the HMM system is normally stable and smooth. The parametric representation of speech gives us good flexibility to modify the speech. However, like all vocoded speech, speech generated from the HMM system often sounds buzzy. It is not easy to draw a simple conclusion on which approach is better, unit selection or HMM. In certain circumstance, one may outperform the other. Therefore, we installed both engines in the platform and delay the decision-making process to a time when users know better what they want do.

4.4 Voice-Morphing Algorithms

Three voice-morphing algorithms, sinusoidal-model based morphing, source-filter model based morphing and phonetic transition, are supported in this platform. Two of them seek to enable pitch, time and spectrum modifications and are used by the unit-selection based systems and HMM-based systems. The third one is designed for synthesis dialect accents with the standard voice in the unit selection based system.

4.5 Sinusoidal-Model Based Morphing

To achieve flexible pitch and spectrum modifications in unit-selection based TTS system, the first morphing algorithm is operated on the speech waveform generated by the TTS system. Internally, the speech waveforms are still converted into parameters through a Discrete Fourier Transforms. To avoid the difficulties in voice/unvoice detection and pitch tracking, a uniformed sinusoidal representation of speech, shown as in Eq. (1), is adopted.

$$S_i(n) = \sum_{l=1}^{L_l} A_l \cdot \cos[\omega_l n + \theta_l] \tag{1}$$

where A_l, ω_l and θ_l are the amplitudes, frequencies and phases of the sinusoidal components of speech signal $S_i(n)$, L_i is the number of components considered. These parameters are obtained as described in [13] and can be modified separately.

For pitch scaling, the central frequencies of all components are scaled up or down by the same factor simultaneously. Amplitudes of new components are sampled from the spectral envelop formed by interpolating A_l. All phrases are kept as before. For formant position adjustment, the spectral envelop forms by interpolating between

A_l is stretched or compressed toward the high-frequency end or the low-frequency end by a uniformed factor. With this method, we can increase or decrease the formant frequencies together, yet we are not able to adjust the individual formant location. In the morphing algorithm, the phase of sinusoidal components can be set to random values to achieve whisper or hoarse speech. The amplitudes of even or odd components can be attenuated to achieve some special effects.

Proper combination of the modifications of different parameters will generate the desired style, speaker morphing targets listed in Table 1. For example, if we scale up the pitch by a factor 1.2-1.5 and stretch the spectral envelop by a factor 1.05-1.2, we are able to make a male voice sound like a female. If we scale down the pitch and set the random phase for all components, we will get a hoarse voice.

4.6 Source-Filter Model Based Morphing

Since in the HMM-based system, speech has been decomposed to excitation and spectral parameters. Pitch scaling and formant adjustment is easy to achieve by adjusting the frequency of excitation or spectral parameters directly. The random phase and even/odd component attenuation are not supported in this algorithm. Most morphing targets in style morphing and speaker morphing can be achieved with this algorithm.

4.7 Phonetic Transition

The key idea of phonetic transition is to synthesize closely related dialects with the standard voice by mapping the phonetic transcription in the standard language to that in the target dialect. This approach is valid only when the target dialect shares similar phonetic system with the standard language.

A rule-based mapping algorithm has been built to synthesize Ji'nan, Xi'an and Luoyang dialects in China with a Mandarin Chinese voice. It contains two parts, one for phone mapping, and the other for tone mapping. In the on-line system, the phonetic transition module is added after the text and prosody analysis. After the unit string in Mandarin is converted to a unit string representing the target dialect, the same unit selection is used to generate speech with the Mandarin unit inventory.

5 Discussions

The conventional TTS applications include call center, email reader, and voice reminder, etc. The goal of such applications is to convey messages. Therefore, in most state-of-the-art TTS systems, broadcast style voices are provided. With the coming age of rich internet applications, we would like to popularize TTS features to more scenarios such as entertainment, casual recording and gaming with our easy-to-access VIP platform. In these scenarios, users often have diverse requirements for voices and speech styles, which are hard to fulfill in the traditional way of using TTS software. With the VIP platform, we can incrementally add new TTS engines, new base voices and new morphing algorithms without affecting users. Such a system is able to provide users enough diversity in speakers, speaking styles and emotions.

In the current stage, new VIPs are created by applying voice-morphing algorithms on provided bases voices. In the next step, we will extend the support to build new voices from user-provided speech waveforms. We also look into opportunities to deliver voice in other applications via our programming interface.

References

1. Wang, W.J., Campbell, W.N., Iwahashi, N., Sagisaka, Y.: Tree-Based Unit Selection for English Speech Synthesis. In: Proc. of ICASSP-1993, Minneapolis, vol.2, pp. 191–194 (1993)
2. Hunt, A.J., Black, A.W.: Unit Selection in a Concatentive Speech Synthesis System Using a Large Speech Database. In: Proc. of ICASSP- 1996, Atlanta, vol. 1, pp. 373–376 (1996)
3. Chu, M., Peng, H., Yang, H.Y., Chang, E.: Selecting Non-Uniform Units from a Very Large Corpus for Concatenative Speech Synthesizer. In: Proc. of ICASSP-2001, Salt Lake City, vol. 2, pp. 785–788 (2001)
4. Yoshimura, T., Tokuda, K., Masuku, T., Kobayashi, T., Kitamura, T.: Simultaneous Modeling Spectrum, Pitch and Duration in HMM-based Speech Synthesis. In: Proc. of European Conference on Speech Communication and Technology, Budapest, vol. 5, pp. 2347–2350
5. Tokuda, K., Kobayashi, T., Masuko, T., Kobayashi, T., Kitamura, T.: Speech Parameter Generation Algorithms for HMM-based Speech Synthesis. In: Proc. of ICASSP-2000, Istanbul, vol. 3, pp. 1315–1318 (2000)
6. Tokuda, K., Zen, H., Black, A.W.: An HMM-based Speech Synthesis System Applied to English. In: Proc. of 2002 IEEE Speech Synthesis Workshop, Santa Monica, pp. 11–13 (2002)
7. Chu, M., Peng, H., Zhao, Y., Niu, Z., Chang, E.: Microsoft Mulan — a bilingual TTS systems. In: Proc. of ICASSP-2003, Hong Kong, vol. 1, pp. 264-267 (2003)
8. Qian, Y., Soong, F., Chen, Y.N., Chu, M.: An HMM-Based Mandarin Chinese Text-to-Speech System. In: Huo, Q., Ma, B., Chng, E.-S., Li, H. (eds.) ISCSLP 2006. LNCS (LNAI), vol. 4274, pp. 223–232. Springer, Heidelberg (2006)
9. Black, A.W., Taylor, P.: Automatic Clustering Similar Units for Unit Selection in Speech Synthesis. In: Proc. of Eurospeech-1997, Rhodes, vol. 2, pp. 601–604 (1997)
10. Chu, M., Zhao, Y., Chang, E.: Modeling Stylized Invariance and Local Variability of Prosody in Text-to-Speech Synthesis. Speech Communication 48(6), 716–726 (2006)
11. Chu, M., Peng, H.: An Objective Measure for Estimating MOS of Synthesized Speech. In: Proc. of Eurospeech-2001, Aalborg, pp. 2087–2090 (2001)
12. Chu, M., Zhao, Y., Chen, Y.N., Wang, L.J., Soong, F.: The Paradigm for Creating Multi-Lingual Text-to-Speech Voice Database. In: Huo, Q., Ma, B., Chng, E.-S., Li, H. (eds.) ISCSLP 2006. LNCS (LNAI), vol. 4274, pp. 736–747. Springer, Heidelberg (2006)
13. McAulay, R.J., Quatieri, T.F: Speech Analysis/Synthesis Based on a Sinusoidal Representation. IEEE Trans. ASSP-34(4), 744–754 (1986)

Using Recurrent Fuzzy Neural Networks for Predicting Word Boundaries in a Phoneme Sequence in Persian Language

Mohammad Reza Feizi Derakhshi and Mohammad Reza Kangavari

Computer engineering faculty, University of science and technology of Iran, I.R. Iran
{m_feizi,kangavari}@iust.ac.ir

Abstract. The word boundary detection has an application in speech processing systems. The problem this paper tries to solve is to separate words of a sequence of phonemes where there is no delimiter between phonemes. In this paper, at first, a recurrent fuzzy neural network (RFNN) together with its relevant structure is proposed and learning algorithm is presented. Next, this RFNN is used to predict word boundaries. Some experiments have already been implemented to determine complete structure of RFNN. Here in this paper, three methods are proposed to encode input phoneme and their performance have been evaluated. Some experiments have been conducted to determine required number of fuzzy rules and then performance of RFNN in predicting word boundaries is tested. Experimental results show an acceptable performance.

Keywords: Word boundary detection, Recurrent fuzzy neural network (RFNN), Fuzzy neural network, Fuzzy logic, Natural language processing, Speech processing.

1 Introduction

In this paper an attempt is made to solve the problem of word boundary detection by employing Recurrent Fuzzy Neural Network (RFNN). This needs a required number of delimiters that should be inserted into the given sequence of phonemes. In so doing, the essential step to be taken is to detect word boundaries. This is the place where a delimiter should be inserted. The word boundary detection has an application in speech processing systems, where a speech recognition system generates a sequence of phonemes which form speech. It is necessary to separate words of the generated sequence before going through further phases of speech processing.

Figure 1 illustrates general model for continuous speech recognition systems [10, 11]. As we can see, at first a preprocessing occurs to extract features. Output of this phase is feature vectors which are sent to phoneme recognition (acoustic decoder) phase. In this phase feature vectors are converted to phoneme sequence. Later, the phoneme sequence enters the "phoneme to word decoder block" where it is converted to word sequence [10]. Finally word sequence is delivered to linguistic decoder phase

J. Jacko (Ed.): Human-Computer Interaction, Part III, HCII 2007, LNCS 4552, pp. 50–59, 2007.

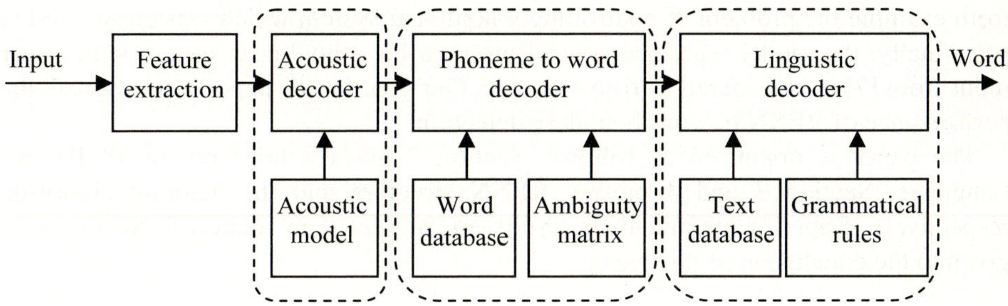

Fig. 1. General model for continuous speech recognition systems [10]

which tests grammatical correctness [10, 12]. The problem under this study is placed in a phoneme to word decoder.

In most of current speech recognition systems, phoneme to word decoding is done by using word database. Within these systems, the word database is stored in structures such as lexical tree or Markov model. However, in this study the attempt is made to look for an alternative method that is able to do decoding without using word database. Although using word database can reduce error rate, it is useful to be independent from word database in some applications; when, for instance, a small number of words in a great volume of speech with large vocabulary (e.g. news) is sought. In such application, it is not economical to make a system with large vocabulary to search for only small number of words. It should be noted that it is necessary to make a model for each word. It is not only unaffordable to construct these models, but the large number of models also require a lot of run time to make a search. While making use of a system which can separate words independent of word database, appears to be very useful since it is possible to make word models of a small number of words and to avoid from unnecessary complications. However, these word models are still needed with a difference that search in word models can be postponed to next phase where word boundaries determined with some uncertainty. Thus, the word which is looked for can be found faster and with a less cost.

Previous works on English language have low performance in this field [3] whereas the works on Persian language seems to have acceptable performance, for there are structural differences between Persian and English language system [15]. (See section 2 for some differences in syllable patterns) Our [8, 9] and others [10] previous works confirm this.

In general, the system should detect boundaries considering all phonemes of input sequence. In order to make the work simple, the problem is reduced to making decision about existence of boundary after current phoneme given the previous phonemes. Since the system should predict existence of boundary after current phoneme it is a time series prediction problem.

Lee and Teng in [1], used five examples to show that RFNN is able to solve time series prediction problems. In the first example, they solve simple sequence prediction problem found in [3]. Second, they solve a problem from [6] in which the current output of the planet is a nonlinear transform of its inputs and outputs with multiple time delay. As third example, they test a chaotic system from [5]. They consider in forth example the problem of controlling a nonlinear system which was considered in [6]. Finally, the model reference control problem for a nonlinear system with linear input from [7] is considered as fifth example. Our goal in this paper is to evaluate the performance of RFNN in word boundary detection.

The paper is organized as follows. Section 2 gives a brief review of Persian Language. Section 3 and 4 present RFNN structure and the learning algorithm respectively. Experiments and their results are presented in section 5. Section 6 is given to the conclusion of this paper.

2 A Brief Review of Persian Language

Persian or Farsi (as called sometimes by some scholar interchangeably) was the language of Parsa people who ruled Iran between 550-330 BC. It belongs to Indo-Iranian branch of Indo-European languages. It became the language of the Persian Empire and was widely spoken in the ancient days ranging from the borders of India in the east, Russia in the north, the southern shore of Persian Gulf to Egypt and the Mediterranean in the west. It was the language of the court of many of the Indian Kings till British banned its use after occupying India in the 18 century [14].

Over the centuries Persian has changed to its modern form and today it is spoken primarily in Iran, Afghanistan, Tajikistan and part of Uzbekistan. It was a more widely understood language in an area ranging from Middle East to India [14].

Syllable pattern of Persian language can be presented as:

$$\text{cv(c(c))}^{1} \tag{1}$$

This means a syllable in Persian has 2 phonemes at its minimum length (cv) and 4 phonemes at maximum (cvcc). Also, it should start with a consonant. In contrast, syllable pattern of English language can be presented as:

$$\text{(c(c(c)))v(c(c(c(c))))} \tag{2}$$

As it can be seen minimum syllable length in English is 1 (a single vowel) while maximum length is 8 (cccvcccc) [13]. Because words consists of syllables, it seems that simple syllable pattern of Persian language makes word boundary detection to be simpler in Persian language [15].

3 Structure of the Recurrent Fuzzy Neural Network (RFNN)

Ching-Hung Lee and Ching-Cheng Teng introduced a 4 layered RFNN in [1]. We used that network in this paper. Figure 2 illustrates the configuration of the proposed RFNN. This network consists of *n* input variables, $m \times n$ membership nodes (*m*-term nodes for each input variable), *m* rule nodes, and *p* output nodes. Therefore, RFNN consists of $n + m.n + m + p$ nodes, where *n* denotes number of inputs, *m* denotes the number of rules and *p* denotes the number of outputs.

[1] C indicates consonant, v indicates vowel and parentheses indicate optional elements.

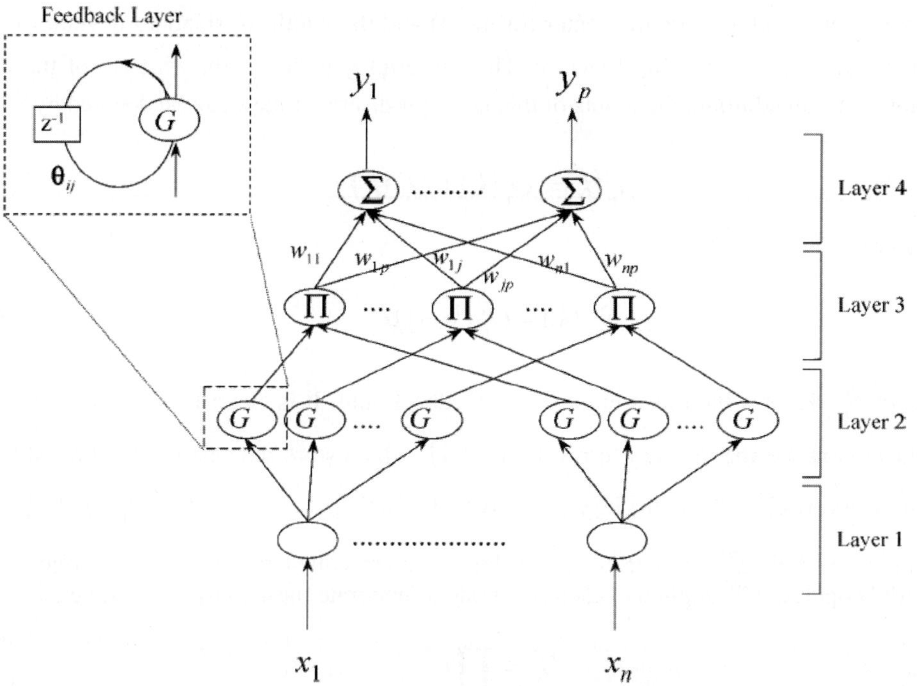

Fig. 2. The configuration of the proposed RFNN [1]

3.1 Layered Operation of the RFNN

This section presents operation of nodes in each layer. In the following description, u_i^k denotes the *i*th input of a node in the *k*th layer; O_i^k denotes the *i*th node output in layer *k*.

Layer 1: Input Layer: Nodes of this layer are designed to accept input variables. So output of these nodes is the same as their input, i.e.,

$$O_i^1 = u_i^1 \tag{3}$$

Layer 2: Membership Layer: In this layer, each node has two tasks simultaneously. First it performs a membership function and second it acts as a unit of memory. The Gaussian function is adopted here as a membership function. Thus, we have

$$O_{ij}^2 = \exp\left\{-\frac{(u_{ij}^2 - m_{ij})^2}{(\sigma_{ij})^2}\right\} \tag{4}$$

where m_{ij} and σ_{ij} are the center (or mean) and the width (or standard deviation) of the Gaussian membership function. The subscript *ij* indicates the *j*th term of the *i*th input x_i. In addition, the inputs of this layer for discrete time *k* can be denoted by

$$u_{ij}^2(k)=O_i^1(k)+O_{ij}^f(k) \tag{5}$$

where

$$O_{ij}^f(k)=O_{ij}^2(k-1).\theta_{ij} \tag{6}$$

and θ_{ij} denotes the link weight of the feedback unit. It is clear that the input of this layer contains the memory terms $O_{ij}^2(k-1)$, which store the past information of the network. Each node in this layer has three adjustable parameters: m_{ij}, σ_{ij}, and θ_{ij}.

Layer 3: Rule Layer: The nodes in this layer are called rule nodes. The following AND operation is applied to each rule node to integrate these fan-in values, i.e.,

$$O_i^3=\prod_j u_{ij}^3 \tag{7}$$

The output O_i^3 of a rule node represents the "firing strength" of its corresponding rule.

Layer 4: Output Layer: Each node in this layer is called an output linguistic node. This layer performs the defuzzification operation. The node output is a linear combination of the consequences obtained from each rule. That is

$$y_j=O_j^4=\sum_{i=1}^{m}u_i^4\ w_{ij}^4 \tag{8}$$

where $u_i^4=O_i^3$ and w_{ij}^4 (the link weight) is the output action strength of the *j*th output associated with the *i*th rule. The w_{ij}^4 are the tuning factors of this layer.

3.2 Fuzzy Inference

A fuzzy inference rule can be proposed as

$$\begin{aligned} R^l: IF\ \ x_1\ is\ A_1^l \ldots x_n\ is\ A_n^l, \\ THEN\ \ y_1\ is\ B_1^l \ldots y_P\ \ is\ B_P^l \end{aligned} \tag{9}$$

RFNN network tries to implement such rules with its layers. But there is some difference! RFNN implements the rules in this way:

$$R^j: \quad IF \ u_{1j} \ is \ A_{1j},\ldots,u_{nj} \ is \ A_{nj} \\ THEN \ \ y_1 \ is \ B_1^j \ldots y_P \ is \ B_P^j \tag{10}$$

where $u_{ij} = x_i + O_{ij}^2(k-1).\theta_{ij}$ in which $O_{ij}^2(k-1)$ denotes output of second layer in previous level and θ_{ij} denotes the link weight of the feedback unit. That is, the input of each membership function is the network input x_i plus the temporal term $O_{ij}^2 \ \theta_{ij}$. This fuzzy system, with its memory terms (feedback units), can be considered as a dynamic fuzzy inference system and the inferred value is given by

$$y^* = \sum_{j=1}^{m} \alpha_j w_j \tag{11}$$

where $\alpha_j = \prod_{i=1}^{n} \mu_{A_{ij}}(u_{ij})$. From the above description, it is clear that the RFNN is a fuzzy logic system with memory elements.

4 Learning Algorithm for the Network

Learning goal is to minimize following cost function:

$$E(k) = \frac{1}{2}\sum_{i=1}^{P}(y_i(k) - \hat{y}_i(k))^2 = \frac{1}{2}\sum_{i=1}^{P}(y_i(k) - O_i^4(k))^2 \tag{12}$$

where $y(k)$ is the desired output and $\hat{y}(k) = O^4(k)$ is the current output for each discrete time *k*.

Well known error back propagation (EBP) algorithm is used to train the network. EBP algorithm can be written briefly as

$$W(k+1) = W(K) + \Delta W(k) = W(k) + \eta\left(-\frac{\partial E(k)}{\partial W}\right) \tag{13}$$

where *W* represents tuning parameters and η is the learning rate. As we know, tuning parameters of the RFNN are *m*, σ, θ and *w*. By applying the chain rule recursively, partial derivation of error with respect to above parameters can be calculated.

5 Experiments and Results

As it is mentioned, this paper tries to solve word boundary detection problem. System input is phoneme sequence and output is existence of word boundary after current phoneme. Because of memory element in RFNN, there is no need to hold previous phoneme in its input. So, the input of RFNN is a phoneme in the sequence and the output is the existence of boundary after this phoneme.

We used supervised learning as RFNN learning method. A native speaker of Persian language is used to produce a training set to train RFNN. He is supposed to determine word boundaries and marked them. The same process was done for test set but boundaries were hidden from the system.

Each of test set and training set consists of about 12000 phonemes from daily speeches in library environment.

As it is mentioned, network input is a phoneme but this phoneme should be encoded before any other process. Thus, to encode 29 phonemes [13] in standard Persian, three methods for phoneme encoding were used in our experiments. These are as follow:

1. Real coding: In this method, each phoneme mapped to a real number in the range [0, 1]. In this case, network input is a real number.
2. 1-of-the-29 coding: In this method, for each input phoneme we consider 29 inputs corresponding to 29 phonemes of Persian. At any time only one of these 29 inputs will set to one while others will set to zero. Therefore, in this method, network input consists of 29 bits.
3. Binary coding: In this method, ASCII code of phoneme used for phonetic transcription, is transformed to binary and then is fed into network inputs. Since only lower half of ASCII characters are used for transcription, 7 bits are sufficient for this representation. Thus, in this method network inputs consists of 7 bits.

Some experiments have been implemented to determine performance of above mentioned methods. Table 1 shows some of the results. Obviously, 1-of-the-29 coding is not only time consuming but also it yields a poor result. When comparing binary with real coding, it is shown that although real coding requires less training time, it has less performance. It is not the case with binary coding. Therefore, binary coding method should be selected for the network. So far, 7 bits for input and 1 bit for output has been confirmed, so, to determine complete structure of the network, the number of rules has to be determined.

The results of some experiments with different number of rules and epochs are presented in Table 2. The best performance considering training time and mean squared error (MSE) is obtained in 60 rules. Although in some cases increasing in rule numbers results in a decrease in MSE, this decrease in MSE is not worth network complication. However, over train problem should not be neglected.

Now, the RFNN structure is completely determined: 7 inputs, 60 rules and one output. So, the main experiment for determining performance of the RFNN in this problem has been done. The RFNN is trained with the training set; then is tested with test set. Network determined outputs are compared with oracle determined outputs.

Table 1. Training time and MSE error for different number of epochs for each coding method (h: hour, m: minute, s: second)

Encoding method	Num. of epochs	Training time	MSE
Real	2	3.66 s	0.60876
Real	20	32.42 s	0.59270
Real	200	312.61 s	0.58830
1 / 29	2	22 m	1
1 / 29	20	1 h, 16 m	1
Binary	2	11.50 s	0.55689
Binary	20	102.39 s	0.51020
Binary	200	17 m	0.46677
Binary	1000	1 h, 24 m	0.45816

Table 2. Some of experimental results to determine number of fuzzy rules (Training with 100 and 500 Epochs)

Number of rules	MSE - 100 Epoch	MSE - 500 Epoch
10	0.5452	0.5431
20	0.5455	0.5449
30	0.5347	0.5123
40	0.5339	0.5327
50	0.4965	0.4957
55	0.4968	0.4861
60	0.4883	0.4703
65	0.5205	0.5078
70	0.5134	0.4881
80	0.4971	0.4772
90	0.5111	0.4918
100	0.4745	0.4543

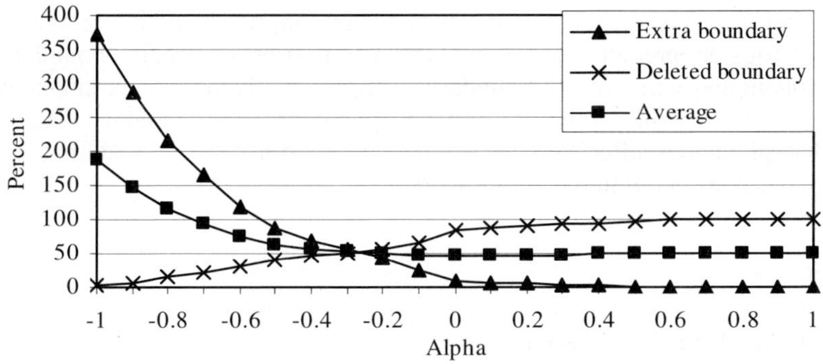

Fig. 3. Extra boundary (boundary in network output, not in test set), deleted boundary (boundary not in network output, but in test set) and average error for different values of α

The RFNN output is a real number in the range [-1, 1]. A hardlim function as follow is used to convert its output to a zero-one output.

$$T_i = \begin{cases} 1 & \text{if } O_i >= \alpha \\ 0 & \text{if } O_i < \alpha \end{cases} \quad (14)$$

where α is a predefined value and O_i determines *i*th output of network. Value one for T_i means existence of boundary and vice versa. Boundaries for different values of α are compared with oracle defined boundaries. Results are presented in Figure 3. It can be seen that the best result is produced when $\alpha = -0.1$ with average error rate 45.95%.

6 Conclusion

In this paper a Recurrent Fuzzy Neural Network was used for word boundary detection. Three methods are proposed for coding input phoneme: real coding, 1-of-the-29 coding and binary coding. The best performance in experimental results, were achieved when the binary coding had been used to code input. The optimum rules number was 60 rules as well.

Table 3. Comparison of results

Reference number	[3]	[8]	[9]	[10]
Error rate (Persent)	55.3	23.71	36.60	34

After completing network structure, experimental results showed average error 45.96% on test set which is an acceptable performance in compare with previous works [3, 8, 9, 10]. Table 3 presents error percentage of each reference. As it is seen, works on English language ([3]) have higher error than Persian language ([8, 9, 10]). Although other Persian works were resulted in lower error rate than ours, but it should be noted that there is a basic difference between our approach and the previous works. Our work tries to predict word boundary; i.e. it tries to predict boundary given previous phonemes while in [8], boundaries is detected given two next phonemes, and in [9], given one phoneme before and one phoneme after boundary. Therefore, it seems that phonemes after boundary have more information about that boundary which will be considered in our future work.

References

1. Lee, C.-H., Teng, C.-C.: Identification and control of dynamic systems using recurrent fuzzy neural networks. IEEE Transactions on Fuzzy Systems 8(4), 349–366 (2000)
2. Zhou, Y., Li, S., Jin, R.: A new fuzzy neural network with fast learning algorithm and guaranteed stability for manufacturing process control. Fuzzy sets and systems, vol.132, pp. 201–216 Elsevier (2002)

3. Harrington, J., Watson, G., Cooper, M.: Word boundary identification from phoneme sequence constraints in automatic continuous speech recognition. In: 12th conference on Computational linguistics (August 1988)
4. Santini, S., Bimbo, A.D., Jain, R.: Block-structured recurrent neural networks. Neural Networks 8(1), 135–147 (1995)
5. Chen, G., Chen, Y., Ogmen, H.: Identifying chaotic system via a wiener-type cascade model. IEEE Transaction on Control Systems, 29–36 (October 1997)
6. Narendra, K.S., Parthasarathy, K.: Identification and control of dynamical system using neural networks. IEEE Transaction on Neural Networks 1, 4–27 (1990)
7. Ku, C.C., Lee, K.Y.: Diagonal recurrent neural networks for dynamic systems control. IEEE Transaction on Neural Networks 6, 144–156 (1995)
8. Feizi Derakhshi, M.R., Kangavari, M.R.: Preorder fuzzy method for determining word boundaries in a sequence of phonemes. In: 6th Iranian Conference on Fuzzy Systems and 1st Islamic World Conference on Fuzzy Systems (Persian) (2006)
9. Feizi Derakhshi, M.R., Kangavari, M.R.: Inorder fuzzy method for determining word boundaries in a sequence of phonemes. In: 7th Conference on Intelligence Systems CIS 2005 (Persian) (2005)
10. Babaali, B., Bagheri, M., Hosseinzade, K., Bahrani, M., Sameti, H.: A phoneme to word decoder based on vocabulary tree for Persian continuous speech recognition. In: International Annual Computer Society of Iran Computer Conference (Persian) (2004)
11. Gholampoor, I.: Speaker independent Persian phoneme recognition in continuous speech. PhD thesis, Electrical Engineering Faculty, Sharif University of Technology (2000)
12. Deshmukh, N., Ganapathiraju, A., Picone, J.: Hierarchical Search for Large Vocabulary Conversational Speech Recognition. IEEE Signal Processing Magazine 16(5), 84–107 (1999)
13. Najafi, A.: Basics of linguistics and its application in Persian language. Nilufar Publication (1992)
14. Anvarhaghighi, M.: Transitivity as a resource for construal of motion through space. In: 32 ISFLC, Sydney University, Sydney, Australia (July 2005)
15. Feizi Derakhshi, M.R.: Study of role and effects of linguistic knowledge in speech recognition. In: 3rd conference on computer science and engineering (Persian) (2000)

Subjective Measurement of Workload Related to a Multimodal Interaction Task: NASA-TLX *vs.* Workload Profile

Dominique Fréard[1,2], Eric Jamet[1], Olivier Le Bohec[1], Gérard Poulain[2], and Valérie Botherel[2]

[1] Université Rennes 2, place Recteur Henri Le Moal
35000 Rennes, France
[2] France Telecom, 2 avenue Pierre Marzin
22307 Lannion cedex, France
{dominique.freard,eric.jamet,olivier.lebohec}@uhb.fr,
{dominique.freard,gerard.poulain,
valerie.botherel}@orange-ftgroup.com

Abstract. This paper addresses workload evaluation in the framework of a multimodal application. Two multidimensional subjective workload rating instruments are compared. The goal is to analyze the diagnostics obtained on four implementations of an applicative task. In addition, an Automatic Speech Recognition (ASR) error was introduced in one of the two trials. Eighty subjects participated in the experiment. Half of them rated their subjective workload with NASA-TLX and the other half rated it with Workload Profile (WP) enriched with two stress-related scales. Discriminant and variance analyses revealed a better sensitivity with WP. The results obtained with this instrument led to hypotheses on the cognitive activities of the subjects during interaction. Furthermore, WP permitted us to classify two strategies offered for error recovery. We conclude that WP is more informative for the task tested. WP seems to be a better diagnostic instrument in multimodal system conception.

Keywords: Human-Computer Dialogue, Workload Diagnostic.

1 Introduction

Multimodal interfaces offer the potential for creating rich services using several perceptive modalities and response modes. In the coming years, multimodal interfaces will be proposed for general public. From this perspective, it is necessary to address methodological aspects of new service developments and evaluations. This paper focuses on workload evaluation as an important parameter to consider in order refining the methodology.

In a multimodal dialoging system, various solutions can be encountered for implementation. All factors of complexity can be combined, such as verbal and non-verbal auditory feedback combined with a graphical view in a gestural and vocal command system. If not correctly designed, multimodal interfaces may easily

J. Jacko (Ed.): Human-Computer Interaction, Part III, HCII 2007, LNCS 4552, pp. 60–69, 2007.

increase user complexity and may conduct to disorientations and overloads. Therefore, an adapted instrument is necessary for workload diagnostic. For this reason, we compare two multidimensional subjective workload rating instruments. A brief analysis of spoken dialogue conditions is presented and used to propose four configurations for information presentation to the subjects. The discrimination of subjects is intended depending on the configuration used.

1.1 Methodology for Human-Computer Dialogue Study

The methodological framework for the study of dialogue is found in Clark's socio-cognitive model of dialogue [2]. This model analyses the process of communication between two interlocutors as a coordinated activity. Recently, Pickering and Garrod [10] proposed a mechanistic theory of dialogue and showed that coordination, called alignment, is achieved by priming mechanisms at different levels (semantic, syntactic, lexical, etc.). This raises the importance of the action-level in the analysis of cognitive activities during the process of communication. Inspired by these models, the methodology used in human-computer dialogue addresses communication success, performance and collaboration. Thus, for the diagnostic, the main indicators concern verbal behaviour (e.g. words, elocution) and general performance (e.g. success, duration).

In this framework, workload is a secondary indicator. For example, Le Bigot, Jamet, Rouet and Amiel [7] conducted a study on the role of communication modes and the effect of expertise. They showed (1) behavioural regularities to adapt to - more particularly experts tended to use vocal systems as tools and produced less collaborative verbal behaviour - and (2) an increase in subjective workload in vocal mode compared to written mode. In the same way, the present study paid attention to all relevant measures. The present paper focuses on subjective workload ratings. Our goal is to analyze objective parameters of the interaction and to manipulate them in different implementations. Workload is used to achieve the diagnostic.

1.2 Workload in Human-Computer Dialogue

Mental workload can be described by the demand placed on user's working memory during a task. Following this view, objective analysis of the task gives an idea of its difficulty. This method is used in cognitive load theory, in the domain of learning [12]. Cognitive load is estimated by the number of statements and productions necessary to handle in memory during the task. This calculation gives a quantitative estimate of task difficulty. The workload is postulated to be a linear function of the objective difficulty of the material, which is questionable.

Some authors focus on the behaviour resulting in temporary overloads. In the domain of human-computer dialogue, Baber et al. [1] focus on the modifications of user's speech production. They show an impact of load increases on verbal disfluencies, articulation rate, pauses and discourse content quality. The goal, for the authors, is to adapt the system's output or intended input when necessary. Detection of overloads is first needed. In this way, a technique using Bayesian networking has been used to interpret symptoms of workload [5]. This technique is used to interpret the overall indicators in the same model. Our goal in this paper is not to enable this kind of detection during a dialogue but to interpret workload resulting from different implementations of an application.

1.3 Workload Measurement

Workload measure can be reached with physiological clues, dual task protocol or subjective instruments. Dual task paradigms are excluded here because the domain of dialogue needs an ecological methodology, and disruption of the task is not desirable for the validity of studies. Physiological measures are powerful for their degree of precision, but it is difficult to select a representative measure. The ideal strategy would be to directly observe brain activity, which is not within the scope of this paper. In the domain of dialogue, subjective measures are more frequently used. For example, Baber et al. [1] and Le Bigot et al. [7] conduct the evaluation with NASA-TLX [3] since this questionnaire is considered as the standard tool for this use in Human Factors literature.

NASA-TLX. The NASA-TLX rating technique is a global and standardized workload rating *"that provides a sensitive summary of workload variations"* [3].

A model of the psychological structure of subjective workload was applied to build the questionnaire. This structure integrates objective physical, mental and temporal demands and their subject related factors into a composite experience of workload and ultimately an explicit workload rating. A set of 19 workload-related dimensions was extracted from this model and a consultation of users was conducted to select the most equivalent to workload factors. The set was reduced to 10 bipolar rating scales. Afterwards, these scales were used in 16 experiments with different kinds of tasks. Correlational and regression analyses were performed on the data obtained. The analyses identified a set of six most salient factors: (1) *mental demand*, (2) *physical demand*, (3) *temporal demand*, (4) *satisfaction* in performance, (5) *effort* and, (6) *frustration* level. These factors are relevant to the first model of the psychological structure of subjective workload.

The final procedure consists of two parts. First, after each task condition, the subject rates each of the six factors on a 20 point scale. Second, at the end, a pair-wise comparison technique is used to weigh the six scales. The overall calculation of task load index (TLX), for each task condition, is a weighted mean that uses the six rates for this condition and the six weights.

Workload Profile. Workload Profile (WP) [13] is based on the multiple resources model, proposed by Wickens [14]. In this model of attention, cognitive resources are organized in a cube divided into four dimensions: (1) *stage of processing* gives the direction: encoding as perception, central processing as thought and production of response. (2) *Modality* concerns encoding. (3) *Code* concerns encoding and central processing. (4) *Response mode* concerns outputs. With this model, a number of hypotheses are possible about intended performance. For example, if the information available for a task is presented with a certain code on a modality and needs to be translated in another code before giving the response, an increase of workload can be intended. The *time share hypothesis* is a second example. It supposes that it is difficult to share resources of an area in the cube between two tasks during the same time interval.

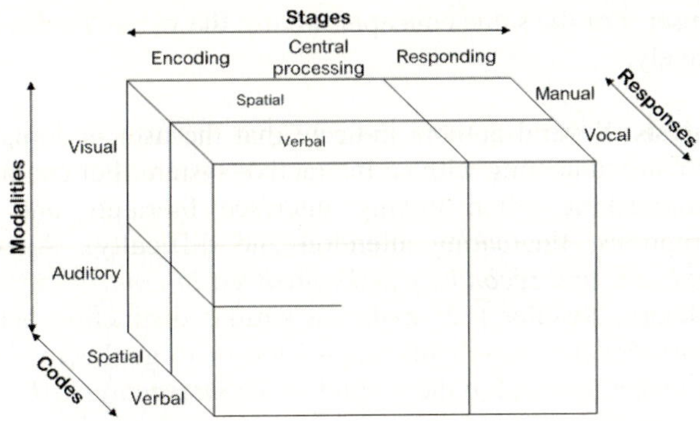

Fig. 1. Multiple resources model (Wickens, 1984)

The evaluation is based on the idea that subjects are able to directly rate (between 0 and 1) the amount of resources they spent in the different resource areas during the task. The original version, used by Tsang and Velasquez [13], is composed of eight scales corresponding to eight kinds of processing. Two are global: (1) *perceptive/central* and (2) *response processing*. Six concern directly a particular area: (3) *visual*, (4) *auditory*, (5) *spatial*, (6) *verbal*, (7) *manual response* and (8) *vocal response*.

A recent study from Rubio, Diaz, Martin and Puente [11] compared WP to NASA-TLX and SWAT. They used classical experimental tasks (Sternberg and tracking) and showed that WP was more sensitive to task difficulty. They also showed a better discrimination of the different task conditions with WP. We aim at replicating this result in an ecological paradigm.

2 Experiment

In Le Bigot et al's study [7] vocal mode corresponded to a telephonic conversation in which the user speaks (voice command) and the system responds with synthesised speech. On the opposite, the written mode corresponded to a chat conversation where the user types via keyboard (verbal commands only) and the system displays the verbal response on the screen. We aim at studying more detailed communication modes. The experiment focused on modal complementarity within output information: the user speaks in all configurations tested and the system responds in written, vocal or bimodal.

2.1 Analysis of Dialogic Interaction

Dialogue Turn: Types of Information. During the interaction, several kinds of information need to be communicated to the user. A categorization has been introduced by Nievergelt & Weydert [8] to differentiate *trails*, which refer to the past actions, *sites*, which correspond to the current action or information to give and *modes*, on the next possible actions. This distinction is also necessary when specifying a vocal system because, in this case, all information has to be given explicitly to the user. For the same concepts, we use the words *feedback*, *response* and *opening*, respectively.

Dual Task Analysis. Several authors indicate that the user is doing more than one single task when communicating with an interactive system. For example, Oviatt et al. [9] consider multitasking when mixing interface literature and cognitive load problems (interruptions, fluctuating attention and difficulty). Attention is shared *"between the field task and secondary tasks involved in controlling an interface"*. In cognitive load theory, Sweller [12] makes a similar distinction between cognitive processing capacity devoted to schema acquisition or to goal achievement. We refer to the first as the *target task* and to the second as the *interaction task.*

2.2 Procedure

Conforming to dual task analysis, we associate feedbacks with openings. They are supposed to belong to the interaction task. Responses correspond to the goal of the application, and they belong to the target task. Figure 2 represents the four configurations tested.

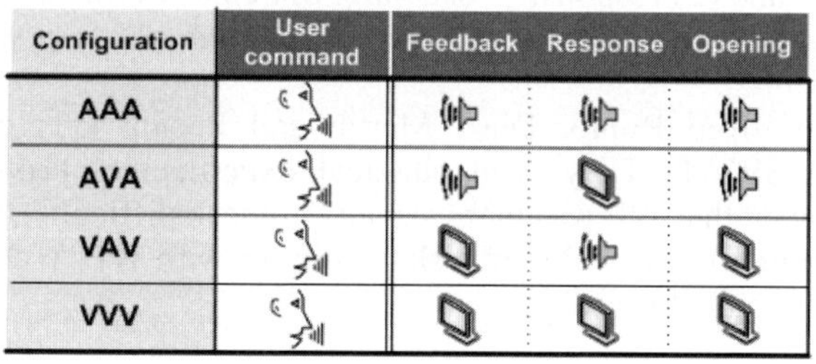

Fig. 2. Four configurations tested

Subjects and Factors. Eighty college students from 17 to 26 years (M=19, 10 males and 70 females) participated in the experiment. They all had little experience with speech recognition systems.

Two factors were tested: (1) *configuration* and (2) automatic speech recognition (ASR) *error during the trial.* Configuration was administered in *between-subjects.* This choice was made to obtain a rating linked to the subject's experience with the implementation of the system rather than an opinion on the different configurations. ASR error trial was *within-subjects* (one with and one without) and counterbalanced across the experiment.

Protocol and System Design. The protocol was *Wizard of Oz.* The system is dedicated to managing medical appointments for a hospital doctor. The configurations differed only in information modality, as indicated earlier. No redundancy was used.

The wizard accepted any word of vocabulary relevant for the task. Broadly speaking, this behaviour consisted in copying an ideal speech recognition model. When no valid vocabulary was used ("Hello, my name's..."), the wizard of Oz sent the auditory message: "I didn't understand. Please reformulate".

The optimal dialogue consisted of three steps: *request*, *response* and *confirmation*. (1) The *request* consisted of communicating two research criteria to the system: the name of the doctor and the desired day for the appointment. (2) The *response* phase consisted of choosing among a list of five responses. In this phase, it was also possible to correct the request ("No. I said Doctor Dubois, on Tuesday morning.") or to cancel and restart ("cancel"...). (3) When a response was chosen, the last phase required a *confirmation*. A negation conducted to a new diffusion of the response list. An affirmation conducted to a message of thanks and dialogue ending.

Workload Ratings. Half of the subjects (40) rated their subjective workload with the original version of the NASA-TLX. The other half rated the eight WP dimensions and two added dimensions inspired from Lazarus and Folkman's model of stress [6]: *frustration* and *loss of control feeling*.

Hypotheses. In contrast to Le Bigot et al [7], no keyboard was used and all user' commands were vocal. Hence, both mono-modal configurations (AAA and VVV) are intended to lead to equivalent ratings and bimodal configurations (AVA and VAV) are intended to decrease workload.

Given Rubio and al's [11] results, WP should provide a better ranking on the four configurations. WP may be explicative when NASA-TLX may only be descriptive. We argue that the overall measurement of workload with NASA-TLX leads to poor results. More precisely, the studies concluded that a task condition was more demanding than the other one [1, 7] and no more conclusions were reached. In particular, no questions emerged from the questionnaire itself giving reasons for workload increases, and no real diagnostic was made on this basis.

2.3 Results

For each questionnaire a first analysis was conducted with a canonical discriminant analysis procedure [for details, see 13] to examine the possibility to discriminate between conditions on the basis of all dependent variables taken together. Afterwards, a second analysis was conducted with ANOVA procedure.

Canonical Discriminant Analysis. NASA-TLX workload dimensions did not discriminate configurations since Lambda Wilks' was not significant (*Lambda Wilk* = 0,533; $F\ (18,88) = 1{,}21; p = .26$).

For WP dimensions a significant Lambda Wilks' was observed (*Lambda Wilk* = 0,207; $F\ (30,79) = 1{,}88;\ p < .02$). Root 1 was mainly composed of *auditory processing* (.18) opposed to *manual response* (-.48). Root 2 was composed of *frustration* (.17) and *perceptive/central processing* (-.46). Figure 3 illustrates these results. On root 1, the VVV configuration is opposed to the three others. On root 2, AAA configuration is the distinguishing feature. AVA and VAV configurations are more perceptive. The VVV configuration is more demanding manually, and the AAA configuration is more demanding centrally (perceptive/central).

ANOVAs. For the two dimension sets, the same ANOVA procedure was applied to the global index and to each isolated dimension. Global TLX index was calculated

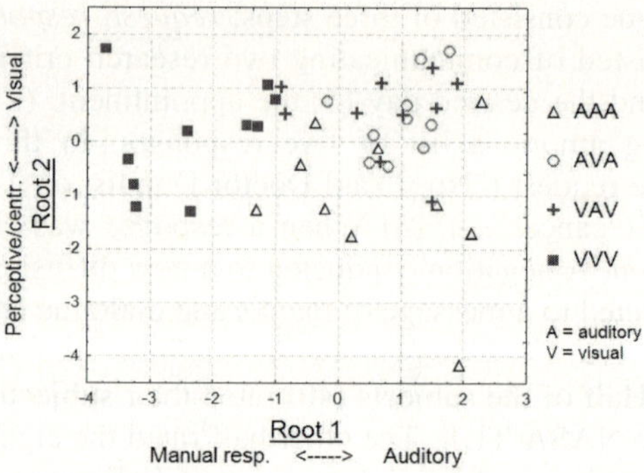

Fig. 3. Canonical discriminant analysis for WP

with the standard weighting mean [3]. For WP a simple mean was calculated including the two stress-related ratings. The plan tested configuration as the categorical factor and trial as a repeated measure. No interaction effect was observed between these factors in the comparisons. Thus, these results are not presented.

Effects of Configuration and Trial with TLX. The configuration produced no significant effect on TLX index ($F(3, 36) = 1{,}104$; $p = .36$; $\eta^2 = .084$) and no significant effect on any single dimension in this questionnaire. The trial gave neither significant effect on the global index ($F(1, 36) = 0{,}162$; $p = .68$; $\eta^2 = .004$) but among dimensions, some effects appeared: ASR error increased mental demand ($F(1, 36) = 11{,}13$; $p < .01$; $\eta^2 = .236$), temporal demand ($F(1, 36) = 4{,}707$; $p < .05$; $\eta^2 = .116$) and frustration ($F(1, 36) = 8{,}536$; $p < .01$; $\eta^2 = .192$); and decreased effort ($F(1, 36) = 4{,}839$; $p < .05$; $\eta^2 = .118$) and marginally satisfaction ($F(1, 36) = 3{,}295$; $p = .078$; $\eta^2 = .084$). Physical demand was not significantly modified ($F(1, 36) = 2{,}282$; $p = .14$; $\eta^2 = .060$). The opposed effect on effort and satisfaction in regard to other dimensions led global index to a weak representativity.

Effects of Configuration and Trial with WP. The configuration was not globally significant ($F(3, 36) = 1{,}105$; $p = .36$; $\eta^2 = .084$) but planed comparisons showed that AVA and VAV configurations gave a weaker mean than VVV configuration ($F(1, 36) = 4{,}415$; $p < .05$; $\eta^2 = .122$). The AAA and VVV configurations were not significantly different ($F(1, 36) = 1{,}365$; $p = .25$; $\eta^2 = .037$). Among dimensions, perceptive/central processing reacted like global mean: no global effect appeared ($F(3, 36) = 2{,}205$; $p < .10$; $\eta^2 = .155$) but planed comparisons showed that AVA and VAV configurations received weaker ratings compared to VVV configuration ($F(1, 36) = 5{,}012$; $p < .03$; $\eta^2 = .139$) ; and AAA configuration was not significantly different to VVV configuration ($F(1, 36) = 0{,}332$; $p = .56$; $\eta^2 = .009$). Three other dimensions showed sensitivity: spatial processing ($F(3, 36) = 3{,}793$; $p < .02$; $\eta^2 = .240$), visual processing ($F(3, 36) = 2{,}868$; $p = .05$; $\eta^2 = .193$) and manual response ($F(3, 36) = 5{,}880$; $p < .01$; $\eta^2 = .329$). For these three ratings VVV configuration was subjectively more demanding compared to the three others.

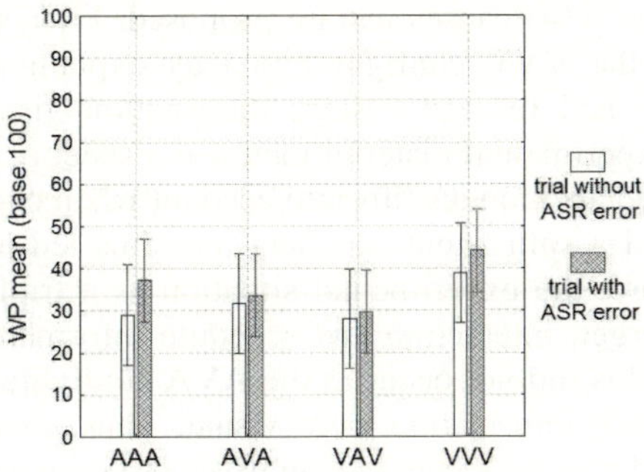

Fig. 4. Comparison of means for WP in function of trial and configuration

The trial with the ASR error showed a WP mean that was significantly higher compared to the trial without error (F (1, 36) = 5,809; $p < .05$; $\eta^2 = .139$). Among dimensions, the effect concerned dimensions related to stress: frustration (F (1, 36) = 21,10; $p < .001$; $\eta^2 = .370$) and loss of control (F (1, 36) = 26,61; $p < .001$; $\eta^2 = .451$). These effects were very significant.

Effect of Correction Mode. The correction is the action to perform when the error occurs. It was possible to say "cancel" (the system forgot information acquired and asked for a new request), and it was possible to directly correct the information needed ("Not Friday. Saturday"). Across the experiment: 34 subjects cancelled, 44 corrected and two did not correct.

A new analysis was conducted for this trial with correction mode as the categorical factor. No effect of this factor was observed with TLX (F (1, 32) = 0,506; $p = .48$; $\eta^2 = .015$). Within dimensions, only effort was sensitive (F (1, 32) = 4,762; $p < .05$; $\eta^2 = .148$). Subjects who cancelled rated a weaker effort compared to those who directly corrected.

WP revealed that cancellation is the most costly procedure. The global mean was sensitive to this factor (F (1, 30) = 8,402; $p < .01$; $\eta^2 = .280$). The ratings implied were visual processing (F (1,30) = 13,743; $p < .001$; $\eta^2 = .458$), auditory processing (F (1,30) = 7,504; $p < .02$; $\eta^2 = .250$), manual response (F (1,30) = 4,249; $p < .05$; $\eta^2 = .141$) and vocal response (F (1,30) = 4,772; $p < .05$; $\eta^2 = .159$).

3 Conclusion

NASA-TLX did not provide information on configuration, which was the main goal of the experiment. The differences observed with this questionnaire only concern the ASR error. Hypotheses have not been reached on user's activity or strategy during the task.

WP provided the intended information about configurations. Perceptive/central processing was higher in mono-modal configurations (AAA and VVV). Subjects had more difficulties in sharing their attention between the interaction task and the target task in mono-modal presentation. Besides, VVV configuration overloaded the three visuo-spatial processors. Two causes can be proposed. First, the lack of perception-action consistency in the VVV configuration may explain this difference. In this configuration, subjects had to read system information visually and to command vocally. Second, the experimental material included a sheet of paper, giving schedule constraints. Subjects had also to take this into account when choosing an appointment. This material generated a split-attention effect and thus led to the increase of load. This led us to reinterpret the experimental situation as a triple task protocol. In the VVV configuration, target, interaction and schedule information were visual, which created the overload. This did not occur in the AVA configuration, where only target information and schedule information were visual. Thus, overloaded dimensions in WP led to useful hypotheses on subjects' cognitive activity during interaction and to a fine diagnostic on the implementations compared.

Regarding workload results, the bimodal configurations look better than mono-modal configurations. But performance and behaviour must be considered. In fact, VAV configuration increased verbosity and disfluencies and led to a weaker recall of the date and time of the appointments taken during the experiment. The best implementation was AVA configuration, which favoured performance and learning, and shortened dialogue duration.

Concerning the ASR error, no effect was produced on resource ratings in WP, but stress ratings responded. This result shows that our version of WP is useful to distinguish between stress and attention demands.

For user modeling in spoken dialogue applications, the model of attention structure, underlying WP, seems more informative than the model of psychological structure of workload, underlying TLX. Attention structure enables predictions about performance. Therefore, it should be used to define cognitive constraints in a *multimodal strategy management component* [4].

References

[1] Baber, C., Mellor, B., Graham, R., Noyes, J.M., Tunley, C.: Workload and the use of automatic speech recognition: The effects of time and resource demands. Speech Communication 20, 37–53 (1996)

[2] Clark, H.H.: Using Language. Cambridge University Press, Cambridge (1996)

[3] Hart, S.G., Staveland, L.E.: Development of NASA-TLX (Task Load Index): Results of empirical and theoritical research. In: Hancock, P. A., Meshkati, N. (eds.) Human mental workload, North-Holland, Amsterdam, pp. 139–183 (1988)

[4] Horchani, M., Nigay, L., Panaget, F.: A Platform for Output Dialogic Strategies in Natural Multimodal Dialogue Systems. In: Proc. of the IUI, Honolulu, Hawaii, pp. 206–215 (2007)

[5] Jameson, A., Kiefer, J., Müller, C., Großmann-Hutter, B., Wittig, F., Rummer, R.: Assessment of a user's time pressure and cognitive load on the basis of features of speech, Journal of Computer Science and Technology (In press)

[6] Lazarus, R.S., Folkman, S.: Stress, appraisal, and coping. Springer, New York (1984)

[7] Le Bigot, L., Jamet, E., Rouet, J.-F., Amiel, V.: Mode and modal transfer effects on performance and discourse organization with an information retrieval dialogue system in natural language. Computers in Human Behavior 22(3), 467–500 (2006)

[8] Nievergelt, J., Weydert, J.: Sites, Modes, and Trails: Telling the User of an interactive System Where he is, What he can do, and How to get places. In: Guedj, R. A., Ten Hagen, P., Hopgood, F. R., Tucker, H. , Duce, P. A. (eds.) Methodology of Interaction, North Holland, Amsterdam, pp. 327–338 (1980)

[9] Oviatt, S., Coulston, R., Lunsford, R.: When Do We Interact Multimodally? Cognitive Load and Multimodal Communication Patterns. In: ICMI'04, State College, Pennsylvania, USA, pp. 129–136 (2004)

[10] Pickering, M.J., Garrod, S.: Toward a mechanistic psychology of dialogue. Behavioral and Brain Sciences, 27 (2004)

[11] Rubio, S., Diaz, E., Martin, J., Puente, J.M.: Evaluation of Subjective Mental Workload: A comparison of SWAT, NASA-TLX, and Workload Profile Methods. Applied Psychology 53(1), 61–86 (2004)

[12] Sweller, J.: Cognitive load during problem solving: Effects on learning. Cognitive Science 12(2), 257–285 (1988)

[13] Tsang, P.S., Velasquez, V.L.: Diagnosticity and multidimensional subjective workload ratings. Ergonomics 39(3), 358–381 (1996)

[14] Wickens, C.D.: Processing resources in attention. In: Parasuraman, R., Davies, D.R. (eds.) Varieties of attention, pp. 63–102. Academic Press, New-York (1984)

Menu Selection Using Auditory Interface

Koichi Hirota[1], Yosuke Watanabe[2], and Yasushi Ikei[2]

[1] Graduate School of Frontier Sciences, University of Tokyo
5-1-5 Kashiwanoha, Kashiwa, Chiba 277-8563
{hirota,watanabe}@media.k.u-tokyo.ac.jp
[2] Faculty of System Design, Tokyo Metropolitan University
6-6 Asahigaoka, Hino, Tokyo 191-0065
ikei@tmit.ac.jp

Abstract. An approach to auditory interaction with wearable computer is investigated. Menu selection and keyboard input interfaces are experimentally implemented by integrating pointing interface using motion sensors with auditory localization system based on HRTF. Performance of users, or the efficiency of interaction, is evaluated through experiments using subjects. The average time for selecting a menu item was approximately 5-9 seconds depending on the geometric configuration of the menu, and average key input performance was approximately 6 seconds per a character. The result did not support our expectation that auditory localization of menu items will be a helpful cue for accurate pointing.

Keywords: auditory interface, menu selection, keyboard input.

1 Introduction

As computers become small and portable, requirement to use such computers all the time to assist users to perform their tasks from the aspect of information and communication. Concept of wearable computer presented a concrete vision of such computers and styles of using them[1].

However, wearable computers still have not been commonly used in our life. One of the reasons is thought to be that the user interface is still not sophisticated enough for it to be used in daily life; for example, wearable key input device is not necessarily friendly for novice users and visual feedback through HMD is sometimes annoying while users' eyes are focusing on objects in real environment.

Some of these problems of the user interface are thought to be solved by introducing auditory interface where information is presented to the user through auditory sensation and interaction with the user is performed based on auditory feedback[2]. Some experimental studies have been carried by ourselves[3,4].

A merit of using auditory interface is that presentation of auditory information is possible simply using headphones. In recent years, many people are using headphones even while they are in public space, and that fact suggests that it can be used for long hours of wearing and listening. Also, headphones are not so weird as HMDs even if they are used in public space.

J. Jacko (Ed.): Human-Computer Interaction, Part III, HCII 2007, LNCS 4552, pp. 70–75, 2007.

A drawback of auditory interface is that the amount of information presented through auditory sensation is generally much less than visual information provided by a HMD. This problem of auditory interface leads us to investigating an approach to improving the informational efficiency of the interface.

One of fundamental idea to solve the problem is an active control of auditory information. If the auditory information is provided passively, the user has to listen to all information that is provided by the system till the end even when the information is of no interest. On the other hand, if the user can select information, the user can skip items that are not required for the user, and it improves informational efficiency of the interface.

In the rest part of this paper, our first-step study on this topic is reported. Menu selection and keyboard input interfaces are experimentally implemented by integrating simple pointing interface with auditory localization, and their performance is evaluated.

2 Auditory Interface System

An auditory display system was implemented for our experiments. The system consists of an auditory localization device, two motion sensors, a headphone, and a notebook PC.

The auditory localization device is a dedicated convolution hardware that is capable of presenting and localizing 16 sound sources (14 from wave data and 2 from white and click noise generators) using HRTF[5]. In the following experiments, HRTF data from KEMAR head[6] was used. The motion sensors (MDP-A3U7, NEC-Tokin) were used to measure the orientation of user's hand and head. The sensor for head was attached to the overhead frame of the headphone, and the other sensor for hand was held by the user. Each sensor has two buttons whose status, as well as motion data, can be read by the PC. The notebook PC (CF-W4, Panasonic) controlled the entire system.

3 Menu Selection

The goal of this study is to clarify completion time and accuracy of menu selection operation. A menu system as shown in Figure 1 is supposed; menu items are located at even intervals of horizontal orientation, and user selects one of them through pointing it by hand motion sensor and pressing a button. The performance of operation was evaluated by measuring completion time and number of erroneous selections performed by the user under different conditions regarding number of menu items (4, 8, 12), angular width of each menu (10, 20, 30deg), with or without auditory localization, and auditory switching modes (direct and overlap); 36 in total combinations.

In case of without auditory localization, the sound source was located in front of the user. Auditory pointer means the feedback of pointer orientation by localized sound, and a repetitive click noise was used as sound source. The auditory switching mode means the way of switching auditory information when the pointer passes

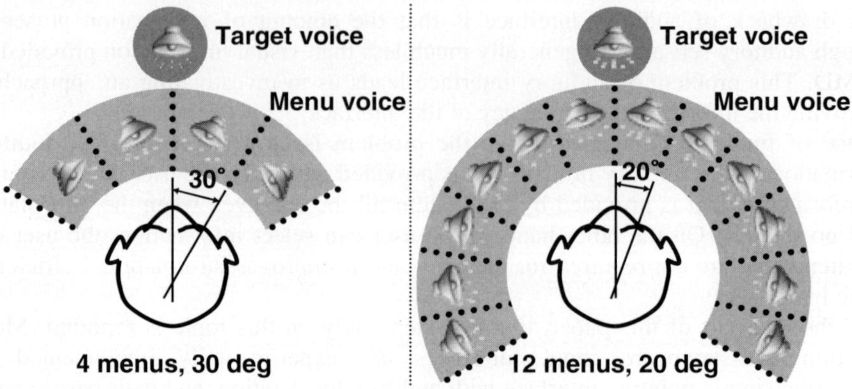

Fig. 1. Menu selection interface. Each menu items are arranged around the user at even angular intervals.

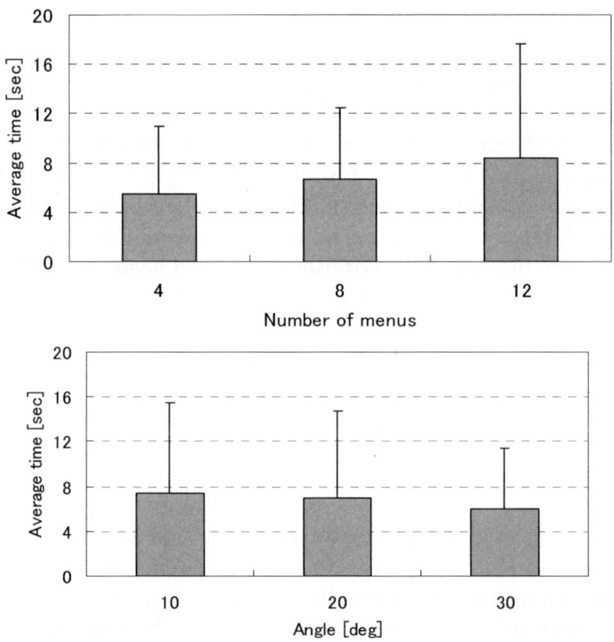

Fig. 2. Average completion time of menu selection. Both increase in the number of menu items and decrease in angular width of each menu item cause the selection task more difficult to perform.

across item borders; in direct mode, the sound source was immediately changed, while in overlap mode, the sound source of previous item continues existing until the end of pronunciation.

To eliminate semantic aspect of the task, vocal data from pronunciation of 'a' to 'z', instead of keywords of practical menus, were used for menu items. Volume of sound was adjusted by the user for comfort. The sound data for menu items were randomly selected but without duplication. The number of subjects was 3, adult persons with normal aural ability. Each subject performed selection for 10 times for each of 36 conditions. The order of condition was randomized.

The average completion time computed for each conditions of the number of items and item angular width is shown in Figure 2. The result suggests that selection task is performed in about 5-9 seconds in average depending on these conditions. Increase in the number of items makes the task more difficult to perform and in both the difference among the average values was statistically significant ($p<0.05$). Decrease in the size of item also makes the task difficult, and the difference was also significant ($p<0.05$). On the other hand, the effect of both auditory localization and auditory presentation mode on the completion time was not made clear ($p>0.05$).

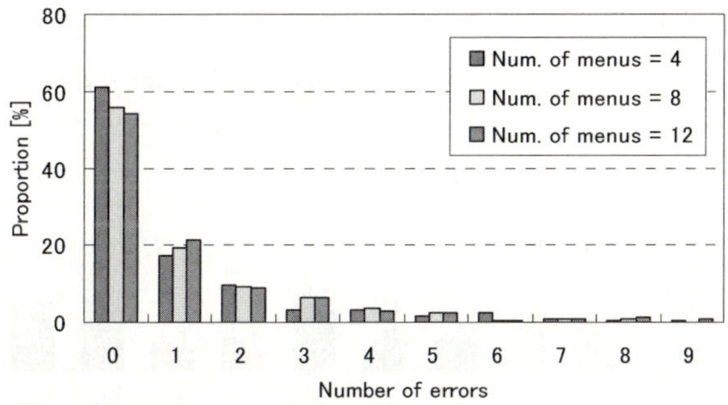

Fig. 3. Number of erroneous selections before selecting collect target item. Only one half of selection operation is performed successfully without retry.

The histogram of number of erroneous selection is plotted in Figure 3. The result suggests that only approximately 50% of selection is completed without error and retry. The success ratio is significantly low if it is compared with similar task using visual feedback. One reason of the result will be because the subjects were instructed to perform the task as fast as possible. The change in the number of menu items caused no noticeable difference in the histogram. Similarly, other conditions had no significant effect on the result.

4 Auditory Keyboard Input

As a more complicated case of menu selection interface, a keyboard input interface was experimentally implemented. Each key is considered as a menu item that is arranged in two-dimensional area as shown in Figure 4.

A map of qwerty keyboard was auditory presented in a similar way to auditory menu interface. In this interface the elevation angle of the pointer is also considered to allow two-dimensional selection. Other framework of the interaction is identical with the menu selection interface. The performance of the key input was measured regarding completion time and number of erroneous selection, under conditions of with and without auditory localization. The angular size of the map was fixed, and direct mode was used as auditory presentation mode.

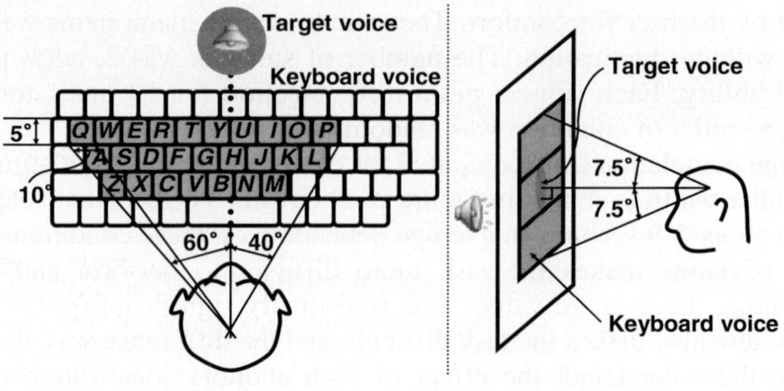

Fig. 4. Auditory keyboard interface. Two-dimensional keyboard layout is mapped to azimuth-elevation space in front of user.

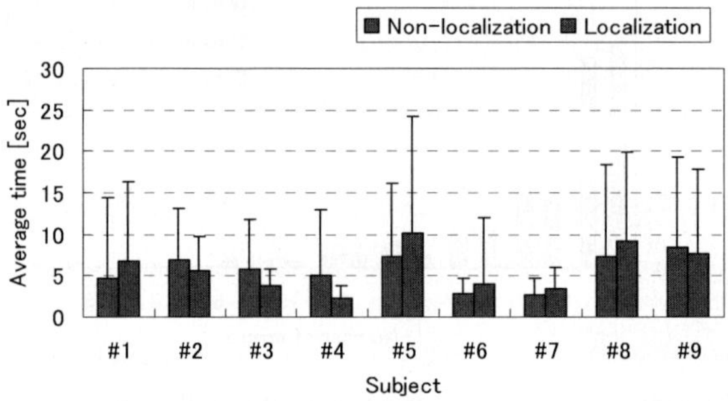

Fig. 5. Completion time of key input operation. There are large differences among individuals. There are some subjects who can better perform the task under the condition with auditory localization.

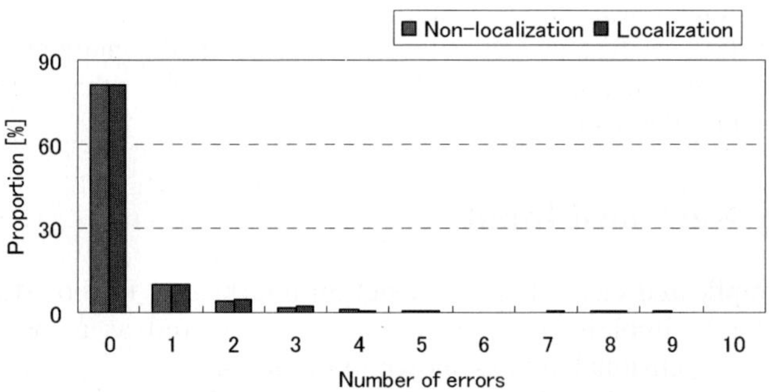

Fig. 6. Number of errors in key input operation. Error ratio of key input task is lower than the menu selection task, probably because the location of each item (or key) is predefined.

The number of subjects was 9, adult persons with normal aural ability. Each subject performed 40 input operations under each localization condition. The target key was randomly chosen from alphabet 26 characters, and order of conditions was also randomized.

The average input completion time was approximately 6 seconds per a character irrelevant to auditory conditions; no significant difference in the completion time between two auditory conditions were found ($p>0.05$). A better performance compared with the menu selection interface is attained despite higher complexity of the task, because the arrangement of items (or keys) is familiar to the subjects. The individual difference of the completion time is shown in Figure 5. The difference may be caused by the difference about how each subject is used to qwerty keyboard.

The histogram about the number of errors is plotted in Figure 6. The result also suggests that more accurate operation is performed than the menu selection interface.

5 Conclusion

In this paper, an approach to auditory interaction with wearable computers was proposed. Menu selection and keyboard input interfaces were implemented and their performance was evaluated through experiments. The result did not support our expectation that auditory localization of menu items will be a helpful cue for accurate pointing. In our future work, we are going to investigate the users' performance in practical situation, such as while walking in the street. Also we are interested in analyzing the reason why auditory localization is not effectively used in the experiments that were reported in this paper.

References

1. Mann, S.: Wearable Computing. A first step toward Personal Imaging, IEEE Computer 30(3), 25–29 (1997)
2. Mynatt, E., Edwards, W.K.: Mapping GUIs to Auditory Interfaces. In: Proc. ACM UIST'92, pp. 61–70 (1992)
3. Ikei, S., Yamazaki, H., Hirota, K., Hirose, M.: vCocktail: Multiplexed-voice Menu Presentation Method for Wearable Computers. In: Proc. IEEE VR 2006, pp. 183–190 (2006)
4. Hirota, K., Hirose, M.: Auditory pointing for interaction with wearable systems. In: Proc. HCII 2003, vol. 3, pp. 744–748 (2003)
5. Wenzel, E.M., Stone, P.K., Fisher, S.S., Foster, S.H.: A System for Three-Dimensional Acoustic 'Visualization' in a Virtual Environment Workstation. In: Proc. Visualization '90, pp. 329–337 (1990)
6. Gardner, W.G., Martin, K.D.: HRTF measurements of a KEMAR dummy head microphone. MIT Media Lab Perceptual Computing Technical Report #280 (1994)

Analysis of User Interaction with Service Oriented Chatbot Systems

Marie-Claire Jenkins, Richard Churchill, Stephen Cox, and Dan Smith

University of East-Anglia
School of Computer Science
Norwich
UK
mcjenkins@gmail.com, mail@richardchurchill.co.uk,
sjc@cmp.uea.ac.uk, djs@uea.ac.uk

Abstract. Service oriented chatbot systems are designed to help users access information from a website more easily. The system uses natural language responses to deliver the relevant information, acting like a customer service representative. In order to understand what users expect from such a system and how they interact with it we carried out two experiments which highlighted different aspects of interaction. We observed the communication between humans and the chatbots, and then between humans, applying the same methods in both cases. These findings have enabled us to focus on aspects of the system which directly affect the user, meaning that we can further develop a realistic and helpful chatbot.

Keywords: human-computer interaction, chatbot, question-answering, communication, intelligent system, natural language, dialogue.

1 Introduction

Service oriented chatbot systems are used to enable customers to find information on large complex websites, which are difficult to navigate. Norwich Union [1] is a very large insurance company offering a full range of insurance products. Their website attracts 50,000 visits a day, with over 1,500 pages making up the website. Many users find it difficult to discover the information they need from website search engine results, the site being saturated with information. The service-oriented chatbot acts as an automated customer service representative, giving natural language answers, and offering more targeted information in the course of a conversation with the user. This virtual agent is also designed to help with general queries regarding products. This is a potential solution for online business, as it is time saving for customers, and allows the company to have an active part in the sale.

Internet users have gradually embraced the internet since 1995, and the internet itself has changed a great deal since then. Email and other forms of online communication such as the messenger programs, chat rooms and forums have become widely spread and accepted. This would indicate that the methods of communication

J. Jacko (Ed.): Human-Computer Interaction, Part III, HCII 2007, LNCS 4552, pp. 76–83, 2007.

involving typing are quite well integrated in online user habits. A chatbot is presented in the same way. Programs such as Windows "messenger" [2] involve a text box for input and another where the conversation is displayed. Despite the simplicity of this interface, experiments have shown that people are unsure as to how to use the system.

Despite the resemblance to the messenger system, commercial chatbots are not widespread at this time, and although they are gradually being integrated in large company websites, they do not hold a prominent role there, being more of an interactive tool or a curiosity rather than a trustworthy and effective way to go about business on the site. Our experiments show that there is an issue with the way that people perceive the chatbot. Many cannot understand the concept of talking to a computer, and so are put off by such a technology. Others do not believe that a computer can fill this kind of role and so are not enthusiastic, largely due to disillusionment with previous and existing telephone and computer technology. Another reason may be that they fear that they may be led to a product by the company, in order to encourage them to buy it. In order to conduct a realistic and useful dialogue with the user, the system must be able to establish rapport, acquire the desired information and guide the user to the correct part of the website, as well as using the appropriate language and having a human-like behaviour. Some systems, such as ours, also display a visual representation of the system in the form of a picture (or an avatar), which is sometimes animated in an effort to be more human-like and engaging. Our research however shows that this is not of prime importance to users. Users expect the chatbot to be intelligent, and expect them to also be accurate in their information delivery and use of language.

In this paper we describe an experiment which involved testing user behaviour with chatbots and comparing this to their behaviour with a human. We discuss the results of this experiment and the feedback from the users.

Our findings suggest that our research must not only consider the artificial intelligence aspect of the system which involves information extraction, knowledgebase management and creation, and utterance production, but also the HCI element, which features strongly in these types of system.

2 Description of the Chatbot System

The system which we named KIA (Knowledge Interaction Agent) was built specifically for the task of monitoring human interaction with such a system. It was built using simple natural language processing techniques. We used the same method used in the ALICE [3] social chatbot system which involves seeking for patterns in the knowledgebase using the AIML technique [4]. AIML (artificial intelligence markup language) is a method based on XML. The AIML method uses templated to generate a response in as natural a way as possible. The templates are populated with patterns commonly found in the possible responses. The keywords are migrated into the appropriate pattern identified in the template. The limitation of this method is that there is not enough variety in the possible answers. The knowledge base was drawn from the Norwich Union website. We then manually corrected errors and wrote in a "chat" section to the knowledge base from which the more informal, conversational utterances could be drawn. The nouns and proper nouns served as identifiers for the utterances and were initiated by the user utterance.

The chatbot was programmed to deliver responses in a friendly, natural way. We incorporated emotive-like cues such as using exclamation marks, interjections, and utterances which were constructed so as to be friendly in tone. "Soft" content was included in the knowledge base giving information on health issues like pregnancy, blood pressure and other such topics which it was hoped would be of personal interest to users. The information on services and products was also delivered using as far as possible the same human-like type of language as for the "soft" content language.

The interface was a window consisting of a text area to display the conversation as it unfolded and a smaller text box for the user to enter text. An "Ask me" button allowed for utterances to be submitted to the chatbot. For testing purposes the "section" link was to be clicked on when the user was ready to change the topic of the discussion as the brief was set in sections. We also incorporated the picture of a woman smiling in order to encourage some discussion around visual avatars. The simplicity of the interface was designed to encouraged user imagination and discussion; it was in no way presented as an interface design solution.

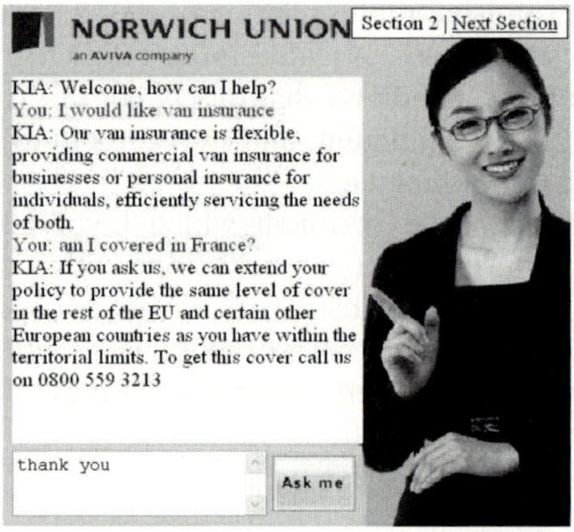

Fig. 1. The chatbot interface design

3 Description of the Experiment and Results

Users were given several different tasks to perform using the chatbot. They conversed with the system for an average of 30 minutes and then completed a feedback questionnaire which focused on their feelings, and reactions to the experience. The same framework was used to conduct "Wizard of Oz" experiments to provide a benchmark set of reactions, in which a human took the customer representative role instead of the chatbot. We refer to this chatbot as the "Human chatbot" (HC).

We conducted the study on 40 users with a full range of computer experience and exposure to chat systems. Users were given a number of to fulfill using the chatbot. These tasks were formulated after an analysis of Norwich Union's customer service system. They included such matters as including a young driver on car insurance, traveling abroad, etc…The users were asked to fill in a questionnaire at the end of the test to give their impressions on the performance of the chatbot and volunteer any other thoughts. We also prompted them to provide feedback on the quality and quantity of the information provided by the chatbot, the degree of emotion in the responses, whether an avatar would help, whether the tone was adequate and whether the chatbot was able to carry out a conversation in general.

We also conducted an experiment whereby one human acted as the chatbot and another acted as the customer and communication was spoken rather than typed. We collected 15 such conversations. The users were given the same scenarios as those used in the human-chatbot experiment. They were also issued with same feedback forms.

3.1 Results of the Experiments

The conversation between the human and HC flowed well as would be expected, and the overall tone was casual but business like on the part of the HC, again as would be expected from a customer service representative. The conversation between chatbot and human was also flowed well, the language being informal but business-like.

1.1 User language

- Keywords were often used to establish the topic clearly such as "I want car insurance", rather than launching into a monologue about car problems. The HC repeated these keyword, often more than once in the response. The HC will also sometimes use words in the same semantic field (e.g. "travels" instead of "holiday").
- The user tends to revert to his/her own keyword during the first few exchanges but then uses the words proposed by the HC. Reeves and Nass [5] state that users respond well to imitation. In this case the user comes to imitate the HC. There are sometimes places in the conversation where at times the keyword is dropped altogether such as "so I'll be covered, right?". This means that the conversation comes to rely on anaphora. In the case of the chatbot-human conversation, the user was reluctant to repeat keywords (perhaps due to the effort of re-typing them) and relied very much on anaphora, which makes the utterance resolution more difficult.

The result of this was that the information provided by the HC was at times incomplete or incorrect and at times there was no answer given at all. The human reacted well to this and reported no frustration or impatience. Rather, they were prepared to work with the HC to try and find the required information.

1.2 User reactions

- Users did however report frustration, annoyance, impatience with the chatbot when it was also unable to provide a clear response or a response at all. It was interesting to observe a difference in users' reaction to similar responses from the HC and the chatbot. If neither was unable to find an answer to their query after several attempts, users became frustrated. However this behaviour was exhibited more slowly with the HC than with the chatbot. This may be because users were aware that they were dealing with a machine and saw no reason to feign politeness, although we do see evidence of politeness in greetings for example.

1.3 Question-answering

- The HC provided not only an answer to the question, where possible, but also where the information was located on the website and a short summary of the relevant page. The user reported that this was very useful and helped them be further guided to more specific information.
- The HC was also able to pre-empt what information the user would find interesting, such as guiding them to a quote form when the discussion related to prices for example, which the chatbot was unable to do. The quantity of information was deemed acceptable for both the HC and the chatbot. The chatbot gave the location of the information but a shorter summary than that of the HC.
- Some questions were of a general nature, such as "I don't like bananas but I like apples and oranges are these all good or are some better than others?" which was volunteered by one user. As well as the difficulty of parsing this complex sentence, the chatbot needs to be able to draw on real-world knowledge of fruit, nutrition etc…To answer such questions requires the use of a large knowledgebase of real-world knowledge as well as methods for organizing and interpreting this information.
- The users in both experiments sometimes asked multiple questions in a single utterance. This led both the chatbot and the HC to be confused or unable to provide all of the information required at the same time.
- Excessive information is sometimes volunteered by the user, e.g. as explaining how the mood swings of a pregnant wife are affecting the fathers' life at this time. A machine has no understanding of these human problems and so would need to grasp these additional concepts in order to tailor a response for the user. This did not occur in the HC dialogues. This may be because users are less likely to voice their concerns to a stranger, than an anonymous machine. There is also the possibility that they were testing the chatbot.

Users may also feel that giving the chatbot the complete information required to answer their question in a single turn is acceptable to a computer system but not acceptable to a human, using either text or speech.

1.4 Style of interaction

- Eighteen users found the chatbot answers succinct and three long-winded. Other users described them as in between, not having enough detail in them or being generic. The majority of users were happy with finding the answer in the sentence rather than in the paragraph as Lin [6] found during his experiments with encyclopedic material. In order to please the majority of users it may be advisable to include the option of finding out more about a particular topic. In the case of the HC, the responses were considered to be succinct and containing the right amount of information. However some users reported that there was too much information.

- Users engaged in chitchat with the chatbot. They thank it for its time and also sometimes wish it “Good afternoon” and “Good morning”. Certain users tell the chatbot that they are bored with the conversation. Others tell the system that this ”feels like talking to a robot”. Reeves and Nass [5] found, that the user expects such a system to have human qualities. Interestingly the language of the HC was also described as “robotic” at times by the human. This may be due to the dryness of the information being made available; however it is noticeable that the repetition of keywords in the answers contributes to this notion.□□□

3.2 Feedback Forms

The feedback forms from the experiment showed that users described in an open text field the tone of the conversation with the chatbot as ”polite”, ”blunt”, ”irritating”, ”condescending”, “too formal”, ”relaxed” and ”dumb”. This is a clear indication of the user reacting to the chatbot. The chatbot is conversational therefore they expect a certain quality of exchange with the machine. They react emotionally to this and show this explicitly by using emotive terms to qualify their experience. The HC was also accused of this in some instances.

The users were asked to rate how trustworthy they found the system to be using a scale of 10 for very trustworthy to 0 for not trustworthy. The outcome was an average rating of 5.80 out of 10. Two users rated the system as trustworthy even though they rated their overall experience as not very good. They stated that the system kept answering the same thing or was poor with specifics. One user found the experience completely frustrating but still awarded it a trust rating of 8/10. The HC had a trustworthiness score of 10/10.

3.3 Results Specific to the Human-Chatbot Experiment

Fifteen users volunteered without elicitation alternative interface designs. Ten of these all included a conversation window, a query box, which are the core components of such a system. Seven included room for additional links to be displayed. Four of the drawings include an additional window for the inclusion of ”useful information”. 1 design included space for web links. One design included disability options such as the choice of text color and font size to be customizable. 5 designs included an avatar. One design included a button for intervention by a human customer service representative.

A common feature suggested was to allow more room for each of the windows and between responses so that these could be clearer. The conversation logs showed many instances of users attacking the KIA persona, which was in this instance the static picture of a lady pointing to the conversation box. This distracted them from the conversation.

3.4 The Avatar

Seven users stated that having an avatar would enhance the conversation and would prove more engaging. Four users agreed that there was no real need for an avatar as the emphasis was placed on the conversation and finding information. Ten stated that having an avatar present would be beneficial, making the experience more engaging and human-like. Thirteen reported that having an avatar was of no real use. Two individuals stated that the avatar could cause “embarrassment”, and may be “annoying”. Two users stated that they thought that having a virtual agent would not help actually included them in their diagrams.

When asked to compare their experience with that of surfing the website for such information, the majority responded that they found the chatbot useful. One user compared it to Google and found it to be “no better”. Other users stated that the system was too laborious to use. Search engines provide a list of results which then need to be sorted by the user into useful or not useful sites. One user stated that surfing the web was actually harder but it was possible to obtain more detailed results that way. Others said that they found it hard to start with general keywords and find specific information. They found that they needed to adapt to the computer’s language. Most users found it to be fast and efficient and generally just as good as a search engine although a few stated that they would rather use the search engine option if it was available. One user clearly stated that the act of asking was preferable to the act of searching. Interestingly a few said that they would have preferred the answer to be included in a paragraph rather than a concise answer.

The overall experience rating ranged from very good to terrible. Common complaints were that the system was frustrating, kept giving the same answers, and was average and annoying. On the other hand some users described it as pleasant, interesting, fun, and informative. Both types of user gave similar accounts and ratings throughout the rest of the feedback having experienced the common complaints.

The system was designed with a minimal amount of emotive behavior.

It used exclamation marks at some points, and more often than not simply offered sentences available on the website, or which were made vaguely human-like. Users had strong feedback on this matter calling the system “impolite”, ”rude”, ”cheeky”, ”professional”, ”warm”, and “human-like”. One user thought that the system had a low IQ. This shows that users do expect something which converses with them to exhibit some emotive behavior. Although they had very similar conversations with the system, their ratings varied quite significantly. This may be due to their own personal expectations. The findings correlate with the work of Reeves and Nass [5]: people are associating human qualities to a machine. It is unreasonable to say that a computer is cheeky or warm for example, as it has no feelings.

Table 1. Results of the feedback scores from the chatbot –human experiment

Experience	0.46	Useful answers	0.37
Tone	0.37	Unexpected things	0.2
Turn-taking	0.46	Better than site surfing	0.43
Links useful	0.91	quality	0.16
emotion	0.23	Interst shown	0.33
Conversation rating	0.58	Simple to use	0.7
Succinct responses	0.66	Need for an avatar	0.28
Clear answers	0.66		

Translating all of the feedback into numerical values between 0 and 1, using 0 as a negative answer, 0.5 as a middle ground answer and 1 as a positive answer, we can clearly see the results. The usefulness of links was voted very positive with a score of 0.91, and tone used (0.65), sentence complexity (0.7), clarity (0.66) and general conversation (0.58) all scored above average. The quality of the bot received the lowest score at 0.16.

4 Conclusion

The most important finding from this work are: that users expect chatbot systems to behave and communicate like humans. If the chatbot is seen to be "acting like a machine", it is deemed to be below standard. It is required to have the same tone, sensitivity and behaviour than a human but at the same time users expect it to process much more information than the human. It is also expected to deliver useful and required information, just as a search engine does. The information needs to be delivered in a way which enables the user to extract a simple answer as well as having the opportunity to "drill down" if necessary. Different types of information need to be volunteered such as the URL where further information or more detailed information can be found, the answer, and the conversation itself. The presence of "chitchat" in the conversations with both the human and the chatbot show that there is a strong demand for social interaction as well as a demand for knowledge.

5 Future Work

It is not clear from this experiment whether an avatar can help the chatbot appear more human-like or make for a stronger human-chatbot relationship. It would also be interesting to compare the use of search engines to that of the chatbot.

It would be interesting to compare the ease of use of the chatbot with a conventional search engine. Many users found making queries in the context of a dialogue useful, but the quality and precision of the answers returned by the chatbot may be lower than what they could obtain from a standard search engine. This is a subject for further research.

Acknowledgements. We would like to thank Norwich Union for their support of this work.

References

1. Norwich Union, an AVIVA company: http://www.norwichunion.com
2. Microsoft Windows Messenger: http://messenger.msn.com
3. Wallace, R.: ALICE chatbot, http://www.alicebot.org
4. Wallace, R.: The anatomy of ALICE. Artificial Intelligence Foundation
5. Reeves, B., Nass, C.: The media equation: how people treat computers, television and new media like real people and places. Cambridge University press, Cambridge (1996)
6. Lin, J., Quan, D., Bakshi, K., Huynh, D., Katz, B., Karger, D.: What makes a good answer? The role of context in question-answering. INTERACT (2003)

Performance Analysis of Perceptual Speech Quality and Modules Design for Management over IP Network

Jinsul Kim[1], Hyun-Woo Lee[1], Won Ryu[1], Seung Ho Han[2], and Minsoo Hahn[2]

[1] BcN Interworking Technology Team, BcN Service Research Group, BcN Research Division, 161 Gajeong-dong, Yuseong-gu, Daejeon, 305-350, Korea
[2] Speech and Audio Information Laboratory, Information and Communications University, Daejeon, Korea
{jsetri,hwlee,wlyu}@etri.re.kr,
{space0128,mshahn}@icu.ac.kr

Abstract. Voice packets with guaranteed QoS (Quality of Service) on the VoIP system are responsible for digitizing, encoding, decoding, and playing out the speech signal. The important point is based on the factor that different parts of speech over IP networks have different perceptual importance and each part of speech does not contribute equally to the overall voice quality. In this paper, we propose new additive noise reduction algorithms to improve voice over IP networks and present performance evaluation of perceptual speech signal through IP networks in the additive noise environment during realtime phone-call service. The proposed noise reduction algorithm is applied to pre-processing method before speech coding and to post-processing method after speech decoding based on single microphone VoIP system. For noise reduction, this paper proposes a Wiener filter optimized to the estimated SNR of noisy speech for speech enhancement. Various noisy conditions including white Gaussian, office, babble, and car noises are considered with G.711 codec. Also, we provide critical message report procedures and management schemes to guarantee QoS over IP networks. Finally, as following the experimental results, the proposed algorithm and method has been prove for improving speech quality.

Keywords: VoIP, Noise Reduction, QoS, Speech Packet, IP Network.

1 Introduction

There have been many related research efforts in the field of improving QoS over IP network for the past decade. Moreover, multimedia quality improvement over IP networks has become an important issue with the development of realtime applications such as IP-phones, TV-conferencing, etc today. In this paper, we try to improve perceptual speech quality over IP network while voice signal is mixed with various noisy signals. Usually, there will be a critical degradation in voice quality when noise deploy to original speech signal over IP network. Perceptual speech with noise signal over IP communication systems requires mutual adaptation process with the guaranteed high quality during conversation on the phone.

J. Jacko (Ed.): Human-Computer Interaction, Part III, HCII 2007, LNCS 4552, pp. 84–93, 2007.

Overall, the proposed noise reduction algorithm is applied the method which is a Wiener filter optimized to the estimated SNR of noisy speech for speech enhancement. The performance of the proposed method is compared with those of the noise reduction methods in the IS-127 EVRC (Enhanced Variable Rate Codec) and in the ETSI (European Telecommunications Standards Institute) standard for the distributed speech recognition front-end. To measure the speech quality, we adopt the well-known PESQ (Perceptual Evaluation of Speech Quality) algorithm. Finally, the proposed noise reduction method is applied with G.711 codec and the proposed method yields higher PESQ scores than the others in most noisy conditions, respectively. Also, according to the necessity of discovering of QoS, we design processing modules in main critical blocks with the message procedures of reporting to measure various network parameters.

The organization of this paper is as follows. Section 2 describes previous approaches on the identification and characterization of VoIP services by using related works. In section 3, we present the methodology of parameters discovering and measuring for quality resource management. In section 4, we propose noise reduction algorithm for applying packet-based IP network and performance evaluation and results are provided in section 5. Finally, section 6 concludes the paper with possible future work.

2 Related Work

For the measurement of network parameters, many useful management schemes proposed in this research areas [1]. Managing and Controlling of QoS-factor in realtime is required importantly for stable VoIP service. An important factor for VoIP-quality control technique involves the rate control, which is based largely on network impairments such as jitter, delay, packet loss rate, etc due to the network congestions [2] [3]. In order to support application services based on the NGN (Next Generation Network), an end-to-end QoS monitoring tool is developed with qualified performance analysis [4].

Voice packets that are perceptually more important are marked, i.e. acquire priority in our approach. If there is any congestion, the packets are less likely to be dropped than the packets that are of less perceptual importance. The QoS schemes which are based on the priority marking are open loop ones and do not make use of changes in the network [5] [6]. The significant factor is that the standard RTCP packet type is defined for speech quality control in realtime without conversational speech quality reporting and managing procedures in detail through VoIP networks. The Realtime Transport Protocol (RTP) and RTP Control Protocol (RTCP) communications use the RTCP-Receiver Report to get back the information of the IP network conditions from RTP receivers to RTP senders. However, the original RTCP provides overall feedback on the quality of end-to-end networks [7]. The RTP Control Protocol Extended Reports (RTCP-XR) are a new VoIP management protocol which defines a set of metrics that contains information for assessing the VoIP call quality by the IETF [8]. The evaluation of VoIP service quality is carried out by firstly encoding the input speech pre-modified with given network parameter values, and then decoded to generate degraded output speech signals. The frequency-temporal filtering combination for an extension method of Philips' audio fingerprinting scheme is introduced to achieve robustness to channel and background noise under the conditions of a real situation [9]. Novel phase noise reduction method is very useful for CPW-based microwave oscillator circuit utilizing a compact planar helical resonator [10]. The amplifier achieves high and constant gain with a wide dynamic input signal range and low noise figure. The performance does not depend on the input signal conditions, whether static-state or transient signals, or whether there is symmetric or asymmetric data traffic on bidirectional transmission [11]. To avoid the complicated psychoacoustic analysis we can calculate the scale factors of the bit-sliced arithmetic coding encoder directly from the signal-to-noise ratio parameters of the AC-3 decoder [12].

In this paper, we propose noise reduction method and present performance results. Also, for discovering and measuring various network parameters such as jitter, delay, and packet loss rate, etc., we design an end-to-end quality management modules scheme with the realtime message report procedures to manage the QoS-factors.

3 Parameters Discovering and Measuring Methodology

3.1 Functionality of Main Processing Modules and Blocks

In this section, we clarify each functionality blocks and modules carried on SoftPhone (UA) for discovering and measuring realtime call-quality over IP network. We design 11 critical modules for UA as illustrated in Fig.1. It comprises in four main blocks and each module is defined as follows:

- SIP Stack Module -

- Analysis of every sending/receiving messages and creation response messages
- Sending to transport module after adding suitable parameter and header for sending message

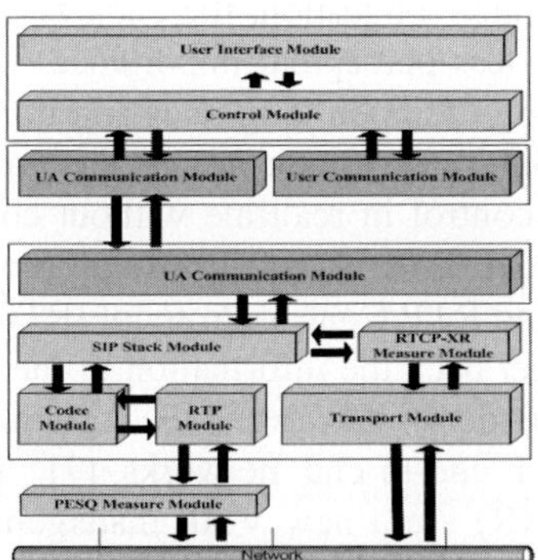

Fig. 1. Main processing blocks for UA (SoftPhone) functionality

- Analysis of parameter and header in receiving message from transport module
- Management and application of SoftPhone information, channel information, codec information, etc.
- Notify codec module of sender's codec information from SDP of receiving message and negotiate with receiver's codec
- Save up session and codec information

- Codec Module –
  - Providing the encoding and decoding function about two different voice codecs (G.711/G.729)
  - Processing of codec (encoding/decoding) and rate value based on SDP information of sender/receiver from SIP stack module
- RTP Module –
  - Sending created data from codec module to other SoftPhone through RTP protocol
- RTCP-XR Measure Module –
  - Formation of quality parameters for monitoring and sending/receiving information of quality parameters to SIP stack/transport modules
- Transport Module -
  - Address messages from SIP stack module to network
  - Address receiving message from network to SIP stack module
- PESQ Measure Module –
  - Measure voice quality by using packet and rate which is received from RTP module and network
- UA Communication Module -
  - In case of requesting call connection, interchange of information to SIP stack module through Windows Mail-Slot and establish SIP session connection
  - Address information to Control module in order to show information of SIP message to user
- User Communication Module -
  - Sending and receiving of input information through UDP protocol.

3.2 Message Report and QoS-Factor Management

In this paper, we propose realtime message report procedures and management scheme between VoIP-QM server and SoftPhones. The proposed method for the realtime message reporting and management consists of four main processing blocks, as illustrated in Fig.2. These four different processing modules implement call session module, UDP communication module, quality report message management module and quality measurement/computation/processing module. In order to control call session, data by call session management module is automatically recorded in database management module according to session establish and release status. All of the call session messages are addressed to quality report message management module by UDP communication. After call-setup is completed, QoS-factor is measuring followed by computation of each quality parameters base on the message processing. Followed by each session establish and release, quality report messages are also recorded in database management module immediately.

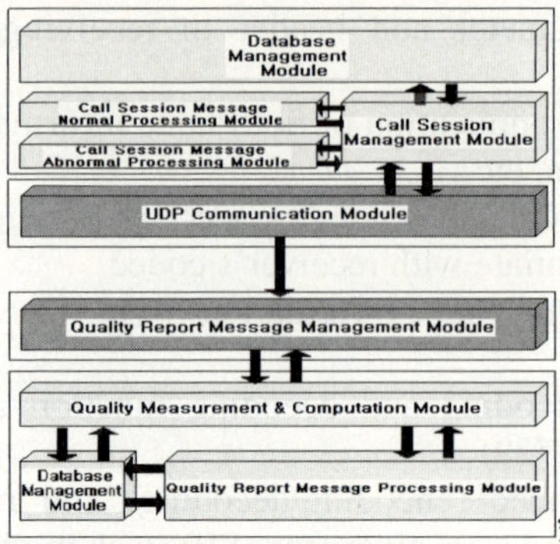

Fig. 2. Main processing blocks for call session & quality management/measurement

3.3 Procedures of an End-to-End Call Session Based on SIP

An endpoint of SIP based Softswitch is known as SoftPhone (UA). That is, SIP client loosely denotes SIP end points where UAs run, such as SIP-phones and SoftPhones. Softswitch performs functions of authentication, authorization, and signaling compression. A logical SIP URI address consists of a domain and identifies a UA ID number. The UAs belonging to a particular domain register their locations with the SIP Registrar of that domain by means of a REGISTER message. Fig. 3 shows SIP based Softswitch connection between UA#1-SoftPhone and UA#2-SoftPhone.

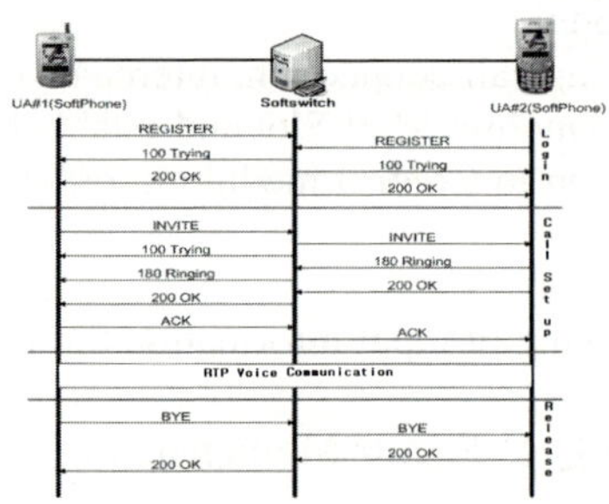

Fig. 3. Main procedures of call establish/release between Softswitch and SoftPhoneï

3.4 Realtime Quality-Fator Measurement Methodology

The VoIP service quality evaluation is carried out by firstly encoding the input speech pre-modified with given network parameter values and then decoded to generate degraded output speech signals. In order to obtain an end-to-end (E2E) MOS between the caller-UA and the callee-UA, we apply the PESQ and the E-Model method. In detail, to obtain the R factors for E2E measurement over the IP network we need to get Id, Ie, Is and Ij. Here, Ij is newly defined as in equation (1) to represent the E2E jitter parameter.

$$R\ factor = R0 - Is - Id - Ij - Ie + A \tag{1}$$

The ITU-T Recommendation provides most of the values and methods to get parameter values except Ie for the G.723.1 codec, Id and Ij. First, we obtain Ie value after the PESQ algorithm applied. Second, we apply the PESQ values to Ie value of R-factor. We measure the E2E Id and Ij from our current network environment. By combining Ie, Id and Ij, the final R factor could be computed for the E2E QoS performance results. Finally, obtained R factor is reconverted to MOS by using equation (2), which is redefined by the ITU-T SG12.

$$\begin{cases} R \le 6.5:\ MOS = 1 \\ 6.5 \le R \le 100:\ MOS = 1 - \frac{7}{1000}R + \frac{7}{6250}R^2 - \frac{7}{1000000}R^3 \\ R \ge 100:\ MOS = 4.5 \end{cases} \quad (2)$$

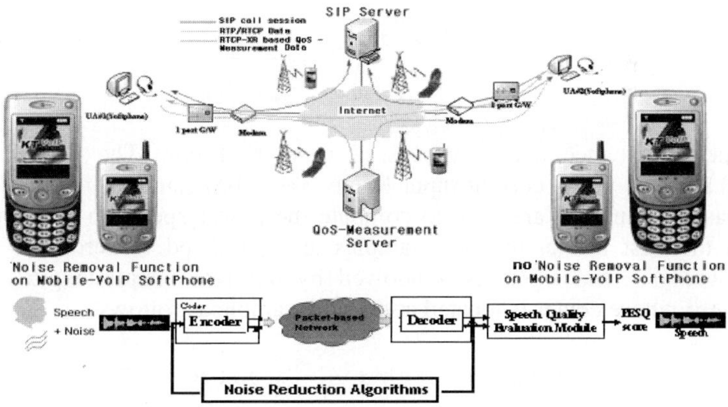

Fig. 4. Architecture for the VoIP system with applying noise removal algorithms

As illustrated in Fig.4, our network includes SIP servers and a QoS-factor monitoring server for the call session and QoS control. We applied calls through the PSTN to the SIP-based SoftPhone, the SIP-based SoftPhone to the PSTN, and the SIP-based SoftPhone to the SIP-based SoftPhone. The proposed noise reduction algorithm is applied to pre-processing method before speech coding and to post-processing method after speech decoding based on single microphone VoIP system.

4 Noise Reduction for Applying Packet-Based IP Network

4.1 Proposed Optimal Wiener Filter

We present a Wiener filter optimized to the estimated SNR of speech for speech enhancement in the VoIP. Since a non-causal IIR filter is unrealizable in practice, we propose a causal FIR (Finite Impulse Response) Wiener filter. Fig. 5 shows the proposed noise reduction process.

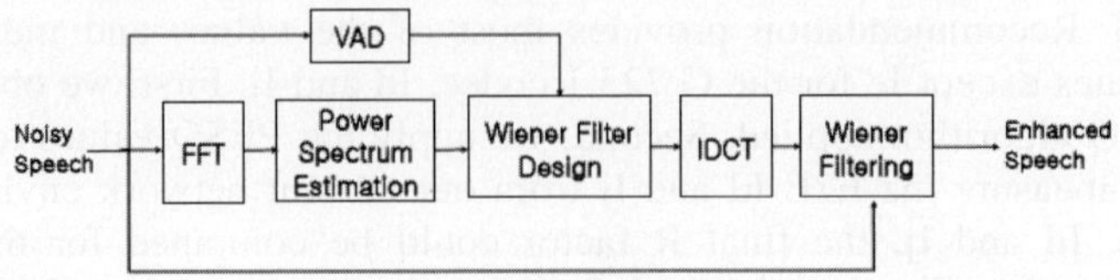

Fig. 5. Procedures of abnormal call establish/release cases

4.2 Proposed Optimal Wiener Filter

For a non-causal IIR (Infinite Impulse Response) Wiener filter, a clean speech signal d(n) , a background noise v(n), and an observed signal x(n) can be expressed as

$$x(n)=d(n)+v(n) \tag{3}$$

The frequency response of the Wiener filter becomes

$$W(e^{j\omega}) = \frac{P_d(e^{j\omega})}{P_v(e^{j\omega}) + P_d(e^{j\omega})} = \frac{\zeta(e^{j\omega})}{1+\zeta(e^{j\omega})} \tag{4}$$

The speech enhancement is processed frame-by-frame. The processing frame having 80 samples is the current input frame. Total 100 samples, i.e., the current 80 and the past 20 samples, are used to compute the power spectrum of the processing frame. In the first frame, the past samples are initialized to zero. For the power spectrum analysis, the signal is windowed by the 100 sample-length asymmetric window w(n) whose center is located at the 70th sample as follows.

$$w(n) = \begin{cases} 0.5(1 - \cos(\frac{2\pi n}{139})); n < 70 \\ \cos(\frac{2\pi(n-70)}{119}); else \end{cases} \tag{5}$$

The signal power spectrum is computed for this windowed signal using 256-FFT. In the Wiener filter design, the noise power spectrum is updated only for non-speech intervals by the decision of VAD (Voice Activity Detection) while the previous noise power spectrum is reused for speech intervals. And the speech power spectrum is estimated by the difference between the noise power and the signal power spectrum. With these estimated power spectra, the proposed Wiener filter is designed. In our proposed Wiener filter, the frequency response is expressed as

$$W(k) = \frac{\zeta^{a}(k)}{|1+\zeta^{a}(k)}, \qquad 0 < a \leq 1 \tag{6}$$

and $\zeta(k)$ is defined by

$$\zeta(k) = \frac{P_d(k)}{P_v(k)} \tag{7}$$

where ζ(k) , P d (k), and P v (k)are the kth spectral bin of the SNR, the speech power spectrum, and the noise power spectrum, respectively. Therefore, filtering is controlled by the parameter α. For ζ(k) greater than one, as α is increased, ζ (k) is also increased while ζ(k) is decreased for ζ(k) less than one. The signal is more strongly filtered out to reduce the noise for smaller ζ (k). On the other hand, the signal is more weakly filtered with little attenuation for larger ζ(k). To analysis the effect of α, we evaluate the performances for α value from 0.1 to 1. The performance is evaluated not for the coded speech but for the original speech in white Gaussian conditions. As α is increased up to 0.7, the performance is improved.

The codebook is trained for deciding the optimal α to the estimated SNR. First, the estimated SNR mean is calculated for the current frame. Second, the spectral distortion is measured with the log spectral Euclidean distance D defined as

$$D = \frac{1}{L}\sqrt{\sum_{k=0}^{L-1}\left[\log\left|X_{ref}(k)\right| - \log\left\{\left|X_{in}(k)\right|W(k)\right\}\right]^2} \quad (8)$$

where k is the index of the spectral bins, L is the total number of the spectral bins, |Xref (k)| is the spectrum of the clean reference signal, and |X in(k)|W(k) is the noise-reduced signal spectrum after filtering with the designed Wiener filter. Third, for each frame, optimal α is searched to minimize the distortion. The estimated SNR means of all bins with the optimal α are clustered by the LBG algorithm. Finally, the optimal α for the cluster is decided by averaging all α in the cluster. When the wiener filter is designed, the optimal α is searched by comparing the estimated SNR mean of all bins with the codeword of the cluster as shown in Fig 6.

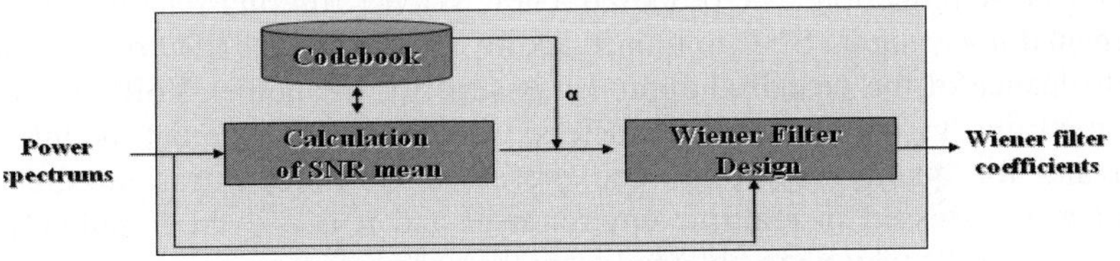

Fig. 6. Design of Wiener Filter by optimal α

5 Performance Evaluation and Results

For the additive noise reduction the noise signals are added to the clean speech ones to produce noisy ones with the SNR of 0, 5, 10, 15, and 20 dB. The total 800 noisy spoken sentences are trained because there are 5 SNR levels, 40 speech utterances, and 4 types of noises. The noise is reduced as pre-processing before encoding the speech in a codec and as post-processing after decoding the speech in a G.711 codec. Final proceeded speech is evaluated by the PESQ which is defined by ITU-T Recommendation P.862 for objective assessment of quality. After comparing an original signal with a degraded one, the output of PESQ provides a score from -0.5 to 4.5 as a MOS-like score. To verify the performance of noise reduction, our results are compared with those of the noise suppression in the IS-127 EVRC and the noise reduction in the ETSI standard. The ETSI noise canceller generates 40 msec buffering delay while there is no buffering delay in the EVRC noise canceller. In Fig. 7 and Fig. 8, the noise reduction performance evaluation results for G.711 for the real-time environment are summarized as the SNR to PESQ. The figures show the average PESQ results in G.711, respectively. In most noisy conditions, the proposed method yields higher PESQ scores than the others.

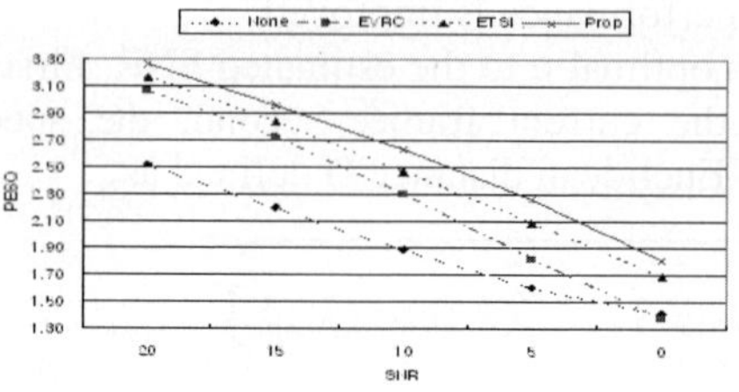

Fig. 7. PESQ score for white Gaussian noise

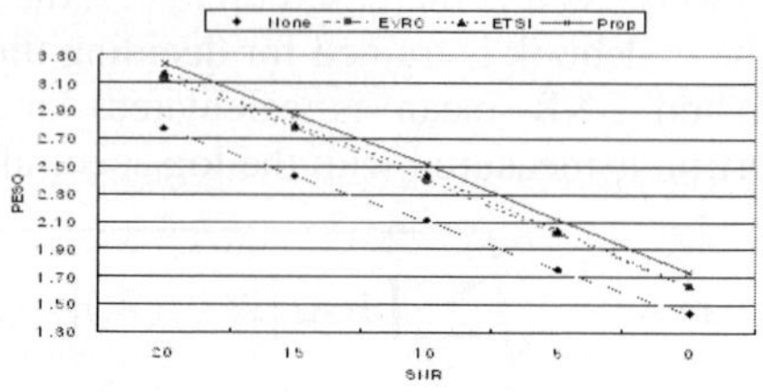

Fig. 8. PESQ score for white Office noise

6 Conclusion

In this paper, the performance evaluation of speech quality confirms that our proposed noise reduction algorithm outperforms more efficiently than the original algorithm in the G.711 speech codec. The proposed speech enhancement is applied before encoding as pre-processing and after decoding as post-processing of VoIP speech codecs for noise reduction. The proposed a new Wiener filtering scheme optimized to the estimated noisy signal SNR to reduce additive noises. The PESQ results show that the performance of the proposed approach is superior to another VoIP system. Also, for the reporting various quality parameters, we design management module for call session and for quality reporting. The presented QoS-factor transmission control mechanism is assessed in realtime environment and it is proved completely by the performance results which are obtained from the experiment.

References

1. Imai, S., et al.: Voice Quality Management for IP Networks based on Automatic Change Detection of Monitoring Data. In: Kim, Y.-T., Takano, M. (eds.) APNOMS 2006. LNCS, vol. 4238, Springer, Heidelberg (2006)
2. Eejaie, R., Handley, M., Estrin, D.: RAP: An End-to-end Rate-based Congestion Control Mechanism for Realtime Streams in the Internet. In: Proc. of IEEE INFOCOM, USA (March 21-25, 1999)
3. Beritelli, F., Ruggeri, G., Schembra, G.: TCP-Friendly Transmission of Voice over IP. In: Proc. of IEEE International Conference on Communications, New York, USA (April 2006)
4. Kim, C., et al.: End-to-End QoS Monitoring Tool Development and Performance Analysis for NGN. In: Kim, Y.-T., Takano, M. (eds.) APNOMS 2006. LNCS, vol. 4238, Springer, Heidelberg (2006)

5. De Martin, J.C.: Source-driven Packet Marking for Speech Transmission over Differentiated-Services Networks. In: Proc. of IEEE ICASSP 2001, Salt Lake City, USA (May 2001)
6. Cole, R.G., Rosenbluth, J.H.: VoIP over IP Performance Monitoring. Journal on Computer Communications Review, 31(2) (April 2001)
7. Schulzrinne, H., Casner, S., Frederick, R., Jacobson, V.: RTP: A Transport Protocol for Real-Time Application. IETF RFC 3550 (July 2005)
8. Friedman, T., Caceres, R., Clark, A.: RTP Control Protocol Extended Reports. IETF RFC 3611 (Novomber 2003)
9. Park, M., et al.: Frequency-Temporal Filtering for a Robust Audio Fingerprinting Scheme in Real-Noise Environments. ETRI Journal 28(4), 509–512 (2006)
10. Hwang, C.G., Myung, N.H.: Novel Phase Noise Reduction Method for CPW-Based Microwave Oscillator Circuit Utilizing a Compact Planar Helical Resonator. ETRI Journal 28(4), 529–532 (2006)
11. Choi, B.-H., et al.: An All-Optical Gain-Controlled Amplifier for Bidirectional Transmission An All-Optical Gain-Controlled Amplifier for Bidirectional Transmission. ETRI Journal 28(1), 1–8 (2006)
12. Bang, K.H., et al.: Audio Transcoding for Audio Streams from a T-DTV Broadcasting Station to a T-DMB Receiver. ETRI Journal 28(5), 664–667 (2006)

A Tangible User Interface with Multimodal Feedback

Laehyun Kim, Hyunchul Cho, Sehyung Park, and Manchul Han

Korea Institute of Science and Technology,
Intelligence and Interaction Research Center,
39-1, Haweolgok-dong, Sungbuk-gu, Seoul, Korea
{laehyunk,hccho,sehyung,manchul.han}@kist.re.kr

Abstract. Tangible user interface allows the user to manipulate digital information intuitively through physical things which are connected to digital contents spatially and computationally. It takes advantage of human ability to manipulate delicate objects precisely. In this paper, we present a novel tangible user interface, SmartPuck system, which consists of a PDP-based table display, SmartPuck having a built-in actuated wheel and button for the physical interactions, and a sensing module to track the position of SmartPuck. Unlike passive physical things in the previous systems, SmartPuck has built-in sensors and actuator providing multimodal feedback such as visual feedback by LEDs, auditory feedback by a speaker, and haptic feedback by an actuated wheel. It gives a feeling as if the user works with physical object. We introduce new tangible menus to control digital contents just as we interact with physical devices. In addition, this system is used to navigate geographical information in Google Earth program.

Keywords: Tangible User Interface, Tabletop display, Smart Puck System.

1 Introduction

In the conventional desktop metaphor, the user manipulates digital information through keyboard and mouse and sees the visual result on the monitor. This metaphor is very efficient to process structured tasks such as word processing and spreadsheet.

The main limitation of the desktop metaphor is cognitive mismatch. The user should be adapted to the relative movement of the virtual cursor which is a proxy of the physical mouse. The user moves the mouse in 2D on a horizontal desktop, but the output result appears on a vertical screen (see Fig. 1(a)). It requires cognitive mapping in our brain between the physical input space and digital output space. The desktop metaphor is still machine-oriented and relatively indirect user interface. Another limitation is that the desktop metaphor is suitable for single user environment in which it is hard for multiple users to share information due to single monitor, mouse and keyboard.

To address these limitations, new user interfaces require direct and intuitive metaphor based on human sensation such as the visual, auditory and tactual sensation and a large display and tools to share information and interaction. In this sense, TUI (Tangible User Interface)[1] has been developed. It allows the user to sense and manipulate digital information physically by our hands.

J. Jacko (Ed.): Human-Computer Interaction, Part III, HCII 2007, LNCS 4552, pp. 94–103, 2007.

(a) (b)

Fig. 1. Desktop system (a) vs. SmartPuck system (b)

In this paper, we introduce SmartPuck system (see Fig. 1(b)) as a new TUI which consists of a large table display based on PDP, a physical device called SmartPuck, and a sensing module.

SmartPuck system bridges the gap between digital interaction based on the graphical user interface in the computer system and physical interaction through which one perceives and manipulates objects in real world. In addition, it allows multiple users to share interaction and information naturally unlike the traditional desktop environment.

The system has some contributions against the conventional desktop system as follows:

- **Multimodal user interface.** SmartPuck has a physical wheel not only to control the detail change of digital information through our tactual sensation but also to give multimodal feedback such as visual (LEDs), auditory (speaker) and haptic (actuated wheel) feedback to the user. The actuated wheel provides various feelings of clicking by modulating the stepping motor's holding force and time in real-time. SmartPuck can communicate with the computer in a bidirectional way to send inputs applied by the user and to receive control commands to generate multimodal feedbacks from the computer through Bluetooth wireless communication. The position of SmartPuck is tracked by the infrared tracking module which is placed on the table display and connected to the computer via USB cable.
- **The PDP-based table display.** It consists of a 50 inch PDP with XVGA (1280x768) resolution for the visual display and table frame to support the PDP (see Figure 1). In order to provide the mobility, each leg of the table has a wheel. Unlike the projection-based display, the PDP-based display does not require dark lighting condition and calibration and avoids unwanted projection on the user's body. We have to consider viewing angle of table display. PDP generally has wider viewing angle than LCD does.
- **Tangible Menus.** We designed "Tangible Menus" which allow the user to control digital contents physically in the similar way that we operate physical devices such as volume control wheel, dial-type lock, and mode selector. Tangible Menus is

operated through SmartPuck. The user rotates the wheel of SmartPuck and simultaneously he feels the status of digital information via sense of touch bidirectionally. For instance, Wheel menu to select one of digital items located along the circle with physical feeling of clicking by turning the wheel of SmartPuck. Dial login menu allows the user to input passwords by rotating the wheel clockwise or count-clockwise.

- **Navigation of Google Earth.** We applied SmartPuck system for Google Earth program and an information kiosk system. The system is used successfully to operate Google Earth program instead of a mouse and keyboard. In order to navigate the geographical information, the user changes the direction of view using various operations by SmartPuck on the table display. The operations include moving, zooming, tilting, rotating, and flying to the target position.

The rest of this paper discusses previous TUIs (Tangible User Interfaces) in Section 2 and then describes SmartPuck system we have developed in Section 3. Section 4 presents Tangible Menus which is new graphical user interfaces based on SmartPuck. We also introduce an application to navigate geographical information in Google Earth. Finally we make the conclusion.

2 Previous Work

TUI (Tangible User Interface) provides an intuitive way to access and manipulate digital information physically using our hands. Main issues in TUI include visual display system to show digital information, physical tools as input devices, and tracking technique to sense the position and orientation of the physical tools.

Tangible media group leaded by Hiroshi Ishii at the MIT Media Lab have presented various TUI systems. Hiroshi Ishii introduced "Tangible Bits" as tangible embodiments of digital information to couple physical space (analog atom) and virtual space (digital information unit, bit) seamlessly [3].

Based on this vision, he has developed several tangible user interfaces such as metaDESK [4], mediaBlocks [5], and Sensetable [6] to allow the user to manipulate digital information intuitively.

Especially, Sensetable is a system which tracks the positions and orientations of multiple physical tools (Sensetable puck) on the tabletop display quickly and accurately. Sensetable puck has dials and modifiers to change the state in real time. Built on the Sensetable platform, many applications have been implemented including chemistry and system dynamics, interface for musical performance, IP network simulation, circuit simulation and so on.

DiamondTouch [7] is a multi-user touch system for tabletop front-projected displays. If the users touch the table, the table surface generates location dependent electric fields, which are capacitively coupled through the users and chairs to receivers.

SmartSkin [8] is a table sensing system based on capacitive sensor matrix. It can track the position and shape of hands and fingers, as well as measure their distance from the surface. The user manipulates digital information on the SmartSkin with free hands.

[9] is a scalable multi-touch sensing technique implemented based on FTIR (Frustrated Total Internal Reflection). The graphical images are displayed via

rear-projection to avoid undesirable occlusion issues. However, it requires significant space behind the touch surface for camera.

Entertaible [10] is a tabletop gaming platform that integrates traditional multi-player board and computer games. It consists of a tabletop display based on 32-inch LCD, touch screen to detect multi-object position, and supporting control electronics. The multiple users can manipulate physical objects on the digital board game.

ToolStone [11] is a wireless input device which senses physical manipulations by the user such as rotating, flipping, and tilting. Toolstone can be used as an additional input device operated by non-dominant hand along with the mouse. The user makes multiple degree-of-freedom interaction including zooming, rotation in 3D space, and virtual camera control. Toolstone allows physical interactions along with a mouse in the conventional desktop metaphor.

3 SmartPuck System

3.1 System Configuration

SmartPuck system is mainly divided into three sub modules: PDP-based table display, SmartPuck, and IR sensing module.

The table display consists of a 50 inch PDP with XVGA (1280x768) resolution for the visual display and table frame to support the PDP. In order to provide the mobility, each leg of the table has a wheel. Unlike the projection-based display, the PDP-based display does not require dark lighting condition and calibration and avoids unwanted projection on the user's body. Fig. 2 shows the system architecture.

SmartPuck is a physical device which is operated by the user's hand and is used to manipulate digital information directly on the table display. The operations include zooming, selecting, and moving items by rotating the wheel, pressing the button, and dragging the puck.

In order to track the absolute position of SmartPuck, a commercial infrared imaging sensor (XYFer system from E-IT) [12] is installed on the table display. It can sense two touches on the display at the same time quickly and accurately.

Fig. 3 shows the data flow of the system. The PC receives the data from SmartPuck and the IR sensor to recognize the user's inputs. SmartPuck sends the angle of the rotation and button input to the PC through wireless Bluetooth communication. The

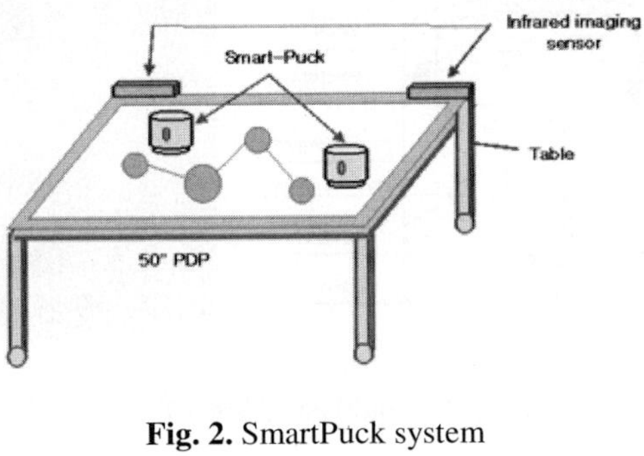

Fig. 2. SmartPuck system

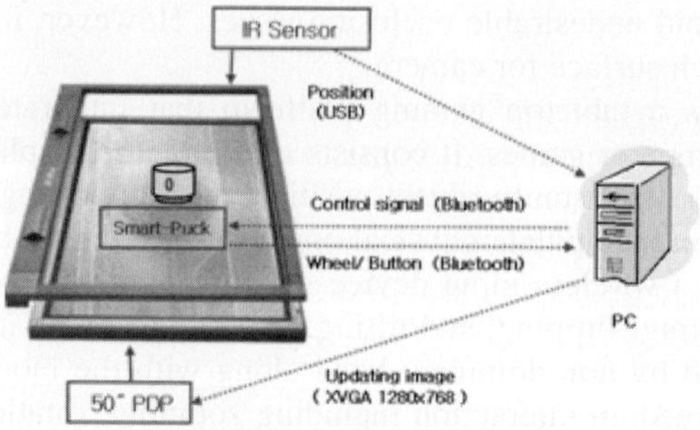

Fig. 3. Data flow of the system

IR sensor sends the positions of the puck to the PC via USB cable. The PC then updates the visual information on the PDP based on the user's input.

3.2 SmartPuck

SmartPuck is a multi-modal input/output device having an actuated wheel, cross-type button, LEDs and speaker as shown in Fig. 4. The user communicates with the digital information via visual, aural, and haptic sensations.

The cross-type button is a 4-way button located on the top of SmartPuck. The combination of button control can be mapped into various commands such as moving or rotating a virtual object vertically and horizontally. When the user spins the actuated wheel, the position sensor (optical encoder) senses rotational inputs applied by the user. At the same time, the actuated wheel gives torque feedback to the user to generate clicking feeling or limit rotational movement.

The LEDs display the visual information saying the status of SmartPuck and the predefined situation. The speaker in the lower part delivers simple effect sounds to the user through auditory channel. The patch is attached underneath the puck to prevent scratches on the display surface.

The absolute position of SmartPuck is tracked by the IR sensor installed on the table and is used for dragging operation.

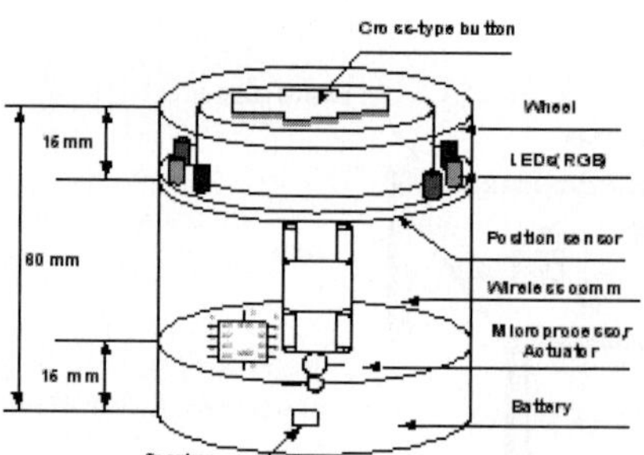

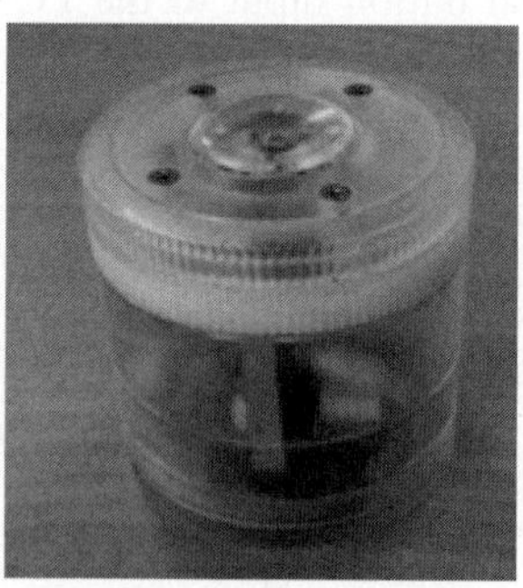

Fig. 4. Prototype of SmartPcuk

4 Tangible Menus

We designed new user interface called "Tangible Menus" operated through SmartPuck. The user rotates the wheel of SmartPuck. At the same time, he/shereceives haptic feedback to represent current status of digital contents in real time. Tangible Menus allows the user to control digital contents physically just as we interact with physical devices.

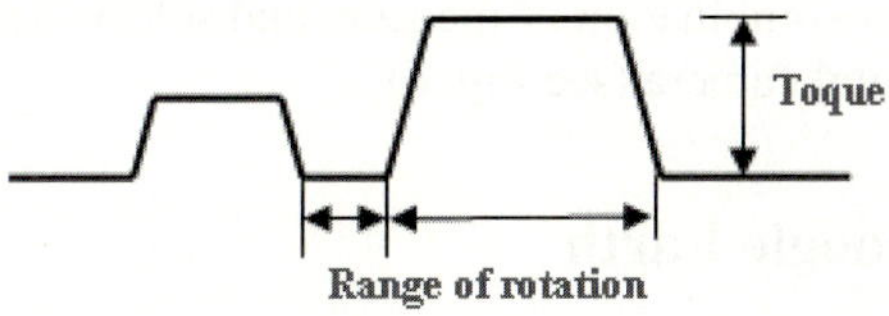

Fig. 5. Haptic modeling by modulating the toque and range of motion

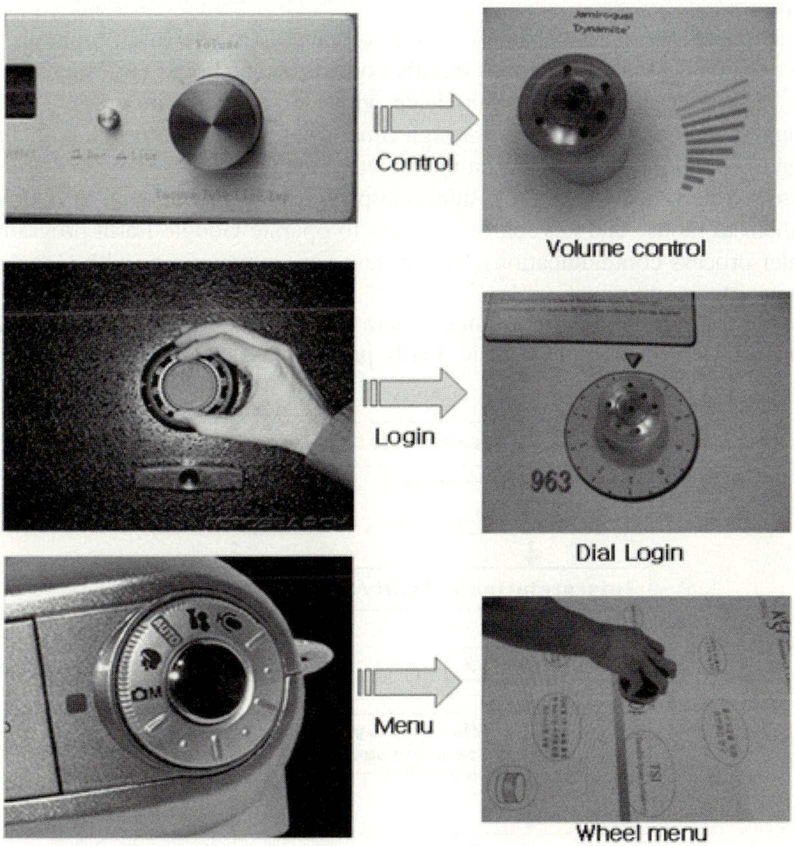

Fig. 6. Physical input modules in real world (left hand side) and tangible menus in digital world (right hand side)

Tangible Menus have different haptic effects by modulating the toque and the range of rotation of the wheel (see Fig. 5). The effects include continuous force effect independent of position, clicking effect, and barrier effect to set the minimum and maximum range of motion. The direction of motion can be either oppose or same direction as the user's motion.

Dial-type operation is common and efficient interface to control physical devices precisely by our hands in everyday life. In Tangible Menus, the user controls the volume of digital sound by rotating the wheel, makes login operation just as we spin the dial to set the number combination of the safe, and selects items in the similar way to the mode dial in a digital camera (see Fig. 6).

5 Navigation of Google Earth

Google Earth is an internet program to search geographical information including the earth, roads, buildings based on satellite images using a mouse and keyboard on the desktop.

In this paper, we use SmartPuck system to operate Google Earth program instead of a mouse and desktop monitor for intuitive operation and better performance.

Fig. 7 shows the steps to communicate with Google Earth program. The system reads inputs applied by the users through SmartPuck system. The inputs include the position of SmartPuck and finger on the tabletop, the angle of the rotation, and button input from SmartPuck. Then the system interprets user inputs through SmartPuck and maps them to mouse and keyboard messages to operate Google Earth program using PC (Inter-process communication). The system can communicate with Google Earth program without additional work.

Basic operations through SmartPuck system are designed to make it easy to navigate geographical information in Google Earth program. They are used to change the

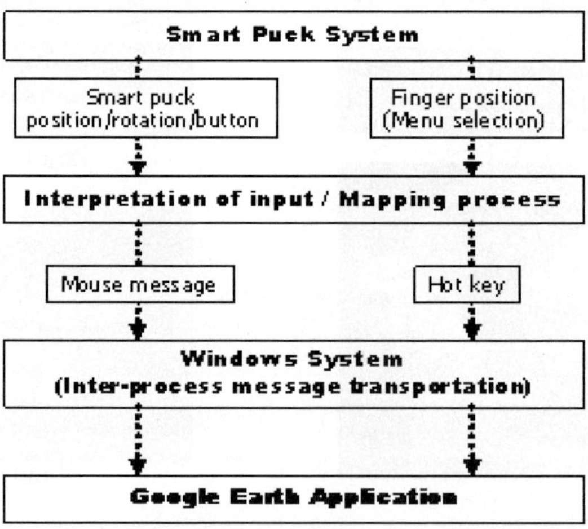

Fig. 7. Software architecture for Google Earth interaction

direction of view by moving, zooming, tilting, rotating, and flying to the target position. We reproduce the original navigation menu in Google Earth program for SmartPuck system. Table 1 shows the mapping between SmartPuck inputs and mouse messages.

Table 1. Mapping from SmartPuck inputs to corresponding mouse messages

Operation	Input of SmartPuck	Mouse message
Moving	Press button & drag the puck	Left button of a mouse and drag the mouse
Zooming	Rotate the wheel	Right button of a mouse and drag the mouse about Y axis
Tilting	Press button & drag the puck	Middle button of a mouse and drag the mouse about Y axis
Rotating	Rotate the wheel	Middle button of a mouse and drag the mouse about X axis
Flying to the point	Press button	Double click the left button of a mouse

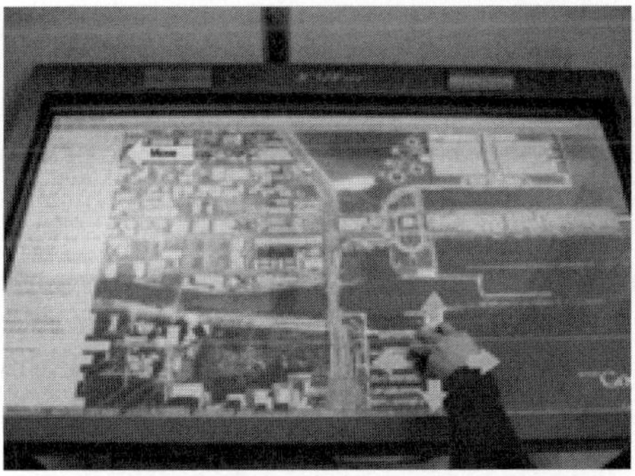
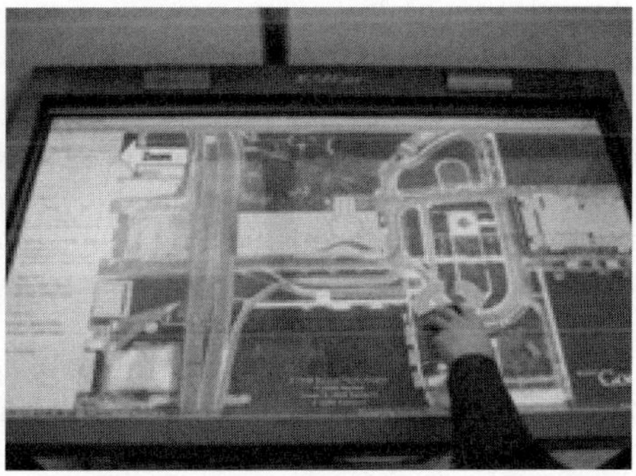

(a) Moving operation (b) Zooming operation

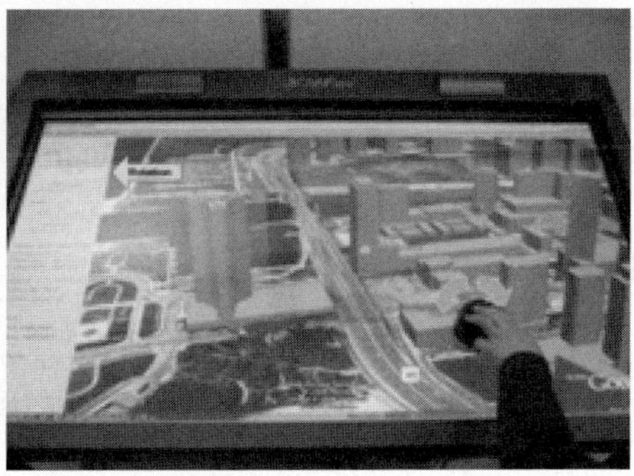

(c) Tilting operation (d) Rotation operation

Fig. 8. Basic operations to navigate 3-D geographical information in Google Earth program through SmartPuck system

For the moving operation, the user places the puck onto the starting point and then drags it toward the desired point on the screen while pressing the built-in button. The scene is moved along the trajectory from the initial to the end points (see Fig. 8(a)). It gives a feeling as if the user manipulates a physical map by his hands. The user controls the level of detail of map intuitively by rotating the physical wheel of the puck clockwise or counter-clockwise to an angle of his choice (see Fig. 8(b)). For moving and zooming operations, the mode is set to Move & Zoom in the graphical menu on the left hand side in the screen.

In order to perform the tilting and rotating operations, the user selects Tile & Rotation mode in the menu before applying the operation by the puck. For tiling the scene in 3D space, the user places the puck on the screen and then moves it vertically while pressing the button. The scene is tilted correspondingly (see Fig. 8(c)). Spinning the wheel rotates the scene in Fig. 8(d).

The graphical menu is added on the left-hand side of the screen instead of the original Google Earth menu which is designed to work with a mouse. By touching the menu by a finger, the user changes the mode of the puck operation and setup in Google Earth program. In addition, the menu displays the information such as the coordinates of touching points, button on/off, and the angle of rotation.

6 Conclusion

We present a novel tangible interface called SmartPuck system which is designed to integrate physical and digital interactions. The user manipulates digital information through SmartPuck on the large tabletop display. SmartPuck is a tangible device providing multi-modal feedback such as visual (LEDs), auditory (speaker), and haptic (actuated wheel) feedback.

The system allows the user to navigate the geographical scene in Google Earth program. Basic operation is to change the direction of view by moving, zooming, tilting, rotating, and flying to the target position by manipulating the puck physically. In addition, we first introduce Tangible Menus which allows the user to control digital contents through sense of touch and to feel the status of digital information at the same time.

For the future work, we apply SmartPuck system to a new virtual prototyping system integrating tangible interface. The user can test and evaluate the virtual 3-D prototype through SmartPuck system providing physical experience.

References

1. Ullmer, B., Ishii, H.: Emerging Frameworks for Tangible User Interfaces. In: Human-Computer Interaction in the New Meillenium, pp. 579–601. Addision-Wesley, London (2001)
2. Google Earth, http://earth.google.com/
3. Ishii, H., Ullmer, B.: Tangible Bits: Towards Seamless Interfaces between People, Bits, and Atoms. In: Proc. CHI 1997, pp. 234–241. ACM Press, New York (1997)
4. Ullmer, B., Ishii, H.: The metaDESK: Models and Prototypes for Tangible User Interfaces. In: Proc. Of UIST 1997, pp. 223–232. ACM Press, New York (1997)

5. Ullmer, B., Ishii, H.: mediaBlocks: Tangible Interfaces for Online Media. In: Ext. Abstracts CHI 1999, pp. 31–32. ACM Press, New York (1999)
6. Patten, J., Ishii, H., Hines, J., Pangaro, G.: Sensetable: A Wireless Object Tracking Platform for Tangible User Interfaces. In: Proc. CHI 2001, pp. 253–260. ACM Press, New York (2001)
7. Han, J.Y.: Low-Cost Multi-Touch Sensing through Frustrated Total Internal Reflection. In: Proc. UIST 2005, pp. 115–118. ACM Press, New York (2005)
8. Rekimoto, J.: SmartSkin: An Infrastructure for Freehand Manipulations on Interactive Surfaces. In: Proc. CHI 2002, ACM Press, New York (2002)
9. Dietz, P.H., Leigh, D.L.: DiamondTouch: A Multi-User Touch Technology. In: Proc. UIST 2001, pp. 219–226. ACM Press, New York (2001)
10. Philips Research Technologies, Enteraible, http://www.research.philips.com/initiatives/entertaible/index.html
11. Rekimoto, J., Sciammarella, E.: ToolStone: Effective Use of the Physical Manipulation Vocabularies of Input Devices. In: Proc. UIST 2000, ACM Press, New York (2000)
12. XYFer system, http://www.e-it.co.jp

Minimal Parsing Key Concept Based Question Answering System

Sunil Kopparapu[1], Akhlesh Srivastava[1], and P.V.S. Rao[2]

[1] Advanced Technology Applications Group, Tata Consultancy Services Limited, Subash Nagar, Unit 6 Pokhran Road No 2, Yantra Park, Thane West, 400 601, India
{sunilkumar.kopparapu,akhilesh.srivastava}@tcs.com

[2] Tata Teleservices (Maharastra) Limited, B. G. Kher Marg, Worli, Mumbai, 400 018, India
dr.pvs.rao@tatatel.co.in

Abstract. The home page of a company is an effective means for show casing their products and technology. Companies invest major effort, time and money in designing their web pages to enable their user's to access information they are looking for as quickly and as easily as possible. In spite of all these efforts, it is not uncommon for a user to spend a sizable amount of time trying to retrieve the particular information that he is looking for. Today, he has to go through several hyperlink clicks or manually search the pages displayed by the site search engine to get to the information that he is looking for. Much time gets wasted if the required information does not exist on that website. With websites being increasingly used as sources of information about companies and their products, there is need for a more convenient interface. In this paper we discuss a system based on a set of Natural Language Processing (NLP) techniques which addresses this problem. The system enables a user to ask for information from a particular website in free style natural English. The NLP based system is able to respond to the query by 'understanding' the intent of the query and then using this understanding to retrieve relevant information from its unstructured info-base or structured database for presenting it to the user. The interface is called UniqliQ as it avoids the user having to click through several hyperlinked pages. The core of UniqliQ is its ability to understand the question without formally parsing it. The system is based on identifying key-concepts and keywords and then using them to retrieve information. This approach enables UniqliQ framework to be used for different input languages with minimal architectural changes. Further, the key-concept – keyword approach gives the system an inherent ability to provide approximate answers in case the exact answers are not present in the information database.

Keywords: NL Interface, Question Answering System, Site search engine.

1 Introduction

Web sites vary in the functions they perform but the baseline is dissemination of information. Companies invest significant effort, time and money in designing their web pages to enable their user's to access information that they are looking for as quickly and as easily as possible. In spite of these efforts, it is not uncommon for a

J. Jacko (Ed.): Human-Computer Interaction, Part III, HCII 2007, LNCS 4552, pp. 104–113, 2007.

user to spend a sizable amount of time (hyperlink clicking and/or browsing) trying to retrieve the particular information that he is looking for. Until recently, web sites were a collection of disparate sections of information connected by hyperlinks. The user navigated through the pages by guessing and clicking the hyperlinks to get to the information of interest. More recently, there has been a tendency to provide site search engines[1] , usually based on key word search strategy, to help navigate through the disparate pages. The approach adopted is to give the user all the information he could possibly want about the company. The user then has to manually search through the information thrown back by the search engine i.e. search the search engine. If the hit list is huge or if no items are found a few times he will probably abandon the search and not use the facility again. According to a recent survey [1] 82 percent of users to Internet sites use on-site search engines. Ensuring that the search engine has an interface that delivers precise[2] , useful[3] and actionable[4] results for the user is critical to improving user satisfaction. In a web-browsing behavior study [7], it was found that none of the 60 participants (evenly distributed across gender, age and browsing experience) was able to complete all the 24 tasks assigned to them in a maximum of 5 minutes per task. In. that specific study, users were given a rather well designed home page and asked to find specific information on the site. They were not allowed to use the site search engine. Participants were given common tasks such as finding an annual report, a non-electronic gift certificate, the price of a woman's black belt or, more difficult, how to determine what size of clothes you should order for a man with specific dimensions.

To provide better user experience, a website should be able to accept queries in natural language and in response provide the user succinct information rather than (a) show all the (un)related information or (b) necessitate too many interactions in terms of hyperlink clicks. Additionally the user should be given some indication in case either the query is incomplete or an approximate answer in case no exact response is possible based on information available on the website. Experiments show that, irrespective of how well a website has been designed, on an average, a computer literate information seeker has to go through at least 4 clicks followed by a manual search of all the information retrieved by the search engine before he gets the information he is seeking[5] . For example, the Indian railway website [2], frequented by travelers, requires as many as nine hyperlink clicks to get information about availability of seats on trains for travel between two valid stations [9].

Question Answering (QA) systems [6][5][4], based on Natural Language Processing (NLP) techniques are capable of enhancing the user experience of the information seeker by eliminating the need for clicks and manual search on the part of the user. In effect, the system provides the answers in a single click. Systems using NLP are capable of understanding the intent of the query, in the semantic sense, and hence are able to fetch exact information related to the query.

---

[1] We will use the phrase "site search engine" and "search engine" interchangeably in this paper.

[2] In the sense that only the relevant information is displayed as against showing a full page of information which might contain the answer.

[3] In the absence of an exact answer the system should give alternatives, which are close to the exact answer in some intuitive sense.

[4] Information on how the search has been performed should be given to the user so that he is better equipped to query the system next time.

[5] Provided of course that the information is actually present on the web pages.

In this paper, we describe a NLP based system framework which is capable of understanding and responding to questions posed in natural language. The system, built in-house, has been designed to give relevant information without parsing the query[6]. The system determines the key concept and the associated key words (KC-KW) from the query and uses them to fetch answers. This KC-KW framework (a) enables the system to fetch answers that are close to the query when exact answers are not present in the info-base and (b) gives it the ability to reuse the KC-KW framework architecture with minimal changes to work with other languages. In Section 2 we introduce QA systems and argue that neither the KW based system nor a full parsing system are ideal; each with its own limitations. We introduce our framework in Section 3 followed by a detailed description of our approach. We conclude in Section 4.

2 Question Answering Systems

Question Answering (QA) systems are being increasingly used for information retrieval in several areas. They are being proposed as 'intelligent' search engine that can act on a natural language query in contrast with the plain key word based search engines. The common goal of most of them is to (a) understand the query in natural language and (b) get a correct or an approximately correct answer in response to a query from a predefined info-base or a structured database.

In a very broad sense, a QA system can be thought of as being a pattern matching system. The query in its original form (as framed by the user) is preprocessed and parameterized and made available to the system in a form that can be used to match the answer paragraphs. It is assumed that the answer paragraphs have also been preprocessed and parameterized in a similar fashion. The process could be as simple as picking selective key words and/or key phrases from the query and then matching these with the selected key words and phrases extracted from the answer paragraphs. On the other hand it could be as complex as fully parsing the query[7] , to identify the parts of speech of each word in the query, and then matching the parsed information with fully parsed answer paragraphs. The preprocessing required would generally depend on the type of parameters being extracted. For instance, for a simple key words type of parameter extraction, the preprocessing would involve removal of all words that are not key words while for a full parsing system it could be retaining the punctuations and verifying the syntactic and semantic 'well-formedness' of the query.

Most QA systems resort to full parsing [4,5,6] to comprehend the query. While this has its advantages (it can determine who killed who in a sentence like "Rama killed Ravana") its performance is far from satisfactory in practice because for accurate and consistent parsing (a) the parser, used by the QA system and (b) the user writing the (query and answer paragraph) sentences should both follow the rules of grammar. If either of them fails, the QA system will not perform to satisfaction. While one can ensure that the parser follows the rules of grammar, it is impractical to ensure this

[6] We look at all the words in the query as standalone entities and use a consistent and simple way of determining whether a word is a key-word or a key-concept.

[7] Most QA systems, available today, do a full parsing of the query to determine the intent of the query. A full parsing system in general evaluates the query for syntax (and followed by semantics) by determining explicitly the part of speech of each word.

from a casual user of the system. Unless the query is grammatically correct – the parser would run into problems. For example

- A full sentence parser would be unable to parse a grammatically incorrect constructed query and surmise the intent of the query[8].
- Parsing need not always necessarily gives the correct or intended result. "Visiting relatives can be a nuisance to him", is a well known example[12], which can be parsed in different ways, namely, (a) visiting relatives is a nuisance to him. (him = visitor) or (b) visiting relatives are a nuisance to him. (him ≠ visitor).

Full parsing, we believe, is not appropriate for a QA system especially because we envisage the use of the system by

- large number of people who need not necessarily be grammatically correct all the time,
- people would wish to use casual/verbal grammar[9]

Our approach takes the middle path, neither too simple not too complex and avoids formal parsing.

3 Our Approach: UniqliQ

UniqliQ is a web enabled, state of the art intelligent question answering system capable of understanding and responding to questions posed to it in natural English. UniqliQ is driven by a set of core Natural Language Processing (NLP) modules. The system has been designed keeping in mind that the average user visiting any web site works with the following constraints

- the user has little time, and doesn't want to be constrained by how he can or can not ask for information[10]
- the user is not grammatically correct all the time (would tend to use transactional grammar)
- a first time user is unlikely to be aware of the organization of the web pages
- the user knows what he wants and would like to query as he would query any other human in natural English language.

Additionally, the system should

- be configurable to work with input in different languages
- provide information that is close to that being sought in the absence of an exact answer
- allow for typos and misspelt words

The front end of UniqliQ, shown in Fig. 1, is a question box on the web page of a website. The user can type his question in natural English. In response to the query,

[8] The system assumes that the query is grammatically correct.

[9] Intent is conveyed; but from a purist angle the sentence construct is not correct.

[10] In several systems it is important to construct a query is a particular format. In many SMS based information retrieval system there is a 3 alphabet code that has to be appended at the beginning of the query in addition to sending the KWs in a specific order.

the system picks up specific paragraphs which are relevant to the query and displays them to the user.

3.1 Key Concept-Key Word (KC-KW) Approach

The goal of our QA system is (a) to get a correct or an approximate answer in response to a query and (b) not to put any constraint on the user to construct syntactically correct queries[11] . There is no one strategy envisaged – we believe a combination of strategies based on heuristics, would work best for a practical QA system. The proposed QA system follows a middle path especially because the first approach (picking up key words) is simplistic and could give rise to a large number of irrelevant answers (high false acceptances), the full parsing approach is complex, time consuming and could end up rejecting valid answers (false rejection), especially if the query is not well formed syntactically. The system is based on two types of parameters -- key words (KW) and key concepts (KC).

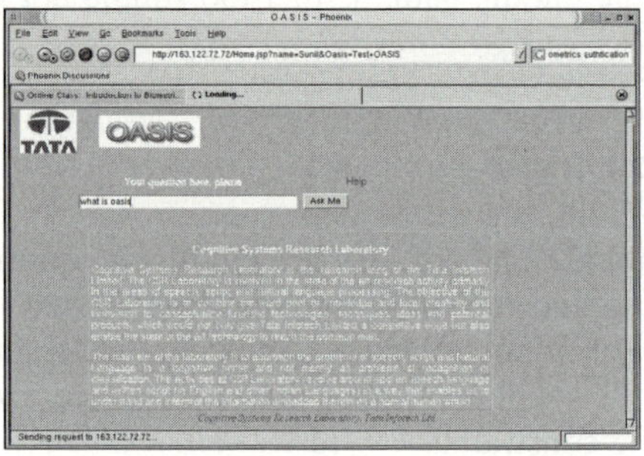

Fig. 1. Screen Shot of UniqliQ system

In each sentence, there is usually one word, knowing which the nature of these semantic relationships can be determined. In the sentence, “I purchased a pen from Amazon for Rs. 250 yesterday” the crucial word is ‘purchase’. Consider the expression, Purchase(I, pen, Amazon, Rs. 250/-, yesterday). It is possible to understand the meaning even in this form. Similarly, the sentence “I shall be traveling to Delhi by Air on Monday at 9 am” implies: Travel (I, Delhi, air, Monday, 9am). In the above examples, the key concept word ‘holds’ or ‘binds’ all the other key words together. If the key concept word is removed, all the others fall apart. Once the key concept is known, one also knows what other key words to expect; the relevant key words can be extracted. There are various ways in which key concepts can be looked at

1. as a mathematical functional which links other words (mostly KWs) to itself. Key Concepts are broadly like 'function names' which carry 'arguments' with them. E.g. KC1 (KW1, KW2, KC2 (KW3, KW4))

   Given the key concept, the nature and dimensionality of the associated key words get specified.

---

[11] Verbal communication (especially if one thinks of a speech interface to the QA system) uses informal grammar and most of the QA systems which use full parsing would fail.

We define the arguments in terms of syntacto-semantic variables: e.g. destination has to be "noun – city name"; price has to be "noun – number" etc.
Mass-of-a-sheet (length, breadth, thickness, density)
Purchase (purchaser, object, seller, price, time)
Travel (traveler, destination, mode, day, time)

2. as a template specifier: if the key concept is purchase/sell, the key words will be material, quantity, rate, discount, supplier etc. Valence, or the number of arguments that the key concept supports is known once the key concept is identified.
3. as a database structure specifier: consider the sentence, "John travels on July 20th at 7pm by train to Delhi". The underlying database structure would be

KeyCon	KW1	KW 2	KW3	KW4	KW5
Travel	Traveler	Destination	Mode	Day	Time
	John	Delhi	Train	July_20	7 pm

KCs together with KWs help in capturing the total intent of the query. This results in constraining the search and making the query very specific. For example, reserve (place_from = Mumbai, place to=Bangalore, class=2nd), makes the query more specific or exact, ruling out the possibility of a reservation between Mumbai and Bangalore in 3rd AC for instance.

A key concept and key word based approach can be quite effective solution to the problem of natural (spoken) language understanding in a wide variety of situations, particularly in man-machine interaction systems.

The concept of KC gives UniqliQ a significant edge over simplistic QA systems which are based on KWs only [3]. Identifying KCs helps in better understanding the query and hence the system is able to answer the query more appropriately. A query in all likelihood will have but one KC but this need not be true with the KCs in the paragraph. If more than one key concept is present in a paragraph, one talks of hierarchy of key concepts[12] . In this paper we will assume that there is only one KC in an answer paragraph.

One can think of a QA system based on KC and KW as one that would save the need to fully parse the query; this comes at a cost, namely, this could result in the system not being able to distinguish who killed whom in the sentence "Rama killed Ravana". The KC-KW based QA system would represent it as kill (Rama, Ravana) which can have two interpretations. But in general, this is not a huge issue unless there are two different paragraphs – the first paragraph describing about Rama killing Ravana and a second paragraph (very unlikely) describing Ravana killing Rama.

There are reasons to believe that humans resort to a key concept type of approach in processing word strings or sentences exchanged in bilateral, oral interactions of a transactional type. A clerk sitting at an enquiry counter at a railway station does not carefully parse the questions that passengers ask him. That is how he is able to deal with incomplete and ungrammatical queries. In fact, he would have some difficulty in dealing with long and complex sentences even if they are grammatical.

[12] When several KCs are present in the paragraph then one KC is determined to be more important than another KC.

3.2 Description

UniqliQ has several individual modules as shown in Fig. 2. The system is driven by a question understanding module (see Fig. 2). (Its first task as in any QA system is preprocessing of the query: (a) removal of stop words and (b) spell checking.) This module not only identifies the intent of the question (by determining the KC in the query) and checks the dimensionality syntax[13] [14] . The intent of the question (the key concept) is sent to the query generation module along with the keywords in the query.

The query module, assisted by a taxonomy tree, uses the information supplied by the question understanding module to specifically pick relevant paragraphs from within the website. All paragraphs of information picked up by the query module as being appropriate to the query are then ranked[15] in the decreasing order of relevance to the query. The highest ranked paragraph is then displayed to the user along with a context dependent prelude to the user. In the event an appropriate answer does not exist in the info-base, the query module fetches information most similar (in a semantic sense) to the information sought by the user. Such answers are prefixed by "You were looking for ....., but I have found ... for you" which is generated by the prelude generating module indicative that the exact information is unavailable. UniqliQ has memory in the sense that it can retain context information through the session. This enables UniqliQ to 'complete' a query (in case the query is incomplete) using the KC-KW pertaining to previous queries as reference.

At the heart of the system are the taxonomy tree and the information paragraphs (info-let). These are fine tuned to suit a particular domain. The taxonomy tree is essentially a word-net [13] type of structure which captures the relationships between different words. Typically, relationships such as synonym, type_of, part_of are captured[16] . The info-let is the knowledge bank (info-base) of the system. As of now, it is manually engineered from the information available on the web site[17] . The info-base essentially consists of a set of info-lets. In future it is proposed to automate this process.

The no parsing aspect of UniqliQ architecture gives it the ability to operate in a different language (say Hindi) by just using a Hindi to English word dictionary[18] . A Hindi front end has been developed and demonstrated [9] for a natural language railway enquiry application. A second system which answers agriculture related questions in Hindi has also been implemented.

---

[13] Dimensionality syntax check is performed by checking if a particular KC has KWs corresponding to an expected dimensionality. For example in a railway transaction scenario the KC reserve should be accompanied by 4 KWs where one KW had the dimensionality of class of travel, 1 KW has the dimensionality of date and 2 KWs have the dimensionality of location.

[14] The dimensionality syntax check enables the system to quiz the user and enable the user to frame the question appropriately.

[15] Ranking is based on a notional distance between the KC-KW pattern of the query and the KC-KW pattern of the answer paragraph.

[16] A taxonomy is built by first identifying words (statistical n-gram (n=3) analysis of words) and then manually defining the relationship between these selected words. Additionally the selected words are tagged as key-words, key-concepts based on human intelligence (common sense and general understanding of the domain).

[17] A infolet is more often a paragraph which is self contained and ideally talks about a single theme.

[18] Traditionally one would need a automatic language translator from Hindi to English.

3.3 Examples

UniqliQ platform has been used in several applications. Specifically, it has been used to disseminate information from a corporate website, a technical book, a fitness book, yellow pages[19] information retrieval [11] and railway [9]/ airline information retrieval. UniqliQ is capable of addressing queries seeking information of various types.

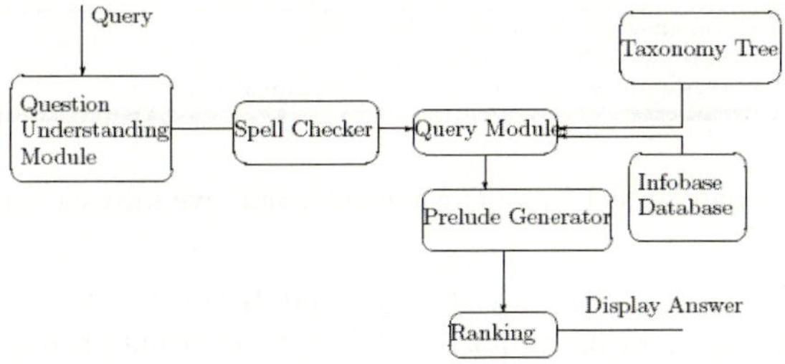

Fig. 2. The UniqliQ system. The database and info-base contain the content on the home page of the company.

Fig 3 captures the essential differences between the current search methods and the system using NLP in the context of a query related to an airline website. To find an answer to the question, "Is there a flight from Chicago or Seattle to London?" on a typical airline website, a user has first to query the website for information about all the flights from Chicago to London and then again query the website to seek information on all the flights from Seattle to London. UniqliQ can do this in one shot and display all the flights from Chicago or Seattle to London (see Fig. 3). Fig. 4 and Fig. 5 capture some of the questions the KC-KW based system is typically able to deal with.

The query "What are the facilities for passengers with restricted mobility?" today typically require a user to first click the navigation bar related to Products and

Ramesh: *Are there any flights from Chicago to London between 6 p.m. and 9 p.m. on Thursday?*
Shyam: *Can you please give me all the flights from Chicago to London which start from Chicago between 6 and 9 PM on Thursday?*

Currently, Ramesh and Shyam have to go the Airline *website ... select the source (Chicago) and destination (London) cities from a drop down menu ... the web page displays all the Chicago-London flights ... Then Ramesh and Shyam have to manually scan the displayed list to get the information they seek. A laborious process ...*
Uniqlic: Displays only the information of flights from Chicago to London which are functional on a Thursday between 6 and 9 PM.

Fig. 3. A typical session showing the usefulness of a NLP based information seeking tool against the current information seeking procedure

[19] User can retrieve yellow pages information on the mobile phone. The user can send a free form text as the query (either as an SMS or through a BREW application on a CDMA phone) and receive answers on his phone.

- Is there a flight from Seattle to Chicago before noon?
- Give me the details of S2-112?
- Please give me the flights from Chicago to London which don't fly on Wednesday?
- Are there flights from Chicago to London on 25/9/2003?

Fig. 4. Some queries that UniqliQ can handle and save the user time and effort (reduced number of clicks)

- Can I carry my pets on my flight from Chicago to London?
- I am 65 years old. Do you provide any concession?
- Would you provide assistance for my 2 years old kid to travel alone?

Fig. 5. General queries that UniqliQ can handle and save the user manual search

services; then search for a link, say, On ground Services; browse through all the information on that page and then pick out relevant information manually. UniqliQ it is capable of picking up and displaying only the relevant paragraph, saving time of the user also saving the user the pain of wading through irrelevant information to locate the specific item that he is looking for!

4 Conclusions

Experience shows that it is not possible for an average user to get information from a web site with out having to go through several clicks and manual search. Conventional site search engines lack the ability to understand the intent of the query; they operate based on keywords and hence flush out information which might not be useful to the user. Quite often the user needs to manually search amongst the search engine results for the actual information he needs. NLP techniques are capable of making information retrieval easy and purposeful. This paper describes a platform which is capable of making information retrieval human friendly. UniqliQ built on NLP technology enables a user to pose a query in natural language. In addition it takes away the laborious job of manually clicking several tabs and manual search by presenting succinct information to the user. The basic idea behind UniqliQ is to enable a first time user to a web page to obtain information without having to surf the web site. The question understanding is based on identification of KC-KW which facilitates using the platform usable for queries in different languages. It also helps in ascertaining if the query has all the information needed to give an answer. The KC-KW approach allows the user to be slack in terms of grammar and works well even for casual communication. The absence of a full sentence parser is an advantage and not a constraint in well delimited domains (such as homepages of a company). Recalling the template specifier interpretation of key concept, it is easy to identify in case any required key word is missing from the query; e.g. if the KC is purchase/sell, the system can check and ask if any of the requisite key words (material, quantity, rate, discount, supplier) is missing. This is not possible with systems based on key words alone.

Ambiguities can arise if more than one key words have the same dimensionality (i.e. belong to the same syntacto-semantic category). For instance, the key concept 'kill' has: killer, victim, time, place etc. for key words. Confusion is possible between killer and victim because both have the same 'dimension' (name of human), e.g. kill who Oswald? (Who did Oswald kill - Kennedy, or who killed Oswald? - Jack Ruby)

Acknowledgments. Our thanks are due to members of the Cognitive Systems Research Laboratory. Several of whom have been involved in developing prototypes to test UniqliQ, the question answering system in various domains.

References

1. http://www.coremetrics.com/solutions/on_site_search.html
2. Indian Rail. http://www.indianrail.gov.in
3. Agichtein, E., Lawrence, S., Gravano, L.: Learning search engine specific query transformations for question answering. In: Proceedings of the Tenth International World Wide Web Conference (2001)
4. AskJeevs http://www.ask.com
5. AnswerBug http://www.answerbug.com
6. START http://start.csail.mit.edu/
7. WebCriteria http://www.webcriteria.com
8. Kopparapu, S., Srivastava, A., Rao KisanMitra, P.V.S.: A Question Answering System For Rural Indian Farmers. In: International Conference on Emerging Applications of IT (EAIT 2006) Science City Kolkata (February 10-11, 2006)
9. Kopparapu, S., Srivastava, A., Rao, P.V.S: Building a Natural Language Interface for the Indian Railway website, NCIICT 2006, Coimbatore (July 7-8, 2006)
10. Koparapu, S., Srivastava, A., Rao, P.V.S.: Succinct Information Retrieval from Web, Whitepaper, Tata Infotech Limited (now Tata Consultancy Services Limited) (2004)
11. Kopparapu, S., Srivastava, A., Das, S., Sinha, R., Orkey, M., Gupta, V., Maheswary, J., Rao, P.V.S.: Accessing Yellow Pages Directory Intelligently on a Mobile Phone Using SMS, MobiComNet 2004, Vellore (2004)
12. http://www.people.fas.harvard.edu/ ctjhuang/lecture_notes/lecch1.html
13. http://wordnet.princeton.edu/

Customized Message Generation and Speech Synthesis in Response to Characteristic Behavioral Patterns of Children

Ho-Joon Lee and Jong C. Park

CS division KAIST, 335 Gwahangno (373-1 Guseong-dong),
Yuseong-gu, Daejeon 305-701, Republic of Korea
hojoon@nlp.kaist.ac.kr, park@cs.kaist.ac.kr

Abstract. There is a growing need for a user-friendly human-computer interaction system that can respond to various characteristics of a user in terms of behavioral patterns, mental state, and personalities. In this paper, we present a system that generates appropriate natural language spoken messages with customization for user characteristics, taking into account the fact that human behavioral patterns usually reveal one's mental state or personality subconsciously. The system is targeted at handling various situations for five-year old kindergarteners by giving them caring words during their everyday lives. With the analysis of each case study, we provide a setting for a computational method to identify user behaviroal patterns. We believe that the proposed link between the behavioral patterns and the mental state of a human user can be applied to improve not only user interactivity but also believability of the system.

Keywords: natural language processing, customized message generation, behavioral pattern recognition, speech synthesis, ubiquitous computing.

1 Introduction

The improvement of robot technology, along with a ubiquitous computing environment, has made it possible to utilize robots in our daily life. These robots would be especially useful as a monitoring companion for young children and the elderly who need continuous care, assisting human caretakers. Their tasks would involve protecting them from various in-door dangers and allowing them to overcome emotional instabilities by actively engaging them in the field. It is thus not surprising that there is a growing interest in a user-friendly human-computer interaction system that can respond properly to various characteristics of a user, such as behavioral pattern, mental state, and personality. For example, such a system would give appropriate warning messages to a child who keeps approaching potentially dangerous objects, and provide alarm messages to parents or a teacher when a child seems to be in an accident.

In this paper, we present a system that generates appropriate natural language spoken expressions with customization for user characteristics, taking into account the fact that human behavioral patterns usually reveal one's mental state or personality subconsciously. The system is targeted at handling various situations for five-year old

J. Jacko (Ed.): Human-Computer Interaction, Part III, HCII 2007, LNCS 4552, pp. 114–123, 2007.

kindergarteners by giving them caring words during their everyday lives. For this purpose, the system first identifies the behavioral patterns of children with the help of installed sensors, and then generates spoken messages with a template based approach. The remainder of this paper is organized as follows: Section 2 provides the related work on an automated caring system targeted for children, and Section 3 analyzes the kindergarten environment and sentences spoken by kindergarten teachers related to the different behavioral patterns of children. Section 4 describes the proposed behavioral pattern recognition method, and Section 5 explains our implemented system.

2 Related Work

Much attention has been paid recently to a ubiquitous computing environment related to the daily lives of children. UbicKids [1] introduced 3A (Kids Awareness, Kids Assistance, Kids Advice) services for helping parents taking care of their children. This work also addressed the ethical aspects of a ubiquitous kids care system, and its directions for further development.

KidsRoom [2] provided an interactive, narrative play space for children. For this purpose, it focused on the user action and interaction in the physical space, permitting collaboration with other people and objects. This system used computer vision algorithms to identify activities in the space without needing any special clothing or devices.

On the other hand, Smart Kindergarten [3] used a specific device, iBadge to detect the name and location of objects including users. Various types of sensors associated with iBadge were provided to identify children's speech, interaction, and behavior for the purpose of reporting simultaneously their everyday lives to parents and teachers.

u-SPACE [4] is a customized caring and multimedia education system for door-key children who spend a significant amount of their time alone home. This system is designed to protect such children from physical dangers with RFID technology, and provides suitable multimedia contents to ease them with natural language processing techniques.

In this paper we will examine how various types of behavioral patterns are used for message generation and speech synthesis. To begin, we analyze the target environment in some detail.

3 Sentence Analysis with the Behavioral Patterns

For the customized message generation and speech synthesis system to react to the behavioral patterns of children, we collected sentences spoken by kindergarten teachers handling various types of everyday caring situations. In this section, we analyze these spoken sentences to build suitable templates for an automated message generation system corresponding to the behavioral patterns. Before getting into the analysis of the sentences, we briefly examine the targeted environment, or a kindergarten.

3.1 Kindergarten Environment

In a kindergarten, children spend time together sharing their space, so a kindergarten teacher usually supervises and controls a group of kindergarteners, not an individual kindergartener. Consequently, a child who is separated from the group can easily get into an accident such as slipping in a toilet room and toppling in the stairs, reported as the most frequent accident type in a kindergarten [5]. Therefore, we define a dangerous place as one that is not directly monitored by a teacher, such as an in-door playground when it is time to study. In addition, we regard toilet rooms, stairs, and some dangerous objects such as a hot water dispenser and a wall socket as a dangerous place too.

It is reported that 5 year old children are very easy to have an accident rather than among 0 to 6 year old children [5]. Thus we collected spoken sentences targeted for 5 year old children with various types of behavioral patterns.

3.2 Sentence Analysis with the Repeated Behavioral Patterns

In this section, we examine a corpus of dialogues for each such characteristic behavioral pattern, compiled from the responses to questionnaire for five kindergarten teachers. We selected nine different scenarios to simulate diverse kinds of dangerous and sensitive situations in the kindergarten targeted for four different children with distinct characteristics. Table 1 shows the profile of four children, and Table 2 shows the summary of nine scenarios.

Table 1. Profile of four different children in the scenario

Name	Gender	Age	Personality	Characteristics
Cheolsoo	Male	5	active	does not follow teachers well
Younghee	Female	5	active	follows teachers well
Soojin	Female	5	active	does not follow teachers well
Jieun	Female	5	passive	follows teachers well

Table 3 shows a part of responses collected from a teacher, according to the scenario as shown in Table 2. It is interesting to note that the teacher first explained the reason why a certain behavior is dangerous in some detail to a child, before just forbidding it. But as it repeated again, she then strongly forbade such a behavior, and finally, scolded the child for the repeated behavior. These three steps of reaction for the repeated behavioral patterns happened similarly to other teachers. From this observation, we adopt three types of sentence templates for message generation for repeated behavioral patterns.

Table 2. Summary of nine scenarios

#	Summary
1	Younghee is playing around a wall socket.
2	Cheolsoo is playing around a wall socket.
3	Soojin is playing around a wall socket.
4	Cheolsoo is playing around a wall socket again after receiving a warning message.
5	Cheolsoo is playing around a wall socket again.
6	Jieun is standing in front of a toilet room.
7	Cheolsoo is standing in front of a toilet room.
8	Jieun is out of the classroom when it is time to study.
9	Cheolsoo is out of the classroom when it is time to study.

Table 3. Responses compiled from a teacher

#	Response
1	영희야! 콘센트는 전기가 흐르기 때문에 그 곳에 물건을 집어 넣으면 아주 위험해요!! (Younghee! It is very dangerous putting something inside a wall socket because the current is live!!!)
2	철수야~ 지난번에 선생님이 콘센트에 물건 집어넣으면 위험하다고 말했지요? 그곳에서 놀지 말고 소꿉영역에서 친구들과 함께 놀아요!! (Cheolsoo~ I said last time that it is very dangerous putting something inside a wall socket! Please go to the playground to play with your friends!)
3	수진아!! 콘센트 근처에서 장난하는 건 아주 위험해요!! 수진이는 똑똑하니까 그곳에서 놀면 안 된다는 거 알지요? 선생님하고 약속!! (Soojin!! It is very dangerous playing around a wall socket!! Because Soojin is smart, I believe you understand why you should not play there! Will you promise me!!
4	철수는 선생님과 약속한 거 잊어버렸어요? 자~ 친구들과 다 같이 약속하자!! (Cheolsoo, did you forget our promise? Let's promise it again together with all the friends!!)
5	철수야! 왜 자꾸 말을 안듣니? 선생님은 철수가 다칠까 봐 걱정이 돼서 그러는 거야!! 철수야 위험하니까 거기서 놀지 마세요!! (Cheolsoo! Why do you neglect my words again and again? I am just afraid that you get injured there. Please do not play over there!!)

To formulate the repetition of children's behavior, we use the attention span of 5 year old children. It is generally well known that the normal attention span is 3 to 5 minutes per year of a child's age [6]. Thus we set 15 to 25 minutes as a time window for repetition, considering personality and characteristics of children.

3.3 Sentence Analysis with the Event

In the preceding section, we have given an analysis of sentences handling repeated behavioral patterns of children. In this section, we focus on the relation between the

Table 4. Different spoken sentences according to the event and behavior

Event	Behavior	Spoken sentence		
none	walking	철수야 (Cheolsoo)	위험하니까 (because it is dangerous)	조심하세요. (be careful)
none	running	철수야 (Cheolsoo)	화장실에서 (in a toilet room)	뛰면 안돼요. (running is forbidden)
slip	walking	철수야 (Cheolsoo)	화장실에서 (in a toilet room)	뛰면 안돼요. (running is forbidden)
slip	running	철수야 (Cheolsoo)		뛰지마. (do not run)

previous events and the current behavior. For this purpose, we constructed a speech corpus as recorded by one kindergarten teacher handling slipping or toppling events and walking or running behavioral patterns of a child. Table 4 shows the variation of the spoken sentences according to the event and behavioral patterns that happened in a toilet room.

If there was no event with a safe behavioral pattern, then the teacher just gave a normal guiding message to a child. But with a related event or dangerous behavior, the teacher gave a warning message to prevent a child from a possible danger. And if the event and dangerous behavioral patterns appeared both, the teacher delivered a strong forbidding message with an imperative sentence form. This speaking style was also observed similarly in other dangerous places such as stairs and playground slide. Taking into account these observations, we propose three types of templates for an automated message generation system. The first one delivers a guiding message; the second one a warning message; and the last one a forbidding message in an imperative form. Next, we move to the sentences with a time flow that is usually related to the schedule management of a kindergartener.

3.4 Sentence Analysis with the Time Flow

In a kindergarten, children are expected to behave according to the time schedule. Therefore, a day care system is able to guide a child to do proper actions during those times such as studying, eating, gargling, and playing. The following spoken sentences shown in Table 5 were also recorded by one teacher, as a part of a day time schedule.

At the beginning of a time schedule, a declarative sentence was used with a timing adverb to explain what have to be done from then on. But as the time goes by, a positive sentence was used to actively encourage expected actions. These analyses lead us to propose two types of templates for behavioral patterns with the time flow. The first one is an explanation of the current schedule and actions to do, similar to the first template as mentioned in Section 3.2. And the second one encourages actions itself with a positive sentence form which is similar to the last template in Section 3.3.

Table 5. Different spoken sentences according to the time flow

Time	Spoken sentence				
13:15	철수야	지금은	양치질하러	갈	시간이에요.
	(Cheolsoo)	(now)	(to gargle)	(to go)	(it is time)
	철수야		양치질하러	갈	시간이에요.
	(Cheolsoo)		(to gargle)	(to go)	(it is time)
	철수야		양치질하러		가자
13:30	(Cheolsoo)		(to gargle)		(let's go)

Before the generation of a customized message for children, we first need to track the behavioral patterns. The following section illustrates how to detect such behavioral patterns of children with wearable types of sensors.

4 Behavioral Pattern Detection

In the present experiment, we use six different kinds of sensors to recognize the behavioral pattern of kindergarteners. The location information recognized by an RFID tag is used both to identify a child and to trace the movement itself. Figure 1 shows pictures of the necklace style RFID tag and a sample detected result. Touch and force information indicates a dangerous behavior of a child with installed sensors around the predefined dangerous objects. The figure on the left in Figure 2 demonstrates the detection of a dangerous situation by the touch sensor. And the figure on the right indicates the frequency and intensity of the pushing event as detected by a force sensor installed on a hot water dispenser. The toppling accident and walking or running behavior can be captured by the acceleration sensor. Figure 3 shows an acceleration sensor attached to a hair band to recognize toppling events, and the shoe to detect a characteristic walking or running behavior. Walking and running behaviors can be assessed by the comparison of the magnitude of an acceleration

Fig. 1. Necklace style RFID tag and detected information

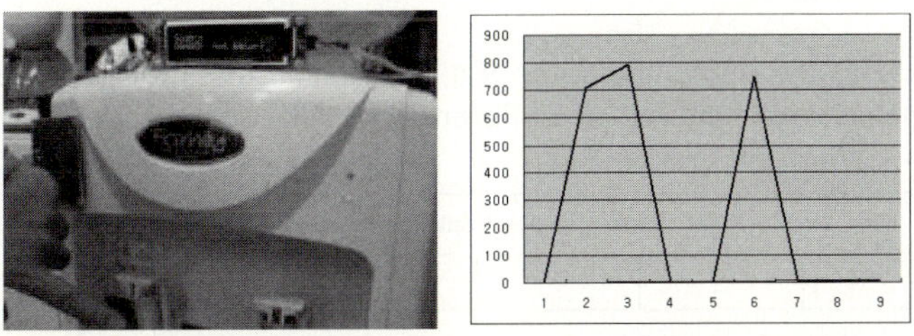

Fig. 2. Dangerous behavior detection with touch and force sensors

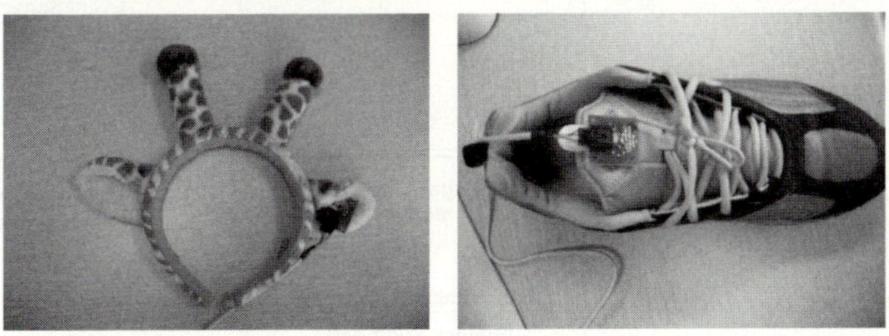

Fig. 3. Acceleration sensor attached hair band and shoe

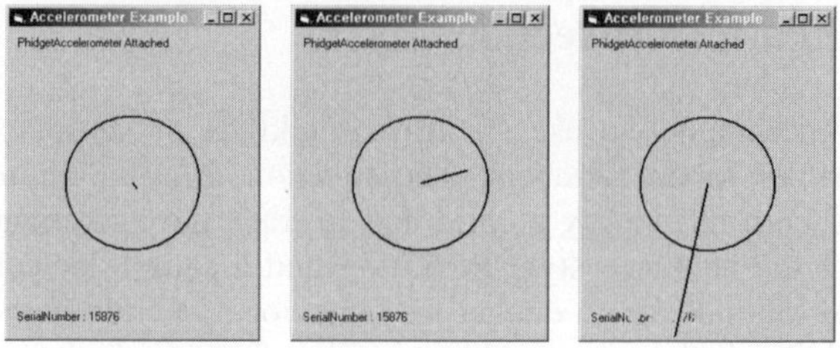

Fig. 4. Acceleration magnitude comparison to determine behavior: stop, walking, running

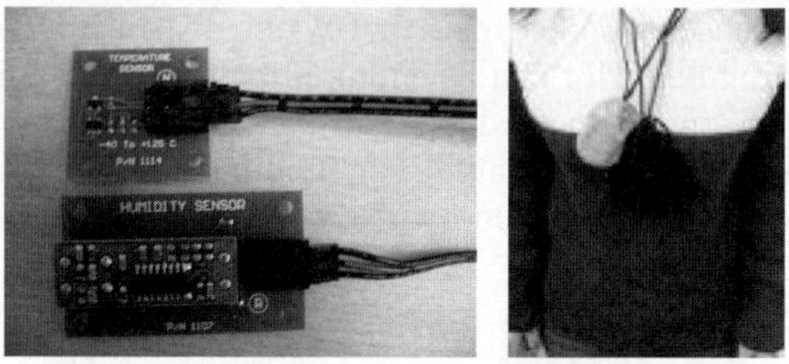

Fig. 5. Temperature and humidity sensors combined with RFID tag

value as shown in Figure 4. We also provide the temperature and humidity sensors to record the vital signs of children that can be combined with the RFID tag as shown in Figure 5.

5 Implementation

Figure 6 illustrates the implementation of a customized message generation system in response to behavioral patterns of children. At every second, six different sensors

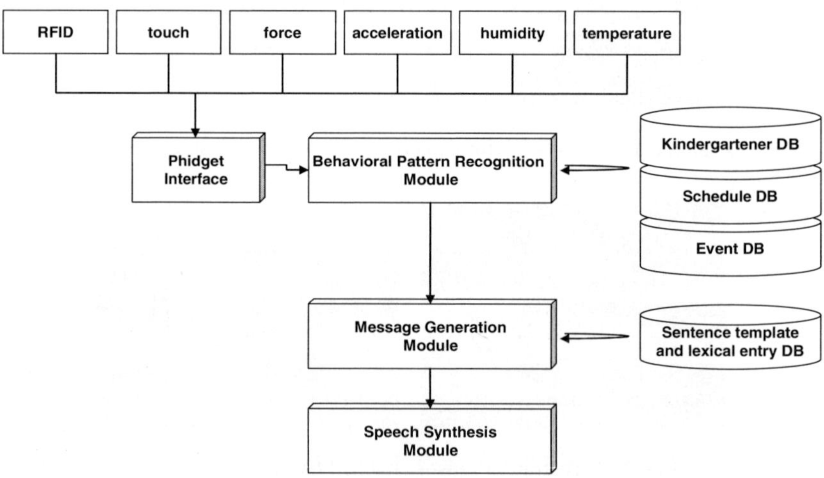

Fig. 6. System overview

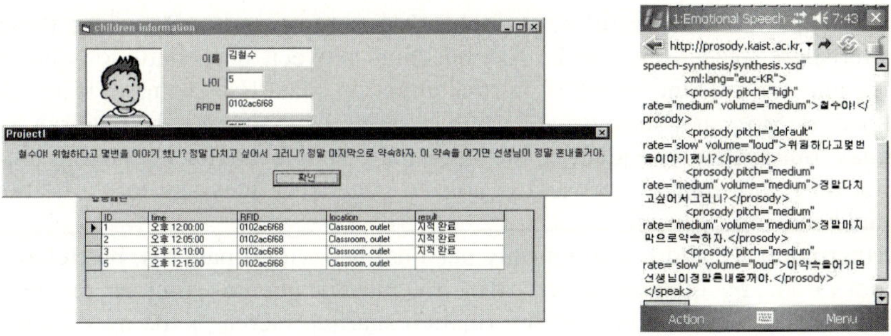

Fig. 7. Generated message and SSML document

report the detected information to the behavioral pattern recognition module through a Phidget interface which is controlled by Microsoft Visual Basic. The behavioral pattern recognition module updates this information to each database managed by Microsoft Access 2003, and delivers the proper type of a message template to the message generation module as discussed in Section 3. Then the message generation module chooses lexical entries for a given template according to the children's characteristics, and encodes the generated message into Speech Synthesis Markup Language (SSML) for a target-neutral application. This result synthesized by a Voiceware text-to-speech system in a speech synthesis module providing a web interface for mobile devices such as PDAs (the figure on the right in Figure 7) and mobile phones. Figure 7 shows the message generation result in response to the behavioral patterns of a child.

6 Discussion

The repetition of behavioral patterns mentioned in Section 3 is a difficult concept to formulate automatically by computer systems or even by human beings, because the usual behavioral pattern appears non-continuously in our daily lives. For example, it is very hard to say that a child who touched dangerous objects both yesterday and today has a serious repeated behavioral pattern, because we do not have any measure to formulate the relation of two separate actions. For this reason, we adopted a normal attention span for children, 15 to 25 minutes for a five-year old child, to describe the behavior patterns with a certain time window. It seems reasonable to assume that within the attention span, children perceive their previous behavior with its reactions of kindergarten teachers. As a result, we implemented our system by projecting the repetition concept to an attention span for customized message generation suitable for the identification of short-term behavioral patterns. To indicate long-term behavioral patterns, we update user characteristics as referred to in Table 1, with the enumeration of short-term behavioral patterns. For example, if a child with neutral characteristics repeats same dangerous behavior patterns ignoring strong forbidding messages within a certain attention span, we update 'neutral' characteristics as 'does not follow well'. It then affects their length of attention span interactively, such as 15 minutes for 'a child who does not follow teachers' directions well', 20 minutes for 'neutral', and 25 minutes for 'a child who follows teachers' directions well'. By using these user characteristics, we can also make a connection between non-continuous behavioral patterns that are over the length of normal attention span. For example, if a child was described as 'does not follow well' with a series of dangerous behavioral patterns yesterday, our system can identify the same dangerous behavior happening today for the first time as a related one, and is able to generate a message to warn about the repeated behavioral pattern.

Furthermore, we addressed not only personal behavioral patterns, but relative past behaviors done by other members also, by introducing an event as mentioned in Section 3.3. This event, a kind of information sharing, increases the user interactivity and system believability by extending knowledge about the current living environment.

During the observation of each case study, we found an interesting point such that user personality hardly influences reactions on behavioral patterns, possibly because our scenarios are targeted only at guidance of kindergarteners' everyday lives. We believe that the apparent relation can be found if we expand target users to more aged people like the elderly, and if we include more emotionally inspirited situations as proposed in the u-SPACE project [4].

In this paper, we proposed a computational method to identify continuous and non-continuous behavioral patterns. This method can be used to find some psychological syndromes such as AHDH (attention deficit hyperactivity disorder) for children as well. It can also be used to identify toppling or vital signal changes such as temperature and humidity in order provide an immediate health care report to parents or teachers, which can be directly applicable for the elderly as well. But for added convenience, a wireless environment such as iBadge [3] should be provided.

7 Conclusion

Generally, it is important for a human-computer interaction system to provide an attractive interface, because simply providing repeated interaction patterns for a similar situation tends to lose one's attention easily. The system must therefore be able to respond differently to the user's characteristics during interaction. In this paper, we proposed to use the behavioral patterns as an important clue for the characteristics of the corresponding user or users. For this purpose, we constructed a corpus of dialogues from five kindergarten teachers handling various types of day care situations to identify the relation between children's behavioral patterns and spoken sentences. We compiled collected dialogues into three groups and found the syntactic similarities of sentences according to the behavioral patterns of children. Also we proposed a sensor based ubiquitous kindergarten environment to detect the behavioral patterns of kindergarteners. We also implemented a customized message and speech synthesis system in response to the characteristic behavioral patterns of children. We believe that the proposed link between the behavioral patterns and the mental state of a human user can be applied to improve not only user interactivity but also believability of the system.

Acknowledgments. This research was performed for the Intelligent Robotics Development Program, one of the 21st Century Frontier R&D Programs, and Brain Science Research Center, funded by the Ministry of Commerce, Industry and Energy of Korea.

References

1. Ma, J., Yang, L.T., Apduhan, B.O., Huang, R., Barolli, L., Takizawa, M.: Towards a Smart World and Ubiquitous Intelligence: A Walkthrough from Smart Things to Smart Hyperspace and UbicKids. International Journal of Pervasive Computing and Communication 1, 53–68 (2005)
2. Bobick, A.F., Intille, S.S., Davis, J.W., Baird, F., Campbell, L.W., Ivanov, Y., Pinhanez, C.S., Schütte, A., Wilson, A.: The KidsRoom: A perceptually-based interactive and immersive story environment. PRESENCE: Teleoperators and Virtual Environments 8, 367–391 (1999)
3. Chen, A., Muntz, R.R., Yuen, S., Locher, I., Park, S.I., Srivastava, M.B.: A Support Infrastructures for the Smart Kindergarten. IEEE Pervasive Computing 1, 49–57 (2002)
4. Min, H.J., Park, D., Chang, E., Lee, H.J., Park, J.C.: u-SPACE: Ubiquitous Smart Parenting and Customized Education. In: Proceedings of the 15th Human Computer Interaction, vol. 1, pp. 94–102 (2006)
5. Park, S.W., Heo, Y.J., Lee, S.W., Park, J.H.: Non-Fatal Injuries among Preschool Children in Daegu and Kyungpook. Journal of Preventive Medicine and Public Health 37, 274–281 (2004)
6. Moyer, K.E., Gilmer, B.V.H.: The Concept of Attention Spans in Children. The Elementary School Journal 54, 464–466 (1954)

Multi-word Expression Recognition Integrated with Two-Level Finite State Transducer

Keunyong Lee, Ki-Soen Park, and Yong-Seok Lee

Division of Electronics and Information Engineering, Chonbuk National University, Jeonju 561-756, South Korea
cpher.inu@gmail.com, {icarus,yslee}@chonbuk.ac.kr

Abstract. This paper proposes another two-level finite state transducer to recognize the multi-word expression (MWE) in two-level morphological parsing environment. In our proposed the Finite State Transducer with Bridge State (FSTBS), we defined Bridge State (concerned with connection of multi-word), Bridge Character (used in connection of multi-word expression) and two-level rule to extend existing FST. FSTBS could recognize both Fixed Type MWE and Flexible Type MWE which are expressible as regular expression, because FSTBS recognizes MWE in morphological parsing.

Keywords: Multi-word Expression, Two-level morphological parsing, Finite State Transducer.

1 Introduction

Multi-word Expression (MWE) is a sequence of several words has an idiosyncratic meaning [1], [2]: *all over, be able to*. If *all over* appears in the sentence sequentially, its meaning can be different from the composed meaning of *all* and *over*. Two-level morphological parsing that uses finite state transducer (FST) is composed with two-level rules and lexicon [3], [4]. Tokenization helps you to break an input sentence up into a number of tokens by the delimiter (white space). It is not easy for MWE to be used as an input directly, because MWE contains delimiter. MWE has a special connection between words, in other words, *all over* has special connection between *all* and *over*. We regard this special connection as a bridge to connect individual word. In surface form, usually a bridge is a white space. We use a symbol '+' in lexical form instead of white space in surface form, and we denominate it Bridge Character (BC). BC enables FST to move another word.

Two-level morphological parsing uses FST. FST needs following two conditions to accept morphemes. 1) FST reaches finial state and 2) there is no remain input string. Also, FST starts from initial state in finite state network (FSN) to analyze a morpheme, and FST does not use previous analysis result. For this reason, FST has a limitation in MWE recognition.

In this paper, we propose extended FST, Finite State Transducer with Bridge State (FSTBS), to recognize MWE in morphological parsing. For FSTBS, we define the special state named Bridge State (BS) and special symbol Bridge Character (BC)

J. Jacko (Ed.): Human-Computer Interaction, Part III, HCII 2007, LNCS 4552, pp. 124–133, 2007.

related with BS. We describe expression method of MWE using the XEROX lexc rule and two-level rule using the XEROX xfst [5], [6], [7].

The rest of this paper is organized as follows; in the next section, we present related work to our research. The third section deals with the Multi-word Expression. In the fourth section, we present Finite State Transducer with Bridge State. The fifth section illustrates how to recognize MWE in two-level morphological parsing. In the sixth section, we analyze our method with samples and experiments. The final section summarizes the overall discussion.

2 Related Work and Motivation

The existing research to recognize MWE has been made on great three fields; classification MWE, how to represent MWE, how to recognize MWE.

One research classified MWE into four sections; Fixed Expressions, Semi-Fixed Expressions, Syntactically-Flexible Expression, Institutionalized phrases [1]. The other research classified MWE into Lexicalized Collocations, Semi-lexicalized Collocations, Non-lexicalize Collocations, Named-entities to recognize in Turkish [8]. Now, we can divide above classification of MWE into Fixed Type (without any variation in the connected words) and Flexible Type (with variation in the connected words).

According to [Ann], "LinGO English Resource Grammar (ERG) has a lexical database structure which essentially just encodes a triple: orthography, type, semantic predicate" [2]. The other method is to use regular expression [9], [10].

Usually, two methods have been used to recognize MWE, one of these, the MWE recognition is finished in tokenization before morphological parsing [5], and another one, it finished in postprocessing after morphological parsing [1], [8]. MWE recognition of Fixed Type is main issue of the preprocessing because preprossesing does not adopt morphological parsing. Sometimes, numeric processing is considered as a field of MWE recognition [5]. In postprocessing by contrast with preprocessing, Flexible Type MWE can be recognized, but there are some overhead to analyze MWE, it should totally rescan the result of morphological parsing and require another rule for the WME.

Our proposed FSTBS has two major significant features. One is FSTBS can recognize MWE without distinction whether fixed or Flexible Type. The other is FSTBS can recognize MWE is integrated with morphological parsing, because lexicon includes MWE which is expressed as regular expression.

3 Multi-word Expression

In our research, we classified MWE by next two types instead of Fixed Type or Flexible Type. One is the expressible MWE as regular expression [5], [11], [12], [13]. The other is the non-expressible MWE as regular expression. Below Table 1 shows the example of the two types.

Table 1. Two types of the MWE

The type of MWE	Example
Expressible MWE as regular expression	*Ad hoc, as it were, for ages, seeing that, ...* *abide by, ask for, at one's finger(s') ends, be going to, devote oneself to, take one's time, try to,....*
Non-expressible MWE as regular expression	*compare sth/sb to, know sth/sb from, learn ~ by heart, ...*

Without special remark, we use MWE as the expressible MWE with regular expression in this paper. We will discuss the regular expression for MWE in the following section. Now we consider that MWE has a special connection state between word and word.

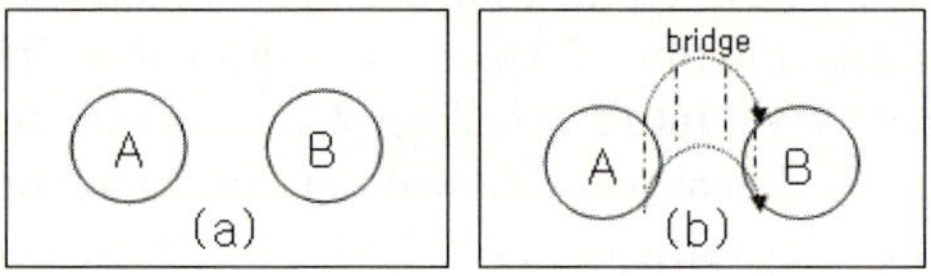

Fig. 1. (a) when *A B* is not MWE, *A* and *B* has no any connection, (b) when *A B* is a MWE, a bridge exists between *A* and *B*

If *A B* is not a MWE as Fig. 1 (a), *A* and *B* are recognized as individual words without any connection between each other, and if *A B* is a MWE as Fig. 1 (b), there is special connection between *A* and *B*, and call this connection *bridge* to connect *A* and *B*. When A = {*at*, *try*}, B = {*most*, *to*}, there is a bridge between *at* and *most*, and between *try* and *to*, because Fixed Type *at most* and Flexible Type *try to* are MWE, but *at to* and *try most* are not MWE, so there is no bridge between *at* and *to*, *try* and *most*. That is, surface form MWE *at most* is appeared as "*at most*" with a blank space but lexical form is "*at BridgeCharacter most*." In second case, *A B* is MWE. Input sentence is *A B*. Tokenizer makes two tokens *A* and *B* with delimiter (blank space). FST recognizes that the first token *A* is one word *A* and the part of MWE with BS. But, FST can not use the information that *A* is the part of MWE. If FST knows this information, it will know that the next token *B* is the part of MWE. FSTBS that uses Bridge State can recognize MWE. Our proposed FSTBS can recognize expressible MWE as regular expression shown above table. That is, non-expressible MWE as regular expression is not treated our FSTBS yet.

3.1 How to Express MWE as Regular Expression

We used XEROX lexc to express MWE as regular expression. Now, we introduce how to express MWE as regular expression. Above Table 1, expressible MWE as regular expression have Fixed Type and Flexible Type. It is easy to express Fixed Type MWE as regular expression. Following code is some regular expressions for Fixed Type MWE, for example, *Ad hoc, as it were and for ages* are shown.

Regular expression for Fixed Type MWE

```
LEXICON Root
  FIXED_MWE #
LEXICON FIXED_MWE
  < Ad "+" hoc > #;
  < as "+" it "+" were > #;
  < for "+" ages > #;
```

The regular expressions of Fixed Type MWEs are so simple, because they are comprised of words without variation. However, the regular expressions of the Flexible Type MWEs have more complexity than Fixed Type MWEs. Words comprising Flexible Type MWE can variable. More over, words are replaced any some words and can be deleted. Take *be going to* for example, there are two sentences "*I am (not) going to school*" and "*I will be going to school*." Two sentences have same MWE *be going to*, but *not* is optional and *be* is variable. In the case of *devote oneself to*, lexical form *oneself* appears *myself, yourself, himself, herself, themselves, or itself* in surface form. Following code is some regular expression for Flexible Type MWE, for example *be going to, devote oneself to* are shown.

Regular expression for Flexible Type MWE

```
Definitions
BeV=[{be}:{am}|{be}:{was}|{be}:{were}|{be}:{being}];
OneSelf=[{oneself}:{myself}|{oneself}:{himself}
          |{oneself}:{himself}|{oneself}:{themselves}
          |{oneself}:{itself}];
VEnd="+Bare":0|"+Pres":s|"+Prog":{ing}|"+Past":{ed} ;
LEXICON Root
   FLEXIBLE_MWE #
LEXICON FLEXIBLE_MWE
< BeV (not) "+" going "+" to > #;
< devote VEnd "+" OneSelf "+" to > #;
```

Although, above code is omitted the meaning of some symbols, but it is sufficient for description of regular expression for Flexible Type MWE. Above mentioned it, such as *one's* and *oneself* are used restrictively in sentence, so we could express these as regular expression. However, *sth* and *sb* are appeared in non-expressible MWE as regular expression can be replaced by any kinds of noun or phrase, so we could not express them as regular expression yet.

4 Finite State Transducer with Bride State

Given a general FST is a hextuple $<\Sigma, \Gamma, S, s_0, \delta, \omega>$, where:

i. Σ denotes the input alphabet.
ii. Γ denotes the output alphabet.
iii. S denotes the set of states, a finite nonempty set.
iv. s_0 denotes the start (or initial) state; $s_0 \in S$.
v. δ denotes the state transition function; δ: S x $\Sigma \rightarrow$ S.
vi. ω denotes the output function; ω: S x $\Sigma \rightarrow \Gamma$.

Given a FSTBS is a octuple <Σ, Γ, S, BS, s_0, δ, ω, έ>, where: from the first to the sixth elements have same meaning in FST.

vii. BS denotes the set of *Bridge State*; BS∈S.

viii. έ denotes function related BS; Add Temporal Bridge (ATB), Remove Temporal Bridge (RTB).

4.1 Bridge State and Bridge Character

We define Bridge State, Bridge Character and Add Temporal Bridge (ATB) function, Remove Temporal Bridge (RTB) function which are related with Bridge State, to recognize MWE connected by a bridge.

Bridge State (BS): BS connects each word in MWE. If a word is the part of MWE, FSTBS can reach BS from it to by Bridge Character. FSTBS shall suspend to resolve its state which is either accepted or rejected until succeeding token is given, and FSTBS operates ATB or RTB selectively.

Bridge Character (BC): Generally, BC is a blank space in surface form and it can be replaced into blank symbol or other symbol in lexical form. On the selection of BC, FSTBS is satisfied by restrictive conditions as follows:

1. BC is just used to connect a word and word in the MWE. That is, a word ∈ $(\Sigma - \{BC\})^+$.
2. Initially, any state does not existing moved by BC from the initial state. That is, state ← $\delta(s_0, BC)$, state ∉ S.

4.2 Add Temporal Bridge Function and Remove Temporal Bridge Function

When some state is moved to BS by BC, FSTBS should operate either ATB or RTB.

Add Temporal Bridge (ATB)

ATB is the function that makes movement from initial state to current BS reached by FSTBS with BC. After FSTBS reaches to BS from any state which is not initial state by next input BC, ATB is a called function. This function makes a temporal bridge and FSTBS uses it in a succeeding token.

Remove Temporal Bridge (RTB)

RTB is the function to delete temporal bridge after moving temporal bridge which is added by ATB. FSTBS calls this function in every initial state to show that finite state network has temporal bridge.

5 MWE in Two-Level Morphological Parsing

Given an alphabet Σ, we define Σ = {a, b, …, z, "+"[1] } and BC = "+". Let $A = (\Sigma - \{``+"\})^+$, $B = (\Sigma - \{``+"\})^+$, then L1 = {*A*, *B*} for Words, and L2 = {*A*"+"*B*}

[1] In regular expression, + has special meaning that is Kleene plus. If you choose + as BC then you should use "+" that denotes symbol plus [5], [11].

for MWE. L is a language L = L1 ∪ L2. Following two regular expressions are for the L1 and L2.

```
RegEx1  = A | B
RegEx2  = A "+" B
```

Regular expression RegEx is for language L.

```
RegEx = RegEx1 ∪ RegEx2
```

Rule0 is two-level replacement rule [6], [7].

```
Rule0²:  "+"  ->  " "
```

Finite State Network (FSN) of Rule0 shown in Fig. 2.

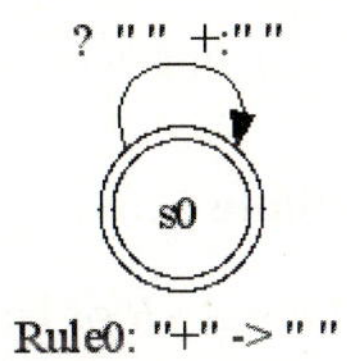

Fig. 2. Two-level replacement rule, *?* is a special symbol denote any symbol. This state transducer can recognize input such as $\Sigma^* \cup$ {" ", +: " "}. In two-level rule +: " " denotes that " " in surface form is replaced with + in lexical form.

FST0 in Fig. 3 shows FSN0 of RegEx for Language L.

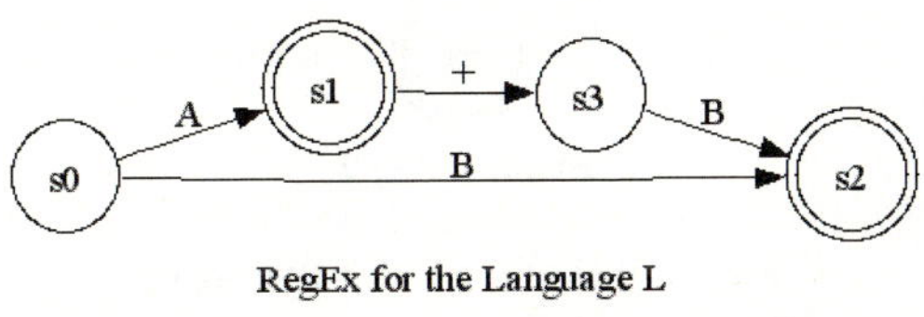

Fig. 3. FSN0 of the RegEx for the Language L. BC = + and $s_3 \in$ BS.

FSN1 = RegEx .o.[3] Rule0. Below showed Fig. 4 is FSN1. FSTBS which uses FSN1 analyzes morpheme. FSN1 is composed two-level rule with lexicon. If the FST uses FSN1 as Fig. 4 and is supplied with *A B* as token by tokenizer, it can recognize *A+B* as MWE from token. However, tokenizer separates input *A B* into two parts *A* and *B* and gives them to FST. For this reason, FST can not recognize *A+B* because *A* and *B* was recognized individually.

---

[2] -> is the unconditional replacement operator. *A* -> *B* denotes that *A* is lexical form and *B* is surface form. Surface form *B* replaces into lexical form *A* [5].

[3] .o. is the binary operator, which compose two regular expressions. This operator is associative but commutative. FST0 .o. Rule0 is not equal Rule0 .o. RST0 [5].

If tokenizer can know that *A B* is a MWE, it can give proper single token "*A B*" without separating to FST. That is, tokenzier will know all of MWE and give it to FST. FST can recognize MWE by two-level rule which only Rule0 is added to. However, it is not easy because tokenizer does not process morphological parsing, so tokenizer can not know Flexible Type MWE, for instance *be going to, are going to, etc*. As it were, tokenizer can know only Fixed Type MWE, for example *all most, and so on, etc*.

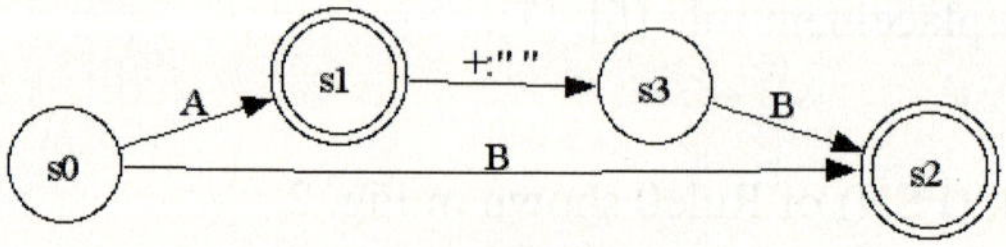

Fig. 4. FSN1 = RegEx .o. Rule0: BC = +:" " and $s_3 \in$ BS.

5.1 The Movement to the Bridge State

We define the Rule1 to recognize MWE *A*+*B* of language L by FST instead of Rule 0.

```
Rule1: "+" -> 0
```

Rule 0 is applied to blank space of surface form. Instead of Rule1 is applied to empty symbol of surface form. FSN of Rule1 shown in Fig. 5.

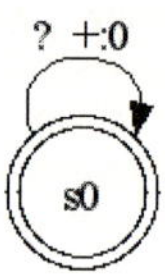

Fig. 5. FSN of the Rule1 ("+" -> 0)

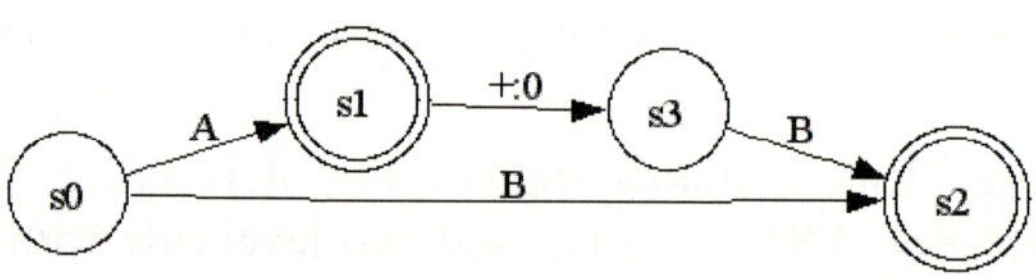

Fig. 6. FSN2: RegEx .o. Rule1. BC = +:0 and $s_3 \in$ BS.

Above shown Fig. 6 is the result FSN of RegEx .o. Rule1. We can see that MWE which can be recognized by FSN2, is the state of moved from *A* by BC. However, when succeeding token *B* is given to FST, FST can not know that precede token move to BS, so FST requires extra function. Extra function ATB is introduced following section.

5.2 The Role of ATB and RTB

Above Fig. 6, we can see that FSN2 has BC = +:0 and BS includes s_3. The Rule1 and proper tokens make FST recognize MWE. As has been point out, it is not easy to make proper tokens for MWE. FST just knows whether a bridge exists or not from current recognized word with given token. Moreover, when succeeding token is supplied for FST, it does not remember previous circumstance whether a bridge is detected or is not. To solve this problem, if a state reaches to BS (s_3), ATB function is performed. Called ATB function connects temporal movement (bridge) to current BS (s_3) using BC for the transition. Fig. 7 shows FSN3 that temporal connection is added by ATB function from current BS.

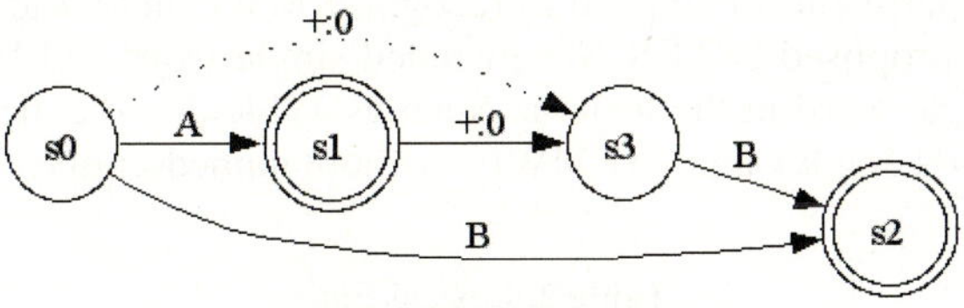

Fig. 7. FSN3: FSN with temporal bridge to BS (s_3). Dotted arrow indicates temporal bridge is added by ATB function.

Such as Fig. 7, when succeeding token is given to FST, transition function moves to s_3 directly: δ (s_0, +:0) → s_3. After crossing a bridge using BC, FST arrives at BS(s_3) and calls RTB which removes a bridge: δ(s_0, +:0) ← 0. If a bridge is removed, FST3 returns to FST2. Reached state by input *B* from BS (s_3) is the final (s2), and since there is no remain input for further recognition, *A*+*B* is recognized as a MWE. Below code is the brief pseudo code of FSTBS.

Brief Pseudo Code of FSTBS

```
FSTBS(token){
  //token ∈ (Σ - {BC})⁺, token = c_k(0<k<n+1)
  //c_0 is the left token boundary
  //c_n+1 is the right token boundary
  //that real surface form is c_k(1≤k≤n)
  state ← s_0
  for(k=0; k≤n+1;k++){
     while(code  ← NextTwoLevelCode(c_k)){
          oldState ← state
          state ← δ(state, code)
          if(state ∈ BS and oldState≠s_0)
             // k == n+1 and code == BC
             AddTemporalBridge(state)
          else if(state ∈ BS and oldState≠s_0)
             // k == 0 and code == BC
```

```
                RemoveTemporalBridge(state)
            else
                do process as a general FST.
        }
    }
}
// AddTmporalBridge is similar to stack push operator
// RemoveTemporalBridge is similar to stack pop
// operator
```

6 Results and Discussion

We performed experiment for English to recognize MWE in two-level morphological parsing using the proposed FSTBS. We included single word and MWE in one Lexicon. We used single word in the lexicon. Such as Table 2, we collected single words from PC-KIMMO's eng.lex and 731 MWEs without named-entity.

Table 2. Lexical Entry

Type	Count	Example
Fixed Type MWE	308	*at most, of course, ...*
Flexible Type MWE	423	*above all, act for, try to, ...*

Lexicon file was compiled as one finite state using lexc of XEROX. English two-level rule and proposed two-level rule (Rule0, Rule1) for MWE was complied using xfst of XEROX. We made one finite state of each complied lexicon finite state and rule finite state by composition. For the evaluation, we used 731 sentences which contained MWE, and tokenizer divided input into tokens without any other processing for MWE.

FSTBS is good to recognition MWE. MWEs were expressed by regular expression, and they are translated finite state network. As good as FST using FSN, FSTBS uses FSN and recognize well too.

7 Conclusions

Morphological parsing system using FST, MWE is recognized preprocessing or postprocessing. They are isolated from morphological parsing. Preprocessing can recognize only Fixed Type without variation. Postprocessing can recognize Fixed Type and Flexible Type. However, it requires additional data.

In this paper, we proposed usable *Finite State Transducer with Bridge State* to recognize MWE in two-level morphological parsing model. We added *Bridge States*, Bridge *Character* and two functions (one is *Add Temporal Bridge* the other is *Remove Temporal Bridge*) to FST for definition of FSTBS.

We classify two types of MWE. They are the *expressible/non-expressible MWE as regular expression*. Our proposed FSTBS can recognize all expressible MWE as regular expression.

Acknowledgments. This work was supported by the second stage of Brain Korea 21 Project.

References

1. Sag, I.A., Baldwin, T., Bond, F., et al.: Multiword Expression: A Pain in the Neck for NLP. In: Gelbukh, A. (ed.) CICLing 2002. LNCS, vol. 2276, pp. 1–15. Springer, Heidelberg (2002)
2. Copestake, A., Lambeau, F. et al.: Multiword Expression: linguistics precision and reusability. In: Proceedings of the 3rd International Conference on Language Resources and Evaluation (LREC), pp. 1941–1947 (2002)
3. Antworth, Evan, L.: PC-KIMMO: A Two-level Processor for Morphological Processor for Morphological Analysis. Summer Institute of Linguistics, Dallas Texas (1990)
4. Karttunen, L.: Constructing Lexical Transducers. In: Proceeding, 16th International Conference on Computational Linguistics, pp. 406–411 (1994)
5. Beesley, K.R., Karttunen, L.: Finite State Morphology. CSLI Publications (2003)
6. Kartunnen, L.: The Replace Operator. In: the Proceeding of the 33rd Annual Meeting of the Association for Computational Linguistics (1995)
7. Kartunnen, L.: Directed Replacement. In: the Proceeding of the 34rd Annual Meeting of the Association for Computational Linguistics, pp. 108–115 (1996)
8. Oflazer, K., Çentinoğlu, Ö., Say, B.: Integrating Morphology with Multi-word Expression Processing in Turkish. In: Second ACL Workshop on Multiword Expressions: Integrating Processing, pp. 64–71 (2004)
9. Segond, F., Breidth, E.: IDAREX: Formal Description of German and French Multi-word Expression with Finite State Technology. Technical Report MLTT-022, Rank Xerox Research Centre, Grenoble Laboratory
10. Segond, F., Tapanainen, P.: Technical Report MLTT-019, Rank Xerox Research Centre, Grenoble Laboratory (1995)
11. Carroll, J., Long, D.: Theory of Finite Automata with an introduction to formal languages. Prentice-Hall International Editions (1989)
12. Cooper, K.D., Torczon, L.: ENGINEERING A COMPILER. Morgan Kaufmann Publishers, San Francisco (2004)
13. Holub, A.I.: Holub: Compiler Design in C. Prentice-Hall, Englewood Cliffs (1990)

Towards Multimodal User Interfaces Composition Based on UsiXML and MBD Principles

Sophie Lepreux[1], Anas Hariri[1], José Rouillard[2], Dimitri Tabary[1], Jean-Claude Tarby[2], and Christophe Kolski[1]

[1] Université de Valenciennes et du Hainaut-Cambrésis, LAMIH – UMR8530, Le Mont-Houy, F-59313 Valenciennes Cedex 9, France
[2] Université de Lille 1, Laboratoire LIFL-Trigone, F-59655 Villeneuve d'Ascq Cedex, France
{sophie.lepreux,anas.hariri,dimitri.tabary, christophe.kolski}@univ-valenciennes.fr, {jose.rouillard,Jean-claude.tarby}@univ-lille1.fr

Abstract. In software design, the reuse issue brings the increasing of web services, components and others techniques. These techniques allow reusing code associated to technical aspect (as software component). With the development of business components which can integrate technical aspect with HCI, the composition issue has appeared. Our previous work concerned the GUI composition based on an UIDL as UsiXML. With the generalization of Multimodal User Interfaces (MUI), MUI composition principles have to be studied. This paper aims at extend existing basic composition principles in order to treat multimodal interfaces. The same principle as in the previous work, based on the tree algebra, can be used in another level (AUI) of the UsiXML framework to support the Multimodal User Interfaces composing. This paper presents a case study on the food ordering system based on multimodal (coupling GUI and MUI). A conclusion and the future works in the HCI domain are presented.

Keywords: User interfaces design, UsiXML, AUI (Abstract User Interface), Multimodal User Interfaces, Vocal User Interfaces.

1 Introduction

The reuse is an important issue in software design, and by extension in interactive software design [2]. Means to support reuse have evolved in the meantime, from modularity to component-based development via object development. So the reuse issue brings the increasing of web services, components and others techniques. These techniques allow reusing code associated to technical aspect (as software component). The reuse can be applied to several steps of the development cycle with the support of three types of component: (1) the code components have a small granularity and are used at the development time; (2) the design components (as proposed by [1]) are used to reuse the known solutions at the design time; (3) the business components have a large granularity and are specific to the domain, they are defined at the

J. Jacko (Ed.): Human-Computer Interaction, Part III, HCII 2007, LNCS 4552, pp. 134–143, 2007.

analysis step. They can be associated to a task in the domain. A goal composition based on tasks was studied by to facilitate the reuse [7]. As these business components can integrate technical aspects with HCI, the composition issue appears.

The Model Based-Development (MBD) appears as a solution adapted to the reuse, the User Interface Definition Language (UIDL) named UsiXML (USer Interface eXtensible Markup Language) respects the MBD principles [8]. This language allows defining the User interface from four levels defined by the CAMELEON Project. UsiXML proposes four steps to define the user interface (cf. Figure 1). The Tasks & Concepts level describes the interactive system specifications in terms of the user tasks to be carried out and the domain objects of these tasks. An Abstract User Interface (AUI) abstracts a Concrete User Interface (CUI) into a definition that is independent of any interaction modality (such as graphical, vocal or tactile). A CUI abstracts a Final User Interface (FUI) into a description independent of any programming or markup language in terms of Concrete Interaction Objects, layout, navigation, and behavior. A FUI refers to an actual UI rendered either by interpretation (e.g., HTML) or by code compilation (e.g., Java).

Multimodality appears as a new technology adopted in the current inhomogeneous environments where several types of users work in different states and interact with a multitude of platforms. Multimodality tries to combine interaction means to enhance the ability of the user interface adaptation to its context of use, without requiring costly redesign and reimplementation. Blending multiple access channels provides new possibilities of interaction to users. The multimodal interface promises to let users choose the way they would naturally interact with it. Users have the possibility to switch between interaction means or to multiple available modes of interaction in parallel.

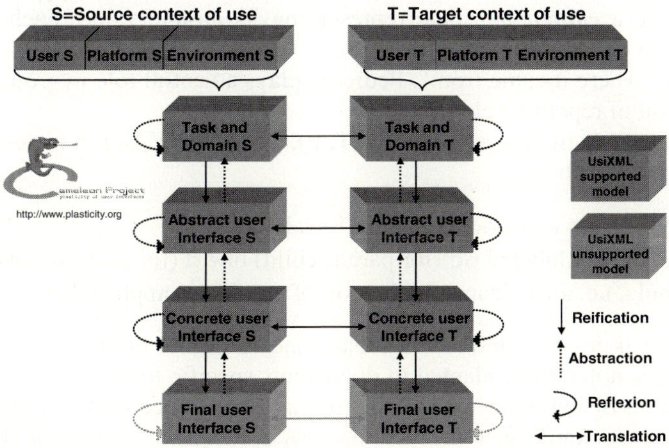

Fig. 1. The four abstraction levels used in the CAMELEON[1] framework

[1] http://giove.isti.cnr.it/cameleon.html

Since a few years, the W3C is working on this aspect and is publishing recommendations concerning a vocal interaction language based on XML, called VoiceXML, which allows describing and managing vocal interactions on the Internet network. VoiceXML is a programming language, designed for human-computer audio dialogs that feature synthesized speech, digitized audio, recognition of spoken and DTMF (Dual Tone Multi-Frequency) key input, recording of spoken input, telephony, and mixed initiative conversations. Its major goal is to bring the advantages of web-based development and content delivery to interactive voice response applications [9, 10, 11].

The second section presents (1) the basic principles of our previous work on the Visual GUI composing based on UsiXML[2], and (2) the new rules to compose user interfaces and in particular multimodal user interfaces. In order to validate the proposed rules, a case study on a food ordering system will be the object of the third section. Finally the paper will conclude with the future works.

2 From GUI Composing to MUI Composing

2.1 Operators at the CUI Level for the GUI Composing

During a previous work, we have proposed composition rules to support GUI composition: each GUI is defined at concrete level of UI definition [4,5]. Since the UI is represented in UsiXML terms and since it is a XML-compliant language (cf. Figure 2), operations could be defined thanks to tree algebra.

In this work, the used notation is based on the data model defined by Jagadish and colleagues [3]. In this model, a data tree is a rooted, ordered tree, such that each node carries data (its label) in the form of a set of attribute-value pairs. Each node has a special, single valued attribute called ***tag*** whose value indicates the type of element. A node may have a ***content*** attribute representing its atomic value. Each node has a virtual attribute called ***pedigree*** drawn from an ordered domain. The pedigree carries the history of "where it came from". Pedigree plays a central role in grouping, sorting and elimination of repetitive elements.

They define a pattern tree as a pair P=(T, F), where T=(V,E) is a node-labelled and edge-labelled tree such that:

- Each node in V has a distinct integer as its label ($i);
- Each edge is either labeled `pc` (for parent-child) or `ad` (for ancestor-descendant);
- F is a formula, i.e. a Boolean combination of predicates applicable to nodes.

This pattern is used to define a database and to define the predicate used in the operations. This notation is adapted to documents specific to interface. Indeed, in the HCI case, the most important is the structure and not the content. For example, it is more important to know that the window has a box as sub-element than that the window has a height equal to 300. So the attributes are stored with the tag. A node is a tag with these attributes and their content. The pattern tree keeps coherent with the variant definition. Another point specific to the database is that the data are in several

[2] http://www.usixml.org

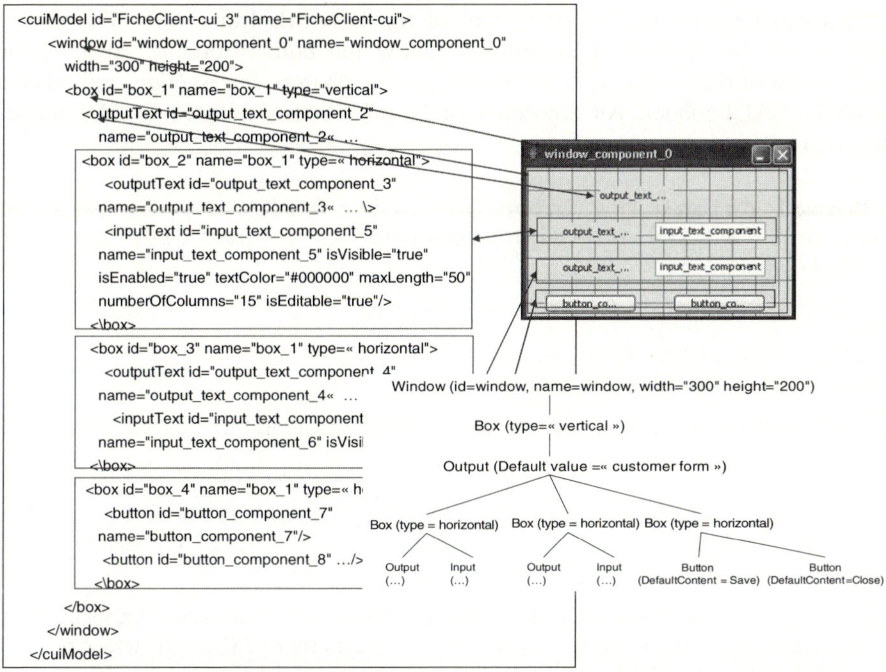

Fig. 2. User interface and its representation in UsiXML and as Tree

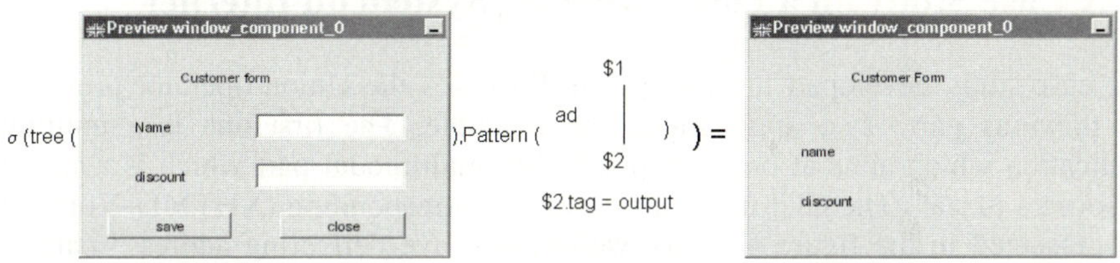

Fig. 3. Example of the *Selection* operator using to select the outputs of the input UI

data trees so the operators use a collection of data trees in input and output. In the HCI case, the input is one (for the unary operators) or two (for the binary operators) XML documents so one or two data trees. The proposed operators to manipulate the CUI model are Similarity, Equivalence, Subset, Set, Selection (cf. Figure 3), Complementary, Difference (Right or Left), Normal Union, Unique Union, Intersection, and Projection. These operations are logically defined on the XML tree and directly performed.

2.2 Adaptation of the Operators at the AUI Level for the Multimodal User Interfaces Composing

If the need is to compose user interface in *Difference* modality then we need to use the upper level as AUI. The same principle as in the previous work based on tree algebra can be used in the other level of the UsiXML framework. The rules are proposed at the AUI level in order to allow the composition at level which is independent of the modality. A set of operators as *Fusion, Intersection*, and others are adapted to AUI model. An algorithm of Normal Union adapted to AUI model is proposed below:

```
Normal Union: The Union operation takes a pair of trees
T1 and T2 as input and produces an output tree as
follows.

Firstly, the root of the output tree T3 is created:

If (T1.$1.tag = T2.$1.tag = abstractContainer) then
T3.$1.tag = abstractContainer

The node in which integrate the second tree is chosen.

If (subtree ti = subtree tj, ti ∈ T1, tj ∈ T2) then

         If (relation (ti-1, ti) = relation (tj-1, tj)=
order independency) then add (ti-1, order independency,
ti, order independency, tj-1,) in T3.

         If (relation (ti-1, ti) = relation (tj-1, tj)=
enabling) then add (abstractContainer AC1 in which
added (ti-1, R1', tj-1), enabling, ti)…
```

3 A Case Study on a Food Ordering System on Internet

The case study developed in this section illustrates the Union operator presented in the previous part. Two applications are available. The first one is a multimodal application which aims at ordering pizza. The multimodal part which is available is "Choose a pizza". The CUI model and its FUI corresponding (XHTML+VoiceXML) are presented in the figure 4 (c, d), while the "Give delivering address" part is not available and can not content vocal modality (this point is discussed in conclusion). The second application is graphical which allows to ordering Chinese food; likewise CUI model and its FUI (in Java) corresponding to the "Choose Meal" task are realized with GrafiXML editor and presented in figure 4 (c, d, e). The AUI (Abstract User Interface) models of each application are developed (Figure 4a and 5a) with the IdealXML editor [6].

The goal is first to obtain a multimodal application allowing to order Chinese food or pizza, and second to reuse the "give delivering address" task from the Chinese food application.

In order to apply the tree algebra operators, the definition needs to be adapted. While the operators applied to the CUI model need to know the structure of the user interface, the operators applied to the AUI model must in addition taking account the relationships. In our example, the tree representations of the two AUI (figure 4a and 5a) are presented in the figure 4b and 5b. In this representation, the relationships are generalized in R1 and R2 in order to treat different possibilities.

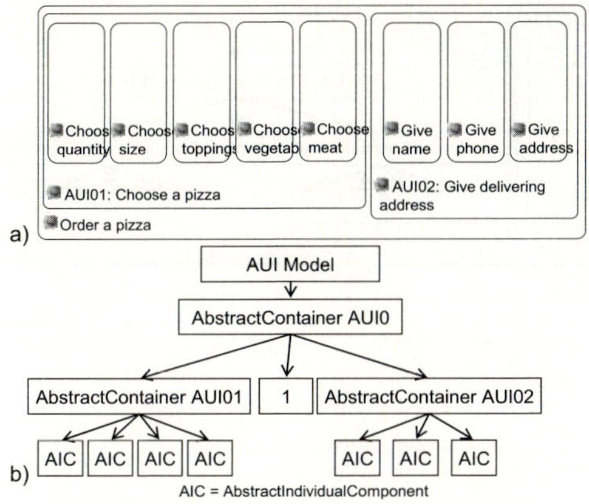


```
<outputText id="Ask_for_pizza_quantity"
        name="Ask_for_pizza_quantity" defaultContent="Quantity:"/>
    <inputText id="pizzaQuantity" name="quantity"
        defaultContent="1"
        voice_prompt="How many pizzas would you like?"
        voice_event_help="Say a number between one and twenty."
        voice_event_nomatch="Sorry I did not understand you."
        voice_event_noinput="You have to pronounce a quantity of
        pizza."/>
       <voice_quantity:grammar>
                <![CDATA[
                    #JSGF V1.0;
                    grammar pizza_quantity;
                    public <quantity> = 1 | 2 | 3 | 4 | 5 | 6 | 7 |
        8 | 9 | 10 | 11 | 12 | 13 | 14 | 15 | 16 | 17 | 18 | 19 | 20
        ;
                ]]>
       </voice_quantity:grammar>
    </inputText>
<outputText id="Ask_for_pizza_size" name="Ask_for_pizza_size"
        defaultContent="Size:"/>
<group voice_prompt="What size would you like?">
        <radioButton id="radiobuttonSize1"
        name="radiobuttonSize" defaultContent="small" />
        <radioButton id="radiobuttonSize2"
        name="radiobuttonSize" defaultContent="medium"/>
        <radioButton id="radiobuttonSize3"
        name="radiobuttonSize" defaultContent="large"/>
        <voice_quantity:grammar>
                <![CDATA[
                    #JSGF V1.0;
                    grammar pizza_size;
                    public <size> = small | medium | large ;
                ]]>
          </voice_quantity:grammar>
c) </group>
```

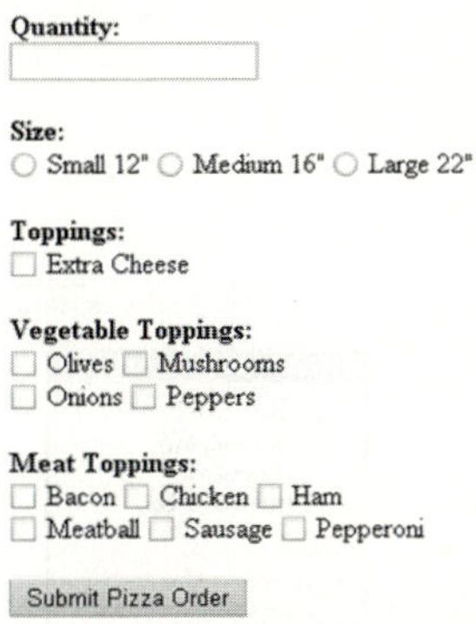

d)

Fig. 4. (a) AUI model of Chinese food ordering application, provided by IdealXML, (b) AUI model in tree representation (c) CUI model extract and (d) FUI associated to the pizza ordering application (Multimodal application but the vocal part is not visible)

If R1 and R2 relationships are "order independency" then the union operator provides a new tree with the three AUIContainers : "Choose a pizza", "Choose Meal" and " Give delivering address" with the relationship "order independency " between these three tasks. The "give delivering address" container (AUI3) was detected as repetitive element in the AUI models and as a result only one of them is reported in the resulting tree.

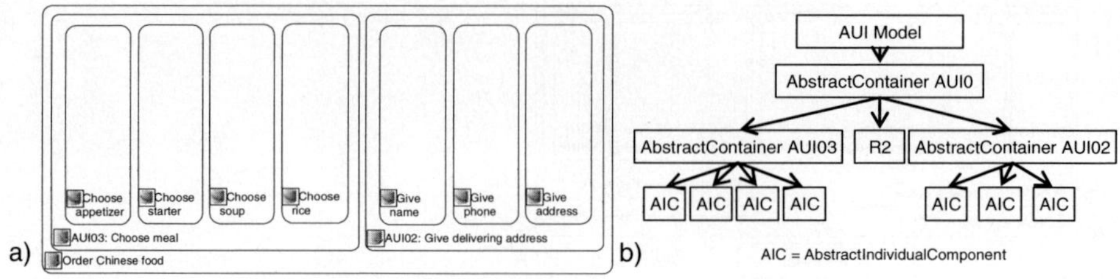


```
<cuiModel id="ChineseFood-cui_12" name="ChineseFood-cui">
    <window id="window_component_0" name="window_component_0"
      defaultContent="Chinese Food Order" width="263" height="491">
      <gridBagBox id="grid_bag_box_1" name="grid_bag_box_1"
        gridHeight="24" gridWidth="13">
          <outputText id="output_text_component_2"
            name="output_text_component_2"
            defaultContent="APPETIZER :"/>
          <checkBox id="checkbox_component_3"
            name="checkbox_component_3"
            defaultContent="Small Fried Shrimp"/>
          <checkBox id="checkbox_component_4"
            name="checkbox_component_4"
            defaultContent="Nicky's Egg Roll"/>
          <checkBox id="checkbox_component_5"
            name="checkbox_component_5"
            defaultContent="Fried Popcorn Shrimp"/>
          <outputText id="output_text_component_6"
            name="output_text_component_6"
            defaultContent="STARTER :" isVisible="true"/>
          <radioButton id="radiobutton_component_7"
            name="radiobutton_component_7"
            defaultContent="Seaweed Soup" isVisible="true"/>
          <radioButton id="radiobutton_component_9"
            name="radiobutton_component_9"
            defaultContent="Hot and Sour Soup"/>
        …
          <button id="button_component_22"
            name="button_component_22"
            defaultContent="Cancel" isVisible="true"/>
          <button id="button_component_23"
            name="button_component_23"
            defaultContent="Order" isVisible="true"/>
      </gridBagBox>
    </window>
</cuiModel>
```

c)

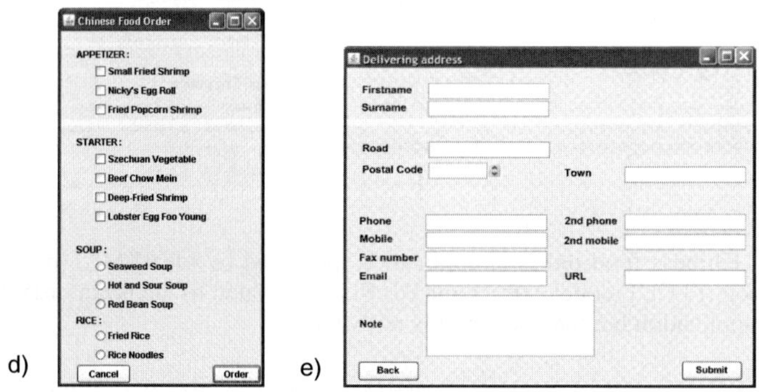

Fig. 5. (a) AUI model of pizza ordering application, provided by IdealXML, (b) AUI model in tree representation (c) CUI model extract and (d) FUI associated to the "Choose meal" sub task and (e) FUI associated to the "Give delivering address" sub task of the Chinese food ordering application (Graphical application); the (c, d, e) elements are provided by GrafiXML[3]

[3] GrafiXML is an editor associated to UsiXML available at http://www.usixml.org

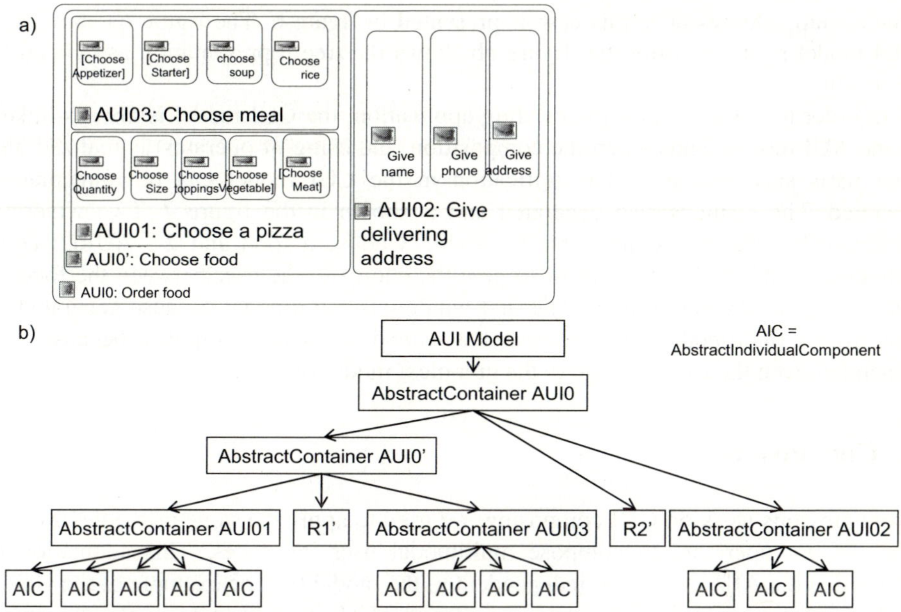

Fig. 6. (a) AUI model result and (b) its tree representation of Union operator

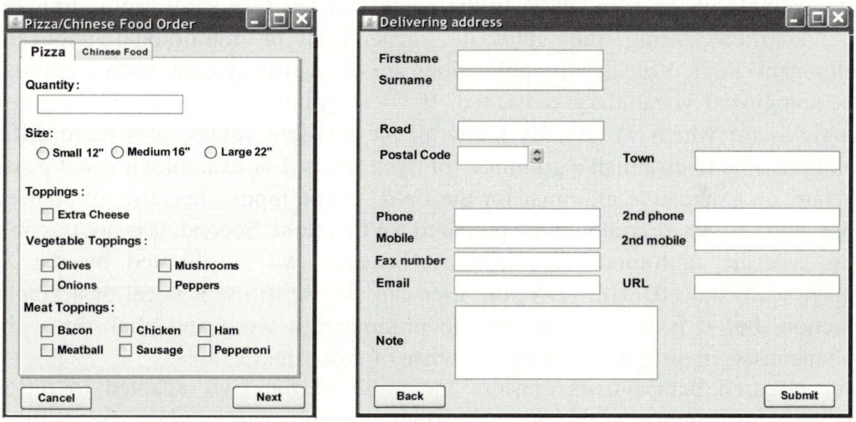

Fig. 7. Resulting FUIs generated from the AUI. In the first window, the first tab is a multimodal reuse from the first application while the second tab is the result from the second application (graphical can be reuse or multimodal must be generated). The second window, corresponding to the common task "Give delivering address", is graphical.

If R1 and R2 are « enabling » relationships, the union operator detects the common part as AUI02 "Give delivering address". As the previous relation is enabling then a new abstractContainer is created (AUI0' and named by the designer). The relation R1' is also chosen by the designer (here order independency) and R2' is enabling relationship. The result in this case is presented in figure 6. The figure 6a shows the AUI model resulting while the figure 6b shows the tree representation associated to the result.

In order to entirely reuse the existing application, the CUI model is always linked to the AUI model. Thus when the composition (the using of operator) is realized, the CUI parts stay available. The reification in the CUI model can be immediately operated. The result is also generated and is shown in the figure 7. Two windows correspond to the two containers: 1 - AU0': Choose a food and 2 - AUI02: Give delivering address. The tags allow to give the choice to the user between the food to choose: Pizza or Chinese food. The first window is Multimodal because generated in part from a multimodal CUI, whereas the second window is graphical because it is generated from the CUI specific to the graphical modality.

4 Conclusion

From previous work on GUI composing, we tried to apply the same principle of using tree algebra operators to compose multimodal user interfaces. This adaptation is realized at the AUI level to be independent to the modality. The example of the Union of two existing interfaces (one GUI and one MUI) was used to apply the union operator. The issue outlines that the previous work can not be used exactly in the same way so a new adaptation is necessary and proposed. The proposal is validated on the example of the case study. In the context of the case study, some limitations were identified during the automatic generation of multimodal applications development. First, VoiceXML applications are described by context-free grammars. Then, recognized vocabulary is limited. If vocal grammars are easy to prepare for input fields for which we already know all the possible values, it is more difficult even impossible to establish a grammar for open fields. For example, it is not possible to prepare an exhaustive grammar for the field "Name input", because, of course, all the possible responses could not be prepared for this field. Second, it is not possible to obtain synergic multimodal applications, because, we are limited by the X+V language [12]. Indeed, with X+V, the user can choose to use a vocal or a graphical interaction, but it is not yet possible to pronounce a word and click on a object simultaneously, in order to combine the sense of those interactions.

Our research perspectives concern the reuse of the CUI adapted to different modalities; for instance let us suppose two applications with similar tasks: if the first one is defined with a graphical CUI and the other one with a vocal + graphical CUI, how the first application (its CUI) could be transformed into a multimodal version?

Acknowledgement. The present research work has been supported by the "Ministère de l'Education Nationale, de la Recherche et de la Technologie», the «Région Nord Pas-de-Calais» and the FEDER (Fonds Européen de Développement Régional) during the projects MIAOU and EUCUE. The authors gratefully acknowledge the support of these institutions. The authors thank also Jean Vanderdonckt for his contribution concerning UsiXML.

References

1. Gamma, E., Helm, R., Johnson, R., Vlissides, J.: Design Patterns: Elements of reusable Object-Oriented Software. Addison Wesley, Massachusetts (1994)
2. Grundy, J.C., Hosking, J.G.: Developing Adaptable User Interfaces for Component-based Systems. Interacting with Computers 14(3), 175–194 (2001)
3. Jagadish, H.V., Lakshmanan, L.V.S., Srivastava, D., Thompson, K.: TAX: A Tree Algebra for XML. LNCS, vol. 2397, pp. 149–164. Springer, Heidelberg (2001)
4. Lepreux, S., Vanderdonkt, J., Michotte, B.: Visual Design of User Interfaces by (De)composition. In: Doherty, G., Blandford, A. (eds.) DSVIS 2006. LNCS, vol. 4323, Springer, Heidelberg (2007)
5. Lepreux, S., Vanderdonckt, J.: Toward a support of the user interfaces design using composition rules. In: Proc. of the 6th International Conference on Computer-Aided Design of User Interfaces, CADUI'2006, Bucharest, Romania, June 5-8, 2006, pp. 231–244. Kluwer Academic Publishers, Boston (2006)
6. Montero, F., Víctor López Jaquero, V.: IDEALXML: An Interaction Design Tool and a Task-based Approach to User Interface Design. In: Proc. of the 6th International Conference on Computer-Aided Design of User Interfaces, CADUI'2006, Bucharest, Romania, June 5-8, 2006, pp. 245–252. Kluwer Academic Publishers, Boston (2006)
7. Nielsen, J.: Goal Composition: Extending Task Analysis to Predict Things People May Want to Do (1994) available at http://www.useit.com/papers/goalcomposition.html
8. Vanderdonckt, J.: A MDA-Compliant Environment for Developing User Interfaces of Information Systems. In: Pastor, Ó., Falcão e Cunha, J. (eds.) CAiSE 2005. LNCS, vol. 3520, pp. 16–31. Springer, Heidelberg (2005)
9. VoiceXML 1.0., W3C Recommendation, http://www.w3.org/TR/voicexml10
10. VoiceXML 2.0., W3C Recommendation, http://www.w3.org/TR/voicexml20
11. VoiceXML 2.1, Working Draft, http://www.w3.org/TR/voicexml21/
12. X+V, XHTML + Voice Profile, http://www.voicexml.org/specs/multimodal/x+v/12

m-LoCoS UI: A Universal Visible Language for Global Mobile Communication

Aaron Marcus

Aaron Marcus and Associates, Inc., 1196 Euclid Avenue, Suite 1F, Berkeley, CA, 94708 USA
Aaron.Marcus@AMandA.com, www.AMandA.com

Abstract. The LoCoS universal visible language developed by the graphic/sign designer Yukio Ota in Japan in 1964 may serve as a usable, useful, and appealing basis for a mobile phone applications that can provide capabilities for communication among people who do not share a spoken language. User-interface design issues including display and input are discussed in conjunction with prototype screens showing the use of LoCoS for a mobile phone.

Keywords: design, interface, language, LoCoS, mobile, phone, user.

1 Introduction

1.1 Universal Visible Languages

Over the centuries, many different theorists and designers have been interested in and proposed artificial, universal sign or visible languages intended for easy learning and use by people all over the world, a kind of visual Esperanto. For example, in the last century, C.K. Bliss in Australia, invented Blissymbolics, [1] a language of signs, and attempted to convince the United Nations to declare Blissymbolics a world auxiliary visible language. Likewise, the graphic designer and sign designer Yukio Ota introduced in 1964 his own version of a universal sign language called LoCoS [5, 6, 7], which stands for Lovers Communication System. The LoCoS language, invented in 1964, was published in a Japanese LoCoS reference book in 1973 [5]. Ota has presented lectures about LoCoS around the world since he designed the signs, and published several articles in English explaining his design, *e.g.*, [6]. The author has written about Ota's work [3], and the author's firm maintains an extranet about LoCoS at this URL: http://www.amanda.com/extranet/extranet_f.html (username: locos, *note: all lowercase*, password: yuki00ta, *note: contains zeros, not o's)*. One of the significant features of LoCoS is that it can be learned in one day. Participants at Ota's lectures have been able to write him messages after hearing about the system and learning the basics of its vocabulary and grammar.

Based on this background, the author's firm worked with Mr. Ota over a period of several months in 2005, and in the ensuing months since then, to design prototypes of how LoCoS could be used on a mobile device. This paper presents an introduction to LoCoS, the design issues presented by trying to adapt LoCoS to a mobile phone use,

J. Jacko (Ed.): Human-Computer Interaction, Part III, HCII 2007, LNCS 4552, pp. 144–153, 2007.

an initial set of prototype screens, and future design challenges. The author and Associates of the author's firm worked with the inventor of LoCoS in early 2005 and subsequently to adapt the language to the context of mobile device use.

1.2 Basics of LoCoS

LoCoS is an artificial, non-verbal, generally non-spoken, visible language system designed for use by any human being to communicate with others who may not share spoken or written natural languages. Individual signs may be combined to form expressions and sentences in somewhat linear arrangements, as shown in Figure 1.

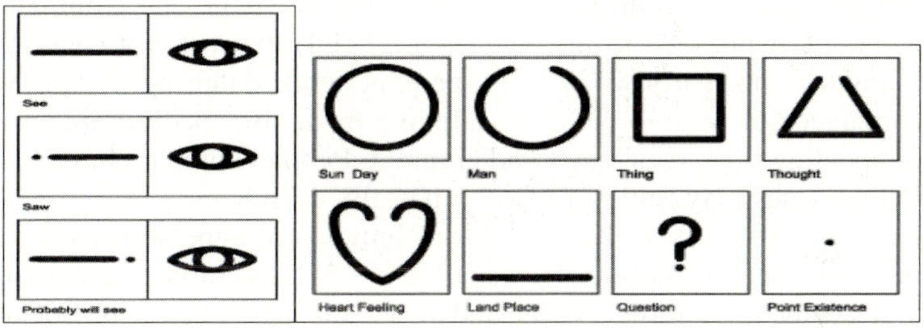

Fig. 1. Individual and combined signs

The signs may be combined into complete LoCoS expressions or sentences, formed by three horizontal rows of square area typically reading from left to right. Note this culture/localization issue: Many, but not all symbols could be flipped left to right for readers/writers used to right-to-left verbal languages. The main contents of a sentence are placed in the center row. Signs in the top and bottom rows act as adverbs and adjectives, respectively. Looking ahead to the possible use of LoCoS in mobile devices with limited space for sign display, a mobile-oriented version of LoCoS can use only one line. The grammar of the signs is similar to English (subject-verb-object). This aspect of the language, also, is an issue for those users used to other paradigms from natural verbal languages.

LoCoS differs from alphabetic natural languages in that the semantic reference (sometimes called "meaning") and the visual form are closely related. LoCoS differs from some other visible languages, *e.g.*, Bliss symbols use more abstract symbols, while LoCoS signs are more iconic. LoCoS is similar to, but different from Chinese ideograms, like those incorporated into Japanese Kanji signs. LoCoS is less abstract in that symbols of concrete objects like a road sign shows pictures of those objects. Like Chinese signs or Kanji, one sign refers to one concept, although there are compound concepts. According to Ota, LoCoS re-uses signs more efficiently than traditional Chinese signs. Note that the rules of LoCoS did not result from careful analysis across major world languages for phonetic efficiency. LoCoS does have rules for pronunciation (rarely used), but audio input/out was not explored in the project to be described for a mobile-LoCoS.

LoCoS has several benefits that would make it potentially usable, useful, and appealing as a sign language displayable on mobile devices. First, it is easy to learn in a progressive manner, starting with just a few basics. The learning curve is not steep, and users can guess correctly at new signs. Second, it is easy to display; the signs are relatively simple. Third, it is robust. People can understand the sense of the language without knowing all signs. Fourth, the language is suitable for mass media and the general public. People may find it challenging, appealing, mysterious, and fun.

2 Design Approaches for m-LoCoS

2.1 Universal Visible Messaging

m-LoCoS could be used in a universal visual messaging application, as opposed to text messaging. People who do not speak the same language can communicate with each other. People who need to interact via a UI (UI) that has *not* been localized to their own language normally would find the experience daunting. People who speak the same language but want to communicate in a fresh new medium may find LoCoS especially appealing, *e.g.*, teen-agers and children. People who may have some speech or accessibility issues may find m-LoCoS especially useful.

Currently the author's firm has developed initial prototype screens showing how LoCoS could be used in mobile devices. The HTML prototype screens have been developed showing a Motorola V505 and a Nokia 7610 phone. A LoCoS-English dictionary was begun and is in progress. Future needs including expanding LoCoS, exploring new, different visual attributes for the signs of LoCoS , including color, animation, and non-linear arrangements (called LoCoS 2.0), and developing the prototype more completely so that it is more complete and interactive.

The assumptions and objectives for m-LoCoS include the following:

For the developing world, there is remarkable growth in the use of mobile phones. China has over 300 million phones, larger than the USA population, and India is growing rapidly. People seem to be willing to spend up to 10% of their income for phones and service, which is often their only like to the world at large. For many users, the mobile phone is the first one that they have ever used. In addition, literacy levels are low, especially familiarity with computer user-interfaces. Thus, if mobile voice communication is expensive and unreliable, mobile messaging may be slower but cheaper, and more reliable Texting may be preferred to voice communication in some social settings. m-LoCoS may make it easier for people in developing countries to communicate with each other and with those abroad. The fact that LoCoS can be learned in one day makes it an appealing choice.

In the industrialized world, young people (*e.g.*, ages 2-25) have a high aptitude for learning new languages and user-interface paradigms. It is a much-published phenomenon that young people like to text-message, in addition to, and sometimes in preference to talking on their mobile phones. In Japan, additional signs, called emoticons have been popular for years. In fact, newspaper accounts chronicle the rise of *gyaru-moji* ("girl-signs") , a "secret" texting language of symbols improvised by Japanese teenage girls. They are a mixture of Japanese syllables, numbers, mathematical symbols , and Greek characters. Even though gyaru-moji takes twice as long for input as standard Japanese, they are still popular. This phenomenon suggests that young people might enjoy sign-messaging using LoCoS. The signs might be unlike anything they have used before, they would be easy to learn, they would be expressive, and they would be aesthetically pleasing. A mobil-device-enabled LoCoS might offer a fresh new way to send messages.

2.2 User Profiles, and Use Scenarios

Regarding users and their use-context, although 1 billion people use mobile phones now, there are a next 1 billion people, many in developing countries, who have never used any phone before. A mobile phone's entire user interface (UI) could be displayed in LoCoS, not only for messaging but for all applications, including voice. For younger users interested in a "cool" or "secret" form of communication in the industrialized world, they would be veteran mobile phone users. LoCoS would be an add-on application, and the success of *gyaru-moji* in Japan, as well as emoticon-use, suggests that a m-LoCoS could be successful. Finally, one could consider the case of travelers in countries that do not speak the traveler's language. Bearing in mind these circumstances, the author's firm developed three representative user profiles and use scenarios for exploring m-LoCoS applications and its UI. Use Scenario 1 concerns the micro-office in a less-developed country: Srini is a man in a small town in India. User Scenario 2 concerns young lovers in a developed country: Jack and Jill, boyfriend and girlfriend, in the USA. Use Scenario 3 concerns a traveler in a foreign country: Jaako is a Finnish tourist in a restaurant in France. Each of these is described briefly below.

Use Scenario 1: Micro-office in a less-developed country. Srini in India lives in a remote village that does not have running water, but just started having access to a new wireless network. The network is not reliable or affordable enough for long voice-conversations, but is adequate for text-messaging. Srini's mobile phone is the only means for non-face-to-face communication with his business partners. Srini's typical communication topic is this: should he go to a next village to sell his products, or wait for the prices to rise?

Use Scenario 2: Young lovers in the USA. Jack and Jill, boyfriend and girl friend, text-message each other frequently, using 5-10 words per message, and 2-3 messages per conversation thread. They think text-messaging is "cool," *i.e.*, highly desirable. They think it would be even "cooler" to send text messages in a private, personal, or secret language not familiar to most people looking over their shoulders or somehow intercepting their messages.

Use Scenario 3: Tourist in a foreign country. Jaako, a Finnish tourist ina restaurant in Paris, France, is trying to communicate with the waiter; however, he and the waiter do not speak a common language. A typical restaurant dialogue would be: "May I sit here?" "Would you like to start with an appetizer?" "I'm sorry; we ran out of that." "Do you have lamb?" All communication takes place via a single LoCoS-enabled device. Jaako and the waiter take turns reading and replying, using LoCoS.

2.3 Design Implications and Design Challenges

The design implications for developing m-LoCoS are that the language must be simple and unambiguous, input must occur quickly and reliably, and several dozen m-LoCoS signs must fit onto one mobile-device screen. Another challenge is that LoCoS as a system of signs must be extended for everyday use. Currently, there are about 1000 signs, as noted in the guidebook published in Japanese [5]. However, these signs are not sufficient for many common use scenarios. The author, working with his firm's associates, estimate that about 3000 signs are required, which is similar to Basic Chinese. The new signs to be added cannot be arbitrary, but should follow the current patterns of LoCoS and be appropriate for modern contexts a half-century after its invention. Even supposedly universal, timeless sign systems like those of Otto Neurath's group's invention called Isotypes [3,7] featured some signs that almost a century later are hard to interpret, like a small triangular shape representing sugar, based on a familiar commercial pyramical paper packaging of individual sugar portions in Europe in the early part of the twentieth century.

Another design challenge for m-LoCoS is that the mobile phone UI itself should utilize LoCoS (optionally, like language switching). For the user in developing countries, it might be the case that telecom manufacturers and service providers might not have localized, or localized well, the UI to the specific users' preferred language. M-LoCoS would enable the user to comfortably rely on a language for the controls and for help. For users in more developed countries, the "cool" factor or the interest in LoCoS would make a m-LoCoS UI desirable. Figure 3 shows an initial sketch by the author's firm for the some signs.

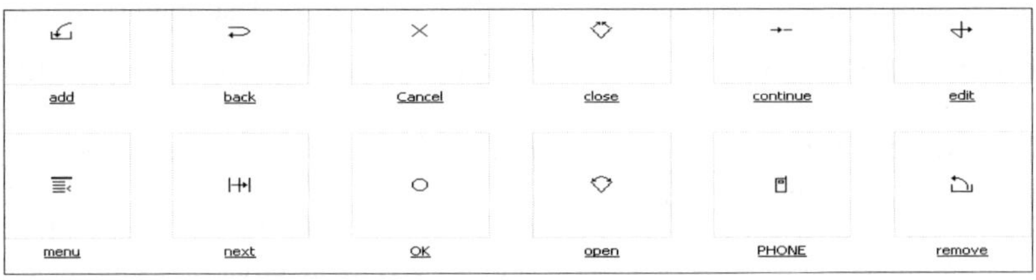

Fig. 2. Sketch of user-interface control signs based on LoCoS

Not only must the repertoire of the current LoCoS signs be extended, but the existing signs must be revised to update them, as mentioned earlier in relation to Isotype. Despite Ota's best efforts, some of the signs are culturally or religiously biased. Of course, it is difficult to make signs that are clear to everyone in the world and are pleasing to everyone. What is needed is a practical compromise that achieves tested success with the cultures of the target users. Examples of current challenges are shown in Figure 4. The current LoCoS sign for "restaurant" might often be mistaken for a "bar" because of the wine glass sign inside of the building sign. The cross as a sign for "religion" might not be understood correctly, thought appropriate, or even be welcome in Moslem countries such as Indonesia.

Another challenge would be to enable and encourage users to try LoCoS. Target users must be convinced to try to learn the visible language in one day. Non-English speakers might need to accommodate themselves to the English subject-verb-object structure. In contrast, in Japanese, the verb comes last, as it does in German dependent phrases. Despite Ota's best efforts, some expressions can be ambiguous. Therefore, there seems to be a need for dictionary support, preferably on the mobile device itself. Users should be able to ask, "what is the LoCoS sign for the X, if any?, or "what does this LoCoS sign mean?"

Fig. 4. LoCoS signs for Priest and Restaurant

In general, displaying m-LoCoS on small screens is a fundamental challenge. There are design trade-offs among the dimensions of legibility, readability, and density of signs. Immediately, one must ask, what should be the dimensions in pixels of a sign? Figure 5 shows some comparative sketches of small signs.

Japanese phones and Websites often seem to use 13 x 13 pixels. In discussions between the author's firm and Yukio Ota, it was decided to use 15 x 15 pixels for the signs. This density is the same as smaller, more numerous English signs. There was some discussions about whether signs should be anti-aliased; unfortunately, not enough was known about support of mobile devices with grayscale pixels to know what to recommend. Are signs easier to recognize and understand if anti-aliased? This issue is a topic for future user research.

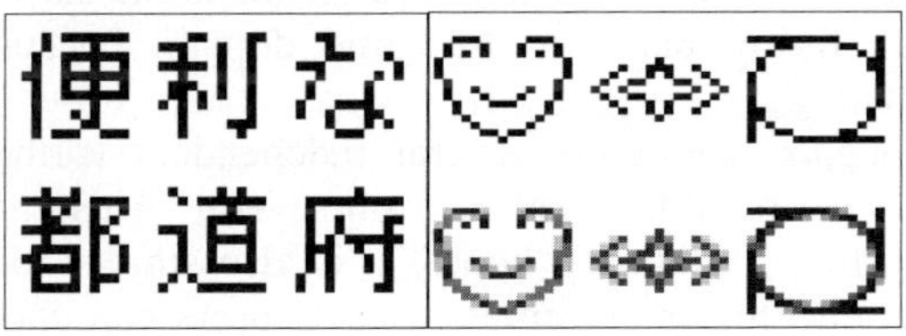

Fig. 5. Examples of signs drawn with and without anti-aliasing

2.4 Classifying, Selecting, and Entering Signs

There are several issues related to how users can enter m-LoCoS signs quickly and reliably. Users may not know for sure what the signs look like. What the user has in mind might not be in the vocabulary yet, or might not ever become a convention. One solution t is to select a sign from a list (menu), the technique used in millions of Japanese mobile phones. Here, an issue is how to locate one of 3,000 signs by means of a matrix of 36 signs that may be displayed in a typical 128 x 128 pixel screen (or a larger number of signs in the larger displays of many current high-end phones).

The current prototype developed by the author's firm uses a two-level hierarchy to organize the signs. Each sign is in of 18 domains of subject matter. Each domein's list of signs is accessible with 2-3 key strokes. 3000 signs divided into 18 domains would yield approximately 170 signs per domain, which could by shown in five screens of 36 signs each. A three-level hierarchy might also be considered. As with many issues, these would have to be user-tested carefully to determine optimum design trade-offs. Figure 6 shows a sample display.

Fig. 6. Sample prototype display of a symbol menu for a dictionary

To navigate among a screen-full of signs to a desired one, numerical keys can be used for eight-direction movement from a central position at the 5-key, which also acts as a Select key. For cases in which signs do not fit onto one screen (*i.e.*, more than 36 signs), the 0-key might be used to scroll upward or downward with one or two taps. There are challenges with strict hierarchical navigation. It seems very difficult to make intuitive the taxonomy of all concepts in a language. Users may have to learn which concept is in which category. Shortcuts may help for frequently-used signs.

In addition, there are different (complementary) taxonomies. Form taxonomies could group signs that look similar (*e.g.*, those containing a circle). Properties taxonomies could group signs that are concrete *vs.* abstract, artificial *vs.* natural, micro-scaled *vs.* macro-scaled, *etc.* Schemas (domains in the current prototype) would group "apple" and "frying pan" in the same domain because both are in the "food/eating" schema.

Most objects/concepts belong to several independent (orthogonal) hierarchies. Might it not be better to be able to select from several? This challenge is similar to multi-faceted navigation in mobile p hones. It is also similar to the "20 Questions" game, but would require fewer questions because users can choose from up to one dozen answers each, not just two choices. Software should sort hierarchies presented to users by most granular to more general "chunking." It is also possible to navigate two hierarchies with just one key press.

A realistic, practical solutions would incorporate context-sensitive guessing of what sign the user is likely to use next. The algorithm could be based on the context of a sentence or phrase the user is assembling, or on what signs/patterns the user frequently selects. Figure 7 illustrates multiple categories selection scheme.

	Concrete	Abstract	Don't know
Man-Made	1	2	3
Naturally -Occurring	4	5	6
Both	7	8	9
Don't Know	*	0	#

Fig. 7. Possible combinations of schema choices for signs

If the phone has a camera, like most recent phones, the user could always write signs on paper and send that image-capture to a distant person or show the paper to a

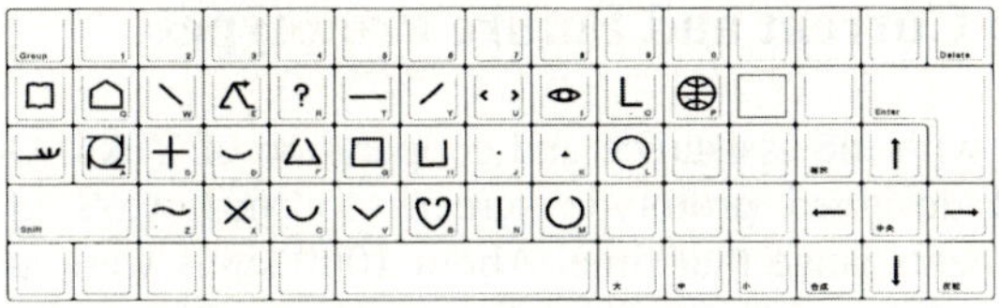

Fig. 8. LoCoS keyboard designed by Yukio Ota

person nearby. However, the user might still require and benefit from a dictionary (in both directions of translation) to assist in assembling the correct signs for a message.

There are other alternatives to navigate-and-select paradigms. For example, the user could actually draw the signs, much like Palm® Graffiti ™, but this would require a mobile device with a touch screen (as earlier PDAs and the Apple iPhone and its competitors provide). One could construct each sign by combining, rotating, and resizing approximately 16 basic shapes. Ota has also suggested another, more traditional approach, the LoCoS keyboard, but this direction was not pursued. The keyboard is illustrated in Figure 8.

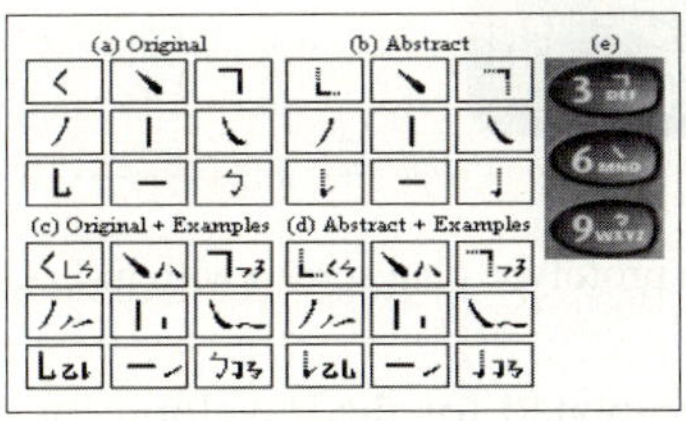

Fig. 9. examples of stroke-order sequential selection from [2]

Still another alternative is the Motorola iTAP® technique, which uses stroke-order sequential selection. In recent years, there have been approximately 320m Chinese phones, with 90m using text messaging in 2003, using sign input via either Pinyin or iTAP. m-LoCoS might be able to use sequential selection, or a mixed stroke/semantic method. Figure 9 shows examples of stroke-order sign usage for Chinese input.

2.5 Future Challenges

Beyond the matters described above, there are other challenges to secure a successful design and implementation of m-LoCoS on mobile devices that would enable visible language communication among disparate, geographically distant users.

For example, the infrastructure challenges are daunting, but seem surmountable. One would need to establish protocols for encoding and transmitting LoCoS over wireless networks. In conjunction, one would need to secure interest and support from telecom hardware manufacturers and mobile communication services.

3 Conclusion: Current and Future Prototypes

The author's firm, with the assistance and cooperation of Yukio Ota, investigated the design issues and designed prototype screens for m-LoCoS in early 2005, with subsequent adjustments since that time. About 1000 signs were assumed for LoCoS, which is not quite sufficient to converse for modern, urban, and technical situations. There is a need for a larger community of users and contributors of new signs. The current prototype is a set of designed screens that have been transmitted as images and show the commercial viability of LoCoS. Figure 10 shows a sample screen.

Literal translation of the "chat"

Joe: where? you

Bill: Restaurant

Joe: I will go there

Bill: happy new year

Fig. 10. Example of a prototype chat screen with m-LoCoS on a mobile phone

Among next steps contemplated for the development of m-LoCoS are to develop an online community for interested students, teachers, and users of LoCoS. For this reason, the author's firm designed and implemented an extranet about LoCoS at the URL cited earlier. In addition, new sign designs to extend the sign set and to update the existing one, ideal taxonomies of the language, working interactive implementations on mobile devices from multiple manufactures, and the resolution of technical and business issues mentioned previously lie ahead. Of special interest to the design community is research into LoCoS 2.0, which is currently underway through Yukio Ota and colleagues in Japan. The author's firm has also consulted with Mr. Ota on these design isues: alternative two-dimensional layouts; enhanced graphics; color of strokes, including solid colors and gradients; font-like characteristics, *e.g.*, thick-thins, serifs, cursives, italics, *etc.*; backgrounds of signs: solid colors, patterns, photos, *etc.*; animation of signs; and additional signs from other international sets, *e.g.*, vehicle transportation, operating systems, *etc.*

m-LoCoS, when implemented in an interactive prototype on a commercial mobile device would be ready for a large deployment experiment, which would provide a context to study its use and suitability for work and leisure environments. The deployment would provide, also, a situation for trying out LoCoS 2.0 enhancements. A wealth of opportunities for planning, analysis, design, and evaluation lies ahead.

Acknowledgements

The author acknowledges the assistance of Yukio Ota, President, Sign Center, and Professor, Tama Art University, Tokyo, Japan. In addition, the author thanks Designer/Analyst Dmitry Kantorovich of the author's firm for his extensive assistance in preparing the outline for this paper and for preparing the figures used in it.

References

1. Bliss, C.K.: Semantography (Blissymbolocs), The book presents a system for universal writing, or pasigraphy, 2nd edn., p. 882. Semantography Publications, Sidney, Australia (1965)
2. Lin, Sears.: Graphics Matters: A Case Study of Mobile Phone Keypad Design for Chinese Input. In: Proc., Conference on Human Factors in Computing Systems (CHI 2005), Extended Abstracts for Late-Breaking Results, Short Papers, Portland, OR, USA, pp. 1593–1596 (2005)
3. Marcus, Marcus, Aaron.: Icons, Symbols, and More, Fast Forward Column. Interactions 10(3), 28–34 (2003)
4. Marcus, Aaron: Universal, Ubiquitous, User-Interface Design for the Disabled and Elderly, Fast Forward Column. Interactions 10(2), 23–27 (2003)
5. Yukio, O.: LoCoS: Lovers Communications System (in Japanese), Pictorial Institute, Tokyo.: 1973. The author/designer presents the system of universal writing that he invented (1973)
6. Yukio, O.: LoCoS: An Experimental Pictorial Language. Icographic, Published by ICOGRADA, the International Council of Graphic Design Associations, based in London, No. 6, pp. 15–19 (1973)
7. Yukio, O.: Pictogram Design, Kashiwashobo, Tokyo, The author presents a world-wide collection of case studies in visible language signage systems, including LoCoS (1987) ISBN 4-7601-0300-7, 1987

Developing a Conversational Agent Using Ontologies

Manish Mehta[1] and Andrea Corradini[2]

[1] Cognitive Computing Lab Georgia Institute of Technology Atlanta, GA, USA
[2] Computational Linguistics Department University of Potsdam, Potsdam, Germany
mehtama1@cc.gatech.edu, andrea@ling.uni-potsdam.de

Abstract. We report on the benefits achieved by using ontologies in the context of a fully implemented conversational system that allows for a real-time rich communication between primarily 10 to 18 years old human users and a 3D graphical character through spontaneous speech and gesture. In this paper, we focus on the categorization of ontological resources into domain independent and domain specific components in the effort of both augmenting the agent's conversational capabilities and enhancing system's reusability across conversational domains. We also present a novel method of exploiting the existing ontological resources along with Google directory categorization for a semi-automatic understanding of user utterance on general purpose topics like e.g. movies and games.

1 Introduction

A growing research community has worked on developing general purpose ontologies [1, 2]. One of the long term goals of the ontology initiatives is to produce common formalisms so that ontologies can be combined together easily for a new domain [3]. The use of ontologies has also become an important step towards the implementation of actual spoken dialog systems [4, 5]. In this respect, this paper reports on the role of ontological resources in a real time system that we developed to simulate an experientially rich interaction between kids and a conversational agent. To create a context, we deployed a 3D-embodied character personifying the fairy tale author Hans Christian Andersen (HCA) and placed him in a graphical representation of his original study. User interaction with the character occurs through spontaneous speech and 2D gesture. The agent's communication channels are synthesized speech coupled with the display of 3D gesture and emotions. HCA domains of discourse include: HCA's fairy tales, his life, the user and his physical appearance and a meta-domain to resolve meta-communication conversational turns during interactive sessions.

Through the paper, we specifically focus on the overall benefits achieved by using ontologies for the development of such a conversational system and present our findings on the following topics:

- Use of ontologies as the underlying common knowledge representation formalism and communication language across the natural language understanding (NLU) and dialog modules.
- Ease and fast development of the dialog system through shared ontological resources across different domains of conversation.

J. Jacko (Ed.): Human-Computer Interaction, Part III, HCII 2007, LNCS 4552, pp. 154–164, 2007.

- Ease of adding new conversation domains, such as e.g. movies and games through a combination of existing ontological resources with Google's directory categorization.

Developing reusable resources is a key challenge for any software application. Ontological reusability across characters and domains depends upon whether the knowledge resources are developed in a generic way. The ability to automatically induce a concept in one character and port it to a new character provides a strong benchmark to test the crafting of ontological resources. For historical characters, where the users are going to address questions regarding their life and physical appearance, concepts for these domains provide a clear case of reuse. We have developed ontological concepts for a characters life and physical appearance that could be used for a new character with little modification. We have also developed properties that are shared across domains. These ontological resources also provide a common representational formalism that simplifies communication across the natural language understanding (NLU) component and dialog modules.

Inside the NLU, the rules that we have defined to detect domain independent dialog acts and properties simplify the addition of new domains to increase the range of discussion topics one could have with the animated agent and not just the topics in its domain of expertise. To the five original domains, we have then added domains like movies and games to provide HCA with the ability to address more general purpose everyday topics. In order to properly capture and understand topics within these new domains during conversation, we utilize Google's directory structure that contains, among other things, updated information and classification of movies and games. For example, if the user asks about a certain computer game that was recently released to the public (and for which we do not have any information in our hand crafted system knowledge base), the NLU uses its internal set of rules to try to classify the question into a dialog act, a property using domain independent rules and an unknown concept which is likely to be the name of the game as it was uttered/typed in by the user. This unknown concept is resolved using Google directory engine. The automatic categorization provided by Google coupled with the domain independent properties and the dialog acts results in an automated representation of the user intent consistent with the current NLU ontological representation formalism.

The rest of the paper is organized as follows. In section 2 we present an overview of the system. We present our natural language understanding module in Section 3. Next, we describe our method of combining existing resources with Google directory categorization to provide a representation for utterances corresponding to general purpose topics. In Section 5, we discuss conversational mover component inside the dialog module that detects the next prospective conversational move of the character. We discuss ontological reusability across different domains in Section 6 and finally conclude with some future directions we are planning to undertake.

2 System Primer

Our framework is a computer game where a player can interact with an embodied character in a 3D world, using spoken conversation as well as 2D gesture. The basic

Fig. 1. HCA in his study

idea behind the game scenario is to have the player communicate with a computer generated representation of the fairytale author Hans Christian Andersen to learn about the writer's life, historical period and fairy tales in an entertaining way that reinforces and support the educational message delivered. There is no visible user avatar as the user perceives the world around him in a first-person perspective. She can explore HCA's study and talk to him, in any order, about any topic within HCA's knowledge domains, using spontaneous speech and mixed-initiative dialog. The user can change the camera view, refer to and talk about objects in the study, and also point at or gesture to them. Typical input gestures are markers like, e.g., lines, points, circles, etc. entered at will via a mouse compatible input device or using a touch-sensitive screen. HCA's domains of discourse are: HCA's fairy tales, his life, his physical presence in his study, the user, HCA's role as gate-keeper for access to the fairy tale world, and the meta-domain of solving problems of meta-communication during speech/gesture conversation. Apart from engaging in conversation on his domain of expertise, the user can discuss everyday topics like movies, games, famous personalities and others using a typed interface.

3 Natural Language Understanding Module

3.1 General Overview

The Natural Language Understanding module (Fig. 2) consists of four main components: a key phrase spotter, a semantic analyzer, a concept finder, and a domain spotter. Any user utterance from the speech recognizer is forwarded to the NLU where a key phrase spotter detects multi-word expressions from a stored set of words labeled with semantic and syntactic tags. This first stage of processing usually is helpful to adjust minor errors due to misrecognized utterances by the Speech recognizer. Key phrases that are domain-related are extracted, and a wider acceptance of utterances is achieved. The processed utterance is sent on to the semantic analyzer. Here, dates, age, and numerals in the user utterance are detected while both the syntactic and semantic categories for single words are retrieved from a lexicon. Relying upon these semantic and syntactic categories, grammar rules are then applied to the utterance to help in performing word sense disambiguation and to create a sequence of semantic and syntactic categories. This higher-level representation of the input is then fed into a set of finite state automata, each associated to a predefined semantic equivalent according to data

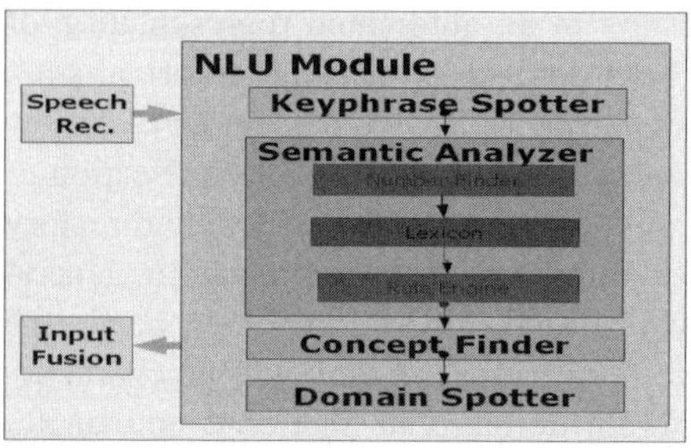

Fig. 2. The main components of the NLU module

used to train the automata. Anytime a sequence is able to traverse a given automaton, its associated semantic equivalent is the semantic representation corresponding to the input utterance. At the same time, the NLU calculates a representation of the user utterance in terms of dialog acts. At the next stage, the concept finder relates the representation of the user utterance, in terms of semantic categories, to the domain level ontological representation. Once semantic categories are mapped onto domain level concepts and properties, the relevant domain of the user utterance is extracted. The domain helps in providing a categorization of the character's knowledge set. The final output in form of concept(s)/subconcept(s) pairs, property, dialog act and domain is sent to the dialog module.

3.2 Rule Sharing

Generic rules are defined inside the semantic analyzer for detecting dialog acts (shown in Fig. 3). These dialog acts provide a representation of user intent like types of question asked (e.g., asking about a particular place or a particular reason), opinion statements (like positive, negative or generic comments), greetings (opening, closing) and repairs (clarification, corrections, repeats) [6]. Rules for detecting these dialog acts are defined based on domain independent syntactic knowledge thereby ensuring that once these rules are hand crafted they can be reused across the different domains of conversation. Altogether in our system we have defined about 300 rules out of which approximately a third of them are domain independent. As explained above, a subset of these domain independent rules is used for detecting the dialog acts and is reused across different domains of conversations. The rest of the domain independent rules are used to detect the domain independent properties (e.g., dislike, like, praise, read, write etc). For instance, general wh-questions about a domain are handled by using the domain independent rules to detect dialog acts and properties while simultaneously domain dependent rules are deployed for detecting the concept present in the user utterance.

A typical rule for detecting a dialog act is of the form:

<aux:all> <hca>:- <question:yes/no> <hca>
apply_at_position :- [beginning]
Number of conditions :- 0

It makes sure that wherever the input sequence "*<aux:all> <hca>*" (occurring e.g. in sentences starting with "*Have you......*", "*Would you......*") is extracted from the user input at the '*beginning*' of a sentence, it is then converted into the sequence "*<question:yes/no> <hca>*". The rule also states that there is no condition which affects its application. In *<aux:all>* the field '*all*' specifies that the rule can be applicable to all the auxiliaries like '*can*', '*shall*' etc. This provides a good generalization mechanism so that the rule needs not be created for all the auxiliaries individually. Table 1 shows an example of processing inside the NLU where this rule is applied to detect the dialog act.

One of the rule for detecting the dialog act '*user opinion*' of type '*negative*' is
<user><aux:all><negative:all> :- <user opinion:negative><subject:user>
apply at position :- [beginning]
Number of conditions :- 0

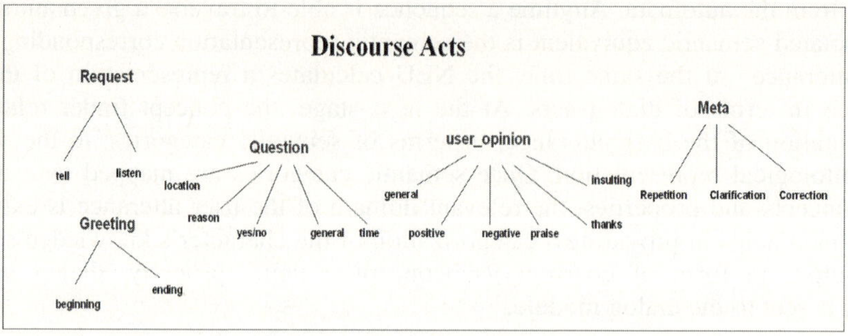

Fig. 3. Examples of different dialog acts that are shared across the domains of conversation

When sentences of the form "*I am not....*", "*I have not....*" are encountered (in this specific case also at the beginning of an input stream), their lexical entries are retrieved from the lexicon and immediately converted into the sequence "*<user><aux:am><negative:not>.....*". The above rule is then applied to rewrite this sequence of categories into "*<user opinion:negative><subject:user>.....*".

Table 1. Pipelined processing across different components inside the NLU

SR output	Do you like your study
Keyphrase Spotter	Do you like your study
Semantic Analyzer	<question:yes/no><verb:like><study:general >
Concept Finder	<dialogact:question><dialogacttype:yes/no> <concept:study><subconcept:general> <property:like>

3.3 Separation of Ontological and Semantic Representations

In a conversational system, the domain knowledge has to be connected to linguistic system levels of organization such as grammar and lexicon. Domain ontology captures knowledge of one particular domain and serves as a more direct representation of the world. Ontological relationships '*is-a*' and '*a-kind-of*' have their lexical counterparts in hyponymy. The part-whole relationships meronymy and holonymy also form hierarchies. This relationship parallelism would suggest that lexical relationships and ontology are the same but a lexical hierarchy might only serve as a basis for a useful ontology and can at most be called an ersatz ontology [8]. Bateman [9] provides an interesting discussion of the relationship between domain and linguistic ontologies. In our architecture, we use two different sets of representations to support the two contrasting objectives of semantic and domain level representation. The role of the concept finder is to provide a link between the two representations. The semantic categories present in the user utterance in the domain are mapped to the domain level concepts and properties through rules defined on the semantic categories. Table 1 shows an example of this mapping.

Inside the NLU, the concept/property representations along with the dialog acts are combined with Google's directory categorization for unknown concepts to achieve a semi-automatic categorization for general purpose topics. We explain on this categorization approach in the next section.

4 Understanding General Purpose Topics Through Google's Directory

Conversational agent research has focused on effective strategies for developing agents that can co-operate with the human participant to solve a task within a given domain. In the framework of our project, we attempt to move from task oriented agents to life-like virtual agents with model of emotion and personality, a sense of humor and social grace, carrying out a mixed initiative conversation on their life, physical appearance and their domain of expertise. In our research, one of the suggested improvements of our first efforts [11] was to increase the range of discussion topics one could have with the animated agent. This raises an interesting challenge of how to cost-effectively develop agents that have sufficient depth to keep the user involved and are able to handle multiple general purpose topics and not just the topics in their domain of expertise. These topics could range from multiple general-purpose subjects like games, movies, current news, famous personalities, food, and famous places. The task of developing conversational agents with abilities to talk about these open-ended domains would be expensive, requiring significant resources. The simplest way to address these topics would have been to handle them with a standard reply "*I don't know the answer*", ignoring them altogether or through shallow pattern matching techniques as illustrated by chat bots like Weizenbaum's seminal ELIZA [12] and Alice [13].

Web directories represent large databases of hand-selected and human-reviewed sites arranged into a hierarchy of topical categories. Search engines utilize these directories to find high-quality, hand-selected sites to add to their database. Users that are searching for a variety of sites on the same topic also find directories helpful by being able to search in only the category that interests them. Google's web directory contains, among other things, classification information about names of movies, games, famous personalities, etc. Making entries for these domains manually in the lexicon would be a labor and time intensive effort. Apart from that, these open ended domains evolve over a period of time. As such they need periodic updates. Thus, using Google's categorization provides an automatic classification method for terms related to these domains. In our architecture, the NLU categorizes the words without a lexical entry and those that are not detected by the keyphrase spotter, into an *unknown* category. The longest unknown sequence of words is combined into a single phrase. These words are sent to the web agent, which uses Google's directory structure to find out whether the unknown words refer to a name of a movie, game, or a famous personality and the corresponding category is returned to the NLU. To illustrate the processing let us assume the user asked "*do you like quake?*". In this case, the NLU marks the word quake as an *unknown* category that, as such, needs further resolution. The temporary output of the NLU is thus a *yes/no-question* dialog act, a property of the kind *like* and an *unknown* category. The *unknown* category is resolved by the web agent into the category game using Google's directory engine (see Fig. 4). Using this newly gathered information, the NLU is capable to pass on to the dialog module a complete output which now consists of a *yes/no-question* dialog act, a property of kind *like*, a concept *game* and a sub concept *quake*. The classification provided by Google along with the properties shared across domains and the dialog acts provides a method to build an automated representation consistent with the current output representation generated by the understanding module. Based on this information, the conversational mover inside the dialog module searches for an appropriate conversational move in response to the original sentence as explained in the next session.

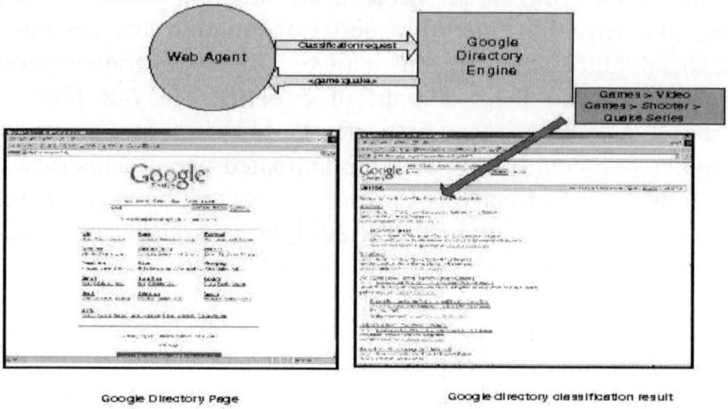

Fig. 4. The unknown category '*quake*' resolved by Google's web directory

5 Conversational Mover

One of the challenges in developing a spoken dialog system for conversational characters is to make system components communicate with each other using a common representation language. This representation language reflects the contradictory ambitions of being rich enough to help encode the personality of the character and general enough so that the formalism doesn't change across characters. At the next stage, inside the dialog module, the output representation from the NLU is used to reason about the next conversational move of the character. This stage of processing is performed inside a module called the conversational mover. For each conversational move of the character, rules are defined using the concept(s)/sub concept(s), property(s)/property type and dialog act/dialog act type pairs delivered by the NLU. This provides a systematic way to connect the user intention to the characters output move. Table 2 shows examples of rules inside the conversational mover. Table 3 provides two examples of processing across different components. Anytime HCA has to produce a response or initiate a new conversational turn on the domain topics, the dialog module selects a contextually appropriate output in accordance with the conversational move produced by this module, the conversational history and the emotional state [7]. The processing after this stage is mainly related to agent's response generation in terms of behavior display, speech generation and its synthesis but it is outside the scope of the paper.

Table 2. Example of two rules inside the conversational mover. XX acts as a placeholder for any *sub_concept* type and allows us to reuse the rule for all the sub concepts.

```
define conv move :- movie_opinion
{
        dialog act :- request or question and
        dialog act type :- listen or general and
        concept :- movie and sub concept: XX and
        property :- like or think
}

define conv move :- famous_personality_knowledge
{
        dialog act :- request or question and
        dialog act type :- listen or general and
        concept :- famous_personality and sub_concept: XX
        property :- know
}
```

6 Ontological Reuse

One of the clear cases of ontological reuse for a historical character is to craft the concepts of his life and physical appearance in a generic way. Figure 5 shows the domain (in)dependent concepts which are currently used in our architecture for HCA life and physical self. The figure also shows general properties which are shared across different domains. To illustrate the reusability of our approach, let us consider some explanatory use cases.

Use case 1: This case represents an utterance which is used by the user to ask about the characters father. The representation from the NLU is independent of a particular character. Similar utterances regarding other family members produce an independent representation with the *sub_concept* slot filled with the corresponding value.

Input: *I want to know a little bit about your father*
NLU: <dialog_act:question>, <dialog_act_type:general>, <concept:family>, <sub_concept:father>

Use case 2: This case represents the use of common properties across different domains. The property *emotion* with property type *scary* is used for the representation across both the utterances belonging to different domain: the first belonging to HCA's fairytales and second one to his physical self.

Input: *Your fairytales are scary*
Domain: fairytale
NLU : <dialog_act:user_opinion>, <dialog_act_type:general> <concept:fairytale>,<sub_concept:general>, <property:emotion>,<property_type:scary>

Input: *You look scary*
Domain: physical self
NLU <dialog_act:user_opinion>, <dialog_act_type:general > <concept:personal_attribute> <sub_concept:self_identity> <property:emotion>, <property_type:scary>

We contend that these reusable portions for the characters life and his physical appearance can save a great deal of development time for a new character.

Table 3. Processing of two utterances inside different components

User: **NLU:** **Google Class. :** **C Mover :**	What do you think about Agatha Christie <dialogact:question><dialogacttype:general> <concept:unknown> <subconcept:agatha_christie> <property:think> <dialogact:question><dialogacttype:general> <concept:famous_personality> <subconcept:agatha_christie> > <property:think> famous_personality_opinion
User: **NLU:** **Google Class. :** **C Mover :**	Do you know about Quake <dialogact:question><dialogacttype:yes/no> <concept:unknown> <subconcept:quake > <dialogact:question><dialogacttype:yes/no> <concept:game> <subconcept:quake> <property:know> famous_personality_opinion

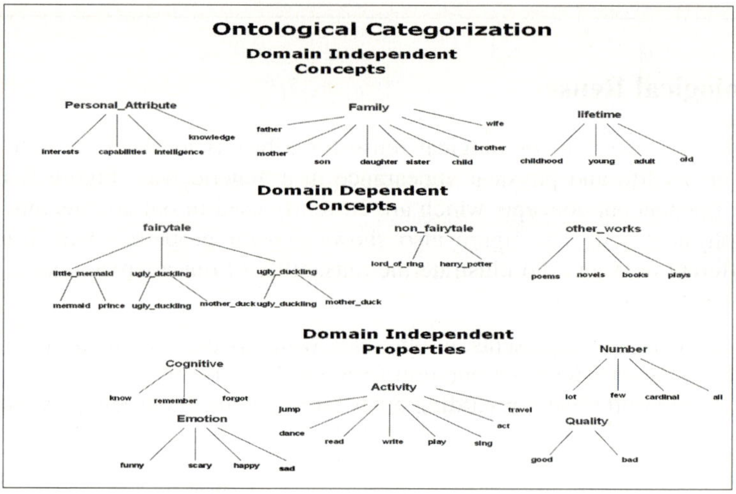

Fig. 5. A set of domain dependent and domain independent concepts and properties

7 Conclusion

In this paper, we discussed the benefits of ontological resources for a spoken dialog system. We reported on the domain independent ontological concepts and properties. These ontological resources have also served as a basis for a common communication language across understanding and dialog modules. We intend to explore what further advantages can be obtained by an ontological based representation and test the reusability of our representation of a characters life and physical appearance through development of a different historical character. For language understanding purposes on topics like movies, games and famous personalities, we have proposed an approach of using web directories along with existing domain independent properties and dialog acts to build a consistent representation with other domain input. This approach helps in providing a semi-automatic understanding of user input for open ended domains.

There have been approaches using Yahoo categories [10] to classify documents using an N-gram classifier but we are not aware of any approaches utilizing directory categorization for language understanding. Our classification approach faces problem when the group of words overlap with the words in the lexicon. For example, when the user says "*Do you like Lord of the rings?*" where the words '*of*' and '*the*' have a lexical entry, their category is retrieved from the lexicon and the only unknown words remaining are '*Lord*' and '*rings*' and the web agent is not able to find the correct category for these individual words. One solution would be to automatically detect the entries, which overlap with the words in the lexicon by parsing the Google directory structure offline and having these entries made in the keyphrase spotter. We plan to solve these issues in the future.

Acknowledgments. We gratefully acknowledge the Human Language Technologies Programme of the European Union, contract # IST-2001-35293 that supported both authors in the initial stage of the work presented in this paper. We also thank Abhishek Kaushik at Oracle India Ltd. for programming support.

References

1. Lenat, B.D.: Cyc: A large-scale investment in knowledge infrastructure. Communication of the ACM 38(11), 33–38 (1995)
2. Philipot, A., Hovy, E.H., Pantel, P.: The omega ontology. In: Proceedings of the ONTOLEX Workshop at the International Conference on Natural Language Processing, pp. 59–66 (2005)
3. Kalfoglou, Y., Schorlemmer, M.: Ontology mapping: the state of the art. Knowledge Engineering Review 18(1), 1–31 (2003)
4. Tsovaltzi, D., Fiedler, A.: Enhancement and use of a mathematical ontology in a tutorial dialog system. In: Proceedings of the IJCAI Workshop on Knowledge Representation and Automated Reasoning for E-Learning Systems, Acapulco (Mexico), pp. 23–35 (2003)
5. Dzikovska, M.O., Allen, J.F., Swift, D.M.: Integrating linguistic and domain knowledge for spoken dialogue systems in multiple domains. In: Proceedings of the IJCAI Workshop on Knowledge and Reasoning in Practical Dialogue Systems, Acapulco (Mexico), pp. 25–35 (2003)
6. Mehta, M., Corradini, A.: Understanding Spoken Language of Children Interacting with an Embodied Conversational Character. In: Proceedings of the ECAI Workshop on Language-Enabled Educational Technology and Development and Evaluation of Robust Spoken dialog Systems, pp. 51–58 (2006)
7. Corradini, A., Mehta, M., Bernsen, N.O., Charfuelan, M.: Animating an Interactive Conversational Character for an Educational Game System. In: Proceedings of the ACM International Conference on Intelligent User Interfaces, San Diego (CA, USA), pp. 183–190 (2005)
8. Hirst, G.: Chapter Ontology and the Lexicon. In: Handbook on Ontologies, pp. 209–230. Springer, Heidelberg (2004)
9. Bateman, J.A.: The Theoretical Status of Ontologies in Natural Language Processing. In: Proceedings of Workshop on Text Representation and Domain Modelling - Ideas from Linguistics and AI, pp. 50–99 (1991)

10. Labrou, Y., Finin, T.: Yahoo! as an ontology: using Yahoo! Categories to describe documents. In: Proceedings of the eighth international conference on Information and knowledge management, pp. 180–187 (1999)
11. Bernsen, N.O., Dybkjær, L.: Evaluation of spoken multimodal Conversation. In: Proceedings of the 6th International Conference on Multimodal Interfaces, pp. 38–45 (2004)
12. Weizenbaum, J.: ELIZA: computer program for the study of natural language communication between man and machine. Communications of the ACM 9, 36–45 (1966)
13. Wallace, R.: The Anatomy of A.L.I.C.E (2002)

Conspeakuous: Contextualising Conversational Systems

S. Arun Nair, Amit Anil Nanavati, and Nitendra Rajput

IBM India Research Lab,
Block 1, IIT Campus, Hauz Khas,
New Delhi 110016, India
arun@cse.iitd.ac.in,{namit,rnitendra}@in.ibm.com

Abstract. There has been a tremendous increase in the amount and type of information that is available through the Internet and through various sensors that now pervade our daily lives. Consequentially, the field of context aware computing has also contributed significantly in providing new technologies to mine and use the available context data. We present *Conspeakuous* – an architecture for modeling, aggregating and using the context in spoken language conversational systems. Since *Conspeakuous* is aware of the environment through different sources of context, it helps in making the conversation more relevant to the user, and thus reducing the cognitive load on the user. Additionally, the architecture allows for representing learning of various user/environment parameters as a source of context. We built a sample tourist information portal application based on the *Conspeakuous* architecture and conducted user studies to evaluate the usefulness of the system.

1 Introduction

The last two decades have seen an immense growth in the variety and volume of data being automatically generated, managed and analysed. The more recent times have seen the introduction of a plethora of pervasive devices, creating connectivity and ubiquitous access for humans. Over the next two decades the emergence of sensors and their addition to available data services for pervasive devices will enable very intelligent environments.

The question we pose ourselves is how may we take advantage of the advancements in pervasive and ubiquitous computing as well as smart environments to create smarter dialogue management systems. We believe that the increasing availability of rich sources of context and the maturity of context aggregation and processing systems suggest that the time for creating conversational systems that can leverage context is ripe. In order to create such systems, complete user-interactive systems with Dialog Management that can utilise the availability of such contextual sources will have to be built.

A best human-machine spoken dialog system is the one that can emulate the human-human conversation. Humans use their ability to adapt their dialog based on the amount of knowledge (information) that is available to them. This ability (knowledge), coupled with the language skills of the speaker, distinguishes

J. Jacko (Ed.): Human-Computer Interaction, Part III, HCII 2007, LNCS 4552, pp. 165–175, 2007.

people that have varied communication skills. A typical human-machine spoken dialog system [10] uses text-to-speech synthesis [4] to generate the machine voice in the right tone, articulation and intonation. It uses an automatic speech recogniser [7] to convert the human response to a machine format (such as text). It uses natural language understanding techniques [9] to understand what action needs to be taken based on the human input. However there is a lot if context information about environment, the domain knowledge and the user preferences that improve the human-human conversation. In this paper, we present *Conspeakuous* – a context-based conversational system that explicitly manages the contextual information to be used by the spoken dialog system. We present a scenario to illustrate the potential of *Conspeakuous*, a contextual conversational system:

Johann returns to his Conspeakuous home after office. As soon as he enters the kitchen, the coffee maker ask him if he wants coffee. The refrigerator overhears Johann answer in the affirmative, and informs him about the leftover sandwich. Noticing the tiredness in his voice, the music system starts playing some soothing music that he likes. The bell rings, and Johann's friend Peter enters and sits on the sofa facing the TV. Upon recognising Peter, the TV switches onto the channel for the game, and the coffee maker makes an additional cup of coffee after confirming with Peter.

The above scenario is just an indication of the breadth of applications that such a technology could enable and it also displays the complex behaviours that such a system can handle. The basic idea is to have a context composer that can aggregate context from various sources, including user information (history, preferences, profile), and use all of this information to inform a Dialog Management system with the capability to integrate this information into its processing. From an engineering perspective, it is important to have a flexible architecture that can tie the contextual part and the conversational part together in an application independent manner, and as the complexity and the processing load of the applications increase the architecture needs to scale. Addressing the former challenge, that of designing a flexible architecture and its feasibility, is the goal of this paper.

Our Contribution. In this paper, we present a *flexible* architecture for developing contextual conversational systems. We also present an enhanced version of the architecture which supports learning. In our design, learning becomes another source of context, and can therefore be composed with other sources of context to yield more refined behaviours. We have built a tourist information portal based on the *Conspeakuous* architecture. Such an architecture allows building *intelligent* spoken dialog systems which support the following:

- The content of a particular prompt can be changed based on the context.
- The order of interaction can be changed based on the user preferences and context.
- Additional information can be provided based on the context.

- The grammar (expected user input) of a particular utterance can be changed based on the user or the contextual information.
- *Conspeakuous* can itself initiate a call to the user based on a particular situation.

Paper Outline. Section 2 presents the *Conspeakuous* architecture. The various components of the system and flow of context information to the voice application are described. In Section 3, we show how learning can be incorporated as a source of context to enhance the *Conspeakuous* architecture. The implementation details are presented in Section 4. We have built a tourist information portal as a sample *Conspeakuous* application. The details of the application and user studies are presented in Section 5. This is followed by related work in Section 6 and Section 7 concludes the paper.

2 *Conspeakuous* Architecture

Current conversational systems typically do not leverage context, or do so in a limited, inflexible manner. The challenge is to design methods, systems, architectures that enables flexible alteration of dialogue flow in response to changes in context.

Our Approach. Depending upon the dynamically changing context, the dialogue task, or the very next prompt, should change. A key feature of our architecture is the separation of the context part from the conversational part, so that the context is not hard-coded and the application remains flexible to changes in context. Figure 1 shows the architecture of Conspeakuous. The Context composer composes raw context data from multiple sources, and outputs it to a Situation composer. A situation is a set or sequence of events. The Situation composer defines situations based on the inputs from the context composer. The situations are input to the Call-flow Generator which contains the logic for generating a set of dialogues (snippets) turn based on situations. The Rule-base contains the context-sensitive logic of the application flow. It details the order of snippet execution as well as the conditions under which they should be invoked. The Call-flow control manager queries the Rule-base to select the snippets from the repository and generates the VUI components in VXML-jsp from them. We discuss two flavours of the architecture: The basic architecture *B-Conspeakuous*, which uses context from the external world, and its learning counterpart *L-Conspeakuous*, which utilises data collected in its previous runs to modify its behaviour.

2.1 *B-Conspeakuous*

The architecture of *B-Conspeakuous* shown in Figure 1 captures the essence of contextual conversational systems. It consists of:

Context and Situation Composer. The primary function of a Context Composer is to collect various data from a plethora of pervasive networked devices avail-

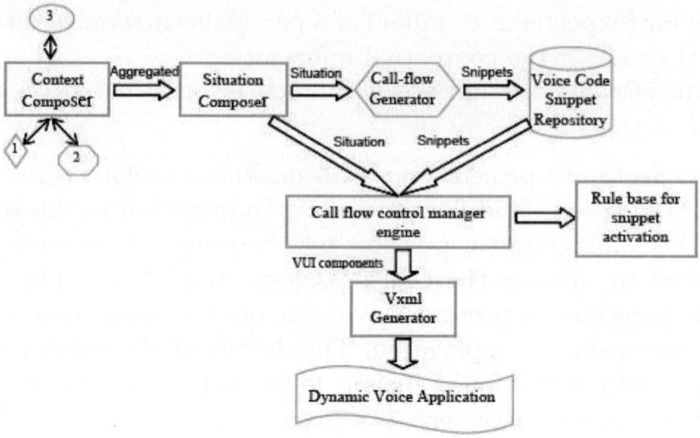

Fig. 1. *B-Conspeakuous* Architecture

able, and to compose it into a useful, machine recognizable form. The Situation Composer composes various context sources together to define situations. For example, if one source of context is temperature, and another is the speed of the wind, a composition (context composition) of the two can yield the effective wind-chill factored temperature. A sharp *drop* in this value may indicate an event (situation composition) of an impending thunderstorm.

Call-flow Generator. Depending on the situation generated by the Situation Composer, the Call-flow Generator picks the appropriate voice code from the repository.

Call-flow Control Manager. This engine is responsible for generating the presentation components to the end-user based on the interaction of the user with the system.

Rule based Voice Snippet Activation. The rule-base provides the intelligence to the Call-flow Control Manager in terms of selecting the appropriate snippet depending on the state of the interaction.

3 Learning as a Source of Context

Now that a framework for adding sources of Context in voice applications is in place, we can leverage this flexibility to add learning. The idea is to log all information of interest pertaining to every run of a *Conspeakuous* application. The logs include the context information as well as the application response. These logs can be periodically mined for "meaningful" rules, which can be used to modify future runs of the *Conspeakuous* application. Although the learning module could have been a separate component in the architecture with the context and situations as input, we prefer to model it as *another source of context*, thereby allowing the output of the learning to be further modified by composing it with other sources of context (by the context composer). This subtlety supports more refined and complex behaviours in the *L-Conspeakuous* application.

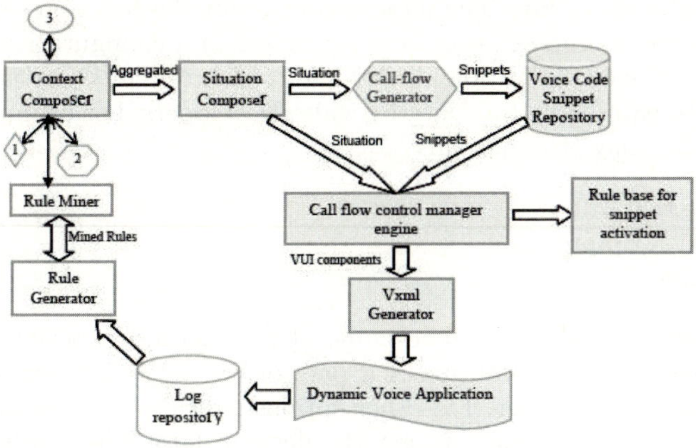

Fig. 2. *L-Conspeakuous* Architecture

3.1 *L-Conspeakuous*

The *L-Conspeakuous* architecture is shown in Figure 2. It enhances *B-Conspeakuous* with support for closed-loop behaviour in the manner described above. It additionally consists of:

Rule Generator. This module mines the logs created by various runs of the application and generates appropriate association rules.

Rule Miner. The Rule Miner prunes the set of the generated association rules (further details in the next section).

4 Implementation

Conspeakuous has been implemented using ContextWeaver [3] to capture and model the context from various sources. The development of Data Source Providers is kept separate from voice application development. As separation between the context and the conversation is a key feature of the architecture, ConVxParser is the bridge between them in the implementation. The final application has been deployed directly on the Web Server and is accessed from a Genesys Voice Browser. The application is not only aware of it's surroundings (context), but is also intelligent to learn from its past experiences. For example, it reorders some dialogues based on its learnings. In the following sections we detail out the implementation and working of *B-Conspeakuous* and *L-Conspeakuous*.

4.1 *B-Conspeakuous* Implementation

With ConVxParser, the voice application developer need only add a stub to the usual voice application. ConVxParser converts this stub into real function calls, depending on whether the function is a part of the API exposed by the Data

Provider Developers or not. The information about the function call, its return type and the corresponding stub are all included in a configuration file read by ConVxParser. The configuration file (with a *.conf* extension) carries information about the API exposed by the Data Provider Developers. For example, a typical entry in this file may look like this:

```
CON_methodname(...)
class: SampleCxSApp
object: sCxSa
```

Here, `CON_methodname(...)` is the name of the method exposed by the Data Provider Developers. The routine is a part of the API they expose, which is supported in ContextWeaver. The other options indicate the *Provider Kind* that the applications need to query to get the desired data. The intermediate files, with a *.conjsp* extension, include queries to DataProviders in forms of stubs of pseudo code. As shown in Figure 3, ConVxParser parses the *.conjsp* files and using information present in the *.conf* files it generates the final *.jsp* files.

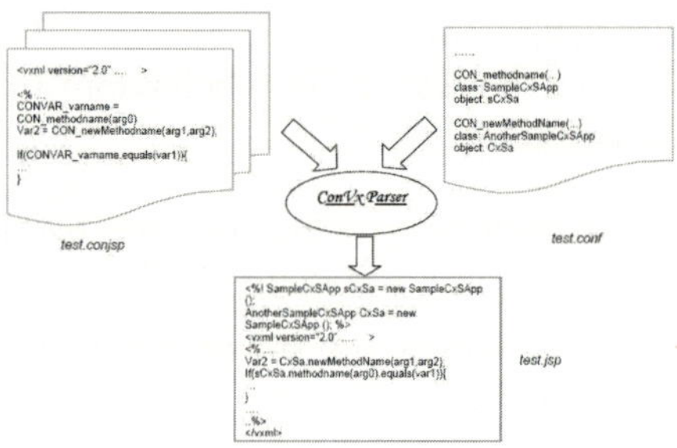

Fig. 3. ConVxParser in *B-Conspeakuous*

The Data Provider has to register a *DataSourceAdapter* and a *DataProvider-Activator* with the ContextWeaver Server [3]. A method for interfacing with the server and acquiring the required data of a specific *provider kind*, is exposed. This forms an entry of the *.conf* file with aforementioned format. The Voice Application Developer creates a *.conjsp* file that includes these function calls as code-stubs. The code-stubs indicate those portions of the code that we would like to be dependent on context. The input to the ConVxParser is both the *.conjsp* file and the *.conf* file. The code-stub that the Application Writer adds may be of the following two types: First, the method invocations are represented by `CON_methodname`. Second, the contextual variables are represented by `CONVAR_varname`.

We distinguish between *contextual* variables and *normal* variables. The meaning of a Normal variable is the same that we associate with any program variable. However, Contextual variables are those, that the user wants to be dependent on some source of context, i.e. represents real time data. There are possibly three

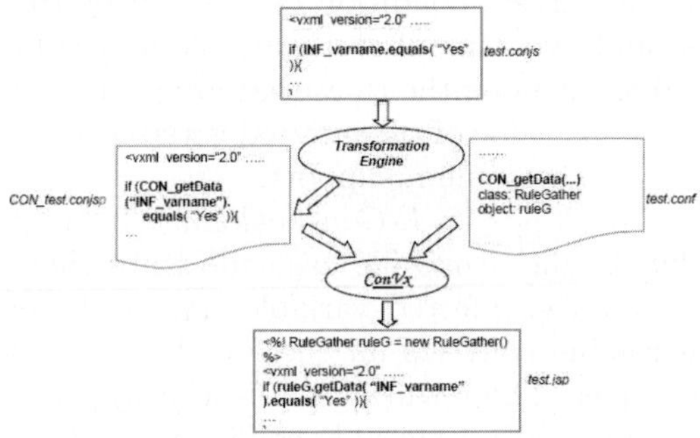

Fig. 4. ConVxParser and Transformation Engine in *L-Conspeakuous*

ways in which the contextual variables and code-stubs can be included in the intermediate voice application. One, where we assign to a *contextual variable* the output of some pseudo-method invocation for some Data Provider. In this case this assignment statement is removed from the final *.jsp* file, but we maintain the method name – contextual variable name relation using a HashMap, so that every subsequent occurrence of that contextual variable is replaced by the appropriate method invocation. This is motivated by the fact that a contextual variable needs to be re-evaluated every time it is referenced, because it represents a real-time data. Second, where we assign the value returned from a pseudo-method invocation that fetches data of some provider kind to a *normal variable*. The pseudo-method invocation to the right of such an assignment statement is converted to a real-method invocation. Third, where we just have a pseudo-method invocation which is directly converted to a real-method invocation.

The data structures involved are mainly HashMaps that are used for maintaining the information about the methods described in the *.conf* file (it saves multiple parses of the file), and for maintaining the mapping between a contextual variable and the corresponding real-method invocation.

4.2 *L-Conspeakuous* Implementation

Assuming that all information of interest has been logged, the Rule Generator periodically looks at the repository and generates interesting rules. Specifically, we run the *apriori* [1] algorithm to generate association rules. We modified *apriori* to support multi-valued items and ranges of values from continuous domains.

In *L-Conspeakuous*, we have yet another kind of variables we call *inferred* variables. Inferred variables are those variables whose values are determined from the rules that the Rule Miner generates. This requires another modification to *apriori*: Only those rules that contain only inferred variables on the right hand side are of interest to us.

The Rule Miner, registered as a Data Provider with ContextWeaver, collects all those rules (generated by Rule Generator) such that, one, their Left Hand

Sides are superset of the current condition (as defined by the current values of the Context Sources) and two, the inferred variable we are looking for must be in their Right Hand Sides. Among the rules that are pruned out using the above stated criteria, we select the value of the inferred variable as it exists in the Right Hand Side of the rule with maximum support.

Figure 4 shows the workings in *L-Conspeakuous*. In addition to the code-stubs in *B-Conspeakuous*, the *.conjs* file has code-stubs that are used to query values that the best suit the inferred variables under the current conditions. The Transformation Engine converts all these code-stubs into stubs that can be parsed by ConVxParser, The resulting file is a *.conjsp* file that is parsed by ConVxParser, which along with a suitable configuration file, gets converted to the required *.jsp* file, which can then be deployed on a compatible Web Server.

5 System Evaluation

We built a tourist information portal based on the *Conspeakuous* architecture and conducted a user study to find out the comfort level and preferences in using a *B-Conspeakuous* and an *L-Conspeakuous* system. The application used several sources of context which includes learning as a source of context. The application suggests places to visit, depending on the current weather condition and past user responses. The application comes alive by adding time, repeat visitor information and traffic congestion as sources of context.

The application first gets the current time from *Time DataProvider*, using which it greets the user appropriately (Good Morning/Evening etc.). Then, the *Revisit DataProvider* not only checks whether a caller is a re-visitor or not, but also provides the information about his last place visited. If a caller is a new caller then the prompt played out is different from that for a re-visitor, who is asked about his visit to the place last suggested. Depending on the weather condition (from *Weather DataProvider*) and the revisit data, the system suggests various places to visit. The list of cities is reordered based on the order of preference of previous customers. This captures the learning component of *Conspeakuous*. The system omits the places that the user has already visited. The chosen options are recorded in the log of the *Revisit DataProvider*. The zone from where the caller is making a call is obtained from the *Zone DataProvider*. The zone data is used along with the congestion information (in terms of hours to reach a place) to inform the user about the expected travel time to the chosen destination. The application has been hosted on an Apache Tomcat Server, and the voice browser used is Genesys Voice Portal Manager.

Profile of survey subjects. Since the *Conspeakuous* system is intended to be used by common people, we invited people such as family members, friends, colleagues to use the tourist information portal. Not all of these subjects are IT savvy, but have used some form of an IVR earlier. The goal is to find whether the users prefer a system that learns user preferences vs. a system that is static. These are educated subjects and can converse in English language. The subjects also have a fair idea of the city for which the tourist information portal has been designed. Thus the subjects had enough knowledge to verify if *Conspeakuous* is providing the right options based on the context and user preferences.

Survey Process. We briefed the *subjects* for about 1 minute to describe the application. Subjects were then asked to interact with the system and give their feedback on the following questions:

- Did you like the greeting that changes with the time of the day ?
- Did you like the fact that the system asks you about your previous trip ?
- Did you like that the system gives you an estimate of the travel duration without asking your location ?
- Did you like that the system gives you a recommendation based on the current weather condition ?
- Did you like that the interaction changes based upon different situations ?
- Does this system sound more intelligent that all the IVRs that you have interacted with before ?
- Rate the usability of this system.

User Study Results. Out of the 6 subjects that called the tourist-information-portal, all were able to navigate with the portal without any problems. All subjects like the fact that the system remembers their previous interaction and converses in that context when they call the system for the second time. 3 subjects liked that the system provides an estimate of the travel duration without having to provide the location explicitly. All subjects like the fact that the system provides the best site based on the current weather in the city. 4 subjects found the system to be more intelligent than all other IVRs that they have used previously. The usability scores given by the subjects are 7, 9, 5, 9, 8 and 7, where 1 is the worst and 10 is the best.

The user studies clearly suggest that the increased intelligence of the conversational system is appreciated by subjects. Moreover, subjects were even more impressed they were told that the *Conspeakuous* system performs the relevant interaction based on the location, time and weather. The cognitive load on the user is tremendously less for the amount of information that the system can provide to the subjects.

6 Related Work

Context has been used in several speech processing techniques to improve the performance of the individual components. Techniques to develop context dependent language models have been presented in [5]. However the aim of these techniques is to adapt language models for a particular domain. These techniques do not adapt the language model based on different context sources. Similarly, there is a significant work in the literature that adapts the acoustic models to different channels [11], speakers [13] and domains [12]. However adaptation of dialog based on context has not been studied earlier.

A context-based interpretation framework, MIND, has been presented in [2]. This is a multimodal interface that uses the domain and conversation context to enhance interpretation. In [8], the authors present an architecture for discourse processing using three different components – dialog management, context tracking and adaptation. However the context tracker maintains the context history of the dialog context and does not use the context from different context sources.

Conspeakuous uses the ContextWeaver [3] technology to capture and aggregate context from various data sources. In [6], the authors present an alternative mechanism to model the context, especially for pervasive computing applications. In the future, specific context gathering and modeling techniques can be developed to handle context sources that affect a spoken language conversation.

7 Conclusion and Future Work

We presented an architecture for *Conspeakuous* – a context based conversational system. The architecture provides the mechanism to use intelligence from different context sources for building a spoken dialog system that is more t in a human-machine dialog. Learning of various user preferences and the environment preferences is also modeled. The system also models learning as a source of context and incorporates this in the *Conspeakuous* architecture. The complexity of voice application development is not compromised since the context modeling is performed as an independent component. The user studies suggest that humans prefer to talk with the machine which can adapt to their preferences and to the environment. The implementation details attempt to illustrate that the voice application development is still kept simple through this architecture. More complex voice applications can be built in the future by leveraging richer sources of context and various learning techniques to fully utilise the power of *Conspeakuous*.

References

1. Agrawal, R., Imielinski, T., Swami, A.: Mining Association Rules between sets of items in Large Databases. In: Proc. of ACM SIGMOD Conf. on Mgmt. of Data, pp. 207–216
2. Chai, J., Pan, S., Zhou, M.X.: MIND: A Context-based Multimodal Interpretation Framework in Conversation Systems. In: IEEE Int'l. Conf. on Multimodal Interfaces, pp. 87–92 (2002)
3. Cohen, N.H., Black, J., Castro, P., Ebling, M., Leiba, B., Misra, A., Segmuller, W.: Building context-aware applications with context weaver. Technical report, IBM Research W0410-156 (2004)
4. Dutoit, T.: An Introduction to Text-To-Speech Synthesis. Kluwer Academic Publishers, Dordrecht (1996)
5. Hacioglu, K., Ward, W.: Dialog-context dependent language modeling combining n-grams and stochastic context-free grammars. In: IEEE Int'l. Conf. on Acoustics Signal and Speech Processing (2001)

6. Henricksen, K., Indulska, J., Rakotonirainy, A.: Modeling Context Information in Pervasive Computing Systems. In: IEEE Int'l. Conf. on Pervasive Computing, pp. 167–180 (2002)
7. Lee, K.-F., Hon, H.-W., Reddy, R.: An overview of the SPHINX speech recognition system. IEEE Transactions on Acoustics, Speech, and Signal Processing 38, 35–45 (1990)
8. LuperFoy, S., Duff, D., Loehr, D., Harper, L., Miller, K., Reeder, F.: An Architecture for Dialogue Management, Context Tracking, and Pragmatic Adaptation in Spoken Dialogue Systems. In: Int'l. Conf. On Computational Linguistics, pp. 794–801 (1998)
9. Seneff, S.: TINA: a natural language system for spoken language applications. Computational Linguistics, pp. 61–86 (1992)
10. Smith, R.W.: Spoken natural language dialog systems: a practical approach. Oxford University Press, New York (1994)
11. Tanaka, K., Kuroiwa, S., Tsuge, S., Ren, F.: An acoustic model adaptation using HMM-based speech synthesis. In: IEEE Int'l Conf. on Natural Language Processing and Knowledge Engineering (2003)
12. Visweswariah, K., Gopinath, R.A., Goel, V.: Task Adaptation of Acoustic and Language Models Based on Large Quantities of Data. In: Int'l. Conf. on Spoken Lang Processing (2004)
13. Wang, Z., Schultz, T., Waibel, A.: Comparison of acoustic model adaptation techniques on non-native speech. In: IEEE Int'l. Conf. on Acoustics Signal and Speech Processing (2003)

Persuasive Effects of Embodied Conversational Agent Teams

Hien Nguyen, Judith Masthoff, and Pete Edwards

Computing Science Department, University of Aberdeen, UK
{hnguyen,jmasthoff,pedwards}@csd.abdn.ac.uk

Abstract. In a persuasive communication, not only the content of the message but also its source, and the type of communication can influence its persuasiveness on the audience. This paper compares the effects on the audience of direct versus indirect communication, one-sided versus two-sided messages, and one agent presenting the message versus a team presenting the message.

1 Introduction

Persuasive communication is "any message that is intended to shape, reinforce or change the responses of another or others." [11]. In other words, in a persuasive communication, a source attempts to influence a receiver's attitudes or behaviours through the use of messages. Each of these three components (the source, the receiver, and the messages) affects the effectiveness of persuasive communication. In addition, social psychology suggests that the *type of communication* (e.g. direct versus indirect) can impact a message's effectiveness [17,5].

The three most recognised characteristics of the source that influence its persuasiveness are *perceived credibility*, *likeability* and *similarity* [14,17]. These are not commodities that the source possesses, but they are the receiver's perception about the source. *Appearance cues* of the source (e.g. a white lab coat can make one a doctor) have been shown to affect its perceived credibility [17]. Hence, there has been a growing interest to use Embodied Conversational Agents (ECAs) in persuasive systems, and to make ECAs more persuasive.

In this paper, we explore persuasive ECAs in a healthcare counseling domain. More and more people use the Internet to seek out health related information [15]. Hence, automated systems on the Internet have the potential to provide users with an equivalence of the "ideal" one-on-one, personalised interaction with an expert to adopt health promoting behaviour more economically and conveniently. Bickmore argued that even if automated systems are less effective than actual one-on-one counselling, they still result in greater impact due to their ability to reach more users (impact = efficacy x reach) [4]. A considerable amount of research has been devoted to improve the efficacy of such systems, most of which focused on personalised content generation with various levels of personalisation [18]. Since one important goal of such systems is to persuade their users to adopt new behaviours, it is also vital that they can win trust and credibility from users [17].In this paper, the ECAs will be fitness instructors, trying to convince users to exercise regularly.

J. Jacko (Ed.): Human-Computer Interaction, Part III, HCII 2007, LNCS 4552, pp. 176–185, 2007.

Our research explores new methods to make automated health behaviour change systems more persuasive using personalised arguments and a team of animated agents for information presentation. In this paper, we seek answers to the following questions:

- *RQ1:* Which type of communication supports the persuasive message to have more impact on the user: *indirect* or *direct*? In the indirect setting, the user obtains the information by following a conversation between two agents: an instructor and a fictional character that is similar to the user. In the direct setting, the instructor agent gives the information to the user directly.
- *RQ2:* Does the use of a team of agents to present the message make it more persuasive than that of a single agent? In the former setting, each agent delivers a part of the message. In the latter setting, one agent delivers the whole message.
- *RQ3:* Is a two-sided message (a message that discusses the pros and cons of a topic) more persuasive than a one-sided message (a message that discusses only the pros of the topic)?

2 Related Work

Animated characters have been acknowledged to have positive effects on the users' attitudes and experience of interaction [7].

With respect to the persuasive effect of adding social presence of the source, mixed results have been found. Adding a formal photograph of an author has been shown to improve the trustworthiness, believability, perceived expertise and competence of a web article (compared to an informal or no photograph) [9]. However, adding an image of a person did not increase the perceived trustworthiness of a computer's recommendation system [19]. It has been suggested that a photo can boost trust in e-commerce websites, but can also damage it [16]. A series of studies found a positive influence of the similarity of human-like agents to subjects (in terms of e.g. gender and ethnicity) on credibility of a teacher agent and motivation for learning (e.g. [3]). Our own work also indicated that the source's appearance can influence his/her perceived credibility, and prominently showing an image of a highly credible source with respect to the topic discussed in the message can have a positive effect on the message's perceived credibility, but that of a lowly credible source can have an opposite effect [13].

With respect to the use of a team of agents to present information, Andre et al [1] suggested that a team of animated agents could be used to reinforce the users' beliefs by allowing us to repeat the same information by employing each agent to convey it in a different way. This is in line with studies in psychology, which showed the positive effects of social norms on persuasion (e.g. [8,12]).

With respect to the effect of different communication settings, Craig et al showed the effectiveness of indirect interaction (where the user listens to a conversation between two virtual characters) over direct interaction (where the user converses with the virtual character) in the domain of e-learning [6]. In their experiment, users significantly asked more questions and memorized more information after listening to a dialogue between two virtual characters. We can argue that in many situations, particularly when we are unsure about our position on a certain topic, we prefer hearing a conversation between people who have opposite points of view on the topic to actually discussing it with someone. Social psychology suggests that in such situations, we find the sources more credible since we think they are not trying to persuade us (e.g. [2]).

3 Experiment 1

3.1 Experimental Design

The aim of this experiment is to explore the questions raised in Section 1. To avoid any negative effect of the lack of realism of virtual characters' animation and voice using Text-To-Speech, we implement our characters as static images of real people with no animation or sound. The images of the fitness instructors used have been verified to have high credibility with respect to giving advice on fitness programmes in a previous experiment [186].

Forty-one participants took part in the experiment (mean age = 26.3; stDev = 8.4, predominately male). All were students on an HCI course in a university Computer Science department. Participants were told about a fictional user John, who finds regular exercise too difficult, because it would prevent him from spending time with friends and family (extremely important to him), there is too much he would need to learn to do it (quite important) and he would feel embarrassed if people saw him do it (quite important).

Participants were shown a sequence of screens, showing the interaction between John and a persuasive system about exercising. The experiment used a between subject design: participants experienced one of four experimental conditions, each showing a different system (see Table 1 for example screenshots):

- *C1: two-sided, indirect, one agent.* The interaction is indirect: John sees a conversation between fitness instructor Christine and Adam, who expresses similar difficulties with exercising to John. Christine delivers a two-sided message: for each reason that Adam mentions, Christine acknowledges it, gives a solution, and then mentions a positive effect of exercise.
- *C2: two-sided, direct, one agent.* The interaction is direct: Christine addresses John directly. Christine delivers the same two-sided message as in Condition C1.
- *C3: one-sided, direct, one agent.* The interaction is direct. However, Christine only delivers a one-sided message. She acknowledges the difficulties John has, but does not give any solution. She mentions the same positive effects of exercise as in Conditions C1 and C2.
- *C4: one-sided, direct, multiple agents.* The interaction is direct and the message one-sided. However, the message is delivered by three instructors instead of one: each instructor delivers a part of it, after saying they agreed with the previous instructor. The message overall is the same as in Condition C3.

A comparison between conditions C1 and C2 will explore research question RQ1: whether direct or indirect messages work better. A comparison between C2 and C3 will explore RQ3: whether one- or two-sided messages work better. Finally, a comparison between C3 and C4 will explore RQ2: whether messages work better with one agent as source or multiple agents.

Table 1. Examples of the screens shown to the participants in each condition

Condition	Screen
C1: two-sided, indirect, one agent	Most importantly, I feel that exercising will prevent me from spending time with my friends and family.   Well, you can make it part of your daily routine. For example, try to take the stairs instead of the elevator, or attend 30-minute lunch time routines in the gym. You would have a lot more energy for your friends and family if you exercised regularly.
C2: two-sided, direct, one agent	 Firstly, it doesn't take as much time as you think. It won't prevent you from spending time with your family and friends. You can make it part of your daily routine. For example, try to take the stairs instead of the elevator, or attend 30-minute lunch time routines in the gym. You would have a lot more energy for your friends and family if you exercised regularly.
C3: one-sided, direct, one agent	 I know that you want to exercise more often, but you also have many reasons for not doing it. But let's look at the positive side. You would have a lot more energy for your friends and family if you exercised regularly.
C4: one-sided, direct, multiple agents	 Christine is right. Besides, you would feel less stressed and have a better mood for the rest of the day. 

We decided to ask participants not only about the system's likely impact on opinion change, but also how easy to follow the system is, and how much they enjoyed it. In an experimental situation, participants are more likely to pay close attention to a system, and put effort into understanding what is going on. In a real situation, a user may well abandon a system if they find it too difficult to follow, and pay less attention to the message if they get bored. Previous research has indeed shown that usability has a high impact on the credibility of a website [10]. So, enjoyment and understandability are contributing factors to persuasiveness, which participants may well ignore due to the experimental situation, and are therefore good to measure separately. Participants answered three questions on a 7-point Likert scale:

- How easy to follow did you find the site? (from "very difficult" to "very easy"),
- How boring did you find the site? (from "not boring" to "very boring"), and
- Do you think a user resembling John would change his/her opinion on exercise after visiting this site? (from "not at all" to "a lot").

They were also asked to explain their answer to the last question.

3.2 Results and Discussion

Figure 1 shows results for each condition and each question. With respect to the likely impact on changing a user's opinion about exercise, a one-way ANOVA test indicated that there is indeed a difference between the four conditions ($p < 0.05$). Comparing each pair of conditions, we found a significant difference between each of C1, C2, C3 on the one hand and C4 on the other ($p<0.05$ for all). Participants' comments confirmed that they thought the multiple agents condition less persuasive, with some mentioning that the use of multiple instructors makes the system almost hectoring in tone and a bit patronizing. The difference between C1 and C2 was not significant, but the trend is for indirect messages to be more persuasive. The difference between C2 and C3 is not significant, but the trend is for two-sided messages to be more persuasive.

With respect to how easy each system is to follow, all four systems scored well on the scale, on average ranging from 5.1 to 6.5 out of 7. This indicates that the users have no difficulty in using any of these alternative, dialog-based user interfaces. Two-sided conditions C1 and C2 were rated on average as easier to follow than one-sided conditions C3 and C4, but only the difference between C2 and C3 was significant ($p<0.05$).

With respect to boredom of each system, two-sided conditions C1 and C2 were rated on average as less boring than one-sided conditions C3 and C4, but this difference was not significant. However, there was a significant correlation between boredom and opinion change (Pearson's correlation = -0.431, $p<0.01$): the more boring the participants found the system, the less impact they thought it would have on the user.

In summary, we conclude the following regarding our research questions:

1. We cannot yet conclude whether indirect communication is more persuasive than direct communication when comparing conditions C1 and C2. The trend is in favour of indirect communication.

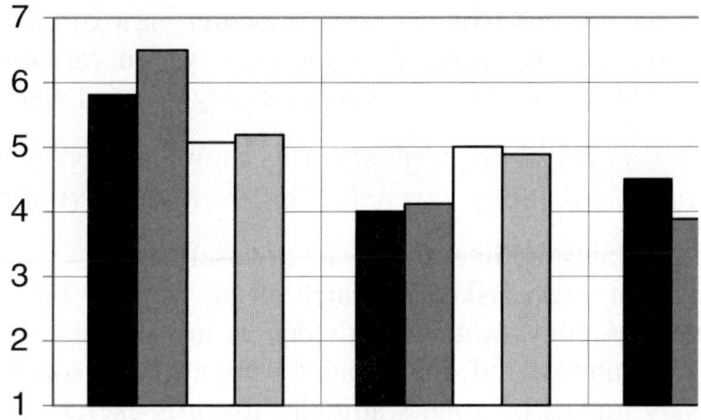

	Easy to Follow	Boredom	Opinion Change
C1: 2-sided, indirect	5.80 (1.55)	4.00 (1.49)	4.50 (1.18)
C2: 2-sided, direct	6.50 (1.08)	4.10 (1.85)	3.90 (1.79)
C3: 1-sided, 1 agent	5.09 (1.81)	5.00 (1.41)	3.45 (1.51)
C4: 1-sided, multiple agents	5.20 (1.75)	4.90 (1.85)	2.20 (1.03)

Fig. 1. The average values and standard deviations of each criterion for each group

2. Surprisingly, the use of a team of agents to present information in this experiment considerably damaged the impact of the persuasive message. Perhaps the fact that all the agents appeared on screen at the same time, made the participants feel hectored and patronised as mentioned by some. An alternative would be to have each agent appear at a different stage of the conversation, re-emphasize what other agents have said and add new supporting information. We may also want to reconsider the way in which one agent supports what another has just said. Currently, this happens via sentences such as "Christine is right". Perhaps it would be better to instead reword the argument Christine has given.
3. The trend in the data suggests that two-sided messages are more persuasive than one-sided ones. This is supported by the two-sided message in C2 being significantly easier to follow than the corresponding one-sided message (C3). It is also supported by the trend in the boredom data, with C2 seeming to be perceived as less boring than C3.

4 Experiment 2

4.1 Experimental Design

The aim of this experiment is to extend and provide an alternative approach to our first experiment. In the previous experiment, participants looked at screenshots of a system. Clearly, this is not as engaging as actually experiencing the system. In this experiment, we tried to give participants a more realistic experience. Instead of screenshots, they watched videos of the system in action. In the previous experiment, we used a between-subject design, and participants only saw one system. In this experiment, we used a within-subject design, with participants comparing between systems, hoping this would lead to a clearer view of what users prefer and regard as more persuasive. We used the same four system variants as in the first experiment, but also added another two, which used only text and were without any agents:

- *C5: two-sided, direct, text only.* This shows the text of the message used in C2.
- *C6: one-sided, direct, text only.* This shows the text of the message used in C3.

The new variants are intended to act as baselines.

Participants were asked to watch all six videos. The user interface was designed such that they could watch each video as many times as they liked. The order of the videos was randomized. Participants were asked to sort the six videos in order of (1) their likely impact on John's attitudes towards exercise, (2) how easy is system is to follow, and (3) boredom. The following section discusses our preliminary results on the basis of thirteen participants (mean age = 28, stDev = 7.7; 4 males, 9 females).

4.2 Results and Discussion

Participants were largely consistent in their judgements on the impact of each system on John's attitudes towards exercise and boredom (Cronbach's alpha=0.58, $p<0.05$, and alpha=.81, $p<0.01$, respectively). However, the same result did not hold for their judgement on how easy to follow each system is.

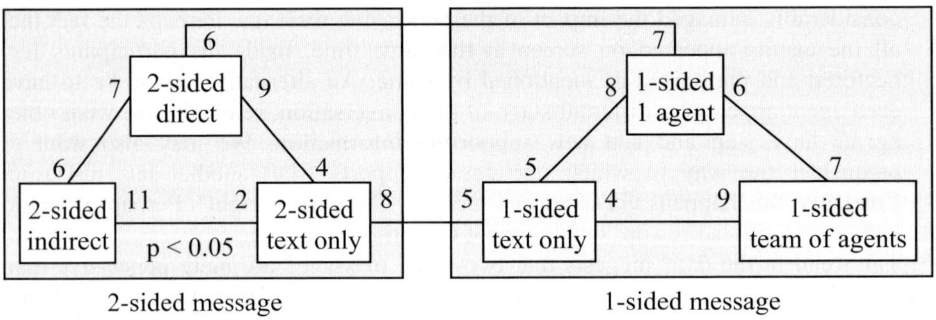

Fig. 2. Number of participants who preferred each system on persuasiveness (Experiment 2)

Figure 2 shows the participants' opinion on persuasiveness when comparing systems pair-wise. Numbers on the line between two systems show how many participants preferred each system. For instance, nine participants preferred the 2-sided, direct system to the 2-sided, text-only system, while four preferred the latter. The trend is for all systems with the agent(s) visible to be perceived as more convincing than their text-only counterparts. However, with the current limited number of participants, only the difference between the two-sided indirect condition and its text-only counterpart has reached statistical significance ($p<0.05$). In Experiment 1, we found trends in favour of indirect messages and 2-sided messages. We do not find these here: participants were evenly divided. Even more surprisingly, in this experiment, the participants liked condition C4 as much as C1, C2, and C3, whilst in Experiment 1, we found a clear, statistically significant difference, with C4 being liked less. This raises the question of whether participants are actually capable

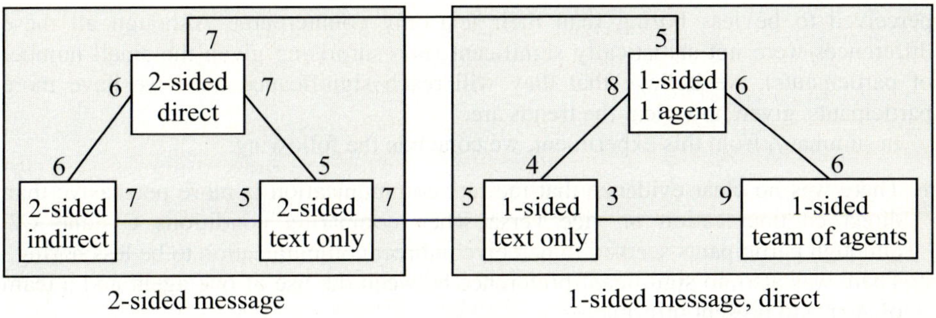

Fig. 3. Number of participants who preferred each system on how easy it is to follow (Exp. 2)

of performing an accurate comparison in persuasiveness when given multiple systems to compare. Perhaps this task makes participants think too much about the differences between systems, while persuasion often takes a peripheral route as well. It may well be that a between-subject design, as in Experiment 1, is more appropriate.

Figure 3 shows the participants' preference on how easy to follow systems are when comparing them pair-wise[1]. Whilst in Experiment 1 we found a trend for 2-sided messages being easier to follow than one-sided messages (with a statistically significant difference between C2 and C3), we do not find a similar result here. There is only a slight trend for 2-sided text only messages being easier to follow than 1-sided text only messages. However, there is a trend that the 1-sided text-only message is harder to follow than 1-sided messages with 1 or more agents.

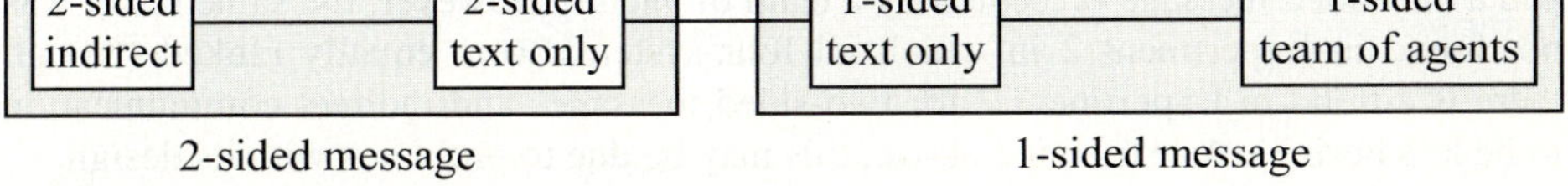

Fig. 4. Number of participants who preferred each system on avoidance of boredom (Exp. 2)

Figure 4 shows the participants' preference on avoidance of boredom when comparing systems pair-wise[2]. As in Experiment 1, we again found a trend for 2-sided messages being less boring than one-sided messages. We also found a trend for the indirect 2-sided message being preferred to the direct one, and the team of agents being preferred to one agent. Furthermore, all the systems with agent(s) visible were

[1] One participant rated all videos as equally easy to follow, so is not included in Figure 3.

[2] Five participants did not complete the task correctly (e.g. one video was rated more than once), and their results are not included in Figure 4.

perceived to be less boring than their text-only counterparts. Although all these differences were not statistically significant (non-surprising given the small number of participants), we believe that they will reach significance once we have more participants, given how clear the trends are.

In summary, from this experiment, we conclude the following:

1. There was no clear evidence that indirect communication is more persuasive than direct communication or vice versa when comparing conditions C1 and C2, although participants seemed to perceive indirect communication to be less boring.
2. There was also no significant preference between the use of one agent and a team of agents to present information.
3. With respect to the persuasiveness of a two-sided message compared to that of a one-sided message, similarly no clear preference was found, although participants seemed to perceive two-sided messages to be less boring.

The lack of results may well be because this experiment was too difficult. Some participants complained that they found it hard to remember and compare six videos. The number not finishing the final question also points in this direction. As mentioned above, a between-subject design may also be more appropriate.

5 Conclusions

This paper has investigated the persuasive effects on the audience's attitudes of direct versus indirect communication, one-sided versus two-sided messages, and one agent presenting the message versus a team presenting the message. Our second experiment suggests that dialog-based systems with the visual appearance of a conversational agent(s) are preferred over systems that use text only, as they are perceived to be more personal and caring, less boring, and to some extent easier to follow. When comparing our four dialog-based systems, we found somewhat conflicting results. Experiment 1 suggested a clear trend in which a two-sided message presented in an indirect communication was the most persuasive, followed by a two-sided message presented in a direct communication, a one-sided message presented by one agent, and a one-sided message presented by a team of agents. However, the same result was not found in Experiment 2 in which all four systems were equally ranked (though there is a trend in Experiment 2 for two-sided messages and indirect communication to be less boring). As explained above, this may be due to problems with its design.

A limitation of our experiments is that they use an indirect form of self-reports where the participants judged the impact of each system on someone else's attitudes (done to ensure the arguments were relevant). Another limitation is the demographic of the participants: predominantly male in Experiment 1 and predominantly female in Experiment 2. Perhaps this has also contributed to the conflicting results.

Further experiments (with more participants) will be carried out to overcome the drawbacks of those presented in this paper, to clarify some conflicting results found and to investigate whether the trends suggested in Experiment 1 are significant. We also plan to implement prototype systems with which the participants can actually interact so that we can measure direct effects of the systems on the participants themselves. In addition, we will explore different ways of using multiple agents, e.g. with agents playing different roles, like doctor and fitness instructor as in [13].

References

1. Andre, E., Rist, T., van Mulken, S., Klesen, M., Baldes, S.: The automated design of believable dialogues for animated presentation teams. In: Cassell, J., Prevost, S., Sullivan, J., Churchill, E. (eds.) Embodied Conversational Agents, pp. 220–255. MIT Press, Cambridge (2000)
2. Aronson, E.: The social animal, Worth (2004)
3. Baylor, A.L., Rosenberg-Kima, R.B., Plant, E.A.: Interface Agents as Social Models: The Impact of Appearance on Females' Attitude Toward Engineering. CHI (2006)
4. Bickmore, T.: Methodological review: Health dialog systems for patients and consumers. Journal of Biomedical Informatics 39(5), 556–571 (2006)
5. Cialdini, R.: Influence: science and practice. Scott, Foresman (1988)
6. Craig, S.D., Gholson, B., Garzon, M.H., Hu, X., Marks, W., Wiemer-Hastings, P., Lu, Z.: Autor tutor and otto tudor. AIED-Workshop on Animated and Personified Pedagogical Agents. Le Mans, France, pp. 25–30 (1999)
7. Dehn, D.M., van Mulken, S.: The impact of animated interface agents: a review of empirical research. International Journal of Human-Computer Studies 52, 1–22 (2000)
8. Fishbein, M., Ajzen, I.: Belief, attitude, intention, and behavior. Addison-Wesley, Reading, MA (1975)
9. Fogg, B.J., Marshall, J., Kameda, T., Solomon, J., Rangnekar, A., Boyd, J., Brown, B.: Web Credibility Research: A Method for Online Experiments and Early Study Results. In: CHI 2001, pp. 295–296 (2001)
10. Fogg, B.J., Soohoo, C., Danielson, D., Marable, L., Stanford, J., Tauber, E.: How do users evaluate the credibility of websites?: A study with over 2500 participants. Designing for user experiences, pp. 1–15 (2003)
11. Miller, G.R.: On being persuaded: Some basic distinctions. In: Roloff, M.E., Miller, G.R. (eds.): Persuasion: New directions in theory and research, pp. 11–28, Sage, Beverly Hills, CA (1980)
12. Nass, C., Reeves, B., Leshner, G.: Technology and roles: A tale of two TVs. Journal of Communication 46(2), 121–128 (1996)
13. Nguyen, H., Masthoff, J.: Is it me or is it what I say? Source image and persuasion (Submitted to conference)
14. O'Keefe, J.D.: Persuasion: theory and research. Sage, Newbury Park, CA (1990)
15. Pew: Internet health resources, Washington, DC, Pew Internet and American Life Project (2003)
16. Riegelsberger, J., Sasse, M.A., McCarthy, J.D.: Shiny happy people building trust? Photos on e-commerce websites and consumer trust. In: Proceedings of CHI 2003. pp. 121–128 (2003)
17. Stiff, J.B., Mongeau, P.A.: Persuasive Communication, 2nd edn. Guilford press (2002)
18. de Vries, H., Brug, J.: Computer-tailored interventions motivating people to adopt health promoting behaviours: Introduction to a new approach, Patient Educ Couns, vol. 36, pp. 99–105 (1999)
19. de Vries, P.: Social presence as a conduit to the social dimensions of online trust. In: Persuasive Technology Conference, pp. 55–59 (2006)

Exploration of Possibility of Multithreaded Conversations Using a Voice Communication System

Kanayo Ogura[1], Kazushi Nishimoto[2], and Kozo Sugiyama[1]

[1] Japan Advanced Institute of Science and Technology, School of Knowledge Science, Asahidai 1-1, Nomi, Ishikawa, 923-1292, Japan
[2] Japan Advanced Institute of Science and Technology, Center for Knowledge Science, Asahidai 1-1, Nomi, Ishikawa, 923-1292, Japan
{k-ogura,knishi,kozo}@jaist.ac.jp

Abstract. Everyday voice conversations require people to obey the turn-taking rule and to keep to a single topic thread; therefore, it is not always an effective way to communicate. Hence, we propose "ChaTEL," a voice communication system for facilitating real-time multithreaded voice communications. ChaTEL has two functions to support multithreaded communications: a function to indicate to whom the user talks and a function to indicate which utterance the user responds to. Comparing ChaTEL with a baseline system that does not have these functions, we show that multithreaded conversations occur more frequently with ChaTEL. Moreover, we discuss why ChaTEL can facilitate multi-threaded conversations based on analyses of users' speaking and listening behaviors.

Keywords: CMC (Computer-Mediated Communication), Multithreaded Conversations.

1 Introduction

In everyday conversations, we usually have to share a single topic thread for a while and talk about something related to the current thread. Moreover, we have to preserve the turn-taking rule: only one person speaks at a time and the others are listeners. Therefore, it is impossible for people who do not have a "turn" to talk about what they want, even if they have an interesting topic or a good idea. As a result, regrettably, they often forget the topic or the idea. Such daily conversation is inefficient.

Since text-based chat systems overcome these restrictions, we can converse in multiple topic threads. Schegloff [1] explained the situation of "schism" related to multiple topic threads in face-to-face conversations. Schism is a situation of divisions of the conversational floor. For example, when four people take part in a conversation, one pair of people converse and the other pair of people converse in the same conversational floor. On the other hand, in text chat conversations, a person who takes part in a conversation can converse in several topic threads at the same time. We define multiple topic threads not as dividing people into several separated groups but as concurrently involving a person in several different topic threads; furthermore, we

J. Jacko (Ed.): Human-Computer Interaction, Part III, HCII 2007, LNCS 4552, pp. 186–195, 2007.

do not think a multiple topic thread is equal to schism in our study. Figure 1 shows examples of a situation of schism and multiple topic threads that we defined in our study.

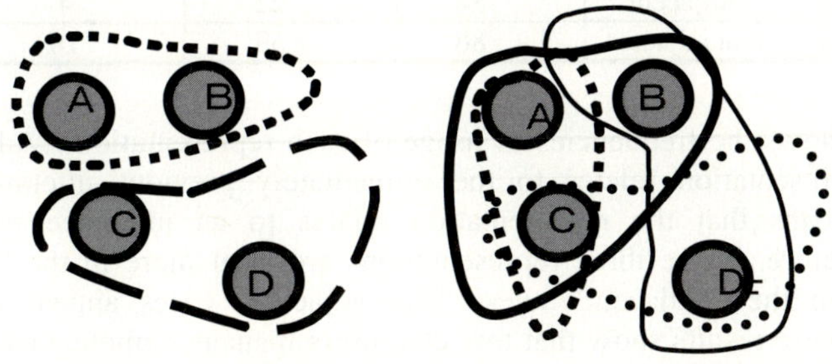

Fig. 1. Examples of schism (left) and multiple topic threads (right)

Based on analyses of text-based chat conversations, we propose a novel voice communication system named "ChaTEL" that allows multithreaded voice communication. The rest of this paper proceeds as follows. Section 2 considers the requirements for enabling us to converse in multiple topic threads with voice based on analysis of a situation of multiple topic threads in text chat conversations. Section 3 explains related works for multithreaded communication systems. Section 4 explains ChaTEL's system set-up. Section 5 describes our experiments to confirm its effects. Section 6 describes our experimental results. Section 7 concludes the paper.

2 Maintaining Multithreaded Conversations in Text-Based Chats

It is very difficult to distinguish simultaneous voice utterances, to memorize them, and to accurately respond to them. Due to such difficulties, we usually have to share a single topic thread. In text-based chats, however, multithreaded conversations are often maintained for a long time. This principally results from the "history of utterances" with which text chat systems are equipped. The history records users' names, messages, and the times messages were sent. They are listed on client application windows. Therefore, users can readily read any utterances and respond to them anytime [2].

In addition, skilled chat users use several special representations to specify receivers and related topics/messages to manage complicated multiple topic threads in text-based chats [3]. Based on analyses of Japanese chat conversations that contain 870 utterances, we found the following three representations for managing multithreads [4]:

1. ">name": specification of receiver(s)
ex.) Are you ready? > Mr. A
2. ">noun": specification of related topic(s)
ex.) I like it very much > chocolate
3. "copy": specification of related phrases in a previous utterance
ex.) I like it very much > chocolate > What a coincidence that you like it so much!

Table 1. Frequencies of usage of each representation

	> name	> noun	copy
Adjacent	**34**	**22**	**4**
Not adjacent	**80**	**58**	**16**

Table 1 shows the frequencies of usage of each representation. "Adjacent" means that the representation relates to the immediately previous utterance, and "Not adjacent" means that the representation relates to an utterance more than two utterances before. These three representations are used more in the "Not adjacent" cases than in the "Adjacent" ones. "Not adjacent" cases appear in multithread situations. These results show that text chat users manage complicated multiple topic threads with these representations to simplify following each thread.

3 Related Works

Few studies have aimed to facilitate multithreaded voice conversations. Berc et al. [5] developed "Pssst," which provides whispering functions for some members in a teleconference using video links. In Pssst, only users of the whispering channel can join both the plenary meeting and the whispering channels. This is an incomplete multithread situation. The users who join only the plenary meeting channel are in the usual single-thread situation. Even those who join the whispering channel can join only two threads. Nishimoto et al. developed "VoiceCafe" [6], an asynchronous teleconference system using voice. Each voice utterance is automatically transcribed by a voice recognition system that analyses the question and answer relations of the utterances. Based on the relations, a tree structure of the relations of the utterances, such as an interface of a BBS system, is automatically constructed. Though this system enables users to converse in multiple topic situations, that is not its principal purpose; the researchers aimed to construct a proper tree structure. Aoki et al. [7] developed an audio space system that allows multiple simultaneous conversations in a conversation space. This system identifies conversation groups based on the turn-taking timing of utterances. Therefore, people in a group can talk in a usual single-thread manner; this system allows multiple single-threaded conversations to exist in a communication space.

4 Our Proposed New Voice Communication System: ChaTEL

We propose a communication system called "ChaTEL" that facilitates multithreaded voice conversations based on findings from text chat analysis. This system is equipped with a "history of conversation" as well as functions that specify receivers of messages and related messages. It is based on server/client architecture identical to typical text chat systems. Using a client, users record voice messages and upload them to the server. A user listens to a message by downloading it from the server.

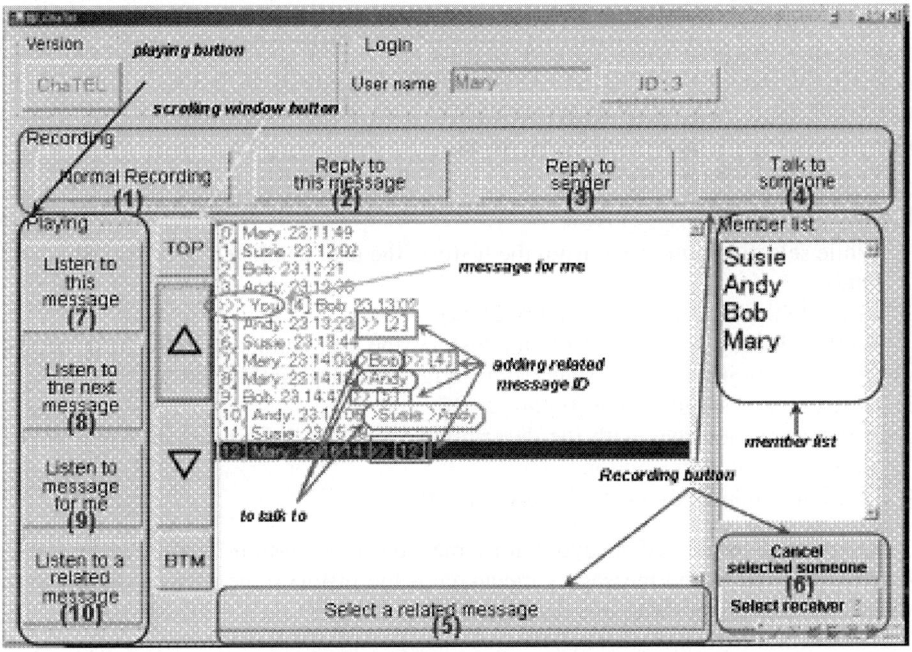

Fig. 2. ChaTEL user interface

Figure 2 shows ChaTEL's user interface. The user wears a headset to talk and to listen to messages. A keyboard is only necessary for inputting a user name for logging in to the system. After logging in, the user can operate all functions by using an LCD display with a touch panel. We prepared the following three ways to record a message:

1. Normal recording

The user can simply record a voice message by pressing the "normal recording" button (Figure 2-(1)). Then the "stop recording" button appears over the entire user interface. After the recording of the message is finished, the user pushes the stop recording button. The recorded voice message is immediately uploaded to the server, and the metadata of the message (ID number, speaker's name, and uploaded time) are dispatched to all clients. Metadata are added at the bottom of the history.

2. Recording by specifying a related message

While selecting a message from the history, the user can record a new message that relates to the selected message by pushing the "Reply to this message" button (Figure 2-(2)). The selected message's ID is added to its metadata recorded by this method, such as ">>[2]," which shows related message IDs.

3. Recording by specifying receiver(s)

After normal recording, the user can specify receivers by selecting a receiver from the member list and pushing the "Select receiver" button (Figure 2-(6)). In addition, after selecting a receiver from the member list, the user can push the "Talk to someone" button (Figure 2-(4)) and record a new message. Otherwise, while selecting a message from the history, the user can record a new message that specifies a receiver by pushing the "Reply to sender" button (Figure 2-(3)). The specified receiver names are added to the message's metadata recorded by such methods as ">Susie>Andy." If the user him/herself is specified as the receiver of a message, the description ">>>You" is added to the top of the message's metadata.

We prepared the following four ways to listen to messages:

1. Listen to this message (Figure 2-(7))
   While selecting a message from the history, the user can listen to it by pushing this button.
2. Listen to the next message (Figure 2-(8))
   While selecting a message from the history, the user can listen to the next message (the message just after the selected message) by pushing this button.
3. Listen to a message for me (Figure 2-(9))
   If there are messages with the description ">>>You," the user can listen only to them by pushing this button.
4. Listen to a related message (Figure 2-(10))

If the message is related to a previous message (description ">>[message ID]" is added at the end of the message's metadata in the history), the user can listen to the related message by pushing this button.

5 User Studies

The aim of the experiments included: 1) to investigate whether multithreaded conversation can be done by voice; 2) to evaluate the usefulness and the effectiveness of the newly added ChaTEL recording/listening functions for facilitating multithreaded conversations; 3) to observe which newly added ChaTEL recording functions are more effective when multithreaded conversations are facilitated; 4) to understand how to record and listen to each message in multithreaded conversations using the newly added ChaTEL recording/listening functions.

We conducted experiments using ChaTEL in four groups that each consisted of four subjects. All subjects were accustomed to text chat, but they had never experienced a PC voice communication system. As a control system, we prepared a "baseline" system equipped only with the following recording/listening functions: "Normal recording," "Listen to this message," and "Listen to the next message." The experiments were conducted in non-face-to-face situations using either ChaTEL or the baseline. Two groups used the baseline system first and then ChaTEL, while the other groups used ChaTEL first then the baseline to eliminate the influence of order.

We prepared four initial topics: "Where do you want to travel?"; "Where are you from?"; "What food do you recommend to others?"; and "What do you want to get now?" We apportioned two of the four topics to each subject; the combinations of topics for the subjects differed. We instructed all users to converse for about 20 minutes using either the baseline system or ChaTEL. We asked them to begin talking about the provided topics and to discuss them completely. However, we allowed them to join other topics that were not assigned and to start talking about any new topics. We sampled the conversation histories, member lists, files of each message, and the log data of all users' actions that contained information on the time that each button was pushed. Based on these data, we analyzed each conversation's thread structures and each user's actions of recording and listening to messages.

6 Results

6.1 Possibility of Multithreaded Conversations Using Voice Communication System

We illustrated the structure of topic-thread relations for each experiment's data to compare ChaTEL and the baseline for degree of occurrence and duration of multithread situations. Figure 3 shows sample diagrams of the structures of topic-thread relations. Several dependent trees as well as branches are found in each tree. A tree corresponds to a topic thread. On the other hand, a branch corresponds to a question and answer pair. Based on Figure 3, we counted the average number of concurrent topic threads and branches per second. The results are shown in Table 2. Additionally, we calculated the duration of multithread situations for all concurrent threads. The results are shown in Table 3.

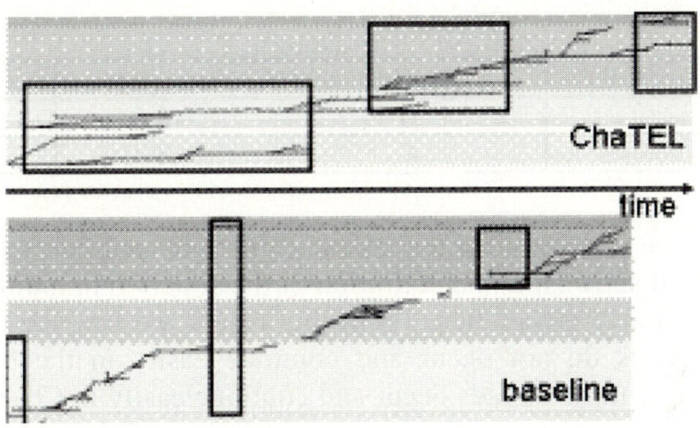

Fig. 3. Sample diagrams of structures of topic thread relations. Rectangles show places where multithreaded conversations occur.

Table 2. Average number of concurrent topic threads and branches per second for baseline and ChaTEL (Both results are significantly different.)

average numbers of concurrent topic threads		average numbers of branches	
baseline	ChaTEL	baseline	ChaTEL
1.20	**1.62**	**1.97**	**2.63**

From Table 2, we can see significantly more concurrent topic threads and branches in ChaTEL than in the baseline. In addition, Table 3 shows that multithreaded situations occur more often and are maintained longer with ChaTEL than with the baseline system in all concurrent threads.

Table 3. Duration of multithread situations for each concurrent thread (sec.)

Numbers of concurrent threads	2 threads	3 threads	4 threads
baseline	**965**	**241**	**0**
ChaTEL	**1418**	**880**	**181**

From these results, we conclude that it is basically possible to concurrently converse on multiple topics with voice communication. Furthermore, the fact that multithreaded situations occur more often and are maintained longer with ChaTEL shows that ChaTEL's newly added recording/listening functions contributed to facilitating multithreaded conversations.

In Section 1, we defined a situation of multithreaded conversations not as division of people who are in the same floor of conversation but as a situation having several threads per user. We examined the number of users in each thread based on conversational histories and diagrams of constructions of topic thread relations when multiple topic threads occur. The results are shown in Table 4.

Table 4. Average Number of conversations for each participant when multiple topic threads occur

Number of participants	2 participants	3 participants	4 participants
baseline	**11**	**8**	**0**
ChaTEL	**6**	**8**	**8**

From Table 4, we can see all users take part in eight multiple topic threads using ChaTEL. This result shows that the definition of the situation in multiple topic threads we explain in Section 1 is satisfied. From this result, we can see that situations of multiple topic threads do not occur and continue easily in the baseline and that situations of multiple topic threads occur and continue easily in ChaTEL. In addition, we conclude that all users in ChaTEL continue to converse in multiple topic threads even if they involve complicated constructions of conversations.

6.2 Usages of Listening/Recording Operations

To see complexity of listening/recording operations, we counted all conversational times and utterances in the baseline and ChaTEL. These results are in Table 5. Moreover, we calculated all times of conversations and all utterances in the baseline and ChaTEL to see frequency of each listening/recording operation. These results are in Tables 6 and 7.

Table 5. all conversation times and utterances in baseline and ChaTEL

	baseline	ChaTEL
All times of conversations (sec)	**5528**	**5689**
All utterances	**339**	**337**

Table 6. Frequency and Ratio of recording operation in ChaTEL

	Frequency	Ratio
Normal recording	**47**	**14.0%**
Recording by specifying a related message	**265**	**78.6%**
Recording by specifying receiver(s)	**25**	**7.4%**
Total	337	100%

From Table 5, we can see there is not much difference between the baseline and ChaTEL in the number of utterances. This result shows that the complexity of listening/recording operations in ChaTEL does not have an influence on the number of utterances and usability of the listening/recording operations.

From Table 6, we can see that users in ChaTEL often use the operation of recording by specifying a related message—nearly 80% of the time. On the other hand, we can see that users use the operation of recording by specifying receiver(s) only 7.4% of the time. In Table 1, users more frequently use the operation of specifying receiver(s) than the operation of specifying a related message in text chat conversations. This result in text chat conversations is in contrast to the results in voice communication systems using baseline and ChaTEL.

Table 7. Frequency and Ratio of listening operations in baseline and ChaTEL

	baseline		ChaTEL	
	frequency	ratio	frequency	ratio
Listen to this message	**595**	**42.6%**	**1002**	**57.0%**
Listen to the next message	**801**	**57.4%**	**737**	**42.0%**
Listen to a message for me	--	--	**1**	**0.1%**
Listen to a related message	--	--	**16**	**0.9%**
Total	1396	100%	1756	100%

From Table 7, we can see that users in the baseline more frequently use the operation of listening to the next message than the operation of listening to this message. On the other hand, we can see that users in ChaTEL more frequently use the operation of listening to this message than the operation of listening to the next message. In addition, we can see that the operation of listening to a message for me and listening to a related message, which are prepared for ChaTEL, have a combined use ratio of only 1%.

6.3 Analysis of How Users Listen to Messages in Multithreaded Conversations

In section 6.2, we saw that users in ChaTEL record messages using operations of recording by specifying a message and receiver(s) at a rate of about 90%. Based on this result, we can expect that users in ChaTEL select operations of listening related to these recording operations. On the other hand, we can expect that users in the baseline listen to messages in order of the history of conversations and that they tend to listen to the newest message users record because they can understand the contents of each message after they listen to a message.

Based on data of actions of listening operations, we examined the distance between a newly listened to message and a previously listened to message (a distance of listening operations) and the distance between a newly listened to message and a newly recorded message (a distance of delay). This result is shown in Table 8.

We explain how to analyze the distances of listening operations and of delay. In distance of listening operations, we consider an operation of listening to be the next message users listen to after the previous message listened to as the standard pattern of listening operations, and we add the score of each listening operation. We use absolute values to descript each point of distance. The following are patterns of listening operations and points. In addition, Table 9 shows the frequencies of patterns of listening operations.

1) NEXT: listening to next message: point = 0
2) REPEAT: listening to the same message: point = -1
3) BACK: listening to n (n>0) utterances forward message: point = -n-1
4) SKIP: listening to n (n>1) utterances next message: point = n-1

In a distance of delay, we calculated the difference between a listened to message ID and a newly recorded message ID as the distance of delay.

Table 8. Avarages of distance of listening and delay (*** shows significant 1% standard)

	baseline	ChaTEL	
Distance of listening	0.49	1.63	***
Distance of delay	1.01	2.53	***

From Table 8, in the baseline, we can see that a distance of listening is near point 0. This result shows that users in the baseline tend to listen to messages in order of the history of conversations. On the other hand, in ChaTEL, we can see that the distance of delay is twice that of the baseline. This result shows that users in ChaTEL can listen to messages besides the newly recorded ones.

Table 9. Averages of frequencies of patterns of listening (*** shows significant 1% standard)

	baseline	ChaTEL	
NEXT	**69.1**	**74.1**	
REPEAT	**4.6**	**6.7**	
BACK	**5.3**	**19.6**	***
SKIP	**9.7**	**16.1**	

From Table 9, we can see that users in ChaTEL tend to listen to past messages distant from the newest recorded message. From Table 8 and Table 9, we can conclude that users in the baseline tend to listen to messages in order of the history of conversations and that users in ChaTEL tend to listen to messages distant from the newest message.

7 Conclusion

In this paper, we proposed a novel communication system named "ChaTEL" to achieve multithreaded voice communication. We equipped ChaTEL with a "history of conversation" as well as functions to specify receivers of messages and related messages; it was based on the findings of our study on text chats where users often converse in a multithreaded manner. Based on user studies we confirmed that ChaTEL facilitates multithreaded voice communication. In addition, users in ChaTEL can listen to messages distant from the newest message without being restricted to the history of conversations. In the future, we plan to improve the system to be used in mobile situations using these results in this study.

Acknowledgement. This research is partly supported by the fund from Kinki Mobile Radio Center Inc., Japan.

References

[1] Schegloff, E.A.: Issues of Relevance for Discourse Analysis: Contingency in Action, Interaction and Co-Participant Context. In: Hovy, E.H., Scott, D. (eds.) Computational and Conversational Discourse, pp. 3–38. Springer, Heidelberg (1996)

[2] Rhyll, V.: Applying membership categorization analysis to chat-room talk, How to Analyse Talk in Institutional Settings: A Casebook of Methods. In: McHoul, A., Rapley, M. (eds.) Continuum, London, pp. 86–99 (2001)

[3] Winiecki, D.J.: Instructional discussion in online education, Practical and research-oriented perspectives. In: Moore, M., Anderson, R.M. (eds.) Handbook of Distance Education, Lawrence Erlbaum Assoc., NJ (2003)

[4] Ogura, K., Ishizaki, M.: The Characteristics of Topic Flow in Chat Conversations, Tech. Report SIG-SLUD, A202-3, Japan Society of Artificial Intelligence, pp. 13–19 (2002)

[5] Berc, L., Gajewska, H., Manasse, M.: Pssst: Side Conversations in the Argo Telecollaboration System. In: Proc. the 8th ACM UIST, pp. 155–156 (1995)

[6] Nishimoto, T., Kitawaki, H., Takagi, H.: VoiceCafe: An Asynchronous Voice Meeting System, Information Technology Letters, LK-005, pp. 273–274 (2003)

[7] Aoki, P.M., Romaine, M., Szymanski, M.H., Thornton, J.D., Wilson, D., Woodruff, A.: The Mad Hatter's Cocktail Party: A Social Mobile Audio Space Supporting Multiple Conversations. In: Proc. ACM CHI 2003, pp. 425–432 (2003)

A Toolkit for Multimodal Interface Design: An Empirical Investigation

Dimitrios Rigas and Mohammad Alsuraihi

School of Informatics, University of Bradford, Richmond Road, Bradford, UK
d.rigas@bradford.ac.uk, mmnalsur@bradford.ac.uk

Abstract. This paper introduces a comparative multi-group study carried out to investigate the use of multimodal interaction metaphors (visual, oral, and aural) for improving learnability (or usability from first time use) of interface-design environments. An initial survey was used for taking views about the effectiveness and satisfaction of employing speech and speech-recognition for solving some of the common usability problems. Then, the investigation was done empirically by testing the usability parameters: efficiency, effectiveness, and satisfaction of three design-toolkits (TVOID, OFVOID, and MMID) built especially for the study. TVOID and OFVOID interacted with the user visually only using typical and time-saving interaction metaphors. The third environment MMID added another modality through vocal and aural interaction. The results showed that the use of vocal commands and the mouse concurrently for completing tasks from first time use was more efficient and more effective than the use of visual-only interaction metaphors.

Keywords: interface-design, usability, learnability, effectiveness, efficiency, satisfaction, visual, oral, aural, multimodal, auditory-icons, earcons, speech, text-to-speech, speech recognition, voice-instruction.

1 Introduction

Interfaces that offer interaction via more than one sense are highly demanded. The auditory system for example has been neglected in the development of user-interfaces [18]. Multimodality is needed for enhancing efficiency and effectiveness of user interface interaction, as well as it is needed for building more satisfactory and friendly interfaces. The aim of this study was to investigate the use of multimodal interaction metaphors (visual, oral, and aural) for improving learnability or the ability to complete tasks from first time use [13] in design environments. The investigation was performed by testing efficiency, effectiveness, and satisfaction of the proposed solutions. In order to perform this investigation, three design toolkits (TVOID, OFVOID, and MMID) offering visual, oral and aural interaction metaphors were built from scratch. An initial survey was used for taking evaluative views about the effectiveness and satisfaction of the interaction metaphors offered in the three toolkits. Then, a multi-group empirical study took place to complete this investigation. The following sections handle this scheme in more detail.

J. Jacko (Ed.): Human-Computer Interaction, Part III, HCII 2007, LNCS 4552, pp. 196–205, 2007.

2 Previous Work

The literature relevant to visual interface design has revealed the existence of usability drawbacks in existing interfaces of the visual-only design environments like cT™ [5], LAD [3], MICE [7], and CO-ED [6]. The heavily focus on conveying information through the visual channel when designing interfaces seems to make them "more and more visually crowded as the user's needs for communication with the computer increases" [17]. This causes the user to experience information overload by which important information may be missed [12]. The visual channel is not the only means that a human perceives information through. Studies on multimedia and its remarkable benefits for furthering the process of learning showed that multimedia can be used as an effective means for learning. A study by Rigas and Memery showed that multimedia helped users to learn more material than only text-and-graphics media, and assisted them in performing different tasks more successfully [22]. In order to solve complexity problems with the current visual user interfaces, Rigas et al [19] suggest that interfaces could be designed in away that visual metaphors communicate the information that 'needs' to be conveyed to the user and the auditory metaphors (earcons) communicate the other part of information (the interaction part) which is used to perform tasks like for example browsing e-mail data. The usability problems: miss-selection and interface intrusion into the task could be solved by employing auditory feedback, namely non-speech audio messages or earcons [1, 2]. The approach is based on using earcons to indicate the currently active graphical metaphor (menu, button, scrollbar, message-box, etc). It was found that the use of combinations of auditory icons, earcons, speech, and special sound effects helped users to make fewer mistakes when accomplishing their tasks, and in 'some cases' reduced the time taken to complete them [21]. The technology currently available for visually impaired users was also investigated, to explore the possibility of using it for enhancing usability of interfaces built for normal users. It was found that the ACCESS Project system by [14], in early 1990s, was pioneer in development of computer-based applications for blinds. It offered an audio-tactile environment for building such applications. Screen readers, which use synthesized speech, and Braille display were found to be the most used tools in blind users' applications. The Emacspeak [15] was the first project that introduced the conceptual-modeled screen reader that unlike traditional screen readers, which read screen contents only, it integrated spoken feedback with application contents. The Image Graphic Reader (IGR) by [16] outlined a procedure for reading charts and graphics for blind students. Haptic-mouse approach was employed after the IGR for reading information of charts and graphics to be, then, represented aurally [24]. A new interesting approach was introduced by [4] discovered that blind users could describe images and colors by listening to musical representations of visual images. Another study towards applying the same approach was carried out by [9] and [10] has given birth to a new invention called the vOICe. It differs from the one was introduced by Cronly-Dillon in that it implements conversion of highly complex video scenes, rather than still images, into sound, with the capability of determining colors. Previous studies have shown that the problems of usability in current user interfaces mainly occur because of lack of experience in designing multimodal interactive interfaces. The guidelines found in [8], [17], [20], [22], [11] have drawn a precise map for enhancing the way of conveying information to the user when using graphical widgets.

3 Experimental Toolkits

Three experimental toolkits were built from scratch using Microsoft Visual C# .NET. Each one of them provided a different set of interaction metaphors for doing the same functionality. These toolkits were developed to find out how learnable each of the implemented interaction metaphors can be, and which toolkit would be the most learnable. The following subsections handle these toolkits in more detail.

3.1 TVOID

TVOID or Typical Visual-Only Interface Designer imitates the style of interaction implemented in most of the existing interface-design systems like Microsoft Visual C# and Java NetBeans IDE. It interacts with the user visually-only with neglect to the other senses like the auditory system. In addition, it interacts with the user via six areas in its main interface, like most of the similar existing systems do. These areas are: menus, toolbar, toolbox, workplace (or drawing-area), properties-table, and status-bar. Figure 1.A shows a screenshot of TVOID.

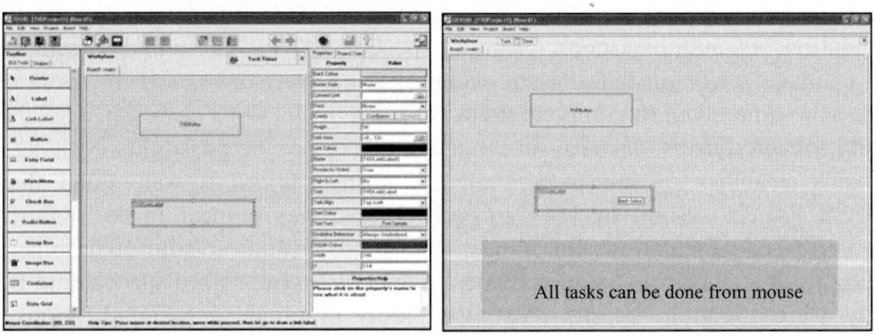

Fig. 1. Screenshots of the Visual-Only Interface Design Toolkits

3.2 OFVOID

OFVOID or On-the-Fly Visual-Only Interface Designer allows the user to do all design-tasks and the other tasks (menu/toolbar tasks) from the workplace area. There is no need for the mouse to leave the workplace area to do any job. The environment is facilitated with a number of time-saving features like, for example, selecting tools while drawing by scrolling over the form (board) being designed. The environment's main interface consists of two parts: menus and workplace. The menus part was added to the environment to show the users the hot-keys required to do the menu/toolbar functions. During the experiments, the users were allowed to use them. Figure 1.B shows a display of this environment.

3.3 MMID

MMID or Multi-Modal Interface Designer provides a combination of visual, vocal and aural interaction. This environment employs speech-recognition and text-to-speech for using it. It also allows the user to interact with the whole environment from the workplace area as the OFVOID environment. However, most of this interaction is through the use of voice-instruction and spoken messages. It adds another modality for interaction with less focus on visual interaction. Figure 2 shows a screenshot of MMID.

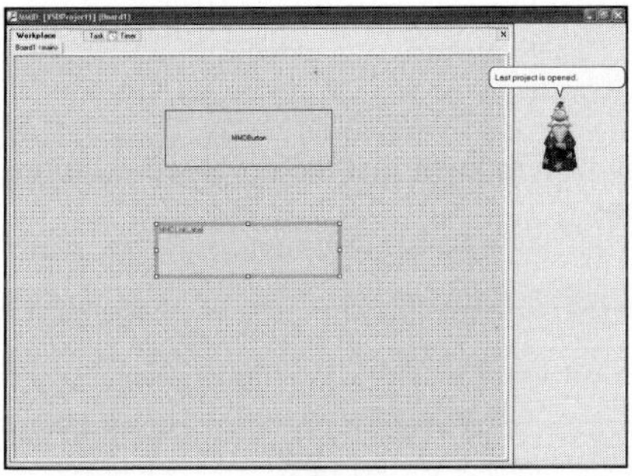

Fig. 2. Screenshot of the Multi-Modal Interface Designer (MMID)

4 Initial Survey

The initial survey aimed at taking users views about effectiveness and satisfaction of the interaction metaphors: auditory icons, earcons, spoken messages, and vocal commands, as solutions to solve some of the common usability problems. Thirty nine users participated in this survey. Their views were found valuable as they gave good impression about using sound (speech and non-speech) for conveying information to users who have no visual imparity. Further more, the initial survey showed to some extent how effective and satisfactory the use of voice-instruction for designing interfaces can be. Figure 3 shows the percentages of users who thought that the solutions implemented for solving the slipping-over buttons and hitting unwanted menu-items usability problems were effective. It also shows the participant's views about effectiveness of visual and spoken help functionality-tags, and the feature implemented for conveying the "current-active-tool" piece of information.

Figure 4 shows that voice-instruction was not much appreciated for tool-selection and drawing. Nonetheless, it can be noticed that the users' views had begun to change as the demonstration went on, and became more optimistic during setting properties by voice.

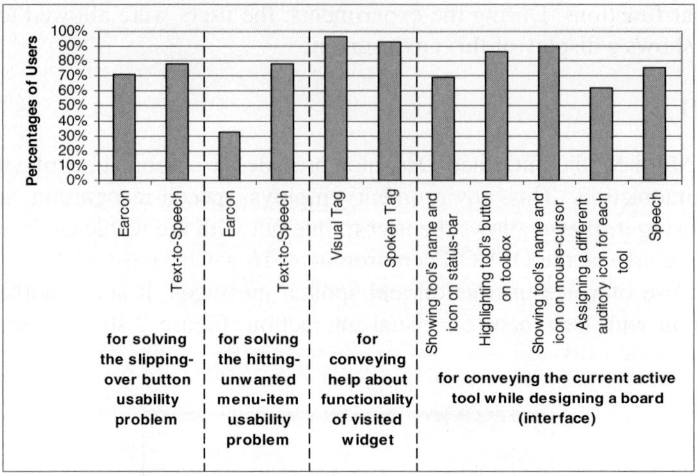

Fig. 3. Percentages of users who thought that the proposed solutions were effective for solving the shown usability problems

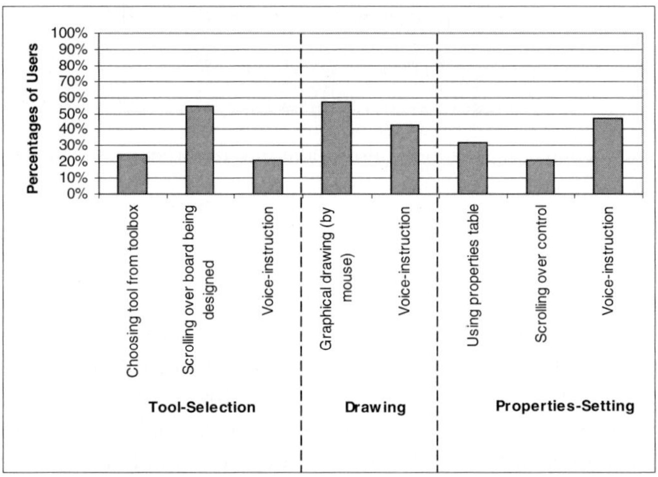

Fig. 4. Percentages of users who liked the demonstrated interaction metaphors for selecting tools, drawing, and setting properties

5 Empirical Multi-group Study

This study aimed at assessing the usability of each of the three design-toolkits to explore the most learnable one in regard to effectiveness, efficiency, and satisfaction. This assessment was fulfilled by testing these environments empirically by three independent groups of users. Each group consisted of 15 users. All the groups were asked to accomplish the same tasks (10 tasks). Each one of the users had attended a 10-minute video training session about the environment he/she was testing before doing the requested tasks. Effectiveness was measured by calculating the percentage of tasks completed successfully by all users and the percentage of functions learned in absence of additional help. Efficiency was measured by timing function learning and task completion for each task in each environment, and counting the number of errors during accomplishment of each task. At end of sessions, the users were asked to give ratings for satisfaction with the tested interaction metaphors.

6 Discussion of Results

During the experiments, it was noticed that the users in Group A, who tried the typical visual-only design environment TVOID expected how to do most of the functions. This environment looked familiar to them because they had experience with similar environments. This experience made them rely primarily on their memory. It made them spend time on recalling how to do particular functions in similar existing systems to be able to do them using TVOID. Expectations of how to do particular functions were incorrect sometimes, which caused the users to find out how to do these functions. In this way, the users who tested TVOID did two things to learn functions: remembering or expecting, and exploring in case of incorrect expectation. This was not the case with the users who tested OFVOID and MMID (Groups B and C). Most of the features in these two environments were new to them, which made them, most of time, head directly to exploring.

Also the results showed that the users in Groups B and C did more mistakes than the users in Group A during accomplishment of the same tasks. However, the difference was found to be not significant at 0.05 ($F = 1.31$, $P = 0.29$). In addition, it was noticed that the users were learning gradually about the interaction metaphors they were using in these two environments every time a task was accomplished. Making mistakes made them more used and familiar to the use of time-saving features and vocal commands. This caused the need for additional help to lessen in these two environments (OFVOID and MMID). Comparing the number of functions learned in absence of additional help under the three environments showed that MMID was the most learnable, and OFVOID was more learnable than the typical visual-only environment TVOID. Figure 5 shows this result.

The users who tested MMID needed less help because most of the vocal commands in the environment were as they expected, recalling that these commands were in the form of simple one-to-three-English phrases. In addition, looking for commands in one categorized list, as a feature in MMID, saved the time for looking for them in different positions, which was the case in the two visual-only environments. The frequent scrolling for selecting a particular tool to be used for drawing or a particular property to be set, in OFVOID, allowed the users to see and learn other tools and other properties on the mouse cursor every time a tool or property was selected. This made the users more familiar to this environment and lessened the need for additional help. The results also showed that the three environments were not as effective as each other. Gathering all vocal commands in one location (e.g. one list) in MMID helped the users in Group C to learn more functions than their counterparts in Groups B and C, who looked for commands in different locations. Also, the use of one interaction metaphor (voice-instruction) in MMID saved the time for the users to decide whether to use menus or toolbar,

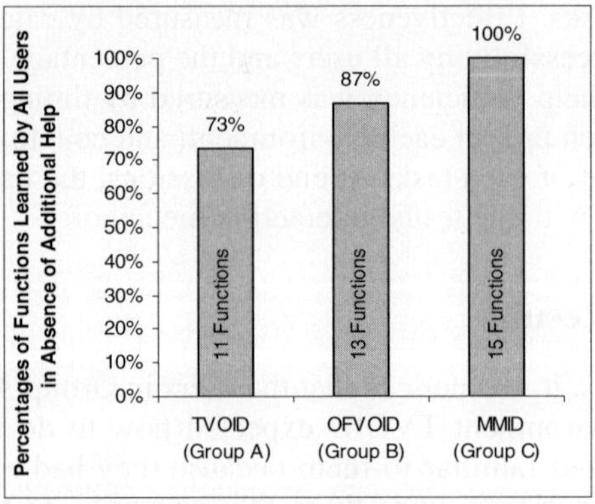

Fig. 5. Percentages calculated for the functions learned in absence of additional help by the users in Groups A (TVOID), B (OFVOID), and C (MMID)

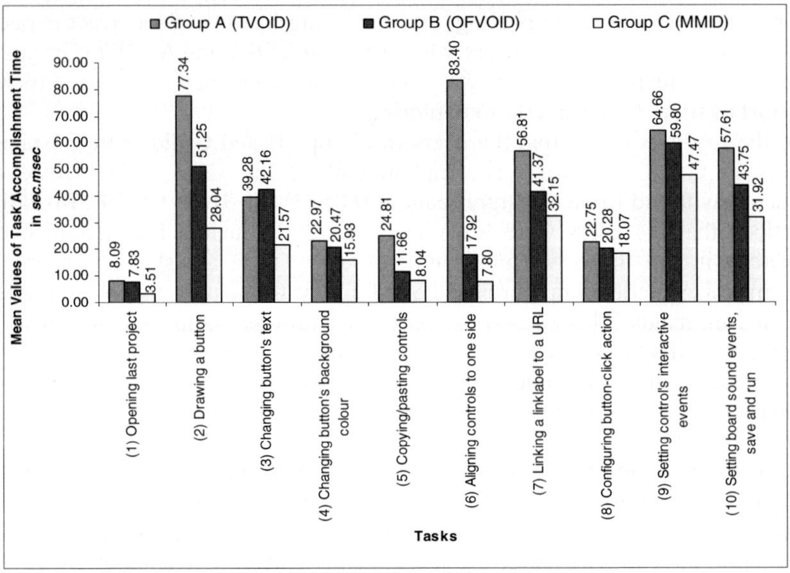

Fig. 6. Mean values of time taken for accomplishing 10 tasks for the first time using TVOID (Group A), OFVOID (Group B) and MMID (Group C)

toolbox or tool-list (by scrolling over board), properties table or properties-list (by scrolling over control), etc which were implemented in the two visual-only environments. The multimodal environment was more efficient in terms of shortening accomplishment time than the two visual-only environments. Figure 6 demonstrates this result. The use of vocal commands saved the time spent in moving the mouse from one position to another and scrolling menus and lists to reach commands in the two visual-only environments. Figure 7 shows the percentages of tasks completed successfully under each of the three environments. The difference between the three

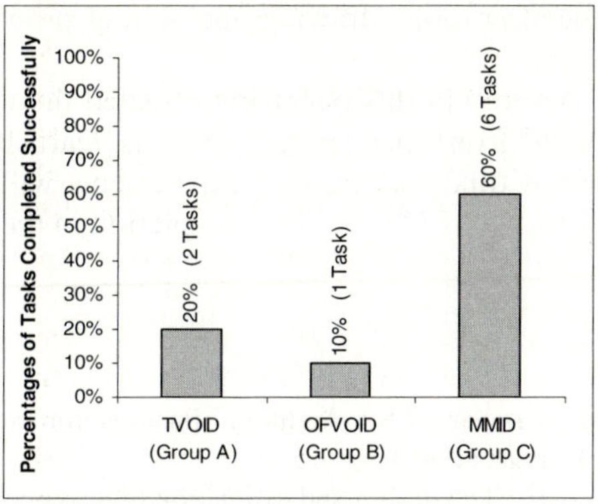

Fig. 7. Percentages of tasks completed successfully in TVOID (Group A), OFVOID (Group B), and MMID (Group C)

environments in this regard was found to be significant (F = 3.80, P = 0.04). The comments that were taken from the users in Group B during testing OFVOID showed that most of them expressed that the saving-time features were the most features they liked. On the other hand, the users who tested MMID (Group C) showed excitement toward designing by voice.

7 Conclusion and Future Research

The aim of this study was to investigate the use of multimodal interaction metaphors (visual, oral, and aural) for improving learnability of interface design environments. The paper presented a quick summary of relevant work. Then, it introduced a usability comparative study between multimodal interaction and visual-only interaction. The investigation started with a preliminary survey that aimed at taking users' views about the effectiveness and satisfaction of the proposed solutions for solving some of the common usability problems. Then an empirical multi-group study was introduced. This study aimed at testing the learnability parameters: effectiveness, efficiency, and satisfaction of a number of interaction metaphors offered by three design toolkits (TVOID, OFVOID, and MMID) built especially for the study. The paper, then, presented the results of these experiments and discussed them.

The study recommends designing design-environments bearing in mind interaction with the least possible mouse movement. A new effectively usable design environment is needed to save designers' time and effort and make them work satisfactorily. The use of time-saving interaction metaphors like instant scrollable lists, short-menus, and vocal commands can save much time during task-accomplishing and facilitate learning of new functions. The interactive mouse cursor was found to be a very good information conveyer as it can be used for showing the current active tool, the mouse coordinates, and the current active property to be set. This solution can extremely save the time for looking for this information in different places (i.e. the toolbox, the status-bar and the properties-table). However, the use of voice-instruction for selecting tools, drawing and setting properties was found to be more efficient and effective.

The empirical work covered in this paper investigated the usability of each of the three design environments from one angle, which is learnability or the ability to accomplish tasks from first time use. Further experiments will take place for testing Experienced User Performance (EUP) of task-completion in the three environments.

References

1. Beaudouin-Lafon, M., Conversy, S.: Auditory illusions for audio feedback. In: ACM CHI'96, Vancouver, Canada (1996)
2. Brewster, S., Clarke, C.V.: The design and evaluation of a sonically-enhanced tool palette. In: ICAD'97, Xerox PARC, USA (1997)
3. Chang, C., Chen, G., Liu, B., Ou, K.: A language for developing collaborative learning activities on World Wide Web. In: Proceedings of 20th International Computer Software and Applications Conference, COMPSAC '96 (1996)
4. Cronly-Dillon, J., Persaud, K.C., Blore, R.: Blind subjects construct conscious mental images of visual scenes encoded in musical form. In: The Royal Society Of London Series B-Biological Sciences, London (2000)
5. Cvetkovic, S.R., Seebold, R.J.A., Bateson, K.N., Okretic, V.K.: CAL programs developed in advanced programming environments for teaching electrical engineering, Education. IEEE Transactions on 37, 221–227 (1994)
6. Finkelstein, J., Nambu, S., Khare, R., Gupta, D.: CO-ED: a development platform for interactive patient education. In: Proceedings International Conference on Computers in Education, 2002 (2002)
7. Guercio, A., Arndt, T., Chang, S.-K.: A visual editor for multimedia application development. In: Proceedings. 22nd International Conference on Distributed Computing Systems Workshops, 2002 (2002)
8. Lumsden, J., Brewster, S., Crease, M., Gray, P.D.: Guidelines for Audio-Enhancement of Graphical User Interface Widgets. In: HCI'2002, London (2002)
9. Meijer, P.: Seeing with sound for the blind: Is it vision? In: Tucson 2002, Tucson, Arizona (2002)
10. Meijer, P.: Vision Technology for the Totally Blind, vol. 2004. Peter Meijer (2004)
11. Oakley, I., McGee, M.R., Brewster, S., Gray, P.D.: Putting the feel in look and feel. In: ACM CHI 2000, The Hague, NL (2000)
12. Oakley, I., Adams, A., Brewster, S., Gray, P.D.: Guidelines for the design of haptic widgets. In: BCS HCI 2002, London, UK (2002)
13. Payne, S.J., Green, T.R.G.: Task-Action Grammars: A Model of the Mental Representation of Task Languages. Human-Computer Interaction 2, 93–133 (1986)
14. Petrie, H., Morley, S., McNally, P., Graziani, P.: Authoring hypermedia systems for blind people. In: IEE Colloquium on Authoring and Application of Hypermedia-Based User-Interfaces, 1995 (1995)
15. Raman, T.V.: Emacspeak-an audio desktop. In: Proceeding IEEE Compcon '97 (1997)
16. Redeke, I.: Image and Graphic Reader. In: Proceedings 2001 International Conference on Image Processing, 2001 (2001)
17. Rigas, D.: Guidelines for Auditory Interface Design: An Empirical Investigation. In: Department of Computer Studies, University of Loughborough, Loughborough, p. 292 (1996)

18. Rigas, D., Memery, D., Yu, H.: Experiments in using structured musical sound, synthesised speech and environmental stimuli to communicate information: is there a case for integration and synergy? In: Proceedings of 2001 International Symposium on Intelligent Multimedia, Video and Speech Processing, 2001 (2001)
19. Rigas, D., Yu, H., Klearhou, K., Mistry, S.: Designing Information Systems with Audio-Visual Synergy: Empirical Results of Browsing E-Mail Data. In: Panhellenic Conference on Human-Computer Interaction. Advances on Human-Computer Interaction, Patras, Greece, 2001 (2001)
20. Rigas, D., Yu, H., Memery, D., Howden, D.: Combining Speech with Sound to Communicate Information in a Multimedia Stock Control System. In: 9th International Conference on Human-Computer Interaction: Usability Evaluation and Interface Design, New Orleans, Luisiana, USA, 2001 (2001)
21. Rigas, D., Hopwood, D., Yu, H.: The Role of Multimedia in Interfaces for On-Line Learning. In: 9th Panhellenic Conference on Informatics (PCI'2003), Thessaloniki, Greece, 2003 (2003)
22. Rigas, D., Memery, D.: Multimedia e-mail data browsing: the synergistic use of various forms of auditory stimuli. In: Proceedings. ITCC 2003. International Conference on Information Technology: Coding and Computing [Computers and Communications], 2003 (2003)
23. Rigas, D.I., Memery, D.: Multimedia e-mail data browsing: the synergistic use of various forms of auditory stimuli. In: Proceedings. ITCC 2003. International Conference on Information Technology: Coding and Computing [Computers and Communications], 2003 (2003)
24. Yu, W., Kangas, K., Brewster, S.: Web-based haptic applications for blind people to create virtual graphs. In: Proceedings. 11th Symposium on Haptic Interfaces for Virtual Environment and Teleoperator Systems, 2003. HAPTICS 2003 (2003)

An Input-Parsing Algorithm Supporting Integration of Deictic Gesture in Natural Language Interface

Yong Sun[1,2], Fang Chen[1,2], Yu Shi[1], and Vera Chung[2]

[1] National ICT Australia, Australian Technology Park
Eveleigh NSW 1430, Australia
[2] School of IT, The University of Sydney,
NSW 2006, Australia
yong.sun@nicta.com.au

Abstract. Natural language interface (NLI) enables an efficient and effective interaction by allowing a user to submit a single phrase in natural language to the system. Free hand gestures can be added to an NLI to specify the referents for deictic terms in speech. By combining NLI with other modalities to a multimodal user interface, speech utterance length can be reduced, and users need not clearly specify the referent verbally. Integrating deictic terms with deictic gestures is a critical function in multimodal user interface. This paper presents a novel approach to extend chart parsing used in natural language processing (NLP) to integrate multimodal input based on speech and manual deictic gesture. The effectiveness of the technique has been validated through experiments, using a traffic incident management scenario where an operator interacts with a map on large display at a distance and issues multimodal commands through speech and manual gestures. The preliminary experiment of the proposed algorithm shows encouraging results.

Keywords: Multimodal chart parsing, Multimodal Fusion, Deictic Gesture, Deictic Terms.

1 Introduction

NLI refers to the interface that allows a user to interact with a system using natural written or spoken language. It enables an efficient and effective interaction by allowing a user to submit a single phrase in natural language to the system. Although NLI is very attractive, it is often difficult to implement it due to the unpredictable nature and ambiguity of natural language. After applying some constrains on the language structures and lexicon, some restricted language interfaces still maintain most of the advantages of NLI; but a user will be required to adapt these restrictions in them. With these facts, an NLI can be redefined as an interface that allows a user to interact with a system using written or spoken language without explicitly learning the commands in it.

Speaking commands to a computer frees up a user's hands for other tasks; and an NLI will be more efficient when combined with other interaction modalities such as,

J. Jacko (Ed.): Human-Computer Interaction, Part III, HCII 2007, LNCS 4552, pp. 206–215, 2007.

hand gesture, body gesture, head gesture and eye gaze etc. By combining speech with other modalities, an NLI can capture the additional cues for disambiguation; and the bandwidth of the interaction between a user and the NLI is broadened.

Free hand gestures can be added to an NLI to specify the referents for deictic terms in speech. With such additional cues, speech utterance length can be reduced, and users need not explicitly specify the referent verbally e.g. "Watch the camera in the section of George street and Eddy avenue" can be reduced by "Watch this camera" <pointing>.

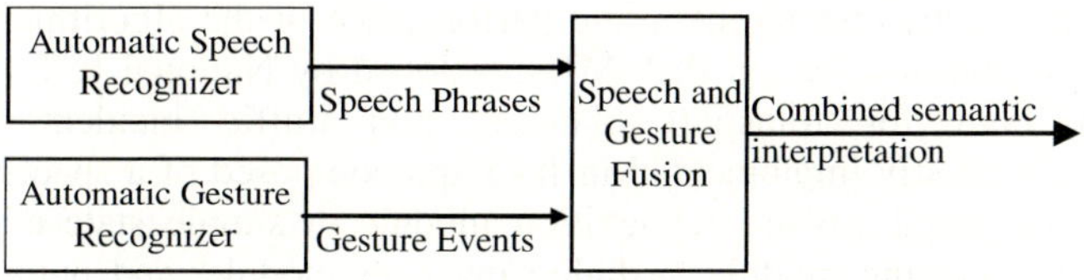

Fig. 1. Integrate Gestures with Speech in Parsing Process

Fig. 1 illustrates a structure to integrate speech with gesture in parsing process in an NLI. This fusion ability allows the system to utilize gesture cues in parsing deictic terms and disambiguation. With this capability, commands such as "Watch this <pointing>" and "Send this <pointing> there <pointing>", are feasible. However, by combining an NLI with other modalities to form a multimodal user interface (MMUI), more challenges emerge.

In MMUI, most multimodal inputs are not linearly ordered. For a multimodal command, multimodal input do not always follow the same order. Different input modalities such as speech and gestures can be used at any time in any order by the user to convey information. For example, in a traffic incident control room, when an operator points to a camera icon on a map and says "play this camera", he/she wants to play a specific camera identified by the hand pointing. The order and timing of when "play this camera" and the pointing gesture occurred and was recognized by speech and gesture recognizers can be different from person to person. The objective of multimodal input parsing, a critical component in an MMUI, is to find the most consistent semantic interpretation when multiple inputs are temporally and/or semantically aligned. In the above example, multimodal parsing should provide as output the joint meaning of both playing the camera and pointing by the hand. The main challenge for multimodal input parsing lies in developing a logic-based or pattern-matching technique that can integrate semantic information derived from different input modalities into a representation with a common meaning.

The multimodal input in our application is discrete, which means it can be individually treated as token in time and modality. Both speech and gesture inputs are recognized as tokens. For example, the phrase 'the end of the street' represents 5 tokens. In one multimodal turn, all multimodal tokens belong to one multimodal utterance. The interpretation of multimodal input, semantic interpretation, is a coherent piece of information for the computer to act upon during human computer interaction.

We propose a new approach termed Mountable Unification-based Multimodal Input Fusion (MUMIF) to integrate gesture with deictic terms in speech. The architecture and implementation of the approach are introduced in [8]. This paper focuses on the parsing algorithm of MUMIF. It can seamlessly integrate individual interpretation provided by speech and gesture recognizers, and provide a joint or combined semantic interpretation of the user's intension. The proposed multimodal chart parsing algorithm is based on chart parsing used in NLP, with the novelties in parsing multimodal inputs. The algorithm provides an alternative method in unification-based multimodal parsing by introducing grammatical consecution conception. To test the effectiveness and performance of the algorithm, we used an MMUI research platform, called PEMMI, developed by National ICT Australia [2]. PEMMI was built for transport planning and traffic incident management applications. It is mostly implemented in Java and composed of a speech recognition module, a vision-based gesture recognition module, a simple state-machine based multimodal input parsing module, a dialog manager module, and output generation module. We removed the state-machine based parsing module in PEMMI and plugged in the integrating module equipped with the proposed algorithm. PEMMI served both as research platform to fine tune the performance of the algorithm, and as a test platform for multimodal parsing evaluation.

2 Related Work

There are two main approaches to integrate speech with gesture inputs in the literature; one is finite-state based and the other is unification-based.

The finite state based approach was adopted in [5]. It uses a finite state device to encode the multimodal integration pattern, the syntax of speech inputs, gesture inputs and the semantic interpretation of these multimodal inputs. Recently, in [7], a similar approach, which utilizes a modified temporal augmented transition network, is reported.

In the unification-based approach, the fusion module applies a unification operation on a speech and gesture input according to a multimodal grammar. It can be found in many documents, such as [4], [6] and [3].

This kind of approach can handle a versatile multimodal command style. However, it suffers from significant computational complexity [5]. Development of the grammar rules requires significant understanding of integration technique.

Unification-based parsing approaches use various algorithms to parsing multimodal input. [4] assumes multimodal input is not discrete and linearly ordered. A multidimensional parsing algorithm runs bottom-up from the input elements, building progressively larger constituents in accordance with the rule set. [3] also assumes multimodal input is not linearly ordered, Multimodal parsing is performed on a pool of elements, where new elements can be added and elements can be removed.

The MUMIF belongs to the unification-based approach. Both [4] and [6] agree the speech and gesture inputs are not linearly ordered. Further, we point out that inputs from one modality are linearly ordered. For example, in "Send this there <pointing1> <pointing2>", pointing1 always precedes pointing2.

With this observation, chart parsing in natural language processing is extended by parsing speech and gesture inputs separately at first, and then combining the parse edges from speech and gesture inputs according to speech-gesture combination rules in a multimodal grammar.

3 Chart Parser

The proposed multimodal parsing algorithm is based on chart parsing in NLP. In NLP, a grammar is a formal system that specifies which sequences of tokens are well formed in the language, and which provides one or more phrase structures for the sequence. For example, **S -> NP VP** says that a constituent of category **S** can consist of sub-constituents of categories **NP** and **VP** [1]. According to the productions of a grammar, a parser processes input tokens and builds one or more constituent structures which conform to the grammar.

A chart parser uses a structure called a *chart* to record the hypothesized constituents in a sentence. One way to envision this chart is as a graph whose nodes are the word boundaries in a sentence. Each hypothesized constituent can be drawn as an *edge*. For example, the chart in Fig. 2 hypothesizes that "hide" is a V (verb), "police" and "stations" are Ns (noun) and they comprise an NP (noun phrase).

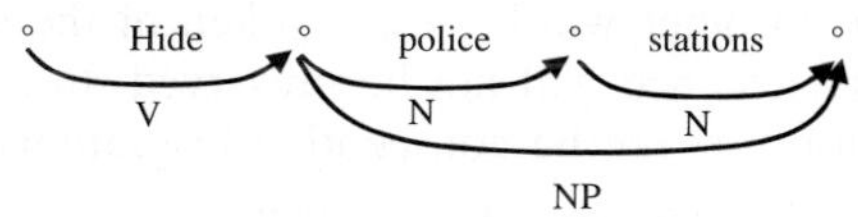

Fig. 2. A chart recording types of constituents in edges

To determine detailed information of a constituent, it is useful to record the types of its children. This is shown in Fig. 3.

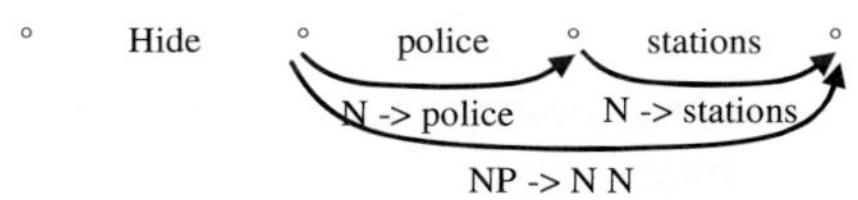

Fig. 3. A chart recording children types of constituents in an edge

If an edge spans the entire sentence, then the edge is called a *parse edge*, and it encodes one or more parse trees for the sentence. In Fig. 4, the verb phrase VP represented as [VP -> V NP] is a parse edge.

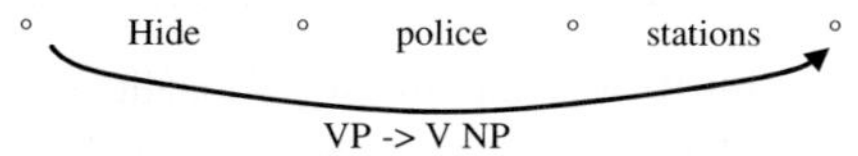

Fig. 4. A chart recording a parse edge

To parse a sentence, a chart parser uses different algorithms to find all *parse edges*.

4 Multimodal Chart Parser

To extend chart parser for multimodal input, the differences between unimodal and multimodal input need to be analyzed.

Speech: ° show ° this ° camera ° and ° that ° camera °

Gesture: ° pointing1 ° pointing2 °

Fig. 5. Multimodal utterance: speech -- "show this camera and that camera" plus two pointing gestures. Pointing1: The pointing gesture pointing to the first camera. Pointing2: The pointing gesture pointing to the second camera.

The first difference is linear order. Tokens of a sentence always follow a same linear order. In a multimodal utterance, the linear order of tokens is variable, but the linear order of tokens from same modality is invariable. For example, as in Fig. 5, a traffic controller wants to monitor two cameras; he/she issues a multimodal command "show this camera and that camera" while pointing to two cameras with the cursor of his/her hand on screen. The gesture pointing1 and pointing2 may be issued before, in-between or after speech input, but pointing2 is always after pointing1.

The second difference is grammar consecution. Tokens of a sentence are consecutive in grammar; in other words, if any token of the sentence is missed the grammar structure of the sentence will not be preserved. In a multimodal utterance, tokens from one modality may not be consecutive in grammar. In Fig. 5, speech -- "show this camera and that camera" is consecutive in grammar. It can form a grammar structure though the structure is not complete. Gesture – "pointing1, pointing2" is not consecutive in grammar. Grammatically inconsecutive constituents are link with a list in the proposed algorithm. "pointing1, pointing2" is stored in a list.

Grammar structures of hypothesized constituents from each modality can be illustrated as in Fig. 6. Tokens from one modality can be parsed to a list of constituents [C1 … Cn] where n is the number of constituents. If the tokens are grammatically consecutive, then n=1, i.e., the Modality 1 parsing result in Fig. 6. If the tokens are not consecutive in grammar, then n>1. For example, in Fig. 6, there are 2 constituents for Modality 2 input.

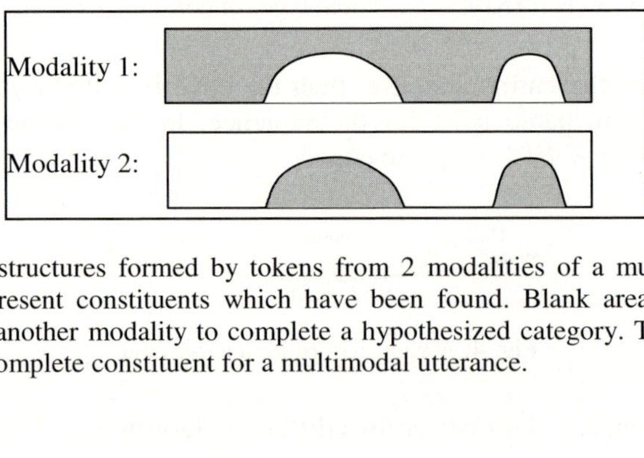

Fig. 6. Grammar structures formed by tokens from 2 modalities of a multimodal utterance. Shadow areas represent constituents which have been found. Blank areas are the expected constituents from another modality to complete a hypothesized category. The whole rectangle area represents a complete constituent for a multimodal utterance.

To record a hypothesized constituent that needs constituents from another modality to become complete, a vertical bar is added to the edge's right hand side. The constituents to the left of the vertical bar are the hypotheses in this modality. The constituents to the right of the vertical bar are the expected constituents from another modality; 'show this camera and that camera' can be expressed as **VP -> V NP | point, point**.

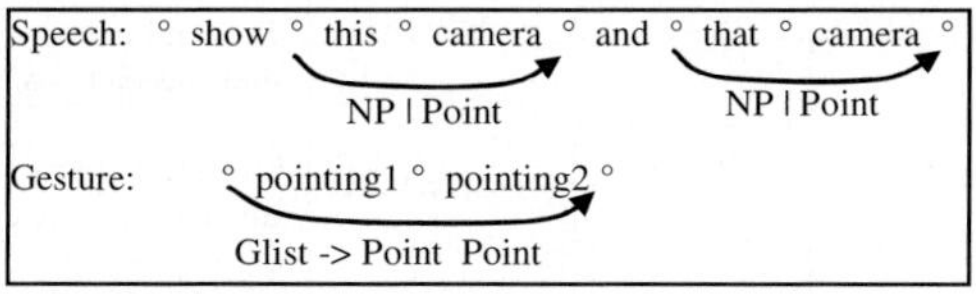

Fig. 7. Edges for "this camera", "that camera" and two pointing gestures

As in Fig. 7, edges for "this camera", "that camera" and "pointing1, pointing2" can be recorded as **NP | Point**, **NP | Point** and **Glist** respectively. Glist is a list of gesture events.

Then, from edges for "this camera" and "that camera", an **NP | Glist** can be derived in Fig. 8.

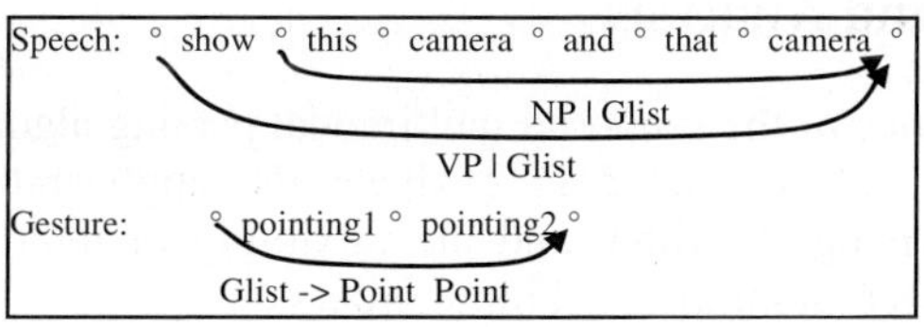

Fig. 8. Parse edges after hypothesizing "this camera" and "that camera" into an NP

Finally, parse edges that cover whole speech tokens and gesture tokens are generated as in Fig. 9. They are integrated to parse edge of the multimodal utterance.

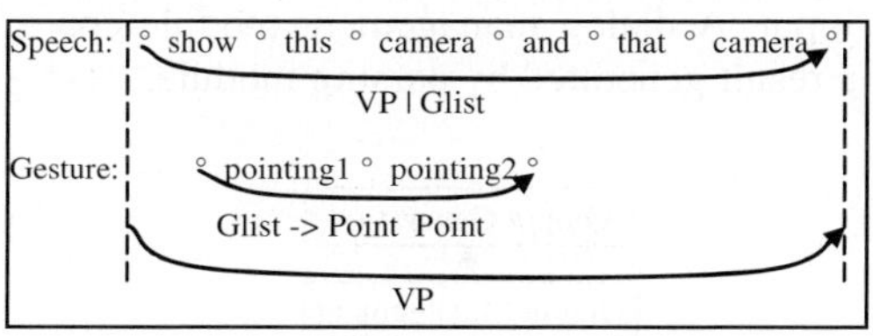

Fig. 9. Final multimodal parse edge and its children

So, a complete multimodal parse edge consists of constituents from different modalities. It has no more expected constituents.

As shown in Fig. 10, in the proposed multimodal chart parsing algorithm, to parse a multimodal utterance, speech and gesture tokens are parsed separately at first, and then the parse edges from speech and gesture tokens are parsed according to speech-gesture combination rules in a multimodal grammar that provided lexical and rules for speech and gesture inputs, and speech-gesture combination rules.

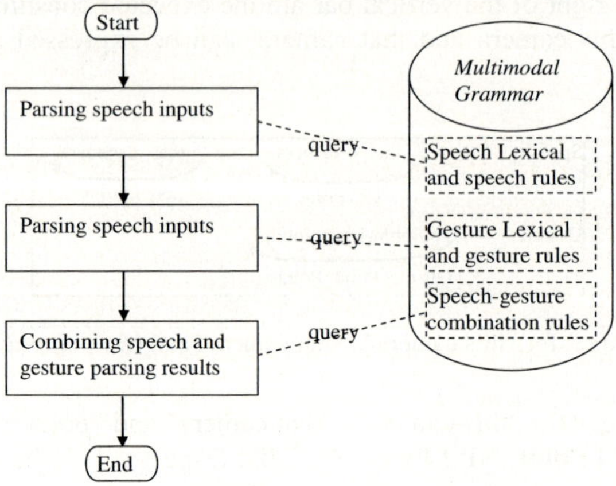

Fig. 10. Flow chart of proposed algorithm

5 Experiment and Analysis

To test the performance of the proposed multimodal parsing algorithm, an experiment has been designed and conducted to evaluate the applicability of the proposed multimodal chart parsing algorithm and the flexibility of multimodal chart parsing algorithm against different multimodal input orders.

5.1 Setup and Scenario

The evaluation experiment was conducted on a modified PEMMI platform. Fig. 11 shows the various system components involved in the experiment. ASR and AGR recognize signals captured by Microphone and Webcam, and provide parsing module with the recognized input. A dialog management module controls output generation according to a parsing result generated by parsing module.

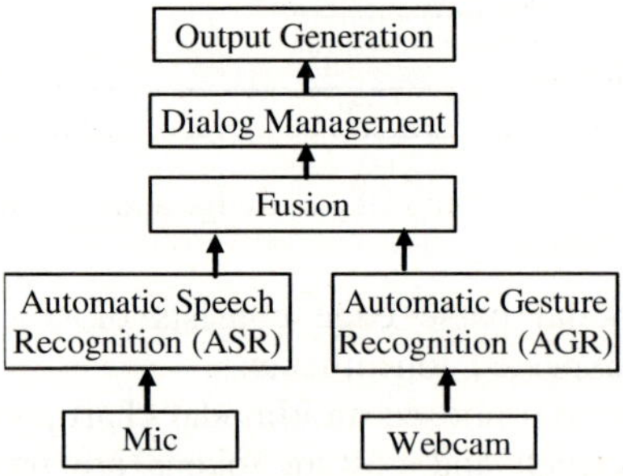

Fig. 11. Overview of testing experiment setup

Fig. 12 shows the user study setup of MUMIF algorithm, which is similar to the one, used in MUMIF experiment. A traffic control scenario was designed within an incident management task. In this scenario, a participant stands about 1.5 metres in front of a large rear-projection screen measuring 2x1.5 metres. A webcam mounted on a tripod, about 1 metre away from the participant, is used to capture manual gestures of the participant. A wireless microphone is worn by the participant.

Fig. 12. User study setup for evaluating MUMIF parsing algorithm

5.2 Preliminary Results and Analysis

During this experiment, we tested the proposed algorithm against a number of multimodal commands typical in map-based traffic incident management, such as

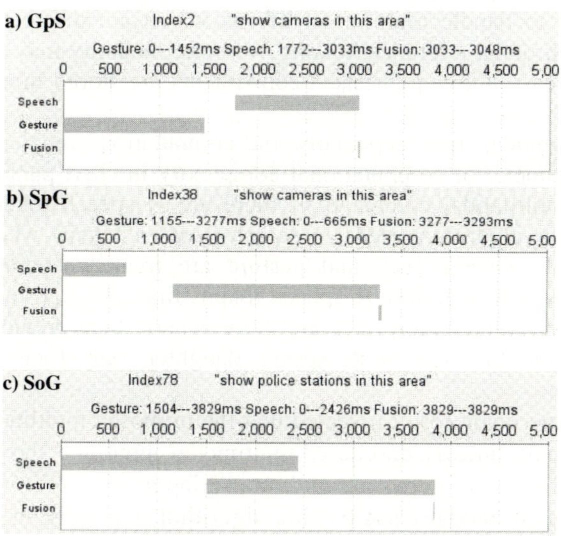

Fig. 13. Three multimodal input patterns

Table 1. Experiment results

Multimodal input pattern	Number of multimodal turns	Number of successful fusion
GpS	17	17
SpG	5	5
SoG	23	23

"show cameras in this area" with a circling/drawing gesture to indicate the area, "show police stations in this area" with a gesture drawing the area and "watch this" with a hand pause to specify the camera to play. One particular multimodal command, "show cameras in this area" with a gesture to draw the area, requires a test subject to issue the speech phrase and to draw an area using an on-screen cursor of his/her hand. The proposed parsing algorithm would generate a "show" action parameterized by the top-left and bottom-right coordinates of the area. In a multimodal command, multimodal tokens are not linearly ordered. Fig. 13 shows 3 of the possibilities of the temporal relationship between speech and gesture: GpS (Gesture precedes speech), SpG (Speech precedes gesture) and SoG (Speech overlaps gesture). The first bar shows the start and end time of speech input, the second for gesture input and the last (very short) for parsing process.

The proposed multimodal parsing algorithm worked in all these patterns (see Table 1).

6 Conclusion and Future Work

The proposed multimodal chart parsing is extended from chart parsing in NLP. By indicating expected constituents from another modality in hypothesized edges, the algorithm is able to handle multimodal tokens which are discrete but not linearly ordered. In a multimodal utterance, tokens from one modality may be consecutive in grammar. In this case, the hypothesised constituents are stored in a list to link them together.

By parsing unimodal input separately, the computation complexity of parsing is reduced. One parameter of computational complexity in chart parsing is the number of tokens. In a multimodal command, if there are m speech tokens and n gesture tokens, the parsing algorithm needs to search in $m+n$ tokens when the inputs are treated as a pool; when speech and gesture are treated separately, the parsing algorithm only needs to search in m speech tokens first and n gesture tokens second. The speech-gesture combination rules are more general than previous approaches. It does not care about the type of its speech daughter, only focus on the expected gestures.

Preliminary experiment result revealed that the proposed multimodal chart parsing algorithm can handle linearly unordered multimodal input and showed its promising applicability and flexibility in parsing multimodal input.

The proposed multimodal chart parsing algorithm is a work in progress. For the moment, it only processes the best interpretation from recognizers. In the future, to develop a robust, flexible and portable multimodal input parsing technique, it will be extended to handle n-best list of inputs. The research of a semantic interpretation possibility can also be a pending topic.

References

1. Bird, S., Klein, E., Loper, E.: Parsing (2005) In http://nltk.sourceforge.net
2. Chen, F., Choi, E., Epps, J., Lichman, S., Ruiz, N., Shi, Y., Taib, R., Wu, M.A.: Study of Manual Gesture-Based Selection for the PEMMI Multimodal Transport Management Interface. In: Proceedings of ICMI'05, October 4–6, Trento, Italy, pp. 274–281 (2005)
3. Holzapfel, H., Nickel, K., Stiefelhagen, R.: Implementation and Evaluation of a Constraint-Based Multimodal Fusion System for Speech and 3D Pointing Gestures. In: Proceedings of ICMI'04, October 13-15, State College Pennsylvania, USA, pp. 175–182 (2004)
4. Johnston, M.: Unification-based Multimodal Parsing. In: Proceedings of ACL'1998, Montreal, Quebec, Canada, pp. 624–630. ACM, New York (1998)
5. Johnston, M., Bangalore, S.: Finite-state multimodal parsing and understanding. In: Proceedings of COLING 2000, Saarbrücken, Germany, pp. 369–375 (2000)
6. Kaiser, E., Demirdjian, D., Gruenstein, A., Li, X., Niekrasz, J., Wesson, M., Kumar, S., Demo.: A Multimodal Learning Interface for Sketch, Speak and Point Creation of a Schedule Chart. In: Proceedings of ICMI'04, October 13-15, State College Pennsylvania, USA, pp. 329-330 (2004)
7. Latoschik, M.E.: A User Interface Framework for Multimodal VR Interactions. In: Proc. ICMI 2005 (2005)
8. Sun, Y., Chen, F., Shi, Y., Chung, V.: A Novel Method for Multi-sensory Data Fusion in Multimodal Human Computer Interaction. In: Proc. OZCHI 2006 (2006)

Multimodal Interfaces for In-Vehicle Applications

Roman Vilimek, Thomas Hempel, and Birgit Otto

Siemens AG, Corporate Technology, User Interface Design
Otto-Hahn-Ring 6, 81730 Munich, Germany
{roman.vilimek.ext,thomas.hempel,birgit.otto}@siemens.com

Abstract. This paper identifies several factors that were observed as being crucial to the usability of multimodal in-vehicle applications – a multimodal system is not of value in itself. Focusing in particular on the typical combination of manual and voice control, this article describes important boundary conditions and discusses the concept of natural interaction.

Keywords: Multimodal, usability, driving, in-vehicle systems.

1 Motivation

The big-picture goal of interaction design is not accomplished only by enabling the users of a certain product to fulfill a task by using it. Rather, the focus should reside on a substantial facilitation of the interaction process between humans and technical solutions. In the majority of cases the versatile and characteristic abilities of human operators are widely ignored in the design of modern computer-based systems. Buxton [1] depicts this situation quite nicely by describing what a physical anthropologist in the far future might conclude when discovering a computer store of our time (p. 319): "My best guess is that we would be pictured as having a well-developed eye, a long right arm, uniform-length fingers and a 'low-fi' ear. But the dominating characteristic would be the prevalence of our visual system over our poorly developed manual dexterity."

This statement relates to the situation in the late 1980s, but it still has an unexpected topicality. However, with the advent of multimodal technologies and interaction techniques, a considerable amount of new solutions emerge that can reduce the extensive overuse of the human visual system in HCI. By involving the senses of touch and hearing, the heavy visual monitoring load of many tasks can be considerably reduced. Likewise, the activation of an action does no longer need to be carried out exclusively by pressing a button or turning a knob. For instance, gesture recognition systems allow for contact-free manual input and eye gaze tracking can be used as an alternative pointing mechanism. Speech recognition systems are the prevalent foundation of "eyes-free, hands-free" systems.

The trend to approach the challenge of making new and increasingly complex devices usable with multimodal interaction is particularly interesting, as not only universities but also researchers in the industrial environment spend increasing efforts in evaluating the potential of multimodality for product-level solutions. Research has shown that the advantages of multimodal interfaces are manifold, yet their usability

J. Jacko (Ed.): Human-Computer Interaction, Part III, HCII 2007, LNCS 4552, pp. 216–224, 2007.

does not always meet expectations. Several reasons account for this situation. In most cases, the technical realization is given far more attention than the users and their interaction behavior, their context of use or their preferences. This leads to systems which do not provide modalities really suited for the task. That may be acceptable for a proof-of-concept demo, but is clearly not adequate for an end-user product. Furthermore the user's willingness to accept the product at face value is frequently overestimated. If a new method of input does not work almost perfectly, users will soon get annoyed and do not act multimodally at all. Tests in our usability lab have shown, that high and stable speech recognition rates are necessary (>90%) for novice users of everyday products. And these requirements have to be met in everyday contexts – not only in a sound-optimized environment! Additionally, many multimodal interaction concepts are based on misconceptions about how users construct their multimodal language [2] and what "natural interaction" with a technical system should look like.

Taken together, these circumstances seriously reduce the expected positive effects of multimodality in practice. The goal of this paper is to summarize some relevant aspects of key factors for successful multimodal design of advanced in-vehicle interfaces. The selection is based on our experience in an applied industrial research environment within a user-centered design process and does not claim to be exhaustive.

2 Context of Use: Driving and In-Vehicle Interfaces

ISO9241-11 [3], an ISO norm giving guidance on usability, requires explicitly to consider the context in which a product will be used. The relevant characteristics of users (2.1), tasks and environment (2.2) and the available equipment (2.3) need to be described. Using in-vehicle interfaces while driving is usually embedded in a multiple task situation. Controlling the vehicle safely must be regarded as the primary task of the driver. Thus, the usability of infotainment, navigation or communication systems inside cars refers not only to the quality of the interaction concept itself. These systems have to be built in a way that optimizes time-sharing and draws as few attentional resources as possible off the driving task. The contribution of multimodality needs to be evaluated in respect to these parameters.

2.1 Users

There are only a few limiting factors that allow us to narrow the user group. Drivers must own a license and thus they have shown to be able to drive according to the road traffic regulations. But still the group is very heterogeneous. The age range goes anywhere from 16 or 18 to over 70. A significant part of them are seldom users, changing users and non-professional users, which have to be represented in usability tests. Quite interestingly older drivers seem to benefit more from multimodal displays than younger people [4]. The limited attentional resources of elderly users can be partially compensated by multimodality.

2.2 Tasks and Environment

Even driving a vehicle itself is not just a single task. Well-established models (e.g. [5]) depict it as a hierarchical combination of activities at three levels which differ in respect to temporal aspects and conscious attentional demands. The topmost strategic level consists of general planning activities as well as navigation (route planning) and includes knowledge-based processes and decision making. On the maneuvering level people follow complex short-term objectives like overtaking, lane changing, monitoring the own car movements and observing the actions other road users. On the bottom level of the hierarchy, the operational level, basic tasks have to be fulfilled including steering, lane keeping, gear-shifting, accelerating or slowing down the car. These levels are not independent; the higher levels provide information for the lower levels. They pose different demands on the driver with a higher amount of mental demands on the higher levels and in increased temporal frequency of the relevant activities on the lower levels [6]. Thus, these levels have to be regarded as elements of a continuum.

This model delivers valuable information for the design of in-vehicle systems which are not directly related to driving. Any additional task must be created in a way that minimizes conflict with any of these levels. To complicate matters further, more and more driver information systems, comfort functions, communication and mobile office functions and the integration of nomad devices turn out to be severe sources of distraction. Multimodal interface design may help to re-allocate relevant resources to the driving task. About 90% of the relevant information is perceived visually [7] and the manual requirements of steering on the lower levels are relatively high, as long as they are not automated. Thus, first of all interfaces for on-board comfort functions have to minimize the amount of required visual attention. Furthermore they must support short manual interaction steps and an ergonomic posture. Finally, the cognitive aspect may not be underestimated. Using in-vehicle applications must not lead to high levels of mental workload or induce cognitive distraction. Research results show, that multimodal interfaces have a high potential to reduce the mental and physical demands in multiple task situations by improving the time-sharing between primary and secondary task (for an overview see [8]).

2.3 Equipment

Though voice-actuation technology has proven to successfully keep the driver's eyes on the road and the hands on the steering wheel, manual controls will not disappear completely. Ashley [9] comes to the conclusion, that there will be fewer controls and that they will morph into a flexible new form. And indeed there is a general trend among leading car manufacturers to rely on a menu-based interaction concept with a central display at the top of the center console and single manual input device between the front seats. The placement of the display allows for a peripheral detection of traffic events while at the same time the driver is able to maintain a relaxed body posture while activating the desired functions. It is important to keep this configuration in mind when assessing the usability of multimodal solutions as the have to fit into this context. Considering the availability of a central display, the speech dialog concept can make use of the "say what you see" strategy [10] to inform novice users about valid commands without time-consuming help dialogs. Haptic or auditory feedback can improve the interaction with the central input device like and reduce visual distraction like for example the force feedback of BMW's iDrive controller [9].

3 Characteristics of Multimodal Interfaces

A huge number of different opinions exist on the properties of a multimodal interface. Different researchers mean different things when talking about multimodality, probably because of the interdisciplinary nature of the field [11]. It is not within the scope of this paper to define all relevant terms. However, considering the given situation in research it seems necessary to clarify at least some basics to narrow down the subject.

The European Telecommunications Standards Institute [12] defines *multimodal* as an "adjective that indicates that at least one of the directions of a two-way communication uses two sensory modalities (vision, touch, hearing, olfaction, speech, gestures, etc.)" In this sense, *multimodality* is a "property of a user interface in which: a) more than one sensory is available for the channel (e.g. output can be visual or auditory); or b) within a channel, a particular piece of information is represented in more than one sensory modality (e.g. the command to open a file can be spoken or typed)." The term sensory is used in wide sense here, meaning human senses as well as sensory capabilities of a technical system.

A key aspect of a multimodal system is to analyze how input or output modalities can be combined. Martin [13, 14] proposes a typology to study and design multimodal systems. He differentiates between the following six "types of cooperation":

- Equivalence: Several modalities can be used to accomplish the same task, i.e. they can be used alternatively.
- Specialization: A certain piece of information can only be conveyed in a specially designated modality. This specialization is not necessarily absolute: Sounds, for example, can be specialized for error messages, but may also be used to signalize some other important events.
- Redundancy: The same piece of information is transmitted by several modalities at the same time (e.g., lip movements and speech in input, redundant combinations of sound and graphics in output). Redundancy helps to improve recognition accuracy.
- Complementarity: The complete information of a communicative act is distributed across several modalities. For instance, gestures and speech in man-machine interaction typically contribute different and complementary semantic information [15].
- Transfer: Information generated in one modality is used by another modality, i.e. the interaction process is transferred to another modality-dependent discourse level. Transfer can also be used to improve the recognition process. Contrary to redundancy, the modalities combined by transfer are not naturally associated.
- Concurrency: Several independent types of information are conveyed by several modalities at the same time, which can speed up the interaction process.

Martin points out that redundancy and complementarity imply a fusion of signals, an integration of information derived from parallel input modes. Multimodal fusion is generally considered to be the supreme discipline of multimodal interaction design. However, it is also the most complex and cost-intensive design option – and may lead to quite error prone systems in real life because the testing effort is drastically increased. Of course so-called mutual disambiguation can lead to a recovery from unimodal recognition errors, but this works only with redundant signals. Thus, great care has to be taken to identify whether there is a clear benefit of modality fusion within the use scenario of a product or whether a far simpler multimodal system without fusion will suffice.

One further distinction should be reported here because of its implication for cognitive ergonomics as well as for usability. Oviatt [16] differentiates between active and passive input modes. Active modes are deployed intentionally by the user in form of an explicit command (e.g., a voice command). Passive input modes refer to spontaneous automatic and unintentional actions or behavior of the user (e.g., facial expressions or lip movements) which are passively monitored by the system. No explicit command is issued by the user and thus no cognitive effort is necessary. A quite similar idea is brought forward by Nielsen [17] who suggests non-command user interfaces which do no longer rely on an explicit dialog between the user and a computer. Rather the system has to infer the user intentions by interpreting user actions. The integration of passive modalities to increase recognition quality surely improves the overall system quality, but non-command interfaces are a two-edged sword: On the one hand they can lower the consumption of central cognitive resources, on the other the risk of over-adaptation arises. This can lead to substantial irritation of the driver.

4 Designing Multimodal In-Vehicle Applications

The benefits of successful multimodal design are quite obvious and have been demonstrated in various research and application domains. According to Oviatt and colleagues [18], who summarize some of the most important aspects in a review paper, multimodal UIs are far more flexible. A single modality does not permit the user to interact effectively across all tasks and environments while several modalities enable the user to switch to a better suited one if necessary. The first part of this section will try to show how this can be achieved for voice and manual controlled in-vehicle applications. A further frequently used argument is that multimodal systems are easier to learn and more natural, as multimodal interaction concept can mimic man-man-communication. The second part of this section tries to show that natural is not always equivalent to usable and that natural interaction does not necessarily imply human-like communication.

4.1 Combining Manual and Voice Control

Among the available technologies to enhance unimodal manual control by building a multimodal interface, speech input is the most robust and advanced option. Bengler [19] assumes, that any form of multimodality in the in-vehicle context will always imply the integration of speech recognition. Thus, one of the most prominent questions is how to combine voice and manual control so that their individual benefits can take effect. If for instance the hands cannot be taken off the steering wheel on a wet road or while driving at high speed, speech commands ensures the availability of comfort functions. Likewise, manual input may substitute speech control if it is too noisy for successful recognition. To take full advantage of the flexibility offered by multimodal voice and manual input, both interface components have to be completely equivalent. For any given task, both variants must provide usable solutions for task completion.

How can this be done? One solution is to design manual and voice input independently: A powerful speech dialog system (SDS) may enable the user to accomplish a task completely without prior knowledge of the system menus used for manual interaction. However, using the auditory interface poses high demands on the driver's working memory. He has to listen to the available options and keep the state of the dialog in mind while interrupting it for difficult driving maneuvers. The SDS has to be able to deal with long pauses by the user which typically occur in city traffic. Furthermore the user cannot easily transfer acquired knowledge from manual interaction, e.g. concerning menu structures. Designing the speech interface independently also makes it more difficult to meet the usability requirement of consistency and to ensure that really all functions available in the manual interface are incorporated in the speech interface.

Another way is to design according to the "say what you see" principle [10]: Users can say any command that is visible in a menu or dialog step on the central display. Thus, the manual and speech interface can be completely parallel. Given that currently most people still prefer the manual interface to start with the exploration of a new system, they can form a mental representation of the system structure which will also allow them to interact verbally more easily. This learning process can be substantially enhanced if valid speech commands are specially marked on the GUI (e.g., by font or color). As users understand this principle quickly, they start using expert options like talk-ahead even after rather short-time experience with the system [20].

A key factor for the success of multimodal design is user acceptance. Based on our experience, most people still do not feel very comfortable interaction with a system using voice commands, especially when other people are present. But if the interaction is restricted to very brief commands from the user and the whole process can be done without interminable turn-taking dialogs, the users are more willing to operate by voice. Furthermore, users generally prefer to issue terse, goal-directed commands rather than engage in natural language dialogs when using in-car systems [21]. Providing them with a simple vocabulary by designing according to the "say what you see" principle seems to be exactly what they need.

4.2 Natural Interaction

Wouldn't it be much easier if all efforts were undertaken to implement natural language systems in cars? If the users were free to issue commands in their own way, long clarification dialogs would not be necessary either. But the often claimed equivalency between naturalness and ease is not as valid as it seems from a psychological point of view. And from a technological point of view crucial prerequisites will still take a long time to solve. Heisterkamp [22] emphasizes that fully conversational systems would need to have the full human understanding capability, a profound expertise on the functions of an application and an extraordinary understanding of what the user really intends with a certain speech command. He points out that even if these problems could be solved there are inherent problems in people's communication behavior that cannot be solved by technology. A large number of recognition errors will result, with people not exactly saying what they want or not providing the information that is needed by the system. This assumption is supported by findings of Oviatt [23].

She has shown that the utterances of users get increasingly unstructured with growing sentence length. Longer sentences in natural language are furthermore accompanied by a huge number of hesitations, self-corrections, interruptions and repetitions, which are difficult to handle. This holds even for man-man communication. Additionally, the quality of speech production is substantially reduced in dual-task situations [24]. Thus, for usability reasons it makes sense to provide the user with an interface that forces short and clear-cut speech commands. This will help the user to formulate an understandable command and this in turn increases the probability of successful interaction.

Some people argue that naturalness is the basis for intuitive interaction. But there are many cases in everyday life where quite unnatural actions are absolutely intuitive – because there are standards and conventions. Heisterkamp [22] comes up with a very nice example: Activating a switch on the wall to turn on the light at the ceiling is not natural at all. Yet, the first thing someone will do when entering a dark room is to search for the switch beside the door. According to Heisterkamp, the key to success are conventions, which have to be omnipresent and easy to learn. If we succeed in finding conventions for multimodal speech systems, we will be able to create very intuitive interaction mechanisms. The "say what you see" strategy can be part of such a convention for multimodal in-vehicle interfaces. It also provides the users with an easy to learn structure that helps them to find the right words.

5 Conclusion

In this paper we identified several key factors for the usability of multimodal in-vehicle applications. These aspects may seem trivial at first, but they are worth considering as they are neglected far too often in practical research. First, a profound analysis of the context of use helps to identify the goals and potential benefit of multimodal interfaces. Second, a clear understanding of the different types of multimodality is necessary to find an optimal combination of single modalities for a given task. Third, an elaborate understanding of the intended characteristics of a multimodal system is essential: Intuitive and easy-to-use interfaces are not necessarily achieved by making the communication between man and machine as "natural" (i.e. human-like) as possible. Considering speech-based interaction, clear-cut and non-ambiguous conventions are needed most urgently.

To combine speech and manual input for multimodal in-vehicle systems, we recommend designing both input modes in parallel, thus allowing for transfer effects in learning. The easy-to-learn "say what you see" strategy is a technique in speech dialog design that structures the user's input and narrows the vocabulary at the same time and may form the basis of a general convention. This does not mean that command-based interaction is from a usability point of view generally superior to natural language. But considering the outlined technological and user-dependent difficulties, a simple command-and-control concept following universal conventions should form the basis of any speech system as a fallback. Thus, before engaging in more complex natural interaction concepts, we have to establish these conventions first.

References

1. Buxton, W.: There's More to Interaction Than Meets the Eye: Some Issues in Manual Input. In: Norman, D.A., Draper, S.W. (eds.) User Centered System Design: New Perspectives on Human-Computer Interaction, pp. 319–337. Lawrence Erlbaum Associates, Hillsdale, NJ (1986)
2. Oviatt, S.L.: Ten Myths of Multimodal Interaction. Communications of the ACM 42, 74–81 (1999)
3. ISO 9241-11 Ergonomic Requirements for Office Work with Visual Display Terminals (VDTs). Part 11: Guidance on Usability. International Organization for Standardization, Geneva, Switzerland (1998)
4. Liu, Y.C.: Comparative Study of the Effects of Auditory, Visual and Multimodality Displays on Driver's Performance in Advanced Traveller Information Systems. Ergonomics 44, 425–442 (2001)
5. Michon, J.A.: A Critical View on Driver Behavior Models: What Do We Know, What Should We Do? In: Evans, L., Schwing, R. (eds.) Human Behavior and Traffic Safety, pp. 485–520. Plenum Press, New York (1985)
6. Reichart, G., Haller, R.: Mehr aktive Sicherheit durch neue Systeme für Fahrzeug und Straßenverkehr. In: Fastenmeier, W. (ed.): Autofahrer und Verkehrssituation. Neue Wege zur Bewertung von Sicherheit und Zuverlässigkeit moderner Straßenverkehrssysteme. TÜV Rheinland, Köln, pp. 199–215 (1995)
7. Hills, B.L.: Vision, Visibility, and Perception in Driving. Perception 9, 183–216 (1980)
8. Wickens, C.D., Hollands, J.G.: Engineering Psychology and Human Performance. Prentice Hall, Upper Saddle River, NJ (2000)
9. Ashley, S.: Simplifying Controls. Automotive Engineering International March 2001, pp. 123-126 (2001)
10. Yankelovich, N.: How Do Users Know What to Say? ACM Interactions 3, 32–43 (1996)
11. Benoît, J., Martin, C., Pelachaud, C., Schomaker, L., Suhm, B.: Audio-Visual and Multimodal Speech-Based Systems. In: Handbook of Multimodal and Spoken Dialogue Systems: Resources, Terminology and Product Evaluation, pp. 102–203. Kluwer Academic Publishers, Boston (2000)
12. ETSI EG 202 191: Human Factors (HF); Multimodal Interaction, Communication and Navigation Guidelines. ETSI. Sophia-Antipolis Cedex, France (2003) Retrieved December 10, 2006, from http://docbox.etsi.org/EC_Files/EC_Files/eg_202191v010101p.pdf
13. Martin, J.-C.: Types of Cooperation and Referenceable Objects: Implications on Annotation Schemas for Multimodal Language Resources. In: LREC 2000 pre-conference workshop, Athens, Greece (1998)
14. Martin, J.-C.: Towards Intelligent Cooperation between Modalities: The Example of a System Enabling Multimodal Interaction with a Map. In: IJCAI'97 workshop on intelligent multimodal systems, Nagoya, Japan (1997)
15. Oviatt, S.L., DeAngeli, A., Kuhn, K.: Integration and Synchronization of Input Modes During Human-Computer Interaction. In: Proceedings of the SIGCHI Conference on Human Factors in Computing Systems, pp. 415–422. ACM Press, New York (1997)
16. Oviatt, S.L.: Multimodal Interfaces. In: Jacko, J.A., Sears, A. (eds.) The Human-Computer Interaction Handbook: Fundamentals, Evolving Technologies and Emerging Applications, pp. 286–304. Lawrence Erlbaum Associates, Mahwah, NJ (2003)
17. Nielsen, J.: Noncommand User Interfaces. Communications of the ACM 36, 83–99 (1993)

18. Oviatt, S.L., Cohen, P.R., Wu, L., Vergo, J., Duncan, L., Suhm, B., Bers, J., Holzman, T., Winograd, T., Landay, J., Larson, J., Ferro, D.: Designing the User Interface for Multimodal Speech and Pen-Based Gesture Applications: State-of-the-Art Systems and Future Research Directions. Human-Computer Interaction 15, 263–322 (2000)
19. Bengler, K.: Aspekte der multimodalen Bedienung und Anzeige im Automobil. In: Jürgensohn, T., Timpe, K.P. (eds.) Kraftfahrzeugführung, pp. 195–205. Springer, Berlin (2001)
20. Vilimek, R.: Concatenation of Voice Commands Increases Input Efficiency. In: Proceedings of Human-Computer Interaction International 2005, Lawrence Erlbaum Associates, Mahwah, NJ (2005)
21. Graham, R., Aldridge, L., Carter, C., Lansdown, T.C.: The Design of In-Car Speech Recognition Interfaces for Usability and User Acceptance. In: Harris, D. (ed.) Engineering Psychology and Cognitive Ergonomics: Job Design, Product Design and Human-Computer Interaction, Ashgate, Aldershot, vol. 4, pp. 313–320 (1999)
22. Heisterkamp, P.: Do Not Attempt to Light with Match! Some Thoughts on Progress and Research Goals in Spoken Dialog Systems. In: Eurospeech 2003. ISCA, Switzerland, pp. 2897–2900 (2003)
23. Oviatt, S.L.: Interface Techniques for Minimizing Disfluent Input to Spoken Language Systems. In: Proceedings of the Sigchi Conference on Human Factors in Computing Systems: Celebrating Interdependence (CHI'94), pp. 205–210. ACM Press, New York (1994)
24. Baber, C., Noyes, J.: Automatic Speech Recognition in Adverse Environments. Human Factors 38, 142–155 (1996)

Character Agents in E-Learning Interface Using Multimodal Real-Time Interaction

Hua Wang[2], Jie Yang[1], Mark Chignell[2], and Mitsuru Ishizuka[1]

[1] University of Tokyo
midi.jie.yang@gmail.com,
ishizuka@miv.t.y-tokyo.ac.jp
[2] University of Toronto
hwang@mie.utoronto.ca,
chignel@mie.utoronto.ca

Abstract. This paper describes an e-learning interface with multiple tutoring character agents. The character agents use eye movement information to facilitate empathy-relevant reasoning and behavior. Eye Information is used to monitor user's attention and interests, to personalize the agent behaviors, and for exchanging information of different learners. The system reacts to multiple users' eye information in real-time and the empathic character agents owned by each learner exchange learner's information to help to form the online learning community. Based on these measures, the interface infers the focus of attention of the learner and responds accordingly with affective and instructional behaviors. The paper will also report on some preliminary usability test results concerning how users respond to the empathic functions and interact with other learners using the character agents.

Keywords: Multiple user interface, e-learning, character agent, tutoring, educational interface.

1 Introduction

Learners can lose motivation and concentration easily, especially in a virtual education environment that is not tailored to their needs, and where they may be little contact with live human teachers. As Palloff and Pratt [1] noted "the key to success in our online classes rests not with the content that is being presented but with the method by which the course is being delivered". In traditional educational settings, good teachers recognized learning needs and learning styles and adjusted the selection and presentation of content accordingly.

In online learning there is a need to create more effective interaction between e-learning content and learners. In particular, increasing motivation by stimulating learner's interest is important. A related concern is how to achieve a more natural and friendly environment for learning. We will address this concern by detecting the attention information from the real-time eye tracking data from each learner and modify instructional strategies based on the different learning patterns for each learner.

J. Jacko (Ed.): Human-Computer Interaction, Part III, HCII 2007, LNCS 4552, pp. 225–231, 2007.

Eye movements provide an indication of learner interest and focus of attention. They provide useful feedback to character agents attempting to personalize learning interactions. Character agents represent a means of bringing back some of the human functionality of a teacher. With appropriately designed and implemented animated agents, learners may be more motivated, and may find learning more fun. However, amusing animations in themselves may not lead to significant improvement in terms of comprehension or recall. Animated software agents need to have intelligence and knowledge about the learner, in order to personalize and focus the instructional strategy.

Figure 1 shows a character agent as a human-like figure embedded within the content on a Web page. In this paper, we use real time eye gaze interaction data as well as recorded study performance to provide appropriate feedback to character agents, in order to make learning more personalized and efficient. This paper will address the issues of when and how such agents with emotional interactions should be used for the interaction between learners and system.

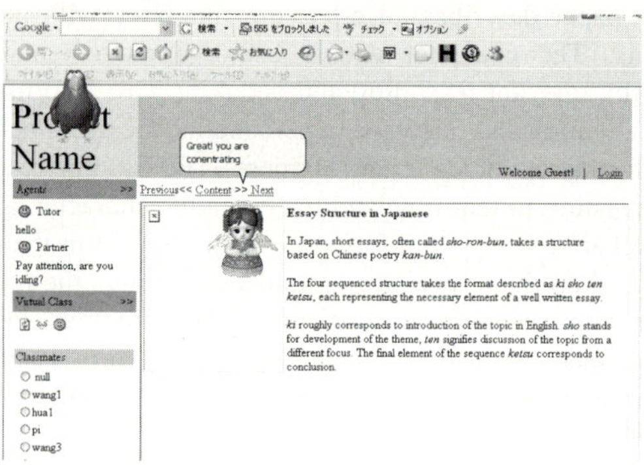

Fig. 1. Interface Appearance 2 Related Work

Animated pedagogical agents can promote effective learning in computer-based learning environments. Learning materials incorporating interactive agents engender a higher degree of interest than similar materials that lack animated agents If such techniques were combined with animated agent technologies, it might then be possible to create an agent that can display emotions and attitudes as appropriate to convey empathy and solidarity with the learner, and thus further promote learner motivation. [2] Fabri et al. [3] described a system for supporting meetings between people in educational virtual environments using quasi face-to-face communication via their character agents. In other cases, the agent is a stand-alone software agent, rather than a persona or image of an actual human. Stone et al. in their COSMO system used a life-like character that teaches how to treat plants [4].

Recent research in student modeling has attempted to allow testing of multiple learner traits in one model [5]. Each of these papers introduces a novel approach towards testing multiple learner traits. Nevertheless, there is not much work on how to make the real-time interaction among different learners, as well as how to interact among different learners with non-verbal information of each learner.

Eye tracking is an important tool for detecting users' attention information and focus on certain content. Applications using eye tracking can be diagnostic or interactive. In diagnostic use, eye movement data provides evidence of the learner's focus of attention over time and can be used to evaluate the usability of interfaces [6] or to guide the decision making of a character agent. For instance, Johnson [7] used eye-tracking to assist character agents during foreign language/culture training. In interactive use of eye tracking for input, a system responds to the observed eye movements, which can serve as an input modality [8].

For the learner's attention information and performance, the ontology base is used to store and communicate learners' data. By using ontology, the knowledge base provides information, both instant and historical, for Empathic tutor virtual class and also the instant communication between agents. Explicit Ontology is easy and flexible to control the character agent.

2 Education Interface Structure

Broadly defined, an intelligent tutoring system is educational software containing an artificial intelligence component. The software tracks students' work, tailoring feedback and hints along the way. By collecting information on a particular student's performance, the software can make inferences about strengths and weaknesses, and can suggest additional work. Our system differs in the way that the interface use real-time interaction with learners resembles the real learning process with teachers) and interact with learners' attention. Figure 2 shows a general system diagram of the system.

In the overview diagram of our system, the character agents interact with learners, exhibiting emotional and social behaviors, as well as providing instructions and guidance to learning content. In addition to input from the user 's text input, input timing, and mouse movement information, etc., feedback about past performance and behavior is also obtained from the student performance knowledge base, allowing agents to react to learners based on that information.

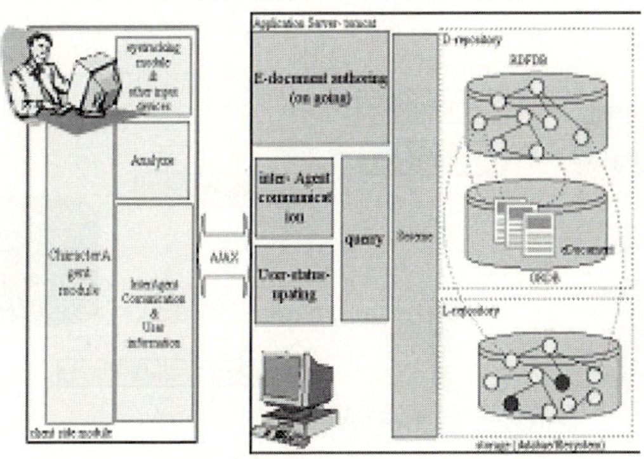

Fig. 2. The system structure

For the multiple learner communication, the system use each learner' character agent to exchange learners' interests, attention information. Each learner has a character agent to represent himself. Besides, each learner's motivation is also linked in the learning process. When another learner has information to share, his agent will come up and pass the information to the other learner. During the interaction among learners, agents detect learner's status and use multiple data channels to collect learner's information such as movements, keyboard inputs, voice, etc.

The functions of character agent can be divided into those involving explicit or implicit outputs from the user, and those involving inputs to the user. In case of outputs from the user, empathy involves functions such as monitoring emotions and interest. In terms of output to the user, empathy involves showing appropriate emotions and providing appropriate feedback concerning the agent's understanding of the users' interests and emotions. Real time feedback from eye movement is detected by eye tracking, and the character agents use this information to interact with learners, exhibiting emotional and social behaviors, as well as providing instructions and guidance to learning content. Information about the learner's past behavior and interests based from their eye tracking data is also available to the agent and supplements the types of feedback and input.

The interface provides the multiple learner environments. The information of each learner is stored with ontology base and the information is sent to character agents. The character agents share the information of the learners according to their learning states. In our learning model, the information from learners is stored in the knowledge base using ontology. Ontology system contains learners' performance data, historical data, and real-time interaction data, etc. in different layers and agents can easily access these types of information and give the feedback to learners.

2.1 Real-Time Eye Gaze Interaction

Figure 3 shows how the character agent reacts to feedback about the learner's status based on eye-tracking information. In this example, the eye tracker collects eye gaze information and the system then infers what the learner is currently attending to. This

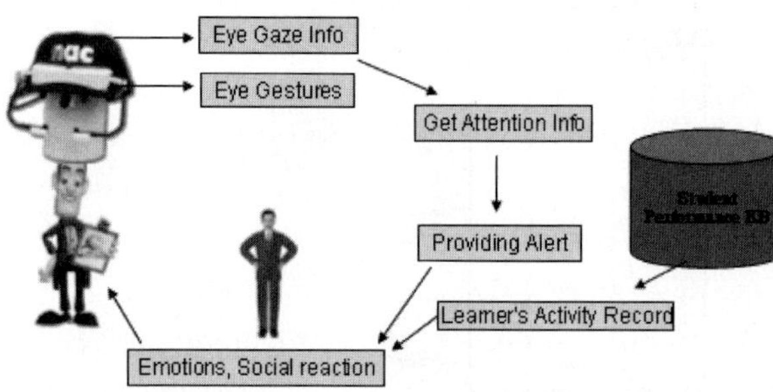

Fig. 3. Real-Time Use of Eye Information in ESA

information is then combined with the learner's activity records, and an appropriate pre-set strategy is selected. The character agent then provides feedback to the learner, tailoring the instructions and emotions (e.g., facial expressions) to the situation.

2.2 Character Agent with Real-Time Interaction

In our system, one or more character agents interact with learners using synthetic speech and visual gestures. The character agents can adjust their behavior in response to learner requests and inferred learner needs. The character agents perform several behaviors including the display of different types of emotion. The agent's emotional response depends on the learner's performance. For instance, an agent shows a happy/satisfied emotion if the learner concentrates on the current study topic. In contrast, if the learner seems to lose concentration, the agent will show mild anger or alert the learner. The agent also shows empathy when the learner is stuck. In general, the character agent interacts between the educational content and the learner. Other tasks of a character agent include explaining the study material and provide hints when necessary, moving around the screen to get or direct user attention, and to highlight information.

The character agents are "eye-aware" because they use eye movements, pupil dilation, and changes in overall eye position to make inferences about the state of the learner and to guide his behavior. After getting learner's eye position information and current area of interest or concentration, the agents can move around to highlight the current learning topic, to attract or focus the learner's attention. For instance, with eye gaze data, agents react to the eye information in real time through actions such as moving to the place being looked at, or by showing the detailed information content for where learners are looking at, etc. ESA can also accommodate multimodal input from the user, including text input, voice input and eye information input, e.g., choosing a hypertext link by gazing at a corresponding point of the screen for longer than a threshold amount of time.

3 Implementation

The system uses server-client communication system to build the multiple learner interface JavaScript and AJAX are used to build the interactive contents which can get real time information and events from learner side. The eye gaze data is stored and transferred using an XML file. The interface uses a two-dimensional graphical window to display character agents and education content. The graphical window interface shows the education content, flash animations, movie clips, and agent behaviors. The Eye Marker eye tracking system was used to detect the eye information and the basic data was collected using 2 cameras facing towards the eye. The learners' information is stored in the form of ontology using RDF files (Figure 4) and the sturdy relationship between different learners can be traced using the knowledge base (Figure 5).

The knowledge base using Ontology is designed and implemented by protégé [9]. Ontology provides the controlled vocabulary for learning domain.

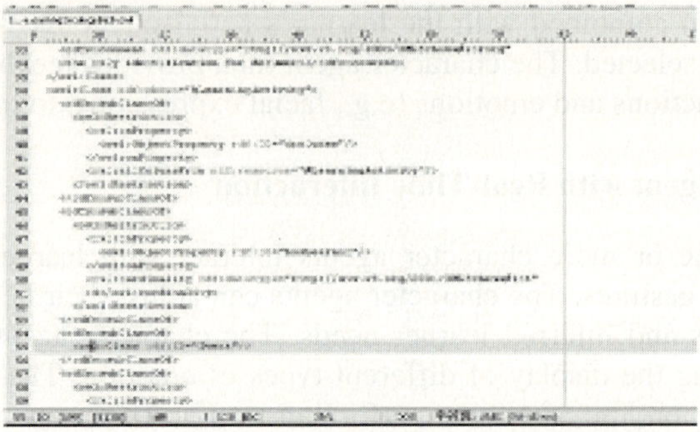

Fig. 4. Learner's Information stored in RDF files

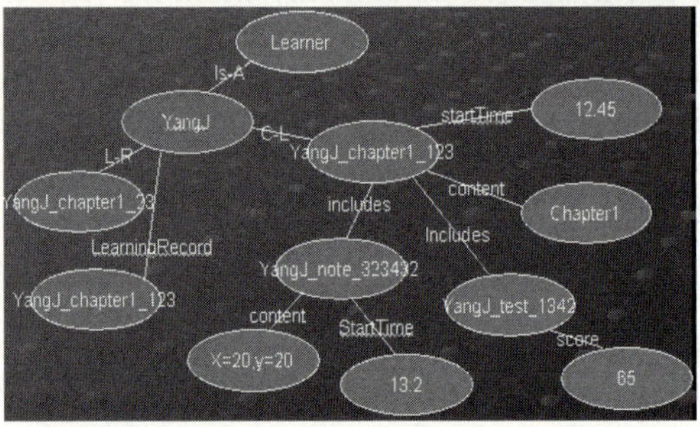

Fig. 5. Relationship among different learners

4 Overall Observations

We carried the informal experiences using the interface after we implement the system. In a usability study, 8 subjects participated using the version of the multiple learners support interface. They learned two series of English lesson. Each learning session lasted about 45 minutes. After the session, the subjects answered questionnaires and commented on the system.

We analyzed the questionnaires and comments from the subjects. Participants felt that the interactions among the learners made them more involved in the learning process. They indicated that the information about how others are learning made them feel more involved in the current learning topic. They also indicated that they found it is convenient to use the character agent in sharing their study information among other learners, which makes them feel comfortable.

Participants in this initial study said that they found the character agents useful and that they listened to the explanation of contents from the agents more carefully than if they had been reading the contents without the supervision and assistance of the character agent. During the learning process, character agents achieve a combination of informational and motivational goals simultaneously during the interaction with learners. For example, hints and suggestions were sometimes used from getting the learners' attention information about what the learner wants to do.

5 Discussions and Future Work

By using the character agents for multiple learners, each learner can get other learning partner's study information, interest, thus they can find the learning partners with similar learning backgrounds and interact with each other. By getting information about learner response, character interfaces can interact with multiple learners more efficiently and provide appropriate feedback. The different versions of character agents are used to observe the different roles in the learning process. In the system, the size, voice, speed of the speech, balloon styles, etc. can be changed to meet different situations. Such agents can provide important aspects of social interaction when the student is working with e-learning content. This type of agent-based interaction can then supplement the beneficial social interactions that occur with human teachers, tutors, and fellow students within a learning community.

Aside from an explicitly educational context, real-time eye gaze interaction can be used in Web navigation. By getting what part of users are more interested in, the system can provide real time feedback to users and help them to get target information more smoothly.

References

1. Palloff, R.M., Pratt, K.: Lessons from the cyberspace classroom: The realities of online teaching. Jossey-Bass, San Francisco (2001)
2. Klein, J., Moon, Y., Picard, R.: This computer responds to learner frustration: Theory, design, and results. Interacting with Computers, 119–140 (2002)
3. Fabri, M., Moore, D., Hobbs, D.: Mediating the Expression of Emotion in Educational Collaborative Virtual Environments: An Experimental Study. Virtual Reality Journal (2004)
4. Stone, B., Lester, J.: Dynamically Sequencing an Animated Pedagogical Agent. In: Proceedings of the 13th National Conference on Artificial Intelligence, Portland, OR, pp. 424–431 (August 1996)
5. Welch, R.E., Frick, T.W.: Computerized adaptive testing in instructional settings. Educational Technology Research and Development 41(3), 47–62 (1993)
6. Duchowski, T.: Eye Tracking Methodology: Theory and Practice. Springer, London, UK (2003)
7. Johnson, W.L., Marsella, S., Mote, H., Vilhjalmsson, S., Narayanan, S., Choi, S.: Language Training System: Supporting the Rapid Acquisition of Foreign Language and Cultural Skills
8. Faraday, P., Sutclie, A.: An empirical study of attending and comprehending multimedia presentations. In: Proceedings of ACM Multimedia, pp. 265–275. ACM Press, Boston, MA (1996)
9. http://protege.stanford.edu

An Empirical Study on Users' Acceptance of Speech Recognition Errors in Text-Messaging

Shuang Xu, Santosh Basapur, Mark Ahlenius, and Deborah Matteo

Human Interaction Research, Motorola Labs, Schaumburg, IL 60196, USA
{shuangxu,sbasapur,mark.ahlenius,deborah.matteo}@motorola.com

Abstract. Although speech recognition technology and voice synthesis systems have become readily available, recognition accuracy remain a serious problem in the design and implementation of voice-based user interfaces. Error correction becomes particularly difficult on mobile devices due to the limited system resources and constrained input methods. This research is aimed to investigate users' acceptance of speech recognition errors in mobile text messaging. Our results show that even though the audio presentation of the text messages does help users understand the speech recognition errors, users indicate low satisfaction when sending or receiving text messages with errors. Specifically, senders show significantly lower acceptance than the receivers due to the concerns of follow-up clarifications and the reflection of the sender's personality. We also find that different types of recognition errors greatly affect users' overall acceptance of the received message.

1 Introduction

Driven by the increasing user needs for staying connected, fueled by new technologies, decreased retail price, and broadband wireless networks, the mobile device market is experiencing an exponential growth. Making mobile devices smaller and more portable brings convenience to access information and entertainment away from the office or home. Today's mobile devices are combining the capabilities of cell phones, text messaging, Internet browsing, information downloading, media playing, digital cameras, and much more. When mobile devices become more compact and capable, the user interface based on small screen and keypad can cause problems. The convenience of an ultra-compact cell phone is particularly offset by the difficulty of using the device to enter text and manipulate data. According to the figures announced by the Mobile Data Association [1], the monthly text messaging in UK broke through the 4 billion barrier for the first time during December 2006. Finding an efficient way to enter text on cell phones is one of the critical usability challenges in mobile industry. Many compelling text input techniques have been previously proposed to address the challenge in mobile interaction design [21, 22, and 41]. However, with the inherent hardware constraints of the cell phone interface, these techniques cannot significantly increase the input speed, reduce cognitive workload, or support hands-free and eyes-free interaction. As speech recognition technology and voice synthesis systems becoming readily available, Voice User Interfaces (VUI) seem to be an inviting solution, but not without problems. Speech recognition

J. Jacko (Ed.): Human-Computer Interaction, Part III, HCII 2007, LNCS 4552, pp. 232–242, 2007.

accuracy remains a serious issue due to the limited memory and processing capabilities available on cell phones, as well as the background noise in typical mobile contexts [3,7]. Furthermore, to correct recognition errors is particularly hard because: (1) the cell phone interfaces make manual selection and typing difficult [32]; (2) users have limited attentional resources in mobile contexts where speech interaction is mostly appreciated [33]; and (3) with the same user and noisy environment, re-speaking does not necessarily increase the recognition accuracy for the second time [15].

In contrast to the significant amount of research effort in the area of voice recognition, less is known about users' acceptance or reaction to the voice recognition errors. An inaccurately recognized speech input often looks contextually ridiculous, but it may phonetically make better sense. For examples, "The baseball game is canceled due to the *under stone* (thunderstorm)", or "Please send the driving directions to *myself all* (my cell phone)." This study investigates users' perception and acceptance of speech recognition errors in the text messages sent or received on cell phones. We aim to examine: (1) which presentation mode (visual, auditory, or visual and auditory) helps the receiver better understand the text messages that have speech recognition errors; (2) whether different types of errors (e.g., misrecognized names, locations, or requested actions) affect users' acceptance; and (3) what are the potential concerns users may have while sending or receiving text messages that contain recognition errors. The understanding of users' acceptance of recognition errors could potentially help us improve their mobile experience by optimizing between users' effort on error correction and the efficiency of their daily communications.

2 Related Work

The following sections explore the previous research with a focus on the three domains: (1) the inherent difficulties in text input on mobile devices and proposed solutions; (2) the current status and problems with speech recognition technology; and (3) the review of error correction techniques available for mobile devices.

2.1 Text Input on Mobile Device

As mobile phones become an indispensable part of our daily life, text input is frequently used to enter notes, contacts, text messages, and other information. Although the computing and imaging capabilities of cell phones have significantly increased, the dominant input interface is still limited to a 12-button keypad and a discrete four-direction joystick. This compact form provides users the portability, but also greatly constrains the efficiency of information entering. On many mobile devices, there has been a need for simple, easy, and intuitive text entry methods. This need becomes particularly urgent due to the increasing usage of text messaging and other integrated functions now available on cell phones. Several compelling interaction techniques have been proposed to address this challenge in mobile interface design. Stylus-based handwriting recognition techniques are widely adopted by mobile devices that support touch screens. For example, Graffiti on Palm requires users to learn and memorize the predefined letter strokes. Motorola's WisdomPen [24] further supports natural handwriting recognition of Chinese and Japanese characters. EdgeWrite [39, 41] proposes a uni-stroke alphabet that enables users to write by moving the stylus along the physical edges and into the corners of a square. EdgeWrite's stroke recognition by detecting the order of the corner-hits can be adopted by other interfaces such as keypad [40]. However, adopting EdgeWrite on cell phones means up to 3 or 4 button clicks for each letter, which makes it slower and less intuitive than the traditional keypad text entry. Thumbwheel provides another solution for text entry on mobile devices with a navigation wheel and a select key [21]. The wheel is used to scroll and highlight a character in a list of characters shown on a display. The select key inputs the high-lighted character. As a text entry method designed for cell phones, Thumbwheel is easy to learn but slow to use, depending on the device used, the text entry rate varies between 3 to 5 words per minute (wpm) [36]. Other solutions have been proposed to reduce the amount of scrolling [5, 22]. But these methods require more attention from the user on the letter selection, therefore do not improve the text entry speed. Prediction algorithms are used on many mobile devices to improve the efficiency of text entry. An effective prediction program can help the user complete the spelling of a word after the first few letters are manually entered. It can also provide candidates for the next word to complete a phrase. An intelligent prediction algorithm is usually based on a language model, statistical correlations among words, context-awareness, and the user's previous text input patterns [10, 11, 14, and 25]. Similar to a successful speech recognition engine, a successful prediction algorithm may require higher computing capability and more memory capacity, which can be costly for portable devices such as cell phones.

The above discussion indicates that many researchers are exploring techniques from different aspects to improve the efficiency of text entry on mobile devices. With the inherent constraints of the cell phone interface, however, it remains challenging to increase the text input speed and reduce the user's cognitive workload. Furthermore, none of the discussed text entry techniques can be useful in a hands-busy or eyes-busy scenario. With the recent improvement of speech recognition technology, voice-based interaction becomes an inviting solution to this challenge, but not without problems.

2.2 Speech Recognition Technology

As mobile devices grow smaller and as in-car computing platforms become more common, traditional interaction methods seem impractical and unsafe in a mobile environment such as driving [3]. Many device makers are turning to solutions that overcome the 12-button keypad constraints. The advancement of speech technology has the potential to unlock the power of the next generation of mobile devices. A large body of research has focused on how to deliver a new level of convenience and accessibility with speech-drive interface on mobile device. Streeter [30] concludes that universality and mobile accessibility are the major advantages of speech-based interfaces. Speech offers a natural interface for tasks such as dialing a number, searching and playing songs, or composing messages. However, the current automatic speech recognition (ASR) technology is not yet satisfactory. One challenge is the limited memory and processing power available on portable devices. ASR typically involves extensive computation. Mobile phones have only modest computing resources and battery power compared with a desktop computer. Network-based speech recognition could be a solution, where the mobile device must connect to the server to use speech recognition. Unfortunately, speech signals transferred over a wireless network tend to be noisy with occasional interruptions. Additionally, network-based solutions are not well-suited for applications requiring manipulation of data that reside on the mobile device itself [23]. Context-awareness has been considered as another solution to improve the speech recognition accuracy based on the knowledge of a user's everyday activities. Most of the flexible and robust systems use probabilistic detection algorithms that require extensive libraries of training data with labeled examples [14]. This requirement makes context-awareness less applicable for mobile devices. The mobile environment also brings difficulties to the utilization of ASR technology, given the higher background noise and user's cognitive load when interacting with the device under a mobile situation.

2.3 Error Correction Methods

Considering the limitations of mobile speech recognition technology and the growing user demands for a speech-driven mobile interface, it becomes a paramount need to make the error correction easier for mobile devices. A large group of researchers have explored the error correction techniques by evaluating the impact of different correction interfaces on users' perception and behavior.

User-initiated error correction methods vary across system platforms but can generally be categorized into four types: (1) re-speaking the misrecognized word or sentence; (2) replacing the wrong word by typing; (3) choosing the correct word from a list of alternatives; and (4) using multi-modal interaction that may support various combinations of the above methods. In their study of error correction with a multi-modal transaction system, Oviatt and VanGent [27] have examined how users adapt and integrate input modes and lexical expressions when correcting recognition errors. Their results indicate that speech is preferred over writing as input method. Users initially try to correct the errors by re-speaking. If the correction by re-speaking fails, they switch to the typing mode [33]. As a preferred repair strategy in human-human conversation [8], re-speaking is believed to be the most intuitive correction method [9,15, and 29]. However, re-speaking does not increase the accuracy of the re-recognition. Some researchers [2,26] suggest increasing the recognition accuracy of re-speaking by eliminating alternatives that are known to be incorrect. They further introduce the correction method as "choosing from a list of alternative words". Sturm and Boves [31] introduce a multi-modal interface used as a web-based form-filling error correction strategy. With a speech overlay that recognizes pen and speech input, the proposed interface allows the user to select the first letter of the target word from a soft-keyboard, after which the utterance is recognized again with a limited language model and lexicon. Their evaluation indicates that this method is perceived to be more effective and less frustrating as the participants feel more in control. Other research [28] also shows that redundant multimodal (speech and manual) input can increase interpretation accuracy on a map interaction task.

Regardless of the significant amount of effort that has been spent on the exploration of error correction techniques, it is often hard to compare these techniques objectively. The performance of correction method is closely related to its implementation, and evaluation criteria often change to suit different applications and domains [4, 20]. Although the multimodal error correction seems to be promising among other techniques, it is more challenging to use it for error correction of speech input on mobile phones. The main reasons are: (1) the constrained cell phone interface makes manual selection and typing more difficult; and (2) users have limited attentional resources in some mobile contexts (such as driving) where speech interaction is mostly appreciated.

3 Proposed Hypotheses

As discussed in the previous sections, text input remains difficult on cell phones. Speech-To-Text, or dictation, provides a potential solution to this problem. However, automatic speech recognition accuracy is not yet satisfactory. Meanwhile, error correction methods are less effective on mobile devices as compared to desktop or laptop computers. While current research has mainly focused on how to improve usability on mobile interfaces with innovative technologies, very few studies have attempted to solve the problem from users' cognition perspective. For example, it is not known whether the misrecognized text message will be sent because it sounds right. Will audible play back improve receivers' comprehension of the text message? We are also interested in what kind of recognition errors are considered as critical by the senders and receivers, and whether using voice recognition in mobile text messaging will affect the satisfaction and perceived effectiveness of users' everyday communication. Our hypotheses are:

Understanding: H1. The audio presentation will improve receivers' understanding of the mis-recognized text message.

We predict that it will be easier for the receivers to identify the recognition errors if the text messages are presented in the auditory mode. A misrecognized voice input often looks strange, but it may make sense phonetically [18]. Some examples are:

[1.Wrong]"How *meant it ticks* do you want me to buy for the white sox game next week?"
[1.Correct] "How *many tickets* do you want me to buy for the white sox game next week?"
[2.Wrong] "We are on our way, will be at *look what the* airport around noon."
[2.Correct] "We are on our way, will be at *LaGuardia* airport around noon"

The errors do not prevent the receivers from understanding the meaning delivered in the messages. Gestalt Imagery theory explains the above observation as the result of human's ability to create an imaged whole during language comprehension [6]. Research in cognitive psychology has reported that phonological activation provides an early source of constraints in visual identification of printed words [35, 42]. It has also been confirmed that semantic context facilitates users' comprehension of aurally presented sentences with lexical ambiguities. [12, 13, 34, 37, and 38].

Acceptance: H2. Different types of errors will affect users' acceptance of sending and receiving text messages that are misrecognized.

Different types of error may play an important role that affects users' acceptance of the text messages containing speech recognition errors. For example, if the sender is requesting particular information or actions from the receiver via a text message, errors in key information can cause confusion and will likely be unacceptable. On the other hand, users may show higher acceptance for errors in general messages where there is no potential cost associated with the misunderstanding of the messages.

Satisfaction: H3. Users' overall satisfaction of sending and receiving voice dictated text messages will be different.

We believe that senders may have higher satisfaction because the voice dictation makes it easier to enter text messages on cell phones. On the other hand, the receivers may have lower satisfaction if the recognition errors hinder their understanding.

4 Methodology

To test our hypotheses, we proposed an application design of dictation. Dictation is a cell phone based application that recognizes a user's speech input and converts the information into text. In this application, a sender uses ASR to dictate a text message on the cell phone. While the message is recognized and displayed on the screen, it will also be read back to the sender via Text-To-Speech (TTS). The sender can send this message if it *sounds* close enough to the original sentence, or correct the errors before sending. When the text message is received, it will be visually displayed and read back to the receiver via TTS as well. A prototype was developed to simulate users' interaction experience with the dictation on a mobile platform.

Participants. A total of eighteen (18) people were recruited to participate in this experiment. They ranged in age from 18 to 59 years. All were fluent speakers of English and reported no visual or auditory disabilities. All participants currently owned a cell phone and have used text messaging before. Participants' experience with mobile text messaging varied from novice to expert, while their experience with voice recognition varied from novice to moderately experienced. Other background information was also collected to ensure a controlled balance in demographic characteristics. All were paid for their participation in this one-hour study.

Experiment Design and Task. The experiment was a within-subject task-based one-on-one interview. There were two sections in the interview. Each participant was told to play the role of a message sender in one section, and the role of a message receiver in the other section. As a sender, the participant was given five predefined and randomized text messages to dictate using the prototype. The "recognized" text message was displayed on the screen with an automatic voice playback via TTS. Participants' reaction to the predefined errors in the message was explored by a set of interview questions. As a receiver, the participant reviewed fifteen individual text messages on the prototype, with predefined recognition errors. Among these messages, five were presented as audio playbacks only; five were presented in text only; the other five were presented simultaneously in text and audio modes. The task sequence was randomized as shown in Table 1:

Table 1. Participants Assignment and Task Sections

Participants Assignment			**Task Section 1**	**Task Section 2**
18~29 yrs	30~39 yrs	40~59 yrs		
S#2(M)	S#8(F)	S#3(M)	Sender	Receiver-Audio, Text, A+T
S#1(F)	S#4(M)	S#14(F)	Sender	Receiver-Text, A+T, Audio
S#7(M)	S#16(F)	S#9(M)	Sender	Receiver-A+T, Audio, Text
S#5(F)	S#6(M)	S#15(F)	Receiver-Audio, Text, A+T	Sender
S#10(M)*	S#17(F)	S#13(M)	Receiver-Text, A+T, Audio	Sender
S#12(F)	S#11(M)	S#18(F)	Receiver-A+T ,Audio, Text	Sender

*S#10 did not show up in the study.

Independent Variable and Dependent Variables. For senders, we examined how different types of recognition errors affect their acceptance. For receivers, we examined (1) how presentation modes affect their understanding of the misrecognized messages; and (2) whether error types affect their acceptance of the received messages. Overall satisfaction of participants' task experience was measured for both senders and receivers, separately. The independent and dependent variables in this study are listed in Table 2:

Table 2. Independent and Dependent Variables

	Independent Variables	Dependent Variables
Senders	1. Error Types: Location, Requested Action, Event/occasion, Requested information, Names.	1. Users' Acceptance 2. Users' Satisfaction
Receivers	1. Presentation Modes: Audio, Text, Audio + Text 2. Error Types: Location, Requested Action, Event/occasion, Requested information, Names.	1. Users' Understanding 2. Users' Acceptance 3. Users' Satisfaction

Senders' error acceptance was measured by their answers to the question "*Will you send this message without correction?*" in the interview. After all errors in each message were exposed by the experimenter, receivers' error acceptance was measured by the question "*Are you OK with receiving this message?*" Receivers' understanding performance was defined as the percentage of successfully corrected errors out of the total predefined errors in the received message. A System Usability Score (SUS) questionnaire was given after each task section to collect participants' overall satisfaction of their task experience.

Procedures. Each subject was asked to sign a consent form before participation. Upon their completion of a background questionnaire, the experimenter explained the concept of dictation and how participants were expected to interact with the prototype. In the Sender task section, the participant was told to read out the given text message loud and clear. Although the recognition errors were predefined in the program, we allowed participants to believe that their speech input was recognized by the prototype. Therefore, senders' reaction to the errors was collected objectively after each message. In the Receiver task section, participants were told that all the received messages were entered by the sender via voice dictation. These messages may or may not have recognition errors. Three sets of messages, five in each, were used for the three presentation modes, respectively. Participants' understanding of the received messages was examined before the experimenter identified the errors, followed by a discussion of their perception and acceptance of the errors. Participants were asked to fill out a satisfaction questionnaire at the end of each task section. All interview sections were recorded by a video camera.

5 Results and Discussion

As previously discussed, the dependent variables in this experiment are: Senders' Error Acceptance and Satisfaction; and Receivers' Understanding, Error Acceptance, and Satisfaction. Each of our result measures was analyzed using a single-factor

ANOVA. F and P values are reported for each result to indicate its statistical significance. The following sections discuss the results for each of the dependent variables as they relate to our hypotheses.

Understanding. Receivers' understanding of the misrecognized messages was measured by the number of corrected errors divided by the number of total errors contained in each message. Hypothesis H1 was supported by the results of ANOVA, which indicates the audio presentation did significantly improve users' understanding of the received text messages ($F_{2,48}$=10.33, p<.001), as shown in Fig. 1a. Age was not one of the independent variables in this study, but was examined for precaution. Fig. 1b shows that users' age has an impact on their understanding of the errors. Compared to the younger groups who also had more experience with mobile text messaging, the older generation had a lower understanding performance ($F_{2,48}$=5.24, p=.009).

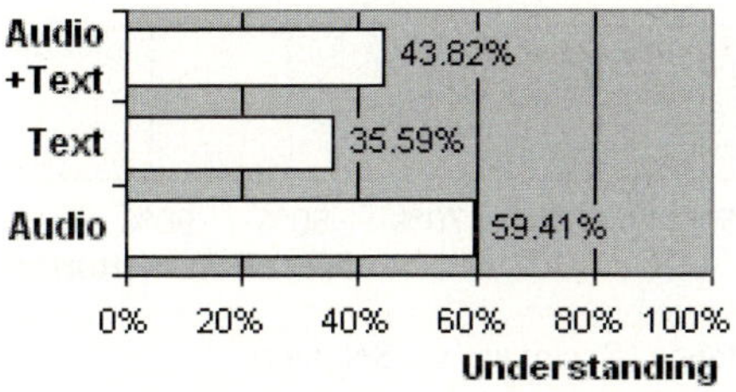

Fig. 1a. Presentation Modes vs. Understanding

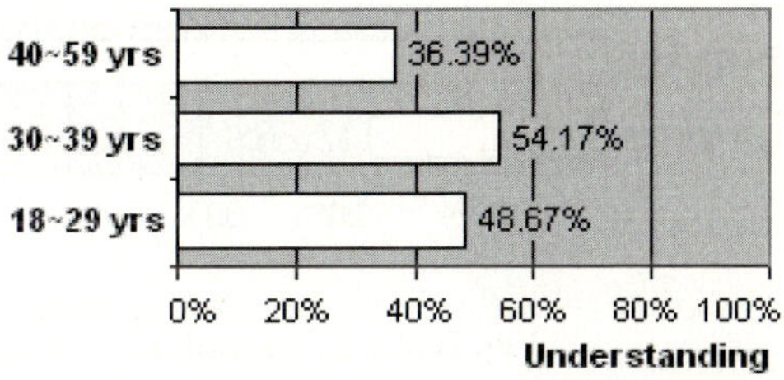

Fig. 1b. Age Groups vs. Understanding

The findings are consistent with many research studies in cognitive psychology. Swinney confirms that prior semantic context facilitates participants' comprehension of aurally presented sentences that contain lexical ambiguities [34]. Luo, Johnson, and Gallo [19] find phonological recoding occurs automatically and mediates lexical access in visual word recognition and reading. Other studies [16, 17] reveal that semantic processing was evident before the acoustic signal was sufficient to identify the words uniquely. These findings indicate that semantic integration can begin to operate with incomplete or inaccurate information.

Acceptance. In our study, senders' error acceptance was measured by their answers to the interview question "Will you send this message without correction?" Receivers' error acceptance was measured by the question "Are you OK with receiving such a message?" after the errors in each message were identified by the experimenter. Hypotheses H2 concerned about the relation between different error types and users' acceptance. As shown in Fig. 2a and 2b, the occurrence of different kinds of errors (see Table 2) had a significant impact on senders' ($F_{4,80}$=3.60, p=.010). and receivers' ($F_{4,250}$=8.92, p<.001) acceptance. Senders showed much lower tolerance for errors in the requested actions and person's names, among the five controlled error types. Receivers indicated a different pattern in acceptance, where they showed significantly higher acceptance for general informative messages regarding upcoming events and occasions. H2 was thus supported by the findings.

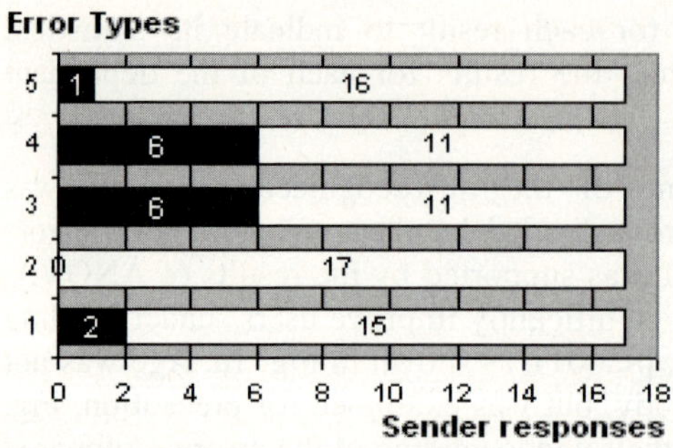

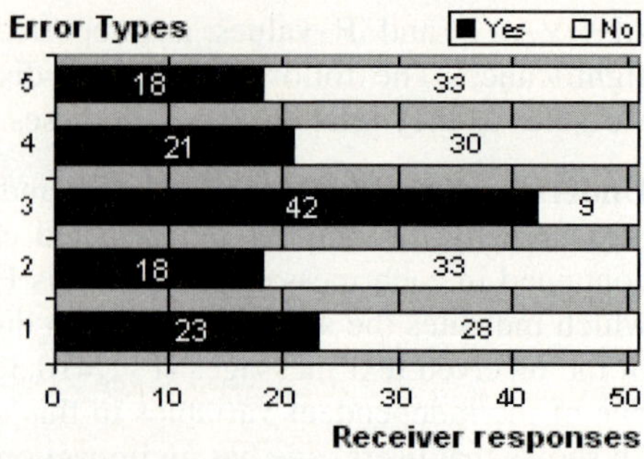

1.Location; **2.**Requested Action; **3.**Event/Occasion; **4.**Requested information; **5.**Person's Name

Fig. 2a. Senders' Error Acceptance

Fig. 2b. Receivers' Error Acceptance

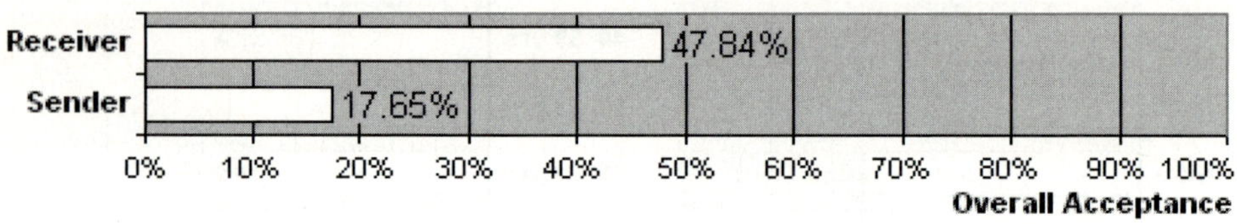

Fig. 2c. Users' Overall Error Acceptance (Receivers vs. Senders)

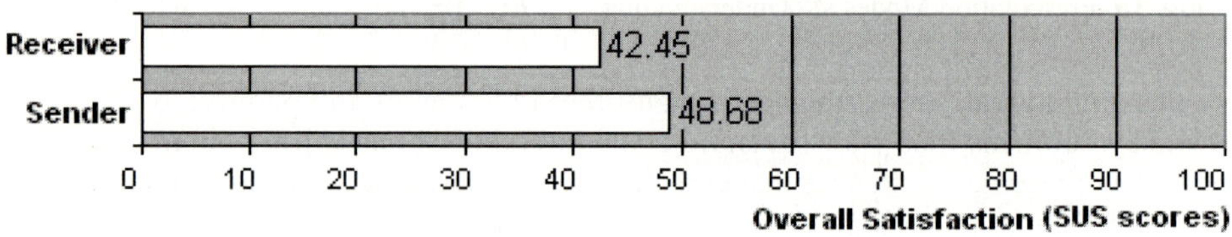

Fig. 3. Users' Overall Satisfaction (Receivers vs. Senders)

A significant difference ($F_{1,66}$=30.01, p<.001) between senders' and receivers' overall acceptance was reported in this study, as shown in Fig.2c. This finding was confirmed by users' debriefing comments during the interview. When sending text messages containing recognition errors, most users were concerned about their self-reflection, as well as the communications needed afterwards to clarify the confusion. As the receiver of misrecognized messages, users gradually developed deciphering skills based on phonetic similarity, common sense, and context of the messages.

Satisfaction. System Usability Scores (SUS) were used in this study to examine users' overall satisfaction with their task experience. As we predicted, the senders reported slightly higher satisfaction than the receivers. A plausible explanation is that senders' dissatisfaction with the inaccurate voice recognition was partially countered by the perceived convenience of entering text with speech input. However, the difference was not significant enough ($F_{1,66}$=1.06, p=.308) to reject the null hypothesis, therefore H3 was not supported by our findings (see results in Fig.3).

An affinity diagram was used in the data analysis of user's comments. Over 1000 incidents were collected and categorized. Some preliminary findings are:

- Users are concerned about the hidden cost associated with miscommunication (e.g., taking the wrong actions, additional time and effort spent on error-decoding, not being able to clarify, etc.)
- Some users showed higher error acceptance for urgent messages so to get the info. out as soon as possible, others showed lower acceptance because they believed words must be accurate in an important message.
- Critical information in a message must be error-free (e.g., when, where, what, who.)
- Users are willing to adapt to the voice recognition system for effective use (e.g., keep messages short and concise, avoid using words that often cause problems, train the voice recognition system to accurately pick up frequently used names, etc.)
- Personality traits and the familiarity between the sender and receiver also affect users' error acceptance in mobile messaging.
- Transfer of training does not work between identification of typing errors and identification of speech recognition errors.

6 Conclusions

This study investigated users' acceptance of speech recognition errors in text messaging. We hypothesized that audio presentation of the misrecognized message would improve receivers' understanding because of the phonetic similarity. We also predicted that different types of errors could affect users' acceptance of the message. Our findings revealed that the audio + text presentation was preferred by most of the users, and the audio playback significantly improved users' understanding. Users indicated overall low acceptance for errors in text messaging. The major concern was the consequence of misunderstanding: a confusing message may trigger a series of follow-up phone calls, which defeats the purpose of quick communication via SMS. This also explains why users showed much lower tolerance for errors in messages that elicit actions or information. In this within-subject study, interestingly, participants showed significantly lower acceptance as a message sender than as a receiver. Although the senders would like to use voice recognition to dictate text messages for convenience and safety concerns, they preferred to correct errors before sending the messages to ensure a clear and efficient communication. In conclusion, our hypotheses were supported by the results from this study. Based on the understanding of users' acceptance and reaction to recognition errors in mobile text messaging, we expect to develop guidelines for the interaction design of dictation to improve its effectiveness as a text input method on mobile devices. However, this study is only a first step towards this direction. Future work should further explore how to control error occurrence in critical information, and how to make error correction easier via a multi-modal interface.

References

Selected References (full references are available at: http://www.geocities.com/shuangxu/HCII2007_Xu.pdf)

3. Alewine, N., Ruback, H., Deligne, S.: Pervasive Speech Recognition. IEEE Pervasive Computing 3(4), 78–81 (2004)
6. Bell, N.: Gestalt imagery: A critical factor in language comprehension. Annals of Dyslexia 41, 246–260 (1991)
13. Frost, R., Kampf, M.: Phonetic recoding of phonological ambiguous printed words. Journal of Experimental Psychology: Learning, Memory, and Cognition 19, 23–33 (1993)
15. Larson, K., Mowatt, D.: Speech error correction: the story of the alternates list. International Journal of Speech Technology, 6(2), 183–194. Memory, and Cognition, 24, 573–592 (2003)
18. Lieberman, H., Faaborg, A., Daher, W., Espinosa, J.: How to wreck a nice beach you sing calm incense. In: Proceedings of Intelligent User Interface'05, pp. 278–280 (2005)
22. MacKenzie, I.S., Soukoreff, R.W.: Text entry for mobile computing: Models and methods, theory and practice. Human-Computer Interaction 17, 147–198 (2002)
27. Oviatt, S., VanGent, R.: Error resolution during multimodal human-computer interaction. In: Proceedings of International Conference on Spoken Language Process (ICSLP'96), pp. 204–207 (1996)
33. Suhm, B., Myers, B., Waibel, A.: Multimodal error correction for speech user interfaces. ACM Transactions on Computer-Human Interaction 8(1), 60–98 (2001)
37. Van Orden, G.C.: A ROWS is a ROSE: Spelling, sound, and reading. Memory and Cognition 15, 181–198 (1987)

Flexible Multi-modal Interaction Technologies and User Interface Specially Designed for Chinese Car Infotainment System

Chen Yang, Nan Chen, Peng-fei Zhang, and Zhen Jiao

Corporate Technology, Siemens Ltd. China, 7 Wangjing Zhonghuan Nanlu, Beijing 100102 P.R. China
{cy.yang,nan.chen,pengfei.zhang,zhen.jiao}@siemens.com

Abstract. In this paper, we present a car infotainment prototype system which aims to develop an advanced concept for intuitive use-centered human machine interface especially designed for Chinese users. In technology aspect, we apply several innovative interaction technologies (most of which are Chinese language specific) to make interaction easier, more convenient and effective. Speech interaction design is especially elaborated in this aspect. While in user interface design aspect, we systematically conducted user investigation to give enlightening clue for better designing logic flow of the system and aesthetic design. Under user-centered design principle and with deep understanding of different interaction technologies, our prototype system makes transition from different interaction modalities quite flexible. Preliminary performance evaluation shows that our system attains high user acceptance.

Keywords: Car Infotainment, Chinese ASR, Chinese TTS, Chinese NLU, Chinese Finger Stroke Recognition, Melody Recognition, User-centered design.

1 Introduction

With the rapid development of China economy, the number of automobiles possessed by common Chinese household is increasing dramatically. The platform which includes navigation, mobile communication, entertainment, and information and services is usually called car infotainment system. With car infotainment system, car nowadays becomes not only a simple transportation vehicle, but more like an integrated information space with multiple functionalities. According to Strategy Analytics, a market analysis company, the China market of car infotainment alone will be worth 4 billion US dollars by the year of 2013. It is thus evident that car information system will be a hot competition focus that can differentiate different vehicles and consequently influencing customers' purchase decision.

As car infotainment system now becomes a complex information space with multiple functionalities. How to design a human-machine interface which can make the operation more effective and intuitive and user-friendly while keeping safety as the top priority is quite important. As we know, car environment is a hands-busy and eyes-busy scenario where drivers should concentrate on the road condition from time

J. Jacko (Ed.): Human-Computer Interaction, Part III, HCII 2007, LNCS 4552, pp. 243–252, 2007.

and time, with hands holding on the steering wheel. Safety is always the major concern under such a scenario. However, usually there is only a limited number of hardware buttons in a car panel. In order to use a function from car infotainment system, a series of buttons need to be pressed. It seems a touch-screen would be better than buttons alone under such circumstances. Even though buttons and touch screen have the highest interaction accuracy, they are quite dangerous to use because they may keep drivers' eyes from the road and drivers' hands away from the steering wheel. Speech interaction provides a better way to communicate with the machine in such a case since it is hand-and-eye free interaction approach.

Chinese character is ideographic, which is quite different from western alphabet system. Chinese input is a difficult issue even if there is a keyboard. Chinese speech recognition and handwriting are known as two simpler ways to input Chinese especially under such a keyboardless scenario. However, each technology has its own pro-and-cons. At present, speech is not robustness enough to noise, and its recognition accuracy is not as high as that of handwriting recognition. However, it is quite suitable for a hands-busy and eyes-busy scenario. Handwriting is robust to environment noise and has a higher accuracy. However, it is not convenient to use when users' hands and eyes are busy. Therefore smooth transition across different interaction modes need to be carefully designed to make the system easier and more effective to use.

Research work has been conducted to study the user interface design related to car infotainment system [1],[2],[3]. However, there is no systematic work done especially for Chinese user groups. In this paper, we report a car infotainment prototype especially designed for Chinese users. This paper is organized as follows: First we describe the functionalities in our prototype system and the underlying concepts. Then, in section 3, interaction technologies background is introduced. Detailed human machine interface design, including speech interaction design is elaborated in section 4, followed by a performance evaluation in Section 5.

2 Function Descriptions and Underlying Concept

Fig. 1 shows our car infotainment prototype system. As to manual interaction, there are a total of 16 hardware buttons, four of which are used as shortcut keys. Touch screen is used in our prototype system.

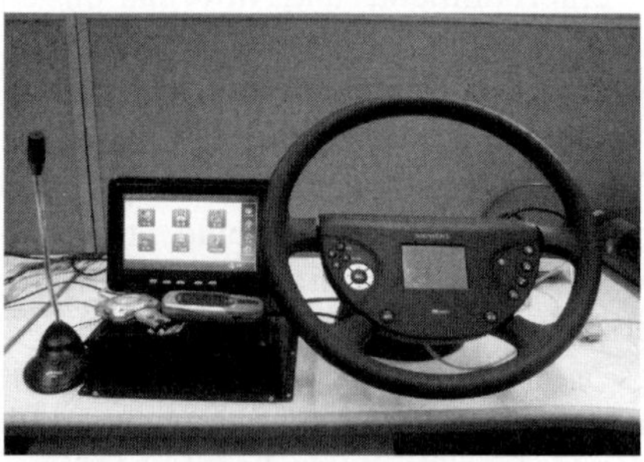

Fig. 1. System appearance

Fig. 2. Main menu

Our car infotainment system has six main functions. It includes GPS navigation, communication (telephone and short message service), entertainment (media player function), personal assistance, car configuration, and network. The main menu of the system is shown in Fig. 2.

With the highly-demanded trend of seamless connection with customer electronics, in communication module, mobile phone can be connected into the platform to place or receive a phone call and receive short message. In entertainment module, there is a function called "My MP3", where external mp3 devices can be plugged into this system and use all the provided interaction technologies to select the songs stored in the mp3 device.

Our system supports multiple interaction modes: all menu items can be speech controlled. In navigation module, Chinese ASR can be used to input the target address by just speaking where to go. As another option, the destination can also be input by our Chinese Finger Stroke recognition engine. In communication module, name dialing is at users' choice when placing a phone call. In the meanwhile, when a short message is received, Chinese TTS engine will read the content of the short message aloud. In entertainment module, users can either directly speak the song's name or hum a little beats of a song to select their favorite songs

3 Multimodal Interaction Technologies

Multimodal interaction technologies are used in our car infotainment prototype system, including buttons, touch-screen, speech, handwriting, and melody recognition. This section will give some introduction on the interaction technologies used in our prototype system.

3.1 Speech Technology

Automatic Speech Recognition
Automatic Speech Recognition (short for ASR) is a technology which can translate the input human sound into a text string [4]. Fig.3 shows the system diagram of an ASR system.

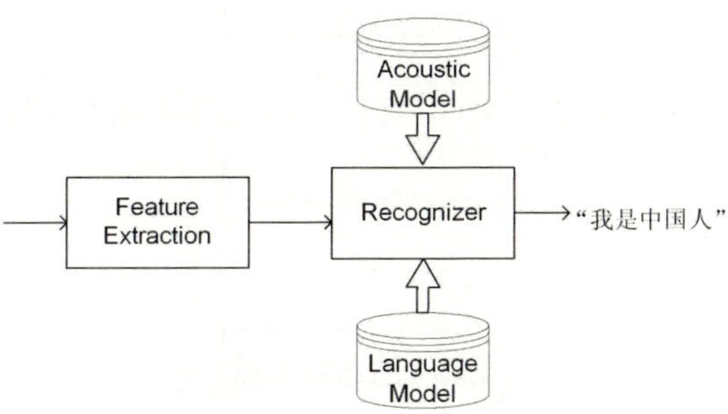

Fig. 3. System diagram of ASR

Given unknown speech, the recognizer can decode the input wave stream into text string with the help of pre-trained acoustic model and language model. Chinese spoken language is monosyllabic and tonal, which is quite different from western languages. Special care should be taken in order to get an acceptable recognition result. While acoustic model part has no much difference from that of other languages, language model part is quite language specific.

Text-to-Speech
Text-to-Speech (short for TTS) is a technology that can generate human-like speech sound according the input text string [4]. Fig. 4 shows the system diagram of a TTS system. There are three modules in a TTS system, that is: text analysis, prosody prediction, and waveform generation. Significant differences of Chinese TTS from other language TTS lie in the first two modules, i.e., TTS preprocessing.

Chinese Natural Language Understanding
Natural Language Understanding (short for NLU) is a technology that can parse the text string and get the meaning or intention of the text string [4],[5]. Speech recognition can only transcribe the input wave stream into text string. With NLU, machine can understand the intention of the text, and corresponding action will be operated. The core of understanding is the representation of semantics. Therefore, this technology is highly language dependent.

3.2 Chinese Finger Stroke Recognition

Most Chinese handwriting recognition is based on character structure [6],[7],[8]. Siemens Limited. China User Interface Design group proposed a new finger stroke recognition system which breaks out of such restriction since the character is now recognized by the stroke orders [9]. In this way, strokes are allowed to be overlapped to each other, which is quite useful when the input pad is too small to input the whole structure of a Chinese character. Fig. 5 shows a simple system diagram of finger stroke recognition engine used in our prototype system.

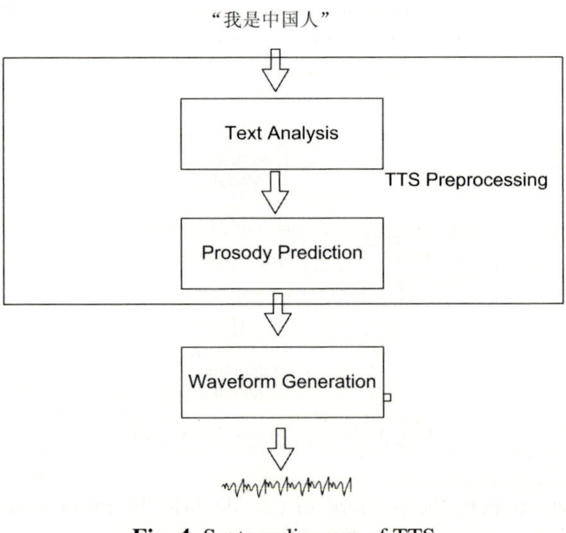

Fig. 4. System diagram of TTS

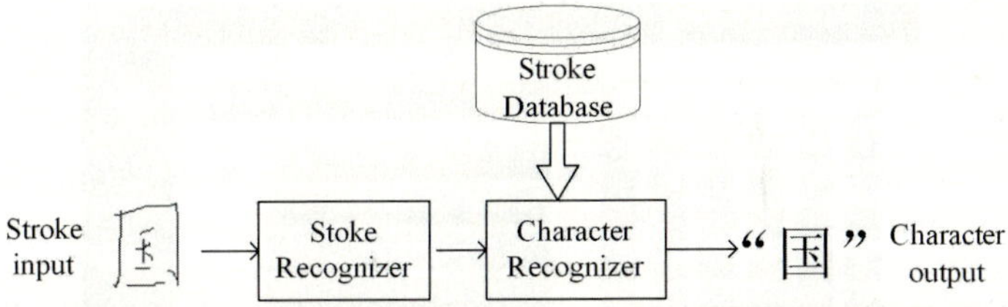

Fig. 5. System diagram of Chinese Finger Stroke Recognition

3.3 Melody Recognition

Music retrieval using the name of a song or a singer is quite familiar to us. However, quite often, we may often encounter such a scenario: you are quite familiar some rhythm and beats of the song, but you can not remember exactly what the song's name is. With the technology named melody recognition, you can easily perform such a task. Typical melody recognition steps include [10],[11].

1. Feature extraction: pitch contour of the music segment is extracted and transcribed as string symbols to be used in following search engine.
2. Search engine: String match is used to find the best alignment between the transcribed music segment and the pre-stored melody database.

4 Human Machine Interface Design

4.1 User Interface Design

In this section, we follow User-centered Design (UCD) procedure to study the Chinese users' typical requirements on the infotainment system, especially the navigation system. The UCD lifecycle starts with users' requirements collection and analysis. The analysis results are used for functional modeling and design. After the prototype is developed, usability evaluation is conducted to collect the users' feedback for the iterative redesign [12].

Chinese drivers have typical driving context, i.e., traffic jam, rules-breaking conditions, overwhelmed traffic indications and signs etc. The specific context may result in typical driving behaviors and requirements from Chinese users. Three main methodologies are used for user investigation: interview, field observation, and focus group. First, thirty drivers were invited to a preliminary short interview to get an overview of the typical driving tasks and their characteristics. Every interview took about thirty minutes. After the interviews, three representative routes in three representative driving contexts (weekday, weekend, and holiday) are selected for the tasks in the field observation, in which twenty filed observations were schemed to discover the habitual interaction language and timing of Chinese users. Then, eight focus groups were held to define function features of the infotainment system and to organize the navigation process.

Fig. 6. Tab label in destination input interface

After conducting systematic user requirement investigation and qualitative and quantitative analysis, we have following interesting findings from Chinese users:

1. Most of the participants mentioned a bad user experience in searching a function in a complicated user interface. They prefer a simple interaction flow
2. Most Chinese users prefer bright color and large icon
3. Most participants think speech is a convenient interaction technology especially in car environment. However they quite concern about the recognition rate. They hope there will be appropriate way to correct the errors when recognition mistakes occur.

Based on the findings, following design strategies are adopted:

1. To make the interaction flow simpler,
1) A tab label is used in destination input interface, where different search approaches, for a instance, all addresses, point of interest (POI), archived addresses are opened by pressing on the their corresponding labels. In this way, traditional vertical interaction depth is smartly transformed to horizontal one. The interface is shown in Fig. 6.
2) Four frequently used functions are put in shortcut key button positions as shown in Fig. 2. This is to ensure to quickly transition from one function to another function
3) Four software buttons are placed in each interface. The text changes according to the interaction result without adding extra interaction levels. For example, in real-time navigation interfaces, the text contents of certain software buttons change at different navigation status, such as at the beginning, in the middle, and at the end of the navigation.

   With all of these considerations, the interaction depth can be controlled within three levels, thus guaranteeing the simple work flow. In this way, users can access to their desired function more quickly.
2. To make the usage of the interface more easily,
1) We design the interaction flow according to the logic from user's perspective. Fore example, in navigation function, the users' main aim is to input a destination and then quickly begin the real navigation function.
2) Self-explaining name of each menu and buttons are carefully chosen to user to understand their functions more easily.

3) Same functions are put in the same position of each interface for quick learning of the system. For example, "return" buttons are always put in the last position of four soft key buttons in each interface. In this way, users can find their desired function more quickly.

In aesthetic design, we use large symbolic icons and bright colors according to the result of user investigation. In order to satisfy Chinese users' preference of personalization interface, we have a theme-changing configuration function for users to change the style of the system outlook in our prototype system.

4.2 Speech Interaction Design

Since speech recognition and natural language understanding technologies do not have as high accuracy as keyboard or buttons, whether the interface with speech technology is effective enough is largely dependent on how well the speech interaction is designed [4]. During the design process, the strength and weakness of speech technologies should be fully aware. Following are the highlights of speech interaction design in our prototype system:

1. Speech is enabled by push-to-talk button and the activation button is put in the car steering wheel to facilitate the use of speech technology;
2. No further confirmation is needed when using the speech function in order to reduce the disturbance to drivers;
3. Speaker-independent technology is utilized to avoid the annoying training process before usage of speech function;
4. Isolated speech recognition grammar is used in command and control scenario to ensure high recognition rate;
5. Dynamic vocabulary and grammar are exploited in different interfaces to enhance the speech recognition rate of each interface;
6. Each speech-enabled icon has a text attached for user easy to know what command should utter;
7. Differentiate the speech-enabled and speech-disabled commands by using different colors;
8. Synthesized speech is used to give feedback of users' each action and to prompt guidance information during navigation;
9. NLU technology is supported in entertainment module to make this interface more user-friendly since recognition accuracy is not crucial to user experience in this function. Instead, by using this technology, users can communicate with the machine with some degree of freedom;
10. Error handling strategy: since speech recognition is not always correct, it is important to have error handling strategy. The most direct way is to support different modes of interaction. In our prototype system, touch screen alone can perform all of the functionalities. And hardware buttons can accomplish frequently used operations. Therefore, if some recognition mistakes occur, users can easily turn back to the previous interface to make corresponding corrections.

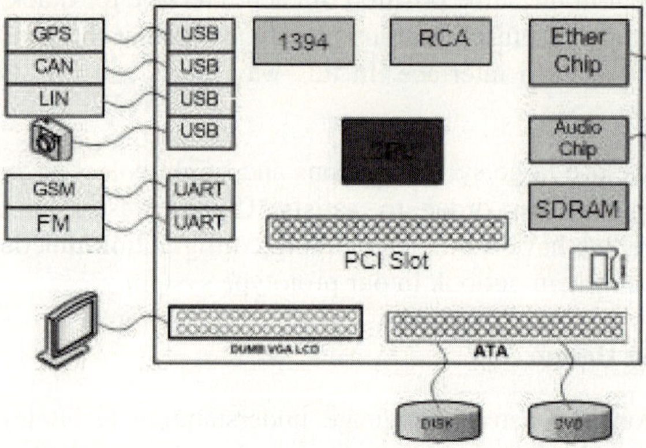

Fig. 7. Hardware layout of the car PC

4.3 Hardware Platform

Our car infotainment prototype system runs on car PC. The motherboard used is VIA EPIA M-Series. Fig. 7 shows hardware layout of the car PC. The fanless VIA Eden processors runs at speeds of up to 1GHz. The motherboard features the VIA CLE266 chipset with embedded MPEG-2 accelerator and integrated 2D/3D graphics core, which ensure smooth DVD playback and a rich overall entertainment experience. The latest high-speed connectivity is supported with IEEE 1394 and USB2.0. This car pc also supports S-Video and RCA TV-Out and 10/100 Ethernet.

5 Evaluation

Preliminary inspection was conducted to test the usability of our car infotainment system prototype. Six people, 3 males and 3 females, participated in the inspection. Their ages range from 24 to 35. The evaluation consists of five dimensions: learnability, efficiency, efficiency, error tolerance and overall satisfaction. Results are shown in Table 1.

Table 1. Performance evaluation

learnability	efficiency	efficiency	error tolerance	overall satisfaction
4.7	4.3	5.0	4.0	4.3

Performance evaluation shows that our system attains high user acceptance. Comprehensive usability test regarding functionalities, interaction and objective satisfaction will be conducted in the next step to further refine the prototype system.

6 Summary

In this paper, we have reported a car information prototype system especially designed for Chinese users. Three main functions, i.e., navigation, entertain, and communication, have been realized in our prototype system at present. With the profound understanding of different interaction technologies (their strength and weakness), innovative multi-modal interaction technologies including Chinese ASR, Chinese TTS, Chinese NLU, Melody recognition, and Chinese Finger Stroke Recognition have been organically applied in the system to make the interaction more effectively and user friendly. In user interface design, we follow the user centered design principle and design the user interface which especially caters for Chinese users' preference. Preliminary evaluation shows that our system has a better user acceptance. Systematic usability test will be conducted in the next step to further refine the prototype system.

Acknowledgement. The authors would like to thank CT IC5 and IC7 of Siemens AG for their great support for this project. The users' requirement analysis is a part of automotive cockpit research work from Ms. Barbara KNAPP. Thanks also go to Junyan CHEN, Rui YANG, Jian NI, Liang ZHANG, Yi-fei Xu, and Heng WANG who contributed a lot to this project. We would also like to thank Wei ZHOU and Ming-hui TIAN for their kind support, and Xiangang QIN and Yanghua LIU for their encouragement and fruitful discussion.

References

1. Ekholm, A.: personal and ubiquitous computing, 6, 153–154 (2002)
2. Akesson, K.P, Nilsson, A.: Designing leisure applications for mundane car-commute. personal and ubiquitous computing 6, 176–187 (2002)
3. Test, J., Fogg, B.J., Maile, M.: CommuterNews: A Prototype of Persuasive In-Car Entertainment. In: Proc. of CHI 2000, pp. 24–25 (2000)
4. Huang, X.-D., Acero, A., Hon, H.-W.: Spoken language Processing - A guide to theory, algorithm and system development. Prentice-Hall, Englewood Cliffs (2001)
5. Allen, J.: Natural Language Understanding, 2nd edn. The Benjamin/Cummings Publishing Company, Menlo Park, CA (1995)
6. Shi, D., Damper, R.I., Gunn, S.R.: Offline Handwritten Chinese Character Recognition by Radical Decomposition. ACM Transactions on Asian Language Information Processing 2(1), 27–48 (2003)
7. Liu, C.L, Jaeger, S., Nakagawa, M.: Online Recognition of Chinese Characters: The State-of-the-Art. IEEE Transactions on Pattern Analysis and Machine Intelligence 26(2), 198–213 (2004)
8. Leung, W.N., Cheng, K.S: A Stroke-order Free Chinese Handwriting Input System Based On Relative Stroke Positions and Back-Propagation Networks. In: Proceedings of the 1996 ACM symposium on Applied Computing, pp. 22–27 (1996)
9. Cao, X.: Chinese Handwriting Recognition Based on Finger Stroke Order, China patent, patent no, 200510066546.8

10. Pardo, B., Birmingham, W.: Query by Humming: How good can it get?. In: Workshop on Music Information Retrieval, SIGIR (2003)
11. Kosui, N., Nishihara, Y., Yamamuro, M., Kushima, K.: A practical query-by-humming system for a large music database. In: Proceedings of the eighth ACM international conference on Multimedia, pp. 333–342 (2000)
12. Vredenburg, K., Isensee, S., Righi, C.: User Centered Design: An Integrated Approach. Prentice-Hall, Inc (2003)

A Spoken Dialogue System Based on Keyword Spotting Technology

Pengyuan Zhang, Qingwei Zhao, and Yonghong Yan

ThinkIT Speech Lab, Institute of Acoustics, Chinese Academy of Sciences
Beijing 100080, P.R. China
{pzhang,qzhao,yyan}@hccl.ioa.ac.cn

Abstract. In this paper, a keyword spotting based dialogue system is described. It is critical to understand user's requests accurately in a dialogue system. But the performance of large vocabulary continuous speech recognition (LVCSR) system is far from perfect, especially for spontaneous speech. In this work, an improved keyword spotting scheme is adopted instead. A fuzzy search algorithm is proposed to extract keyword hypotheses from syllable confusion networks (CN). CNs are linear and naturally suitable for indexing. To accelerate search process, CNs are pruned to feasible sizes. Furthermore, we enhance the discriminability of confidence measure by applying entropy information to the posterior probability of word hypotheses. On mandarin conversational telephone speech (CTS), the proposed algorithms obtained a 4.7% relative equal error rate (EER) reduction.

1 Introduction

Research on spoken dialogue systems and their real-world applications have attracted increased attention in recent years [1]. For spoken dialogue applications it is critical to understand the user's requests accurately, since the rest of the system acts based on this recognized result [2]. On the other hand, the performance of current large vocabulary continuous speech recognition (LVCSR) systems is far from perfect, especially for spontaneous speech. In this paper, we focus our interest on the study of recognition strategy obtained during the utterance understanding process. A keyword-based approach is employed to understand spontaneous speech.

The task of keyword spotting is to detect a set of required words in the input continuous speech [3]. It is desirable to achieve the highest possible keyword recognition rate, while minimizing the number of false keyword insertions. A syllable confusion matrix (SCM) is adopted to extract keywords in this paper. The quality of SCM has an obvious influence on the performance of keyword spotting. Based on traditional approaches, we propose an improved SCM. Furthermore, we enhance the discriminability of confidence measure by applying entropy information to the posterior probability of word hypotheses.

The remainder of the paper is structured as follows: Section 2 presents an overview of system framework. In section 3, we introduce the keyword spotting scheme. Experiment results are presented in section 4 followed by the conclusions in Section 5.

J. Jacko (Ed.): Human-Computer Interaction, Part III, HCII 2007, LNCS 4552, pp. 253–261, 2007.

2 Overview

The basic architecture of a spoken dialogue system is illustrated in Fig. 1 [4]. Generally, a spoken dialog system consists of two parts: utterance understanding part and utterance generation part. When receiving a user utterance, the system behaves as follows [5]:

(1) The keyword spotting system receives a user utterance and outputs keyword hypotheses.

(2) The keyword hypotheses are passed to the semantic analyzer. Semantic analyses are performed to convert them into a meaning representation, often called a semantic frame.

(3) The discourse understanding component receives the semantic frame, refers to the current dialogue state, and updates the dialogue state.

(4) The dialogue manager refers to the updated dialogue state, determines the next utterance, and outputs the next content to be delivered as a semantic frame. The dialogue state is updated at the same time so that it contains the content of system utterances.

(5) The surface generator builds the system response, typically as a surface expression (text sentence).

(6) The speech synthesizer generates the system voice using a text-to-speech (TTS) conversion system.

This paper concerns the keyword spotting module of this spoken dialogue system. A novel keyword spotting scheme is proposed to extract keyword hypotheses from syllable confusion networks (CNs).

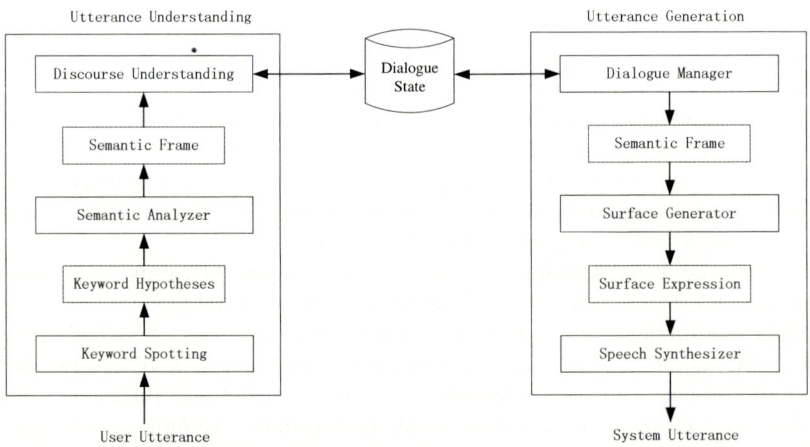

Fig. 1. Module structure of a spoken dialogue system

3 Keyword Spotting Scheme

In our keyword spotting system, search space is built on total Chinese syllables, not specifically for keywords. Syllable recognition is performed without any lexical constraints.

Given a spoken input, a very large lattice is generated firstly. A clustering algorithm is used to translate syllable trigram lattice into a CN [6]. The CN has one node for each equivalence class of original lattice nodes and adjacent nodes are linked by one edge per word hypothesis. We extract keywords from CNs. Generally, confusion matrix is adopted to achieve higher recognition rate in speech recognition system [7-9]. Based on traditional approaches, we generate SCM based on CNs. Entropy information based posterior probability is also applied to reject false accepts.

3.1 Generation of Syllable Confusion Matrix

Confusion matrix is often used for similarity measure. In Mandarin, every character is spoken in a monosyllabic manner. Most of Chinese characters can be expressed by about 1276 syllables which consist of a combination of 409 base syllables and 4 tones. In this work, we build a base syllable confusion matrix which has only 409 entries.

Generally, the syllable confusion matrix is calculated using a syllable recognizer, which recognizes 1-best syllable sequences instead of words [8]. It can be described as the following steps:

(1) Canonical syllable level transcriptions of the accent speech data should be obtained firstly.

(2) A standard Mandarin acoustic recognizer whose output is syllable sequence will be used to transcribe those accent speech data.

(3) With the help of dynamic programming (DP) technique, these recognized syllable sequence are aligned to the canonical syllable level transcriptions. Regardless of insertion and deletion errors, substitution errors are considered. Given a canonical syllable S_m and an aligning hypothesis S_n, we can compute confusion probability:

$$P(S_n \mid S_m) = \frac{count(S_n \mid S_m)}{\sum_{i=1}^{N} count(S_i \mid S_m)} . \tag{1}$$

where $count(S_n \mid S_m)$ is the number of S_n which is aligned to S_m. N is the total syllable number in our dictionary.

However, there is a conceptual mismatch between decoding criterion and confusion probability evaluation. Given an input utterance, a Viterbi decoder is used to generate the best sentence. But it does not ensure that each syllable is the optimal one. Instead of 1-best syllable hypotheses, we generate confusion matrix from CNs. N-best hypotheses of each slice are considered. Fig. 2 describes an example of CN. For schematic description, we give top 4 hypotheses in each slice. Corresponding canonical syllable is also presented.

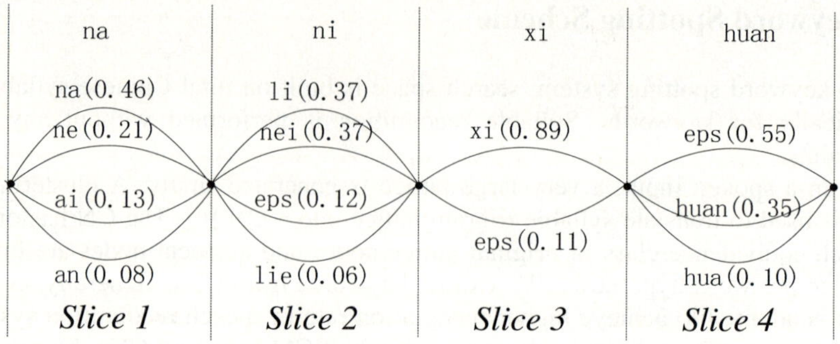

Fig. 2. An example of syllable confusion network

In order to assess whether a CN provides more information than 1-best recognition result, the syllable error rate (SER) on evaluation set is computed. As Table 1 shows, SER of CNs drops significantly compared with 1-best recognition result. That is to say, CNs provide us more effective information.

Table 1. SER of CNs and 1-best recognition result

Methods	SER [%]
1-best recognition result	49.5
CNs	27.1

Recognizer output voting error reduction (ROVER) technology is adopted to align CN and canonical recognition results [10]. We select special slices to generate the confusion matrix. Given a canonical syllable S_m, only slices including S_m are considered. A classification function $\beta(k)$ is defined as:

$$\beta(k)=\begin{cases}1 & \text{if } S_m \text{ is a most probable syllable in the } k^{\text{th}} \text{ slice} \\ 0 & \textit{others}\end{cases} \quad . \tag{2}$$

Then, confusion probability can be expressed as:

$$P(S_n \mid S_m)=\frac{\sum_{k=1}^{C}\beta(k)count(S_n \mid S_m)}{\sum_{i=1}^{N}\sum_{k=1}^{C}\beta(k)count(S_i \mid S_m)} \quad . \tag{3}$$

where C is the number of slices in training data, N is the number of syllables in dictionary.

Table 2 presents an example of a confusion matrix. Value in each bracket is the confusion probability between syllables. Obviously, the summation over each row is 1.

Table 2. An example of syllable confusion matrix

ba	ba (0.419)	la (0.074)	ma (0.056)	da (0.043)	...
cai	cai (0.286)	chai (0.107)	tai (0.101)	can (0.088)	...
gen	gen (0.244)	geng (0.106)	ge (0.055)	gou (0.035)	...
lan	lan (0.267)	nan (0.092)	luan (0.062)	lai (0.058)	...
mei	mei (0.416)	nei (0.055)	men (0.051)	lei (0.049)	...
...	...	...	...	...	...

3.2 Fuzzy Keyword Search

Fig.3 describes the block diagram of fuzzy keyword search. For a fast retrieval, arcs of CNs are indexed efficiently. Syllable name and associated posterior probability are also labeled with each arc. In order to exactly locate occurrences of a keyword, we improve the algorithm to record the most probable time information of the syllable in each arc. Moreover, SCM is adopted to improve keyword recognition rate. With the CN and SCM, keyword hypotheses are generated according to the relevance score.

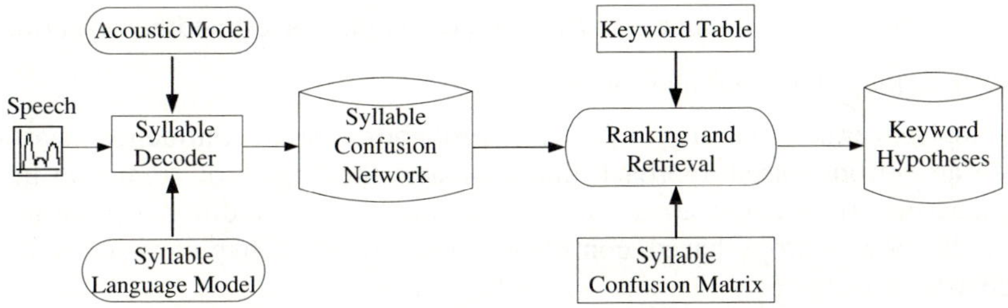

Fig. 3. Block diagram of fuzzy keyword search

In this work, each equivalence class in the CN is defined as a slice. Then CN can be represented as a slice vector $S_N = \{s_1, ..., s_n, ..., s_N\}$. Let the syllable sequence of a keyword Q_M be $\{q_1, ..., q_m, ..., q_M\}$, syllable relevance score $C(m,n)$ is defined as:

$$C(m,n) = \log\{(1-\alpha)p(q_m \mid s_n, O) + \alpha P_{conf}(m,n)\} . \quad (4)$$

$$P_{conf}(m,n) = \sum_{\{\varphi_i \mid \varphi_i \in s_n, \varphi_i \in SimSet(q_m)\}} p(\varphi_i \mid s_n, O) p(q_m \mid \varphi_i) . \quad (5)$$

where $p(q_m \mid s_n, O)$ is the posterior probability, α is a weighting factor, $P_{conf}(m,n)$ is the confusion probability which is simplified by considering q_m 's most similar syllables. $SimSet(q_m)$ and $p(q_m \mid \varphi_i)$ are provided by the SCM. The keyword relevance score is calculated by averaging cumulative dynamic programming (DP) score of underlying syllables. The search procedure is to match syllable sequence Q_M with partial slices from the start position of S_N to the end.

3.3 Calculating the Entropy Information

CN is a linear graph transformed from syllable lattice, which aligns links in the original lattice and transforms the lattice into a linear graph in which all paths pass through all nodes. To determine whether a keyword is correct or not, it might be helpful to take all the other arcs in the same slice into account. The posterior probability included in the confusion network is a good confidence measure. Besides posterior probabilities, entropy information obtained in the CN is drawing more attentions in recent years, where not only words in the best path but also words in competing paths are used in computing the probabilities [11, 12].

Entropy measures the difference of posterior probabilities among syllables in the CN, and ambiguity of syllable identity can be better captured by entropy than the posterior probability alone. Entropy for a slice is defined as:

$$E(s_n) = -\sum_{i=1}^{m} p(l_i \mid s_n, O) \log p(l_i \mid s_n, O) \ . \tag{6}$$

where l_i is the syllable in slice s_n, $p(l_i \mid s_n, O)$ is the corresponding posterior probability, m is the syllable number of s_n.

To emphasize the reliability of posterior probability based confidence measure, we propose an entropy-based approach that evaluates the degree of confusion in confidence measure. By incorporating entropy information into traditional posterior probability, the new entropy-based confidence measure of a hypothesized syllable is defined as:

$$C_{entropy}(q_m) = (1-\beta)C(m,n) + \beta E(s_n) \ . \tag{7}$$

Deriving word level scores from syllable scores is a natural extension of the confidence measure. Generally, logarithmic mean is adopted to calculate word confidence. The formula can be written as:

$$CM\left(W\right) = \frac{1}{M}\sum_{m=1}^{M} C_{entropy}(q_m) \ . \tag{8}$$

where M is the number of syllables in w.

4 Experiments

We conducted experiments using our real time keyword spotting system. Acoustic model is trained using train04, which is collected by Hong Kong University of Science and Technology (HKUST) [13]. SCM adopted in this paper are generated using 100 hour mandarin conversational telephone speech (CTS).

4.1 Experimental Data Description

The algorithms proposed in this paper were evaluated on 2005_eval which was provided by HTRDP (National High Technology Research and Development Program). All the data are recorded through landline telephone with local service in real world with environmental noise. All utterances are mandarin conversational speech, but with obvious dialect accent. Speech data are sampled at the rate of 8 kHz with 16 bit quantization. The evaluation set includes 1543 utterances from 14 speakers and the length totals up to 1 hour. 100 keywords were selected randomly as the keyword list. 80 percent is two-syllable Chinese words and others are three-syllable words.

4.2 Experiment Results

A common metric to evaluate the keyword spotting is its equal error rate (EER) which is obtained from the threshold that gives equal false acceptance rate (FA) and false rejection rate (FR). The FA fits the case in which an incorrect word is accepted, and the FR fits the case of rejecting the correct word.

$$FA = \frac{num.of\ incorrect\ words\ labelled\ as\ accepted}{num.\ of\ incorrect\ words}\ .$$

$$FR = \frac{num.of\ correct\ words\ labelled\ as\ rejected}{num.\ of\ keywords * hours\ of\ testset * C}\ .$$

where C is a factor which scales the dynamic range of FA and FR on the same level. In this paper, C is set to 10.

Table 3. Effect of two different syllable confusion matrixes

Beam	α	SER [%]	SGD	EER SCM-1 [%]	EER SCM-2 [%]	Relative reduction [%]
0.001	0.01	27.1	18.6	32.7	32.4	0.9
0.01	0.03	30.9	8.9	32.2	31.2	3.1
0.05	0.05	37.2	4.3	35.4	34.9	1.4
0.10	0.10	41.5	3.1	37.4	36.2	3.2

Table 4. EER comparison of different methods

Methods	EER [%]
CN+SCM-1	32.2
CN+SCM-2	31.2
CN+SCM-2+Entropy	30.7

CNs are pruned to contain only those arcs whose posterior probabilities are within a pruning threshold with respect to the best one in each slice. The experiments of two SCMs are summarized in Table 3. The values of syllable graph density (SGD) are also provided. SCM-1 represents the SCM based on 1-best recognition result. SCM-2 is generated based on CN. These results clearly indicate that SCM-2 has more positive impact with different pruning beam. It's interesting to note that when pruning beam increased from 0.001 (without pruning) to 0.1, the relative equal error rate (EER) reduction of using SCM-2 over SCM-1 is ranged from 0.9% to 3.2%. Optimal weighting factor α is increased in consistence.

Table 4 describes the EER performance of various techniques proposed in this paper. As we can see, the improved confusion matrix provides an EER reduction of up to 3.1% in relative. When entropy information is applied, EER has a 4.7% relative reduction.

5 Conclusions

In this paper, we have presented an improved keyword spotting scheme which is applied to a dialogue system. Syllable CNs are applied to extract keyword hypotheses. An improved SCM is also introduced into our keyword spotting scheme. Entropy information is integrated into posterior probability-based confidence measure to reject false accepts. Experiments show that algorithms proposed in this paper achieve 4.7% EER relative reduction.

Acknowledgements. This work is (partly) supported by Chinese 973 program (2004CB318106), National Natural Science Foundation of China (10574140, 60535030), and Beijing Municipal Science & Technology Commission (Z0005189040391).

References

1. Carlson, R., Hirschberg, J., Swerts, M.: Error Handling in Spoken Dialogue Systems. Speech Communication, pp. 207–209 (2005)
2. Akyol, A., Erdogan, H.: Filler Model Based Confidence Measures for Spoken Dialogue Systems: A Case Study for Turkish. ICASSP2004, pp. 781–784 (2004)
3. Heracleous, P., Shimizu, T.: A Novel Approach for Modeling Non-keyword Intervals in a Keyword Spotter Exploiting Acoustic Similarities of Languages. Speech Communication, pp. 373–386 (2005)

4. Higashinaka, R., et al.: Evaluating Discourse Understanding in Spoken Dialogue Systems. ACM Transactions on Speech and Language Processing, 1–18 (2004)
5. Higashinaka, R., Sudoh, K., Nakano, M.: Incorporating Discourse Features into Confidence Scoring of Intention Recognition Results in Spoken Dialogue Systems. Speech Communication, pp. 417–436 (2006)
6. Mangu, L., Brill, E., Stolcke, A.: Finding Consensus Among Words: Lattice-based Word Error Minimization. Eurospeech, pp. 495–498 (1999)
7. Moreau, N., Kim, H-K., Sikora, T.: Phonetic Confusion Based Document Expansion for Spoken Document Retrieval. ICSLP, pp. 542–545 (2004)
8. Liu, M., et al.: Mandarin Accent Adaptation Based on Context-independent/Context-dependent Pronunciation Modeling. In: Proc. ICASSP 2000, pp. 1025–1028 (2000)
9. Yi, L., Fung, P.: Modelling Pronunciation Variations in Spontaneous Mandarin Speech. ICSLP 2000, pp. 630–633 (2000)
10. Fiscus, J.G.: A Post-processing System to Yield Reduced Word Error Rates: Recognizer Output Voting Error Reduction (ROVER). In: Proceedings of IEEE ASRUWorkshop: Santa Barbara, pp. 347–352 (1997)
11. Chen, T-H., Chen, B., Wang, H-M.: On Using Entropy Information to Improve Posterior Probability-based Confidence Measures. In: International Symposium on Chinese Spoken Language Processing, pp. 454–463 (2006)
12. Xue, J., Zhao, Y.: Random Forests-based Confidence Annotation Using Novel Features from Confusion Network. ICASSP 2006, pp. 1149–1152 (2006)
13. http://www.ldc.upenn.edu/

Part II

Adaptive, Intelligent and Emotional User Interfaces

Dynamic Association Rules Mining to Improve Intermediation Between User Multi-channel Interactions and Interactive e-Services

Vincent Chevrin[1] and Olivier Couturier[2]

[1] Laboratoire Trigone/LIFL, CUEEP, Bâtiment B6 Cité Scientifique, 59655 Villeneuve d'Ascq Cedex France
vincent.chevrin@univ-lille1.fr
[2] Centre de Recherche en Informatique de Lens (CRIL) – IUT de Lens Rue de l'université, SP 18 62307 Lens Cedex France
couturier@cril.univ-artois.fr

Abstract. This paper deals with multi-channel interaction managing thru an intermediation between channels and Interactive e-Services (IeS). After work on modeling and theoretical framework, we implemented a platform: Ubi-Learn, which is able to manage this kind of interaction thru an intermediation middleware based on a Multi-Agents System (MAS): Jade. The issue addressed here is linked to the way you choose a channel depending on the user's task. First, we have encoded several ad hoc rules (tacit knowledge) into the system. In this paper, we present our new approach based on association rules mining approach which allows us to propose automatically several dynamic rules (explicit knowledge).

Keywords: Interactive e-Services, Intermediation, association rules mining.

1 Introduction

The rapid spreading of wireless phone and data devices and the development of intelligent communications networks and middleware enable emergence of ubiquitous computing. To manage this new concept, we work both on the designing of Interactive e-Services (IeS) and on the intermediation between these IeS and the channels for interaction with the users (customers, learners, etc.). Our works have driven us towards two directions for the design of future multi-channel flexible interactive e-Services: (1) The complex interactions allowed by the right combination of channels or/and interaction modalities (i.e. language vs. direct manipulation). The coupling of these elements is done dynamically, depending on the user contexts and organization rules [6]; (2) The use of such or such channel or also set of channels is depending on the task done by the user. Knowing if a channel is adapted to a task in a certain context is very complex. In this paper, we propose an adapted solution which is to use a data mining algorithm allowing to extract particular knowledge called explicit knowledge. Nowadays, experts can not tackle a large amount of data. So, data mining method can help them in order to discover new information.

J. Jacko (Ed.): Human-Computer Interaction, Part III, HCII 2007, LNCS 4552, pp. 265–274, 2007.

At a conceptual level, we worked on a theoretical model of communication between human and organizations through channels, and we have built a taxonomy allowing, amongst other things, to select the best channel to use according to the context of the interaction. Finally, this taxonomy has helped us to formulate a definition of a channel. This paper deals with our recent works as regards the determination of rules allowing to choose the best channel into a given situation[1]. Thus, we introduce a Data Mining Agent (called DMA) which generates the dynamic rules set. Our first proposition is based on Association Rules Mining (ARM) such as "If *Antecedent* Then *Conclusion*" which constitutes an adapted solution to solve it. This task is a major issue in Data Mining (DM) which is an active research domain to face the increasing number of large databases. A set of association rules is mainly generated depending on two user-specified metrics: *support* and *confidence*. These metrics allow us to judge rules quality in order to inject them in the process of Ubi-Learn. The main originality of our proposition is to generate dynamic rules from the context. According to the context, we can regenerate rules both at design time and at runtime. For instance, the following rule {if (*Age*<30 AND *Occupation*="Computer scientist" AND Service="e-mail access" AND …) then *AdequatChannel*="PDA"} indicates that the preferred channel of a computer scientist under thirty years old is the PDA for the service…, etc. Then, these rules are used by a software agent (Rules Agent), which manages several adaptation levels (see Fig. 3).

2 Theoretical Works Around Channels Properties

2.2 An Analyze and Predictive Model of Channels Properties

Our previous works [2], [13] led us to consider three points of view about multi-channel interaction: (1) A more "interactional" approach where the channels intervene into complex cognitive processes between two people engaged more or less directly into a joint activity; (2) An approach that we call "Theory of Information", where the channels are characterized by their intrinsic properties, such as their symbolic representation possibilities, the media richness, and the adequacy to the user's task;

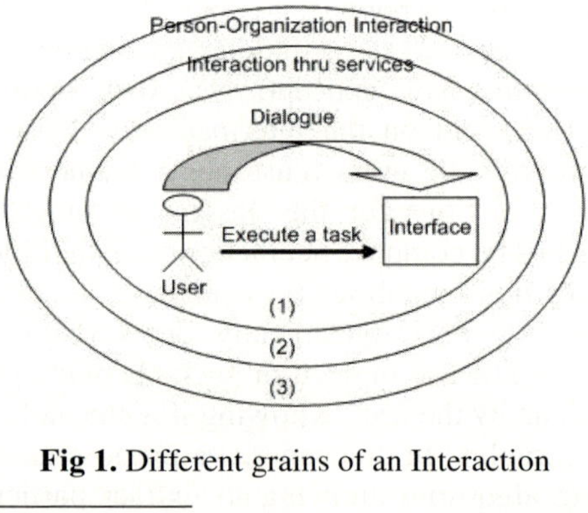

Fig 1. Different grains of an Interaction

[1] A situation is characterized by the contexts of interaction (user profile, rules of the organization, etc.) and the task(s) executed.

(3) An approach of the "acceptance" of the media by the user, whatever his adaptation to the media is. These three points of view correspond to two distinct theoretical fields one related to "Media" and another related to the adequacy between the task done and the media used. Moreover, it is essential to distinguish several views (cf. **Fig 1**) of an interaction at a granularity level:

- At thin grain ((1) on **Fig 1**), the interaction is like a situation where the user executes a task thru an electronic media[2]. This is an "interactional" approach, where the channels characteristics will have an incidence on the interaction and where the "Theory of Information" will have an important role. In this framework, the task adequacy is also an important aspect. Modeling the interaction level means we will be able to do a qualitative measurement of the using of such or such media according to its properties and according to the user task.
- At a larger grain ((2) on **Fig 1**), there are more constraints to the interaction. Indeed, this one is into an intermediation between some channels and services. So, it is necessary to take care of all the channel's properties, such as the networks, hardware, etc., but also the interaction context[3]. In this case, this is at this level that the taxonomy presented in the next section will be relevant;
- At the higher grain ((3) on **Fig 1**), this is the case of a Person-Organization Interaction. Here, it is necessary to add organization rules and policies. In this field, this is the "acceptance" aspect that will be relevant[4].

According to us, it is necessary to study these three points of view in order to characterize Person-Organization Interactions well. This step will allow us to be able to predict the channel to use according to the user's task and according to the global interaction context. The complexity of the multi-channel interaction being huge, we established a theoretical framework. Then, we discuss about the main points allowing to propose this framework. More details about this could be found in [3].

2.2 The Cooperation Inside the Cognitive Interaction

Works in the field of the psycholinguistic led by Clark, Brennan, and other colleagues [9], [8]. Their major interrogation was around the main properties of the communication. Their conclusions show obviously that this act needs collaboration between the interlocutors: *"The lesson is that communication is a collective activity. It requires the coordinated action of all the participants. Grounding is crucial for keeping that coordination on track."* [8]. Clark evokes the concept of joint activity which as means it is necessary to have at least two persons for an interaction. According to him, a joint activity is defined like activities set which imply more than one participant. Moreover, the atomic component of the activity is the action: an activity progresses towards its objective thru several joint actions. In addition, for collaboration and coordination, participants need to share several information, Clark calls that the common ground. According to him, there are two kinds of common ground: the personal and the communal. This common ground must evolve during the

[2] There are the two first points at the beginning of this section.

[3] There is several definition of context. We will discuss about this point in another section.

[4] This is the third and last point at the beginning of this section.

different communications. These updates need a process in order to be efficient: the Grounding. Clark defines grounding as: *"…to ground a thing, is to establish it as a part of common ground well enough for current purposes".* That means the participants work together to reach a mutual knowledge. Clark and Brennan have studied grounding thru different media (phone, e-mail, etc.). It seems that the effort needed to communicate is different according to the media used. They have determined eight constraints or properties and eleven costs related to the different media. **Table 1** shows the different properties. In this paper we will not discuss about the costs that we do not use in the works presented here.

Table 1. Constraints related to a communication between two participants

Co-presence	A and B share the same physical environment
Visibility	A and B are visible to each other
Audibility	A and B use speaking to communicate
Co-temporality	B receives at roughly the same time as A produces
Simultaneity	A and B can send and receive at once and simultaneously
Sequentiality	A's and B's turns cannot get out of sequence
Reviewability	B can review A's messages
Revisability	A can revise messages for B

According to Clark, *it* is the Least Collaborative Effort, which helps two participants to choose the best media in a given situation. The persons choose the media that reduces more the collaborative effort [7]. According to him, this means that during a communication, each participant tries to minimize his/her collaboration effort – the work that the two participants do is done thru a mutual acceptation of the collaboration. Some works in HCI are also based on grounding, such as [15].

2.3 The Social Aspect of the Channels

In this section, we will introduce the Media Richness Theory (MRT), and one of its critics led us to introduce the Theory of Media Synchronicity. The first assumption of this theory is that organizations process information to reduce uncertainty and equivocally [10]. Uncertainty is defined as *"the difference between the amount of information required to perform the task and the amount of information already possessed by the organization."* Equivocally is defined as the ambiguity of the task, caused by conflicting interpretations about a group situation or environment. Therefore, when equivocally is high, an individual does not know what questions to ask and when uncertainty is high the group knows the question but lacks the necessary information. In conclusion, as information increases, uncertainty and equivocally decrease. The second assumption of this theory is commonly used media in organizations works better for certain tasks than others. Specifically, [10] concluded that written media was preferred for unequivocal messages while face-to-face media was preferred for messages containing equivocally. They present a media richness hierarchy which incorporates four media classifications; face-to-face, telephone, addressed documents, and unaddressed documents. The richness of each media is based on four criteria shown in **Table 2**.

Table 2. Media properties from MRT

Feedback	Media capacity to support rapid bidirectional communication
Symbol variety	All signs allowing communication, verbal or not are likely to improve communication
Language variety	Using of different languages (scientist, etc.) allows to enrich the communication
Personal focus	Transcription of sentiments, emotions growth the medias richness

The richest communication medium is face-to-face meetings followed by telephone, e- mail, and memos and letters. But several points contradict that, let us take the example of e-mail and face-to-face: (1) in e-mail, we can add videos, pictures, files, etc.; (2) e-Mails become familiar (signature, personalization of the messages, etc.); (3) in e-Mail, the social presence is less strong, and this may be easier to talk with teachers, bosses, etc.

Moreover, this theory does not into account the context and the user's task. Dennis and Valacich [12] give some limitation of the MRT (Some empirical tests doing on the MRT show these limitations, in particular with recent electronic media), and propose some improvements. So they propose the Theory of Media Synchronicity. In this field, synchronicity means that two persons work together on a same activity at the same time and have a shared "concentration". They propose five media properties, characterizing the communication between these two people, and on the basis of the MRT. This is shown in **Table 3**.

Table 3. Media properties from the Theory of Media Synchronicity (TSM)

Feedback	Properties from MRT (the same signification)
Symbol variety	Properties from MRT (the same signification)
Concurrency	This is the number of communication at the same time (on the same media)
"Rehearsability"	Capacity to read again a message before send it
"Reprocessability"	Capacity re-examine the messages in the communication context

We can report that two interaction approaches, one like grounding from psycholinguistic, and the other from social psychology, present some analogies. The concepts of "concentration" and grounding have undoubtedly common roots.

2.4 Starting Point of Our Theoretical Framework

The study of these theories allows us to synthesize several channel properties that we have synthesized in **Table 4**. This tableau shows the relations which we highlighted between the different models, concepts and theories. Thus, for the moment, we proposed nine properties allowing to characterize a channel or a set of channels (Symbol variety, Feedback, Simultaneity, Sequentiality, Reviewability, Revisability, Personal focus, Language variety, Concurrency). Obviously, these properties are not enough to characterize a channel. To complement these works, we have built a taxonomy of the used channels inside a personalized interaction.

These works were already presented [5]. So our taxonomy includes our theoretical model with the different properties of the channels. For more details on this taxonomy see [3]. Thus, our theoretical framework, with the taxonomy allow us to characterize

Table 4. Relations between the different properties from the different models and theories

Grounding	MRT	TSM
Co-presence	Symbol variety	Symbol variety
Visibility		
Audibility		
Co-temporality	Feedback	Feedback
Simultaneity	*	*
“Sequentiality”	*	*
"Reviewability"	*	“Rehearsability”
"Revisability"	*	“Reprocessability”
Co-presence	Personal focus	*
*	*	Concurrency
Co-presence	Language variety	*
Visibility		*
Audibility		*

both a situation and the available channels, i.e. to do a given task, the user needs some properties, we can map these properties with the different channels properties, and choose the most adapted to the situation. Thus, we can be predictive concerning the channel to use in a given situation. Other models could help us in the future to improve this framework, such as the Task Acceptance Model (TAM) [11] and the Task-Technology Fit (TTF) [14]. TAM and FIT are often associated, and the strong idea, for us, here, is that the user must stay free, as far as possible, about the choice of the channels used to do his/her task. For the moment, we do not take into account these models in our modeling, but rather during the experimentation phases. Here, we are closer to a social approach. In the next section, we discuss this aspect. In the next section, we briefly present our platform Ubi-Learn, which manages the multi-channel interactions thru an intermediation between IeS and channels.

3 Our Software Architecture

3.1 Overview

Fig 2 shows the intermediation between e-Services delivered by the organization and the user via the use of different channels synchronously or asynchronously. Ubi-Learn were already presented in [4]. In these works, we also presented the intermediation

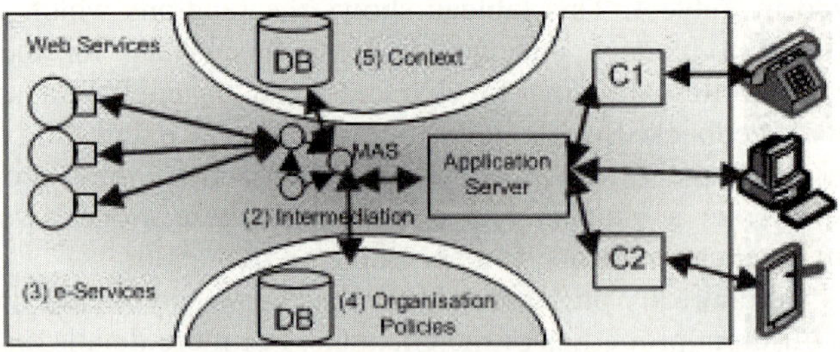

Fig 2. Simplified view of our software architecture (Ubi-Learn)

middleware implemented in Ubi-Learn, in the next section, we briefly remind it. In this figure, C1 and C2 represent the channel adaptation systems.

3.2 The Intermediation Middleware of Ubi-Learn

Fig. 3 shows that an intermediation uses several levels: the e-Service Composition; the Channel determination; the Quality of Service (QoS); the format that we call the Quality of Interaction (QoI) by analogy with the QoS; and finally the persistence of data. These different levels influence the intermediation and obviously, the composition and the adaptation of the e-Services, but also the capacity to choose the best channel for a particular IeS. It is important to notice that, in **Fig. 3**, all agents performing the actions are represented as a single agent whereas, to implement one agent of the figure, there could be a hierarchy of concrete Jade agents (e.g. a factory, a manager, etc.). In [4] we presented in details the four levels.

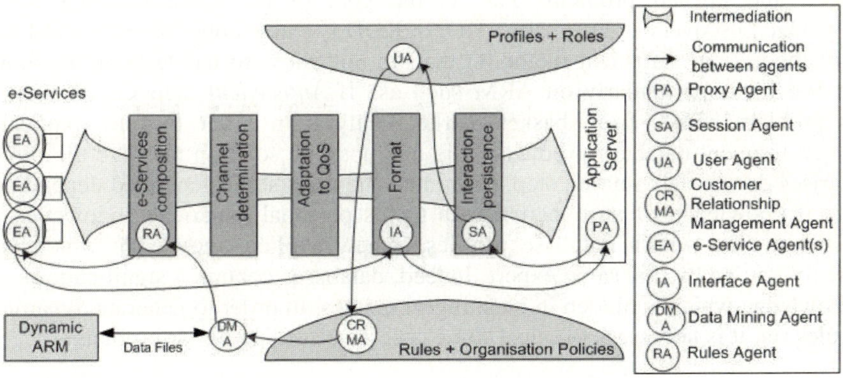

Fig. 3. Conceptual and technical view of our middleware

Here, briefly, and to summarize, we can describe the global running of the middleware from the **Fig. 3**: a customer accesses the Application Server through several channels. This server sends the user request to the *PA*. This agent creates a *SA* specific both to the user and the channel and is responsible for the persistence of each intermediation. Then, the request passes through *UA* (manages the user preferences, roles, etc.) and *CRMA* (manages the organization policies). These agents take the contexts into account. Afterwards, the *RA* executes a particular composition of the e-Services according to the channels in use. The *RA* sends a request to the appropriate *EA*, and the latter sends an XML flow (representing an abstract representation of the e-SI) to the *IA*. This agent sends the *ML flow (XHTML, WML or VoiceXML) to the *PA*, which sends these data back to the Application Server. And the latter transmits the *ML flow to the right channel. In the next section, we introduce our solution to generate rules (automatically and dynamically).

4 Dynamic Rules Generation

One drawback of the previous work is the static rules set which is fixed by experts. Consequently, these rules constitute the tacit knowledge of the expert. We wish to generate dynamically these rules set thanks to well-known data mining algorithms. In this case, the generated knowledge is explicit because it is the result of an algorithm. Among the current data mining methods, we wish to use the association rules mining (ARM) which is one of the possible solutions allowing to solve our problem by establishing logical relations between criteria. One of advantages is that the formalism is similar compared to current static rules.

4.1 Association Rules Generation

4.1.1 Motivations

In front of the increasing number of large databases, extracting useful information is a difficult and opened problem. This is the goal of an active research domain: Knowledge Discovery in Databases (KDD). KDD is a new hope for companies which use methods (e.g. statistical methods) that do not allow to tackle large amounts of data. We focus particularly on ARM such as "If *Antecedent* then *Conclusion*" [1]. This problem comes from basket market analysis in order to find implications between frequent database products. It is one possible solution to solve the problem and arises during data mining step. Currently, the rules set is generated depending on the tacit knowledge of an expert thanks to his personal experience. However, it is possible to find within database profiles, a new explicit knowledge which is not currently known by this same expert. Indeed, databases contain a significant quantity of knowledge which is hidden in meaningful masses. In order to generate dynamically the rules set, it is necessary to select some criteria according to our problem.

4.1.2 Definition

ARM [1] can be divided into two subproblems: the generation of the frequent itemsets lattice and the generation of association rules. Let $|I| = m$ the number of items, the search space to enumerate all possible frequent itemsets is equal to 2^m, and so exponential in m [1] and let $|T| = n$ the number of transactions. Let $I = \{a_1, a_2, \ldots, a_m\}$ be a set of items, and let $T = \{t_1, t_2, \ldots, t_n\}$ be a set of transactions establishing the database, where every transaction t_i is composed of a subset $X \subseteq I$ of items. A set of items $X \subseteq I$ is called *itemset*. A transaction t_i contains an itemset X in I, if $X \subseteq t_i$.

4.2 Methodology

In a first way, we realized a feasibility study in order to exploit existing tools. The Data Mining Agent (DMA) receives data (provided a binary matrix from the User Agent and the CRM Agent, thru data files). The DMA use an ARM algorithm (into Dynamic ARM[5] (DARM), see **Fig. 3**) to tackle these data files. When its task is finished, the Data Mining Agent retrieves rules from the DARM, and sort the right out the bad at a syntactic level (we keep only one channel in conclusion, etc.).

[5] DARM contains an ARM algorithms package.

Nevertheless, this agent should collaborate with a human being expert with the domain (this part is not show on the **Fig. 3**), which chooses the relevant rules at a semantic level. For each task, a rules set is generated by an ARM and for each of them, we selected one kind of rules such as "If *Customers' criteria* then *Channel"*. In these rules, *Customers' criteria* could be given by the context of interaction, the user's profile, etc. The quantity of these criteria can be easily infinite. Thus, it is difficult to generate these rules and sort them. These kinds of rules constitute the explicit knowledge which is relevant in this case. Consequently, they are inserted in the middleware, more precisely in the Rules Agent and the Data Mining Agent (see **Fig. 3**). After this task done, Data Mining Agent sends the selected rules to the Rules Agent thru a XML file. This agent update its knowledge base thanks to this rules set. The starting point of an ARM algorithm is a binary matrix ($m*n$). Intersection of a transaction (customer) and an item (criteria) is equal to 1 if the item is contained in the transaction. Criteria include customers' data and communication channels. Thanks to this matrix, it is possible to run an ARM which generates dynamically our rules set. Typical ARM is sufficient to obtain the rules set such as *apriori* [1].

5 Conclusions and Further Works

During a Person-Organization Interaction, choosing the best channel in a given situation is complex. All the different situations can not be exhaustively numbered. Indeed, these situations are too numerous (infinity) to be formalized. To solve this issue, we have worked on a theoretical framework to formalize the concept of channel and we have proposed both a taxonomy and a definition of the channel concept. This framework enables us to characterize all imaginable situations of Person-Organization Interaction, whatever the different contexts, the user, the task done, etc. and propose different rules allowing to choose best channel depending on the situation. In this paper, we argue the issue of the dynamic rules generation. According to us, the link we have made between two areas both Human Computer Interaction and Association Rules Mining for the purpose of the management of context-aware applications is original and relevant in this case. Indeed, these rules are as "If *Users criteria* then *channels*" where the users' criteria are given by the situation (context, task, etc.). Such we have said before, these criteria could be infinite. That is why we proposed to exploit a data mining solution to give some relevant rules to determine the best channel in a given situation. Currently, we work on a small sample of people to generate a compact rules set. However, our first experimentations show that the number of generated rules is large but results are encouraging because several rules are relevant. In order to refine the quality of generated rules, it is necessary to widen this sample. We can also see if the analysis of a large sample is possible in this area. To experiment it, we are realizing a form allowing to retrieve a consistent data set.

Acknowledgments. The authors are thankful to the MIAOU and EUCUE programs (French Nord Pas-de-Calais Region) and the UE funds (FEDER) for providing support for this research. Moreover, this work has been partly supported by the "Centre National de la Recherche Scientifique" (CNRS), the "IUT de LENS" and the "Université d'Artois".

References

1. Agrawal, R., Mannila, H., Srikan, R., Toivonen, H., Verkamo, A.I.: Fast discovery of association rules, Advances in knowledge discovery and data mining, American Association for Artificial Intelligence, pp. 307–328 (1996)
2. Bourguin, G., Derycke, A., Tarby, J.C.: Beyond the Interface: Co-Evolution inside Interactive Systems – A proposal founded on Activity Theory. In: Proceedings of IHM-HCI 2001 conference, Lille France, 10-14 september 2001, People and computer XV – Interaction without Frontiers, Blandford, Vanderdonckt, Gray. (eds) pp. 297–310. Springer, Heidelberg (2001)
3. Chevrin, V.: L'interaction Usagers/Services, multimodale et multicanale: une première proposition appliquée au domaine du e-Commerce. PhD in Computer Science. UST Lille. France (2006)
4. Chevrin, V., Sockeel, S., Derycke, A.: An Intermediation Middleware for supporting Ubiquitous Interaction in Mobile Commerce. In: ICPS'06, IEEE International Conference on Pervasive Services 2006 Lyon (2006)
5. Chevrin, V., Rouillard, J., Derycke, A.: Multi-channel and multi-modal interactions in E-marketing: Toward a generic architecture for integration and experimentation. In: HCI International conference, Las Vegas, Lawrence Erlbaum editors, 10 pages (June 2005)
6. Chevrin, V., Derycke, A., Rouillard, J.: Some issues for the Modelling of Interactive E-Services from the Customer Multi-Channel Interaction Perspectives, EEE 05 International. In: IEEE international conference on e-Technology, e-Commerce and e-Service, pp. 256–259. IEEE Press, Hong Kong (2005)
7. Clark, H.: Using Language. Cambridge University Press, Cambridge (1997)
8. Clark, H., Brennan, S.: Grounding in Communication. In: Resnick, L.B., Levine, J. M., Teasley, S.D. (eds.): Perspectives on Socially Shared Cognition (1991)
9. Clark, H., Schaefer, E.F.: Contributing to discourse. Cognitive Science 13, 259–294 (1989)
10. Daft, R.L., Lengel, R.H.: Information Richness: A New Approach to Managerial Behavior and Organization Design. In: Staw, B. M., Cummings, L. L. (eds.): Research in Organizational Behavior vol. 6, pp. 191–233 (1984)
11. Jr Davis, F.D.: A Technology Acceptance Model for Empirically Testing New End-User Systems: Theory and Results, Unpublished Doctoral Dissertation, Massachusetts Institute of Technology (1985)
12. Dennis, A.R., Valacich, J.S.: Rethinking Media Richness: Towards a Theory Of Media Synchronicity. In: Proceedings of the 32nd Hawaii International Conference on System Sciences (1999)
13. Derycke, A., Rouillard, J., Chevrin, V., Bayart, Y.: When Marketing meets HCI: Multi-channel customer relationships and multimodality in the personalization perspective. In: HCI International 2003 Heraklion, Crete, Greece, 2003, vol. 2 , pp. 626–630 (2003)
14. Goodhue, D.L.: Understanding User Evaluations of Information Systems, Management Science 41(12), 1827–1844 (1995)
15. Traum, D.R.: On Clark and Schaefer's Contribution Model and its applicability to Human-Computer Collaboration. In: proceedings of COOP'98 Workshop on Use of Clark's Models of Language for the design of Cooperative Systems (May 1998)

Emotionally Expressive Avatars for Chatting, Learning and Therapeutic Intervention

Marc Fabri, Salima Y. Awad Elzouki, and David Moore

Faculty of Information and Technology, Leeds Metropolitan University, UK
{m.fabri,s.elzouki,d.moore}@leedsmet.ac.uk

Abstract. We present our work on emotionally expressive avatars, animated virtual characters that can express emotions via facial expressions. Because these avatars are highly distinctive and easily recognizable, they may be used in a range of applications. In the first part of the paper we present their use in computer mediated communication where two or more people meet in virtual space, each represented by an avatar. Study results suggest that social interaction behavior from the real-world is readily transferred to the virtual world. Empathy is identified as a key component for creating a more enjoyable experience and greater harmony between users. In the second part of the paper we discuss the use of avatars as an assistive, educational and therapeutic technology for people with autism. Based on the results of a preliminary study, we provide pointers regarding how people with autism may overcome some of the limitations that characterize their condition.

Keywords: Emotion, avatar, virtual reality, facial expression, instant messaging, empathy, autism, education, therapeutic intervention.

1 Introduction

The word avatar comes from the Sanskrit language and can be translated as *God's Incarnation on Earth*. In the virtual reality community, avatars are 3D humanoid characters inhabiting virtual space, with varying degrees of animation and behavioral abilities. Avatars typically represent humans who visit the space *virtually*. Each visitor controls their avatar and is aware of other visitors' avatars and their actions [3].

In this paper we present our work on emotionally expressive avatars. Our avatars are able to show expressions corresponding to the following emotions: happiness, disgust, sadness, surprise, anger and fear [cf. 12]. These avatars are animated and highly distinctive in their appearance. Because humans are so adept at reading facial expressions in the real world, any avatar that plausibly displays emotions in a virtual world can be utilized in a range of applications.

In the first part of the paper we discuss the use of avatars in computer mediated communication. We have developed and tested an Instant Messaging tool called the *Virtual Messenger,* which allowed two users to virtually enter a meeting place in order to communicate and collaborate on a given task. Users see each others' virtual representations and chat with each other, as well as visibly express emotions via their

J. Jacko (Ed.): Human-Computer Interaction, Part III, HCII 2007, LNCS 4552, pp. 275–285, 2007.

animated avatar heads. We develop an evaluation framework for the user's subjective experience and discuss study results.

In the second part of the paper we then look into a potential application area for the Virtual Messenger, or for tools derived from the interaction paradigm employed. People with autism often display behavior that is considered socially or emotionally inappropriate [15], and find it hard to relate to other people [40]. There is evidence that virtual environment technology can address some of these impairments [5,6,31].

However, any technology using avatars has to be designed so that people with autism can readily understand the avatar's expressions, and potentially ascribe a mental and emotional state to the avatar. We present results from a study that explored the extent to which children and youth with autism could recognize, and make inferences from, emotions displayed by a humanoid avatar. The positive findings support the optimism that such avatars could be used effectively as a) an assistive technology such as the Virtual Messenger to help people with autism to circumvent their social isolation, b) as a means of educating the person with autism where the avatar may in some sense become a "teacher", and c) as actors in virtual reality role-playing where people with autism may practice their mind-reading skills.

1.1 Why Emotions Are Important

From the real world we know that whenever one interacts with another person, both monitor and interpret each others emotional expressions. Argyle [2] argued that that the expression of emotion, in the face or through the body, is part of a wider system of natural human communication that has evolved to facilitate social life. Emotions can also have an influence on cognitive processes, including coping behaviors such as wishful thinking, resignation, or blame-shifting [21]. Findings in psychology and neurology suggest that emotions are also an important factor in decision-making, problem solving, cognition and intelligence in general. Picard [37] pointed out that the emotional state of others influences not only our own emotional state, but directly the decisions we make. Another area where emotions can be critical is that of learning. It has been argued that the ability to show emotions and empathy through body language is central to ensuring the quality of tutor-learner and learner-learner interaction [7]. Acceptance and understanding of ideas and feelings, criticizing, silence, questioning – all involve non-verbal elements of interaction [27]. Emotions can motivate and encourage, they can help us achieve things [7].

2 Avatars for Chatting – The Virtual Messenger

The 'Virtual Messenger' is a communication tool designed to allow two spatially separated users to meet *virtually* and discuss a topic (Fig. 1). It is probably best described as an Instant Messaging tool with the added facility of representing interlocutors as avatars. The tool allowed investigating how a user's experience is different when the avatars representing users are emotionally expressive, as opposed to being non-expressive. Giving virtual characters expressive abilities has long been considered beneficial as it potentially leverages the observer's real-life experience with social interaction [37,8]. A choice of six avatar heads was available, each capable of displaying the "universal" facial expressions of emotion *happiness*, *surprise*, *anger*, *fear*, *sadness* and *disgust* [12] and a neutral face. Expressions were designed to be highly distinctive and recognizable [14]. All characters were based on identical animation sequences to ensure consistence and validity.

Fig. 1. The Virtual Messenger Interface

2.1 Experimental Setup

The Virtual Messenger was evaluated in a between-groups experiment conducted in pairs. Participants were given a classic survival scenario (*You are stranded in the desert about 50 miles from the nearest road...)* and had to debate what course of action would be best for their survival. During the experiment, their only means of communication was the Virtual Messenger. There were two versions of the Virtual Messenger tool, corresponding to the experimental conditions:

1. **Condition (NE):** Users could click on emoticons which then appeared in the chat log of both participants. Participants were represented by avatars, but there was no change in avatar appearance other than random idle animations such as blinking.
2. **Condition (EX):** Featured the same emoticons and avatar representations. When a user clicked an emoticon, it appeared in the chat log and also caused their avatar in the partner's messenger window to display that emotion.

By making *emotional expressiveness* the intervention, we were able to investigate its effect on the user's experience. Conditions were assigned to participant pairs, i.e. interlocutors either could both use their avatar's expressions, or neither of them could.

2.2 Evaluation Framework

In order to evaluate the user's experience effectively, we introduced the concept of **"richness of experience"** and hypothesized that a user's experience is richer when avatars are emotionally expressive, compared to non-expressive avatars. It was postulated that a richer experience would manifest itself through:

1. More **involvement** in the task
2. Greater **enjoyment** of the experience
3. A higher sense of **presence** during the experience
4. A higher sense of **copresence**

In addition to these four measures, participants were observed during the experiment, and given the opportunity to comment on any aspect of their experience after the task was completed. These qualitative measures formed an important part of the data analysis. At the time of the experiment no comparable study combining all four factors of *richness* existed. Various researchers have looked at these in isolation [39,29,38,17,20] and their interpretations informed the definition and the choice of evaluation tools. Below we explore each characteristic in detail:

1. **Involvement:** Defined here as an objective measure of the number of user-initiated actions and communications taking place. These were automatically recorded.
2. **Enjoyment:** Designers of consumer products have long been aware of the potential that quantifying *enjoyment* and *pleasurability* of use can yield for a product's success [25,22]. We used Nichols' [32] mood adjective checklist, a self-report tool specifically designed for measuring aspects of interaction in virtual reality systems.
3. **Presence:** Defined as *"a psychological state in which the individual perceives oneself as existing within an environment"* [4]. Several instruments for measuring presence were available varying from technological [41] to psychological, introspective approaches [39]. We used the fully validated 43-item ITC-SOPI questionnaire [29] because of its generic applicability. ITC-SOPI considers four distinct factors of presence: a) Being in a physical space other than the actual place one is in (spatial), b) the user's interest in the presented content (engagement), c) believability and realism of the content (naturalness), and d) .negative physical effects of the experience such as headaches or eyestrain.
4. **Copresence:** Refers to the sense of being together with another person in a computer-generated environment, sometimes also referred to as *social presence* [20,39]. For the Virtual Messenger investigation, other researchers [17,38] were followed by measuring the phenomenon of copresence via a short post-experiment questionnaire covering aspects of space, togetherness and responsiveness.

2.3 Results and Analysis

32 volunteers took part in the study. They were aged 21-63 with equal gender split (average age 28.2 years, stdev 13.4). Participants were computer literate, well educated and skilled in the use of keyboard and mouse. Few had experience of using console games, virtual reality, or other 3D applications. Several had used Instant Messaging tools before. In summary, results confirmed that the avatar faces used were effective and efficient. It is worth looking at each measure in detail because not all characteristics of richness did produce equally conclusive results:

1. **Involvement:** Sessions lasted between 8 and 35 minutes (average 21.2) excluding questionnaires. (EX) participants were significantly more involved in the task ($p<0.05$). They wrote considerably more messages, messages were longer, nearly twice as many items were moved, and there was 8 times more use of emoticons.
2. **Enjoyment:** High enjoyment scores were recorded in both conditions (averaging 71.22% for (EX) and 72.01% for (NE)). The difference was not statistically significant (one-way ANOVA, $p<0.05$).
3. **Presence:** The subjective sense of presence was consistently high across both conditions with no significant difference between the two conditions overall, or when testing for individual factors (one-way ANOVA, $p<0.05$). As an indication,

presence scores for the (EX) condition were 3.06 (Spatial), 3.61 (Engagement), 2.61 (Naturalness) and 1.63 (Negative Effects), all based on a 5-item Likert scale.

4. **Copresence:** Participants using expressive avatars (EX) reported a significantly higher sense of copresence ($F(1,32)=3.5$, $p<0.05$). Average scores were 4.13 for condition (EX), and 3.73 for (NE), again based on a 5-item Likert scale.

2.4 Discussion

Whilst *involvement* and *copresence* showed significantly higher scores in the (EX) condition (supporting the hypothesis), the *enjoyment* and *presence* showed no significant difference in response to the two conditions. The consistently high *enjoyment* scores can arguably have been influenced by the novelty of the application.

When looking at quantitative factors in combination with the qualitative data, interesting patterns emerged: The greater activity under condition (EX) which was logged as well as visually observed could be attributed to a *richer* experience. However, the way these discussions developed would have been counter-productive in a real life-threatening situation. (NE) acted in a more task-oriented and efficient way. It is possible that the introduction of emotional expressiveness may not be appropriate for all types of avatar applications, or in all communication contexts, as they may distract users from the task at hand. An alternative possibility is that by focusing on emotional expressions alone the environment may become "hyper-emotional", leading to a distracting rather than constructive collaborative experience.

There was a tendency by some participants to mimic emotions displayed by their partners. This was particularly relevant to the (EX) condition where it affected predominantly the happiness expression. The mimicry of communicative cues is well-documented for real life social interaction, typically as a regulator of trust and rapport [26,28]. Imitative behavior is also considered a good indicator for the existence of empathy [34]. From the observations we infer that such mimicry may have taken place during the task, when participants appeared to have copied their partner's facial expressions. This in turn may have led to more *likeability* between partners as they sensed that there was an interlocutor who *empathized* with them, which is congruent with post-experimental feedback by these participants. There is, then, some evidence that mechanisms fostering the emergence of empathy in the real world may apply equally to interaction through the Virtual Messenger, despite the somewhat artificial setup. It is quite conceivable that deliberate use of mimicking in future system has the potential to be a useful means of communication – and potentially persuasion.

In the next section we consider the further application of emotionally expressive avatars, such as those used here. Our main concern is to find ways to help people with autism overcome at least some of the limitations that characterize their condition.

3 Avatars for Learning and Therapeutic Intervention

Wing [40] considers autism involving a "triad of impairments": 1) A social impairment: the person with autism finds it hard to relate to and empathize with other people; 2) a communication impairment: the person with autism finds it hard to understand and use verbal and non-verbal signals, and may display behavior considered socially or emotionally inappropriate [15]; and 3) a tendency towards rigidity and inflexibility in thinking, language and behavior. Research suggests that this triad is underpinned by a "theory of mind deficit" [24]: people with autism may have difficulty understanding other people's mental and emotional state, or ascribing such a state to themselves. Given this understanding of autism, we argue that virtual reality systems utilizing emotionally expressive avatars can potentially benefit people with autism in three ways – as an assistive technology, as an educational technology, and as a means of helping address any Theory of Mind deficit.

3.1 Avatars as an Assistive Technology

Concerning its potential role as an *assistive technology*, our argument is that people with autism may be able to use the Virtual Messenger to communicate more fruitfully with other people. This is important since people with autism may experience social exclusion because they find it difficult to make friends [6]. Indeed, the difficulty to relate socially to other people is seen as a hallmark of autism [33]. Any means of addressing these issues, we argue, is therefore worthy of investigation. Tools such as the Virtual Messenger have the potential to enable communication that is simpler and less threatening to people with autism than its face-to-face equivalent, thereby avoiding many of the potential pitfalls [35]. The direct and active control over interactions may also increase confidence of people who otherwise feel out of control in social situations [35]. Users can communicate at their own pace and, if needed, slow down the rate of interaction in order to gain time to think of alternative ways of dealing with a particular situation. Thus, tools like the Virtual Messenger can potentially help people with autism who cannot or do not wish to come together physically, but who wish to discuss common interests. It may provide a means by which people with autism can communicate with others, and thus circumvent, at least in part, their social and communication impairment and sense of isolation.

3.2 Avatars as an Educational Technology

Concerning the potential *educational* use of the Virtual Messenger, the idea is to use the technology as a means of educating the user with autism, possibly in an attempt to help overcome their autism-specific "deficits". Thus the conversational partner of a user with autism may be in some sense their "teacher". One specific way in which this might be used is for the purposes of practice and rehearsal of events in the "real world", for example a forthcoming school visit, family gathering or interview.

Programmes that allow people with autism to practice social skills are often advocated, partly on the grounds that social impairments can affect general educational progress [1]. The argument for the use of avatar-based communication in such programmes is that it enables social skills to be practiced and rehearsed in realistic settings in real time [6,35,36]. Tools like the Virtual Messenger offer a safe and controlled environment which can be used repeatedly under the same conditions in order to learn appropriate social rules, without having to deal face-to-face with other people [6]. Users' interactions can be recorded and used for subsequent educational discussion. This creates an opportunity for people with autism to learn by making mistakes but without suffering the real consequence of their errors.

3.3 Addressing Theory of Mind Issues

Another interesting possibility is that of using tools like the Virtual Messenger to help people with autism with any Theory of Mind (ToM) deficit. Although the status of this alleged deficit is controversial, with for example some research suggesting that the perception of emotions in others is not systematically or specifically deficient in people with autism [19], many advocate its explicit teaching [e.g. 24,33]. It is argued [24] that children with autism can be successfully taught to interpret mental states.

We argue, then, that tools like the Virtual Messenger can potentially play a valuable role concerning ToM. Being able to express their emotions through a choice of appropriate facial expressions for their avatars., and being required to interpret the emotions displayed by their interlocutors' avatars, may help address the ToM issue in users with autism. McIlhagga and George [30] suggest that users who see other avatars' behavior and facial expressions may build a model of the emotional state of the underlying agent or user. Enabling people with autism to work in such environments provides them, in principle at least, with an opportunity to practice their mind reading skills and address ToM issues.

4 Avatars for People with Autism – An Exploratory Study

In order to investigate whether and how people with autism may interact with emotionally expressive avatars, we conducted a preliminary study with two aims: to establish whether a) the chosen avatars were readily recognizable, and b) participants could relate events in simple social scenarios to the relevant emotions. We developed a single-user computer system, incorporating avatar representations for 4 emotions – *happy, sad, angry, frightened* – and involving 3 stages [5]. It should be noted that the development of the system happened in parallel to the Virtual Messenger development. While the action units underlying all facial expressions were identical in the two systems, for technical reasons different avatar models were used.

In **Stage 1** the avatar representations of the 4 emotions were sequentially presented in isolation. Users were asked to select the emotion they think is being displayed, from a list. In a second activity, users were told that a particular emotion is being felt and asked to select the avatar head they believe to correspond to that emotion. These two activities form part of a standard procedure to establish the baseline of emotion recognition [24]. **Stage 2** attempts to elicit the possible emotions in the context of a simple social scenario (Fig. 2). It requires users to predict the likely emotion caused by certain events. In **Stage 3** of the system the user is given an avatar representation of one of the emotions and asked to select which of a number of given events they think may have caused this emotion. Throughout the system, the avatar "face" is used as the means of attempting to portray the emotions. A problematic issue when developing the system concerned the range of emotions to consider. The literature suggests that there are 6 *universal* expressions of emotion [12] as used with the Virtual Messenger. However, autism researchers [18] argue that it is debatable when and if children utilize all 6 emotions. Instead, work with individuals with autism tends to concentrate on a subset of emotions. While subsets vary in the literature, we followed [24] and used *happy, sad, angry* and *frightened*.

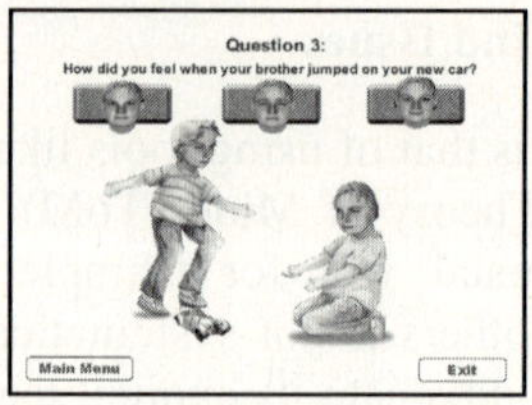

Fig. 2. Stage 2 of the system

4.1 Results and Discussion

The study involved school-aged participants with a diagnosis of autism. Of 100 potential UK-based participants contacted, 34 replied. 18 participants were reported as children with Aspergers Syndrome and 16 as children with severe autism. The age range was from 7 to 16 years (mean 9.96). 29 participants were male, 5 female.

Each participant was sent a pack consisting of a CD containing the system outlined above, a blank diskette, a questionnaire asking participants for their views about the software, a parent questionnaire asking for the participant's age and autism diagnosis, and for the parent's views about the software, brief instructions and a stamped addressed envelope. Participants were asked to work through the 3 stages of the system described above. The software logged their work onto the diskette. Once the task was completed, participants and their parents were each asked to fill in the questionnaires. The diskette with log data and the questionnaires were then returned.

Results from analyzing the log files suggest that, for all but one of the questions, the participants were demonstrating responses significantly above those expected by chance. Of the 34 participants, 30 were able to use the avatars at levels demonstrably better than chance. Concerning the four participants who did not demonstrate a significant difference from chance, it appears that these participants had a real difficulty in understanding the emotional representation of the avatars. These four participants were in the group that described themselves as having severe autism as opposed to Aspergers Syndrome. In general, however, for the participants who responded, there is very strong evidence that the emotions of the avatars are being understood and used appropriately.

5 Summary and Further Work

We have outlined two empirical studies concerning emotionally expressive avatars. The first investigates how the ability to express and perceive emotions during a dialogue between two individuals in the *Virtual Messenger* tool affects their experience of the given virtual world scenario. The study has also led to the development of guidelines for making emotionally expressive avatars effective and efficient [see 13]. The second study can be seen as an application of the first study to the specific potential user group of people with autism. We believe that this study gives grounds for optimism that avatars can help addressing one or more of the impairments of people with autism.

We are currently conducting a third empirical study to investigate whether and how the avatars used in the Virtual Messenger are recognizable, and their emotional expressions understandable to children with more severe autism. By studying the pre-validated emotion representations with such a user group, we are arguably testing the standard in extremis, and hence potentially enabling the standard to be strengthened. This is an example of an "off-shoot" argument for assistive technology – lessons from the use of the technology in extraordinary human computer interaction might lead to helpful development of the technology for "general" use [11,23]. Similarly, our work can be expected to contribute towards clarifying the noted lack of guidance in the literature [cf. 18] regarding how children might understand the behavior of virtual characters and their emotional signals.

Much remains to be done, therefore, and we hope that the studies reported in this paper may play a part in moving forward the important area of emotional expressiveness in avatar-based communications, as well as the use of avatars as an educational and therapeutic tool.

References

1. Aarons, M., Gittens, T.: Autism: A social skills approach for children and adolescents. Winslow Press, Oxford (1998)
2. Argyle, M.: Bodily Communication, 2nd edn. Methuen, New York (1988)
3. Bailenson, J., Blascovich, J.: Avatars. Encyclopedia of HCI. Berkshire, pp. 64–68 (2004)
4. Blascovich, J.: Social influence within immersive virtual environments. In: Schroeder, R. (ed.) The Social Life of Avatars. CSCW Series, pp. 127–145. Springer, London (2002)
5. Cheng, Y.: An avatar representation of emotion in collaborative virtual environment technology for people with autism. PhD thesis, Leeds Metropolitan University, UK (2005)
6. Cobb, S., Beardon, L., Eastgate, R., Glover, T., Kerr, S., Neale, H., Parsons, S., Benford, S., Hopkins, E., Mitchell, P., Reynard, G., Wilson, J.: Applied virtual environments to support learning of social interaction skills in users with Aspergers Syndrome. Digital Creativity 13(1), 11–22 (2002)
7. Cooper, B., Brna, P., Martins, A.: Effective Affective in Intelligent Systems – Building on Evidence of Empathy in Teaching and Learning. In: Paiva, A. (ed.) Affective Interactions. LNCS (LNAI), vol. 1814, pp. 21–34. Springer, London (2000)
8. Cowell, A., Stanney, K.: Manipulation of non-verbal interaction style and demographic embodiment to increase anthropomorphic computer character credibility. International Journal of Human-Computer Studies 62, 281–306 (2005)
9. Dautenhahn, K., Woods, S.: Possible Connections between bullying behaviour, empathy and imitation. In: Proceedings of Second International Symposium on Imitation in Animals and Artifacts, pp. 68–77, AISB Society (2003) ISBN 1-902956-30-7
10. Desmet, P.M.A.: Measuring emotion: development and application of an instrument to measure emotional responses to products. In: Blythe, M.A., Monk, A.F., Overbeeke, K., Wright, P.C. (eds.) Funology: from usability to enjoyment, pp. 111–123. Kluwer, Dordrecht (2003)
11. Edwards, A.: Extra-ordinary human-computer interaction. Cambridge University Press, New York (1995)
12. Ekman, P., Friesen, W.V.: Facial Action Coding System. Consulting Psych. Press (1978)

13. Fabri, M.: Emotionally expressive avatars for collaborative virtual environments. PhD Thesis, Leeds Metropolitan University, UK (2006)
14. Fabri, M., Moore, D., Hobbs, D.: Mediating the Expression of Emotion in Educational CVEs. International Journal of Virtual Reality, Springer, London, 7(2), 66–81 (2004)
15. Frith, U.: Autism: Explaining the Enigma. Blackwell, Oxford (1989)
16. Garau, M., Slater, M., Pertaub, D., Razzaque, S.: The responses of people to virtual humans in an Immersive Virtual Environment. Presence, vol. 14(1), pp. 104–116. MIT Press, Cambridge (2005)
17. Garau, M.: The Impact of Avatar Fidelity on Social Interaction in Virtual Environments. PhD Thesis, University College London (2003)
18. George, P., McIlhagga, M.: The communication of meaningful emotional information for children interacting with virtual actors. In: Paiva, A.M. (ed.) Affective Interactions. LNCS (LNAI), vol. 1814, pp. 35–48. Springer, Berlin (2000)
19. Gepner, B., Deruelle, C., Grynfeltt, S.: Motion and emotion: A novel approach to the study of face processing by young autistic children. Journal of Autism and Developmental Disorders 31, 37–45 (2001)
20. Gerhard, M.: A Hybrid Avatar/Agent Model for Educational Collaborative Virtual Environments. PhD Thesis, Leeds Metropolitan University, UK (2003)
21. Gratch, J., Marsella, S.: Evaluating a computational model of emotion. Journal of Autonomous Agents and Multi-Agent Systems 11(1), 23–43 (2005)
22. Hassenzahl, M.: The effect of perceived hedonic quality on product appealingness. International Journal of Human-Computer Interaction 13(4), 481–499 (2001)
23. Hobbs, D.J., Moore, D.J.: Human computer interaction. FTK Publishing, London (1998)
24. Howlin, P., Baron-Cohen, S., Hadwin, J.: Teaching Children with Autism to Mind-Read: A Practical Guide for Teachers and Parents. John Wiley and Sons, New York (1999)
25. Jordan, P.W.: Designing Pleasurable Products. Taylor and Francis, London (2000)
26. Kendon, A.: Movement coordination in social interactions. Acta Psych 32(2), 101–125 (1970)
27. Knapp, M.L., Hall, J.A.: Nonverbal Communication in Human Interaction, 3rd edn., Holt, Rinehart and Winston (1992)
28. LaFrance, M.: Posture Mirroring and Rapport. In: Davis, M. (ed.): Interaction Rhythms: Periodicity in Communicative Behavior, pp. 279–298 (1982)
29. Lessiter, J., Freeman, J., Keogh, E., Davidoff, J.D.: A Cross-Media Presence Questionnaire: The ITC Sense of Presence Inventory. Presence, MIT Press, Cambridge 10(3) (2001)
30. McIlhagga, M., George, P.: Communicating Meaningful Emotional Information in a Virtual World. In: Paiva, A., Martinho, C. (eds.): Proceedings of International Workshop on Affect in Interactions, Siena, Italy, pp. 150–155 (1999)
31. Moore, D.J., Cheng, Y., McGrath, P., Powell, N.J.: CVE technology for people with autism. Focus on Autism and Other Developmental Disabilities 20(4), 231–243 (2005)
32. Nichols, S.: Virtual Reality Induced Symptoms and Effects (VRISE): Methodological and Theoretical Issues. PhD Thesis, University of Nottingham, UK (1999)
33. Ozonoff, S., Miller, J.: Teaching Theory of Mind. Journal of Autism and Developmental Disorders 25, 415–433 (1995)
34. Paiva, A., Dias, J., Sobral, D., Aylett, R., Sobreperez, P., Woods, S., Zoll, C., Hall, L.: Caring for Agents and Agents that Care. In: Proceedings of International Conference on Autonomous Agents and Multi-Agent System, New York, USA (2004)
35. Parsons, S., Mitchell, P., Leonard, A.: Do adolescents with autistic spectrum disorders adhere to social conventions in virtual environments? Autism 9, 95–117 (2005)

36. Parsons, S., Mitchell, P., Leonard, A.: The use and understanding of VE by adolescents with autistic spectrum disorders. J of Autism and Developmental Disorders 34(4), 449–466 (2004)
37. Picard, R.: Affective Computing. MIT Press, Cambridge (1997)
38. Schroeder, R., Steed, A., Axelsson, A., Heldal, I., Abelin, A., Wideström, J., Nilsson, A., Slater, M.: Collaborating in Networked Immersive Spaces. Computers and Graphics 25(5), 781–788 (2001)
39. Slater, M.: Measuring Presence: A Response to the Witmer and Singer Presence Questionnaire. Presence, MIT Press, Cambridge, 8(5), 560–565 (1999)
40. Wing, L.: The Autism Spectrum Constable, London (1996)
41. Witmer, B.G., Singer, M.J.: Measuring Presence in Virtual Environments: a Presence Questionnaire. Presence, MIT Press, Cambridge, 7(3), 225–240 (1998)

Can Virtual Humans Be More Engaging Than Real Ones?

Jonathan Gratch[1], Ning Wang[1], Anna Okhmatovskaia[2], Francois Lamothe[3], Mathieu Morales[3], R.J. van der Werf[4], and Louis-Philippe Morency[5]

[1] University of Southern California
[2] McGill University
[3] Ecole Spéciale Militaire de St-Cyr
[4] University of Twente
[5] Massachusetts Institute of Technology

Abstract. Emotional bonds don't arise from a simple exchange of facial displays, but often emerge through the dynamic give and take of face-to-face interactions. This article explores the phenomenon of rapport, a feeling of connectedness that seems to arise from rapid and contingent positive feedback between partners and is often associated with socio-emotional processes. Rapport has been argued to lead to communicative efficiency, better learning outcomes, improved acceptance of medical advice and successful negotiations. We provide experimental evidence that a simple virtual character that provides positive listening feedback can induce stronger rapport-like effects than face-to-face communication between human partners. Specifically, this interaction can be more engaging to storytellers than speaking to a human audience, as measured by the length and content of their stories.

1 Introduction

Emotion is often studied as something that arises within an individual's head and "leaks" to the outside world through their nonverbal behavior (Ekman, 1992), possibly leading to better communication and coordination with sensitive observers (R. Frank, 1988; Keltner & Haidt, 1999). But emotion sometimes seems to emerge from the space between individuals. For example, feelings of antagonism may arise as facial expressions and postures are exchanged, as "one person's gradual leaning forward first leads to withdrawal until ground is held" (Parkinson, 2001). In such a fashion, feelings may arise, not from each individuals' understanding of how the interaction relates to their personal beliefs and desires (as argued by many theories and computational models of emotion, e.g., Ellsworth & Scherer, 2003; Gratch & Marsella, 2004; Neal Reilly, 1996), but via interpersonally distributed cognition where "neither person's separate cognitive processes can entirely explain the resulting co-regulated reaction" (Fogel, 1993 in Parkinson, 2001).

Rapport is one crucial characteristic of successful interactions that seems to emerge outside of conscious awareness through the subtle interplay of nonverbal emotional signals. Cappella (1990) states rapport to be "one of the central, if not *the* central, constructs necessary to understanding successful helping relationships and to explaining the development of personal relationships." Rapport is correlated with characteristic

J. Jacko (Ed.): Human-Computer Interaction, Part III, HCII 2007, LNCS 4552, pp. 286–297, 2007.

nonverbal behaviors in face-to-face interactions. Participants seem tightly enmeshed in something like a dance. They rapidly detect and respond to each other's movements. Tickel-Degnen and Rosenthal (1990) equate rapport with behaviors indicating positive emotions (e.g. head nods or smiles), mutual attentiveness (e.g. mutual gaze), and coordination (e.g. postural mimicry or synchronized movements). Rapport is argued to underlie social engagement (Tatar, 1997), success in negotiations (Drolet & Morris, 2000), improving worker compliance (Cogger, 1982), psychotherapeutic effectiveness (Tsui & Schultz, 1985), improved test performance in classrooms (Fuchs, 1987) and improved quality of child care (Burns, 1984).

Two lines of research suggest that virtual characters could establish rapport with humans, and thereby attain rapport's beneficial influence over communication, persuasion and learning. On the one hand, studies suggest that rapport can be experimentally induced or disrupted by altering the presence or character of contingent nonverbal feedback (eg., Bavelas, Coates, & Johnson, 2000; Drolet & Morris, 2000). On the other hand, research on the social impact of virtual characters suggests that people, in some sense, treat virtual characters as if they were real people, and exhibit many of the subtle social influences that arise in human-to-human interaction (Kramer, Tietz, & Bente, 2003; Nass & Reeves, 1996). "Embodied conversational agents" have attempted to generate nonverbal cues together with speech, but only a few have addressed the technical challenges of establishing the tight reciprocal feedback associated with rapport. For example, Neurobaby analyzes speech intonation and uses the extracted features to trigger emotional displays (Tosa, 1993). More recently, Breazeal's Kismet system extracts emotional qualities in the user's speech (Breazeal & Aryananda, 2002). Whenever the speech recognizer detects a pause in the speech, the previous utterance is classified (within one or two seconds) as indicating approval, an attentional bid, or a prohibition. This recognition feature is combined with Kismet's current emotional state to determine facial expression and head posture. People who interact with Kismet often produce several utterances in succession, thus this approach is sufficient to provide a convincing illusion of real-time feedback. Only a few systems can interject meaningful nonverbal feedback *during* another's speech and these methods usually rely on simple acoustic cues. For example, REA will execute a head nod or paraverbal (e.g., "mm-hum") if the user pauses in mid-utterance (Cassell et al., 1999). Some work has attempted to extract extra-linguistic features of a speakers' behavior, but not for the purpose of informing listening behaviors. For example, Brand's voice puppetry work attempts to learn a mapping between acoustic features and facial configurations inciting a virtual puppet to react to the speaker's voice (Brand, 1999). Although there is considerable research showing the benefit of such feedback on human to human interaction, there has been almost no research on their impact on human to virtual human rapport (cf. Bailenson & Yee, 2005; Cassell & Thórisson, 1999).

There is some reason to believe, however, that, at least in certain contexts, a virtual human could promote more rapport than might be found in normal human-to-human interactions. Rapport is something that typically develops over time as inhibitions break down and partners begin to form emotional bonds. Strangers rarely exhibit the characteristic positivity, mutual attention or nonverbal coordination seen amongst friends (Welji & Duncan, 2004). Virtual humans, in contrast, can be programmed to produce such behaviors from the very beginning of an interaction. Further, some researchers have suggested that virtual humans may be inherently less threatening than other forms of social interaction due to their game like qualities and the inherent unreality of the virtual worlds they inhabit (Marsella, Johnson, & LaBore, 2003; Robins, Dautenhahn, Boekhorst, & A. Billard, 2005). Alternatively, people might find an immediately responsive agent disconcerting or insincere, working against the establishment of rapport. In this article, we assess the potential of the RAPPORT AGENT to create more engagement and speech fluency than might be found between typical strangers. In the study presented here, we test the hypothesis that a virtual human could be more engaging than a human listener.

The next section describes the technical capabilities of the RAPPORT AGENT. We then describe a study that assesses the engagement and speech fluency of story tellers speaking to a positive active listening agent, an unresponsive agent or an unfamiliar human listener. We conclude with a general discussion and future thoughts.

2 Rapport Agent

The RAPPORT AGENT (Figure 1) was designed to establish a sense of rapport with a human participant in "face-to-face monologs" where a human participant tells a story to a silent but attentive listener (Gratch et al., 2006). In such settings, human listeners can indicate rapport through a variety of nonverbal signals (e.g., nodding, postural mirroring, etc.) The RAPPORT AGENT attempts to replicate these behaviors through a real-time analysis of the speaker's voice, head motion, and body posture, providing rapid nonverbal feedback. Creation of the system is inspired by findings that feelings of rapport are correlated with simple contingent behaviors between speaker and listener, including behavioral mimicry (Chartrand & Bargh, 1999) and backchanneling (e.g., nods, see Yngve, 1970). The RAPPORT AGENT uses a vision based tracking system and signal processing of the speech signal to detect features of the speaker and then uses a set of reactive rules to drive the listening mapping displayed in Table 1. The architecture of the system is displayed in Figure 2.

To produce listening behaviors, the RAPPORT AGENT first collects and analyzes the speaker's upper-body movements and voice. For detecting features from the participants' movements, we focus on the speaker's head movements. Watson (Morency, Sidner, Lee, & Darrell, 2005) uses stereo video to track the participants' head position and orientation and incorporates learned motion classifiers that detect head nods and shakes from a vector of head velocities. Other features are derived from the tracking data. For example, from the head position, given the participant is seated in a fixed chair, we can infer the posture of the spine. Thus, we detect head gestures (nods, shakes, rolls), posture shifts (lean left or right) and gaze direction.[1]

Acoustic features are derived from properties of the pitch and intensity of the speech signal, using a signal processing package, LAUN, developed by Mathieu Morales. Speaker pitch is approximated with the cepstrum of the speech signal (Oppenheim & Schafer, 2004) and processed every 20ms. Audio artifacts introduced by the motion of the Speaker's head are minimized by filtering out low frequency noise.

[1] Note that some authors have argued that higher-level patterns of movement may play a more crucial role in the establishment of rapport and would be overlooked by this local approach (Grammer, Kruck, & Magnusson, 1998; Sakaguchi, Jonsson, & Hasegawa, 2005).

Speech intensity is derived from amplitude of the signal. LAUN detects speech intensity (silent, normal, loud), range (wide, narrow), questions and backchannel opportunity points (derived using the approach of Ward & Tsukahara, 2000).

Recognized speaker features are mapped into listening animations through a set of authorable mapping language. This language supports several advanced features. Authors can specify contextual constraints on listening behavior, for example, triggering different behaviors depending on the state of the speaker (e.g., the speaker is silent), the state of the agent (e.g., the agent is looking away), or other arbitrary features (e.g., the speaker's gender). One can also specify temporal constraints on listening behavior: For example, one can constrain the number of behaviors produced within some interval of time. Finally, the author can specify variability in behavioral responses through a probability distribution of different animated responses.

These animation commands are passed to the SmartBody animation system (Kallmann & Marsella, 2005) using a standardized API (Kopp et al., 2006). SmartBody is designed to seamlessly blend animations and procedural behaviors, particularly conversational behavior. These animations are rendered in the Unreal Tournament™ game engine and displayed to the Speaker.

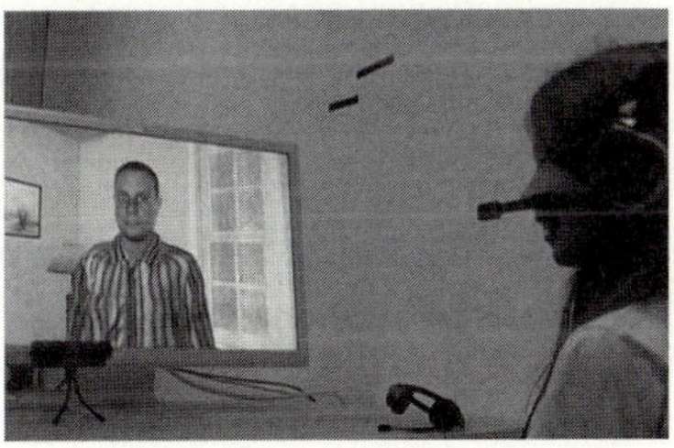

Fig. 1. A child telling a story to the RAPPORT AGENT

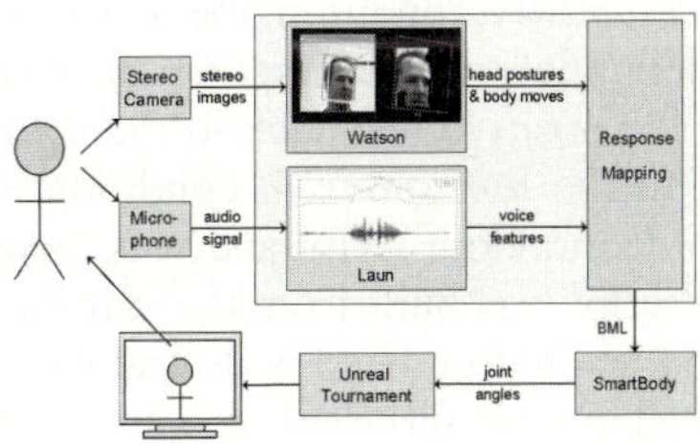

Fig. 2. Rapport Agent architecture

Table 1. Rapport Agent Mapping

Silence → gaze up/straight
Raised loudness → head nod
Backchannel → head nod
Ask question → head nod
Speaker shifts posture → mimic
Speaker gazes away → mimic
Speaker nods or shakes → mimic

3 Evaluation

Experimental Setup: In evaluating these hypotheses, we adapted the "McNeill lab" paradigm (McNeill, 1992) for studying gesture research: a speaker explains to a listener a previously watched film clip. As people can be socially influenced by a virtual character whether or not they believe it represents a real person (Nass & Moon, 2000), we used a cover story to make the subjects believe that they were interacting with a real human. Participants were told that the purpose of the study was to evaluate an advanced telecommunication device, specifically a computer program that accurately captures all movements of one person and displays them on the screen (using an Avatar) to another person. In line with the cover story, it was explained that we were interested in comparing this new device to a more traditional telecommunication medium such as video camera, which is why one of the participants was seated in front of the monitor displaying a video image, while the other saw a life-size head of an avatar (see Figure 3).

The subjects were assigned[2] to one of three conditions labeled respectively "face-to-face", "responsive" and "unresponsive." In all conditions, subjects sat across a table, separated by 8 feet (Figure 3). In a *face-to-face* condition, the listener and speaker could see each other (the screen and monitors in Figure 3 were removed). In the *responsive* and *unresponsive* conditions, the Speaker and the Listener were separated by a screen and didn't see each other directly. Rather, the Listener could hear the Speaker and see a video image of him/her. The Speaker could see an avatar on the monitor, sized to approximate the same field-of-view as the face-to-face condition. In the *responsive* condition, the avatar was controlled by the Rapport Agent, as described earlier. The Avatar therefore displayed a range of nonverbal behaviors intended to provide positive feedback to the speaker and to create an impression of active listening. In the *unresponsive* condition, the Avatar's behavior was controlled by a pre-recorded random script and was independent of the Speaker's or Listener's behavior. The script was built from the same set of animations as those used in responsive condition, excluding head nods and shakes. Thus, the Avatar's behavioral repertoire was limited to head turns and posture shifts.

Fig. 3. Experimental setup. The Listener (left) sees a video image of the Speaker (right). The Speaker sees an Avatar allegedly displaying the Listener's movements. Stereo cameras are installed in front of both participants (Listener data is ignored but stored for data collection/analysis).

Subjects. The participants were 48 adult volunteers from the University of Southern California's Institute for Creative Technologies. Two subjects were excluded from analysis due to an unforeseen interruption of experimental procedure. The final

[2] Subjects were not randomly assigned to the three conditions. Rather, the responsive and unresponsive conditions were part of an earlier study (Gratch et al., 2006). Here, we contrast face-to-face subjects with these earlier results. This methodological choice does limit the strength of our conclusions (see Section 5).

sample size was 46: 16 in a responsive and 12 in an unresponsive condition, 18 in face-to-face condition.

Procedure: Each subject participated in an experiment twice: once in a role of the Speaker and once as the Listener. The order was selected randomly.

While the Listener waited outside of the room, the Speaker watched a short segment of a Sylvester and Tweety cartoon, after which s/he was instructed to describe the segment to the Listener. The participants were told that they would be judged based on the Listener's story comprehension. The Speaker was encouraged to describe the story in as much detail as possible. In order to prevent the Listener from talking back we emphasized the distinct roles assigned to participants, but did not explicitly prohibit the Listener from talking. No time constraints were introduced.

After describing the cartoon (while the Speaker was sitting in front of the Avatar), the Speaker was asked to complete a short questionnaire collecting the subject's feedback about his experience with the system. Then the participants switched their roles and the procedure was repeated. A different cartoon from the same series, and of similar length, was used for the second round.

At the end of the experiment, both participants were debriefed. The experimenter collected some informal qualitative feedback on their experience with the system, probed for suspicion and finally revealed the goals of the study and experimental manipulations.

Dependent Variables: Engagement was indexed by total time it took the subject to tell the story and total number of words in the subject's story (independent of individual differences in speech rate).

To assess conversational fluency, we used two groups of measures: speech rate and the amount of speech disfluencies (Alibali, Heath, & Myers, 2001). Speech rate was indexed by the overall speech rate (all words per second) and the fluency speech rate (lexical and functional words per second). Amount of disfluencies was indexed by the disfluency rate (disfluencies per second) and the disfluency frequency (a ratio of the number of disfluency to total word count).

Subjective sense of rapport was measured through self-report using the forced-choice questionnaire items: "Did you feel you had a connection with the other person?" and "Did you think he/she [the listener] understood the story completely?". Additionally, the questionnaire included several open-ended questions, which were used as a source of qualitative data.

Thus the hypotheses were operationalized in terms of these measured variables, in the following ways:

- H1a: Total time to tell the story will be longest in the *responsive* condition, followed by the *face-to-face* and then the *unresponsive* condition.
- H1b: The recorded stories will be the longest in the *responsive* condition in terms of total word count followed by the *face-to-face* condition and then the *unresponsive* condition.
- H2: The disfluency rate will be the highest in the *unresponsive* condition followed by the *face-to-face* condition and then the *responsive* condition.
- H3: The subjects in *face-to-face* condition are most likely to report a sense of rapport on the questionnaire, followed by *responsive* condition and then *unresponsive* condition.

Results: The Tukey test was used to compare responses pairewise across the 3 conditions[3]. To satisfy the independence assumption required for the statistical analyses we conducted, analyses were conducted on speakers' data only. Table 2 summarizes the significant differences in duration and interaction fluency.

From Table 2, we can see that speakers in the *responsive* condition spoke longer and used more words than those in *unresponsive* and *face-to-face* condition. This result is consistent with H1a and H1b with the exception that the difference between the *face-to-face* and *unresponsive* conditions did not reach significance. However, this result demonstrates that speakers are more engaged when speaking to the responsive agent than to a real human listener.

In terms of disfluency, there are significant differences among three conditions in terms of speaker's disfluency rate, with speakers in the *unresponsive* condition having the highest disfluency rate. There are no significant differences between speakers in *face-to-face* and *responsive* condition. This is only partially consistent with H2: the speaker interacting with a real human listener didn't display more disfluency than those interacted with responsive agent, contrary to our predictions.

We further analyzed the different causes of disfluency. We counted the number of pause filler and incomplete words in the speech. There was no significant difference in number of pause fillers among the three conditions, but speakers in *unresponsive*

Table 2. Engagement and disfluency of speech

Variable	Responsive	Face-to-Face	Unresponsive
Duration (in seconds)	189.86_a	101.61_b	94.26_b
Number of Words Spoken	481.00_a	288.89_b	273.33_b
Number of Relevant Words[1]	456.13_a	277.44_b	251.33_b
Overall Speech Rate	2.62_a	2.91_a	2.94_a
Disfluency Rate[2]	0.1258_a	0.1130_a	0.2044_b
Number of Pause Fillers[3]	17.63_a	8.11_a	19.67_a
Pause Fillers Rate	$9.44E\text{-}2_a$	$8.57E\text{-}2_a$	$17.91E\text{-}2_b$
Number of Incomplete Words[4]	7.25_a	3.33_a	2.33_a
Incomplete Words Rate	$3.13E\text{-}2_a$	$2.73E\text{-}2_a$	$2.53\ E\text{-}2_a$
Number of Prolonged Words[5]	10.88_a	3.22_b	2.83_b
Prolonged Words Rate	$5.69\ E\text{-}2_a$	$3.68E\text{-}2_a$	$3.12E\text{-}2_a$

[1] Number of Relevant Words = n – pf - iw (n = Number of words spoken, pf = Number of Pause Fillers, iw = Number of Incomplete Words)
[2] Disfluency Rate = (pf + iw)/d (pf = Number of Pause Fillers, iw = Number of Incomplete Words, d = Duration)
[3] Example of Pause Fillers: "um" and "er".
[4] Example of Incomplete Words: "univers-".
[5] Example of Prolonged Words: "I li::ke it", where ":" signifies lengthened vow "i".
[Note] Means in the same row that do not share subscripts differ at $p < .05$ in the Tukey honestly significant difference comparison.

[3] Data from Responsive and Unresponsive conditions was analyzed and published before. This is a secondary analysis on the data set with additional data from face-to-face condition.

condition used significantly more pause fillers per second than the *face-to-face* and *responsive* conditions. No differences were found in either total number of incomplete words or frequency of incomplete words among three conditions. Also speakers in *responsive* condition used significantly more prolonged words than *face-to-face* and *unresponsive* condition, but there's no significant difference in prolonged words rate among these three conditions.

Contrary to H3, there are no significant differences emerged on self-report of rapport among speakers from different conditions. This may have been a byproduct of the low reliability of the self-report measure, e.g. each measure is a single item scale.

4 Discussion

The main hypothesis (H1) that a virtual human could be more engaging than a human listener was supported, suggesting that such technology can serve, both as a methodological tool for better understanding human-computer interaction, and as a means to establish rapport and its associated a range of socially desirable consequences, including improved computer-mediated learning and health interventions.

Contrary to our predictions (H2), however, face-to-face interactions did not differ significantly in disfluency with those with the RAPPORT AGENT, suggesting a more nuanced relationship between feedback, engagement, and fluency. The literature suggests that rapport serves as a mediating factor: contingent nonverbal feedback promotes rapport, which in turn, promotes beneficial social outcomes such as engagement and speech fluency. Rather, this result is more consistent with linguist theories that argue that nonverbal feedback such as head nods serve a variety of functions based on context. For example, Allwood and Cerrato (2003) argue that head nods serve a rapport-like function, conveying that the listener is paying attention. In contrast, nods can also convey semantically relevant information: that specific content was received or to show attitudinal reactions such as agreement or refusal. One could argue that the former function is more important for engagement, whereas the latter is more important for fluency (see also Bavelas et al., 2000; Cassell & Thórisson, 1999).

Indeed, anecdotal observations are consistent with the interpretation of Allwood and Cerrato (2003). Many head nods seem to be interpreted as an "I'm paying attention" signal that helps promote engagement. We further suspect that it is the frequency, rather than the timing of such gestures that are important for promoting this function. Indeed, the responsive agent generated far more head nods than human listeners. On the other hand, some agent gestures were clearly interpreted as conveying semantic meaning, and many speech disfluencies seemed to arise from the apparent inappropriateness of meaning conveyed by these gestures. Consider the following exchange taken from one of the speakers in the responsive condition: "... and the cat overhears this, and, so, Sylvester goes upstairs dressed as a bellhop [agent: shakes head] [speaker pauses] YES[emphatically], [speaker pause/smile] uh, so, uh, the, he knocks on the door." The agent detected a head shake as the speaker spoke "bellhop" (she actually made a slight side-to-side movement with her head at that moment) and attempted to mimic this gesture. This was interpreted as disagreement by the listener, causing the speaker to apparently lose her train of thought. We suspect such "inappropriate semantic feedback" is responsible for the higher disfluency rate in the responsive condition when compared to face-to-face interaction.

Though our findings on engagement are tantalizing, several methodological factors qualify the generality of our findings and must be considered before attempting to translate them into specific applications. Subjects were not assigned randomly across conditions – the face-to-face condition was run separately and after the other conditions. Thus, we cannot strictly rule out the impact of other incidental factors that might have systematically changed in this condition (e.g., weather, time of year). Additionally, subjects in the responsive and unresponsive conditions were led to believe they were speaking to a human controlled avatar, whereas the behaviors were, in fact, controlled by an intelligent agent. Several studies suggest that people will show similar social effects even if they are aware they are interacting with an agent, although the effects tend to be attenuated (Nass & Moon, 2000). Findings on self report did not reach significance, perhaps do to the lack of precision of our questionnaire (subsequent studies are using a licker scale), however several authors have noted that virtual characters often produces measurable behavioral effects even though subjects may not register awareness of these influences through self-report (Bailenson et al., 2005). Finally, the unresponsive condition varied both the contingency and the frequency of behaviors (e.g., the unresponsive agent did not nod). As the absence of behavior also communicates information, we cannot say definitively if it is the presence or contingency that promotes engagement. A larger study is currently underway that should address these methodological concerns and tease apart the factors that contributed to the observed effect.

This study focused on engagement and speech fluency; however rapport is implicated in a number of social effects including enhanced feelings of trust, greater persuasiveness and greater cooperation during negotiations. It should be straightforward to assess the impact of agent behavior on these other factors. For example, Frank, et. al (1993), showed that short face-to-face interactions enhance subsequent cooperation on simple social games (e.g., Prisoner's Dilemma). An obvious extension to the current study is to include a subsequent negotiation game as an indirect measure of trust/cooperation.

A key limitation of the RAPPORT AGENT is its reliance on "mindless feedback" (i.e., it does not actually understand any of the meaning of the speaker's narrative). While this feedback can be quite powerful, it is insufficient for most potential applications of virtual humans. Such rapid, automatic feedback could be integrated with more meaningful responses derived from an analysis of the user's speech but there are several technical obstacles must be overcome. Most speech recognition systems operate in batch mode and only extract meaning several hundred milliseconds after an utterance is complete. We have begun to experiment with continuous speech recognition but this considerably lowers the word accuracy rate. Even if text can be rapidly recognized, techniques for extracting useful meaning typically requires complete sentences. To provide this type of within utterance feedback we see in rapportful interactions, systems would have to rapidly detect partial agreement, understanding or ambiguity at the word or phrase level. We are unaware of any such work. Thus, systems that attempt to create the rapid contingent feedback associated with rapport (e.g., technological advances in incremental speech understanding), must find a way to integrate delayed semantic feedback with the more rapid generic feedback that can be provided by systems like the RAPPORT AGENT.

As this research advances, it will be important to develop a more mechanistic understanding of the processes that underlie rapport and social engagement. Although it is descriptive to argue that rapport somehow emerges in "the space between individuals," this observation is not that helpful when trying to construct a computational model of the process. Clearly, rapportful experiences are emotional experiences, but the specific emotion judgments underlying such experiences elude us. Scherer points one way forward (Scherer, 1993), arguing that subtle nonverbal cues are appraised (consciously or nonconsciously) with respect to each participants own needs, goals and values. For example, subtle cues of engagement may covey to the speaker that they are a good storyteller, and impacts their self-concept or self-esteem. We therefore regard an investigation of the appraisals that underlie feelings of rapport or engagement as an important subject for future research.

Although work on "virtual rapport" is in its early stages, these and related findings give us confidence that virtual characters can create some of the behavioral and cognitive correlates of successful helping relationships. We have explored factors related to effective multi-modal interfaces and assessed these properties in terms of explicit specific social consequences (i.e., engagement and fluency). Findings such as this can inform our understanding of the critical factors in designing effective computer-mediated human-human interaction under a variety of constraints, (e.g., video conferencing, collaboration across high vs. low bandwidth networks, etc.) by helping to identify crucial factors that impact social impressions and effective interaction. Given the wide-ranging benefits of establishing rapport, applications based on such techniques could have wide-ranging impact across a variety of social domains.

Acknowledgements. We thank Wendy Treynor for her invaluable help in data analysis. This work was sponsored by the U.S. Army Research, Development, and Engineering Command (RDECOM), and the content does not necessarily reflect the position or the policy of the Government, and no official endorsement should be inferred.

References

1. Alibali, M.W., Heath, D.C., Myers, H.J.: Effects of visibility between speaker and listener on gesture production: some gestures are meant to be seen. Journal of Memory and Language 44, 169–188 (2001)
2. Allwood, J., Cerrato, L.: A study of gestural feedback expressions. In: Paper presented at the First Nordic Symposium on Multimodal Communication, Copenhagen (2003)
3. Bailenson, J.N., Swinth, K.R., Hoyt, C.L., Persky, S., Dimov, A., Blascovich, J.: The independent and interactive effects of embodied agent appearance and behavior on self-report, cognitive, and behavioral markers of copresence in Immersive Virtual Environments. PRESENCE: Teleoperators and Virtual Environments 14, 379–393 (2005)
4. Bailenson, J.N., Yee, N.: Digital Chameleons: Automatic assimilation of nonverbal gestures in immersive virtual environments. Psychological Science 16, 814–819 (2005)
5. Bavelas, J.B., Coates, L., Johnson, T.: Listeners as Co-narrators. Journal of Personality and Social Psychology 79(6), 941–952 (2000)
6. Brand, M.: Voice puppetry. In: Paper presented at the ACM SIGGRAPH (1999)

7. Breazeal, C., Aryananda, L.: of Affective Communicative Intent in Robot-Directed Speech. Autonomous Robots 12, 83–104 (2002)
8. Burns, M.: Rapport and relationships: The basis of child care. Journal of Child Care. 2, 47–57 (1984)
9. Capella, J.N.: On defining conversational coordination and rapport. Psychological Inquiry 1(4), 303–305 (1990)
10. Cassell, J., Bickmore, T., Billinghurst, M., Campbell, L., Chang, K., Vilhjálmsson, H., et al.: Embodiment in Conversational Interfaces: Rea. In: Paper presented at the Conference on Human Factors in Computing Systems, Pittsburgh, PA (1999)
11. Cassell, J., Thórisson, K.R.: The Power of a Nod and a Glance: Envelope vs. Emotional Feedback in Animated Conversational Agents. International Journal of Applied Artificial Intelligence 13(4-5), 519–538 (1999)
12. Chartrand, T.L., Bargh, J.A.: The Chameleon Effect: The Perception-Behavior Link and Social Interaction. Journal of Personality and Social Psychology 76(6), 893–910 (1999)
13. Cogger, J.W.: Are you a skilled interviewer? Personnel Journal 61, 840–843 (1982)
14. Drolet, A.L., Morris, M.W.: Rapport in conflict resolution: accounting for how face-to-face contact fosters mutual cooperation in mixed-motive conflicts. Experimental Social Psychology 36, 26–50 (2000)
15. Ekman, P.: An argument for basic emotions. Cognition and Emotion 6, 169–2000 (1992)
16. Ellsworth, P.C., Scherer, K.R.: Appraisal processes in emotion. In: Davidson, R.J., Goldsmith, H.H., Scherer, K.R. (eds.) Handbook of the affective sciences, pp. 572–595. Oxford University Press, New York (2003)
17. Fogel, A.: Developing through relationships: Origins of communication, self and culture. Harvester Wheatsheaf, New York (1993)
18. Frank, R.: Passions with reason: the strategic role of the emotions. W. W. Norton, New York (1988)
19. Frank, R.H., Gilovich, T., Regan, D.T.: The evolution of one-shot cooperation: an experiment. Ethology and Sociobiology 14, 247–256 (1993)
20. Fuchs, D.: Examiner familiarity effects on test performance: implications for training and practice. Topics in Early Childhood Special Education 7, 90–104 (1987)
21. Grammer, K., Kruck, K.B., Magnusson, M.S.: The courtship dance: Patterns of nonverbal synchronization in opposit-sex encounters. Journal of Nonverbal Behavior 22, 3–29 (1998)
22. Gratch, J., Marsella, S.: A domain independent framework for modeling emotion. Journal of Cognitive Systems Research 5(4), 269–306 (2004)
23. Gratch, J., Okhmatovskaia, A., Lamothe, F., Marsella, S., Morales, M., van der Werf, R., et al.: Virtual Rapport. In: Paper presented at the 6th International Conference on Intelligent Virtual Agents, Marina del Rey, CA (2006)
24. Kallmann, M., Marsella, S.: Hierarchical Motion Controllers for Real-Time Autonomous Virtual Humans. In: Paper presented at the 5th International Working Conference on Intelligent Virtual Agents, Kos, Greece (2005)
25. Keltner, D., Haidt, J.: Social Functions of Emotions at Four Levels of Anysis. Cognition and Emotion 13(5), 505–521 (1999)
26. Kopp, S., Krenn, B., Marsella, S., Marshall, A., Pelachaud, C., Pirker, H., et al.: Towards a common framework for multimodal generation in ECAs: The behavior markup language. In: Paper presented at the Intelligent Virtual Agents, Marina del Rey, CA (2006)
27. Kramer, N.C., Tietz, B., Bente, G.: Effects of embodied interface agents and their gestural activity. In: Paper presented at the Intelligent Virtual Agents, Kloster Irsee, Germany (2003)

28. Marsella, S., Johnson, W.L., LaBore, C.: Interactive pedagogical drama for health interventions. In: Paper presented at the Conference on Artificial Intelligence in Education, Sydney, Australia (2003)
29. McNeill, D.: Hand and mind: What gestures reveal about thought. The University of Chicago Press, Chicago, IL (1992)
30. Morency, L.-P., Sidner, C., Lee, C., Darrell, T.: Contextual Recognition of Head Gestures. In: Paper presented at the 7th International Conference on Multimodal Interactions, Torento, Italy (2005)
31. Nass, C., Moon, Y.: Machines and mindlessness: Social responses to computers. Journal of Social Issues 56(1), 81–103 (2000)
32. Nass, C., Reeves, B.: The Media Equation. Cambridge University Press, Cambridge (1996)
33. Neal Reilly, W.S.: Believable Social and Emotional Agents (Ph.D Thesis No. CMU-CS-96-138). Carnegie Mellon University, Pittsburgh, PA (1996)
34. Oppenheim, A.V., Schafer, R.W.: From Frequency to Quefrency: A History of the Cepstrum. IEEE Signal Processing Magazine, pp. 95-106 (September 2004)
35. Parkinson, B.: Putting appraisal in context. In: Scherer, K., Schorr, A., Johnstone, T. (eds.) Appraisal processes in emotion: Theory, methods, research, pp. 173–186. Oxford University Press, London (2001)
36. Robins, B., Dautenhahn, K., Boekhorst, R.t., Billard, A.: Robotic Assistants in Therapy and Education of Children with Autism: Can a Small Humanoid Robot Help Encourage Social Interaction Skills? Special issue, Design for a more inclusive world of Universal Access in the Information Society, 4(2) (2005)
37. Sakaguchi, K., Jonsson, G.K., Hasegawa, T.: Initial interpersonal attraction between mixed-sex dyad and movement synchrony. In: Anolli, L., Duncan Jr, S., Magnusson, M.S., Riva, G. (eds.): The hidden structure of interaction: from neurons to culture patterns. Amsterdam (2005)
38. Scherer, K.: Comment: interpersonal expectations, social influence, and emotion transfer. In: Blanck, P.D. (ed.) Interpersonal Expectations: theory, research, and applications, pp. 316–333. Combridge University Press, Paris (1993)
39. Tatar, D.: Social and personal consequences of a preoccupied listener. Stanford University, Stanford, CA (1997)
40. Tickle-Degnen, L., Rosenthal, R.: The Nature of Rapport and its Nonverbal Correlates. Psychological Inquiry 1(4), 285–293 (1990)
41. Tosa, N.: Neurobaby. ACM SIGGRAPH, 212–213 (1993)
42. Tsui, P., Schultz, G.L.: Failure of Rapport: Why psychotheraputic engagement fails in the treatment of Asian clients. American Journal of Orthopsychiatry 55, 561–569 (1985)
43. Ward, N., Tsukahara, W.: Prosodic features which cue back-channel responses in English and Japanese. Journal of Pragmatics 23, 1177–1207 (2000)
44. Welji, H., Duncan, S.: Characteristics of face-to-face interactions, with and without rapport: Friends vs. strangers. In: Paper presented at the Symposium on Cognitive Processing Effects of 'Social Resonance' in Interaction, 26th Annual Meeting of the Cognitive Science Society (2004)
45. Yngve, V.H.: On getting a word in edgewise. In: Paper presented at the Sixth regional Meeting of the Chicago Linguistic Society (1970)

Automatic Mobile Content Conversion Using Semantic Image Analysis

Eunjung Han[1], Jonyeol Yang[1], HwangKyu Yang[2], and Keechul Jung[1]

[1] HCI Lab., School of Media, College of Information Technology,
Soongsil University, 156-743, Seoul, S. Korea
{hanej,yjyhorse,kcjung}@ssu.ac.kr
[2] Department of Multimedia Engineering, Dongseo University, 617-716, Busan, S. Korea
hayang88@hanmail.net

Abstract. An approach to knowledge-assisted semantic offline content re-authoring based on an automatic content conversion (ACC) ontology infrastructure is presented. Semantic concepts in the context are defined in ontology, text detection (e.g. connected component based), feature (e.g. texture homogeneity), feature parameter (e.g. texture model distribution), clustered feature (e.g. k-manes algorithm). We will show how the adaptation of the layout can facilitate browsing with mobile devices, especially small-screen mobile phones. In a second stage we address the topic of content personalization by providing a personalization scheme that is based on the ontology technology. Our experiment shows that the proposed ACC is more efficient than the existing methods in providing mobile comic contents.

1 Introduction

The recent progress in mobile devices has resulted to a rapid increase of the available amount of various contents. Various contents are used in a wide range of applications in areas (e.g. game, music, comic, e-book) on the mobile devices. Personal digital assistants (PDAs) with networking functionality are now packaged with various contents that are commercially available for cellular phones and two-way pagers. Several research projects [1-5] proposed systems that automatically convert web-based documents that was designed for desktop viewing into formats appropriate for viewing in mobile devices. In [6], present a user study on how users interact with a mobile image browser with basic functions. Thus, a lot of on/off-line contents are being converted into mobile contents. The recent trend is that comic contents are largely demanded and became one of the most popular and profitable mobile contents. However, the existing mobile comic contents inflicted many problems owing to the small display area on mobile devices [1], and processors consume much time in generating images that is fitted for the screen since the comic contents on mobile devices are manually produced by computer software such as Adobe Photoshop. But a complicated relation at the regulation of many objects/ agent/ devices at the creation should support high-label mutual application.

In [7], the web page is reformatted on the basis of page annotation. The re-authoring technique proposed in [8], required web pages to have sections and section

J. Jacko (Ed.): Human-Computer Interaction, Part III, HCII 2007, LNCS 4552, pp. 298–307, 2007.

headers, which however, are rarely used in web page authoring today. In [9-12], the authors discussed the problem of image annotations based on ontology facilitate keyword based image retrieval. In [13] propose a framework for retrieving art images in various aspects using an ontology-based method is introduced.

In this paper, an approach to knowledge-assisted semantic offline content[1] re-authoring based on an automatic content conversion (ACC) ontology infrastructure is presented. We describe the ACC system to efficiently provide mobile comic contents on the small screen. In order to create automatically mobile comic book fitting for mobile devices, splitting a comic and extracting texts must be considered. The general system architecture, Fig.1 demonstrates how a comic book can be re-authored for a smaller display. Especially, we also consider a semantic structure of a frame since it includes important contexts of comic. When the fitted image is provided on mobile devices, it can be scale-downed if it is bigger than the size of mobile screen. Semantic concepts in the context are defined in ontology, feature (e.g. texture homogeneity), feature parameter (e.g. texture model distribution), clustered feature (e.g. k-manes algorithm). Therefore, the ACC extracts the text using (e.g. connected component) analysis [2] before the image is minimized since users can not understand the excessively minimized text. Lastly, the ACC provides fitted frame images without texts on mobile devices, and locates the extracted text at the bottom of the screen. Semantic Web technologies are used for knowledge representation in the resource description framework schema (RDFS) language [14]. F-logic [15] rules are defined to describe how frame splitting, features, feature clustering, aiming at the ACC corresponding to the semantic concepts defined in the ontology. This supports flexible and managed execution of various devices application and comic book in images analysis tasks. Hereby, it can convert automatically off-line comic contents to mobile comic contents (Fig.1).

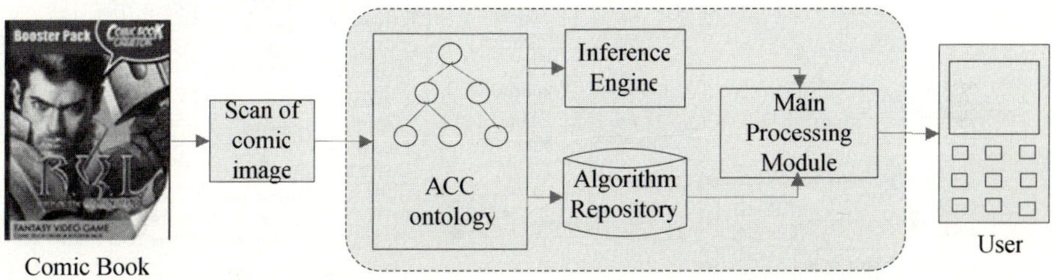

Fig. 1. Overall system architecture

The remainder of the paper is organized as follows. In section 2, a detail description of the proposed knowledge-assisted analysis system ACC ontology is given. Sections 3 and 4 describe the developed ontology framework and its application to the mobile comic content the form respectively. Experimental results are presented in Section 5. Finally, conclusions are drawn in Section 6.

[1] Comic book of offline content.

[2] The text is located in the balloon, and the regions of the figure in the frame are connected to each other.

2 ACC Ontology

In order to implement the knowledge-assisted approach described in the *ACC ontology* is constructed. The *ACC ontology* is used to support the analysis of each various comic images. Comic image segment depends on their frame splitting and text extraction which are used to select the most appropriate algorithms for the analysis process. Consequently, the development of the proposed analysis ontology deals with the following concepts (RDFS classes) and their analogy properties, as illustrated in Fig.2.

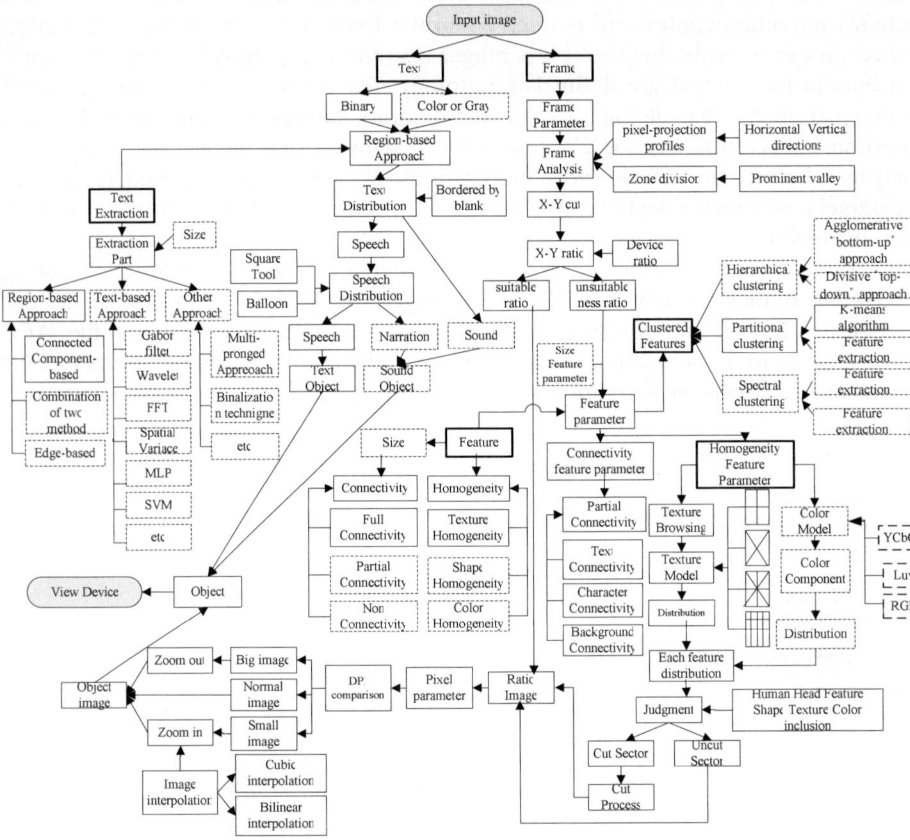

Fig. 2. ACC ontology system architecture

- Class *Text*, information divides *square tool* and *balloon*, speech distribution is ripped into *speech, narration and sound.* We locate the extracted text to the bottom of the screen. Through this process, we endow the consistency to each of comic image content and can support the readability of comic contents.

- Class *Text extraction*: used to model the extraction process, which consists of three stages (*Region-based Approach, Text-based Approach and Other Approach*). Based on the assumption that the text is located at the center of the *Speech* on white background, we extract the text using a *connected components* algorithm. First, in order to extract the text efficiently, we convert the cut image into the binary image using thresholding. Then we extract the text from the binary image using *region-based approach.*
- Class *Feature:* the superclass of each pixel features associated with each object. It is superclassed to *connectivity*, *homogeneity* and *size*. The connectivity and homogeneity classes are further subclass to *text connectivity*, *character connectivity*, *background connectivity* and *texture homogeneity* classes respectively. *Texture homogeneity* extraction of the intensity and texture vectors corresponding to each pixel. These will be used along with the spatial features in the following stages.
- Class *Feature Parameter,* which denotes the actual qualitative descriptions of each corresponding feature. It is subclassed according to the defined features, i.e., to *Connectivity Feature Parameter*, *Homogeneity Feature Parameter* and *Size Feature Parameter.*
- Class *Feature Distribution* represent information about the type of *judgment* distribution *cut section*, *uncut sector* and the *Pixel Paramete*r for its Size regulation.
- Class *Frame,* image in x- and y-axis splitting after information about the device ratio of judgment distribution *suitable ratio*, *unsuitable ratio*.
- Class *Clustered feature:* used to model the clustered features subclassed to *Hierarchical clustering, Partition clustering and Spectral clustering*. The superclass of the available processing algorithms to be used during the image feature clustering.

3 Mobile Comic Image Processing

We propose an ACC for providing efficiently and quickly mobile comic contents. In order to create automatically mobile comic contents fitting for mobile devices, splitting a comic and extracting texts must be considered. Comic splitting is a stage for eliminating non-important regions of comics, and is necessary to effectively display the comic on the small size of the mobile screen. Text extracting is necessary to prevent the text from excessively minimized comics when the comic contents are displayed on the small screen. We mainly deal with a method for comic splitting and briefly deal with a method for texts extracting because texts are easily extracted based on our assumptions that texts are located at the center of the balloon including a white background. In a stage for comic splitting, it is an important problem to determine whether any regions of the comic are semantic regions or not because the non-semantic regions are not necessary to display it on the small screen. It contains 2 layers with interconnected steps to perform an automatic image conversion suitable for small screen devices.

Page Layout Analysis. The ACC cuts tentatively the page into the frames using *X-Y recursive cut algorithm*[3]. Then, to customize the cartoon contents in mobile devices, ACC splits definitely the frame into the frame images fitted to the screen size of mobile devices. Especially, we also consider a semantic structure of a frame since it includes important contexts of cartoon. When the fitted image is provided on mobile devices, it can be scale-downed if it is bigger than the size of mobile screen. [16]. This mask can be used for model-based selection of semantic frame for which the homogeneity attribute is described in the ontology by the *Texture Homogeneity* class and additionally the connectivity attribute is described by the *Full-Connectivity* class.

Fig. 3. Splitting the frames from the comic image

Semantic region clustering. A self-organizing feature map (SOFM) is used for a semantic clustering tool to produce the image contents fitting for the small screen. It is a clustering method useful for variety types of comic images as a prerequisite stage for preserving semantic meanings. In a stage for comic splitting, it is an important problem to determine whether any regions of the comic are semantic regions or not because the non-semantic regions are not necessary to display it on the small screen.

Supervised neural networks such as MLP to preserve the semantic meanings need a previous knowledge about the desired output [2]. However, it is difficult to adopt supervised networks to cluster any regions of image because great numbers of textures appear in various comics drawn by a variety of maker or writer. Although the existing methods for clustering without a supervisor have two main ways which are a hierarchical approach such as a tree dendrogram and a portative approach as *k*-mean algorithm, they have a significant drawback which needs much computational time when using the hierarchical approach and make implicit assumptions on the form of clusters when using the portative approach [102]. We use a SOFM [67] to cluster similar texture information[4] which is used to represent the comic images, and use agglomerative clustering method to automatically segment the clustered SOFM. This

[3] Comics consist of the frames.

[4] Texture information which is useful for gray-scale image segmentation give us a good clue for semantic analysis.

approach performs the clustering without any external supervision due to the unsupervised network, and reduces computational time because the segmentation is performed on 2D space of the SOFM.

Texture information is used as features for representing semantic objects, and is extracted within each overlapping blocks, and are used as an input for the SOFM to cluster the similar texture information. Agglomerative clustering is then used to automatically segment the learnt 2D SOFM space based on inter-cluster distance [27]. Fig. 4 shows a block diagram of our approach for clustering. Computing distances and merging two clusters are continually achieved until minimum distance has smaller value than given threshold (Fig.5).

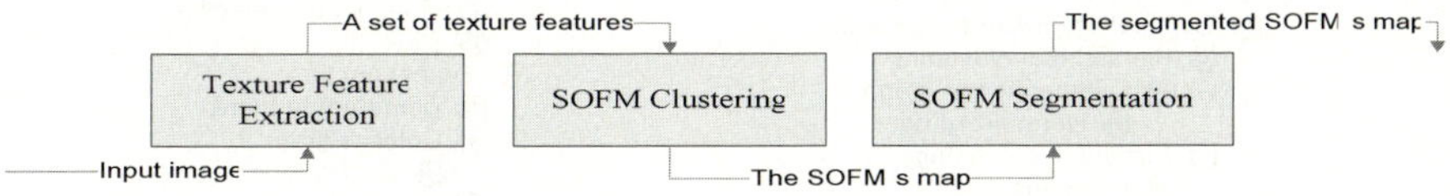

Fig. 4. Block diagram for clustering using SOFM

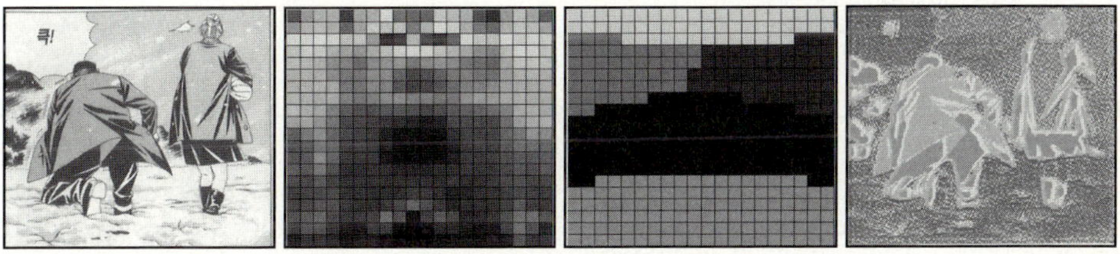

(a) (b) (c) (d)

Fig. 5. Clustered image on 2D SOFM space: (a) input image, (b) clustered SOFM image, (c) segmented image (d) result image

4 ACC Knowledge Infrastructure

Following the proposed methodology, the ACC ontology described in section 2 and image analysis described in section 3 can be applied to the form specific ontology. For this purpose, a form specific ontology is needed to provide the comic book image form and mobile devices knowledge of the suitable forms. Figure 6 shows a snapshot of the protégé-2000 ontology editor with the species hierarchy [17]. The mapping of the generic content rules to form specific ones is quite straightforward and derives directly from the ACC methodology detailed in section 2. As follow from section 2, frame cut is the first step for mobile content automatic conversion of any of the frames. Consequently, a rule of the first category without any condition is used to add X-Y recursive cut in the frame parameter.

IF X-Y ratio == Device ratio
THEN suitable ratio = X-Y ratio
ELSE unsuitableness ratio = X-Y ratio

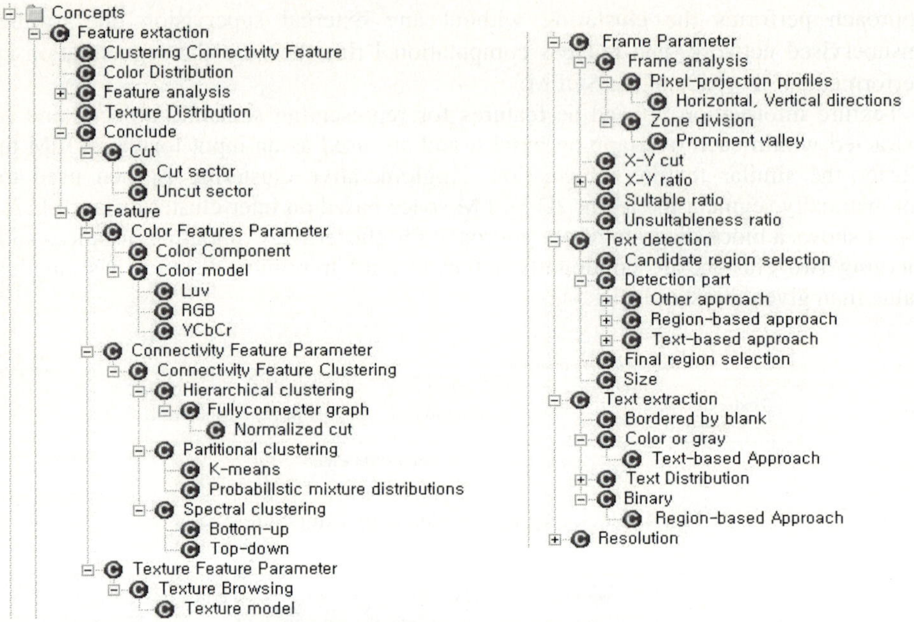

Fig. 6. Overall classes of the tool's RDFS browser: The provide various mobile comic content out of off-line book

This contains a comic image of the RDFS browser part of the tool we developed. In Fig.7, see the description of the RDFS class passive agent, a subclass of subject matter description.

5 Experimental Results

We perform to convert the 30-comic pages into mobile comic contents using each method. Table 1 is the executing times for converting the 30 comic book pages using each method. Especially, it takes over 10 minutes to convert the comic book using the existing methods because a comic book usually has over 100 pages. On the other hand, it takes about 1.5 minutes to convert the comic book using the ACC ontology.

Table 1. Result for executing times of converting the 30 comic books pages using each method

	The Existing Methods	ACC
Executing Times	10 (min)	1.5 (sec)

To make the frame images fitted to the screen size of mobile devices, the ACC cuts tentatively the page into the frames. We expect that if a comic book page consists of 5 frames, the 30 comic pages will divide into over the 150 pieces. However, we knew that the 30 comic book pages were divided into 120 pieces using the ACC ontology through the experiment. The rest of 30 pages were not divided as shown in Fig. 8. If the frame overlaps other frames (Fig. 7(a)) or an image exists on the outline of frame (Fig. 7(b)), they were not divided.

(a) (b)

Fig. 7. Comic pages, which can not be split into the frames: (a) the frame, which exists in the other frame, (b) the frame of which outline is split by the image

Fig. 8 shows our application. A comic book is scanned by scanner, it is turned into bitmap images, and scanned image are stored into a folder having a name of the comic book. If a producer loads the folder, a scanned image is displayed, and next images of the folder are displayed when completing one loop for one scanned image. Dividing frames are sequentially displayed, and an image expressing non-overlapping 5×5 size blocks on a clustered image of frames using *K-means algorithm* is displayed. Finally, we approximately eliminate the non-semantic regions using analyzing the clustered result images in x- and y-axis, the semantic region images are displayed, and both the result images and the text images are saved into storages of algorithm repository. Fig. 9 shows result images which extract the semantic region.

(a) (b) (c)

Fig. 8. Semantic region results: (a) input frames, (b) images to analyze the semantic region with blocks, (c) semantic region results

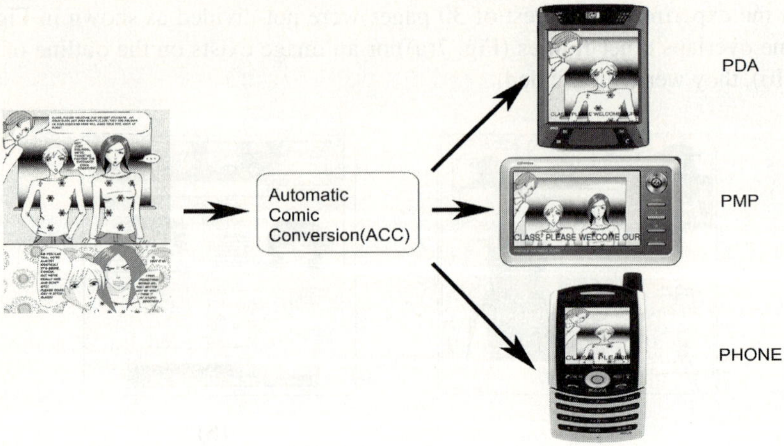

Fig. 9. Our ACC ontology application

6 Conclusions

In this paper, an approach to knowledge-assisted semantic comic books re-authoring based on a mobile comic contents ontology infrastructure is presented. The main difficulties in manual conversion from off-line comic images into mobile comic contents are time consuming and expensive. To solve the problems, we proposed the system which converts automatically the existing comic contents into mobile comic contents.

As future works, we will cover the enhancement for more image feature extraction and object detection techniques of semantic as shown. Evaluation of retrieval performance of our scheme needs further investigation. In addition to this, we will research about effective and cheap provision of mobile comic contents through continuous development of the automatic conversion system.

Acknowledgements. This work was supported by the Soongsil University Research Fund.

References

1. Chen, Y., Ma, W.Y., Zhang, H.J.: Detecting Web Page Structure for Adaptive View-ing on Small Form Factor Devices. In: Proc. of the International WWW Conference Budapest, Hungary. ACM 1-58113-680-3/03/0005, pp. 225–233 (2003)
2. Bickmore, T., Girgensohn, A., Sullivan, J.W.: Web Page Filtering and Re-Authoring for Mobile Users. Computer Journal 42(6), 534–546 (1999)
3. Chua, H.N., Scott, S.D., Choi, Y.W., Blanchfield, P.: Web-Page Adaptation Framework for PC & Mobile Device Collaboration. In: Proc. of 19 th International Conference on AINA'05, vol. 2, pp. 727–732 (2005)

4. Anderson, C.R., Domingos, P., Weld, D.S.: Personalizing Web Sites for Mobile Users. In: Proc. of the 10th International WWW Conference (2001)
5. Bickmore, Schilit, B.: Digestor: Device-independent access to the world wide web. In: Intl. WWW Conference (1997)
6. Xie, X., Liu, H., Goumaz, S., Ma, W.Y: Learning user interest for image browsing on small-form-factor devices. In: Proc. of the SIGCHI Conf. on Human factors in computing systems, pp. 671–680 (2005)
7. Hori, M., Kondoh, G., Ono, K., Hirose, S., Singhal, S.: Annotation-Based Web Content Transcoding. In: Proc. of WWW-9, Amsterdam, Holland (2000)
8. Bickmore, T.W., Schilit, B.N.: Digestor: Device-independent Access to the World Wide Web. In: Proc. of the 6th WWW Conference, pp. 655-663 (1997)
9. Schreiber, A.T., Dubbeldam, B.: Ontology-based photo annotation. IEEE Intelligent Systems (2001)
10. Schreiber, A., Blok, I.: A Mini-experiment in Semantic Annotation. In: Horrocks, I., Hendler, J. (eds.) ISWC 2002. LNCS, vol. 2342, pp. 404–408. Springer, Heidelberg (2002)
11. Hollink, L., Schreiber, T, A., Wielemaker, J., Wielinga, B.: Semantic Annotation of Image Collections. In: Proc. of the KCAP'03 Workshop on Knowledge Capture and Semantic Annotation, Florida (2003)
12. Hu, B., Dasmahapatra, S., Lewis, P., Shadbolt, N.: Ontology-Based Medical Image Annotation with Description Logics. IEEE ICTAI'03, pp. 03–05 (2003)
13. Jiang, S., Huang, T. Gao, W.: An Ontology-base Approach to Retrieve Digitized Art Image. In: Proc. of the WI'04 IEEE/WIC/ACM International Conference on 20-24, pp. 131–137 (2004)
14. Brickley, D., Guha, R.V.: RDF Schema Specification 1.0, W3C Recommendation, (2004) Available http://www.w3.org/TR/rdfschema
15. Angele, J., Lausen, G.: Ontololgies in F-logic. In: International handbooks on Information systems, Berlin, Germany (2004)
16. Han, E.J., Jun, S.K., Park, A.J., Jung, K.C.: Automatic Conversion System for Mobile Cartoon Contents. In: Proc. of the ICADL'05 International Conference, vol. 3815, pp. 416–423 (2005)
17. http://protege.stanford.edu/

History Based User Interest Modeling in WWW Access

Shuang Han, Wenguang Chen, and Heng Wang

School of Electronics Engineering and Computer Sciences, Peking University
hs@graphics.pku.edu.cn

Abstract. WWW cache stores user's browsing history, which contains large amount of information that may be accessed again but not yet added to user's favorite page folder. The existed www pages can be used to abstract user's interest and predicts user interaction. By that means, a model that describes user's interest is needed. In this paper, we discuss two methods about www-cache, data mining and user interest: simple user interest model and real time two-dimensional interest model. Moreover, the latter is described in detail and applied to user interest modeling. An experiment is performed on 20 users' interest data sets, which shows real time two-dimensional interest model is more effective in www cache modeling.

Keywords: www cache, user interest, interest model, data mining.

1 Introduction

As World Wide Web becomes more common in people's lives, the continuously increasing amount of information poses challenges for Web users to find useful information from web data lack of regular order. Sometimes an individual user needs to discover valid information from history web pages over again. However, the disorder storage of web information makes it rather hard. Therefore, it is necessary to bring a method to get user's favorite web pages in history. A user interest model that abstracts user interest and predicts user interaction is constructed based on log record. In this paper, we propose to obtain user's access preference by history based user interest modeling. Two methods are performed in our experiment on 20 users' interest data sets. Then the two methods are measured in consistent way, which shows real time two-dimensional interest model is more effective in www cache modeling.

2 History Based User Interest Modeling in WWW Access

2.1 Method Overview

There are several methods about www-cache, data mining and user interest. Traditional www-cache methods store the most highly accessed web pages. To abstract user interest, *simple user interest model* [1] described user interest through the definition (term, weight), in which weight represents the importance of term. The main idea of building *simple user interest model* is to calculate weight of term. Early *simple user interest model* takes the frequency of term in hyper text as weight of term

J. Jacko (Ed.): Human-Computer Interaction, Part III, HCII 2007, LNCS 4552, pp. 308–312, 2007.

[2][3][4]. Improved *simple user interest model* defines the term set T as $\{t_1, t_2, ..., t_m\}$, the text set in www cache D as $\{d_1, d_2, ..., d_n\}$. The improved calculation of weight of term is given as

$$Node(t_i).weight = idf_i \sum_{j=1}^{n} stf_{ij} . \quad (1)$$

Where idf_i represents reverse-text frequency of term t_i in D while df_i represents the text frequency of term t_i in D (only one count for each text), and stf_{ij} represents the frequency of term t_i in d_j, considering both places and tags of t_i in d_j.

Simple user interest model method is text-based data mining method [2][5]. However, *simple user interest model* ignored the important relationship among interests. To solve this problem, a *real time two-dimensional interest model* [6] was proposed.

The property of real time in *real-time two-dimensional interest model* can show the user's current interest states. And the inferential relations between interests are well considered in the model. This model is not the simple extension of the simple interest model, but the round improvement of the model and its related algorithm.

Our main work is to get user's favorite web pages in history through *real time two-dimensional interest model*, so as to make it more convenient for user to find useful information.

2.2 Real-Time Two-Dimensional Interest Model

User interest can be described both one-dimensionally and two-dimensionally, respectively related to "how important a single interest is in the interest set of a user" and "the successive relationship between two interests". We take the former as Interest Node, the latter as Interest Rule. *Real-time two-dimensional interest model* is mainly based on them.

We collected 20 users' interest data sets provided by 20 different users as experimental materials. For each user, we build real-time two-dimensional interest model to predict his past browsing interest. Therefore, we need to get both Interest Node and Interest Rule for each user.

Exactly like the one in *simple user interest model*, *Interest Node* is a binary group (term, weight), where weight represents the importance of interest term. Weights of *Interest Nodes* are calculated through mining of text information in the www cache, so as to obtain the term that shows user's interest. Then the favorite web pages will be picked out. Primary calculation of weight of *Interest Node* follows the expression (1).

However, every newly visited web page will cause the recalculation of all *Interest Nodes*. Therefore, *Interest Nodes* need to be updated in real-time. Also, the relationship among one-dimensional interests is significant for interest prediction. As a result, *Interest Rules*, which keep passages between interests, are proposed. To obtain *Interest Rules*, we need the existing dependence among web pages in www cache: the existing passages from one page to another. The turning from current web page to another is what we call "browsing trends", according to which a Trend Matrix can be generated, by which we create the *Interest Library* that keeps all *Interest Rules*, with their weights calculated using the *Trend Matrix*. Assume at time *t*, user is browsing page S_i ; at the next time *t+1*, user might choose:

① Keep browsing page S_i
② Click the addresses on page S_i then turn to one or more other pages
③ Click the "go back" button so as to return to the page last visited
④ Enter new address or open a new page in favorite folder

Pages in www-cache can be represent by directed graph *G=(V,E)*, in which pages are abstracted as nodes, the hyperlink relationship among pages as directed edges. We take α , β , χ and δ to represent the 4 trends user might choose as described above, where they meet $0 < \alpha, \beta, \chi, \delta < 1$, $\alpha + \beta + \chi + \delta = 1$. In this case, the *Trend Matrix Q* can be defined as follows:

$$Q = (q_{ij})_{n \times n},\ q_{ij} = \begin{cases} \alpha, & i = j \\ \beta, & (v_i, v_j) \in E \\ \chi, & (v_j, v_i) \in E \\ \delta, & others \end{cases} . \tag{2}$$

With the generation of *Trend Matrix*, *Interest Library* for each user can be built up. As a result, *Interest Nodes* will be updated in real-time. The *Interest Library* can be updated every other time, which is up to the user.

Until here, we can get our primary *real-time two-dimensional interest model*. However, the whole *Interest Library* will result in a huge needed disk space up to 20TB[1] that can't be afforded by normal users. Therefore, we have to roughen user interest. The set of all interest terms *T* is partitioned into disjoint union of equivalence classes according to the equivalence relation on *T*, *Interest Node* converts to *Rough Interest Node*, and *Interest Rule* converts to *Rough Interest Rule*, which greatly reduces space of *Interest Library* storage. Now the *real-time two-dimensional interest model* can be built in reality.

Finally, while building *real-time two-dimensional interest model*, all of web pages are treated equally, concealing the different importance of different web pages, which should be handled differently. The hypertext link relationship among web pages contains a large amount of underlying language meaning, helpful for the automatic analyzing of user interest. Individual web page's value can be judged, based on the defined value commonly adopted as PageRank (see reference [1]).

2.3 Obtaining User Interest

Since we've got *real-time two-dimensional interest model*, 20 users' interest can be concluded (calculated? determined by computation). With the existed *Interest Node* and *Interest Library*, at the moment user refreshes the improved history web page list, the conjectured favorite pages will be moved to top. Sequence of pages is decided by real-time-updated *Interest Nodes*. User's *Interest Nodes* are sorted by their weights. The location of every single page of each user depends on its key words' location in sequenced *Interest Node* set. Order of page is decided by weight of page. Calculation of weight of page S_j is given by

$$S_j.weight = \sum (stf_{ij} \cdot RoughNode(C_i).weight) . \quad (3)$$

To avoid unnecessarily unimportant calculation, we don't have to consider every *Interest Node* while calculating. Only a few *Interest Nodes*, which are evidently of greater importance than others take part in calculation. Beforehand, we take these *Interest Nodes* as concerned interest set *IS*. In this case, the expression can be modified as

$$S_j.weight = \sum_{C_i \in IS} (stf_{ij} \cdot RoughNode(C_i).weight) . \quad (4)$$

2.4 Experimental Results

Considering that there is no strict preference on web pages, user's preference is usually rough. Assume that user's interest can be divided into 5 levels, 20 users manually classify their history web pages by 5 levels, which we keep as benchmark. 5 values are given to the 5 levels of user interest: 1, 2, 3, 4, 5. As for web page S_i, we take its value *L(i)*. The lower the value of a single page is, the more interest the user shows in this page.

Then we apply both *simple user interest model* and *real time two-dimensional interest model* to obtain user interest. For each model, we compare the sorted history web page sequence with pages marked by users. In the web page sequence, if one page shows in front of the other page which owns a lower value, we call it *Rank Reversal*, by which we will judge the efficiency of each model. We define *Rank Reversal* of the whole web page sequence as

$$RR = \sum_i \sum_{j<i, L(j)>L(i)} (L(j) - L(i)) . \quad (5)$$

Also, we define total *Rank Reversal* as RR_{total} . *RR* can be standardized as $\frac{RR}{RR_{total}}$. Therefore, the precision of modeling is measured by

$$P = 1 - \frac{RR}{RR_{total}} . \quad (6)$$

Fig.1 shows results of 20 users in both *simple user interest model* and *real time two-dimensional interest model*. The precisions (P) of 20 users in *real time two-dimensional interest model* are mostly higher than the ones in *simple user interest model*.

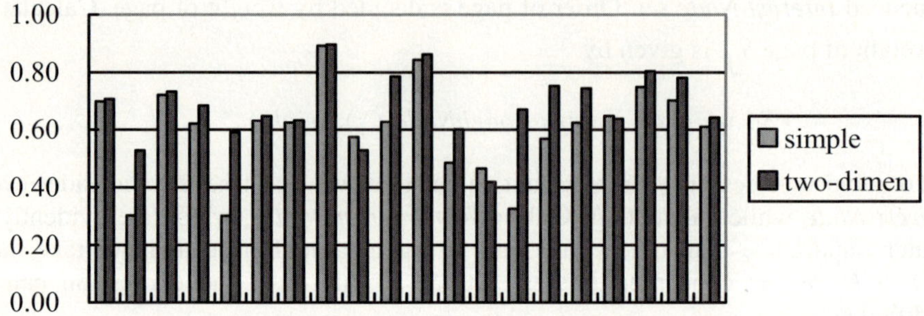

Fig. 1. Comparison of two models.

3 Conclusion

In this paper, we propose to obtain user's access preference by history based user interest modeling. Both simple user interest model and real time two-dimensional interest model are applied in our experiment on 20 users' interest data sets. Experimental results show that history based user interest modeling is helpful in obtaining user's access preference. Furthermore, real time two-dimensional interest model is more effective than simple user interest model in www cache modeling.

Acknowledgments. This study is supported by the Natural Science Foundation of China under Grant No.60473100.

References

1. Brin, S., Page, L.: The anatomy of a large-scale hypertextual www search engine. In: Proceedings of 7th world wide www Conference (www'98), Brisbane, Australia, pp. 107–117 (1998)
2. Bao-Wen, X., Wei-Feng, Z., Chu, W.C., Hong-Ji, Y.: Application of data mining in WWW pre-fetching. In: Proceedings of IEEE MSE, Tai Wan, 2000, pp. 372–377 (2000)
3. Wei-Feng, Z., Bao-Wen, X., Chu, W.C., Hong-Ji, Y.: Data mining algorithms for WWW pre-fetching. In: Proceedings of the 1st International Conference on WWW Information Systems Engineering (WISE'2000), Hong Kong, China, pp. 34–38 (2000)
4. Wei-Feng, Z., Bao-Wen, X., Song, W., Hong-Ji, Y.: Pre-fetching WWW pages through data mining based prediction. Journal of Applied System Studies, Cambridge International Science Publishing, England, 3(2), 366–371 (2002)
5. Jia-Hui, H., Xiao-Feng, M., et al.: Research on www mining. Journal of Computer Research and Development,(in Chinese) 38(4) , 405–414 (2001)
6. Bao-Wen, X., Wei-Feng, Z.: www cache based model of users' real time two-dimensions interest. Chinese Journal of Computers 27(4), 461–470 (2004)

Development of a Generic Design Framework for Intelligent Adaptive Systems

Ming Hou[1], Michelle S. Gauthier[2], and Simon Banbury[2]

[1] Defence Research & Development Canada
Ming.Hou@drdc-rddc.gc.ca
[2] CAE Professional Services Canada
{mgauthier,sbanbury}@cae.com

Abstract. A lack of established design guidelines for intelligent adaptive systems is a challenge in designing a human-machine performance maximization system. An extensive literature review was conducted to examine existing approaches in the design of intelligent adaptive systems. A unified framework to describe design approaches using consistent and unambiguous terminology was developed. Combining design methodologies from both Human Computer Interaction and Human Factors fields, conceptual and design frameworks were also developed to provide guidelines for the design and implementation of intelligent adaptive systems. A number of criteria for the selection of appropriate analytical techniques are recommended. The proposed frameworks will not only provide guidelines for designing intelligent adaptive systems in the military domain, but also broadly guide the design of other generic systems to optimize human-machine system performance.

Keywords: design guidance, design framework, intelligent adaptive interface, intelligent adaptive system.

1 Introduction

Computer-based systems assist operators in a myriad of mental and physical activities (e.g., decision support systems, automation, expert systems, and information fusion), to varying degrees of autonomy (e.g., tool, aid, associate, autonomous agent), and sophistication (e.g., assistant, associate or coach). There is a need to develop a unified framework to describe these conceptual approaches using consistent and unambiguous terminology. In addition, a lack of integration between the Human Factors (HF) and Human Computer Interaction (HCI) communities has increased the propensity for terminology to become ambiguous and misleading when applied globally. Furthermore, there are no established design guidelines for advanced operator interfaces used by decision-makers dynamically managing enormous amount of data and information in a complex and networked environment (e.g., World Wide Web or network centric warfare). In order to redefine the field in question, it is necessary to develop a framework of design guidelines encompassing both HF and HCI approaches. Defence Research & Development Canada (DRDC) has completed a project focused on developing theoretical concepts and preliminary guidelines for designing an agent-based interface system [1] [2]. The aim of this paper is to examine existing approaches in the

J. Jacko (Ed.): Human-Computer Interaction, Part III, HCII 2007, LNCS 4552, pp. 313–320, 2007.

design of intelligent adaptive systems. A unified framework to describe design approaches using consistent and unambiguous terminology was developed.

2 Methodology

Relevant literature was collected from scientific, defence, government, and internet-based sources pertaining to intelligent adaptive systems. The obtained literature was categorized into four topic areas: conceptual and project-related framework (68); analytical techniques (32); design principles and considerations (113); and psychological and behaviorally-based implementations (24). All articles were then classified in terms of Level of Experimentation, Peer Review, Domain Relevance and Literature Review Area. The literature was collated and reduced according to appropriate selection criteria. Table 1 details the number of articles classified according to the level of experimentation involved (i.e., conceptual study with no evaluation, single laboratory-based evaluation, single simulator- or field-based evaluation, and multiple laboratory-, field- or simulator-based evaluations), degree of peer review (i.e., none, conference proceedings and journal article), and proximity, and therefore relevance, to military domains (i.e., basic, business, industrial and military). These results demonstrate that the breadth of articles reviewed is sufficient, as a large number of articles have been used in all four topic areas.

Table 1. Number of references used in the literature review grouped by level of experimentation, peer review and domain relevance

	Level of Experimentation				Peer Review			Domain Relevance			
	Conceptual	Single Lab Evaluation	Single Sim/Field Evaluation	Multiple Evaluation	None	Conference	Journal	Basic	Business	Industrial	Military
Total	63	27	39	29	47	88	24	36	14	20	90

3 Intelligent Adaptive Systems

3.1 Automation and Interface

Traditionally, there have been two main thrusts of research and development addressing problems associated with operators working under conditions of excessive workload (e.g., sub-optimal task performance, error, and loss of situation awareness). The first body of research originated from the HF community, and was aimed at assessing the effects of adaptable automation on operator performance and workload within error-critical domains, such as aviation and industrial process control. The second approach originated from the HCI community, and consisted of research assessing the effects of adaptable operator machine interfaces (OMIs) on operator performance within relatively more harmless domains, such as word processing and web browsing.

Despite the obvious similarity between the HF and HCI research into intelligent adaptive systems, there is a paucity of research concerned with integrating these two research streams. This is an unfortunate oversight, as the lack of integration of these research streams creates potential for confusion over terminology.

3.2 Intelligent Adaptive Systems (IAS)

Capable of context-sensitive communication with the operator, intelligent adaptive systems (IAS) are a synergy of intelligent adaptive automation and intelligent adaptive interface technologies. IAS technologies currently under construction operate at the level of Assistant (e.g., Germany's CASSY/CAMMA programs [3], France's Co-pilote Electronique program [4]), Associate (e.g., USAF Pilots' Associate [5]) and US Army Rotorcraft Pilots' Associate programs [6], and Coach (e.g., the United Kingdom's Cognitive Cockpit program [7]).

Technological advances in both Artificial Intelligence and the physiological monitoring of human performance have the potential for enabling higher levels of intelligent support. Thus, in future, IAS will be considered fully integrated, intelligent systems that take on agent-like properties, rather than conventional systems with a discrete automation control centre. Future IAS will be able to: a) respond intelligently to operator commands, and provide pertinent information to operator requests; b) provide knowledge-based state assessments; c) provide execution assistance when authorized; d) engage in dialogue with the operator, either explicitly or implicitly, at a conceptual level of communication and understanding; and, e) provide the operator with a more useable and non-intrusive interface by managing the presentation of information in a manner appropriate to the content of the mission [8].

4 Generic Conceptual Framework for IAS

After reviewing the approaches concerned with the design of an intelligent adaptive system, a generic conceptual framework was developed. It has the following four components, which are common to all conceptual frameworks:

- *Situation Assessment and Support System.* Comprises functionality relating to real-time mission analysis, automation, and decision support in order to provide information about the objective state of the aircraft/vehicle/system within the context of a specific mission, and uses a knowledge-based system to provide assistance (e.g., automate tasks) and support to the operator.
- *Operator State Assessment.* Comprises functionality relating to real-time analysis of the psychological, physiological and/or behavioural state of the operator in order to provide information about the objective and subjective state of the operator within the context of a specific mission.
- *Adaptation Engine.* Utilizes the higher-order outputs from Operator State Assessment and Situation Assessment systems, as well as other relevant aircraft/vehicle/system data sources, to maximize the goodness of fit between aircraft/vehicle/system state, operator state, and the tactical assessments provided by the Situation Assessment system.

- *Operator Machine Interface (OMI).* The means by which the operator interacts with the aircraft/vehicle/system in order to satisfy mission tasks and goals; also the means by which, if applicable, the operator interacts with the intelligent adaptive system.

All four components operate within the context of a *closed-loop* system: a feedback loop re-samples operator state and situation assessment following the adaptation of the OMI and/or automation (see Figure 1).

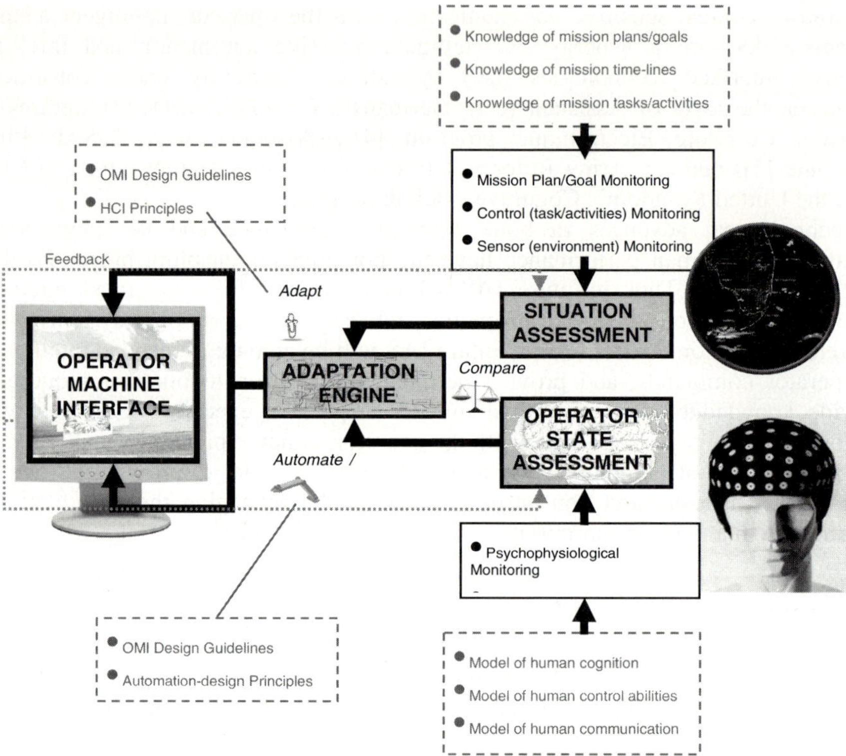

Fig. 1. Generic Conceptual Framework for Intelligent Adaptive Systems

5 Generic Framework for the Development of IAS

One of the most recent and comprehensive attempts to generate a design and development framework for intelligent adaptive systems was done by Edwards [9]. Edwards examined a variety of theoretical approaches to generate a generic, integrated and comprehensive framework for the development of an intelligent, adaptive, agent-based system for the control of Uninhabited Aerial Vehicles. These design approaches are CommonKADS (Knowledge Acquisition and Design Structuring) [10], IDEF (Integrated Computer Aided Manufacturing Definition) standards [11], Explicit Models Design (EMD) [12], Perceptual Control Theory (PCT) [13], and Ecological Interface Design (EID) [14].

The framework provides a comprehensive and efficient means of developing intelligent adaptive systems. The output of these processes is the construction and specification of a number of models that are used to construct an intelligent adaptive system:

- *Organization Model.* This model incorporates knowledge relating to the organizational context that the knowledge-based system is intended to operate in (e.g., command and control (C2) structures, Intelligence Surveillance, Target Requisition and Reconnaissance - ISTAR etc.);
- *Task Model.* This model incorporates knowledge relating to the tasks and functions undertaken by all agents, including the operator;
- *Agent Model.* This model incorporates knowledge relating to the participants of the system (i.e., computer and human agents), as well as their roles and responsibilities;
- *User Model.* This model incorporates knowledge of the human operator's abilities, needs and preferences;
- *System Model.* This model incorporates knowledge of the system's abilities, needs, and the means by which it can assist the human operator (e.g., advice, automation, interface adaptation);
- *World Model.* This model incorporates knowledge of the external world, such as physical (e.g., principles of flight controls), psychological (e.g., principles of human behaviour under stress), or cultural (e.g., rules associated with tactics adopted by hostile forces);
- *Dialogue/Communication Model.* This model incorporates knowledge of the manner in which communication takes place between the human operator and the system, and between the system agents themselves;
- *Knowledge Model.* This model incorporates a detailed record of the knowledge required to perform the tasks that the system will be performing; and,
- *Design Model.* This model comprises the hardware and software requirements related to the construction of the intelligent adaptive system. This model also specifies the means by which operator state is monitored.

Operationally, Edwards' framework illustrates the sequential process by which the models described above are created (see Figure 2). Indeed, common to all approaches reviewed in this document are the following system functions:

- Modified OMI to handle the interaction and dialogue between the operator and the systems agents (e.g., tasking interface manager);
- Tracking of operator goals/plans/intent (and progress towards them);
- Monitoring of operator state;
- Monitoring of world state; and,
- Knowledge of the effects of system advice, automation and/or adaptation on operator and world state (i.e., closed-loop feedback).

Furthermore, the models described here can also be mapped onto the generic conceptual framework described in Section 4 (see Figure 1). The association of Figures 1 and 2 indicates that: the User Model enables physiological monitoring of the operator; the Task, System, and World Models enable the monitoring of mission plan/goal completion, tasks/activities, as well as entities and objects in the external environment; the Knowledge Model enables the system to provide advice to the operator, automate tasks, or adapt the OMI; and that the Dialogue Model enables the interaction between the system and the operator. This shows the implementation of the generic conceptual framework. Figure 2 also illustrates each of the models with the relevant tools/methods/techniques relating to the design of intelligent adaptive systems, specifically:

- *Cognitive Analysis Methodologies.* Contribute to the construction of the Task, Agent and User Models;
- *Task Analysis Methodologies.* Contribute to the construction of the Task, Agent and System and World Models;
- *Human-Machine Function Allocation and Agent-based Design Principles.* Contribute to the construction of the Agent, Dialogue and Communication Models;
- *Human-Machine Interaction and Organization Principles.* Contribute to the construction of the Dialogue and Communication Models;

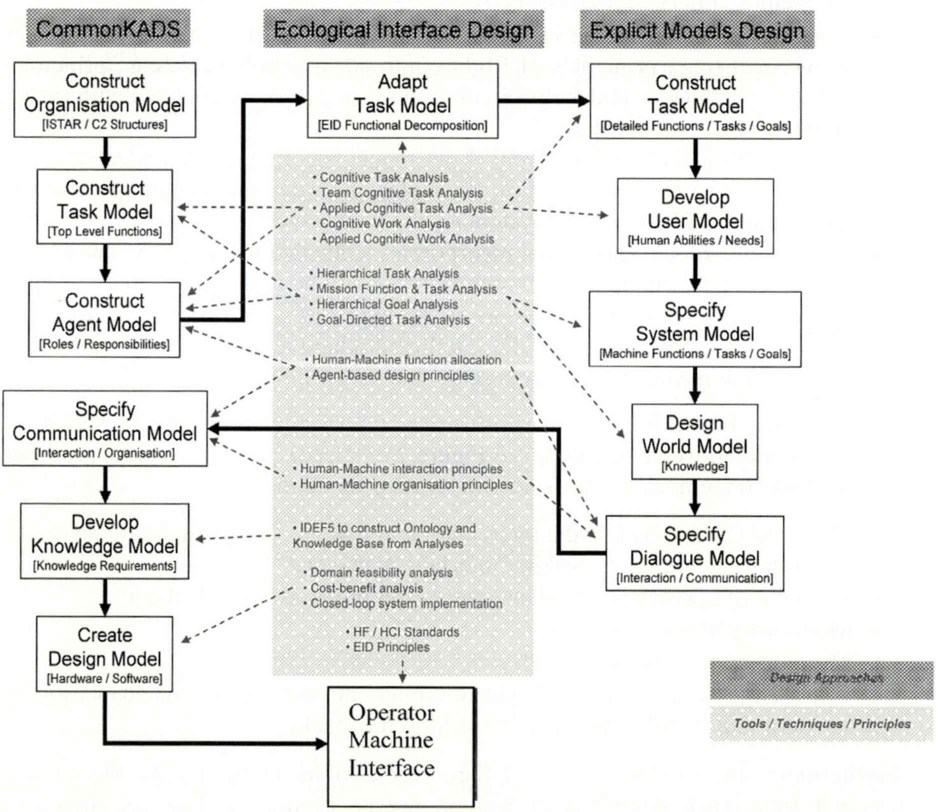

Fig. 2. Generic Framework for the Development of Intelligent Adaptive Systems

- *IDEF5 Guidelines*. Contribute to the construction of the ontology and knowledge base. This is then used to enumerate the knowledge captured by the analysis process;
- *Domain Feasibility, Cost-Benefit Analysis and Principles for Closed-Loop Implementation*. Contribute to the construction of the Design Model, including the means by which operator state is monitored; and,
- *Human Factors and Human Computer Interaction Principles.* Contribute to the construction of the OMI and related systems. The design process might also include principles from Ecological Interface Design.

Most of the tools/techniques/methodologies are generic (i.e. context independent) and scalable. The selection of the analysis tools is less critical as they are for the most part adjustable, and can be (and sometimes must be) modified to suit the domain. In addition, approaches can be combined to play to their strengths and mitigate weaknesses. There are a number of criteria that can be used to determine which of the analysis and design tools, techniques and methodologies described can be used for the design and development of a specific intelligent adaptive system. These criteria are:

- Project constraints: schedule and budget.
- Domain: complexity, criticality, uncertainty, and environmental constraints (particularly relevant to the choice of operator state monitoring systems).
- Operator: consequences of error and overload, what kind and quantity of support is needed, who needs to be in control (particularly relevant in combat domains).
- Tasks: suitability for adaptation, assistance or automation.

6 Conclusion

An extensive literature review has been conducted to examine approaches related to the design of intelligent adaptive systems. A unified framework to describe these approaches using consistent and unambiguous terminology was developed. It integrates design methodologies from both HCI and HF fields and provides generic conceptual guidance for the design of intelligent adaptive systems including human-machine interfaces. In addition, generic design guidance for the implementation of the conceptual framework was also generated to guide detailed analyses of system component models with associated analytical tools. A number of criteria for the selection of appropriate analytical techniques were also recommended. The proposed frameworks will not only provide guidance for designing intelligent adaptive systems in military domain, but also guide other generic systems to optimize human-machine system performance.

References

1. Hou, M., Koberiski, R., Brown, M.: Intelligent Adaptive Interfaces for the Control of Multiple UAVs. Augmented Cognition: Past, Present, and Future (Special Issue), Journal of Cognitive Engineering and Decision Making (In press). Human Factors and Ergonomics Society, Santa Monica, CA (2007)

2. Hou, M., Kobierski, R.: Operational Analysis and Performance Modeling for the Control of Multiple UAVs from An Airborne Platform. In: Cook, N.J., Pringle, H., Pedersen, H., Connor, O. (eds.) Advances in Human Performance and Cognitive Engineering Research. Human Factors of Remotely Operated Vehicles, vol. 7, pp. 267–285. Elsevier, New York, NY (2006)
3. Gerlach, M., Onken, R.: CASSY- The electronic part of the human-electronic crew. In: Proceedings of the 3rd international workshop on human-computer teamwork (Human-Electronic Crew: Can we trust the team?). Cambridge, UK, 27-30 September 1994 (1995)
4. Joubert, T., Sallé, S.E., Champigneux, G., Grau, J.Y., Sassus, P., Le Doeuff, H.: The Copilote Electronique project: First lessons as explanatory development starts. In: Proceedings of the 3rd international workshop on human-computer teamwork (Human-Electronic Crew: Can we trust the team?) Cambridge, UK, 27-30 September 1994 (1995)
5. Miller, C. A., Riley, V.: Achieving the Associate Relationship: Lessons learned from 10 years of research and design. In: Proceedings of the 3rd international workshop on human-computer teamwork (Human-Electronic Crew: Can we trust the team?) Cambridge, UK, 27-30 September 1994 (1995)
6. Taylor, R.M., Bonner, M.C., Dickson, B., Howells, H., Miller, C., Milton, N., Pleydell-Pearce, K., Shadbolt, N., Tennison, J., Whitecross, S.: Cognitive cockpit engineering: Coupling functional state assessment, task knowledge management, and decision support for context-sensitive aiding. In: McNeese, M.D., Vidulich, M.: Cognitive systems engineering in military aviation environments: Avoiding cogminutia fragmentosa. Human Systems Information Analysis Center State-of-the-art Report 02-01. Wright-Pattern Air Force Base, OH: Human Systems Information Analysis Center, pp. 253–312 (2002)
7. Miller, C., Hannen, M.: User Acceptance of An Intelligent User Interface: A Rotorcraft Pilot's Associate Example. In: Maybury, M.T. (ed.) Proceedings of the 4th International conference on intelligent user interfaces, pp. 109–116. ACM Press, New York, NY (1998)
8. Egglestone, R.G., Whittaker, R.D.: Work-centred support system design: Using frames to reduce work complexity. In: proceedings of the 46th Human Factors and Ergonomics Society Conference, Baltimore (2002)
9. Edwards, J.L.: A Generic, Agent-Based Framework for the Design and Development of UAV/UCAV Control Systems. Technical Report (W7711-037857/001/TOR), Prepared by Artificial Intelligence Management and Development Corporation (AIMDC) for Defence R and D Canada Toronto (2004)
10. Schereiber, G., Akkermans, H., Anjewierden, A., de Hoog, R., Shadbolt, N., Van de Velde, W., Wielinga, W.: Knowledge Engineering and Management: The CommonKADS Methodology. MIT Press, Cambridge, Massachusetts (2000)
11. National Institute of Standards and Technology, Integrated Definition for Function Modeling (IDEF0). National Technical Information Service, Springfield, VA (1993a)
12. Edwards, J.L.: Distributed Artificial Intelligence and Knowledge-based Systems. In: Steusloff, H.U. (ed.), Distributed Systems Modelling Emphasized Object-Orientation. Technical Report AC/243 (Panel 11) TR/s. North Atlantic Treaty Organization Defence Group (1994)
13. Powers, W.T.: A Hierarchy of Control. In: Roberson, R. J., Powers, W. T. (eds.) Introduction to modern psychology: the control theory view. The Control Systems Group Inc., Gravel Switch, KY, pp. 59–82 (1990a)
14. Vicente, K.J., Rasmussen, J.: Ecological Interface Design: theory foundations. IEEE Transactions on Systems, Man, and Cybernetics SMC-22, 589–606 (1992)

Three Way Relationship of Human-Robot Interaction

Jung-Hoon Hwang[1], Kang-Woo Lee[2], and Dong-Soo Kwon[1]

[1] Mechanical Engineering, Korea Advanced Institute of Science and Technology, Guseong-Dong, Yuseong-Gu, Daejeon, Korea
[2] School of Media, Sungsil University, Sangdo-Dong, Dongjak-Gu, Seoul, Korea
hwangjh@kaist.ac.kr, kangwooster@gmail.com, kwonds@kaist.ac.kr

Abstract. In this paper, we conceptualize human-robot interaction (HRI) such that a 3-way relationship among a human, robot and environment can be established. Various interactive patterns that may occur are analyzed on the basis of shared ground. The model sheds light on how uncertainty caused by lack of knowledge may be resolved and how shared ground can be established through interaction. We also develop measures to evaluate the interactivities such as an Interaction Effort, Interaction Situation Awareness using the information theory as well as Markovian transition. An experiment is carried out in which human subjects are asked to explain or answer about objects through interaction. The results of the experiments show the feasibility of the proposed model and the usefulness of the measures. It is expected that the presented model and measures will serve to increase understanding of the patterns of HRI and to evaluate the interactivity of HRI system.

Keywords: Human-Robot Interaction, Shared Ground, Metrics, Interaction Effort, Interaction SA.

1 Introduction

Robots are expected to provide various services in our daily lives and to actively interact with ordinary people rather than only robot experts. A great deal of effort is being exerted to develop communication and coordination systems between humans and robots in order to realize an efficient, collaborative, and affective relationship. In this paper, our research goal lays on the development of a formal model of HRI as well as measures based on the model. Scholtz[1] presented role model of human operator in the interaction with robot. Dautenhahn[2] presented various levels of interaction between human user and service robot. We attempt to construct the model of 3-way relationship between human, robot, and their surrounding environment using information theoretic approach. Conventionally, Artificial Intelligence (AI) has focused the linkage between an intelligent system and its environment, whereas Human-Computer Interaction (HCI) or Human Machine Interaction (HMI) has focused on the linkage between human user and artificial system. These linkages have been independently studied in those areas. However, as a robot moves in our daily environment and frequently interacts with ordinary people, a robotic system is

J. Jacko (Ed.): Human-Computer Interaction, Part III, HCII 2007, LNCS 4552, pp. 321–330, 2007.

demanded not only to be intelligent but also to be communicative. In this sense, the linkage between human, robot and environment are interwoven in HRI, and our research focuses on how a shared ground is established on these three variables.

Second research goal is the development of measure based on the model. In spite of increasing efforts in the measurement of human-robot interaction, the research on HRI still suffers from a lack of a general evaluation method or metric. Steinfeld et al.[3] pointed the necessity of common metrics to measure system performance, operator performance, and robot performance in HRI, and raised issues of common metrics in a diverse range of human robot applications such as navigation, perception, and management. So, our research extends to develop the measures that evaluate the interactivity of HRI. These measures are designed to show whether agents share a ground or not, whether the interacting state is converged into a shared ground state, and how much interaction effort are required to form the shared ground. With these theoretical model and measures, an experiment is carried out in which one subject of a paired group is asked to explain a presented object, while the other is asked to answer what it might be. The experiment showed results that provide sound insight of our approach.

2 Formalization of Human-Robot Interaction

HRI can be expressed in terms of a three-way relationship among a human, robot, and environment. One way to formalize this three-way relationship is based on information theory, in which three variables, the knowledge of humans, the knowledge of robots, and environment, can be formalized with entropy and mutual information.

2.1 Modeling of Human-Robot Interaction with Information Theory

In Fig. 1 the relationship between the knowledge possessed by human user (U), the knowledge possessed by robot (R) and environmental object (E) is formalized with entropy and mutual information. Entropy H denotes the uncertainty of a variable. Mutual information I is the shared portion of two or more variables and can be considered as a common ground between the variables. Using these concepts, the relationships are expressed as given in Fig. 1.

Fig. 1 also shows that human-robot interaction can be decomposed into various areas that are shared by each party and those that are not shared. Each area is closely related to the patterns of interaction, since the interaction pattern varies according to the ground occupied by the agents.

2.2 Uncertainties That Need to Be Resolved

In order to improve the interactivity between human and robot, it is necessary to resolve the uncertainty caused by discrepancies in the agents' knowledge. The uncertainty from the robot's viewpoint is the area obtained by subtracting the total entropy of $\mathrm{H}(R)$ from $\mathrm{H}(U,E,R)$.

$$\mathrm{H}(U,E \mid R) = \mathrm{H}(U,E,R) - \mathrm{H}(R) \ . \tag{1}$$

The uncertainty from the robot's viewpoint ($H(U,E \mid R)$) can be divided into three parts – $H(U \mid R,E)$, $H(E \mid U,R)$, and $I(U;E \mid R)$. For each case, the robot may be required to remove the uncertainty in order to interact with the other agent.

For example, the uncertainty $H(U \mid R,E)$ is the unknown portion about the human user to the robot. The interaction process between robot *R* and user *U*, to reduce the uncertainty of $H(U \mid R,E)$ and increase the shared information of $I(U;R \mid E)$, is the robot's learning process about the user. If a home service robot finds something while cleaning a room, it can ask the user what the object is and what it should do with the object. The user teaches the robot the name of the object, the place where it has to be moved, and how it should be handled. Instructive teaching and a learning process between a human and a robot can be a solution to resolve the problem of uncertainty caused by robot's lack of knowledge, and can improve collaboration between the user and robot.

In contrast to the robot's uncertainty, the human user's uncertainty is expressed by $H(R,E \mid U) = H(U,R,E) - H(U)$, which is decomposed into three parts, $H(R \mid U,E)$, $H(E \mid U,R)$, and $I(R;E \mid U)$.

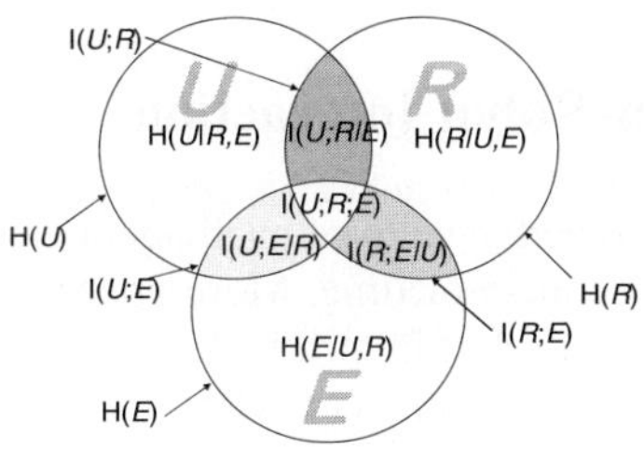

Fig. 1. Three-way relationship between U, R and E. The uncertainties in HRI are expressed with entropy, mutual information, and conditional entropy.

2.3 Interaction Process Model

From the interaction patterns for each agent to reduce its uncertainty, interaction can be seen as a process of reducing the uncertainty of each agent and establishing shared ground with other agent. As interaction between human and robot occurs more frequently, dynamic changes in ground formation are expected to accompany.

The establishment of shared ground through the interaction between two agents can be a sequential process in which an agent's state can be represented in terms of one of the regions referred to above, and this may correspond to each agent's mental model (or belief) about himself or herself and partner. That is, whenever an interaction occurs, each agent can take an action or reaction based on his/her mental model. However, in order to efficiently communicate with each other, the knowledge states of the agents should converge into shared ground $I(U;R;E)$. The sequential process of the interaction can be modeled with our approach.

The interaction process of each agent is modeled as a state transition diagram. The regions in the diagram of the three-way relationship can be mapped to the states of each agent. Since an agent can share a ground with others only after it has the ground,

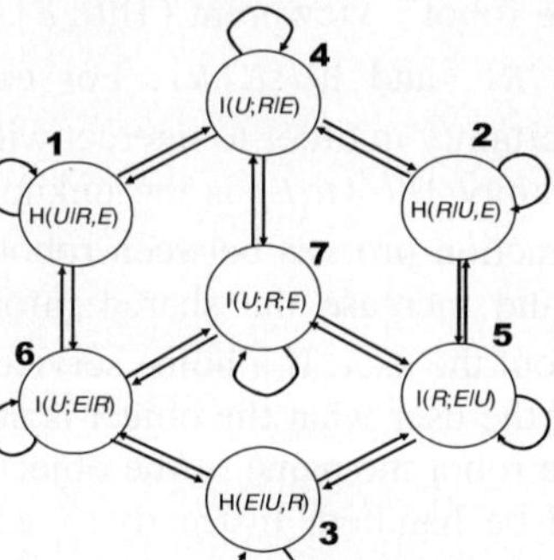

Fig. 2. State Transition Diagram of the HRI Process Model. Each region of Fig. 1 is mapped into each state of state transition diagram.

the state transition can only occur between regions that are adjoined with a line. The state transition diagram of the interaction process is connected as shown in Fig. 2.

3 Measure of Human-Robot Interaction

As described above, the knowledge state of each agent can be evolved and converged through interaction over the course of time. More generally, we can conceptualize the interaction between human and robot in terms of a state transition over time. With this model, we have derived several measures of HRI.

3.1 Markov Chain Model of HRI Process

If the interaction has a set of states composed of $s_1, s_2, \ldots, s_m$ at each moment of the time $t_1, t_2, \ldots, t_n$, we can describe the probability of state S_i that occurs on the nth interaction (trial) given that a sequence of S has occurred on the previous jth interaction as follows:

$$p(t_n = s_i \mid s_{n-1}, \ldots, s_{n-j} = S) = b \quad . \tag{2}$$

If the conditional probability of x_i is independent of all states in the sequence except the very previous state s_j, then

$$p(t_n = s_i \mid s_{n-1}, \ldots, s_{n-j} = S) = p(t_n = s_i \mid s_{n-1}) \quad . \tag{3}$$

The sequential process with this property is termed a Markov chain. Our interaction process model is assumed to be a Markov chain as other researches [4, 5]. Thus, the model of the HRI process can be characterized with a state transition matrix.

3.2 Weighted Entropy with State Transition

Our conceptual framework of HRI is extended in order to develop a measure of interactivity between human and robot. In our approach, entropy, which is a measure of the amount of uncertainty, is used. This entity provides a quantification of uncertainty and randomness in the system. In this case, the system is a model of the HRI process. In order to measure goal-directed activities, Belis and Guiasu[6] introduced utility u_i of a state with its probability p_i to entropy. The information given by the state s_i having a probability of p_i and a utility u_i is

$$I = -k \sum_{i=1}^{n} u_i p_i \log p_i \tag{4}$$

Using this weighted entropy method with proper utilities, we can estimate whether interaction states are converged into a shared ground or how fast the designed interaction can reach the shared ground state using our approach. The utilities of the weighted entropy are decided as shown in equation (5). The probability value of each state transition is used in calculating the utility value since the larger probability has greater influence on converging to the shared ground state.

When state transition occurs from S1 to S2,

$$u_i = \begin{cases} -1 \times p_i & \text{if S2 is the goal state or closer to the goal state than S1} \\ 1 \times p_i & \text{Otherwise} \end{cases} \tag{5}$$

3.3 Measuring Interaction Effort and Interaction Situation Awareness (SA)

Interaction between two agents is efficient if they are in a state of shared ground, whereas additional efforts are required to understand each other if they are not in a state of shared ground. The amount of effort in understanding the other's interactivity is proportional to the amount of uncertainty in the interactivity. Eq. (6) describes this relation.

$$I_{IE} = k \left(\sum_{P_{ij} \in M} P'_{ij} P'_{ij} \log P'_{ij} - \sum_{P_{ij} \in L} P'_{ij} P'_{ij} \log P'_{ij} \right) + C \tag{6}$$

in which C is a constant value that is calculated constantly with the number of positive directional probabilities M and the number of non-positive directional probabilities L to make the minimum value of I_{IE} is zero. k is a normalization factor. The equation can be decomposed into two terms representing the probability of the state transition directed to state 7 (shared ground state) and the probability not directed to state 7, respectively.

In order to interact properly, an agent must understand what the other agent wants or says, and react according to the response of the other agent. For example, if the receiver does not understand the message delivered by the sender, the sender should re-explain its intention or provide more information about the message. We call this as interaction situation awareness (SA[7]). The Interaction SA can be measured if we adopt the components corresponding to the states of an agent's understanding about the other agent from the state transition matrix. For example, P_{35} is the probability that an agent comes to know that the other agent knows something. Using these components, we can calculate the Interaction SA in terms of the difference between the probability of the state transition in which an agent is aware of the other agent's action and the probability of the state transition in which an agent is not aware. The measure of Interaction SA of each agent is given by equation (7). M_{SA} of the first term is the group of probabilities that an agent comes to know the situation. L_{SA} of second term is the group of probabilities such that an agent still does not know the situation. C_{SA} is a constant value that is calculated constantly with the number of M_{SA} and L_{SA} to make the minimum value of I_{SA} is zero. k_{SA} is a normalization factor.

$$I_{SA} = k_{SA}\left(\sum_{P_{ij} \in M_{SA}} P'_{ij} P'_{ij} \log P'_{ij} - \sum_{P_{ij} \in L_{SA}} P'_{ij} P'_{ij} \log P'_{ij} \right) + C_{SA} \tag{7}$$

The measure of the situation awareness can be independently applied to each agent. In the case of HRI, we can measure a user's awareness about a robot system and a robot's awareness about a user, respectively. These two measures can be used to evaluate the interactivity of a designed HRI, and to improve the interactivity of the robot system.

4 Interaction Case Study

An experiment was designed to test the proposed interaction model and the measures of interaction. The interaction process of information transfer between two human agents was applied. Since an intelligent service robot be targeted to interact with people as a human interact with another. Hence human-human interaction (HHI) is a good preliminary test-bed to verify the proposed model of HRI.

4.1 Experiment Procedure

In the experiment, thirty human subjects from the Korea Advanced Institute of Science and Technology (KAIST) and Yonsei University participated. Subjects were asked to carry out a 'questioning and answering' task in which one of the two subjects explained about an object, and the other answered what it might be. During the task the questioner was allowed to provide further explanation if the answerer could not correctly answer. The answerer was allowed to express whether he/she could understand the explanation.

The objects used in the experiment were hardware such as a gear box, milling blade, ball bearing, etc. These materials are familiar to students majoring in mechanical engineering, but may not be familiar to students of social science or art. Based on the subjects' major and years, they were classified into two different groups – expert and novice. Furthermore, subjects were paired into one of 3 groups – expert – expert paired group (E-E group), novice – novice paired group (N-N group) and novice – expert paired group (N-E group).

In the experiment, two subjects were located in a chamber as shown in Fig. 3. The experimental materials were displayed on the desk so both subjects could see them. The subjects of each pair took different roles (i.e., one subject as a questioner), and then switched their roles (i.e., a questioner would then become an answerer) after completing the explanation once. A trial of the task was completed if an answerer correctly responded and the questioner pressed a button. The next trial would start and continue until all items were correctly answered. During the experiment, subjects

Fig. 3. Scene from the experiment. Various objects from mechanical engineering are used.

were allowed to use only linguistic expressions. No gestures were allowed. The whole experimental process was recorded with a camcorder. The experiment is run by a computer program without any interruption from the experimenter.

4.2 Evaluation of Subject's State

After the experiment, the states of each agent were evaluated and classified by analyzing the video records. Since the internal state of an agent cannot be observed directly, it must be inferred from observations. Therefore, operational definitions are needed to classify the state of each agent. The operational definitions for the states are given as follows:

- No shared ground about a particular object between a questioner and answerer is assumed before an interaction occurs. The asker is assumed to be in state (6) in which he has the knowledge of the object, while the respondent is assumed to be in state (3).
- The questioner is assumed to be in state (7) about the object with the answerer while waiting for the answer after querying about a particular object.

4.3 The Results

4.3.1 State Transition Probability for Three Different Paired Groups

The state transition probability matrixes for three different paired groups were obtained from the evaluation process. First, in the E-E group, the interactions between subjects were mainly in the shared ground state (7), while in the N-N group, they were mainly in state 5 or 6, which means he/she has a ground alone. Interesting results are obtained for the N-E group: The state transition probability matrix of the N-E group is very similar to that of the novice group.

$$P_{N-N}[3,5,6,7;5,6,7]=\begin{bmatrix}0.467 & 0.533 & 0.000\\ 0.812 & 0.000 & 0.187\\ 0.000 & 0.811 & 0.189\\ 0.141 & 0.070 & 0.789\end{bmatrix},\ P_{E-E}[3,5,6,7;5,6,7]=\begin{bmatrix}0.714 & 0.286 & 0.000\\ 0.629 & 0.000 & 0.371\\ 0.000 & 0.556 & 0.444\\ 0.091 & 0.074 & 0.835\end{bmatrix}$$

and $P_{N-E}[3,5,6,7;5,6,7]=\begin{bmatrix}0.500 & 0.500 & 0.000\\ 0.811 & 0.000 & 0.189\\ 0.000 & 0.713 & 0.287\\ 0.160 & 0.080 & 0.760\end{bmatrix}$

4.3.2 Comparing Interaction Effort Between Groups

The result above indicates that the E-E group could easily establish shared ground during the interaction, whereas the other groups had difficulty in establishing shared ground. Therefore, we may expect that the E-E group requires less effort in the interaction than the other two groups. To estimate how much interaction efforts are required in the differently paired groups, the interaction efforts are summarized with other indices in Table 1. The results showed that the averaged interaction effort value (0.379) in the E-E group is less than the value (0.625) of the N-N group and the value (0.621) of the N-E group. The differences (t-test, $p < .05$ for the E-E group and N-N group, and E-E group and N-E group) between groups are statistically significant. However, no significant difference (t-test $p > 0.2$) was found between the N-N group and the N-E group. The other measures of required time and turns per each trial showed similar results that supported the results of the interaction efforts between groups.

4.3.3 Comparing Interaction SA Between Groups

As shown in Table 2, N-N group and E-E group show a large difference in the measure of Interaction SA. This difference originates from the difference in expertness. Comparing N-N group with N-E group, the novices do not show a large difference (t-test $p = 0.6289$ for agent B in N-E group vs. agent A in N-N group, $p = 0.5824$ for agent B in N-E group vs. agent B in N-N group). However, comparing E-E group with N-E group, the measures of some experts show differences with others (t-test $p = 0.0396$ for agent A in E-E group vs. agent A in N-E group).

From these results, it is known that the novices show similar Interaction SA regardless of the opponent's expertness while the measure of Interaction SA of the experts can be changed by the opponent's expertness. The spectrum of information that the novice can express and understand is narrow while the spectrum of information that the expert can express and understand is wide, thus possibly accounting for this difference.

Table 1. Measure of Interaction Effort, time, and turns

	Average of the Measure of Interaction Effort	Time per a trial (sec)	Turns per a trial
N-N group	0.625	45.3	13.9
E-E group	0.376	31.2	7.1
N-E group	0.621	38.7	12.9

Table 2. Measure of Interaction SA

	Agent A	Agent B
N-N group	0.623	0.619
E-E group	0.495	0.517
N-E Group*	0.561	0.639

*Experts were Agent A and novices were Agent B in the N-E Group.

4.3.4 Discussion on the Results

In general various aspects of the interaction in the different groups have been investigated using our measure. The difference between groups was found in terms of how much interaction effort is required or whether an agent understood the state of the other, etc. The results indicated that the N-N and N-E groups required more interaction effort to share common grounds, whereas the E-E group needed less interaction effort to share common grounds. Hence, the interaction in the E-E group is more efficient than in the other groups. The measure of state awareness also showed similar results, but provided additional information about the relative interactivity between expert and novice. That is, the expert's understanding about other's state (or situation) was better than the novice's during the interaction. This implies that expertise related to the objects contributed to efficient interaction.

However, the difference between the groups cannot simply be attributed to the amount of knowledge. LeFrance[8] pointed out that experts have not only more knowledge, but also have structured knowledge that can be easily accumulated and accessed. Moreover, experts are able to access a problem more abstractly, but novices superficially treat a problem. Therefore, during the interaction, experts can deal with more information than novices can. However, inequality of expertise levels interferes with communication during the interaction. The message delivered by a novice contains superficial or partial information of the object, and thus does not facilitate understanding well. Similarly, the message delivered by an expert contains more abstract or specialized information, and thus a novice has difficulty understanding the message.

5 Conclusions

In this paper, a formal model of human-robot interaction is developed based on information theory, and attempts are made to explain the dynamics of interactions in terms of a three-way relationship. In addition, the interactivities are classified in terms of what grounds the three variables of U, R, E share. Throughout the formalization, patterns of interactivity were discovered that might occur in actual human-robot interactions. Any uncertainty caused by a discrepancy between the two knowledge systems must be resolved in order to maximize task performance. A formal model of human-robot interaction could describe the sequence of interaction processes and make it possible to model and predict the interaction process.

We also developed measures to evaluate the performance of interacting agents in terms of interaction effort and interaction situation awareness. In the experiment, it was demonstrated that the proposed measures are effective in measuring the interactivity. Furthermore interesting aspects of interaction were found through comparisons of three different groups through the experiment. We expect that the measures of interaction effort and situation awareness will be helpful in analyzing and enhancing the interaction process.

Acknowledgments. This work was partially supported by the Intelligent Robotics Dev. Program of the 21C Frontier R&D Programs funded by the Ministry of Commerce, Industry and Energy of Korea.

References

1. Scholtz, J.: Theory and Evaluation of Human Robot Interactions. In: The 36th Annual Hawaii International Conference on System Sciences (2003)
2. Dautenhahn, K., Werry, I.: Issues of Robot-Human Interaction Dynamics in the Rehabilitation of Children with Autism. In: The Sixth International Conference on the Simulation of Adaptive Behavior (2000)
3. Steinfeld, A., Fong, T., Kaber, D., Lewis, M., Scholtz, J., Schultz, A., Goodrich, M.: Common Metrics for Human-Robot Interaction. Human-Robot Interaction, Salt Lake City, Utah (2006)
4. Raush, H.L.: Process and Change-A Markov Model for Interaction. Family Process 11, 275–298 (1972)
5. Williams, J.D., Young, S.: Partially observable Markov decision processes for spoken dialog systems. Computer Speech and Language 21, 393–422 (2007)
6. Belis, M., Guiasu, S.: A quantitative-qualitative measure of information in cybernetic systems. IEEE Transactions on Information Theory 14, 593–594 (1968)
7. Endsley, M.R.: Towards a theory of situation awareness in dynamic systems. Human Factors 37, 32–64 (1995)
8. LaFrance, M.: The Quality of Expertise: Implications of Expert-Novice Difference for Knowledge Acquisition. SIGART Newsletter, Number 108, Knowledge Acquisition Special Issue, 6–14 (1989)

MEMORIA: Personal Memento Service Using Intelligent Gadgets

Hyeju Jang, Jongho Won, and Changseok Bae

Post PC Research Group, Digital Home Research Division,
Electronics and Telecommunications Research Institute,
161 Gajeong-dong, Yuseong-gu, Daejeon, 305-700, Korea
{hjjang,jhwon,csbae}@etri.re.kr

Abstract. People would like to record what they experience to recall their earlier events, share with others, or even hand down to their next generations. In addition, our environment has been getting digitalized and the cost of storing media has been being reduced. This has led research on the life log that stores people's daily life. The research area includes collecting experience information conveniently, manipulating and recording the collected information efficiently, and retrieving and providing the stored information to users effectively. This paper describes a personalized memory augmentation service, called MEMORIA, that collects, stores and retrieves various kinds of experience information in real time using the specially designed wearable intelligent gadget (WIG).

Keywords: Intelligent Gadget, Smart Object, Personalized Service, Memory Assistant System, Memory Augmentation Service.

1 Introduction

People seem to have a tendency to record their lives. While keeping diary on the paper or in the computer before, people record and share their lives more actively with the help of electronic machines in the digital era. The representative recording media such as personal homepages and blogs enable people to express their feelings, to give their opinions, and to contain information they are interested in. In addition, digital cameras are prevailed all over now, which record not only images but also moving pictures of personal information. When, where, and what a person did are recorded as images or videos with text information in the form of metadata such as an exchangeable image file format (EXIF) or annotated information. These data can be said that people volunteer to make them with intention.

What's more, information recorded automatically by the power of digital era is also increasing. Closed-circuit televisions (CCTVs) in everywhere record our movement. Where, when, and how much a person spend with a credit card, when and whom a person talked with on the phone, which e-mail a persona received and sent are recording in a digital way. The recorded forms of these kinds of information from our lives are called life logs.

J. Jacko (Ed.): Human-Computer Interaction, Part III, HCII 2007, LNCS 4552, pp. 331–339, 2007.

To collect these kinds of various information of the life log from people's daily life, researches for adding the ability of collecting and processing information on the objects are ongoing. One of them is an effort to provide the intelligence into every object with the name of the smart object. In this paper, we use a smart object called a wearable intelligent gadget (WIG) that has the information processing capability. It can be carried or worn at hand in daily life such as a wallet, a bag, and a necklace. WIGs are able to play various roles like collecting information or transmitting data to others.

This paper describes a personalized memory augmentation service model using WIGs, called MEMORIA. It is a real-time application that exploits WIGs, which collect and save experience data and provide users with user friendly interfaces for data retrieval. The service can provide users to recall their past memories, and also strengthens and enhances their memories.

MEMORIA is differentiated from others in that it is a real-time online service. Real-timeness is much more practical especially to the people who need monitoring services such as patients with dementia because it can provide immediate status updates. In addition, MEMORIA expands the possibility of a new business model using WIGs. With the wearable, reconfigurable, and scalable features, it is possible to create a various kinds of services which are more personalized as the trend in the ubiquitous computing era.

2 Related Works

As the personal service areas, recently there has been much research related to the "Life Log" to record everyday experience information. They mainly focus on how to sense personal experience information, how to log such sensed information, and how to query or retrieve the necessary information from the logged data.

The life log video system led by Prof. Aizazwa from Tokyo university used brain wave, movement, recognizing face, position, time, internet, log of using application programs as the factors managing memories [1]. As memory information of a person, not only video and audio but also daily life information recorded from various wearable sensors is used.

The representative example of research using WIGs is TTT(Things That Think) project in MIT [2]. In this project, many researches are being done for the development of thinking objects. For instance, attaching information processing device to objects, attracting people's eyes, recognizing people's voice, and providing information users want is possible in "Invisible Media". MIT also developed bYOB(Build Your Own Bag) which can grab outside environment and service intellectually, a smart bag [3].

Nokia developed and provided Lifeblog connecting to their cellular phones, which is a PC based software [4]. Users save contents made with Nokia cellular phones, or video they take a photograph with their interests using Lifeblog through wireless network. Saved information can be shared with other users if they want. The target of Lifeblog is mainly video and text data, it's still difficult to support other information like environment, the reaction of a living body, and movement.

Microsoft is developing a lifelog service using SenceCam and MyLifeBits Viewer. Users bring SenseCam and collect experience information. Collected information is saved and managed in MyLifeBits which is a PC based application [5].

Canada Queens University's eyeBlog is the system which saves and shows user's video information automatically [6]. EyeBlog measures people's gaze information using a wearable wireless gaze sensor, ECSGlasses(Eye-Contect Sensing Glasses). Using this, it records 1:1 conversation and recorded information can be shown through web. Video is automatically recorded based on user's interests. For example, if it catches somebody looking at the user with ECSGlasses, it thinks that's 1:1 conversation and records the conversation with video. Moreover, it's also possible for users to record the conversation manually with buttons. Newly recorded videos are saved in a certain directory of a web server, web contents are automatically manipulated and uploaded to the blog. Then, users can watch video contents built using preview function. eyeBlog is also an example of using Web 2.0.

3 System Design of MEMORIA

3.1 Wearable Intelligent Gadget (WIG)

WIG is a wearable platform which is reconfigurable, scalable, and component-based. It can be equipped, carried as a personal accessory, or in a certain case, implanted internally into a body. It is used to gather various kinds of personal information, and that can process those gathered information to provide specially personalized services for the ubiquitous computing environment. It also can be installed on diverse ubiquitous environments to gather various environmental information to provide more adequate personal services by analyzing and combining with those information.

For the hardware point of view, WIG consists of a base block and device blocks. The base block is equipped with a processor, a memory, a network, a power and a stack-able interface. The device block consists of a sensor and a stack-able interface. The function of WIG depends on the type of device blocks, and the function of a device block depends on the sensor equipped. WIG can be only a base block itself, or one base block stacked with multiple device blocks.

For the software point of view, WIG consists of a light-weighted operating system and a WIG middleware. The WIG middleware has a component-based modular architecture for the reconfigurability and the scalability. It also allows the logical and physical grouping. The physical grouping is a set of WIGs that compose the physical PAN or BAN, and the logical grouping is a set of WIGs that are grouped by a common attribute.

As shown in Fig. 1, WIG consists with the hardware platform, the software platform, as well as the WIG toolkit.

The WIG toolkit is a set of tools consisted with the hardware toolkit, API, and various utilities that support the WIG hardware platform manufacturers, service developers, and service providers, respectively.

For more details of WIG, refer to [7].

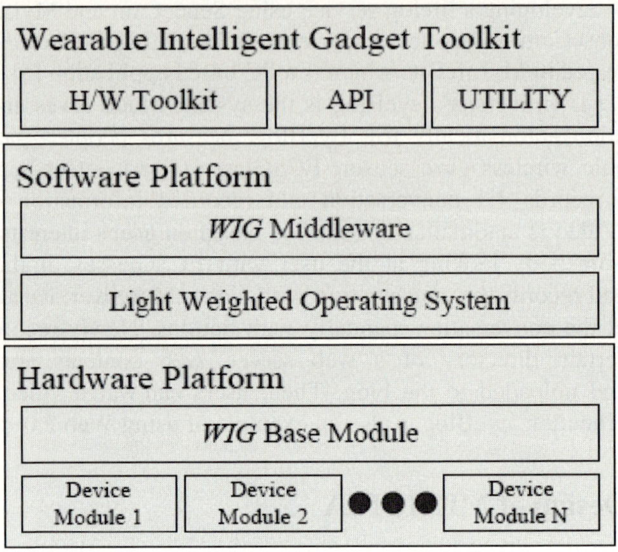

Fig. 1. Wearable Intelligent Gadget (WIG) architecture

3.2 Service Environment of MEMORIA

MEMORIA is based on the client-server architecture, which consists of a life log server, logging clients, service clients, and a web server. The life log server (LLS) stores and manages many kinds of data obtained from different logging clients, and provides service clients with relevant data to user queries in real-time. The logging clients gather user-centric information and log it to LLS. The service clients interact with users and request information to LLS if needed according to the user query. The web server enables LLS to be integrated with various web-based services.

MEMORIA is a real-time service that exploits gadgets, which collect, save and provide experience data to users through user interfaces for data retrieval. MEMORIA saves and retrieves various experience data simultaneously. For it, it should work under the ubiquitous computing environment which is connected with wire-wireless network. In other words, it saves a lot of various data in the remote server in real-time and get the necessary data from the remote server.

Fig. 2 shows the service environment of MEMORIA. It consists of Life log server which saves and manages various data and retrieve the queried data, logging gadgets which collect various personal data and deliver to the life log server, service gadgets which interact with users and show the information provided by the life log server, and web server which provide various web-based services together with the life log server. And, WIGs as the logging gadgets and service gadgets can compose WIG network as a PAN (Personal Area Network) or a BAN (Body Area Network).

MEMORIA integrates largely two kinds of services, a logging service and a retrieving service. The former collects personal data and saves into the remote logging server, and the latter retrieves and provides data users find.

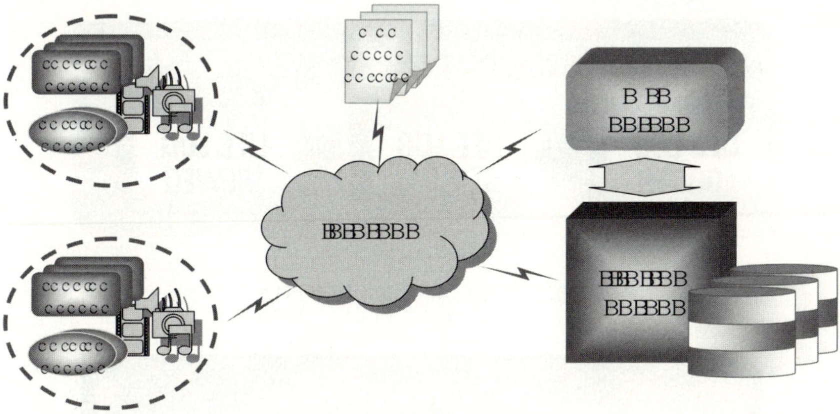

Fig. 2. Service environment of MEMORIA

The process of a logging service includes both logging gadgets collecting personal experience data and sending to the remote life log server in real time, and the life log server saving the given data. To do it, the life log server becomes a server that provide a interface to save experience data, and the logging gadgets be the clients that saves the collected data to the server.

The process of a retrieving service also includes two services. One is the service for service gadgets people have to get the query and to request the relevant data to the life log server, and the other is the service for the life log server to retrieve the relevant experience data and give them to the service gadgets. To do it, they also have a client/server architecture, which the life log server provide an interface which the service gadgets.

3.3 Design of MEMORIA

MEMORIA is a memory augmentation service to trace user's location and scenery information. The logging and service clients are corresponding to the WIGs, called logging gadgets (LGs) and service gadgets (SGs), respectively. WIGs for MEMORIA are all equipped with a ZigBee module for establishing BAN. In addition to LGs and SGs, network gadgets (NGs) that have the wireless Ethernet functionality are used to communicate between LGs and LLS.

Fig. 3 describes the system of MEMORIA. It consists of three parts: Life log logger, Life log server, and Life log viewer. They are corresponding to a logging WIG, a life log server, and a service WIG, respectively.

WIGs are able to be reconstituted and to work together. It means it supports reorganization of service components as well as of hardware.

In this section, the three parts of the MEMORIA system will be explained.

1) Life Log Logger: Fig. 4 shows the life log logging system for the service of MEMORIA. The logger collects GPS and image data with time information in real time which device module of each gadget can process, filters invalid data, and transfers the data to the remote life log server using the interface of the life log server. The kinds of data can be expanded according to the kinds of device modules.

Fig. 3. The system of MEMORIA

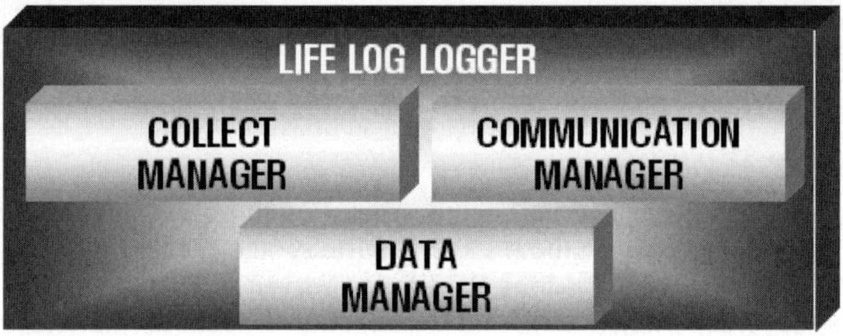

Fig. 4. Life Log Logger of MEMORIA

Keeping track of user's location and scenery information, LGs have a GPS module that follows the NMEA 0183 protocol and a camera module that produces JPEG images. They gather GPS and image data, and log them with their system time to synchronize both.

2) Life Log Server: Life log server logs data from the life log logger, process user queries from the life log viewer and gives the retrieved data to the viewer. It supports multiple connections of logging gadgets, service gadgets, and web servers. It also provides interfaces with the logger and viewer.

LLS is implemented on a Fedora Core 5 Linux. It consists of a log, query, DB, and session managers as shown in Fig. 5. The session manager is responsible for managing the connection of both connection-oriented and connectless clients with the thread based multi-processing capability. The db manager maintains DBMS used to handle both metadata of LLS and the indexing information of the logged data. The log manager handles the actual logging process, and the query manager processes client's queries.

3) Life Log Viewer: Fig. 6 shows the SG for the service of MEMORIA, which is also called Life Log Viewer. The viewer plays a role of user interaction and provides search interface for users. It can help users retrieve the experience data using the interface of the life log server. It also manages query and user information from user's input.

Life log viewer has a user interface which can connect life log server and retrieve information a user queries. It transmits user queries to the life log server in real time and provide retrieved information to the users in real time. A user keeps records in a life log server using his portable WIG. Then, he uses a device which support service providing to retrieve his own experience information.

SGs, currently used with an ultra mobile PC, provide the web-based graphical user interface for ease of use.

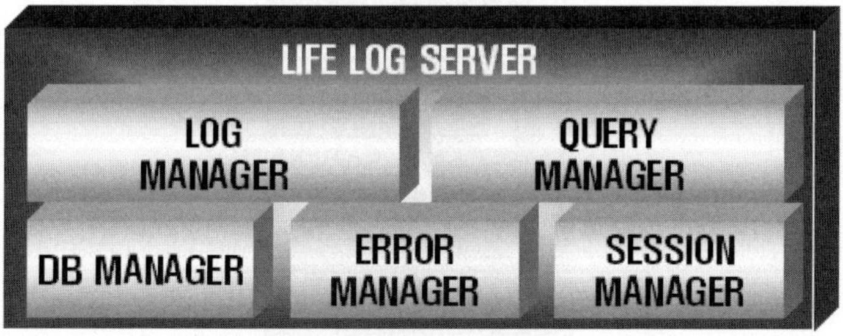

Fig. 5. Life Log Server of MEMORIA

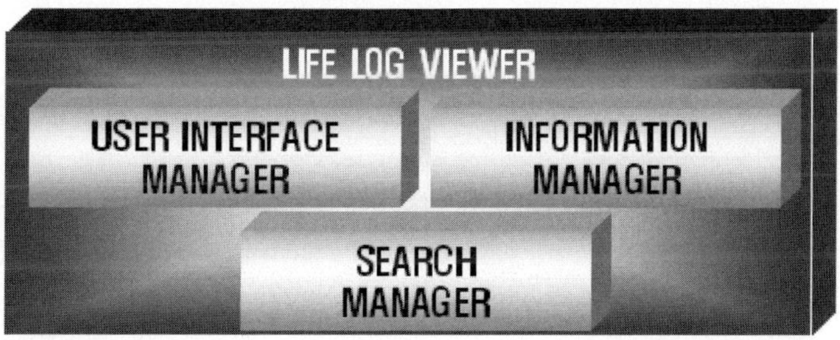

Fig. 6. Life Log Viewer of MEMORIA

4 Result

Fig. 7 describes a model equipped with devices for life log logging. A camera for image and video data is as her necklace, and a GPS receiver is on her arm as a bracelet. Life log is recorded using these kinds of gadgets which can be equipped naturally as daily accessories as a model in Fig. 7.

Fig. 8 shows a user interface of MEMORIA viewer which support time-based information retrieval and the result of retrieval. In the picture, A is a bar for a time-based query, so that a user can enter. B and C indicate where a user used to be, and D represents the information at each point. E describes what he/she saw at that point.

As the picture shows, a user can retrieve experience from a specific point for certain duration. It keeps records of position information of users and what users see and hear in the life log server. Users can access the server whenever they need, and retrieve memories. In other words, a user can recall memories from the map and the images retrieving the life log server.

Fig. 7. A Model Equipped with Logging Gadgets

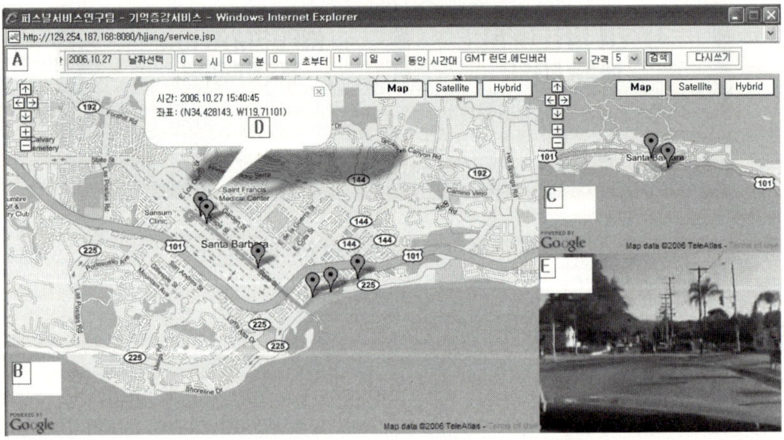

Fig. 8. The User Interface of MEMORIA Life Log Viewer

5 Conclusion

This paper deals with a personal memento service based on the life log that stores personal experience information, called MEMORIA. It is an example service using wearable intelligent gadgets (WIGs) and life log. WIG is one of smart objects. It has the capability of collecting and processing information, and can be installed or attached into every object we use in our daily life. By wearing accessories attached with WIG, wearer's experience information can be collected without any attention of the wearer, and recorded into a life log in real-time. The collected information can very vary depending on the WIGs attached. Example of them can be what the WIG wearer has seen, hear, and talk, where the wearer has been, etc. MEMORIA that uses these kinds of personal information to provide a personal memory augmentation is a new service paradigm that can be adapted for the ubiquitous computing service environment. As a result, it can be adapted to various memory augmentation service areas such as assisting dementia patients or monitoring people who need a continuous cares.

Currently, we focus on enhancing and extending MEMORIA by adding wearer's activity information by using WIGs that collects and processes wearer's movement information. With the movement information, we believe that activity based memory augmentation services can be possible.

References

1. Tancharoen, D., Yamasaki, T., Aizawa, K.: Practical Experience Recording and Indexing of Lfe Log Video. In: Proc. of CARPE 2005, Singapore, pp. 61–66 (November 2006)
2. MIT's Things That Think Home Page http://ttt.media.mit.edu/
3. Nanda, G.: Accessorizing with Networks: The Possibilities of Building with Computational Textilies, Master Thesis, MIT (2005)
4. Cherry, S.: Total Recall: A Microsoft Researcher is Determined to Record Everything About His Lfe, IEEE Spectrum, 24–30 (November 2005)
5. Gemmel, J., Bell, G., Lueder, R.: My Life Bits: A Personal Database for Everything. Communications of ACM 2006, 49(1) (2006)
6. Dickie, C., Vertegaal, R., et al.: Augmenting and Sharing Memory with eyeBlog. In: Proc. of Carpe 2004, New York, USA, October 2004, pp. 105–109 (2004)
7. Won, J., Lee, K.H., Bae, C.: Wearable Intelligent Gadgets for Personalized Service. In: Proc. of International Conference of Ubiquitous Information Technology (ICUT 2007), Dubai, United Arab Emirates (February 2007)

A Location-Adaptive Human-Centered Audio Email Notification Service for Multi-user Environments

Ralf Jung and Tim Schwartz

Saarland University, Computer Science Department, Stuhlsatzenhausweg, 66123 Saarbrücken, Germany
{rjung,schwartz}@cs.uni-sb.de

Abstract. In this paper, we introduce an application for a discreet notification of mobile persons in a multi-user environment. In particular we use the current user position to provide a personalized email notification with non-speech audio cues embedded in aesthetic background music. The notification is done in a peripheral way to avoid distration of other people in the surrounding.

Keywords: Auditory Display, Ambient Soundscapes, Indoor Positioning.

1 Introduction

In our everyday life, people feel the need to be reachable in every situation. To guarantee this reachability, people make use of a variety of technologies, e.g. computers and mobile phones. A problem arises when a message or a phone call reaches the user and he must be notified about this event. In the context of a mobile phone this will usually be done by ring tones or vibration.

These types of notification have several disadvantages in situations like a business meeting. Not only is the lack of privacy a big disadvantage because attendees will know who received the message, but also the people`s attention in the room will be distracted from their current work. Even by switching off the ring tone and using the vibration alarm, the vibration could be audible (especially when the phone is lying on the desk) or the owner may not recognize the notification since the phone is in his jacket. The distraction problem raises from the fact that a notification signal is a "stand-alone" cue, that means the natural noise environment has a different sound type than the notification signal. The challenge is to increase the privacy by disguising the personal notification audio cue, which has the effect that nobody in the room can assign an appearing cue to the target person.

Our approach is to build up an artificial sound environment, the *ambient soundscape*, which is in our case a piece of non-speech easy listening music. This soundscape can be seen as an auditive envelope in which notification signals (in our case an instruments that fit into the composition) can be seamlessly integrated.

In our conference scenario, we assume a group of business men in a presentation who must be reachable the whole time or are waiting for an important email.

Registered users enter the conference room with their PDA that is equipped with an RFID reader card. The first user triggers the aforementioned ambient soundscape

J. Jacko (Ed.): Human-Computer Interaction, Part III, HCII 2007, LNCS 4552, pp. 340–348, 2007.

after his PDA receives the signal of one of the RFID tags that are mounted at the ceiling of the room. If an important email arrives (currently found out by keyword-matching of incoming emails), the current position of the user in the room will be determined by the PDA. These location coordinates will be send via wireless LAN to the system which determines the loudspeaker that is the nearest to the user. After knowing the position of the target person, his preselected favorite notification instrument (e.g. guitar) will be seamlessly mixed into the background music. To achieve this, a variety of musical constraints have to be considered whereas one of the most important constraint is the right point in time in which the notification instrument can be mixed into the soundscape without destroying the composition.

Unlike using the PDA loudspeakers for playing the notification signal, the use of the room speakers avoid the source detection of the notification signal. Not only the distraction can be avoided but also the privacy will be increased, because only the target person knows his personal notification instrument that he selected. Since the instrument fits into the composition other people will perceive the notification as part of the composition and not as a notification cue.

2 Related Work

Hudson and Smith designed a non-speech audio system that provides a preview of incoming emails by combining sample sounds [1]. The “audio glance” gives an overview of four important properties of a received message by coding information into the notification sound. First, the optional preamble sound is used for announcing messages that are classified as important. The sound of the main audio icon gives information about the message category, e.g. sender information in which the sample length represents the size of the mail body. For whom the mail is appointed to (single or group of users) is coded in the recipients icon and the finishing optional content flags announced mails where a keyword matching test for header or body is positive. The playback of the resulting sound could distract other people that are in the same room in which the notification takes place. Users can also receive their audio glance while they are away from their desk by holding up a color coded card in front of a camera. For multi-user environments, concurrently played samples could produce a confusing sound.

The Nomadic Radio [2] uses contextual audio cues on a wearable hands-free SoundBeam neckset for providing information. The scaleable audio interface remotes services and messages e.g. for email, news broadcasts and calendar events with wireless LAN and a telephony infrastructure. The interaction device is mounted on the shoulder of the user and is connected with a mini-portable PC that is also worn by the user. Messages are announced depending on the current user conversation context via speech and rendered spatial audio cues. Wearing such an additional special device that has only the function to receive auditive notifications could be hindering and reduce the acceptance. We decided to use standard PDAs for our notification system because the spread and popularity of PDAs increased in the last years.

3 The Ambient Email Notification Service

Our claim to build a user centered notification service made a variety of demands on the architecture. Figure 1 gives a rough design overview of the four fundamental elements: *Positioning System*, *eMail Server*, *Sound Repository* and *SAFIR* (Spatial Audio Framework for Instrumented Rooms) that are used for the Ambient Email Notification service (*AeMN*). In the graphical administration interface the user has the choice whether he wants to use the stationary or the mobile notification. The first one makes sense if the user stays at his desk. He can authenticate himself with his name and his password. The location of his personal desk and the email account login information are internally stored in an xml file on the AeMN server. The alternative is the mobile version where the user´s PDA is already registered and used for finding out his current position. We assume that each user has his own PDA, so we don`t need a manual authentication. In both cases the user has the possibility to enter a personal keyword for filtering incoming messages by their subject line. Incoming messages of registered users are periodically checked by email agents that run on the AeMN server.

After authentication, the user can select an ambient soundscape that ought to be played as the background sound. The system checks the sound repository for appropriate notification signals that can be integrated into the background soundscape as notification audio cues. After selecting his personal notification instrument, e.g. guitar or drums, the appropriate wav sound file will be retrieved from the sound repository and audio objects will be generated in the spatial audio system SAFIR [3].

AeMN recognizes when one or more registered users enter the room and automatically starts the selected backgound soundscape and the login process for checking the user accounts on the email server. The selected audio notification cues will be precached. If a user receives a new email that passed the filter successfully, the coordinates of the current user position that are computed by his PDA will be matched to the spatial audio system coordinates (listener position) and the notification cue will be seamlessly integrated into the soundscape. The loudspeaker that is nearest to the target person plays the notification cue with slightly increased volume to ease the perception. The notification can be stopped by pressing a button at a small user interface that is running on the PDA or at the administration interface on the desktop computer in case of the stationary version.

In the following we will give a more detailed overview of the structure and functionality of the sound repository and the positioning system.

3.1 Ambient Notification with Personalized Audio Cues

The main problem of traditional "stand alone" notification signals is the distraction of all present persons especially in multi-user environments. To introduce more privacy and confidentiality, we decided to integrate the notification signals with respect to the musical composition seamlessly into a background soundscape (see also [4]). The two musical components, namely the soundscapes and the notification instruments, were composed and recorded by ourselves. The compositions fulfill some perceptional constraints such as the auditive Gestalt laws [5], [6] and the consideration of the volume of the instruments that are well-known in musicology to influence the

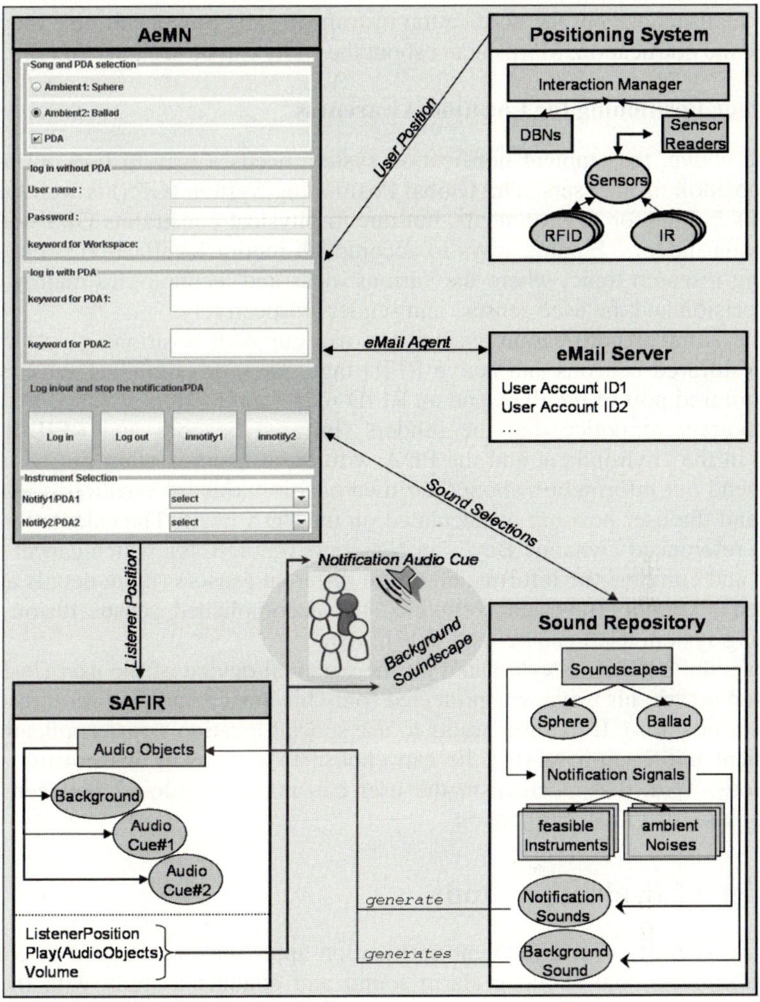

Fig. 1. Design Overview of the Audio Email Notification Architecture

perception process. The user has the possibility to choose a soundscape that matches his personal preferred music style and an instrument or ambient noise (natural sounds e.g. sea gull voices or flowing water) that he can easily recognize.

The notification cues can be mixed into the corresponding soundscape at certain points in time. We are obliged to this restriction to guarantee a fluent integration. Because of the fact that each user can select his personal instrument, other attendees will not be able to associate an instrument to a specific user even if they recognize the new cue. The personal instrument will seamlessly leave the soundscape if the user informs the system by pressing a button on his PDA or desktop GUI that he percepted the notification.

The effectiveness of the peripheral perception with our acoustical notification system was successfully tested in a user study with 25 persons where we especiallychecked whether the users percept the notification instruments and how much time they need to recognize the notification. More details about the study can be seen Section 4.

3.2 Indoor Positioning for Location Awareness

As stated above, the ambient notification system needs a way to find out about the current position of the users. The Global Positioning System (GPS) is well known for such tasks in outdoor environments, but due to physical constraints GPS normally is not working indoors. Finding ways to accomplish indoor localization is currently an interesting research topic, where the various ideas and technologies mainly differ in costs, precision and the used sensors and senders respectively.

For the ambient notification system, we use our own positioning system that is based on infrared beacons and active RFID tags. The corresponding sensors are the built in infrared port of the PDA and an RFID reader card that is attached to the PDA. It is important to notice that the senders (infrared beacons and RFID tags) are installed in the environment and the PDA with the sensors is worn by the user. The senders send out information about their own position, this information is read by the sensors and the user position is calculated on the PDA itself. The calculation is done with geo referenced Dynamic Bayesian Networks (geoDBNs), which cancel out false readings and combine the information of the different sensors (more details about geo referenced Dynamic Bayesian Networks, the accomplished sensor fusion and the positioning system itself can be read in [7], [8]).

Because the position is calculated on the personal device of the user (instead of a centralized server) his privacy is protected (only his device and the user himself know the current position). If the user wants to use special location aware applications, like the ambient notification service, he can choose to give away his position to these applications. With this mechanism the user can make a trade-off between privacy, benefit of and trust in an application.

4 Design of Evaluation Study

To test the viability of our ambient notification approach, we decided to compare it against a conventional acoustic alarm sound and conduct a study with the aim of answering the following two questions: For each kind of notification we want to know how often a notification is recognized (Efficiency) and with what delay the subjects react (Reaction time).

We recruited 25 participants (five women and twenty men) at ages from 20 to 35 years. Most of them had a background in either computer science or music.

4.1 Setup of the Study

The study was carried out in an instrumented room equipped with spatial audio hardware providing output through eight speakers mounted in a circular arrangement under the ceiling.

In this way, we were able to position the different parts of the soundscape and the specific notification instruments independently of each other. In addition to this, we prepared a computer with the test software. The study consisted of three parts with an overall duration of 30 minutes.

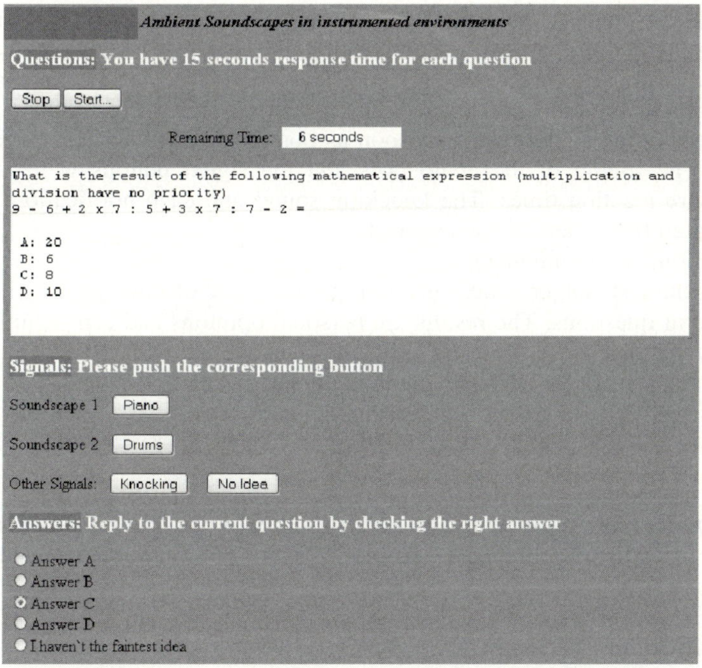

Fig. 2. Screenshot of the Computational Test

(1) Introduction and sound presentation (15 minutes)
In an explanatory text the subject was first introduced to the topic of the study and the test procedure and then given the opportunity to ask questions until we could ensure the tasks were fully understood. Subsequently, the subjects learned two personal notification signals and the corresponding soundscapes as well as the conventional alarm sound by repeated listening.

(2) Computer-based test (10 minutes)
The test environment included a question window, a signal button area and a radio button area for possible answers (see Figure 2). We prepared two recorded and prearranged soundscapes in which the notification instrument (learned by the subject in the introductory phase) and the conventional alarm sound appeared randomly. The task for the subject was to press the corresponding signal button after recognition of a notification signal as soon as possible. To prevent subjects from focusing on the background soundscape and to distract them from the auditive stimulus, they had to answer mathematical questions under time pressure. As a result of their increased cognitive load, the subjects perceived the audio signals in a rather peripheral way. In ambient soundscape *AS01*, the piano was the relevant notification instrument. In the second soundscape *AS02* we chose the drums as the audio cue. In contrast to the melody-dominated piano, the drums in AS02 are more rhythmically oriented. As a salient but natural traditional acoustic alarm signal we added a knocking sound randomly to both soundscapes. The volume of salient audio cues is important for the recognition process and we took great care to play the

knocking sound at the same volume level as the notification instruments, but while these were part of the composition and matched its overall rhythmic and melodic structure, the knocking stood outside of the overall composition. The two soundscapes were played in a row. Users were told to push the corresponding signal button as soon as possible when they perceived an audio cue. The timing of the audio cues and the signal buttons were recorded to measure reaction times. The knocking sound and each notification instrument appeared five times for each subject.

(3) Questionnaire (5 minutes)
After the test, subjects were given a questionnaire of three pages with different styles of questions. The results are personal opinions and can be influenced by many factors. Thus we only used the questionnaire for retrieving additional information, not for deriving quantitative data.

4.2 Results

Our main interest was whether the proposed notification system works efficiently (and potentially more peripheral than traditional audio notification systems). We also looked at the reaction time and some additional information extracted from the questionnaire.

4.2.1 Notification Efficiency

Over the course of all 25 subjects, there were 125 piano and 125 drum cues. Of these, 98 piano and 109 drum cues were recognized and identified by the subjects. The standard deviation of the rate for the drum signal with a value of 0,162 is lower than the piano value (0.244) and clearly lower than the knocking deviation (0,286).

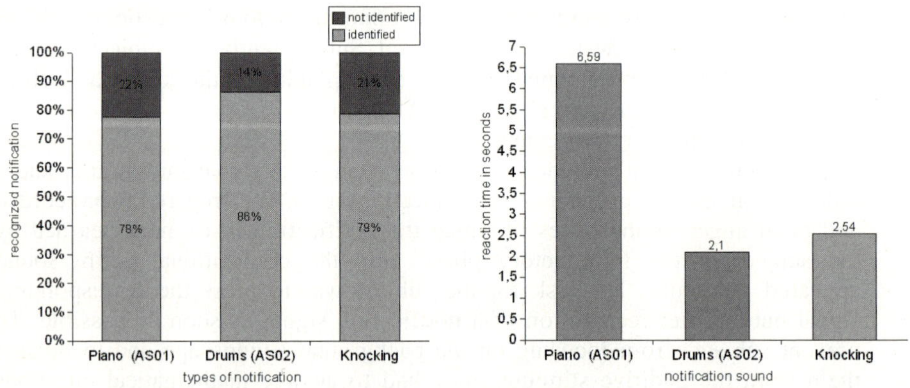

Fig. 3. Overall Notification Efficiency (left) and Overall Reaction Time (right)

This suggests that the more rhythmical drums are easier to identify than the a melodical instrument like the piano. Compared to the conventional alarm signal (knocking), the efficiency is surprisingly high (Fig. 2). Especially the drum notification in AS02 surpassed the knocking sound by seven percent and proved to be the most efficient of the three notification types.

4.2.2 Reaction Time

We were also interested in the delay between the notification appearance and the act of pressing the button (Fig. 3). Subjects had to perceive the audio signal, identify it and press the corresponding signal button on the screen. We found out that the average reaction time for piano notifications was higher on average (6,59 seconds) than the reaction time for drum (2,1 seconds) and knocking notifications (2,54 seconds).

We observed all subjects during the test and took notes whether they first answered the current question or first pressed the signal button. We found out that there seemed to be two types of perception:

- *Immediate Perception.* The subject recognized the audio signal in the first five seconds after its appearance. The audio cue was focused immediately after the stimulus perception.
- *Memorized Perception.* The test person pressed the button after the audio signal had already disa.ppeared. The reason for this phenomenon was an effect often described with the words "I think I have heard a signal". In general, subjects which had stated in the questionnaire that they were difficult to distract form their current work had a longer reaction time or missed notifications completely.

5 Conclusions and Future Work

We introduced an ambient notification service that works with personalized audio cues and that adapts to the position of the user with the help of his PDA. Occuring events, in our case an incoming email where the subject line matches a preselected keyword, can be announced by enhancing a background soundscape with a personal cue that is played near the user`s current position with increased volume. This type of unobtrusive notification gives us the chance to follow a low-level privacy approach. Areas of applications are shops where employees can receive information (e.g. a cashier is needed in the point of sale area) and at the same time the background soundscape would have a comfortable effect on the customers.

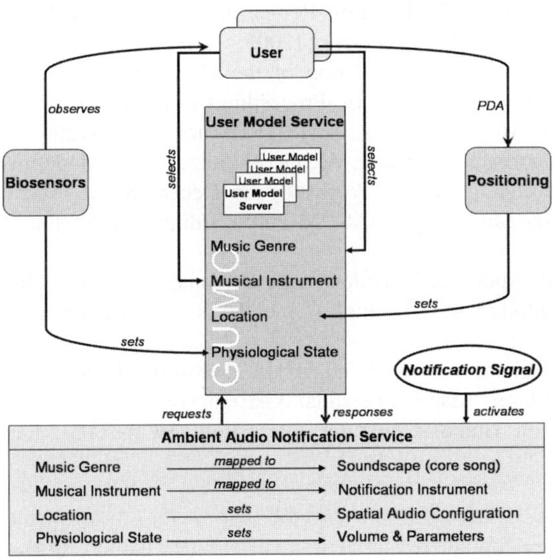

Fig. 4. User Model Integration for Ambient Audio Notification

The future work includes the connection to the General User Model Ontology GUMO [9], [10] to provide a more adaptive and flexible notification service for instrumented rooms (Figure 4). The enhanced personalization features will include the position of the user, his personal music style and favorite instruments and his physical state that we will try to find out with biosensors connected to the user [11]. The individual settings can then be accessed via http requests when the user enters a room.

References

1. Hudson, S.E., Smith, I.: Electronic Mail Previews Using Non-Speech Audio. In: CHI '96: Conference companion on Human factors in computing systems, New York, NY, USA, pp. 237–238. ACM Press, New York (2006)
2. Sawhney, N., Schmandt, C.: Nomadic Radio: Scaleable and Contextual Notification for Wearable Audio Messaging. In: CHI '99: Proceedings of the SIGCHI conference on Human factors in computing systems, pp. 96–103. ACM Press, New York, NY, USA (1999)
3. Schmitz, M., Butz, A.: Safir: Low-Cost Spatial Audio for Instrumented Environments. In: Proceedings of the 2nd International Conference on Intelligent Environments, Athens, Greece (2006)
4. Butz, A., Jung, R.: Seamless User Notification in Ambient Soundscapes. In: IUI '05: Proceedings of the 10th international conference on Intelligent user interfaces, pp. 320–322. ACM Press, New York, NY, USA (2005)
5. Camurri, A., Leman, M.: Gestalt-Based Composition and Performance in Multimodal Environments. In: Joint International Conference on Cognitive and Systematic Musicology, pp. 495–508 (1996)
6. Reybrouck, M.: Gestalt Concepts and Music: Limitations and Possibilities. In: Joint International Conference on Cognitive and Systematic Musicology, Brugge, Belgium, pp. 57–69 (1997)
7. Brandherm, B., Schwartz, T.: Geo Referenced Dynamic Bayesian Networks for User Positioning on Mobile Systems. In: Strang, T., Linnhoff-Popien, C. (eds.) LoCA 2005. LNCS, vol. 3479, pp. 223–234. Springer, Berlin, Heidelberg (2005)
8. Schwartz, T., Brandherm, B., Heckmann, D.: Calculation of the User-Direction in an Always Best Positioned Mobile Localization System. In: Proceedings of the International Workshop on Artificial Intelligence in Mobile Systems (AIMS), Salzburg, Austria (2005)
9. Heckmann, D., Schwartz, T., Brandherm, B., Kroener, A.: Decentralized User Modeling with UserML and GUMO. In: Proceedings of the Workshop on Decentralized, Agent Based and Social Approaches to User Modelling, (DASUM 2005), Edinburgh, Scotland, pp. 61–65 (2005)
10. Jung, R., Heckmann, D.: Ambient Audio Notification with Personalized Music. In: Proceedings of Workshop on Ubiquitous User Modeling (UbiqUM'06), Riva del Garda, Italy, pp. 16-18 (2006)
11. Brandherm, B., Schultheis, H., von Wilamowitz-Moellendorff, M., Schwartz, T., Schmitz, M.: Using Physiological Signals in a User-Adaptive Personal Assistant. In: Proceedings of the 11th International Conference on Human-Computer Interaction (HCII-2005), Las Vegas, Nevada, USA (2005)

Emotion-Based Textile Indexing Using Neural Networks

Na Yeon Kim, Yunhee Shin, and Eun Yi Kim*

Department of Internet and Multimedia Engineering, Konkuk Univ., Korea
{yeon0830,ninharsa,eykim}@konkuk.ac.kr

Abstract. This paper proposes a neural network based approach for emotion based textile indexing. Generally, the human emotion can be affected by some physical features such as color, texture, pattern, and so on. In the previous work, we investigated the correlation between the human emotion and color or texture. Here, we aim at investigating the correlation between the emotion and pattern, and developing the textile indexing system using the pattern information. Therefore, the survey is first conducted to investigate the correlation between the emotion and the pattern. The result shows that a human emotion is deeply affected by the certain pattern. Based on that result, an automatic indexing system is developed. The proposed system is composed of feature extraction and classification. To describe the pattern information in the textiles, the wavelet transform is used. And the neural network is used as the classifier. To assess the validity of the proposed method, it was applied to recognize the human emotions in 100 textiles, and then our system produced the accuracy of 90%. This result confirmed that our system has the potential to be applied for various applications such as textile industry and e-business.

Keywords: Emotion recognition, neural networks, pattern recognition, feature extraction, wavelet transform.

1 Introduction

For a given product or object, predicting human emotions is very important in many business, scientific and engineering applications. In particular, the emotion-based textile indexing has been considerable attention, as it can be applicable to the E-business and furthermore help pattern designer. In current, the textiles are manually annotated by human experts in the current, which cause a huge amount of time and effort. To reduce the cost and time, automatic indexing system should be developed to classify the textiles based on the emotional features. However, it is difficult to directly predict the human emotion from the textiles, due to the ambiguity of human emotion. For example, when seeing the images in Fig. 1, some may feel 'romantic' and some may tells that it is dynamic.

Therefore, it is an important issue to find the correlation between the human emotion and physical features such as color, texture and shape information included

* Corresponding author: Tel.: +82–2–450–4135, Fax: +82-2-450-4135.

J. Jacko (Ed.): Human-Computer Interaction, Part III, HCII 2007, LNCS 4552, pp. 349–357, 2007.

Fig. 1. Examples of textile images

in the textile images. Related to this issues, some works have been investigated [1-3]. Kobayashi have investigated how the color and patterns affect human emotion based on the survey. Although they showed the correlation between some physical features and human emotions, they did not provide the automated system to extract the physical features from the textiles and analyze the features. In the previous work, we developed the automatic indexing system using color and textures [3]. The system works well on classifying the textiles for some emotions, however it has limitation to be generally used for all the emotion groups of Kobayashi.

Here, we aim at investigating the correlation between the emotion and pattern, and developing the textile indexing system using the pattern information. Therefore, the survey is first conducted to investigate the correlation between the emotion and the pattern. The result indicates that the human emotions are deeply dependent on the patterns included in the textile. Therefore, the pattern recognition system using traditional machine learning is used for developing automatic indexing system. The proposed system is composed of feature extraction and classification. To describe the pattern information in the textiles, the wavelet transform is used. And the neural network is used as the classifier.

To assess the validity of the proposed method, it was applied to recognize the human emotions in 100 textiles, and then our system produced the accuracy of 90%. This result confirmed that our system has the potential to be applied for various applications such as textile industry and e-business.

This paper is organized as follows. Section 2 shows the data collection and analysis for investigating the correlation between the emotion and the pattern. And the proposed indexing system is described in Section 3. Section 4 shows experimental results, and the conclusion are followed.

2 Data Collection and Analysis

In this work, our goal is to investigate how the pattern information in textiles affects human emotions, and developing the textile indexing system based on the results. For this, the survey is first conducted. The process is performed by two steps: data collection and data analysis.

From the Pattern-Book [1], we collected 220 textile images, and then, classify them into nine groups according to their pattern. In the results, textile images are classified

[1] Meller, Susan, "Textile designs : 200 years of European and American patterns for printed fabrics organized by motif, style, color, layout", Harry N. Abrams, 1991.

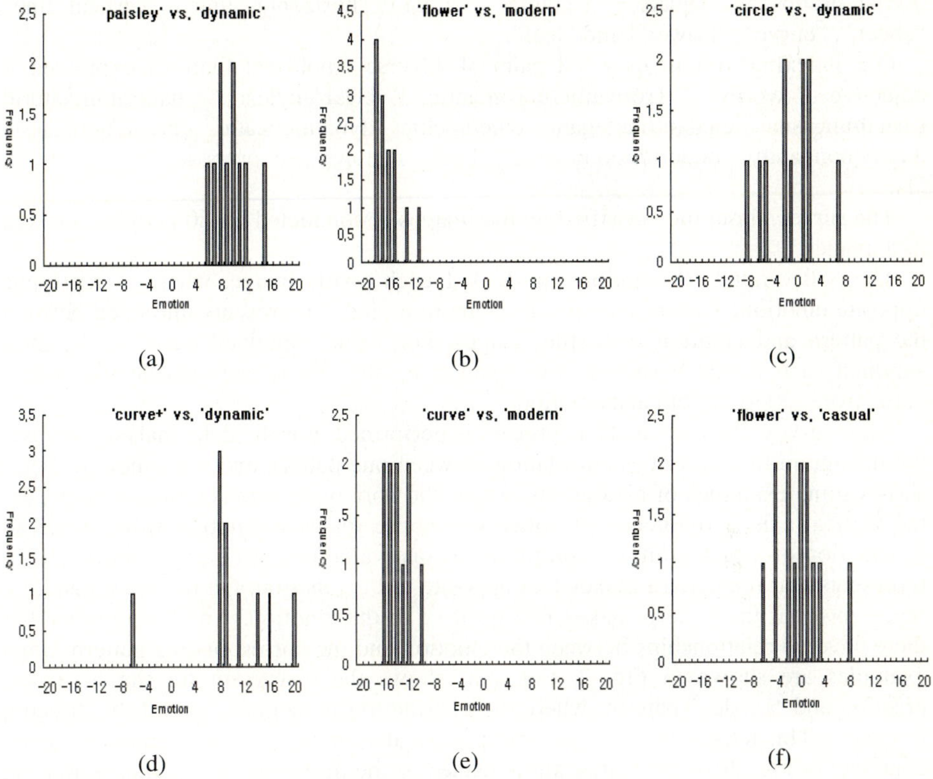

Fig. 2. The histograms to show the correlation of a pattern and an emotion: (a) paisley vs. dynamic (b) flower vs. modern (c) circle vs. dynamic (d) curve vs. dynamic (e) curve vs. modern (f) flower vs. casual

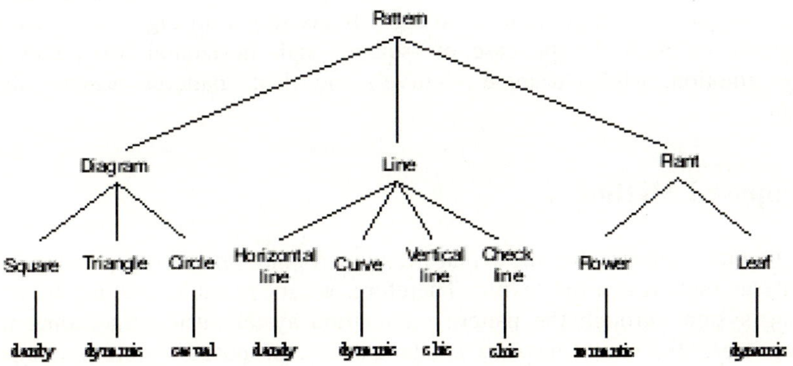

Fig. 3. A graph structure representing the correlation of pattern and emotion

9-type groups as "square", "triangle", "circle", "horizontal line", "vertical line", "check", "curve", "flower", and "leaf".

Our indexing system uses ten pairs of adverse emotional features expressed as adjective words: {romantic/unromantic, clear/unclear, natural/unnatural, casual/uncasual, elegant/inelegant, chic/unchic, dynamic/static, classic/nonclassic, dandy/nondandy, modern/nonmodern}. These features are proposed by Kobayashi [1].

The survey about the classified textile images is conducted on 20 peoples, for total 220 images.

The pollee rated 10 emotions to -1, 0, 1 each textile image, where -1 represents opposite emotion, 1 represents positive emotion, and 0 represents unrelated between the pattern and emotion in textile images. For values obtained each textile, these summed each textile based on investigation results. Thus, each textile has integer value from -20 to 20 for each emotion.

After survey, the data analysis process is performed. For the data analysis, we used the histogram that describes correlation between one pattern and one emotion. Fig. 2 shows some examples of histograms, where the horizontal axis is emotion value, and the vertical axis is frequency of pollee's response for each emotion value. Here the distribution of a histogram is represented as one value out of (+), (-), and 0. The (-) represents that the pattern makes feel opposite to the emotion. On the other hand, (+) represents that the pattern makes feel positive to the emotion. And 0 represents that there have no relationships between the emotion and the corresponding pattern. Some examples are shown in Fig. 2. Fig. 2(a) shows the histogram for the 'dynamic' emotion and 'paisley' pattern, where the distribution is inclined toward the direction of the (+). This tells us that the 'paisley' pattern affects the 'dynamic' emotion. On the contrary, in Fig. 2(b), the histogram is leaned to the direction of (-). This shows that 'flower' pattern makes feel opposite emotion to 'modern'. And a histogram is distributed around 0 as shown in Fig. 2(c), then, it shows that there have no relationships between the emotion and the corresponding pattern.

Through these analyses, we find the fact that the human emotions are deeply dependent on the patterns included in the textile. Fig. 3 illustrates these correlations between the pattern and emotion as tree graph. As shown in Fig. 3, each pattern has the specific emotion. In the case of 'square' and 'horizontal line', they present 'dandy' emotion, while 'triangle', 'curve', and 'leaf' patterns present 'dynamic' emotion.

3 Proposed Method

In the previous section, we show that the human emotions are deeply dependent on the patterns included in the textile. Therefore, we try to build emotion-based textile indexing system through the pattern recognition system using traditional machine learning. Here, the neural network is adapted. The proposed system is composed of feature extraction and classification. To describe the pattern information in the textiles, the wavelet transform is used. And the neural network is used as the classifier.

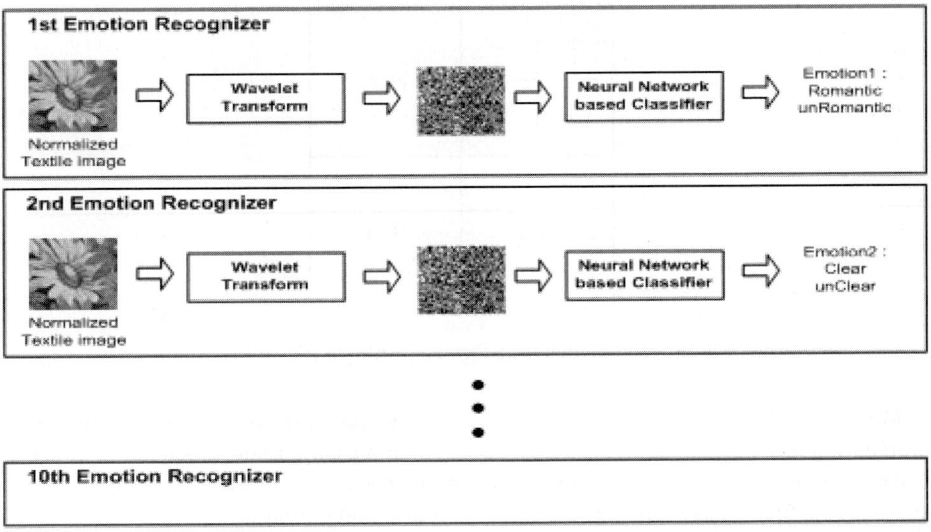

Fig. 4. The NN-based recognizer for a specific emotion

Fig. 4 shows the outline of the proposed system, where it is composed of 10 NN-based systems to recognize the respective human emotions. Each recognizer classifies textile image according to correlation of inputted image.

3.1 Feature Extraction

Generally, a pattern can be described as a combination of texture, edge, and color. Therefore, we use a wavelet transform. The wavelet transform provides successive approximations to the image by down-sampling and have the ability to detect edges during the high-pass filtering. The wavelet transform decomposes to 4 sub-blocks as LL, LH, HL, and HH as shown in Fig. 5 [4]. LL is involving the textual content, while the other sub-blocks are involving edge information for vertical, horizontal and diagonal orientations.

In our method, the LL level is again decomposed into 4 sub-blocks using wavelet transform. This process is iterated 6 times, so that 24 sub-blocks are created. Then, from each block the following parameters are calculated.

$$M(I) = \frac{1}{N^2} \sum_{i=0}^{N-1} \sum_{j=0}^{N-1} I(i, j) \tag{1}$$

$$\mu_2(I) = \frac{1}{N^2} \sum_{i=0}^{N-1} \sum_{j=0}^{N-1} (I(i, j) - M(I))^2 \tag{2}$$

$$\mu_3(I) = \frac{1}{N^2} \sum_{i=0}^{N-1} \sum_{j=0}^{N-1} (I(i, j) - M(I))^3 \tag{3}$$

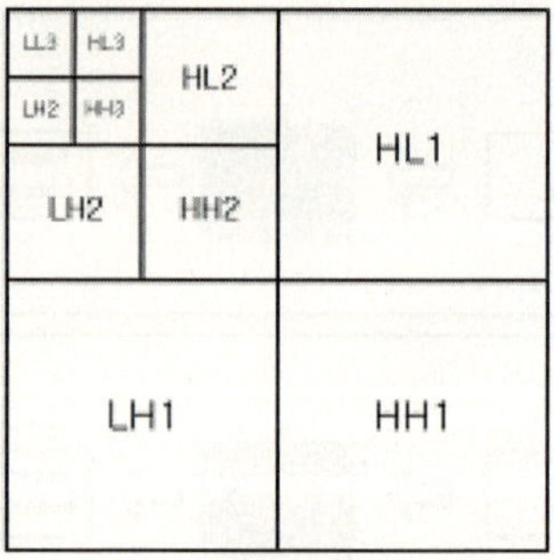

Fig. 5. The wavelet transformed results of a 2-D image

Given *NxN* image, Eq. (1) represents average value, and Eqs. (2) and (3) represent momentum each 2 and 3 dimension. Due to created total 24 sub-blocks after 6-levels wavelet transform, 72 parameters are created. These are used as the input of the classifier that recognizes the pattern information in some textiles.

3.2 NN Based Recognizer

In this paper, the proposed system uses multilayer perceptron (MLP) as a classifier [5-7]. The network is composed of input layer, hidden layer, and output layer. The adjacent layers are fully connected. We use NNs composed of total 72 input nodes and 1 output node from 24 sub-blocks obtained by 6-level wavelet transform. And the number of hidden nodes is determined by the experiment.

Our system uses pattern *(I, d)*, to train the network where *I* is textile image, and *d* is emotion value manually labeled in the textile image. The NNs are trained using the back-propagation algorithm (BP). The input layer receives the wavelet transformed values of 64 x 64 textile image. The output value of hidden node is obtained from the dot product of the vector of input values and the vector of the weights connected to the hidden node. It is then presented with the output nodes. The weights are adjusted by training with a back-propagation algorithm in order to minimize the sum of squared error during the training session.

The output value of NNs is normalized to 0~1. And if the output value is bigger than 0.5, the system decides that the image includes the corresponding emotion. Otherwise, the system decides the opposite emotion or nothing.

4 Experimental Results

To assess the validity of the proposed method, the proposed indexing system has been tested with 220 captured textile images. For the respective textile images, twenty peoples were selected to manually annotate according to the emotions that they feels from the images. Then 120 images of 220 collected images were used for training the NNs and the others were used for test. In this work, the parameters of NN were fixed as follows: error rate is fixed to 0.02, momentum to 0.5, and iteration to 5000.

Fig. 6 illustrates the classified results by the proposed system. Figs. 6(a) and (b) show examples of the classified results as emotion 'chic' and 'unchic' respectively. As can shown Fig. 6(a), the emotion of 'chic' is labeled at the textiles with patterns of 'vertical line' and 'check line', while the emotion of 'unchic' is labeled at the textiles with patterns of 'geometries' in Fig. 6(b). And Figs. 6(c) and (d) show examples of the classified results as emotion 'dandy' and 'non-dandy' respectively. As can shown Fig. 6(c), the emotion of 'dandy' is labeled at the textiles with patterns of 'horizontal line' and 'square', on the other hands, the emotion of 'non-dandy' is labeled at the textiles with patterns of 'curve' and 'geometries of curve type' in Fig. 6(d).

These results prove that the correlation between emotion and pattern described in Fig. 3 is true. Also, these show that our NN-based recognizer is successfully worked.

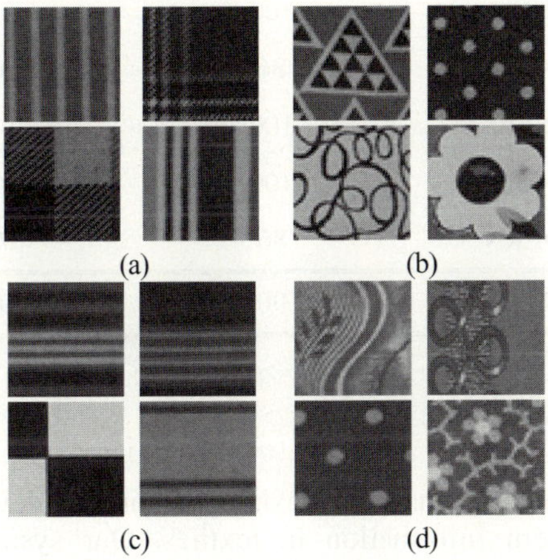

Fig. 6. The examples of emotion recognition results: (a) The emotion of 'chic', (b) The emotion of 'unchic', (c) The emotion of 'dandy', (d) The emotion of 'non-dandy'

The performance of the proposed system is summarized in Table 1. For analysis of performance two measures are used such as precision and recall. These are defined as follows.

$$precision(\%) = \frac{\#\ of\ correctly\ detected\ textile\ image}{\#\ of\ detected\ textile\ image} \times 100 \quad (4)$$

$$recall(\%) = \frac{\#\ of\ correctly\ detected\ textile\ image}{\#\ of\ textile\ image} \times 100 \quad (5)$$

The proposed system shows the precision of 98% and the recall of 90% on average. This result confirmed that our system has the potential to be applied for various applications such as textile industry and e-business.

Table 1. The performance analysis of the proposed recognition system (%)

	Wavelet Transform	
	recall	precision
ROMANTIC	79	100
CLEAR	86	100
NATURAL	86	100
CASUAL	79	100
ELEGANT	100	100
CHIC	100	100
DYNAMIC	86	100
CLASSIC	100	100
DANDY	100	100
MODERN	86	78
AVERAGE	90	98

5 Conclusion

In this paper, a new emotion based indexing system was developed that label each textile using the pattern information in textiles. Our system is component two modules: feature extraction and classification. To describe the pattern information in the textiles, the wavelet transform was used. And the neural network was used as the classifier.

To assess the validity of the proposed method, it was applied to recognize the human emotions in 100 textiles, and then our system produced the precision of 98% and the recall of 90%. This result confirmed that our system has the potential to be applied for various applications such as textile industry and e-business.

Acknowledgments. This work was supported by the Technology Infrastructure Foundation Program funded by the Ministry of Commerce, Industry and Energy, South Korea.

References

1. Shigenobu Kobayashi, COLOR IMAGE SCALE, Kodansha (1991)
2. Soen, T., Shimada, T., Akita, M.: Obgective Evaluation of Color Design, Color Res. Appl., vol. 12, pp. 187–194 (1987)
3. Kim, E.Y., Kim, S.-j., Koo, H.-j., Jeong, K., Kim, J.-i.: Emotion-based Textile Indexing using Colors and Texture. In: Wang, L., Jin, Y. (eds.) FSKD 2005. LNCS (LNAI), vol. 3613, pp. 1077–1080. Springer, Heidelberg (2005)

4. Li, H., Doermann, D., Kia, O.: Automatic Text Detection and Tracking in Digital Video, IEEE Transactions on Image Processing, vol. 9(1) (January 2000)
5. Haykin, S.: Neural Networks a comprehensive foundation, 2nd edn., Prentice Hall, Englewood Cliffs, pp.10-13, pp.156-173 (1999)
6. Bauer, H.-U., Geisel, T.: Dynamics of signal processing in feedback multilayer perceptrons. In: Proc. Int. Joint Conf. Neural Networks, pp. 131-136 (1990)
7. Brown, M., An, P.C., Harris, C.J., Wang, H.: How biased is your multi-layer perceptron?, in World Congr. Neural Networks, pp. 507-511 (1993)

Decision Theoretic Perspective on Optimizing Intelligent Help

Chulwoo Kim and Mark R. Lehto

School of Industrial Engineering, Purdue University, West Lafayette, IN 47907, USA
{kim218,lehto}@purdue.edu

Abstract. With the increasing complexity of systems and information overload, agent technology has become widely used to provide personalized advice (help message) to users with their computer-based tasks. The purpose of this study is to investigate the way to optimize advice provided by the intelligent agent from a decision theoretic perspective. The study utilizes the time associated with processing a help message as the trade-off criterion of whether to present a help message or not. The proposed approach is expected to provide guidance as to where, when and why help messages are likely to be effective or ineffective by providing quantitative predictions of value of help messages in time.

Keywords: intelligent agent, intelligent help, decision theoretic perspective, help optimization.

1 Introduction

The increasing complexity of systems and information overload makes an assistance system an essential component of a software system. Computer interfaces are having more and more functionality, and the limitations of computer development will be how to enable the computers to know what the users want the computers to do [1]. As indicated in the production paradox [2], novice users try to perform tasks with a computer system almost immediately without knowing how to do them, resulting in frustrations with the system. As a way of overcoming these problems, agent technology has become widely used to provide personalized assistance to users with their computer-based tasks. The role of intelligent agents as an advice provider has been advocated [1, 3, 4].

The difficulty of providing advice (help messages) is that there are several possible answers to the problems based on limited inputs or no appropriate cues. Given that it is impossible to develop a perfect intelligent agent which always provides an appropriate help message, it is important to develop a framework to trade off among various variables related to selecting the right sort of help message. The traditional approach to providing advice is to provide the most likely or suitable advice suggested by the implemented algorithm. The problem with this approach is that it does not properly consider the cost and benefit of the advice. As the scheme of

J. Jacko (Ed.): Human-Computer Interaction, Part III, HCII 2007, LNCS 4552, pp. 358–365, 2007.

trading off the cost and benefit of the advice, expected utility has been proposed [3] and used in some intelligent help systems using subjective cost and benefit functions. Although the decision theoretic optimization based on the expected utility (cost) provides a powerful and flexible tradeoff mechanism, users or domain experts have to be directly asked about their preferences to develop a cost (utility) function. Domain-specific learning techniques have been used occasionally, but most practitioners parameterize the cost function and then engage in a laborious and unreliable process of hand-tuning [5].

This study investigates the way of optimizing the provision of a help message with the assumption that the cost and value of a help message can be measured in terms of time.

2 Literature Review

2.1 Intelligent Agent

The intelligent agent is generally defined as a hardware or software-based computer system with autonomy, social ability, reactivity, and pro-activeness [6, 7]:

- Autonomy: agents act without the direct interruption of human users, and have some control over their behaviors;
- Social ability: agents interact with other agents or human users using some type of communication language;
- Reactivity: agents perceive their environment and respond to changes;
- Pro-activeness: agents show goal-directed behavior by taking the initiative

The basic function of intelligent agents is to provide personalized assistance to users with their computer-based tasks.

Although the intelligent agent technology provides a promising future, it still has problems for its fullest adoption to the interface design. The debate on the advantages and disadvantages of intelligent agents and direct manipulation [8] has highlighted differing views on the most promising opportunities for user interface innovation [3]. One group has expressed optimistic opinions for refining intelligent-interface agents with suggestions that research should focus on developing more powerful tools for understanding a user's intention and taking automated actions. Another group has shown concerns that the efforts should be directed toward tools and metaphors that improve users' ability to understand and directly manipulate systems and information.

[9] summarizes problems associated with the user-initiated approach and the system-initiated approach, and argue the adequacy of the mixed approach. The problems of the user-initiated approach can be summarized in three aspects: 1) the user-initiated approach is often ineffective; 2) the user-initiated approach is often inefficient in that it makes no use of information about the user and the task progress; and 3) users handle their tasks without necessarily optimizing the solution due to the cost of learning. The challenges faced by the system-initiated approach can be

summarized in three aspects: 1) it is often inappropriate since the correct identification of a user's goal is not always possible; 2) the major challenge is the timing of advice; and 3) users tend to have predictability and the control of the system.

Two approaches have been studied to overcome the limitations of the user-initiated and system-initiated approaches: the mixed initiative approach and the advice approach. The mixed initiative approach indicates a creative integration of direct manipulation and automation [3]. [3] argues that the mixed initiative approach could provide a different kind of user experience characterized by more natural collaborations between users and computers, rather than advocating one approach over the other.

The advice approach is to consider computer systems as an advisor to provide people with suggestions, help and assistance, and users decide whether to use them or not [1]. A key idea in achieving the transition from a *command* structure to a more flexible and collaborative one will be the development of computer interfaces based on the idea of *advice*. This study focuses on the advice giving aspect of the intelligent agent.

2.2 Decision Theoretic Perspective

The decision theoretic perspective provides a more fundamental explanation of how and why more or less information might be transmitted, in particular situations, that takes into consideration both uncertainty and the outcome of the consequences occurred [10]. The basic idea is that the amount of information transmitted can be determined by taking into consideration user knowledge, uncertainty, and the outcome of the consequences incurred. It indicates that the amount of information transmitted is not necessarily the index of a better intelligent agent. In most cases, it can be assumed that the more information transmitted the better. However, this is not always true because the amount of information transmitted doesn't take into consideration the cost and benefits of the help messages provided by the intelligent agents. Especially in the information overloaded environment such as the computer systems of these days, the problem is when and how much information or how many messages the agent needs to present to the user.

There has been a recent trend to use decision theoretic optimization, of which the objective is to minimize the expected cost and maximize expected utility for designing a user interaction interface [5, 11, 12]. The basic idea of decision theoretic optimization for designing intelligent agents is that a proposed action will be taken only when the agents believe that the action has greater expected value than inaction [11]. The approach used in developing these systems involves manual preference elicitation methods by directly or indirectly asking for users' subjective ratings on the preference or by domain experts. Although decision-theoretic optimization provides a powerful and flexible approach for these systems, the accuracy of the underlying utility function determines the success of these systems [5].

3 Expected Time-Based Optimization Framework

3.1 Classification of User Needs

The way that the intelligent help agents respond to the user needs represents the proactiveness of the intelligent help agents. The intelligent help agents are required to provide proactive help, not just respond passively to the user's requests. In the traditional signal detection theory, a signal indicates an event or object that needs to be identified. With this definition in mind, the user's need for help can be considered as a signal in the context of using the intelligent help agents.

There are two cases where the user needs help. The first case is the system-driven need where the system considers certain information may be helpful to the user. As indicated in [9], users often do not look for needed help probably because users do not have experience or skills to find the needed information. If the system recognizes that certain information may assist the user to complete the user's task, the system should provide help messages. Help messages that may shorten task completion time or help messages that indicate problematic situations are the examples representing the system-driven need.

The second case is the user-driven need that the user recognizes certain information is needed. The agent is supposed to provide help messages to the user when the user looks for help because the user does not know what to do or how to do the user's task. In traditional systems, the user uses a help function which provides a list of help messages related to operations of the systems. The intelligent agent approach is to provide help messages autonomously based on the user's context. If the user is doing the user's task without any problem, the user does not need this type of help so that the agent should not provide any help messages.

The agent's actions of providing a help message can be categorized depending on the user need as summarized in Table 1. Correct identification indicates that the agent provides a help message when the user needs it. False alarm indicates that the agent does not provide a help message when the user needs it. Miss indicates that the agent provides a help message when the user does not need it. Correct rejection indicates that the agent does not provide a help message when the user does not need it.

Table 1. Classification of help messages

	s (User need)	n (No user need)
S (Help message)	Correct Identification	False Alarm
N (No help message)	Miss	Correct Rejection

3.2 Cost of Help

The above classification only involves the identification of user needs without the relevance of a help message being considered. The Correct Identification only indicates that the agent identifies the user need at the right time. Although the system correctly identifies the user need, it would not be helpful if the system provides a message which is irrelevant or costs more to process than without the message. Providing an irrelevant message causes extra time to process the help message without assisting the user. Presenting a message at the wrong time will not be helpful since a message at the wrong time is considered an irrelevant one.

Although there are several considerations for help message presentation, the usefulness of a help message can be evaluated from the utilitarian perspective. Assuming that the use of a computer system depends on the utilitarian aspect of the system, time can be a good measure of the system performance. Although relevance can be an important standard of determining accuracy of the help system, a relevant help message which the user already knows is not considered helpful since the message only increases the user's task completion time with the extra time to process the help message. The introduction of time is beneficial in that it can explain why even a correct, relevant message can be useless and undermines user performance. The basic concept of this approach is supported by the GOMS model [13]. [13] consider that tasks can be described as a serial sequence of cognitive operations and the time associated with operations can be approximated. By analyzing time associated with processing a help message, we can decide whether to provide a help message or not.

To complete a task, the user is supposed to perform several subtasks. There is not only one way of performing a task so that at each decision point, the user decides which subtask to perform. The amount of time devoted to each routine varies, so it is desirable to provide a help message in the way that the help message reduces the amount of time required to complete the user's task. The type of help message that guides the user to a shorter route will be beneficial in that the user can wisely select the subsequent subtask. Some help messages can even help the user to skip some subtasks. The help messages when there is only one route may not be helpful, only causing extra time to read the messages.

3.3 Optimization of Help

Given that cost can be assigned to the outcome, the optimal help threshold can be assessed using the expected utility of each action [11]. The help should be given when the probability that the user needs help exceeds the optimal help threshold. With time being the utility of each action, the expected utility of presenting a help message or presenting no message can be expressed in the time associated with each action. Since it is difficult to calculate the time associated with processing a help message without considering the task performance time, the expected time of presenting a help message and presenting no help message is estimated using the total task performance time.

The expected time of presenting a message and presenting no message can be calculated as shown below:

$$ET(message) = P_s * T_{HIT} + (1-P_s) * T_{FA}$$
$$= P_s * (T_{Task} + T_{Message\_HTT} - T_{Saved}) + (1-P_s)(T_{Task} + T_{Message\_FA}) \quad (1)$$
$$ET(no\_message) = P_s * T_{MISS} + (1-P_s) * T_{CR}$$
$$= P_s * T_{Task} + (1-P_s) * T_{Task}$$
$$= T_{Task}$$

Where:

P_s = the probability of a signal (help)

T_{CR} = cost of a correct rejection (the system does not provide a help message when help is not needed)

$= T_{Task}$

T_{FA} = cost of a false alarm (the system provides a help message when help is not needed)

$= T_{Task} + T_{Message\_FA}$

T_{HIT} = cost of a correct identification (the system provides a help message when help is needed)

$= T_{Task} + T_{Message\_HTT} - T_{Saved}$

T_{MISS} = cost of a missed signal (the system does not provide a message when help is needed)

$= T_{Task}$

T_{Task} = Time needed to complete a task without a help message

T_{Saved} = Time saved by a help message

$T_{Message\_HIT}$ = Timetoprocessa helpmessagewhenthesystemprovidesa helpmessage whenhelpis needed

$T_{Message\_FA}$ = Time to process a help message when the system provides a message when help is not needed

The expected task performance time of presenting a help message is the summation of the times associated with processing a help message and performing a task with a help message. The time to process a help message does not only include the time to read the message but also the time associated with performing the suggestion in the message and the remedy action if the suggestion in the message is wrong. The basic assumption of the equation is that the time to process a help message varies according to whether it is a correct identification or a false alarm. The user will be more likely to follow the suggestion in the help message if the message is provided when the user needs help. The expected time of presenting no help message is exactly same as the task performance time since there is no change.

The optimal help threshold probability can be calculated as shown below:

$$ET(message) = ET(no\_message)$$
$$P_s(T_{Task} + T_{Message\_HTT} - T_{Saved}) + (1-P_s)(T_{Task} + T_{Message\_FA}) = T_{Task} \quad (2)$$
$$P_s^* = \frac{T_{Message\_FA}}{T_{Saved} + T_{Message\_FA} - T_{Message\_HTT}}$$

The help message should be provided when the probability that the user needs help exceeds the optimal threshold probability (P_s^*).

4 Conclusion

This study proposed the decision theoretic framework of optimizing the provision of a help message considering time as its cost and value. Although there are multiple purposes for providing advice such as increasing accuracy, increasing user confidence, etc., the purpose of reducing time required to complete a task is more appropriate for many tasks which are not safety-related or not critical. Many tasks that people do every day using their computers would belong to this category. By assigning the time associated with processing a help message provided by an intelligent agent as cost, The proposed approach would provide guidance as to where, when and why help messages are likely to be effective or ineffective by utilizing quantitative predictions of value and cost of intelligent help messages in time.

Future studies can be directed toward implementing the proposed approach in the real system and test if the proposed approach can save time and improve user satisfaction.

References

1. Lieberman, H.: Interfaces that give and take advice. In: Carroll, J.M. (ed.) Human-Computer Interaction in the New Millennium, pp. 475–485. ACM Press/ Addison-Wesley, N.Y (2001)
2. Carroll, J., Rosson, M.B.: Paradox of the active user. In: Carroll, J.M. (ed.) Interfacing thought: cognitive aspects of human-computer interaction, pp. 80–111. MIT Press, Cambridge, MA (1987)
3. Horvitz, E.: Uncertainty, Action, and Interaction: In Pursuit of Mixed-Initiative Computing. Intelligent Systems, IEEE Computer Society, pp. 17-20 (September / October 1999)
4. Virvou, M., Kabassi, K.: Evaluating an intelligent graphical user interface by comparison with human experts. Knowledge-Based Systems 17, 31–37 (2004)
5. Gajos, K., Weld, D.S.: Preference elicitation for interface optimization. In: Proceedings of the 18th annual ACM symposium on User interface software and technology, Seattle, WA, USA, pp. 173 –182 (2005)
6. Wooldridge, M.: Intelligent agents. In: Weiss, G. (ed.) Multiagent systems, a modern approach to distributed artificial intelligence, pp. 27–78. MIT Press, Cambridge, MA (1999)
7. Klusch, M.: Information agent technology for the Internet: A survey. Data. and Knowledge Engineering 36, 337–372 (2001)
8. Shneiderman, B., Maes, P.: Direct manipulation vs. interface agents. Interactions 4(6), 42–61 (1997)
9. Mao, J., Leung, Y.W.: Exploring the potential of unobtrusive proactive task support. Interacting with Computers 15, 265–288 (2003)

10. Lehto, M.R.: Optimal warnings: an information and decision theoretic perspective. In: Wogalter, M.S. (ed.) The handbook of warnings, pp. 89–108. Erlbaum, Mahwah, NJ (2006)
11. Horvitz, E.: Principles of mixed-initiative user interfaces. In: Proceedings of the ACM SIGCHI, Pittsburgh, PA, pp. 159–166. ACM Press, New York (1999)
12. Zhou, M.X., Wen, Z., Aggarwal, V.: A graph-matching approach to dynamic media allocation in intelligent multimedia interfaces. In: Proceedings of the 10th international conference on Intelligent user interfaces, San Diego, California, pp. 114-121 (2005)
13. Card, S.K., Moran, T.P., Newell, A.: The Psychology of Human-Computer Interaction. Lawrence Erlbaum, Hillsdale, N.J (1983)

Human-Aided Cleaning Algorithm for Low-Cost Robot Architecture*

Seungyong Kim, Kiduck Kim, and Tae-Hyung Kim

Department of Computer Science and Engineering, Hanyang University
1271 Sa 1-Dong, Ansan, Kyunggi-Do, 426-791, South Korea
{kimsy,kdkim,tkim}@cse.hanyang.ac.kr

Abstract. This paper presents a human-aided cleaning algorithm that can be implemented on low-cost robot architecture while the cleaning performance far exceeds the conventional random style cleaning. We clarify the advantages and disadvantages of the two notable cleaning robot styles: the random and the mapping styles, and show the possibility how we can achieve the performance of the complicated mapping style under the random style-like robot architecture using the idea of human-aided cleaning algorithm. Experimental results are presented to show the cleaning performance.

Keywords: Cleaning robots, Random style cleaning, Mapping style cleaning, Human-robot interaction.

1 Introduction

Since the application of household service robots has been restricted to nonessential tasks, the proliferation of the robot markets has been limited so far contrast to that of the industrial robot applications. In order to be of practical value, we may have to answer a basic question, "what does the robot do?" Recently, an autonomous robotic vacuum cleaner has a clear answer to the question and becomes one of the most successful killer applications that widen the horizon of household service robots. It simply cleans floors. Albeit simple, the cleaning robot delivers a practical importance to consumer electronics industry, but it challenges technical and economic problems [1]. Thus, the robot cleaner would not be able to be successful in the market, without having a proper compromise between the two problems. If we stress on a technical problem, we may end up with a high-cost intelligent robot, but of little economic value. If we pursue an economic value, the final product may not clean well enough.

Traditionally and academically, many researches on the cleaning algorithm are based on the existence of navigation maps for a cleaning floor [2, 3]. Creating and managing such a map would play a pivotal role for the robot to find its cleaning paths and particular locations to move. Robots should recognize proper landmarks using an expensive vision sensor, stores those image points to map database with coordinates.

* This research has been supported by the Ministry of Education and Human Resources Development, S. Korea, under the grant of the second stage of BK21 project.

J. Jacko (Ed.): Human-Computer Interaction, Part III, HCII 2007, LNCS 4552, pp. 366–375, 2007.

The map building process is complicated enough. Moreover, although the mapping and navigation process is completed, the method raises a localization problem [4, 5], which is more difficult one because it is expensive to compensate the moving aberration due to friction, slipping, and unorthodox floor conditions. Dead-reckoning [4], Markov localization [6], and Monte Carlo localization [7] are some of approaches to deal with the problem. The mapping and navigation based approach would be technically possible to construct a truly intelligent cleaning robot in unknown and unstructured environments, albeit expensive.

On the other hand, if we decide to sacrifice the utmost cleaning efficiency, which is not that critical to housekeeping chores like cleaning, we may build a robot at a modest price, where the architecture is equipped with a modest microprocessor, minimum number of motors, and with a limited set of sensors like bump sensor, cliff and wall sensors. What about maps? No need. Its mobility is based on a random walk. Simply to be random, we may not need an expensive vision sensor or complex actuators for navigating maps. Roomba [8, 9] by iRobot, Inc., is a pioneering product in this random style robot, and Roboking by LG Electronics and Trilobite by Electrolux are one of those as well. The complexity is intentionally minimized yet they do clean well up to the users' expectations. A home service robot in this style was recorded as the first significant commercial success due to its simplicity in terms of cleaning operations at modest price.

Nonetheless, they used to clean the same area repeatedly while other part of the area remained unclean for a quite long time. In this paper, we present a human-aided cleaning algorithm for the better cleaning efficiency like map-based approach yet with low-cost robot architecture like Roomba. Navigation map building, autonomous path finding, and automatic localization problems are all important computation problems for machine intelligence, but the higher cost and complexity of such system is too much for floor cleaning robots. Note that human beings can do better for the area partitioning than machine. Moreover, the users are familiar with the interior shape of their home. In this work, we can parameterize the operational behavior of cleaning robot. At one extreme of human-robot interactions, if we do not teach anything about the cleaning space, the robot is supposed to move around the space randomly as Roomba does. At another extreme, if we teach every details about the moving information, the robot repeat what people do to clean their floor; the robot mimics housemaids. There is a wide spectrum of robot operations between the two extremes. For example, people may point out every one and each of turning points in a polygonal cleaning space, instead of dragging the robot to the entire cleaning space, and then the robot would be able to do the rest by automatically filling the space defined by the given set of edges. Designing the cleaning algorithm for the division of works between human beings and robots, we can achieve the two conflicting goals of low-cost robot architecture and cleaning efficiency as much as we can. The heart of our approach is to make a division of roles between human being and machine.

The remainder of the paper is organized as follows. Section 2 briefly describes the background of robot driving systems and their required set of sensors. In Section 3, we identify the set of robot instructions in our *human-aided cleaning algorithm* and

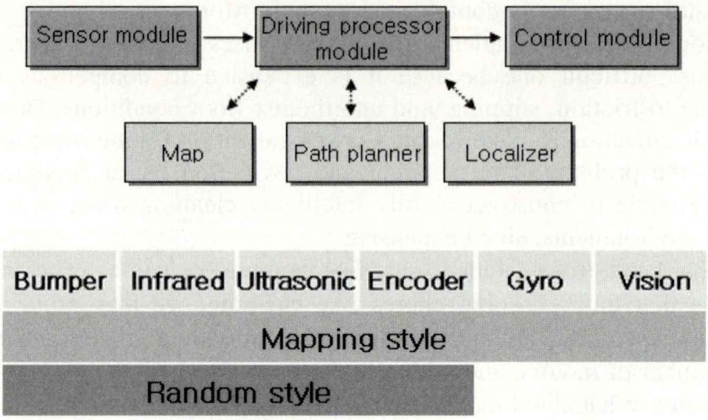

Fig. 1. Robot driving system and various sensors

present our approach in general. To show the behavioral performance of our approach, we conducted experiments for diverse shapes of cleaning space with proper information from human beings, and compared them with that of Roomba. We used the Player/Stage simulator [10, 11] developed at the University of Southern California on Linux Fedora 3.0 with kernel version 2.6.9-1.667. The experimental results are discussed in Section 4. We conclude the paper in Section 5.

2 Background

There are two contrasting robot driving systems as shown in Fig. 1: the random style and the mapping style. The cleaning robot comprise a *sensor module* that manages a plurality of sensors, a *driving processor module* that processes cleaning algorithms based on the inputs from various sensors, and a *control module* that executes control instructions from the processor module via an actuator. The random style driving system consists of these three components. The mapping style robot additionally comprises a map that is built and used for navigation, a path planner that routes a whole path in a cleaning area, and a localizer that periodically estimates and corrects the current position when friction and slipping happen. The number and the type of the sensors are quite different among various cleaning robots, but gyro and vision sensors are normally employed only for the mapping style. Our approach essentially requires an ultrasonic[1] sensor for distance measurement, a gyro sensor for angle measurement, and an encoder for moving distance measurement. Possibly an infrared sensor can be included for cliff and staircase detection. We do not need an expensive vision sensor that is only used for map building and localization. Normal sensor configuration is summarized in Fig. 1, and our approach needs a gyro sensor additionally, comparing to the random style.

[1] Normally, a laser sensor is more accurate for the measurement, but more expensive.

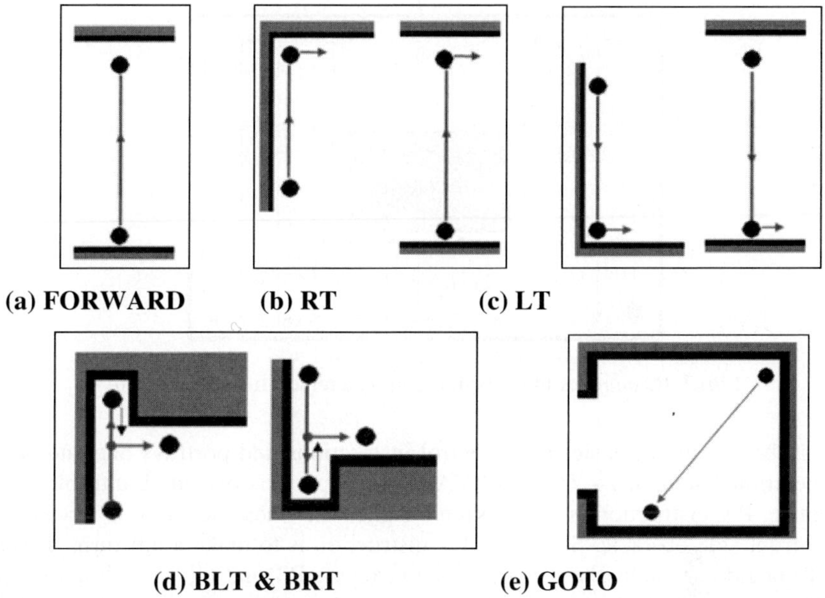

Instruction	Description	Instruction	Description
`FORWARD`	Go straight	`BLT`	Make backwardly left turn
`RT`	Make right turn	`BRT`	Make backwardly right turn
`LT`	Make left turn	`GOTO`	Go to the next work point

Fig. 2. Basic robot control instructions

3 Human-Aided Cleaning Algorithm

As presented in the previous section, there are two robot driving styles: random and mapping. The random style robot can be built on inexpensive components and operate in simple but creative ways [8]. The main thrust of the human-aided cleaning algorithm is to perform like the mapping style robot, but with almost same robot architecture as the random style; our robot algorithm does not provide a mechanism for path planning and localization facilities but get provided the essential intelligence with a proper interaction from the human users who are familiar with the cleaning floor situations. The seemingly magical high performance comes right from the human-robot interactions. In this section, we present the overall architecture of our approach and clarify what human beings should provide to the robot.

3.1 Overall Architecture

The human-aided cleaning algorithm consists of three components: basic control instruction sets, region filling algorithm from the mapping style [3], and a list of necessary hardware components.

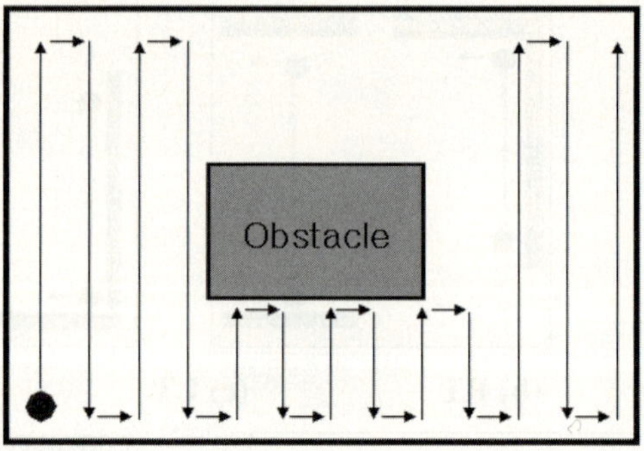

Fig. 3. Basic robot movement based on a region filling algorithm

Fig. 2 shows our six basic robot control instructions and portrays one and each of their operational semantics. The FORWARD instruction is executed until blocked by an obstacle. RT instruction is for making a right turn when the robot is blocked by a left and front side obstacle. Similarly, LT instruction is to make a left turn. If there is only a front side obstacle, the robot is able to execute RT and LT according to a given control program implementation. BLT is to make a left turn backwardly, that is effectively to make a right turn from the original moving direction after having run into a narrow alley. BRT is to make a right turn backwardly in order to escape from an alley. Finally, the GOTO instruction is to move directly from an endpoint of a cleaning section to a starting point of another one without performing a cleaning job. Cleaning sections are partitioned for the purpose of cleaning efficiency based on information from human users.

These six instructions can suffice to implement the cleaning robot movement that is similar to a region filling algorithm as shown in Fig. 3. From a specific starting point, the robot keeps moving up and down until it reaches to an obstacle. After it gets into an area that is limited by an obstacle, the movement is confined to the below of the obstacle. The upper part is remained not traveled. The pseudo-code representation for the region filling algorithm is shown in Fig. 4. The default instruction is FORWARD so the program does not have to specify it to the robot explicitly. Region filling algorithm is only used within a particular cleaning section. Human users provide the robot with the most reasonable section partitioning information so we can safely assume that it knows how the entire cleaning area is comprised of smaller cleaning sections that is to be cleaned based on the region filling algorithm.

3.2 Human-Robot Interaction

Region filling algorithm based robot movement is performed based on the space information that is provided by a human user: the starting point of the current cleaning section, the relative coordinate information for the cleaning space, and the moving distance and angle for the next cleaning section. A cleaning space can be partitioned to multiple cleaning sections for higher cleaning performance. A cleaning section is always rectangular. Thus, if there is a cleaning section partitioned with an obstacle like in Fig. 3, there can be a region that is not covered by our cleaning robot

```
// F:front, L:left, R:right
enum collision_type{
  Nothing =0,
  F,
  FL,
  FR,
  FLR
};

enum movement_template{
  Forward =0,
  RT,
  LT,
  BRT,
  BLT,
  GoTo,
};

for( ; ;)
{
  if( is_this_region_complete() )
  {
    if( next_region_check() )
    {
      movement = Goto;
    }
    else{
      break;
    }
  }

switch(movement){
  case Forward:
    switch(collision){
      case Nothing:
        /* straight forward */
        break;
      case F:
      case FR:
      case FL:
      case FLR:
        if( /* upside? */){
          if( /* FR || FLR */ ){
            movement = BLT;
          }else
            movement = RT;
        }else { /* down side */
          if( /* FL || FLR */ ){
            movement = BRT;
          }
          else
            movement = LT;
        }
        break;
    }
    break;
    .
    .
    .
} // end switch
// end for
```

Fig. 4. Pseudo-code representation for a region filling algorithm

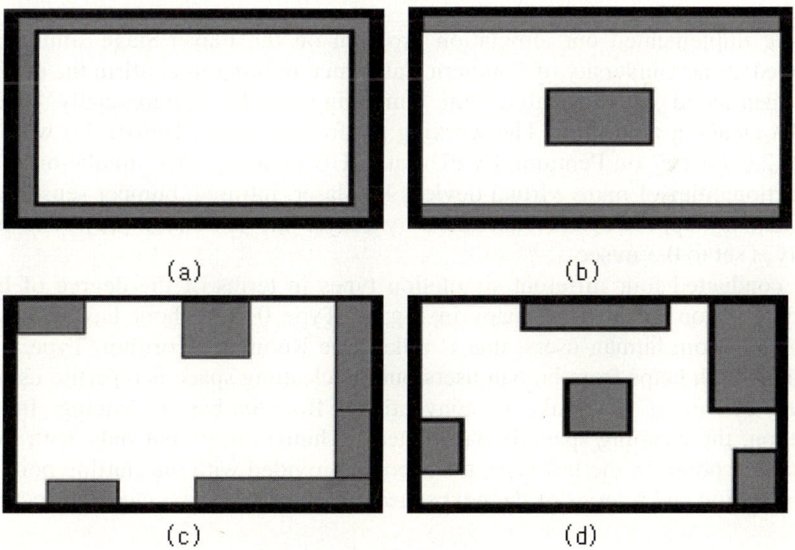

Fig. 5. Four different maps used in the simulation experiment

since the region filling algorithm is applied to one and each of those sections. Human users are responsible for the most reasonable partitioning for cleaning efficiency.

Completed at a section, the robot is directed to move directly to the starting point of the next cleaning section using the GOTO instruction with distance and angle parameters. The number of repetitions in a cleaning section can be decided arbitrarily depending on dirtiness.

Unlike the mapping method, our cleaning robot does not have to make computational efforts to come up with the cleaning space information, and the information is provided by a human user. A creative way of human-robot interaction is required to conveniently let the robot know about the cleaning space information consisting of the rectangular shape of sections and the cleaning sequence of those sections. The design of such interfacing method is beyond the scope of this paper, since the primary purpose of our research in this paper is to corroborate the usefulness of the human-aided cleaning algorithm, as shown in the next section.

4 Experimental Results

In our simulation experiment, we use four different maps from the simplest form without any obstacles to a complicated one with randomly placed obstacles as shown in Fig. 5. The cleaning area is represented by white areas in the figure. The room size excluding the area by obstacles is 8.2m X 4.5m. Cleaning performance will be represented by the progress percentage with regard to the cleaning area in a given time span and by the elapsed time to finish a given cleaning task.

4.1 Experiment Environment

We have implemented our simulation program on the Player/Stage simulator [10] developed at the University of Southern California, in order to confirm the efficacy of the human-aided cleaning algorithm comparing to the commercially successful Roomba cleaning algorithm. The working platform is Linux Fedora 3.0 with kernel version 2.6.9-1.667 on Pentium 4 CPU with 1GB memory. Our simulation relies on the functionalities of many virtual devices like laser, infrared, bumper sensors and so forth, that is supported and confirmed by Player 2.0 simulator [11]. The moving velocity is set to 0.3 m/sec.

We conducted four different simulation types in terms of the degree of human-robot interaction to the four maps in Fig. 5. Type 0 is without having any extra information from human users, that is alike pure Roomba algorithm. Type 1 is still without enough helps from human users but the cleaning space is bipartite using only two sets of virtual walls like in conventional Roomba-based cleaning. In type 2 simulation, the cleaning space is partitioned by human users but only with the very first starting point. In the last type, the robot is provided with the starting point of the starting section and a series of the next starting points of the next cleaning sections.

4.2 Results

Fig. 6. shows the progress percentage of cleaned area for four different types of maps that are applied to by four different human-robot interaction modes. We just limit the time interval up to 10 minutes because there is not much progress after then. For

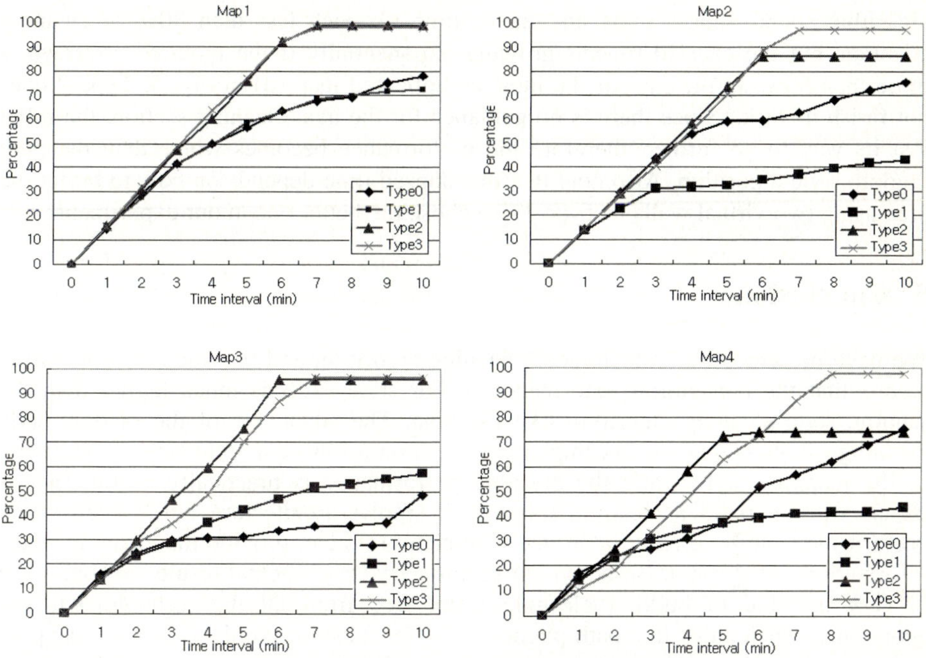

Fig. 6. Progress percentage of cleaned area

map 1	Complete coverage (%)			
	30	60	90	95
Type0	2	6	20	82
Type1	3	6	18	31
Type2	2	4	6	7
Type3	2	4	6	7

map 2	Complete coverage (%)			
	30	60	90	95
Type0	3	6	21	48
Type1	3	33	42	70
Type2	2	5	don't	don't
Type3	2	5	7	7

map 3	Complete coverage (%)			
	30	60	90	95
Type0	3	12	55	93
Type1	4	21	24	29
Type2	2	4	6	6
Type3	3	5	7	7

map 4	Complete coverage (%)			
	30	60	90	95
Type0	4	8	33	90
Type1	3	36	52	58
Type2	2	4	don't	don't
Type3	3	5	7	8

Fig. 7. Elapsed time to complete given coverages

example, as we can see in the figure, Type 2 and Type 3 operations are finished within 8 minutes while Type 0 and Type 1 show very gentle slope after 7 or 8 minutes so they need more than 60 minutes to reach 95% coverage of the given cleaning area.

We also measured the elapsed time to reach certain amount of cleaned area. As shown in Fig. 7, the random style algorithm (Type 0 and Type 1) and human-aided algorithm spend almost same amount of time to reach less than 30% of cleaning coverage but the elapsed time is growing exponentially if the required coverage is more than 50%. In the case of the most complicated map (d) in Fig. 5, Type 2 does not finish its task.[2] Since there is no guidance for the next cleaning section, the robot lost its way to go further, therefore the performance becomes worse than the pure random style algorithm. Also note that the elapsed time depends on how to bisect the area using two virtual walls in Type 1; we chose the better one in our experiment.

5 Conclusion

We have presented the human-aided cleaning algorithm and provided the simulation results that the behavioral performance of our style exceeds much higher than the random style cleaning algorithm like Roomba. The advantage of the random style cleaning robots is that we can implement them on a low-cost architecture comparing to the mapping style while the cleaning performance is practically useful. In this paper, we can build a cleaning robot with similar architecture but its behavioral performance can be greatly improved if human users can provide the cleaning space information to the robot. Based on our preliminary experimental results, we believe it is very possible to build a cleaning robot free from all the technological and economical difficulties like path planning and localization problems for the mapping style cleaning robots. We are going to further explore the simplification of basic robot instruction sets that can be implemented with the minimized sensing and driving modules. We are also working on the most convenient way of human-robot interactions that may lead to high cleaning performance.

References

1. Fiorono, P., Prassler, E.: Cleaning and Household Robots: A Technology Survey. Autonomous Robots 9, 51–92 (2000)
2. Elfes, A.: Sonar-Based Real-World Mapping and Navigation. IEEE Journal of Robotics and Automation RA-3(3), 249–265 (1987)
3. Oh, J., Choi, Y., Park, J., Zheng, Y.: Complete Coverage Navigation of Cleaning Robots Using Triangular-Cell-Based Map. IEEE Transactions on Industrial Electronics, 51(3), 718–726 (2004)
4. Tsai, C-C.: A Localization System of a Mobile Robot by Fusing Dead-reckoning and Ultrasonic Measurements, IEEE Instrumentation and Measurement Technology Conference, pp. 144–149 (1998)
5. Neira, J., Tardos, J., Horn, J., Schmidt, G.: Fusing Range and Intensity Images for Mobile Robot Localization. IEEE Transactions on Robotics and Automation 15(1), 53–76 (1999)
6. Fox, D., Burgard, W., Thrun, S.: Active Markov Localization for Mobile Robots, Robotics and Autonomous Systems, vol. 25 (1998)
7. Dellart, F., Fox, D., Burgard, W., Thrun, S.: Robust Monte Carlo Localization for Mobile Robots. In: Proc. Of National Conference on Artificial Intelligence, vol. 128 (2001)

[2] In map 2 (Fig. 5 (b)) map 4 (Fig. 5 (d)), Type 2 terminates its task at 86.4% and 73.82%, respectively.

8. Jones, J.: Robots at the Tipping Point: The Road to the iRobot Roomba. IEEE Robotics and Automation Magazine 13, 76–78 (2006)
9. Fortizzi, J., DiSalvo, C.: Robots Service Robots in the Domestic Environment: A Study of the Roomba Vacuum in the Home, ACM Annual Conference on Human Robot Interaction, pp. 258–265 (2006)
10. Gerkey, B., Vaughan, R., Howard, A.: The Player/Stage Project: Tools for Multi-Robot and Distributed Sensor Systems. In: Proceedings of the International Conference on Advanced Robotics, pp. 317–323 (2003)
11. Collett, T., MacDonald, B., Gerkey, B.: Player 2.0: Toward a Practical Robot Programming Framework. In: Proceedings of the Australasian Conference on Robotics and Automation (2005)

The Perception of Artificial Intelligence as "Human" by Computer Users

Jurek Kirakowski, Patrick O'Donnell, and Anthony Yiu

Human Factors Research Group, UCC, Cork Enterprise Centre
Cork, Ireland
jzk@ucc.ie, p.odonnell@student.ucc.ie, yiucw@mac.com

Abstract. This paper deals with the topic of 'humanness' in intelligent agents. Chatbot agents (e.g. Eliza, Encarta) had been criticized on their ability to communicate in human like conversation. In this study, a CIT approach was used for analyzing the human and non-human parts of Eliza's conversation. The result showed that Eliza could act like a human as if it could greet, maintain a theme, apply damage control, react appropriately to cue, offer a cue, use appropriate language style and have a personality. It was non human insofar as it used formal or unusual treatment of language, failed to respond to a specific question, failed to respond to a general question or implicit cue, evidenced time delays and phrases delivered at inappropriate times.

Keywords: chatbot, connectionist network, Eliza, Critical Incident Technique, humanness.

1 Introduction

There is a potentially diverse range of applications for intelligent agents in software use. Such agents have a part to play in domains such as user interfaces, the negotiation of information retrieval and organization, and electronic purchasing. These agents represent the active use of weak Artificial Intelligence units in computer use in general. The search engine "Encarta", devised by Microsoft, is a good example which demonstrates some of the applications associated with these kinds of agents. The software uses Natural Language Processing (NLP) in order to give the program ability to carry out sophisticated information retrieval tasks. This stems from the capacity of sophisticated NLP programs to parse the typed requests of human users and approach an "understanding" of these requests in terms of keywords which can then be used to search the web for relevant information and parse the resulting text in order to construct a response to a request.

"Encarta" offers an attractive user interface because it can parse, analyse and produce natural language utterances. This allows the program to produce relevant responses to human utterances in natural language form. It is this aspect of NLP agents that is the concern of this paper. In theory, a powerful enough NLP agent could offer a hugely attractive form of Human Computer Interaction in that computer use could be mediated by an agent that behaves as though it can understand instructions that are typed in by human users and respond in kind with natural-seeming utterances.

J. Jacko (Ed.): Human-Computer Interaction, Part III, HCII 2007, LNCS 4552, pp. 376–384, 2007.

The point has been raised that in order to communicate with computers, humans must learn the language of computers and that computers are, at present, incapable of communicating by using human languages [8]. The prospect of an NLP agent that is powerful enough to deal with human languages would radically change this state of affairs.

There are several ways of approaching the problem of building a software engine that has to deal with human language utterances. Since an agent that is successful in this task is essentially a form of Artificial Intelligence, it seems fitting to begin by describing the traditional approach to AI and how it relates to this problem. Traditional AI approaches rely on a Strong Physical Symbols System approach (SPSS), whereby a series of symbols is given to the engine in question, the symbols are manipulated in some logical manner within the engine and a series of symbols is given as output [7]. There are several problems attendant on these approaches, both in general and in the specific case of language processing. A general criticism of SPSS approaches is that of symbol grounding [6]. The problem is essentially that of how a system that depends on the manipulation of virtual symbols can ever ascribe any kind of meaning to those symbols, except in terms of other arbitrary symbols thus defined themselves. Another problem that is of particular interest with regards to the question of language is the problem of emergent problem spaces as associated with these types of systems. This consists of attempts by the engine to generate all possible solutions to a problem once posed, and an inability to choose the most likely solution from amongst the other contenders. This problem is especially relevant to language processing as it is a task that must occur in real time, and any attempt by a language engine to test each individual solution before choosing the correct one will be time consuming. The classic example of this type of problem in language processing comes from attempts to build sentence parsers along this line. The engine, when tested, generated five possible meanings for the sentence "Time flies like an arrow" [1].

The second prominent approach in contemporary Artificial Intelligence is the connectionist approach (also referred to as parallel distributed processing or the neural net approach). There are at least three unique features that make a connectionist network a powerful system for handling human conversation: namely superpositioning, intrinsic context sensitivity, and strong representational change. [3] Firstly, two representations are said to be fully superposed when the resources used to represent item 1 are co-extensive with those used to represent item 2. The natural mechanism of connectionist learning and superpositioning storage yield a system that will extract the statistical central tendency of an exemplar. This is usefully seen as embodying prototype-style knowledge representation. The network extracts various feature complexes and thus comes to encode information not just about specific exemplars but also about the stereotypical features set displayed in the training data. The network can generalise novel case sensibly by dint of its past training.

Secondly, the connectionist network concept can also display intrinsic context sensitivity. The most radical description of this would be that connectionist system does not involve computations defined over symbols. Instead, any accurate picture of the system's processing will have to be given at the numerical level of unites, weights and activation-evolution equations, while the symbolic-manipulating computational description will at most provide a rough guide to the main trends in the global behaviour of the system [3]. The network can then learn to treat several inputs, which result in subtly different representational states, as prompting outputs which have much in common.

Thirdly, a connectionist network can show strong representational change. Fodor [4] suggested concept learning can only consist in the triggering of innate representational atoms or the deployment of such atoms in a "generate and test" learning style. According to [3] this is weak representational change as the product necessarily falls within the expressive scope of the original representational base. The connectionist network on the other hand, can acquire knowledge without the benefit of any such resource. For example the NETtalk [10] and the past-tense learning network [9] both begin with a set of random connection weights and learn about a domain "from scratch".

Connectionist models however have a similar grounding problem as the SPSS approach does. Connectionist models explain symbols by a series of context-sensitive connections. The process itself does not 'bottom-out' or come to a definition that is *not* prone to context infection. In additional, there is a problem in systematicity [5] in that a connectionist network can fail to process sentences with constituents in novel syntactic position and at a novel level of embedding when processing includes determining the word's semantic role.

The symbol grounding problem is the problem of representing meaning in a system of purely arbitrary symbols. One approach to robotics and AI in general that may be able to address this problem involves dodging the question of representation altogether. Wallis [11] discusses the possibility of producing agents that can exhibit all the characteristics of an intelligent agent (intention, planning etc.) without using any more representation "than a microwave oven would." Wallis' stance is informed by Brooks' [2] approach to robotics, wherein robots can be developed that behave in an autonomous, intelligent fashion without any bona fide "understanding" of their own behaviours or why they are performing them. The essential tenet that underlies this approach is that an agent's intelligent behaviour arises out of an interaction between the agent and its environment, in the service of achieving some goal. Reflective reasoning about the environment, the goal or the behaviour by the agent is not necessary for the behaviour to be described as intelligent. The agents that exhibit this type of architecture can perform behaviours that can be described as intelligent without possessing any capacities that we would describe as "intelligence" because their actions make sense within their environment with regards to the satisfaction of some goal. Thus, if it is possible to produce a chatbot that has no representation of meaning but can behave as though it did (i.e. seem to understand utterances and interact with users), then users would be forced to conclude that its conduct within a dialogue was "intelligent". The earliest types of chatbot programs, that scan for keywords and match responses, can be seen as non-representational chatbot agents. It is intended to examine the way in which one of these agents will interact with users, and how it might be possible to improve on its ability to be regarded as an agent that produces intelligent language behaviour. What is interesting is whether a non-representational approach such as this can be brought to bear in an arena such as language, a system of representational symbols.

It is not appropriate in this paper to attempt to select between these three approaches to the architecture of a natural language machine. No doubt in the end the "best" approach will be a hybrid of some kind and there are problems of principle as well as of implementation. We note that in the past research has taken a particular technology as a given and focussed on the application. We propose to turn the problem round.

That is, it is intended to do a much more "requirements" orientated survey, to identify what aspects of speech comprehension and production by software agents characterise them as being "inhuman" in the eyes of computer users and which aspects are characteristic of human language behaviour. It may later be appropriate to discuss which types of programs and architectures are best equipped to support the type of behaviours seen as quintessentially "human". In other words, the research question addressed in this paper is: when users interact with an agent that is equipped to process human language and respond with utterances of its own, what kind of mistakes can the program make that a human wouldn't and that make the dialogue between user and agent seem unnatural.

2 Method

In the experiment fourteen college-aged participants were asked to interact with an Eliza-style computer program (chatbot) for three minutes and then to participate in the elicitation of critical incidents with a transcript of their session. The program was based on the classic Eliza design with two important differences. Firstly, there was no mechanism that retained previous phrases entered by the user which could be used to re-start a stalled conversation (eg: "Tell more more about [a previous utterance]".) This was for theoretical reasons as will be discussed later. Secondly, there was a mechanism which enabled the chatbot to switch contexts on detecting particular words. Thus if the chatbot detected the word "music" the whole list of trigger phrases and responses changed to a music-orientated set.

A qualitative approach incorporating the Critical Incidents Technique (CIT) and content analysis of responses is involved in this study. At the end of this interaction, the participants were presented with a printed transcript of the dialogue and asked to highlight instances of the conversation that seemed particularly unnatural (up to three examples) and then to report why this was so. The same was done for up to three examples of speech that did seem convincing. The data produced by the critical incident technique were content analysed, with user responses being sorted by theme. The data coding was cross-checked independently by another individual. Inter-rater reliability of approx. 0.53 was obtained in the first pass. Items on which there was disagreement were discussed and placed in mutually agreeable categories with the assistance of a third independent rater. We are reasonably sure that the categories that have emerged represent reproducible aspects of the data set.

3 Results

The various themes that were produced during the content analysis were as follows. Firstly, under the heading of unconvincing characteristics-

- *Fails to maintain a theme once initiated.* In that, once a theme emerged in the dialogue, the chatbot failed to produce statements relevant to that theme in the following section of the dialogue.
- *Formal or unusual treatment of language.* Some statements in the chatbots database seemed overly stiff and formal or used unusual words and language.

- *Failure to respond to a specific question.* Users would ask for a specific piece of information, such as asking the chatbot what its favourite film might be, and receiving no answer.
- *Fails to respond to a general question or implicit cue.* Users offer the chatbot a cue (in the form of a general question, like "How are you?", or offer a cue in the form of a statement, like "Tell me about yourself." Or "Let's talk about films then.") and receive an irrelevant response.
- *Time delay.* A fairly cosmetic fault, users felt that the chatbot responded too quickly to a detailed question or too slowly to a courtesy.
- *Phrases delivered at inappropriate times, with no reference to preceding dialogue.* Where generic type phrases did not fit into the conversation in a natural way, or the chatbot responds to an inappropriate key phrase, with a resulting nonsequitur.

Under the heading of convincing aspects of the conversation-

- *Greetings.* Several participants identified the greeting as a human-seeming characteristic.
- *Maintains a theme.* When the chatbot introduced a theme and was successful at producing a few statements that were relevant to that theme, users found this convincing.
- *Damage control.* When the chatbot produced a breakdown in communication (for any of the reasons mentioned earlier) and then produced a statement that seemed to apologise for the breakdown or seemed to redirect the conversation in a more fruitful direction, users found this a convincingly human trait.
- *Reacts appropriately to cue.* Users found it convincing when the chatbot responded appropriately to a cue such as "How are you?" or "Tell me about yourself."
- *Offers a cue.* Users found it convincing when the chatbot offered a cue for further discussion, such as "What do you want to talk about?" or offered a range of topics for discussion.
- *Language style.* Users found conversational or colloquial English to be convincing.
- *Personality.* The fact that the chatbot was given a name (in fact, even users who did not report the inclusion of a name as convincing referred to it as a "Sam" or a "he") suggests that users wish to assign a personal agency to the chatbot even in the teeth of discrepant knowledge.

4 Discussion

This research focuses on requirement and not any kind of implementation. For now it is enough to identify what traits in the bot-human interaction make it different to human-human interaction and how best these shortcomings might be addressed. Indeed, a reassuring symmetry emerges in the themes identified by users as being convincing or not: maintaining a theme is convincing, while failure to do so is unconvincing, formal or unusual language is unconvincing while colloquial or conversational English is the opposite. Reacting appropriately to a cue is human while failing to a react to one isn't. Delivering an unexpected phrase at an inappropriate time does not impress, but damage control statements can rectify the situation. It is time to address each feature of the bot-human dialogue in a little more detail.

4.1 Maintenance of Themes

One of the factors, upon which the success or failure of the program to appear human seems to depend, is its ability (or lack thereof) to maintain a conversational theme once introduced. The Eliza-style chatbot used in this trial has no memory of a conversation as such (it operates on a first order Markov process, whereby each token is generated in response to the token immediately preceding, with no reference to the accumulated tokens, in this case token = utterance and accumulated tokens = the whole dialogue). This does not preclude it from maintaining a theme however; indeed several participants reported its ability to do so as a convincing feature of its dialogue. The means by which this is accomplished (given that the program has no "memory" of the conversation) is now described.

The chatbot used was unlike the classic Eliza program in that as well as having specific phrases activated by the presence of a keyword, the program could activate a whole database of phrases in response to a key phrase that are specifically related to that phrase (for example, an inventory of keyword-response pairs that are related to music can be prompted by the word "music").

Thus, the program has access to a database of phrases that are most likely to be relevant to the theme raised. At present, failure to maintain a theme that has activated one of these databases may be due to the fact that these databases contain all the same generic response phrases and keyword-response pairs as the general text database that serves as the default set of responses. This makes the likelihood that a theme-relevant phrase is activated lower than if the specialised databases were to contain theme-relevant phrases only. Thus, a means of improving the ability of this program to maintain a theme in conversation might be to enlarge the number of theme relevant keyword-response pairs in these databases and remove most of the generic keyword-response pairs from these "themed" databases.

4.2 Failure to Respond to a Specific Question

This problem, essentially, is a question of how much information is contained in the program's memory and whether or not it can be accessed. Thus, if a person were to ask the program "What is the capital of France?" and the program did not have the information required, the program seems less human. There is no easy way to solve this problem. The solutions are to give the program a large enough database of information to be able to cope with most information requests of this kind (this approach suffers from the fact that the database is still a finite resource and almost certainly contains less information than a human would be expected to) or to grant the program access to the internet and equip it with a more powerful means of parsing information requests so that it can then establish the exact nature of a request and search for the relevant data on the internet. This first solution is brute force and is probably most relevant to a personal-use "humanised" AI, with a role as a user-interface for small-scale personal computer use, while the second is the type of approach that might be associated with a general information retrieval agent such as Microsoft's "Encarta".

4.3 Responding to Social Cues

This category covers the failure or success of the program to react appropriately to a social cue such as "How are you?" or "Tell me about yourself." Some of these cues can be treated in a similar way to the information requests dealt with above, in that an appropriate response can be matched, from a database, to a specific cue.

4.4 Formal and Colloquial Language

In general, formal language was regarded as being an unconvincing trait of the program's, with casual or colloquial language being preferred. Replacing formal phrasings with casual equivalents is a relatively minor adjustment that can be made to improve the program's performance. It is worth bearing in mind however that this trial involved a chatbot that was geared towards free conversation as opposed to being a helper agent in a structured task. In other circumstances, language style might not be a consideration for users at all, or perhaps even more formal and precise language might be preferred (eg in making a financial transaction.)

4.5 Greetings and Personality

Some users reported that certain surface details involved in the chatbot's dialogue made it seem more human by their very presence. The fact that the bot "introduced itself" at the beginning of the dialogue and was given a human name for the trial influenced people into regarding it as slightly more human. This is separate from the functional issues involved in recognizing conversational breakdown and issuing damage repair, and is probably more related to personal preferences.

4.6 Offers a Cue

The chatbot was deemed to be very "humanlike" when it offered cues on which users could elaborate. The possibility has already been raised of including more cues which are designed to elicit clarification in situations where the chatbot does not have enough information to respond appropriately to a cue. This promotes information exchange between the user and the chatbot and is likely to reduce ambiguity and allow the chatbot to react more reliably to user-statements.

4.7 Phrases Delivered at Inappropriate Times

This is an enduring problem of the Eliza style keyword-response chatbot, generic phrases are produced which do not fit well into the conversation, or a keyword prompts a response that is inappropriate in the context it is used. The first problem can be caused when the generic "placeholder" phrase is a poor one. In the case of the second problem, the chatbot might produce an inappropriate phrase due to the fact that it is insensitive to context. A word which means one thing in a certain context, and which prompts an appropriate response, might mean something completely different in a different context and the same response, when prompted, will no longer be appropriate. Some suggestions for remedying this problem are to equip the program with statements that ask for clarification and to refine the types of keywords that prompt particular responses. In addition, a chatbot that relies on a connectionist architecture may well be more sensitive to context than the model described here and may thus be able to select appropriate responses with a high degree of accuracy.

4.8 Damage Control

In certain situations, the chatbot seemed to be offering to change the topic of conversation after a particular line of conversation broke down, or to try and clarify previous statements. This is a further example of the kind of information-exchange that can occur between users and agents. Not only does this ability seem to make the chatbot appear more human, it would be a valuable ability to develop in any of the major potential applications of chatbots as helpful agents. This type of capability would allow for a more refined search when using information-retrieval agents. In personal computer user-interfaces, this kind of information-exchange opens up the possibility for the agent to make suggestions as regards computer-use.

With regards to the method of analysis employed in this study, it is intended to discuss the level to which the Critical Incident Technique was an appropriate tool of assessment in this trial. The benefits of the Critical Incident Technique as regards this study were as follows:

- Rare events were noted as well as common events, thus the situation in which bot-human interaction could break down and then be retrieved by the bot in a damage control exercise did not occur in all or most of the dialogues but it was identified alongside more common shortcomings of the bot nonetheless.
- Users were asked to focus on specific instances of communication breakdown (as opposed to being allowed to offer the vague opinion that the dialogue "felt wrong") and this allows for a more precise focus on individual problem areas (such as being able to treat "failure to answer a specific question" as a separate problem to "failure to respond to a general question or cue").

However, some shortcomings of the Critical Incident Technique as used in this trial were as follows:

- There is no indication as to the relative severity of failures by the bot to appear human. In other words, it is difficult to tell if users found the agent's inability to maintain a conversational theme a more serious problem than the delivery of unexpected and inappropriate phrases during the dialogue, or even if there is a degree of individual difference involved in which characteristics of the bot's conversation-style are pertinent to its seeming human.
- This method of analysis requires a focus on specific incidents of success or failure and is not particularly sensitive to context. This trial involved a simulated conversation, in which context would be important in establishing whether or not the dialogue seemed natural and though participants are asked to describe the events that lead up to a critical incident as part of their report, some information regarding the context of the conversation as a whole is probably missed.

References

1. Bobrow, D.: Syntactic Analysis of English by Computer – A Survey, tech report 1055, BBN (1963)
2. Brooks, R.A.: Intelligence without representation. Artificial Intelligence 47, 139–159 (1991)
3. Clark, A.: Associative Engine: Connectionism, Concepts, and Representational change. Bradford Book; London, England (1993)
4. Fodor, J.: Representations: Philosophical Essays on the Foundations of Cognitive Science. MIT Press, Cambridge (1981)
5. Hadley, R.F: Systematicity in connectionist language learning. Mind. and Language 9, 247–272 (1994)
6. Harnad, S.: The Symbol Grounding Problem. Physica D 42, 335–346 (1990)
7. Newell, A., Simon, H.A.: Computer science as empirical inquiry: Symbols and search. Commun. Assoc. Comput. Machinery 19, 111–126 (1976)
8. Pinker, S.: The Language Instinct. Penguin. London, p. 193 (1994)
9. Rumelhart, D., McClelland, J.: On learning the past tense of English verbs' in Parallel Distributed Processing: Exploration in the Microstructure of Cognition, vol. 2. MIT Press, Cambridge (1986)
10. Sejnowski, T., Rosenberg, C.: NETtalk: A Parallel Network That Learns to Read Aloud. Technical report JHU/ECC-86/01, John Hopkins University (1986)
11. Wallis, P.: Intention without representation, Philosophical Psychologyy, vol. 17(2) (2004)

Speaker Segmentation for Intelligent Responsive Space

Soonil Kwon

Korea Institute of Science and Technology, Intelligence & Interaction Research Center
P.O. BOX 131,Cheongryang,
Seoul 130-650, Korea
soonil@kist.re.kr

Abstract. Information drawn from conversational speech can be useful for enabling intelligent interactions between humans and computers. Speaker information can be obtained from speech signals by performing Speaker Segmentation. In this paper, a method for Speaker Segmentation is presented to address the challenge of identifying speakers even when utterances are very short (0.5sec). This method, involving the selective use of feature vectors, experimentally reduced the relative error rates by 27–42% for groups of 2 to 16 speakers as compared to the conventional approach for Speaker Segmentation. Thus, this new approach offers a way to significantly improve speech-data classification and retrieval systems.

Keywords: Speaker Segmentation, Speaker Recognition, Intelligent Responsive Space (IRS), Human Computer Interaction (HCI).

1 Introduction

Human Computer Interaction (HCI) technology has brought about a number of exciting and challenging applications. One of the applications showing significant promise is the development of Intelligent Responsive Space. Intelligent Responsive Space provides intelligent services and natural interfaces based on the information obtained by monitoring the behaviors, speech, and identities of interactive persons. Recently the development of intelligent interaction technology has focused on intelligent meeting technology as the physical object of Intelligent Responsive Space [1]. In intelligent meeting technology, Speaker Segmentation is very helpful for identifying the participants at meetings, transcribing the dialog at meetings, and providing related documents and the contents of meetings [2][3][4].

The conventional method for Speaker Segmentation is to use Gaussian Mixture Models (GMMs) of speech spectral features to identify a speaker with the minimum probability of error. In this case, segmentation performance depends highly on the amount of data available for recognizing speakers [5]. Experimental evidence has shown that utterances need to be long enough to ensure adequate speaker discrimination [6]. However, in some applications, it is necessary to operate with short speech segments. In spontaneous speech interactions such as telephone conversations and meetings, short utterances lasting an average of about 0.5 seconds

J. Jacko (Ed.): Human-Computer Interaction, Part III, HCII 2007, LNCS 4552, pp. 385–392, 2007.

(e.g., ``Yes", ``No", or ``Sure") occur frequently [7]. A smaller data set is usually more susceptible to segmentation errors since some feature vectors are more likely to skip the boundaries of short utterances. Therefore, a new Speaker Segmentation method was proposed for this study which excluded the consideration of the particular feature vectors which potentially cause segmentation errors.

The proposed method was experimentally evaluated. In actual conversations such as meetings and debates, the number of participants varies. Thus, in this study, four different groups consisting of 2, 4, 8 and 16 participants were tested. In addition, three lengths of utterances (0.5, 1, 2 seconds) were used for the experiments. Each utterance consisted of spontaneous speech from telephone conversations. Experimental results showed that the study method achieved consistently higher accuracy than the conventional method.

The rest of this paper is organized as follows: Section 2 explains the conventional Speaker Segmentation method; section 3 describes the proposed method; section 4 describes the experiments and discusses results; Conclusions and future plans are described in section 5.

2 Basics of Speaker Segmentation

Speaker Segmentation identifies the speaker of each speech segment. In other words, speech signals are indexed according to the speaker at each time unit. Speaker Segmentation can be regarded as the continuous and sequential execution of Speaker Identification. While speech recognition catches what a person is saying, Speaker Identification identifies the person who is talking.

Speaker Identification is essentially a kind of voice-pattern recognition problem. The system decides who the person is among a group of people. To do this, speech data for people in a group are collected as a training step. From this data, statistical speaker models are built. The model-based method uses a probabilistic formulation of feature space to measure the similarity between two vector sets. The Gaussian model is a basic parametric model. The Gaussian Mixture Model, a weighted sum of some Gaussian distributions, has been found to be effective for developing a speaker model. Model training is accomplished by using the Estimate Maximize (EM) algorithm. The next step in speaker identification is the task of comparing an unidentified utterance with the training models and making the identification. The goal of the identifying process is to choose the speaker model with the minimum probability of error [3][4][6][8].

To train speaker models and execute Speaker Identification and Speaker Segmentation, speech information needs to be analyzed by the short-time spectrum. Cepstral processing is useful to extract features from the speech signal. In addition, the filter bank method analyzes the speech signal through a bank of band-pass filters covering the available range of frequencies. The Mel Frequency Cepstral Coefficient (MFCC) can be obtained by transforming as follows:

- take the Fast Fourier Transform (FFT).
- take the magnitude.
- take the log: result is real valued and symmetric.

- warp the frequencies according to the mel scale.
- take the inverse Fast Fourier Transform.

The mel scale is based on non-linear human perception of sound frequency in which the higher frequency band is compressed since it is regarded as less important for the understanding of sounds than the lower frequency band.

The conventional method for Speaker Segmentation is similar to the conventional Speaker Identification method. The difference between the two methods is whether the procedure is continuously executed or not. To identify the speaker of each segment, speaker models are trained for each participant in a conversation. The set of data (input vectors) from each segment is then used to identify speakers via previously trained speaker models. Based on the Maximum Likelihood criterion, each segment of input data is sequentially mapped to the model of a certain speaker.

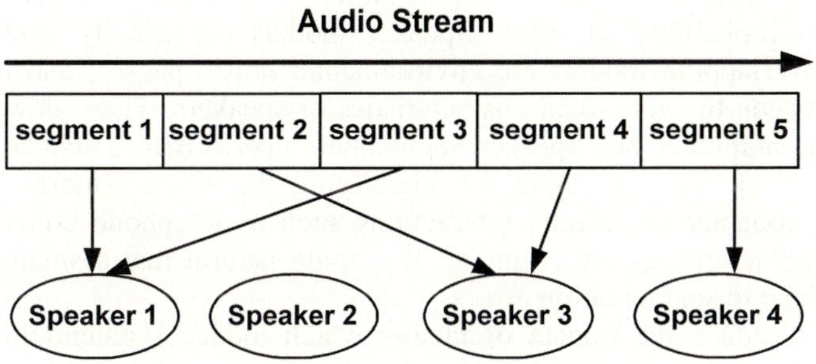

Fig. 1. Illustration of Speaker Segmentation

Fig. 1 shows that continuous speech data such as spoken dialogues and broadcast news can be divided into respective segments identifiable to certain speakers. A long segment is useful for improved Speaker Segmentation performance as it includes more information about the speakers and thus makes identification more accurate. However, it is apt to miss speaker changes that may occur within a segment. To solve this problem, a smaller segment size can be used. However, this requires a refined speaker change detection process to improve precision.

The length of the segment can be either variable or static. In variable length segmentation, the speech stream is divided into different lengths depending on several factors such as pauses and background changes. Pauses are an important consideration in speaker change analysis. In the middle of speaking, people usually breathe. Speaker changes are not likely to occur between these breathing points. The pause point is defined as a certain period within which the energy of a signal stays below the threshold. However, static segmentation assumes a fixed length. A static segmentation is attractive since it is computationally simple, but care has to be taken when choosing the length of segments. Too short a segment may not provide adequate data for analysis, while a longer segment may miss a speaker change point.

Speaker change detection is a very important step in accurate Speaker Segmentation. However, it is not easy to detect speaker changing points due to the lack of data, the variability of speech signal, and environmental noise. More sophisticated algorithms may overcome these difficulties. However, a good method for detecting speaker change has not yet been developed. To improve the speaker change detection algorithm, we can incorporate other features representing the speed and habit of speaking that have not been deeply explored yet. Multi-modal features, such as expression, emotion, gaze, and gesture, can also be useful in improving the performance of speaker change detection.

In this paper, speaker change detection is not considered because the focus is segmentation, and it is assumed that speakers do not change within a segment. For segmentation, the fixed-amount of data is extracted by a sliding window without overlapping.

3 New Method for Speaker Segmentation

A conventional method of Speaker Segmentation is to choose a speaker model with the minimum probability of error. Speaker models are usually overlapped. The reasons for overlapping models are environmental noise, pauses, and unpredictable similarity between the acoustical characteristics of speakers. These unwanted factors result in segmentation errors. Speaker Segmentation performance also depends highly on the amount of data available for identifying the voice patterns of speakers. However, in spontaneous speech interactions such as telephone conversations and meetings, short utterances are common. It is quite natural that a smaller data set is more susceptible to segmentation errors.

In order to reduce the impact of factors which induce segmentation errors, the proposed method split each speaker model into two: non-overlapped and overlapped models. Fig. 2 shows an illustration of one-dimensional speaker-model splitting in which there are two speakers: speaker 1 and speaker 2. Dotted lines represent conventional speaker models, and solid lines represent the new speaker models discussed in this paper. Speaker 1-a is the non-overlapped model of speaker 1, Speaker 1-b is the overlapped model of speaker 1, Speaker 2-a is the non-overlapped model of speaker 2, and Speaker 2-b is the overlapped model of speaker 2. A is the decision boundary of speaker 1 and speaker 2. Two conventional speaker models are split into 4 new speaker models to detect and eliminate undesirable factors.

For splitting speaker models, conventional speaker-models (GMMs) were first trained with sets of speaker-specific speech data (training vectors). Next, using the Maximum Likelihood criterion with the speaker models built in the previous step, we classified the training vectors for each speaker into two categories (non-overlap and overlap) since there could have been some vectors falsely identified if competing speaker models overlapped. In the last step of training, based on the reclassified training vectors, two models for each speaker were reconstructed: non-overlapped and overlapped speaker models [7].

For example, assume there are S single-speaker speech data sets. With feature vectors extracted from these data, we trained speaker models, Mi, where $i=1,\ldots,S$. Then we categorized feature vectors from each speaker data into non-overlapped and overlapped vectors using the Maximum Likelihood criterion as follows [7]:

- x_j: j-th input vector, $j=1,\ldots,N$.
- $I_j = arg\ max\ Pr(x_j \mid M_i),\ i=1,\ldots,S,\ j=1,\ldots,N.$

- If I_j is a correct speaker index, $x_j \rightarrow P$ (a vector set of a non-overlapped category).
- Else $x_j \rightarrow Q$ (a vector set of a overlapped category).

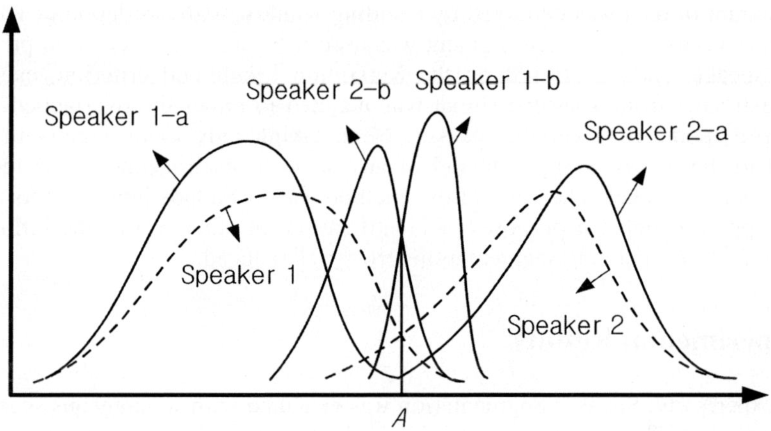

Fig. 2. Illustration of model splitting

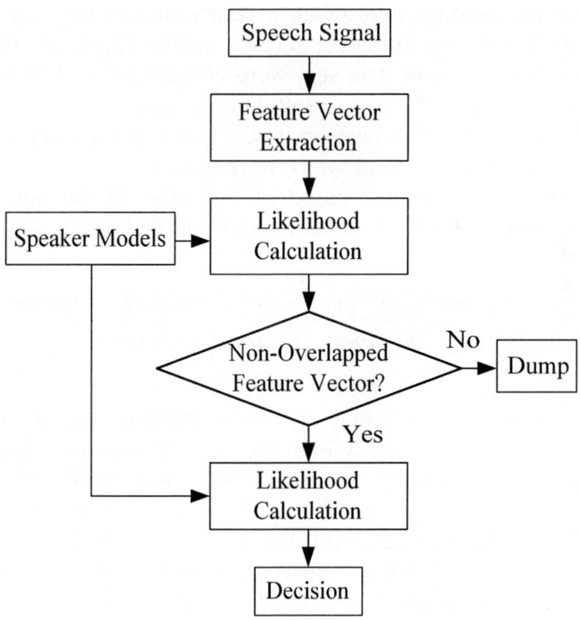

Fig. 3. Block diagram of Speaker Segmentation Procedure

After feature vector categorization, we reconstructed the speaker models. For each speaker *i*, we built two models, non-overlapped (MP_i) and overlapped (MQ_i), with the vectors of P and Q, respectively. Using the pairs of speaker models, we selected the feature vectors that would determine Speaker Segmentation.

As seen in Fig. 3, continuous speech data such as spoken dialogues and broadcast news need to be divided into respective segments of speakers. For segmentation, the fixed-amount of data was extracted by a sliding window with overlapping. The set of data (input vectors) from each segment was used to identify speakers with previously trained speaker models. Based on the Maximum Likelihood criterion, each input vector extracted from a speech signal was mapped to either the overlapped or non-overlapped model of a certain speaker. Next, taking only input vectors that were mapped to the non-overlapped model of any speaker, each segment was identified with a specific speaker. The point of this method was to exclude input vectors mapped to overlapped models for purposes of identification. In other words, the influence of common features inducing segmentation errors was reduced.

4 Experimental Results

In this experiment, Speaker Segmentation was executed with spontaneous speech data sets obtained from telephone conversations. The length of short utterances was 0.5, 1, and 2 seconds. We conducted experiments with 1 and 2 second utterances to compare with 0.5 second cases. Usually there are a varying number of people participating in conversations such as meetings and debates. Hence, in this experiment, data from 4 groups composed of varying numbers of participants (2, 4, 8, 16 persons) were examined. Twenty five different data sets were created for each group. Each speech data set was artificially made of 16 short utterances. For example, for an experiment with 0.5 second utterances of 4 participants, 25 test speech set, consisting of 16 utterances of 4 participants (8 second long), were used.

The performance was calculated based on the ratio of the number of correctly identified segments to the number of total segments as follows:

$$Error \quad rate = \frac{Number \quad of \quad correctly \quad identified \quad segments}{Number \quad of \quad total \quad segments} . \tag{1}$$

Experimental results showed that the new method tested in this research consistently achieved higher accuracy than the conventional method. It is interesting to observe that the new method outperformed the conventional GMM method for all the utterance lengths considered. In Fig. 4, the range of difference in the absolute error rate between the GMM (baseline) and the new method ranged from 3.2% to 8.4% absolute (27.4% to 42% relative error rate) with respect to the various number of participants (speakers) in the case of 0.5 sec utterances. The error rate of our method with 0.5 sec utterances (8.8%) was almost the same as the error rate of the conventional method (baseline) with 2 sec utterances (9.5%) in the case of a group with 4 participants. This means that the conventional method requires utterances approximately 4 times longer than the new method to achieve approximately the same level of accuracy.

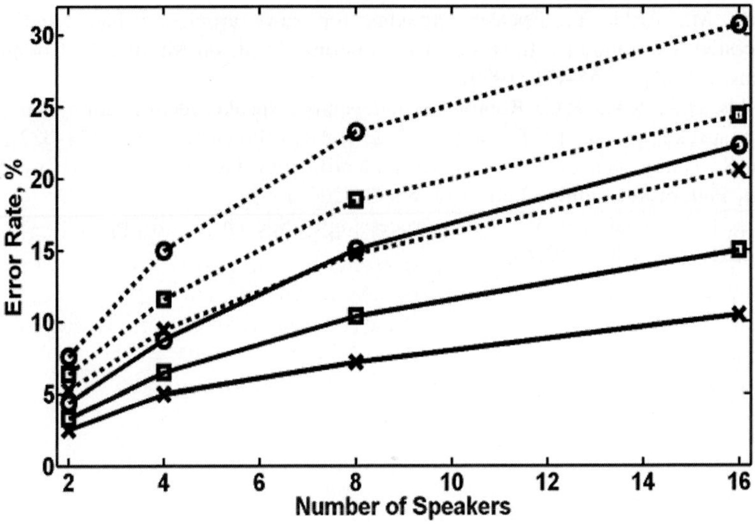

Fig. 4. Measured error rate of Speaker Segmentation with respect to the lengths of utterances, the number of speakers, and the methods of Speaker Segmentation (solid lines for the baseline method and dotted lines for the new method; **O** for 0.5 sec of utterances, □ for 1.0 sec, and **x** for 2.0 sec)

5 Conclusion

This paper examined a new Speaker Segmentation method designed to reduce identification errors. This method was useful for Speaker Segmentation by identifying speakers from short utterances. It also made it possible to detect the boundaries of short utterances. These results indicate that Speaker Segmentation can be applied to spontaneous speech in human-to-human, human-to-robot, and human-to-computer interactions. Future work should focus on the further refinement of identification methods in natural data streams, such as meetings and broadcast news.

References

1. Park, J.-H., Yeom, K.-W., Ha, S., Park, M.-W., Kim, L.: An overview of intelligent responsive space in tangible space initiative technology. In: Proc. Internt. Workshop on the Tangible Space Initiative (3rd), pp. 523–531 (2006)
2. Busso, C., Hernanz, S., Chu, C.-W., Kwon, S., Lee, C., Georgiou, P.G., Cohen, I., Narayanan, S.: Smart room: participant and speaker localization and identification. In: Proc. IEEE Internat. Conf. on Acoustics, Speech, and Signal Processing, 2005, vol. 2, pp. 1117–1120 (2005)
3. Campbell, J.P.: Speaker recognition: A tutorial. Proc. IEEE 85, 1436–1462 (1997)
4. Kwon, S., Narayanan, S.: Unsupervised Speaker Indexing Using Generic Models. IEEE Trans. on Speech and Audio Processing 13(5) part 2, 1004–1013 (2005)

5. Nishida, M., Ariki, Y.: Speaker indexing for news articles, debates and drama in broadcasted TV programs. In: Proc. IEEE Internat. Conf. on Multimedia Computing and Systems, vol. 2, pp. 466-471 (1999)
6. Reynolds, D.A., Rose, R.C.: Robust text-independent speaker identification using Gaussian mixture speaker models. IEEE Trans. on Speech Audio Processing 3(1), 334–337 (1995)
7. Kwon, S., Narayanan, S.: Robust speaker identification based on selective use of feature vectors. Pattern Recognition Letters 28, 85–89 (2007)
8. Rabiner, L.R., Schafer, R.W.: Digital Processing of Speech Signals, pp. 476–489. Prentice Hall, Englewood Cliffs (1978)

Emotion and Sense of Telepresence: The Effects of Screen Viewpoint, Self-transcendence Style, and NPC in a 3D Game Environment

Jim Jiundc Lee

Graduate Institute of Communication Studies
National Chiao Tung University, Taiwan
jiulee@mail.nctu.edu.tw

Abstract. Telepresence, or the sense of "being there", has been discussed in the literature as an essential, defining aspect of a virtual environment, including definitions rooted in behavioral response, signal detection theory, and philosophy, but has generally ignored the emotional aspects of the virtual experience. The purpose of this study is to examine the concept of presence in terms of people's emotional engagement within an immersive mediate environment. Three main theoretical statements are discussed: a). Objective telepresence: display viewpoint; b). Subjective telepresence: emotional factors and individual self-transcendence styles; c). Social telepresence: program-controlled entities in an on-line game environment. This study has implications for how research could be conducted to further our understanding of telepresence. Validated psychological subjective techniques for assessing emotions and a sense of telepresence will be applied. The study results could improve our knowledge of the construct of telepresence, as well as better inform us about how a virtual environment, such as an online game, can be managed in creating and designing emotional effects.

Keywords: Computer game, emotion, self-transcendence style, telepresence.

1 Theoretical Background

1.1 Virtual Environment

Applications of virtual reality technology to advance various fields such as education, communication, health, training, entertainment and the military, have gained extremely high attention recently. In the past, a virtual environment was commonly defined as "electronic simulations of environments experienced via the mounted eye goggles and wired clothing enabling the end user to interact in realistic three-dimensional situations." (Coates, 1992) This definition, however, appears to only be useful for system vendors but not for researchers. Based on this definition, a virtual environment becomes solely a collection of media and machines. As a result, it might hinder the attempt to reveal embedded characteristics that might substantially impact the interaction process in the virtual environment. Imagination and illusory space have

J. Jacko (Ed.): Human-Computer Interaction, Part III, HCII 2007, LNCS 4552, pp. 393–400, 2007.

been frequently discussed in the literature as two primary factors in constructing the virtual experience. The former is directed by the users' cognitive processes, while the latter emphasizes a space in which consensual hallucination, mutual acceptance and make-believe can be triggered. Apparently, both depend on the user's mental operations. The experience of virtual reality should in fact be discussed from the user's subjective perspective.

It is thus more appropriate to define virtual reality as "a real or simulated environment which is mediated through media and the individual's mental construction to enable telepresence experiences."

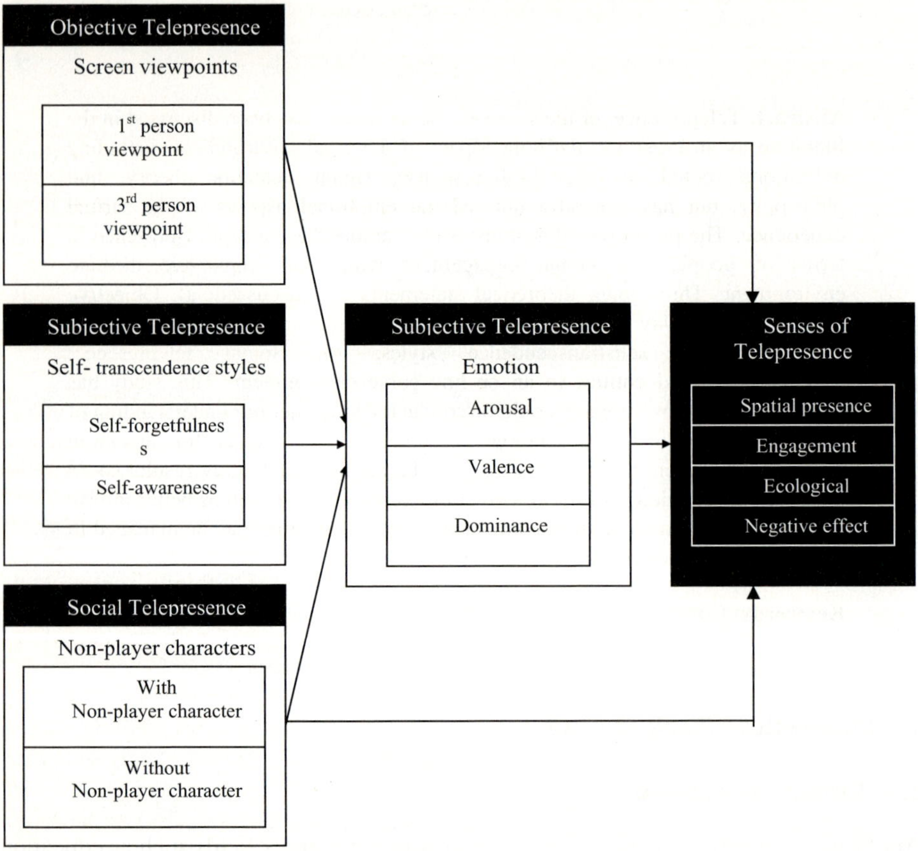

Fig. 1. Research Conceptual Model

1.2 Telepresence

Telepresence, or the sense of "being there", has been recognized in the literature as an essential, predicted element of an immersion experience. Telepresence is the generic perception of the surrounding environment which involves automatic or controlled mental processes. In other words, virtual realities reside in a user's consciousness

(Steuer, 1995). Factors influencing the sense of telepresence can be categorized in terms of three dimensions: (a) objective telepresence, (b) subjective telepresence, and (c) social telepresence (Schloerb, 1995; Heeter, 1992). Objective telepresence refers to physical facilities or stimuli which allow users to interact with the environment. Subjective telepresence refers to users' characteristics including mental processes and the cognitive tendency to suspend disbelief. Social telepresence refers to the sense of the co-existence of other intelligent beings, even if those beings might only seem intelligent or are just program-generated (Biocca, 1997). In the present study, objective, subjective, and social telepresence will be examined respectively in terms of screen viewpoint, emotion, self- transcendence style, and non-player character (see Figure 1).

1.2.1 The Screen Viewpoints

In a 3D online game environment, the screen viewpoint (1st or 3rd) is one of the most important environmental factors that might affect subjective senses of telepresence (Tarr, Williams, Hayward, and Gauthier, 1998). The 1st and 3rd person viewpoints in computer games are often used to describe camera viewpoints. The 1st person viewpoint sets the player's screen display to be the same as the way in which his / her avator sees in the game world. In a sense, it casts players directly into the game environment. As for using the 3rd person viewpoint, players either look over the shoulder of, or look down from certain degrees on, his / her avator to interact with the game world. Rollings and Adams (2003) indicated that although the 1st person viewpoint might efficiently immerse gamers into a virtual environment, its limited 30 degrees of field vision is quite different from human eyes which provide up to 120~180 degrees of field vision. Some important cues or information about the surrounding environment might thus be missed and cause serious cognitive problems. In contrast, the 3rd person viewpoint provides players with a wider field vision allowing them to be aware of situations in front of them, as well as to collect information from the rear and both sides. This is considered to provide great help to players, in particular during their tactical thinking (Fabricator, Nussbaum, and Rosas, 2002). However, this viewpoint might also engender the player's role to switch between actor and observer, which causes inevitable break-down of the immersion experience. Whether the 1st person viewpoint or the 3rd person viewpoint could enhance a higher sense of telepresence remains largely unknown.

1.2.2 Self-transcendence Style and Emotion

Roberts, Smith, and Pollock (2000) proposed three individual factors that might contribute to the sense of telepresence: imagination, emotion, and willing suspension of disbelief. Among these three, emotion and willing suspension of disbelief have been identified by many scholars (Freeman, Avons, Meddis, Pearson, and IJsselsteijn,1999; Freeman, Avons, Pearson, and IJsselsteijn, 2000; Stacy and Jonathan, 2002; Broach, Page, Jr., Wilson,1995, 1997; Ravaja et al., 2004) for their superior effects, especially in a 3D virtual environment. Emotion can highly affect individuals' cognitive activities, which in turn deepens their flow experiences. Willing suspension of disbelief is an individual's conscious will and subconscious tendency to accept or exclude environmental stimuli. Emotion and willing suspension of disbelief will be investigated respectively in terms of dimension theory of emotion (arousal, valence, dominance) and Self-transcendence styles (Self-forgetfulness vs. Self-awareness)(Cloninger, Przybeck, & Svrakic,1993) for their strengths in affecting a sense of telepresence.

1.2.3 On-Player Character

A game-based environment is designed to encourage a high degree of human interaction with the indigenous non-player characters (NPC), as players encounter prototypical social contexts or scenarios. As in examples like the most popular game genre at present, Role Playing Games (RPGs), a large part of the narrative action is dependant on the interactivity of synthetic characters. Players will confront different types of encounters which are designed to trigger or to direct an anticipated plot during the course of the campaign. Therefore, players' emotional responses, either positive or negative, are profoundly involved in the action and affective state of NPCs with the game (McCollum, Barba, Santarelli, and Deaton, 2004).

NPCs can be broadly divided into four categories (Louchart and Aylett, 2003): combat, problem-solving, information-gathering, and social. Among these four NPCs, the combat NPC is the one that can significantly affect players' emotional responses. The combat NPCs are action encounters which represent minor or significant threats to players. Players have to fight or bypass them in order to survive or advance to the next level. They will be used as one of the independent variables to measure players' emotional responses, as well as their sense of telepresence.

In sum, the present study aims to examine how an individual might sense telepresence through the mutual interaction between internal and external factors in a 3D game environment. Variables of the personal point of view (objective telepresence), self-transcendence styles (subjective telepresence), and combat NPC (social telepresence) will be compared for their effects on the subject's emotional responses and senses of telepresence. To investigate the hypotheses, the present study generated the following research questions:

- Will different screen viewpoints affect players' emotional responses and senses of telepresence?
- Will players' self-transcendence styles affect their emotional responses and senses of telepresence?
- Will combat NPCs affect players' emotional responses and senses of telepresence?
- Will players' emotional responses affect their senses of telepresence?
- Will the interaction effects among screen viewpoints, players' self-transcendence styles, and combat NPCs affect players' emotional responses and senses of telepresence?

2 Methodology

2.1 Study Design

Adopted from a shooting computer game called Unreal Tournament 2003, four experimental environments (1st person viewpoint without combat NPC, 1st person viewpoint with combat NPC, 3rd person viewpoint with combat NPC, 3rd person viewpoint without combat NPC) were developed. Unreal Tournament 2003 allows game developers to customize and modify the game to create needed gameplay modes which include adding combat NPCs and changing screen viewpoints.

There were three independent variables - the screen viewpoints (1st and 3rd person viewpoints), self-transcendence styles (self-forgetfulness and self-awareness), the combat NPC (with or without), and two dependent variables – emotional responses (arousal, valence, dominance), and senses of telepresence (spatial presence, engagement, ecological validity, negative effect) in the present study.

2.2 Subjects

A two-step procedure was administrated to select appropriate subjects. To prevent the effects caused by the event of causal or core players, subjects with moderated gameplay experience were required for the present study. A Gamer Dedication Questionnaire based on Ip and Adams's (2002) 15 factors of gamer classification was managed in the first stage to filter out causal and core players. Only subjects whose gamer-dedication scores fell between 46-55 were allowed to proceed to the next stage. At the second stage, subjects received an 11-item Self-transcendence Inventory (Cloninger, , Przybeck, Svrakic, and Wetzel, 1994) to identify their self-awareness or self-forgetfulness styles. As a result, 22 self-awareness subjects and 24 self-forgetfulness subjects participated in this experiment. Ages ranged from 21 to 24.

2.3 Procedure

Upon arrival, subjects were given the Gamer Dedication Questionnaire and Self-transcendence Inventory to identify their gameplay experiences and styles. Then, the researcher randomly assigned these subjects into four groups: 1st person viewpoint with combat NPC (1st VP + NPC), 1st person viewpoint without combat NPC (1st VP), 3rd person viewpoint with combat NPC (3rd VP + NPC), 3rd person viewpoint without combat NPC (3rd VP). Each group included approximate numbers of self-forgetfulness and self-awareness subjects. Based on Grabe, Spitzer, and Freyberger's (1999) findings, gender difference has very low correlation with these two styles (Wilks's lambda = 0.95, F = 1.85, df = 7, 223, p = 0.08) and thus was not considered as a significant issue in this study. According to the assigned group, a tutorial web page was loaded onto the subject's computer screen and started a 5-minute practice session to master the interface operation. When they had no more further questions, subjects proceeded to the formal experiment stage. They were required to execute a search task to find 6 virtual pieces of equipment. After completing the search task, subjects moved on to answer the Self-Assessment Manikin (Lang, 1995) and the ITC-Sense of Presence Inventory (ITC-SOPI)(Lessiter, Freeman, Keogh, and Davidoff, 2001) which respectively measured their emotional responses (arousal, valence, dominance) and senses of telepresence (spatial presence, engagement, ecological validity, negative effect). The average length of time needed to complete the experiment was 45 minutes.

3 Results and Discussion

The MANOVA model was applied first to test the three main effects of the independent variables as well as the interaction effects among the three on the dependent variables. One-way analysis of variance (ANOVA) was carried out to analyze the data further once the significant main effect of interfaces or cognitive styles was found. Since the data of the present study currently is still under collection, the results reported here are not the final findings.

The MANOVA analyses yielded two significant main effects: self-transcendence styles (Wilks' Lambda = .779, p= .045) and screen viewpoints (Wilks' Lambda = .661, p = .026), and the interaction effects between the two (Wilks' Lambda = .773, p = .039) on the dependent variables for subjects' emotional responses and senses of telepresence. Further analyses of ANOVA results are reported as follows.

The 1st person viewpoint affected players' arousal (p=.034) and valence emotions (p=.047) significantly more than did the 3rd person viewpoint.

The 1st person viewpoint affected players' sense of engagement (p=.038) and ecological validity (p=.008) significantly more than did the 3rd person viewpoint.

Self-forgetfulness players felt significantly more arousal (p=.030) and dominance (p=.031) emotions than self-awareness players.

Self-forgetfulness players sensed significantly more spatial presence (p=.006) engagement (p=.043), ecological validity (p=.050), and felt fewer negative effects (p=.039) than self-awareness players.

With the 1st person viewpoint, self-forgetfulness players appeared to have significantly higher arousal (p=041) and valence (p=.050) emotions than self-awareness players.

With the 1st person viewpoint, self-forgetfulness players appeared to sense significantly higher spatial presence (p=.005), engagement (p=.042), and ecological validity (p=.049) than self-awareness players.

With the 3rd person viewpoint, self-forgetfulness players appeared to sense significantly higher engagement (p=044), ecological validity (p=.050), and felt fewer negative effects (p=.017) than self-awareness players.

Players' self-transcendence styles have significantly more margin effects than the screen viewpoints on arousal emotion (p=.046) and spatial presence (p=.042), but less effect on ecological validity (p=.022).

Although no significant result was found, players' arousal emotion seemed to tend to correlate with senses of spatial presence (p=.061) and engagement (p=.057).

In general, the pilot results so far are consistent with previous study conclusions (Draper, Kaber, and Usher, 1998; Barfield and Weghorst, 1993; Prothero and Hoffman, 1995; Schuemie et al., 2000). The field of view (screen viewpoints) and individual cognitive tendencies of allocating attention resources (self-transcendence styles) to the mediated environment are the two important components which highly affect arousal and valence emotions, and which might further trigger players' senses of spatial presence, engagement, and ecological validity. The final study results will focus on unfolding more detailed information about the relationships among telepresence factors, which hopefully might provide implications for computer game developers to successfully create a virtual environment which is both enjoyable and immersible.

References

1. Barfield, W., Weghorst, S.: The sense of presence within virtual environments: A conceptual framework. In: Salvendy, G., Smith, M. (eds.) Human-computer interaction: Applications and case studies, pp. 699–704. Elsevier, Amsterdam (1993)
2. Biocca, F., Levy, M.: Communication applications of virtual reality. In: Biocca, F., Levy, M. (eds.) Communication in the age of virtual reality, pp. 127–158. Lawrence Erlbaum Associates, Hillsdale, NJ (1995)
3. Broach, V.C., Jr Page, T.J., Wilson, D.: Television programming and its influence on viewers ' perceptions of commercials: the role of program arousal and pleasantness. Journal of Advertising 24(4), 45–50 (1995)
4. Broach, V.C., Jr Page, T.J., Wilson, R.D.: The Effects of Program Context on Advertising Effectiveness. In: Wells, W.D. (ed.) Measuring Advertising Effectiveness, pp. 203–214. Lawrence Erlbaum Associates, Mahwah, NJ (1997)
5. Cloninger, C.R., Svrakic, D.M., Przybeck, T.R.: A psychobiological model of temperament and character. Archives of General Psychiatry 50, 975–990 (1993)
6. Cloninger, C.R., Przybeck, T.R., Svrakic, D.M., Wetzel, R.D.: The temperament and Character Inventory (TCI). Center for Psychobiology of Personality, St. Louis, MO (1994)
7. Coates, G.: Program from Invisible Site—a virtual sho, a multimedia performance work. In: presented by George Coates Performance Works, San Francisco, CA (March 1992)
8. Draper, J.V., Kaber, D.B., Usher, J.M.: Telepresence. Human Factors 40, 354–375 (1998)
9. Fabricatore, C., Nussbaum, M., Rosas, R.: Playability in action videogames: A qualitative design model. Human-Computer Interaction 17(4), 311–368 (2002)
10. Freeman, J., Pearson, D.E., Ijsselsteijn, W.A.: Effects of sensory information and prior experience on direct subjective ratings of presence. Presence: Teleoperators and Virtual Environments 8(1), 1–13 (1999)
11. Freeman, J., Avons, S.E., Meddis, R., Pearson, D.E., IJsselsteijn, W.A.: Using behavioural realism to estimate presence: A study of the utility of postural responses to motion stimuli. Presence: Teleoperators and Virtual Environments, 9(2) (2000)
12. Gerhard, M., Moore, D., Hobbs, D.: An Experimental Study of the Effects of Presence in Collaborative Virtual Environments. In: Proceeding of the International Conference on Intelligent Agents for Mobile and Virtual Media, Bradford, UK (2001)
13. Gibson, J.J.: The Ecological Approach to Visual Perception. Houghton Mifflin Co, Boston (1979)
14. Grabe, H., Spitzer, C., Freyberger, H.J.: Relationship of dissociation to temperament and character in men and women. The. American Journal of Psychiatry 156, 1811–1831 (1999)
15. Heeter, C.: Being There: The Subjective Experience of Presence. Presence: Teleoperators and Virtual Environments 1(2), 262–271 (1992)
16. Ip, B., Adams, E.: From casual to core – A statistical mechanism for studying gamer dedication. Gamasutra (June 5 2003), Last retrieved on January 2005 from http://www.gamasutra.com/features/20020605/ip_pfv.htm
17. Koda, T.: Agents with faces: The effects of personification. In: Proceeding of HCI (1996)
18. Lang, P.J.: The emotion probe: studies of motivation and attention. American Psychologist 50, 372–385 (1995)
19. Lessiter, J., Freeman, J., Keogh, E., Davidoff, J.D.: A Cross-Media Presence Questionnaire: The ITC Sense of Presence Inventory. Presence: Teleoperators and Virtual Environments 10(3), 282–297 (2001)

20. Louchart, S., Aylett, R.: Solving the narrative paradox in VEs - Lessons from RPGs. In: Rist, T., Aylett, R., Ballin, D., Rickel, J. (eds.) IVA 2003. LNCS (LNAI), vol. 2792, pp. 244–249. Springer, Heidelberg (2003)
21. McCollum, C., Barba, C., Santarelli, T., Deaton, J.: Applying a cognitive architecture to control of virtual non-player characters. In: Proceedings of the 2004 Winter Simulation Conference (2004)
22. Prothero, J.D., Hoffman, H.G.: Widening the field of view increases the sense of presence in immersive virtual environments. Technical Report TR-95-2, Human Interface Technology Lab (1995)
23. Ravaja, N., Saari, T., Salminen, M., Laarni, J., Holopainen, J., Järvinen, A.: Emotional response patterns and sense of presence during video games: Potential criterion variables for game design. In: Proceedings of NordCHI 2004, Tampere, Finland, pp. 23–27 (2004)
24. Roberts, L.D., Smith, L.M., Pollock, C.M.: U r a lot bolder on the net (2000)
25. Shyness and internet use. In: Crozier, W.R. (ed.): Shyness: Development.
26. consolidation and change. Routledge, New York, pp.121–138
27. Rollings, A., Adams, E.: Andrew Rollings and Ernest Adams on Game Design. New Riders, USA (2003)
28. Schloerb, D.W.: A Quantitative Measure of Telepresence. Presence: Teleoperators and Virtual Environments 4(1), 64–80 (1995)
29. Schuemie, M.J., Bruynzeel, M., Drost, L., Brinckman, M., de Haan, G., Emmelkamp, P.M.G., van der Mast, C.A.P.G.: Treatment of acrophobia in virtual reality: A pilot study. In: Broeckx, F., Pauwels, L. (eds.), Conference Proceedings Euromedia 2000. May 8–10, Antwerp, Belgium, pp. 271–275 (2000)
30. Stacy, M., Jonathan, G.: A Step Towards Irrationality: Using Emotion to Change Belief. In: Proceedings of the 1st International Joint Conference on Autonomous Agents and Multi-Agent Systems, Bologna, Italy (2002)
31. Steuer, J.: Defining virtual reality:Dimensions determining telepresence. In: Biocca, F., Levy, M.R. (eds.) Communication in the age of virtual reality, pp. 33–56. Lawrence Erlbaum Associates, Hillsdale, NJ (1995)
32. Takeuchi, A., Naito, T.: Situated facial displays: Towards social interaction. In: Proceeding of CH'95 Human Factors in Computing Systems, Addison-Wesley, London (1995)
33. Tarr, M.J., Williams, P., Hayward, W.G., Gauthier, I.: Three-dimensional object Recognition is viewpoint-dependent. Nature Neuroscience 1, 275–277 (1998)

Emotional Interaction Through Physical Movement

Jong-Hoon Lee[1,2], Jin-Yung Park[1], and Tek-Jin Nam[1]

[1] Collaboration and Interaction Design Research Lab.
Department of Industrial Design, Korea Advanced Institute of Science and Technology,
373-1, Guseong-dong, Useong-gu, Daejeon, Korea
[2] INNOIZ Inc., Seoul, Korea
{rniro,vanilla0,tjnam}@kaist.ac.kr

Abstract. As everyday products become more intelligent and interactive, there are growing interests on the methods to improve emotional value attached to the products. This paper presents a basic method of using temporal and dynamic design elements, in particular physical movements, to improve the emotional value of products. To utilize physical movements in design, a relation framework between movement and emotion was developed as the first step of the research. In the framework, the movement representing emotion was structurized in terms of three properties; velocity, smoothness and openness. Based on this framework, a new interactive device, 'Emotion Palpus', was developed, and a user study was also conducted. The result of the research is expected to improve emotional user experience when used as a design method or directly applied to design practice as an interactive element of products.

Keywords: Emotion, Physical Movement Design, Interaction Design, Interactive Product Design, Design Method.

1 Introduction

Advanced technology has reduced the limitations in making products. Companies pay more attention to the customer's diverse needs and lifestyles. The emotional value of the product, which can improve user experiences in HCI, is becoming more important for the success of products.

The conventional and representative design method to enhance the emotional value of the product is to advance its aesthetic form. This is usually done by applying design principles for the organization of ordinary design elements, such as form, material and color. So far, the design elements have been mainly visual and static.

However, as products are getting intelligent and more interactive by advanced technology, new design elements have emerged. One kind is the dynamic and temporal design elements. Especially physical movement is an interesting dynamic element for expressing functional or emotional status of products. For example, in everyday life, a fluttering leaf in a storm calls a distressing feeling, and a slowly moving pendulum weight looks courteous and generous. Physical movement can easily attract people's attention by visually changing its surroundings and can be independently expressed in the tangible space unlike graphical movement.

J. Jacko (Ed.): Human-Computer Interaction, Part III, HCII 2007, LNCS 4552, pp. 401–410, 2007.

Nevertheless, it is hard to represent its scale or shape due to the 3 dimensional form and material of the product, and difficult to implement it mechanically due to physical limitations. Detailed design methods of utilizing physical movement for emotional value of product, however, hasn't been thoroughly studied.

The objective of this study is to investigate the method of using dynamic design elements, particularly physical movement, to improve the emotional value and expression of a product. To do this, we first analyzed the related work of movement application by literature review. The relationship between emotion and movement in the existing studies was investigated, and in-depth characteristics of emotion and movement were studied to reify the relationship. Then, we conducted field research for the development of the relationship. From the result of the basic research, a relation framework between emotion and movement was developed. To apply the framework in product design and human computer interaction, we developed a new interactive device that can express the emotion of a product. Evaluating the framework using the device and developing application scenario were conducted.

2 Related Work of Movement Application

In the visual communication design field, various studies have conducted meaningful effects of integrating dynamic movement with static images. Vaughan(1997) proposed that understanding motion expression of performance art can be helpful in applying movement as a design element in GUI [1]. Uekita(2000) introduced the method of improving emotion by designing the movement of Kinetic Typography [2]. These studies, though, haven't presented the detail method to design movements for a certain emotion. In the product design field, some studies show application examples using movement as a design element. Weerdesteijn(2005) applied movements for the education assistant device that enables children to learn emotional expression through their body [3]. Physical movements have also been proposed applying to a communication device [4] or ambient display [5], [6]. Even though these works tried to utilize movement as a design element in various ways, few have studied the systematic methods or application of physical movement as a design element.

The way to apply movement to product design can be divided in two parts: one is to let the product itself move, and the other is to provide a separate moving part to the product. Even though few examples of applying movement to the product itself, such as Tanks Tail[1] and Nabaztag[2], have been commercialized recently, these stay on the level of using movement for people's concentration.

In the non-design fields, more works have been done to understand and represent the relationship between movement and emotion, but it is still difficult to find a proper example of applying movement to design from these studies [7], [8], [9]. Therefore, to design efficient physical movements, it is essential to study embodying the relationship between emotion and movement of various fields. Additionally, the study of utilizing this for practical development of products from the design perspective is necessary as well.

---

[1] http://www.k-wako.co.jp/enter/tail.html

[2] http://www.nabaztag.com/vl/FR/index.html

3 Theoretical Background of Relation Between Emotion and Movement

3.1 The Formal Components of Movement

Movement consists of several formal components. Kepes and Moholy-Nagy, polytechnic engineers, classified them as following [10];

1) Rhythm: intervals of time between a motion and the next motion
2) Beat: rhythmical flow or rhythmic pace.
3) Sequence: relating to both rhythm and beat, explaining time based events
4) Direction: generated when an object has sequential movement in space

Aside from these four, path, volume, and speed are frequently referred as well.

3.2 The Characteristic of Emotion

In order to structurally understand the relationship between multifaced emotion and movement, it is important to understand the criteria in classifying emotion.

In the studies of emotion, sections of emotion are classified by Basic Categories and Multidimensional Categories. The former is grouping similar emotions within discrete categories, while the latter is distinguished by emotion space with various axis of more than 2-dimension[3]. Here, emotion space is generated by bi-polar dimensions, where each axis has two opposing adjectives as the emotion scale.

The most representative one of diverse multidimensional models is the Circumplex Model. The generalized model of the existing Circumplex Models by Russell is composed with Pleasantness axis and Activation axis [11]. These two emotion components were selected for the foundation of structuralizing the relationship between movement and emotion.

3.3 The Emotion-Movement Relation Framework

The Literature Study Analysis for the Emotion-Movement Relation
The speed of movement is related to 'Activation', so faster movement can present more activated emotion [9]. Boone and Cunningham(2001)[7] deduced the relationship between volume and sequence of movement. He mentioned that big and smooth movement was presented from pleasant or joyful emotion, and dreadful or sorrowful emotion caused shrinking movement. Negative emotion brought about jerky movements in uneven beats as well.

We applied these results to two emotion components of the Circumplex Model; 'Activation' is related to speed and volume of movement, and both ends of the 'Pleasantness' axis are related to smooth or jerky movement.

The Field Study Analysis by In-Depth Interview
A field study was conducted to interpret the connection between movement and emotion in the literature study. All participants were choreographers who create

[3] Kim, J., Moon, J., Designing towards emotional usability in customer interface-strustworthiness of cyber-banking system interfaces, Interacting with Computers, Vol. 10, pp. 1-29, 1998.

movement for performance or dance directors who teach dancing. They had in-depth interview with questionnaires about emotional representation through movements in their field[4]. The result of the interview shows that emotions distinguished by 'Activation' and 'Pleasantness' in the Circumplex Model can be expressed as formal components of movement, such as speed, sequence, rhythm, and volume.

The Emotion-Movement Relation Framework
Based on the preliminary researches, an Emotion-Movement relation framework was developed. Settled rhythm and beat can be integrated as 'Velocity', and sequence and uneven rhythm can be interpreted as 'Smoothness'. Direction and volume are combined as 'Openness' including constriction and expansion.

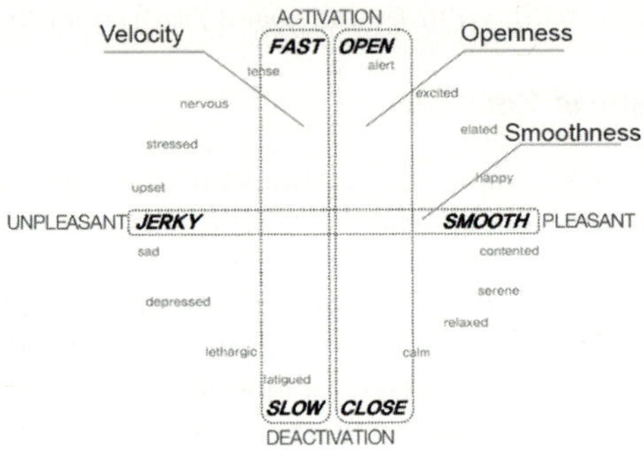

Fig. 1. The Emotion-Movement Relation Framework

Fig. 1 is the framework to design relevant physical movements for emotional expression, proposed in this study. After defining the relative emotion scales on each axis and combining proper degree of three movement components, the intended emotion is finally presented.

4 Application Prototype: Emotion Palpus

4.1 Concept of Emotion Palpus

In order to explore how this framework can be used in a new interactive product or in existing products by adding physical movement features, we developed a new interactive device called Emotion Palpus. It is a physical device that can generate physical movements to express various emotions. Its movement speed and movement type can be controlled to adjust 'Velocity' and 'Smoothness' of the framework, so it can be used as a prototyping and test platform. Its metaphor is from a palpus of living

[4] The interview had progressed for two hours per a day from the 18th of June to the 20th of June in 2006. Twenty interviewees were selected among the professional, who have more than 20 years work experience. One director of Korean dance co. and two ballet teachers participated separately.

creatures (insects, snails and so on). It helps communicate through moving feelers, attached to existing products, such as PC monitors, telephones, and audio devices.

In addition to the hardware prototype, software interface was also developed to enable the user to make emotional movements by controlling velocity, smoothness, and openness of the physical object's movement. Fig. 2 shows its system structure.

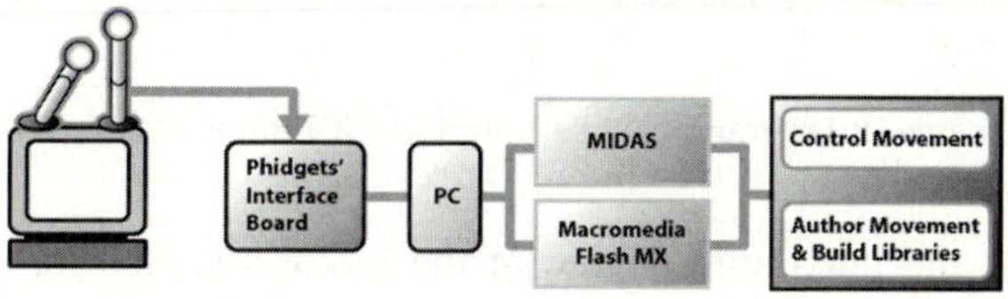

Fig. 2. The System structure of Emotion Palpus

4.2 Components and Implement

1) Hardware

The hardware part has a simple shape to minimize other aspects like form, which can influence emotion. It has a bar-shaped structure, consisting of three servo-motors, which were used for vertical piston movement with a spring, back-and-forth and right-and-left movement with two joints (Fig. 3). This hardware is used to express various movements while minimizing structural restrictions.

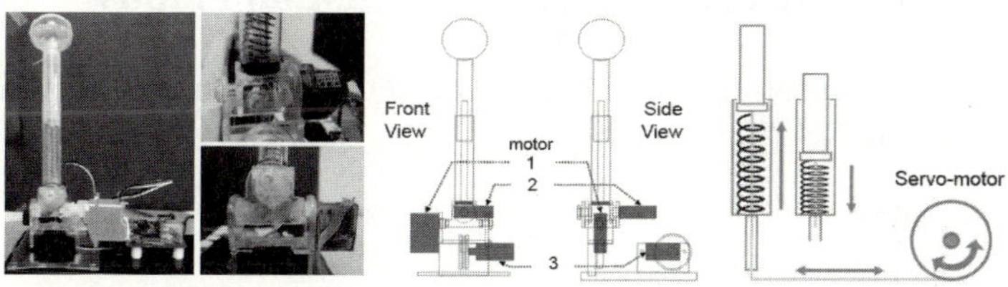

Fig. 3. The hardware prototype of Emotion Palpus and its structure drawing

The horizontal movement generated by the rotation of servo-motors is swapped to vertical movement, and piston movement is embodied by coiled spring. The rotating movements back-and-forth and right-and-left are presented by the rotation to the X-axis and the rotation to the Y-axis in the 3-dimensional space. To connect the hardware with the PC, two '4-Motor PhidgetServo' interfaces by Phidgets[5] were used.

2) Software

The software part of Emotion Palpus is to control the movement of hardware through GUI on the screen. The movement made by a user can be saved and reused. A user can easily present speed, openness and smoothness by controlling the angle of the servo-motors on the time-line graph in its user interface. To control three servo-motors of a device, each motor can be controlled with a modular controller (Fig. 4).

[5] Phidgets Inc., PhidgetsTM, http://www.phidgets.com

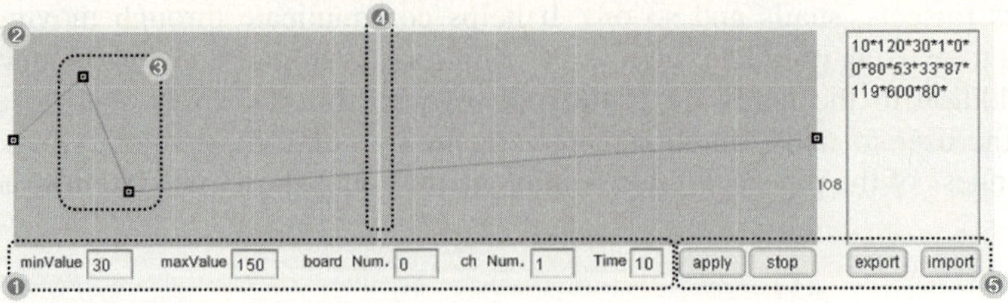

Fig. 4. One modular graphical user interface of Emotion Palpus's software

- Input area: the maximum degree of the motor's angle, the minimum degree, the interface board number, channel number, running time.
- Work place: the area to control the angle graph on the time-line
- The graph editor: the graph representing angle degree at the point
- Time bar
- Action buttons: play, pause, output of text code, input of text code

Flash 8.0 and MIDAS, interactive prototyping tools, were used for the embodiment of the software module and the motor-control. MIDAS supports components that can help install complex hardware with simple scripts and control interface boards with Flash.

5 Evaluation of the Framework with Emotion Palpus

We conducted two experiments with Emotion Palpus to verify the validity of the Emotion-Movement Relation Framework.

5.1 Experiment 1

Experiment Design

The purpose of the first experiment was to know the relation between two elements of emotion and three elements of movement. The emotional effect from the movement elements –velocity, openness and smoothness– was examined and analyzed.

- Velocity: 5 levels to differentiate each time of a circular movement basis
- Openness: 5 levels to differentiate width and height of a circular movement basis
- Smoothness: 5 levels of circular movement without acceleration to movement with four accelerations

15 movements with Emotion Palpus were used, representing different levels of each element (Fig. 5). For each level, 15 movie clips (740x480) were randomly presented with Windows Media Player on a 19 inch monitor display. Participants consisted of university students from 21 to 26 years old, 6 males and 4 females. All of them are novices at movement design.

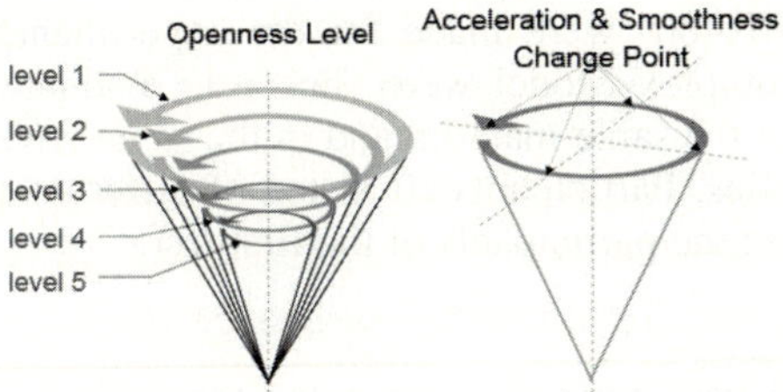

Fig. 5. The levels of 'Openness' and the change point of 'Acceleration and Smoothness'

Procedure
5 levels per each movement of all were provided and repeatedly presented three times. After watching one movie representing a level, participants selected the most appropriate emotion from the list in the questionnaire.

Result
The experiment was evaluated the relationship between emotion and movement element: velocity, openness and smoothness. The relationship of emotion and velocity or smoothness of movement was statistically significant with (F=99.538, p=.000) and (F=14.570, p=.000) from the each result of one-way ANOVA test. Because both velocity and emotion categories were ranking scales, we conducted the correlation analysis through the Spearman correlation coefficient. As a result, velocity has correlation with the 'Activation' axis of emotion on the positive direction (=.930, >.01). For smoothness, positive correlation with 'Pleasantness' was shown (=.760, >.01) However, no significant effect was found for openness (F=.587, p>0.05).

5.2 Experiment 2

Experiment Design
The purpose of the second experiment was to validate that the emotion from the framework can be properly recognized by the movement elements on the framework. The 16 stimuli were selected with Emotion Palpus: eight for levels of velocity-smoothness combination and eight for levels of openness-smoothness combination. Fig. 6 shows eight areas of emotions intended from them.

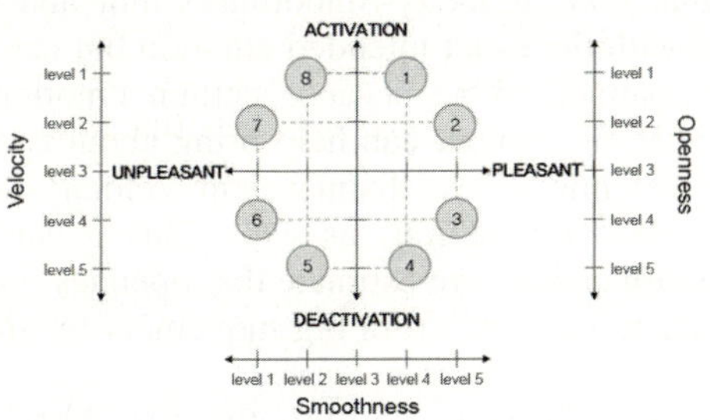

Fig. 6. Eight areas of the intended emotions in the Emotion-Movement Relation Framework

16 Movie clips (740x460) were made for the experimental stimuli. 16 emotion adjectives on the Circumplex Model were chosen to evaluate each movement. The test was conducted with the same material and in the same environment with the first, except for the movie clips. Participants consisted of different people but in the same age or gender range with the participants of the first test.

Procedure
Each of the 16 stimuli was iteratively presented three times. Participants wrote the answer in the questionnaire sheet right after watching each movie clip.

Result
The results from a Velocity-Smoothness and Openness-Smoothness are shown in Fig. 7. In the left graph of Fig. 8, the selection rate of the intended emotion for high or low level of velocity unit is relatively high, whereas the selection rate of the intended emotion for middle level is low. This shows that velocity has significant influence on emotion. In the right graph, the answers are relatively spread out by and large.

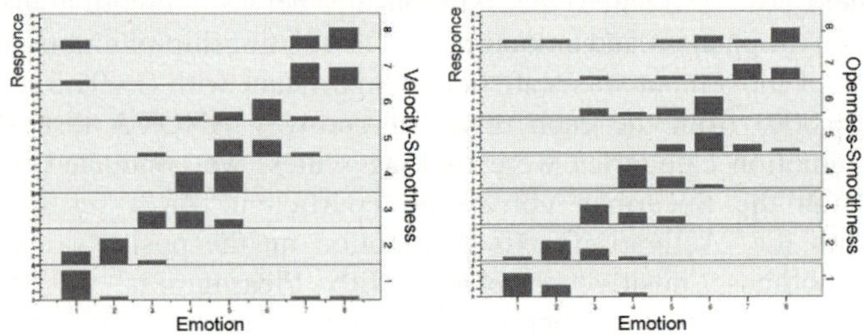

Fig. 7. The selection distribution graph of the intended emotions for 'Velocity-Smoothness' and 'Openness-Smoothness'

5.3 Discussion

As velocity and smoothness each show effective correlation in the first experiment with the 'Activation' axis and the 'Pleasantness' axis, the Emotion-Movement relation framework is validated. However, openness didn't show effective correlation with the framework from the result of the first experiment. The result of the second experiment presents that both Velocity-Smoothness unit and Openness-Smoothness unit do not correspond with the exact intended emotion but can influence round about the emotion. This is assumed to be because certain emotions were simply tested without any context. Specific context can help bring about certain emotions. Even if the Openness-Smoothness unit is less distinct than Velocity-Smoothness unit, it can lead to some of the intended emotions as well. This means openness affects the 'Activation' axis. From this result, we estimate that openness can be more effective at the moment of changing movement, from big movement to small movement or from small to big.

The result of the two experiments certifies the possibility of presenting relevant emotions in the intended area, compounding movement elements. This suggests that Emotion Palpus can be effectively utilized when designing expected emotions based on the framework.

Towards Affective Sensing

Gordon McIntyre[1] and Roland Göcke[2]

[1] Department of Information Engineering, Research School of Information Sciences and Engineering, Australian National University,
[2] NICTA Canberra Research Laboratory*,
Canberra, Australia
gordon.mcintyre@anu.edu.au, roland.goecke@nicta.com.au
http://users.rsise.anu.edu.au/~gmcintyr/index.html

Abstract. This paper describes ongoing work towards building a multimodal computer system capable of sensing the affective state of a user. Two major problem areas exist in the affective communication research. Firstly, affective states are defined and described in an inconsistent way. Secondly, the type of training data commonly used gives an oversimplified picture of affective expression. Most studies ignore the dynamic, versatile and personalised nature of affective expression and the influence that social setting, context and culture have on its rules of display. We present a novel approach to affective sensing, using a generic model of affective communication and a set of ontologies to assist in the analysis of concepts and to enhance the recognition process. Whilst the scope of the ontology provides for a full range of multimodal sensing, this paper focuses on spoken language and facial expressions as examples.

1 Introduction

As computer systems form an integral part of our daily life, the issue of user-adaptive human-computer interaction systems becomes more important. In the past, the user had to adapt to the system. Nowadays, the trend is clearly towards more human-like interaction through user-sensing systems. Such interaction is inherently multimodal and it is that integrated multimodality that leads to robustness in real-world situations. One new area of research is affective computing, i.e. the ability of computer systems to sense and adapt to the affective state (colloquially 'mood', 'emotion', etc.)[1] of a person. According to its pioneer, Rosalind Picard, 'affective computing' is computing that relates to, arises from, or deliberately influences emotions [1]. Affective sensing attempts to map measurable physical responses to affective states. Several studies have successfully mapped strong responses to episodic emotions. However, most studies take place in a controlled environment, ignoring the importance that social settings, culture and context play in dictating the display rules of affect.

* National ICT Australia is funded by the Australian Government's Backing Australia's Ability initiative, in part through the Australian Research Council.

[1] The terms affect, affective state and emotion, although not strictly the same, are used interchangeably in this paper.

J. Jacko (Ed.): Human-Computer Interaction, Part III, HCII 2007, LNCS 4552, pp. 411–420, 2007.

In a natural setting, emotions can be manifested in many ways and through different combinations of modalities. Further, beyond niche applications, one would expect that affective sensing must be able to detect and interpret a wide range of reactions to subtle events. In this paper, a novel approach is presented which integrates a domain ontology of affective communication to assist in the analysis of concepts and to enhance the recognition process. Whilst the scope of the ontology provides for a full range of multimodal sensing, our work to date has concentrated on sensing in the audio and video modalities, and the examples given relate to these. The remainder of the paper is structured as follows. Section 2 explains the proposed framework. Section 3 gives an overview of the ontologies. Section 4 details the application ontology. Section 5 explains the system developed to automatically recognise facial expressions and uses it as an example for applying the ontologies in practice. Finally, Section 6 provides a summary.

2 A Framework for Research in Affective Communication

The proposed solution consists of 1) a generic model of affective communication; and 2) a set of ontologies. An ontology is a statement of concepts which facilitates the specification of an agreed vocabulary within a domain of interest. The model and ontologies are intended to be used in conjunction to describe

1. affective communication concepts,
2. affective computing research, and
3. affective computing resources.

Figure 1 presents the base model on the example of emotions in spoken language. Firstly, note that it includes speaker and listener, in keeping with the Brunswikian lens model as proposed by Scherer [2]. The reason for modelling attributes of both speaker and listener is that the listener's cultural and social presentation vis-`a-vis the speaker may also influence judgement of emotional content. Secondly, note that it includes a number of factors that influence the expression of affect in spoken language. Each

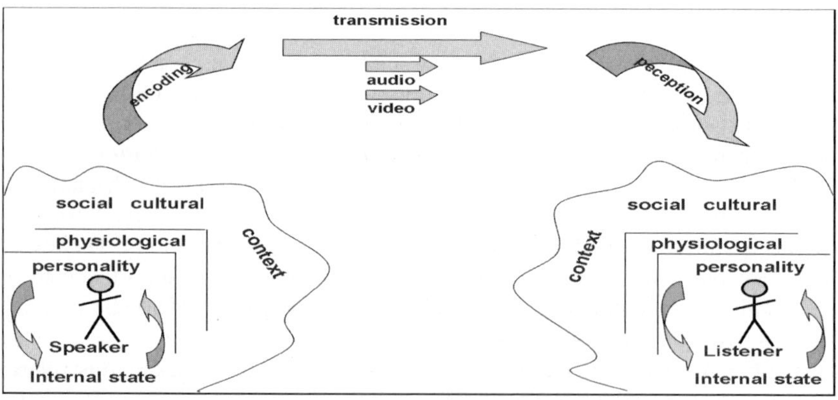

Fig. 1. A generic model of affective communication

of these factors is briefly discussed and motivated in the following. More attention is given to context as this is seen as a much neglected factor in the study of automatic affective state recognition.

2.1 Factors in the Proposed Framework

Context. Context is linked to modality and emotion is strongly multimodal in the way that certain emotions manifest themselves favouring one modality over the other [3]. Physiological measurements change depending on whether a subject is sedentary or mobile. A stressful context such as an emergency hot-line, air-traffic control, or a war zone is likely to yield more examples of affect than everyday conversation. Stibbard [4] recommends *"...the expansion of the data collected to include relevant non-phonetic factors including contextual and inter-personal information."* His findings underline the fact that most studies so far took place in an artificial environment, ignoring social, cultural, contextual and personality aspects which, in natural situations, are major factors modulating speech and affect presentation. The model depicted in Figure 1 takes into account the importance of context in the analysis of affect in speech.

Recently, Devillers et al. [5] included context annotation as metadata to a corpus of medical emergency call centre dialogues. Context information was treated as either task-specific or global in nature. The model proposed in this paper does not differentiate between task-specific and global context as the difference is seen merely as temporal, i.e. pre-determined or established at "run-time".

Other researchers have included "discourse context" such as speaker turns [6] and specific dialogue acts of greeting, closing, acknowledging and disambiguation. Inclusion in a corpus of speaker turns would be useful but annotation of every specific type of dialogue act would be extremely resource intensive.

The HUMAINE project [7] included a proposal that at least the following issues be specified:

- Agent characteristics (age, gender, race)
- Recording context (intrusiveness, formality, etc.)
- Intended audience (kin, colleagues, public)
- Overall communicative goal (to claim, to sway, to share a feeling, etc.)
- Social setting (none, passive other, interactant, group)
- Spatial focus (physical focus, imagined focus, none)
- Physical constraint (unrestricted, posture constrained, hands constrained)
- Social constraint (pressure to expressiveness, neutral, pressure to formality)

but went on to say, "It is proposed to refine this scheme through work with the *HUMAINE databases as they develop.*" Millar et al. [8] developed a methodology for the design of audio-video data corpora of the speaking face in which the need to make corpora re-usable is discussed. The methodology, aimed at corpus design, takes into account the need for speaker and speaking environment factors. In contrast, the model presented in this paper treats agent characteristics and social constraints separate to context information. This is because their effects on discourse are seen as separate topics for research. It is evident that

1. Context is extremely important in the display rules of affect;
2. Yet, defining context annotation is still in its infancy.

Agent characteristics. As Scherer [2] points out, most studies are either speaker oriented or listener oriented, with most being the former. This is significant when you consider that the emotion of someone labelling affective content in a corpus could impact the label that is ascribed to a speaker's message. The literature has not given much attention to the role that agent characteristics such as personality type play in affective presentation which is surprising when one considers the obvious difference in expression between extroverted and introverted types. Intuitively, one would expect a marked difference in signals between speakers. One would also think that knowing a person's personality type would be of great benefit in applications monitoring an individual's emotions. At a more physical level, agent characteristics such as facial hair, whether they wear spectacles, and their head and eye movements all affect the ability to visually detect and interpret emotions.

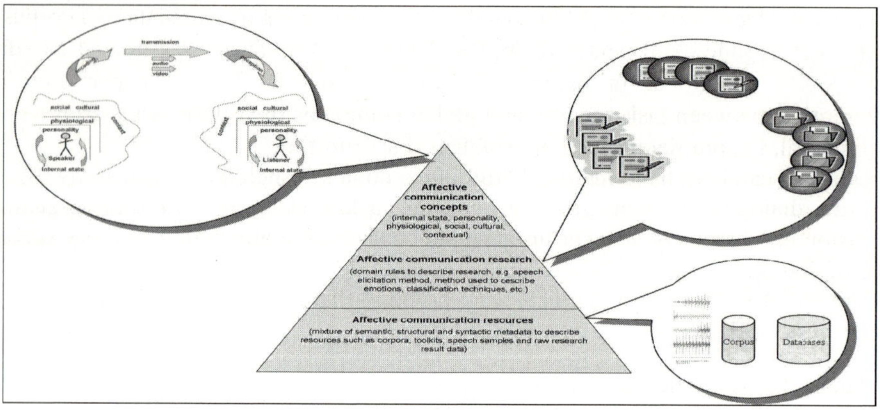

Fig. 2. A set of ontologies for affective computing

Cultural. Culture-specific display rules influence the display of affect [3]. Gender and age are established as important factors in shaping conversation style and content in many societies. Studies by Koike et al. [9] and Shigeno [10] have shown that it is difficult to identify the emotion of a speaker from a different culture and that people will predominantly use visual information to identify emotion. Putting it in the perspective of the proposed model, cognisance of the speaker and listener's cultural backgrounds, the context, and whether visual cues are available, obviously influence the effectiveness of affect recognition.

Physiological. It might be stating the obvious but there are marked differences in speech signals and facial expressions between people of different age, gender and health. The habitual settings of facial features and vocal organs determine the speaker's range of possible visual appearances and sounds produced. The configuration of facial features, such as chin, lips, nose, and eyes, provide the visual cues, whereas the vocal tract length and internal muscle tone guide the interpretation of acoustic output [8].

Social. Social factors temper spoken language to the demands of civil discourse [3]. For example, affective bursts are likely to be constrained in the case of a minor relating to an adult, yet totally unconstrained in a scenario of sibling rivalry. Similarly, a social setting in a library is less likely to yield loud and extroverted displays of affect than a family setting.

Internal state. Internal state has been included in the model for completeness. At the core of affective states is the person and their experiences. Recent events such as winning the lottery or losing a job are likely to influence emotions.

2.2 Examples

To help explain the differences between the factors that influence the expression of affect, Figure 2 lists some examples. The factors are divided into two groups. On the left, is a list of factors that modulate or influence the speaker's display of affect, i.e. cultural, social and contextual. On the right, are the factors that influence production or detection in the speaker or listener, respectively, i.e. personality type, physiological make-up and internal state.

Modulating factors			Production and detection factors		
Cultural	**Social**	**Context**	**Agent Characteristics**	**Physiological**	**Internal State**
Speaker's vis-à-vis listener's age and gender Language Customs Race	Education Familiarity/ rapport with listener Gender	Group situations Ambient conditions Dialogue turn Familiarity with system Sedentary/active Overt/covert Location	Extrovert/ Introvert Authoritarian/ control freak Child vs elderly Appearance, eg spectacles, facial hair, head and eye movement	Voice quality Child vs elderly Gender Illness/ Infirmity Impairment Vocal tract length Skin colour	Recent events, eg lottery wins, losses

Fig. 3. Use of the model in practice

3 A Set of Ontologies

The three ontologies described in this paper are the means by which the model is implemented and are currently in prototype form. Figure 3 depicts the relationships between the ontologies and gives examples of each of them. Formality and rigour increase towards the apex of the diagram. The types of users are not confined solely to researchers. There could be many types of users such as librarians, decision support systems, application developers and teachers.

3.1 Ontology 1 - Affective Communication Concepts

The top level ontology correlates to the model discussed in Section 2 and is a formal description of the domain of affective communication. It contains internal state, personality, physiological, social, cultural, and contextual factors. It can be linked to external ontologies in fields such as medicine, anatomy, and biology. A fragment of the top-level, domain ontology of concepts in shown in Figure 4.

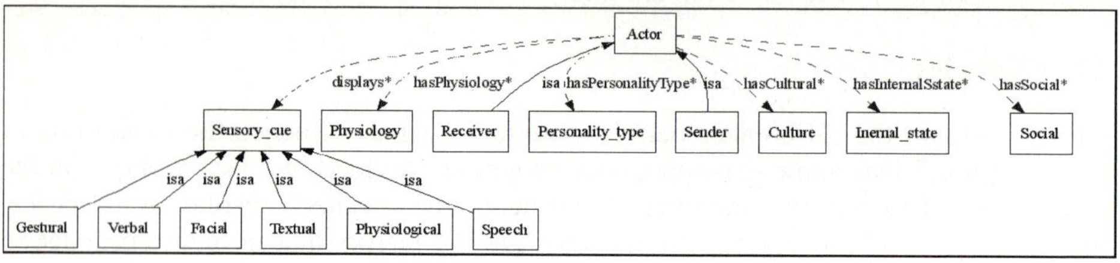

Fig. 4. A fragment of the domain ontology of concepts

3.2 Ontology 2 - Affective Communication Research

This ontology is more loosely defined and includes the concepts and semantics used to define research in the field. It has been left generic and can be further subdivided into an affective computing domain at a later stage, if needed. It is used to specify the rules by which accredited research reports are catalogued. It includes metadata to describe, for example,

- classification techniques used;
- the method of eliciting speech, e.g. acted or natural; and
- manner in which corpora or results have been annotated, e.g. categorical or dimensional.

Creating an ontology this way introduces a common way of reporting the knowledge and facilitates intelligent searching and reuse of knowledge within the domain. For instance, an ontology just based on the models described in this paper could be used to find all research reports where:

SPEAKER(internalState='happy',
physiology='any',
agentCharacteristics='extrovert',
social='friendly',context='public',
elicitation='dimension')

Again, there are opportunities to link to other resources. As an example, one resource that will be linked is the Emotion Annotation and Representation Language

(EARL) which is currently under design within the HUMAINE project [11]. EARL is a XML-based language for representing and annotating emotions in technological contexts. Using EARL, emotional speech can be described either using a set of forty-eight categories, dimensions or even appraisal theory. Examples of annotation elements include "Emotion descriptor" - which could be a category or a dimension, "Intensity" - expressed in terms of numeric values or discrete labels, "Start" and "End".

3.3 Ontology 3 - Affective Communication Resources

This ontology is more correctly a repository containing both formal and informal rules, as well as data. It is a combination of semantic, structural and syntactic metadata. This ontology contains information about resources such as corpora, toolkits, audio and video samples, and raw research result data. The next section explains the bottom level, application ontology used in our current work in more detail.

4 An Application Ontology for Affective Sensing

Figure 5 shows an example application ontology for affective sensing in a context of investigating dialogues. During the dialogue, various events can occur, triggered by one of the dialogue participants and recorded by the sensor system. These are recorded as time stamped instances of events, so that they can be easily identified and distinguished. In this ontology, we distinguish between two roles for each interlocutor: sender and receiver, respectively. At various points in time, each interlocutor can take on different roles. On the sensory side, we distinguish between facial, gestural, textual, speech, physiological and verbal[2] cues. This list, and the ontology, could be easily extended for other cues and is meant to serve as an example here, rather than a complete list of affective cues. Finally, the emotion classification method used in the investigation of a particular dialogue is also recorded.

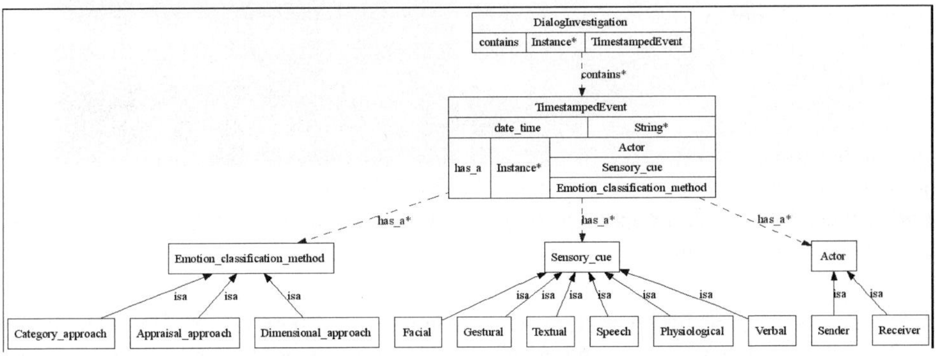

Fig. 5. An application ontology for affective sensing

[2] The difference between speech and verbal cues here being spoken language versus other verbal utterings.

We use this ontology to describe our affective sensing research in a formal, yet flexible and extendible way. In the following section, a brief description of the facial expression recognition system developed in our group is given as an example of using the ontologies in practice.

5 Automatic Recognition of Facial Expressions

Facial expressions can be a major source of information about the affective state of a person and they are heavily used by humans to gauge a person's affective state. We have developed a software system – the Facial Expression Tracking Application (FETA) [12] – to achieve automatic facial expression recognition. It uses statistical models of the permissible shape and texture of faces as found in images. The models are learnt from labelled training data, but once such models exist, they can be used to automatically track a face and its facial features. In recent years, several methods using such models have been proposed. A popular method are the Active Appearanc e Models (AAM) [13]. AAMs are a generative method which model non-rigid shape and texture of visual objects using a low-dimensional representation obtained from applying principle component analysis to a set of labelled data. AAMs are considered to be the current state-of-the-art in facial feature tracking and are used in the FETA system, as they provide a fast and reliable mechanism for obtaining input data for classifying facial expressions.

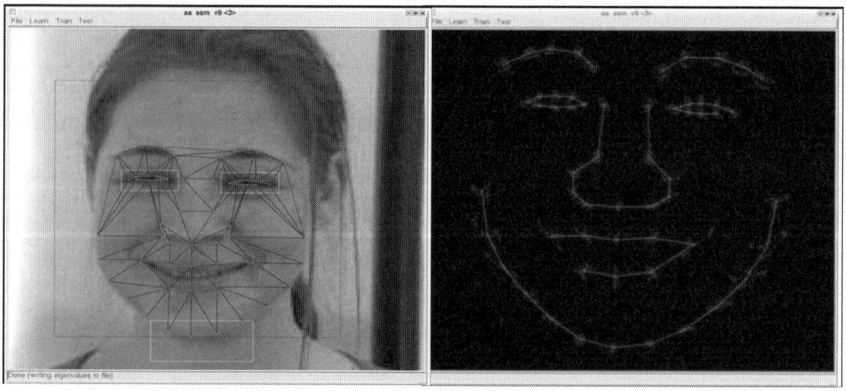

Fig. 6. Left: An example of an AAM fitted to a face from the FGnet database. Right: Point distribution over the training set.

As a classifier, the FETA system uses artificial neural networks (ANN). The ANN is trained to recognise a number of facial expressions by the AAM's shape parameters. In the work reported here, facial expressions such as neutral, happy, surprise and disgust are detected. Other expressions are possible but the FGnet data corpus [14] used in the experiments was limited to these expressions. As this paper is concerned with a framework for affective computing, rather than a particular method for affective sensing and a set of experiments, we omit experimental results of the automatic facial expression recognition experiments, which the interested reader can find in [12].

In the domain ontology of concepts, we would list this work as being on the facial sensory cue with one person present at a time. As the data in the FGnet corpus is based on subjects being asked to perform a number of facial expressions, it would be recorded as being acted emotions in the ontology. Recordings were made in a laboratory environment, so the context would be 'laboratory'. One can easily see how the use of an ontology facilitates the capture of important metadata in a formalised way. Following the previous example of an application ontology, we would record the emotion classification method (by the corpus creators) as being the category approach. The resources provided in the FGnet corpus are individual images stored in JPEG format. Due to space limits in this paper, we will not describe the entire set of ontologies for this example. The concept should be apparent from the explanation given here.

6 Conclusions and Future Work

We have presented ongoing work towards building an affective sensing system. The main contribution of this paper is a proposed framework for research in affective communication. This framework consists of a generic model of affective communication and a set of ontologies to be used in conjunction. Detailed descriptions of the ontologies and examples of their use have been given. Using the proposed framework provides an easier way of comparing methodologies and results from different studies of affective communication. In future work, we intend to provide further example ontologies on our web-page. We will also continue our work on building a multimodal affective sensing system and plan to include physiological sensors as another cue for determining the affective state of a user.

References

1. Picard, R.: Affective Computing. MIT Press, Cambridge (MA), USA (1997)
2. Scherer, K.: Vocal communication of emotion: A review of research paradigms. Speech Communication 40(1–2), 227–256 (2003)
3. Cowie, R., Douglas-Cowie, E., Cox, C.: Beyond emotion archetypes: Databases for emotion modelling using neural networks. Neural Networks 18(4), 371–388 (2005)
4. Stibbard, R.: Vocal expression of emotions in non-laboratory speech: An investigation of the Reading/Leeds Emotion in Speech Project annotation data. PhD thesis, University of Reading, United Kingdom (2001)
5. Devillers, L., Vidrascu, L., Lamel, L.: Challenges in real-life emotion annotation and machine learning based detection. Neural Networks 18(4), 407–422 (2005)
6. Liscombe, J., Riccardi, G., Hakkani-T"ur, D.: Using context to improve emotion detection in spoken dialog systems. In: Proceedings of the 9th European Conference on Speech Communication and Technology EUROSPEECH'05.Lisbon, Portugal, vol. 1, pp. 1845–1848 (September 2005)
7. HUMAINE: http://emotion-research.net/ (Last accessed 26 October 2006)

8. Millar, J., Wagner, M., Goecke, R.: Aspects of Speaking-Face Data Corpus Design Methodology. In: Proceedings of the 8th International Conference on Spoken Language Processing ICSLP2004, Jeju, Korea, vol. II, pp. 1157–1160 (October 2004)
9. Koike, K., Suzuki, H., Saito, H.: Prosodic Parameters in Emotional Speech. In: Proc. 5th International Conference on Spoken Language Processing ICSLP'98, Sydney, Australia, ASSTA, vol. 2, pp. 679–682 (December 1998)
10. Shigeno, S.: Cultural similarities and differences in the recognition of audio-visual speech stimuli. In: Mannell, R., Robert-Ribes, J. (eds.): Proceedings of the International Conference on Spoken Language Processing ICSLP'98, Sydney, Australia, ASSTA, vol. 1, pp. 281–284 (December 1998)
11. Schröder, M.: D6e: Report on representation languages (Last accessed 26 October 2006) http://emotionresearch.net/deliverables/D6efinal
12. Arnold, A.: Automatische Erkennung von Gesichtsausdrücken auf der Basis statistischer Methoden und neuronaler Netze. Masterthesis, University of Applied Sciences Mannheim, Germany (2006)
13. Cootes, T., Edwards, G., Taylor, C.: Active Appearance Models. In: Burkhardt, H., Neumann, B. (eds.) ECCV 1998. LNCS, vol. 1407, pp. 484–498. Springer, Heidelberg (1998)
14. Wallhoff, F.: Facial Expressions and Emotion Database. Technische Universität München (Last accessed 6 December 2006) http://www.mmk.ei.tum.de/waf/fgnet/feedtum.html

Affective User Modeling for Adaptive Intelligent User Interfaces

Fatma Nasoz[1] and Christine L. Lisetti[2]

[1] School of Informatics, University of Nevada Las Vegas
Las Vegas, NV, USA
nasoz@egr.unlv.edu

[2] Department of Multimedia Communications, Institut Eurecom
Sophia-Antipolis, France
lisetti@eurecom.fr

Abstract. In this paper we describe the User Modeling phase of our general research approach: developing Adaptive Intelligent User Interfaces to facilitate enhanced natural communication during the Human-Computer Interaction. Natural communication is established by recognizing users' affective states (i.e., emotions experienced by the users) and responding to those emotions by adapting to the current situation via an affective user model. Adaptation of the interface was designed to provide multi-modal feedback to the users about their current affective state and to respond to users' negative emotional states in order to compensate for the possible negative impacts of those emotions. Bayesian Belief Networks formalization was employed to develop the User Model to enable the intelligent system to appropriately adapt to the current context and situation by considering user-dependent factors, such as: personality traits and preferences.

Keywords: User Modeling, Bayesian Belief Networks, Intelligent Interfaces, Human Computer Interaction.

1 Introduction and Motivation

The field of Human-Computer Interaction (HCI) is defined as "a discipline concerned with the design, evaluation and implementation of interactive computing systems for human use and with the study of major phenomena surrounding them" [20] and Maybury [28] defines optimal human-computer interactions as ones where users are able to perform complex tasks more quickly and accurately, thus improving user satisfaction.

While interacting with an intelligent system each user's responses are different from other users [33]. This makes it necessary to build *user models* that will enable the system to record relevant user information in order to interact with its users appropriately. A User Model is defined as "the description and knowledge of the user maintained by the system" [33]. An adaptive system should modify the user model as the individual user changes, because each user differs from other users and the same specific user may change while s/he is interacting with the system.

J. Jacko (Ed.): Human-Computer Interaction, Part III, HCII 2007, LNCS 4552, pp. 421–430, 2007.

Conventional user models are built on the knowledge level of the users about the specific context, what their skills and goals are, and the self-report about what they like or dislike. The applications of this traditional user modeling include student modeling [2] [10] [29] [36], news access [3], e-commerce [16], and health-care [37].

However, none of these conventional models accommodates a very important component of human intelligence: *Affect and Emotions*. People do not only emote, but they also are affected by their emotional states. Emotions influence various cognitive processes in humans (perception and organization of memory [5], categorization and preference [38], goal generation, evaluation, and decision-making [12], strategic planning [24], focus and attention [14], motivation and performance [8], intention [17], communication [4] [15], and learning [19]), as well as their interactions with computer systems [35]. The influence of affect on cognition and human-computer interaction increases the necessity in developing intelligent computer systems that understand users' emotional states, learn their preferences and personality, and respond accordingly.

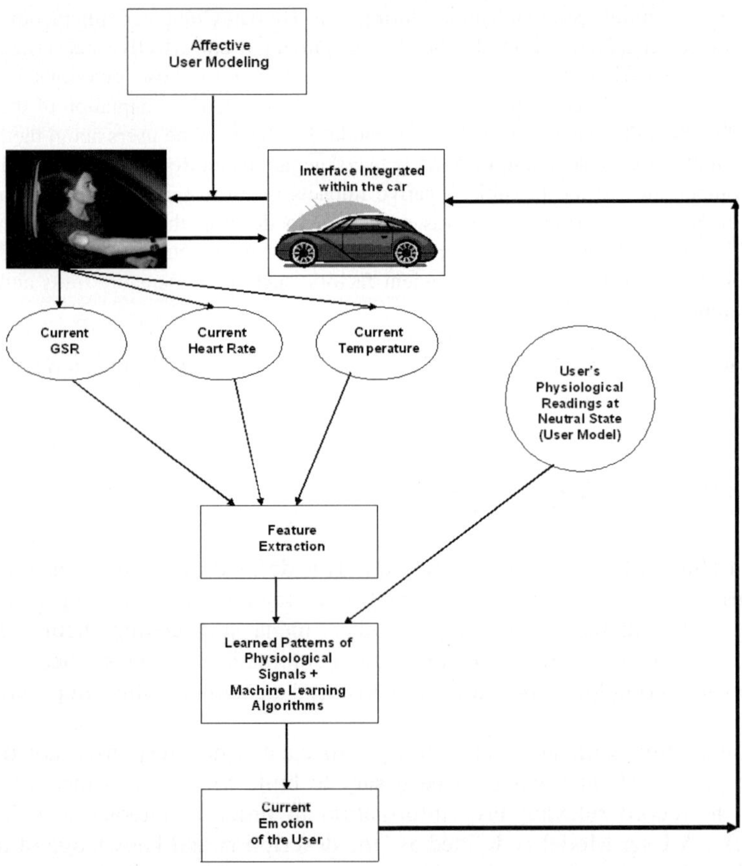

Fig. 1. User Modeling Integrated with Emotion Recognition

The main objective of our research is to create Adaptive Intelligent User Interfaces that achieve the goals of human-computer interaction defined by Maybury [28] by performing real-time emotion recognition and adapting to the affective state of the user depending on the user dependent specifics such as personality traits or users' preferences and the current context and application. Although there are several possible applications of such systems, our current research interest focuses on the *Driving Safety* application. Previous research suggests that automobile drivers emote while driving in their cars [22] and their driving is affected by their negative emotions/states [18] [22] including anger, frustration, panic, boredom, or sleepiness. We aim to enhance driving safety with adaptive intelligent car interfaces that can recognize and adapt to the drivers' negative affective states.

We have been designing and conducting various in-lab and virtual reality experiments to elicit emotions from the participants and collect and analyze their physiological data in order to map human's physiological signals to their emotions [25] [26] [27] [30] [31]. After recognizing the user's emotion and giving feedback to her about her emotional state, the next step is adapting the intelligent system to the user's emotional state by also considering the current context and application and user dependent specifics, such as user's personality traits. Bayesian Belief Networks formalization was employed to create these user models in order to enable the intelligent system to adapt to user and application dependent specifics. Figure 1 represents our overall approach to the adaptive interaction of intelligent systems, by integrating emotion recognition from physiological signals with affective user modeling, in the specific case of driving safety application.

2 Related User Modeling Research

In the recent years, there has been a significant increase in the number of attempts to build user models that include affect at some level in the user model. Carofiglio and de Rosis' project [6] discusses the effect of emotions on an argumentation in a dialog, and models how emotions are activated and how the argumentation is adapted accordingly using Belief Networks. In the model, the user interacting with the system's agent is represented as the receiver. For example when a positive emotion "hope" is activated, the intensity of this emotion is influenced by the receiver's belief that a specific event will occur to self in the future, the event that the belief is desirable, and the belief that this situation favors achieving the agent's goal. The model represents both logical and emotional reasoning in the same structure. The model evaluates every candidate argument applying simulative reasoning by focusing on the current state of the dialog and by guessing the effect of the candidate on the receiver of argument. The difficulties encountered in some cases when classifying the argumentation as being 'rational' or 'emotional' increased the authors' belief in the importance of including emotional factors while creating natural argumentation systems. In this approach the assessment of the emotion is performed in the Bayesian Belief Network by activation of related cognitive components.

Affect and Belief Adaptive Interface System (ABAIS), created as a rule-based system by Hudlicka and McNeese [21], assesses pilots' affective states and active beliefs and takes adaptive precautions to compensate for their negative affects. The architecture of this system is built on i) sensing the user's affective state and beliefs (User State Assessment Module), ii) inferring the potential effects of them on the user's performance (Impact Prediction Module), iii) selecting a strategy to compensate, and finally (Strategy Selection Module) iv) implementing this strategy (Graphical User Interface[GUI]/Decision Support System[DSS] Adaptation Module). Sensing the user's affective state and beliefs is defined as the most critical of the whole structure and it receives various data about the current user to identify his current affective state (e.g. high anxiety) and his beliefs (e.g. hostile aircraft approaching). The potential effects (generic effects and the task-specific effects) (e.g. task neglect) of the user's emotions and beliefs are inferred in the Impact Prediction Module using a rule-based reasoning. Rule-based reasoning is also used when selecting a counter strategy (e.g. present reminder of neglected tasks) to compensate the negative effects on the user's performance and finally the selected strategy is implemented in the GUI/DSS Module by using a rule-based reasoning to consider the individual pilot preferences.

Conati's [9] probabilistic user model, which was based on Dynamic Decision Networks (DDN), was built to represent the emotional state of users while interacting with an educational game by also including causes and effects of the emotion, as well as user's personality and goals. Probabilistic dependencies between causes, effects, and emotional states and their temporal evolution are represented by DDNs. DDNs are used due to their capability of modeling uncertain knowledge and environments to change over time.

Assessing users' emotional states is a very important component in both Hudlicka and McNeese's [21] and Conati's [8] models; however, none of these studies actually perform emotion recognition. Overall objective if our research is to perform both emotion recognition and appropriate interface adaptation and combine them in the same system. The adaptive intelligent user interface described in this article combines both the emotion recognition process and the modeling of user dependent factors such as emotions and personality traits.

3 Bayesian Belief Networks

Bayesian Belief Network (BBN) [34] is a directed acyclic graph, where each node represents a random discrete variable or uncertain quantity that can take two or more possible values. The directed arcs between the nodes represent the direct causal dependencies among these random variables.

The conditional probabilities that are assigned to these arcs determine the strength of the dependency between two variables. A Bayesian Belief Network can be defined by specifying:

1. Set of random variables: $\{X_1, X_2, X_3, ... X_n\}$.

2. Set of arcs among these random variables. The arcs should be directed and the graph should be acyclic. If there is an arc from X_1 to X_2, X_1 is called as the parent of X_2 and X_2 is called as the child of X_1.

3. Probability of each random variable that is dependent on the combination of its parents. For a random variable X_i, the set of its parents is represented as par(X_i), and the conditional probability of X_i is defined as:

$$P(X_i \mid par(X_i))$$

4. If a node has no parents unconditional probabilities are used.

Unlike the traditional rule-based expert systems, BBNs are able to represent and reason with uncertain knowledge. They can update a belief in a particular case when new evidence is provided.

3.1 User Modeling with Bayesian Belief Networks

The Bayesian Belief Network representation of the User Model that records related affective user information in the driving environment is shown in Figure 2.

User model for the driving safety application is built as a decision support system. There are various parameters that would affect the optimal action that should be chosen by the adaptive interface. Some of the parameters (i.e. nodes) of the BBN are:

- Emotional state of the driver (represented by E, with 6 states: anger, frustration, panic, boredom, sleepiness, and non-negative);
- Driver's personality traits (represented by P, with 5 states: agreeable, conscientious, extravert, neurotic, open to experiments);
- Driver's age (represented by A, with 4 states: below 25, 25-40, 40-60, and above 60);
- Driver's gender (represented by G, with 2 states: female and male);
- Safeness of the current state (represented by S, with 2 states: no accident and accident).

Personality trait, age, and gender were chosen to be included in the model since previous studies suggest that they have influence on how people drive. For the model, possible emotions and states that a driver can experience are chosen as: Anger, Frustration, Panic, Boredom, and Sleepiness and their influence on one's driving are mentioned in section 1.

Personality traits of the driver were included in the user model, because previous studies suggest that personality differences result in different emotional responses and physiological arousal to the same stimuli [23], and the preferences of a person are affected by her personality [32]. Questionnaires can be used in order to successfully identify a driver's personality. Five-Factor-Model was chosen to determine the personality traits [11]. Following are the personality traits based on the Five-Factor-Model:

- Neuroticism (High neuroticism leads to violent and negative emotions and interferes with the ability to handle problems)
- Extraversion (High extravert people work in people oriented jobs, while low extravert people mostly work in task oriented jobs)
- Openness to experience (Open people are more liberal in their values)

- Agreeableness (High agreeable people are skeptical and mistrustful)
- Conscientiousness (High conscientious people are hard-working and energetic) [11].

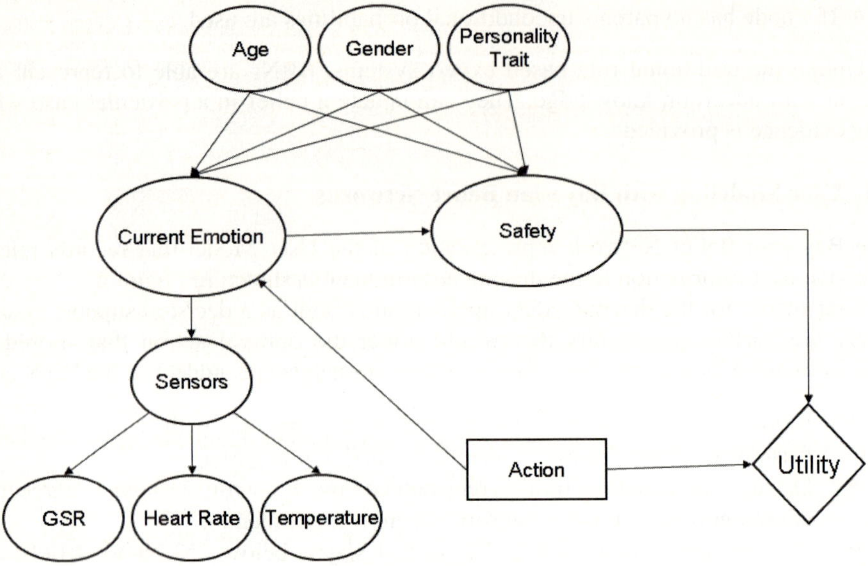

Fig. 2. Bayesian Belief Network Representation of Driver Model

These personality traits also influence the way people are driving. Celler et al.'s study [7] show that Agreeableness have slight negative correlation with the number of driving tickets and Arthur and Graziano's study [1] showed that people with low Conscientiousness level have higher risk of being in a traffic accident.

Age and gender also have effect on people's driving [13]. Younger drivers are at a greater level of crash involvement (with a distinguished difference between 18-19-years- olds and 25-years-olds), more likely to take risks, they tend to show increased level social deviance, display the highest driving violation rates, and associate a lower level of risk perception, whereas older drivers tend to show a greater frequency of drowsy driving and tend to more likely suffer from visual impairments that affect their driving [13]. When it comes to gender differences, men are more likely to have accidents because of rule violations, and they make up majority of the aggressive drivers. Women on the other hand, are more likely to involve in crashes caused by perceptual or judgmental errors and they have lower driving confidence [13].

The node *Action* (represented by A) represents the possible actions (states) that can be taken by the interface. These actions include:

- Change the radio station
- Suggest the driver to stop the car and rest

- Roll down the window
- Suggest the driver to do a relaxation exercise
- Tell the driver to calm down
- Make a joke
- Splash some water on the driver's face

The node Utility (represented by U) represents the possible outcomes of the interface's chosen action in terms of an increase in the safety of the driver. This node is called the *utility node*, and the outcomes are called *utilities*. The three possible outcomes are:

- -1 (decrease in safety, i.e. decrease in probability for no accident),
- 0 (no change),
- 1 (increase in safety, i.e. increase in probability for no accident)

For example, if the driver was angry and the interface's action was suggesting the driver to do a relaxation exercise, and if this made the driver angrier, the outcome is negative 1. The variables determining this outcome are *Safety* and *Action*.

The posterior probability for *Safety* is calculated and it is used to calculate the *expected utility* of choosing each action. The action yielding the highest expected utility is chosen as the interface's action. The formula for the posterior probability of each state of *Safety* is given by:

$$P(S_i \mid E,P,A,G) = \frac{P(E,P,A,G \mid S_i)P(S_i)}{P(E,P,A,G \mid S_1)P(S_1) + P(E,P,A,G \mid S_2)P(S_2)} \quad (1)$$

Table 1. Actions with highest expected utility for different cases

Emotion	Personality Trait	Age	Gender	Safety	Interface Action
Anger (95%)	Conscientious (85%)	40-60	Female	Accident (14%)	Relaxation technique
Anger (70%)	Neurotic (90%)	Below 25	Male	Accident (6%)	Make a Joke
Sleepiness (95%)	Conscientious (95%)	25-40	Female	Accident (12%)	Suggest stopping the car and resting
Sleepiness (88%)	Neurotic (85%)	Below 25	Female	Accident (9%)	Change the radio station

The formula for the expected utility of each action is given by:

$$EU(A_i) = U(S_1, A_i)P(S_1 \mid E, P, A, G) + U(S_2, A_i)P(S_2 \mid E, P, A, G) \tag{2}$$

The reason for choosing Bayesian Belief Networks formalization to represent the user model in driving environment was BBN's ability to represent uncertain knowledge and to update a belief in a particular case when new evidence is provided.

3.2 Results

The driver model created with BBN for was tested by assigning various combinations of events with different probabilities to the network's variables. Table 1 shows the optimal action of the interface chosen by the BBN in four different cases.

4 Discussion

The strength of adaptive user interfaces lies in the fact that they are able to adapt to different users and different interactions based on the models that are built for users. An important component that influences users' interaction with computer systems is the user itself. Human-computer interaction is affected by various user dependent factors such as emotional states and personality traits. For this reason we built an adaptive user model with Bayesian Belief Network to record relevant affective user information.

User modeling is a very important part of adaptive interaction; however it is a difficult task especially when the existing real data is very limited. Affective knowledge is specifically restricted in the domain of driving safety. Currently our model is not complete due to the fact not all the functional dependencies can be calculated because of lack of enough real data. Our user model will be completed as a result of a collaborative effort of experts from the fields of Psychology and Transportation by determining the causal dependencies among the variables.

References

1. Arthur, W., Graziano, W.G.: The five-factor model, conscientiousness, and driving accident involvement. Journal of Personality 64, 593–618 (1996)
2. Barker, T., Jones, S., Britton, J., Messer, D.: The Use of a Co-operative Student Model of Learner Characteristics to Configure a Multimedia Application. User Modeling and User.-Adapted Interaction 12, 207–241 (2002)
3. Billsus, D., Pazzani, M.J.: User Modeling for Adaptive News Access. User. Modeling and User-Adapted Interaction 10, 147–180 (2000)
4. Birdwhistle, R.: Kinesics and Context: Essays on Body Motion and Communication. University of Pennsylvania Press (1970)
5. Bower, G.: Mood and Memory. American Psychologist 36(2), 129–148 (1981)
6. Carofiglio, V., de Rosis, F.: Combining Logical with Emotional Reasoning in Natural Argumentation. In: Proceedings of 9th International Conference on User Modeling - Assessing and Adapting to User Attitudes and Affect: Why, When, and How?, Pittsburgh, PA, pp. 9–15 (June 2003)

7. Cellar, D.F., Nelson, Z.C., Yorke, C.M.: The Five-Factor Model and Driving Behavior: Personality and Involvement in Vehicular Accidents. Psychological Results 86, 454–456 (2000)
8. Colquitt, J.A., LePine, J.A, Noe, R.A.: Toward an integrative theory of training motivation: A meta-analytic path analysis of 20 years of research. Journal of Applied Psychology 85, 678–707 (2000)
9. Conati, C.: Probabilistic Assessment of User's Emotions in Educational Games. Journal of Applied Artificial Intelligence - special issue on Merging Cognition and Affect in HCI 16(7-8), 555–575 (2003)
10. Corbett, A., McLaughlin, M., Scarpinatto, S.C.: Modeling Student Knowledge: Cognitive Tutors in High School and College. User Modeling and User-Adapted Interaction 10, 81–108 (2000)
11. Costa, P.T., McCrae, R.R.: The Revised NEO Personality Inventory (NEO PI-R) professional manual. Psychological Assessment Resources, Odessa, FL (1992)
12. Damasio, A.: Descartes' Error. Avon Books, New-York, NY (1994)
13. Department of Transport: International review of the individual factors contributing to driving behavior. Technical report, Department for Transport (October 2003)
14. Derryberry, D., Tucker, D.: Neural Mechanisms of Emotion. Journal of Consulting and Clinical Psychology 60(3), 329–337 (1992)
15. Ekman, P., Friesen, W.V.: Unmasking the Face: A Guide to Recognizing Emotions from Facial Expressions. Prentice Hall, Inc, New Jersey (1975)
16. Fink, J., Cobsa, A.: A Review and Analysis of Commercial User Modeling Servers for Personalization on the World Wide Web. User Modeling and User-Adapted Interaction 10, 209–249 (2000)
17. Frijda, N.H.: The Emotions. Cambridge University Press, New York (1986)
18. Fuller, R., Santos, J.A. (eds.): Human Factors for Highway Engineers. Elsevier Science, Oxford, UK (2002)
19. Goleman, D.: Emotional Intelligence. Bantam Books, New York (1995)
20. Hewett, T., Baecker, R., Card, S., Gasen, J., Mantei, M., Perlman, G., Strong, G., Verplank, W.: ACM SIGCHI, Curricula for Human-computer Interaction. Report of the ACM SIGCHI Curriculum Development Group, ACM (1992)
21. Hudlicka, E., McNeese, M.D.: Assessment of User Affective and Belief States for Interface Adaptation: Application to an Air Force Pilot Task. User Modeling and User-Adapted Interaction 12, 1–47 (2002)
22. James, L.: Road Rage and Aggressive Driving. Prometheus Books, Amherst, NY (2000)
23. Kahneman, D.: Arousal and attention in: Attention and Effort, pp. 28–49. Prentice-Hall, Englewood Cliffs, N.J (1973)
24. Ledoux, J.: Brain Mechanisms of Emotion and Emotional Learning. Current Opinion in Neurobiology 2, 191–197 (1992)
25. Lisetti, C.L., Nasoz, F.: MAUI: A Multimodal Affective User Interface. In: Proceedings of the ACM Multimedia International Conference, Juan les Pins, France (December 2002)
26. Lisetti, C.L., Nasoz, F.: Using Non-invasive Wearable Computers to Recognize Human Emotions from Physiological Signals. EURASIP Journal on Applied Signal Processing - Special Issue on Multimedia Human-Computer Interface 11, 1672–1687 (2004)
27. Lisetti, C.L., Nasoz, F.: Affective Intelligent Car Interfaces with Emotion Recognition for Enhanced Driving Safety (*Invited). In: Proceedings of 11th International Conference on Human-Computer Interaction, July 2005, Las Vegas, Nevada, USA (2005)

28. Maybury, M.T.: Human Computer Interaction: State of the Art and Further Development in the International Context - North America (Invited talk). In: International Status Conference on MTI Program, Saarbruecken, Germany (October 26-27, 2001)
29. Millan, E., Perez-de-la Cruz, J.L.: A Bayesian Diagnostic Algorithm for Student Modeling and its Evaluation. User Modeling and User-Adapted Interaction 12, 281–330 (2002)
30. Nasoz, F., Lisetti, C.L.: MAUI avatars: Mirroring the User's Sensed Emotions via Expressive Multi-ethnic Facial Avatars. Journal of Visual Languages and Computing 17(5), 430–444 (2006)
31. Nasoz, F., Alvarez, K., Lisetti, C.L., Finkelstein, N.: Emotion Recognition from Physiological Signals for Presence Technologies. International Journal of Cognition, Technology, and Work – Special Issue on Presence 6(1) (2003)
32. Nass, C., Lee, K.M.: Does computer-generated speech manifest personality? An experimental test of similarity-attraction. In: Proceedings of the CHI 2000 Conference, The Hague, The Netherlands (April 1-6, 2000)
33. Norcio, A.F., Stanley, J.: Adaptive Human-Computer Interfaces: A Literature Survey and Perspective. IEEE Transactions on Systems, Man, and Cybernetics 19(2), 399–408 (1989)
34. Pearl, J.: Probabilistic Reasoning in Expert Systems: Networks of Plausible Inference. Morgan Kaufmann Publishers, Inc., San Francisco (1988)
35. Reeves, B., Nass, C.I: The Media Equation: How People Treat Computers, Television, and New Media Like Real People and Places. Cambridge University Press, Cambridge
36. Selker, T.: A Teaching Agent that Learns. Communications of the ACM 37(7), 92–99 (1994)
37. Warren, J.R., Frankel, H.K., Noone, J.T.: Supporting special-purpose health care models via adaptive interfaces to the web. Interacting with Computers 14, 251–267 (2002)
38. Zajonc, R.: On the Primacy of Affect. American Psychologist 39, 117–124 (1984)

A Multidimensional Classification Model for the Interaction in Reactive Media Rooms

Ali A. Nazari Shirehjini

Fraunhofer-Institute for Computer Graphics,
Darmstadt, Germany
ali.nazari@igd.fraunhofer.de
http://www.igd.fhg.de/igd-a1/

Abstract. We are already living in a world where we are surrounded by intelligent devices which support us to plan, organize, and perform our daily life. Their number is constantly increasing. At the same time, the complexity of the environment and the number of intelligent devices must not distract the user from his original tasks. Therefore a primary goal is to reduce the user's mental workload. With the emergence of newly available technology, the challenge to maintain control increases, while the additional value decreases. After taking a closer look at enriched environments, there will come up the question of how to build a more intuitive way for people to interact with such an environment. As a result the design of proper interaction models appears to be crucial for AmI systems. To facilitate the design of proper interaction models we are introducing a multidimensional classification model for the interaction in reactive media rooms. It describes the various dimensions of interaction and outlines the design space for the creation of interaction models. By doing so, the proposed work can also be used as a meta-model for interaction design.

1 Classification of Interaction Paradigms for Ambient Intelligence

In the field of Human-Environment-Interaction one can differentiate between various interaction paradigms that can be classified in multiple dimensions themselves (see figure 3).

1.1 Who Takes the "Initiative"? The System or the User?

One of the most important dimensions is named Initiative. Following our model, an interaction can be explicit, implicit, or mixed. But in general, Human-Environment-Interaction is divided in two classes: explicit and implicit interaction [10]. Within the scope of an explicit interaction the user takes the initiative to manage and manipulate the environment. The user can decide when to perform which activity. An example of explicit interaction is to turn on the lights of your room using the manual switches. Another example is to control your slide presentation using natural gesture or touching the desired display.

In contrast to the explicit interaction approach, by an implicit interaction actions can also be performed automatically. In such a case the environment takes the

J. Jacko (Ed.): Human-Computer Interaction, Part III, HCII 2007, LNCS 4552, pp. 431–439, 2007.

initiative to perform an activity. The user does not determine when what happens. Instead, users are observed to understand their current behaviour and situations. In other words, the decision is influenced by the user's behaviour. Therefore, they are interacting with the environment in an implicit manner because they deliver implicit inputs which are required to make decisions. An implicit interaction can happen reactively or pro-actively. By a reactive interaction the environment responds immediately to a current situation change or to an event. By a pro-active interaction the environment analyzes the future needs of the user. To meet those needs required actions will be performed in advance.

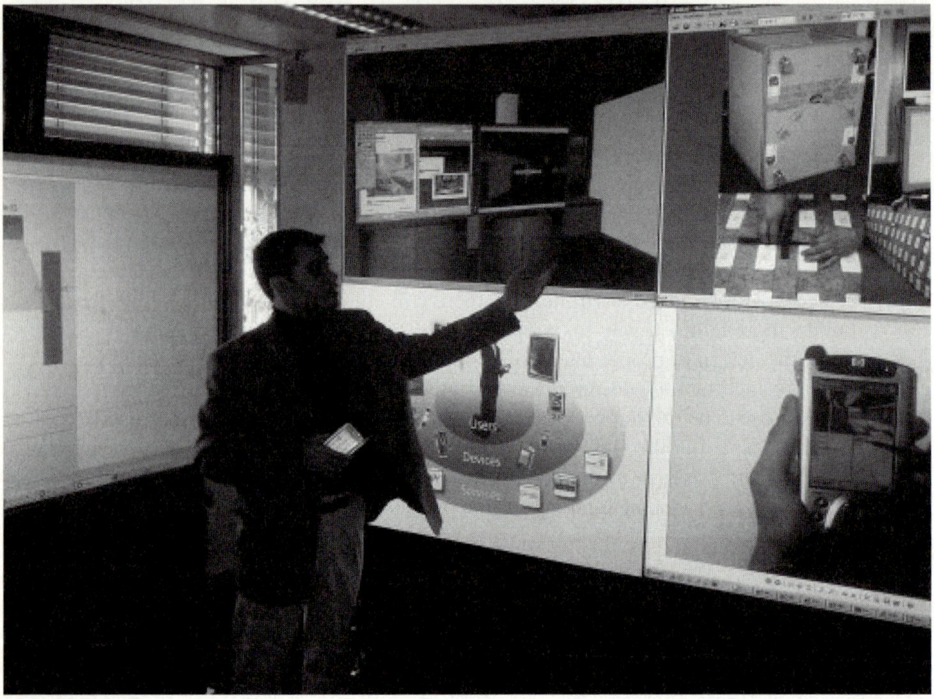

Fig. 1. The PECo system [4] allows for explicit interaction with the environment using a mobile controller assistant

When analyzing the implicit interaction approach one major challenge comes up. It is the lack of control. Several works reported already that people do not accept a full-adaptive and over-automated environment [2]. Instead, users should always be in control [3]. Another challenge of implicit interaction – when deploying it for complex AmI-E – is the lack of a system face [2]. This makes it difficult for users to build an appropriate mental model about the system [1] and to understand the automated (re)actions of their intelligent environment. Another challenge is the missing ability of users to override the default behaviour of the system. Beside these challenges, rich input from environment is necessary for truly intelligent (i.e. meaningful and appropriate) behaviour. This requires truly highly-developed context-awareness techniques (models, sensing technologies, reasoning . . .) which is one of the current challenges of Ambient Intelligence. But Human-Environment-Interaction can also consist of a combination of both implicit and explicit interaction to overcome abovementioned challenges. Such a hybrid interaction provides both explicit and implicit access to Ambient Intelligence Environments (AmI-E) at the same time. By doing so, the user can for example use an explicit assistant to interact with adaptive environments (see fig. 1). While the adaptive environment provides reactive interaction with air conditioning and lighting devices the user uses explicit remote control assistants to manage his presentation. Due the concurrent nature of this hybrid approach, interaction conflicts can exist. Here, an important issue is the conflict resolution and interaction synchronization of concurrent environment control at a semantically level. It should be avoided that an implicit interaction system can perform activities which would effect the environment in a opposite manner as intended by the user when he had recently interacted with his environment using an explicit assistance system. The major scientific challenge is to handle arising conflicts, opposed actions, or inappropriate automatisms of the adaptive environment.

The overall approach of a hybrid interaction is shown in the figure 2. It combines the benefits of implicit and explicit interaction. At the one hand, this will allow the user to "stay in the loop" because there is always the possibility to access the environment via the explicit assistant system. At the other hand, the user is supported by the implicit system. The benefits of automation remain. The problem of an over-automation would not exist any more, because the user will be able to decide which activities are permitted for an implicit interaction. Inappropriate pro-activities can be reversed using the explicit assistant thus the usability of the system will increase.

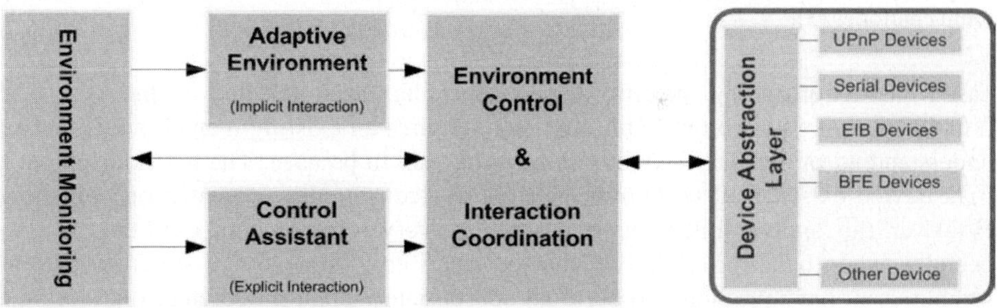

Fig. 2. Overall approach of the PECo system [4] is to provide a hybrid interaction through combination of explicit 3D-based assistant and adaptive environment

1.2 Goal, Functions and the Corresponding "Strategy Development"

What is the level of detail of the user's commando expressions? Does he want very specific functions to be performed on specific devices? Or is he talking at a higher level about his goals which should be achieved by available devices whereby the devices themselves decide how to achieve his goals?

Within the dimension of "Goals and functions" interaction systems are classified using the user's commando expressions. For example a user can express "switch on that specific light at the end of the room" (see fig. 6). This corresponds to a function

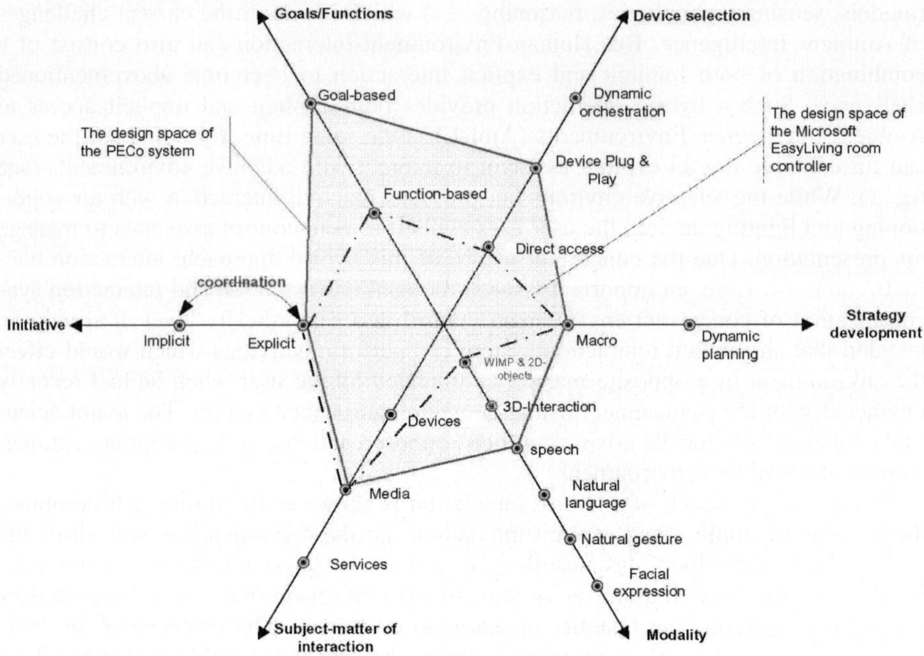

Fig. 3. This figure shows a multidimensional model for the classification of Human- Environment-Interaction. Additionally, it compares the design space of two different interaction systems; a 3D-based, mobile environment controller assistant [4] against the Microsoft EasyLiving room controller [5].

based interaction with a specific device which has been selected by the user. The function here is "switch on". This approach requires an existing mental model and an understanding of existing devices and how they are to be used. The user knows that a light device exists. And he knows the light device provides a "switch on" function. However, this approach is difficult to apply for very complex composed devices. Especially, when handling an interconnected smart environment as a smart device ensemble users have problems to build an appropriate mental model and to choose the right function they need to achieve their goal [6].

In contrast to this approach, one can also just ask the environment to adjust his environment to become "brighter". The environment will decide how to achieve this goal, i.e. which set of functions to execute. This corresponds to a goal-based explicit interaction with the environment [7, 1]. In this example the goal is "brighter". The environment can achieve this by opening the blind shutters or by using a dimmer or a switch (see fig. 4). The environment will determine the strategy (set of functions) to achieve the goal and will also assign those functions to available devices. The user will not care more which devices to choose. Therefore, users will not be faced with the complexity of the environment. However, users must be also able to interact based on functions. This is because of the mental model of the users. Most of them think in

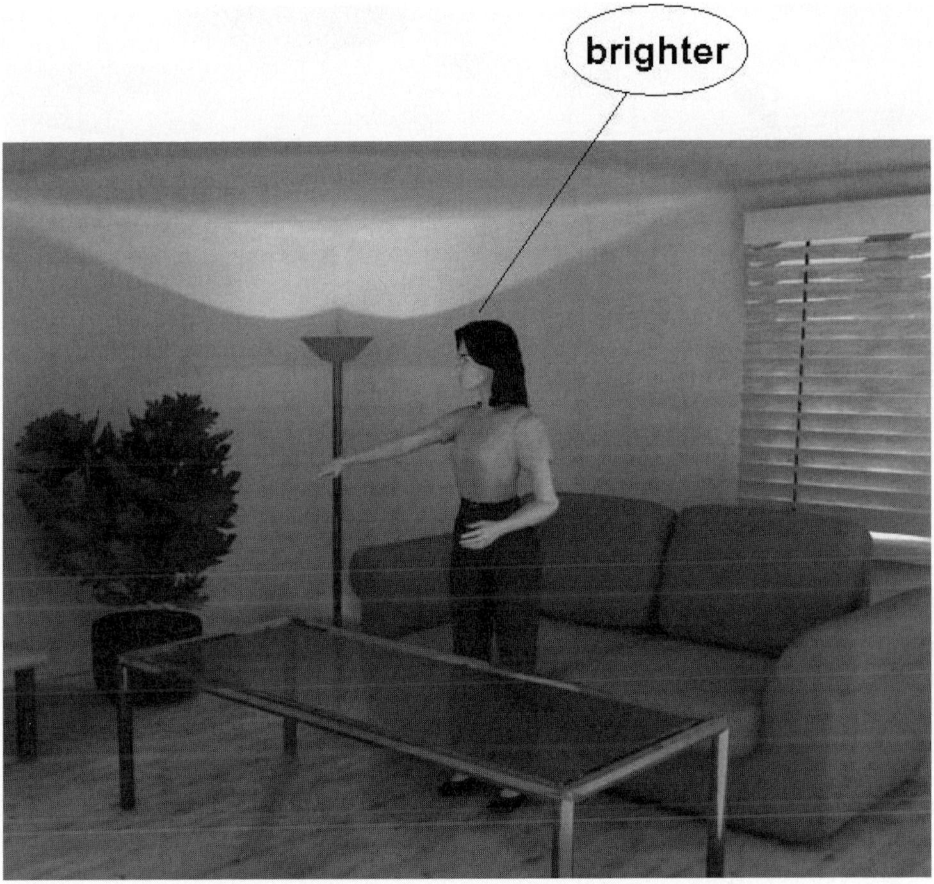

Fig. 4. Goal-based interaction with AmI-E (Source: EMBASSI)

terms of functions and therefore prefer a function-based interaction. Only when the technology becomes fully invisible – which is implausible – they begin to express goals instead of functions [6].

On the dimension of "Strategy-Development" Human-Environment-Interaction distinguishes between static and dynamic strategy-generation. Macros for example always achieve a given goal by using the same set of functions. For example to make "brighter" the above example environment (see fig. 4) a macro would always open the blind shutter. Another macro could discover all the devices of the type "binary light" and turning on all of them. However, this approach will not be able to make use of new device types. For example, if the environment becomes enriched by several dimmers the aforementioned macro can not consider them. The opposite approach would be a dynamic strategy-generation which takes environment's capabilities and user's preferences into account. Then this strategy can be mapped on the functions of

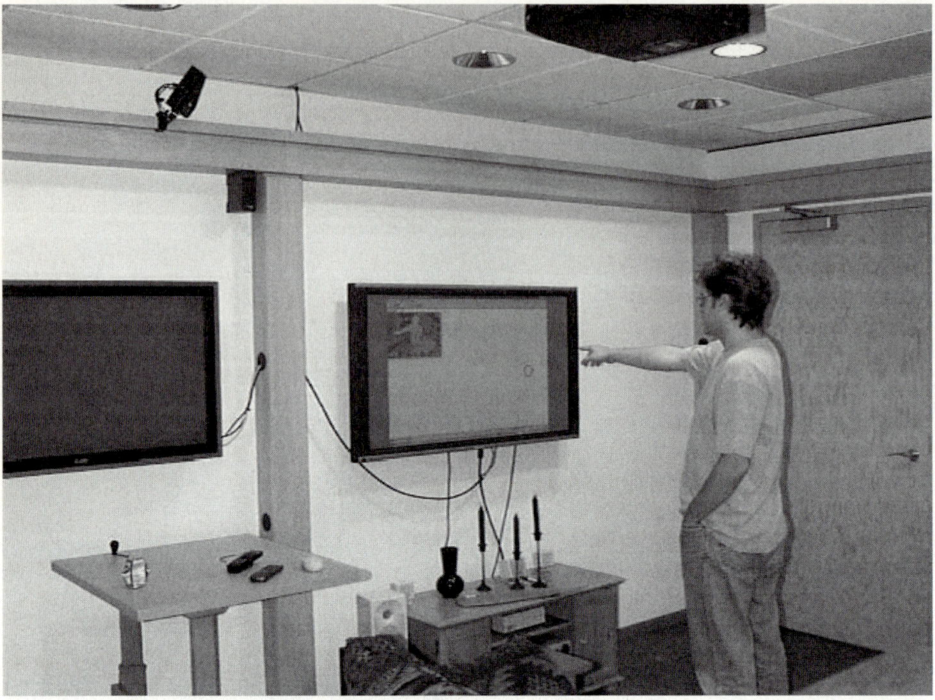

Fig. 5. Explicit gesture-based interaction with services (Source: EasyLiving project)

a dynamically created ensemble of devices. In this approach, even a combination of binary lights, blind shutters and dimmers could be considered to achieve the goal of the user.

1.3 "Device Selection": How Does the User Perceive his Environment? as Several Inter-connected Devices or as a Dynamic Device Ensemble?

Regarding the dimension of device selection there are two possibilities how the user can interact with the environment. For the first one, the user directly selects the device with the proper features in order to perform the desired function (see fig. 6).

For the second one, the devices organize themselves and decide which one will actually performing the operation (see fig. 4). Especially, for a goal-based interaction such a self-organizing and dynamic device selection is useful. Additionally, the user changes his mental perception from a group of independent devices to an environment filled with interconnected devices. As a result he will not longer express his goals to one particular device, but to the environment itself [6]. One example for a function-based, device-oriented Human-Environment-Interaction would be pointing at a display and saying "next picture" (see fig. 5). In a more dynamical form of interaction, a user would merely specify the abstract type of a device for the desired function.

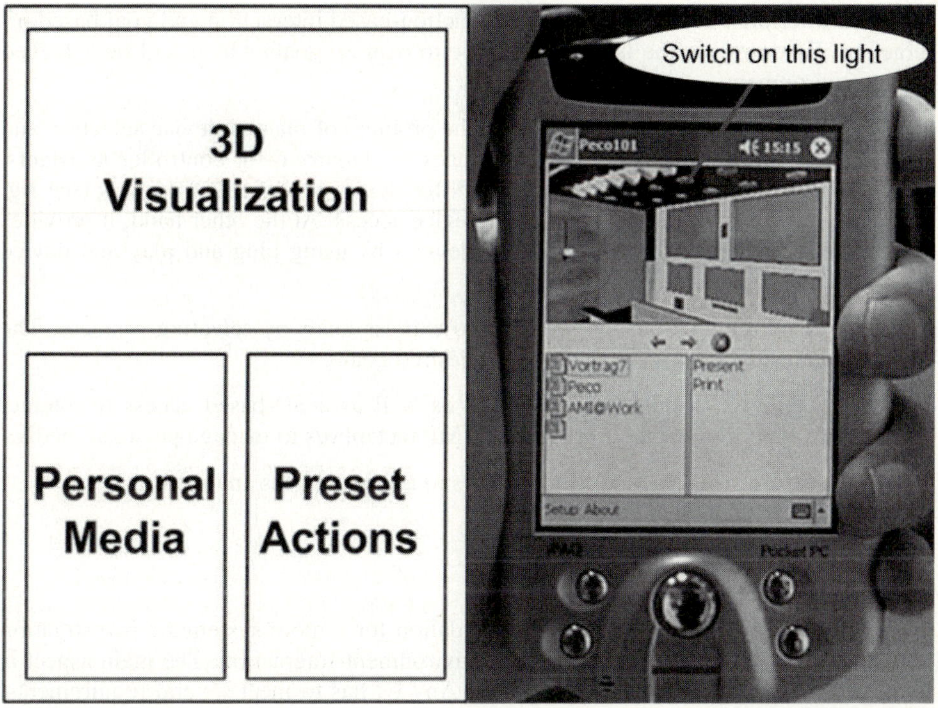

Fig. 6. The PECo-system uses a 3D-based interface to provide access to complex multimedia environments

1.4 Interaction Modalities and the Subject-Matter of Interaction

For classifying Human-Environment-Interaction this dimension expresses different forms of interaction modalities (e.g., for user input and system feedback). A classic example would be the traditional 2D GUI (WIMP).

On another dimension, the Human-Environment-Interaction distinguishes different types of interaction subject-matters (interaction with device, media, or service). Depending on the object type you want to interact with, the intuitively of a specific metaphor or the usability of a modality for user input can be very different. For example a speech commando based interaction with a forecast service in a driving situation may be very intuitive. In contrast, the same modality would not be usable for device selection or document browsing in a presentation scenario.

2 An Example for the Present Classification Model

Within this chapter we use the presented model to classify the PECo system (see fig.6). The interaction model of the PECo system is described in detail in [4]:

Initiative: PECo follows a hybrid approach as described in chapter 1.1. It provides an explicit environment control and mechanisms for interaction synchronization and conflict management.

Goals / Functions: PECo provides both function-based interaction and goal based interaction. By doing so, the user will be able to express goals which will be achieved by the environment.

Device selection: Especially, it addresses the problem of manual device selection and the complex nature of existing user interfaces for environment controller assistants. To overcome this, it deploys 3D metaphors for device selection and access (see fig. 6). At the one hand, it allows for a direct device access. At the other hand, it provides macros which dynamically consider new devices by using plug and play and device discovery mechanisms.

Strategy development: enables the user to express goals by selecting a macro. The macro contains the strategy to achieve the desired goal.

Modality: PECo provides a speech-based as well as a 3D-based access to interact with adaptive environments. It provides WIMP metaphors to manage personal media.

Subject-matter: of interaction PECo allows to access devices and media.

3 Conclusion

The model we just presented forms a foundation for a more systematic investigation and classification of concept for Human-Environment-Interaction. The main aspect is its segmentation into multiple dimensions. Any UI has to meet several requirements, which depend on the user's domain and the supported activities. During development of basic interaction concepts, our model offers formal criteria for deciding which interaction paradigm suits most. Of course there are already other existing classification models for Human-Environment-Interaction [8–11]. But in contrast to [9] and [8], our model gives a deeper and more detailed insight of Human-Environment-Interaction.

References

1. Kirste, T.: Smart environments and self-organizing appliance ensembles. In: Aarts, E., Encarnação, J.L. (eds.) True Visions, Springer, Heidelberg (2006)
2. Rehman, K., Stajano, F., Coulouris, G.: Interfacing with the invisible computer. In: NordiCHI '02: Proceedings of the second Nordic conference on Human-computer interaction, New York, NY, USA, pp. 213–216. ACM Press, New York (2002)
3. Aarts, E., Encarnação, J.L: True Visions: The Emergence of Ambient Intelligence. Springer, Heidelberg (2006)
4. Shirehjini, A.A.N.: A novel interaction metaphor for personal environment control: Direct manipulation of physical environment based on 3d visualization. In: Computers and Graphics, Special Issue on Pervasive Computing and Ambient Intelligence, vol. 28, pp. 667–675. Elsevier Science, Amsterdam (2004)
5. Braumitt, B., Meyers, B., Krumm, J., Kern, A., Shafer, S.: EasyLiving: Technologies for Intelligent Environments. In: Handheld and Ubiquitous Computing, 2nd Intl. Symposium (2000)

6. Sengpiel, M.: Mentale modelle zum wohnzimmer der zukunft, ein vergleich verschiedener user interfaces mittels wizard of oz technik. Diploma thesis, FU Berlin, Berlin, Germany (2004)
7. Yates, A., Etzioni, O., Weld, D.: A reliable natural language interface to household appliances. In: Proceedings of the 2003 international conference on intelligent user interfaces, pp. 189–196. ACM Press, New York (2003)
8. Sheridan, T.B.: Task Allocation and Supervisory Control. Handbook of Human-Computer-Interaction, pp. 159–173 (1988) ISBN 0444818766
9. Schmidt, A., Kranz, M., Holleis, P.: Interacting with the ubiquitous computer: towards embedding interaction. In: sOc-EUSAI '05: Proceedings of the 2005 joint conference on Smart objects and ambient intelligence, New York, NY, USA, pp. 147–152. ACM Press, New York (2005)
10. Köppen, N., Nitschke, J., Wandke, H., van Ballegooy, M.: Guidelines for developing assistive components for information appliances - Developing a framework for a process model. In: Proceedings of the International Workshop on Tools for Working with Guidelines (TFWWG), Biarritz, France, October 2000, Springer, Heidelberg (2000)

An Adaptive Web Browsing Method for Various Terminals: A Semantic Over-Viewing Method

Hisashi Noda[1], Teruya Ikegami[1], Yushin Tatsumi[2], and Shin'ichi Fukuzumi[1]

[1] System Platform Software Development Division, NEC Corporation
[2] Internet Systems Research Laboratories, NEC Corporation

Abstract. This paper proposed a semantic over-viewing method. This method extracts headings and semantic blocks by analyzing a layout structure of a web page and can provide a semantic overview of the web page. This method allows users grasp the overall structure of pages. It also reduces the number of operations to target information to about 6% by moving along semantic blocks. Additionally, it reduces the cost of Web page creation because of adapting one Web page content to multi-terminals. The evaluations were conducted in respect to effectiveness, efficiency and satisfaction. The results confirmed that the proposed browser is more usable than the traditional method.

Keywords: cellular phone, mobile phone, non-PC terminal, remote controller, web browsing, overview.

1 Introduction

Ubiquitous computing has enabled people to communicate at any time and any place. Besides PCs, terminals capable of browsing Web pages, such as mobile phones, PDAs, TV sets, car navigation systems, and information appliances, are growing increasingly diverse. In a conventional way, Web creators make pages for each specific terminal. Thereby, additional cost is needed to create and to maintain the pages. For solving this, research on terminal-adaptive User Interface (UI), which does not depend on the size of display area and input device with terminals, has been studied. For instance, techniques converting Web pages designed for PCs to pages for specific mobile terminal [Britton] have been proposed, and techniques parsing Web pages and providing adapted displays [Chen] [Baudisch] [Baluja] have been researched. Furthermore, mobile browser techniques can directly view Web pages designed for PCs on a mobile phone [Opera] [Parush].

However, these conventional techniques have problems: users cannot easily grasp a page's overview because of smaller display size or resolution, and they reach target information with too many operations due to simple input device.

Our goal is to propose an adaptive UI which allows users to browse Web pages on mobile terminal with small screen and simple input device with keeping high usability only when making pages for PCs. In various types of terminals, this paper focuses on the mobile phone because it is the typical case.

J. Jacko (Ed.): Human-Computer Interaction, Part III, HCII 2007, LNCS 4552, pp. 440–448, 2007.

2 Problems of Terminal-Adaptive UI

2.1 Problems from the User's Point of View

When browsing web pages for PC on mobile phone, there were several traditional methods such as converting tags from PC's to mobile phone's, and directly browsing web pages for PC on mobile phone (called a mobile browser).

However, from the user's point of view, these traditional methods have two problems.

(1) Difficulty of grasping overall structure
Because an only small part of page can be displayed, users cannot grasp an overall structure of the page and cannot understand the position of each piece of information on the whole.

(2) Low operability
In addition to a small screen, because users cannot use a pointing device, e.g. a mouse, they must require many operation steps for reaching target information.

2.2 Problems from the Content Provider's Point of View

From the content provider's point of view, when content providers create web pages for each type of terminal, the cost of creation and maintenance are necessary for each terminal.

To overcome these problems, this paper proposes an adaptive UI which allows users to browse Web pages on mobile terminal with small screen and simple input device with keeping high usability only when making pages for PCs. This paper defines usability as effectiveness, efficiency and satisfaction in the definition of ISO9241-11[ISO]. Effectiveness is defined as that users can access desired information for PCs' Web page on mobile phone. Efficiency is defined as less operation steps. Satisfaction is defined as more positive answers by subjective evaluation.

3 Novel Terminal-Adaptive UI

3.1 Semantic Over-Viewing Method

First, regarding the problem of grasping an overall structure, we featured a minified image for mobile phones to allow users to get the entire picture. However, with an only simple minified image, the smaller image prevents them from seeing details. Hence, we designed that headings is exploited and presented to showing users detailed information.

In addition to the minified image, a detailed view was provided to display detailed contents. With transition between this detailed view and the minified view, a zooming in/out technique was applied since it is more commonly used. With the traditional straightforward zooming, however, a display is not always desired, and adjustments to positioning of display are necessary, when magnifying. These adjustments are the critical problem because non-PC does not involve direct pointing. Thereby, zooming in/out by unit of a semantic block makes it possible to magnify and minify in the more desired position and to reduce the user's adjustment of the position.

Second, solving of the low operability requires a support method for moving within a page. Indeed, there is a method with which users can jump between a certain distances. However, the method needs user's adjustments of the position for them to reach a desired target because with it they have to jump without considering the structure of the page. As mentioned above, with non-PC terminal it is the critical problem. To overcome the problem, we presented a jumping method by unit of a semantic block for improving the operability.

On the basis of this idea mentioned above, this paper proposed a method which analyzes a structure of web pages, presents the headings on the minified image, zooms in/out and jumps by unit of the semantic block, called a semantic over-viewing method. A whole browser including semantic over-viewing method is called a semantic browser.

3.2 Design of Semantic Overview

This sub-section describes design of overview. Specifically, it explains extraction of headings and semantic blocks, and layout design of overview and detailed view.

3.2.1 Extraction of Headings and Semantic Blocks

Realizing a semantic over-viewing method requires extracting semantic blocks and headings. Hence, our layout analysis technique [Tatsumi] was applied. The layout analysis engine analyzes display elements which were rendered (e.g. position and color) in addition to structure of HTML elements so that the analyzed layout is fit for human sense. Figure 1 illustrates an image of our layout analysis.

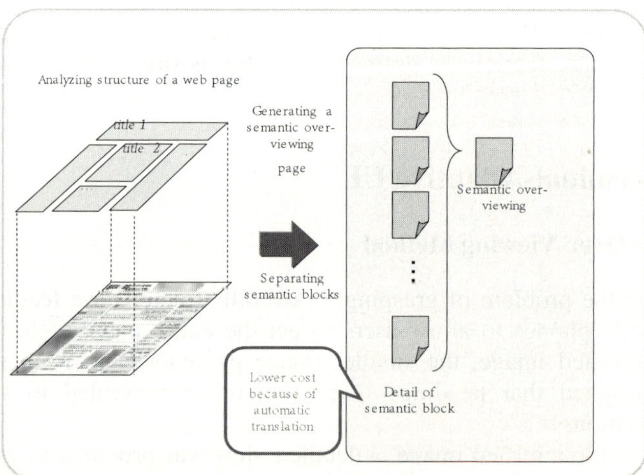

Fig. 1. Image of Layout Analysis

In this paper, a semantic block is a piece of layout with a certain size which is reflected by the page structure. The block includes some display elements. These blocks correspond to green areas in Fig. 1. The heading is the representative of the content of page, what we call headline, cross-head and subheading. The headings are shown as "title1" and "title2" in Fig. 1.

3.2.2 Overview and Detailed View

Figure 2(a) shows a screen shot of the overview. A minified image is displayed. This is a sample where the block "services" is selected. The selected block is bounded by a blue rectangle.

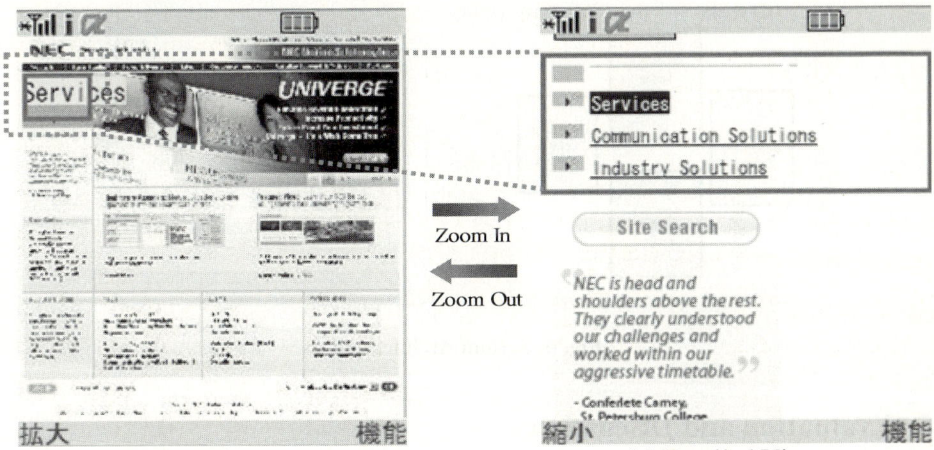

(a) Overview (b) Detailed View

Fig. 2. Examples of Screen Shot

Figure 2(b) shows a screen shot of detailed view. This is a sample where users jumped into the block of "services". The aim of the detailed view is for users to get the detailed information. W adopted a display type without horizontal-scrolling such as a mobile browser because text information is more readable than a display type with horizontal-scrolling.

Although the layout of the detailed view differs from that of the overview, an animation of a frame of zooming helps users understand the relation between detailed view and overview.

4 Implement

4.1 System Architecture

The system was composed of a server and client. The server was implemented in C++ and Java Servlet. The client was implemented in java application for mobile phone. The system architecture is shown in Fig 4.

On the server-side, a layout analysis engine obtains a page designed for PCs and analyzes the page. Next, a page making/dividing section converts tags for PCs to those for mobile phones. A client server communication section sends HTML texts and images to the client-side. On the client-side, a pre-load control section loads images in the background. An overview image creation section creates an overview image from the analysis. A zooming control section controls zooming in and out based on user's operation, and translates between the overview and the detailed view smoothly with animation. A HTML rendering section renders HTML element (e.g. a tag, img tag, input tag).

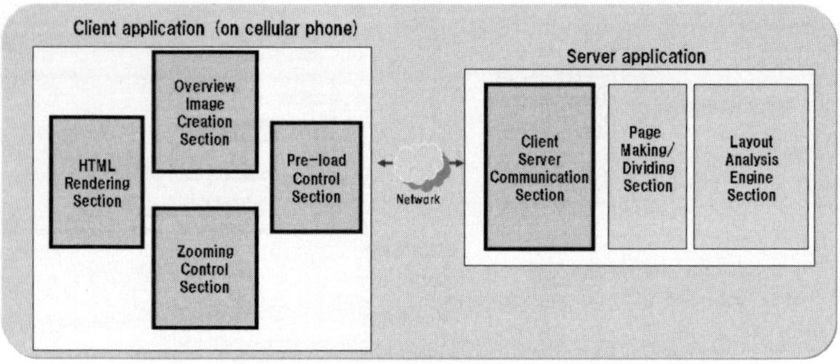

Fig. 4. System Architecture

5 Evaluation and Discussion

This section describes evaluation of the proposed method. As defined in section 2, the evaluation was conduced in respect to efficiency, satisfaction and effectiveness.

5.1 Evaluation of Efficiency

Efficiency is defined as less operation steps. An experiment actually measured the number of clicks while subjects started at the top of the web page and reached the center of the page. Specifically, the number of the clicks on the proposed browser was compared with that on the mobile browser for the web pages which were top 10 on access (e.g. Yahoo, MSN, and Amazon). The results show that the mobile browser needed 187 clicks on average. In contrast, our proposed method needed average 12 clicks. The number of clicks with the proposed method was only 6% on average compared with the traditional method. The proposed browser is significantly efficient.

5.2 Evaluation of Satisfaction

Satisfaction is defined as more positive answers on the subjective evaluation as a higher ratings. We evaluated user's satisfaction for the actual users and extracted advantages and issues on the semantic browser on the following procedures.

5.2.1 Subjects

Fifteen employees engaged in an IT company aged to twenties to forties were recruited. All of the subjects have experienced browsing PC pages on the mobile browser. Regarding the frequency for this access, "a few times a month" is eleven (79%), "a few times a week" is three (21%), and "every day" is one (7%).

5.2.2 Procedure

The subjects used freely for one month and a half. After trial use of our semantic browser, they answered the subjective evaluation. The questionnaires included three aspects: the total convenience of the semantic browser, the convenience of the semantic over-viewing method and operability.

5.2.3 Results

The results on the total convenience of the semantic browser are shown in fig. 5. Positive answers account for 60% and negative answers for 40%. The positive answer is more than the negative. Consequently, we judged that the semantic browser was positively evaluated by the subjects on the total convenience.

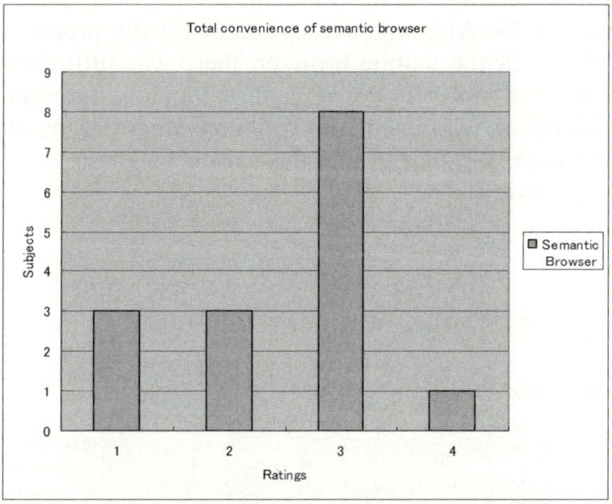

Fig. 5. Result of total convenience of semantic browser

The results on convenience of semantic over-viewing method were shown in Fig. 6. As a general trend, positive answers were 53% and negative were 47%. Little difference exists between the positive answer and the negative although the positive answer was a little more.

One of the two subjects who evaluated "not very convenience" answered "too late". Another subject answered "lower readability". One of the reasons for the low readability was due to poor image compressing algorithm when generating over-view images. Regarding delayed response, both the two subjects also rated "too late" on response. We recognized that the delayed response and low resolution downgraded the subject's ratings.

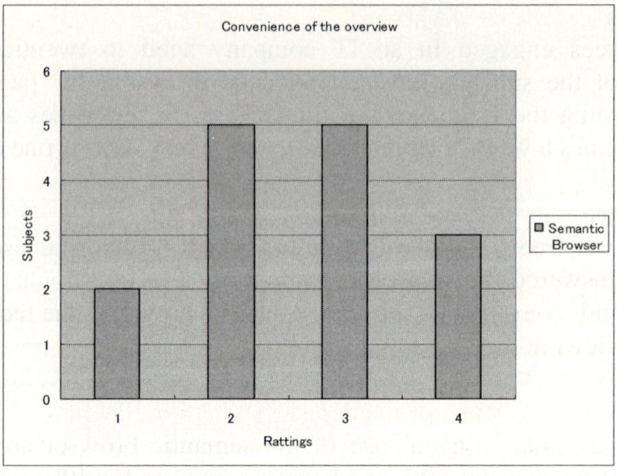

Fig. 6. Result of convenience of the overview

Figure 7 shows that the results on operability compared with mobile browser. The ratings tend to be low. Average ratings for semantic browser were 2.13 and those for mobile browser were 1.73. Although average rates for the proposed browser were a little higher than those for the mobile browser, there was little difference among the two. Three subjects rated “not very convenient of semantic browser”. The two of the three subjects are identical, who rated "not very convenient of the overview". The one subject did not comment. We judged that the reason for these low rates is similar on convenience of the overview.

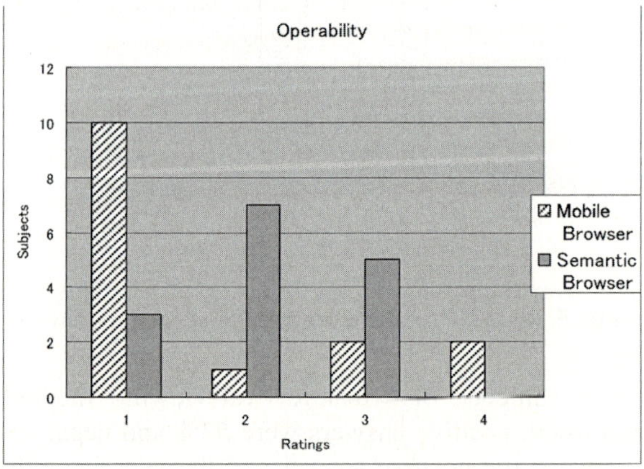

Fig. 7. Result of operability

5.3 Evaluation of Effectiveness

Effectiveness is defined as that users can access desired information through the overview. For effectiveness, evaluations on a user study and about accuracy of layout analysis were conducted.

5.3.1 Evaluation on User Study

All subjects reached the detailed view using the overview. Furthermore, on questionnaires, no one answered that she or he did not know how to use. These results confirmed that all subjects achieved the goal.

5.3.2 Accuracy of Layout Analysis

Evaluation experiment was conducted to investigate an accuracy of our layout analysis method in which headings determined by users and those extracted by the method were compared for 166 evaluation pages. The accuracy is 71.4%.

The inconsistency is divided into two patterns: excess of headings or deficiency of them. The analysis engine was designed to extract more headings. Even if too many headings are extracted, users can confirm the content within the overview selectively and they do not have to translate the detailed view. We recognized the browser had no problem in practical use.

Consequently, since they can reach all detailed views and archive the goal, the proposed browser was effective.

6 Conclusion

This paper proposed an adaptive-UI using a semantic over-viewing method. This method extracts headings and semantic blocks by analyzing a layout structure of a web page. By using the information, it can provide a semantic overview of the web page. This method allows users grasp the overall structure of pages. The features of the method are as follows.

- It reduces the number of operations to target information to about 6% by moving along semantic blocks
- It reduces the cost of Web page creation because of adapting one Web page content to multi-terminals
- It proves more usable than the mobile browser by the evaluation for effectiveness, efficiency and satisfaction

In the future work, we will plan to improve the response on semantic browser. This work also extends a task besides browsing such as navigation between pages.

References

Baluja, S.: Browsing on Small Screens: Recasting Web-Page Segmentation into an Efficient Machine learning Framework. In: Proceedings of the 15th International Conference on World Wide Web (WWW2006), pp. 33–42 (May 2006)

Baudisch, P., Xie, X., Wang, C., Ma, W.Y.: Collapse-to-Zoom: Viewing Web Pages on Small Screen Devices by Interactively Removing Irrelevant Content. In: Proceedings of the 17th annual ACM Symposium on User Interface Software and Technology(UIST2004), pp. 91–94 (October 2004)

Britton, K.H., Case, R., Citron, A., Floyd, R., Li, Y., Seekamp, C., Topol, B., Tracey, K.: Transcoding: Extending e-business to new environment. IBM SYSTEMS JOURNAL 40(1), 153–178 (2001)

Chen, Y., Ma, W.Y., Zhang, H.: Detecting Web Page Structure for Adaptive Viewing on Small Form Factor Devices. In: Proceedings of the 12th International Conference on World Wide Web (WWW2003), pp. 225–233 (May 2003)

ISO - Ergonomic requirements for office work with visual display terminals (VDTs): -Part 11: Guidance on Usability, ISO9241-11 (1998)

Opera - Opera Software, cited (7/3/2007) http://www.opera.com/

Tatsumi, T., Asahi, T.: Analyzing Web Page Headings Considering Various Presentation. In: Proceedings of the 14th International Conference on World Wide Web (WWW2005), pp. 956–957 (May 2005)

Parush, A., Yuviler-Gavish, N.: Web Navigation Structures in Cellular Phones: the depth/breadth trade-off issue. International Journal of Human-Computer Studies 60, 753–770 (2004)

Evaluation of P2P Information Recommendation Based on Collaborative Filtering

Hidehiko Okada and Makoto Inoue

Kyoto Sangyo University
Kamigamo Motoyama, Kita-ku, Kyoto 603-8555, Japan
hidehiko@ics.kyoto-su.ac.jp

Abstract. Collaborative filtering is a social information recommendation/ filtering method, and the peer-to-peer (P2P) computer network is a network on which information is distributed on the peer-to-peer basis (each peer node works as a server, a client, and even a router). This research aims to develop a model of P2P information recommendation system based on collaborative filtering and evaluate the ability of the system by computer simulations based on the model. We previously proposed a simple model, and the model in this paper is a modified one that is more focused on recommendation agents and user-agent interactions. We have developed a computer simulator program and tested simulations with several parameter settings. From the results of the simulations, recommendation recall and precision are evaluated. Findings are that the agents are likely to overly recommend so that the recall score becomes high but the precision score becomes low.

Keywords: Multi agents, P2P network, information recommendation, collaborative filtering, simulation.

1 Introduction

Several information recommendation and filtering methods have been developed for solving the problem of information overloads [1-3]. One of the methods is collaborative filtering [4]. The method can discover information that a user does not yet know but other users (whose profiles are similar to the user in some point of view) know. An advantage of the method over content-based filtering methods is that collaborative filtering does not require analyses of information contents: precise semantic analysis of information contents is usually difficult for computer systems. Collaborative filtering can be applied to personalized recommendations. There will be two variations of such recommendation systems that utilize collaborative filtering on computer networks: a server-client based one and a peer-to-peer (P2P) based one [5-7]. The latter benefits its scalability and flexibility.

To evaluate effectiveness of an application system on a large-scale P2P network, a large number of nodes must participate in the evaluation, but obtaining the participation and cooperation of the large number of nodes in a short period of time is usually difficult. Instead of evaluating the system in the real world, it will be effective

J. Jacko (Ed.): Human-Computer Interaction, Part III, HCII 2007, LNCS 4552, pp. 449–458, 2007.

to pre-evaluate the system by developing a simulator. Related researches have developed P2P network simulators (e.g., [8]), but a simulator for P2P information distribution systems based on collaborative filtering is still a research challenge. We previously proposed a model of P2P information recommendation system based on collaborative filtering [9]. In this paper, we propose a modified model that is more focused on recommendation agents and user-agent interactions. We have developed a computer simulator program to evaluate the ability of recommendation agents based on our model. By using the program, we have tested simulations with several parameter settings. From the results of the simulations, the ability of agents is evaluated.

2 P2P Information Recommendation Model Based on Collaborative Filtering

The basic idea of our simulation model is as follows. First, a P2P network includes several nodes (computers), and a user uses a computer that works as a node in the P2P network (Fig.1). Each user periodically receives recommendations of some data items from an agent that serves for the user. An agent determines which items to recommend by collaborative filtering with some neighbor nodes. Of the items recommended by an agent, a user accepts those which meet his/her preference and rejects the others.

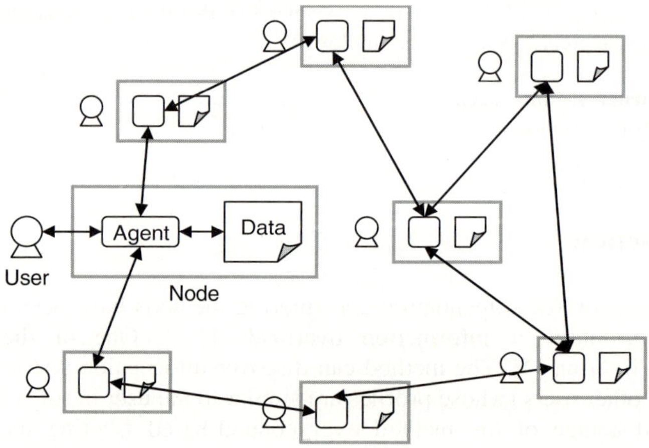

Fig. 1. Nodes, Users and Agents in a P2P Network

Based on this idea, our system model consists of the following components.

- Network model
- Data model
- Agent model
- User model

2.1 Network Model

Suppose a P2P network consists of N nodes (computers). Each node has a list of neighbor nodes with which the node can communicate. The node lists are updated when agents communicate with each other: when an agent A1 of a node N1 communicate with another agent A2 of another node N2, A1 (A2) merges the node list of A2 (A1) node with the node list of its own node. Fig. 2 shows an example. The left part of the figure shows that agent A1 initiates to communicate with agent A2 (A1 can find A2 because N2 is included in the node list of N1). The right part of the figure shows that node lists of N1 and N2 are updated: the underlined nodes are added from the list of partner node. A2 adds N1 in the list of N2 because A2 detects N1 by this communication and N1 is not included in the list of N2. As shown in this example, an agent can find new nodes on the network each time the agent communicates with another agent. Thus, the agent becomes able to search for data to recommend from more neighbor nodes.

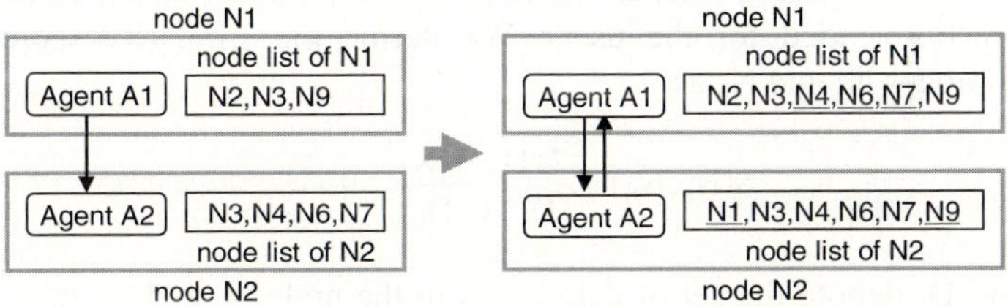

Fig. 2. Example of Node Lists Updated by Agents

2.2 Data Model

Suppose there are D data items in total, and each item belongs to a data category with some degree. In the case where data items are musical ones, the categories can be blues, classical, pop, jazz, etc. Table 1 shows an example of data items and membership scores of the items to data categories. In this example, date item D1 belongs to data category C1 completely and not to C2 and C3 at all: the membership scores are in [0, 1] and the higher the score is, the more the data item belongs to the data category.

The vector of category membership scores is attached to each data item as metadata.

2.3 Agent Model

The most important component in our system model is the agent model, because the design of agents determines the ability of the recommendation system. Each node includes a recommendation agent that serves for the user of the node. Each agent periodically recommends data items determined by collaborative filtering with some neighbor nodes.

Table 1. Example of Data Items and Their Membership Scores to Data Categories

Data Item	Data Category			
	C1	C2	C3	...
D1	1.0	0.0	0.0	...
D2	0.0	1.0	0.5	...
D3	1.0	1.0	0.0	...
...	...	...	...	...

An agent of a node first selects some nodes in the current node list. The nodes can be selected, for example, randomly, based on the past selection history, or based on similarity scores (described next) at the last communication. Then, the agent communicates with each agent in the selected nodes, checks the data in each selected node, and calculates similarity score between its own node and each selected node. The similarity scores are used for the collaborative filtering: the more similar set of data items a neighbor node has, the more probable the data items includes useful ones for the user of its own nodes (i.e., the more probable the data items includes items that should be recommended for the user). We define the similarity score $S(N_a, N_b)$ between two nodes N_a and N_b as

$$S(N_a, N_b) = \frac{2|D_a \cap D_b|}{|D_a| + |D_b|} . \quad (1)$$

where D_a and D_b denote the set of data items in the node N_a and N_b respectively and $|X|$ denotes the number of data items in the set X. The score S becomes the largest 1.0 in the case the two nodes have the same data items and becomes the smallest 0.0 in the case $D_a \cap D_b = \Phi$.

The agent then extracts data items that the selected nodes have but its own node does not yet have, and determines which of the extracted items to recommend based on a probability defined as a function of the similarity score: a data item found in a neighbor node with a larger/smaller similarity score is recommended with higher/lower probability. Fig. 3 shows examples of the recommendation probability function. In the case of (a), an item found in a node with similarity score x is recommended with the probability x. In the case of (b) and (c), an item found in a node with smaller similarity is recommended with much less probability (zero if $S < 0.5$ in the (c) case). Thus, the design of this function characterizes agent recommendation behavior.

2.4 User Model

Each user periodically receives recommendations of data items (that the user does not yet have) from an agent that serves for the user. In the real world, a user will accept some of the recommended data items that meet his/her preference (the accepted items are added to the data set of his/her own nodes) and will reject the others. To simulate this user behavior, users' implicit preferences on the data items are denoted as preference score vectors in our user model. The user preference vectors are similar to

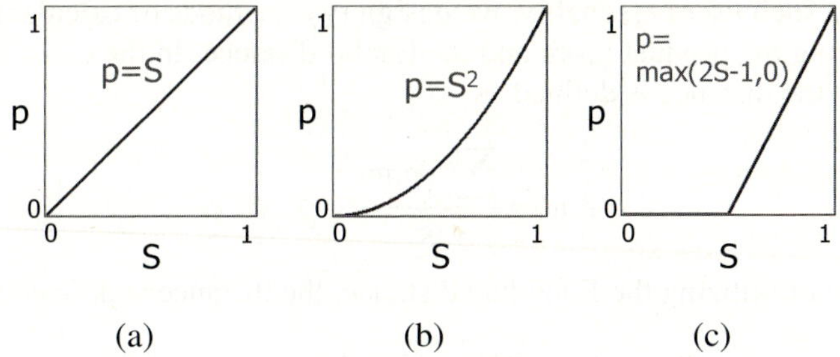

Fig. 3. Examples of Recommendation Probability Function

Table 2. Example of Users and Their Preference Scores on Data Categories

User	Data Category			
	C1	C2	C3	...
U1	1.0	0.0	0.0	...
U2	0.0	0.3	0.8	...
U3	0.2	1.0	0.0	...
...	...	...	...	...

the category membership vectors of data items. Table 2 shows an example of users and preference scores of the users on data categories. In this example, user U1 prefers data category C1 to the maximum degree and not C2 and C3 at all: the preference score is in [0, 1] and the higher the score is, the more the user prefers the data category.

Note that the user preference vector of each user is *implicit* so that an agent does not know the preference vector of the user: our model of recommendation system does not require users to express (i.e., input to the system) their preferences on data categories. The user preference vectors are used only to simulate the user behavior of data item acceptance/rejection.

Based on the preference vector of a user and the membership vector of a data item, a distance value of the two vectors is calculated to evaluate the degree to which the data item meets the user's preference. The method of calculating the distance characterizes users' personality. Suppose the user U1 in Table 2 receives the recommendation of data items D1, D2 and D3 in Table 1.

- Suppose U1 minds whether data items belong much to categories he/she prefers much (C1) but *does not mind* whether the items belong to categories he/she prefers little (C2 and C3). In this case, U1 will accept D1, *D3* and reject D2. We denote this type of user as user type 1.
- Suppose U1 minds whether data items belong much to categories he/she prefers much (C1) and *also minds* whether the items belong little to categories he/she prefers little (C2 and C3). In this case, U1 will accept only D1 and reject D2, *D3*. We denote this type of user as user type 2.

To simulate such user personality, we design two methods of calculating the vector distance utilizing the product score and the Euclid distance. In the case of utilizing the product score, the distance is defined as

$$d(\vec{p}, \vec{m}) = \frac{\sum_{i=1}^{c} p_i m_i}{c} . \tag{2}$$

and in the case of utilizing the Euclidian distance, the distance is defined as

$$d(\vec{p}, \vec{m}) = \frac{\sqrt{\sum_{i=1}^{c} (p_i - m_i)^2}}{c} . \tag{3}$$

where $\vec{p} = \{p_1, p_2, \ldots\}$ is the user preference vector, $\vec{m} = \{m_1, m_2, \ldots\}$ is the membership vector of a data item, and c is the number of data categories.

In the case of utilizing the product score, a user accepts data items of which $d(\vec{p}, \vec{m})$ is larger than a threshold value, or accepts a data item at a probability defined as a monotonically non-decreasing function of $d(\vec{p}, \vec{m})$. The value of $d(\vec{p}, \vec{m})$ does not increase for data categories of which the user does not prefer at all (i.e., $p_i = 0$). Thus, this variation can simulate the type 1 users.

On the other hand, in the case of utilizing the Euclidian distance, a user accepts data items of which $d(\vec{p}, \vec{m})$ is smaller than a threshold value, or accepts a data item at a probability defined as a monotonically non-increasing function of $d(\vec{p}, \vec{m})$. The value of $d(\vec{p}, \vec{m})$ can increase for some data category c* even though a user does not prefer c* at all (i.e., $p_{c*}=0$): $(p_{c*} - m_{c*})^2 > 0$ if $p_{c*} \neq m_{c*}$. Thus, this variation can simulate the type 2 users.

3 Evaluation of Recommendation Ability by Simulation

We have developed a computer simulator program to evaluate the ability of P2P information recommendation based on our model. By using the program, we have tested simulations with several parameter settings. From the results of the simulations, the ability of agents in our model is evaluated. Recall and precision can be used as metrics of the ability in information recommendations [10]. The metrics are defined as follows.

$$\text{Recall} = \frac{|D_{rec} \cap D_{rel}|}{|D_{rel}|} . \tag{4}$$

$$\text{Precision} = \frac{|D_{rec} \cap D_{rel}|}{|D_{rec}|} . \tag{5}$$

where D_{rec} is the set of data items a user has been *rec*ommended and D_{rel} is the set of data items the user can accept if recommended (i.e., *rel*evant items).

The following shows an example of the simulation designs. The basic parameters are designed as shown in Table 3.

Table 3. Example of Basic Simulation Parameter Design

Number of users (nodes)	100
Total number of data items	100
Number of initial data items for each user	5
Number of data categories	8
Number of nodes an agent communicates for a try of recommendation	3

Each of the 100 users is randomly either the type 1 or 2 user. A preference vector for a user is designed so that p_i = 1.0 for a randomly selected category and p_i is a random value in [0, 0.3] for the other seven categories. This design simulates a situation in which each user prefers one of the eight categories very much and not the other seven categories so much.

The number of data items is also 100. A membership vector of each item is designed in the same way as a preference vector: m_i = 1.0 for a randomly selected category and m_i is a random value in [0, 0.3] for the other seven categories. This design simulates a situation in which each data item belongs to one of the eight categories very much and not the other seven categories so much. Thus, the relevant data item set D_{rel} for a user is likely to include items of which m_x = 1.0 for the category x where p_x =1.0. In this design, the 100 users and the 100 data items are likely to be categorized into eight groups.

The set D_{rel} for a user is determined as follows. The distance $d(\vec{p},\vec{m})$ is calculated 100 times for a single user and the 100 data items. If the user is type 1, $d(\vec{p},\vec{m})$ is based on the vector product so that the value $d(\vec{p},\vec{m})$ becomes *larger* as a data item meets the preference of the user more. The maximun value of $d(\vec{p},\vec{m})$ among the 100 data items are calculated (d_{max}), and D_{rel} for the user is determined as the set of data items of which $d(\vec{p},\vec{m}) \geq 0.9 * d_{max}$. In the same manner, D_{rel} for a type 2 user is determined. If the user is type 2, $d(\vec{p},\vec{m})$ is based on the Euclid distance so that the value $d(\vec{p},\vec{m})$ becomes *smaller* as a data item meets the preference of the user more. The minimum value of $d(\vec{p},\vec{m})$ among the 100 data items are calculated (d_{min}), and D_{rel} for the user is determined as the set of data items of which $d(\vec{p},\vec{m}) \leq 0.3 * d_{min}$. The threshold factors 0.9 and 0.3 are determined so that $|D_{rel}|$ becomes around 10 to 15.

Data items that each user initially has are five items randomly selected from D_{rel} of the user. In the initial state, the similarity score $S(N_a, N_b)$ between two nodes N_a and N_b is determined by these five items in N_a and N_b.

Suppose each of the 100 users receives recommendation once a specific interval of time: it is defined as one cycle that all users receive recommendation once in a random order. For a try of recommendation, an agent randomly selects three nodes in the current node list and determines data items to recommend by collaborative filtering with the three nodes.

As the recommendation probability function that characterizes agent behavior, the function in Fig 3(a) is applied. The simulation continued until no user accepted one or more items in two successive cycles.

The result of simulation with the above design is shown in Figs. 4, 5 and Table 4. Fig. 4 shows the number of users who accepted some of the recommended items and the total number of data items accepted by the users. This trial of simulation continued to 63 cycles. The maximum and mean numbers of accepting users in a cycle were 22 and 8. In average, 1.2 items were accepted per accepting user in a cycle. These values seem relatively small: this will be because, in this simulation, the 100 users (nodes) are implicitly categorized into 8+ groups and the number of nodes an agent communicates for a try of recommendation is small (three: see Table 3). Fig. 5 and Table 4 show the results of recommendation recall and precision. Fig 5(a) & Table 4(a) show the results for type 1, and Fig 5(b) & Table 4(b) show the results for type 2. A plot in Fig. 5 represents a value of recall or precision for a user (the threshold value of $d(\vec{p}, \vec{m})$ is not the same even for the users of the same type because the preference vector $\vec{p}$ is not the same).

It should be noted that D_{rel} includes data items a users initially has: these items are the relevant ones but not the recommended ones. In the calculation of recall and precision scores, these initial items are removed from D_{rel}.

Findings from the results in Fig. 5 and Table 4 are as follows.

- The agents recommended very well in terms of recall. For both type 1 and 2 users, the mean recall scores were 0.98.
- On the other hand, the agents did not recommend so well in terms of precision. In the best case the precision score was 1.0 (so that no irrelevant item was recommended to the user) but in the worst case the score was 0.11. The average precision score was 0.75 (or 0.72) for type 1 (or 2) users, which was smaller than the average recall scores.

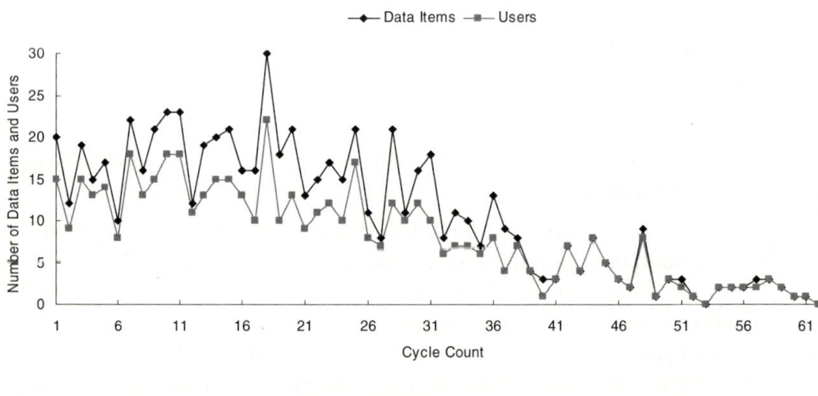

Fig. 4. Numbers of Accepting Users and Accepted Data Items

We tested additional trials of simulations in which the recommendation probability function p(S) was changed from that in Fig. 3(a) to Fig. 3(b) and Fig. 3(c), but the results were similar to the above: high scores of recall and lower scores of precision

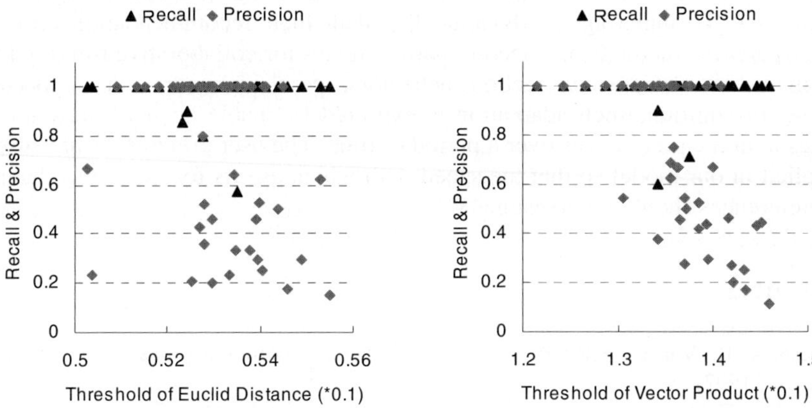

(a) Type 1 Users (b) Type 2 Users

Fig. 5. Recall and Precision Scores for Each User

Table 4. Statistics of Recall and Precision Scores

	ave	S.D.	max	min
Recall	0.98	0.067	1.0	0.57
Precision	0.75	0.32	1.0	0.15
F	0.80	0.25	1.0	0.26

(a) Type 1 Users

	ave	S.D.	max	min
Recall	0.98	0.071	1.0	0.60
Precision	0.72	0.30	1.0	0.11
F	0.79	0.24	1.0	0.20

(b) Type 2 Users

than recall scores. It was worse still that recall scores could be smaller in the cases (b) and (c) than in the case (a) because in the cases of (b) and (c) the recommendation probability becomes smaller.

These results indicate that agents in our P2P recommendation system model are likely to overly recommend. We find that future research should include improvements in the design of agents for better precision.

4 Conclusion

In this paper, we proposed a model of P2P information recommendation based on collaborative filtering. The model is a modified one from the model we proposed before. We have developed a computer simulator of recommendation network system based on the model. The ability of recommendation agents was evaluated by analyzing results of simulations with experimental system parameter designs. It is found that the agents are likely to overly recommend so that the recall score becomes high but the precision score becomes low. Improvement in the agent design for better precision is a research challenge in our future work.

A promising solution to the challenge is the design of agent adaptation to behaviors of their user. To make agents dynamically adapt their recommendation probability functions and the methods of selecting partner nodes for collaborative filtering to logs of their users' acceptance/rejection behaviors, precision scores are expected to improve. In addition, such adaptation is expected to enable agents follow temporal changes in users' preferences over a period of time. The user preferences are supposed as implicit in our model so that the speed with which agents follow to the changes in user preferences should be investigated.

References

1. Resnick, P., Varian, H.R.: Recommender Systems. Communications of the ACM 40(3), 56–58 (1997)
2. Riecken, D.: Introduction: Personalized Views of Personalization. Communications of the ACM 43(8), 26–28 (2000)
3. Konstan, J.A.: Introduction to Recommender Systems: Algorithms and Evaluation. ACM Transactions on Information Systems 22(1), 1–4 (2004)
4. Goldberg, D., Nichols, D., Oki, B.M., Terry, D.: Using Collaborative Filtering to Weave an Information Tapestry. Communications of the ACM 35(12), 61–70 (1992)
5. Oram, A. (ed.): Peer-to-peer: Harnessing the Benefits of a Disruptive Technology. O'Reilly and Associates (2001)
6. Lethin, R.: SPECIAL ISSUE: Technical and Social Components of Peer-to-peer Computing - Introduction. Communications of the ACM 46(2), 30–32 (2003)
7. Androutsellis-Theotokis, S., Spinellis, D.: A Survey of Peer-to-peer Content Distribution Technologies. ACM Computing Surveys 36m(4), 335–371 (2004)
8. Yanagihara, T., Iwai, M., Tokuda, H.: Designing and Implementing a Simulator for P2P Networks, Special Interest Groups on System Software and Operating System. Information Processing Society of Japan(in Japanese) 2002(60), 157–162 (2002)
9. Okada, H.: Simulation Model of P2P Information Distribution based on Collaborative Filtering. In: Proc. 11th Int. Conf. on Human-Computer Interaction (HCI International 2005), CD-ROM (2005)
10. Herlocker, J.L., Konstan, J.A., Terveen, L.G., Riedl, J.T.: Evaluating Collaborative Filtering Recommender Systems. ACM Transactions on Information Systems 22(1), 5–53 (2004)

Understanding the Social Relationship Between Humans and Virtual Humans

Sung Park and Richard Catrambone

School of Psychology and Graphics, Visualization, and Usability Center (GVU)
Georgia Institute of Technology
gtg116s@mail.gatech.edu, rc7@prism.gatech.edu

Abstract. Our review surveys a range of human-human relationship models and research that might provide insights to understanding the social relationship between humans and virtual humans. This involves investigating several social constructs (expectations, communication, trust, etc.) that are identified as key variables that influence the relationship between people and how these variables should be implemented in the design for an effective and useful virtual human. This theoretical analysis contributes to the foundational theory of human computer interaction involving virtual humans.

Keywords: Embodied conversational agent; virtual agent; animated character; avatar; social interaction.

1 Introduction

Interest in virtual humans or embodied conversational agents (ECAs) is growing in the realm of human computer interaction. Many believe that interfaces based on virtual humans have great potential to be beneficial. Anthropomorphizing an interface means adding human-like characteristics such as speech, gestures, and facial expressions. These components can be very effective and efficient at conveying information and communicating emotion. The human face, especially, is powerful in transmitting a great deal of information efficiently [9]. For example, a virtual human with a confused face might be better (e.g., faster) at letting a user know that the virtual human does not understand the user's command than simply displaying "I don't understand" on the screen. The text requires the user to read, which might be disruptive to the main task the user is involved in [7].

Virtual humans can work as an assistant, such as a travel agent or investment advisor, and help with tasks that require managing vast amounts of information [7]. Personified interfaces are also known to be engaging and appropriate for entertainment tasks [15]. In clinical settings, virtual humans can be useful as well (for a review, see [11]). Some studies noted that exposure to a virtual audience might be helpful in diminishing the fear of public speaking [1]. Virtual humans have also been adopted in the development of virtual classroom scenarios for the assessment and treatment of Attention Deficit Hyperactivity Disorder (ADHD) [21].

J. Jacko (Ed.): Human-Computer Interaction, Part III, HCII 2007, LNCS 4552, pp. 459–464, 2007.

Interest in understanding the social dimension of the interaction between users and virtual humans is growing in the research field. Some research suggests that there is a striking similarity between how humans interact with one another and how a human and a virtual human interact. For example, a study by Nass, Steuer, and Tauber [19] claimed that individuals' interactions with computers are fundamentally social. Their evidence suggests that users can be induced to elicit social behaviors (e.g., direct requests for evaluations elicit more positive responses, other-praise is perceived as more valid than self-praise) even though users assume machines do not possess emotions, feelings, or "selves".

In order to examine the social dimension of the interaction between users and virtual humans, we survey a range of human-human relationship models and research that might provide insights to understanding the social relationship between humans and virtual humans.

2 Social Interaction with Virtual Humans

An understanding of the nature of human relationships might provide insights to the social aspects of the interaction people can have with virtual humans. People build and maintain relationships through a combination of verbal and nonverbal behaviors within the context of face-to-face conversation. The relationship is formed based on a dyadic interaction where a change in the behavior and the cognitive and emotional state of a person produces a change in the state of the other person [14]. However, in the human-virtual human relationship, this change will mostly occur in the human's state because the virtual human typically takes an assistant or advisory role.

Because relationships are often defined in terms of what people do together, it is important to survey the types of tasks people might do with a virtual human. A virtual human can help with tasks ranging from one-time tasks to tasks that require a larger amount of time or that are done on multiple occasions (see Table 1).

Table 1. Different types of tasks a virtual human might assist (human interacting with virtual human) or people might do together (human interacting with human) distinguished by the length of the interaction

	Short Term Interaction	Long Term Interaction
Human Interacting With Virtual Human	• Providing information or facts (e.g., displaying information from a kiosk booth) • Providing recommendations for a simple task (e.g., which items to pack for a trip to a foreign country) • Helping carry out a simple procedure (e.g., editing a document)	• Assisting a user through a month-long health behavior change program [4] • Teaching a user some skill that requires several or many sessions
Human Interacting With Human	• Service encounter	• Tasks that form a service relationship (i.e., customer – service provider) • Tasks that form an advisor-advisee relationship (e.g., graduate student – advisor)

2.1 Service Relationship (Buyer-Seller Relationship)

A good deal of research about social relationships has been done at both ends of the time spectrum. Tasks done in a shorter time frame with a virtual human can be influenced by studies of service interactions defined as a service *encounter* where there are no apparent expectations of future interactions. This is differentiated from a service *relationship*, where a customer expects to interact with the service provider again in the future. Interestingly, a marriage metaphor has been used to make contributions to the understanding of the service relationship [8]. This enabled us to explore how relationships develop and change, the importance of social/relational elements (e.g., trust, commitment), and cooperative problem solving.

One such important variable in the marriage metaphor is expectation. Expectation relates to behaviors that contribute to the outcome (e.g., a partner behaving in a cooperative and collaborative manner) and the outcomes themselves [3]. Partners might improve interaction by either altering expectations on desired outcomes or by altering expectations on how they would interact. With virtual humans, users' expectations are certainly different from when they interact with traditional windows and icons. Users expect more social behavior and more flexibility, yet at the same time, they are well aware of the capabilities and the limitations of virtual humans. Xiao [25] claimed that expectations or perceptions of users on virtual humans are subject to enormous individual differences. For this reason, Xiao further emphasizes the importance of flexibility in virtual human design. We think that providing sufficient training or practice with the virtual human might provide the opportunity and time for users to adjust their expectations of what they can achieve through the interaction and how to best interact with virtual humans.

In a service relationship, communication behaviors influence problem-solving efficacy. This includes *nondefensive listening*, paying attention to what a partner is saying while not interrupting; *active listening*, summarizing partner's viewpoint; *disclosure*, sharing of ideas and information, direct stating of point of view; and *editing*, interacting politely and not overacting to negative events [6]. One partner's communication behavior will influence the other partner's. For example, a failure to edit negative emotions will result in the expression of reciprocal negativity from the other partner [8]. In another example, a unilateral disclosure of information or ideas can elicit reciprocal disclosure from the other's partner. The nature of the tasks determines the nature of communication between users and virtual humans. The design of a communication method should be a deliberate one. When a task requires disclosure of a user's view on a certain event, it is probably a good idea to provide virtual human's (i.e., designer's) view first and ask one in return.

Expectations, communications, and appraisals (how one might evaluate the other) all influence the longer-term outcomes of the relationship such as satisfaction, trust, and commitment. Most marketing studies mentioned that service providers should put emphasis on these variables to extend their relationship with their customers [17]. Designers who are specifically developing virtual humans for a long-term relationship should be mindful of these factors.

2.2 Advisor-Advisee Relationship

Another long-term relationship that has been studied rigorously is the advisor-advisee relationship. Advice-giving situations are interactions where advisors attempt to help the advisees find a solution for their problems [18] and to reduce uncertainty [24]. Finding a solution or making a decision is social because information or advice is provided by others.

Research on advice taking has shown that decisions to follow a recommendation are not based on an advisee's assessment of the recommended options alone [13] but also on other factors such as characteristics of the advisee, the advisor, and the situation. For example, advisees are more influenced by advisors with a higher level of trust [24], confidence [23], and a reputation for accuracy [26].

Trust is the expectation that the advisor is both competent and reliable [2]. Trust cannot emerge without social uncertainty (i.e., there must be some risk of getting advice that is not good for the advisee); trust can also reduce uncertainty by limiting the range of behavior expected from another [16]. Bickmore and Cassell [5] implemented a model of social dialogue between humans and virtual humans and demonstrated how it has an effect on trust.

Confidence is the strength with which a person believes that an opinion or decision is the best possible [20]. Higher confidence can act as a cue to expertise and can influence the advisee to accept the advice. With virtual humans, a confident voice, facial expression, and tone of language might increase the acceptance of the virtual human's recommendations.

Another factor in this relationship is the emotional bond or rapport. Building rapport is crucial in maintaining a collaborative relationship. Studies showed a significant emotional bond between therapist and client [12], between supervisor and trainee [10], and between graduate advisor and student [22]. It might be interesting to examine if rapport between humans and virtual humans varies as a function of the length of the relationship, display of affect by the agent, and the type of task.

There are factors in a human-virtual human relationship that are likely to have a different weighting relative to a human-human relationship. For example, the human-human advisor-advisee relationship can have monetary interdependency. The advisor might receive profits from advisee's decision or suffer loss of reputation or even job security [24]. The decision making process is affected by this monetary factor which does not exist in a human-virtual human advisory relationship. In another example, studies showed that advisors (e.g., travel agents, friends) conducted a more balanced information search than the advisee; however, when presenting information to their advisee, travel agents provided more information supporting their recommendation than conflicting with it [13]. Assuming virtual humans provide objective and balanced information to the users, this might favor virtual humans over humans in some advisor-advisee relationships.

3 Conclusion

Our review surveyed a range of human-human relationship models and research that might provide insights to understanding the social relationship between humans and virtual humans. We specifically considered two long-term relationship models: the service and advisor-advisee relationship model. We delved into various social constructs (expectations, communication, trust, etc.) that are identified as key variables that influence the relationship between people and how these variables should be implemented in the design for an effective and useful virtual human. This theoretical study contributes to the foundational theory of human computer interaction involving virtual humans.

References

1. Anderson, P., Rothbaum, B.O., Hodges, L.F.: Virtual reality exposure in the treatment of social anxiety. Cognitive and Behavioral Practice 10, 240–247 (2003)
2. Barber, B.: The logic and limits of trust. Rutgers University Press, NJ (1983)
3. Benun, I.: Cognitive components of martial conflict. Behavior Psychotherapy 47, 302–309 (1986)
4. Bickmore, T., Picard, R.: Establishing and maintaining long-term human-computer Relationships. ACM Transactions on Computer-Human Interaction 12(2), 293–327 (2005)
5. Bickmore, T., Cassell, J.: Relational agents: a model and implementation of building user trust. In: Proc. CHI 2001, pp. 396–399. ACM Press, New York (2001)
6. Bussod, N., Jacobson, N.: Cognitive behavioral martial therapy. Counseling Psychologist 11(3), 57–63 (1983)
7. Catrambone, R., Stasko, J., Xiao, J.: ECA user interface paradigm: Experimental findings within a framework for research. In: Pelachaud, C., Ruttkay, Z. (eds.) From brows to trust: Evaluating embodied conversational agents, pp. 239–267. Kluwer Academic/Plenum Publishers, NY (2004)
8. Celuch, K., Bantham, J., Kasouf, C.: An extension of the marriage metaphor in buyer-seller relationships: an exploration of individual level process dynamics. Journal of Business Research 59, 573–581 (2006)
9. Collier, G.: Emotional Expression. Lawrence Erlbaum Associates, Hillsdale, NJ (1985)
10. Efstation, J., Patton, M., Kardash, C.: Measuring the working alliance in counselor supervision. Journal of Counseling Psychology 37, 322–329 (1990)
11. Glantz, K., Rizzo, A., Graap, K.: Virtual reality for psychotherapy: current reality and future possibilities. Psychotherapy: Theory, Research, Practice, Training 40, 55–67 (2003)
12. Horvath, A., Greenberg, L.: Development and validation of the working alliance inventory. Journal of Counseling Psychology 36, 223–233 (1989)
13. Jonas, E., Schulz-Hardt, S., Frey, D., Thelen, N.: Confirmation bias in Sequential information search after preliminary decisions: An expansion of Dissonance theoretical research on selective exposure to information. Journal of Personality and Social Psychology 80, 557–571 (2001)
14. Kelly, H.: Epilogue: An essential science. In: Kelly, H., Berscheid, A., Christensen, J., Harvey, T., Huston, G., Levinger, E., McClintock, L., Peplau, L., Peterson, D. (eds.) Close Relationships, pp. 486–503. Freeman, NY (1983)
15. Koda, T.: Agents with faces: A study on the effect of personification of software agents, Master's thesis, Massachusetts Institute of Technology, Cambridge, MA (1996)
16. Kollock, R.: The emergence of exchange structures: an experimental study of uncertainty, commitment, and trust. American Journal of Sociology 100, 313–345 (1994)
17. Lee, S., Dubinsky, A.: Influence of salesperson characteristics and customer emotion on retail dyadic relationships. The International Review of Retail, Distribution and Consumer Research, 21–36 (2003)

18. Lippitt, R.: Dimensions of the consultant's job. Journal of Social Issues 15, 5–12 (1959)
19. Nass, C., Steuer, J., Tauber, E.: Computers are social actors. In: Proc. CHI 1994, pp. 72–78. ACM Press, New York (1994)
20. Peterson, D., Pitz, G.: Confidence, uncertainty, and the use of information. Journal of Experimental Psychology: Learning, Memory, and Cognition 14, 85–92 (1988)
21. Rizzo, A., Buckwalter, J., Zaag, V.: Virtual environment applications in clinical neuropsychology. In: Proceedings in IEEE Virtual Reality, 63–70 (2000)
22. Schlosser, L., Gelso, C.: Measuring working alliance in advisor-advisee relationships in graduate school. Journal of Counseling Psychology 48(2), 157–167 (2001)
23. Sniezek, J., Buckley, T.: Cueing and cognitive conflict in judge-advisor decision making. Organizational Behavior and Human Decision Processes 62, 159–174 (1995)
24. Sniezek, J., van Swol, L.: Trust, confidence, and expertise in a judge-advisor system. Organizational Behavior and Human Decision Processes 84, 288–307 (2001)
25. Xiao, J.: Empirical studies on embodied conversational agents. Doctoral dissertation, Georgia Institute of Technology, Atlanta, GA (2006)
26. Yaniv, I., Kleinberger, E.: Advice taking in decision making: Egocentric discounting and reputation formation. Organizational Behavior and Human Decision Processes 83, 260–281 (2000)

EREC-II in Use – Studies on Usability and Suitability of a Sensor System for Affect Detection and Human Performance Monitoring

Christian Peter[1], Randolf Schultz[1], Jörg Voskamp[1], Bodo Urban[1], Nadine Nowack[2], Hubert Janik[2], Karin Kraft[2], and Roland Göcke[3,*]

[1] Human-Centered Interaction Technologies, Fraunhofer IGD Rostock, J. Jungius Str. 11, 18059 Rostock, Germany
{cpeter,rschultz,voskamp,urban}@igd-r.fraunhofer.de
[2] Chair of Complementary Medicine University of Rostock, E. Heydemann Str. 6, 18057 Rostock, Germany
{nadine.nowack,karin.kraft,hubert.janik}@med.uni-rostock.de
[3] NICTA Canberra Research Laboratory & RSISE, Australian National University, Canberra ACT 0200, Australia
roland.goecke@nicta.com.au

Abstract. Interest in emotion detection is increasing significantly. For research and development in the field of Affective Computing, in smart environments, but also for reliable non-lab medical and psychological studies or human performance monitoring, robust technologies are needed for detecting evidence of emotions in persons under everyday conditions. This paper reports on evaluation studies of the EREC-II sensor system for acquisition of emotion-related physiological parameters. The system has been developed with a focus on easy handling, robustness, and reliability. Two sets of studies have been performed covering 4 different application fields: medical, human performance in sports, driver assistance, and multimodal affect sensing. Results show that the different application fields pose different requirements mainly on the user interface, while the hardware for sensing and processing the data proved to be in an acceptable state for use in different research domains.

Keywords: Physiology sensors, Emotion detection, Evaluation, Multimodal affect sensing, Driver assistance, Human performance, Cognitive load, Medical treatment, Peat baths.

1 Introduction

Emotions are currently discovered by numerous researchers in different fields of research and are regarded to be a potential key to many problems unsolved or observations not understood up to now. This includes designers of physical or

* National ICT Australia is funded by the Australian Government's Backing Australia's Ability initiative, in part through the Australian Research Council.

J. Jacko (Ed.): Human-Computer Interaction, Part III, HCII 2007, LNCS 4552, pp. 465–474, 2007.

artificial objects, human-computer interaction researchers, interface designers, human-human communication specialists, phone service companies, marketing specialists, therapists for mental or physical discomforts or illnesses or, more general, people concerned about the well-being of other people. But also in the traditionally emotion-aware sciences, emotions get renewed attention due to the increased availability of novel technologies in this field. Among the multitude of possibilities for measuring emotion, cf. [11], the number of exploitable emotion channels for unobtrusive emotion monitoring is small. When mobile or at least non-lab acquisition of emotion-related physiological parameters is needed, the choices are very limited.

While facial expressions are one of the most obvious manifestations of emotions [8], their automatic detection is still a challenge (see [6]), although some progress has been made in recent years [1, 9]. Problems arise especially when the observed person moves about freely, since facial features can only be observed when the person is facing a camera. A similar problem arises with speech analysis, which requires a fairly constant distance between microphone and speaker (see [6]). Gesture and body movement/posture also contain signs of emotions, but still are not sufficiently enough investigated to provide for robust emotion recognition. Emotion-related changes of physiological parameters have been studied for a long time (e.g. [3, 4, 7, 10, 14]) and thereby presently can be considered to be the most investigated and best understood indicators of emotion. It is hence assumed that physiology sensors can become a good and reliable source on emotion-related data of a user, despite their disadvantage of needing physical contact.

There are various commercial systems available for measuring emotion-related peripheral physiological parameters, such as Thought Technologies' Procomp family, Mindmedia's Nexus device, Schuhfried's Biofeedback 2000 x-pert, or BodyMedia's SenseWear system. However, those systems have been developed for medical or psychological studies which usually take place in fixed lab environments, or for sportsmen who have lower requirements on time resolution and availability of the data than most HCI applications have. Having realised the shortcomings of commercial systems, the scientific community also developed prototypical sensor systems for unobtrusive measuring physiological states. These are mainly feasibility studies with in part very interesting sensor placements and application ideas [2, 12, 15, 16].

This paper reports on evaluation studies of one of those. The EREC sensor system developed at Fraunhofer IGD Rostock allows to wirelessly measure heart rate, skin conductance, and skin temperature. The evaluations have been performed independently by two groups and covered 4 different application fields. In a medical environment, the emotion-related physiological reactions on peat baths were examined. The second study investigated human performance in sports, and a third dealt with driver assistance issues. The fourth report gives account on inclusion of the EREC system into a multimodal affective sensing approach.

Section 2 describes the improvements of the used versions of the system compared to the initial system described in [15]. This is followed by the evaluation reports in Section 3. A summary and outlook in Section 4 conclude the paper.

2 System Overview of the EREC-II Sensor System

The EREC system consists of two parts. The sensor unit uses a glove to host the sensing elements for skin resistance and skin temperature. It also collects heart rate data from a Polar heart rate chest belt and measures the environmental air temperature. The base unit is wirelessly connected to the sensor unit, receives the pre-validated sensor data, evaluates them, stores them on local memory and/or sends the evaluated data to a processing host. In the following, more details are given in comparison to the EREC-I system described in [15]:

(a)

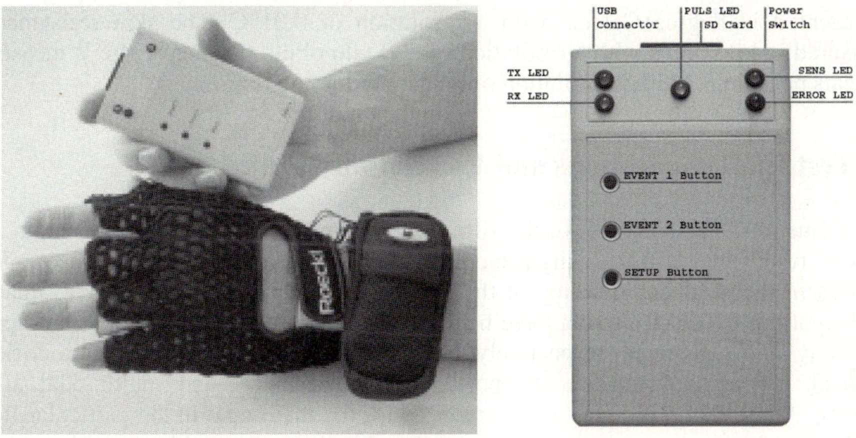

(b)

Fig. 1. (a) In EREC-II the sensing circuitry is stored in a wrist pocket, making the glove lighter and improving ventilation. (b) Base unit of EREC-IIb.

2.1 EREC-II Sensor Unit

The sensor unit is functionally identical to that of EREC-I, with small changes to the circuit layout. The sensing elements are fixed now on a cycling glove. As shown in Figure 1(a), the sensor circuitry is not integrated in the glove, but put into a small wrist pocket. Connection between sensing elements and circuitry is established by a thin cable and a PS/2 shaped socket. As with EREC-I, the skin conductivity sensor is implemented two-fold. The skin temperature is taken at two different positions as well and integrated in one sensor, leading to higher accuracy and higher resolution. Also in the sensor unit, the ambient air temperature near the device is measured as already done with EREC-I. Skin temperature as well as skin conductivity are sampled 20 times per second each. Heart rate is still measured using Polar technology.

Data are sent out by the heart rate sensor immediately after a beat has been detected. All collected data are immediately digitized and assessed for sensor failure as was done in the EREC-I system. Based on the evaluation results, output data are prepared, wrapped into the EREC protocol and fitted with a CRC check sum. The data are then sent out by the integrated ISM-band transmitter.

2.2 EREC-II Base Unit

The base unit has undergone a major re-design (see Figure 1(b)). It has now a pocket-size case, no display, and uses an SD card for storing data permanently. There is still the possibility of a serial connection to a PC. The user interface consists of light emitting diodes (LEDs) for communicating different sensor and system states, and push buttons for the user to mark special events. As with EREC-I, sensor data are received from the sensor unit, transport errors are assessed (CRC), and reliability checks are performed each time new data are received. Validated data are sent out immediately to a connected PC and stored on the memory card at an average rate of 5 Hz. All data are made available in engineering units. The skin temperature is represented in degree Celsius with a resolution of 0.01°C. The skin resistance is measured in kilo ohms with a resolution of 300 kilo ohms. The heart rate is measured in beats per minute with a resolution of 1 beat per minute (bpm).

3 Test Implementations and Evaluation Studies

Over time, different versions of the EREC-II system have been developed and tested in field tests. They differ in slight modifications of the hardware in the base unit as well as in the software running on the base unit's microcontroller. Four evaluation studies of the EREC-II system have been performed independently by two groups in Germany and Australia, respectively. The studies covered the application fields medical, human performance in sports, driver assistance, and multimodal affect sensing. All studies were real-world studies with the main goal in the particular field. Evaluating the sensor system was a by-product kindly performed by or with the local staff. This section describes shortly the particulars of the different versions and, in more detail, the studies and their evaluation results.

3.1 EREC-IIa

System Particulars. EREC-IIa is the first version of the EREC-II series. Serial communication to a PC can be established by a RS232 connection. However, the SUB-D socket for the serial connection has been replaced by a miniUSB socket to save space in both the casing and on the printed circuit board. It can also be seen as a step towards a USB connection between PC and base unit. Data are stored on a SD card. The same data format and writing procedure is used as with the EREC-I system. Still, the memory card needs to be pre-formatted and has to contain an empty file which is then filled by the controller with sensor data in a proprietary file format.

The user interface of the device consists of 3 LEDs which use simple flash codes to signal different states. For instance, slow flashing of the sensor LED indicates that all sensors are working correctly, while fast flashing indicates failure of at least one sensor, with increasing flash frequency for an increasing number of failing sensors. This approach allows to use a few LEDs to deliver much information, which is beneficial for battery life. Two push buttons allow for simple user input, for instance, to mark special events. EREC-IIa can be seen in figure 1.

Evaluation. This study was performed over a period of 8 weeks by the Chair of Complementary Medicine of the University of Rostock, Germany, at the rehabilitation clinic "Moorbad Bad Doberan" (Bad Doberan, Germany) which has broad and long-standing experience in the application of peat in the treatment of various diseases.

Physiological response to peat baths
Hot peat is used for various medical indications such as relief of pain and general improvement of chronic skeletal and rheumatic diseases as well as gynaecological and dermatological problems. So far only subjective qualitative and unsystematic reports on the emotional reactions during and after a peat bath exist. Therefore, the study has been performed to investigate emotion-related physiological reactions of healthy persons in a single session of a peat bath and to obtain quantified evidence for their changes during this session. During the study, peat baths were performed as usual: 20 minutes peat bath (40.5°C), warm shower, and 20 minutes of rest. For study purposes, an additional 10 minutes for answering questionnaires were added at the beginning and the end of the bathing session. Thereby one session lasted for about one hour.

Electro-cardiographic (ECG) data were collected by a Holter monitor, and skin temperature and skin resistance measurements where gathered with the EREC-IIa system. The latter also recorded the room temperature near the sensors. At the beginning of the session, the subject put on the sensor glove and the ECG electrodes were fitted on the upper side of the left and right distal forearms. During the peat bath, only the subject's head and the distal forearms were outside the peat, with the hands resting on a handrest. Thereby, a fairly comfortable position was achieved for the test person.

Generally, all test persons felt comfortable and found the glove easy to put on and off. The light, meshed fabric on the top side of the glove allowed for good air ventilation around the hand and, hence, avoided a local increase of the temperature caused by the glove. However, the leather part at the palm was fairly stiff which made it difficult for subjects with thin fingers to maintain proper contact between electrodes and skin. This problem could be answered by either providing gloves in different sizes, or by using gloves of a material which is thinner and more elastic than this actual model.

We also experienced bad skin conductance readings at the beginning of the session with most subjects. One assumption is that this may be due to very dry skin of the particular test persons, which changed over time during the session. In this case, the sensitivity of the sensing circuitry should be adaptable or even self-adapting to the actual conditions. Another explanation would be that the material of the electrodes is not suitable for continuous use over several weeks. Being exposed to human sweat, a chemically aggressive substance, the metallic surface of the electrodes is subject to corrosion which leads to deterioration of sensing results. In this case, a chemically more resistant material should be chosen for the electrodes, or other techniques for measuring electro dermal activity (EDA) should be found.

The data collection unit is very neat and handy. Having LEDs indicating the system being operational and showing any problems that might occur is nice and assuring. However, just 2 flashing LEDs for indicating many different states is sub-optimal in our view. Even more problematic was the use of the red LED. It was used for indicating SD card errors, sensor errors, bad wireless connection, and a warning on low battery status. This was not only difficult to memorize but also, as a consequence, led to the experimenter feeling helpless and fearful for the data each time the red light was on. We think that more LEDs would be beneficial, for instance one for each sensor type, one for battery life, and one for the quality of the wireless connection. The push buttons for indicating different states were very helpful as they allowed to mark events during the session which attention had to be paid to in the data evaluation. They could be handled easily and were safe from unintended use.

Storing the data on an exchangeable SD card is a very good idea and helps to perform several tests in a row without the need of saving data on a PC between sessions. However, preparation of the SD cards for use in the EREC-IIa system is not acceptable for the non-technical user. It required the experimenter to first format the SD card on the PC, and then to create an empty file of sufficient size on the SD card using a dedicated program. Particularly the need of calculating the size of the empty file caused extra stress since the experimenter was constantly worried that the size was not sufficiently big and valuable data being lost, while on the other hand a big file resulted in inconvenient long reading times in the EmoChart analyser. An improvement would be to let the EREC system create the files as needed, freeing the user from technical considerations and fears.

Finally, the idea of synchronized collection of EDA, skin temperature and room temperature data by use of a sensor glove is considered very useful as it provides a new and easy way to collect emotion-related time-synchronized physiological data.

3.2 EREC-IIb

System Particulars. EREC-IIb has been developed based on first experiences with EREC-IIa. It now features a real USB connection for the serial communication to the PC using the virtual COM port mode to allow existing RS232-based software for online analysis of sensor data. The SD card still needs to be formatted before being inserted into the system, but the controller now creates itself files in the proprietary file format, one file per session. The user interface has been changed slightly by providing more LEDs and better interpretable flash codes but is otherwise identical to EREC-IIa.

Multimodal Affective Sensing Approach. The NICTA Vision Science, Technology and Applications (VISTA) group is interested in measuring and analysing physiological sensor data from a perspective of monitoring human performance as well as improved human-computer interaction (HCI) in the long term. In the following, a brief overview of these activities is given, which are driven by both applications and general research issues. We believe that only a multimodal, multi-sensor approach can truly deliver the robustness required in real-world applications, and supplying computer systems with the capability to sense affective states is important for developing intelligent systems. In terms of modalities, our research is focussed on using audio, video, and physiological sensors.

In the audio modality, we use features such as fundamental frequency F0, energy, and speed of delivery to gain insights into evidence of affective states in spoken language. Recently, we proposed a new, more comprehensive model of affective communication and a set of ontologies which provide a rigorous way of researching affective communication [13]. In the video modality, we use active appearance models (AAM) to track the face of users and its facial features [5]. AAMs are a popular method for modelling the shape and texture of non-rigid objects (e.g. faces) using a low dimensional representation obtained from applying principle component analysis to a set of labelled video data. We combine AAMs with artificial neural networks to automatically recognise facial expressions. Finally, we use the EREC-II sensor glove system for measuring physiological responses related to affective states. Galvanic skin response, heart rate and skin temperature are of particular interest to us and these measures are all provided by the EREC-II system.

In our experience, both experimenters and test subjects find the glove system easy to use and comfortable to wear. From a user's point of view, the glove does not prevent a 'normal' use of the hand. The system being integrated into a glove has the advantage that it is very lightweight and that it is comfortable to wear even for longer periods of time. We found that having the sensor circuitry in a separate unit which is attached to the wrist is acceptable in many application areas, in particular when the wearer is sitting, for example, while working on a computer. However, for more mobile application scenarios, it would be advantageous to have a more compact unit that is integrated with the sensor glove. We experienced occasional problems with the heart rate sensor whose transmission was not always received by the sensor circuitry. We see potential for further improvements in terms of the reliability of the transmission in this area. Overall, we found the sensors to work reliably and the entire system to be robust and very useful in our applications, which we describe in the following.

Evaluation. EREC-IIb has been evaluated at the National ICT Australia (NICTA) Canberra Research Laboratory, Australia, who use the system since November 2006. The evaluation results stated here have been obtained over a period of 5 weeks in two different studies.

Human Performance Monitoring

In a joint project with the Australian Institute of Sports (AIS), Canberra, Australia, we investigate how state-of-the-art camera technology in the infrared range of the electro-magnetic spectrum can be used to measure performance indicators that were so far only accessible by physiological sensors. Near-infrared (NIR) cameras can be tuned to wavelengths specifically relevant to human haemoglobin, which is the carrier of oxygen in blood, so that haemoglobin levels can be measured in a non-invasive way. Similarly, far-infrared cameras (FIR) can visualise thermal energy emitted from an object, e.g. a human body. We use FIR cameras to measure the surface temperature of athletes, map these onto a 3D model of the athlete's body and determine the heat source using finite-element methods.

In this project, the EREC-II sensor glove system is used as a ground-truthing device because it allows to measure physiological parameters directly. In the experiments, an AIS athlete sits on a cycling ergometer during a training interval and data are recorded from the EREC-II system, the NIR and FIR cameras. During an analysis of the training interval, the performance indicators derived from the video data is compared with the data from the physiological sensors as well as data from blood samples. The test subjects in the experiments have found the EREC-II sensor glove comfortable to wear and reported no particular problem with it. Our goal is to develop a non-invasive measurement system that allows for an easy, non-invasive way of measuring an athlete's performance indicators. For future versions of the EREC system, we would like to see an optional pulse oximeter (SpO2 sensor) being integrated. The project is currently in the experimental phase.

Affective Sensing for Improved HCI

We also investigate multimodal HCI systems that are capable of sensing the affective state of a user and that monitor this state or take it into account in the actions of the HCI system. The application background here are driver assistance systems that aid the driver in their driving task. Vehicle drivers have to perform many cognitive tasks at the same time and one of the major sources for accidents is 'cognitive overload'. Another danger is driver drowsiness which is particularly relevant for long-distance and night-time driving.

In our experimental vehicle, we have placed cameras that look at both the road and surroundings outside the car as well as monitor the driver. While facial feature tracking and eye blink detection are one way of detecting drowsiness, we had no way of measuring physiological parameters before the EREC-II system was incorporated. Ultimately, one would like the sensors in the EREC-II system to be integrated into the steering wheel, rather than having to wear a sensor glove, but for an experimental vehicle the setup is acceptable. Measuring the heart rate, galvanic skin resistance and skin temperature give direct cues about the affective state of the driver and can be used to improve the reliability of drowsiness detection systems. The test subjects in our experiments found no problem in wearing the glove while driving. Current work in this project focuses on the integration of sensor data from the EREC-II system and video system in a multimodal system.

4 Summary and Outlook

This paper reported on design aspects and evaluation studies of the EREC-II system for measuring affect-related physiological parameters. The evaluations have been performed independently by two groups in Germany and Australia, respectively. The evaluations can be summarized as follows:

The design of the sensor system as consisting of a lightweight glove and a wrist pocket is fine. Particularly the meshed fabric at the top of the glove was rated very comfortable by all subjects. The palm side of the glove being made of leather has been experienced as pleasant by some subjects (sports), as acceptable by others (automobile and multimodal affect sensing), and as sub-optimal for persons with slim hands and fingers. The latter was mainly due to the material being too stiff to maintain proper contact to the skin.

For the electronics being put into a separate wrist pocket, it was acceptable for all applications. However, integration into the glove has been suggested by all studies.

The system has been considered easy to use after a number of adjustments were made to the initial design. Particularly, the handling of the SD card and related file management have been a problem at first which could be alleviated in version IIb. Occasional problems occurred with the pulse sensor which could be alleviated by changing the placement of the pulse receiver away from the battery pack.

The system proved to be robust and reliable. An experienced lack of confidence in the reliability of the system was due to sub-optimal usage of LEDs representing the system and sensor states.

Based on these results, the following improvements are envisioned for the next development phase:

- Other material for the glove will be sought and evaluated. Also, different sizes will be provided where needed. Integration of the electronics into the glove will be evaluated. Since processing electronics inside the glove will increase weight and stiffness of the glove as well as producing heat and hindering air circulation, this seems to be an option only for selected application fields.
- The heart rate detection needs to be improved. We will investigate new ways here as well as look for ways to improve the currently used technology. Skin resistance electrodes will get a more resistant surface, for instance of silver/silver chloride as used with conventional medical devices. This will alleviate sensor fouling and lead to improved readings for EDA. Adaptation or even self-adaptation of skin resistance sensors to the actual range of measurement values is an issue also to be addressed in following versions.
- The user interface needs to be further improved. Particularly the usage of LEDs for indicating system states and sensor and communication errors needs to be separated. This will be addressed in the next version.

Concluding, it can be said that developing sensor systems for physiological parameters is a challenging undertaking. First, there proved to be huge inter-personal variations in the range of physiology readings, particularly for EDA. Second, different scenarios have different requirements on the design of the system, and common requirements are rated with different priorities by different user groups. It was also found that users in different research domains have a different understanding of what technology should do and is capable of doing, which also results in different requirements on the user interface of hard- and software.

We conclude that sensor systems for real-world applications need either be domain-specific, i.e. dedicated to an application field or even scenario, or very adaptable.

Acknowledgements

We would like to thank the evaluation teams for sacrificing their time, coping with the shortcomings of the system, and providing such extensive feedback. We also would like to thank the persons who volunteered for the studies.

References

1. Aleksic, P.S., Katsaggelos, A.K.: Automatic Facial Expression Recognition Using Facial Animation Parameters and Multi-Stream HMMs. IEEE Trans. on Information Forensics and Security 1(1), 3–11 (2006) (2005)
2. Anttonen, J., Surakka, V.: Emotions and heart rate while sitting on a chair. In: Proceedings of the SIGCHI conference on Human factors in computing systems, CHI 2005, pp. 491–499. Portland, Oregon, USA (April 2005)
3. Ax, A.: The physiological differentiation between fear and anger in humans. In: Psychosomatic Medicine, vol. 55(5), pp. 433–442, The American Psychosomatic Society (1953)
4. Branco, P., Firth, P., Encarnacao, L.M., Bonato, P.: Faces of Emotion in Human-Computer Interaction. In: Proceedings of the CHI 2005 conference, Extended Abstracts, pp. 1236–1239. ACM Press, New York (2005)
5. Cootes, T.F., Edwards, G., Taylor, C.J., Burkhardt, H., Neuman, B.: Active appearance models. In: Burkhardt, H., Neumann, B. (eds.) ECCV 1998. LNCS, vol. 1407, pp. 484–489. Springer, Heidelberg (1998)
6. Cowie, R., Douglas-Cowie, E., Tsapatsoulis, N., Votsis, G., Kollias, S., Fellenz, W., Taylor, J.G.: Emotion recognition in human computer interfaces. IEEE Signal Processing Magazine 18(1), 32–80 (2001)
7. Ekman, P., Levenson, R. W., Friesen, W.: Autonomic Nervous System Activity Distinguishes among Emotions. In Science, vol. 221(4616), pp. 1208–1210, The American Association for Advancement of Science (1983)
8. Ekman, P., Davidson, R.J. (eds.): The Nature of Emotion: Fundamental Questions. Oxford University Press, New York (1994)
9. Fasel, B., Luettin, J.: Automatic Facial Expression Analysis: A Survey. Pattern Recognition 36(1), 259–275 (2003)
10. Herbon, A., Peter, C., Markert, L., van der Meer, E., Voskamp, J.: Emotion Studies in HCI – a New Approach. In: Proceedings of the 2005 HCI International Conference, Las Vegas, vol. 1, CD-ROM (2005) ISBN 0-8058-5807-5
11. Hudlicka, E.: Affect Sensing and Recognition: State-of-the-Art Overview. In: Proceedings of the 2005 HCI International Conference, Las Vegas. vol. 11. CD-ROM (2005)
12. Lee, Y.B., Yoon, S.W., Lee, C.K., Lee, M.H.: Wearable EDA Sensor Gloves using Conducting Fabric and Embedded System. Engineering in Medicine and Biology Society, 2006. EMBS '06. In: 28th Annual International Conference of the IEEE. Supplement, pp. 6785–6788 (2006)
13. McIntyre, G., Goecke, R.: Researching Emotions in Speech. In: Proceedings of the Eleventh Australasian International Conference on Speech Science and Technology SST2006, Auckland, New Zealand, pp. 264–269 (December 2006)
14. Palomba, D., Stegagno, L.: Physiology, Perceived Emotion and Memory: Responding to Film Sequences. In: Birbaumer, N., Öhman, A. (eds.) The Structure of Emotion, pp. 158–168. Hogrefe and Huber Publishers, Toronto (1993)
15. Peter, C., Ebert, E., Beikirch, H.: A Wearable Multi-Sensor System for Mobile Acquisition of Emotion-Related Physiological Data. In: Proceedings of the 1st International Conference on Affective Computing and Intelligent Interaction, Beijing, pp. 691–698. Springer, Heidelberg (2005)
16. Picard, R.W., Scheirer, J.: The Galvactivator: A Glove that Senses and Communicates Skin Conductivity. In: Proceedings from the 9th International Conference on Human-Computer Interaction, August 2001, New Orleans, LA, pp. 1538–1542 (2001)

Development of an Adaptive Multi-agent Based Content Collection System for Digital Libraries

R. Ponnusamy and T.V. Gopal

Dept. of Computer Science & Engg., College of Engg., Anna University
Chennai -600025, India

Abstract. Relevant digital content collection and access are huge problems in digital libraries. It poses a greater challenge to the digital library users and content builders. In this present work an attempt has been made to design and develop a user-adaptive multi-agent system approach to recommend the contents automatically for the digital library. An adaptive dialogue based user-interaction screen has also been provided to access the contents. Once the new contents are added to the collection then the system should automatically alert appropriate user about the new content arrivals based on their interest. The user interactive Question Answering (QA) system provides enough knowledge about the user requirements.

Keywords: Question Answering (QA) systems, Adaptive Interaction, Digital Libraries, Multi-Agent System.

1 Introduction

Digital Libraries are modern social and virtual institutions for information collection, preservation and dissemination to be distributed across the world. The Web Digital Library is one such information environment and is distributed, large, open and heterogeneous in nature. Relevant digital content collection building and access are huge problems in these digital libraries. It poses a greater challenge to the digital library users as well as to the content builders. On account of huge variety of digital collections providers, the content developer has to spend considerable time and effort for identification of the digital content in the web as well as from the service providers; to standardize the digital content collection is the major problems.

In the Indian Institute of Science (IISc) different departments are taking initiative to develop a research literature repository to provide on-line materials and contents. These repositories are expected provide on-line research literature/contents to various science/engineering researchers. These repositories store all the research literatures viz. research papers, theses, e-books, web-blogs and technical reports submitted by students and scholars as well as collected from different web portals. These literatures are classified and stored in different department servers/repositories. The collection building and management in these repositories happen in the regular interval. In order to collect the literature to establish and update these repositories in the specific topic or area, say for example of computing literature has to be done in the manual method.

J. Jacko (Ed.): Human-Computer Interaction, Part III, HCII 2007, LNCS 4552, pp. 475–485, 2007.

The content manager has to explicitly go to the related web to collect the needed content. Instead the content manager expects a system that has to automatically search and present/recommend the specific set of literature on the desktop from the Web. This is called as automatic content collection management [1]. In this case the automatic relevant information collection from different content provider's web portal is the most important problem to be solved. Most of the retrieval system just retrieves the passive results (retrieve a set of articles) at the time of searching. It is not able to retrieve the literature if the new literature has been added to the system on a later period of time. The main advantage of recommendation system is that it is able to recommend a set of newly added literature actively even after the searching is over. In this system an automatic alert system has been designed to alert the existing users based on their profiles whenever the new content is added to the library.

Some of the serious usability problems in e-learning and other web digital libraries are [2] failure to relate the real – world experience of the user, poor presentation of key information and lack of accessibility even in the most basic sense. The concept oriented relevant information communication system is the long standing dream of the information and cognitive scientist. The primary expectation is that if the user presents any of the phrase or keyword, then the system must be able to identify the related concepts also. That is the system must be able to identify semantically relevant idea of the user. The user interface must be in a meaningful user-centric way in order to improve the quality and to solve the above said problems. There are two critical things very much important for automatic content collection management system. First one is based on the relativity algorithm or methodology and the second one is the user-interface design. In this present approach a LSA based algorithm is used to support the relevant recommendation or content identification. Secondly the user personalization [9, 11] is the way for the user-centric computing. One of the important issues that assist the fast, relevant and economical content identification of information from the Internet is to build a relevant content collection. This user personalization involves a process of gathering user-information during interaction with the user, which is then used to deliver appropriate content services, tailored to make the user's needs. This experience is used better to serve the customer by anticipating needs, making the interaction efficient and satisfying both parties and to build a relationship between them that encourage the content manager/customer to come again for subsequent operations.

The user personalization can be realized in many user profile models [9], and the user-personal agent [15] is an instrument in processing these user personal modeling. The user profile model determines the information processing. Interface agents [10, 12, 13, 15, 17], also known as personal agents are autonomous software entities that provide assistance to users. These agents act as human assistance, collaborating with the user in the same work environment and becoming more efficient as they learn about user interests, habits and preferences. Instead of user-initiated interaction via commands and/or direct manipulation, the user is engaged in a cooperative process in which both human and software agents initiate communication, monitor events and perform tasks. Also, there are many such agents [12-18] developed in different environments. An attempt has been made by Daniela Godoy and Analia

Amandi to design [12,16] a personal searcher using intelligent agents. Their extension of work involves a user profiling architecture [16] for textual based agents. In another attempt they developed a user association rule to learn user assistance requirements. D. Cordero and his team members have developed an Intelligent Agent for generating personal newspapers [13].

The main user-interface agent interaction personalization issues [18] are (i) discovering the type of assistance each user wants. (ii) Learning the particular assistance requirements, (iii) users have different contexts of analyzing users' tolerance to agents' errors, (iv) discovering when to interrupt the user, (v) discovering how much control the user wants to delegate to the agent and to prove the means to provide simple explicit user feedback, (vi) providing the means to capture as much implicit feedback, (vii) providing the means to control and inspect agent behavior. Total personalization is not just to interact with the user to get some feedback but to understand the user completely and accordingly establish various sophisticated actions such as warnings or suggestions or actions without the interference of the user. The system also designed to have a Question Answering (QA) system to understand the content manager/user to build the relevant content for collection building.

Shahram Rahimi and Norman F. Carver [8] have identified a suitable domain-specific multi-agent architecture to distributed information integration. Similarly current information sources are independent and information agents are developed separately. To reduce the level of information processing each agent is designed to provide expertise on a specific-topic by drawing on relevant information from other information agents in the related knowledge domains. Every information agent contains ontology of its domain, its domains model and its information source models. Each concept matrix together with the ACM classification represents the ontology. The ontology consists of descriptions of objects and relationships (noun, verb phrases). The model provides a semantic description of the domain, which is used extensively for processing query.

In this present work, an attempt is made to design and develop a domain specific (subject specialist) multi-agent system to support the content collection and to recommend the relevant content. This system is specially designed to aid the researchers/students/content managers to collect the standard on-line contents from distributed web portals and to recommend/alert the same to various related users working in that field. The domain specific agent is able to self-proclaim the related content that the user is seeking about the specific area. Subsequently the same information is recommended to the user. Also, the user interface agent is designed to understand the user and is able to initiate different actions under various circumstances.

Section 2 explains the architecture, component and functionality of the multi-agent based content collection management system. Section 3 explains the user modeling and user interface design. Section 4 presents the ACM CR Classification and Automated Concept-Matrix Formulation method. Section 5 presents the method used for concept relativity analysis. Section 6 gives the implementation as well as experiment results. Section 7 concludes this paper.

2 Self-proclamative Multi-agents Based Automatic Content Collection Building Systems

In this multi-agent system every individual agent is designed to the specific domain (Specific Subject) apart from the agents to be used for the user-interaction. The domain-specific agent will take-care of the identification of documents related to the specific area. These domain-specific agents are able to travel to different web servers or able to query the web servers to collect the required information.

A phrase-extraction component will perform the task of technical phrase extraction. A concept dictionary is attached to the system to provide a reference to the phrase-extraction component. After extracting the technical phrases from the documents, it formulates the concept-matrix. This concept matrix later used for concept relativity analysis to identify whether the collected document belongs to particular category or not. If the document belongs under certain category then it will be collected and put-up on respective repository. Otherwise, it also tries to find the likely relativity with other specific categories. This is performed through the phrase-vector-term cosine function. Every agent in the multi-agent system maintains a phrase-vector table for major categories. If it identifies relativity with its neighbor or adjacent agents then it self-proclaims such information to its neighbor about their relativity of the documents. The domain-specific agents are able to travel to various servers with the phrase-extraction component. The user-interface agents are designed to learn the user through user interaction. It is able to classify the user under different category and this information is given to the central server moderator. The moderator resides in the central server generates a message to various users about the arrival of new document and informs the respective users.

2.1 Domain-Specific Agents

In the present design there are eleven such agents, which are designed to do the concept matching at the individual first level hierarchy. For every subject at the first top level it is designed with a specific agent. Such an agent is taking care of the concept comparison and identification of relevant documents related to the categories. The dispatcher informs about the arrival of the new web servers or portals information through the blackboard system. Immediately the domain specific agents are actively involved to get the web server information from the blackboard and perform the concept relativity analysis to identify the related documents that are stored in that web portal or server. The concept relativity analysis is performed through the Latent Semantic Analysis. After identifying the specific documents, the individual domain-specific agents store the document in the specific repository. Then the same is alerted to the user through the user interface agent.

2.2 Phrase-Extraction Component

The phrase extraction component attached with every-domain specific agent. As soon as the domain-specific agent gets the new document from the web servers or portal it passes the same to the phrase extraction component. This phrase-extraction component performs a list of preprocessing steps. These preprocessing steps involve stop-word elimination, phrase comparison and phrase matching. The phrase comparison through the concept dictionary is provided with the system. It is also doing the phrase matching to eliminate the slight differences and it will record the new phrases in the concept dictionary. After extracting the phrase, the system will frame the concept-matrix. Other than the central server there exists a phrase extraction component in every individual domain-specific agent.

2.3 Concept Dictionary

It provides a list of concepts required to run the system. At the initial stages while starting up the system a list of independent concepts taken from ACM computing review classification index, keywords as well as using the words and phrases of Microsoft on-line computer dictionary. The user through the user interface agent to provide systems ontology enters these phrases and words. Later additions of concepts will automatically take-place after the identification of new technical phrases. Usually it considers the occurrences of the words and phrase for the new phrase addition.

2.4 User-Interface Agent

User-Interface Agent provides various facilities to learn about the user. These facilities include Login system, Search screen, Concept Dictionary, Document Recommendation window, User-Interaction Window and Help window. This login system allows the system to identify the user for user personalization. It is normally designed with a username and password. The search screen gives the facility for text-input entry screen for document search, additional and related term entry. Second component is the concept dictionary as explained the previous section. Third one is the recommendation window, which recommends different types of new documents related to the user-interested area as soon as the user login to the system. Also this interface has the option to upload a new document in the servers. If a new document comes into the system then it will be informed through the blackboard. Immediately the category of that document identified through classification system. Then the system also recommends that document to the related user. The user interaction system will interact to the user to get more information related to search if the user is of interactive type. A special option is provided to do a rational search, which means that the system does not consider the user profile and it will go for searching of its own. At last the help system gives various details about the operations of the system. The complete design of this user interface system is explained in Section 3.

2.5 Blackboard

This is a shared memory, which stores and exchanges the query as well as the messages required for different servers and agents. The individual domain-specific agents are permitted to read/write the content of this shared memory. After identification new phrases from the collected document the domain specific agent writes the phrases in this shared memory. Then every domain-specific agent takes those phrases to update its concept-dictionary.

2.6 Moderator/Dispatcher

It is a simple component that is used to reduce the message flow increase in the system. A single moderator exists in every central server. The arrival of the new web portal information to the system needs to be informed to the agents explicitly. This moderator or dispatcher takes care of this work. It maintains the list of all agents working in the different areas. As soon as it gets the information about the new document arrival then it automatically generates a message to the different users through the user interface agent.

3 User Modeling and User Interface Agent Design

In the present system design the user-access matrix is employed to represent the user's intention that consists of a set of phrases, which expresses at least a partial intention. This is built in adapting the user by means of different methods. The user adaptation is done through the user profile and the user search history is a part of this user profile. The system is designed to learn the user's behavior and accordingly behaves in the environment. The method of user classification is presented in section 3.1 and the complete method of building this user access matrix is explained in the following sub-section 3.2. After building the user access matrix the system performs the concept relativity analysis to bring the information that is very much related to the concept. The process of the concept matrix building and concept relativity analysis is explained in section 4 and the process of concept relativity analysis is explained in section 5.

3.1 User Classifications

The system is designed to identify the various behaviors of different user to adapt the strategy for the recommendation. Sixteen different types of strategies are considered for various users in conformity of their behavior. The first question is about the interest of the user to interact with the agent or not. Sometimes the user may hide the agent and hesitates to interact with the user. An option is given to hide the agent. Second question is about the interest to listen to the agent's suggestion or not. When the user hides the agent then he/she will be warned about the impact. If the user keeps continuously hiding the agent then the user assumed to ignore the warnings and suggestions. Third is patience of the user to give complete information to the agent. The user screen has the option to enter the additional/equivalent string to represent the searcher's intention. If the user enters this information it is assumed that he/she is patient enough to listen to the agent. Fourth is the intention of the agent to take its own decision. Based on the users understanding the system decides different strategies for recommendation and searching. The agent's strategy for information, recommendation and searching is given below. This information is learned over a period of time. But, normally while starting up, the agent has the assumption that it has full freedom to take decisions of its own.

1. Agent has to search using the global profiles and using user personal profile collected through the search history. It will not give any recommendations and warnings and does not like to recommend the information to the user. It will do simple search.

2. Agent can interact with user and so it can get some information while searching, but it will not suggest or recommend any information while searching, because the user is not patient enough to listen to the recommendations and warnings.

Similarly the other fourteen choices are decided and accordingly it decides the different types of user's choice and actions. If the user wishes to interact with the system then one can use Question Answering system [3-7]. A question corpus database is designed with this system to adapt the various users.

3.2 A Method for User Personal Profile Building

The main components of user profiles are User-Name, User-Id, User-Type, User-Subject Categories and User-Access Matrix. Initially the user enters the User-Subject Categories and later on it will be automatically updated by the system. The user-interested subjects' hierarchies (User-Subject Categories) are also learned by the system and the same is used for the future searching and is recorded in the user profile. The method of building the concept matrix will differ in different circumstances. These methods are explained in the following section.

1. In this first method of building the user-access matrix is built using the user presented search strings. If the user presents related terms that is also included in the matrix. The user access matrix is also similar to the concept matrix, but we call it as the user-access matrix because it represents the user intension. There will be one user-access matrix used for one user.
2. In this second case, after presenting the search query its category is also recorded in the history. If the new query is related to previous one then those related phrases from that query is also added and search. If search history is not available then the global search profile is taken for the first time searching.
3. The method of user type prediction is explained in the subsection 3.1. This user profile normally represents the various subject interests of the user and the type of the user. The Global subject profile is used to explain the different type of general subject concepts and their related items. Most of the time the subject that the user refers is not very much clear. The reason is that the subject matters cannot be simply expressed by one or more keywords or phrases. In such a situation, the system needs to track the user-interest through previous history; otherwise it needs interaction with the user. But, many times the user is not patient enough to interact with the system to answer all the queries the agent asks for. This is attributed to user understanding over a period of time. It basically understands the type of the user and accordingly it takes different types of recommendations or retrieval strategy [17]. After understanding various types of users, types of retrieval mechanisms are employed for content collection.

As soon as the user query is entered into the interface system, the system will perform the concept relativity analysis to identify the fourth-level sub-hierarchy concept topic. On this process the phrases and words in the user-query are first extracted and then it will be related to the various keywords and phrases of all the fourth-level sub-hierarchy categories using Latent Semantic Analysis (method of performing the latent semantic analysis and concept relative analysis is given in section 5). The most related concept hierarchies are identified and then these areas are recorded as the related areas to the user. In this case of our present design the system always gives a chance to do a rational search. The user interface provides a check box to indicate the rational search and the user can indicate it through this option. That is the system also does the search without looking into the user-personal profiles. Important critical part of the interface design always keeps track of the interest of the user and then issues the warning if it tries to access the ambiguities terms or tries to travel in different or new direction by checking the user adaptability. The adaptive ness of the user is understood through different ways. Normally the general subject hierarchy itself gives sufficient information about the hierarchy and the relativity of the system. It can be taken as the general global profile for the whole system design.

4 ACM CR Classifications and Automated Concept Matrix Formulation

The complete ACM CR classification tree hierarchy is given in http://www.acm.org/class/1998/ccs98.html [19]. In this present work we wish to add more number of concepts/phrases at every fourth level sub-hierarchy. Each and every document is represented as a concept and every concept is represented thorough a concept matrix. Concept matrix contains a list of technical phrases. The system will automatically add any number of concepts at this level. The classification and extraction of technical phrases to construct a concept matrix is the very critical task, for which we use the list of ACM proper noun index, Keyword index. Apart from this we also use a list of words and phrases from Microsoft on-line computer dictionary. The phrase extractor agent automatically extracts using these words and phrases, an additional set of words and phrases. The occurrences of all these phrases are taken and then the relativity between the list of index and newly extracted phrase is taken into account in order to include the particular technical phrase in the concept matrix. These phrases are also stored in the concept dictionary and used for the future usage. Normally while extracting the technical phrases from the list of complete phrases extracted from the query, we will just see the occurrence of these independent words and phrases in those list and select those phrases as the technical phrases.

5 Paper Preparation Method for Concept-Pattern Relativity

Latent Semantic Analysis (LSA) is a theory and method for representing the contextual usage of meaning of phrase relative ness by statistical computations applied to a large corpus of text. Phrase and passage meaning representation derived by LSA have been found to be capable of simulating a variety of human cognitive phenomena. After processing a large sample of machine-readable language, LSA exhibits the phrases, either taken from the original corpus or new, as points in a very high dimensional semantic space.

In this case it is represented as a conceptual matrix and it also permits one to infer about the relation of expected contextual usage of phrases. LSA applies a Singular Value Decomposition (SVD) to the matrix; this is a form of a factor or more properly the mathematical generalization of which factor analysis is a special case.

SVD is a powerful technique employed for solving a linear system of equations **AX=B**, in M equations of N unknowns with M > = < N in order to get unique set of solutions; a set of singular solutions, infinite number of solutions; non trivial solutions or trivial solutions based upon the nature of the coefficient matrix A, whatever maybe the vectors X, B. Concepts of rank, null space, range space of linear algebra are essential in formulating the computer program for any practical problem in conformity with the decomposition of the matrix A

$$[A] = [U][W][V^T]$$

in the usual notation when more equations than the unknowns are given, relevant solutions can also be obtained by least squares method.

After the reconstruction of the original matrix we find the correlation between required user-concept matrix and the existing document in the sub-hierarchy. If the correlation is high then documents are retrieved and presented to the user. The same process is repeated for all agents. If none of them find good correlation in its sub-hierarchy it is proclaimed that the information is not available in the hierarchy.

The main issue while using the LSA is the size of the matrix very much high and the system is not able to process is sometimes. In order to avoid this situation and keep the matrix under control every time only a set of five to ten documents alone are alternatively taken for relativity analysis.

6 Simulation Experiments and Results

The system is simulated using apache web servers. All these servers are hosted with IBM Tehiti server to run the Aglets [20]. The subject-specific agent, phrase-extraction component and user interfaces agent are developed using this aglets. There are four such Apache web servers that are hosted and one of them acts as a central server that runs the moderator, black-board and central concept dictionary. An Agent Transfer Protocol (ATP) is used to communicate with these different agents. Aglet uses a technique called serialization to transmit data on the heap and to migrate the interpretable byte-code. These aglets are supporting message passing and broadcasting. Each aglet is integrated with the functional components of this architecture. The blackboard system is shown as the explicit component and is implemented through using standard java serialization. For the domain specific aglets (Agents) initially the user has to specify the training sample document either from the local machine or from the web through user-interface aglet. Each domain specific aglets is designed to learn the concept-matrix of that specific hierarchy. The training documents are indicated with specific category-hierarchy and this is considered as global subject profile. After the training is over, the query is given to the system through user interface screen and this is preprocessed and then the user access matrix is framed as recorded and passed to blackboard. Then the moderator broadcasts the message to all the domain-specific aglets about the arrival of new query and every domain-specific aglet gets the query and processes it to recommend the set of documents related to the given user query. Normally every user is logged in to the system through proper login. All the user details are recorded and the user-profile is built as explained in Section 3.

In these experiments, the ACM CR classification system at the fourth-level hierarchy there exists nearly 1120 categories and the present system is trained with few documents under each category. To evaluate this approach all the servers are hosted with sum of 2682 documents collected through Internet. Later the multi-agent system is performing the automatic content collection and the same is alerted to the required users. Then the precision of these systems is measured with 100 alerts/documents. In order to evaluate the effectiveness of automatic content collection system a well-known precision measure is used. This is given by

$$\text{Precision} = \frac{\text{Number of Collected Documents that are Relevant}}{\text{Total Number of Documents Collected}}$$

Based on the measurement pertaining to precision the relevant documents are collected from few web servers for testing as given in figure 1. It is found in the graph that precision indicated in the vertical direction shows the increasing tendency justifies relevant content collection.

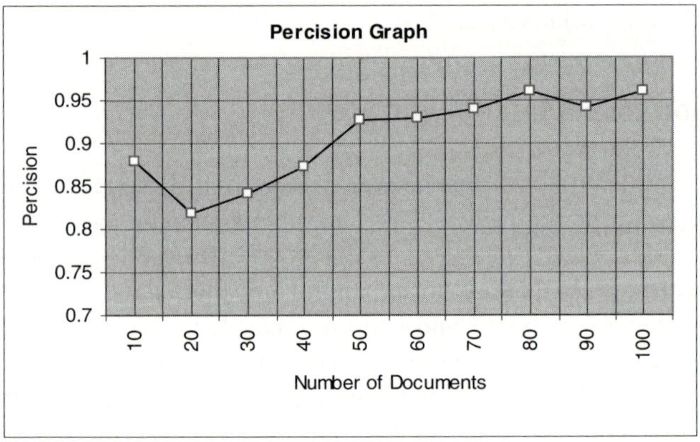

Fig. 1. Precision for content collection system

7 Conclusion

An attempt is made in this paper to design and develop an adaptive multi-agent framework for automatic electronic content collection using ACM CR classification hierarchy. This work has revealed that the Latent Semantic Analysis along with concept matrix setup enables one to identify the related concepts effectively and to understand the user intention. The initial system is setup with a few set of predefined words and phrases and later on it acquires all the set of phrases. It also yields good results in terms of concept relativity.

References

1. Knowledge and Content Technologies http://cordis.europa.eu/ist/kct/
2. Frontend.com – Usability Engineering and Interface Design, Why people can't use e learning, what the e learning sector needs to learn about usability (May 2001)
3. Ahrenberg, L., et al.: Coding Schemes for Studies of Natural Language Dialogue, In: AAAI - Spring Symposium (1995)
4. Flycht-Eriksson, A.: Dialogue and Domain Knowledge Management in Dialogue Systems. In: Proceedings of the First SIGdial Workshop on Discourse and Dialogue (2000)
5. Jönsson, A., Dahlbäck, N.: Distilling dialogues - A method using natural dialogue corpora for dialogue systems development. In: Proceedings of 6th Applied Natural Language Processing Conference, pp. 44–51 (2000)
6. Degerstedt, L., Jönsson, A.: A Method for Iterative Implementation of Dialogue Management http://www.ida.liu.se/ arnjo/papers/eurospeech-01.pdf
7. Dahlback, N., Jonsson, A.: Knowledge sources in spoken dialogue systems. In: Proceedings of Eurospeech '99, Budapest, Hungary (1999)
8. Rahimi, S., Carver, N.F.: A Multi-Agent Architecture for Distributed Domain-specific Information Integration. In: Proc. Of the 38th Hawaii Intl. Conference on System Sciences (2003) http://www.ieee.org
9. Bonett, M.: Personalization of Web Services: Opportunities and Challenges, Ariadne Issue 28 http://www.ariadne.ac.uk/issue28/personalization/intro.html
10. Gururaj, R., Sreenivasa Kumar, P.: Survey of User Profile Models for Information Filtering System, CIT (2004)
11. Liu, F., Yu, C.: Senior Member, Personalised Web Search for Improving Retrieval Effectiveness, IEEE Trans. On Knowledge and Data Engineering, 16(1) (January 2004)
12. Godoy, D., Amandi, A.: Personal Searcher: An Intelligent Agent for Searching Web Pages
13. Cordero, D., Roldan, P., Schiafino, S., Amandi, A.: Intelligent Agents Generating Personal Newspapers
14. Schiaffino, S., Amandi, A.: Using Association Rules to Learn Users' Assistance Requirements. In: Proceddings ASAI 2003, Argentine Symposium on Artificial Intelligence – Buenos Aires, Argentina (September 2003)
15. Fleming, M., Cohen, R.: User Modeling in the Design of Interactive Interface Agents
16. Godoy, D., Amandi, A.: A user Profiling Architecture for Textual-Based Agents
17. Armentano, M., Godoy, D., Amandi, A.: An empirical study in agent based interface issues, Technical Report
18. Schiaffino, S., Amandi, A.: User-interface agent interaction: Personalization issues, Int. Jour. Human Computer Studies vol. 60, pp. 129–148 (2004) http://www.elseviercomputerscience.com
19. ACM Computing Classification System www.acm.org/class/1998
20. www.trl.ibm.co.jp/aglets

Using Content-Based Multimedia Data Retrieval for Multimedia Content Adaptation

Adriana Reveiu, Marian Dardala, and Felix Furtuna

Academy of Economic Studies, 6 Romana Place, Bucharest, Romania
{reveiua,dardala,titus}@ase.ro

Abstract. The effective retrieval and multimedia data management techniques to facilitate the searching and querying of large multimedia data sets are very important in multimedia applications development. The content-based retrieval systems must use the multimedia content to represent and to index data. The representation of multimedia data supposes to identify the most useful features for representing the multimedia content and the approaches needed for coding the attributes of multimedia data. The multimedia content adaptation realize the multimedia resources manipulation, respecting the specific quality parameters, function on the limits required by networks and terminal devices. The goal of the paper is to identify a design model for using content-based multimedia data retrieval in multimedia content adaptation. The goal of this design is to deliver the multimedia content in various networks and to different types of peripheral devices, in the most appropriate format and function on specific characteristics.

Keywords: multimedia streams, content based data retrieval, content adaptation, media type.

1 Introduction

The development of multimedia applications, from the last years, due to the exponential growth of the Internet had as consequence a great usage of multimedia data. As a result, the importance of the researches in multimedia technologies field had been increasing. Because of the features and characteristics of multimedia data, their management and querying techniques are unlike than those of traditional data. Multimedia data is heterogeneous from many points of view: some data is time dependent and the other is time independent, multimedia data uses different formats for data representing, some data is structured and some data is represented as unstructured or as semi-structured streams of data, some data can be transferred remotely in a short time and the others needs a large period to be transferred.

In contrast with text-based systems, multimedia applications include powerful descriptions of human thinking in video, audio, animations and images. [1] But it is a big gap between how the users think about the reality and the physical representation of multimedia data. Users want to access multimedia data at the object level, but multimedia-retrieval systems tend to represent multimedia data based on their low-level characteristics such as color, patterns, textures and shapes, with no combination between these features and no way to represent automatically the human thinking

J. Jacko (Ed.): Human-Computer Interaction, Part III, HCII 2007, LNCS 4552, pp. 486–492, 2007.

issue. The representation of multimedia data according with human's perspective is difficult to be realized and it isn't a system that can provide automated identification or classification of objects from multimedia data streams. [2]

2 Media Type in Retrieval Context

We use the *media type* concept to refer the multimedia data types in a unitary way. Media type includes the following multimedia data types: image, animation, sound and video streams. We used the media type and their components to make classifications in the indexing process.

From the temporal point of view, media type elements can be classified in:

- static components – the multimedia data without a temporal component, as example the image,
- dynamic components – that are time dependent, like animation, sound and video streams.

From visual point of view, there are:

- media components that use display resources, like image, animation and video,
- media components that don't need display resources, like sound component.

Continuous multimedia data like video and audio suppose the usage of some specific concepts like data streams, temporal composition, time schedule and synchronization.

Theses concepts are distinct from those used in conventional data models and as a consequence, they cannot be used in content-based multimedia management systems in the same format.

In media type can be defined operations like:

- *open* that could be used to read information from an existing file or from a capturing device, like: a scanner for static images, microphone for audio stream, webcam for video sequence,
- *close* for the file or device.

For temporal data stored in the files can be defined operations like: *play* for media sequence starting, *stop* for media sequence finishing and *pause* to interrupt media sequence and to continue from the same point. In the fig. 1 we defined an object-oriented model for media type.

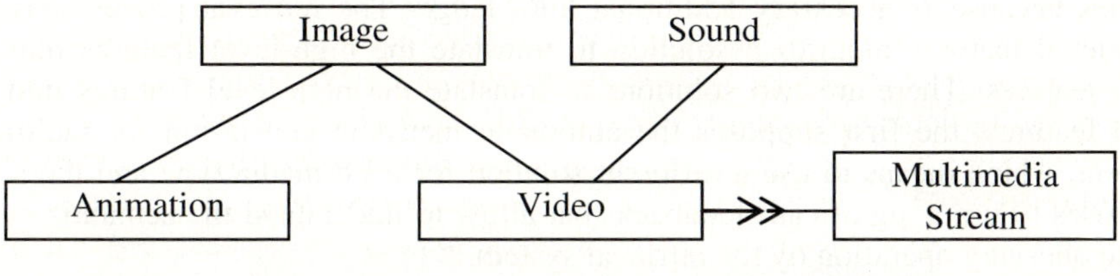

Fig. 1. Object-oriented model of media type

There are two kinds of relations between defined classes:

- the relations symbolized by —— describe the inheritance relations,
- the relation symbolized by —>>— describe a collection relation.

The efficient modeling of multimedia data is critical in content-based multimedia data retrieval. The design issues for an efficient multimedia data model must include:

- support for rich conceptual content,
- the possibility to represent the most important static and dynamic aspects of multimedia data,
- including the knowledge of low-level data,
- isolating the user from the low-level data representation.

3 Content-Based Retrieval and Management Techniques in Multimedia Applications

Before the usage of content-based retrieval techniques, multimedia data was annotated using text characteristics that allows to access and to classify the multimedia data using text-based searching. But, because of the huge amount of multimedia data and because of the diversity of multimedia data types used in actual applications, the traditional text-based querying proves its limits.

The content-based multimedia data retrieval is useful in many application areas like: products and services advertising, real-time systems that use multimedia data, globalization of multimedia data access – "anywhere and anytime", providing multimedia data upon request, assisted training, medical diagnosis, video indexing, multimedia digital libraries, information searching on the Internet and so on.

The content-based retrieval systems must use the multimedia content to represent and to index data. The representation of multimedia data supposes to identify the most useful features for representing the multimedia content and the approaches needed for coding the attributes of multimedia data.

The multimedia content features can be classified into low-level and high-level features. [3]

The *low-level features* are the multimedia content characteristics that could automatically be extracted or detected like: components' color, shape, bounds, texture, bandwidth or pitch. Theses features are used to recognize and to classify the multimedia content.

The *high-level features* are semantic characteristics of multimedia content and suppose to add semantics to multimedia content. It is difficult to process high-level queries because is necessary additional knowledge. The retrieval process based on high-level features requires a solution to translate the high-level features into low-level features. There are two solutions to translate the high-level features into low-level features: the first supposes the automatic metadata generation for multimedia content, which means to use a different solution for each media type and the second supposes to use a significant feedback that allow to understand the semantic context of the querying operation by the retrieval system.

The low-level and high-level multimedia content features extracted can be used to multimedia content adaptation process.

Successful storage and access of multimedia data require analysis of the following issues:

- Efficient representation of multimedia components and storage in a database,
- Proper indexing architecture for the multimedia databases,
- Proper and efficient technique to query data in multimedia database systems.

4 Multimedia Content Adaptation

The growth of multimedia data consumers is influenced by network technologies development together with the newest communication protocols and with the growing of networks' bandwidth. Despite of technological developments, it is no way to guarantee the quality of service of final users, when heterogeneous devices and networks are used.

A promising solution is the alternative offered by the dynamic adaptation principle for multimedia content and multimedia data quality to the level available in the network. As example, a user asks for a high level video sequence, but the terminal equipment access limits force the user to play the video sequence at a low level resolution. So that, to adapt the multimedia content, the system must contain information regarding users' profile.

Multimedia content adaptation became recently a research subject. The former solutions used for content delivery, like file download and multimedia sequence streaming are over fulfilled. File download supposes to store on a local computer the whole multimedia file before its playing and multimedia sequence streaming allows progressively data playing when there is available as much resources as necessary. Both solutions have important disadvantages. To download resources before displaying is time consuming and need a large storage space at the final receptor. The multimedia data streaming reduce the time needed for download and minimize the storage space needed, but depend on the network conditions when play the resources. So, it is almost impossible to guarantee the services quality at delivery because of heterogeneous nature of the Internet.

4.1 Solutions for Multimedia Content Adaptation

Content adaptation process has as a goal to manipulate multimedia resources, respecting the specific quality parameters, function on the limits required by used networks and terminal devices heterogeneity [4].

In the adaptation process we will take into consideration the following solutions: scaling, transcoding and transmoding.

The scaling supposes to use the mechanisms for eliminating or modifying some parts of resources so that to reduce their quality, having the goal to satisfy receiver capacities and needs. The scaling options depend on the data coding format. The scaling has as an effect to obtain data in the format used by source data.

The transcoding supposes to transform the resource from one coding format in another, so it is necessary to decode and to code the resource in another format. The transcoding can be a partial decode process and a coding operation using various parameters, but in the some coding format.

The transmoding supposes to process one resource from a multimedia format in another format, such as to transform a video sequence in images or an image into a text format. The content adaptation is made up by modifying the media object quality so that it can be delivering in the network function on the available bandwidth and then can be presented on the terminal by satisfying the users' constraints and terminal's access facilities.

4.2 Practical Options for Multimedia Content Adaptation

Function on the place where content adaptation is made up; there are some practical options for content adaptation:

- Adaptation by the supplier,
- Adaptation by the receiver,
- Adaptation at the network level.

Adaptation by the supplier supposes to realize resource adaptation at the server level and it is realized function on the terminal and/or network characteristics. The characteristics are detected in a former transaction. After a successful adaptation, the transmitter sends to receiver, its version of adapted resource. This action need the usage of server computing power and adds a delay between the client request and resource delivery by the server. Furthermore, the usage of multicast scenarios, the delivery of the same information to devices with different capacities, it is not allowed in this case because the server must create different versions for one resource, one for each class of devices, leading to the growing of storage requirements at the server level.

Adaptation by the receiver supposes to take the decision about what and how to be adapted, at the terminal level, even if the adaptation could be made in another place, in a proxy node, for example. It is not recommendable to realize the adaptation at the final user because at this place the adaptation could fail because of insufficient client resources and because of additional network bandwidth needed.

Both methods can be viewed as nontransparent adaptation techniques because final nodes and communication protocols are implied during the adaptation process.

Adaptation at the network level is a transparent adaptation method in which only the network, transport system is responsible for adaptation.

Low level adaptation methods that could be used for qualitative adaptation are dependent by data codification format.

4.3 Techniques for Multimedia Content Adaptation

The main techniques that could be used for multimedia content adaptation are:

Temporal adaptability offer adaptation mechanisms by changing the resource in time, by using a subset of the initial resource.

Spatial adaptability refers to the adaptation regarding spatial resolution of the resource. Spatial adaptability has as effect, the growing of the resource's resolution comparing with the basic level.

Quantification modifies the quantification resource parameters by reducing the resolution, for example, having as goal to reduce the data volume.

Color adaptation is a special kind of adaptability, used for multimedia data with a visual component. The goal is to modify the frequency or quantification of multimedia data, like in the case of an image file in which it is modified the chrominance and is kept the image luminance.

5 Design a Multimedia Content Adaptation System Using Data Retrieval

This section considers the adaptation of multimedia content using a content-based multimedia data retrieval system. There are several processes involved in multimedia content adaptation using data retrieval. The four main steps are multimedia data parsing, indexing, content-based retrieval and adaptation.

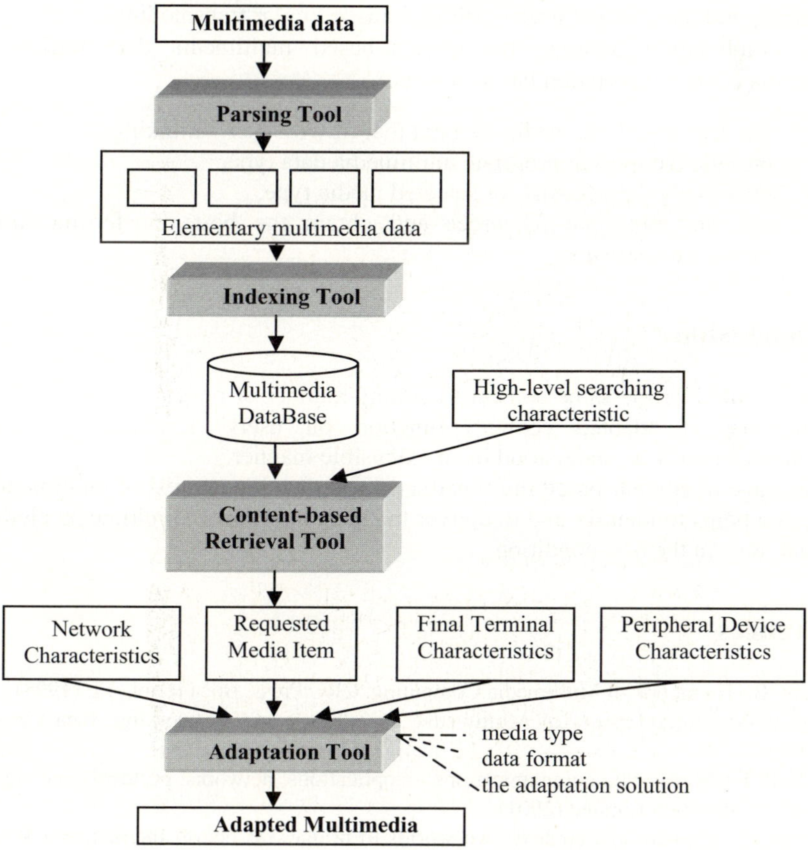

Fig. 2. Process of multimedia data adaptation using content-based data retrieval

The *parsing* refers to the process of segmenting and classification of continuous multimedia streams and consists in three tasks: multimedia streams segmentation into elementary multimedia elements, extracting low-level features from the elementary elements and modeling of content.

The *indexing* process supposes to store the extracted segments and their content in the database or in another data management system.

The *content-based retrieval* relies on parsing and indexing of multimedia data streams. Fig. 2 summarizes the whole process of multimedia data adaptation using content-based data retrieval.

The *adaptation* process uses the results from content-based retrieval process and the characteristics of networks and/or peripheral devices used by each final user and provide the multimedia content adapted using the most appropriate technique for those characteristics.

The adaptation process supposes to select the appropriate media type, the best data format, the location for doing adaptation (supplier, receiver or network level), what kind of adaptation fit the contextual requirements (temporal, spatial or color adaptation) and the solution used (scaling, transcoding or transmoding).

The combination between the content-based multimedia data retrieval and multimedia content adaptation has as results:

- the delivery of the media element that fit with user's thinking,
- provide the most appropriate multimedia data type,
- provide the best format for selected media type,
- use the minimum resources and obtain the best transferring time for multimedia streams.

6 Conclusion

The idea to deliver the same content to a large number of people will be replaced by the delivery of adapted content, function on users' terminal and network characteristics must be understood in an extensible manner.

The usage of content-based multimedia data retrieval in context of multimedia data adaptation helps to identify and to deliver the most appropriate multimedia element to the final user, in the best condition.

References

1. Furht, B.: Handbook of Multimedia Computing. CRC Press, Boca Raton, FL (1998)
2. Pagani, M.: Encyclopedia of Multimedia Technology and Networking, Idea Group Inc. (2005)
3. Halsall, F.: Multimedia communications – applications, networks, protocols and standards, Pearson Education Limited (2001)
4. Pereira, F.: Content and context: two worlds to bridge. In: Fourth International Workshop on Content-Based Multimedia Indexing, CBMI, Riga- Letonia (2005)
5. Kosch, H.: Distributed Multimedia Database Technologies Supported by MPEG-7 and MPEG-21, Auerbach Publications (2004)

Coping with Complexity Through Adaptive Interface Design

Nadine Sarter

University of Michigan
Department of Industrial and Operations Engineering
Center for Ergonomics
1205 Beal Avenue
Ann Arbor, MI 48109
U.S.A.
sarter@umich.edu

Abstract. Complex systems are characterized by a large number and variety of, and often a high degree of dependency between, subsystems. Complexity, in combination with coupling, has been shown to lead to difficulties with monitoring and comprehending system status and activities and thus to an increased risk of breakdowns in human-machine coordination. In part, these breakdowns can be explained by the fact that increased complexity tends to be paralleled by an increase in the amount of data that is made available to operators. Presenting this data in an inappropriate form is crucial to avoiding problems with data overload and attention management. One approach for addressing this challenge is to move from fixed display designs to adaptive information presentation, i.e., information presentation that changes as a function of context. This paper will discuss possible approaches to, challenges for, and effects of increasing the flexibility of information presentation.

Keywords: interface design, adaptive, adaptable, complex systems, adaptation drivers.

1 Introduction

Complex systems are characterized by a large number and variety of parts and by a high degree of dependency – both spatial and temporal – between subsystems. They tend to involve unfamiliar, unplanned, and often invisible or incomprehensible sequences of events as well as common-mode connections where a subsystem serves more than one other component of the system. This complexity, in combination with coupling, has been shown to lead to difficulties with anticipating, monitoring and comprehending system status and activities and thus to an increased risk of breakdowns in the performance of joint human-machine systems. In part, these breakdowns can be explained by the fact that the growth in complexity of modern technologies is paralleled by an increase in the amount of data that is needed by, and available to, operators. Presenting this data in an inappropriate form is crucial to avoid

J. Jacko (Ed.): Human-Computer Interaction, Part III, HCII 2007, LNCS 4552, pp. 493–498, 2007.

problems with data overload and attention management. One proposed approach for addressing this challenge is to move from fixed display designs to adaptive information presentation, i.e., information presentation that changes as a function of context, to ensure that the right information is provided at the right time and in the right format for a given task and situation. Some examples of adaptive user interfaces that have been developed and fielded already include systems that help users sort e-mail, fill out repetitive forms, or help menus that adapt to the user's stress or proficiency level (e.g., Picard, 1997; Trumbly et al., 1994).

This paper will discuss possible approaches to, challenges for, and effects of increasing the flexibility of information presentation. In particular, the benefits and shortcomings of system-initiated adaptation versus user-controlled adaptability will be discussed and compared. Next, possible drivers of display adaptation will be reviewed and discussed. Among the drivers that have been proposed in the literature are user states and characteristics which include personal preferences, experience, fatigue, and alertness/arousal. Capabilities and limitations of human information processing may also be considered, such as perceptual thresholds, timesharing abilities, and crossmodal links in attention. Other possible drivers of adaptation are norms/standards of the work environment, modality appropriateness, task demands, and environmental conditions. Some empirical findings to date on the effects of different forms of display adaptation on system awareness, workload, joint system performance, user trust, and system acceptance will be reviewed.

2 Adaptive or Adaptable Interface Design

The need for moving from fixed display design to context-dependent information representation is widely acknowledged. However, the proper locus of control over the adaptation of an interface continues to be a matter of debate (e.g., Billings, 1997; Billings and Woods, 1994; Hancock and Chignell, 1987; Scerbo, 1996). One important distinction has been made between adaptive and adaptable interfaces. Adaptive interfaces adjust primarily on their own (but sometimes allow for some user control) to changing tasks contexts and demands whereas adaptable designs allow users (but not the system) to change the presentation of information according to their needs and preferences. As with most design choices, either approach involves benefits and risks.

Adaptive designs have the advantage of not imposing additional task demands on the operator and thus not risking the creation of "clumsy automation" (Wiener, 1989) where the automation provides the most support when the user is not busy but fails to assist the user, or even gets in the way, during periods of high task load. In the context of multimodal interface design, for example, Reeves et al. (2004) suggest that a user profile could be captured and determine interface settings. Similarly, Buisine and Martin (2003) propose to adapt multimodal system settings to observed user preferences for a given task and leave the modality choice to the user only when no preference evolves.

Challenges for adaptive interface design include the need for identifying and properly implementing appropriate drivers of display change for a given task environment. Adaptive systems also need to be designed such that the user is informed, in a data-driven fashion, about (system-generated changes in) the currently active interface configuration without adding to the already existing problem of data overload. It is well known that high levels of automation can reduce operator awareness of system dynamics (e.g., Kaber et al., 1999; Sarter and Woods, 2000; Sarter et al., 1997) since humans tend to be less aware of changes that are under the control of another agent than when they make the changes themselves (Wickens, 1994).

For the same reason, adaptable designs involve a considerably lower risk of confusion since the user is in control of changes in information presentation. Once the user initiates a change, he/she will look for confirming feedback in a top-down manner. Due to the perception of increased control, he/she will also likely perceive a higher level of trust in the system. These increased levels of trust and control, however, come at the price of imposing an additional task – interface management. First, the user is required to realize the need for adaptation. For various reasons, failures can occur at this stage. The user may be experiencing high levels of task load and thus not be able to assess critically the appropriateness of the interface settings. Also, even in the absence of high workload and possible time pressure, the user may not be the best judge of the desirable interface setup (Andre and Wickens, 1995, October)). Once the need for change is realized, the operator needs to determine how to adjust the interface properly. For example, it may become apparent that the scale of a map display needs to be changed. However, identifying the proper scale may require experimentation and thus distract the user from the main task at hand. Finally, the user needs to identify and use the proper controls to achieve the desired settings.

The above considerations suggest that, instead of adopting one or the other approach to flexible interface design, it may be more useful to develop a hybrid solution which, at times, allows the system to control display settings but, at other times, supports the user in intervening or overriding system-generated adaptations. Such an approach would help achieve a proper balance between flexibility, predictability, and workload. One example of this approach in the area of control automation in the aviation domain is the work by Inagaki, Takae, and Moray (1999) who have shown that the best decisions about aborting a takeoff were made when pilot and the automation shared control.

3 Adaptation Drivers

If the decision is made to develop a system-controlled adaptive interface for at least some operational circumstances, the identification of appropriate drivers is critical. Among the drivers for display adaptation that have been proposed in the literature are user states and characteristics which include personal preferences, experience, fatigue, and alertness/arousal (e.g., Hollnagel and Woods, 2005; Schmorrow and Kruse, 2002). Capabilities and limitations of human information processing also need to be included in the determination of variations in information display. Perceptual thresholds, timesharing abilities, and crossmodal links in attention can be used to decide on the proper type and timing of signal presentation (e.g., Ferris et al., 2006; Spence and Driver, 1997). Crossmodal spatial and temporal links in attention have recently received considerable attention. They can lead to unwarranted and undesired re-orientation of attention in one modality to the location of unrelated signals in a different sensory channel (spatial links) or to the failure to notice a cue in one modality if it follows a signal in a different modality within certain time windows (temporal links).

Yet other proposed drivers of adaptation include norms/standards of the work environment, modality appropriateness (i.e., the need to match a display modality to a particular type of information – such as the use of visually presented information for spatial tasks), task demands (e.g., the need for information integration, the dual nature of tasks involving both individual and collaborative activities, and time pressure), and environmental conditions (e.g., ambient noise levels).

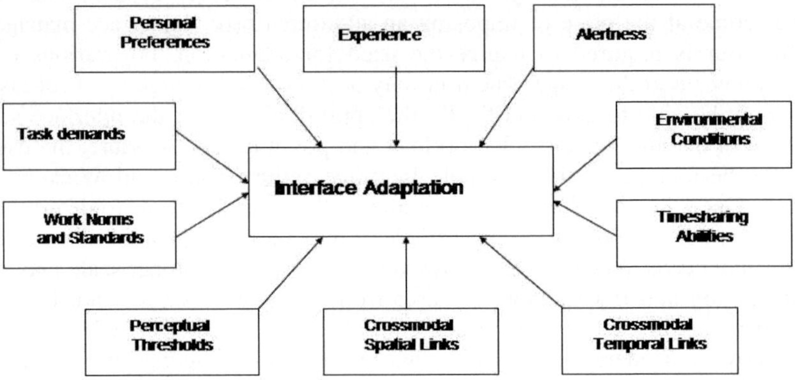

Fig. 1. Proposed Drivers of Interface Adaptation

The appropriateness of the above drivers depends, in part, on the domain for which an interface is designed. For example, the use of personal preferences can be counterproductive in collaborative work domains (e.g., Ho and Sarter, 2004). Also, gaps in our understanding of various aspects of information processing as it occurs in complex environments hamper our ability to vary appropriately the nature and timing of information presentation. Research needs in this area abound, such as the importance of a better understanding of crossmodal spatial and temporal links and constraints between vision, hearing, and touch. Most work to date has examined these issues in the context of spartan laboratory environments, and thus the applicability of findings to the design of real-world interfaces is questionable. Among the many unresolved questions are the exact nature of modality assymmetries (such as apparently opposite effects of crossmodal spatial links between visual-auditory and visual-tactile stimulus combinations) and the proper timing of crossmodal cues to avoid attentional blink and inhibition of return problems (e.g., Ferris and Sarter, Revised manuscript submitted).

Among the challenges for implementing these drivers in real-world contexts is the need to sense online the presence/variation of some of these factors. For example, considerable efforts are under way to identify the most appropriate physiological measures of alertness, fatigue, and workload (such as gaze direction, pupil diameter, EEG, heart rate, or blood pressure).

4 Concluding Remarks

The need for more flexible context-sensitive interface designs is widely acknowledged. Much less agreement has been reached, however, on the proper approach to, and implementation of, adaptive and/or adaptable displays. This paper discussed some of the benefits and disadvantages of these two approaches and their possible combination, possible drivers for adaptive interface design, and research needs to determine the proper implementation of these drivers. The conference presentation will provide more detail on these issues and present recommendations for the design of adaptive and adaptable displays.

Acknowledgments. The preparation of this manuscript was supported, in part, by a grant from the Army Research Laboratory (ARL), under the Advanced Decision Architecture (ADA) Collaborative Technology Alliance (CTA) (grant #DAAD 19-01-2-0009; CTA manager: Dr. Mike Strub; project manager: Sue Archer) and by a grant from the National Science Foundation (grant #0534281; Program Manager: Dr. Ephraim Glinert).

References

1. Billings, C.: Aviation automation: The search for a human-centered approach. Erlbaum, Mahwah, NJ (1997)
2. Billings, C.E., Woods, D.D.: Concerns about adaptive automation in aviation systems. In: Mouloua, M., Parasuraman, R. (eds.) Human performance in automated systems: current research and trends, pp. 264–269. Erlbaum, Hillsdale, NJ (1994)
3. Buisine, S., Martin, J-C.: Design principles for cooperation between modalities in bi-directional multimodal interfaces. In: Proceedings of the CHI 2003 workshop on Principles for multimodal user interface design, Ft. Lauderdale, Florida (2003)
4. Ferris, T., Penfold, R., Hameed, S., Sarter, N.B.: Crossmodal links in attention: Their implications for the design of multimodal interfaces in complex environments. In: Proceedings of the 50th Annual Meeting of the Human Factors and Ergonomics Society. San Francisco, CA (October 2006)
5. Ferris, T.K., Sarter, N.B.: Crossmodal links between vision, audition, and touch in complex environments (Manuscript submitted 2007)
6. Ho, C.-Y., Sarter, N.B.: Supporting synchronous distributed communication and coordination through multimodal information exchange. In: Proceedings of the 48th Annual Meeting of the Human Factors and Ergonomics Society. New Orleans, LS (September 2004)
7. Hollnagel, E., Woods, D.D.: Joint cognitive systems: Foundations of cognitive systems engineering. CRC Press, Boca Raton, FL (2005)
8. Inagaki, T., Takae, Y., Moray, N.: Automation and human-interface for takeoff safety. In: Proceedings of the 10th International Symposium on Aviation Psychology, pp. 402–407 (1999)
9. Kaber, D., Omal, E., Endsley, M.: Level of automation effects on tele-robot performance and human operator situation awareness and subjective workload. In: Mouloua, M., Parasuraman, R. (eds.) Automation technology and human performance: Current research and trends, pp. 165–170. Erlbaum, Mahwah, NJ (1999)

10. Picard, R.: Does HAL cry Digital Tears: Emotions and computers. In: Stork, D.G. (ed.) HAL's Legacy, MIT Press, Cambridge, MA (1997)
11. Reeves, L.M., Lai, J., Larson, J.A., Oviatt, S., Balaji, T.S., Buisine, S., Collings, P., Cohen, P., Kraal, B., Martin, J.-C., McTear, M., Raman, T.V., Stanney, K.M., Su, H., Wang, Q.-Y.: Guidelines for multimodal user interface design. Communications of the ACM 47(1), 57–59 (2004)
12. Sarter, N.B., Woods, D.D., Billings, C.E.: Automation surprises. In: Salvendy, G. (ed.) Handbook of Human Factors and Ergonomics, 2nd edn., pp. 1926–1943. Wiley, New York, NY (1997)
13. Sarter, N.B., Woods, D.D.: Teamplay with a powerful and independent agent: A full-mission simulation study. Human Factors 42(3), 390–402 (2000)
14. Scerbo, M.W.: Theoretical perspectives on adaptive automation. In: Parasuraman, R., Mouloua, M. (eds.): Automation and Human Performance, LEA, pp. 37–63 (1996)
15. Schmorrow, D.D., Kruse, A.A.: DARPA's augmented cognition program: Tomorrow's human computer interaction from vision to reality: Building cognitively aware computational systems. In: IEEE 7th Conference on Human Factors and Power Plants, Scottdale, AZ (2002)
16. Spence, C., Driver, J.: Cross-modal links in attention between audition, vision, and touch: Implications for interface design. International Journal of Cognitive Ergonomics 1(4), 351–373 (1997)
17. Trumbly, J.E., Arnett, K.P., Johnson, P.C.: Productivity gains via an adaptive user interface. Journal of Human-Computer Studies 40, 63–81 (1994)
18. Wickens, C.: Designing for situation awareness and trust in automation. In: Proceedings of the IFAC Conference. Baden-Baden, Germany, pp. 174–179 (1994)
19. Wiener, E.L.: Human factors of advanced technology (glass cockpit) transport aircraft. Technical Report 117528. CA: NASA Ames Research Center, Moffett Field (1989)
20. Andre, A.D., Wickens, C.D.: When users want what's not best for them. Ergonomics in Design, 10–14 (1995)

Region-Based Model of Tour Planning Applied to Interactive Tour Generation

Inessa Seifert

Department of Mathematics and Informatics,
SFB/TR8 Spatial Cognition
University of Bremen, Germany
seifert@informatik.uni-bremen.de

Abstract. The paper addresses a tour planning problem, which encompasses weakly specified constraints such as different kinds of activities together with corresponding spatial assignments such as locations and regions. Alternative temporal orders of planed activities together with underspecified spatial assignments available at different levels of granularity lead to a high computational complexity of the given tour planning problem. The paper introduces the results of an exploratory tour planning study and a Region-based Direction Heuristic, derived from the acquired data. A gesture-based interaction model is proposed, which allows structuring the search space by a human user at a high level of abstraction for the subsequent generation of alternative solutions so that the proposed Region-based Direction Heuristic can be applied.

1 Introduction

Planning of different activities in an unfamiliar environment is a spatial task people are more or less often challenged with. Consider for example planning of a journey to a foreign city or a country. Before starting a journey, travelers have to agree on what they are going to do, i.e., different kinds of activities, together with where and when the activities will take place. Usually, the original considerations regarding the kind as well as the temporal order of activities together with corresponding locations are known only partially and at different levels of granularity: for example visiting of sightseeing attractions in a particular city, a part of a country, or swimming at a sea coast. Since most journeys are constrained in time, travelers have to consider how durations of alternative activities and time required for covering the distances between multiple destinations fit into the given temporal scope of a journey. Dealing with multiple spatio-temporal configurations und reasoning about various constraints is a cognitively demanding task [5].

On the one hand the illustrated problem domain encompasses partially specified activities together with spatial assignments, which are available at different levels of granularity or underspecified. And on the other hand, to compile a journey which our traveler enjoys means to find a solution out of different possible alternatives which fulfills such important criteria like the traveler's personal preferences, moods or even emotions. Since the personal criteria regarding the solution quality are difficult or

J. Jacko (Ed.): Human-Computer Interaction, Part III, HCII 2007, LNCS 4552, pp. 499–507, 2007.

even impossible to formalize, the given problem solving task cannot be totally outsourced to a computational constraint solver. To provide assistance with such type of Partially Unfomalized Constraint Satisfaction Problems (PUCP) we pursue in our recent work [11] a collaborative assistance approach, which requires the user's active participation in the given problem solving task [9].

Since the spatio-temporal planning task is now shared between an artificial assistance system and a user, the problem domain is separated into *hard constraints*, for example a temporal scope of a journey, specific locations, and types of activities, and *soft constraints*, for example, personal preferences. An assistance system supplies a user with alternative solutions that fulfill the specified hard constraints. However, depending on the number of constraints left unspecified, we face the problem of high computational complexity as well as the problem of the obtained solution space becoming sufficiently large [12].

In our previous work we proposed a Region-based Representation Structure, which allows for specification of spatial and temporal constraints at different levels of granularity and generation of alternative solutions [10]. In [11] we proposed the region-based heuristics, which requires specific temporal order of activities and herewith are very well suited for modification of existing solutions at different levels of granularity. Yet, underspecified temporal order of activities drives the system to the limits of performance and hardly acceptable response times. The pioneering work of Krolak and colleagues demonstrated how the computational complexity of another spatial problem, namely the classical Traveling Salesman Problem, could be reduced using human-machine interaction. The search space has been structured by a human and herewith prepared for the subsequent computations performed by an artificial system [6].

Although a weakly specified tour planning problem is for the most of the people a cognitively demanding and time consuming task, they do manage to produce a single or a limited set of solutions for a given problem in a tolerable amount of time. To identify the underlying cognitive processes and problem solving strategies we conducted an exploratory study.

The paper introduces a gesture-based interaction model, which is based on the Region-based Model of Spatial Planning derived from the analysis of the acquired empirical data. The proposed interaction model provides users with operations that resemble the identified spatial problem solving strategies. The operations allow for pruning of significant parts of the search space and applying of the Region-based Direction Heuristic (RDH). The RDH doesn't require a predefined temporal order of activities and allows for efficient generation of alternative solutions. This paper represents a promising approach for solving computationally complex problems using human-machine interaction.

2 Tour Planning Problem

To plan a tour through a foreign country means to find a feasible temporal order of activities and corresponding routes under consideration of spatial and temporal constraints. An activity is defined by its type (*what)*, duration (*how long)* and a spatial

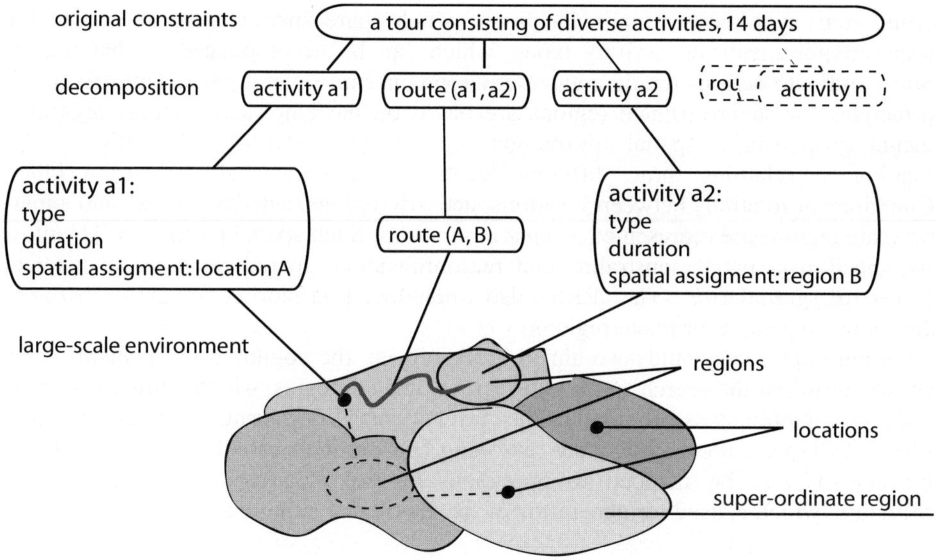

Fig. 1. Representation of the tour planning problem

assignment *(where)* ([2], [11]). Depending on the knowledge available at the beginning of the planning process, the initial set of activities and routes is underspecified (see Fig. 1).

Usually, at the beginning of the planning process spatial assignments are known only partially, i.e., defined at different levels of granularity: for example a particular location, a region, a part of the country, or left unspecified. An activity type can include a set of one of more possible options for activities, like swimming, or hiking, or also left unspecified.

Spatial constraints represent partially specified spatial assignments of the planned activities, and routes between them. We consider temporal constraints, which encompass an overall scope of a journey together with the condition that subsequent activities don't overlap with each other in time. An assistance system is responsible for instantiation of alternative spatial assignments as well as alternative temporal orders of activities. To solve the given tour planning problem means to find all possible spatio-temporal configurations consisting of different variations of activities, corresponding spatial assignments, and routes between them.

2.1 Region-Based Representation Structure

In our previous work [11] we introduced a collaborative spatial assistance system, which operates on a Region-based Representation Structure [10], and allows for interactive specification and relaxation of spatial constraints at different levels of granularity. The RRS is a graph-based knowledge representation structure, which encompasses a spatial hierarchy consisting of locations, activity regions and super-ordinate regions. Locations are associated with specific activity types and represent nodes of the graph, which are connected with each other via edges carrying distance costs. Activity regions contain locations, which share specific properties, like the user's requirements on activity types, which can be accomplished in that region. Super-ordinate regions divide a given environment into several parts. The structuring principles for super-ordinate regions are based on the empirical findings regarding mental processing of spatial information (e.g., [7], [13], and [4]). The RRS includes topological relations: how different locations are connected with each other. Containment relations between locations, activity regions, activity regions and super-ordinate regions are represented as *part-of* relations. Such spatial partnomies [1] allow for specifying spatial constraints and reasoning about spatial relations at different levels of granularity. The RRS also includes neighboring relations between corresponding super-ordinate regions.

In our exploratory study we aimed at identifying the cognitive mechanisms, such as structuring of the search space into regions, and strategies, which allow for solving the given planning task efficiently. The current contribution brings together both lines of research and demonstrates how reasoning and problem solving strategies utilized by humans can be mapped to operations on the Region-based Representation Structure, which is used for generation of the alternative solutions.

3 Region-Based Model of Tour Planning

Due to limitations of the cognitive capacity of the human mind people developed sophisticated strategies to deal with complex problems by dividing them into sub-problems [8] and solve them operating at different levels of abstraction [3].

The fine-to-coarse planning heuristic provides analysis and description of human strategies when performing a route-planning task, i.e., finding a path from one specific location to another specific location in a regionalized large-scale environment [14]. The heuristic operates on a hierarchically organized knowledge representation structure. The structure encompasses different abstraction levels, like places and regions. The route-planning procedure is executed simultaneously at different levels of granularity: information regarding close distances is activated at a fine level, i.e. places, whereas the information regarding far distances is represented at a coarse level, i.e., regions.

Based on the assumptions, that (1) mental knowledge is hierarchical and (2) regions help to solve spatial problems more efficiently, we conducted an exploratory study. The study aimed at asserting the role of regionalization in weakly specified tour planning problems.

3.1 Tour Planning Study

During the experiment subjects were asked to plan and provide a description of an individual journey to two imaginary friends, who intended to travel about the given environment. As an unfamiliar large-scale environment we chose Crete, which is a famous holiday island in Greece. The participants had to consider the following constraints: a journey had to start and end at the same location, cover 14 days, and encompass a variety of different activities. The participants were provided with a map, which was annotated with symbols representing different activity types. During the study, the participants had to accomplish the following tasks: 1) produce a feasible order of activities with concrete locations and routes between them, 2) draw the resulting route on the map, 3) describe the decisions they made by advising imaginary friends how to solve such tour planning problems. We analyzed the descriptions as well as the features of the produced tours, such as the shape resulting from selected routes. The results allow us to derive the following assumptions regarding the underlying problem solving strategies.

3.2 Regionalization

Humans solve such kind of planning problems using different levels of abstraction [3]. The analysis of the descriptions revealed, that the participants divided the given environment into several super-ordinate regions according to the salient structural features of the environment. The salient features are topographical properties such as landscapes, sea coast, and major cities. Herewith, the super-ordinate regions build the highest level of abstraction. The subjects identified attractions situated in super-ordinate regions and made a decision, which super-ordinate regions were worth visiting.

3.3 Region-Based Direction Strategy

Since mental regions may have only vague boundaries, Fig. 2 provides a schematic illustration of a separation of a given environment into several regions according to its salient structural features, e.g., major cities and landscapes. Additionally, the structuring principles based on cardinal directions, reported by [7], were applied (Fig. 3).

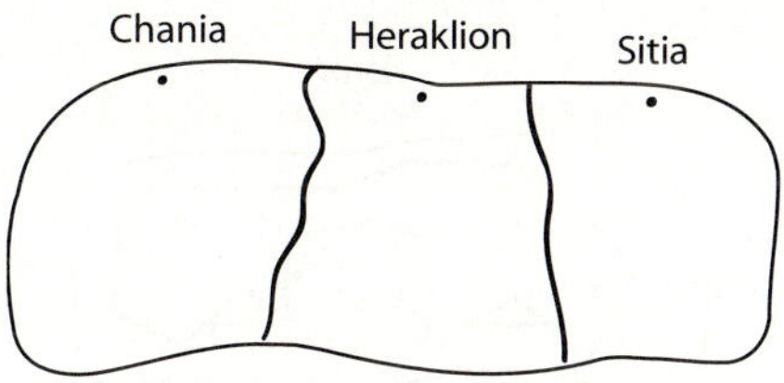

Fig. 2. Division in 3 parts

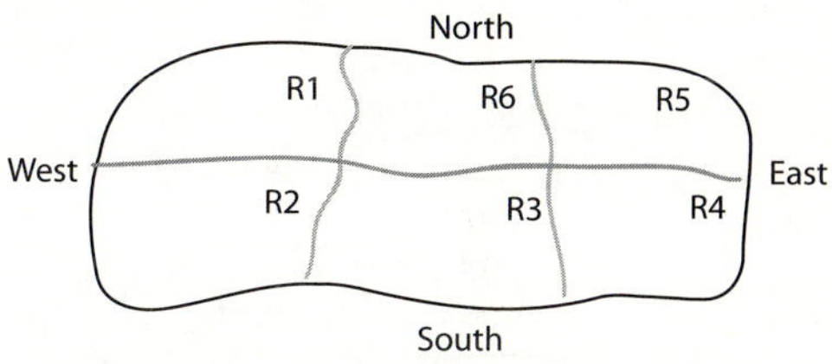

Fig. 3. Regions resulting from cardinal directions

Such regions build the highest level of abstraction. After that the subjects searched for the attractions situated in the high-level regions, and if required cluster the attractions into smaller regions, e.g., sea coast, which share specific properties, such as vicinity of towns or specific landscapes.

While selecting the appropriate locations, the subjects put high-level regions in a particular order (see Fig. 4): e.g., getting from the northern part of the island to the south coast. Due to the cognitive model of planning [3] a human is capable of changing his plan at different levels of abstraction at any point at time. That means that the order of current and subsequent high-level regions influence the planning process at a finer level of granularity (see Fig. 5), and the other way round, decisions made on the finer level impact the order of the high-level regions.

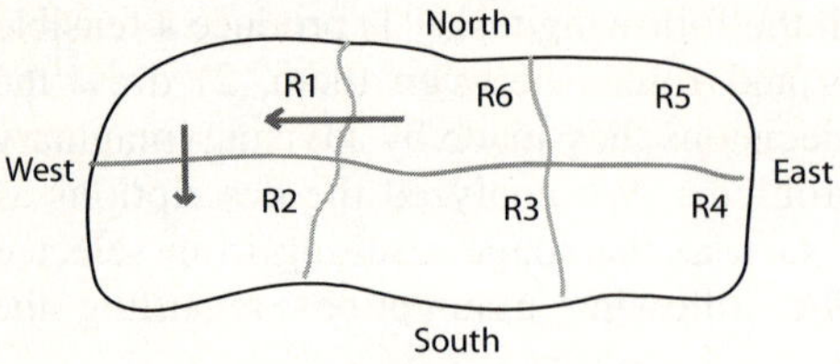

Fig. 4. High-level order relations

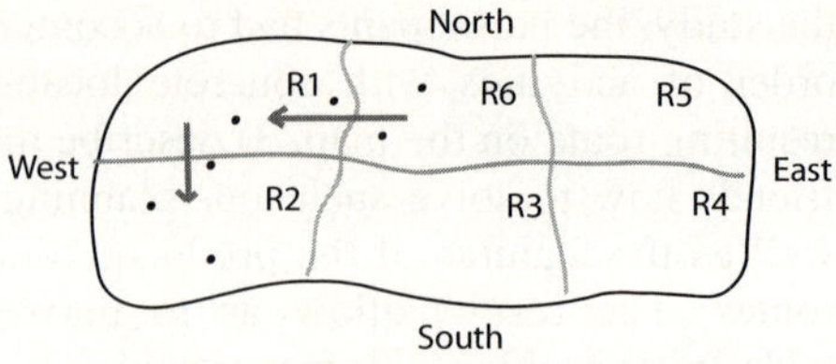

Fig. 5. Selection of locations

3.4 Region-Based Direction Heuristic

The region-based direction heuristic utilizes the direction relations between the neighboring super-ordinate regions, e.g., super-ordinate region R1 in the west of super-ordinate region R6 (see Fig. 4). To implement the RDH we extended the neighboring relations between the super-ordinate regions of the Region-based Representation Structure with corresponding cardinal directions. The edges between different locations, which represent nodes of the hierarchical region-based graph, have to be also supplemented with direction information between the nodes.

Now, the super-ordinate regions are related to each other by neighboring relations, e.g., R6 is neighbor of R1, R3, R5 and cardinal directions between the neighboring regions: West(R6, R1), South(R6, R3), East(R6, R5). The generation of alternative tours is implemented as a depth-first search algorithm, which considers the direction information between subsequent super-ordinate regions when selecting appropriate nodes, e.g., R6, R1, R2, R3, R6 (see Fig 6., Fig. 7).

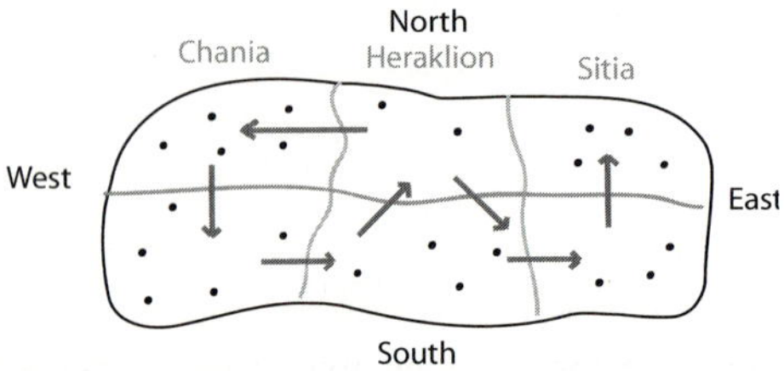

Fig. 6. High-level order of regions

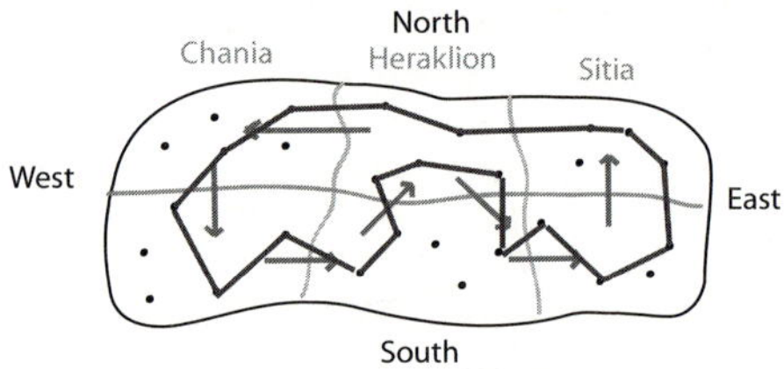

Fig. 7. Tour resulting from the high-level order of the super-ordinate regions

To preserve the high-level course of a tour, which is defined by the order of the super-ordinate regions each current node *node n* and a subsequent *node n+1* should satisfy the following criteria:

1. *Node n* and *node n+1* belong to the same super-ordinate region, or *node n+1* belongs to the next super-ordinate region from the ordered set of super-ordinate regions.
2. Each node is visited only once.

3. The selection of the subsequent *node n+1* depends on the direction relation between the subsequent super-ordinate regions, i.e., the coarse direction.
4. First, the nodes are selected, which presume the direction of the subsequent super-ordinate regions.
5. If no nodes can be found which correspond to the direction relation that holds between two subsequent super-ordinate regions, the algorithm starts with instantiation of slight deviations from the course of the journey.
6. The opposite direction to the direction between two subsequent super-ordinate regions is tried as the last opportunity.
7. Nodes, which are situated in the last super-ordinate region, presume the direction relation between the last pair of super-ordinate regions.

The proposed search heuristics allow the efficient generation of trips. Nevertheless, an assistance system needs the user's input to start with the generation procedure. In the next section we introduce an interaction model, which arose from the described exploratory study. The interaction model resembles the described problem solving steps and allows for utilizing of the proposed heuristics.

4 Interactive Tour Planning

The assistance system operates on a touch screen device equipped with a pen-like pointing device. Such pointing devices have also additional buttons, to provide the functionality of the right, middle and left buttons of a conventional computer mouse. The following figures demonstrate the selection of spatial assignments at different levels of granularity. The constraints are represented as a list of activities, which are defined by an activity type, duration, and a spatial assignment.

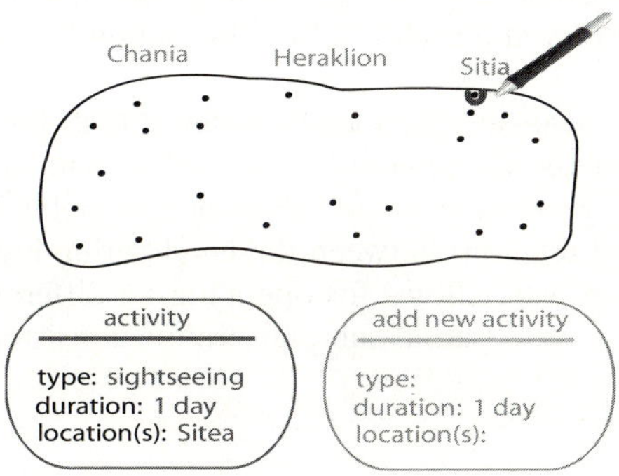

Fig. 8. Selection of a fixed location

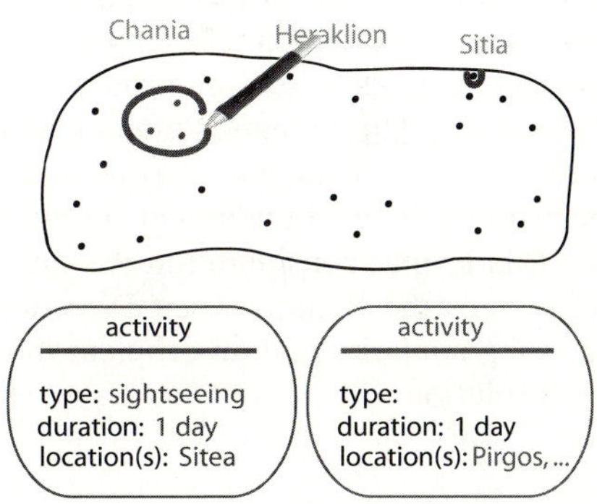

Fig. 9. Selection of a user-specific region

Figure 8 illustrates a definition of a fixed location with a specific activity type. Figure 9 demonstrates a selection of a user-specific region, which is considered as a set of optional locations for a specified activity.

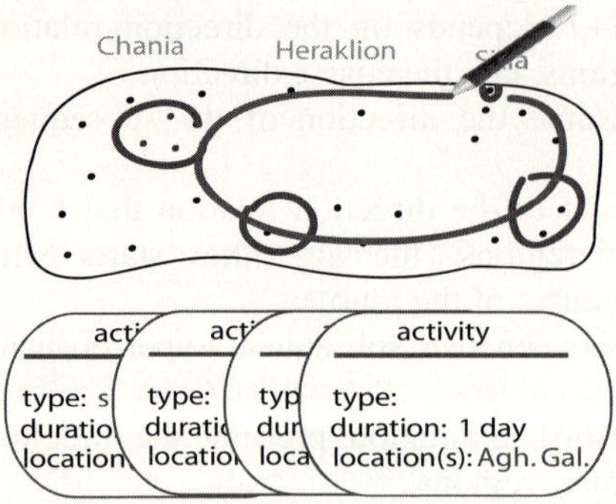

Fig. 10. Setting up the high-level order of super-ordinate regions

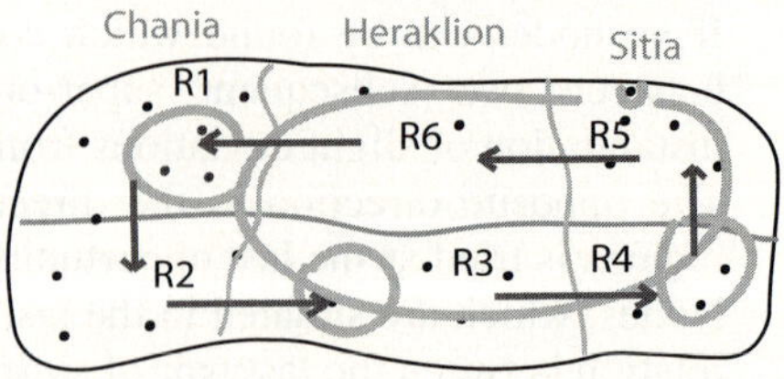

Fig. 11. Internal representation of the user-defined order of the super-ordinate regions

Figure 10 illustrates the definition of a high-level order of the super-ordinate regions. Figure 11 shows the corresponding internal representation of the assistance system: R5, R6, R1, R2, R3, R4, R5, which are used for the generation of alternative solutions.

5 Conclusion

In the scope of the paper we demonstrated how human-machine interaction can be employed for solving computationally complex problems. In our pervious work we proposed the cognitively motivated Region-based Representation Structure, which resembles the hierarchical mental knowledge representation. The current contribution introduced a gesture-based interaction model, which operates on the RRS and allows not only for definition of constraints at different levels of granularity, but also for preparation of the search space by a human user at a high-level of abstraction for the subsequent constraint solving procedure.

Due to non deterministic human planning behavior, the specific order of high-level regions can be changed during the process of planning. The RRS and the demonstrated interaction model allows for generation of sub-tours at any point in time. Taking into consideration the direction relations between the neighboring high level regions the Region-based Direction Heuristic allows for operating on different levels of granularity and an efficient integration of partial sub-plans into a consistent overall solution.

Acknowledgments

I gratefully acknowledge financial support by the German Research Foundation (DFG) through the Transregional Collaborative Research Center SFB/TR 8 Spatial Cognition (project R1-[ImageSpace]). I also want to thank Thora Tenbrink, who helped to design and conduct the introduced exploratory studies. Special thanks to Zhendong Chen and Susan Träber, who help to conduct the experiments and evaluate the data.

References

1. Bittner, T., Stell, J.G.: Vagueness and Rough Location. Geoinformatica 6, 99–121 (2002)
2. Brown, B.: Working on problems of tourist. Annals of Tourism Research 34(2), 364–368 (2007)
3. Hayes-Roth, B., Hayes-Roth, F.: A Cognitive Model of Planning. Cognitive Science 3, 275–310 (1979)
4. Hirtle, S.C.: The cognitive atlas: using GIS as a metaphor for memory. In: Egenhofer, M., Golledge, R. (eds.) Spatial and temporal reasoning in geographic information systems, pp. 267–276. Oxford University Press, Oxford (1998)
5. Johnson-Laird, P.N.: Mental models. Harvard University Press, Cambridge, MA (1983)
6. Krolak, P., Felts, W., Marble, G.: A Man-Machine Approach Toward Solving the Traveling Salesman Problem. Communications of the ACM 14(5), 327–334 (1971)
7. Lyi, Y., Wang, X., Jin, X., Wu, L.: On Internal Cardinal Direction Relations. In: Cohn, A.G., Mark, D.M. (eds.) COSIT 2005. LNCS, vol. 3693, pp. 283–299. Springer, Heidelberg (2005)
8. Newell, A., Simon, H.A.: Human problem solving. Prentice Hall, Englewood Cliffs, NJ (1972)
9. Schlieder, C., Hagen, C.: Interactive layout generation with a diagrammatic constraint language. In: Habel, C., Brauer, W., Freksa, C., Wender, K.F. (eds.) Spatial Cognition II. LNCS (LNAI), vol. 1849, pp. 198–211. Springer, Heidelberg (2000)
10. Seifert, I., Barkowsky T., Freksa, C.: Region-Based Representation for Assistance with Spatio-Temporal Planning in Unfamiliar Environments. In: Gartner, G., Cartwright, W., Peterson, M.,P.: Location Based Services and TeleCartography, Lecture Notes in Geoinformation and Cartography, pp. 179–191, Springer, Heidelberg (2007)
11. Seifert, I.: Collaborative Assistance with Spatio-Temporal Planning Problems. In: Spatial Cognition 2006. LNCS, Springer, Heidelberg (to appear)
12. Stamatopoulos, P., Karali, I., Halatsis, C.: PETINA - Tour Generation Using the ElipSys Inference System. In: Proceedings of the ACM Symposium on Applied Computing SAC '92, Kansas City, pp. 320–327 (1992)
13. Tversky, B.: Cognitive maps, cognitive collages, and spatial mental models. In: Campari, I., Frank, A.U. (eds.) COSIT 1993. LNCS, vol. 716, pp. 14–24. Springer, Heidelberg (1993)
14. Wiener, J.M.: PhD Thesis, University of Tübingen, Germany: Places and Regions in Perception, Route Planning, and Spatial Memory (2004)

A Learning Interface Agent for User Behavior Prediction

Gabriela Şerban, Adriana Tarţa, and Grigoreta Sofia Moldovan

Department of Computer Science
Babeş-Bolyai University,
1, M. Kogălniceanu Street, Cluj-Napoca, Romania
{gabis,adriana,grigo}@cs.ubbcluj.ro

Abstract. Predicting user behavior is an important issue in *Human Computer Interaction* ([5]) research, having an essential role when developing intelligent user interfaces. A possible solution to deal with this challenge is to build an *intelligent interface agent* ([8]) that learns to identify patterns in users behavior. The aim of this paper is to introduce a new agent based approach in predicting users behavior, using a probabilistic model. We propose an intelligent interface agent that uses a supervised learning technique in order to achieve the desired goal. We have used *Aspect Oriented Programming* ([7]) in the development of the agent in order to benefit of the advantages of this paradigm. Based on a newly defined evaluation measure, we have determined the accuracy of the agent's prediction on a case study.

Keywords: user interface, interface agent, supervised learning, aspect oriented programming.

1 Introduction

Nowadays, computers pervade more and more aspects of our lives, that is why an interactive software system has to be able to adapt to its users. Adaptability is possible to achieve by intelligent interface agents that learn by "watching over the shoulder" ([8]) of the user and by detecting regularities in the user's behavior.

Human-Computer Interaction ([5]) is a discipline that deals with improving user interfaces. Graphical user interfaces are still hard to learn for inexperienced users. Intelligent User Interface agents are a way of solving this problem, for example by guiding users through a given task.

Interface agents are autonomous semi-intelligent systems that employ artificial intelligence techniques in order to provide assistance to a user dealing with a particular application. Their autonomy is provided by the capability of learning from their environment.

Aspect Oriented Programming (AOP) is a new programming paradigm that addresses the issues of *crosscutting concerns* ([7]). A crosscutting concern is a feature of a software system whose implementation is spread all over the system. An aspect is a new modularization unit that corresponds to a crosscutting concern. The aspects are integrated into the system using a special tool called *weaver*.

J. Jacko (Ed.): Human-Computer Interaction, Part III, HCII 2007, LNCS 4552, pp. 508–517, 2007.

In this paper we propose a new approach in predicting users behavior (sequences of user actions) using an interface agent, called **LIA** (Learning Interface Agent), that learns by supervision. In the training step, **LIA** agent monitors the behavior of a set of real users, and captures information that will be stored in its knowledge base, using Aspect Oriented Programming. Aspect Oriented Programming is used in order to separate the agent from the software system.

Based on the knowledge acquired in the training step, **LIA** will learn to predict the sequence of actions for a particular user. Finally, this prediction could be used for assisting users in their interaction with a specific system. Currently, we are focusing only on determining accurate predictions. Future improvements of our approach will deal with enhancing **LIA** with assistance capability, too.

The main contributions of this paper are:

- To develop an intelligent interface agent that learns using an original supervised learning method.
- To present a theoretical model on which our approach is based.
- To define an evaluation measure for determining the precision of the agent's prediction.
- To use *Aspect Oriented Programming* in the agent development.

The paper is structured as follows. Section 2 presents our approach in developing a learning interface agent for predicting users behavior. An experimental evaluation on a case study is described in Section 3. Section 4 compares our approach with existing ones. Conclusions and further work are given in Section 5.

2 Our Approach

In this section we present our approach in developing a learning interface agent (**LIA**) for predicting users behavior. Subsection 2.1 introduces the theoretical model needed in order to describe the agent behavior given in Subsection 2.2. The overall architecture of **LIA** agent is proposed in Subsection 2.3.

2.1 Theoretical Model

In the following, we will consider that **LIA** agent monitors the interaction of users with a software application $\mathcal{SA}$, while performing a given task $\mathcal{T}$. We denote by $\mathcal{A}$ the set $\{a_1, a_2, \ldots, a_n\}$ of all possible actions that might appear during the interaction with $\mathcal{SA}$. An action can be: pushing a button, selecting a menu item, filling in a text field, etc.

During the users interaction with $\mathcal{SA}$ in order to perform $\mathcal{T}$, user traces are generated. A *user trace* is a sequence of user actions. We consider a *user trace successful* if the given task is accomplished. Otherwise, we deal with an *unsuccessful* trace.

Currently, in our approach we are focusing only on *successful* traces, that is why we formally define, in the following, this term.

Definition 1. ***Successful user trace***
Let us consider a software application $\mathcal{SA}$ and a given task $\mathcal{T}$ that can be performed using $\mathcal{SA}$. A sequence $t = < x_1, x_2, \ldots, x_{k_t} >$, where

- $k_t \in \mathbb{N}$, *and*
- $x_j \in \mathcal{A}, \ \forall 1 \le j \le k_t$

*which accomplishes the task $\mathcal{T}$ is called a **successful user trace**.*

In Definition 1, we have denoted by k_t the number of user actions in trace t. We denote by $\mathcal{ST}$ the set of all *successful user traces.*

In order to predict the user behavior, **LIA** agent stores a collection of *successful user traces* during the training step. In our view, this collection represents the *knowledge base* of the agent.

Definition 2. ***LIA's Knowledge base – $\mathcal{KB}$***
Let us consider a software application $\mathcal{SA}$ and a given task $\mathcal{T}$ that can be performed using $\mathcal{SA}$. A collection $\mathcal{KB} = \{t_1, t_2, \ldots, t_m\}$ of successful user traces, where

- $t_i \in \mathcal{ST}, \ \forall 1 \le i \le m$,
- $t_i = < x_1^i, x_2^i, \ldots, x_{k_i}^i >, \forall x_j^i \in \mathcal{A}, \ 1 \le j \le k_i$

*represents the **knowledge base** of **LIA** agent.*
We mention that m represents the cardinality of $\mathcal{KB}$ and k_i represents the number of actions in trace t_i $(\forall 1 \le i \le m)$.

Definition 3. ***Subtrace of a user trace***
*Let $t = < s_1, s_2, \ldots, s_k >$ be a trace in the knowledge base $\mathcal{KB}$. We say that $sub_t(s_i, s_j) = < s_i, s_{i+1}, \ldots, s_j >$ $(i \le j)$ is a **subtrace** of t starting from action s_i and ending with action s_j.*

In the following we will denote by $\|t\|$ the number of actions (length) of (sub) trace t. We mention that for two given actions s_i and s_j $(i \ne j)$ there can be many subtraces in trace t starting from s_i and ending with s_j. We will denote by $\mathcal{SUB}(s_i, s_j)$ the set of all these subtraces.

2.2 LIA Agent Behavior

The goal is to make **LIA** agent capable to predict, at a given moment, the appropriate action that a user should perform in order to accomplish $\mathcal{T}$.

In order to provide **LIA** with the above-mentioned behavior, we propose a supervised learning technique that consists of two steps:

1. Training Step
During this step, **LIA** agent monitors the interaction of a set of real users while performing task $\mathcal{T}$ using application $\mathcal{SA}$ and builds its knowledge base $\mathcal{KB}$ (Definition 2). The interaction is monitored using AOP.

In a more general approach, two knowledge bases could be built during the training step: one for the successful user traces and the second for the unsuccessful ones.

2. Prediction Step

The goal of this step is to predict the behavior of a new user *U,* based on the data acquired during the training step, using a probabilistic model. After each action *act* performed by *U*, excepting his/her starting action, **LIA** will predict the next action, $a_r (1 \le r \le n)$, to be performed, with a given probability $P(act, a_r)$, using $\mathcal{KB}$.

The probability $P(act, a_r)$ is given by Equation (1).

$$P(act, a_r) = \max\{P(act, a_i), 1 \le i \le n\}. \tag{1}$$

In order to compute these probabilities, we introduce the concept of *scores* between two actions. The score between actions a_i and a_j, denoted by $score(a_i, a_j)$ indicates the degree to which a_j must follow a_i in a successful performance of $\mathcal{T}$. This means that the value of $score(a_i, a_j)$ is the greatest when a_j should immediately follow a_i in a successful task performance.

The score between a given action *act* of a user and an action a_q, $1 \le q \le n$, $score(act, a_q)$, is computed as in Equation (2).

$$score(act, a_q) = \max\left\{\frac{1}{dist(t_i, act, a_q)}, 1 \le i \le m\right\}, \tag{2}$$

where $dist(t_i, act, a_q)$ represents, in our view, the *distance* between two actions *act* and a_q in a trace t_i, computed based on $\mathcal{KB}$.

$$dist(t_i, act, a_q) = \begin{cases} length(t_i, act, a_q) - 1 & \text{if } \exists sub_{t_i}(act, a_q) \\ \infty & otherwise \end{cases}. \tag{3}$$

$length(t_i, act, a_q)$ defines the minimum distance between *act* and a_q in trace t_i.

$$length(t_i, act, a_q) = min\{\ \|s\| \mid s \in \mathcal{SUB}_{t_i}(act, a_q)\ \}. \tag{4}$$

In our view, $length(t_i, act, a_q)$ represents the minimum number of actions performed by the user *U* in trace t_i, in order to get from action *act* to action a_q, i.e., the minimum length of all possible subtraces $sub_{t_i}(act, a_q)$.

From Equation (2), we have that $score(act, a_q) \in [0,1]$ and the value of $score(act, a_q)$ increases as the *distance* between *act* and a_q in traces from $\mathcal{KB}$ decreases.

Based on the above *scores*, $P(act, a_i), 1 \le i \le n$, is computed as follows:

$$P(act, a_i) = \frac{score(act, a_i)}{\max\{score(act, a_j) \mid 1 \le j \le n\}}. \tag{5}$$

In our view, based on Equation (5), higher probabilities are assigned to actions that are the most appropriate to be executed.

The result of the agent's prediction is the action a_r that satisfies Equation (1). We mention that in a non-deterministic case (when there are more actions having the same maximum probability P) an additional selection technique can be used.

2.3 LIA Agent Architecture

In Fig. 1 we present the architecture of **LIA** agent having the behavior described in Section 2.2.

In the current version of our approach, the predictions of **LIA** are sent to an *Evaluation Module* that evaluates the accuracy of the results (Fig. 1). We intend to improve our work in order to transform the agent in a personal assistant of the user. In this case the result of the agent's prediction will be sent directly to the user.

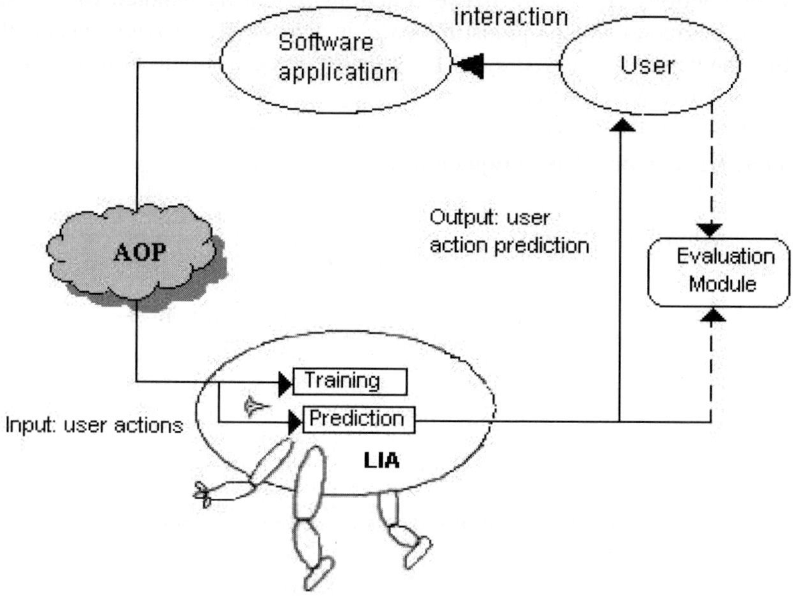

Fig. 1. LIA agent architecture

The agent uses AOP in order to gather information about its environment. The AOP module is used for capturing user's actions: mouse clicking, text entering, menu choosing, etc. These actions are received by **LIA** agent and are used both in the training step (to build the knowledge base $\mathcal{KB}$) and in the prediction step (to determine the most probable next user action).

We have decided to use AOP in developing the learning agent in order to take advantage of the following:

- Clear separation between the software system $\mathcal{SA}$ and the agent.
- The agent can be easily adapted and integrated with other software systems.

- The software system $\mathcal{SA}$ does not need to be modified in order to obtain the user input.
- The source code corresponding to input actions gathering is not spread all over the system, it appears in only one place, the *aspect*.
- If new information about the user software system interaction is required, only the corresponding aspect has to be modified.

3 Experimental Evaluation

In order to evaluate **LIA's** prediction accuracy, we compare the sequence of actions performed by the user U with the sequence of actions predicted by the agent. We consider an action prediction accurate if the probability of the prediction is greater than a given threshold.

For this purpose, we have defined a quality measure, $ACC(\mathbf{LIA}, U)$, called *ACCuracy*. The evaluation will be made on a case study and the results will be presented in Subsection 3.3.

3.1 Evaluation Measure

In the following we will consider that the training step for **LIA** agent was completed. We are focusing on evaluating how accurate are the agent's predictions during the interaction between a given user U and the software application $\mathcal{SA}$. Let us consider that the user trace is $t_U = < y_1^U, y_2^U, \ldots, y_{k_U}^U >$ and the trace corresponding to the agent's prediction is the following: $t_{LIA}(t_U) = < z_2^U, \ldots, z_{k_U}^U >$. For each $2 \le j \le k_U$, **LIA** agent predicts the most probable next user action, z_j^U, with the probability $P(y_{j-1}^U, z_j^U)$ (Section 2.2). The following definition evaluates the accuracy of **LIA** agent's prediction with respect to the user trace t_U.

Definition 4. ***ACCuracy of LIA agent prediction - ACC***
The accuracy of the prediction with respect to the user trace t_U *is given by* Equation (6).

$$ACC(t_U) = \frac{\sum_{j=2}^{k_U} acc(z_j^U, y_j^U)}{k_U - 1}, \tag{6}$$

where

$$acc(z_j^U, y_j^U) = \begin{cases} 1 & \text{if } z_j^U = y_j^U \text{ and } P(y_{j-1}^U, z_j^U) > \alpha \\ 0 & \text{otherwise} \end{cases}. \tag{7}$$

In our view, $acc(z_j^U, y_j^U)$ indicates if the prediction z_j^U was made with a probability greater than a given threshold α, with respect to the user's action y_{j-1}^U. Consequently, $ACC(t_U)$ estimates the overall precision of the agent's prediction regarding the user trace t_U.

Based on Definition 4 it can be proved that $ACC(t_U)$ takes values in [0, 1]. Larger values for *ACC* indicate better predictions.

We mention that the accuracy measure can be extended in order to illustrate the precision of **LIA**'s prediction for multiple users, as given in Definition 5.

Definition 5. ***ACCuracy of LIA agent prediction for Multiple users - ACCM***
Let us consider a set of users, $\mathcal{U}=\{U_1,\ldots,U_l\}$. *Let us denote by* $\mathcal{UT}=\{t_{U_1},t_{U_2},\ldots,t_{U_l}\}$ *the set of successful user traces corresponding to the users from* $\mathcal{U}$. *The accuracy of the prediction with respect to the user* U_i *and his/her trace* t_{U_i} *is given by* Equation (8):

$$ACCM(\mathcal{UT})=\frac{\sum_{i=1}^{l} ACC(t_{U_i})}{l}. \tag{8}$$

where $ACC(t_{U_i})$ *is the prediction accuracy for user trace* t_{U_i} *given in* Equation (6).

3.2 Case Study

In this subsection we describe a case study that is used for evaluating **LIA** predictions, based on the evaluation measure introduced in Subsection 3.1.

We have chosen for evaluation a medium size interactive software system developed for faculty admission. The main functionalities of the system are:

- Recording admission applications (filling in personal data, grades, options, particular situations, etc.).
- Recording fee payments.
- Generating admission results.
- Generating reports and statistics.

For this case study, the set of possible actions $\mathcal{A}$ consists of around **50** elements, i.e., $n \approx 50$. Some of the possible actions are: filling in text fields (like first name, surname, grades, etc.), choosing options, selecting an option from an options list, pressing a button (save, modify, cancel, etc.), printing registration forms and reports.

The task $\mathcal{T}$ that we intend to accomplish is to complete the registration of a student. We have trained **LIA** on different training sets and we have evaluated the results for different users that have successfully accomplished task $\mathcal{T}$.

3.3 Results

We mention that, for our evaluation we have used the value **0.75** for the threshold α. For each pair (training set, testing set) we have computed ACC measure as given in Equation (6). In Table 1 we present the results obtained for our case study. We mention that we have chosen **20** user traces in the testing set. We have obtained accuracy values around **0.96**.

Table 1. Case study results

Training dimension	ACCM
67	0.987142
63	0.987142
60	0.987142
50	0.982857
42	0.96

As shown in Table 1, the accuracy of the prediction grows with the size of the training set. The influence of the training set dimension on the accuracy is illustrated in Fig. 2.

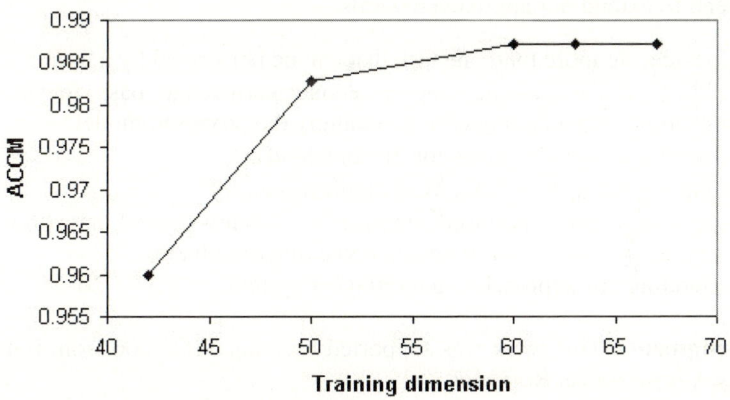

Fig. 2. Influence of the training set dimension on the accuracy

4 Related Work

There are some approaches in the literature that address the problem of predicting user behavior. The following works approach the issue of user action prediction, but without using intelligent interface agents and AOP.

The authors of [1-3] present a simple predictive method for determining the next user command from a sequence of Unix commands, based on the Markov assumption that each command depends only on the previous command. The paper [6] presents an approach similar to [3] taking into consideration the time between two commands.

Our approach differs from [3] and [6] in the following ways: we are focusing on desktop applications (while [3] and [6] focus on predicting Unix commands) and we have proposed a theoretical model and evaluation measures for our approach.

Techniques from machine learning (neural nets and inductive learning) have already been applied to user traces analysis in [4], but these are limited to fixed size patterns.

In [10] another approach for predicting user behaviors on a Web site is presented. It is based on Web server log files processing and focuses on predicting the page that a user will access next, when navigating through a Web site. The prediction is made using a training set of user logs and the evaluation is made by applying two measures. Comparing with this approach, we use a probabilistic model for prediction, meaning that a prediction is always made.

5 Conclusions and Further Work

We have presented in this paper an agent-based approach for predicting users behavior. We have proposed a theoretical model on which the prediction is based and we have evaluated our approach on a case study. Aspect Oriented Programming was used in the development of our agent.

We are currently working on evaluating the accuracy of our approach on a more complex case study.

We intend to extend our approach towards:

- Considering more than one task that can be performed by a user.
- Adding in the training step a second knowledge base for unsuccessful executions and adapting correspondingly the proposed model.
- Identifying suitable values for the threshold α .
- Adapting our approach for Web applications.
- Applying other supervised learning techniques (neural networks, decision trees, etc.) ([9]) for our approach and comparing them.
- Extending our approach to a multiagent system.

Acknowledgments. This work was supported by grant TP2/2006 from Babeş-Bolyai University, Cluj-Napoca, Romania.

References

1. Davison, B.D., Hirsh, H.: Experiments in UNIX Command Prediction. In: Proceedings of the Fourteenth National Conference on Artificial Intelligence, Providence, RI, p. 827. AAAI Press, California (1997)
2. Davison, B.D., Hirsh, H.: Toward an Adaptive Command Line Interface. In: Proceedings of the Seventh International Conference on Human Computer Interaction, pp. 505–508 (1997)
3. Davison, B.D., Hirsh, H.: Predicting Sequences of User Actions. In: Predicting the Future: AI Approaches to Time-Series Problems, pp. 5–12, Madison, WI, July 1998, AAAI Press, California. In: Proceedings of AAAI-98/ICML-98 Workshop, published as Technical Report WS-98–07 (1998)

4. Dix, A., Finlay, J., Beale, R.: Analysis of User Behaviour as Time Series. In: Proceedings of HCI'92: People and Computers VII, pp. 429–444. Cambridge University Press, Cambridge (1992)
5. Dix, A., Finlay, J., Abowd, G., Beale, R.: Human-Computer Interaction, 2nd edn. Prentice-Hall, Inc, Englewood Cliffs (1998)
6. Jacobs, N., Blockeel, H.: Sequence Prediction with Mixed Order Markov Chains. In: Proceedings of the Belgian/Dutch Conference on Artificial Intelligence (2003)
7. Kiczales, G., Lamping, J., Menhdhekar, A., Maeda, C., Lopes, C., Loingtier, J.-M., Irwin, J.: Aspect-Oriented Programming. In: Aksit, M., Matsuoka, S. (eds.) ECOOP 1997. LNCS, vol. 1241, pp. 220–242. Springer, Heidelberg (1997)
8. Maes, P.: Social Interface Agents: Acquiring Competence by Learning from Users and Other Agents. In: Etzioni, O. (ed.) Software Agents — Papers from the 1994 Spring Symposium (Technical Report SS-94-03), pp. 71–78. AAAI Press, California (1994)
9. Russell, S., Norvig, P.: Artificial Intelligence - A Modern Approach. Prentice-Hall, Inc., Englewood Cliffs (1995)
10. Trousse, B.: Evaluation of the Prediction Capability of a User Behaviour Mining Approach for Adaptive Web Sites. In: Proceedings of the 6th RIAO Conference — Content-Based Multimedia Information Access, Paris, France (2000)

Sharing Video Browsing Style by Associating Browsing Behavior with Low-Level Features of Videos

Akio Takashima and Yuzuru Tanaka

Meme Media Laboratory, West8. North13, Kita-ku
Sapporo Hokkaido, Japan
{akiota,tanaka}@meme.hokudai.ac.jp

Abstract. This paper focuses on a method to extract video browsing styles and reusing it. In video browsing process for knowledge work, users often develop their own browsing styles to explore the videos because the domain knowledge of contents is not enough, and then the users interact with videos according to their browsing style. *The User Experience Reproducer* enables users to browse new videos according to their own browsing style or other users' browsing styles. The preliminary user studies show that video browsing styles can be reused to other videos.

Keywords: video browsing, active watching, tacit knowledge.

1 Introduction

The history of video browsing has been changing. We used to watch videos or TV programs passively (Fig. 1. (1)), then select videos on demand (Fig. 1. (2)). There are increasingly more opportunities to use video for knowledge work, such as monitoring events, reflecting on physical performances, or analyzing scientific experimental phenomena. In such ill-defined situations, users often develop their own browsing styles to explore the videos because the domain knowledge of contents is not useful, and then the users interact with videos according to their browsing style (Fig. 1. (3)) [1]. However, such kind of tacit knowledge, which is acquired through user's experiences [2], has not been well managed. The goal of our research is to share and reuse tacit knowledge in video browsing (Fig. 1. (4)). This paper focuses on a method to extract video browsing styles and reusing it.

To support video browsing process, numerous studies which focus on content based analysis for retrieving or summarizing video had been reported [3][4]. The content based knowledge may include semantic information of video data, in other words, generally accepted assumptions. For example, people tend to pay attention to goal scenes of soccer games, or captions on news program include the summary or location of the news topic, etc. Thus, this approaches only work on the specific purposes (e.g. extracting goal scenes of soccer games as important scenes) which are assumed beforehand. Several studies have been reported that address using users' behavior to estimate preferences of the users in web browsing process [5]. On the other hand, little is reported in video browsing process.

J. Jacko (Ed.): Human-Computer Interaction, Part III, HCII 2007, LNCS 4552, pp. 518–526, 2007.

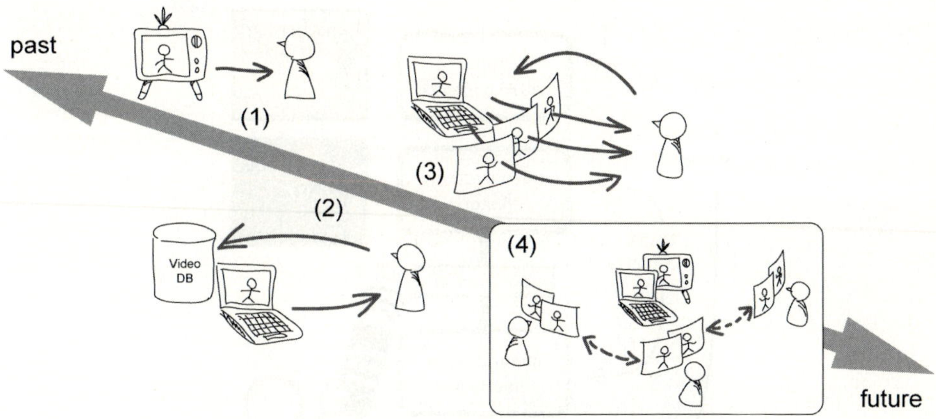

Fig. 1. The history of video browsing has been changing. We used to watch videos or TV programs passively (1), and then select videos on demand (2). Now we can interact with videos according to our own browsing style (3), however, we could not share these browsing styles. We assume that sharing them leads us to the next step of video browsing (4), especially in knowledge work.

In the area of knowledge management systems, many studies have been reported [6]. As media for editing and distributing and managing knowledge, Meme Media have been well known in the last decade [7]. However, target objects for reusing or sharing have been limited to the resources which are easily describable such as functions of software or services of web applications. In this work, we extend the area of this approach to more human side which treats indescribable resources such as know-how or skills of human behavior, in other words, tacit knowledge.

2 Approach

This paper focuses on a method to extract video browsing styles and reusing it. We assume the following characteristics in video browsing for knowledge work:

- People often browse video in consistent, specific manners
- User interaction with video can be associated with low-level features of the video

While user's manipulation to a video depends on the meanings of the content and on how the user's thought is, it is hard to observe these aspects. In this research, we tried to estimate associations between video features and user manipulations (Fig. 2). We treat the low-level features (e.g., color distribution, optical flow, and sound level) as what are associated with user manipulation. The user manipulation indicates changing speeds (e.g., Fast-forwarding, Rewinding, and Slow Playing). Identifying associations from these aspects, which can be easily observed, means that the user can grab tacit knowledge without domain knowledge of the content of the video.

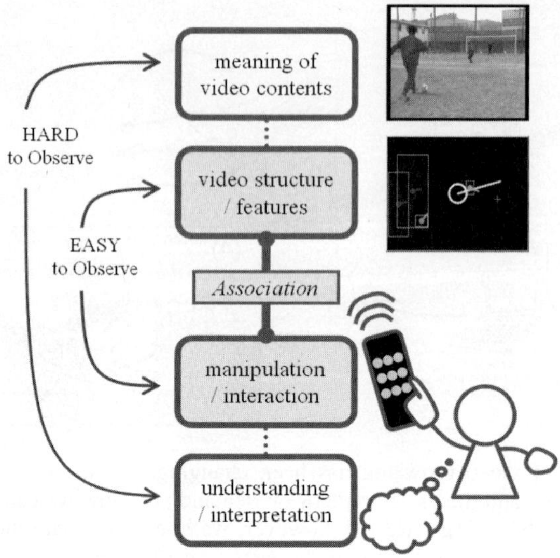

Fig. 2. While users' manipulations may depend on the meaning of the contents or users' understandings of the videos, it is difficult to observe these aspects. Therefore, we tried to estimate associations between easily observable aspects such as video features and user manipulations.

3 The User Experience Reproducer

3.1 System Overview

To extract associations between users' manipulations and low-level video features, and to reproduce browsing style for other videos, we have developed a system called the User Experience Reproducer.

The User Experience Reproducer consists of the Association Extractor and the Behavior Applier (Fig. 3).

The Association Extractor identifies relationships between low-level features of videos and user manipulation to the videos. The Association Extractor needs several training videos and the browsing logs by a particular user on these videos as input. To record the browsing logs, the user browses training videos using the simple video browser, which enables user to control playing speed. The browsing logs possess the pairs of a video frame number and the speed at which the user actually played the frame. As low-level features, the system analyzes more than sixty properties of each frame such as color dispersion, mean of color value, number of moving objects, optical flow, sound frequency, and so on. Then the browsing logs and the low-level features generate a classifier that determines the speed at which each frame of the videos should be played. In generating the classifier, we use WEKA engine that is a data mining software [8].

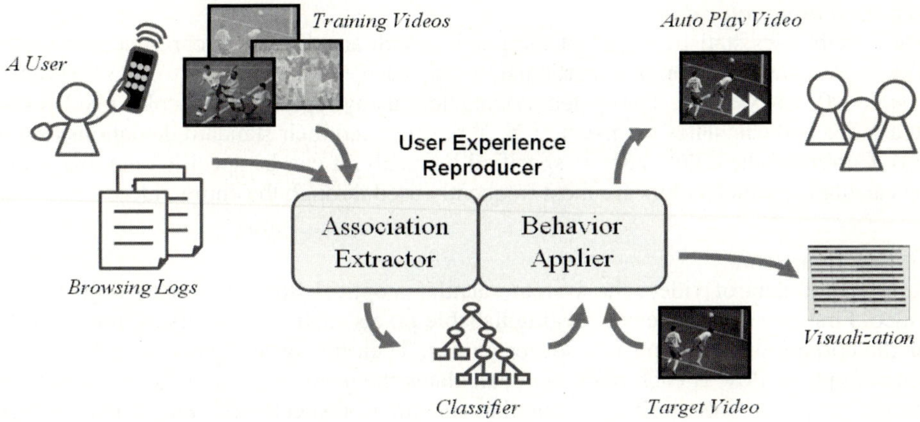

Fig. 3. *The User Experience Reproducer* consists of *the Association Extractor* and *the Behavior Applier. The Association Extractor* calculates associations using browsing logs and the low-level video features, and then creates a classifier. *The Behavior Applier* plays target video automatically based on the classification with the classifier.

The Behavior Applier plays the frames of a target video automatically at each speed in accordance with the classifier. The Behavior Applier can remove outliers from the sequence of frames, which should be played at the same speed, and also can visualize whole applied behavior to each frame of the video.

3.2 The Association Extractor

The Association Extractor identifies relationships between low-level features of video and user manipulation to the videos then generates a classifier. In this section we describe more details about the low-level features of video and user manipulations which are currently considered in the Association Extractor.

Low-level features of video

Video data possesses a lot of low-level features. Currently, the system can treat more than sixty features. These features are categorized into five aspects as follows:

- Statistical data of color values in a frame
- Representative color data
- Optical flow data
- Number of moving objects
- Sound levels

Statistical data of color values in a frame

As a most simple low-level feature, we treat the statistical data of color values in each frame of a video, for example, the mean and the standard deviation of Hue, Saturation, and Value (Brightness).

Representative color data
The system uses statistical data of the pixels which are painted a representative color. The representative color is a particular color space set beforehand (e.g. 30<H<=50, 80<S<=90, 75<V<=95). The system counts how many representative color pixels exist in a frame and calculates the mean of X, Y position and their standard deviations (Fig. 4 (a)). Currently, the color space is specified manually, it can be specified automatically by calculating which colors are most frequently used through the entire video.

Optical flow data
As dynamic data of video, the system calculates optical flow of moving objects in a video. First, the system detects distinguishable pixels such as contours of human body or the corners of a goal post in soccer games. Then the system calculates the vector data of optical flow at each point, and calculates the mean angle and the magnitude of vector values in the twelve rectangular sub areas respectively (Fig. 4 (b)). These values may represent not only states of moving objects but also camera motions.
The number of the distinguishable pixels is also one of the features.

Number of moving objects
The system can detect moving object and then counts the number of objects according to its size (Fig. 4 (c)). If the video consistently records the same objects, each detection

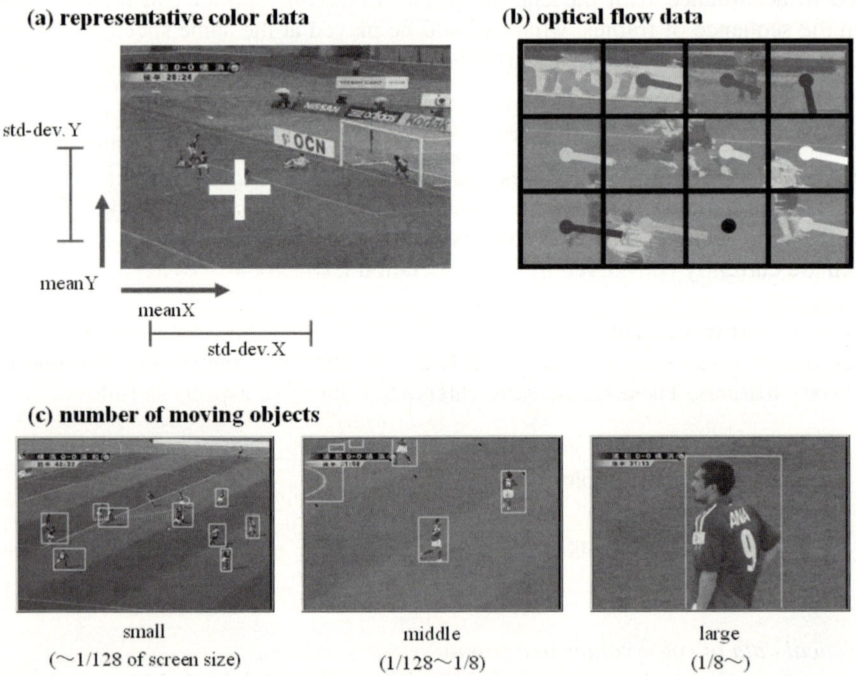

Fig. 4. The system makes associations between users' browsing speeds and low-level video features such as representative color data (a), optical flow data (b), and number of moving objects (c)

of a small object means that it may have been recorded in a wide angle and each detection of a large object means the opposite case.

Sound levels
Sound levels are divided into ten groups based on its frequency (e.g. 0-32Hz, 32-64Hz, ..., 8000-10000Hz) and used as low-level features. If the video includes sound data, it can be one of good features of the video.

User manipulations
To record the browsing logs, the user browses training videos using the simple video browser, which enables user to control playing speed. We categorized the patterns of changing playing speeds into three types based on the patterns frequently used in informal user observation [9]. The three types are as follows:

- Skip
- Re-Examine
- Others

Skip
We regard the browsing with the speed higher than the normal playing speed (1.0x) as a skipping behavior.

Re-Examine
In exploring video, a user could re-check and focus on a frame that has just passed during browsing. When the pattern is made from forwarding at less than normal speed after the rewinding, we regard it as a re-examine behavior

Others
The speeds which are not described above are categorized into this class.

To avoid any conflict, we set the priority in the order of Re-Examine, Skip, and then Others.

3.3 The Behavior Applier

The Behavior Applier plays the frames of a target video automatically at each speed in accordance with the classifier.

Mapping from User Manipulation into Auto Play Speed
The user manipulations are categorized into three types described above, and the classifier tries to associate each video frame of a target video into these three types.

We designed the mapping from three types of behaviors into specific speeds (Fig. 5). The skip behavior is reproduced as faster playing (5.0x). The others are reproduced as playing at a normal speed. The re-examine behavior is reproduced as slower playing (0.5x).

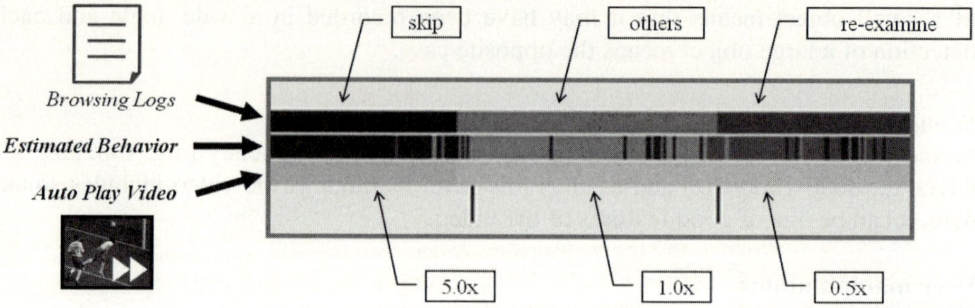

Fig. 5. This visualization shows that how target video will play at a various speeds. The three belts are indicates video data, in other words, accumulated video frames from left to right. The first belt indicates a browsing log of a video which used for training the classifier. The second belt shows estimated behaviors for a target video. In this figure, the same video is used as the one of training video and the target video for confirmation. Therefore the first and the second belt should be ideally the same. The third belt indicates the noise reduced version of the second belt. The target video will play at each speed written in the bottom of this figure.

4 User Study

We conducted a preliminary user study to extract and reuse one's browsing style.

Setting

In this study, we used ten 5min. soccer game videos for training a classifier, and two 5min. soccer game videos for applying the browsing style and for playing automatically. The number of recorded soccer games is three and the training videos are some fragments of these games. The target videos are not included in training videos. We observed two subjects so that the process described above was conducted twice. Each subject is a normal computer user and asked to explore the training videos to find interest scenes of soccer games. After the system generates the classifiers for each of the users, the users watch two target videos playing automatically through each classifier, and then asked their impression.

Overview of the results

In training phase, subjectA tried to re-examine (rewind then play at less than normal speed) particular scenes, which show players gathering in front of goal post or show a player kicking the ball to the goal. In addition, he skipped out-of-play scenes and scenes do not display goal post. SubjectB tended to skip out-of-play scenes of the games.

Through the Behavior Applier, each subject saw the target videos playing automatically in accordance with their own browsing style. The trial of subjectA played nearly 80% of important (for subjectA) scenes at a slower speed. The trial of SubjectB skipped nearly 70% of out-of-play scenes. These percentages were calculated by measuring duration of these scenes manually. The results of informal interview tell that both subjects got satisfaction from the target videos, which are automatically played.

5 Discussion

5.1 Results of the User Study

In our user study, we tried to quantize how many scenes which are meaningful for a user are detected. Although, it is not easy to describe whether the applied browsing behavior by the system constitutes a perfect fit for the user's particular needs, it seems possible to reuse tacit knowledge in video browsing without any domain knowledge of the contents.

The results of the user study might be too good. We think there are two reasons. First, the data which are used for training a classifier and playing target video are not sufficiently large. Although these videos are not the same, the videos are recorded by one TV station, so that the conditions of low-level features might not be so different. Secondly, the browsing styles were very consistent because the two subjects both had their own browsing style at least for soccer games. If the subjects have not browsed video so consistently, the result might be worse.

Kind of attribute for association
In this work, the Association Extractor considers more than sixty features to generate a classifier. Video data has more and more features that we can observe, and we think that the result will be better if the system can treat more features.

On the other hand, we categorized users' manipulations into some meaningful patterns such as skipping and re-examining then we use only three categories to be associated with a lot of low-level features. It is because that the system may not generate any associations if both sides (user behavior and video features) have a lot of attributes. Estimating several patterns of browsing behavior [10] is one of our future work to regard users' manipulations as low-level actions.

6 Conclusion

How people interact with text and images in everyday life involves not only simple naive information-receiving processes but also complex knowledge-construction processes. Videos as knowledge materials are no exception. In video browsing especially for knowledge work, sharing and reusing know-how of video browsing plays crucial role in solving problems. In this paper, we described a way of reusing such knowledge without any domain knowledge of videos.

We plan to conduct additional experiments and to develop a framework that allows users to combine several video browsing styles to obtain a composite style.

References

1. Yamamoto, Y., Nakakoji, K., Takashima, A.: The Landscape of Time-based Visual Presentation Primitives for Richer Video Experience. In: Costabile, M.F., Paternó, F. (eds.) INTERACT 2005. LNCS, vol. 3585, pp. 795–808. Springer, Heidelberg (2005)
2. Polanyi, M.: Tacit Dimension, Peter Smith Pub Inc. (1983)

3. Nakamura, Y., Kanade, T.: Semantic analysis for video contents extraction—spotting by association in news video. In: Proceedings of the fifth ACM international conference on Multimedia, Seattle, pp. 393–401 (1997)
4. Ekin, A., Tekalp, A.M., Mehrotra, R.: Automatic soccer video analysis and summarization. IEEE Trans. on Image Processing 12(7), 796–807 (2003)
5. Seo, Y., Zhang, B.: Learning user's preferences by analyzing web-browsing behaviors. In: Proceedings of International Conference on Autonomous Agents, pp. 381–387 (2000)
6. Alavi, M., Leidner, D.E.: Knowledge management systems: issues, challenges, and benefits. Journal of Commun. AIS, AIS, Atlanta, GA, 1(2) (1999)
7. Tanaka, Y.: Meme Media and Meme Market Architectures: Knowledge Media for Editing, Distributing, and Managing Intellectual Resources. IEEE Press, New York (2003)
8. WEKA: http://www.cs.waikato.ac.nz/ml/weka/
9. Takashima, A., Yamamoto, Y., Nakakoji, K.: A Model a Tool for Active Watching: Knowledge Construction through Interacting with Video. In: Proceedings of INTERACTION: Systems, Practice and Theory, pp. 331–358 (2004)
10. Syeda-Mahmood, T., Ponceleon, D.: Learning video browsing behavior and its application in the generation of video previews. In: Proceedings of the ninth ACM international conference on Multimedia, pp. 119–128 (2001)

Adaptation in Intelligent Tutoring Systems: Development of Tutoring and Domain Models

Oswaldo Vélez-Langs[1,2] and Xiomara Argüello[1]

[1] TESEEO Group
Universidad del Sinú
Montería - Colombia
[2] Universidad Rey Juan Carlos
Madrid - Spain
oswaldo.velez.langs@urjc.es, xarguello@hotmail.com

Abstract. This paper describes the aspects kept in mind for the development of the tutoring and domain models, of an Intelligent Tutoring System (ITS), where the instruction type that will give the tutoring system, the pedagogic strategies and the structure of the course are established. Also is described the software development process and their principal functions. This work is part of the research project that involves the adaptation process of the interfaces into Intelligent Tutoring Systems at the University of Sinu's TESEEO Research Group ([2]). The final objective of this work is to provide mechanisms for the design and development of system interfaces for tutoring/training, those are effective and at the same time modular, structured, configurable, flexible and adaptable.

Keywords: Adaptive Interfaces, Tutoring Model, Domain Model, Tutoring Intelligent Systems, Instructional Cognitive Theory.

1 Introduction

The accelerated rhythm of change presented in all the levels in our society, has placed in evidence the need to tighten the relation between teachers and students, in such a way that be fortified and that be done increasingly more real, contextualized and active. This has involved to that each one of the actors involved in the teaching-learning process performs new roles and acquire greater commitments.

Since the introduction of the information technologies in the teaching-learning process, the development of systems has been seeking to support all the process, since the so much perspective of the teacher one as of the student. In this search have been elaborated systems that, though they have served as additional component of the process, they do not pass to be multimedia tools that are limited to expose to student the concepts of determined subject in one static way and in many occasions little attractive. From there that, the evolution of the information systems applied in the education has been increasingly more innovative, since the point of view of the

J. Jacko (Ed.): Human-Computer Interaction, Part III, HCII 2007, LNCS 4552, pp. 527–534, 2007.

design, navigability and usability so much for the administrator as for the user of the systems. The introduction of Internet in this environment has brought as consequence that the developers of these technologies implement Web applications that use simple interfaces and easy navigation.

Under these premises we have oriented our research toward the development of Web Adaptive Intelligent Interfaces, establishing user models that permit to the tutorial system be adapted to different students using adequate pedagogical strategies to each student style, seeking thus to fortify the existing relation between the technology and the learning process. For example the Honey and Munford [1] studies reveal that the learning depends on various personal factors that practically every individual possesses an own style and that this does not always remain invariable but can change with the time and to depend on the context of the educational tasks. Taking in account the experience of the studies before mentioned that promote the improvement of the quality of the education by means of the personalized learning, we examine the characteristics of some learning styles models in order to selecting the most appropriate one for the adaptation of the proposed system.

In our work the domain model of tutoring system is a fundamental piece, therefore is from the evaluation and feedback, that the system will be able to identify the degree of meaning that the student has respect to the course or thematic, and to leave from the results, to evaluate the tutoring strategy and its own performance, according to the student preferences and learning styles. The domain model is converted thus in the link among the user model (Description of the learning style and student preferences) and the tutoring model (Description of the processes and tools to utilize during the teaching).

Therefore to achieve the evaluation of the knowledge meaning, a contents design is required, that permit to tutoring system to know to priori a navigation map of the course and the fundamental concepts that the student should signify. To structure the course that will give the system, we have developed a simple web application, the content editor (EDC), which is a tool in which the content of the same one is described step by step, entering each nucleus and sub-nucleus, with the respective pre-requisite and co-requisite and from this description, that will carry out the educational one by means of the EDC, the system will extract the path rules through that they will describe the sequence that should continue the student.

We are waiting that our work contribute in the improvement of teaching–learning process of our students, be a tool of educational support, and that become a pillar of development of these technologies in the region like an alternative solution to the difficulties that should face the present student; mainly the homogeneous form as is transmitted thc knowledge without attending to the individual differences.

2 Tutoring Model

When any system is personalised, is important have clear that a fundamental part is the user model, which in our case, they are supported in the Kolb learning cycle [2], Honey and Mumford learning styles[1] and in the Witkin cognitive theory [3,4], which is studied in [5]; but also one must keep in mind that, for a system as the we are proposing, another very important aspect is the tutoring model, where the pedagogical strategies are established and the type of instruction that will be used (depending on the learning style preferred by the student), also to this it concerns all the referring problems in the development of the curriculum or the program content and the teaching way, the same is involved with the selection and the sequence of the teaching material and the tools and components for instruction.

This model is based in the cognitive learning theories; these theories are very influential in the practice of the instructional design. The cognitive learning theory [6,7,8] generally corresponds to the rationalist philosophy and often seems compatible with the main principles in the constructivism. The difference of the cognitive theory compared with behaviour theory is that the cognitivists do a lot more emphasis in factors of the apprentice and little to the factors in the environment. That is the reason that we support our research in this trend, specifically in the Robert Gagné theory [9,10,11].

2.1 Robert Gagné Cognitivist Theory

This theory establishes that there are different types or levels of learning. The key aspect in this classification is that each level requires different type of instruction. Gagné [9,10] identifies 5 main categories of learning: Verbal information, Intelectual skills, Cognitiv strategies, and attitudes.

For each learning type are necessary different external and internal conditions. For example, so that the cognitive strategies are learned, there should be opportunity to practice the development of new solutions to the problems; to learn attitudes; the apprentice should be exposed to a credible model or with persuasive arguments. Also, Gagné describes five conditions or factors, that influence in the learning: Reception and registration of the information by means of the senses, Storage and recovery in the short and long time memory, Perception and expectations, Trial of the information and Executive control of cognition / executive strategies.

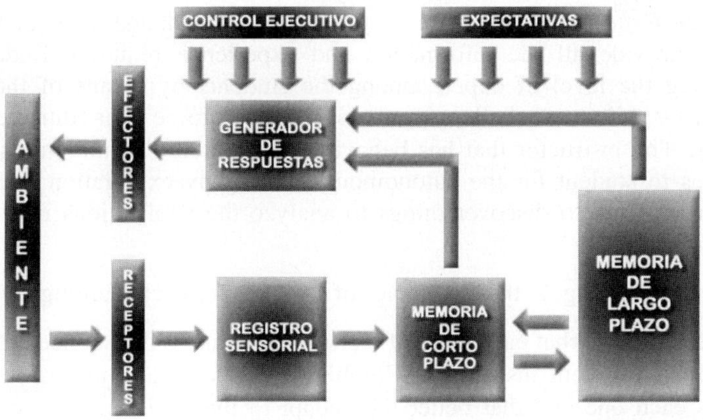

Fig. 1. Basic model of learning from Gagné

The Fig. 1show like Gagné [13] understands the learning process. The model is extensively accepted for the process of design. The instructional designer sees his role as a supplier of environmental stimuli, carefully created to facilitate the long-range retention when the information enters the long-range memory, this is related to the existing information and worked with the pre-existing scheme, the instruction then measures the answer of the apprentice, which reflects the manipulation of the information that does the brain.

2.2 Tutor Roles

It is possible to affirm that the learning style is equal to teaching style. This has a clear consequence, if the instructor does not understand the relation between the teaching and learning styles, he teaches in an unconscious way according to his own style of learning. t turns out to be fundamental that the tutor, on the one hand identify its form to learn and by another know the styles of its students to adapt better its style of teaching al style of learning of those.

In our case, is important to clarify, that once identifying the levels of preference by each one of the styles of learning, the system will assume the roles according to each style, according to the priority of the same one.

We will utilize the definitions of relation among the Kolb and Money learning styles, and the roles for the tutor established in [14]. The four basic roles of the tutor, that the system will assume once identifying the style of learning of greater preference, are defined like:

- ***Tutor***. This instructor type is a model to follow, teaches providing the necessary knowledge so that the students can think and to act. Applies the rule: Teaching through the personal example.
- ***Motivator***. This instructor provides practical exercises, mixing real situations with virtual so that the students can create experiences and to reflect on them. The fundamental objective is to develop in the students the capacity for the independent action, the initiative and the responsibility.
- ***Knowledge Expert***. The instructor should possess knowledge in an area of specific work, to provide all the information and experience required. Endeavours for maintaining the level of expert among the students by means of the unfold of knowledge detailed and challenging them to that reinforce their competences.
- ***Curiosity.*** The instructor that has behaviour as promoter of the curiosity, assigns challenges to student for the autonomous learning by exploration and discovery. The instructor aid to discover things to analyze the applications in complex and new situations.

We define in the Fig. 2, the basic roles of the tutor for each learning style:

Then is established that each style of learning of Honey-Alonso, needs two roles of the tutor for its efficient instruction, Combining the tools and materials of learning that utilizes each one and that better they adapt to their predominant style, without forgetting other activities and strategies that promote and maximize the other styles.

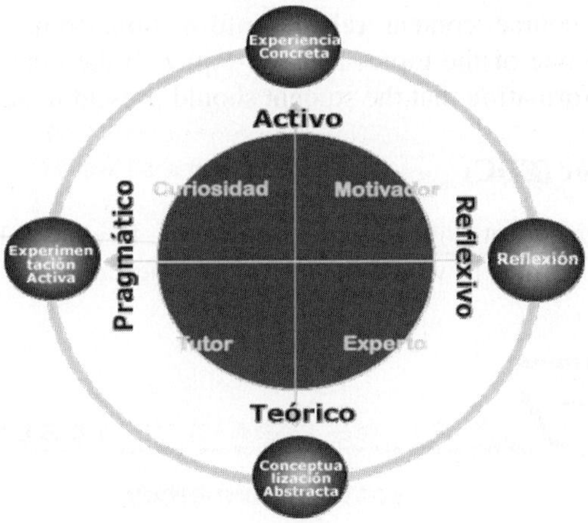

Fig. 2. Tutor Basic roles and their relation with Kolb learning cycles and learning styles of Honey-Alonso

3 Domain Model

The key to obtain improvement in the teaching-learning process is based in teaching the students how to learn in a significant way. In order to implementing this strategy, should be permitted to the student:

- To organize and/or to express new ideas.
- To understand and/orr y/o clarify concepts
- Deep in explanations.
- Increasing the retention of ideas and concepts.
- Processing, to organize and to prioritize the information.
- Integrating new elements to its base of know-how in a significant way.

And last but not least, to identify erroneous concepts. In our Intelligent Interface model this is a key aspect, from evaluation and feedback, the tutoring system could be to identify the learning grade that has the student and from results, to evaluate the tutoring strategy and their performance related to the adaptation level taking in account student preferences.

The domain model is the link between user model and tutoring model, therefore to achieve the evaluation of the learning of the knowledge, a contents design is required, that permit to tutoring system a priori know a course navigation map and the fundamental concepts that the student should to learn.

It is thus, like the domain model can be understood as the formal representation of the contents of the subject or course. Here the general structure is established, the description of the content of the subject that will do the educational one, which will be validated after to have defined the topics and sub-topics order in the area or course, in order that the tutoring system a priori has a navigation map.

In this model is involved the course organization and the actors and objects in the teaching–learning process: the teacher, who is the one that manages the course, the course that is the course content related information, topic, shows the specific information of each one of the topics and sub-topics in the content; evaluation, That are exercises and information that the student should present to advance al next topic.

3.1 Contents Editor (EDC)

To structure the course that will give the system, we have developed a simple web application, which is a tool in which the content of the same one is described step by

Fig. 3. Course Creation

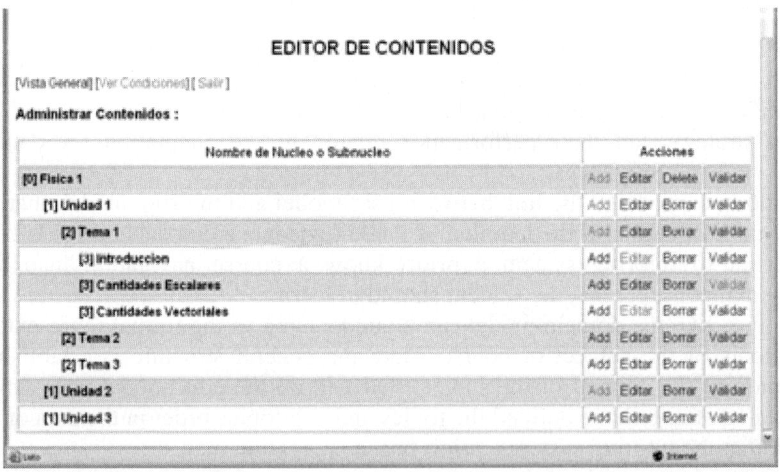

Fig. 4. Hierarchical structures of contents

step, incorporating each topic and sub-topic, with its respective pre-requisites and co-requisites (Fig. 3).

From this description, that will realize the tutor, the system will extract the travel rules through that will describe the sequence that should continue the student. The tutor establishes the content of the subject differentiating the following sections: units, topics, sub-topics and concepts. Initially al to create the course, the tutor will define the units that are in it. Continued it will indicate the topics and sub-topics pertaining to each unit and finally will enunciate the main concepts, . This it will be seen represented by the system as is illustrated in the Fig. 4.

Once it structured the course, the tutor should validate the restrictions for the concepts that understand each unit, establishing the type of relation among them. In agreement with the domain, will exist concepts that will do part of various sub-topics at time (Fig.5); is for this that depending on the results of an evaluation of the pre-concepts, the system will design the navigation with those contents that the student does not know or that still not know.

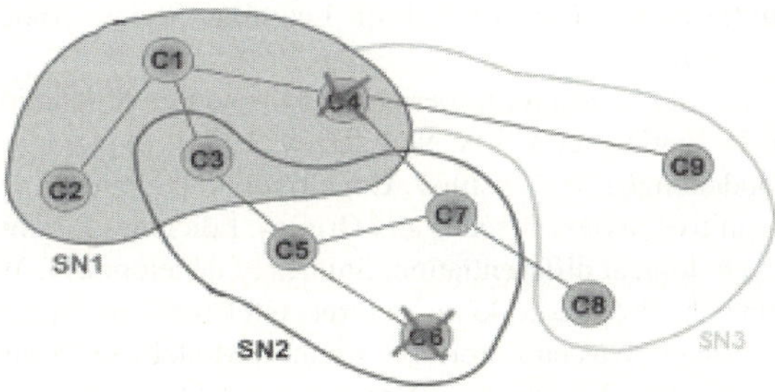

Fig. 5. Concepts distributed by topics

Then the evaluations will be able to do by topics and they will have as an objective to discover if the student has related the concepts; on another hand the games, exercises, discussions and other will have as end to discover if the concept is learned or not . This is another adaptation way that will implement our system, showing to each student the contents that in reality he needs to learn.

The previous thing, will be the final exit of all the adaptation process that will carry out the system; that is to say, after detected the predominant learning style, the system, according to it established in the tutoring model, chooses the roles of the tutor that should implement, as well as the tools and materials of adequate learning, and keeping in mind the structure of the definite course previously for the tutor, they will be presented to the student the contents of the subject according to their inclinations and preferences.

4 Conclusions

Keep in mind the goal of promoting learning, more active, effective and significative, our group is developing one intelligent and adaptive tutor system, based in personality aspects and in the cognitive instructional theory. With the conjunction of these, a tool will be obtained that support al student during the acquisition of the knowledge, in a way personalized, being adapted to its individual form of learning.

The process described will be carry out, in the first place, through the identification of the style of predominant learning in each student, where the intention is that the system adapt to this, and present to him the contents of the subject of the most adequate form, keeping in mind inclinations and preferences marked by the learning style preferred, without forgetting those characteristics dictated by the other styles.

With this mechanism we are looking for that the student have a more active role in his education and that the tutoring system guide and re-direct its process of in a efficient way for the learning. We are trying to use Evolutionary Computation paradigm for the machine learning process that automated the user profile detection scheme [15].

References

1. Honey, P., Mumford, A.: The Manual of Learning Styles. Maidenhead, Berkshire. Ardingly House (1986)
2. Kolb, D.A.: Experiential Learning: Experience as the source of learning and development. Prentice Hall P T R, Englewood Cliffs, New Jersey (1984)
3. Witkin, H., Goodenough, A.: Estilos Cognitivos. Naturaleza y orígenes. Spanish translation of: Cognitive Styles: Essence and Origins. Ediciones Pirámide. Madrid (1991)
4. Witkin, H.A.: Psychological differentiation: Studies of development, Wiley, New York.
5. Aguado, J., Aldana, J.: Propuesta de un Entorno Inteligente de Aprendizaje basado en el Uso de Interfaces Adaptativas en Entornos Virtuales: Modelo de Usuario (in spanish). Msc thesis in Computer Science Engineering. Universidad del Sinú, Montería (2006)
6. http://hsc.csu.edu.au/pro_dev/teaching_online/how_we_learn/cognitive.html
7. McGriff, S.J.: http://www.personal.psu.edu/faculty/s/j/sjm256/portfolio/kbase/Theories&Models/theoryintro.html
8. McGriff, S.J.: http://www.personal.psu.edu/faculty/s/j/sjm256/portfolio/kbase/Theories&Models/Cognitivism/cognitivism.html
9. Kearsley, G.: http://tip.psychology.org/gagne.html
10. http://www.ittheory.com/gagne1.htm
11. Bostock, S.: Keele University (July 2005) http://www.keele.ac.uk/depts/cs/ Stephen_Bostock/docs/atid.htm
12. http://www.ittheory.com/condit.htm
13. Gagné, R.M., Driscoll, M.P.: Essentials of Learning for Instruction. 2nd edn. (1988)
14. Muñoz-Seca, B., Silva-Santiago, C-V.: Acelerando el aprendizaje para incrementar la productividad y competitividad: El directivo educador (in spanish) (2000)
15. Velez-Langs, O.E., de Antonio, A.: Intelligent Tutoring Systems Interfaces Adaptation Process Using Aspects of Personality and Learning Style. WSEAS Transactions on Advances in Engineering Education 3(2), 175–182 (2006)

Confidence Measure Based Incremental Adaptation for Online Language Identification

Shan Zhong, Yingna Chen, Chunyi Zhu, and Jia Liu

Department of Electronic Engineering,
Tsinghua University,
Beijing 100084, China
zhongshan00@mails.tsinghua.edu.cn

Abstract. This paper proposes an novel two-pass adaptation method for online language identification by using confidence measure based incremental language model adaptation. In this system, we firstly used semi-supervised language model adaptation to solve the problem of channel mismatch, and then used unsupervised incremental adaptation to adjust new language model during online language identification. For robust adaptation, we compare three confidence measures and then present a new fusion method with Bayesian classifier. Tested on the RMTS(Real-world Multi-channel Telephone Speech) database, experiments show that using semi-supervised language model adaptation, the target language detection rate rises from 73.26% to 80.02% and after unsupervised incremental language model adaptation, an extra rise over 3.91% (from 80.02% to 83.93%) is obtained.

Keywords: Language Identification, Language Model Adaptation, Confidence Measure, Bayesian Fusion.

1 Introduction

Nowadays, with the development of speech recognition system, many material uses have been proposed. Language identification (LID) is a technique to identify the language being spoken from a sample of speech by an unknow speaker.

As the global economic community expands, there is an increasing need for automatic spoken language identification services.Many techniques have been develeped rapidly for this task,such as Parallel Phone Recognizer followed by Language Modeling (PPRLM) [1], Gaussian Mixture Model (GMM) classifier [2], and so on [3]. But there is a common problem with all of these techniques. How our system runs robustly with the mismatch of different microphones, telephone channels, accent, background noises, and so on. Sometimes the mismatch will be pestilent in the real-world tasks. To solve this problem, we propose a novel two-pass adaptation system for online robust language identification by using confidence measure based incremental language model adaptation.

The paper is organized as follow. In section 2 we describe three confidence measures (CMs) in detail, and then fusing them with Bayesian classifier. Section 3

J. Jacko (Ed.): Human-Computer Interaction, Part III, HCII 2007, LNCS 4552, pp. 535–543, 2007.

discusses our language model adaptation methods. Experiment results are shown in Section 4 followed by the conclusion given in section 5.

2 Bayesian Fusion of Confidence Measures

In speech recognition, CMs are used to evaluate the reliability of recognition results. Comparing to Gaussian model classifier or max-likelihood classifier, the CM based method is more robust and with better performance in practical LID tasks.

In our LID system, with the difference of online garbage models, three kinds of CMs are employed. We described and compared these three CMs, and then presented a new CM fusion method by using Bayesian classifier. The experiment results will be given later.

2.1 Best_Lan Confidence Measure (CM_{BS})

CM_{BS} is the difference between the log-likelihood of the first and second candidates in a N-best decoding approach, normalized by the length of the utterance.

$$C(L_i, X) = \frac{1}{n}[\log(P(X|L_i)) - \log(P(X|L_j))] \ . \tag{1}$$

where X represents the observed vector sequence, n stands for the frames of the utterance, L_i is the first candidate language and L_j represents the second.

This measure is a simple but classical confidence measure when the N-best decoding is available. Because the garbage model of the second candidate is the most competitive one, the confidence score can well distinguish the languages.

2.2 Avg_Lan Confidence Measure (CM_{AVG_N})

The idea of CM_{AVG_N} is similar to CM_{BS}, but it calculates the distance between the first candidate language and the average of the residual N-best candidates.

$$C(L_i, X) = \frac{1}{n_i}\log(P(X|L_i)) - \frac{1}{N-1}\sum_{j=1, j\neq i}^{N}\frac{1}{n_j}\log(P(X|L_i)) \ . \tag{2}$$

To use CM_{AVG_N}, we can get better use of the information of the decoding result by arithmetical average of the N-best candidates. But from the physical model, it is obvious that the candidates with higher matching scores should be more competitive to the identification result. To deal with this problem, the third algorithm is shown below.

2.3 Post_Lan Confidence Measure (CM_{POST})

The posterior probability $P(L|X)$ is a splendid confidence score when the observed speech vector sequence is X. By the Bayesian rule, $P(L|X)$ can be split up as follows:

$$P(L|X) = \frac{P(X|L)P(L)}{P(X)} = \frac{P(X|L)P(L)}{\sum_i P(X|L_i)P(L_i)} . \tag{3}$$

If L is viewed as equal, $P(L|X)$ can be expressed:

$$P(L|X) = \frac{P(X|L)}{\sum_i P(X|L_i)} . \tag{4}$$

Here, the posterior probability confidence measure is constructed by the N-best candidates $\sum_i P(X|L_i)$. If $\sum_i P(X|L_i)$ is considered as the online garbage model, the third confidence measure is proposed as CM_{POST}:

$$C(L_i, X) = \frac{1}{n_i}\log P(X|L_i) - \log\sum_{j=1}^{N}\exp\left(\frac{1}{n_j}\log P(X|L_j)\right) . \tag{5}$$

2.4 Bayesian Fusion of Confidence Measures (CM_{fusion})

Since the three CMs are of different information, better performance will be achieved after merging them together. These works are CM combining, shown in Fig.1. Recent efforts on CM combining include linear discriminant analysis (LDA) based CM combining [4], support vector machine (SVM) classifier [5], boosting [6], and others.

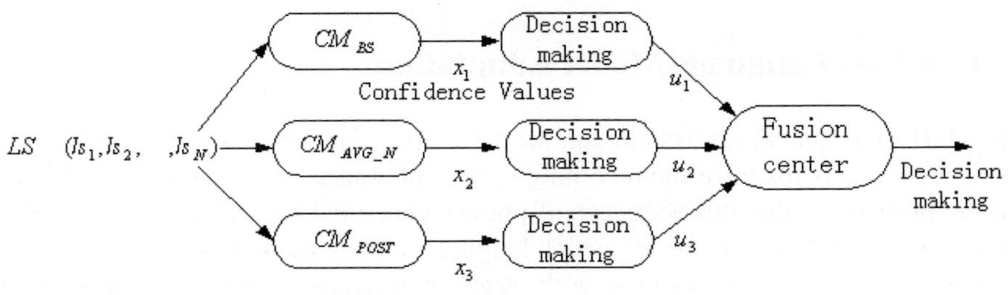

Fig. 1. Bayesian fusion of confidence measures

We apply the Bayesian classifier in which individual CMs are used as features for making a decision whether the recognition result is correct or incorrect as described in [7]. This approach is concerned about the estimation of the two classes and finds Bayes optimal decision boundary. From the Bayesian classification rule in binary cases, the following decision rule is expressed as:

$$\begin{cases} \omega_1 & if \quad \dfrac{P(x_1, x_2, \cdots, x_N | \omega_1)}{P(x_1, x_2, \cdots, x_N | \omega_0)} > Th \\ \omega_0 & if \quad \dfrac{P(x_1, x_2, \cdots, x_N | \omega_1)}{P(x_1, x_2, \cdots, x_N | \omega_0)} < Th \end{cases} . \tag{6}$$

where $x_i = j, j \in \{0,1\}$ means that the ith individual decision chooses the class ω_j. If we assume the independence of local decisions, then the left-hand side of the (6) can be factored as:

$$\prod_{S_1} \frac{P(x_i = 1 | \omega_1)}{P(x_i = 1 | \omega_0)} \prod_{S_0} \frac{P(x_i = 0 | \omega_1)}{P(x_i = 0 | \omega_0)} = \prod_{S_1} \frac{1 - P_{M_i}}{P_{F_i}} \prod_{S_0} \frac{P_{M_i}}{1 - P_{F_i}} . \tag{7}$$

where $s_k = \{i | u_i = k\}$ is the set of local decisions for ω_k. P_{M_i} and P_{F_i} represent the probabilities of miss and of false alarm of the ith local decisions, respectively. Substituting (7) into (6) and taking the logarithms leads to:

$$\begin{cases} \omega_1 & if \quad \sum_{i=1}^{N} [x_i \log \dfrac{1 - P_{M_i}}{P_{F_i}} + (1 - x_i) \log \dfrac{P_{M_i}}{1 - P_{F_i}}] > Th \\ \omega_0 & if \quad \sum_{i=1}^{N} [x_i \log \dfrac{1 - P_{M_i}}{P_{F_i}} + (1 - x_i) \log \dfrac{P_{M_i}}{1 - P_{F_i}}] < Th \end{cases} . \tag{8}$$

which is a weighted voting of local decision reflecting the reliability of each local decision maker.

3 Two-Pass Language Model Adaptation

The PPRLM is our basic system for the LID task [8]. The front-end HMM based phone recognizers tokenize the incoming speech utterance into a sequence of phones, and the probability that this sequence of phones generated by each language model is calculated. Finally, we can decide which language it is by the scores.

Thus the decoding sequences with high confidence scores can be used for adaptation. In our LID system, two parts of adaptation are contained. One is for the front-end phone recognizer, and the other is for the language model. Nevertheless, experiments show that language model adaptation is much more effective than the adaptation of phone recognizer, with the need of less adaptation data and clearly lower computation cost at the meanwhile [9]. Because it is very appropriate for our online adaptation system, this paper is focused on the language model adaptation.

During language model adaptation, the language of each adaptation data has to be recognized first. Then, each speech utterance in the adaptation data set is decoded to several phone sequences automatically through each phone recognizer. As a result, the transcriptions of each speech utterance for its corresponding language models that follow each phone recognizer are gained. Finally, we use these new transcriptions to build an adapted language model with the linear merging method. For a word w_i in n-gram history h, with parameter λ,

$$P^{s+a}(w_i \mid h) = \lambda P^s(w_i \mid h) + (1-\lambda)P^a(w_i \mid h) \ . \tag{9}$$

where $0<\lambda<1$ is the weight of the source model s and $1-\lambda$ is the weight of new adaptation model a. In fact, it can just be viewed as a maximum a posterior (MAP) adaptation strategy, given observation sample x, the MAP estimate is obtained as the model of the posterior distribution of θ denoted as $g(\cdot \mid x)$

$$\theta_{MAP} = \arg\max_{\theta} g(\theta \mid x) \ . \tag{10}$$

3.1 Semi-supervised Language Model Adaptation

Different from supervised LM adaptation, semi-supervised LM adaptation means that only the languages of the adaptation data are available (see Fig.2). The transcriptions of each speech utterance for its corresponding language models which follow each phone recognizer are gained from front-end phone recognizers.

Giving the exact transcription of each speech utterance by manual work needs great patience and also great deal of time. But an experienced listener can estimate the language of the speech very easily and quickly. So the semi-supervised LM adaptation is effective, and its workload is reasonable.

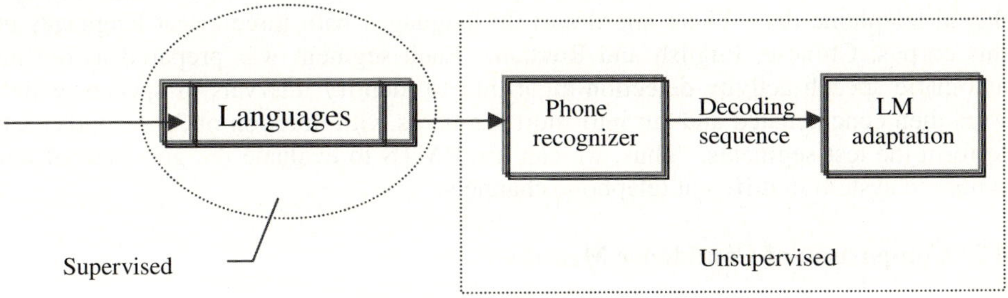

Fig. 2. Block diagram of semi-supervised LM adaptation

3.2 Confidence Measure Based Online Unsupervised Language Model Adaptation

After the semi-supervised LM adaptation, the performance has been greatly improved. But we can get further improvement by online unsupervised LM adaptation [10]. During the adaptation shown in Fig.3, we first send the incoming unknown speech utterance into our PPRLM system, and then use the language scores with high confidence to guide the model adaptation. A threshold for confidence score is set in order to ensure that almost all the utterance used for adaptation are correctly recognized.

Because of the online unsupervised adaptation, the LM is matching the testing domain step by step. Compared with the initial input utterance, the data tested later provide better accuracy. So after the whole testing process, the LM is optimized. In our LID system, the optimal LM is used to re-estimate the input utterance to get an additional accuracy improvement.

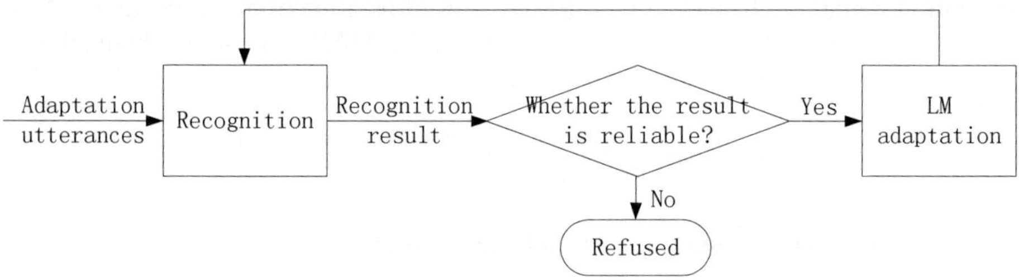

Fig. 3. Block diagram of CM based online unsupervised LM adaptation

4 Experimental Results

4.1 Speech Corpus

Real-world Multi-channel Telephone Speech (RMTS) is a speech corpus collected from different telephone channels in real-life phone-call situation. All the data come from one side of conversation and are presented as standard 8-bit 8 kHZ mu-law digital telephone data. There are almost 30 languages with three target languages in this corpus: Chinese, English and Russian. Each segment was prepared to use an automatic speech activity detection algorithm to identify intervals of speech, which were then concatenated and cut into short segments with duration of 35 seconds each to form the test segments. Thus, we can use RMTS to evaluate the goodness of our proposed system in different telephone channels.

4.2 Comparison of Confidence Measures

Fig.4 shows that CM_{BS} outperforms CM_{AVG_N} and CM_{POST}. It is because that CM_{BS} stands for the distinction of the most competitive two candidates. CM_{POST} is approximate to the posterior probability by sufficient models. But actually in our experiment, only three garbage models are offered. That is why CM_{POST} does not perform well here.

The experiment indicates us how to adjust the weighting factors when fusing the above three CM. CM with better detection rate should have larger weight. With the well adjusted parameters, CM_{fusion} greatly improves the detection performance and gets the best result. So the following unsupervised LM adaptation experiment is based on CM_{fusion}.

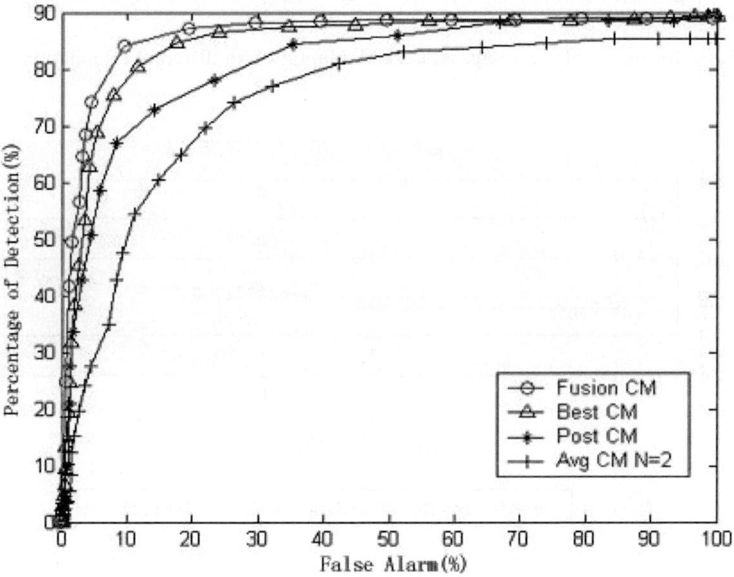

Fig. 4. Language detection rates with different confidence measures

4.3 Language Model Adaptation

In our LM adaptation process, semi-supervised LM adaptation is first used in three different telephone channels. Fig.5 shows that after the process, the detection rate of the target language rises from 73.26% to 80.02%, and the average rises from 70.85% to 77.45%.

In the course of testing, the online unsupervised LM adaptation works. Illustrated in Fig.6, at fist, the adaptation is inconspicuous for the sparseness of the data accumulated. But as the test data accumulated,3 hours in the experiment, the LM is matching the testing domain and the detection rate rises gradually. An extra rise of the target language detection rate over 3.91% (from 80.02% to 83.93%) is obtained, and the average over1.91% (from 77.45% to 79.36%).

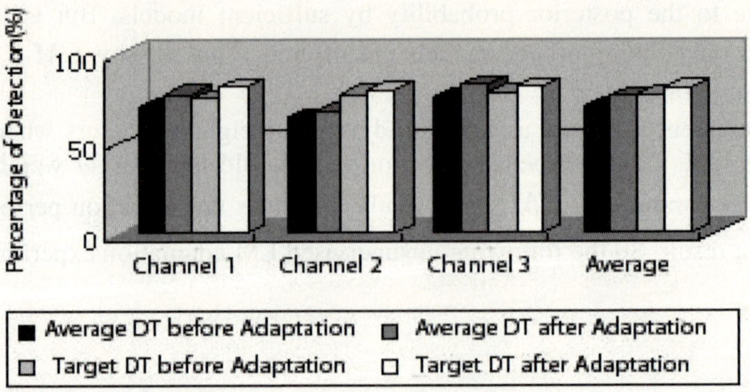

Fig. 5. Performance of semi-supervised LM adaptation in different telephone channels

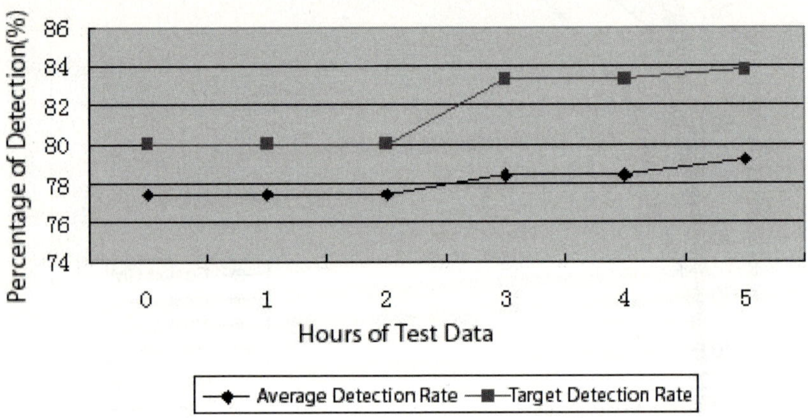

Fig. 6. Detection rates during online unsupervised LM adaptation

5 Conclusions

This paper presented an improved two-pass adaptation method for online language identification by using confidence measure based incremental language model adaptation. The experiments results show that this method can clearly improve the system performance, and make it more robustly in different channels. However, we should be careful in choosing good CM features for combining so as not to raise the estimation problem. For further improvement, our future work will apply this method not only to the language model, but also to the acoustic model.

Acknowledgements. This project is supported by the National Natural Science Foundation of China (NSFC) (60572083).

References

1. Muthusamy, Y.K., Barnard, E., Cole, R.A.: Reviewing automatic language identification. IEEE Trans. Signal Proc. Magn 11(4), 33–41 (1994)
2. Torres-Carrasquillo, P.A., Reynolds, D.A., Jr Deller, J.R.: Language identification using Gaussian mixture model tokenization. In: Proc. ICASSP '02, vol. 1, pp. 757–760 (2002)
3. Zissman, M.A., Berkling, K.M.: Automatic language identification. Speech Communication 35(1-2), 115–124 (2001)
4. Kamppari, S., Hazen, T.: Word and phone level acoustic confidence scoring. In: Proc. ICASSP '00, Istanbul, Turkey, pp. 5–9 (2000)
5. Zhang, R., Rudnicky, A.: Word level confidence annotation using combinations of features. In: Proc. EUROSPEECH '01, Aalborg, Denmark, pp. 2105–2108 (2001)
6. Moreno, P.J., Logan, B., Raj, B.: A boosting approach for confidence scoring. In: Proc. EUROSPEECH '01, Aalborg, Denmark, pp. 2109–2112 (2001)
7. Kim, T-Y., Ko, H.: Bayesian fusion of confidence measures for speech recognition, Signal Processing Letters, IEEE, vol. 12(12), pp. 871–874 (December 2005) Digital Object Identifier 10.1109/LSP.2005.859494
8. Shizhen, W., Jia, L., Runsheng, L.: Language Identification Using PPRLM with Confidence Msasures. In: Proceeding of ICSP2004, pp. 683–686 (2004)
9. Chen, Y., Liu, J.: Language Model Adaptation and Confidence Measure for Robust Language Identification. In: Proceeding of ISCIT 2005, vol. 1, pp. 270–273 (2005)
10. Bacchiani, M., Roark, B.: Unsupervised Language Model Adaptation. In: IEEE International Conference on Acoustics, Speech and Signal Processing - Proceedings, vol. 1, pp. 236–239 (2003)

Study on Speech Emotion Recognition System in E-Learning

Aiqin Zhu[1] and Qi Luo[2]

[1] College of Urban and Environment Science,Central China Normal University, Wuhan, 430079, Hubei, China

[2] Wuhan University of Science and Technology Zhongnan Branch Wuhan, 430223, Hubei, China

Qiluo1982@yahoo.com.cn

Abstract. Aiming at emotion deficiency in present E-Learning system, speech emotion recognition system is proposed in the paper. A corpus of emotional speech from various subjects, speaking different languages is collected for developing and testing the feasibility of the system. The potential prosodic features are first identified and extracted from the speech data. Then we introduce a systematic feature selection approach which involves the application of Sequential Forward Selection (SFS) with a General Regression Neural Network (GRNN) in conjunction with a consistency-based selection method. The selected features are employed as the input to a Modular Neural Network (MNN) to realize the classification of emotions. Our simulation experiment results show that the proposed system gives high recognition performance.

Keywords: E-learning, SFS, GRNN, MNN, Affective computing.

1 Introduction

E-Learning uses modern educational technologies to implement an ideal learning environment through integrating the information technology into curriculum, which can embody the learning styles of students' main-body function, reform the traditional teaching structure and the essence of education thoroughly [1].

Although the current E-Learning systems have many merits, many of them only treat advanced information technology as simple communication tools, and release some learning contents and exercises in the network [2]. This kind of movable textbook or electronic textbook is indifferent to the learners, which lacks of the interaction of emotion. Besides, this kind of learning materials without using of the superiority of interactive multimedia technology and displaying the function of network effectively, which leads to the phenomenon of emotion deficiency in the current E-Learning system.

Emotion deficiency refers to the separation among students and teachers, students and students, which make students and teachers, students and students can't carry on face to face communicating promptly like conventional education. Thus, some learning problems of the learners in the learning process can't be solved and

J. Jacko (Ed.): Human-Computer Interaction, Part III, HCII 2007, LNCS 4552, pp. 544–552, 2007.

perplexity of the psychology can't get help. If students gaze at indifferent computer screens for a long time, they do not feel the interactive pleasure and emotion stimulation, and they may have antipathy emotion.

Affective computing is a hot topic in Artificial intelligence, it is computing that related to, arise from, or deliberately influence emotion [3], which is firstly proposed by Professor Picard at MIT in 1997. Affective computing consists of recognition, expression, modeling, communicating and responding to emotion [4].In this components, emotion recognition is one of the most fundamental and important modules. It is always based on facial and audio information.

In the field of HCI, speech is primary to the objectives of an emotion recognition system, as are facial expressions and gestures. It is considered a powerful mode to communicate intentions and emotions. This paper explores methods by which an E-learning System can recognize human emotion in the speech signal. Basing on it, the corresponding emotion encouragement and compensation is provided according to the specific emotion state. Teaching strategies and learning behaviors are adjusted according to learners' emotion state. Thus, it could help the learners to solve emotion deficiency in E-learning system essentially.

In the past few years, a great deal of research has been done to recognize human emotion using audio information. In the paper [5], the authors explored several classification methods including the Maximum Likelihood Bayes classifier, Kernel Regression and K-nearest Neighbors, and feature selection methods such as Majority Voting of Specialist. However, the system was speaker dependent, and the classification methods had to be validated on a completely held-out database. In [6], the authors proposed a speaker and context independent system for emotion recognition in speech using neural networks. The paper examined both prosodic features and phonetic features. Based on these features, one-class-in-one (OCON) and all-class-in-one (ACON) neural networks were employed to classify human emotions. However, no feature selection techniques were used to get the best feature set, and the recognition rate was only around 50%.

In this paper, we present an approach to language-independent machine recognition of human emotion in speech. The potential prosodic features are extracted from each utterance for the computational mapping between emotions and speech patterns. The discriminatory power of these features is then analyzed using a systematic approach, which involves the combination of SFS [7], GRNN [8] and consistency-based selection method. The selected features are then used for training and testing a modular neural network. Standard neural network and K-nearest Neighbors classifiers are also investigated for the purpose of comparative studies.

2 Speech Emotion Recognition System in E-Learning

The structure of speech emotion recognition system is shown in Figure 1. It consists of seven modules: speech input, preprocessing, spectral analysis, feature extraction, feature subset selection, modular neural network for classification, and the recognized emotion output.

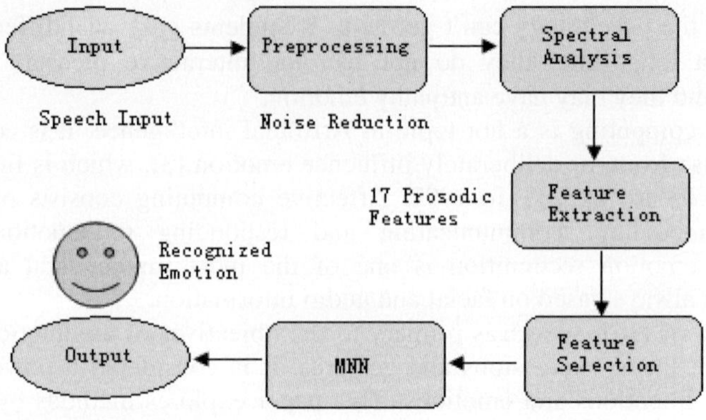

Fig. 1. The structure of speech emotion recognition system

2.1 Data Acquisition

In order to build an effective language-independent emotion recognition system and test its feasibility, a speech corpus containing utterances that are truly representative of an emotion was recorded. Our experimental subjects were provided with a list of emotional sentences, and were directed to express their emotions as naturally as possible by recalling the emotional happening, which they had experienced in their lives. The data were recorded for six classes: happiness, sadness, anger, fear, surprise and disgust. Since our aim is to develop a language in dependent system, subjects from different language backgrounds are selected in this study. The speech utterances were recorded in English, Chinese. Over 500 utterances, each delivered with one of six particular emotions, were recorded at a sampling rate of 22050 Hz, using a single channel 16-bit digitization.

2.2 Preprocessing

The preprocessing prepares the input speech for recognition by eliminating the leading and trailing edge. The volume is then normalized to improve detection by the spectrogram generator. Unvoiced sounds are cut if they appear dominant in the signal. A noise gate with a delay time of 150 ms and a threshold of 0.05 is used to remove the small noise signal caused by digitization of the acoustic wave. The threshold is the amplitude level at which the noise gate starts to open and let sound pass. A value of 0.05 is selected empirically through the observation of background static“hiss” in the quiet parts of sections.

2.3 Spectral Analysis and Feature Extraction

Previous works have explored several features for classifying speaker affect: phoneme and silence duration, short-time energy, pitch statistics and so on. However, as prosody is believed to be the primary indicator of a speaker’s emotional state, we choose prosodic features of speech for emotion analysis. A total number of 17 prosodic features are extracted by analyzing the speech spectrogram. These 17 possible candidates are listed in Table 1.

Table 1. 17 Prosodic Features

Feature	Description
1	Pitch range (normalized)
2	Pitch mean (normalized)
3	Pitch standard deviation (normalized)
4	Pitch median (normalized)
5	Rising pitch slope maximum
6	Rising pitch slope mean
7	Falling pitch slope maximum
8	Falling pitch slope mean
9	Overall pitch slope mean
10	Overall pitch slope standard deviation
11	Overall pitch slope median
12	Amplitude range (normalized)
13	Amplitude mean (normalized)
14	Amplitude standard deviation (normalized)
15	Amplitude median (normalized)
16	Mean pause length
17	Speaking rate

3 Feature Selection

The ultimate goal of feature selection is to choose a number of features from the extracted feature set that yields minimum classification error. In this study, we propose the adoption of an efficient one-pass selection procedure, the sequential forward selection (SFS) approach that incrementally constructs a sequence of feature subsets by successively adding relevant features to those previously selected. To evaluate the relevancy of the subsets, we adopt the general regression neural network (GRNN). In this section, we first analyze the discrimination power of the 17 extracted features using the SFS method with GRNN. We then discuss some limitations of GRNN as the number of selected features grows, and introduce a consistency based selection [9] as a complementary approach.

3.1 Sequential Forward Selection

The SFS is a bottom-up search procedure where one feature at a time is added to the current feature set. At each stage, the feature to be included in the feature set is selected among the remaining available features, which have not been added to the feature set. So the new enlarged feature set yields a minimum classification error compared to adding any other single feature. If we want to find the most discriminatory feature set, the algorithm will stop at a point when adding more features to the current feature set increases the classification error. For finding the order of the discriminatory power of all potential features, the algorithm will continue until all candidate features are added to the feature set. The order in which a feature is added is the rank of feature's discriminatory power.

3.2 General Regression Neural Network

The GRNN is then used to realize the feature selection criteria in measuring classification error. The GRNN is a memory based neural network based on the estimation of a probability density function. The main advantage of the GRNN over the conventional multilayer feed-forward neural network is that, unlike the multilayer feed-forward neural network which requires a large number of iterations in training to converge to a desired solution, GRNN needs only a single pass of learning to achieve optimal performance in classification. In mathematical terms, if we have a vector random variable *x*, a scalar random variable *y*, let *X* be a particular measured value of *x*, then the conditional mean of *y* given *X* can be represented as:

$$\hat{Y}(X) = \frac{\sum_{i=1}^{n} Y_i \exp(-\frac{D_i^2}{2\sigma^2})}{\sum_{i=1}^{n} \exp(-\frac{D_i^2}{2\sigma^2})} \quad (1)$$

Where D_i^2 is defined as

$$D_i^2 = (X - X_i)^T (X - X_i). \quad (2)$$

In the above equation (1), *n* denotes the number of samples. *Xi* and *Yi* are the sample values of the random variable *x* and *y*. The only unknown parameter in the above equation is the width of the estimating kernel σ. However, because the underlying parent distribution is not known, it is impossible to compute an optimum value of σ for a given number of observations. So we have to find the σ value on an empirical basis. A leave-one-out cross validation method is used to determine the σ value that gives the minimum error.

3.3 Experimental Results Using SFS and GRNN

By applying SFS/GRNN, the discriminatory power of the 17 candidate features is determined in an order of {1,13,17,4,8,9,3,16,6,7,15,14,12,5,2,11,10}. The mean square error versus the feature index is plotted in Figure 2.

The abscissa in Fig. 2 corresponds to feature order number. From the curve above, we can observe that the minimum mean square error occurs at the point where the top 11 features are included, which correspond to the feature numbers {1,13,17,4,8,9,3,16 ,6,7,15}. However, we can also observe that when the feature index number is greater than 9, the error curve is almost flat. A possible interpretation of this outcome is that due to the approximation nature of the GRNN modeling process which does not incorporate any explicit trainable parameters, it will be increasingly difficult for the network to characterize the underlying mapping beyond a certain number of features due to the limited number of training samples and their increasing sparseness in high-dimensional spaces. Thus, the order of features beyond the minimum point may not necessarily reflect their actual importance. We therefore need to consider more carefully about the relevance of those features around and beyond the minimum. An alternative approach is suggested in the next section to review the effectiveness of features from the point where the error curve begins to flatten.

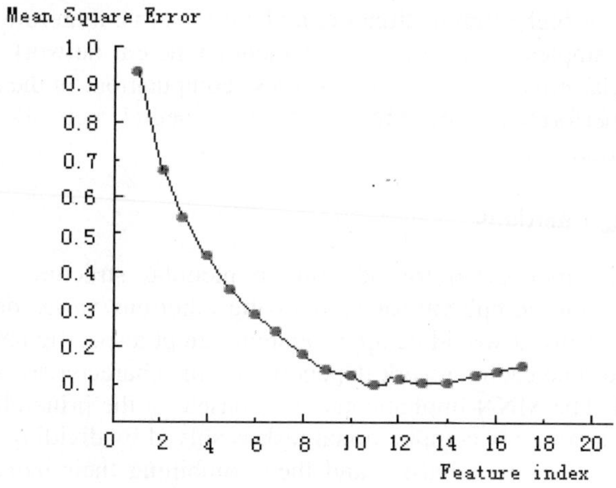

Fig. 2. Error Plot for SFS/GRNN

3.4 Consistency-Based Feature Selection

In this paper, we use a consistency-based approach as a complementary approach to evaluate the relevance of features around and beyond the minimum error point. The consistency measure of each feature is computed by:

$$c = \frac{mean \cdot \text{int}\, er - class \cdot dis\, \text{tan}\, ce}{mean \cdot \text{int}\, ra - class \cdot dis\, \text{tan}\, ce} \cdot \quad (3)$$

Where the distances are the space of the features under consideration. A given feature is said to have a large discrimination power if its intra-class distance is small and interclass distance is large. Thus, a greater value of the consistency implies a better feature.

3.5 Experimental Results Using Consistency-Based Selection

By computing the consistency measure for the features around and beyond the minimum point using equation (3), we find that feature 2 has the highest consistency measure. The consistency ranking of the next top three features is the same as achieved by SFS/GRNN. These features are 6, 7, and 15. As a result, we choose four highly consistency features, namely {2, 6, 7, 15}. Using the combined SFS/GRNN and consistency-based method, we get a total of 12 features. These 12 features are used as input to the MNN which will be described in the next section.

4 Experiment and Conclusion

In this section, we present a modular neural network (MNN) architecture, which effectively maps each set of input features to one of the six emotional categories. It should be noted that although we use a GRNN for feature selection, but GRNN has the disadvantage of high computational complexity, and is, therefore not suitable for evaluating new samples. Thus we apply a modular neural network based on back-propagation for classification which requires less computation. In the experiments, we compared the performance of MNN, Standard neural network and K-nearest Neighbors classifier.

4.1 Recognizing Emotions

In this study, the motivation for adopting a modular structure is based on the consideration that the complexity of recognizing emotions varies depending on the specific emotion. Thus, it would be appropriate to adopt a specific neural network for each emotion and tune each network depending on the characteristic of each emotion to be recognized. The MNN implementation is based on the principle of "divide and conquer", where a complex computational task is solved by dividing it into a number of computationally simple subtasks, and then combining their individual solutions. Modular architecture offers several advantages over a single neural network in terms of learning speed, representation capability, and the ability to deal with hardware constraints. The architecture of the MNN used in this study in shown in Figure 3. The proposed hierarchical architecture consists of six sub-networks, where each sub-network specializes in a particular emotion class. In the recognition stage, an arbitration process is applied to the outputs of sub-network to produce the final decision.

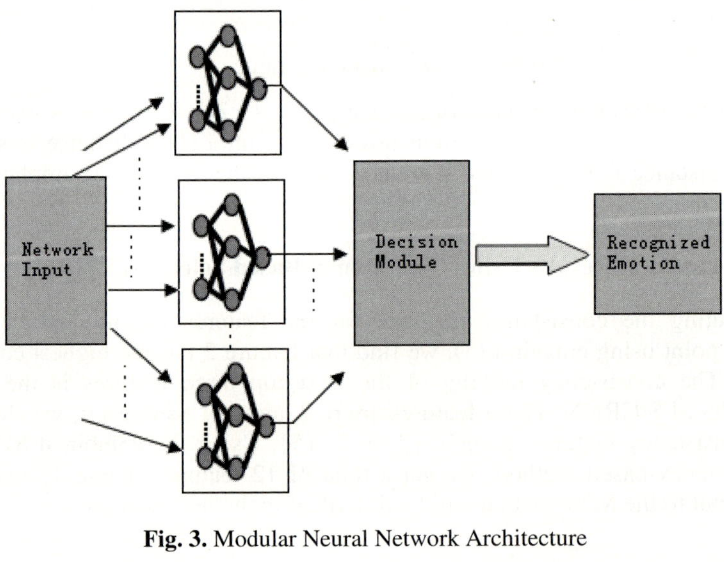

Fig. 3. Modular Neural Network Architecture

4.2 Recognition Results

The experiments we performed are based on speech samples from seven subjects, speaking four different languages. A total of 580 speech utterances, each delivered with one of six emotions were used for training and testing. The six different emotion labels used are happiness, sadness, anger, fear, surprise, and disgust. From these samples, 435 utterances were selected for training the networks and the rest were used for testing.

We investigated several approaches to recognize emotions in speech. A standard neural network (NN) was first used to test all the 17 features and the 12 selected features. The number of input nodes equals to the number of features we used. Six output nodes, associated with each emotion and a single hidden layer with 10 nodes were used. A learning process was performed by the back propagation algorithm. The system gives an overall correct recognition rate of 77.24% on 17 features and 80.69% on 12 selected features.

In the second experiment, we examined the K-nearest Neighbors classifier (KNN) on the 12 selected features. Leave one- out cross validation was used to determine the appropriate k value. This classifier gives the overall recognition rate of 79.31%.

Finally, we tested the proposed modular neural network (MNN) by using the 12 selected features. The architecture of the network was the same as depicted in figure 3. Each subnet consisted of a 3-layered feed-forward neural network with one 12 element input vector. Each sub-network was trained in parallel. It is also noted that the modular network was able to learn faster than the standard neural network. Furthermore, the classification performance was improved with the added benefit of computational simplicity. This approach achieves the best overall classification accuracy of 83.31%.

4.3 Discussion and Conclusion

The comparison of the recognition results using different approaches is shown in Figure 4. The number that follows each classifier corresponds to the dimension of the input vector. The results show that, by applying SFS/GRNN in conjunction with a consistency-based selection method, the performance of the system was greatly

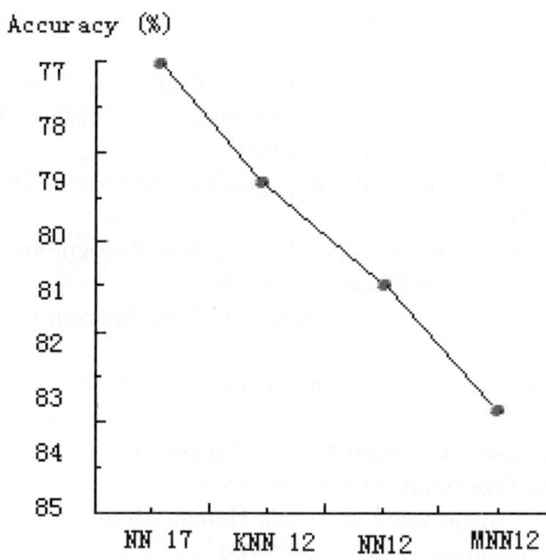

Fig. 4. Comparison of the Recognition Results

improved. It also demonstrates that the proposed modular neural network produces a noticeable improvement over a standard neural network and a K-nearest Neighbors classifier which has been adopted in some of the other literatures. The time for training a set of sub-networks in MNN was also much less than for a large standard NN. This leads to efficient computation and better generalization.

In this paper, we have presented an approach to language independent machine recognition of human emotion in speech. We have investigated the universal nature emotion and its vocal expression. Although language and cultural background have some influence on the way in which people express their emotions, our proposed system has demonstrated that the emotional expression in speech can be identified beyond the language boundaries.

The results of these experiments are promising. Our study shows that prosodic cues are very powerful signals of human vocal emotions. In the future, multi-module emotion recognition including facial and other features such as gesture will be studied [10]. This complementary relationship will help in obtaining higher emotion recognition accuracy. I wish that this article's work could give some references to certain people.

Acknowledgment

The research work in this paper was supported by Natural Science Foundation of Wuhan University of Science and Technology Zhongnan Branch.

References

1. Kekang, H.: E-Learning Essence- information technology into curriculum. E-education Research 105(1), 3–4 (2002)
2. Jijun, W.: Emotion deficiency and compensation in distance learning. Chinese network education (2005)
3. Picard, R.W.: Affective Computing. MIT Press, Cambridge (1997)
4. Picard, R.W.: Affective Computing, Challenges. Cambridge. International Journal of Human Computer studies 59(1), 55–64 (2003)
5. Dellaert, F., Polzin, T., Waibel, A.: Recognizing Emotion in Speech. In: Proceedings of the ICSLP '96 (1996)
6. Nicholson, J., Takabashi, K., Nakatsu, R.: Emotion Recognition in Speech Using Neural Network. Neural Information Processing (1999)
7. Kittler, J.: Feature Set Search Algorithms. Pattern Recognition and Signal Processing, 41–60 (1978)
8. Specht, D.F.: A general regression neural network. IEEE Trans. Neural Networks 2(6), 568–576 (1991)
9. Wu, M.: Dynamic resource allocation via video content and short-term statistics. In: IEEE Int. Conf. on Image Processing, vol. III, pp. 58–61 (2000)
10. Cai, Q., Mitche, A., Aggarwal, J.K.: Track Human Motion in an Indoor Environment. In: Proc.of 2nd Intl.Conf.Image Processing (2003)

Part III
Gesture and Eye Gaze Recognition

How Do Adults Solve Digital Tangram Problems? Analyzing Cognitive Strategies Through Eye Tracking Approach

Bahar Baran, Berrin Dogusoy, and Kursat Cagiltay

Computer Education and Instructional Technologies,
Middle East Technical University, 06531 Metu/Ankara
{boztekin,bdogusoy,cagiltay}@metu.edu.tr

Abstract. Purpose of the study is to investigate how adults solve tangram based geometry problems on computer screen. Two problems with different difficulty levels were presented to 20 participants. The participants tried to solve problems by placing seven geometric objects into correct locations. In order to analyze the process, the participants and their eye movements were recorded by an Tobii Eye Tracking device while solving the problems. The results showed that the participants employed different strategies while solving problems with different difficulty levels

Keywords: Tangram, problem solving, eye tracking, spatial ability.

1 Introduction

Spatial ability is directly related to individuals' daily life experiences. Therefore, using visualization based activities in science and mathematics curriculum is supported by educators. Olkun (2003) [10] identified spatial visualization as the mental manipulation of objects and their parts in two-dimensional and three-dimensional spaces. Other researchers define it as the ability to mentally restructure of manipulate the components of the visual stimulus and involves recognizing, retaining and recalling configurations when the figure or parts of the figure are moved [4]. Linn and Petersen (1985) defined spatial ability as representing, transforming, generating and recalling symbolic, nonlinguistic information (pp.1482) [8]. They classified three types of spatial ability: mental rotation, spatial perception and spatial visualization. They defined mental rotation as ability to rotate a two or three-dimensional figure rapidly and accurately [3]. Spatial perception related to orientation of an individual's own body and high spatial perception requires overcoming distracting information [7]. Spatial visualization involves complicated, multistep manipulation of spatially presented information [7].

Tangram, a well-known Chinese puzzle, allows people form over 1000 patterns from seven geometric pieces. Indeed, in Mathematics, tangram is used to help learners to develop their spatial abilities [10], [11]. Kennedy and Tipps (1994) argued that

J. Jacko (Ed.): Human-Computer Interaction, Part III, HCII 2007, LNCS 4552, pp. 555 – 563, 2007.

materials made even the most difficult mathematical concepts easier to understand. In addition, they are more understandable for the learners specially bridging between abstract concepts to real objects. Tooke, Hyatt, Leigh, Snyder and Borda (1992) [12] claimed that Mathematics is better learned when the learners have more experiences in manipulations. As stated by Ben-Chaim, Lappan and Houang (1989), [2] visualization provide the learners additional strategies potentially enriching their problem solving repertoire.

In our study, the term spatial ability is used to describe mental manipulation of 2D geometric objects including activities such as rotation of geometric objects, perceiving the geometric objects' space (big or small) and creating new geometric objects by combination of other figures. The assigned problem solving task is to create a tangram object with seven geometric objects. Problem solving is defined as any goal directed sequence of cognitive operations [1]. The main goal behind the idea of problem solving is to seek different solution angles within the problem solver's knowledge which is basically constituted in the memory [5]. This study aims to explore adults' 2D problem solving abilities with digital tangram. The main research question with the sub questions is,

How do participants solve digital tangram problems with different difficulty levels?

- ❖ How do eye fixation durations of the participants differ according to difficulty levels of the geometric figures?
- ❖ How do the participants' eye fixation counts change according to difficulty levels of the geometric figures?
- ❖ How do the participants' task completion durations change according to difficulty levels of the geometric figures?
- ❖ How do the participants' transition numbers between screens change according to difficulty levels of the geometric figures?
- ❖ What are the behaviors patterns of the participants while they are solving the digital problems?

2 Methodology

Twenty graduate students, between 20 to 30 years of age, participated to this study. They used digital tangram software to solve two different problems, with different complexity levels. Participants were first allowed to play with an easy figure to become familiar with the software. After they felt comfortable with the controls, they proceeded to the actual tasks.

The participants were asked to make patterns like a bird and crow. (Fig. 1. Level 1: First problem and geometric objects to solve puzzles. Level 2: Second problem and geometric objects to solve puzzles. level 1 and level 2). For the easy puzzle (level 1), the placement of the pieces is discernible and rotating some of the pieces is required. For the more difficult level (level 2), the places of the pieces are not so obvious when

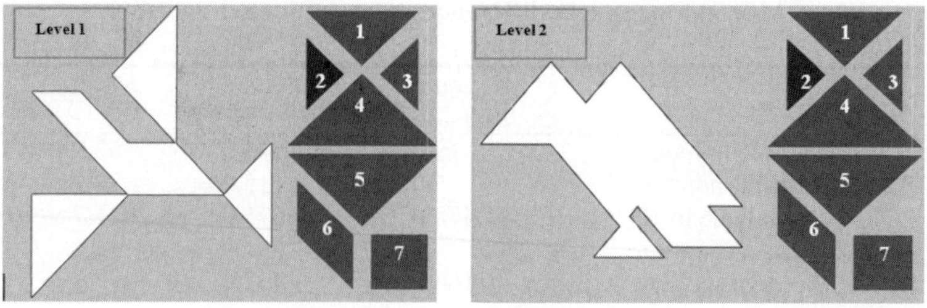

Fig. 1. Level 1: First problem and geometric objects to solve puzzles. Level 2: Second problem and geometric objects to solve puzzles.

compared to the easy one. We defined two sections on the screen under the Area of Interests (AOIs) category. The first part, left side of the screen which is named after 'problem part', consists of a specific figure that the participants have to create. The second part, right part of the screen, which is named after 'geometric objects', consists of different geometric objects (triangle, square, parallelogram) to create the certain figure on the pattern screen. Geometric objects part was numbered by the researchers to be used in the result section.

The participants and their eye movements were recorded by a Tobii Eye Tracking device while solving the problems. In this study, we had two independent variables 'Figure complexity' (level 1 and 2) and 'Screen Differences' (problem and geometric objects screens). In addition there were five dependent variables; 'Time to First Fixation', 'Fixation count (number of fixations)', 'Average fixation duration (millisecond)', 'Transition (number of transitions)' and 'Task completion duration (seconds)'. Time to first fixation is defined as time from the beginning of the recording until the respective AOIs were first fixated upon. Fixation count is defined as number of fixations in the respective AOIs. Average fixation duration is defined as the average length of all fixations during all recordings on the respective AOIs. Transition number is the number of eye switching between the two sections of the screen (from problem screen to geometric objects screen and vice versa. Task completion duration is the time that the participants completed the task with success.

3 Results

3.1 Differences Between Level 1 and Level 2

It was investigated whether or not there is a significant difference between different difficulty levels of problems. The results showed that there is a significant difference between two levels, $t(38)=-2.794$, $p=.01$ for fixation count, $t(38)=-2.914$, $p=.008$ for task completion duration and for transition number, $t(38)=-2.037$, $p=.049$. However, there is no significant difference for average fixation duration and time to first fixation (Table 1).

Table 1. Mean score differences between level 1 and 2

		Minimum	Maximum	Mean	Std. Deviation
Level 1	Task completion	18.0	145.0	62.7	32.6
	Transfer number	5.0	115.0	36.9	29.9
	Time to 1st fixation	478.0	5075.0	2021.7	1227.0
	Average fixation duration	166.0	437.0	297.2	75.4
	Fixation count	15.0	185.0	68.7	43.8
	Transitions	5.0	115.0	36.9	29.9
Level 2	Task completion	27.0	329.0	128.6	95.7
	Transfer number	10.0	228.0	67.3	59.6
	Time to 1st fixation	383.0	8032.0	2117.4	1865.3
	Average fixation duration	152.0	420.0	286.1	62.5
	Fixation count	20.0	404.0	148.4	119.7
	Transitions	10.0	228.0	67.3	59.6

3.2 Differences Between Problem and Geometric Objects Screens

The results were investigated whether there is a significant difference between participants' focus on the problem and geometric objects Area of Interest (AOI) screens according to their fixation count, average fixation duration and time to first fixation (Table 2).

For the level 1, there is a significant difference between problem and geometric objects screens based on participants' fixation count, average fixation duration , $t(38) = 4.28$, $p = .000$, $t(38) = 3.06$, $p = .004$ respectively.

For the level 2, there is a significant difference between problem and geometric objects screens based on participants' fixation count, average fixation duration $t(38) = 3.98$, $p = .001$, $t(38) = 3.57$, $p = .001$, respectively.

When we investigated the level differences for the problem screen, there is a significant difference between level 1 and 2 based on fixation count and gaze duration, $t(38) = -2.96$, $p = .007$, $t(38) = -3.11$, $p = .005$ respectively. However, there is no significant difference between level 1 and 2 based on participants' average fixation duration for the problem screen. In detailed, when mean scores were investigated it was clear that mean of fixation count has increased from level 1 to level 2.

Additionally, when we examined the level difference on the geometric objects screen, there is no significant difference between level 1 and level 2 for participants' fixation counts and average fixation durations. However, it can be seen that the mean scores of the participants' fixation count has increased from level 1 to level 2 for the geometric objects screen.

Moreover, for verifying the data, the hotspot data were also investigated (Fig. 2). Analyzing the hot spots of the screen is a powerful technique to understand the gaze behavior and for better visualization of the eye movements of the participants. The most focusing area was colored as red while others green.

Table 2. Mean score differences between problem and geometric objects screens

		Screen	Mean	Std. Deviation
Level 1	Fixation count	problem	103.1	65.2
		geometric objects	35.1	27.9
	Average fixation duration	problem	342.1	118.1
		geometric objects	252.1	57.2
Level 2	Fixation count	problem	238.7	193.9
		geometric objects	58.6	56.9
	Average fixation duration	problem	331.4	99.8
		geometric objects	241.0	52.9

When we investigated the hotspots of the first problem (a bird), the participants focused on the head of the bird composing a small triangle and a parallelogram. Moreover, it was clear that participants tended to focus on the problem screen rather than the geometric objects screen for this level.

For the second problem (a crow), the hotspots of the participants showed that they focused on the discernible pieces than the not obvious ones. For this figure, the most fixated place was the leg of the crow and similarly for level 1, participants tended to focus on the problem part than the geometric objects. However, when the two levels were analyzed together in terms of the focusing areas of the participants, we see that when the complexity level increases the participants had a tendency to focus on the problem screen more than the geometric objects screen.

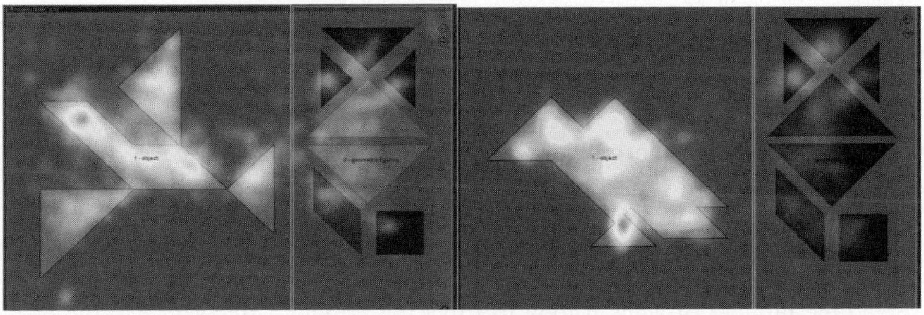

Fig. 2. The participants' focusing places on the level 1 and 2

3.3 Behavior Patterns for Level 1

Gaze replies of the participants were watched and investigated to understand how they had been solved the first problem. Figure 3 shows how the participants placed seven geometric objects in seven steps. Initially, the participants began to place from big and discernible parts than the inconspicuous ones. That is most of the participants placed geometric objects 4 and 5 (Fig. 1) in the beginning. Another explicit result was that the parallelogram was placed in the fourth step. The participants preferred to place small parts after most of the figures were placed. For example, most of the participants placed the object 4 at the first step. This may show that participants generally focused on the particular objects rather than the overall picture. Parallel to this findings, most of the participants placed the object 3 (small object) at the seventh step. Also, the object 7 was never used in step1 and 2. This behavior pattern of the participants may be interpreted as an inductive approach because they solved the problem by mainly focusing on particular objects rather than general figure (Fig.3).

The maximum time required to solve the problem was 145 seconds (see Table 1), nine out of 20 participants made mistakes while solving the problem. A total of 11 mistakes were done. These participants generally put some figures to wrong places. The parallelogram had been the most difficult figure and most participants could not place this part in the first try.

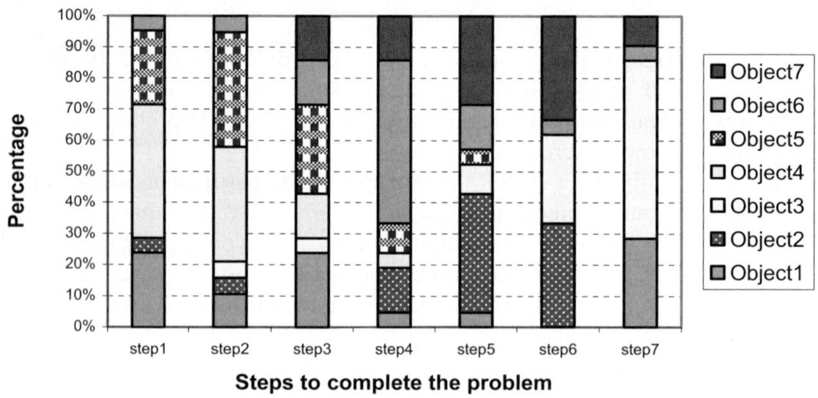

Fig. 3. Behavior patterns for the level 1

3.4 Behavior Patterns for the Level 2

The participants solved the problem 2 in three different ways (Fig. 4). In detail, 10 participants solved it by the strategy 1 and eight participants solved by the strategy 2. The remaining two participants solved the problem by the strategy 3.

For the second problem, a specific behavior pattern could not be observed. Its complex nature made more than one solution possible. However, the researchers observed the number of steps it took to solve the problem. According to the results, the participants solved the problem in 15 steps on the average. Maximum step count to solve problem was 34 and minimum was seven. Only three participants solved the problem in seven steps with no mistake. Furthermore, the most difficult objects were big triangles (geometric objects 4 and 5, see Fig. 1) and participants tried 51 times to find the correct place for these geometric objects. After these geometric objects the most difficult objects to place were geometric objects 1 and 7. Especially, the geometric object 7 (the square) was the hardest handled piece. It was observed that

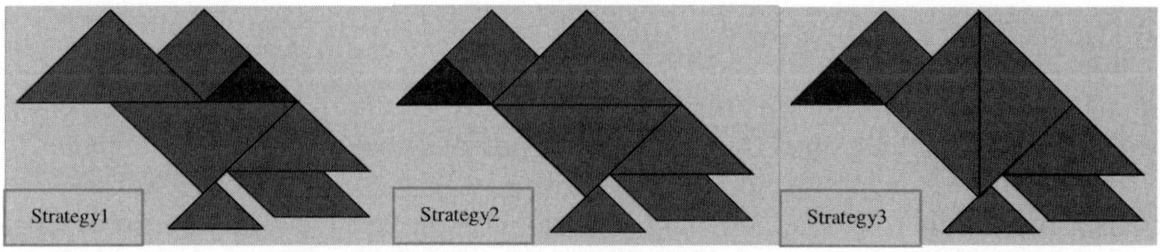

Fig. 4. Three solution strategy for the level 2

the participants had difficulties to rotate this geometric object. They needed to rotate the square 45° clockwise for placing this geometric object properly. It was observed that the participants realized it later than the placement of other geometric objects.

4 Conclusion and Discussion

Eye-tracking data showed that participants tended to choose different strategies while solving problems with different difficulty levels. The results showed that there are significant differences between level 1 and level 2 in accordance with the task completion duration and transition number. These results are interpreted as there might be a relationship among problem solving process, complexity level of the task and number of eye transitions between screens. As an expected result of this study, in case of the complexity level increase, the problem solving process is affected and fixation count, task completion duration and transition number are increased, too. Also, the increase in transition number increase may be interpreted as a mental process emerged and in the problem solving process the increase of complexity level is directly related with the task completion duration.

According to the AOIs results, the participants focused especially on the problem screen rather than on the geometric objects screen. In addition, when it was compared the level 1 to level 2 problem screens, the participants focused on the problem screen especially for the level 2'. When the two levels of the geometry problems were investigated, the reason for finding difference between the problem and geometric objects screen among participants may be related with the tendency to focus on the problem part for finding a solution. Additionally, as in the Table 2, when the complexity level increases, the number of focusing on the problem screen was increased, too. This is obvious that the participants inclined to focus on the problems screen as the complexity level increased. Although the results indicated that there was not a significant difference between level 1 and level 2 in terms of the focusing on geometric objects screen, hotspot data showed that participants focused more on level 2's geometric objects part than on the level 1's. Furthermore, there was a significant difference between participants in terms of focusing on problem screen between the first and second problems. It was clear that participants generally focused on the problem part comparing with the geometric objects when the complexity level is increased. Learners generated different strategies for different problems like inductive or deductive approaches. In problem 1, it was easy to recognize the objects rather than the overall picture because of the discernible parts in the problem. For this reason, they had a tendency to place the bigger and discernible objects before the small objects. However, in the second problem the participants needed to think about the relationship between objects and their places for comprehending the whole picture and solve the problem. For this reason, they tried to see the overall picture rather than focusing on individual objects. This may be an evidence that the participants had chosen to follow a deductive approach.

Also, there might be a relationship between complexity level and the individuals' cognitive process like formation of new strategies. Participants may choose deductive strategies for the complex problem and they may choose strategies that are more inductive for the easier problems. This might be a clue to understand learners' problem solving strategies and whether there is a relationship between the task complexity and focus place of the participants on the screen.

As seen in the behavior pattern data and hotspot data, the participants tended to focus on the big and discernible objects than the vague ones. This might be an evidence for describing the problem solving process in terms of putting the objects in correct position since the participants placed the discernible objects firstly and inconspicuous ones later than the other objects. Also, this result is supporting the reason behind placing parallelogram lastly as its position was not clearly seen. Almost all participants had difficulty while placing the square and the reason that lay beneath might be related to the rotation problems of this object.

While solving the problem in the level 2, it was investigated that the participants followed three different strategies. In the first steps of the problem, the participants tended to place the discernible and big objects in the screen like the problem in level1. However, as it was seen in the findings, the participants had difficulties while placing these big objects that they had tried to place the objects 4 and 5 for 51 times. The participants might carry the first problem solving strategy that they used in level1 to the problem in level2. However, when they examined that the solution was not efficient, they changed their strategy and developed different strategies for solving the problem.

People have a tendency to use the familiar strategies that they used before, in the process of solving a problem but these previously known solving strategies may not be efficient in every condition. For this reason, it should be reminded by the educators to try different solution strategies. Also, in this process educators need to give some clues about developing strategies in regards of problem solving. Lastly, if digital tangrams are considered to be used in educational settings, as much as possible various solving strategies have to be presented to learners. The more diverse examples are given, the more successful applications are solved with tangrams in terms of accustoming to the problems.

5 Limitations and Future Studies

In this study, the sample size of the study is at the lowest limit of experimental studies. Therefore, this study may be repeated with a wider sampling especially with participants from diverse backgrounds. Furthermore, in another study, children needs to participate to the study for generalizing the results among different age groups and this may help to the educators in terms of using the digital tangrams in the educational platforms effectively. Moreover, it can be investigated what the possible differences are between participants in regards to use digital tangrams and hand made tangrams.

Acknowledgements. This study was supported by TUBITAK under grant SOBAG 104K098 and METU Human Computer Interaction research group (http://hci.metu.edu.tr).

References

1. Anderson, J.R., Boyle, C.B., Reiser, B.J.: Intelligent tutoring systems. Science 228, 456–462 (1985)
2. Ben-Chaim, D., Lappan, G., Houang, R.T.: The role of visualization in the middle school curriculum. Focus on Learning Problems in Mathematics 11, 49–60 (1989)
3. Black, A.A.: Spatial ability and earth science conceptual understanding. J. of Geoscience Education 53(4), 402–414 (2005)
4. Bodner, G., Guay, R.: The Purdue Visualization of Rotations Test. The. Chemical Educator 2(4), 1–17 (1997)
5. Chiev, W., Wang, Y.: Formal description of the cognitive process of problem solving. In: ICCI'04 (2004)
6. Kayhan, E.B.: Investigation of high school students' spatial Ability. Unpublished Ms thesis. Metu, Ankara (2005)
7. Kennedy, L.M., Tipps, S.: Guiding children's learning of mathematics, 7th edn. Wadsworth, Belmont, CA (1994)
8. Linn, M.C., Petersen, A.C.: Emergence and characterization of sex differences in spatial ability: A meta-analysis. Child Development 56, 1479–1498 (1985)
9. Matlin, M.W.: Cognition, 2nd edn. Harcourt Brace and Company (1998)
10. Olkun, S.: Comparing Computer versus Concrete Manipulative in Learning 2D Geometry. J. of Comp. in Math. and Sci. Teaching. 22(1), 43–56 (2003)
11. Olkun, S., Altun, A., Smith, G.: Computers and 2D geometric learning of Turkish fourth and fifth graders. British J. of Educ. Tech. 36(2), 317–326 (2005)
12. Tooke, D.J., Hyatt, B., Leigh, M., Snyder, B., Borda, T.: Why aren't manipulatives used in every middle school mathematics classroom? Middle School J. 24, 61–62 (1992)

Gesture Interaction for Electronic Music Performance

Reinhold Behringer

Leeds Metropolitan University, Headingley Campus, Leeds, LS6 3QS, UK
r.behringer@leedsmet.ac.uk

Abstract. This paper describes an approach for a system which analyses an orchestra conductor in real-time, with the purpose of using the extracted information of time pace and expression for an automatic play of a computer-controlled instrument (synthesizer). The system in its final stage will use non-intrusive computer vision methods to track the hands of the conductor. The main challenge is to interpret the motion of the hand/baton/mouse as beats for the timeline. The current implementation uses mouse motion to simulate the movement of the baton. It allows to "conduct" a pre-stored MIDI file of a classical orchestral music work on a PC.

Keywords: Computer music, human-computer interaction, gesture interaction.

1 Introduction

In the minds of many people, the worlds of "classical music" and "computer science" have no intersection. However, there are several areas in which these two fields approach each other. Computers can be used as a tool for automatically generating music, as an aid for the conventional human composition process, or as tools for performance, where their large capabilities in the acoustic processing, e.g. sound synthesis and design are employed. The musical avant-garde has embraced these capabilities and has used computers since the 1950s to generate novel music, for example based on strict mathematical principles for human players (Xenakis [1]) or for directly performing music [2]. Software tools, applications, and frameworks (such as CSound and Max/MSP) have been developed for making these capabilities available to composers. The standardization of communication between synthesizers and computers by the MIDI (Musical Instrument Digital Interface) standard (1983) [3] brought the use of computers in music composition and performance into the mainstream of music production.

1.1 Large Number of Parameters for Music and Sound

The use of computers provides infinite possibilities for the creation of sounds, no longer limited by the physical constraints of conventional acoustic music instruments but solely by the computing power and memory of the computer system in use. They can control electronic synthesizers or act themselves as synthesizers. One of the possibilities is to create "virtual instruments" which are simulations of sound creation mechanisms based on true physical principles. However, to access the vast number of

J. Jacko (Ed.): Human-Computer Interaction, Part III, HCII 2007, LNCS 4552, pp. 564–572, 2007.

possibilities and parameters for the creative use of synthesizers and virtual instruments is often not intuitive to the player. A musician can learn how to play conventional music instruments and express very subtle nuances of musicality. But using the computer as a musical instrument for expressive live play is in general quite difficult, due to the large number of parameters to be controlled simultaneously and due to the non-standardized interfaces to such computer music systems. As a consequence, "electronic" music generated by computer-controlled synthesizers often lacks the aesthetic quality of human live music play [4], because of an insufficient control of all possible sound creation parameters. This is also true in general for most electronic synthesizers which are mainly controlled by buttons, knows, and sliders. This interface paradigm has been transferred to computer-controlled synthesizers, as the Graphical User Interface (GUI) of music software systems often emulates this synthesizer operation of a one-on-one controller mapping. An exception is the Theremin, which operates on the principle that the position of the player's body relative to an antenna is directly translated into the creation of a sound, based on analog electronics principles. This allows the player to directly interact with the generated sound in an intuitive way, enabling the player to shape the sound with intuitive musicality. There have been many adaptations of this technique into software interfaces for computer simulations of the Theremin principle (e.g. [5]), simulating the effect of the interaction for the sound creation [6]. However, the acoustic possibilities of the Theremin are limited to monophonic music (unless several Theremins would be combined) and to the unique continuous pitch change of this instrument.

1.2 Sampled Instrumental Sounds

These shortcomings of synthesizers and computer interfaces have prevented the widespread use of computer technologies in the performance of traditional non-avant-garde classical music. A step forward has been the introduction of sampled sounds, based on recordings of acoustic instruments. This of course limits the freedom of the sound creation process to the production of "naturalistic" instrument sounds. But this removes from the player the burden of creating a musically pleasing sound, as the recorded instruments naturally have incorporated centuries of musical heritage and experience in them. Examples of such sample libraries of orchestral instruments are the Vienna Symphonic Library [7] or the Garritan Orchestra Libraries [8]. The number of parameters for the sound generation is significantly reduced in these libraries, because the various playing techniques have been recorded as separate sample sets. To change from one sample to another can be easily mapped to a single keystroke and hence can be executed very rapidly. Shaping the sound can be achieved with very few parameters, as the main sound characteristics are in the pre-recorded samples. This can be used for a real-time performance given by a human player of a particular sampled instrument.

1.3 Music Timeline

With these sampling techniques of reproducing the sound of acoustic instruments, it is possible to create "natural" and realistic sounding renditions of classical orchestral works. This broadens the application of computers in the musical context away from music types which made specific use of the inherent sound characteristics of synthesized sounds and computerized rendition. However, there is still one big hurdle in the creation of renditions of traditional classical music: to create a "musical" aesthetically pleasing time flow of the music rendition. A music performance by a human instrumentalist has often subtle deliberate tempo variations, which are intuitively generated by the player. If the player is in a live performance and plays the instrument, then this timeline is generated naturally. However, if a music part is created "offline" as a rendition by programming a sequence of music events (notes, controller chances, etc.) using a (software) sequencer, then the programmer has to create this timeline manually, either by editing tempo variations or deviations from the musical beat.

In this paper we address the issues of creating such an offline music timeline intuitively, using gesture interaction, as used by orchestra conductors.

2 Related Work

Since the mid 1980s, much research and development has been done in the area of interaction with music instruments, in order to make the capabilities of computer music available for the music creation and performance process.

Already in the 1960s, Max Mathews had experimented with a light-pen [9] for using graphical interaction as a composition tool. He later developed the radio baton [10] for allowing improvising and conducting music, based on 3D tracking of radio frequency tracking emitted from the baton. Other early conducting systems have been developed in the 1980s [11][12].

Teresa Marrin Nakra's "Conductor Jacket" [13][16] is a complete system worn by an orchestra conductor for interacting with a computer system. The "Digital Baton" in this system was also used in MIT's "Brain Opera" [14]. It is comprised of 3 sensor systems: an IR LED at the baton's tip, an array of 5 force sensitive resistor strips at the grip handle, and 3 orthogonal 5G accelerometers [15]. The visual tracking was done through the IR LED which emits modulated (20 kHz) light, detected by a 2D position-sensitive photodiode. Also magnetic tracking can be used as a simple interface for orchestra conducting, as demonstrated by Schertenleib et al. [17]. An infrared baton that is actively emitting IR for tracking by triangulation has been used in conducting demonstrations such as the "Personal Orchestra" by Borchers et al. [18]. Common to these systems is that they are not completely seamless and require the conductor to either wear devices and sensors, use specialized batons, or move in a specific location relative to a receiving device.

A large area of research is how sensor data from those interfaces can be mapped into acoustic or musical parameters (e.g. [19]). Research has shown that more complex mapping schemes which allow simultaneously controlling several parameters with a reduced number of control input, allow the user to do more complex tasks [20]. This cross-coupling of several parameters actually emulates real acoustic instruments, in which such a cross coupling frequently occurs: the input controls often act on several sound parameters simultaneously.

3 Concept

The idea of our approach of an interface between a musician / conductor and an electronic computer-controlled synthesizer is to leverage from the repertoire of gestures that have been employed in the interaction of the conductor with a traditional orchestra. This will allow that the timeline for a synthesizer rendition can be created naturally, enabling the musician to create an aesthetically pleasing musical performance recording. There is a set of pre-defined gestures which the orchestra conductor executes in order to synchronize orchestra players and to tell the orchestra members how to play their music part [17]. The information conveyed by the conductor is basically tempo (beat) and "expression". The latter one is a complex set of parameters, mostly consisting of instructions on loudness and phrasing. Some of this is conveyed not only by hand motion but also by facial expressions, using the whole range of human-human interaction for conveying the musical intent of the conductor to the orchestra members.

3.1 Elements of Conducting an Orchestra

The goal of this research project is not to exploit the facial interaction (at this time) of the conductor with the orchestra, but rather to focus solely on the gestural interaction. In this section we briefly will revisit a few essentials of traditional conducting [21]. The main parameter conveyed through the hand motion is the beat of the music tempo. A long vertical motion from top to bottom indicates the first beat in a measure. Vertical hand motion indicates the pace of the music to be played, and the beat itself (rhythmic pulse, ictus) is by convention on the lower bounce of the hand. In other words: the beat is characterized by the sudden change in direction of the hand motion at the bottom of the motion.

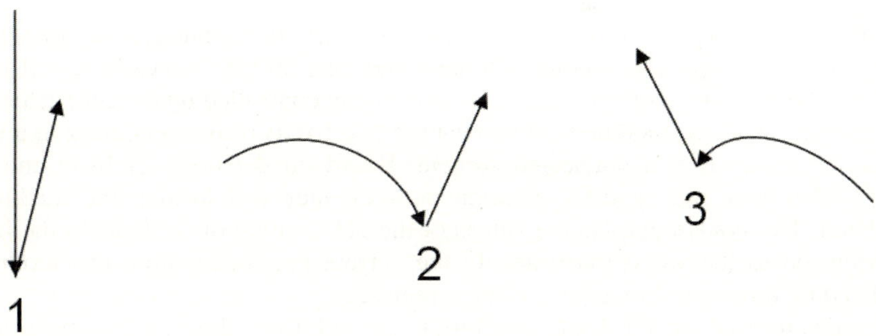

Fig. 1. Motion of the conductor's hand of a THREE beat: the numbers indicate the beat within the measure. The ictus is at the deflection of the hand motion (change of direction from down to up = bouncing).

In Fig. 1, the standard figure for conducting a THREE beat is shown [21]. The initial motion is from the top downward. The first beat is at the bounce of the motion at the bottom. The hand then raises up, only to move down again to create the 2nd bounce (beat #2). The third beat is again a bottom bounce, but higher up. From there, the hand returns back to the upper default location, for indicating the next bar.

3.2 Mapping of Conductor Hand Motion

Based on the conductors' practice, the following seems a reasonable approach to map the hand gestures to recognition:

- The longest vertical down motion indicates the beginning of a bar.
- The beats are the time when the inversion of motion direction between downward and upward occurs (bounce at the lower end).
- The amplitude of the hand motion – both in vertical and horizontal direction – is mapped to the overall volume of the music.
- In a more sophisticated version, the "hemisphere" of the predominant hand position can indicate the parts of the orchestra to which the conducting gestures are addressed. This is done by conductors to highlight individual instrument groups and could be used in the same way for an automatic separation of those groups of synthesizer instruments.

The tempo can be computed from the time duration between two beat points. This will give only a coarsely quantized tempo map, as a new tempo would only be determined at those ictus inflection points. However, in a real performance the tempo can change between the beats, indicated by a slowing hand motion. In order to bridge these gaps between beats which can be in the order of 200 ms to 2 seconds [4], it is necessary to continuously monitor the hand motion and to derive a suitable mapping onto the resulting tempo.

4 System Architecture

The development of the envisioned system is done in modules. The system will analyze the motion of the conductor's hand and play an electronically stored music file (in MIDI format), with the tempo and expression controlled by the conductor.

The visual tracking module is observing the two hands of the conductor in a video stream, obtained from a connected camera. Based on detection of hand and face (using color cues and expected relation between face and hands), the tracking is initialized. The system outputs the values of the 2D location of the hand in the image synchronized to the video framerate. In the current implementation, this module is simulated by mouse motion over a given screen area.

In order to recreate the hand position at any arbitrary time and to increase the "resolution" to the required smallest musical time (5ms), a spline algorithm creates a smooth representation of the motion. This allows to interpolate the location and the time of the beats at a higher resolution than the video frame sampling.

An analysis is done to detect the beginning of a bar (longest vertical stretch of motion) and the beat (velocity zero-transition at lower end). These values lead to the tempo which is sent to the synthesizer module.

An optional module for acoustic tracking can be connected, to provide feedback from the sound/audio of other ensemble players [22][23]. Currently, such a module is not being integrated, but the architecture provides input for this. This would basically be a score follower, comparing the captured audio with the expected audio.

In order to compensate for lag and latency (processing time), it is necessary to extrapolate from the current measurements to the current time.

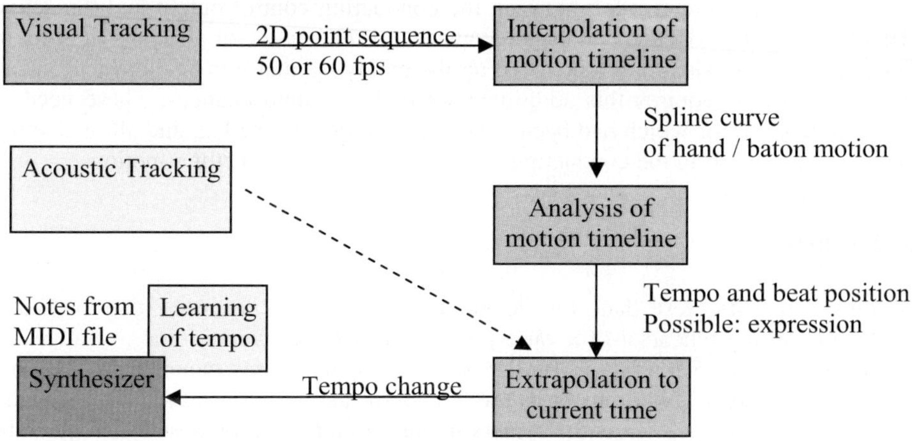

Fig. 2. Architecture for conduction a MIDI file

Since the MIDI event storing is usually done in musical time, that is in measures and bars, there needs to be a translation of the beat interval time (real time) into musical time – this happens through the tempo. Based on the beat timing, this tempo is computed and sent to the synthesizer. The synthesizer is playing a pre-stored MIDI file ("score") and uses the tempo to adapt the replay speed. From the conducting amplitude, the volume can be derived and sent to the synthesizer.

Since the tempo in a classical music piece can vary quite significantly, it is difficult to predict the tempo with the lag compensation correctly: in most cases it will be right, however in cases of a sudden tempo change, the prediction / extrapolation of the tempo will be not correct, if it is plainly extrapolated from past tempo chances. Therefore, it is necessary to embed the expected tempo changes into the MIDI file. In practice, at the first run the MIDI file does have a "standard" default tempo. As the music piece is played for the first time, the tempo captured from the conducting is stored and placed into the MIDI file as a reference tempo. At the next runs, this tempo map allows a more correct prediction of the tempo variations.

5 Implementation

The system is being implemented on Windows XP, using the Windows32 APIs and DirectX for replay of a MIDI file. The software modules have been written in C++ for fast real-time operation.

Since it is important to use a precise timing, the Windows high precision timer was used instead of the multimedia timer.

There are two types of tempo changes which are computed as a consequence of the beat detection: the "true" tempo change, based on the detected beat. These tempo changes are stored and synchronized to the MIDI file timer, so that a new replay of the MIDI file (without conducting) will result in the timing of the conducted timeline. In order to reproduce the live replay as it is being conducted, another tempo needs to be computed: as there is a lag between the conducting control output and the actual MIDI file play, the MIDI file is usually "ahead" of the conductor analysis. In order to compensate and to slow down or speed up the replay, so that it is again synchronized to the conductor, requires this additional set of live tempo changes. These need to compensate the error which had been created by the processing lag, and allow that the sounding music during the conducting is in sync with the conductor's motion.

6 Results

To obtain realistic test data for development, we have recorded two orchestra conductors during rehearsal of a variety of classical music works – the overall video data covers about 15 hours on MiniDV tape. The camera was mounted on a tripod, behind the orchestra, facing towards the conductor above the heads of the orchestra members. This viewpoint puts the camera in place of a regular orchestra member. The zoom lens of the camera was set so that the arms of the conductor fill the image in extreme moments.

This data collection has partially been transferred to a hard disk and reduced to 320x240 pixels – this resolution is deemed to be a good compromise between precision requirement and computation time economy.

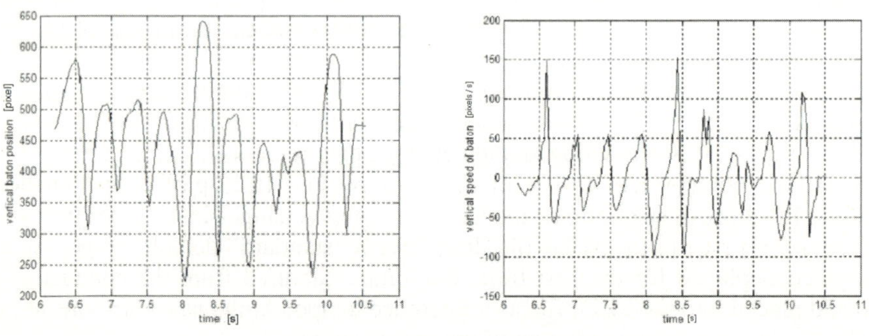

Fig. 3. Left: Vertical baton/hand motion. Right: vertical speed of the hand/baton.

From previous experiments [24], we have obtained the following typical hand / baton motion patter shown in Fig. 3 (solely the vertical motion component). It clearly can be seen how the bar detection and the beat detection can be done by analyzing these motion patterns.

We have implemented the replay of standard orchestral MIDI files with complex structure and many control parameter events. One example is Johann Strauss' waltz

"At the Blue Danube". We hope to have the system ready for HCI 2007in order to show a demonstration of the capabilities.

7 Conclusions and Outlook

There is still a lot to do until a system for capturing the conductor's gestures through computer vision can be used reliably in a situation where an electronic instrument is supposed to play in an orchestral example together with human players. At the time of the submission of this paper, our prototype was not yet in a state for us to make an assessment of the suitability for such an envisioned application. However, such a system is feasible, and the current state of technology is mature enough to envision that such a system can be built.

There are many possible applications of such a system:

- Professional musicians (soloists) will be enabled to rehearse their part of a performance at home, using an automatic computer-controlled accompaniment system, in a "music-minus-one" fashion, but with an automatically adaptable timeline of the accompanying other instruments, fitting to the interpretation of the soloist.
- Music could be written specifically for a piece for "orchestra and synthesizer" where the synthesizer part would be played by a computer. This would raise the computer into the status of an individual orchestra member, playing an electronic instrument according to the instructions of the conductor.
- This system could also be used in education and training, to teach facts about music, interpretation, and performance.
- Such a system could be developed into an application giving "hobby home conductors" the ability to give individual performances within their home.

References

1. Xenakis, I.: Musiques Formelles (1963), reprinted Paris, Stock (1981)
2. Doornbusch, P.: The Music of CSIRAC, Australia's first computer music. Common Ground (2005)
3. Heckroth, J.: Tutorial on MIDI and Music Synthesis. MIDI Manufacturers Association Inc. (2001) (accessed 12 February, 2007) http://www.midi.org/about-midi/tutorial/tutor.shtml
4. Dannenberg, R.B.: Music Understanding by Computer. 1987/88 Computer Science Research Review, Carnegie Mellon School of Computer science, pp. 19–28 (1988)
5. Bolas, M., Stone, P.: Virtual mutant theremin. In: Int. Computer Music Conference, San Jose, CA, USA, pp. 360–361 (1992)
6. Theremin World: (accessed 14 February, 2007) http://www.thereminworld.com/software.asp
7. Vienna Symphonic Library: (accessed 15 February, 2007) http://www.vsl.co
8. Garritan Orchestral Libraries: (accessed 15 February, 2007) http://www.garritan.com
9. Mathews, M.V., Rosler, L.: Graphical Language for the Scores of Computer-Generated Sound. In: Perspectives of New Music, pp. 92–118 (1968)
10. Boulanger, R.C., Mathews, M.V.: The 1997 Mathews radio-baton and improvisation modes. In: Proc. of ICMC 1997, Thessaloniki (1997)

11. Brill, L.M.: A Microcomputer based conducting system. Computer Music Journal 4(1), 8–21 (1980)
12. Haflich, F., Burnds, M.: Following a Conductor: the Engineering of an Input Device. In: Proc. of the 1983 International Computer Music Conference, San Francisco (1983)
13. Marrin Nakra, T.: Immersion Music: A Progress Report. 2003. In: Int. Conf. On New Interfaces for Musical Expression (NIME), May 22-24, Montreal (2003)
14. Paradiso, J.A.: The Brain Opera Technology: New Instruments and Gestural Sensors for Musical Interaction and Performance. Journal of New Music Research 28(2), 130–149 (1998)
15. Marrin Nakra, T., Paradiso, J.A.: The Digital Baton: a Versatile Performance Instrument. In: Proc. of the 1997 International Computer Music Conference, San Francisco, pp. 313–316 (1997)
16. Marrin, T.A.: Towards an Understanding of Musical Gesture: Mapping Expressive Intention with the Digital Baton. MSc thesis, MIT, Boston (1996)
17. Schertenlaib, S., Gutierrez, M., Vexo, V., Thalmann, D.: Conducting a virtual orchestra. IEEE Multimedia 11(3), 40–49 (2004)
18. Borchers, J.O., Samminger, W., Mühlhäuser, M.: Personal Orchestra: conducting audio/video music recordings. In: Proc. of Wedelmusic, Darmstadt (2002)
19. Rovan, J.B., Wanderley, M.M., Dubnov, S., Depalle, P.: Instrumental Gestural Mapping Strategies as Expressivity Determinants in Computer Music Performance. In: Wanderley, M., Battier, M. (eds.) Trends in Gestural Control of Music, Ircam, Paris (2000)
20. Hunt, A., Wanderley, M.M., Paradis, M.: The importance of parameter mapping in electronic instrument design. In: Proc. of the 2002 Conference on New Instruments for Musical Expression (NIME), Dublin, Ireland (2002)
21. Green, E.A.H.: The Modern Conductor, 6th edn. Prentice Hall, Upper Saddle River, New Jersey (1997)
22. Vercoe, B.: Teaching your computer how to play by ear. In: Proc. of 3rd Symposium on Arts and Technology (1991)
23. Dannenberg, R.B., Grubb, L.: Automated accompaniment of musical ensembles. In: Proc. of the 12th National Conference on Artificial Intelligence, AAAI, pp. 94–99 (1994)
24. Behringer, R.: Conducting Digitally Stored Music by Computer Vision Tracking. In: 1st Int. Conf. on Automated Production of Cross Media Content for Multi-Channel Distribution (AXMEDIS), Florence (2005)

A New Method for Multi-finger Detection Using a Regular Diffuser

Li-wei Chan, Yi-fan Chuang, Yi-wei Chia, Yi-ping Hung, and Jane Hsu

Graduate Institute of Networking and Multimedia
Department of Computer Science and Information Engineering
National Taiwan University
hung@csie.ntu.edu.tw

Abstract. In this paper, we developed a fingertip finding algorithm working with a regular diffuser. The proposed algorithm works on images captured by infra-red cameras, settled on one side of the diffuser, observing human gestures taken place on the other side. With diffusion characteristics of the diffuser, we can separate finger-touch from palm-hover events when the user interacts with the diffuser. This paper contributes on: Firstly, the technique works with a regular diffuser, infra-red camera coupled with an infra-red illuminator, which is easy to deploy and cost effective. Secondly, the proposed algorithm is designed to be robust for casually illuminated surface. Lastly, with diffusion characteristics of the diffuser, we can detect finger-touch and palm-hover events, which is useful for natural user interface design. We have deployed the algorithm on a rear-projection multi-resolution tabletop, called I-M-Top. A video retrieval application using the two events on design of UIs is implemented to show its intuitiveness on the tabletop system.

Keywords: Multi-Finger Detection, Intuitive Interaction.

1 Introduction

Work with displays in life size, direct manipulation using bare hand gesture is more nature and more like how people interact with the real world. Recently, researchers have been studying on design of user interface on digital surfaces such as interactive wall and tabletop. Among which, many works are based on the visual hand gesture recognition techniques. Obviously, for applications that need for complex operations and rich interactions, a finger-level gesture recognition technique is necessary.

In this paper, a fingertip finding algorithm applied with a regular diffuser is proposed. The algorithm works on images captured by infra-red cameras, settled on one side of the diffuser, observing human gestures taken place on the other side. On user's hands approaching the diffuser lighted by the infra-red illuminator, the camera observes reflection left by the hands to do further recognition. The installation is quiet simple, cost-effective and flexible to deploy with digital surface achieved by either front or rear projection.

The proposed algorithm is able to separate fingertip interactions into two events: finger-touch (figure 1a-1c) and palm-hover (finger 1d) events. Finger-touch event

J. Jacko (Ed.): Human-Computer Interaction, Part III, HCII 2007, LNCS 4552, pp. 573–582, 2007.

refers to the fingertips are contacting the surface and palm-hover event refers to the user's palms are hovering over the display surface. The two kinds of events can be used in designing user interfaces reacting accordingly. For example, when the user's palms approach the display surface, the content beneath the palms can change accordingly so as to give more specific selections for upcoming fingertip actions.

2 Related Work

Previous researches working on finger tracking on interactive wall or tabletop systems using computer vision techniques have exploited ways of installations. These works can differ in how cameras installed to observe human hand gestures. In one kind of installations, the camera is settled to be able to directly observe the hand gestures [2-5, 7, 8, and 10], so clear hand shape segmentations are expected for analysis. In [2], their work presented a robust finger tracking algorithm by using single camera, but they cannot distinguish whether the user's fingers touch the surface. In [10], the work proposed analyzing finger shadows shown on the surface to detect finger-touch events. With the use of two cameras, these works [4, 5, and 7] can track fingers and detect finger-touch event on the surface.

Another installation is to have cameras installed behind a transparent sheet, and to observe hand gestures through the surface. In [1], they use an infra-camera and infra-red illuminator placed on one side of a diffuser. The installation in their work is similar to ours, but they only provide palm-level recognition, so only simple operations were presented. Working with two cameras, TouchLight [6] proposed an effective fingertip finding approach by using stereo information, but a special diffuser, HoloScreen, is required. FTIR[9] is another work with excellent performance to track multiple fingertips when the users place hands on the surface, but hovering fingertips are not detectable in their setting.

3 Design and Implementation

In this work, we have developed a multi-finger finding algorithm working with a regular diffuser. A sample installation applying the proposed algorithm is shown in figure 1. The infra-red camera coupled with an infra-red illuminator is settled on one side of the diffuser, observing human gestures taken place on the other side. On user's hands approaching the diffuser, the camera observes reflection left by the hands to do further recognition. The same installation was also found in [1], but they only provide palm-level recognition, so only simple operations were presented. There are several reasons making fingertip recognition behind a diffuser a difficult problem. First, since the diffuser dilutes the reflection with the distance, we can not expect a clear silhouette of hand to be segmented by simply a threshold. Second, it is usually hard to produce a uniform illuminated surface without calibration, so some algorithm tries to well segment hand shape on a region of the surface can be failed on other regions. Third, with a high degree of change in hand gesture, the observed reflection can be in freeform, which leads a simple matching-based approach easily locate fake fingertips.

We roughly classify hand gestures into four cases as shown in figure 2. In the first three cases, fingertips touching the surface are expected identified. In the last case, the hand hovers over the surface, but the reflection on it is still observable, though vague. In this case, no fingertip should be found. The proposed algorithm works well in all the cases.

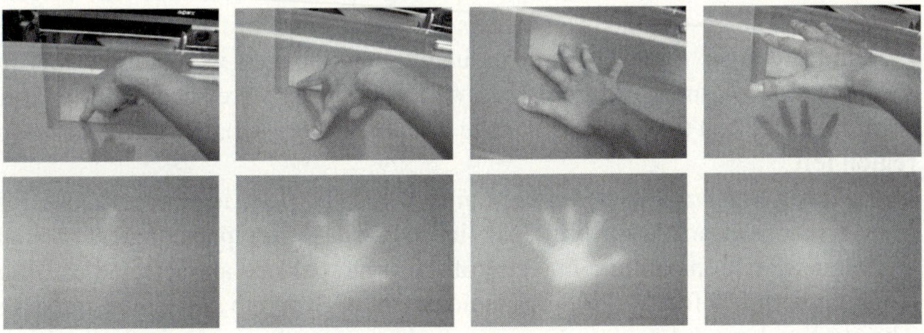

(a) (b) (c) (d)

Fig. 1. Four cases of close-up views of hand gestures taken placed on the surface. The first row shows the gesture types. The second row shows the corresponding observations taken by infrared camera.

Finding Fingertips. Considering a user puts hands on the digital surface (figure 1a-1c), the contact areas of the hands would leave strong reflection, while the other parts dilute with distance away the surface. As a result, the intensity is much solid inside the contact areas, declines rapidly on the boundaries, and finally, shown smooth for the rest. By using the knowledge, our algorithm consists of following steps. First, potential areas are extracted by applying background subtraction. Second, a mathematical morphological opening operation is used to extract watershed from the subtracted images. The watershed is then used to separate finger parts reflection from the rest. For each finger part reflection, we calculate its principal axis and pick points around then two ends of the axis as the candidate positions. At last, fingertip template matching and middle finger removal are used to reject fake candidates. By several rejection steps concatenated, we can effectively locate only a few position candidates for proceeding sophisticated and maybe time-consuming verifications like template matching. The proposed processes well work on a surface suffering non-uniform illumination. For more detail, we describe each step on the following. Refer to finger 2 to find some results produced in each step.

(a) *Background subtraction*: we first extract potential areas by applying background subtraction.
(b) *Separating finger and palm parts reflection by a morphological opening*: since the contact areas left by hands usually have strong reflection, we separate finger part reflection from palm part reflection by using a morphological opening with a structure element having its size larger than a normal finger and smaller than a palm. We define a normal fingertip pattern with r as the radius of circular

fingertip (figure 2e). The size of the structure element for opening is set twice of *r*. The 2nd Column in figure 2 shows the palm parts of reflection after opening in four cases of gestures. In the implementation, we use a template having a square of 17x17 pixels with a circle whose radius r is 5 pixels.

(c) *Identifying finger part reflection*: we apply a difference operation between subtraction images and results after opening operation, to extract the finger part reflection. The resulting difference is then dichotomized to the finger regions. Identifying finger region greatly reduces potential area where fingertips might locate. The 3rd column in figure 2 shows finger regions are successfully extracted in all cases. Noted that, for the 4th case gesture, (figure 2d), there will be no finger region left.

(d) *Calculating principal axis for each finger part region*: in this step, we further reduce potential area to a principal line by using principal component analysis technique. Positions around one end of the principal line are selected as fingertip candidates and to form a group. Candidates in each group are scored in next step. The survived candidate with best matched score in the group is then selected as fingertip. The direction of principal line is considered as the orientation of the fingertip which will be used in tracking fingertips and allocating fingertips to palms in the next section. The principal lines of finger regions are augmented to potential areas as shown in 3rd column in figure 2. This step reduces the search space from a region to a handful points.

(e) *Rejecting fake fingertips by pattern matching and middle finger removal*: after previous steps, only a few fingertip candidates are passed. In this step, we verify fingertip candidates by using 1) fingertip matching, and 2) middle finger removal, which are two heuristic borrowed from [3] and modified to suit our case. In this step, we verify fingertip candidates using subtracted image (1st column in figure 2). In the process of fingertip matching, for each candidate, a template-sized region located at the candidate's position in the subtracted image is copied, and referred as fingertip patch. We then binarize the patch by a threshold set as the average of max and min intensity in the patch. Next, we compute sum of absolute difference between the patch and fingertip template. Candidates with low scores are discarded. In the implementation, we set the score threshold as $0.8*\pi*r^2$. In the process of middle finger removal, if pixels on the edge of fingertip patch coexist in the diagonal direction, then it is not on the fingertip and is removed. Final results are shown in last column in the finger 2.

Tracking fingertips. We use Kalman filter technique to track the position and velocity for fingertips. A simple strategy is used to assign detection results (observations) to Kalman trackers. After detection phase finished, each observation creates a searching area to find the nearest tracker according the distance between the observation and the trackers' position predictions. If no tracker is found in its searching area, the observation then creates itself a Kalman tracker. Trackers with on observation fed more than several consequent frames are discarded. With the high detection frames per second, the simple strategy works well.

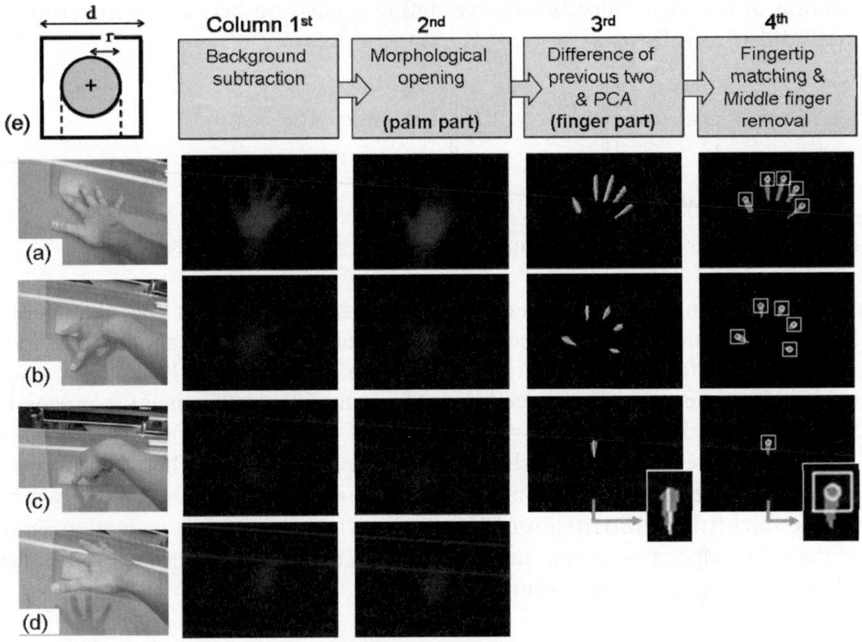

Fig. 2. The images produced during and after processing. Icons labeled (a), (b), (c), and (d) are four cases of gestures. Produced images for each case are arranged in corresponding row. Icon (e) is the fingertip template used in the process. First three columns collect intermediate results during processing. The last column shows the final results.

Finding palms. To find palms, we analyze the palm part reflection as in 2nd column in figure 2. Since the reflection left by contact fingertips are removed after the grayscale morphological opening applied, strong reflection remains in palm part reflection is mainly left by placed palm or hovering palm. We use the heuristic that dichotomizes the image by a threshold selected as three quarter of max intensity of the reflection. A connected component operation is then applied to the binary image. Mean positions for each component with its size larger than a predefined value is picked as detected palm.

Allocating fingertips to corresponding palms. In this section, we describe several steps to associate tracked fingertips to corresponding palms. In general, each palm might have several fingertips associated. Palms with no fingertip associated are users having their hands hovering over the diffuser.

In order to find corresponding palm p^* for each fingertip f, following information is required: (1) a pair of fingertip position and direction $<f^{pos}, f^{dir}>$, (2) a set of palm candidates within proximity of the fingertip $\{p_1, p_2, .. p_s\}$ and their positions $\{p_1^{pos}, p_2^{pos}, .. p_s^{pos}\}$, and (3) a set of unit vectors gives directions from p_i^{pos} to f^{pos} and recorded as $\{p_1^{dir}, p_2^{dir}, .. p_s^{dir}\}$. The association of fingertips and palms is based on two observations. First, the fingertip would be in proximity of its own palm p^*. Second, the included angle between f^{dir} and p^{*dir} would be small. Figure 5 shows an illustration of the idea. Specifically, we define a measure between a fingertip and a palm candidate as follow:

$$m = \arg_i \min\left\{\left\| f^{pos}, p_i^{pos} \right\| \times \left(1 - \cos\left(A(f^{dir}, p_i^{dir})\right)\right)\right\},$$

$$p^* = p_m,$$

where $A(f^{dir}, p_i^{dir})$ computes the included angle between directions f^{dir} and p_i^{dir}.

Performance Evaluation. To demonstrate the effectiveness of the algorithm, we include an evaluation on frames per second versus number of fingers simultaneously sliding on the surface. Our experiment was done on a Pentium IV 2.4Ghz machine with 512MB of memory. The video stream from the infra-red camera is processed at 360x240 pixel resolution, covering a full view of the surface (106 cm x 76 cm.). In the figure 3, the resulting curve shows a sub-linear relationship between frames per second and number of fingers simultaneously sliding on the surface. While we have not done careful optimization of the codes, the current implementation achieves more than 70 frames per second in average when single finger shown on the surface and 35 frames per second in ten-finger case.

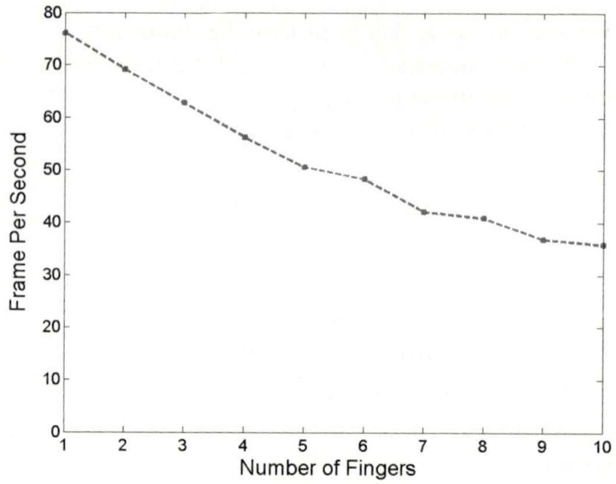

Fig. 3. The average frames per second versus the number of fingers moving on the surface

4 Application Demonstration

We have developed the proposed finger detection algorithm on a personal tabletop system, named i-m-top. A video retrieval application on the tabletop system is also implemented to help users find interested videos from a large video database. The user is allowed to issue queries, manipulate retrieved results, and feed positive videos back by using barehanded interactions.

4.1 I-M-Top

I-m-top is an interactive rear-projection multi-resolution personal tabletop system (figure 6) which has a diffuser as its tabletop surface. The system includes two projectors, one named foveal projector and the other named peripheral projector, to present a multi-resolution display on the tabletop. The presented display consists of one foveal region on a part of the tabletop in front of the user, and one peripheral region covering the whole tabletop. With the multi-resolution design, the user can have detailed perception in the foveal region while retain overall view of the whole space in the peripheral region. For the detection part, the system has an infra-red camera coupled with an infra-red illuminator installed under the tabletop, observing users' hand gestures taken place on the tabletop. The detection results are then fed to applications of the system.

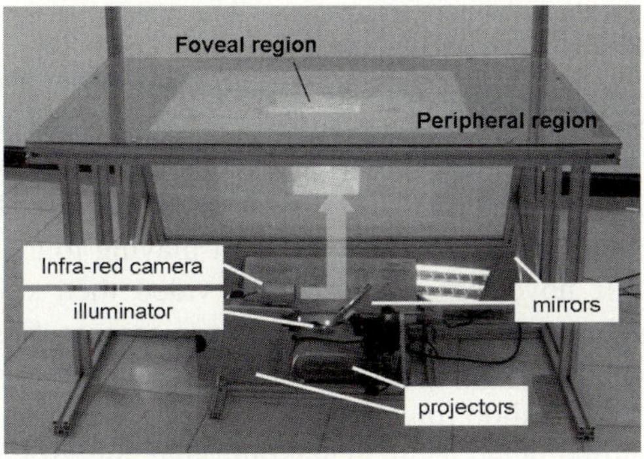

Fig. 4. A shot of i-m-top, an interactive rear-projection multi-resolution tabletop system

4.2 A Sample Application – Video Retrieval System

In the following we give a brief introduction to the video retrieval system and more detail description on three main functions for the users to operate with.

When the user issues a query, the application starts by retrieving videos from database and arranges them on two vertical walls in a 3D scene as shown in figure 7. In the center of the space is a transparent plate covered by foveal projection. Videos more relevant to the query are arranged closer to the plate and presented with higher resolution, so the user can easily see and manipulate them. On the contrary, irrelevant videos are arranged over the peripheral region to also give the user a rough view. If interested, the user can drag them onto the plate to obtain a detailed perception of video content. Under the plate are three scrollbars, with which the user can manipulate video walls at will. With the benefits of multi-resolution display, we have larger display region to present more video results to the user at a time. By using fingertips and hovering palms, the user can find interest videos easily. More specifically, we describe three main functions of the application in the following:

1. *Issue queries*: for this function, we make a virtual keyboard. In the initial, the virtual keyboard is enveloped into a button as figure 2(a). When the button is

Fig. 5. The artist's sketch of the video retrieval system. Retrieved videos are presented on the two vertical walls. The video plate in the center gives an area to present detailed video content and to keep positive videos for relevance feedback. The scrollbars on the bottom and top allow users to slide video walls in and out, up and down.

touched by fingertips, the virtual keyboard spreads out. The user then uses fingertips to hit the keys to key in a searching question. Once the "Enter" key pressed, the query is sent out, and the virtual keyboard is enveloped again.

2. *Browse videos*: After query issued, retrieved videos are then arranged on the vertical walls and presented with still key shots. If the user has a palm hovering over a video, the video then turns flat and start playing to give the user a preview of video content. If hovering palm left, the video then stops and backs to its original state. For interest video results, the user can use fingertips to drag them out of the walls as *figure 4(a)*, place on the center plate, and see them clearly. On the bottom, the user can slide fingers on scrollbars placed on two sides and middle of the area, sliding two video walls in and out separately or both. By sliding walls, the use is allowed to have videos in the peripheral region moving into foveal region, or to make video results which are initially invisible flying into the screen *(figure)*. Moreover, the scroll bar on the top is for users to move the two walls up and down.
3. *Feedback positive videos:* videos left on the center plate are considered been selected as positive results, the user can press the button on the leftmost of operation area to issue a feedback. New results then replace the videos of the walls.

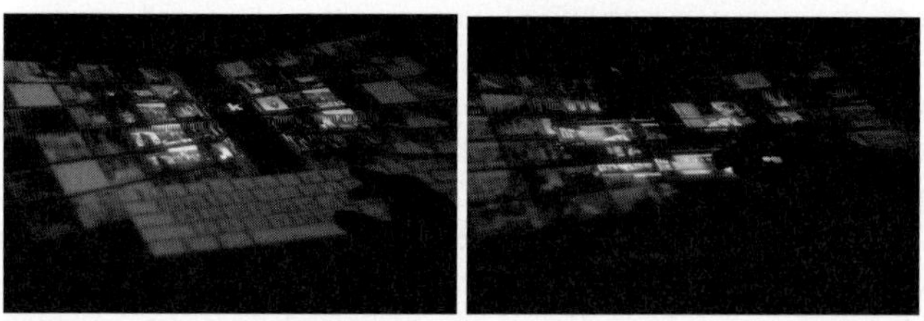

Fig. 6. The left image shows the user is typing on the virtual keyboard. The right image is the user previews a video by having a hovering palm over it.

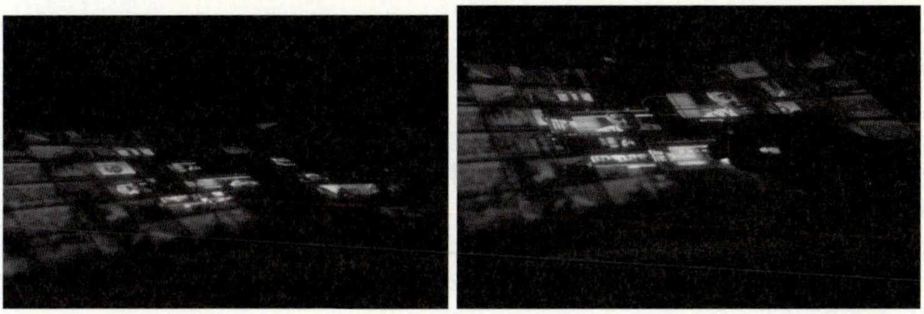

Fig. 7. The user moves fingertips on the scrollbar. The video walls are sliding in, showing more videos onto the surface.

5 Conclusion

In this work, we introduced a multi-fingertip finding algorithm that works with a regular diffuser, an infra-red camera coupled with an infra-red illuminator. The algorithm is capable of detecting finger-touch event and palm-hover events when the user interacts with the diffuser. Our experimental results have shown that the performance produces more than 70 frames per second in single-finger case and more than 35 frames per second in ten-finger case. This is important when multi fingers simultaneously operating on the surface to be able to obtain fluent interactions. The installation is quiet simple, cost-effective and flexible to deploy with digital surface achieved by either front or rear projection.

Acknowledgments. This work was supported in part by the grants of NSC 95-2422-H-002-020 and NSC 95-2752-E-002-007-PAE.

References

1. Rekimoto, J., Matsushita, N.: Perceptual Surfaces: Towards a Human and Object Sensitive Interactive Display. In: Proceedings of ACM Workshop on Perceptive User Interfaces (PUI 1997) (1997)
2. Hardenberg, C.V., Berard, F.: Bare-hand human-computer interaction. In: Proceedings of the ACM Workshop on Perceptive User Interfaces (PUI), Orlando, Florida (2001)
3. Koike, H., Sato, Y., Kobayashi, Y.: Integrating paper and digital information on EnhancedDesk: a method for realtime finger tracking on an augmented desk system. In: ACM Trans. Computer.-Human Interact (CHI 2001) vol. 8(4), pp. 307–322 (2001)
4. O'Hagan, R.G., Zelinsky, A., Rougeaux, S.: Visual gesture interfaces for virtual environments. Interacting with Computers 14(3), 231–250 (2002)
5. Corso, J., Burschka, D., Hager, G.: The 4D Touchpad: Unencumbered HCI With VICs. IEEE Workshop on Computer Vision and Pattern Recognition for Human Computer Interaction (CVPR-HCI) (June 2003)
6. Wilson, A.: TouchLight: An Imaging Touch Screen and Display for Gesture-Based Interaction. In: International Conference on Multimodal Interfaces (ICMI 2004) (2004)
7. Malik, S., Laszlo, J.: Visual Touchpad: A Two-handed Gestural Input Device. In: Proceedings of the ACM International Conference on Multimodal Interfaces (ICMI (2004) pp. 289–296 (2004)

8. Letessier, J., Bérard, F.: Visual Tracking of Bare Fingers for Interactive Surfaces. In: ACM Symposium on User Interface Software and Technology (UIST 2004), Santa Fe, New Mexico, USA (2004)
9. Han, J.Y.: Low-Cost Multi-Touch Sensing through Frustrated Total Internal Reflection. In: Proceedings of the 18th Annual ACM Symposium on User Interface Software and Technology (UIST 2005) (2005)
10. Wilson, A.D.: PlayAnywhere: A Compact Interactive Tabletop Projection-Vision System. In: ACM Symposium on User Interface Software and Technology (UIST 2005), Seattle (October 2005)

Lip Contour Extraction Using Level Set Curve Evolution with Shape Constraint

Jae Sik Chang[1], Eun Yi Kim[2], and Se Hyun Park[3,*]

[1] Computer Science Dept., University of California, Santa Barbara, CA, USA
jschang@cs.ucsb.edu

[2] School of Internet and Multimedia, NITRI[**], Konkuk Univ., Seoul, Korea
eykim@konkuk.ac.kr

[3] School of Computer and Communication, Daegu Univ., Daegu, Korea
Tel.: +82 53 850 6637
sehyun@daegu.ac.kr

Abstract. In this work, a novel method for lip contour extraction based on level set curve evolution is presented. This method takes not only color information but also lip contour shape constraint represented by a distance function between the evolving curve and parametric shape model. In this method, the curve is evolved by minimizing an energy function that incorporates shape constraint function as internal energy, while previous curve evolution methods use a simple smoothing function. The new shape constraint function prevents the curve from evolving to arbitrary shapes occurred due to weak color contrast between lip and skin regions. Comparisons with other method are conducted to evaluate the proposed method. It showed that the proposed method provides more accurate results than other methods.

1 Introduction

Due to wide-ranging applications such as speech recognition, speaker verification, and face modeling, etc., there has been substantial research in the area of lip contour extraction. So far, a lot of lip contour extraction approaches have been presented and studied, yet it is still considered as an unresolved problem. The main difficulty of the lip contour extraction is low color contrast between the lip and the face skin for unadorned faces [1, 2].

Various kinds of method for lip contour extraction have been proposed in the literature and the methods can be categorized into two major kinds: image segmentation and parametric model fitting methods.

The first kind method segments image into lip and background regions using various segmentation techniques such as clustering, level set active contour model, etc. [2, 3]. The methods often use non-parametric contour representations such as binary image and level sets. These representations are useful to describe the complex shape.

---

* Corresponding author.

** Next-Generation Innovative Technology Research Institute.

J. Jacko (Ed.): Human-Computer Interaction, Part III, HCII 2007, LNCS 4552, pp. 583–588, 2007.

However, they often generate arbitrary shapes not like lip mainly due to the lack of shape limitations.

The second kind method evolves a parametric model to fit contour of lip in a given image, which generally use control points or parametric functions such as b-spline and polynomials[1]. The methods are easy to generate a contour like a lip and use for the various applications due to their fixed number of parameters that limit the shape of contours. However, they sometimes excessively simplify or abstract the contours, so that they are difficult to describe the complex shaped contour.

In this paper, we propose a novel lip contour extraction method based on level set curve evolution using shape constraint. The method combines the advantages of the parametric and non-parametric contour representation. In this method, the curve is evolved by minimizing an energy function that incorporates shape constraint function as internal energy, while previous curve evolution methods use a simple smoothing function. The new shape constraint function prevents the curve from evolving to arbitrary shapes occurred due to weak color contrast between lip and skin regions. Comparisons with other method are conducted to evaluate the proposed method. It showed that the proposed method provides more accurate results than other methods.

The rest of this paper is organized as follows. In Section 2, illustrates how to formulate a lip contour detection problem as an energy minimization problem, and the minimization scheme is shown in Section 3. Experimental results are presented in Section 4. Finally, conclusions are presented in Section 5.

2 Problem Formulation

2.1 MAP Estimation

$S=\{s: 1\leq s \leq M_1 \times M_2\}$ denotes the $M_1\times M_2$ lattice. Let $g = \{g_s\}$be the input image defined by S, wherein g_s is a random variable at a pixel s that takes a photometric feature differently selected according to the target object. Here, the input image g is composed of the object regions R, and background region, R^c. Let $\vec{\gamma}(p):[0,1]\rightarrow\Re^2$ be a closed planar curve. Then, g can be separated by $\vec{\gamma}$ into the region enclosed by $\vec{\gamma}$, $R_{\vec{\gamma}}$, and its complement region, $R^c_{\vec{\gamma}}$. Thus, $R_{\vec{\gamma}}$ and $R^c_{\vec{\gamma}}$ have a common boundary $\vec{\gamma}$, i.e. $\vec{\gamma}=\partial R_{\vec{\gamma}}=\partial R^c_{\vec{\gamma}}$, where ∂R is the boundary of region R. Let $\omega(\vec{\gamma})=\{\omega_s(\vec{\gamma})\mid\omega_s(\vec{\gamma})\in\Lambda\}$ denote the label configurations defined in S, wherein $\omega_s(\vec{\gamma})$ is a random variable taking a value in the label set $\Lambda = \{\lambda, \lambda^c\}$.

Object extraction can then be achieved by finding the curve $\vec{\gamma}$ that best separates the object and the background. Since a maximum a posteriori (MAP) is used as the optimality criterion, the present aim is to identify $\vec{\gamma}$ that maximizes the following posterior distribution for a fixed input image g.

$$\vec{\gamma}^* = \arg\max_{\vec{\gamma}} P(\omega(\vec{\gamma})\mid g) \approx \arg\max_{\vec{\gamma}} P(g\mid\omega(\vec{\gamma}))P(\omega(\vec{\gamma})) \tag{1}$$

A posteriori probability is divided into a prior probability $P(\omega(\vec{\gamma}))$ and likelihood function $P(g\mid\omega(\vec{\gamma}))$.

Since the respective likelihood function of a random field can be reduced to a product of the local likelihood function of random variables on the field, the MAP estimation can be represented by the following equation:

$$\vec{\gamma}^* = \arg\max_{\vec{\gamma}} \left\{ \prod_{s \in R_{\vec{\gamma}}} \left[P(g_s \mid \omega_s(\vec{\gamma}) = \lambda) \right] \times \prod_{s \in R^c_{\vec{\gamma}}} \left[P(g_s \mid \omega_s(\vec{\gamma}) = \lambda^c) \right] \times P(\omega(\vec{\gamma})) \right\} . \quad (2)$$

By substituting the obtained likelihood function and prior probability to Eq. 2, the MAP estimation is formulated as the minimization of the following function:

$$\vec{\gamma}^* = \arg \min_{\vec{\gamma}} E(\vec{\gamma}) \quad (3)$$

, where $E(\omega)$ is called *a posterior energy function* and defined as

$$\begin{aligned} E(\vec{\gamma}) &= -\sum\nolimits_{R_{\vec{\gamma}}} \log\left[P(g_s \mid \omega_s(\vec{\gamma}) = \lambda) \right] \\ &- \sum\nolimits_{R^c_{\vec{\gamma}}} \log\left[P(g_s \mid \omega_s(\vec{\gamma}) = \lambda^c) \right] - \log P(\omega(\vec{\gamma})) . \end{aligned} \quad (4)$$

Finally, the object contour in the current frame is obtained by finding the curve $\vec{\gamma}$ to minimize the posteriori energy function of Eq. 4.

2.2 A Prior Probability

In this research, shape constraint using a distance function between the curve and parametric shape model is used as prior to prevent the arbitrary shaped results. Thus prior probability can be represented as follows:

$$-\log P(\omega(\vec{\gamma}) = Dist(\vec{\gamma}, C) \quad (5)$$

To describe lip shape, we use 4-cubic curves(C_{UL}, C_{UR}, C_{LL} and C_{LR}) as the parametric lip shape model, in which each cubic curve describes upper-left, upper-right, lower-left and lower-right lip contours, respectively, as shown in Fig. 1. And the distance function between the curve and parametric shape model is defined as follows:

$$Dist(\vec{\gamma}, C) = \int_{\vec{\gamma}} \left| y(\vec{\gamma}(p)) - C_{A(\vec{\gamma}(p))}(x(\vec{\gamma}(p)) \right| dp , \quad (6)$$

where $x(\cdot)$ and $y(\cdot)$ are the x and y coordinates of the given point, respectively, and $C_{A(\vec{\gamma}(p))}(\cdot)$ is the y coordinate of a cubic curve C_A at the given x coordinate and $A(\cdot)$ is the area where the given point belongs, for example UL, UR, LL or LR.

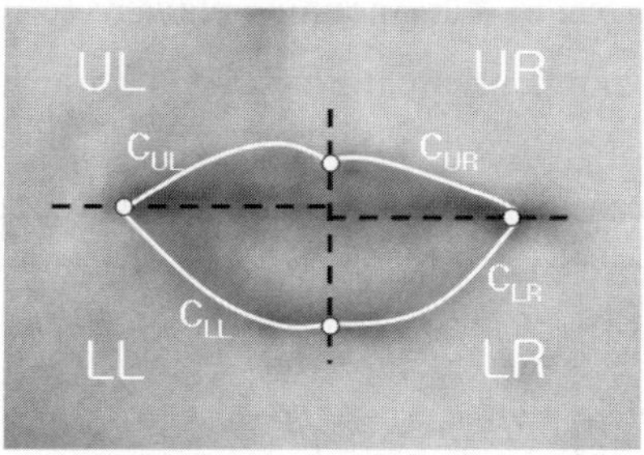

Fig. 1. Parametric lip shape model

2.3 Likelihood Probabilities

We assumed that the region around lip in an image consists of two regions with approximately constant intensities of color, and the likelihoods can be represented as follows [3]:

$$-\sum_{R_{\vec{\gamma}}} \log[P(g_s \mid \omega_s(\vec{\gamma}) = \lambda)] - \sum_{R_{\vec{\gamma}}^c} \log[P(g_s \mid \omega_s(\vec{\gamma}) = \lambda^c)]$$
$$= \lambda_1 \int_{inside(\vec{\gamma})} |h(x,y) - c_1|^2 dxdy + \lambda_2 \int_{outside(\vec{\gamma})} |h(x,y) - c_2|^2 dxdy. \quad (7)$$

In Eq. 7, individual terms are squares of intensity differences between the pixel (x, y) and the mean of inside and outside regions, respectively. The Eq. 7 is minimized since the sum of the color intensity deviations of inside and outside regions are minimized. It separates the region around lip into two different colored regions, lip and skin regions.

Thus, the curve evolution is performed by minimization of the following energy function using level set method [3]:

$$E(c_1, c_2, \vec{\gamma}, C) = \mu \cdot Dist(\vec{\gamma}, C)$$
$$+ \lambda_1 \int_{inside(\vec{\gamma})} |h(x,y) - c_1|^2 dxdy + \lambda_2 \int_{outside(\vec{\gamma})} |h(x,y) - c_2|^2 dxdy, \quad (8)$$

where $\vec{\gamma}$ is the evolving curve, C is the parametric shape model, c_1, c_2 are the averages of h inside $\vec{\gamma}$ and respectively outside $\vec{\gamma}$, $h(x,y)$ is a pseudo hue [1] at pixel (x,y) of a given image, and μ, λ_1, λ_2 are constants.

3 Level Set Curve Evolution

The aim of this paper is to find a lip boundary curve. Let $\vec{\gamma}(p) : [0,1] \to \Re^2$ be a closed planar curve that we use as boundary of the lip region R. To minimize the posterior energy function, we take the steepest descent with respect to $\vec{\gamma}$. For any point $\vec{\gamma}(p)$ on the curve $\vec{\gamma}$, the motion equation can be written as

$$\frac{d\vec{\gamma}(p)}{dt} = -\frac{\partial E(\vec{\gamma})}{\partial \vec{\gamma}(p)}, \quad (9)$$

where the right-hand side is (minus) the functional derivative of the energy [4, 5].

Accordingly, the motion equation for a point $\vec{\gamma}(p)$ can be defined as

$$\frac{d\vec{\gamma}(p)}{dt} = [\lambda_1 (h((x,y) - c_2)^2 - \lambda_2 (h(x,y) - c_1)^2] \vec{n}(\vec{\gamma}(p)) - \mu \cdot Dist(\vec{\gamma}, C) \vec{n}(\vec{\gamma}(p)), \quad (10)$$

where $\vec{n}(x)$ is the unit normal to $\vec{\gamma}$ at x pointing outward from $R_{\vec{\gamma}}$.

We represent curve $\vec{\gamma}$ implicitly by the zero level set of function ϕ: $\Re^2 \to \Re$, with the region inside $\vec{\gamma}$ corresponding to $\phi > 0$ [3, 6, 7]

Accordingly, Eq. 10 can be rewritten by the following equation, which is a level set evolution equation [3, 6, 7]:

$$\frac{d\phi(s)}{dt} = \left(\lambda_1 (h((x,y) - c_2)^2 - \lambda_2 (h(x,y) - c_1)^2\right) \|\nabla\phi\| + \mu \cdot Dist(\vec{\gamma}, C) \|\nabla\phi\|. \quad (11)$$

The stopping criterion is satisfied when the difference of the number of pixel inside contour ($\vec{\gamma}$) is less than a threshold value chosen manually.

Finally, the proposed lip contour extraction algorithm is shown in Fig. 2.

1. Set up initial contour that enclose lip and repeat Steps 2 to 3 until terminal condition is satisfied.
2. Evolve curve using level sets.
3. Filter small area and holes using connected component analysis.
4. Update parametric model from the evolving curve by the least square method.
5. Output the curve.

Fig. 2. The lip contour extraction algorithm

4 Experimental Results

The experiments are performed on frontal faces include various lip shapes. And comparisons with Chan's method [3] are conducted to evaluate the proposed method.

The (a) of the Fig. 3 images are show initial curves, (b) shows lip contour extracted by proposed method, (c) shows final parametric cubic curves and (d) shows the lip contour extracted by Chan's method.

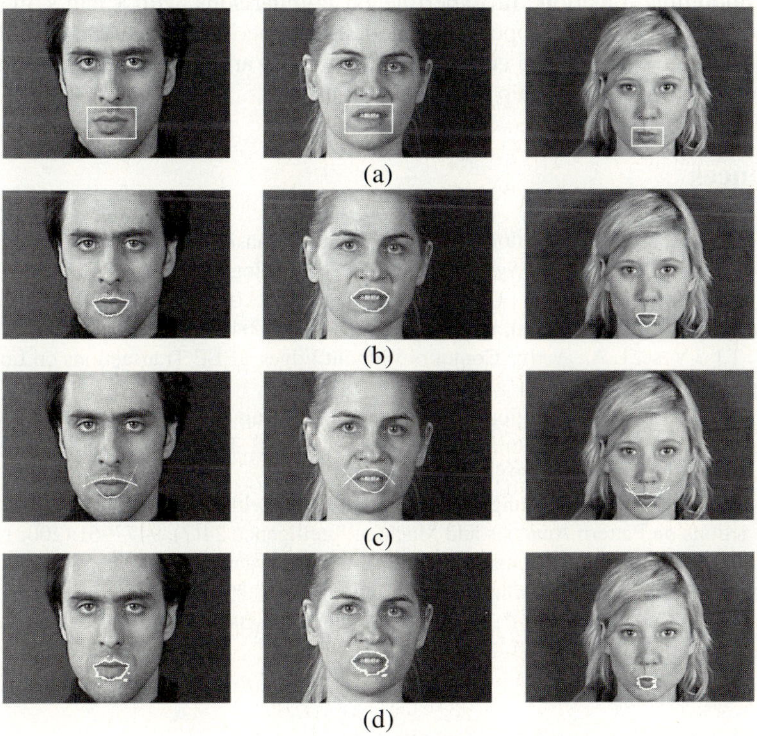

Fig. 3. Results of the lip contour extractions: a) initial curves, b) proposed method, c) parametric curves, d) Chan's method

The first image of Fig. 3 shows a face that includes closed lip. As shown in Fig. 3, the proposed method provides more superior results than Chan's method. The Chan's method results some noises because of a beard around lip. However, the proposed method results accurate lip contour without the noises. The second image shows the experiments on open mouse. As shown in the second image, the results avoid the hole between upper and lower lips, even though the region has different color from lips. It is because the curve evolved from the initial curve located outside of lip. Anyway, in even this case, Chan's method results jagged contour and noises while the proposed method detects accurate lip contour. And an experiment on pursed lips is shown in the third image of Fig. 3. The experiment approves that the proposed method detect more accurate contours of pursed lips than Chan's method.

5 Conclusions

In this paper, we proposed a novel lip contour extraction method based on level set curve evolution using shape constraint. The method combined the advantages of the parametric and non-parametric contour representation. In this method, the curve was evolved by minimizing an energy function that incorporates shape constraint function using parametric lip contour model, while previous curve evolution methods use a simple smoothing function. In experiments, comparisons with Chan's method are conducted to evaluate the proposed method. The experiments results showed that the proposed method prevents the curve from evolving to arbitrary shapes occurred due to weak color contrast between lip and skin regions.

References

1. Eveno, N., Caplier, A., Coulon, P.: Accurate and Quasi-Automatic Lip Tracking. IEEE Transactions on Circuits and Systems for Video Technology 14(5), 706–715 (2004)
2. Leung, S., Wang, S., Lae, W.: Lip Image Segmentation Using Fuzzy Clustering Incorporating an Elliptic Shape Function, vol. 13(1), pp. 51–62 (2004)
3. Chan, T.F., Vese, L.A.: Active Contours Without Edges. IEEE Transactions on Image Processing 10(2), 266–277 (2001)
4. Zhu, S.C., Yuille, A.: Region Competition: Unifying Snakes, Region Growing, and Bayes/MDL for Multiband Image Segmentation. IEEE Transactions on Pattern Analysis and Machine Intelligence 18(9), 884–900 (1996)
5. Mansouri, A.: Region Tracking via Level Set PDEs without Motion Computation. IEEE Transactions on Pattern Analysis and Machine Intelligence 24(7), 947–961 (2002)
6. Osher, S., Scthian, J.A.: Fronts propagating with curvature-dependent speed: Algorithms based on Hamilton-Jacobi Formulation. J.Comput. Phys. 79, 12–49 (1988)
7. Caselles, V., Catte, F., Coll, T., Dibos, F.: A geometric model for active contours in image processes. Numer. Math. 66, 1–31 (1993)

Visual Foraging of Highlighted Text: An Eye-Tracking Study

Ed H. Chi, Michelle Gumbrecht, and Lichan Hong

Palo Alto Research Center
3333 Coyote Hill Road, Palo Alto, CA 94304 USA
{echi,hong}@parc.com, mgumbrec@stanford.edu

Abstract. The wide availability of digital reading material online is causing a major shift in everyday reading activities. Readers are skimming instead of reading in depth [Nielson 1997]. Highlights are increasingly used in digital interfaces to direct attention toward relevant passages within texts. In this paper, we study the eye-gaze behavior of subjects using both keyword highlighting and ScentHighlights [Chi et al. 2005]. In this first eye-tracking study of highlighting interfaces, we show that there is direct evidence of the von Restorff isolation effect [VonRestorff 1933] in the eye-tracking data, in that subjects focused on highlighted areas when highlighting cues are present. The results point to future design possibilities in highlighting interfaces.

Keywords: Automatic text highlighting, dynamic summarization, contextualization, personalized information access, eBooks, Information Scent.

1 Introduction

Digital workspaces need to support productive reading, since it is an essential activity in the understanding of the collective records of human existence. Vannaver Bush's lasting legacy is to ask us to understand how computers can help readers be more productive in interacting with published records [5]. Increasingly, as readers evolve into skimmers [12], we need methods for directing users to the most relevant regions on the page. One of the major ways to do this is through highlights and annotations.

There are some existing works in understanding the creation and use of annotations in both paper and electronic forms [11,18,8]. In particular, the use of highlights for reviewing and recall of specific information has been suggested in a number of different systems [3,9,21,14]. Popular search engines such as Yahoo! and Google have now implemented keyword highlighting capabilities in their browser plug-in toolbars. Recently, we introduced a technique called ScentHighlights that not only highlights keywords, but also highlights sentences if they contain conceptual keywords that are highly relevant to the topics expressed by search keywords [7].

While highlights are generally thought to increase user performance in skimming, the field still lacks a detailed understanding of the way in which highlights affect user behavior. We are interested in understanding how highlighting interfaces affect user visual foraging behavior during page skimming.

J. Jacko (Ed.): Human-Computer Interaction, Part III, HCII 2007, LNCS 4552, pp. 589–598, 2007.

In the field of educational psychology and instruction, there are some interesting research in understanding the role of underlining and highlighting as an effective encoding and reviewing process during learning [13,15,19]. Some researchers point to the von Restorff isolation effect [20] as a possible controversial explanation for users' visual foraging behavior. As applied to highlights, the ***von Restorff isolation effect*** suggests that readers "*(a) tend to focus on* and *(b) learn what is marked*, whether the information is important or not" [13, emphasis added]. Notice that there are two parts to this definition: (a) an attention effect and (b) a learning effect. Existing research appears to confirm the learning effect, while there has been no evidence of the attention effect. That is, readers seem to have increased recall in the presence of highlights, confirming the learning effect, but existing literature does not show why that learning is happening. Researchers have inferred that readers pay more attention to items that are isolated against a homogeneous background, regardless of its semantic appropriateness, but have no physical evidence of this claim.

Our goal is to confirm this inference while understanding the visual foraging behavior of readers in the presence of highlights. To our knowledge, our research is the first eye-tracking analysis of highlighting techniques. In detailed coding of eye traces, we found regularities in users' visual foraging behavior. The contribution of this paper is to provide direct eye-tracking evidence of the von Restorff isolation effect in highlighting interfaces. Users indeed are more likely to pay attention to highlighted areas and performed accordingly.

2 Related Work

Despite the pervasiveness of highlighting as a technique in graphical interfaces, we know surprisingly little about the way users visually forage for information in the presence of highlights on pages. Woodruff et al. [21] and Olston and Chi [14] studied the effectiveness of their interfaces and found subjects were faster using their interfaces than non-highlighted versions. However, these studies do not explain why these highlighting interfaces work, nor do they identify or explain the changes in reader strategy or behavior.

Existing educational psychology literature on highlighting or underlining offers two potential explanations. One explanation advocates the potential benefits of the encoding process during the act of underlining. That is, actually performing the underlining will increase recall of the information. While the existence of this benefit is less than clear, some argue that the benefits of student-generated underlining is due to the levels of processing theory, in that "information which is processed at deeper levels through elaboration is ultimately remembered better" [13].

Another explanation focuses on the so-called von Restorff isolation effect [20], which states that an item isolated against a homogenous background will be more likely to be attended to and remembered. Indeed, while there is contradictory evidence regarding the effectiveness of performing underlining and highlighting during study, research by Nist and Hogrebe [13] and Peterson [15] seems to agree that the von Restorff isolation effect could be used to explain students' performance. Students appear to learn what is marked, whether the information is important or not.

Silvers and Kreiner [19] provided the strongest evidence to date. They showed that even when given advanced warning of the inappropriateness of pre-existing highlights, subjects' performance was affected by the highlights in reading comprehension tests. While the von Restorff isolation effect might partially help explain reader performance, existing studies do not contain actual reading behavior data to confirm that readers pay more attention to highlighted areas.

In this paper, we show the first eye-tracking results that provide direct evidence of the von Restorff isolation effect for highlighting interfaces. Readers' attention is directed to highlighted areas, regardless of their appropriateness to the task. These findings have deep implications for highlighting interfaces in general.

3 ScentHighlights

Recently, Chi et al. [7] introduced ScentHighlights, which automatically highlights both keywords and sentences that are conceptually related to a set of search keywords. Fig. 1 is a screenshot of the ScentHighlights technique along with some eye trace data. For the purpose of skimming, the technique provides a way to automatically highlight potentially relevant passages.

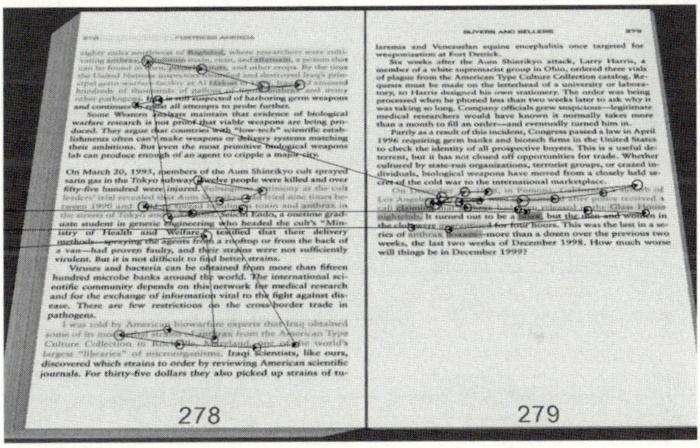

Fig. 1. Eye trace data for a subject performing visual foraging using ScentHighlights. The beginning of each eye trace is marked by red fixation circles, gradually giving way to darker reds as time advances; blue marks the end portion of the eye trace. (Subject 2 – Task 11 – Question 10).

We perform the conceptual highlighting by computing what conceptual keywords are related to each other via word co-occurrence and spreading activation. Spreading activation is a cognitive model developed in psychology to simulate how memory chunks and conceptual items are retrieved in the brain [2]. This model is suitable for our purpose of identifying related keywords and sentences. Details of the method are found in a previous publication [7].

We illustrate how ScentHighlights can help readers locate relevant passages with a realistic scenario here. The scenario below is based on *Biohazard* by Ken Alibek [1], a non-fiction retelling of his experiences working on biological weapons in the former

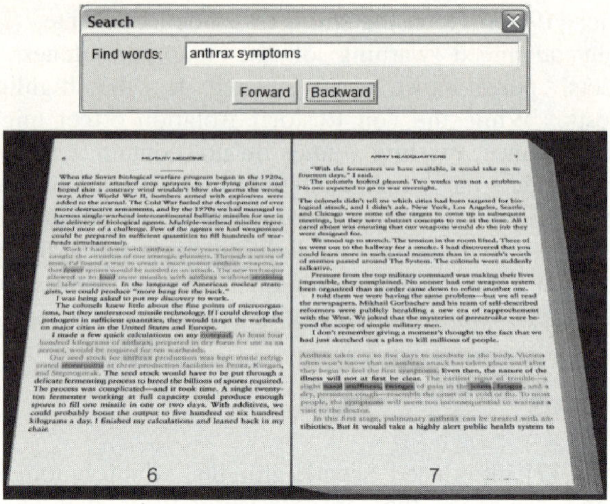

Fig. 2. (a: top) keyword search box; (b: bottom) highlights obtained for "anthrax symptoms"

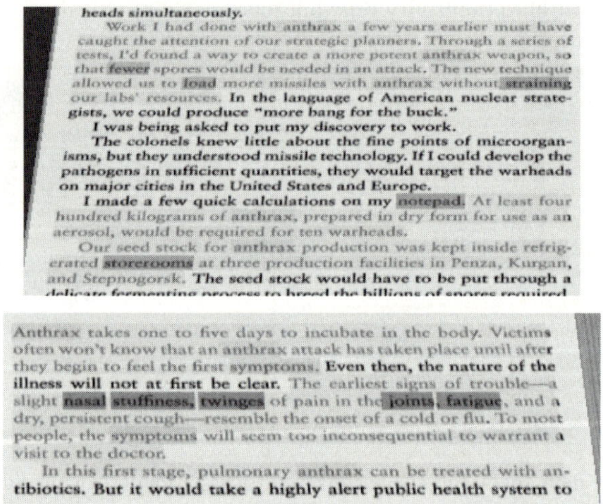

Fig. 3. (a: top) Zoomed detail of the highlights on left page; (b: bottom) Zoomed detail of the highlights on right page

Soviet Union. Suppose we are looking to find out the symptoms of anthrax. We first type the keywords "anthrax symptoms" into the search box (Figure 2a). Searching forward from the beginning of the book produces the result shown in Figure 2b.

The system identified three profitable regions to examine. Zooming up to the relevant passages that were highlighted on the left page shows that Alibek had worked on creating an anthrax weapon (Fig. 3a). The conceptual keywords that caused the sentences to be highlighted are highlighted in grey, distinguished from the exact keyword matches shown in pastel-like colors. The boundaries of the highlighted sections are defined by sentences, as the algorithm attempts to highlight the top 3-5 most relevant sentences.

The spreading activation process produced highlights that were relevant to the task at hand. Zooming up to the relevant sections that are highlighted on the right side of the page gives us the information we were seeking (Fig. 3b).

We see that the anthrax symptoms are *nasal stuffiness, twinges of pain in joints, fatigue, and a dry persistent cough.* Searching forward or turning to each new page will continue to produce highlights that are only relevant to the search keywords.

The ScentHighlights technique enables novel interactive browsing of electronic text in which users' attention is guided toward the most relevant sentences according to some user interest. We now turn our attention to the experiments used to understand how highlighting changes visual foraging behavior.

4 Method

4.1 Study Design

We were interested in determining whether having highlighting on a page would affect users' reading strategy and eye movement patterns, as compared to having no highlighting present.

We used a 12 X 3 mixed design. All participants completed 12 questions but we counterbalanced the order such that each presentation order was unique. Each question was presented within one of three conditions (the within-subjects variable): No Highlighting; Keyword Highlighting; and ScentHighlights. All participants received four questions in each of the three conditions.

Our goals were to examine the effect of condition and type of highlighting on eye-gaze behavior for each task (a between-subjects comparison), as well as to determine general eye movement patterns for each of the three conditions (a within-subjects comparison). **Participants:** Six participants (4 males, 2 females) were recruited from within our company. All were full-time employees who volunteered their time to participate. **Study Stimuli:** We used twelve questions adapted from a study that compared index searches through a physical copy of *Biohazard* versus an electronic text version [6]. The questions were written in school exam style by a former researcher who had not read the book. A sample of questions are "Where did Alibek marry his wife Lena Yemesheva?" and "What year did open air testing at Rebirth Island stop?"

We created the presentation pages by taking screenshots, one for each condition. For the Keyword and ScentHighlights conditions, we determined a set of keywords taken from the text of the task questions, which were then used to determine the highlighting patterns.

4.2 Study Procedure

Participants used a Dell Optiplex GX270 desktop computer equipped with two NEC MultiSync LCD 2080UX+ 20-inch monitors located side-by-side. After we obtained consent, participants put on a SMI head-mounted eye-tracker. We conducted the adjustment and calibration processes, and we used the EyeLink Intelligent Eye

Tracking System to handle eye-tracking functions. The SMI eye-tracker has a sampling rate of 250Hz, with an average error of 0.5-1.0 degree of visual angle.

Participants were then trained on the different types of highlighting that they would encounter by looking at a set of sample pages. We showed them sample pages for all three conditions. As participants examined the pages, we explained the meaning of the different colors used in highlighting: blue and green for topical keywords; grey for semantic or conceptual similarity; and yellow sentences were the top-rated sentences relevant to the search terms. We then showed them how to use Weblogger [16], a program used to control timing. The Weblogger box also contained controls for connecting to the eye-tracking system, calibrating, and drift correcting, as well as displaying the current task question. Weblogger also recorded all eye-tracking and browsing activity. We placed Weblogger on the left-hand monitor such that it would not interfere with the page display area.

Participants were presented with 12 questions. Each question was a factual question that could be answered from the information presented within the pages. Participants were instructed to read and comprehend the question prior to starting the timer on Weblogger. They were instructed to read only the presented pages to find the answer. When participants found the answer, they were to stop the Weblogger timer and give the answer. The experimenter then gave feedback on the accuracy of the answer. We performed a manual drift correction between tasks to adjust for any eye-tracking errors that may have occurred.

5 Results and Discussion

5.1 Accuracy and Response Time

Participants differed in the accuracy of their answers in the three conditions. Participants using ScentHighlights achieved perfect accuracy (M=1.00), followed by No Highlighting (M=0.92), and Keyword Highlighting (M=0.79).

The mean response times for each condition were No Highlighting: M = 44.5 sec.; Keyword Highlighting: M = 29.6 sec.; and ScentHighlights: M = 26.7 sec. We conducted statistical tests using the natural log transformations of the raw data, and we compared mean response times among conditions and found no significant differences due to the large subject variances.

5.2 Eye Fixation Movement Pattern Coding

Eye movement patterns during reading are extensively studied in the psychology literature [10,17]. These eye-tracking studies show that eye movements advance in discrete chunks. Readers' eyes stop and fixate on some characters before another saccade moves to the next set of characters or another part of the page. Each fixation lasts 190ms on average. **Eye fixation** patterns, therefore, are the main measure of behavior in past eye-tracking research.

For each of the 72 trials, we coded the eye movement behavior data according to a simple coding scheme. We analyzed each fixation individually, logging the entire eye movement behavior into a large spreadsheet. We logged the first eye fixations and the

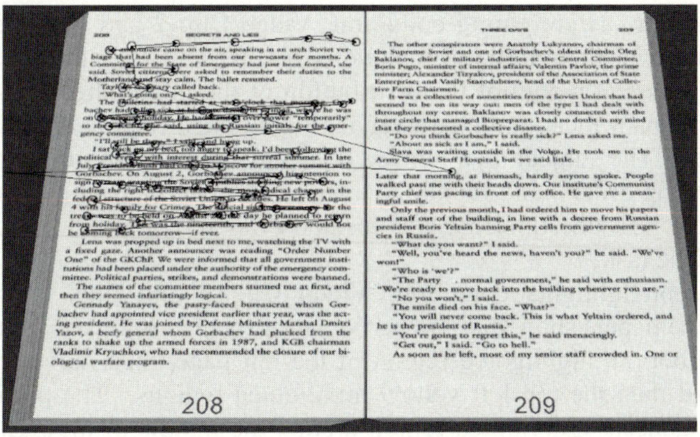

Fig. 4. This eye trace depicts a prototypical sequential reading behavior with the No Highlighting condition, where the answer was found near the middle of the left page. (Participant 3 – Task 9 – Question 3).

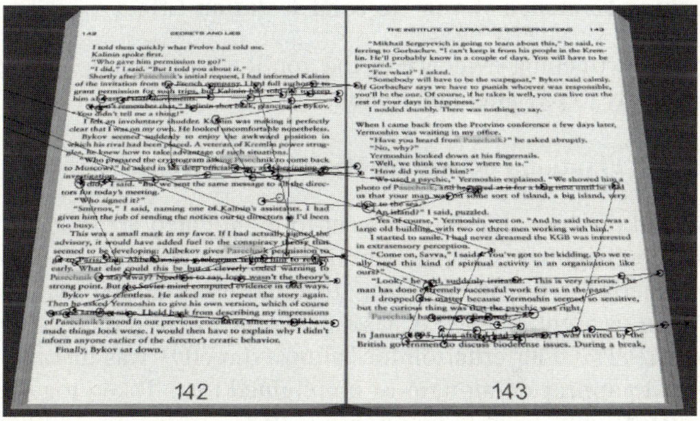

Fig. 5. This eye trace depicts a good strategy using the Keyword Highlighting condition. The participant first scanned the middle of both pages, then skimmed over the highlighted regions quickly, before finding the answer near the bottom right. (Participant 6 – Task 5 – Question 5).

initial eye behavior. We also logged the number of fixations that were spent inside and around a highlighted area and the total number of fixations for the entire task.

Here we present sample eye-tracking traces for each of the three conditions. Red fixation circles mark the beginning of each eye trace, gradually giving way to darker reds as time advances; blue marks the end portion of the eye trace. For the No Highlighting condition, Video Clip 1 and Fig. 4 demonstrate prototypical eye-gaze behavior[1]. We can see that the participant scanned the text sequentially in reading order, starting from the top-left corner of the page. Eventually, the subject found the answer in the middle of the left page. Luckily, the answer was not at the bottom of the right page!

---

[1] The video clips are at: http://www-users.cs.umn.edu/~echi/misc/foraging-highlighting.mov

For the Keyword Highlighting condition, Video Clip 2 and Fig. 5 show that the subject scanned over the middle of the two pages initially. We inferred that the user was building a mental model of the distribution of the highlighted areas. In reading order, the participant then skimmed over the highlighted regions from top to bottom on the left page. The subject then jumped over to the bottom of the right page (which was not in reading order!) and found the answer. The participant double-checked the answer with the task question that was located off-screen (on the left-hand monitor) before ending the task.

For the ScentHighlights condition, Video Clip 3 and Fig. 1 (located at the beginning of the paper) show that the participant first read in reverse reading order by skimming the bottom highlighted region of the left page, then moved quickly to the left middle and then the top left yellow highlighted regions. The participant finally settled on the densely highlighted region around the middle of the right page, where the answer was located. Notice that the participant could have performed even faster if s/he had quickly scanned over the entire screen first to decide which of the four highlighted regions to pay attention to first.

5.3 Eye-Tracking Evidence of von Restorff Isolation Effect

We found direct eye-tracking evidence of the von Restorff isolation effect in our data. Users are more likely to pay attention to highlighted areas and performed accordingly.

5.3.1 Initial User Fixation Focused on Highlighted Areas

We wanted to find out how often users went to highlighted areas at the beginning of the task. With ScentHighlights, users went directly to highlighting **10** out of 24 times (41.7%). Our criterion for "directly" was that the users' initial eye fixation had to appear on an item of highlighted text. Users "almost" went directly to highlighting **7** out of 24 times (29.2%). Our criterion for "almost directly" was that the users' second eye fixation had to appear on an item of highlighted text. Taken together, users who read with ScentHighlights went to highlighting **70.8%** of the time within the first two eye fixations.

With Keyword Highlighting, users went directly to highlighting **3** out of 24 times (12.5%). Our criterion here is that the initial fixation had to either appear on a highlighted keyword or in the neighboring areas of highlighted words. We determined this "*neighboring area*" to be located within the same line of text, or closely above or below the line containing the highlighted item. Users "almost" went directly to highlighting **3** out of 24 times (12.5%). Our criterion for "almost" is that the users' second eye fixation had to appear on or in the neighboring area of a highlighted keyword. Taken together, users who read with Keyword Highlighting went near highlighted keywords **25%** of the time within the first two eye fixations.

5.3.2 Users Fixated on Highlighted Areas Heavily

We found that users fixated on highlighted areas heavily. For the ScentHighlights condition, 1184 fixations out of a total of 2259 fixations are spent within the highlighted areas. In other words, a staggering **52.4%** of the fixations are spent on highlighted sentences or keywords.

Users who read with Keyword Highlighting spent 1107 fixations out of a total of 2565 fixations near neighboring areas of highlighted keywords (**43.2%**). Here the definition of "neighboring area" is the same as the description in the previous section.

Taken together, these two pieces of evidence directly confirmed that users tended to focus on highlighted areas. At the beginning of the task, subjects were attracted by highlighted keywords and sentences within the first two fixations (which is roughly within the first half second). Moreover, users focused on the highlights by spending roughly half of their fixations on the highlighted areas.

6 Conclusion

As reading evolve more toward skimming rather than in-depth reading, readers need effective ways to direct their attention. In this paper, we reported results from an eye-tracking study that compared user visual foraging behavior under different highlighting conditions: No Highlighting, Keyword Highlighting, and a highlighting technique called ScentHighlights [7]. ScentHighlights attempt to highlight not only the search keywords, but also sentences and words that are highly conceptually relevant to the topic [7]. We provided the first eye-tracking validation of the von Restorff isolation effect for highlights. The von Restorff isolation effect says that an item isolated against a homogenous background will be more likely to be attended to and remembered. This puts to rest some past confusion in the literature regarding various potential explanations for the effectiveness of underlining [13,15]. We found that roughly half of the fixations were in highlighted regions, and subjects' eyes were drawn to highlighted regions initially.

The results reported here have immediate application to popular interfaces such as the search result listings returned by web search engines. Web searchers need to digest large amounts of material quickly. Search result pages could be highlighted using ScentHighlights. Tools such as Browster [4], which enables readers to mouse-over hyperlinks to obtain a quick read of the distal page, could be enhanced with highlights.

Although highlighting had become rather common, there had been limited understanding of the visual foraging behavior of users reading highlighted text. Some knowledge of the process of reading is needed by, at least, the practitioners who design reading interfaces. Our hope is that we have closed some of the gaps between the theory and the practice of the use of highlights in graphical interfaces.

Acknowledgements. The user study portion has been funded in part by contract #MDA904-03-C-0404 to Stuart K. Card and Peter Pirolli under the ARDA NIMD/ARIVA program. We thank the UIR group for suggestions and comments.

References

1. Alibek, K., Handelman, S.: Biohazard. Delta Publishing, New York (1999)
2. Anderson, J.R., Pirolli, P.L.: Spread of Activation. Journal of Experimental Psychology: Learning, Memory and Cognition 10, 791–798 (1984)

3. Boguraev, B., Kennedy, C., Bellamy, R., Brawer, S., Wong, Y.Y., Swartz, J.: Dynamic presentation of document content for rapid on-line skimming. In: Proc. AAAI Symposium on Intelligent Text Summarization, Stanford, CA, pp. 118–128 (1998)
4. Browster.: (Accessed March 2006) http://www.browster.com
5. Bush, V.: As we may think. The Atlantic Monthly 176(1), 101–108 (1945)
6. Chi, E.H., Hong, L., Heiser, J., Card, S.K.: eBooks with Indexes that Reorganize Conceptually. In: Proc. CHI2004 Conference Companion, pp. 1223–1226. ACM Press, New York (2004)
7. Chi, E.H., Hong, L., Gumbrecht, M., Card, S.K.: ScentHighlights: highlighting conceptually-related sentences during reading. In: Proc. 10th International Conference on Intelligent User Interfaces, pp. 272–274. ACM Press, New York (2005)
8. Churchill, E., Trevor, J., Bly, S., Nelson, L., Cubranic, D.: Anchored Conversations. In: Proc. CHI 2000, pp. 454–461. ACM Press, New York (2000)
9. Graham, J.: The Reader's Helper: A Personalized Document Reading Environment. In: Proc. CHI 1999, pp. 481–488. ACM Press, New York (1999)
10. Just, M.A., Carpenter, P.A.: A theory of reading: From eye fixations to comprehension. Psychological Review 87(4), 329–354 (1980)
11. Marshall, C.C.: Annotation: from paper books to the digital library. In: Proc. of DL '97, pp. 131–140. ACM Press, New York (1997)
12. Nielson, J.: How Users Read on the Web. Useit.com Alertbox (1997) (Accessed March 2006) http://www.useit.com/alertbox/9710a.html
13. Nist, S.L., Hogrebe, M.C.: The role of underlining and annotating in remembering textual information. Reading Research and Instruction 27(1), 12–25 (1987)
14. Olston, C., Chi, E.H.: ScentTrails: Integrating Browsing and Searching on the Web. ACM Transactions on Computer-Human Interaction 10(3), 177–197 (2003)
15. Peterson, S.E.: The Cognitive Functions of Underlining as a Study Technique. Reading Research and Instruction 31(2), 49–56 (1992)
16. Reeder, R.W., Pirolli, P., Card, S.K.: Web-Eye Mapper and WebLogger: Tools for analyzing eye tracking data collected in web-use studies. In: Proc. CHI2001, pp. 19–20. ACM Press, New York (2001)
17. Robeck, M.C., Wallace, R.R.: The Psychology of Reading: An Interdisciplinary Approach, 2nd edn. Lawrence Erlbaum, Hillsdale, NJ (1990)
18. Schilit, B.N., Golovchinsky, G., Price, M.N.: Beyond Paper: Supporting Active Reading with Free Form Digital Ink Annotations. In: Proc. of CHI '98, pp. 249–256. ACM Press, New York (1998)
19. Silvers, V.L., Kreiner, D.S.: The effects of pre-existing inappropriate highlighting on reading comprehension. Reading Research and Instruction 36(3), 217–223 (1997)
20. Von Restorff, H.: Uber die Wirkung von Bereichsbildungen im Spurenfeld (The effects of field formation in the trace field). Psychologie Forschung 18, 299–334 (1933)
21. Woodruff, A., Faulring, A., Rosenholtz, R., Morrison, J., Pirolli, P.: Using Thumbnails to Search the Web. In: Proc. CHI 2001, pp. 198–205. ACM Press, New York (2001)
22. Zellweger, P.T., Bouvin, N.O., Jehøj, H., Mackinlay, J.D.: Fluid Annotations in an Open World. In: Proc. Hypertext 2001, pp. 9–18. ACM Press, New York (2001)

Effects of a Dual-Task Tracking on Eye Fixation Related Potentials (EFRP)

Hiroshi Daimoto[1], Tsutomu Takahashi[2], Kiyoshi Fujimoto[2], Hideaki Takahashi[1,3], Masaaki Kurosu[1,3], and Akihiro Yagi[2]

[1] Department of Cyber Society and Culture, The Graduate University for Advanced Studies, Japan
[2] Department of Psychology, Kwansei Gakuin University, Japan
[3] National Institute of Multimedia Education, Japan

Abstract. The eye fixation related brain potentials (EFRP) associated with the occurrence of fixation pause can be obtained by averaging EEGs at offset of saccades. EFRP is a kind of event-related brain potential (ERP) measurable at the eye movement situation. In this experiment, EFRP were examined concurrently along with performance and subjective measures to compare the effects of tracking difficulty during a dual-task. Twelve participants were assigned four different types of a tracking task for each 5 min. The difficulty of tracking task is manipulated by the easiness to track a target with a trackball and the easiness to give a correct response to the numerical problem. The workload of the each tracking condition is different in the task quality (the difficulty of perceptual motor level and/or cognitive level). As a result, the most prominent positive component with latency of about 100 ms in EFRP was observed under all tracking conditions. The amplitude of the condition with the highest workload was smaller than that of the condition with the lowest workload, while the effects of the task quality and the correspondency with the subjective difficulty in incremental step were not recognized in this experiment. The results suggested that EFRP was an useful index of the excessive mental workload.

1 Introduction

In this research, the application range of eye fixation related potentials (EFRP) to measure mental workload in a dual-task tracking was investigated. EFRP is obtained by averaging the electro-encephalogram (EEG) locked to the point in time of the offset of the saccadic eye movements, derived from the electro-oculogram (EOG). The most prominent component which is called lambda response changes with visual properties of visual stimulus [3] and attention [7]. EFRP has been applied to many situations in ergonomics. Daimoto et al. [1] showed that the EFRP amplitude decreased after a monotonous manual tracking task (60 min) which was divided into 12 blocks compared with that of before the task. After the task, participants reported that they were tired and were tedious of a boring task. It might be able to conclude that EFRP decrease in amplitude by fatigue. Takeda et al. [4] also showed that the EFRP amplitude decreased after a long time proof reading task (300 min) which

J. Jacko (Ed.): Human-Computer Interaction, Part III, HCII 2007, LNCS 4552, pp. 599–604, 2007.

consisted of five blocks. However, these ergonomic studies do not classify the workload whether it is the perceptual motor (hand-motor level) and cognitive (memory-thinking level). The purpose of present paper is to examine the variation of EFRP that is measured during a dual-task tracking task with different types of workload.

2 Methods

2.1 Participants

Participants were 10 students at Kwansei Gakuin University and 2 working people between the ages 21 and 34 volunteered to participate in the present experiment. They had normal or corrected-to-normal vision. Informed consent was obtained after the procedures were explained. One participant was excluded from the analysis of data because of the lambda response was not clear. The analysis of data was performed for 11 participants.

2.2 Task and Procedure

After placement of electrodes, each participant with the head moderately fixed by a head rest sat on a chair in front of the 100-inch display which was placed at a distance of 274 cm from the eyes of the participants. Participants were assigned four different types of a tracking task for each 5 minutes. It was defined by the difficulty of manual motor (with or without target speed shift) and calculation (with or without addition). A primary task was to track a target stimulus (small circle = 0.63 in diameter) which move random directions at every two seconds without running out of a square frame (4.12° on a side) by trackball. The easy tracking condition was to track a target at a speed of 2.51 °/s (low speed only). The difficult tracking condition was to track a target at a speed of 2.51°/s and 5.64°/s (high speed mixed). The high speed state was synchronized exactly with a figure presentation (1 sec at intervals of 2sec) at the peripheral field (30° > the gray field of Fig.1 > 10°) on the positive screen (black and white) of a 100 inch display

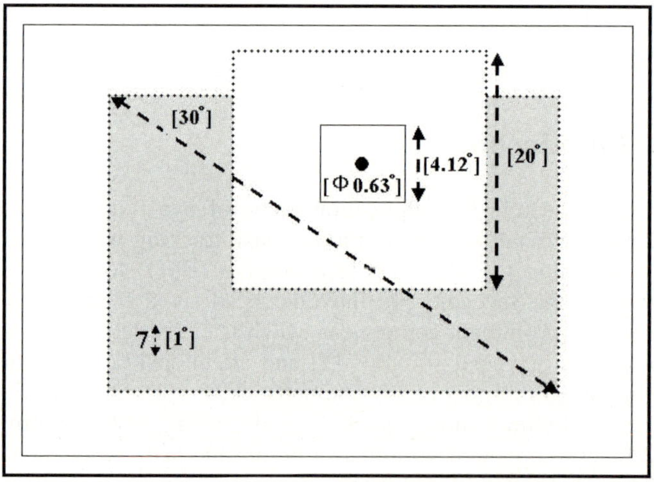

Fig. 1. Settings of manual tracking task

(see Fig.1). When the target stimulus was deviated from the square frame, the black colour of the displayed things (a target stimulus, a square frame, and a figure) were turned the colour red.

The secondary task was to utter a randomised single-digit figure (0-9) which was presented at a random position in the peripheral field. The easy utterance condition was to utter a single-digit figure simply which they looked at. The difficult utterance condition was to utter a single-digit figure (ones digit) that was made an addition to a prior figure.

Table 1 indicates the combination of the two different kinds of workload in each condition. The conditions were: (1) A, the task is the easy tracking and the easy utterance; (2) B, the task is the easy tracking and the difficult utterance; (3) C, the task is the difficult tracking and the easy utterance; (4) D, the task is the difficult tracking and the difficult utterance.

The within subject design was used in this experiment. The implementation order of each condition was counterbalanced. Saccadic eye movements were elicited under all conditions because of presentation of a single-digit figure at a peripheral field.

A questionnaire in a range of seven-point about the subjective concentration and fatigue was conducted after all tracking conditions. Moreover the questionnaire for subjective order of the difficulty was conducted at the last

2.3 Recording

The EEG was recorded at occipital site (Oz) according to the international 10-20 system referred to linked ear lobes. The ground lead was attached to the midline forehead. Eye movements were recorded by means of EOG. A pair of electrodes was placed at the outer canthi of eyes for the horizontal EOG. Another pair of electrodes was placed at the infra- and the supraorbital to the left eye for the vertical EOG. The EEG and EOGs were amplified with AC differential amplifiers at a low frequency time constant of 0.08 Hz and a high frequency cutoff of 30 Hz. The signals were digitised every 2 ms and recorded on a hard disk. EEG and EOG were measured during whole tracking task. EEG was averaged at offset of saccades in order to obtain EFRP. When noises or artifacts (e.g. eye blinks, muscle potentials) got mixed with the EEG data, it was cancelled from averaging data automatically.

Performance was recorded for every condition in terms of the tracking errors and the utterance errors. The tracking errors were the number of deviations from a square frame. The utterance errors were the number of incorrect utterances of a single-digit figure. The utterance behaviors (voice and face) of the participants were recorded by a video camera.

3 Results

Table 1 shows the results derived from questionnaire, performance, and physiological assessments in each condition. The mean values of all items are calculated.

3.1 Questionnaires

The rating of subjective concentration and fatigue were submitted to two-factor ANOVAs (perceptual motor vs. cognitive) with repeated measures. The two-factor

Table 1. Combination of the two different kinds of workload and results (mean value) of each measurement in each condition

	A	B	C	D
Perceptual motor workload	without	without	with	with
Cognitive workload	without	with	without	with
Score of concentration	4.55	4.36	4.73	4.64
Score of fatigue	2.64	3.18	3.36	3.55
Order of difficulty	4.00	2.27	2.64	1.09
Frequency of tracking error	7.73	10.45	59.45	68.45
Frequency of utterance error	0.27	4.55	0.55	5.45
Amplitude of EFRP (P100)	6.96	5.50	5.13	5.26
Number of the averaging	98.09	148.27	106.55	125.45

ANOVAs revealed significant main effects of the condition on the rating of fatigue ($F_{1,10} = 7.11$, $p < 0.05$). Further analysis by Turkey's HSD test revealed that the rating fatigue in the B, C, and D conditions were significantly increased than that of the A condition (A vs. B, $p < 0.05$; A vs. C, $p < 0.01$; A vs. D, $p < 0.01$). Though there were no significant condition differences in the rating of subjective concentration, participants were relatively concentrated on the task of the four conditions.

The order of difficulty in each condition was different significantly (A vs. B and C vs. D, $p < 0.01$ [Wilcoxon signed-rank test]). Feelings of difficulty in order was first = D, second = B and C, third = A. All participants reported that A condition was the most easy. Most participants reported that D condition was the most difficult.

3.2 Performance and Errors

As in Table 1, tracking errors occur frequently in the conditions with perceptual motor workload. Utterance errors occur frequently in the conditions with cognitive workload. The frequency of tracking error and utterance error were submitted to two-factor ANOVAs (perceptual motor vs. cognitive) with repeated measures. The two-factor ANOVAs revealed significant main effects of the perceptual motor workload on the frequency of tracking error ($F_{1,10} = 103.15$, $p < 0.01$) and the cognitive workload on the frequency of utterance error ($F_{1,10} = 36.85$, $p < 0.01$). Further analysis by Turkey's HSD test revealed that the frequency of tracking errors in the C and D conditions was significantly higher than those of the A and B conditions ($p< 0.01$), and the frequency of utterance errors in the B and D conditions were significantly higher than those of the A and C conditions ($p< 0.01$).

3.3 Eye Fixation Related Potentials

Table 1 shows the mean value of the peak amplitude of EFRP and the number of averaging EEG. The amplitude of A condition is larger than those of the other conditions. Fig. 2 shows grand averaged wave of EFRPs over 11 participants from the

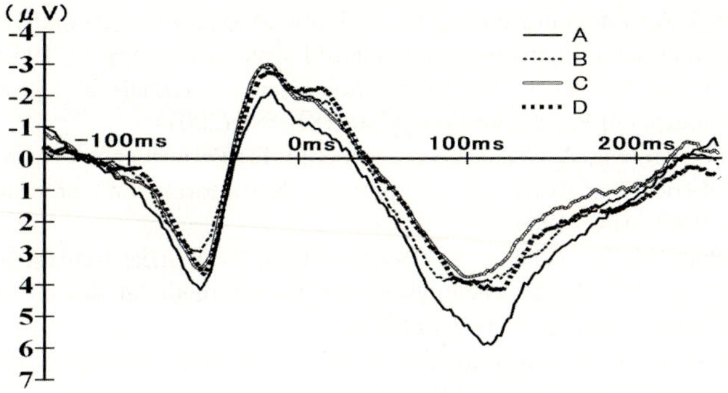

Fig. 2. Grand averaged wave of EFRPs in four conditions

electrode site at Oz under the four conditions. 0 ms indicates offset of the saccade. The amplitude of A condition is larger than that of the D condition significantly (A vs. D, $p < 0.02$ [Wilcoxon signed-rank test]).

4 Discussion and Implications

After offset of saccade, EFRP was obtained from most participants. In the A condition the mental workload is the smallest, the amplitude of EFRP during the dual-task tracking was not decreased in comparison with the D condition which was accompanied with the excessive mental workload about perceptual motor and cognitive problems. While the effects of the task quality (perceptual motor vs. cognitive) and the correspondency with the subjective difficulty in incremental step were not recognized in this experiment. The result indicates that the amplitude of EFRP decreases when it is above their processing capacities excessively, even when they are concentrated on the task. Though Yagi et al. [6] found that EFRP increased in amplitude during an attractive task, it has to be considered that there is a certain limit in the variation of EFRP.

Past findings [2][5] in similar ergonomic studies on the auditory ERP shows that the amplitude of P300 decreases with the level of the mental workload in the primary task. However, it is hard to measure P300 in the field because of a noise and a restriction of eye movements. On the other hand, it is possible to measure EFRP in the noise environment under free saccade situations. Thus, EFRP is applicable as an index of mental workload in the various fields.

References

1. Daimoto, H., Suzuki, M., Yagi, A.: Effects of a monotonous tracking task on eye fixation related potentials. The Japanese Journal of Ergonomics[in Japanese] 34, 59–65 (1998)
2. Isreal, J.B., Chesney, G.L., Wickens, C.D., Donchin, E.: P300 and tracking difficulty: evidence for multiple resources in dual-task performance. Psychophysiology 17, 259–273 (1980)

3. Kazai, K., Yagi, A.: Integrated effect of stimulation at fixation points on EFRP (eye-fixation related brain potentials). International Journal of Psychophysiology 32, 193–203 (1999)
4. Takeda, Y., Sugai, M., Yagi, A.: Eye fixation related potentials in a proof reading task. International Journal of Psychophysiology 40, 181–186 (2001)
5. Wickens, C.D., Kramer, A., Vanasse, L., Donchin, E.: Performance of concurrent tasks: A psychophysiological analysis of reciprocity of information processing resources. Science 221, 1080–1082 (1983)
6. Yagi, A., Sakamaki, E., Takeda, Y.: Psychophysiological measurement of attention in a computer graphic task. In: Proceedings of the 5th International Scientific Conference of Work With Display Unit, pp. 203–204 (1997)
7. Yagi, A.: Visual signal detection and lambda responses. Electroencephalography and Clinical Neurophysiology 52, 604–610 (1981)

Effect of Glance Duration on Perceived Complexity and Segmentation of User Interfaces

Yifei Dong, Chen Ling, and Lesheng Hua

University of Oklahoma
Norman, OK
{dong,chenling,hua}@ou.edu

Abstract. Computer users who handle complex tasks like air traffic control (ATC) need to quickly detect updated information from multiple displays of graphical user interface. The objectives of this study are to investigate how much computer users can segment GUI display into distinctive objects within very short glances and whether human perceives complexity differently after different durations of exposure. Subjects in this empirical study were presented with 20 screenshots of web pages and software interfaces for different short durations (100ms, 500ms, 1000ms) and were asked to recall the visual objects and rate the complexity of the images. The results indicate that subjects can reliably recall 3-5 objects regardless of image complexity and exposure duration up to 1000ms. This result agrees with the "magic number 4" of visual short-term memory (VSTM). Perceived complexity by subjects is consistent among the different exposure durations, and it is highly correlated with subjects' rating on the ease to segmentation as well as the image characteristics of density, layout, and color use.

Keyword: Visual Segmentation, Perceptual Complexity, Rapid Glance.

1 Introduction

Graphic user interface (GUI) is the major means that human interacts with computer at present. To display large-volume and heterogeneous data and functionalities, a GUI is often organized in multiple displays in form of windows, pages, or tabs or even spread out in several screens. In a complex task such as air traffic control (ATC), users have to browse or flip through multiple displays, and read popup messages from emergent events or periodical notification. Rapid perception is required in these scenarios for users to make fast and accurate response.

How well can human perceive visual information at a quick glance? Studies show that observers can recognize real-world scene in a single glance [6] and can acquire object- or scene-level information within 500ms [2]. Similar result shows that subjects can accurately assess the aesthetics of web pages in merely 50ms [4]. It is tempting to conjuncture that the same phenomenon occurs in the perception of GUI since it is also visual perception. But GUI images are very different from real-world scenes: GUI objects are mostly artificial and abstract therefore require training for users to recognize them. The spatial relation between the GUI objects is not necessarily

J. Jacko (Ed.): Human-Computer Interaction, Part III, HCII 2007, LNCS 4552, pp. 605–614, 2007.

mapped to the physical world. There are much fewer types of GUI objects than physical objects, leaving less room for contrast between adjacent or even hierarchical objects. These differences may slow down the perception of GUI. On the other hand, however, there are also some factors that make the perception of GUI faster: Overlap between GUI objects is rare; many GUIs follow common design guidelines and patterns; and people are getting more and more familiar with the common visual language. Therefore, both positive and negative factors exist to affect the performance of rapid perception of GUI.

Here we are interested with the functional (rather than emotional as in [4]) characteristics of rapid perception of GUI. The focused activity is visual segmentation: an early stage perceptual process by which the visual system forms objects by grouping or binding locations and features out of the visual information [1,12]. In addition to the glance duration, another variable in consideration is the metrics of information complexity [13]. The objectives of this study are to investigate whether the segmentation quality of GUI display within short glances is the same as that by longer glance; whether human perceive complexity different after different durations of exposure; and whether perceived complexity and performance of segmentation are related.

2 Theoretical Background

2.1 Visual Segmentation

One of the most basic issues in visual perception is "perceptual segregation" or "segmentation", i.e., which parts of the visual information belong together and thus form separate objects [1,12]. Segmentation can be based on many visual features: lines, shapes, or contrast in brightness, color, texture, granularity, and spatial frequency.

Feature integration theory [8,9], Treisman distinguishes the features of objects with the objects themselves. A two-step model is used to illustrate the mechanism of visual information processing. The first step is a parallel process in which the visual features of objects in the environment are processed together. This process does not depend on attention. The second step is a serial process in which features are combined to form objects. The serial process is slower than the first parallel process, especially when there are large number of objects. Two higher-level cognitive activities may help feature combination at this stage: Focused attention can "glue" forming unitary objects from the available feature to the location of the object; and stored knowledge about the characteristics of familiar objects can direct features combination toward these objects. In the absence of focused attention or relevant stored knowledge, features will combine randomly, providing "illusory conjunctions".

2.2 Information Complexity

Xing proposed three dimensions for information complexity: quantity, variety, and relation [13]. The *quantity* dimension describes the number of visual objects on a display. It affects the second step of serial visual processing more than the first step of parallel processing. The metric for this dimension is number of fixation groups, which is similar to Tullis's concept of overall density, i.e., the percentage of available character spaces being used on the screen [11]. The *variety* dimension is related to the first step of parallel processing with segmentation and pop-out. Visual features including distinctive colors, luminance contrast, spatial frequency, size, texture, and motion signals play a key role in this complexity dimension. Too many or too few visual features can lead to difficulty in segmentation. The *relation* dimension is also related to the second step of serial processing and deals with detailed processing of information. It depends on the relationship of visual stimuli with its surrounding stimuli. It can be best measured by clutter. This concept is dimension to Tullis's local density concept which is related to the number of filled character spaces near other characters [11].

3 Methodology

3.1 Participants

Six subjects aged 20-26 participated in this experiment, including 4 males and 2 females. All subjects have normal or corrected-to-normal vision and normal color vision. Students who might be sensitive to images (e.g., art, architecture, computer imaging majors) were not excluded in order to avoid any potential influence. The entire experiment procedure took approximately one hour and fifteen minutes.

3.2 Equipment

Twenty screenshot images of web pages and software interfaces, of which four are from air traffic control (ATC) displays, were evaluated in this study. The images were selected based on two criteria: (1) they do not belong to well-known web sites or interfaces of software (to reduce the possible influence of familiarity on evaluations); (2) the stimuli sets need to cover a wide range of visual features in order to be representative. These twenty images were separated into two sets of ten images with similar collective characteristics.

All images were shown on the screen with resolution of 1024x768 pixels in 24-bit true color. A webcam was used to record the segmentation drawing actions of the subjects.

3.3 Procedure

The experiment consisted of three tasks. Before the first task, subjects accepted training about the definition of segmentation and complexity with image examples. There were three sessions in the first task with one of three exposure durations, 100ms, 500ms, and 1000ms for each session. (The arrangement of the experimental condition is discussed in the next section.) At the beginning of each session, two images were used for practice. With the two practice trials, the subjects were primed for the exposure duration for the experiment runs, when the images were displayed with random order. After each image had been shown on the screen with brief exposure time, the subjects were instructed to draw the objects that they had remembered of the image on a drawing sheet. They were encouraged to speak out aloud while they drew. After drawing, the subjects were asked to report any visual features that they remembered for any objects. They were then asked to choose the complexity rating of the image from 1 to 5. The procedure repeated for each of the 10 images in the image set. The second session followed immediately after the first session, where subjects were shown another 10 images in another image set for another exposure duration, and were asked to draw the objects, describe the visual features, and give the complexity rating. After the second session, a five-minute break was administered to reduce the fatigue. Then in the third session, the same images as shown in the first session were shown again on the screen for another exposure duration, and subjects carried the same tasks out of drawing objects and rating complexity. During the first task, the recorder recorded all the hand movements on the drawing sheet and the verbal report of subjects for later data analysis.

In the second task, subjects ranked the 10 images as they saw in session 1 and 3 in the first task from simple to complex. And in the third task, the images that they just ranked were shuffled, and subjects filled out a survey for each image on the complexity rating and image characteristics including ease of segmentation, local density, overall density, color use, and layout. They also drew out their segmentation of each image again while looking at the image.

After the experiment sessions, the experimenter counted number of objects based the drawing sheets and recording. An object was taken into account if it was placed at the right location or its relative position with the adjacent valid objects was correct.

3.4 Experimental Design

A within-subject design was used. Every subject carried out three tasks in sequence. To avoid or reduce the learning effect, a Latin-square design was used (see Table 1). The independent variable is the exposure duration, and the dependent variable is the complexity ratings and number of remembered objects by the subjects.

Table 1. Latin square experimental design

	Duration (first task)			Second task	Third task
	100ms	500ms	1000ms	Ranking	Survey
Image set 1	S1 S3 S6	S2 S3 S5	S1 S4 S5	S1 S3 S5	S1 S3 S5
Image set 2	S2 S4 S5	S1 S4 S6	S2 S3 S6	S2 S4 S6	S2 S4 S6

4 Results and Analysis

4.1 Descriptive Statistics

The subjects gave complexity rating and drew the objects after three exposure durations and during the survey. The data is compared across these four levels (Table 2) and are plotted in Figure 1. The trend shows that the perceived complexity for images is the highest at 100ms, and decreased to the lowest level at 500ms. It increased a little at 1000ms, and maintains at the same level in the survey. As for the performance of segmentation, subjects were able to detect more objects as the duration increases.

Table 2. Descriptive statistics of complexity rating and objects derived of 20 Images

Exposure Duration	Complexity Rating		#Objects Derived	
	M	SD	M	SD
100ms	3.62	0.922	3.28	1.050
500ms	3.25	0.950	3.47	1.157
1000ms	3.38	0.960	3.97	0.901
survey	3.40	1.078	4.83	1.768

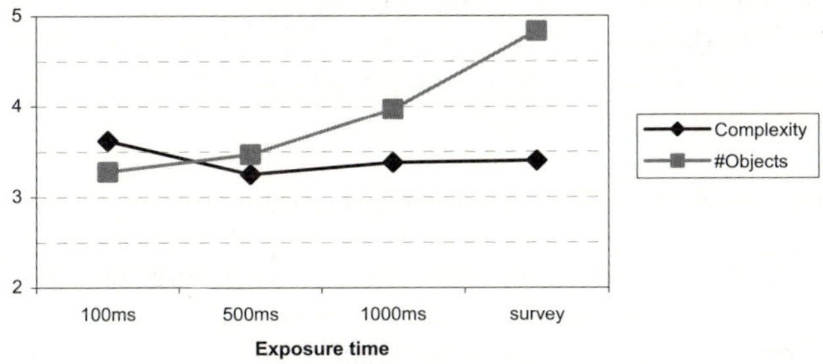

Fig. 1. Complexity rating and number of objects for three durations and survey

The degree of agreement among complexity rankings given by all six subjects for both sets of images were calculated with Kendall's coefficient of concordance. The degree of agreement were high among the subjects for both images sets (W=0.7899, p<0.0001 for 10 images in Set 1; W=0.9280, p<0.0001 for 10 images in Set 2). It implies that the perceived level of complexity is consistent among all subjects. Since the subjects also gave complexity ratings on the images, a ranking was derived based on the average complexity rating in the surveys. When this overall ranking were included with the ranking by each subject, the degree of agreement was also high (W=0.7690, p<0.0001 for 10 images in Set 1; W=0.9364, p<0.0001 for 10 images in Set 2).

4.2 ANCOVA Analysis

ANCOVA analyses were performed on the number of objects drawn by the subjects after three exposure durations to see whether the numbers of detected objects are significantly different from each other. Because the number of existing objects of images can directly affect the number of objects drawn by the subjects, this number was used as covariate. The number of existing objects of images is calculated based on the average number of objects reported by subjects in the survey. ANCOVA reveals significant effect of exposure duration on the number of objects drawn by the subjects (F=9.18, p=0.0002). Post-hoc analysis showed that the number of objects drawn after 1000ms is significantly larger than those with 100 ms and 500ms. There is no significant difference between the number of objects drawn with 100ms and 500ms.

Similar ANCOVA analysis was also performed on the complexity ratings of three durations and the survey with number of existing objects as covariate. The exposure duration is not significant in affecting the perceived complexity.

The recording reveals that with longer exposure time, subjects described the features more accurately and remembered more details about the objects. When the duration increases from 100ms to 500ms, although there is no significant augment in number of objects, but subjects described more features (such as colors, images, and shapes) than in 100ms. At 100ms duration, subjects were often seen reporting certain colors on the image, but pointed out wrong location for the color. According to the feature integration theory by Treisman [8,9], this phenomenon of "illusory conjunction" indicates that visual features are stored in the feature map and have not been bound to specific visual object yet. With more exposure time, serial attention starts to act as "glue" to bind the features to the objects, hence the precise and detailed description. When the duration increases from 500ms to 1000ms, there is significant augment in number of derived objects, the added parts are the detailed parts that are difficult to capture in 100ms or 500ms.

4.3 Correlation Analysis and Multiple Regression

A correlation analysis was run between the complexity ratings that subjects gave after three exposure durations and in the survey when they had sufficient time to evaluate the image. All correlation relationships are significant and fairly strong (around 0.70) except between ratings given at 100ms and 500ms. A correlation analysis was also run among all the items in the final survey (Table 3). The complexity rating is significantly correlated with all items, which warrant further multiple regression analysis.

Table 3. Correlation between complexity ratings and image characteristics

(n=60)	r	p
Number of Existing Objects	0.31	0.0154
Ease of segmentation	0.46	0.0002
Color use	-0.51	0.0001
Layout	-0.45	0.0003
Local density	0.41	0.0011
Overall density	0.49	0.0001

A multiple regression analysis was run based on the survey data to see how the perceived complexity in the survey can be accounted for by each of the image characteristics. 48.32% of variation in complexity of the image can be accounted for by overall density (β=0.33, p=0.01), layout of image (β=-0.29, p=0.07), local density (β=0.11, p=0.45), color (β=-0.19, p=0.21), number of existing objects (β=0.10, p=0.18), and ease of segmentation (β=0.09, p=0.47) together.

Higher overall density is found associated with higher perceived complexity. Because the overall density is directly related to number of fixation group in an image, the perceived complexity is significantly affected by the number of fixation groups, which is one of important perception metrics by Xing [13]. Local density is also significantly correlated with the complexity rating. Local density describes the clutterness of the display, and corresponds to the relation dimension in the perception metrics [13]. Better layout of the image also gives rise to less perceived complexity.

The negative sign in color implies that the worse the color use is in an image, the higher the perceived complexity is. To reduce the complexity of display, better layout design, less overall and local density are important.

4.4 Relationship Between Number of Existing Objects and Complexity

Based on the average segmentation derived from the survey, the images were divided into two types, those with less than 4 existing objects (n=10), and those with more than 4 existing objects (n=10). Figure 2 shows the relationship between exposure duration and the complexity ratings for images with different existing objects. Images with more objects have higher perceived complexity at all durations.

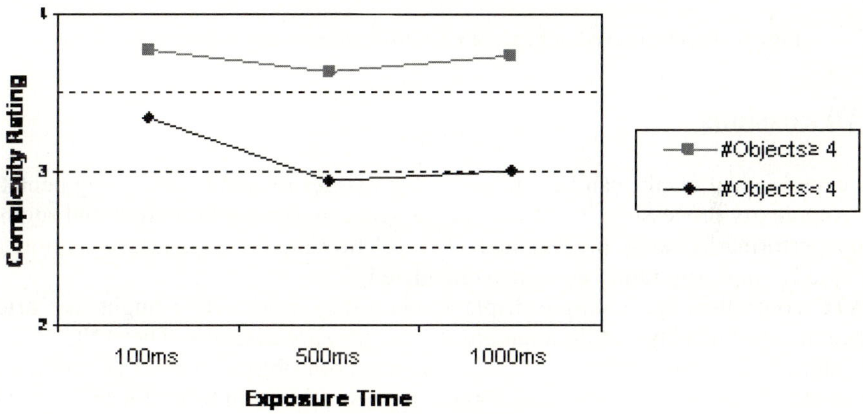

Fig. 2. Complexity rating of images with different total objects after 3 durations

For both types of images, the complexity rating drops as the exposure time increases from 100ms to 500ms, and slightly rebounds from 500ms to 1000ms. This can be explained by that longer exposure helped subjects make sense of the images. The declining slope is steeper for images with fewer objects because there is less information to process. When subjects were given more time, they began to process the logical relation between objects, increasing the dimension of complexity.

4.5 Relationship Between Number of Derived Objects and Ease of Segmentation

It is possible that the ease of segmentation may affect how subject perform their segmentation tasks. We divided the 20 images to those easy to segment (survey rating <3, n=15), and those hard to segment (survey rating >3, n=5), and analyzed the average objects derived at three durations.

The trend shown in Figure 3 is quite intriguing. For easy-to-segment images, more objects were derived in 1000ms than 500ms intervals, yet there is not much difference between 100ms and 500ms. For hard-to-segment images, the trend is reversed: more objects were derived in 500ms than 100ms, but there is not much difference between 500ms and 1000ms. We could not come up with a convincing explanation for the difference. More detailed analysis on the nature of the different increases is under way.

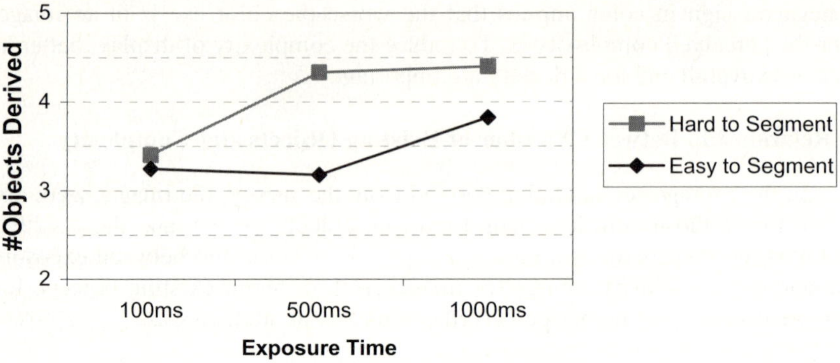

Fig. 3. Objects derived of hard- or easy-to-segment images after 3 durations

5 Discussions

The experimental results can help to understand issues related to image segmentation and complexity processing. The relationship between exposure duration and segmentation performance were investigated. The relationship between segmentation and perceived complexity rating were also elucidated.

ATC controllers use multiple displays when they work. They might just briefly glance at other displays while attending to the primary displays. The ANCOVA results shows significant difference between numbers of objects derived at 1000ms and the shorter durations of 100ms and 500ms. It suggests that in order for the controller to perform visual segmentation reliably, a lower limit of 1000ms delay is needed before a display is refreshed. Some of the most complex screenshots used in this experiment are taken from real ATC displays. Longer exposure time is expected for controllers to correctly parse those interfaces.

The experimental results demonstrate the relationship among the three dimensions of the information complexity: quantity, variety, and relation proposed by Xing [13]. The complexity rating is significantly related to all three dimensions. The multiple regression result demonstrated that three of these dimensions can account for nearly 50% of variation of the perceptual complexity.

The number of objects derived by segmentation falls in the range of 3-5, which agrees with the commonly accepted capacity for visual short term memory (VSTM). The serial feature binding process requires more time. Therefore our results show that more accurate and detailed description were given for 1000 ms. Segmentation is a pre-attentive bottom up activity with parallel processing, whereas complexity rating involve conscious decision making and assessment, which is a top-down activity. The rating is fairly consistent among 100ms, 500ms, 1000ms, and survey results. A general pattern shown is that subjects gave the highest complexity rating at 100ms. With this exposure time, the visual information has not been fully processed. The higher-level assessment of this incomplete information processing leads to higher level of complexity.

Several interesting issues emerged from the experiment. One is the meaning of "complexity". Although subjects were instructed to rate the perceptual complexity, they usually still wanted to make sense out of the image, and considered those familiar or easier to analyze as less complex. Indeed, the definition of the adjective "complex" in Merriam-Webster Dictionary is both objective (composed of two or more parts) and subjective (hard to separate, analyze, or solve), indicating that the link between the two is already deeply embedded in human language and thinking.

Another interesting phenomenon is that the wide use of GUI over two decades has conditioned the users to certain habits in perceiving interfaces. For example, subjects routinely missed the top bar even if it occupies large area and is in high contrast to the objects below. The reason might be that many web sites use that area for advertisement (hence the users actively ignore it), or that the top area is reserved for relatively static components like title bar, menu bar, and toolbar (hence the users are not motivated to view it). This phenomenon is not obvious in other border areas.

When subjects recalled the objects after 100ms, sometimes they remarked that they remembered there was something somewhere but could not remember what it was. This is consistent with the known fact that critical processes involved in object recognition are remarkably fast, occurring within 100-200ms of stimulus presentation. However, it may take another 100ms for subsequent processes to bring this information into awareness [10].

The subjects never tried to segment textual areas even in the longest 1000ms and when the text is formatted with prominent visual cues such as blank lines, bigger font size and different style. We may thus infer that textual variation is not a good way to catch attention in the context of rapid glance.

Screenshot images from real software applications instead of artificially constructed images are used as stimuli in this study. The advantage of this design is that the stimuli are authentic, but its disadvantage is that it is hard to control prior knowledge and isolate significant variables from numerous visual features.

Acknowledgement. This study was supported in part by the Civil Aerospace Medical Institute, Federal Aviation Administration (FAA), with the grant entitled as "*Investigating Information Complexity in Three Types of Air Traffic Control (ATC) Displays.*" We express our sincere appreciation to the FAA grant monitor Dr. Jing Xing for her contribution to the original design of the study

References

[1] Eysenck, M.W., Keane, M.: Cognitive Psychology: A Student's Handbook. 4th edn. Psychology Press (2000)

[2] Fei-Fei, L., Iyer, A., Koch, C., Perona, P.: What do we perceive in a glance of a real-world scene? Journal of Vision, 7(1):10, 1–29 (2007) http://journalofvision.org/7/1/10/, doi:10.1167/7.1.10

[3] Julesz, B.: Experiments in the visual perception of texture. Scientific American 212, 38–48 (1975)

[4] Lindgaard, G., Fernandes, G., Dudek, C., Brown, J.: Attention web designers: You have 50 milliseconds to make a good first impression! Behaviour and Information Technology 25(2), 115–126 (2006)

[5] Luck, S.J., Vogel, E.K.: The capacity of visual working memory for features and conjunctions. Nature 390, 279–281 (1997)

[6] Oliva, A.: Gist of the scene. In: Itti, L., Rees, G., Tsotsos, J.K. (eds.) The Encyclopedia of Neurobiology of Attention, pp. 251–256. Elsevier, San Diego, CA (2005)
[7] Quinlan, P.T., Wilton, R.N.: Grouping by proximity or similarity? Competition between the Gestalt principles in vision. Perception 27, 417–430 (1998)
[8] Treisman, A.M.: Features and objects: The fourteenth Bartlett memorial lecture. Quarterly Journal of Experimental Psychology 40A, 201–237 (1988)
[9] Treisman, A.: Perceiving and re-perceiving objects. American Psychologist 47, 862–875 (1992)
[10] Treisman, A.M., Kanwisher, N.G.: Perceiving visually presented objects: recognition, awareness, and modularity. Current Opinion in Neurobiology 8(2), 218–226 (1998)
[11] Tullis, T.: An evaluation of alphanumeric, graphic, and color information display. Human Factors 25, 541–550 (1981)
[12] Vecera, S.P., Farah, M.J.: Is visual image segmentation a bottom-up or an interactive process? Perception and Psychophysics 59(8), 1280–1296 (1997)
[13] Xing, J.: Measures of information complexity and the implications for automation design. Washington, DC: Federal Aviation Administration; No: DOT/FAA/AM-04/17 (2004)

Movement-Based Interaction and Event Management in Virtual Environments with Optical Tracking Systems

Maxim Foursa and Gerold Wesche

Fraunhofer Institut für Intelligente Analyse- und Informationssyteme
Virtual Environments, 53754 Sankt Augustin, Germany
{Maxim.Foursa,Gerold.Wesche}@iais.fraunhofer.de

Abstract. In this paper we present our experience in using optical tracking systems in Virtual Environment applications. First we briefly describe the tracking systems we used, and then we describe the application scenarios and present how we adapted the scenarios for the tracking systems. One of the tracking systems is markerless, that means that a user doesn't have to wear any specific devices to be tracked and can interact with an application with free hand movements. With our application we compare the performance of different tracking systems and demonstrate that it is possible to perform complex actions in an intuitive way with just small special knowledge of the system and without any specific devices. This is a step forward to a more natural human-computer interface.

Keywords: tracking systems, virtual environments, application scenarios, interaction techniques.

1 Introduction

Position and orientation tracking is a very important topic in Virtual Environments (VE). Tracking technologies allow to render perspectively correct scenes and to interact with 3-D objects. Different approaches are used to solve the tracking problem each of them having its own advantages and limitations. Mechanical tracking devices measure position and orientation by using a direct mechanical connection between a reference point and the target. Electromagnetic tracking devices function by measuring the strength of the magnetic fields generated by sending electricity through three small wire coils, oriented perpendicular to one another. These three coils are embedded in a small unit that is attached to whatever the system needs to be tracked - typically, the user. Acoustic tracking devices use ultrasonic (high-frequency) sound waves for measuring the position and orientation of target objects. They consist of three high frequency sound wave emitters in rigid formation that forms the source for three receivers which are also present in a rigid arrangement on the user. Optical tracking devices used in virtual environments are for tracking position and orientation of a user's head and a stylus. Basically, they come in two variants. In the first one, one or several cameras are mounted on top of the head-mounted display (HMD), and a set of infrared LEDs (Light Emitting Diodes) is placed above the head at fixed locations in the environment. In the alternative setup, the cameras are mounted on the ceiling or

J. Jacko (Ed.): Human-Computer Interaction, Part III, HCII 2007, LNCS 4552, pp. 615–624, 2007.

on a fixed frame and a few LEDs are placed at fixed and known positions on HMD or shutter glasses. Inertial Tracking Devices apply the principle of conservation of angular momentum and allow the user to move around in a comparatively large working volume since there is no hardware or cabling between the computer and the tracking device ([1], [2], [3]).

As mentioned, each tracking technology has its own pluses and minuses. For example with a mechanical or magnetic system, the user has to be linked to a measurement instrument by cable or a mechanical linkage, which is not very comfortable; mechanical systems are very precise and have low latency. Magnetic and acoustic tracking systems suffer from different sources of distortions. Optical tracking systems can work fast over a large area and be comfortable to use, but they are limited by intensity of light sources and they require "line of sight" from emitter to receiver. As high quality precise optical systems are quite expensive, we have developed a relatively cheap system based on commodity hardware, which meets the requirements of user-VE-user interaction - IR-Tracking System [4]. In the next paragraphs we will briefly consider the system and describe our interaction paradigm.

Although the system we developed is an optical one and does not have cables connecting the user and his devices to other systems it still has interaction devices and the user has to hold them in his hands and know how to operate with them. The next step would be a tracking system, which doesn't require any specific devices. We participated in the development of the HUMODAN tracking system [5], which is able to track movements of up to 20 reference points of a human body without any markers. The system itself doesn't have any interaction paradigm and we had to develop our own application specific ones. So after description of IR-tracking system and our experience in using it we briefly present the HUMODAN Tracking System, our interaction techniques and compare the HUMODAN system with our IR-Tracking System and electromagnetic one.

2 A Simple IR Tracking System

Compared to high-end infrared tracing systems such as the expensive ART infrared optical tracking system [16], which can deliver very accurate results, our system is much more cost-effective and insensitive to frequent usage. Our system uses active infrared markers at the devices and therefore can be used with passive cameras that are less expensive than e.g the professional ART cameras.

The system was originally designed at FhG-IAIS for a CAVE [6] and a Stereowall [7] VE systems to replace a regular electromagnetic system with a lot of cables by a cableless one. The system employs three near-infrared monochrome cameras JAI-M50IR, equipped with 6 mm lenses and infrared filters and it is installed on a frame above a reflective screen (see Fig. 1). These cameras are attached to an RGB frame grabber. The output from the frame grabber is one image with the size 769x570 that contains synchronized output from all the cameras in R, G and B planes. The scanning speed of the cameras is 25 fps. This output is processed on a workstation with Pentium 4 2.2 GHz processor using specially developed software on the MS Windows platform. For separation of objects to track we are using active infrared

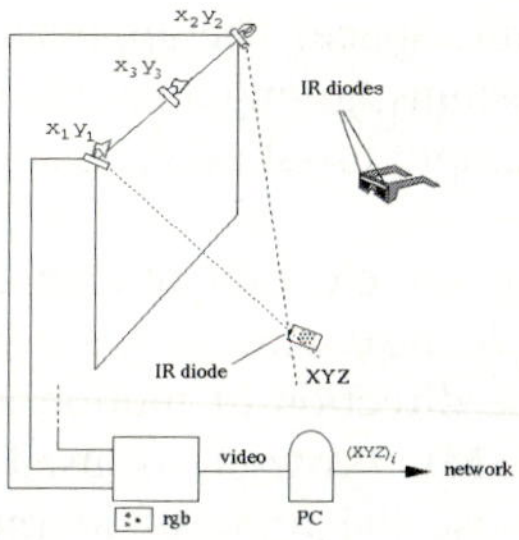

Fig. 1. Tracking system setup

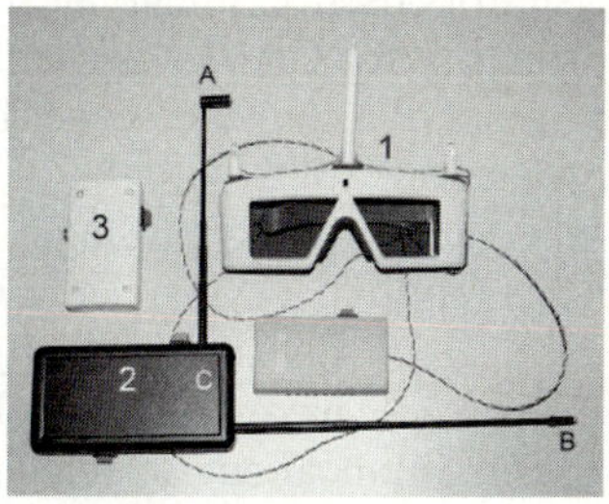

Fig. 2. Devices for tracking with LEDs: 1- active stereo glasses with three LEDs; 2 – infrared stylus with three LEDs (A, B and C); 3 – one LED device.3 Applications

beacons. With the infrared filters installed the cameras are practically not sensitive to normal light and can work in both dark and light environments.

We used three devices to track (see Fig. 2): a pointer with one LED emitter (3), shutter glasses with three LEDs (1) and a stylus with three LED emitters (A, B and C) with a telescopic tube (2) - for better direction reconstruction. The third LED (C) is not visible on the image since it is installed from the right side; it is working only when user presses and holds the button on the top of the stylus. The power supply for the devices is a 9V battery. The direct current is constant and can be varied from 5 mA to 50 mA. For calibration of the system we used a calibration target with more than 30 points measured in a coordinate system by using a theodolite. First we applied the Tsai algorithm [8] to get internal camera parameters and radial distortion coefficient and then we used Faugeras method [9] to calibrate the tracking syst8em in the coordinate system of our virtual reality installation. Here are the most important characteristics of the system: speed of image processing (update rate): 25 fps; accuracy of marker position reconstruction: 5mm; accuracy of angle tracking for glasses: 3° and accuracy of angle tracking for stylus: below 1°; latency: about 60 ms; tracked devices: LEDs, up to six; hardware price (frame grabber, three cameras, lenses, filters, cables): $4000. The system is described in details in [9]. We used the tracking system with several applications; one of them has been developed specially for the system. Below we present our experience in using the system with the applications.

2.1 Virtual Planetarium

Virtual Planetarium [11] is an educational application in virtual environment, intended for teaching and demonstration of fundamental astronomy and astrophysics. The application uses special methods to display the astronomical objects realistically, as they are visible by astronauts of a real spacecraft, preserving correct visible sizes of all objects for any viewpoint and using 3D model based on real astronomical data and images. The model represents 3200 brightest stars, 30 objects in the Solar System, including 9 main planets and their largest satellites, an interactive map of constellations, composed of ancient drawings, a database, describing astronomical objects textually and vocally in English and German languages. Stereoscopic projection system is used to create an illusion of open cosmic space. The application is destined primarily for CAVE-like virtual environment systems, giving a perception of complete immersion into the scene, but also works in simple installations using a single wall projection.

Regular navigation in CyberStage is performed using an electromagnetic 3D pointing device (stylus), or joystick/mouse in more simple installations. User can manipulate by a green ray in a virtual model, choosing the direction of motion and objects of interest. A navigation panel, emulating an HTML browser, is used to display the information about selected objects and to choose the route of journey. Navigation is based on the following principles: simple pointing to a sky object displays its description on the panel; selection of item in the lists of planets/constellations on the panel initiates the motion to the planet or switches on/off the constellation; rotation of stylus and pressing its button are used for manual navigation; short click to the stylus' button initiates or stops the motion, with 1 sec period of acceleration. If the button is pressed and held, the rotation of stylus changes the orientation of the observer, also with a small damping.

In case of using the IR Tracking system, the user has just to change the name of the tracking system in the start script of the application and start the tracking server - the listening daemon prepares the data for the application in the same format, as the electromagnetic system does. Head-tracking works the same way as normal electromagnetic tracking, though it is more comfortable to wear the glasses without cables. The stylus is calibrated in the way, that a user sees the green ray as it is emitted by a user's hand. But since we used for the construction of the ray points A and B (see fig. 2), to perceive the stylus as prolongation of the hand, the plane formed by the two antennas with LEDs should be perpendicular to the ground. Here is the summary of the usage of IR system with the application: it is possible to perform all above mentioned actions designed for the electromagnetic system; it is more comfortable to use the cableless devices; there are some limitations in using the system: the stylus should be below the glasses, the user should not move out of the tracked volume, the user should get used to unusual behavior of the green ray in some cases.

2.2 Free-Form Sketching

We chose one of our most complex applications that has a high degree of interactivity and requires direct 3D interaction, which means that, in order to manipulate a virtual object, the user points to it with his hands, using a tracked input device. In case of IR tracking, the user can interact in a way that no cables hinder his movements.

The Free-form modeling application [12] allows designing simple free form models by constructing a network of curves. Within loops in the curve network, surfaces can be fit in. Designers can work on their virtual models in the same way as they would in a real situation, by applying two-handed interaction: the non-dominant hand holds the model in a way that will allow the dominant hand to carry out the editing functions in the right places. In this application Cubic B-Spline curves are drawn with a stylus, edited and automatically integrated into the existing network. Also available are functions like smoothing, sharpening and dragging, providing the designer with a potent interface that is easy to use, at the same time masking the complex mathematical representation of the Spline curves and surfaces. New free-hand drawn curves are being integrated into the existing network in the following way: points of intersection are being predetermined on net-curves that are being approached by a new curve. The final curve approximates the drawn curve and interpolates the points of intersection. Curve drawing as well as curve modification tools (e.g. smoothing, deforming), which all rely on direct 3D interaction, are supported. Additionally, basic CAD functions (copy, move, delete) are available.

The actual purpose of the network of curves is to define the boundary of surface parts, i.e. the user has to image the model in terms of contour curves. Therefore, surface construction is achieved the following way: In each closed loop of curve pieces a part of the surface can be fit in. This is initiated, using the surface construction tool, by pointing into the loop with the input device and generating the corresponding event (i.e. pressing a button of moving the other hand to the side). In case a closed loop has been found it is highlighted and a surface part appears.

Fig. 3. Free-form modeling with regular electromagnetic (*left*) and IR Tracking (*right*) systems

Normally an electromagnetic tracking system has been used (Fig 3, left image). An additional device was used to switch between tools (in the left hand; Fig 3, left image).

In case of using IR Tracking system we had to do some changes in the interface and the interaction works as follows:

- Tool selection: move the ray of the stylus inside of the sphere in the upper-right corner (see Fig.3, right image), press the button. The tool selector is then shown (blue squares on the Fig. 3, right image). Move the ray of the stylus to the required tool - the corresponding square is then highlighted.
- Curve drawing: select the curve drawer. Move the pointer to the position where the curve is supposed to start. Move the pointer with the button pressed. When the curve is supposed to end, release the button.
- Curve deformation: select the desired tool (smoother/sharpener/warper). Select the curve by moving the pointer. To activate the tool press the button. The warper moves around the curve, following the hand. For smoothing and sharpening, no special control is needed except selecting a curve.
- Surface creation and deletion: select the tool. Move the pointer to the location of the loop of curve pieces or to the surface part, respectively. The selected object is highlighted. Initiate surface creation or removal by the button on the stylus.

Regarding the simplicity and cost effectiveness of the IR tracking solution, most tasks could be performed in a reasonable way. In particular, we recognized the following characteristics:

- It is possible to perform all above mentioned actions designed for the electromagnetic system;
- It is more comfortable to use the cableless devices;
- There are some limitations in using the system: the stylus should be below the glasses, the user should not move out of the tracked volume, the user should get used to unusual behavior of the green ray in some cases;
- The accuracy of the IR Tracking system is lower than of the electromagnetic one and it leads to less stable work with the system: e.g. sometimes if the user wants to draw a long curve, he can create the curve in the desired form just from the second or third attempt.

From this we conclude that for creation tasks, such as drawing and connecting curves, the accuracy of the IR tracking system is probably not sufficient. However, for any kind of constrained based interaction, the advantages of cableless interaction can be fully utilized. In these cases, the free hand movement is mapped to the object modification in an indirect manner. Consider e.g. curve smoothing, where the user only points along the curve and therefore only activates or deactivates an automatic shaping process.

2.3 Music Composition Assistant

In order to demonstrate the best features of the IR Tracking system we have developed the following simple application. The idea of the application is based on sonification of 3D movements. By using the device 3 from Fig. 2 a user can create sound events in the following way:

- the user selects the center of a volume, where s/he feels most comfortable;
- when s/he presses a button of the device, two notes are generated, depending on the distance of the device from the selected center on Y and X directions with resolution 1.5 cm per half-tone (see Fig. 4); when a user releases the button, no sound is generated; when X or Y of the device equals zero, then just one tone is generated;
- the user can change the volume of the sound by moving the tracked device higher (increase volume) or lower (decrease volume).

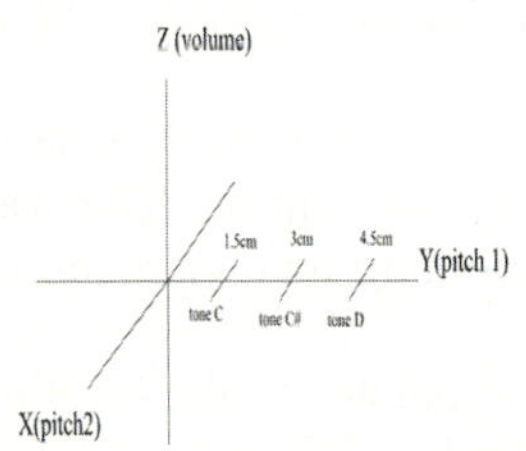

Fig. 4. Sonification of movements

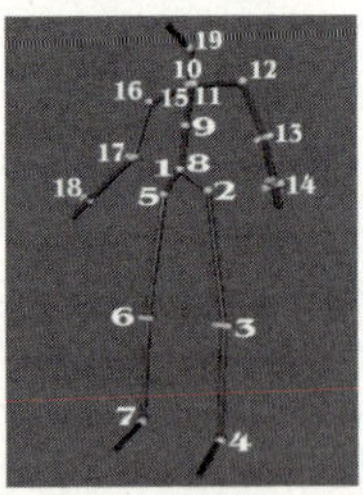

Fig. 5. Human model

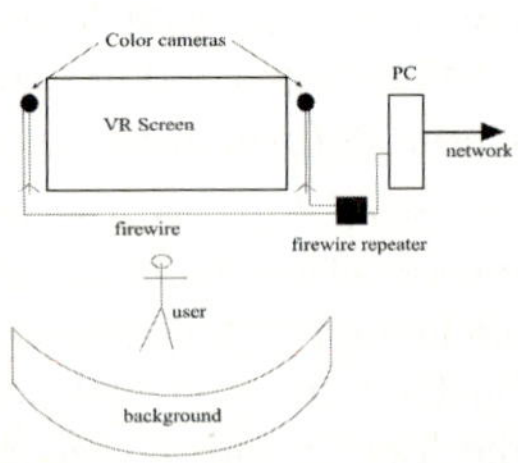

Fig. 6. HUMODAN system setup

If the user is working with two such devices, he can produce four tones simultaneously. With some training a user can produce his own melodies by just moving his hands. Our experiments have shown that this can be very exiting, especially for people who are not familiar with music composition and for kids - the easiness of the process makes it very attractive. This application can work even with a tracking system with worse accuracy - one has just to change to resolution.

3 A Markerless Optical Tracking System

3.1 The HUMODAN System

HUMODAN is an innovative system developed by a consortium of companies ([5], [13,] [14]) for automatic recognition and animation of human motion in controlled environments. The most relevant and distinctive feature of this system with respect to existing technologies is that the tracked individual does not wear any type of marker or special suit and neither has any other sensors. This allows the system to be highly useful in a wide range of technological areas, like for example TV production, tele-presence, immersive and collaborative interactivity storytelling, medicine diagnose support, tele-operation, education and training.

We participated in the system development and integration into our VR-framework. The integrated system is shown in Fig.7 with the following main modules:

- ARS: automatic reconstruction system, it includes: calibration module; MTS: motion tracking and segmentation; BPM: biomechanical processing module.
- VR-framework: listen daemon; virtual character module; virtual environment module.

The calibration process is based on a chessboard calibration method [15], in which internal and external parameters of cameras are calculated. Motion tracking and segmentation is the kernel of the whole system and is based on a new matching method, which uses Mumford-Shah segmentation functional [16]. The matching process can reconstruct in 3D up to twenty reference points of human upper-body (see Fig 5): it tracks several clearly visible reference points of human body (as hands, head and shoulders) and uses additional methods to detect other points. BPM module helps the matching process by applying geometrical restrictions to reconstructed movements of human joints. The interface described in 2.2 is used to transmit the data to the graphic server with the Avango VR-framework, though the format of the transmitted data is the following:

Frame N:
Joint-name-i: X_i Y_i Z_i Rx_i Ry_i Rz_i, i=0..19

where **N** is the number of reconstructed frame, X_i Y_i Z_i Rx_i Ry_i Rz_i - translation and rotation parameters of joint **i**. Listening daemon pre-processes the data and the movements of the tracked user are then mapped onto a virtual character and used in the application.

The HUMODAN vision system employs two color firewire cameras AVT Marlin F033C working with resolution 320x240 and equipped with 6mm lenses. The cameras are connected to a PC via a firewire repeater, the PC is running under OS Windows 2000 or XP. ARS receives the videos from the cameras using DirectX 9.0 drivers for firewire and it transmits the reconstructed information to the graphic server. Green background is installed behind the user to help the segmentation and matching algorithms of the ARS. Lighting condition in the room of the VR installations is a very critical issue. Illumination should neither be too bright, as it will prevent the user from seeing the projections rendered by the VR framework, nor too dark, to allow the ARS to find and reconstruct user's skeleton.

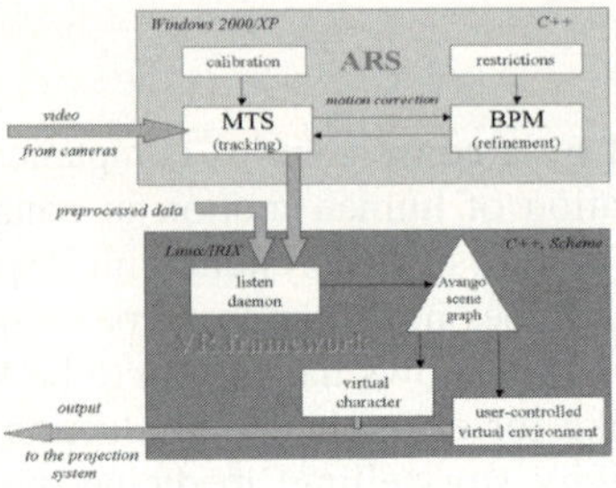

Fig. 7. HUMODAN system integrated into a VR-framework

Fig. 8. Free-form modeling with HUMODAN tracking system

Here are the most important characteristics of the system: speed of image processing (update rate): 20 fps; accuracy of hands' position reconstruction: 1cm; latency: about 100 ms; tracked points: up to six, hardware price (frame grabber, three cameras, lenses, filters, cables): $4000.

More detailed information and the references to numerous publications describing different aspects and methods used in the HUMODAN system can be found in [14]. The system has been presented to the public for the first time during the IEEE VR 2005 conference in Bonn, Germany, March 13-16 2005.

4.2 The demonstrators In order to challenge the HUMODAN tracking system, we chose the free form modeling application described in 3.2. In the HUMODAN version, the user can interact hands-free, and no cables hinder his movements. In the following, we describe the modifications we made to support cableless, and moreover, markerless interaction, and we describe to what degree our expectations were fulfilled.

We developed a distributed version of the free-form modeling application : it works on two separate Responsive Workbench [6] installations, A, and B. At workbench A, the HUMODAN tracking system is used to track the position of the hands for all input purposes (see Fig. 7), whereas an electromagnetic tracking system is used for head tracking. This is needed to achieve a perspectively correct rendering for the main user, who wears stereo glasses. The curve and surface tools described below at workbench A rely directly on the position of the hands, without using markers or input devices. At workbench B, an electromagnetic tracking system is used for head tracking and for the hands as well (see Fig. 3, left image). A stylus and a similar device held in the left hand are used for all input actions. In addition to that, the user at the Workbench B sees an avatar of the user of Workbench A.

The collaborative design application uses, at workbench A, both hands as input "devices". At workbench B, standard 3D input devices, which are electromagnetically tracked, are used. The hands act as manipulators for curve drawing, curve deformation, and surface creation. Furthermore, the hands perform all system control tasks, i.e. they switch between the available tools. The hands are used in the following way:

- Tool selection: repeatedly move the left hand upwards until the desired tool is selected. Each time the hand reaches a certain height level, the tool is switched.
- Curve drawing: select the curve drawer. Then, position the right hand (the drawing hand) at the position where the curve is supposed to start. Move the left hand sideward to the left in order to activate drawing. Sweep out the curve with the right hand. When the curve is supposed to end, remove the left hand from the left area.
- Curve deformation: select the desired tool. Use the same method to activate curve deformation as used for curve drawing. The warper moves around the curve, following the hand. For smoothing and sharpening, no control of the right hand is needed except selecting a curve.
- Surface creation and deletion: move the right hand to the location of the loop of curve pieces or to the surface part, respectively. The selected object is highlighted. Initiate surface creation or removal by reaching to the left side with the left hand.

3.2 Usability of the Sketching System with Markerless Tracking

In general it was possible to perform all above-mentioned actions. However, it turned out that due to low accuracy of reconstruction of hands' position, it was quite difficult to draw connecting curves using just the camera based hand tracking. Therefore, in the distributed demonstrator, the curves can be drawn at workbench B, using the electromagnetic tracked pen. At the same time, at workbench A, the user moves his/her right hand in order to fit in a surface part, to select and deform a curve, and triggers his/her actions with the left hand as described. Creation tasks are much easier to perform with a sufficiently accurate input device, whereas manipulation tasks can be quite easily performed by using just the hands, since many tasks are strongly constrained. For example, due to the energy minimization of the variational modeling module, deforming a curve will always create a somehow visually pleasing result.

The HUMODAN system is a new paradigm to interact in virtual environments. The best characteristics are: real-time, non-invasive, biomechanical correct, low cost in software and hardware. However, the accuracy and stability of the system has to be improved.

4 Conclusion

In this work we presented our experience in using optical tracking systems in Virtual Environment applications. We briefly described the tracking systems we used, our application scenarios and the way we adapted the scenarios for the tracking systems. We compared the performance of the marker-based and markerless system and came to the conclusion, that with low-cost and easy-to-use optical systems users can use nearly the same interactive possibilities, however the systems still lack the performance (i.e. accuracy) needed in some applications (i.e. virtual surgery). As a consequence, the most demanding interaction tasks, which include creation and drawing of objects, could not be accomplished in a satisfactory way; probably also many system control tasks. On the other hand, most other interaction tasks, in particular constrained based manipulation, benefit from lightweight, easy-to-handle input devices, and even more benefit from free-hand interaction.

Acknowledgments. The work has been supported by European IST (IST-2001-32202) and Russian Foundation for Basic Research (05-07-90382) programs.

References

1. Mulder, A.: Human movement tracking technology. Technical report, School of Kinesiology, Simon Fraser University (1994)
2. Youngblut, C., Johnson, R.E., Nash, S.H., Wienclaw, R.A., Craig A. W.: Review of Virtual Environment Interface Technology, Institute for Defense Analysis (1996)
3. Meyer, K., Applewhite, H.L., Biocca, F.A.: A Survey of Position Trackers. Presence: Teleoperators and Virtual Environments, 1(2) (1992)
4. Foursa, M.: Real-time infrared tracking system for Virtual Environments: from ideas to a real prototype. In: VEonPC2002 Workshop proceedings, pp. 85–93 (2002)
5. Perales, F.J., Buades, J.M., Mas, R., Varona, X., Gonzalez, M., Suescun, A., Aguinaga, I., Foursa, M., Zissis, G., Touman, M., Mendoza, R.: A New Human Motion Analysis System Using Biomechanics 3D models. In: ACM SIGGRAPH 2004 conference proceedings, Los Angeles, California (August 2004)
6. Eckel, G., Göbel, M., Hasenbrink, F., Heiden, W., Lechner, U., Tramberend, H., Wesche, G., Wind, J.: Benches and Caves. In: Bullinger, H.J., Riedel, O. (eds.) Proc. 1st Int. Immersive Projection Technology Workshop, Springer, London (1997)
7. Brusentsev, P., Foursa, M., Frolov, P., Klimenko, S., Matveyev, S., Nikitin, I., Niktina, L.: Virtual Environment Laboratories based on Personal Computers: Principles and Applications. In: VEonPC2002 Workshop proceedings (2002)
8. Faugeras, O.D., Toscani, G.: The calibration problem for stereo. In: Proceedings of IEEE Computer Vision and Pattern Recognition (1986)
9. Foursa, M.: Real-time infrared tracking system for Virtual Environments. In: ACM SIGGRAPH VRCAI 2004, conference proceedings, pp. 427–430 (2004)
10. Tramberend, H.: Avocado: A Distributed Virtual Reality Framework. In: Proc. of the IEEE Virtual Reality (1999)
11. Nikitin, I., Göbel, M., Klimenko, S.: Virtual Planetarium: educational application in Virtual Environment. In: VEonPC 2001, Workshop proceedings, pp. 53–66 (2001)
12. Wesche, G.: A User Interface for Free Form Shape Design at the Responsive Workbench. Journal of Computing and Information Science in Engineering 4, 178–185 (2004)
13. Aguinaga, I., Suescun, A., Foursa, M., Mendoza, R., Zissis, G., Perales, F., Touman, M.: HUMODAN project overview. In: ACM SIGGRAPH VRCAI 2004, conference proceedings (2004)
14. HUMODAN project web-page http://www.humodan.com
15. Heikkila, J., Silven, O.: A Four-Step Camera Calibration Procedure with Implicit Image Correction. In: Proc. of IEEE Computer Vision and Pattern Recognition, pp. 1106–1112 (1997)
16. Buades, R., et al.: A New Method for Detection and Initial Pose Estimation Based on Mumford-Shah Segmentation Functional, vol. 2652, pp. 117–125, Springer-Verlag, Heidelberg (2003) (last access: February 23, 2007) www.ar-tracking.de

Multiple People Gesture Recognition for Human-Robot Interaction

Seok-ju Hong, Nurul Arif Setiawan, and Chil-woo Lee*

Intelligent Image Media & Interface Lab, Department of Computer Engineering,
Chonnam National University, Gwangju, Korea
Tel.: 82-62-530-1803
seokju@image.chonnam.ac.kr, arif@image.chonnam.ac.kr,
leecw@chonnam.ac.kr

Abstract. In this paper, we propose gesture recognition in multiple people environment. Our system is divided into two modules: Segmentation and Recognition. In segmentation part, we extract foreground area from input image, and we decide the closest person as a recognition subject. In recognition part, firstly we extract feature point of subject's both hands using contour based method and skin based method. Extracted points are tracked using Kalman filter. We use trajectories of both hands for recognizing gesture. In this paper, we use the simple queue matching method as a recognition method. We also apply our system as an animation system. Our method can select subject effectively and recognize gesture in multiple people environment. Therefore, proposed method can be used for real world application such as home appliance and humanoid robot.

Keywords: Context Aware, Gesture Recognition, Multiple People.

1 Introduction

Recently, People prefer new input method such as eye blinks, head motions, or other gestures to traditional computer input devices such as mouse, joystick, or keyboard. Gesture recognition technology is more important than any method since it support instinctive input method. Also it is useful in multiple people environment for home appliance. Currently, there are no researches which focused on gesture recognition in multiple people situation. Most researches are focusing on gesture recognition in single person and multiple people tracking.

First we describe multiple people tracking technology. Multiple people tracking research consist of deterministic and stochastic method. In deterministic method, objects are modeled by color histogram representation, texture, appearance and objects shape such as edgelet. And then tracking is performed by matching process in hypothesized search area [1-4]. This method has a disadvantage that object's movement is fast or discontinuous. Stochastic method use probability to estimate new position of objects based on certain feature [5-7]. But this method needs a lot of computational cost so the numbers of people tracked is limited.

---

* Corresponding author.

J. Jacko (Ed.): Human-Computer Interaction, Part III, HCII 2007, LNCS 4552, pp. 625–633, 2007.

Next we describe gesture recognition technology. Skin color based method use only skin information [8]. But it has a disadvantage that skin extraction will fail in case of complex background and illumination change. Contour based method use distance from body center point to both hand points for recognizing gesture [9]. This method is limited to recognition's number since it only uses distance information. 3D based method use 3d model of human body [10]. But it has a disadvantage such as complicated calculation cost and large database construction. Most of these works only focused on single person gesture recognition.

In this paper we deal with gesture recognition in multiple people. First of all we will define gesture and context. In segmentation part we process multiple people tracking and subject decision. In recognition part we extract feature point of body in decided subject. For extracting feature point we use two methods such as contour based method and skin based method. For recognizing gesture we use queue matching method. We also introduce animation system as an application. Finally we will show experimental result and conclusion. Our system architecture is shown in Fig. 1.

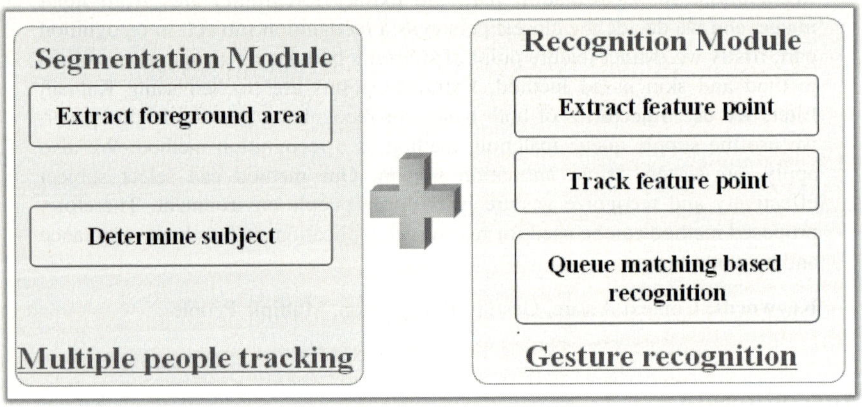

Fig. 1. System architecture (Segmentation module and Recognition module)

2 Context Aware Gesture Definition

In this section we define gesture which is used in our system. Next, we define each individual person's state from input image. Finally we describe state transition model for selecting subject.

2.1 Definition of Gesture

Mankind expresses his mind using eye blink, body movement, or sound. Specifically both hands' movement is used for expressing gesture. So gesture can be analyzed by using movement of both hands. We can not define all gestures used by people. Therefore, we define five gestures for human-robot interaction as shown in Fig. 2. Each gesture meaningfully separated into each other.

Fig. 2. Definition of Gestures (come here, stops, shake hands, heart, bye bye)

2.2 Definition of State

"Context" is consisting of many situations such as illumination, number of people, temperature, noise and so on. In this paper, we define the "context" as intention state between human and computer. We selected speed and distance as intention of behaviors. According to these factors, state will be decided as shown in Table 1. The speed decides [Walking] or [Running] and the distance of behavior is most important factor since it decides to apply gesture recognition algorithm.

Each person has an only one state per every frame. Each state change using state transition model as shown Fig. 3. We assume that there are 3~4 people in input image. If one person going closer, we decide the person as a subject. If a subject decided, we extract feature point from subject's area. In next section, we describe how to extract feature point and how to recognize gesture.

Table 1. Definition of states

State	Definition
Null	Person is not exist.
Object	Person is detected.
Walking	Person is detected, and he/she is walking.
Running	Person is detected, and he/she is running.
Recognition Enabled	Person is detected, and he/she is closer or doing specific gesture.

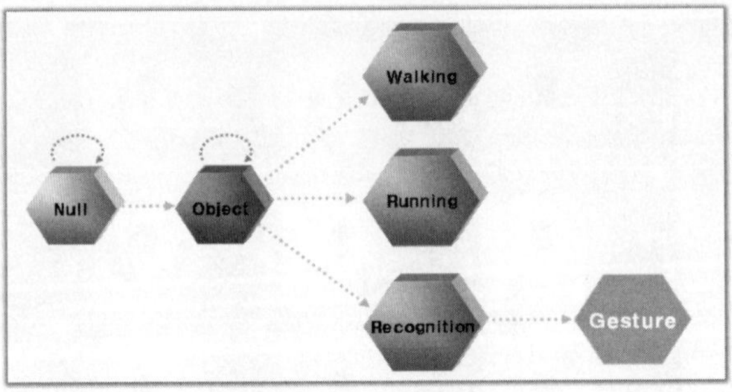

Fig. 3. State transition model of our system

3 Feature Extraction Method

In this paper, we extract area of both hands and head. Segmentation process use Gaussian mixture model in improved HLS space [11]. We use two methods for extracting feature area. First method is contour based method. Second method is skin based method. In this section, we describe these methods and tracking method.

3.1 Contour Based Method

In segmentation process, we extract subject's silhouette from input image. We must eliminate noise since silhouette image has a many noise. To remove this noise we apply dilation operation as shown equation 1. Contour line data is easily extracted from binary image data. We use OpenCV library for extracting contour. It retrieves contours from the binary image and returns the number of retrieved contours. We can get contour line to connect retrieved contour points. Contours can be also used for shape analysis and object recognition.

$$A \oplus B = \{z \mid [(\hat{B})_z \cap A] \subseteq A\} \tag{1}$$

Fig. 4. Contour based method (input image, segmentation result, feature point result, wrong extracting feature point)

After extracting contour, we extract feature point for using contour based method. First we define three points of body (Left Hand-LH, Right Hand-RH, and Head Point-HP). [LH] point is the lowest X coordinate of contour result. [RH] point is the highest

X coordinate of contour result. [HP] point is the lowest Y between [LH] and [RH]. Extracted points will use for recognizing gesture.

This method has an advantage that calculation cost is simple. But these extract wrong points since both hands are occluded in body area as shown in Fig. 4. To solve this problem we must estimate points when position of both hands is change quickly.

3.2 Skin Based Method

Skin is an important factor for extracting both hands and head. There are many methods how to extract skin from image. In this paper we use to extract skin from YCBCR image. First of all, we apply mask in segmentation silhouette image and then we can get only subject area. And then we convert masked RGB image into YCbCr image. If we apply defined threshold in YCbCr image, we can get skin result image as shown Fig. 5.

Fig. 5. Skin based method (input image, segmentation result, masked segmentation image, extracted skin result image)

For recognizing gesture we must decide both hands position from skin result image. Both hands position can get x-y coordinate from x-y projection. Intersection of x projection and y projection is position of both hands and head. Our result can show in Fig. 6.

Skin based method has lower calculation cost than contour based method. Also this method can detect both hands points when both hand s occluded. But this method arise problem when illumination change. Also this must apply another skin threshold for different human race.

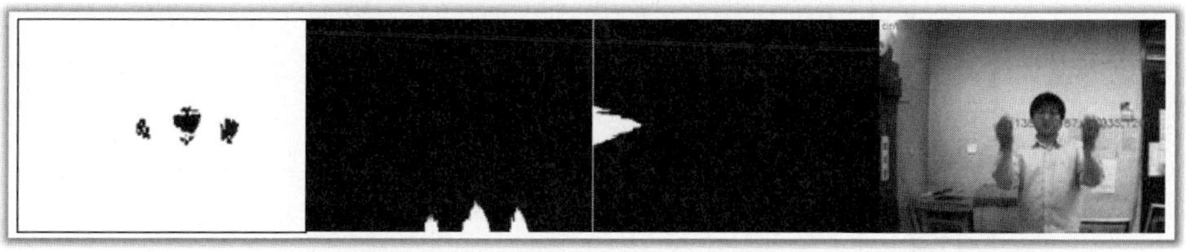

Fig. 6. Extracted skin result image, x projection image. y projection image, feature point

3.3 Feature Tracking Using Kalman Filter

In this paper, we use a Kalman filter for tracking both hands. The Kalman filter is a set of mathematical equations that provides an efficient computational (recursive)

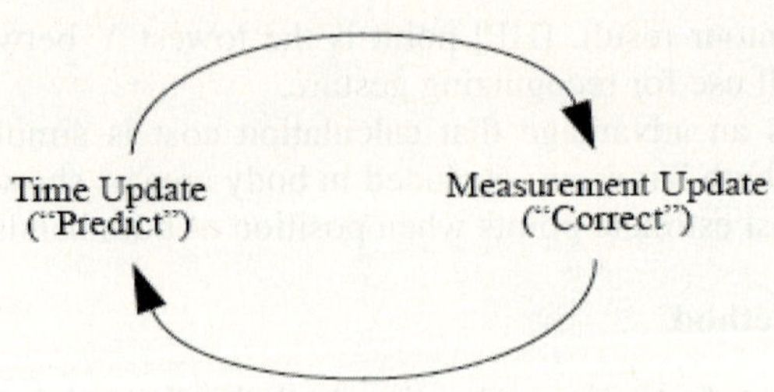

Fig. 7. Kalman filter algorithm architect

solution of the least-squares method. The filter is very powerful in several aspects: it supports estimations of past, present, and even future states, and it can do so even when the precise nature of the modeled system is unknown.

The Kalman filter estimates a process by using a form of feedback control: the filter estimates the process state at some time and then obtains feedback in the form of (noisy) measurements. As such, the equations for the Kalman filter fall into two groups: time update equations and measurement update equations. The time update equations can also be thought of as predictor equations, while the measurement update equations can be thought of as corrector equations. Indeed the final estimation algorithm resembles that of a predictor-corrector algorithm for solving numerical problems as shown below in Fig. 7.

4 Gesture Recognition Using Queue Matching

The gesture contains user's intentions in motions of whole body. Especially, trajectories of hands include more intentions. So, we adopt the different recognition

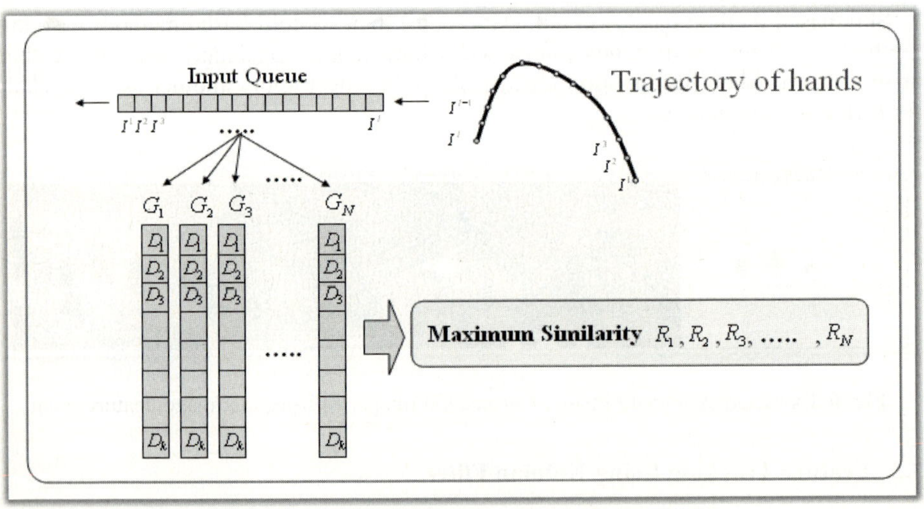

Fig. 8. Queue matching method for recognizing gesture

method which uses trajectories of hands as features. Many researchers have tried to develop the matching algorithm for the trajectories in a number of ways. Generally, the methods are used for recognition of handwritten character. But, it is not effective to apply into the gesture recognition, because it is difficult to decide the start and end point of meaningful gestures. Therefore, many researchers are continuing to study about the problems, Gesture Spotting [9].

In this paper, we propose the simple queue matching method instead of gesture spotting algorithm if the gestures are not complicated. And this method has the advantage in fast to process and easy to implement.

The basic concept of this algorithm is as follows. Assume that the model set M has N models. Also, direction vectors represent the trajectories of hands, and these vectors are stored continuously in each gesture models.

We can get directional vectors from each frame. And, input queue with the length I is a set of these vectors. If the meaningful gesture of subject is in the input queue, it can be assumed that this queue includes the subject's intention. And then, input queue is compared with each model gesture. Finally, we can decide the gesture, as a recognition result. In next section we introduce our system as an application.

5 Application: Animation System

In this paper we use our system as an animation generation system. From input image we construct 3D body model in virtual space. 3D body model has a similar appearance with subject. Also this model has a similar action with subject's action.

To construct animation system, we use feature point from gesture recognition system. These points used for estimating human body point. Extracted feature points have many noises from general environment. We use NURB algorithm for eliminating noise. And we estimate each body joint position using Inverse Kinematics. To estimate correctly, we use information such as human anatomy, previous frame information and collision process. Finally, we estimate body point using extracted feature point and end-effector.

To represent 3D model, first we construct 3D virtual space in animation system. Gesture recognition system send to animation system feature point information. We can get animation system similar doing input gesture.

Fig. 9. Implemented animation system

6 Future Work

The experiment was taken on 2 PCs with 3.0 GHz Intel Pentium 4 CPU and 512MB RAM. We used Bumblebee of Point Grey for extracting stereo information. The system is written in Visual C++ 6.0 based on OpenCV 1.0. Fig. 6 shows results of extracted feature points and gesture recognition result.

Contour based method has a problem when both hands are occluded in body area. For example, both hands position go wrong when [heart] and [bye bye]. Skin based method extract good position in every gesture. It is shown robust result when both hands are occluded in body area. But skin is failed when illumination change.

We have a problem since we use only 2 dimensional data for recognizing gesture. For example, we can not recognize both hands upward and both hands upward in round fashion. This can recognize gestures if we use 3 dimensional data instead of 2 dimensional data. And our system can not make trajectory information when subject doing [shake hands gesture] and subject doing [bye bye gesture]. To solve this problem, we must use time information and movement information of specific area. If we use a convex hull algorithm for extracting feature point, we can have a simple calculation cost and accurate feature points.

Fig. 10. Contour based gesture recognition result(come here, stop, shake hands, heart, bye bye)

Fig. 11. Skin based gesture recognition result(come here, stop, shake hands, heart, bye bye)

Also we have a problem when subject is changed. Subjects have a little different trajectory information of gesture. To solve this problem, we assign a personal ID. Our system recognizes a personal ID, and it uses a model gesture of ID as a model gesture.

In this paper, we proposed gesture recognition in multiple people environment. Our system is divided into two modules – segmentation module and gesture recognition module. Also our system can change subject if subject entered. And then our system tracked feature points using Kalman filter. Finally, our system can recognize gesture using simple queue matching.

In this paper, we propose animation system using implemented gesture system. This system can make 3D information of human. We can get automated animation in future.

Our method can use general interface of robot. If it solve previous problem, intelligent robot can communicate with mankind naturally.

Acknowledgments. This research has been supported in part by MIC & IITA through IT Leading R&D Support Project and Culture Technology Research Institute through MCT, Chonnam National University, Korea.

References

1. Zhao, T., Nevatia, R.: Tracking Multiple Humans in Crowded Environment. In: Proceedings of CVPR 2004, pp. 1063–6919 (2004)
2. Wu, B., Nevatia, R.: Detection of Multiple, Partially Occluded Humans in a Single Image by Bayesian Combination of Edgelet Part Detectors. In: Proceedings of ICCV 2005, vol. 1, pp. 90–97 (2005)
3. Haritaoglu, I., Harwood, D., Davis, L.S.: W4: Real-Time Surveillance of People and Their Activities. IEEE Transactions on Pattern Analysis and Machine Intelligence 22(8), 809–830 (2000)
4. Siebel, N.T, Maybank, S.: Fusion of Multiple Tracking Algorithms for Robust People Tracking. In: Heyden, A., Sparr, G., Nielsen, M., Johansen, P. (eds.) ECCV 2002. LNCS, vol. 2353, pp. 373–387. Springer, Heidelberg (2002)
5. Franc, J.B., Fleuret, o., Fua, P.: Robust People Tracking with Global Trajectory Optimization. In: Proceedings of CVPR 2006, vol 1, pp. 744–750 (2006)
6. Nguyen, H.T., Ji, Q., Smeulders, A.W.M.: Robust multi-target tracking using spatio-temporal context. In: Proceedings of CVPR 2006, vol. 1, pp. 578–585 (2006)
7. Han, J., Award, G.M., Sutherland, A., Wu, H.: Automatic Skin Segmentation for Gesture Recognition Combining Region and Support Vector Machine Active Learning, In: Proceedings of FGR 2006, pp. 237–242 (2006)
8. Li, H., Greenspan, M.: Multi-scale Gesture Recognition from Time-Varying Contours. In: Proceedings of ICCV 2005, vol 1, pp. 236–24 (2005)
9. Lee, S-W.: Automatic Gesture Recognition for Intelligent Human-Robot Interaction. In: Proceedings of FGR 2006, pp. 645–650 (2006)
10. Setiawan, N.A., Hong, S-j., Lee, C-w.: Gaussian Mixture Model in Improved HLS Color Space for Human Silhouette Extraction. In: Proceedings of ICAT 2006, pp. 732–741 (2006)
11. http://www.sourceforge.net/projects/opencvlibrary

Position and Pose Computation of a Moving Camera Using Geometric Edge Matching for Visual SLAM

HyoJong Jang[1], GyeYoung Kim[1], and HyungIl Choi[2]

[1] School of Computing, Soongsil University, Korea
{ozjhj114,gykim11}@ssu.ac.kr
[2] School of Media, Soongsil University, Korea
hic@ssu.ac.kr

Abstract. A prerequisite component of a autonomous mobile vehicle system is the self localization ability to recognize its environment and to estimate where it is. Generally, we can determine the position and the pose using homography approach, but it has errors especially in simultaneous change of position and pose. In this paper, we proposed position and pose computation method of a camera through analysis of images obtained from camera equipped mobile robot. Proposed method is made up of two steps. First step is to extract feature points and matching in sequential images. Second step is to compute the accurate camera position and pose using geometric edge matching. In first step, we use KLT tracking to extract feature points and matching in sequential images. In second step, we propose an iterative matching method between predicted edge models through perspective transform using the result calculated by homography of the matched feature points and generated edge models in correspond points till there is no variation in matching error. For the purpose of the performance evaluation, we performed the test to compensate the position and the pose of the camera installed in wireless-controlled vehicle with the video sequence stream obtained at 15Hz frame rate and show the experimental results.

Keywords: vSLAM, Perspective Transformation, KLT tracking, Geometric Edge Matching.

1 Introduction

Location information provides the most important clue for recognition of the situation which a robot or automatic guided vehicle is faced with, or the job that the user wants to do. The feature expression method is sometimes given in a very simple form such as points or lines or a more complex pattern or 3D environment model at other view points or times[1][2]. These vision-based techniques enable more accurate localization by linking with dead reckoning for error correction of measuring instruments, or with inertial sensor, ultrasound or laser-based sensors through sensor fusion[3].

To solve those problems, this paper proposed the method of computing camera position and pose from the location predicted by perspective transformation and the

J. Jacko (Ed.): Human-Computer Interaction, Part III, HCII 2007, LNCS 4552, pp. 634–641, 2007.

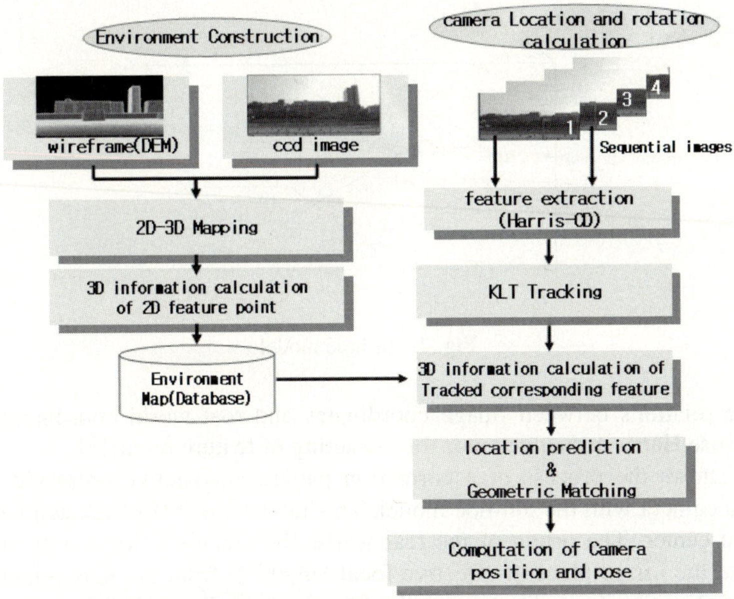

Fig. 1. Proposed System Overview

relations of feature points determined through the KLT (Kanade-Lucas-Tomasi) tracking between sequential images. Fig. 1 shows the schematic diagram of the proposed system.

2 Methodology

2.1 Acquisition of 3D Information for Construction of Environment Map

The initial position and pose of the camera received from GPS include errors. Therefore, to figure out in which location the 2D feature points in the camera's field of view are located in a 3D space, a 3D DEM(Digital Elevation Model) was obtained based on the initial position and pose with consideration given to sensor errors. The used DEM is 3D topographical information which includes the location and elevation information in 1m interval with the experiment area limited to 300m x 300m. To register the acquired DEM with the sensor image, the DEM data were read to create a wireframe with mesh structure consisting of the vertexes of rectangles, which is then moved to top, bottom, left, and right for registration.

After registration using visual clues as described above, the picking method was used, which is a well-known 3D graphic technique to obtain and store the 3D position of each feature point of the sensor image.

2.2 Prediction of Feature Points Using Perspective Transformation

In order to extract the feature points from the images acquired from the CCD camera and recalculate the 3D location of the camera by registering them, we must accurately

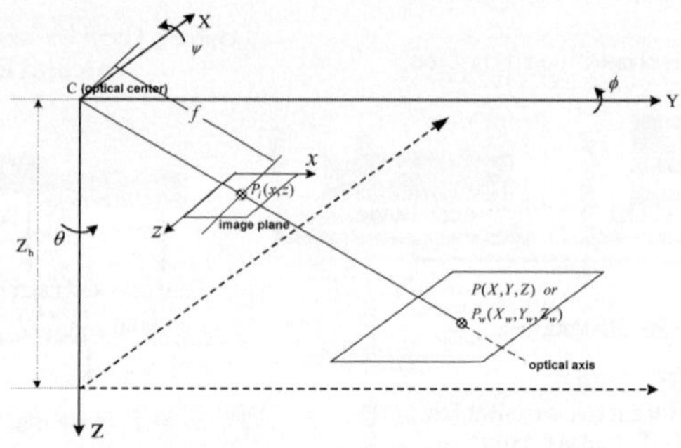

Fig. 2. pin-hole model

define the relations between image coordinates and real world coordinates. In this paper, we use Harris corner detector for extracting of feature points[4].

Fig. 2 shows the process of a correction pattern perspective projected to image plane by a camera with the pin-hoe model. This model consists of image plane and C, the optical center. The origin of the real world coordinates is located at the camera center, and the image plane at effective focal length (f) from the lens center, and the real world object at $Z=Z_h$. The pan angle (θ) represents the angle between the optical axis projected to the plane where Z=0 and the Y axis, while the tilt angle (φ) represents the angle between the optical axis and the Z axis, and the swing angle (ψ) represents the plane where Y=0 and the X axis. To define the transformation relations between the real world coordinates (X, Y, Z) and the image coordinates (x, z), we drew the Z axis for the pan angle θ so that the X-Z plane will be parallel to the x-z plane, and rotate the Y axis by the tilt angle φ to obtain the coordinates (X', Y', Z'). Now, the relations between the position in the (X, Y, Z) coordinates and the (X', Y', Z') coordinates of a point in a 3D space can be defined by the following expression[5].

$$\begin{bmatrix} X' \\ Y' \\ Z' \end{bmatrix} = R \cdot \begin{bmatrix} X \\ Y \\ Z \end{bmatrix} = \begin{bmatrix} \cos\theta & \sin\theta & 0 \\ -\cos\varphi\sin\theta & \cos\varphi\sin\theta & \sin\varphi \\ \sin\varphi\sin\theta & -\sin\varphi\cos\theta & \cos\varphi \end{bmatrix} \begin{bmatrix} X \\ Y \\ Z \end{bmatrix} \tag{1}$$

Now, we will consider the transformation relations between the (X', Y', Z') coordinates with both pan and tilt angles at 0 and the image coordinates (x, z). The following expression can be inferred from the perspective transformation based on the pin-hole model.

$$\begin{aligned} x &= f\frac{X'}{Y'} = f\frac{X\cos\theta + Y\sin\theta}{-X\cos\phi\sin\theta + Y\cos\cos\theta + Z\sin\phi} \\ y &= f\frac{Z'}{Y'} = f\frac{X\sin\phi\sin\theta - Y\sin\phi\cos\theta + Z\cos\phi}{-X\cos\phi\sin\theta + Y\cos\phi\cos\theta + Z\sin\phi} \end{aligned} \tag{2}$$

The above expression shows the transformation relations between the (X, Y, Z) coordinates and the (x, z) coordinates without consideration of swing angle. Now, in consideration of the swing angle ψ between the image coordinates (x, z) and the real world coordinates (X, Y, Z), a point in the (X, Y, Z) space is projected to the image coordinates in accordance with the following expression:

$$\begin{bmatrix} x' \\ z' \end{bmatrix} = \begin{bmatrix} \cos\psi & \sin\psi \\ -\sin\psi & \cos\psi \end{bmatrix} \begin{bmatrix} x \\ z \end{bmatrix} \tag{3}$$

2.3 Feature Point Tracking Using KLT Method

We can predict the location of feature points after movement if we extract feature points from CCD images, and then apply the changes of camera position and pose input from homography method and the perspective transformation described above. If homography method has no error, the predicted location must be identical to the feature point moved from the original image. However, as homography has errors especially in simultaneous change of position and pose, the errors accumulate over time, resulting in great differences from the actual values[6]. Therefore, this study tracked the predicted location of the feature point and the actual changing position of the feature point to correct the errors of homography method through the correlations between two geometric edge models. To track the location of the feature point moving in sequential images, the KLT feature point tracking method based on the Newton Rapson method proposed by Tomasi and Kanade was used[7]. The intensity pattern of the images change toward more complex rotation according to the camera movement. In this case, the intensity value of the point (x, y) at time t and time t+τ in the sequential images can be expressed as the following relationship:

$$I(x, y, t+\tau) = I(x-\Delta x, y-\Delta y, t) \tag{4}$$

Here, the displacement between two sequential images can be expressed as (Δx, Δy). Consequently, we can find the location at time t+τ from the location of the point at time t. Expression (5) can be derived from Expression (4), which can be rewritten as Expression (6) which is the well-known KLT tracking equation.

$$\left(\iint_W gg^T \omega A_r\right) = \iint_W [A(v) - B(v)] g\,\omega dA_r \tag{5}$$

$$Zd = e \tag{6}$$

Here, Z is identical to gradient matrix, and e can be obtained from the sum of the differences of intensity values in the w areas of the two windows. Therefore, we can get the final displacement d by solving this equation.

2.4 Camera Position and Pose Computation by Geometric Matching

There must be at least 3 feature points for registration, which is based on the theory that three or more points measured for two coordinate systems are required to get one unique measurement value from the calculation of the relations between two coordinate systems through the measurement of a point indicated in two different coordinate systems.[8] Although it is possible to increase the number of feature points to improve accuracy, real time processing becomes difficult if the number of learning models and calculations increase.

For an accurate calculation of correction value, in this paper, we propose Y-type edge model. It can be reduce the error that reveals in case of calculation of 3 dimensional camera position and pose through 2 dimensional correspondences of feature points.

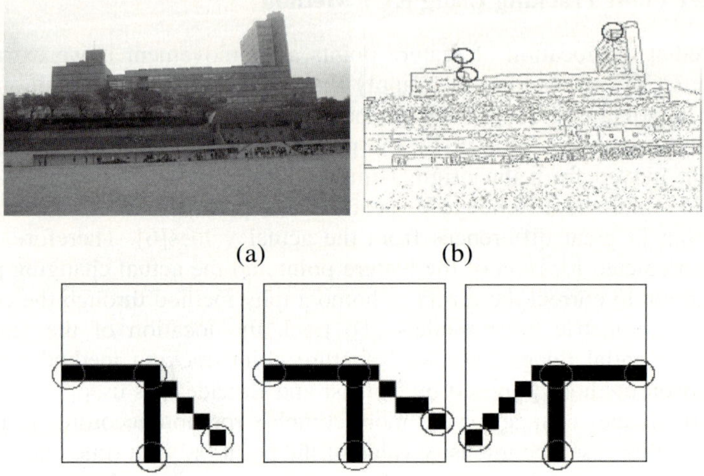

(c)

Fig. 3. Example of Y-type Edge model

Fig. 3 shows the example of Y-type edge model. The edge image (b) is obtained by using LoG operator. (c) is examples of Y-type edge model from (b) and they can be constructed as follows: first of all, If the center corner point of Y-type edge model at t time, intersection points obtained from the boundary of 11×11 window region at the center. Therefore, usually Y-type edge model is made up of three intersection points and a center point. If the locations of feature points in Y-type edge models are predicted through perspective transformation, and the feature points are tracked from sequential images, the position and pose of the camera that minimizes the sum of the differences of distance between Y-type edge models of two frames are recalculated by Expression (7).

$$\underset{\Delta X,\Delta Y,\Delta Z,\Delta\theta,\Delta\varphi,\Delta\psi\pm\alpha}{\arg\min}\left(\sum_{i=1}^{n}\sqrt{(YEdge_{t+1}^{i}-YEdge_{p}^{i})^{2}}\right) \tag{7}$$

Here, $YEdge_{t+1}^{i}$ is the Y-type edge model of ith correspondence point at time t+1, and $YEdge_{p}^{i}$ is the predicted Y-type edge model of ith correspondence point at time t. Accordingly, we can determine the position (X, Y, Z) and pose (θ, ϕ, ψ) of the camera in such a manner that the sum of the displacements between the tracked and predicted

Y-type edge model by Expression (7). And, in Expression (7), $YEdge^{i}_{t+1} - YEdge^{i}_{p}$ is defined by Expression (8).

$$
\begin{aligned}
&YEdge^{i}_{t+1} - YEdge^{i}_{p} = \\
&\alpha \sum_{k=1}^{3} \sqrt{(\underline{\nabla}(Corner^{i}_{t+1}, Y^{k_{component}}_{t+1}) - \underline{\nabla}(Corner^{i}_{p}, Y^{k_{component}}_{p}))^{2}} \\
&\beta \sum_{k=1}^{3} \sqrt{(dist(Corner^{i}_{t+1}, Y^{k_{component}}_{t+1}) - dist(Corner^{i}_{p}, Y^{k_{component}}_{p}))^{2}}
\end{aligned}
\tag{8}
$$

Here, we defined α is 0.6 and β is 0.4 in this paper. And, Expression (8) shows in Fig.4

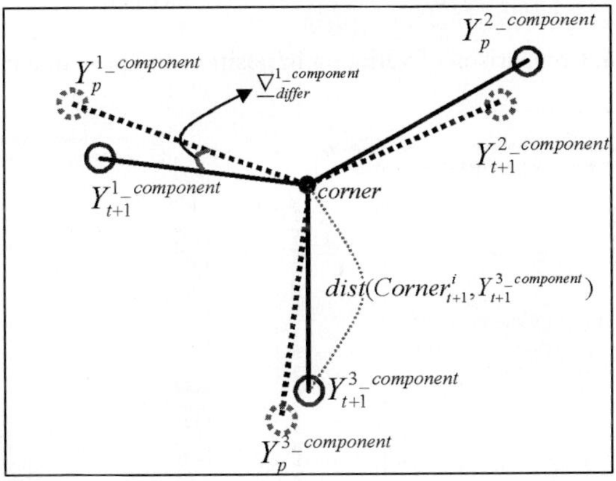

Fig. 4. Matching example of Y-type edge model

(a) Frame #1 (b)Frame #75 (c)Frame #150

Fig. 5. Result of extracted corner point

Fig. 5 shows the corner points extracted from frames #1, #75, and #150 among the image frames input in real time. For discrimination of corner points, Harris corner response value was used and stored in the list.

The graphs (a), (b) in Fig. 6 show how close to the actual values with the recalculated values using proposed method than the homography method.

Graph (a), (b) in Fig.6 compares the recalculated values by using proposed method with the values calculated homography method and actual values. And graph (a), (b) in Fig.7 show the cumulative errors of the position and pose. As shown in these

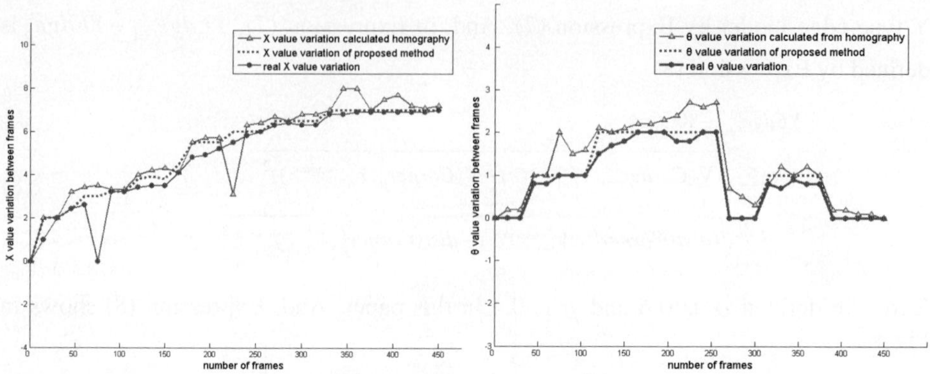

(a) (b)

Fig. 6. Comparison of variation in position and pose of a camera

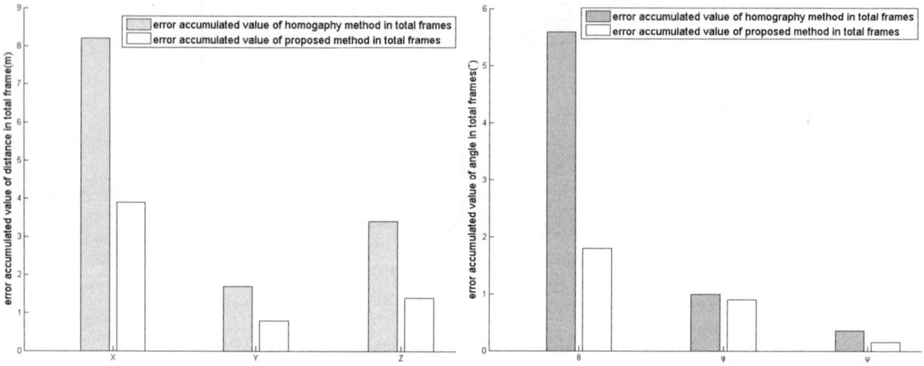

(a) (b)

Fig. 7. Comparison of accumulative errors in total frames

graphs, homography method errors accumulated over time and caused large differences at last. The position error was less than 1m at first, but accumulated and increased up to 12m after a certain time, while the cumulative pose error was about 9 degrees at the maximum. The proposed error correction method decreased these cumulative errors from 12m to 4m for position and 9 to 1.8 degrees for pose. And finally, according to Fig.6 and Fig.7, we can see that proposed method outperformed homography method.

4 Conclusions and Suggestions for Future Studies

This study proposed a computation method for the position and pose of camera installed in a wireless-controlled experimental vehicle using the vision-based registration using perspective transformation and KLT tracking without ground reference points, and evaluated its performance through experiment. The proposed method corrects the camera position and pose from the relation between the Y-type edge models predicted by perspective transformation using the location and pose changes calculated homography method and the Y-type edge models tracked by the KLT tracking method from sequential images.

In the experiment, when the input sequential images moved or rotated over a certain degree, the proposed could not track the feature points. Therefore, in the future, we need to study on the algorithm for determining the searching range of feature points in a variable manner according to environmental changes and also on the feature point searching method that is more robust against pose. Furthermore, the used feature points were sensitive to illumination and not robust against illumination changes that occur suddenly between sequential frames. To complement this shortcoming, we need to consider using color space that is more robust against illumination changes.

Acknowledgements. This work was supported by the Korea Research Foundation (KRF-2006-005-J03801).

References

1. Talluri, R., Aggarwal, J.K.: Image/map correspondence for mobile robot self-location using computer graphics. IEEE Trans. Patt. Anal. Mach. Intel. 15(6), 597–601 (1993)
2. Colis, C.I., Trahanias, P.E.: A framework for visual landmark identification based on projective and point-permutation invariant vectors. Robotics and Autonomous Systems 35, 37–51 (2001)
3. Cramer, S.M., Haala, D.: Direct Georeferencing Using GPS/Inertial Exterior Orientations For Photogrammetric Applications, International Archivers of Photogrammetry and Remote Sensing, Part B3, XXXI, 198–205 (2000)
4. Harris, C., Stephens, M.: A combined corner and edge detector. In: Forth Alvey Vision Conference, Menchester, UK, pp. 147–151 (1988)
5. Haralick, R.M.: Determination camera parameters from the perspective projection of a rectangle. Pattern Recognition 22(3), 225–230 (1989)
6. Prince, S.J.D., Xu, K., Cheok, A.D.: Augmented reality camera tracking with homographies. IEEE Computer Graphics and Application 22(6), 39–45 (2002)
7. Tomasi, C., Kanade, T.: Detection and Tracking of Point Features, Carnegie Mellon University Technical Report CMU-CS-91-132 (April 1991)
8. Horn, B.K.P.: Closed-form solution of absolute orientation using unit quaternions. Journal of the Optical Society of America 4, 629–642 (1987)

“Shooting a Bird”: Game System Using Facial Feature for the Handicapped People

Jinsun Ju, Yunhee Shin, and Eun Yi Kim

Department of Internet and Multimedia Engineering, Konkuk Univ., Korea
{vocaljs,ninharsa,eykim}@konkuk.ac.kr

Abstract. This paper presents a novel computer game system that controls a game using only the movement of human’s facial features. Our system is specially designated for the handicapped people with severe disabilities and the people without experience of using the computer. Using a usual PC camera, the proposed game system detects the user’s eye movement and mouse movement, and then interprets the communication intent to play a game. The game system is tested with 42 numbers of people, and then the result shows that our game system should be efficiently and effectively used as the interface for the disabled people.

Keywords: Augmented game, HCI, Facial feature tracking, neural network.

1 Introduction

Recently, computer games using traditional interface such as a keyboard and a mouse have been replaced by new game paradigm such as body-interaction games. The body-interaction games use human’s gestures to control a game, which makes the players feel more realistic enjoyment and actual feelings. From now on, various interfaces based on human gestures have been developed to provide the natural communication in between players and game systems. Some systems use the hand gestures as the input to control a game and some systems use the full-body motions.

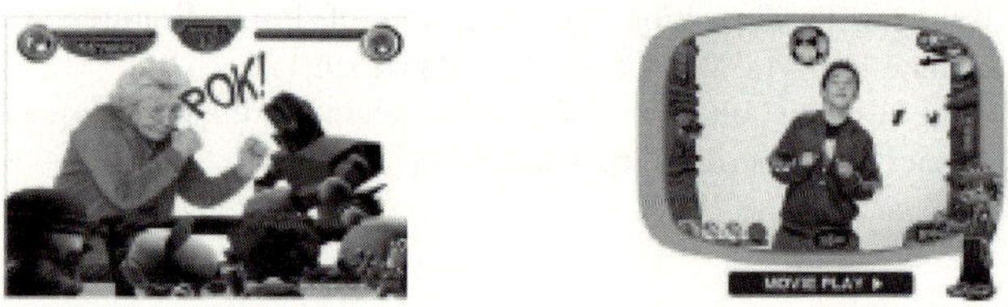

(a) (b)

Fig. 1. (a) and (b) Eyetoy™ game system

Although such systems are well worked on the people without physical disabilities, they can not be applied to the handicapped people. For the handicapped people, the game system with general interface that adaptable to the people with various physical disabilities should be developed.

J. Jacko (Ed.): Human-Computer Interaction, Part III, HCII 2007, LNCS 4552, pp. 642–648, 2007.

Accordingly, this paper presents a novel computer game system that controls a game using only the movement of human's facial features. Our system is specially designated for the handicapped people with severe disabilities and the people without experience of using the computer. Using a usual PC camera, the proposed game system detects the user's eye movement and mouse movement, and then interprets the communication intent to play a game.

The game system is tested with 42 numbers of people, and then the result shows that our game system should be efficiently and effectively used as the interface for the disabled people.

The organization of the paper is as follows. Section 2 gives an overview of our game system. Section 3 describes our game module ("Shooting a bird") Section 4 describes our interface (feature detector, feature tracker, mouse controller). Experimental results are presented in Section 5 and the final conclusions are made in Section 6.

2 Overview the Game System

The outline of the proposed game system is demonstrated in Fig. 2. Fig. 2(a) shows our game system, which consists of a PC camera and a computer. The PC camera, which is connected to the computer through the USB port, supplies 30 color images of size 320×240 per second. The computer is a PentiumIV–3GHz with the Window XP operating system.

Fig.4(b) overviews of our game system. The game is made using FLASH(version MX 2004), and is one of the shooting games where a user hits randomly flying bird with a gun. A player controls the cursor by his (or her) eye movement and fires a gun by opening his mouth. Our game movements of a player are detected and tracked in the interface modular, which will be described in Section 4 in detail.

Our game movements of a player are detected and tracked in the interface modular, which will be described in Section 4 in detail.

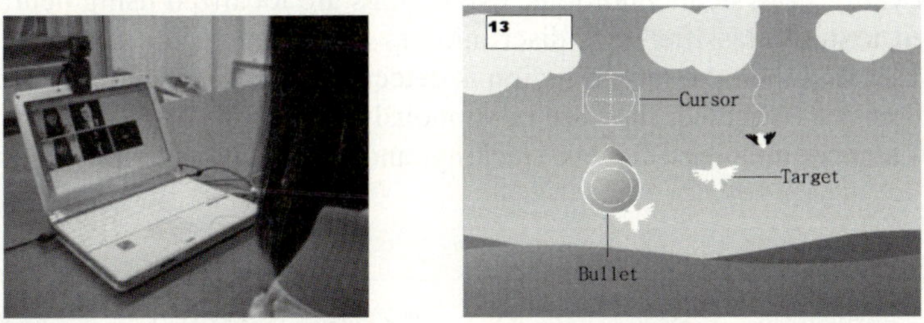

(a) (b)

Fig. 2. "Shooting a bird game" (a) hardware architecture (b) Shot of "shooting a bird"

3 Game Module

Fig.3 shows a shot of our game system. The game is made using FLASH(version MX 2004).The game is one of the shooting games where a user hits randomly flying bord

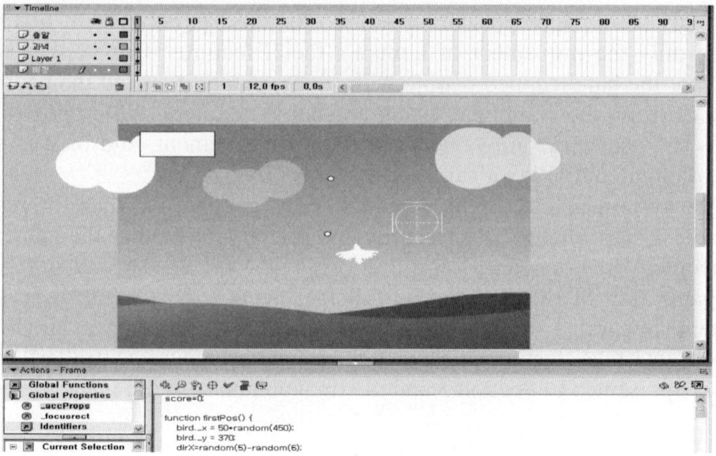

Fig. 3. shot of "shooting a bird"

with a gun. The game consists of three parts. 1) Characters movement. 2) a movement of background. 3) Calculated score. A player controls the cursor by his (of her) eye movement and fires a gun by opening his mouth. These movements of a player are detected and tracked in the interface modular.

4 Interface Module

Fig.4 demonstrates the interface module, which consists of facial feature detector, facial feature tracker and mouse controller. The facial feature detector firstly extracts user's face from the background using skin-color model, and then localizes user's eyes and mouth from the face region. To be robust to the complex background and users with various physical conditions, eye regions are localized using neural network (NN)-based texture classifier that discriminates the facial region into eye class and non-eye class, and then the mouth region is detected based on edge information. Once these features are extracted, they are continuously tracked by facial feature tracker: a mean-shift algorithm is used for eye tracking, and a template matching is used for the

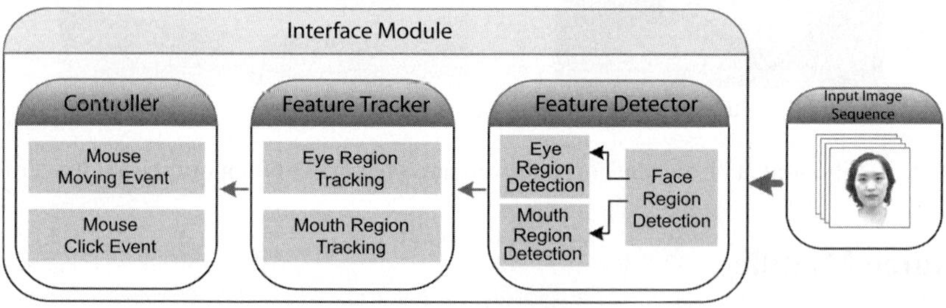

Fig. 4. The interface to use eye and mouse movement

mouth tracking. Based on the tracking results, mouse operations such as movement or click are implemented in a mouse controller. Our system moves the cursor to the point at which the user gazed on the display, and then fires the gun to that point if he opens and closes his mouth.

4.1 Facial Feature Detector

In facial feature detector, given an image sequence, the regions of the face and facial features are detected automatically. The facial region is first obtained using skin-color and then, the eye regions are localized by a neural network (NN)-based texture classifier that discriminates each pixel in the extracted facial regions into the eye-class and non-class using the texture property. And then mouth is localized by edges information within the search region estimated using several heuristic rules based on eye position. The detection results are delivered to feature tracker.

4.2 Facial Features Tracker

In facial feature tracker, it tracks eyes and mouth. Once the eye and mouth regions are localized in feature detector, they are continuously and correctly tracking by mean-shift algorithm and template matching, respectively.

Fig. 5 shows the results of the facial features tracking, where the facial features are drawn out white for the better viewing. As can be seen in Fig. 5 the facial features are accurately tracking. The extracted facial features have been drawn white for better viewing. The features are tracked throughout the 100 frames and not lost once.

Fig. 5. Tracking result of facial features

4.3 Mouse Control Module

The computer translates the user's eye movements into the mouse movements by processing the images received from the PC camera. Then the processing of a video sequence is performed by the proposed facial features tracking system. The system determines the center of eyes in the first frame as the initial coordinates of mouse, and then computes it automatically in subsequent frames. The coordinates of mouth region and eye regions in each frame are sent to the operating system through Window functions. Mouse point is moved according to eye movement.

5 Experimental Results

We use these facial features tracking method as an interface to control the game system. Twenty handicapped peoples tested our system. Fig.6 shows the snapshot to play a game. A player was playing our game using his (or her) facial features. Fig.8 is a player controls the cursor by his (or her) eye movement and fires a gun by opening his mouth. These movements of a player are detected and tracked in the interface modular. Based on the results, it does the mouse operations such as movement or click.

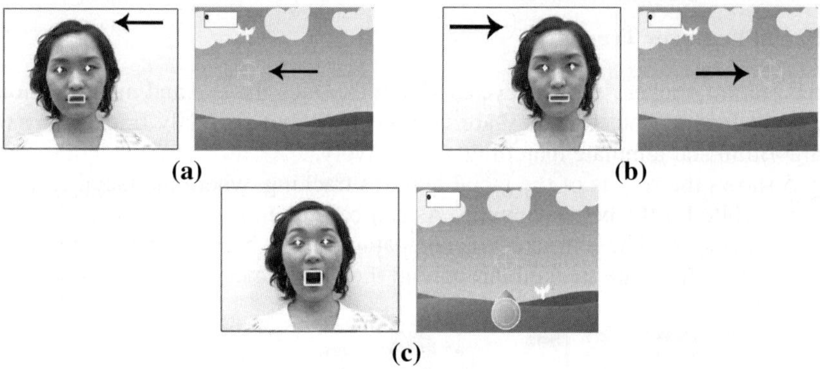

Fig. 6. The interface using our game system

Table 1. "Shooting a bird" Game test result (s)

	The people Non-disabled users		The People Disabled users	
	Mean	Deviation	Mean	Deviation
Shooting a bird game	95.25	14.02	188.94	76.56
Standard Mouse	48.6	3.14	-	-

Table 1 presents the averages times to be taken to shooting 10-birds in the "shooting a bird" game. To show the effectiveness of the game system, it was applied to the disabled users. As the disabled users cannot move their hands, they tested with only our interface system. There are two interesting points in this table. In case of non-disabled users, the average time taken to play the game with the standard mouse was the faster than the proposed interface. Then, the first noticeable point is that the deviation of our interface is larger than one of standard mouse. This difference is resulted in the fact that they are accustomed to standard mouse but they are poor to using our interface. Consequently, that result tells us that the computational time can be reduced if they would practice using our game system. The second interesting point is that the deviation in the disabled users is larger than one of the non-disabled users when playing the game with our interface system. This difference was the same reason as with the first case. Most of the non-disabled users are accustomed to playing a computer game, while a small number of disabled users have experienced the computer game. That is, the time to play a game could be rapidly reduced if the disabled users would have the sufficient practice.

Moreover, to assess the validity of the proposed system for disabled users, it was applied to the "spelling board."

Table 2. Spelling board result (*s*)

	Group 1		Group 2	
	Mean	Deviation	Mean	Deviatio n
Eye Mouse[]	30.6	4.76	63.94	32.11
Proposed method	16.95	4.19	37.12	18.40
Standard Mouse	8.4	0.44	×	×

In this experiment, the clicking event was mainly involved, like the "Shooting a bird" game system. The timing results for the experiments are summarized in table 2.

The two experiment results show that our systems are effectively used for the disabled users.

Consequently, the experiment with proposed interface showed that it has a potential to be used as generalized user interface in many applications.

6 Conclusions

In this paper, we implemented the game system for the handicapped people using multiple facial features detection and tracking as PC-based HCI system. The proposed game system has worked very well in a test database and cluttered environments with 42-people. Then it is accurately detected and tracked to facial features regardless of disabilities or not and also is robust to the time-varying illumination and less sensitive to the specula reflection of eyeglasses.

In experiment is compared the proposed method with standard mouse respectively. The experimental results show that our system should be efficiently and effectively used as the interface for the disabled people. Also our system has a potential to be used as generalized user interface in many application.

Acknowledgments

This work was supported by Seoul R&BD Program in Korea.

References

1. Sharma, R., Pavlovic, V.I., Huang, T.S.: Toward multimodal human-computer interface. Proceedings of the IEEE 86, 853–869 (1998)
2. Scassellati, B.: Eye finding via face detection for a foveated, active vision system. American Association for Artificial Intelligence (1998)
3. Hornof, A., Cavender, A., Hoselton, R.: EyeDraw: A System for Drawing Pictures with Eye Movements. ACM SIGACCESS Accessibility and Computing, Issue 77-78 (2003)
4. Kim, E.Y., Kang, S.K. (eds.): ICCSA 2006. LNCS, vol. 3982, pp. 1200–1209. Springer, Heidelberg (2006)
5. Lyons, M.L.J.: Facial Gesture Interfaces for Expression and Communication. In: IEEE International Conference on Systems, Man, Cybernetics, vol. 1, pp. 598–603 (2004)
6. Jie, Y., DaQuan, Y., WeiNa, W., XiaoXia, X., Hui, W.: Real-time detecting system of the driver's fatigue. In: ICCE International Conference on Consumer Electronics, 2006 Digest of Technical Papers. pp. 233–234 (2006)
7. Schiele, B., Waibel, A.: Gaze Tracking Based on Face-Color. School of Computer Science. Carnegie Mello University (1995)
8. Chan, a.d.c., Englehart, K., Hudgins, B., Lovely, D.F.: Hidden markov model classification of myoeletric signals in speech. IEEE Engineering in Medicine and Biology Magazine 21(4), 143–146 (2002)
9. Comaniciu, D., Ramesh, V., Meer, P.: Kernel-Based Object Tracking. IEEE Trans. Pattern Analysis and Machine Intelligence 25(5), 564–577 (2003)
10. Olson, C.F.: Maximum-Likelihood Template Matching. In: Proc. IEEE Conf. Computer Vision and Pattern Recognition, vol. 2, pp. 52–57 (2000)
11. Shin, Y., Kim, E.Y.: Welfare Interface Using Multiple Facial Feature Tracking. In: Sattar, A., Kang, B.-H. (eds.) AI 2006. LNCS (LNAI), vol. 4304, pp. 453–462. Springer, Heidelberg (2006)

Human Pose Estimation Using a Mixture of Gaussians Based Image Modeling

Do Joon Jung, Kyung Su Kwon, and Hang Joon Kim

Department of Computer Engineering, Kyungpook National University
702-701, 1370, Sangyuk-dong, Buk-gu, Daegu, Korea
{djjung,kskwon,hjkim}@ailab.knu.ac.kr
http://ailab.knu.ac.kr

Abstract. In this paper, we propose an approach toward body parts representation, localization, and human pose estimation from an image. In the image, the human body parts and a background are represented by a mixture of Gaussians, and the body parts configuration is modeled by a Bayesian network. In this model, state nodes represent pose parameters of an each body part, and arcs represent spatial constraints. The Gaussian mixture distribution is used to model the prior distribution for the body parts and the background as a parametric model. We estimate the human pose through an optimization of the pose parameters using likelihood objective functions. The performance of the proposed approach is illustrated on various single images, and improves the human pose estimation quality.

Keywords: Human Pose Estimation, Mixture of Gaussians, Bayesian Network.

1 Introduction

Human pose estimation of an image is one of the critical tasks in many computer vision applications such as surveillance, perceptual user interfaces, augmented reality, and smart rooms. In the last decade, there has been a great deal of interest in methods for human pose estimation and analysis of human body motion in the research field such as robot imitation, gesture recognition, sign language recognition, and activity recognition etc.[1][2][3][4]. Human pose estimation is challenging task due to the ambiguity caused by body articulation, loose clothing, and self-occlusion between body parts. In general, human body part representation and localization are key steps toward human pose estimation, and articulated human can be represented as assemblies of rigid body parts.

There have been a significant number of methods for human pose estimation. We can classify those methods into two main approaches. The top-down approach makes samples in a high dimensional space and fully models self-occlusion [5][6]. It does not incorporate bottom-up part identification, and is inappropriate without a strong pose prior. The bottom-up approach identifies the body parts, and then assembles them into the best configuration [7][8][9][10]. Recently, Roberts et al. [9] introduced a human pose estimation method using partial configurations and probabilistic regions. In the method, a part-based description of human pose from single images of

J. Jacko (Ed.): Human-Computer Interaction, Part III, HCII 2007, LNCS 4552, pp. 649 – 658, 2007.

people is described. It is able to perform estimation efficiently in the presence significant background clutter, large foreground variation, and self-occlusion.

In this paper, we also focus on body part representation, localization and human pose estimation in a bottom-up approach. The body part and background are modeled through mixture of Gaussians, and human pose is estimated using optimization from likelihood objective function. We estimate the 2-D human pose within a probabilistic framework, and formulate the human pose estimation to optimization problem. This approach can achieve reliable performance when the distribution of colors within the human body parts follows the assumed model or distribution.

In this paper, we are only interested in a human upper body configuration. The body configuration is modeled by a Bayesian network where the nodes denote body part and the arcs encode constraints among them.

2 Human Pose Estimation

In this section, the method used to estimate human pose in an image is introduced. Our goal is to find an optimal body joints that best describes the status of a human pose based on color images. We assume the human pose estimation problem within a probabilistic framework, and the task is to optimize pose parameters from image observations.

2.1 Image Modeling

We consider that an image consists of two parts: human body part and a background part. The body parts and background become accomplished with the clusters. In the clusters of 2D points, there are 2D spatial means and covariance matrices. In our work, the body parts and a background spatial statistics are described from point of their second-order properties, for computational convenience we it will be able to interpret this in a Gaussian model [11]. Therefore, each body parts and a background are represented by a Gaussian distribution, and all the parts in the image are represented by a Gaussian mixture model. We focus here on the color feature and spatial information. Each body parts and a background have a spatial (x, y) and color (R, G, B) element. The color is expressed from inside RGB color space. The spatial and color distributions are assumed to be independent. Therefore, each pixel is represented by a five-dimensional feature vector. We utilize both color and spatial information in a Gaussian representation of the human body for pose estimation. For human pose estimation, we use a person model which consists of six body parts. We consider just a human upper body configuration in the person model. Because we interest in upper body human poses like Figure 1 (a). The body parts are head, torso, two upper arms and two lower arms. In the image plane, we assume the human body parts as a set of ellipsoids like Figure 1 (b). Each ellipsoid represents a support of Gaussian particulars, mean color and spatial layout. For representation of human, representation of body parts with their relationship are used widely and also us it uses. Because pose estimation method using a representation of whole body human pose hard to work with condition of the different light and the human pose.

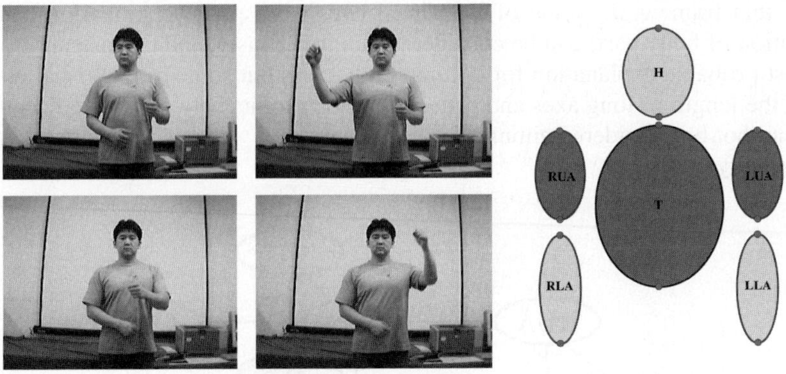

(a) (b)

Fig. 1. Color images with a human model: (a) sample color images, (b) a human model (Red circle points represent the link point of body parts. The link points are two maximum distance points from the center).

According to variation of the spatial layout of body parts in the image plane, the likelihood of body parts are changed. We will find the best spatial layout of body part through maximum likelihood.

2.2 Human Modeling Based on Bayesian Network

A Bayesian network or Bayesian belief network is, a form of probabilistic graphical model, directed acyclic graph of nodes representing variables and arcs representing dependences relations among the variables [12]. Bayesian networks provide a rigorous framework for combining semantic and sensor-level reasoning under conditions of uncertainty [13][14]. In this paper, a human body configuration is modeled by a Bayesian network as shown in Figure 2. Each random variable X_i represents the pose parameter of body part *i*. We model the spatial relationships between the body parts using a Bayesian network. These spatial relationships are known a priori, and used to create the network architecture. In Figure 2, the circles represent network nodes, and the directed arcs of circles indicate statistical dependencies between nodes. In the network, empty circles encode observation of variables, and filled-in circles encode estimation of variables, $P(X|e)$. Abbreviations are: H = head, T = torso, RUA = right upper arm, LUA = left upper arm, RLA = right lower arm, LLA = left lower arm. There are 6 variables in the each node denoted by empty circles as follows, X = { X_1, …, X_6 }. These variables are discrete or have been transformed to discrete variables.

X_1 : 2D center position of body part.
X_2 : an aspect ratio of body part.
X_3 : a length of long axis.
X_4 : 2D position of upper joint of body part.
X_5 : 2D position of lower joint of body part.
X_6 : a degree of tilt between the main axis (in the "height" direction)

Under this framework, some of the visual cues (ex. spatial information and color information of body part) can be considered simultaneously, and consistently to arrive at a most probable explanation for optimal body parts but some of the visual cues (ex. ratio of the length of long axes and distance of body joints between two adjacent body parts) can not be considered simultaneously. Therefore, we consider these visual cues consecutively.

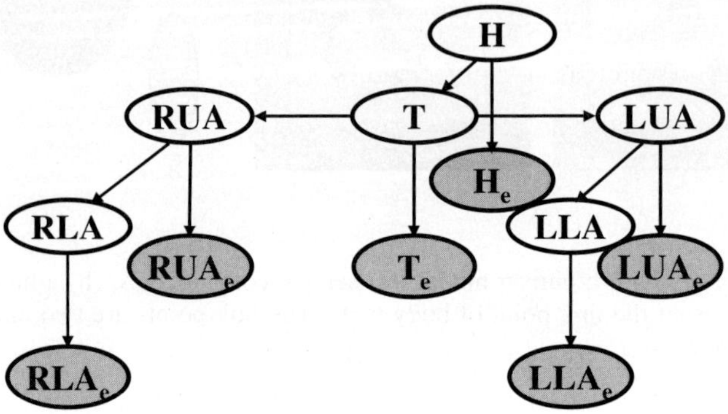

Fig. 2. Bayesian network for the human upper body pose estimation

2.3 Optimization of Pose Parameters

We model the human pose using Bayesian network. Our goal is optimization of the Bayesian network which is described the best human pose. We denote the set of state nodes as $S = \{s_1 ... s_6\}$, and the set of evidence nodes as $E = \{e_1 ... e_6\}$. We also denote a state at node i as s_i, evidence at the corresponding evidence node as e_i. We use two kinds of likelihood objective function for optimization of Bayesian network.

First, there is an objective function for evaluation of body part likelihood, $P(e_i \mid s_i)$. As described in section 2.1, each body parts and a background are represented by a Gaussian distribution and all the parts in the image are represented by a Gaussian mixture model. Using learned model, each pixel of the original image is affiliated with the most probable Gaussian, providing for a probabilistic image segmentation map (Figure 3 (c)). We define the body part likelihood, $P(e_i \mid s_i)$ as follows.

$$P(e_i \mid s_i) = \frac{1}{Z} \sum_{k=1}^{Z} \frac{1}{(2\pi)^{D/2} |\Sigma_i|^{1/2}} \exp\left(-\frac{1}{2} (x_k - \mu_i)^T \Sigma_i^{-1} (x_k - \mu_i) \right), \tag{1}$$

Where, Z is the number of pixels in the segmentation map for body part i, and D is dimensionality of feature space. $\mathbf{x}_k$ is a feature vector of a pixel within a segment i, $\boldsymbol{\mu}_i$ and $\boldsymbol{\Sigma}_i^{-1}$ are mean vector and inverse covariance matrix of feature space for body part i, learned form the manually labeled images, respectively.

According to the spatial layout of the body part, the segmentation result is different. Therefore, in the first objective function, we will find the best spatial layout of body part which generates the best segmentation map.

Second, there is an objective function for relation of two state nodes $P(s_i \mid s_{i-1})$. The $P(s_i \mid s_{i-1})$ represents a relation between state node s_i and parent state node s_{i-1}. We define a proportion measurement and a distance measurement. Thereafter, we convert these to a probabilistic measurement. The probabilistic, proportion, and distance measurements are as follows.

$$P(s_i \mid s_{i-1}) = \frac{C}{1 + \exp(E_1(s_i \mid s_{i-1}) + E_2(s_i \mid s_{i-1}))}, \tag{2}$$

Where C is a normalization coefficient. $E_1(s_i \mid s_{i-1})$ is a proportion measurement about body sizes and $E_2(s_i \mid s_{i-1})$ is a distance measurement about body joints between two adjacent body parts, respectively.

$$E_1(s_i \mid s_{i-1}) = \frac{\| \bar{r}_{i,i-1} - \frac{X_3^{S_i}}{X_3^{S_{i-1}}} \|}{\sigma_{i,i-1}^2}, \quad E_2(s_i \mid s_{i-1}) = \frac{\| X_4^{S_i} - X_5^{S_{i-1}} \|}{X_3^{S_i}}, \tag{3}$$

Where $\| \cdot \|$ is the Euclidean distance, $\bar{r}_{i,i-1}$ is a mean ratio and $\sigma_{i,i-1}^2$ is a variance of the length of long axes between two adjacent body parts learned from the manually labelled images. $X_3^{S_i}$ and $X_3^{S_{i-1}}$ are length of long axis of state node s_i and s_{i-1}, respectively. $X_4^{S_i}$ is 2D position of upper joint and $X_5^{S_{i-1}}$ is 2D position of lower joint of state node s_i and s_{i-1}, respectively.

We represent each body part by an ellipsoid with rotation, the body parts and their relations are modeled the Bayesian network. The states node of Bayesian network is optimized with objective function as mentioned above.

For adjusting the different size of body parts according to the different user and different view, we initialize a state node for head pose using face detection algorithm [15] and optimize the other states node sequentially.

First, the initial pose can be estimated by using face detection algorithm in the given image. Then, we adjust the human pose by changing the variables(X_1, …, X_3) of the Bayesian network model which becomes the maximum probability.

We optimize the states node sequentially. After optimized the state node for the torso, an optimization is performed for state nodes for left upper arm and left lower arm. Optimization of left arm can be evaluated as sum of left upper arm and left lower arm. Another states node also optimized sequentially.

(a) (b) (c)

Fig. 3. (a) Input image, (b) human model, (c) image segmentation map

3 Experimental Results

We tested our algorithm on two kinds of dataset. One is a collection of captured images with people performing meaningful gesture from a gesture-based game control system [16]. Experimental environment of the system was the laboratory room where possible noises were existed and the lighting condition was changing. The other dataset we use is a collection of sports news photographs of football players collected from the internet. We are focusing on middle resolution image, where a person's upper body length is more than 120 pixels.

For applying the proposed approach to the images, we divided the images to two groups, one group images used to learning and the other group images used to testing. In the learning process, the background Gaussian model parameters are learned by observing the scene with people. Because we hard to take background information in a single image. Therefore, the distribution of color in the whole image is more easily for background learning. Gaussian models parameters for each body parts are learned from hand-segmented body parts. The people of two groups of images for learning and testing wear a cloth of the same color, in our experimentation. The size of the body is different among uses. First, initial size of body in the Bayesian network model comes to give with statistical value of learning data. Then, the initial head position can be estimated by the face detection algorithm. Thereafter, we adjust the model by searching the pose parameters which becomes the maximum likelihood with the input image. Figure 4 shows initialize of Bayesian network model parameters.

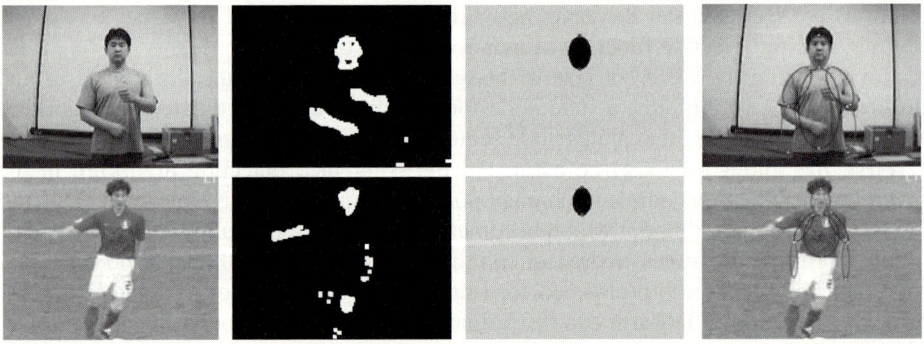

(a) (b) (c) (d)

Fig. 4. Model initialize with input frame: (a) input frame, (b) candidate face (skin color region), (c) detected face, (d) visualization of model initialization (focus on face region)

The projection of the Bayesian network model was matched against the extracted body parts. Since the estimation with the best body parts match is not always the most likely body pose. Figure 5 shows the body parts matching and pose estimation results.

When an arm observed in front of the torso, the proposed approach shows good performance. Figure 6 show an example of pose estimation error. Errors occurred mostly in occlusion situations or more subtle situations, such as when two hands are too close together.

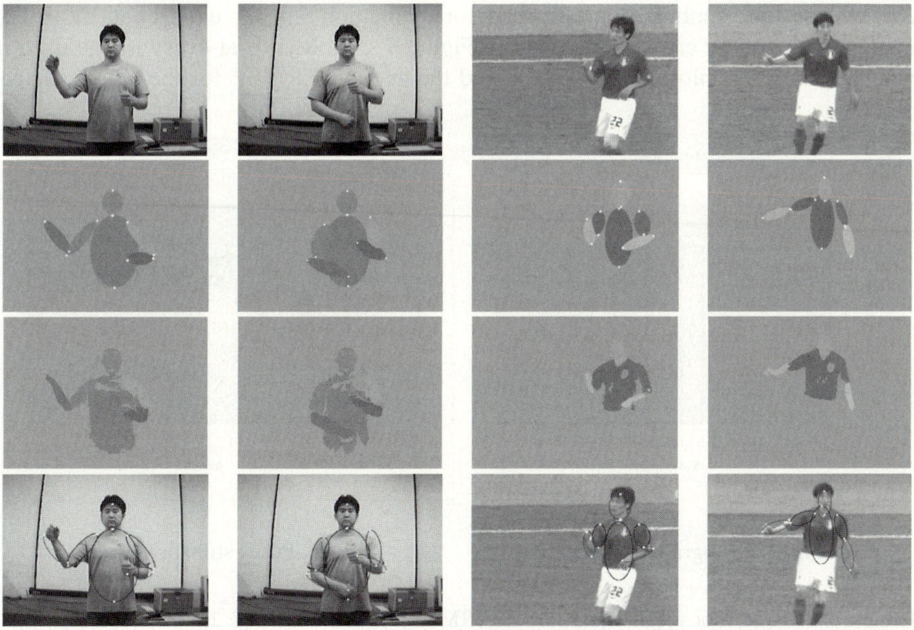

Fig. 5. Pose estimation results. First row: input images, second row: optimized human model, third row: segmentation map, forth row: pose estimation result.

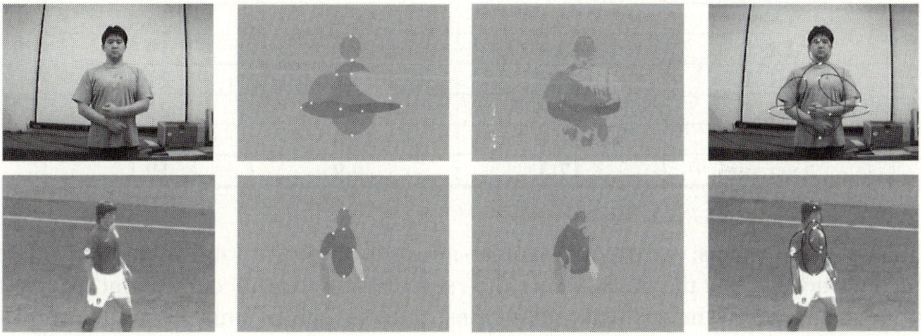

(a) (b) (c) (d)

Fig. 6. Pose estimation error: (a) input frame, (b) optimized human model, (c) segmentation map, (d) pose estimation result

For evaluation, we compare the estimated body joint positions with the manually annotated position in the image. In an image, we compute the 2D Euclidean distance error for the ith joint, denoted by e_t^i. We then compute the RMSE (Root Mean Square Error) for that frame, denoted by $RMSE_t$ as follows.

$$RMSE_t = (\frac{1}{N}\sum_{i=1}^{N}(e_t^i)^2)^{1/2}, \tag{4}$$

Where N is the number of joints used for evaluation (in our experiment N = 12). Histograms of these errors are shown in Figure 7. The RMSE at every image used in experimentation is plotted in Figure 8 and the averaged RMSE for the whole images is given in Table 1.

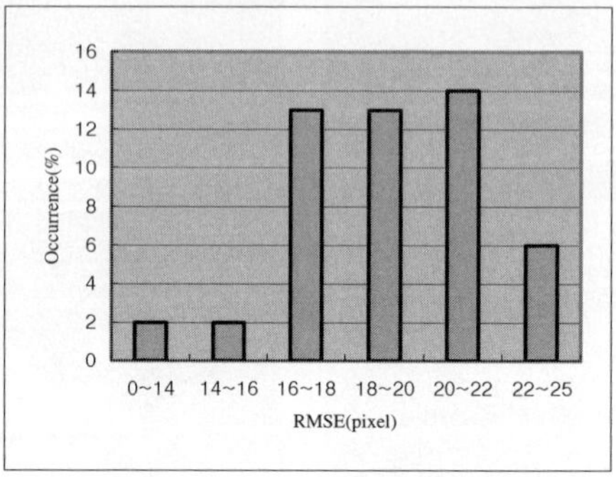

Fig. 7. Histogram of RMSE

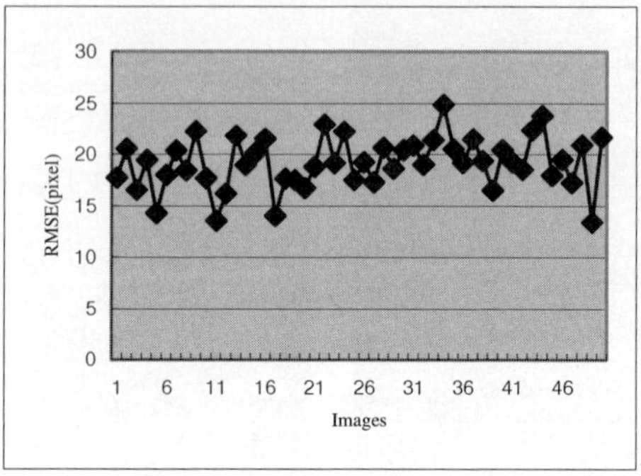

Fig. 8. Pose estimation error

Table 1. Average root mean square errors (RMSE) of the estimated 2D pose for each body parts and for the body pose (e.g., LUA refers to left-upper-arm)

	Gesture Player	Foot Player	Averages
Head	**13.5**	**15.6**	**14.6**
Torso	**14.3**	**18.4**	**16.4**
LUA	**16.4**	**21.6**	**19.0**
LLA	**18.5**	**24.1**	**21.3**
RUA	**19.9**	**24.2**	**22.1**
RLA	**21.2**	**22.0**	**21.6**
Averages	**17.3**	**20.9**	**19.1**

In our experiments, we found error in about 19% of the total images under test. This does not include the cases where the estimation is roughly correct but inaccurate. Errors occur mostly in occlusion situations or more subtle situations, such as when two hands are too close together. We are now working on adding more features (texture, motion) to the method in order to deal with some difficult situations.

4 Conclusions

In this paper, we proposed an approach toward body parts representation, localization and human pose estimation from an image. Our goal is to find a best configuration of human upper body pose from an image. The human body part and a background are represented by a mixture of Gaussians and the body part is modeled by a Bayesian network. In this model, state nodes represent pose parameters of an each body part and arcs represent spatial constraints. The Gaussian mixture distribution is used to model the prior distribution for the body part and the background as a parametric model. We estimated the human pose through an optimization of the pose parameters. The pose parameters are optimized likelihood objective function. We evaluated the performance of the proposed approach using ground truth method on variety single images. As a result, the proposed approach can automatically label upper body pose from images and improved the human pose estimation quality. This approach can achieve reliable performance when the distribution of colors within the human body parts follows the assumed model or distribution.

Acknowledgements

This research was supported by grant No.R05-2004-000-11494-0 from Korea Science & Engineering Foundation.

References

1. Acosta, C., Calderon, A., Hu, H.: Robot Imitation from Human Body Movement. In: Proceedings of the AISB '05, Third International Symposium on Imitation in Animals and Artifacts, pp. 1–9 (2005)
2. Park, H.S., Kim, E.Y., Kim, H.J.: Robot Competition Using Gesture Based Interface. In: 18th International Conference on Industrial and Engineering Application of Artificial Intelligence and Expert Systems (IEA/AIE 2005), pp. 131–133 (2005)
3. Ong, S.C.W., Ranganath, S.: Automatic sign language analysis: a survey and the future beyond lexical meaning. IEEE Transactions on Pattern Analysis and Machine Intelligence 27, 873–891 (2005)
4. Ben-Arie, J., Wang, Z., Pandit, P.: Human activity recognition using multidimensional indexing. IEEE Transactions on Pattern Analysis and Machine Intelligence 24, 1091–1104 (2002)
5. Deutsher, J., Davison, A., Reid, I.: Automatic partitioning of high dimensional search spaces associated with articulated body motion capture. In: Proceedings of the 2001 IEEE Computer Society Conference on Computer Vision and Pattern Recognition, vol. 2, pp. 669–676 (2001)
6. Sminchisescu, C., Triggs, B.: Covariance scaled sampling for monocular 3D body tracking. In: Proceedings of the 2001 IEEE Computer Society Conference on Computer Vision and Pattern Recognition, vol. 1, pp. 447–454 (2001)
7. Ramanan, D., Forsyth, D.A.: Finding and tracking people from the bottom up. In: Proceedings of the 2001 IEEE Computer Society Conference on Computer Vision and Pattern Recognition, vol. 2, pp. 467–474 (2003)
8. Gao, J., Shi, J.: Multiple frame motion inference using belief propagation. In: Proceedings of the Sixth IEEE International Conference on Automatic Face and Gesture Recognition, pp. 875–880 (2004)
9. Roberts, T.J., McKenna, S.J., Ricketts, I.W.: Human Pose Estimation using Learnt Probabilistic Region Similarities and Partial Configurations. In: Pajdla, T., Matas, J(G.) (eds.) ECCV 2004. LNCS, vol. 3024, pp. 291–303. Springer, Heidelberg (2004)
10. Mori, G., Ren, X., Efros, A.A., Malik, J.: Recovering Human Body Configurations: Combining Segmentation and Recognition. In: Proceedings of the 2004 IEEE Computer Society Conference on Computer Vision and Pattern Recognition, vol. 2, pp. 326–333 (2004)

11. Wren, C.R., Azarbayejani, A., Darrell, T., Pentland, A.P.: Pfinder: Real-Time Tracking of the Human Body. IEEE Transactions on Pattern Analysis and Machine Intelligence 19, 780–785 (1997)
12. Jordan, M.I.: Learning in Graphical Models. MIT press, Cambridge (1998)
13. Cowell, R.G., Dawid, A.P., Lauritzen, S.L., Spiegelhalter, D.J.: Probabilistic Networks and Expert Systems. Springer, NY (1999)
14. Pearl, J.: Probabilistic Reasoning in Intelligent Systems: Networks of Plausible Inference. Morgan Kaufmann, San Mateo, CA (1998)
15. Jung, D.J., Lee, C.W., Kim, H.J.: Detection and Tracking of Face by a Waling Robot. In: Iberian Conference on Pattern Recognition and Image Analysis, pp. 500–507 (2005)
16. Park, H.S., Kim, E.Y., Jang, S.S., Kim, H.J.: Recognition of Human Action for Game System. In: 13th International Conference on AI, Simulation, Planning in High Autonomy Systems, pp. 100–108 (2004)

Human Motion Modeling Using Multivision

Byoung-Doo Kang[1], Jae-Seong Eom[1], Jong-Ho Kim[1], Chul-Soo Kim[1], Sang-Ho Ahn[2], Bum-Joo Shin[3], and Sang-Kyoon Kim[1]

[1] Department of Computer Science, Inje University, Kimhae, 621-749, Korea
{dewey,jseom,lucky,charles,skkim}@cs.inje.ac.kr
[2] Department of Electronics and Intelligent Robotic Engineering, Inje University, Kimhae, 621-749, Korea
elecash@inje.ac.kr
[3] Department of Biosystem Engineering, Pusan National University, Miryang, 627-706, Korea
bjshin@pusan.ac.kr

Abstract. In this paper, we propose a gesture modeling system based on computer vision in order to recognize a gesture naturally without any trouble between a system and a user using real-time 3D modeling information on multiple objects. It recognizes a gesture after 3D modeling and analyzing the information pertaining to the user's body shape in stereo views for human movement. In the 3D-modeling step, 2D information is extracted from each view by using an adaptive color difference detector. Potential objects such as faces, hands, and feet are labeled by using the information from 2D detection. We identify reliable objects by comparing the similarities of the potential objects that are obtained from both the views. We acquire information on 2D tracking from the selected objects by using the Kalman filter and reconstruct it as a 3D gesture. A joint of each part of a body is generated in the combined objects. We experimented on ambiguities using occlusion, clutter, and irregular 3D gestures to analyze the efficiency of the proposed system. In this experiment, the proposed gesture modeling system showed a good detection and a processing time of 30 frames per second, which can be used in a real-time.

1 Introduction

In the existing intelligent-home system, a smart-home-based home networking technology and technologies for interaction between the system and a user have been studied. These researches provide the same service without discrimination between users. However, upcoming smart home analyzes the user's needs through various intelligent interfaces by being connected organically in real life situations. Therefore, in order to provide these intelligent context-recognition application services, information on human morphology is required. To acquire this information various methodologies have been studied to represent human gestures more realistically and conveniently. Gesture recognition begins with finding out automatically determining information on the shape change of each body part with time. There are two methods in gesture recognition technology: one uses a 2D image sequence and the other uses 3D data.

J. Jacko (Ed.): Human-Computer Interaction, Part III, HCII 2007, LNCS 4552, pp. 659–668, 2007.

By using a 2D image sequence, acquiring information on the various states becomes difficult due to loss of data, such as in the case of occlusion[1]-[4]. However, the 3D technology has been actively studied vigorously and its practical use for applications such as image reconstruction or animation has expanded as it uses multiple objects and information acquired from a various view, although its calculation is complex and it has difficulty to extracting a proper parameter[5]-[14].

In existing researches, a human hand, foot, and dynamic and static physical shape changes of the human body have been measured using a sensor in order to recognize a gesture completely. A typical method employing mechanical sensor is the use of sensing technology, such as data glove and magnetic sensors[5]-[8]. Because these methods can obtain accurate data by measuring the articulation angle and spatial location directly, they have been used in the field of virtual reality systems. However, these sensing-based systems cause inconvenience to users since they transfers data using a sensing based mechanism. There is a marker-free motion capture method that generates motion data while acting independently of any particular devices[9]-[16]. This method is used to acquire motion information on a certain body part of an actor-based vision system. This actor-based system has been well studied because it does not cause inconvenience to an actor due to the attachment of the device or any restriction due to it, although a detailed drawing is low comparing to sensing based technology. The marker-free motion capture method has simple operation and searches for the end effectors of all the bodies because it uses color information. It performs 3D modeling after estimating an articulation position that is not extracted from the information on the end effectors extracted from detailed images of a body[14],[16]. This problem constrains the user, and therefore this method cannot be adapted to a natural environment such as a sensor home. Li[13] suggested a method to require a special space like a blue screen studio because it requires a simple background although it does not require the user to be in a special position for initialization.

Sundaresan [14] suggested a method to do not require the storage of the initial background of the user's initial position, but it cannot acquire information on all the user's actions because it models a simple movement of the upper part of the body. Therefore, a 3D modeling system that recognizes the user's position should have an organic interface between the system and the user without a sensing mechanism. In other words, it needs a 3D modeling technology about a human body based on vision that is not restricted to an initialization employing a special position or a limited studio environment. In particular, we provide a basis for technology to develop context-aware gesture recognition capability for use in smart-home-based computer vision systems.

2 Human motion modeling

The existing researches stored previously obtained information to determine a human region and extract it; they considered an initial position and a gap image along with the current image to record the current position. If the initial position is used to extract a body region, the body region is acquired more accurately but its practicable scope is reduced.

In this paper, we increase efficiency and decrease user convenience. Fig. 1 shows the main structure of the system. To extract a human region, we extract the difference image between the previous and a current images; subsequently, we extract the human region candidates using the current image edge and AND bit operation. Generally, if a human movement disappears, a human region cannot be extracted. Although the movement decreases, we maintain a threshold so as to retain the human region. If there is movement under the threshold value, the human region without movement is restored by replacing it with a previous image.

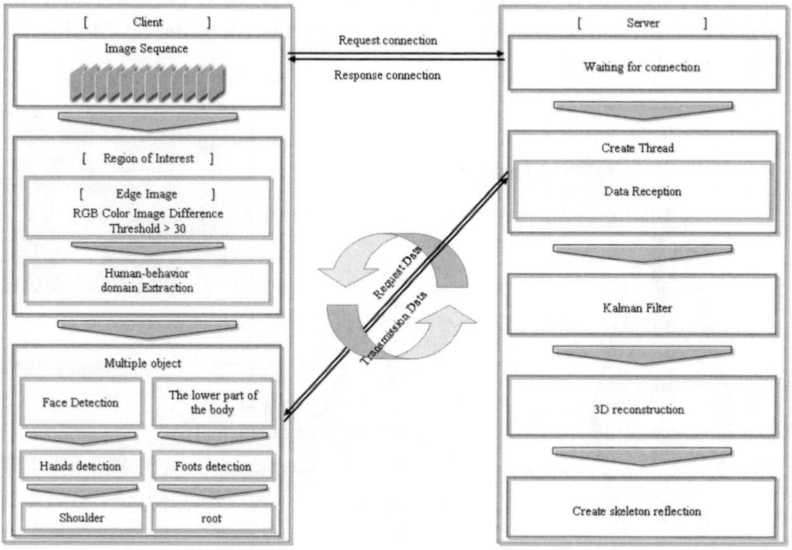

Fig. 1. Main structure for human motion modeling using multivision

This system extracts a skin blob from the extracted human region candidates in order to extract their face and hands, and it extracts the skin blob within the threshold value Cr after transforming an RGB color value into an YCbCr region. Because the extracted skin blob is far away from the camera and small in size, its size is changed for extraction. The position information of the extracted skin blob is acquired through blob labeling. The face and hands are judged on the basis of size, position information, and distance information of each blob.

In the case that a person approaches to a camera, if value difference is over threshold human pants region color is extracted. After transforming the extracted color into YCbCr, a leg candidate is selected by presenting a similar color on the screen. Because it is difficult to judge a particular foot from the leg candidates, only a leg part is extracted by the AND bit operation from the difference image edge and a pant color region.

In this paper, we used two clients and one server to transform a 2D image to a 3D image. One camera is connected to each client, and the position information of the face, human body, and foot that is acquired is transferred to a server through a socket. 2D coordinates are transformed to 3D coordinates by a balance matching method.

2.1 The Face Detection

Among the extracted skin blobs of the human candidates, the largest blob having appropriate distance information and position information is extracted as the face. To increase the face detection rate from an image sequence, the detector must guarantee a high detection rate. Fig. 2 shows the structure of a face detector using principal component analysis (PCA) and support vector machine (SVM)[17],[18]. The data collector accumulates the values of Haar-like features. The feature space is then transformed into the principal component space. Selected features from the principal component space are used as the feature vectors for the SVM. In the next step, the SVM classifier is trained with the training patterns. In the last step, the SVM classifier classifies regions into faces and non faces [19].

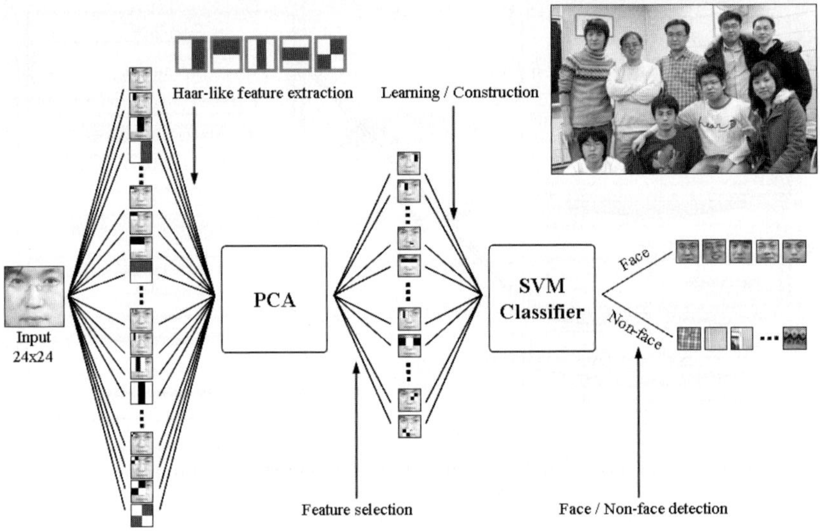

Fig. 2. Primary structure for face detection

2.2 The Reconstruction Method of the Segmented Difference Image

A difference image of each frame between the previous image and a current images is extracted in order to extract the human region. The difference image extracts changes when the value of the transformed color is greater than the threshold value after comparing the previous image with the current image, and it activates the region possessing the difference. The larger the movement of an extracted difference image, the larger the change a region of the difference image as compared to an after image and light source, Therefore, it is difficult to decide the body region. An edge image is acquired by extracting the current edge in order to accurately extract the human region, and the difference image is acquired by a gap between the previous and the current images. If the edge and a difference images are presented by a logical product, a more accurate human region can be extracted; an edge is extracted through the difference image.

(a) (b) (c) (d)

Fig. 3. Extraction of a human region (a) Original image (b) Canny edge (c) RGB difference image (d) AND bit operation

2.3 The Extraction of Skin Blob

Face and hand candidates are extracted by extracting a color similar to the skin color on the screen. RGB color is transformed into YCbCr color, the color that exists in the scope of value Cr skin color is regarded as the skin color and the skin blob is extracted. When extracting a skin blob, the skin color is detected within the human area extracted by an edge difference image in order to extract the most profitable blob in a body part (see Fig.4 (a)). The extracted skin blob is transformed into a convenient size so as to extract it through an expansion operation, and the position information is obtained through blob labeling.

2.4 Hands Detection

For the skin blobs extracted from the human candidates, (except in the case of faces), after calculating the approximate distance from a face of propriety of distance and acquiring position information of both the hands, a hand is extracted. Fig. 4 shows the result of the hands detection.

(a) (b) (c)

Fig. 4. Results of the hand detection (a) Skin blob image (b) AND bit operation (c) Hands detection

2.5 Feet Detection

When a person approaches the camera, if the difference in the screen is greater than the threshold, the color of the human pant region is extracted. After transforming the extracted color into an YCbCr color, the leg candidates are selected by presenting a color similar to that of the extracted pant color on the screen, as shown in Fig. 5. Because it is difficult to identify a foot from among the leg candidates, the lower part of the body is extracted (as in Fig. 5) by using AND bit operation from the difference image edge of Fig. 4 (a) and the pant color region of Fig. 5 (c).

All the potential candidate regions are established without distinction between the right foot and the left foot. To identify a foot region, a group that has two feet tags is searched. The analysis using tag information is similar to that in the hand case.

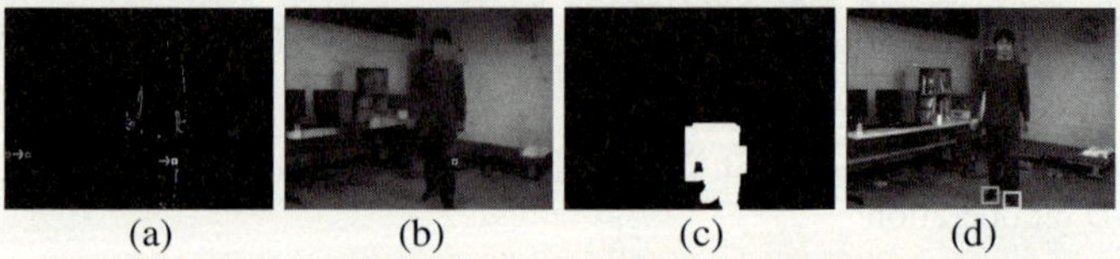

Fig. 5. Result of feet detection (a) AND bit operation, searching the position of pants (b) Detection the color of pants in the morphology image (c) The region of the pants (d) Feet detection

2.6 Kalman Filter

The Kalman filter analyzes a body part acquired from the previous frame, decides the 2D position, and predicts the movement in the next frame. Because it knows the movements of each body part, it is possible to divide the movements into right- and left-hand movement and to predict the position, although the body part may disappear or occlusion may occur[20].

The state vector of the Kalman filter uses static information from the multiple objects detectors and dynamic information between frames. For efficient multiple objects tracking, the Kamlan filter requires a setting of an appropriate trace model. We set the state vector as the center coordinates (x, y) of the detected multiple objects and the quantity of change $(\Delta x, \Delta y)$ between previous and current frames.

2.7 Parallel Camera Model

When two cameras are operated in parallel, this camera model is mainly used to avoid complicated calculations and geometrical transformations being structure that optical axis runs parallel being arranged.

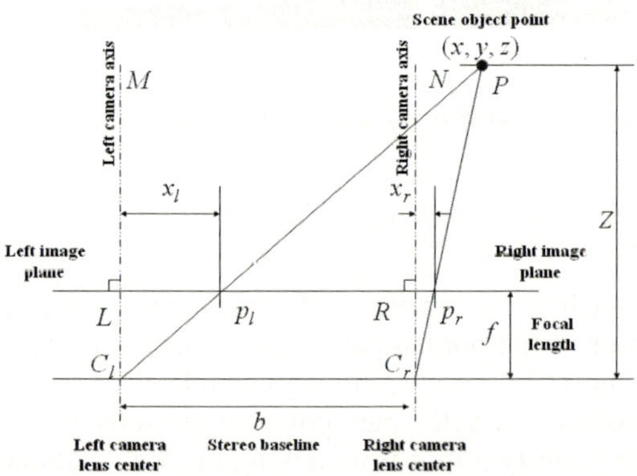

Fig. 6. Relation between depth and change in parallel camera model

The position P of an object is observed at points p_l and p_r in the right and left reflex aspect, respectively, as shown in Fig. 6. If we assume that the starting point of the coordinate command there is on the left side of the lens center, we can compare $p_l LC_l$ with a similar triangle PMC_l.

Fig. 7 (a) shows the detection results using the left camera and (b) shows those for the right camera. We can calculate z and obtain the 3D reconstruction; we obtain a result such as the one shown in (c) by using both these images[21],[22].

(a) Left camera (b) Right camera (c) Skeleton

Fig. 7. Result of 3D reconstruction

3 Experimental Results

Our 3D modeling system is implemented using Visual C++ on a 3.0 GHz Pentium IV PC with a Microsoft Windows operating system. Fig. 8 shows the experimental environment. We use a two-camera (HYVISION HVR-2030C) system. The distance between the cameras is 1m and the distance from the camera to the man is 3m. The processing time for 30 frames was 1s.

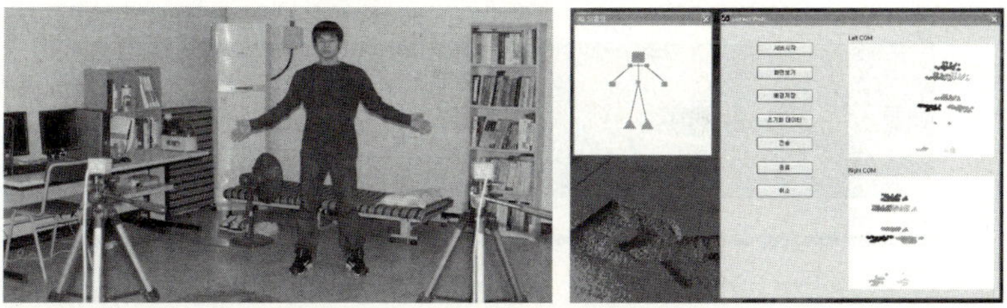

Fig. 8. Experimental environment

We used a two-client and one-server system to reconstruct the 3D image from the stereo camera for the multicamera network. Each of the cameras are linked to a client. The proposed system transmits the face, hands, and feet instantaneous 2D position information acquired by the server using the appropriate camera. The server transforms the 2D coordinate information into 3D coordinates by using the parallel camera model.

To analyze the conformity of the performance without an initialization process, a person who walks naturally enters the camera's visual field at various positions. In Fig. 9, we can observe that detection and reconstruction progress well from the pretreatment steps to the skeleton generation.

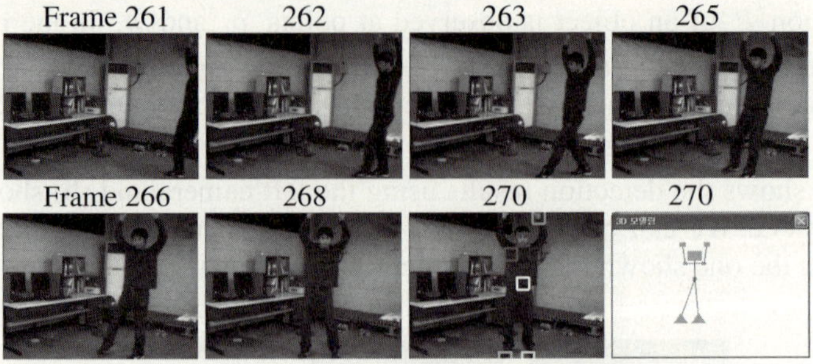

Fig. 9. Experiment in which man raises his hand and enters the camera's visual field

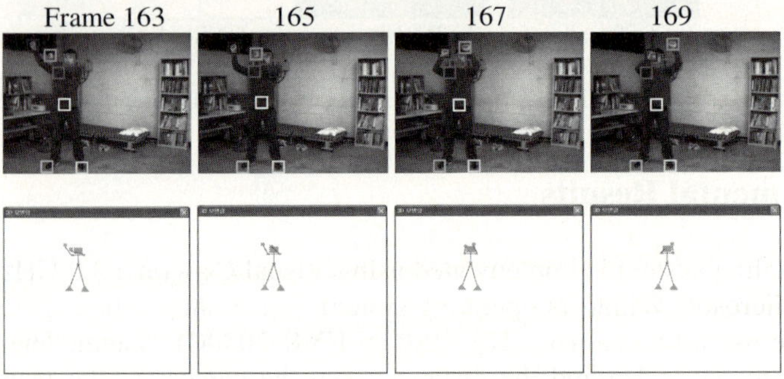

Fig. 10. Results of the occlusion test (the position that raises hand on heads)

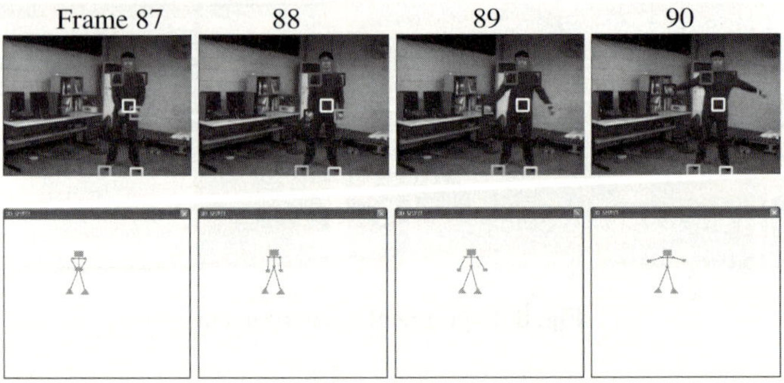

Fig. 11. Results of the occlusion test (the position that Spread after gather hands)

Fig. 10 is the experiment result in which a man raises his hand and enters the camera's visual field. From the observed results of the experiment, the detection and conformity are good.

Fig. 10 shows the experimental result for occlusion. The proposed system correctly detects and tracks the arms and hands covering the face. Because our system is improved tracking performance at process that Kalman filter predicts and controls. From the experimental results in Fig. 10 and 11, it can be observed that detection is good in the case where two hands are near each other.

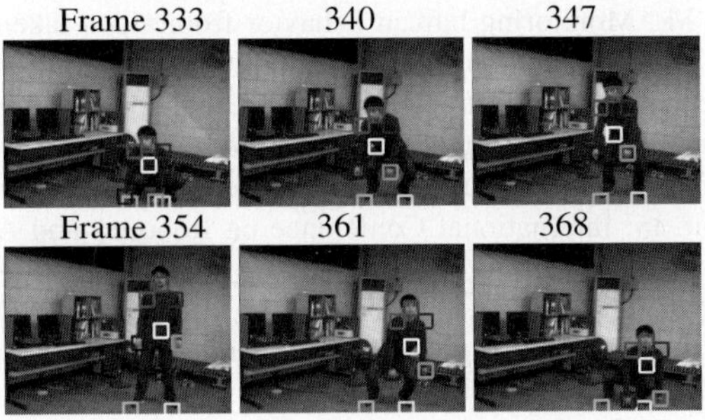

Fig. 12. Results of the ambiguity test

Fig. 12 shows the experimental result for an ambiguous case. From the experimental result, we can see that search correctly (left hand, right hand, left foot, right foot) without ambiguity.

4 Conclusion

In this paper, we propose a gesture modeling system based on computer vision in order to recognize a gesture naturally without any problems arising between the system and the user by using real-time 3D-modeling information on multiple objects. In the image processing field, a difference image is widely used because it reduces the system load and can be programmed easily by a few operations. However, the various types of noises processing problems occur, and the threshold is adjusted accordingly to improve the detection performance. In order to resolve these problems, we proposed the reconstruction method involving the segmented difference image. We designed our system to divide the image into the upper and lower parts of the body. The reconstruction method of the segmented difference image calculates division region's changes apart. When moved multiple object stopped, we solve the problem that do not detect partially because we replace division region of the previous frame.

Although the proposed method detects multiple objects efficiently, its performance will be enhanced if the system is designed to segment more regions according to the dynamic quality of multiple objects. Furthermore, our system can even detect the speed variation of the multiple objects because we can locally adjust the threshold; it can deal well with the position of the body and can be used in many applications such as in a smart homes.

References

1. Venkatesh Babu, R., Ramakrishnan, K.R.: Recognition of human actions using motion history information extracted from the compressed video. Image and vision computing 22, 597–607 (2004)
2. Aggarwal, J.K., Cai, Q.: Human motion analysis: a review. Computer Vision and Image Understanding 73(3), 428–440 (1999)

3. Ayers, D., Shah, M.: Monitoring human behavior from video taken in an office environment. Image and Vision Computing 19, 833–846 (2001)
4. Davis, J.: Hierarchical motion history images for recognizing human motion. IEEE Workshop on Detection and Recognition of Event in Video, 39–46 (2001)
5. Tanie, H., Yamane, K., Nakamura, Y.: High Marker Density Motion Capture by Retroreflective Mesh Suit. In: International Conference on Robotics and Automation, pp. 2884–2889 (2005)
6. Hashi, S., Tokunaga, Y., Yabukami, S., Toyada, M., Ishiyama, K., Okazaki, Y., Arai, K.I.: Development of real-time and highly accurate wireless motion capture system utilizing soft magnetic core. IEEE Transactions on Magnetics 41, 4191–4193 (2005)
7. Miller, N., Jenkins, O.C., Kallmann, M., Mataric, M.J.: Motion capture from inertial sensing for untethered humanoid teleoperation. In: IEEE/RAS International Conference on Humanoid Robots, vol. 2, pp. 547–562 (2004)
8. Yabukami, S., Kikuchi, H., Yamaguchi, M.: Motion Capture System of Magnetic Makers Using Three-Axial Magnetic Field Sensor. IEEE Transactions on magnetics 36, 3646–3648 (2000)
9. Wren, C.R., Azarbayejani, A., Darrell, T., Pentland, A.P.: Pfinder: Real-Time Tracking of the Human Body. Pattern Analysis and Machine Intelligence 19, 780–785 (1997)
10. Date, N., Arita, D., Yonemoto, S., Taniguchi, R.: Performance Evaluation of Vision-based Real-time Motion Capture. In: Proceedings of the International Parallel and Distributed Processing Symposium, vol. 8 (2003)
11. Moeslund, T.B., Granum, E.: Multiple Cues used in Model-Based Human Motion Capture. Automatic Face and Gesture Recognition, pp. 362–367 (2000)
12. Esteban, C.H., Schmitt, F.: Silhouette and stereo fusion for 3D object modeling. Computer Vision and Image Understanding 96, 367–392 (2004)
13. Li, L., Hilton, A., Illingworth, J.: A relaxation algorithm for real-time multiple view 3D-tracking. Image and vision computing 20, 841–859 (2002)
14. Sundaresan, A., Chellappa, R.: Markerless Motion Capture using Multiple Cameras. Computer Vision for Interactive and Intelligent Environment, pp. 15–26 (2005)
15. Saito, H., Baba, S., Kimura, M., Vedula, S., Kanade, T.: Appearance-Based Virtual View Generation of Temporally-Varying Events from Multi-Camera Images in the 3D Room. IEEE Transactions on, 5, 303–316 (2003)
16. Cheung, K.M., Baker, S., Kanade, T.: Shape-From-Silhouette Across Time Part II: Applications to Human Modeling and Markerless Motion Tracking. International Journal of Computer Vision, 63, 225–245 (2005)
17. Johnson, R.A., Wichern, D.W.: Applied Multivariate Statistical Analysis, pp. 356–395. Prentice-Hall, Englewood Cliffs (2002)
18. Vapnik, V.: The Nature of Statistical Learning Theory, 2nd edn. Springer, Heidelberg (2001)
19. Kang, B.D., Kim, J.H., Kim, S.K., et al.: Effective Face Detection using a Small Quantity of Training Data. In: Chang, L.-W., Lie, W.-N. (eds.) PSIVT 2006. LNCS, vol. 4319, pp. 553–562. Springer, Heidelberg (2006)
20. Welch, G., Bishop, G.: An Introduction to the Kalman filter. University of North Carolina at Chapel Hill, Department of Computer Science, TR 95-041 (2004)
21. Jain, R., Kasturi, R., Schunck, B.G.: Machine vision, pp. 289–298. McGraw-Hill, Inc., New York (1995)
22. Sonka, M., Hlavac, V., Boyle, R.: Image processing analysis and machine vision. PWS, 441–507 (1998)

Real-Time Face Tracking System Using Adaptive Face Detector and Kalman Filter

Jong-Ho Kim[1], Byoung-Doo Kang[1], Jae-Seong Eom[1], Chul-Soo Kim[1], Sang-Ho Ahn[2], Bum-Joo Shin[3], and Sang-Kyoon Kim[1]

[1] Department of Computer Science, Inje University, Kimhae, 621-749, Korea
{lucky,dewey,jseom,charles,skkim}@cs.inje.ac.kr
[2] Department of Electronics and Intelligent Robotic Engineering, Inje University, Kimhae, 621-749, Korea
elecash@inje.ac.kr
[3] Department of Biosystem Engineering, Pusan National University, Miryang, 627-706, Korea
bjshin@pusan.ac.kr

Abstract. In this paper, we propose a real-time face tracking system using adaptive face detector and the Kalman filter. Basically, the features used for face detection are five types of simple Haar-like features. To only extract the more significant features from these features, we employ principal component analysis (PCA). The extracted features are used for a learning vector of the support vector machine (SVM), which classifies the faces and non-faces. The face detector locates faces from the face candidates separated from the background by using real-time updated skin color information. We trace the moving faces with the Kalman filter, which uses the static information of the detected faces and the dynamic information of changes between previous and current frames. In this experiment, the proposed system showed an average tracking rate of 97.3% and a frame rate of 23.5 frames per s, which can be adapted into a real-time tracking system.

1 Introduction

Recently, computer vision has been actively studied in a variety of fields.

In particular, face detection is being studied as the basic technology for face recognition and face tracking.

Using computer vision a face detection system detects a human face in real-time. Users only stare at a camera, and hence, it does not require physical contact from users and lessen the user's denial. Further, such a system can detect a face in a natural situation.

Human faces do not have fixed information as is the case with nonliving objects, instead, they possess various features such as facial expression, race, age, gender, hair style. Information is given by these features as well as mechanical features of light and of the camera, and therefore, there exist various face detection methods that have been studied.

J. Jacko (Ed.): Human-Computer Interaction, Part III, HCII 2007, LNCS 4552, pp. 669–678, 2007.

A face detection method is divided into a local feature-based method[1] and a template based method[2]. The local feature-based method is based on the existence or nonexistence of unique facial features and the correlation of the positions of the eyes, a nose, and a mouth. This method shows a high recognition value when only one person is present in an image and the eyes, nose and mouth in the images are clear. However, it requires a considerable number of operations because it executes a scanning process using a multi scale window to detect faces of various-size in a given image.

The template-based method is divided into a shape-based method[2] and color-based method[3]. The shape based method studies face images, creates a standard template, applies a window or classifier to the input images, compares the images with the template, and detects the facial region. However, it cannot work efficiently when some part of the face is hidden by another face or shadow or the face is inclined to one side.The color-based method creates a skin color model using previously trained images and detects a face from these images by using the skin color. Color-based information has a fast processing time and detects a face image accurately with regularized value and fewer calculations. However, it is sensitive to the intensity and direction of light and cannot detect correctly when the background color and skin color are similar.

To solve these problems, we propose a real-time face tracking method using an adaptive face detector and the Kalman filter.

The face detector is constructed based on simple Haar-like features, PCA[4], and SVM[5]. The detector has acceptable detection speed and it is not affected to a large extent by the size of the training dataset. As such, it works well with a small quantity of training data. We can trace a moving face with the Kalman filter that uses static information from the face detector and dynamic information of changes between the previous and current frames.

The proposed system performs better face detection because it uses effective features selected from simple Haar-like features with PCA. The SVM classifier, which works well with the binary classification of faces and non-faces, also contributes toward better face detection. The Kalman filter, which has the best prediction ability, makes it possible for the system to trace faces efficiently using the face detector.

Furthermore, the face detector does not work for the entire image in a frame but it works only for face candidates that are separated by real-time updated skin-color information. This improves the processing time and decreases the mis-detection rate.

2 Overview of Face Tracking System

Fig. 1 shows the primary structure of our face tracking system.

In the classifier construction step, the proposed system extracts Haar-like features from the learning images, and subsequently extracts efficient features from them using PCA : these are then user as the SVM learning data and form an SVM face classifier. In the skin color detection step, the proposed system extracts face candidates using real-time updated skin color information. Lastly, it tracks the detected face by using the Kalman Filter.

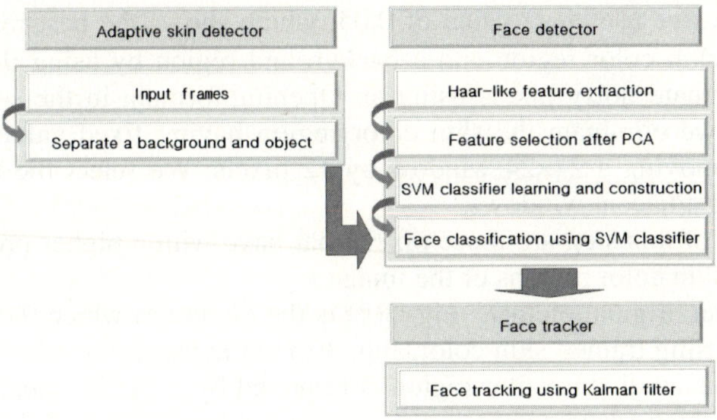

Fig. 1. Primary structure for face tracking

3 The Adaptive Skin Detection Algorithm

3.1 Training the Skin Color

The skin color training using 100 sets of faces and hands after manually segmenting the skin region. These images were captured using a PC camera and collected from the internet. Fig. 2 shows the skin color training images used in this study.

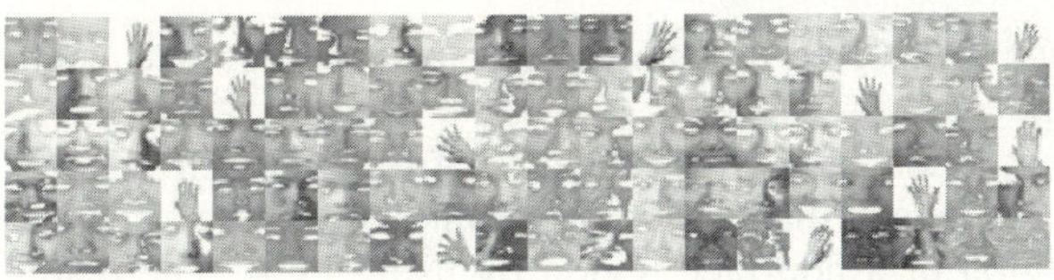

Fig. 2. skin color training images used in this study

3.2 Detection of Skin Pixels

In this step, we detect the skin color regions from the images by using trained skin color. Among these regions a region whose position is not changed in the next frame is not regarded as a face candidate. Only if we are able to compare the change in the position of a skin-color region in the current frame from that in the previous frame can we mathematically reconstruct skin color information, for example, as given by Eq.1.

$$S_{n+1} = (1-\alpha) \bullet S_n + \alpha \times S_m \quad (1)$$

- S_{n+1} is the new skin color for the next frame.
- S_n is the skin color region in the current frame.
- S_m is the in-motion pixels of the skin color.
- α is the weight for merging two frames.(0.05)

In this study, we use an α value of 0.05, which shows the best result. Moreover, we separate a skin color region and a background region by using the updated skin color. We eliminate noisy pixels using an Opening formula in the separated image. Subsequently, we eliminate the skin color region having fixed value from the face candidates by moving a 24×24 window by 12 pixels. We select the face candidates after combining adjacent windows.

The outputs of this step are those pixels that have with a higher probability of belonging to the skin color regions of the image.

Fig. 3(a) is an original picture. Fig. 3(b) is the picture in which the face candidate is detected by using trained skin color. Fig. 3(c) is the picture in which the skin color is updated and a small skin color region is removed by a 24×24 window. Fig. 3(d) is the final selected face candidates.

(a) (b) (c) (d)

Fig. 3.

4 Construction of Face Detector

In this step, a face is detected by using a detector from the face candidates obtained in the previous step.

First, the detector detects Haar-like features from a face image.

Then, it selects features that can be used to judge whether a detected Haar-like feature is a face region or a non-face region by using PCA. The feature space is transformed into the principal component. The features selected from the principal component space are used as feature vectors of the SVM.

In the last step, an SVM classifier divides the face candidates into a face image and a non-face image using a trained pattern.

4.1 Feature Extraction

The face detector is based on the simple rectangular features that were presented by Viola and Jones[6]. It measures the differences between the regional averages at various scales, orientations, and aspect ratios. The rectangular features can be rapidly evaluated at any scale (see fig. 4). However, these features require very large training datasets. Therefore, after analyzing the principal components, we select only the useful features from each of the five rectangular features. These selected features are used as a feature vector for the SVM. The experiments demonstrate that they provide

Fig. 4. Haar-like features used in this study

useful information and improve the performance of accurate classification when small training datasets are used.

We used 12 principal components that explain features having a cumulative explanation rate greater than 90%. From these 12 principal components, we selected 288 useful features from the entire range of the 162,336 simple Haar-like features. Fig. 5 shows the 288 useful features selected by using PCA. Consequently, a training image is converted to 288 values corresponding to these useful features, and our SVM classifier uses this input vector having of 288 dimensions for training.

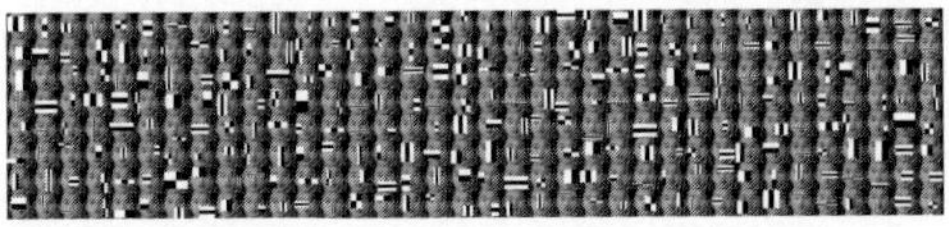

Fig. 5. The 288 useful features selected for this study

4.2 Training of Classifier

The training data were 1000 face images and 1000 non-face images randomly selected from the MIT CBCL face data set[7]. Each image was normalized to 24×24 pixels.

Fig. 6 gives an overview of the detection progress, which comprises simple feature extraction, feature analysis, and classifier construction. Firstly, from the simple Haar-like features, useful features are selected by using PCA. Training images, as shown in fig. 5, are converted into input vectors having 288 dimensions with the selected features. The SVM classifier uses these input vectors for training.

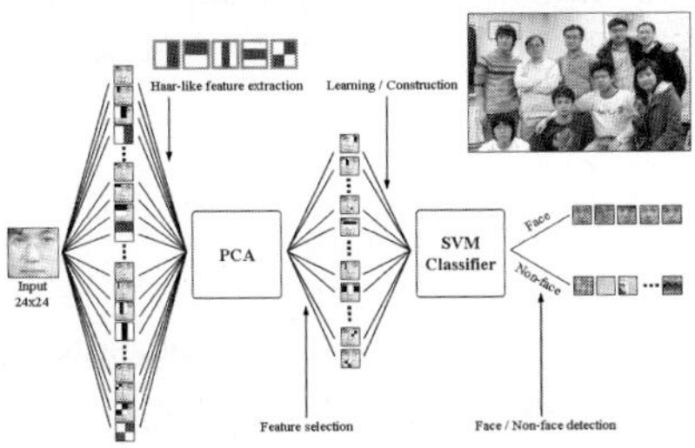

Fig. 6. Primary structure for face detection

5 Face Tracking with Kalman Filter

In this paper, we used the Kalman filter[8] to reduce the cost of operation and improve the tracking rate in the sequence of video images. The state vector of the Kalman filter uses static information from the face detector and dynamic information between frames.

For efficient multiple objects tracking, the Kamlan filter requires a setting of an appropriate trace model. We set the state vector as the center coordinates (x, y) of the detected face and the quantity of change $(\Delta x, \Delta y)$ between previous and current frames.

The state vector of the Kalman filter in time t is defined as:

$$\mathbf{x}(t) = [x, y, \Delta x, \Delta y]^T, \tag{2}$$

The Kalman filter assumes that the system state vector, $x(t)$, evolves according to time as:

$$\mathbf{x}(t+1) = \Phi(t)\mathbf{x}(t) + w(t) \tag{3}$$

where $w(t)$ is a zero mean Gaussian noise with covariance $\mathbf{Q}(t)$.

$$\mathbf{Q}(t) = \begin{bmatrix} 0 & 0 & 0 & 0 \\ 0 & 0 & 0 & 0 \\ 0 & 0 & 1 & 0 \\ 0 & 0 & 0 & 1 \end{bmatrix} \tag{4}$$

The measurement vector is given by:

$$\mathbf{z}(t) = \mathbf{H}(t)\mathbf{x}(t) + v(t) \tag{5}$$

where $v(t)$ is another zero mean Gaussian noise factor, with covariance $\mathbf{R}(t)$.

The covariance $\mathbf{R}(t)$ is defined as

$$\mathbf{R}(t) = \begin{bmatrix} 1 & 0 \\ 0 & 1 \end{bmatrix} \tag{6}$$

We assumed that faces move with uniform speed and linear direction. The state transition matrix $\mathbf{\Phi}(t)$ is defined as follows:

$$\mathbf{\Phi}(t) = \begin{bmatrix} 1 & 0 & 1 & 0 \\ 0 & 1 & 0 & 1 \\ 0 & 0 & 1 & 0 \\ 0 & 0 & 0 & 1 \end{bmatrix} \tag{7}$$

The input vector is a four-dimensional vector that uses the center coordinates of the multi object and changes of the x, y, Δt, Δt axis. Therefore, the measurement matrix $\mathbf{H}(t)$ is defined as:

$$\mathbf{H}(t) = \begin{bmatrix} 1 & 0 & \Delta t & 0 \\ 0 & 1 & 0 & \Delta t \\ 0 & 0 & 1 & 0 \\ 0 & 0 & 0 & 1 \end{bmatrix} \tag{8}$$

The error is calculated using the margin of the measurement z_k and the prediction $\mathbf{H}_k x_{k/k-1}$ of the previous step, the estimate is updated using the Kalman gain of the k state as a weight, and calculate the optimal estimate $x_{k/k}$ finally.

6 Experimental Results

The proposed face tracking system was developed using Visual C++ on a 2.4GHz P4 PC with a Microsoft Windows operating system. To evaluate our system, we experimented with face detection and tracking on various video sequences. The video sequences were collected from various sources such as the Open-Video website[9], captured video from TV broadcasts, Boston University IVC Head Tracking Video Set[10], and PC cameras.

6.1 The Result of Skin Color Detection According to the Rate of Trained and Updated Skin Color

Fig. 7 shows a true positive rate and false negative rate depending on the merging weight value α of Eq.1.

True positive means that the skin color regions are correctly recognized as skin color regions, while false negative means that the background regions are incorrectly recognized as skin color regions.

When the value of α was near 0, the initial skin color value was not updated and some of the background regions incorrectly recognized as the skin color regions never shift to the background regions. On the contrary, when the value of α was near 1, the skin color value changed excessively to such an extent that mis-recognition rate increased. Experimentally, we used 0.05 as the value of α and this shows the best result.

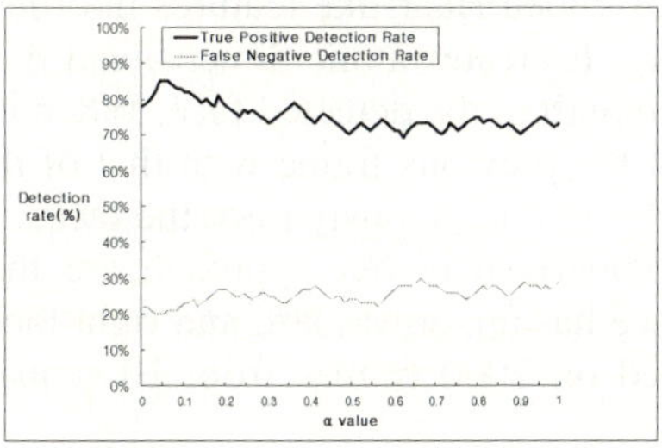

Fig. 7. Detection rate according to the Value of α

6.2 Tracking Experiment for Images Obtained Under Various Conditions

Figs. 8 (a) and (b) shows the face detection and tracking results from sequences under various conditions. As shown in fig. 8(a), although face detection fails due to non-inclusion of rotated faces in the training of the face detector, face tracking is possible.

Fig.8 (b) shows successful face tracking in which occlusion occurs locally in the face region.

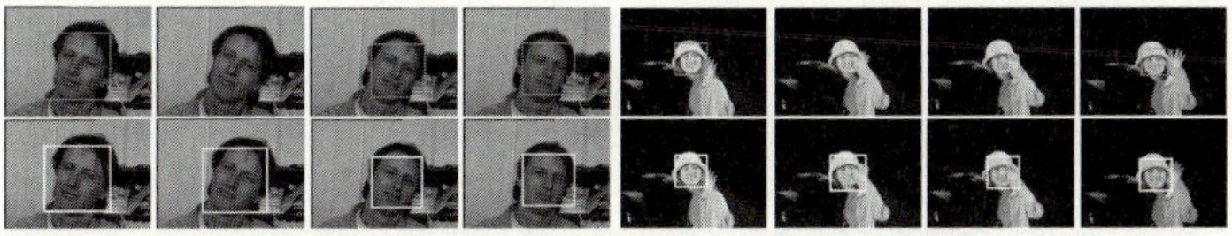

(a) (b)

Fig. 8. (a) Results of face tracking in a heavily rotated face and (b) local occlusion sequence

Fig. 9 shows examples of detecting a non-face region as a face region when the face candidates are not assigned by a skin color. However, we detect only a face region completely such as in fig. 10 by limiting the face detection region to face candidates.

Fig. 9. Examples of recognizing a non-face image as a face image

Fig. 10. Examples of detecting a face image from face candidates

6.3 Comparison with Related Works

To compare our tracking system with related works, we selected a method from among the various tracking methods. This method[11] uses Viola-Jones's basic features and Lienhart's[12] extended Haar-like features in order to increase the detection rate of various facial poses. It creates a one-dimensional deformable face graph after subdividing the eyes and mouth in the detected face. When it fails to detect the face, it matches the face graph of the previous frame with that of the current frame by using DP(Dynamic Programming) to continuously trace the faces.

The steps used for comparison in our approach are the same as those used in method. The input sequence has up, down, left, and right face poses and frequent light changes. We experimented on 2000 frames from 10 sequences, and the results are listed in Table 1.

Table 1. The comparison of the obtained results using our system and those obtained using method[11]

	Method[11]				Our Approach			
Sequence	**D.F.**	**D.R. (%)**	**T.F.**	**T.R. (%)**	**D.F.**	**D.R. (%)**	**T.F.**	**T.R. (%)**
#1 (jam5.avi)	33	83.5	0	100	12	94.0	0	100
#2 (jary.avi)	38	81.0	0	100	40	80.0	8	96.0
#3 (jim2l.avi)	47	76.5	16	92.0	20	90.2	4	98.0
#4 (llrx.avi)	104	48.0	40	80.0	47	76.5	12	94.0
#5 (llm1.avi)	30	85.0	0	100	14	93.0	0	100
#6 (vam7.avi)	76	62.0	24	88.0	35	82.6	3	95.5
#7 (jam9.avi)	84	58.0	12	94.0	37	81.4	5	97.5
#8 (llm1r.avi)	35	82.5	5	97.5	50	72.0	12	94.0
#9 (llm4.avi)	90	55.0	20	90.0	24	87.8	5	97.5
#10 (mll6.avi)	31	84.5	0	100	8	96.0	0	100
Total	**689**	**71.6**	**117**	**94.2**	**287**	**85.4**	**49**	**97.25**

(D.F.: Detection fail, D.R.: Detection rate, T.F.: Tracking fail, T.R.: Tracking rate)

When we apply our method to an image(#8), the track rate is less than that of method[11]. For face candidates the face image is not detected accurately because the face is hidden by a shadow.

However, for the sequences of up, down, left, and right facial movements, such as #7 and #9, our system generally showed a higher tracking rate. In particular, our system

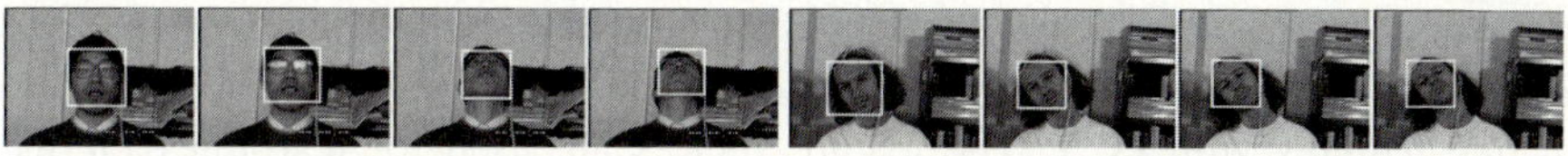

Fig. 11. Tracking result for sequences #4 and #6

Table 2. The comparison results for face detection from an entire image with those from face candidates

Sequence	Face detection from an entire image D.R. (%)	T.R. (%)	F.P.S	Face detection from face candidates D.R.(%)	T.R. (%)	F.P.S.
#1 (jam5.avi)	94.0	100	19	94.0	100	23
#2 (jary.avi)	83.6	94.4	18	80.0	96.0	24
#3 (jim2l.avi)	90.2	97.8	20	90.2	98.0	24
#4 (llrx.avi)	75.8	89.6	19	76.5	94.0	25
#5 (llm1.avi)	93.0	100	19	93.0	100	23
#6 (vam7.avi)	82.6	95.5	21	82.6	95.5	22
#7 (jam9.avi)	81.4	97.2	20	81.4	97.5	24
#8 (llm1r.avi)	75.0	93.2	21	72.0	94.0	25
#9 (llm4.avi)	87.8	94.6	20	87.8	97.5	24
#10 (mll6.avi)	96.0	100	19	96.0	100	25
Total	**85.9**	**96.2**	**19.7**	**85.4**	**97.3**	**23.5**

(D.R.: Detection rate, T.R.: Tracking rate, F.P.S. : Frames Per Second)

was much better than method[11] in which the front of the face does not appear during the given time and the face is extremely rotated (sequences #4 and #6) when the sequence involved a moving face(sequences #1 and #3) as shown in fig. 11.

Table 2 shows the results obtained from the detection of a face from an entire image and from face candidates by using skin color.

Face detection in the skin color regions show greater improvement in processing time, detection rate, and mis-detection rate then those for the entire image as shown in fig.4. In particular, the processing time is improved by more than 20% as compared to the case when the skin color region is not applied. This is because the system detects a face not from entire images but from face candidates, and it shows an improvement in the mis-detection rate of incorrect recognition of a background as a face because the system filters a possible face recognition region from the background.

In the experiment, a detector combining skin color with PCA and SVM showed an average detection rate of 85.4%. A tracking system showed an average tracking efficiency 97.3% by employing a detector that guarantees high detection rates and optimum face position through the prediction process of the Kalman filter. Moreover, it showed a processing time of 23.5 frames per s, which can be adapted into a real-time processing system.

7 Conclusion

In this paper we proposed a real-time face detection system to track a face from various input images that have illumination changes, complex backgrounds, various facial movements, and various poses.

Firstly, we designed an effective face detector using PCA and SVM. The useful features that discriminate between faces and backgrounds are extracted from simple Haar-like features with PCA. The feature vectors are used for learning patterns for SVM, which is appropriate for binary classification. The Kalman filter for tracking uses the face positions in each frame, which is the result of the face detector and changes in face position between frames, as the parameters for the state vector. The prediction process of the Kalman filter presents an optimal face position prediction for the next frame. Furthermore, the proposed system detected face candidates using real-time updating of changes in skin color information with position, improved the processing time, and decreased the incorrect detection rate by detecting a face from face candidates. Consequently, we implemented a tracking system combining an adaptive face detector with a high detection rate and the prediction ability of Kalman filter to obtain synergy.

In the experiment, we obtained an average tracking rate of 97.3% and 23.5 frames per s on sequences of 320×240 pixel images that are available in a real-time system.

However, it is difficult to track a face when the light is dim, the face is rotated quickly, and when some part of the face is continuously hidden.

Therefore, we are trying to study the detection of a face in various situations and how to tracking a face using several cameras when other objects hide some part of the face or when people rotate their face quickly.

References

1. Park, T., Park, S.K, Park, M.: An effective method for detecting facial features and face in human-robot interaction. Information Sciences 176, 3166–3189 (2006)
2. Brunelli, R., Poggio, T.: Face recognition: Features versus Templates. IEEE Trans PAMI. 15, 1042–1052 (1993)
3. Hsu, R.L., Abdel-Mottaleb, M., Jain, A.K.: Face detection in color images. IEEE transaction on Pattern Analysis and Machine Intelligence 24(5), 696–706 (2002)
4. Johnson, R.A., Wichern, D.W.: Applied Multivariate Statistical Analysis, pp. 356–395. Prentice-Hall, Englewood Cliffs (2002)
5. Vapnik, V.: The Nature of Statistical Learning Theory, 2nd edn. Springer, Heidelberg (2001)
6. Viola, P., Jones, M.J.: Robust Real-Time Face Detection. International Journal of Computer Vision 57(2), 137–154 (2004)
7. MIT CBCL - Face Database http://www.ai.mit.edu/projects/cbcl/
8. Welch, G., Bishop, G.: An Introduction to the Kalman filter. University of North Carolina at Chapel Hill, Department of Computer Science, TR 95-041 (2004)
9. Open-Video http://www.open-video.com
10. Boston University IVC Head Tracking Video Set http://www.cs.bu.edu/groups/ivc/
11. Yao, Z., Li, H.: Tracking a Detected Face with Dynamic Programming. Image and Vision Computing 24(6), 573–580 (2006)
12. Lienhart, R., Maydt, J.: An Extended Set of Haar-like Features for Rapid Object Detection. IEEE Int'l Conf. Image Processing 1, 900–903 (2002)

Kalman Filtering in the Design of Eye-Gaze-Guided Computer Interfaces

Oleg V. Komogortsev and Javed I. Khan

Perceptual Engineering Laboratory, Department of Computer Science, Kent State University, Kent, OH, USA 44242
okomogor@cs.kent.edu, javed@kent.edu

Abstract. In this paper, we design an Attention Focus Kalman Filter (AFKF) - a framework that offers interaction capabilities by constructing an eye-movement language, provides real-time perceptual compression through Human Visual System (HVS) modeling, and improves system's reliability. These goals are achieved by an AFKF through identification of basic eye-movement types in real-time, the prediction of a user's perceptual attention focus, and the use of the eye's visual sensitivity function and eye-position data signal de-noising.

Keywords: Human Visual System Modeling, Kalman Filter, Human Computer Interaction, Perceptual Compression.

1 Introduction

There is a significant amount of research being conducted in the area of eye-tracking. An eye-tracker is a web-camera-like device that provides information about the location of the user's eye-gaze. Eye-gaze can be used as a direct input to a computer. Eye-tracking technology has recently become non-intrusive and more appealing to the user.

There are many advantages of eye-based input. Eye-movements are essentially faster than the current popular methods of input, plus each person naturally looks at the desired destination before any other action is taken [2]. In addition, the control-to-display relationship for an eye-tracking device is already established in our brain [1]. For motion-impaired people an eye-tracker is extensively used as an input device to a computer. Eye tracking data provides the means for perceptual compression as well. Perceptual compression uses properties of the Human Visual System (HVS) to provide content compression that is imperceptible to the viewer. The perceptual compression can be applied as bandwidth reduction of the video stream or the computational burden reduction for the 3D-based content. Interactive and content compression components make eye-tracking extremely attractive in the design of future interfaces and in the production and distribution of multimedia streams.

In this paper we propose an Attention Focus Kalman Filter (AFKF) framework that merges together the paradigms of interaction, compression and noise removal.

J. Jacko (Ed.): Human-Computer Interaction, Part III, HCII 2007, LNCS 4552, pp. 679–689, 2007.

2 Previous Work

Jakob [1] has proposed an eye-gaze-based interaction interface. The activation of the interface components was done through eye-fixation detection. Different interface actions were performed by specific eye-fixation durations. A computer application was designed to test the proposed interface. It was reported that the interface accuracy was comparable to the touch screen displays rather than a mouse, but the system provided an impression of responding to the user's intention rather than explicit input.

Perceptual compression was investigated previously for still images by Tsumura et. al. [9], Stelmach and Tam [10]; for real-time video by Komogortsev and Khan [4,5,6,7]; for 3D content by Murphy and Duchowsky [11].

Eye-movement detection by the Kalman Filter was proposed by Sauter et. al. [8]. Sauter used the innovations generated by a Kalman Filter to identify the eye-movements called saccades. Grindiger [5] used a Kalman Filter to identify different eye-movement types following the idea proposed by the Sauter. Gridinger's implementation used a mouse-generated signal as a testbed for saccade detection. The saccade detection parameters proposed by Gridinger allowed the construction of a well-behaved saccade detection filter.

3 Human Visual System

3.1 Basic Eye-Movements

There are three major types of eye-movements that are exhibited by the Human Visual System during the perception of multimedia and interaction with the interface components.

1. Fixation: - "eye movement which stabilizes the retina over a stationary object of interest" [4]. Eye-fixations are accompanied by drift, small involuntary saccades and tremor. A human's eye perceives the highest quality picture during an eye-fixation.
2. Saccades: - "rapid eye movements used in repositioning the fovea to a new location in the visual environment" [4]. Usually saccades transition the HVS from one eye-fixation to another. The HVS is blind during a saccade .
3. Smooth pursuit: - eye movement that develops when the eyes are tracking a moving visual target. The quality of vision varies during smooth pursuit eye-movements.

3.2 Human Visual System Sensitivity

A visual sensitivity function allows us to perform multimedial compression through the knowledge of current eye-gaze position. The formula was discussed in our previous work in [7].

4 Kalman Filtering

The Kalman filter is a recursive estimator that is used for computing a future estimate of the dynamic system state from a series of incomplete and noisy measurements. A

Kalman Filter minimizes the mean of the squared estimate error, between the prediction of the system's state and the measurement. Only the estimated state from the previous time step and the new measurements are needed to compute the new estimate for the current dynamic system's state.

A Kalman filter works with a dynamic system that is modeled by an n-by-1 state vector that is updated through this discrete time equation:

$$x_{k+1} = Ax_k + Bu_k + w_k \tag{4.1}$$

In the equation above, **A** is an n-by-n state transition matrix, **B** is an n-by-m optional control input matrix, which relates control vector m-by-1 $\mathbf{u_k}$ to the dynamic system's state $\mathbf{x_k}$. **w** is an n-by-1 process noise vector with covariance $\mathbf{Q_k}$.

We should note that here lower-case, bold letters denote vectors, and upper-case, bold letters denote matrices.

Every dynamic system's state has a j-by-1 observation/measurement vector:

$$z_k = Hx_k + v_k \tag{4.2}$$

H is a j-by-n observation model matrix which maps the true state into the observed space. $\mathbf{v_k}$ is an observation noise j-by-1 vector with covariance $\mathbf{R_k}$.

The Discrete Kalman filter has two distinct phases which are used to compute the next dynamic system state's estimate.

Predict

project the state vector ahead:

$$\hat{x}_{k+1}^{-} = A\hat{x}_k + Bu_{k+1} \tag{4.3}$$

project the error covariance matrix ahead:

$$P_{k+1}^{-} = AP_k A^T + Q_k \tag{4.4}$$

The predict phase uses the state estimate information from the past time step to produce an estimate for the future state.

Update

compute the Kalman gain:

$$K_{k+1} = P_{k+1}^{-} H^T (HP_{k+1}^{-} H^T + R_k)^{-1} \tag{4.5}$$

update the estimate of the state vector with a measurement z_k:

$$\hat{x}_{k+1} = \hat{x}_{k+1}^{-} + K_{k+1}(z_{k+1} - H\hat{x}_{k+1}^{-}) \tag{4.6}$$

update the error covariance matrix:

$$P_{k+1} = (I - K_{k+1}H)P_{k+1}^{-} \tag{4.7}$$

Once the future system's state becomes current, the new measurement information is used to refine the predictions made in the predict phase, which allows the Kalman Filter to come to the more precise dynamic system's state estimate.

5 Attention Focus Kalman Filter Design

We model HVS as a system that has two state vectors $x_k = \begin{bmatrix} \theta_x(k) \\ \dot{\theta}_x(k) \end{bmatrix}$ and $y_k = \begin{bmatrix} \theta_y(k) \\ \dot{\theta}_y(k) \end{bmatrix}$. $\theta_x(k)$ represents the horizontal and $\theta_y(k)$ represents vertical eye position on the screen. $\dot{\theta}_x(k)$, $\dot{\theta}_x(k)$ represent the horizontal and vertical eye-velocity, respectively, at the time k. The state transition matrix is $A_k = \begin{bmatrix} 1 & \Delta t \\ 0 & 1 \end{bmatrix}$.

where Δt is the system's eye-gaze sampling interval. The observation matrix for both state vectors is: $H_k = [1 \quad 0]$

The standard deviation for the instrument noise relates to the accuracy of the eye-tracker equipment and is bounded by one degree of the visual angle, thus making the standard deviation of measurement noise $R_k = \delta_v^2 = 1°$.

In the scenario when the eye-position signal is corrupted $R_k = \delta_v^2 = 1000°$ The standard deviation of the process noise, in our case the noise inside of the eye, has to do with three eye-sub-movements during an eye-fixation: drift, small involuntary saccades and tremor. Among those three, involuntary saccades have the highest amplitude - around half of the visual angle. We create an upper boundary of 1° as a system's noise estimation and use the following covariance matrix for the system's noise process: $Q_k = \begin{bmatrix} \delta_w^2 & 0 \\ 0 & \delta_w^2 \end{bmatrix}°$ where $\delta_w^2 = 1°$ represents the variance of the HVS noise.

6 Designing Interaction with AFKF

Eye Movement Detection by AFKF

Saccade detection was performed through the method proposed by Sauter [8]. Chi square test monitors the difference between predicted and observed eye-velocity:

$$\chi^2 = \sum_{i=1}^{p} \frac{(\dot{\theta}_i^- - \dot{\theta}_i)^2}{\delta^2} \tag{6.1}$$

where $\dot{\theta}_i^-$ is the predicted eye-velocity computed with Equation 4.3 and $\dot{\theta}_i$ is the observed eye-velocity. δ is the standard deviation of the measured eye-velocity during the sampling interval under consideration. Once a certain threshold of the χ^2 is achieved a saccade is detected (value of 150 is used in our system). It was reported by Giringer that the filter behaves better if the standard deviation δ is a constant. Our experiments use values $\delta^2 = 1000$ and p=5 proposed by Giringer.

We have developed a function to map the value of χ^2 to the amplitude of the corresponding saccade. The development of such a function is possible due to the fact that HVS uses phasic (fast) eye-muscle fibers with high motoneuronal firing rate for large saccades and tonic (slow) eye-muscle fibers with lower motoneuronal firing rate for the saccades of lesser amplitude [6]. This mechanism ensures different rate of rise of eye-muscle force for the saccades of various amplitudes providing higher acceleration to the eye globe during saccades of high amplitude. We have derived the function matching saccade amplitude to the value by empirical testing. Let A_{sac_deg} represent the amplitude of a saccade measured in degrees, then:

$$A_{sac\_amp} = -0.000024\chi^6 + 0.0536\chi^4 + 1.5 \quad (6.2)$$

Once the amplitude of the saccade is determined the duration of the saccade is calculated through the equation developed by Carpenter [12].

$$D_{sac\_dur} = (2.2A_{sac\_amp} + 21)/1000 \quad (6.3)$$

D_{sac_dur} is saccade duration measured in seconds.

Eye-fixation detection analysis is performed on updated through the AFKF eye-positions (Equation 4.6). If the eye velocity threshold did not exceed 0.5 deg/sec for a specified period of time (minimum 100 msec.), then an eye-fixation was detected.

Smooth pursuit was detected when the eye-position sample was not a part of an eye-fixation or a saccade and the eye-velocity did not exceed 140 deg/sec (the termination condition for smooth pursuit).

6.2 Eye-Movement-Based Interaction Language

Eye-movement language can be created by identifying basic eye-movement types and using them as tokens for more complex language structures. The spatial and temporal information for each language token combined with content and context information has to be considered before each sentence is evaluated into a specific command. The challenge in the eye-movement language design is due to the fact that humans usually do not use their eye-movements to control the environment. The HVS consists of eye-movements that can be intentionally controlled and ones that cannot. As an example, an eye-fixation is a voluntary eye movement - each of us can look at a point of interest and examine it at will. The length of this examination can be varied voluntarily as well. Saccadic eye movements can be voluntary and can be involuntary. If we move our eyes from one point of the screen to another point, the saccadic eye movements involved would be voluntary. If we are looking at the screen and something catches our attention in the periphery, then the HVS moves to the new target with involuntary saccades. Smooth pursuit eye-movements are involuntary. The interaction approach proposed by Jacobs [1] is to use eye-fixations of different durations to manipulate various interface components. In the implementation of our system, we use eye-fixation tokens with a length of 500 msec. to select the interface components. The smooth pursuit tokens were used to center the object of interest on the screen.

7 Perceptual Compression with AFKF

Feedback Loop Delay

The feedback loop delay T_d is the period of time between the instant the eye position is detected by an eye-tracker and the moment when a perceptually compressed image is displayed. The delay existence disrupts the eye-gaze-based systems due to uncertainty that it brings [7].

Perceptual Attention Focus Window
Our system compensates for the feedback loop delay by constructing a Perceptual Attention Focus Window (W^{PAW}) [7]. Figure 1 present W^{PAW} diagram.

Enhanced Perceptual Attention Window
This paper introduces Enhanced Perceptual Attention Window (W^{EPAW}) that has a better performance than W^{PAW}.

The most significant shifts in eye-position happen during saccades. Once a saccade is detected through a chi-square test, the saccade amplitude and duration are calculated using Equations 6.2 and 6.3. The eye-movement trajectory during a saccade is predicted by Robinson's model [13].

$$\theta_{sac}(t) = \theta(t) + A_{sac\_amp}(20t + 0.24e^{-83t} - 0.24) \tag{6.1}$$

where A_{sac_amp} is the amplitude of the saccade calculated from Equation 6.2, t=0 is the onset of the saccade, $\theta(t)$ is eye-position at the beginning of the saccade. At the end of the saccadic eye-movement Human Visual System takes at least 200 msec. or longer to calculate the next saccade target [12]. This assumption allows us to place W^{EPAW} center during the saccade and for additional 200 msec. after the saccade at the coordinates provided by Robinson's model. In all other cases the W^{EPAW} center coordinates are calculated through the prediction done by AFKF:

$$x_{EPAW\_center}(k) = \dot{\theta}_x^-(k - T_d) \quad y_{EPAW\_center}(k) = \dot{\theta}_y^-(k - T_d) \tag{6.2}$$

The future predicted eye-speed is calculated as:

$$V_{EPAW\_FPES\_x}(k) = \sum_{i=m}^{k} \frac{\sqrt{(x_{EPAW\_center}(i - T_d) - \theta_x(i - T_d))^2}}{k - m} \tag{6.3}$$

where $\theta_x(i - T_d)$ is the observed eye-gaze position by the eye tracker.

W^{EPAW} model transforms visual sensitivity function discussed earlier into more complex function which was presented in our previous work [7].

8 Experiment Setup

Equipment
The proposed system was implemented with Applied Science Laboratories eye-tracker model 504. The system was tested with a 24 inch flat screen monitor and a Core Duo E6600 powered computer with 2GB of RAM.

Interaction
The interaction capabilities of the AFKF where tested by playing the World of Warcraft video game. World of Warcraft is a massively multiplayer online role-playing game with a dynamic virtual 3D environment. A player creates an in game avatar that he or she controls. The avatar interacts with the environment by moving around in a virtual world, selecting different objects, and trading or destroying those objects. The mouse cursor in the game was controlled by the AFKF-generated eye-movement language tokens described in Section 6. The project was implemented

under the *World of Warcraft Percept Interface* name using the Microsoft Foundation Class Library (MFC); more details are available at [3].

Perceptual Compression

The system's perceptual compression capabilities were tested with the following MPEG-2 video clip:

Shamu: This video captures an evening performance of Shamu at a Sea World, during night time under a tracking spotlight. The video consists of several moving objects: Shamu, the trainer, and the crowd. Each object is moving at different speeds during various periods of time. The background of the video was constantly moving due to the fact that the camera was trying to follow Shamu.

Participants

The experiments were conducted with one male subject with normal vision.

9 Results

Signal Noise Removal

Eye-tracker eye-position data was classified as noisy when the eye-tracker failed to report proper eye-position. The failure to identify proper eye-position usually happens due to the subject's jerky head movements, changes in the content's lighting, etc. When the eye-position cannot be properly identified the eye-tracker reports it with negative eye-position values. In this case the AFKF uses the signal noise measurement covariance matrix defined in Section 4.

An example of noise removal by the AFKF is presented in Figure 2.

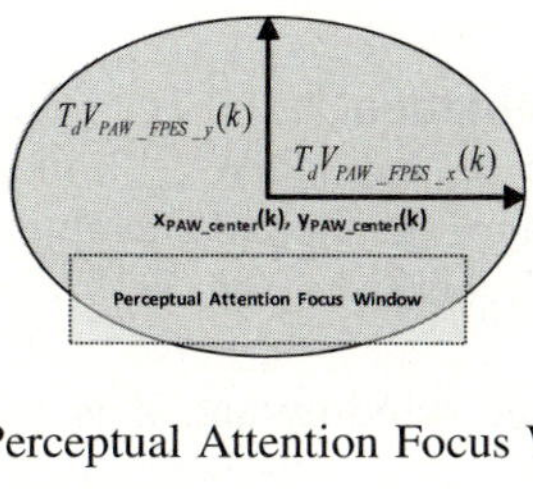

Fig. 1. Perceptual Attention Focus Window diagram

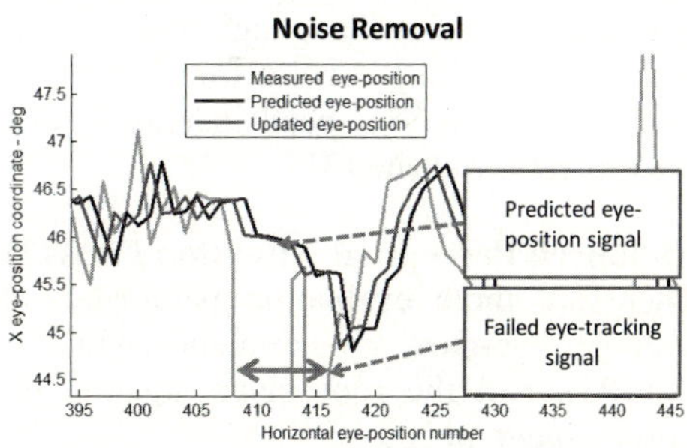

Fig. 2. Eye-tracker signal de-tracker signal de-tracker signal

Interaction

It was possible to interact with the World of Warcraft game using eye-movement language tokens generated by the AFKF and described in Section 6. Selection of an object inside the game is presented by Figure 3. Through eye-movement interaction

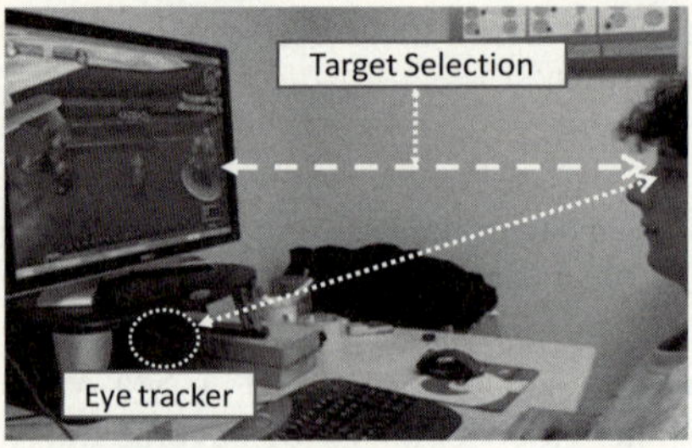

Fig. 3. Target selection byan eye-fixation token generated by the AFKF

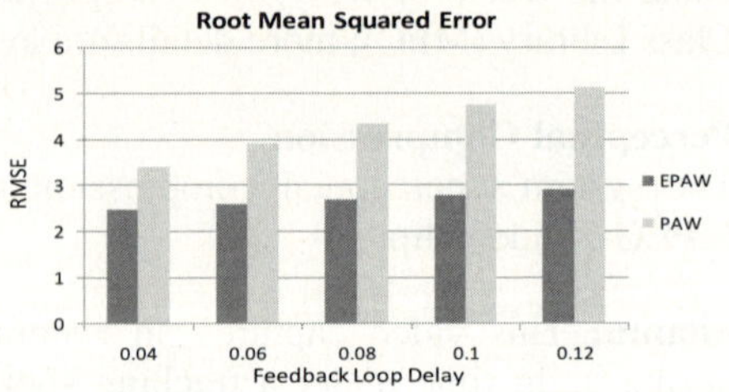

Fig. 4. W^{EPAW} vs. W^{PAW}. Root Mean Squared Error estimation.

the game environment feels more alive: the world talks back when you look at it. The selection of objects is done much faster than through the use of mouse and it feels as the system anticipates the user's intentions.

Several difficulties were encountered during the system's testing as well. 1) The Midas touch problem described by Jacob [1] - no matter what you look at it gets activated. It becomes annoying when you would like to inspect something rather than activate it. This problem can probably be solved by changing the eye-fixation token's activation lengths for different types of menus and objects. 2) It was hard to select very small menu items inside the game due to the fact that the eye-tracker accuracy is around 1°. 3) The slippage in eye calibaration.The recalibration was usually required after 5 minutes in order to restore the accuracy of the eye-tracking. 4) Another problem is that a player would like to do several things simultaneously such as select objects, use different spells or character abilities to interact with these objects (e.g. trade, destroy), and move around. Previously simultaneous actions were possible through the use of a keyboard and mouse, but executing the same sequence of actions with eye-movement language tokens requires more time. This issue can be partially resolved by adding a voice input to the interface. With such multichannel inputs the interface interaction speed increases considerably. More information is available at the project's website [3].

Enhanced Perceptual Attention Focus Window Evaluation

There are three evaluation parameters that we use to validateW^{EPAW} model: the average eye-gaze containment (AEGC), the average perceptual resolution gain (APRG), and the root mean squared error (RMSE) between the W^{EPAW} and the observed eye-position.

The RMSE measures the quality of the constructed window and it is calculated using the following formula:

$$RMSE_{EPAW}(k)=\sum_{i=m}^{k}\frac{\sqrt{(x_{EPAW\_center}(i)-\theta_x(i))^2}}{k-m} \tag{9.1}$$

where $x_{PAW\_center}(i)$ is the center of the W^{PAW} at the time k, $\theta_x(i)$ is the horizontal eye-position at the time i, m is the beginning of the sampling interval (m=T_d in our system's case) and k is the end of the sampling interval (full experiment length). The RMSE shows how close the predicted W^{PAW} center is to the actual eye-position.

Average Eye-Gaze containment

The AEGC is a percentage of the eye-position samples contained within the W^{EPAW}.

$$AEGC(k) = \frac{100}{k-m}\sum_{i=m}^{k} GAZE^{EPAW}(i) \tag{9.2}$$

The variable $GAZE^{EPAW}(i)$ equals one when the ith eye-position is inside of the W^{EPAW}, and it equals zero otherwise. The AEGC includes all of these types of the eye-movements: eye-fixations, saccades, and smooth pursuit. As we have investigated in our previous research, the AEGC provides a more conservative estimation than does the average eye-fixation containment.

Average Perceptual Resolution Gain

The actual amount of bandwidth and computational burden reduction when using the W^{PAW} depends on these two parameters: the size of the area which requires high quality coding (W^{PAW}) and the visual degradation of the periphery. the APRG mathematically estimates the amount of perceptual compression, but the actual implementation numbers may differ.

$$APRG(k) = \frac{H * W * (k-m)}{\sum_{i=m}^{k} \int_0^W \int_0^H S_i(x, y)dxdy} \tag{9.3}$$

$S_i(x, y)$ – is the eye sensitivity function. One degree of visual angle is added to each dimension of the W^{PAW}. This is done to address the situation when the center of an eye-fixation falls on the boundary of the W^{PAW} - an eye can see approximately one degree of visual angle with highest quality from the center of an eye-fixation. This approach assures that the viewer will not see the degradative effect if the W^{PAW} contains this eye-fixation. W and H are the width and height of the visual image.

Evaluation parameters

<u>Root Mean Squared Error:</u> Figure 4 shows the RMSE values for the W^{PAW} constructed previously in [7] and the Enhanced Perceptual Attention Focus Window designed in Section 7. W^{EPAW} performed much better for all delay scenarios, reducing RMSE by up to 2° per sampling interval.

<u>Average Eye-Gaze Containment:</u> Figure 5 presents the AEGC value achieved by the W^{EPAW} for different delay scenarios. In all cases the AEGC is higher than 90%. For a 0.1 sec. delay and higher the AEGC is close to 100%. This result means that the perceptual compression is going to be completely unnoticed by the AFKF system's user.

<u>Average Perceptual Resolution Gain</u>: Figure 6 presents the APRG value achieved by the W^{EPAW} for different delay scenarios. The highest APRG value of 2.3 was achieved by the lowest feedback loop delay scenario of 40 msec. The size of the W^{EPAW} grows considerably when the delay is increased. The increase in delay decreases the compression factor of perceptual compression. For example, delay values of more than 0.12 sec. produce an APRG close to 1, indicating than no compression is possible. The higher APRG value the higher is bandwidth reduction and computational burden reduction. The exact numbers will depend on how visual sensitivity function is mapped to the specific encoding scheme.

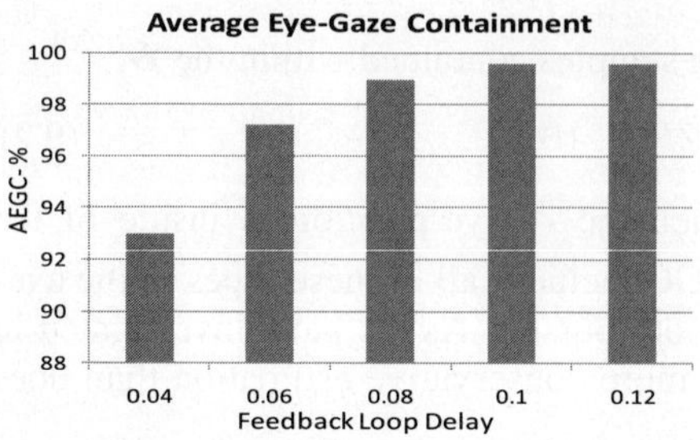

Fig. 5. Average Eye-Gaze Containment achieved by the WEPAW for various feedback delay values

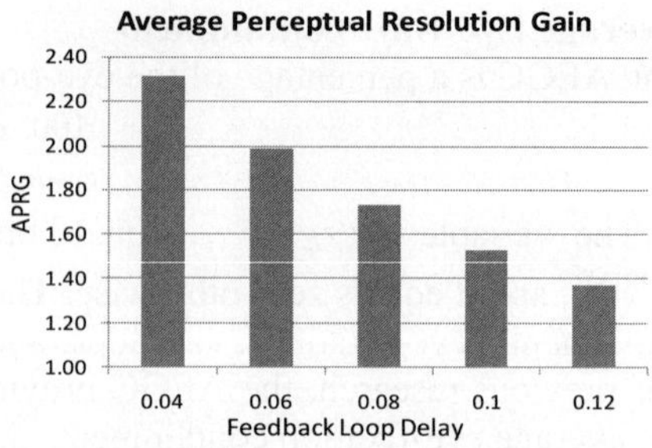

Fig. 6. Average Perceptual Resolution Gain achieved by the WEPAW for various feedback delay values

10 Conclusion

The human computer interaction world is rapidly growing. The community searches for new methods and inputs to provide a more natural, seamless way of communication. Eye-tracking technology can be successfully used to substitute or enhance already existing interaction models and provide more ubiquitous interactive environments.

In this paper we have designed the Attention Focus Kalman Filter framework that removes the noisy signal from the eye-position data stream, creates eye-movement language tokens for interaction, and provides the means for perceptual compression.

The advantage of the proposed framework is the fact that it is equipment- and media- independent. Any eye-tracker vendor can use the AFKF to improve the accuracy of the eye-tracking signal.

The eye-movement language can be applied to any eye-gaze-based interface by adjusting the detection and triggering parameters. We successfully tested the interaction capabilities of the eye-movement language in [3].

The concept of a Perceptual Attention Focus Window can be applied to any visual content by mapping the visual sensitivity function to a specific codec. The potential provided by perceptual compression is high, especially for the scenarios where loop delay values are low.

References

[1] Jacob, R.J.K.: Eye tracking in advanced interface design, Virtual environments and advanced interface design. Oxford University Press, Inc., New York, NY (1995)

[2] Ware, C., Mikaelian, H.T.: An Evaluation of an Eye Tracker as a Device for Computer Input. In: Proc. ACM CHI+GI'87 Human Factors in Computing Systems Conference pp. 183–188 (1987)

[3] Komogortsev, O.: World of Warcraft Percept Interface http://www.cs.kent.edu/ okomogor/ wowpercept/wowpercept.htm

[4] Duchowski, A.T.: Eye Tracking Methodology: Theory and Practic. Springer, London, UK (2003)

[5] Grindinger, T.: Eye Movement Analysis and Prediction with the Kalman Filter, Masters thesis, Computer Science, Clemson University, Clemson, SC, USA (August 2006)

[6] Bahill, A.T.: Development, validation and sensitivity analyses of human eye movement models. CRC Critical Reviews in Bioengineering 4, 311–355 (1980)

[7] Komogortsev, O., Khan, J.: Perceptual Multimedia Compression based on the Predictive Kalman Filter Eye Movement Modeling. In: Proceedings of the Multimedia Computing and Networking Conference (MMCN'07), San Jose, pp. 1–12 (January 28 – February 1, 2007)

[8] Sauter, D., Martin, B.J., Di Renzo, N., Vomscheid, C.: Analysis of eyetracking movements using innovations generated by a Kalman filter. Med. Biol. Eng. Comput 29, 63–69 (1991)

[9] Norimichi, T., Chizuko, E., Hideaki, H., Yoichi, M.: Image compression and decompression based on gazing area. In: Human Vision and Electronic Imagin, SPIE (April 1996)

[10] Stelmach, L.B., Tam, W.J.: Processing image sequences based on eye movements. In: Proc. SPIE 2179, 90–98 (1994)

[11] Murphy, H., Duchowski, A.T.: Gaze-Contigent Level Of Detail Rendering. Eurographics 2001 (2001)

[12] Carpenter, R.H.S.: Movements of the Eyes, pp. 56–57. Pion, London (1977)

[13] Robinson, D.A.: Models of the saccadic eye movement control system. Kybernetic 14, 71 (1973)

Human Shape Tracking for Gait Recognition Using Active Contours with Mean Shift

Kyung Su Kwon[1], Se Hyun Park[2], Eun Yi Kim[3], and Hang Joon Kim[1]

[1] Department of Computer Engineering, Kyungpook National Univ., Korea
{kskwon,hjkim}@ailab.knu.ac.kr
[2] School of Computer and Communication, Daegu Univ., Korea
sehyun@daegu.ac.kr
[3] Department of Internet and Multimedia Engineering, Konkuk Univ., Korea
eykim@konkuk.ac.kr

Abstract. In this paper, we present a human shape extraction and tracking for gait recognition using geodesic active contour models(GACMs) combined with mean-shift algorithm. The active contour models (ACMs) are very effective to deal with the non-rigid object because of its elastic property, but they have the limitation that their performance is mainly dependent on the initial curve. To overcome this problem, we combine the mean-shift algorithm with the traditional GACMs. The main idea is very simple. Before evolving using level-set method, the initial curve in each frame is re-localized near the human region and is resized enough to include the targe object. This mechanism allows for reducing the number of iterations and for handling the large object motion. Our system is composed of human region detection and human shape tracking. In the human region detection module, the silhouette of a walking person is extracted by background subtraction and morphologic operation. Then human shape are correctly obtained by the GACMs with mean-shift algorithm. To evaluate the effectiveness of the proposed method, it is applied the common gait data, then the results show that the proposed method is extracted and tracked efficiently accurate shape for gait recognition.

Keywords: Human Shape Tracking, Geodesic Active Contour Models, Mean Shift, Gait Recognition.

1 Introduction

During the decades, the gait recognition has recently has received many attentions from computer vision researchers [1-5]. The human gait recognition is the process of identifying individuals by way of their walking at a distance [1]. It has many applications such as visual surveillance, security management, smart interface, and the human identification. The major issue related to the gait recognition is to generate the accurate human shapes. Generally, the human gait is determined by their weight, limb length, habitual posture and so on [2]. To use these features in gait recognition, the technique should be firstly developed to extract and track the human shape.

J. Jacko (Ed.): Human-Computer Interaction, Part III, HCII 2007, LNCS 4552, pp. 690–699, 2007.

However, it is difficult problem as the human shape is deformed variously in an image sequence and also includes discontinuous and dim edge [6].

Recently, active contour models (ACMs) have been increasingly used in object extraction and tracking. ACMs are effective to describe the elastic properties of the non-rigid objects, so that can provide the detailed analysis of the shape deformation during the human is moving through the whole video sequences.

In this paper, we present a human shape extraction and tracking for gait recognition using geodesic active contour models (GACMs) combined with mean-shift algorithm. The GACMs are specially designed to overcome the major drawback of the ACMs that the performance is higly dependent on the initial curve [7]. The main idea is very simple. Before evolving using level-set method, the initial curve in each frame is re-localized near the human region and is resized enough to include the targe object.

Fig. 1 shows the overview of the proposed system, which is composed of human region detection and human shape tracking. In the human region detection, the silhouette of a walking person is extracted by background subtraction and morphologic operation. Thereafter, in the human shape tracking, the human shape is correctly obtained by the GACMs with mean-shift algorithm. The tracking is performed by two steps: curve localization step and curve deformation step. When given the initial curve of the current frame from the object contour of the previous frame, the initial curve is firstly localized near the target object using mean-shift algorithm, and then it is deformed using a level-set method.

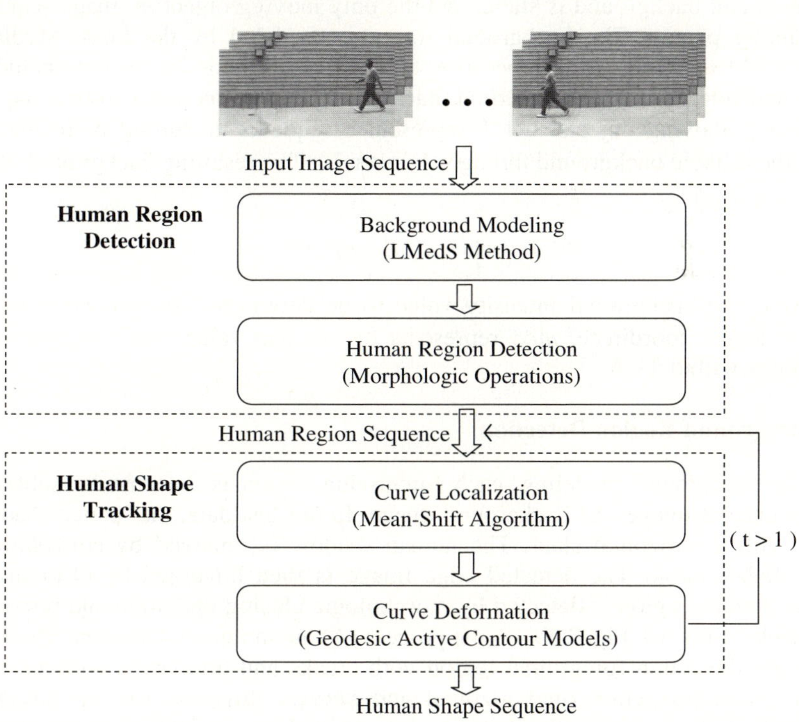

Fig. 1. Overview of the proposed method

To evaluate the effectiveness of the proposed method, it is applied the common gait data [8] which include a walking person. Experiment results show that the proposed method is extracted and tracked efficiently accurate shape for gait recognition.

The remainder of this paper is organized as follows. Section 2 describes the human region detection. Section 3 describes the human shape extraction and tracking. Experimental results are presented in Section 4. Finally, the conclusion is drawn in Section 5.

2 Human Region Detection

In this section, we firstly present the human region detection algorithm for getting shape information of a walking person from each frame of an image sequence. This is the preprocessing phase of human tracking. And it is composed two steps: background modeling and human region detection.

2.1 Background Modeling

To extract the human region, background subtraction based change detection in between the current image and background image is adopted. We have assumed that the camera and background is static, and the only moving object in image sequences is a walking person. The background image is modeled by the Least Median of Squares (LMedS) method [9] because, the used gait data [8] is not included a background image. Using this method, background can be modeled from a sequence of including moving objects. Let I represent a sequence including N images. We can get the reliable background through N over 70. The resulting background $B(i, j)$ can be computed by

$$B(i, j) = \min_{q} med_{t}(I_{ij}^{t} - q)^2, \tag{1}$$

where q is the background intensity value to be determined for the pixel location (i, j) on image coordinate, med represents the median value, and t represents the frame index within $1-N$.

2.2 Foreground Region Detection

After the background modeling, each foreground region is detected by subtraction between current image and background image. In our test data, the human shadow is existed with a horizontal slant. The human shadow is removed by convolution of vertical Sobel mask. The detected edge image is then binarized by Ostu method. Accurate human region is detected by morphologic closing operation and removal of inner black points [6]. Fig. 2 shows the process of human region detection. Thereafter, we can get the rough foreground region with cracks and dim edges without human shadow. After projection on horizontal and vertical direction for the foreground region, gained range of region projection is used to determine initial curve's position (the centroid) and size of GACMs.

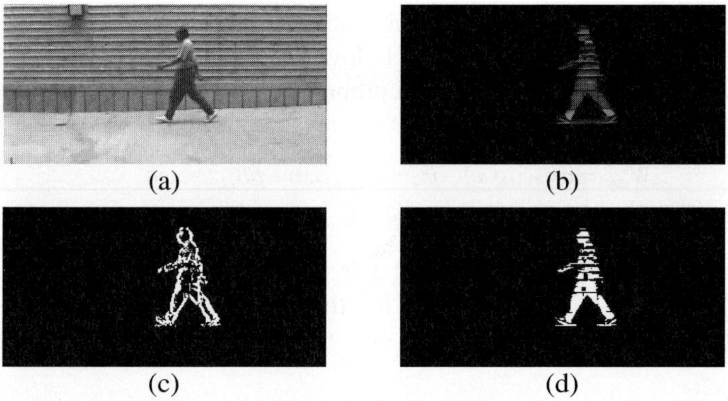

Fig. 2. The procedure of human region detection: (a) an original image, (b) the result of background subtraction, (c) an edge image after performing the vertical Sobel operation, (d) a foreground image without human shadow

3 Human Shape Tracking

After human region is detected, GACMs combined with a mean-shift algorithm for human shape tracking is used. In general, the ACMs are very effective to extract the boundary of the non-rigid object. Howere, they have the limitation that their performance is mainly dependent on conditions of the initial curve such as location and size. To solve this problem, we present a method of human shape tracking using a GACM and a mean-shift algorithm. In this method, the tracking process is achieved by two steps: curve localization step and curve deformation step. In first step, a mean-shift algorithm is used to move the initial curve near the human region. And the re-localized init curve is resized enough to include the target region. In the second set, the curve is deformed by a level-set method.

3.1 Curve Localization Using Mean-Shift

The mean-shift algorithm is a nonparametric technique that climbs the gradient of a probability distribution to find the nearest dominant mode [10]. This algorithm has recently been used as an efficient technique for object tracking [11]. In this paper, a mean-shift algorithm to replace the curve location in every frame excepted the first frame is used. And the curve location is determined by the number of pixels belong to human region in search window. The human region is represented by a binary foreground image $F(i, j)$.

The mean-shift algorithm iteratively replace the search window location (the centroid) until the moving distance of window below the threshold. The search window location is simply computed as follows [12, 13]:

$$x = M_{10} / M_{00} \quad \text{and} \quad y = M_{01} / M_{00}, \tag{2}$$

where M_{ab} is the $(a+b)th$ moment as defined by

$$M_{ab}(W) = \sum_{i,j \in W} i^a j^b F(i, j).$$

The object location is obtained by successive computations of the search window location (i, j). The center of search window W is initialized with the center of the initial curve. And its size is updated in proportional to the amount of object's motion at each frame as follows:

$$W_{width} = \max(\alpha(|m_x^t - m_x^{t-1}| - B_{width}), 0) + \beta B_{width} \quad \text{and}$$
$$W_{height} = \max(\alpha(|m_y^t - m_y^{t-1}| - B_{height}), 0) + \beta B_{height}, \tag{3}$$

where α and β is a constant, and the t is the frame index. Fig. 3 shows the curve localization by mean-shift algorithm. After the initial curve is localized, to completely surround the target region, the initial curve firstly is resized to outward of human region.

(a) (b) (c)

Fig. 3. Curve localization: (a) the result of curve evolving in the first frame, (b) the init curve in the second frame, and (c) the result of curve re-localization in the second frame

3.2 Curve Deformation Using Level-Set

Then the re-localized and scaled curve is deformed until it matches the human boundary using GACs. The GACMs was proposed by Vicent Caselles as a geometric alternative for snakes with the object of finding the curve $C(q)$ that minimizes the following energy [12]:

$$E(C) = \int_0^1 g(|\nabla I(C(q)|)|C'(q)|dq, \tag{4}$$

where $C'(q)$ is the partial derivative of curve, q is its parameter and $g(.)$ is a monotonically decreasing function such as a Gaussian and delta function.

The object boundary detection is to finding the curve that best take into account image characteristics. In order to minimize the energy E, the steepest-descent method, Euler-Lagrange equation is used. According to it, the curve evolution equation is derived as following:

$$C_t = g(|\nabla I|)k\vec{N} - (\nabla g(|\nabla I|)\vec{N})\vec{N}, \tag{5}$$

where k is the Euclidean curvature, $\vec{N}$ is the unit inward normal vector and t denotes the time as the contour evolves.

The geodesic curve equation (5) was implemented using level-set technique. We represent curve C implicitly by the zero level-set of function $u: \Re^2 \rightarrow \Re$, with the region inside C corresponding to $u > 0$. Accordingly, Eq. (5) can be rewritten by the following equation, which is a level-set evolution equation [7]:

$$u_t = g(|\nabla I|) k |\nabla u| + \nabla g(|\nabla I|) |\nabla u| \tag{6}$$

The unit inward normal vector $\vec{N}$ and the curvature value k is estimated from the level-set function u as following:

$$\vec{N} = -\frac{\nabla u}{|\nabla u|}, \quad k = div\left(\frac{\nabla u}{|\nabla u|}\right).$$

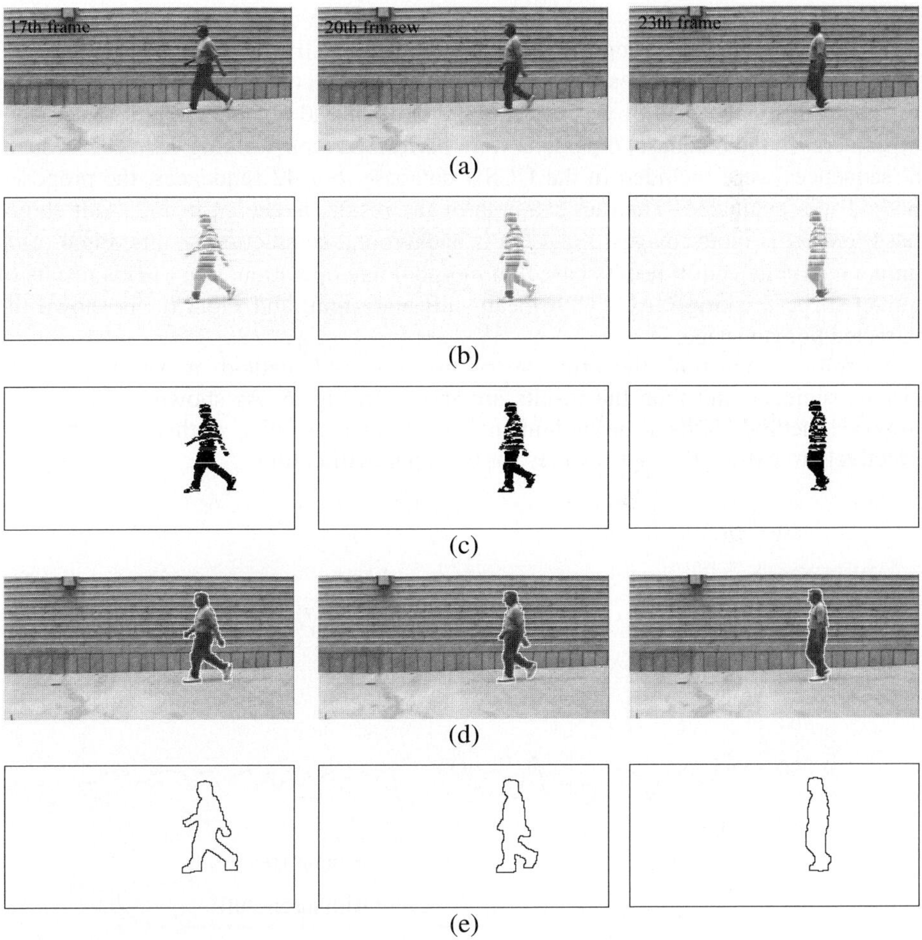

Fig. 4. Results of human region detection and shape tracking: (a) the input images, (b) the background subtraction results, (c) the human region detection results, (d) the human shape tracking results, (e) the extracted human shape is shown

To set up the initial level set values, we use a Euclidian distance mapping technique which is computed Euclidian distance between each pixel of the image and initial curve's centroid. And the evolving area is determined by narrow band approach, which is defined around the latest contour position and the level-set function is updated only within a set of narrow band pixels. The curve evolving is terminated when the difference of the number of pixel inside contour C is less than a threshold value chosen manually.

4 Experimental Results

The proposed system was implemented using MS Visual C++ 6.0 and Intel's OpenCV beta3.1. The computer is a PentiumIV-2.8GHz with the Windows XP operation system. The proposed system was evaluated on the UCSD database [8]. The image size is a 320×160. It was taken in the outdoor and obtained at a distance from the camera. In the database, 6 persons were performed their walking 7 times. As such, 42 sequences were included in the UCSD database. For 42 sequences, the proposed method was evaluated. Then an example of the results is shown in Fig. 4. It shows that Fig.4 (a) is input images, Fig.4 (b) is background subtraction results, Fig.4 (c) is human region detection results based on morphologic operation, Fig.4 (d) is results of human shape tracking GACs with mean-shift algorithm, and Fig.4 (e) is shown the extracted human shape.

To fully demonstrate the effective of the proposed method, it was tested with various subjects, and then the results are shown in Fig. 6. As shown in Fig. 6, the proposed method yields accurate human shape tracking results, so that it can be used effectively to extract the gait features for human identification.

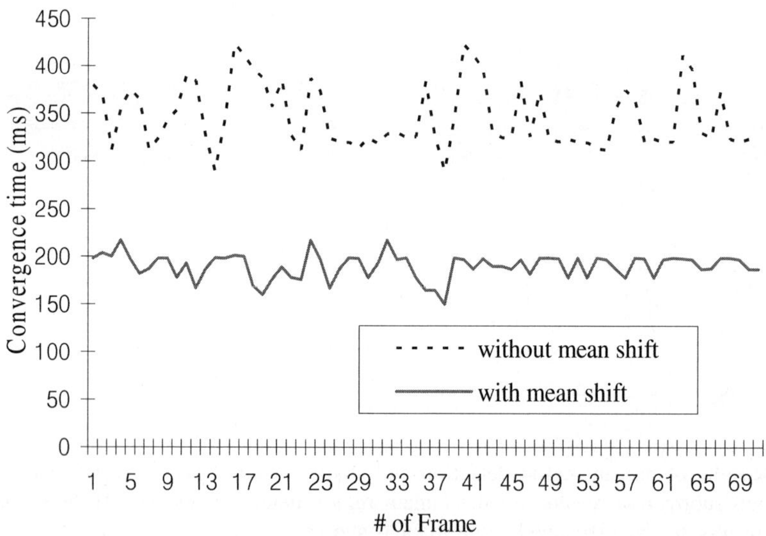

Fig. 5. Comparison of two methods in term of convergence time

(a) the person #2 (25th, 28th and 28th frame)

(b) the person #4 (33th, 36th and 37th frame)

(c) the person #6 (33th, 36th and 37th frame)

Fig. 6. Results of human shape tracking on the other subjects: (a), (b) and (c) are a subject of UCSD database, respectively

To quantitatively assess of validity of the proposed human shape tracking method, we compare the results between the proposed method using mean-shift algorithm and the method only using GACMs without mean-shift algorithm. The comparison in term of convergence speed on a sequence is shown in Fig.5. In the proposed method, the curve evolving function is fast converged because initial curve is re-localized neared the human region using mean-shift algorithm. Due to it, the method only using ACM takes larger time to track the human shape than the proposed method.

Consequently, the proposed method yields accurate human shape tracking, so that it can be used effectively to extract the gait features for human identification.

5 Conclusions

In this paper, we presented a human shape extraction and tracking method for gait recognition using geodesic active contour models (GACMs) combined with mean-shift algorithm. Our system consists of two modules: the human region detection and the human shape tracking. In the human region detection module, the silhouette of a walking person is extracted by background subtraction and morphologic operation. Then human shapes are correctly obtained by the GAC with mean-shift algorithm. The main idea is very simple. Before evolving using level-set method, the initial curve in each frame is re-localized near the human region and is resized enough to include the target object. To evaluate the effectiveness of the proposed method, it was applied the common gait data, then the results showed that the proposed method is extracted and tracked efficiently accurate shape for gait recognition.

Acknowledgments

This work was supported by the Korea Research Foundation Grant (KRF-2006-331-D00545).

References

1. Wang, L., Ning, H., Tan, T., Hu, W.: Automatic Gait Recognition Based on Statistical Shape Analysis. IEEE Transaction on Image Processing, 1120–1131 (2003)
2. Lee, L., Grimson, W.: Gait analysis for recognition and classification. In: Proceedings of the International Conference on Automatic Face and Gesture Recognition, pp. 155–162 (2002)
3. Collins, R., Cross, R., Shi, J.: Silhouette-based Human Identification from Body Shape and Gait. In: Proceedings of the International Conference on Face and Gesture Recognition, pp. 366–371 (2002)
4. Vega, I., Sarkar, S.: Statistical Motion Modell Based on the Change of Feature Relationships: Human Gait-Based Recognition. IEEE Transactions on Pattern Analysis and Machine Intelligence, 1323–1328 (2003)
5. Sarkar, S., Phillips, P.J., Liu, Z., Vega, I.R., Grother, P., Bowyer, K.: The HumnaID Gait Challenge Problem: Data Sets, Performance and Analysis. IEEE Transactions on Pattern Analysis and Machine Intelligence, 162–177 (2005)
6. Liu, L., Zhang, S., Zhang, Y., Ye, X.: Human Contour Extraction Using Level Set. In: Proceedings of the International Conference on Computer and Information Technology pp. 608–612 (2005)
7. Paragios, N., Deriche, R.: Geodesic Active Contours and Level Sets for the Detection and Tracking of Moving Objects. IEEE Transactions on Pattern Analysis and Machine Intelligence, 266–279 (2000)
8. Little, J., Boyd, J.: Recognizing People by Their Gait Description via Temporal Moments. Videre 1(2), 1–33 (1998)
9. Yang, Y., Levine, M.: The Background primal sketch: An approach for tracking moving objects. Mach. Vis. Applicant, 17–34 (1992)

10. Kim, K.I., Jung, K., Kim, H.J.: Texture-Based Approach for Text Detection in Image Using Support Vector Machines and Continuously Adaptive Mean Shift Algorithm. IEEE Transactions on Pattern Analysis and Machine Intelligence, 1631–1639 (2003)
11. Jaffre, G., Crouzil, A.: Non-rigid Object Localization From Color Model Using Mean Shift. In: Proceedings of the International Conference on Image Processing, vol. 3, pp. 317–319 (2003)
12. Caselles, V., Kimmel, R., Sapiro, G.: Geodesic Active Contours. In: Proceedings of IEEE the International Conference on Computer Vision, pp. 694–699 (1995)

Robust Gaze Tracking Method for Stereoscopic Virtual Reality Systems

Eui Chul Lee[1], Kang Ryoung Park[2], Min Cheol Whang[2], and Junseok Park[3]

[1] Dept. of Computer Science, Sangmyung University, 7 Hongji-dong, Jongro-Ku, Seoul, Republic of Korea
oryong@smu.ac.kr

[2] Division of Digital Media Technology, Sangmyung University, 7 Hongji-dong, Jongro-Ku, Seoul, Republic of Korea
{parkgr,whang}@smu.ac.kr

[3] Electronics and Telecommunications Research Institute, 161 Gajeong-Dong, Yuseong-gu, Daejon, Republic of Korea
parkjs@etri.re.kr

Abstract. In this paper, we propose a new face and eye gaze tracking method that works by attaching gaze tracking devices to stereoscopic shutter glasses. This paper presents six advantages over previous works. First, through using the proposed method with stereoscopic VR systems, users feel more immersed and comfortable. Second, by capturing reflected eye images with a hot mirror, we were able to increase eye gaze accuracy in a vertical direction. Third, by attaching the infrared passing filter and using an IR illuminator, we were able to obtain robust gaze tracking performance irrespective of environmental lighting conditions. Fourth, we used a simple 2D-based eye gaze estimation method based on the detected pupil center and the 'geometric transform' process. Fifth, to prevent gaze positions from being unintentionally moved by natural eye blinking, we discriminated between different kinds of eye blinking by measuring pupil sizes. This information was also used for button clicking or mode toggling. Sixth, the final gaze position was calculated by the vector summation of face and eye gaze positions and allowing for natural face and eye movements. Experimental results showed that the face and eye gaze estimation error was less than one degree.

1 Introduction

Recently, stereoscopic virtual reality (VR) systems have been widely used. Also, to make users feel more immersed, interested and comfortable within these VR systems, additional input devices (haptic devices, eye trackers, etc.) have been tried and applied [1–5]. However, when users have to wear semi-transparent shutter glasses to see stereoscopic displays, they may experience inconvenience when trying to use an input device such as a keyboard, a mouse, a haptic device, and so forth. Also, when using eye trackers, eye images cannot be seen through semi-transparent shutter glasses since the eyes can be hidden.

For example, in previous research on eye tracking, researchers used a gaze tracking system based on remote mono or stereo cameras that were able to pan, tilt and zoom.

J. Jacko (Ed.): Human-Computer Interaction, Part III, HCII 2007, LNCS 4552, pp. 700–709, 2007.

Yoo *et al.* used two cameras that were also able to pan and tilt, with wide and narrow view lenses and multi-infrared illuminators [6]. However, this method could not be applied to stereoscopic VR environments, because the exterior cameras could not capture eye images, and the infrared illuminators could not illuminate eye regions. Shih *et al.* analyzed the three-dimensional eye structure with a stereo camera and multiple light sources [7]. However, due to the above mentioned problems, this method also could not be applied to the stereoscopic VR environments.

In our previous work, we proposed a gaze tracking method by analyzing the three dimensional analysis of a human eye [21]. But, this method could not be applied to our system, because this method is suitable to a HMD environment and required so many operations caused by three dimensional analyses and using multiple illuminators.

In our other previous works, we used a similar eye tracking module compared with proposed system [17][19][20]. But, since this method was also suitable to a HMD environment, we could not use this method in the stereoscopic VR environments. In details, they did not consider the facial movement. The research [18] tracked both the facial and eye movement by vision-based method. However, it takes the complicated algorithm and additional illuminators on eyeglass to track the facial movement.

To overcome these problems, it is necessary to attach an eye gaze tracking camera below the shutter glasses as in our previous research [22]. However, because the camera captured eye regions in a slanted direction (due to the discrepancy between the glasses and the camera coordinates), the vertical resolution and consequent vertical accuracy of eye gaze tracking were prone to degradation.

Therefore, in this paper, we propose a new eye tracking method that works by attaching an eye tracking module (including a camera, an infrared illuminator and a hot mirror) and capturing eye images free from vertical distortion and resolution degradation. In addition, to eliminate errors caused by facial movements, we used the Polhemus sensor instead of a face tracking camera in our experiments, because eye features were not visible through the shutter glasses when using a face tracking camera.

2 The Proposed Method

Fig.1 shows the proposed method in a stereoscopic VR environment. This method was based on the following policies. First, we used a monocular camera with a single lens. Second, we used an infrared illuminator, an infrared passing filter and a hot mirror. Third, we compensated for the errors caused by facial movements or rotations during the gaze tracking process based on vectors calculated with a Polhemus sensor.

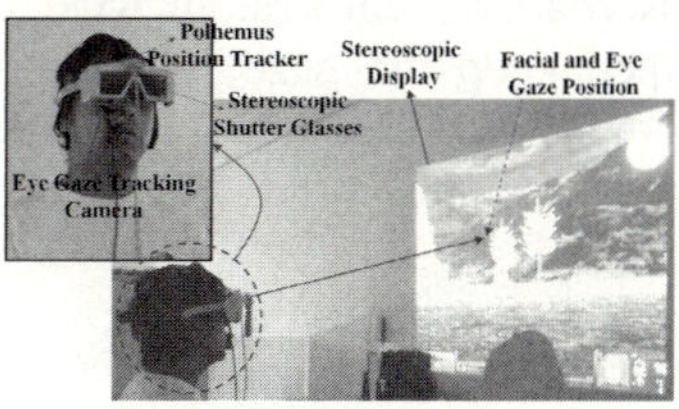

Fig. 1. Overview of the proposed method in a stereoscopic VR environment [18]

2.1 Proposed Gaze Tracking System

As shown in Fig. 2, the proposed method consisted of stereoscope shutter glasses [8], a small USB camera [9], one IR-LED (850nm), a hot mirror which reflected infrared light and passed visible light [10] and a Polhemus position tracking sensor [11].

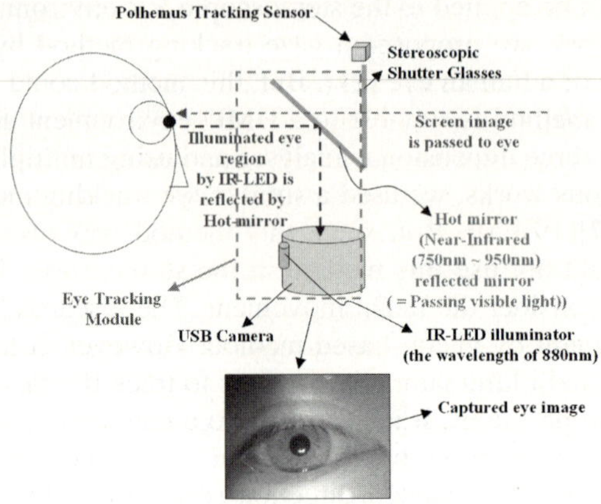

Fig. 2. Overview of the proposed face and eye gaze tracking system [17-20]

The shutter glasses were indispensable for viewing stereoscopic displays. Therefore, we used a small gaze tracking module and attached it to the space between the glasses and a given user's eye. Through this scheme, since the distance between the camera and the user's eye was so close, we were able to capture images at high spatial resolution. Also, the camera was able to capture images that were not affected by the semi-transparent lenses of the shutter glasses.

To acquire an accurate pupil area, we used an infrared LED [12]. Since this IR-LED had a wavelength of 880nm and a wide (36°) illumination angle, we were able to capture appropriate eye images that showed clear edges between pupils and irises.

Also, we used a hot mirror which reflected infrared lights and other visible lights. By using this specialized mirror, users were able to see screen images. The camera was also able to capture illuminated eye regions, as shown in Fig. 2.

Next, we attached an infrared (> 700nm) passing filter [13] to the lens of the camera, so that the system was not affected by environmental lighting conditions. In addition, by using invisible infrared lights, users did not experience 'dazzling' effects on their eyes. Also, since we used a USB camera, an ADC (analog to digital converter) was not required. This helped keep the gaze tracking system from becoming too heavy. For eye image capturing, we used a spatial resolution of 640×480 pixels with a frame rate of fifteen frames per second.

2.2 Detecting the Accurate Center of the Pupil

In general, when a perfect circular shape is projected onto the CCD plane of a camera based on the perspective transform [15], the projected shape is not actually a perfect circle but a distorted ellipse, as shown in Fig. 3. Therefore, we propose an accurate pupil detection algorithm. Although we first carried out circular edge detection, we also had to perform additional calculations. In iris recognition systems, researchers have commonly used the circular edge detection algorithm for segmenting pupil and iris regions [14]. However, this method was not suitable because it only works when the shape of the pupil is assumed to be a perfect circle.

Therefore, secondly, we defined a local area based on the initial center of each pupil acquired with circular edge detection. Then, since the pupil area showed a low grey level region compared with other areas [15], we binarized the local area by using a meaningful threshold value based on Gonzalez's method [15].

Third, we carried out morphological operations in order to fill in the hole (glint [16]) produced by specular reflections. These morphological operations included several erosions and dilations. Finally, through binarizing the local area, we were able to estimate the accurate center of the pupil.

However, when users blinked their eyes, our system was not able to estimate pupil areas, as shown in Fig. 4. When users closed their eyes, the initial center of each pupil was not measured correctly, as shown in Fig. 4 (a). Therefore, the number of black pixels obtained during the local binarization process was small compared with when the user's eye was open, as shown in Fig. 4 (b). Therefore, we used a heuristically-defined threshold of the number of black pixels (1257) to judge whether the user's eye was closed or not. If the system decided that the user's eye was closed, we used the pupil center which was acquired from the previous image frame.

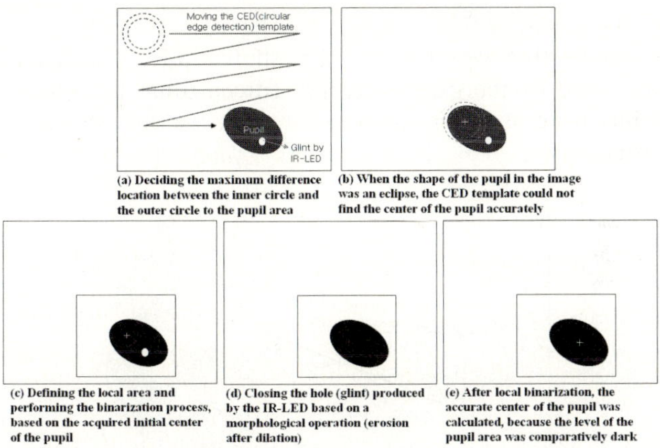

Fig. 3. Procedures used for detecting the accurate center of the pupil [17][19]

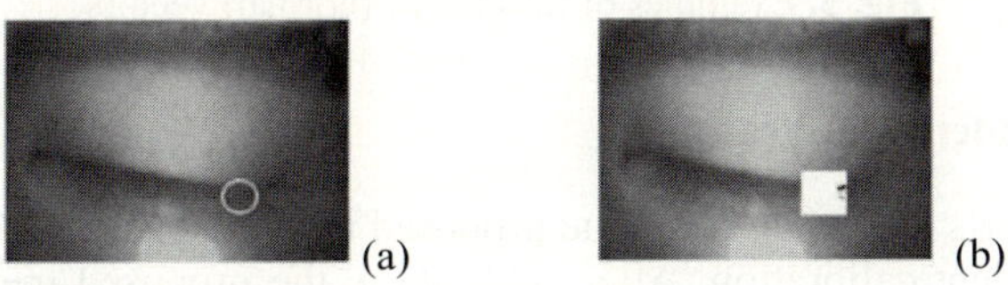

Fig. 4. Local binarization when eyes were blinked. (a) When the eye was closed, the initial center of the pupil was detected with circular edge detection. (b) Local binarization based on the initial center [17].

2.3 Calculating the Facial Gaze Point

In our system, we compensated for eye tracking results based on facial movements or rotations. The acquired data type obtained from the Polhemus tracking sensor was (x, y, z, θ, α, β). (x, y, z) represents the geometric offset between the receiver and the coil sensor. (θ, α, β) represents the angular offset between the receiver and the coil sensor. By using this data, we were able to easily calculate not only the normal facial vectors but also the intersection point with the monitor plane. The equations for calculating the normal facial vectors and the intersection point are as follows:

$$(\theta,\alpha,\beta)=(\theta_1,\alpha_1,\beta_1)-(\theta_2,\alpha_2,\beta_2) \tag{1}$$

In Eq. (1), (θ_1, α_1, β_1) represents a previous directional angle. (θ_2, α_2, β_2) represents a current directional angle. By subtracting one of these from the other, we were able to calculate the angular variation between the previous and current angles.

$$\begin{bmatrix} x' \\ y' \\ z' \\ 1 \end{bmatrix} = \begin{bmatrix} \cos\alpha\cdot\cos\beta & \sin\beta & -\sin\alpha\cdot\cos\beta & 0 \\ -\cos\theta\cdot\cos\alpha\cdot\sin\beta+\sin\theta\cdot\sin\alpha & \cos\theta\cdot\cos\beta & -\sin\alpha\cdot\cos\theta\cdot\sin\beta+\sin\theta\cdot\cos\alpha & 0 \\ -\sin\theta\cdot\sin\beta\cdot\cos\alpha+\cos\theta\cdot\sin\alpha & -\sin\theta\cdot\cos\beta & \sin\alpha\cdot\sin\theta\cdot\sin\beta+\cos\alpha\cdot\cos\theta & 0 \\ 0 & 0 & 0 & 1 \end{bmatrix} \begin{bmatrix} x \\ y \\ z \\ 1 \end{bmatrix} \tag{2}$$

Assuming that the initial direction ratio (x, y, z) was (0, 0, 1), the next direction ratio was calculated as Eq. (2):

$$\frac{x-x_2}{x'}=\frac{y-y_2}{y'}=\frac{z-z_2}{z'} \tag{3}$$

Finally, the gaze vectors were calculated as shown in Eq. (3). Arrival points on the screen were calculated by the gaze vectors at fifteen times per second. These calculated arrival points were used for compensating for eye gaze errors caused by facial movements or rotations.

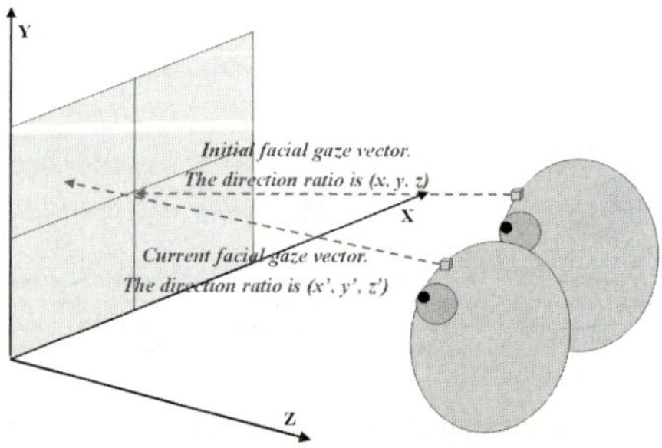

Fig. 5. Examples of facial gaze (normal) vectors

2.4 User-Dependent Calibration

To track each user's eye when using the proposed method, each user first had to complete user-dependent calibration. After calibration, the proposed method was able to calculate each user's eye gaze positions on a screen based on the calibrated centers of the pupil. When a user viewed the four corner points of the screen, the four centers of the pupil were seen, as shown in Fig. 6 (a).

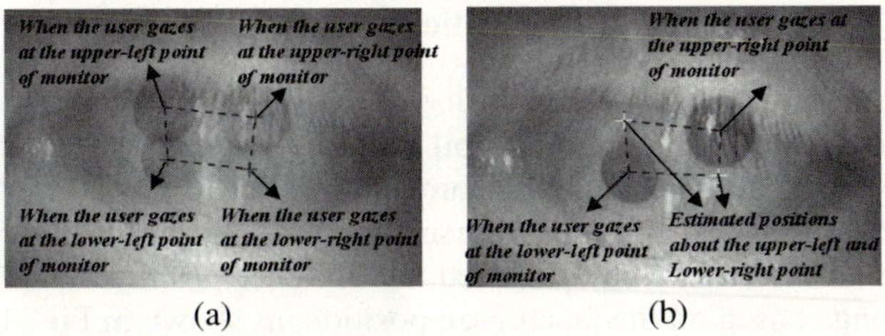

Fig. 6. Estimating the centers of two pupils by using two calibrated points. (a) Merged image using the centers of four pupils when the user gazed at the four corner points of the monitor. (b) Merged image using the centers of two pupils (marked with a red cross) when the user gazed at the two corner points of the monitor, and the estimated centers of two pupils (marked with a yellow cross) [17].

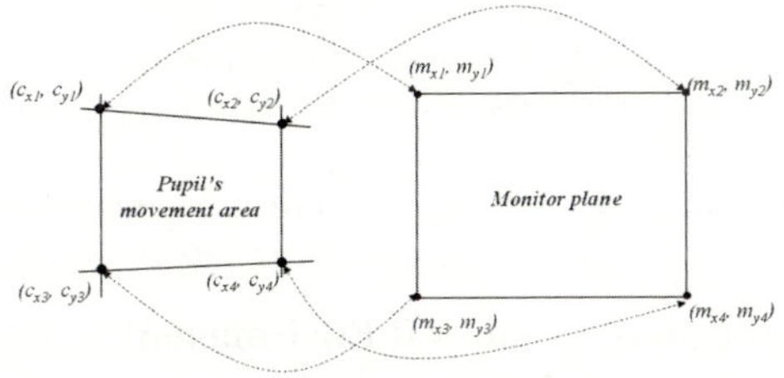

Fig. 7. Conceptual diagram of the Geometric transform process [15][17][19][20]

However, the four stages of user-dependent calibration can cause inconvenience for users. Thus, we reduced the number of stages to two. By using this method, after calibration, we were able to estimate the other two points based on the relationship between the facial location (as estimated by the Polhemus tracking sensor) and the monitor location. The estimation results are as shown in Fig. 6 (b).

After user-dependent calibration, the centers of four pupils were mapped to the monitor plane based on the Geometric transform process [15]. The Geometric transform process refers to the method of setting the relationship between a tetragon and a rectangle, as shown in Fig. 7. One center (c_{xc}, c_{yc}) in the pupil's movement area (as shown in Fig. 7) was calculated to one gaze position (m_{xc}, m_{yc}) of the monitor plane based on Eq. (4)~(7):

$$m_{x1} = a \cdot c_{x1} + b \cdot c_{y1} + c \cdot c_{x1} \cdot c_{y1} + d \tag{4}$$

$$m_{y1} = e \cdot c_{x1} + f \cdot c_{y1} + g \cdot c_{x1} \cdot c_{y1} + h \tag{5}$$

$$\begin{bmatrix} m_{x1} & m_{x2} & m_{x3} & m_{x4} \\ m_{y1} & m_{y2} & m_{y3} & m_{y4} \\ 0 & 0 & 0 & 0 \\ 0 & 0 & 0 & 0 \end{bmatrix} = \begin{bmatrix} a & b & c & d \\ e & f & g & h \\ 0 & 0 & 0 & 0 \\ 0 & 0 & 0 & 0 \end{bmatrix} \begin{bmatrix} c_{x1} & c_{x2} & c_{x3} & c_{x4} \\ c_{y1} & c_{y2} & c_{y3} & c_{y4} \\ c_{x1}c_{y1} & c_{x2}c_{y2} & c_{x3}c_{y3} & c_{x4}c_{y4} \\ 1 & 1 & 1 & 1 \end{bmatrix} \tag{6}$$

$$\begin{bmatrix} a & b & c & d \\ e & f & g & h \\ 0 & 0 & 0 & 0 \\ 0 & 0 & 0 & 0 \end{bmatrix} \begin{bmatrix} c_{xc} \\ c_{yc} \\ c_{xc}c_{yc} \\ 1 \end{bmatrix} = \begin{bmatrix} m_{xc} \\ m_{yc} \\ 0 \\ 0 \end{bmatrix} \tag{7}$$

2.5 Merging Eye and Facial Gaze Positions

Assuming that there were no facial movements, we were easily able to calculate gaze positions based on the four acquired pupil centers. However, in reality, since facial movements continuously occurred, we compensated for the calculated gaze position on the screen based on the measured intersection position of the screen as defined by the gaze vectors. For that, we compensated the eye gaze position by defining the gazing available range based on the facial gaze position, as shown in Fig. 8.

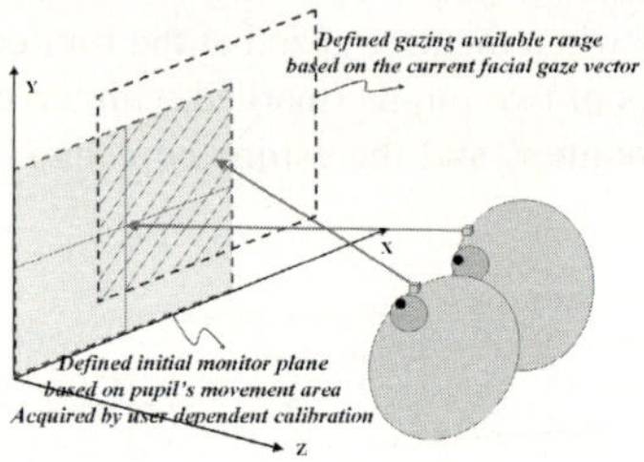

Fig. 8. Gazing available range accordance with gaze vectors

2.6 Applications to the Stereoscopic VR Environment

Estimated gaze information is generally used to perform two commands. The first one is a 'navigation command' and the other one is a 'pointing command'. For these commands, we implemented two interface modes. The first mode was the 'composite mode', in which we divided the stereoscopic screen into nine areas, as shown in Fig. 9. When the user's gaze point existed in the 'navigation zone', the screen view was moved according to the user's gaze point (like a mouse-dragging mode). However, when the gaze point was in the 'pointing zone', the view was not moved and the gazed object was selected according to a pen-pointing mode in a tablet pad. The second interface was the 'toggle mode' in which the navigation and pointing commands were mutually changed by eye blinking for a predetermined time period (more than one second). In the experiment, we performed a subjective evaluation (such as measuring levels of interest, immersion, sickness, etc) of the composite and toggle modes.

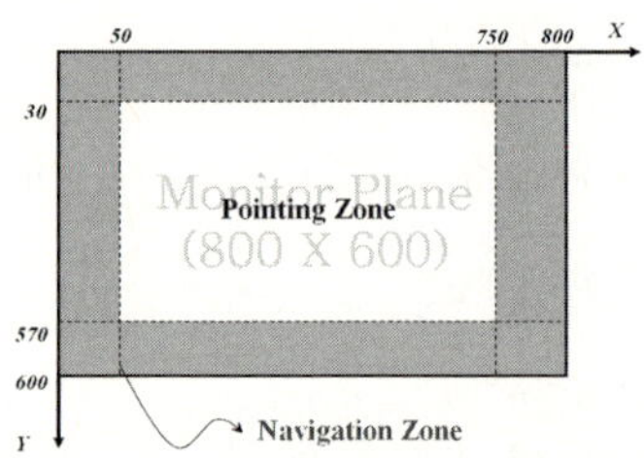

Fig. 9. Allocating areas of the monitor plane with a spatial resolution of 800*600 pixels. The centered white area is the 'pointing zone' and the outer grey area is the 'navigation zone' [20].

3 Experimental Results

Our gaze detection algorithm was tested with a Pentium-IV 2.4 GHz CPU. To measure accuracy, we performed the following test. A total of fifty users were asked to gaze at twelve specific points, as shown in Fig. 10. The test was iterated twenty times.

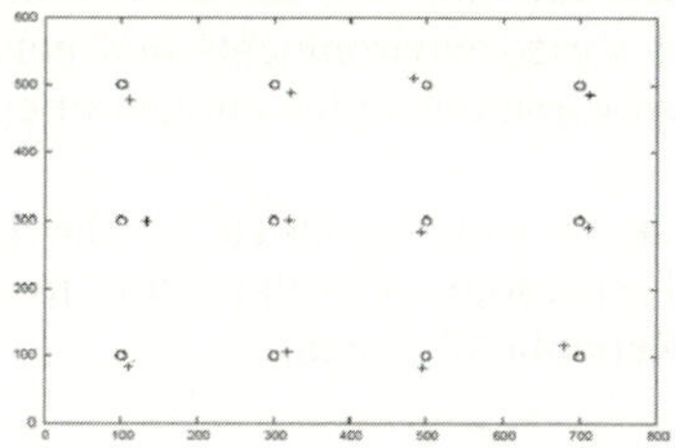

Fig. 10. Examples of gaze detection results when using the proposed method. (Reference points are marked with "○" and estimated gaze points are marked with "+").

Experimental results showed that the average gaze detection error was about 0.95°, as shown in Fig. 10. In the next experiment, we measured the levels of interest and immersion of the proposed method compared with those when using a conventional mouse system. Also, we measured sickness levels when users executed stereoscopic VR applications by using the proposed method. Experimental results are shown in Fig. 11. The results of the subjective experiments show that the proposed method led to greater levels of interest and immersion than those obtained when using a conventional mouse system. Also, the sickness rate was reduced after a few minutes.

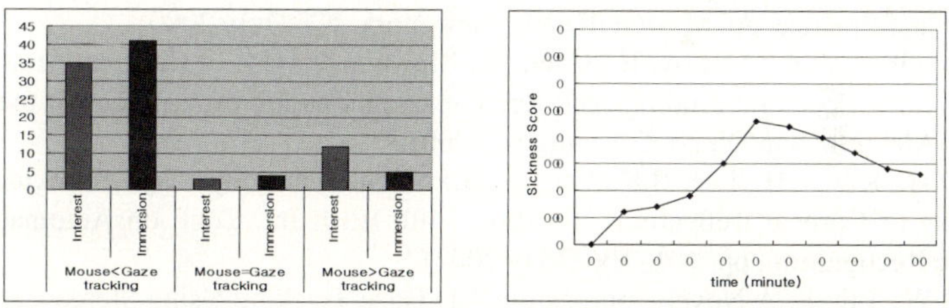

(a) (b)

Fig. 11. Subjective results of about fifty persons. (a) Survey results in terms of levels of interest and immersion. (b) Time lapses and changes in sickness levels (average values) [17][20][22].

4 Conclusions

In this paper, we have presented a new gaze tracking method for stereoscopic VR systems. In order to estimate gaze positions on stereoscopic screens, we designed an eye tracking module and we attached this eye tracking module to the space between the stereoscopic shutter glasses and the user's eye. Also, to compensate for errors caused by facial movements or rotations, we used a Polhemus tracking sensor. In the user-dependent calibration stage, we proposed a method of minimizing the stages of calibration. Experimental results showed that the gaze estimation error of our proposed method was less than one degree. Also, as shown in the results obtained with subjective surveys, levels of interest and immersion when using the proposed method were higher than those when using a conventional mouse system. Also, when using the proposed method, the initial sickness levels were lower and there was less accordance with time lapses after a few minutes. In future work, we plan to measure gaze detection accuracy in more varied environments and enhance accuracy in terms of lens distortion and individual variations of the amount of eyeball rotation.

Acknowledgement. This study was supported by the project titled "Five Senses Information Processing Technology Development for Network Based Reality Service" funded by ETRI, Republic of Korea.

References

1. Bar-Cohen, Y., Mavroidis, C., Bouzit, M., Dolgin, B., Harm, D., Kopchok, G., White, R.: Virtual Reality Robotic Operation Simulations Using MEMICA Haptic System. In: Smart-Systems 2000: The International Conference for Smart Systems and Robotics for Medicine and Space Applications, September 6 to 8, 2000b, Houston, Texas (2000)
2. Hurmuzlu, Y., Ephanov, A., Stoianovici, D.: Effect of a Pneumatically Driven Haptic Interface on the Perceptional Capabilities of Human Operators, Presence, MIT Press, vol. 7(3), pp. 290–307 (1998)
3. Kenaley, G.L., Cutkosky, M.R.: Electrorheological Fluid-Based Robotic Fingers With Tactile Sensing. In: Proceedings of the 1989 IEEE International Conference on Robotics and Automation, Scottsdale AR, pp. 132–136 (1989)
4. Duchowski, A.T., Vertegaal, R.: Course 05: Eye-Based Interaction in Graphical Systems: Theory and Practice. ACM SIGGRAPH, New York, NY (July 2000)
5. Gramopadhye, A.K., Melloy, B., Chen, S., Bingham, J.: Use of Computer Based Training for Aircraft Inspectors: Findings and Recommendations. In: Proceedings of the HFES/IEA Annual Meeting, San Diego, CA (August 2000)
6. Yoo, D.H., Kim, J.H., Lee, B.R., Chung, M.J.: Non-contact Eye Gaze Tracking System by Mapping of Corneal Reflections. In: Proc. Fifth IEEE Int. Conf. on Automatic Face and Gesture Recognition, pp. 101–106 (May 2002)
7. Shih, S.W., Liu, J.: A Novel Approach to 3-D Gaze Tracking Using Stereo Cameras, IEEE Transactions on Systems, Man and Cybernetics, Part B, vol. 34(1), pp. 234–245 (February 2004)
8. Accessed on (January 10, 2007) http://www.vrdis.com/eng/eng_pro/etc_60gx.html
9. CRID=2204,CONTENTID=10556, Accessed on (January 10, 2007) http://www.logitech.com/index.cfm/products/details/KR/KO
10. Accessed on (January 10, 2007) http://www.ndcinfrared.com/tfodhot.aspx
11. Accessed on (January 10, 2007) http://polhemus.com/?page=Motion_Fastrak
12. Lee, S.J. et al.: A Study on Fake Iris Detection based on the Reflectance of the Iris to the Sclera for Iris Recognition, ITC-CSCC 2005, Jeju Island, South Korea, pp. 1555–1556 (July 4-7, 2005)
13. Accessed on (January 10, 2007) http://www.kodak.com/global/en/professional/support/techPubs/f13/f13.pdf

14. Daugman, J.: How Iris Recognition Works, IEEE Transaction on Circuits and System for Video Technology, 14(1) (2004)
15. Gonzalez, R.C., Woods, R.E.: Digital Image Processing, 2nd edn. pp. 587–591. Prentice-Hall, Inc, Englewood Cliffs (2002)
16. Lee, E.C., Park, K.R., Kim, J.H.: Fake Iris Detection By Using the Purkinje Image. In: ICB'06. LNCS, vol. 3832, pp. 397–403. Springer, Heidelberg (2006)
17. Lee, E.C., Park, K.R.: A Study on Manipulating Method 3D Game in HMD Environment by using Eye Tracking. Journal of the Institute of Electronics Engineers of Korea (submitted)
18. Lee, E.C., Park, K.R., Whang, M.C., Lim, J.S.: Near Infra-red Vision-based Facial and Eye Gaze Estimation Method for Stereoscopic Display System. In: 10th International Federation of Automatic Control (IFAC), Ritz-Carlton Hotel, Seoul, Korea, September 4-6, 2007 (accepted for publication 2007)
19. Lee, E.C. et al.: System and Method for Tracking Gaze, US patent pending
20. Lee, E.C., Park, K.R.: Manipulating character's view direction of three dimensional first person shooting game by using gaze tracking in HMD environment. In: 2nd Next Generation Computing Conference, KINTEX, Ilsan, Korea (November 16-17, 2006)
21. Lee, E.C., Park, K.R.: A Study on Eye Gaze Estimation Method Based on Cornea Model of Human Eye. In: Lecture Notes in Computer Science (MIRAGE, INRIA Rocquencourt, France, March, 28–30, 2007 (accepted for publication 2007)
22. Lee, E.C., Park, K.R.: 3D View Controlling by Using Eye Gaze Tracking in First Person Shooting Game. Journal of Korea Multimedia Society, 8(10) (October 2005)

EyeScreen: A Gesture Interface for Manipulating On-Screen Objects

Shanqing Li, Jingjun Lv, Yihua Xu, and Yunde Jia

School of Computer Science and Technology, Beijing Institute of Technology, Beijing, China
{shanqingli,kennylanse,yihuaxu,jiayunde}@bit.edu.cn

Abstract. This paper presented a gesture-based interaction system which provides a natural way of manipulating on-screen objects. We generate a synthetic image by linking images from two cameras to recognize hand gestures. The synthetic image contains all the features captured from two different views, which can be used to alleviate the self-occlusion problem and improve the recognition rate. The MDA and EM algorithms are used to obtain parameters for pattern classification. To compute more detailed pose parameters such as fingertip positions and hand contours in the image, a random sampling method is introduced in our system. We describe a method based on projective geometry for background subtraction to improve the system performance. Robustness of the system has been verified by extensive experiments with different user scenarios. The applications of picture browser and visual pilot are discussed in this paper.

1 Introduction

Vision-based analysis and interpretation of hand gestures has become an active research topic of computer vision and human computer interaction (HCI) in recent years. Compared with traditional interaction devices such as keyboards, mice and joysticks, gesture-based interfaces have two obvious advantages. Firstly, gesture interface provides a more natural and direct approach to interact with virtual objects in HCI. Secondly, 3D information of gestures recovered by stereo vision techniques can be used to supply 3D inputs in applications of intelligent interaction and augmented reality.

Many vision-based interaction system have been developed in recent years [1~6]. Segen and Kumar [1] described a multi-dimensional hand gesture interface system and its use in interactive spatial applications. The system acquires input data from two cameras that look at the hand, recognizes three gestures and tracks the hand in 3D space. Zhang et al. [2] presented a Visual Panel system using an arbitrary quadrangle panel as user interface. The system provides flexible and robust interaction through tracking the panel and a tip pointer. Corso et al. [3] built a 4D Touchpad platform based on the Visual Interface Cues (VICs) framework. The system supplements 3D

J. Jacko (Ed.): Human-Computer Interaction, Part III, HCII 2007, LNCS 4552, pp. 710–717, 2007.

physical interaction with an additional temporal dimension, in which predefined sequences of VICs are used to trigger interaction events. Malik and Laszlo [4] proposed a Visual Touchpad system that allows fluid two-handed interactions with computers. The system acquires the 3D position of a user's fingertip with two cameras, and simulates the mouse clicks by detecting contact of user's fingertips with a panel surface. Wilson and Oliver [6] presented a perception-based user interface called GWINDOWS. The depth information recovered by two cameras is used to enhance automatic object detection and tracking robustness. The speech recognition is also integrated in the system to perform several basic window management tasks.

In the previous paper [7], we have described a vision-based interaction system called EyeScreen. The system uses multi-view images from two cameras to tracks an index finger and detects the clicking action of the fingertip. Several simple gestures are recognized to verify the proposed recognition algorithm. In this paper, we define a common used gesture set to manipulate virtual on-screen objects for actual applications. After the gesture is recognized, a random sampling method is presented to obtain more detailed pose parameters such as fingertip positions and hand contours. In order to improve the system performance, a method based on projective geometry for background subtraction is also introduced in this paper. We have successfully realized two interesting applications of picture browser and visual pilot based on our interaction system.

2 Calibration and Background Subtraction

We follow the system configuration in [7]: two cameras are mounted in front of a screen to capture multi-view images covering the full screen, as shown in Fig.1. The interaction space is defined as the common field of view of the two cameras. In the space, users can interact with the on-screen objects using their own hand gestures.

The projective transformations between (left and right) image planes and screen plane can be described by two homography matrices $\boldsymbol{H}_{LS}$ and $\boldsymbol{H}_{RS}$ respectively. Given

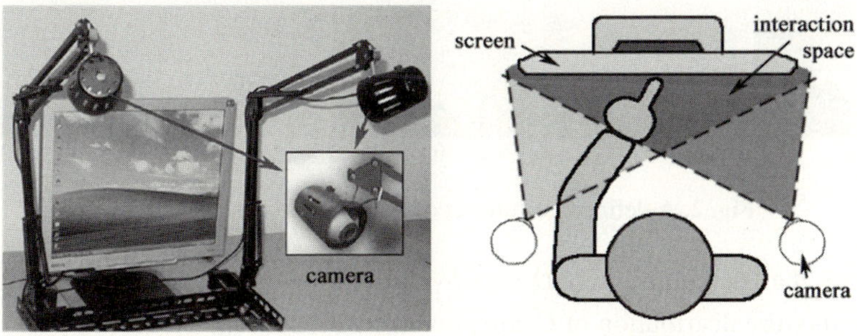

(a) (b)

Fig. 1. (a) System configuration, (b) Interaction using EyeScreen an arbitrary point P_S(x, y) in the screen plane, its corresponding points in the left and right image $P_L(x_L, y_L)$ and $P_R(x_R, y_R)$ can be calculated by

$$P_L \cong \boldsymbol{H}_{LS} P_S \tag{1}$$

$$P_R \cong \boldsymbol{H}_{RS} P_S \tag{2}$$

where $\cong$ means equal up to a scale factor, $\boldsymbol{H}_{LS}$ and $\boldsymbol{H}_{RS}$ are 3x3 homography matrices. During the calibration procedure, a chessboard image is rendered on the screen providing pairs of corresponding points to compute the $\boldsymbol{H}$ matrices.

To subtract images displayed on the screen, we provide an effective approach based on projective geometry which is independent of illumination changes. From Equation (1) and (2), we get

$$P_L = \boldsymbol{H}_{LS} \boldsymbol{H}_{RS}^{-1} P_R \tag{3}$$

According to Equation (3), we can transform all points in the right image to the left image plane: $P_L' = \boldsymbol{H}_{LS} \boldsymbol{H}_{RS}^{-1} P_R$. If the scene point P_S is on the screen, we have $P_L' = P_L$; otherwise, $P_L' \neq P_L$. So we subtract the regions corresponding to images displayed on the screen by a simple thresholding method, which can efficiently improve the robustness of hand region segmentation.

3 Gesture Recognition

An appearance-based learning approach is applied for gesture recognition in our system. Five common used gestures are defined to manipulate on-screen objects, as shown in Fig. 2. We first subtract the background using the algorithm described in Section 2 and segment hand regions from video images with a skin-color model. And then, we obtain principle components of gesture patterns using the PCA method and map feature vectors to a most relevant space for pattern classification. Finally, the Expectation Maximization (EM) algorithm is used to estimate the parameters of the mixture density model.

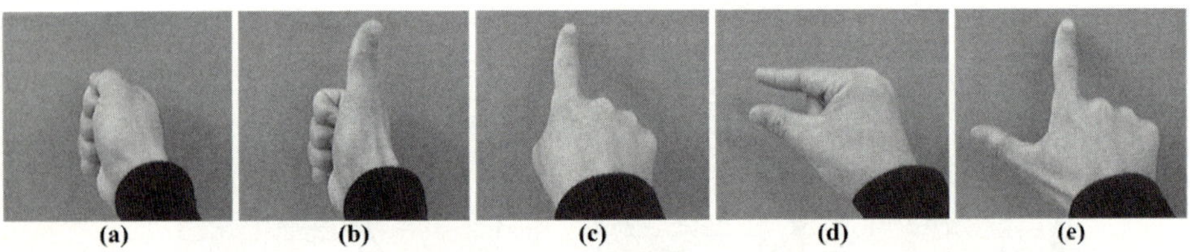

Fig. 2. A defined gesture set of five common used gestures

Assume that a sample set $D = \{x_1, \cdots, x_N\}$ was drawn independently from a Gaussian mixture distribution of $\boldsymbol{C}$ components, which is represented as

$$p(x \mid \Theta) = \sum_{j=1}^{C} p(x \mid c_j, \Theta) p(c_j \mid \Theta) \tag{4}$$

where $\Theta = \{(\alpha_j, \mu_j, S_j) \mid j \in [1, C]\}$.

After the EM training converges, we obtain the parameters of the mixture model, and then generate a Bayesian classifier for gesture recognition. For an input pattern x, the discriminant function is defined as

$$g_j(x) = p(c_j \mid x) = \frac{p(x \mid c_j)\alpha_j}{\sum_{l=1}^{C} p(x \mid c_l)\alpha_l} \tag{5}$$

For gesture recognition, the ambiguity caused by the self-occlusion problem is still a challenge after decades of research. Using multi-view images is an effective way to alleviate such problems. In our system, synthetic images linking two-view images are used to recognize gestures. The recognition rate for five gestures defined in Fig. 2 is 97.69% when synthetic images are used, and 84.76% with left images, 86.33% with right images, respectively. The experimental results show that this approach can improve the recognition rate about 10%.

4 Pose Parameters Computation

For some applications, we need the recognized gesture type as well as more detailed pose parameters such as fingertip positions and hand contours. The gesture type can be obtained from the procedure of gesture recognition described in Section 3. In order to compute the parameters of gestures in Fig. 2(c, d, e), a random sampling method is applied in our system. The contour models represented by B-spline curves are indicated by black curves in Fig. 3. We make an assumption that the gesture's movement obeys the rules of rigid body motion, so the shape contour of gestures can be represented by a shape-space vector:

$$S = [P_x, P_y, \alpha_x(\cos\theta - 1), \alpha_y(\cos\theta - 1), -\alpha_y \sin\theta, \alpha_x \sin\theta]^T \tag{6}$$

where P_x and P_y are the translation parameters, α_x and α_y are the scaling parameters, θ is the rotation angle.

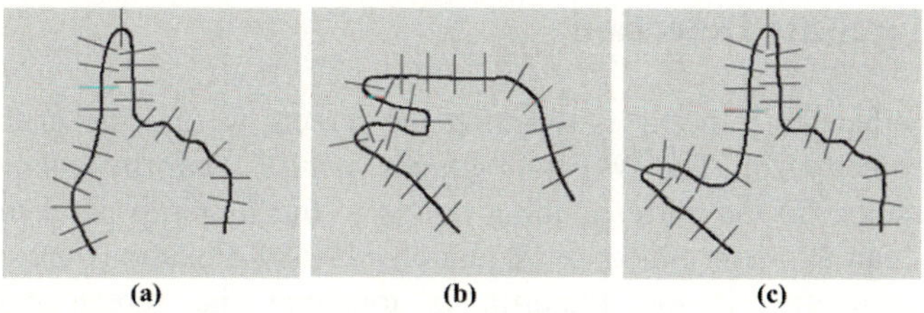

Fig. 3. Contour models of gestures, the B-spline curve is indicated by black curves and the red lines represent normal lines to the curve at control points

After the gesture types have been determined by gesture recognition procedure, a sample set $\{S_n, n = 1, \cdots, N\}$ is generated according to the specific gesture type around the hand regions in the video images, where N is the number of samples. To obtain the state vector of a specific gesture, we first compute the confidence π_n for each sample, and then define the mean of all samples as the estimation of the state vector.

The procedure of computing confidence includes the following steps: (1) detect the edges by applying a canny filter on the video images; (2) search for the edge pixels along the normal lines to the curve at control points (the normal lines are indicated by red lines in Fig. 3); (3) select the shortest distance d_i between the detected edge pixels and the control point, and then compute the confidence by

$$\pi_t^{(n)} = exp\left(- \sum_{i=1}^{N} \frac{d_i^2}{2\sigma^2} \right) \tag{7}$$

The state vector of the specific gesture is estimated by

$$\varepsilon(S) = \sum_{n=1}^{N} \pi_n \cdot S_n \tag{8}$$

From the calculated state vector, we can recover the gesture contour and then obtain the fingertip position. The detection results are shown in Fig. 4.

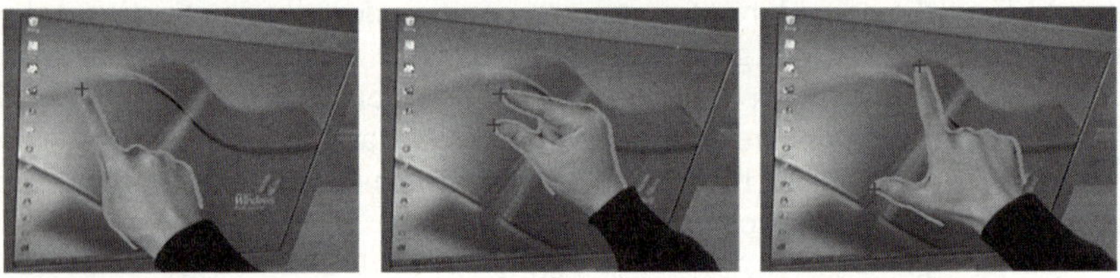

(a) (b) (c)

Fig. 4. The results for pose parameters computation (hand contour is represented by green curves, and the fingertips are indicated by red crosses)

5 Touching State Detection

To detect whether the fingertip is touching the screen, we use the method based on projective geometry [7]. The two homography matrices can be obtained from the calibration results. So the corresponding points to the fingertip pixel in the left and right images can be determined by Equation (1) and Equation (2). According to perspective geometry, if the fingertip is touching the screen plane, its two corresponding points in the screen plane will locate at the same position, as shown in Fig. 5(a); otherwise they locate at different positions, as shown in Fig. 5(b). So the touching state detection problem can be converted as measuring the distance between these two corresponding points. When the distance is less than a given threshold, we know that the fingertip is touching the screen.

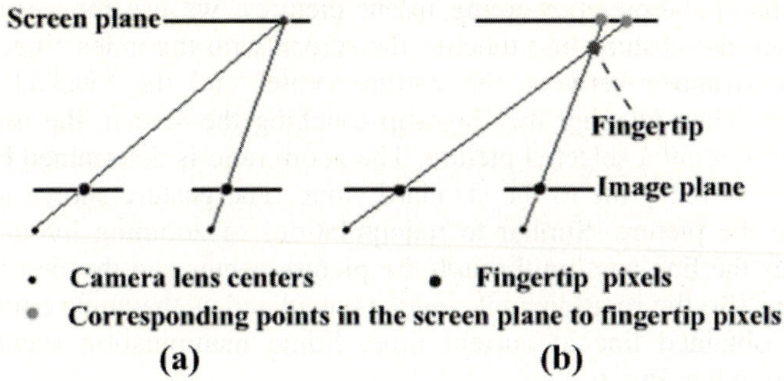

Fig. 5. Diagrams for touching state detection, (a) The fingertip is touching the screen plane, twoorresponding points are at the same location, (b) The fingertip is above the screen plane, two corresponding points are at different locations

6 Applications

Based on the defined gesture set and our interaction system, we discuss two applications of picture browser and visual pilot game in this section. Picture browser enables the users to directly move, zoom in/out and rotate the images on the screen by their own hand gestures. In the visual pilot game, actual manipulations are simulated to control the fighter using hand gestures.

6.1 Picture Browser

Three gestures from the defined gesture set are used to realize the picture browser which can move, zoom in/out and rotate the selected picture in a more natural and direct way. The pinch gesture shown in Fig. 2(d) is used to move the picture and the destination position is defined as the mean value of two fingertip positions. To

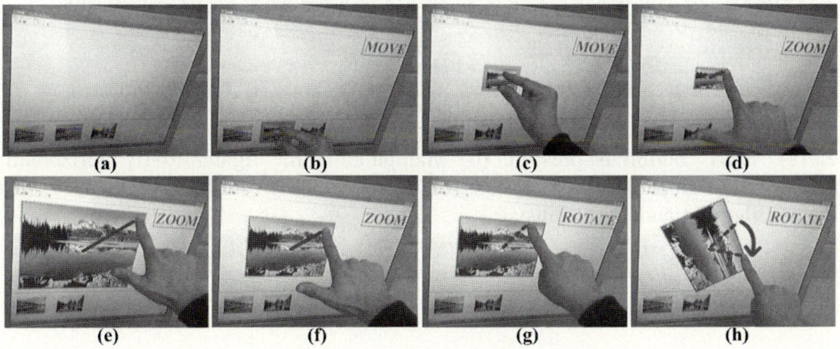

Fig. 6. (a) The initialized interface, (b) Ready to move a picture, (c) Move the picture by the pinch gesture, (d) Ready to zoom in/out the picture, the standard distance is represented by a solid red line, (e), (f) Zoom in/out the picture, (g) Ready to rotate the picture, the base line is represented by a dashed red line, (h) Rotate the picture, the rotation angle and direction is indicated by a red arrow

achieve the manipulation of zooming in/out pictures, we use the gesture shown in Fig. 2(e). When the gesture first touches the screen with the index finger, the system calculates the distance between the picture center and the touched point as the standard value. Then keeping the fingertip touching the screen, the user moves the gesture to zoom in/out a selected picture. The zoom ratio is determined by the ratio of the distance at current time to the standard value. The gesture shown in Fig. 2(c) is used to rotate the picture. Similar to manipulations of zooming in/out pictures, the system defines the line passing through the picture center and the first touched point as the base line. So the rotation angle can be calculated as the angle between the base line and the obtained line at current time. Some manipulation scenes of picture browser are shown in Fig. 6.

6.2 Visual Pilot

Applying touching state detection and gesture recognition techniques, we designed a vision-based interaction game called "Visual Pilot", which allows a user to manipulate a virtual fighter naturally by hand gestures. The pointing gesture shown in Fig. 2(c) is employed to control the game menus. The touching action on buttons by the index fingertip can be robustly detected using our system. We use the two gestures shown in Fig. 2(a) and Fig. 2(b) to control the flight of the fighter and launch missiles, respectively. Some snapshots of playing the game are given in Fig. 8.

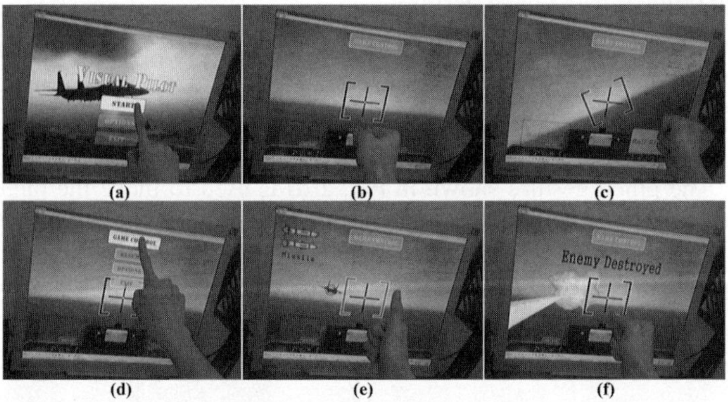

Fig. 7. (a) "Start" button is pressed; (b) Manipulating the fighter to fly horizontally; (c) Manipulating the fighter to roll clockwise; (d) "Game Control" button is pressed; (e) Ready to launch a missile; (f) Launching a missile

7 Conclusion

EyeScreen is a robust vision-based interaction system which provides a more natural and direct way of manipulating on-screen objects by hand gestures for HCI. In this paper, we obtain the hand pose parameters by gesture recognition and a random sampling method. A background subtraction method based on projective geometry is introduced to improve the system performance. Two interesting applications have been successfully realized. The system has a wide application foreground in digital entertainment, intelligent interaction and augmented reality.

Currently, EyeScreen provides robust tracking and gesture recognition for a single hand. In our future work, interactions involving two hands will be developed to improve the usability of our system. Besides, utilization of 3D information can be integrated in the Eyescreen system to enhance the robustness.

Acknowledgments. This work was partially supported by the National Natural science Foundation (No.60473049) of China and Chinese High-Tech (863) Program.

References

1. Segen, J., Kumar, S.: Gesture VR: Vision-Based 3D Hand Interface for Spatial Interaction. In: The sixth ACM international conference on Multimedia (1998)
2. Zhang, Z.,Wu, Y., Shan, Y.,Shafer, S.: Visual Panel: Virtual Mouse, Keyboard and 3D Controller with an Ordinary Piece of Paper. In: ACM workshop on PUI (2001)
3. Corso, J.J., Burschka, D., Hager, G.D.: The 4D Touchpad: Unencumbered HCI With VICs. In: IEEE Workshop on Computer Vision and Pattern Recognition for Human Computer Interaction (2003)
4. Malik, S., Laszlo, J.: Visual Touchpad: A Two-handed Gesture Input Device. ICMI (2004)
5. Oka, K., Sato, Y., Koike, H.: Real-time Tracking of Multiple Fingertips and Gesture Recognition for Augmented Desk Interface Systems. In: Proceedings of IEEE Conference on Automatic Face and Gesture Recognition, pp. 429–434 (2002)
6. Wilson, A., Oliver, N.: GWindows: Towards Robust Perception-Based UI. In: IEEE Workshop on Computer Vision and Pattern Recognition for Human Computer Interaction (2003)
7. Xu, Y., Li, S., Jia, Y.: EyeScreen: A Gesture-Based Interaction System. In: IEEE International Conference on Signal and Image Processing (2006)

GART: The Gesture and Activity Recognition Toolkit

Kent Lyons, Helene Brashear, Tracy Westeyn,
Jung Soo Kim, and Thad Starner

College of Computing and GVU Center
Georgia Institute of Technology
Atlanta, GA 30332-0280 USA
{kent,brashear,turtle,jszzang,thad}@cc.gatech.edu

Abstract. The **G**esture and **A**ctivity **R**ecognition **T**oolit (GART) is a user interface toolkit designed to enable the development of gesture-based applications. GART provides an abstraction to machine learning algorithms suitable for modeling and recognizing different types of gestures. The toolkit also provides support for the data collection and the training process. In this paper, we present GART and its machine learning abstractions. Furthermore, we detail the components of the toolkit and present two example gesture recognition applications.

Keywords: Gesture recognition, user interface toolkit.

1 Introduction

Gestures are a natural part of our everyday life. As we move about and interact with the world we use body language and gestures to help us communicate, and we perform gestures with physical artifacts around us. Using similar motions to provide input to a computer is an interesting area for exploration. Gesture systems allow a user to employ movements of her hand, arm or other parts of her body to control computational objects.

While potentially a rich area for novel and natural interaction techniques, building gesture recognition systems can be very difficult. In particular, a programmer must be a good application developer, understand the issues surrounding the design and implementation of user interface systems and be knowledgeable about machine learning techniques. While there are high level tools to support building user interface applications, there is relatively little support for a programmer to build a gesture system. To create such an application, a developer must build components to interact with sensors, provide mechanisms to save and parse that data, build a system capable of interpreting the sensor data as gestures, and finally interpret and utilize the results.

One of the most difficult challenges is turning the raw data into something meaningful. For example, imagine a programmer who wants to add a small gesture control system to his stylus–based application. How would he transform the sequence of mouse events generated by the UI toolkit into gestures?

J. Jacko (Ed.): Human-Computer Interaction, Part III, HCII 2007, LNCS 4552, pp. 718–727, 2007.

Most likely, the programmer would use his domain knowledge to develop a (complex) set of rules and heuristics to classify the stylus movement. As he further developed the gesture system, this set of rules would likely become increasing complex and unmanageable. A better solution would be to use some machine learning techniques to classify the stylus gestures. Unfortunately doing so requires extensive domain knowledge about machine learning algorithms.

In this paper we present the **G**esture and **A**ctivity **R**ecognition **T**oolkit (GART), a user interface toolkit designed to abstract away many machine learning details so an application programmer can build gesture recognition based interfaces. Our goal is to allow the programmer access to powerful machine learning techniques without requiring her to become an expert in machine learning. In doing so we hope to bridge the gap between the state of the art in machine learning and user interface development.

2 Related Work

Gestures are being used in a large variety of user interfaces. Gesture recognition has been used for text input on many pen based systems. ParcTab's Unistroke [8] and Palm's Graffiti are two early examples of gesture based text entry systems for recognizing handwritten characters on PDAs. EdgeWrite is a more recent gesture based text entry method that reduces the amount of dexterity needed to create the gesture [11]. In Shark2, Kristensson and Zhai explored adding gesture recognition to soft keyboards [4]. The user enters text by drawing through each key in the word on the soft keyboard and the system can recognize the pattern formed by the trajectory of the stylus through each letter. Hinckley et al. augmented a hand–held with several sensors to detect different types of interaction with the device (recognizing when it is in position to take a voice note, powering on when it is picked up, etc) [3]. Another use of gesture is as an interaction technique for large wall or tabletop surfaces. Several systems utilize hand (or finger) posture and gestures [5,12]. Grossman et al. also used multi-finger gestures to interact with a 3D volumetric display [2].

From a high level, the basics of using a machine learning algorithm for gesture recognition is rather straightforward. To create a machine learning model, one needs to collect a set of data and provide descriptive labels for it. This process is then repeated many times for each gesture and then repeated again for all of the different gestures to be recognized. The data is used by a machine learning algorithm and is modeled via the "training" process. To use the recognition system in an application, data is again collected. It is then sent through the machine learning algorithms using the models trained above and the label of the model most closely matching the data is returned as the recognized value.

While conceptually this is a rather simple process, in practice it is unfortunately much more difficult. For example, there are many details in implementing most machine learning algorithms (such as dealing with limited precision), many of which may not be covered in machine learning texts. A developer might use one a machine learning software package created to encapsulate a variety of algorithms such as Weka [1] or Matlab. An early predecessor to this work, the Georgia Tech Gesture Toolkit (GT^{2}k), was designed in a similar vein [9]. It was designed around Cambridge University's speech recognition toolkit (CU–HTK) [13] to facilitate building gesture based applications. Unfortunately, GT^{2}k requires the programmer to have extensive knowledge about the underlying machine learning mechanisms and leaves several tasks such as the collection and management of the data to the programmer.

3 GART

The Gesture and Activity Recognition Toolkit (GART) is a user interface toolkit. It is designed to provide a high level interface to the machine learning process facilitating the building of gesture recognition applications. The toolkit consists of an abstract interface to the machine learning algorithms (training and recognition), several example sensors and a library for samples.

To build a gesture based application using GART, the programmer first selects the sensor she will use to capture information about the gesture. We currently support three basic sensors in our toolkit: a mouse (or pointing device), a set of Bluetooth accelerometers, and a camera sensor. Once a sensor is selected, the programmer builds an application that can be used to collect training data. This program can be either a special mode in the final application being built, or an application tailored just for data collection. Finally, the programmer instantiates the base classes from the toolkit (encapsulating the machine learning algorithms, and library) and sets up the callbacks between them for data collection or recognition. The remainder of the programmer's coding effort can then be devoted to building the actual application of interest and using the gesture recognition results as desired.

3.1 Toolkit Architecture

The toolkit is composed of three main components: *Sensors*, *Library*, and *Machine Learning*. *Sensors* collect data from hardware and may provide post–processing. The *Library* stores the data and provides a portable format for sharing data sets. The *Machine Learning* component encapsulates the training and recognition algorithms. Data is passed from the sensor and machine learning components to other objects through callbacks. The flow of data through the system for data collection involves the above three toolkit components and the application (Figure 1). A sensor object collects data from the physical sensors and distributes it. The sensor will likely send raw data to the application for visualization as streaming video, graphs, or for other displays. The sensor also bundles a set of data with its labeling information into a sample. The sample is sent to the library where it stored for later use. Finally, the machine learning component can pull data from the library and use it to train the models for recognition. Figure 2 shows the data flow for a recognition application. As before, the sensor can send raw data to the application for visualization or user

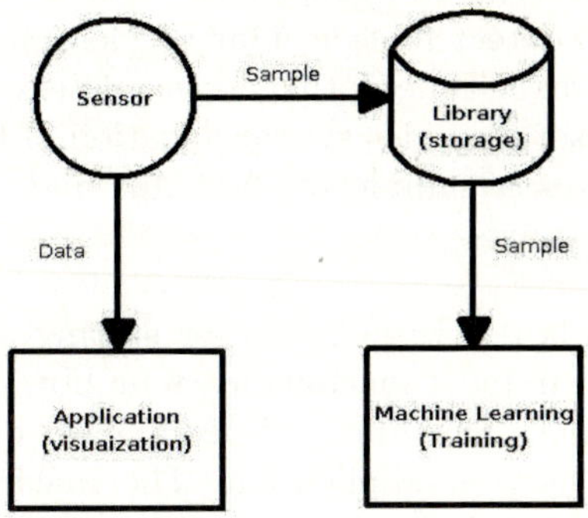

Fig. 1. Data collection

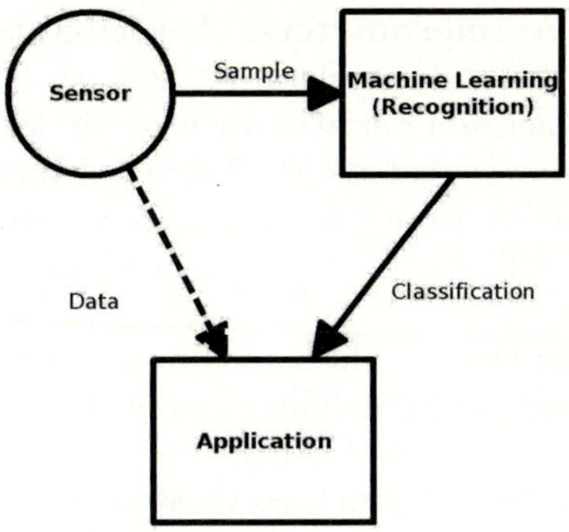

Fig. 2. Gesture recognition

feedback. The sensor also sends samples to the machine learning component for recognition, and recognition results are sent to the application.

Sensors. Sensors are components that interface with the hardware, collect data, and may provide parsing or post–processing of the data. Sensors are also designed around an event–based architecture that allows them to notify any listeners of available data. The sensor architecture allows for both synchronous or asynchronous reading of sensors.

Our toolkit sensors support sending data to listeners in two formats: samples and plain data. Samples are well defined sets of data that represents gestures. A sample can also contain meta information such as gesture labels, a user name, time stamps, notes, etc. Through a callback, sensors send samples to other toolkit components for storage, training, or recognition. The toolkit has been designed for extensibility particularly with respect to available sensors. Programmers can generate new sensors by inheriting from the base sensor class. This class provides event handling for interaction with the toolkit. The programmer can then implement the sensor driver and any necessary post–processing. The toolkit supports event based sensors as well as polled sensors and it streamlines data passing through standard callbacks. Three sensors are provided with the toolkit:

- **Mouse:** The Mouse sensor provides an abstraction for using the mouse as the input device for gestures The toolkit provides three implementations of the mouse sensor. MouseDragDeltaSensor generates samples which are composed of Δx and Δy from the last mouse position. The MouseDragVectorSensor generates sample which consists of the same information in polar coordinates (θ and radius from the previous point). Finally, MouseMoveSensor is similar to the vector drag sensor, but does not segment the data using mouse clicks.
- **Camera:** The SimpleImage sensor is a simple camera sensor which reads input from a USB camera. The sensor provides post–processing that tracks an object based on a color histogram. This sensor produces samples that are composed of the (x, y) position of the object in the image over time.

- **Accelerometers:** Accelerometers are devices which measure static and dynamic acceleration and can be used to detect motion. Our accelerometer sensor interfaces with small wearable 3 axis Bluetooth accelerometers we have created [10]. The accelerometer sensor provides synchronization of the data from multiple sensors and generates a sample of Δx, Δy, and Δz indicating changes in acceleration for each axis.

Library. The library component in the toolkit is responsible for storing and organizing data. This component is not found in most machine learning libraries but is a critical portion of a real application. The library is composed of a collection of samples created by a data collection application. The machine learning component then uses the library during training as the source of labeled gestures. The library also provides methods to store samples in an XML file.

Machine Learning. The machine learning component provides the toolkit's abstraction for the machine learning algorithms and is used for modeling data samples (training) and recognizing gesture samples. During training, it loads samples from a given library, trains the models, and returns the results of training. For recognition, the sensor sends samples to the machine learning object which in turn sends a result to all of its listeners (the application). A result is either the label of the classified gesture or any errors that might have occurred. One of the main goals of the toolkit was to abstract away as many of the machine learning aspects of gesture recognition as possible. We have also provided defaults for much of the machine learning process. However, at the core of the system are hidden Markov models (HMMs) which we currently use to model the gestures. There has been much research supporting the use of HMMs to recognize time series data such as speech, handwriting and gesture recognition. [7,6,10].

The HMMs in GART are provided by CU-HTK [13]. Our HTK class wraps this software which provides an extensive framework for training and using hidden Markov models (HMMs), as well as a grammar based infrastructure. GART provides the high level abstraction of our machine learning component and integration into the rest of the toolkit. We also have an options object which keeps track of the necessary machine learning configuration information such as the list of gesture to be recognized, HMM topologies, and models generated by the training process.

While the toolkit currently uses hidden Markov models for recognition, the abstraction of machine learning component allows for expansion. These expansions could include other popular techniques such as neural networks, decision trees or support vector machines. An excellent candidate for this expansion would be the Weka machine learning library, which includes implementations for a variety of different algorithms [1].

3.2 Code Samples

The basics of setting up a new application using the toolkit components described above requires relatively little code. To set up a new gesture application the programmer needs to create a set of options (using the defaults provided by the toolkit) and a library object. The programmer then initializes the machine learning component, HTK, with the options. Finally a new sensor is created.

```
Options myOpts=new GARTOptions();
Library myLib= myOpts.getLibrary();
HTK htk=new HTK(options);
Sensor=new MySensor();
```

For data collection, the programmer needs to connect the sensor to the library so it can save the samples.

```
sensor.addSensorSampleListener(library);
```

Finally for recognition, the programmer configures the sensor to send samples to the HTK object for recognition. The recognition results are then sent back to the application for use in the program.

```
sensor.addSensorSampleListener(htk);
htk.addResultListener(myApplication);
```

The application may also want to listen to the sensor data to provide some user feedback about the gesture as it is happening (such as a graph of the gesture).

```
sensor.addSensorDataListener(myApplication);
```

Finally, the application may need to provide some configuration information for the sensor on initialization and it may need to segment the data by calling startSample() and stopSample() on the sensor.

GART was developed using the Java JDK 5.0 from Sun Microsystems. It has been tested in the Linux, Mac OS X, and Windows environments. The core GART system requires CU–HTK, free software that may be used to develop applications, but not sold as part of a system.

4 Sample Applications

We have built several different gesture recognition applications using our toolkit. Our first set of applications demonstrate the capabilities of each sensor in the toolkit, and here we will discuss the WritingPad application. Virtual Hopscotch is more fully featured and was built by a student in our lab that had no direct experience with the development of GART.

The WritingPad is an application that uses our mouse sensor. It allows a user to draw a gesture with a mouse (or stylus) and have it recognized by the system. To create a gesture, the user depresses the mouse button, draws the intended shape, and releases the mouse button. This simple system uses the toolkit to recognize a few different handwritten characters and some basic shapes.

The application is composed of three objects. The first object is the main WritingPad application which initializes the program, instantiates the needed GART objects (MouseDragVectorSensor, Library, Options and and HTK) and connects these for training as described in Section 3.2. This object also creates the main application window and populates it with the UI components (Figure 3).

At the top is an area for the programmer to control the toolkit parameters needed to create new gestures. In a more fully featured application, this functionality would either be in a separate program or hidden in a debug mode. On the left is an area used to label new gestures. Next, there is a button to save the library of samples and another button to train the model. Finally at the top right, there is a toggle button that changes the application state between data collection and recognition modes. The change in modes is accomplished by calling a method in the main WritingPad object which alters the *sensor* and *result* callbacks as described above (Section 3.2). In recognition mode, this object receives the results from the machine learning component and opens a dialog box with the label of the recognized gesture (Figure 3). A more realistic application would act upon the gesture to perform some other action. Finally, the majority of the application window is filled with a CoordinateArea, a custom widget that displays on-screen user feedback. This application demonstrates the basic components needed to use mouse gestures.

The Virtual Hopscotch application is a gesture based game inspired by the traditional children's game, Hopscotch. This game was developed over the course of a weekend by a student in our lab who had no prior experience with the toolkit. We gave him instructions to create a game using two accelerometers and our applications that demonstrate the use of the different sensors. From there, he designed and implemented the game.

The Virtual Hopscotch game consists of a scrolling screen with squares displayed to indicate how to hop (Figure 4). The player wears our accelerometers on her ankles and follows the game making different steps or jumps (right foot hop, left foot hop, and jump with both feet). As the squares scrolls into the central rectangle, the application starts sampling and the player performs her hop gesture. If the gesture is recognized as correct, the square changes color as it scrolls off the screen and the player wins points. Figure 4 show the game in action. The blue square in the center is the indication that the player should stomp on her left foot. The two squares just starting to show at the top of the screen are the next move to be made, in this case jumping with both feet.

For Writing pad, the majority of application code (approximately 300 lines) is devoted to the user interface. In contrast, only a few dozen lines are devoted to

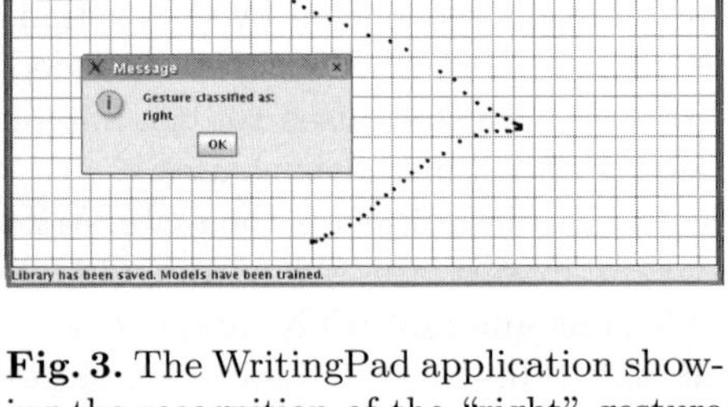

Fig. 3. The WritingPad application showing the recognition of the "right" gesture

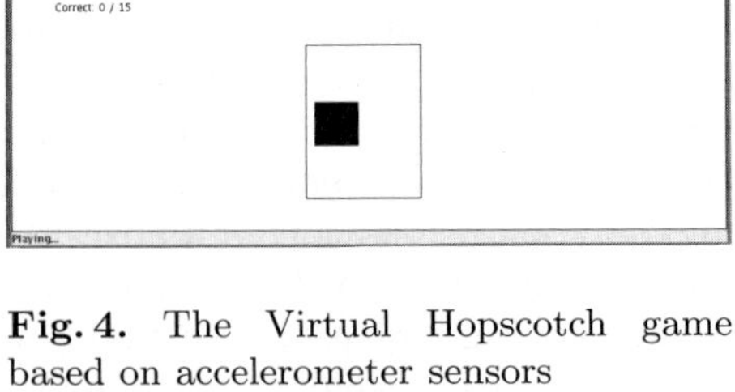

Fig. 4. The Virtual Hopscotch game based on accelerometer sensors

gesture recognition. Similarly, Virtual Hopscotch has a total of 878 lines of code and again, most of which are associated with the user interface. Additional code was also created to manage the game infrastructure. Of the six classes created, three are for maintaining game state. The other three have direct correspondence to the WritingPad example. There is one class for the application proper, one for the main window and one for the game visualization.

5 Discussion

Throughout the development of GART, we have attempted to provide a simple interface to gesture recognition algorithms. We have distilled the complex process of implementing machine learning algorithms down the essence of collecting data, providing a method to train the models, and obtaining recognition results. Another important feature of the toolkit is the components that support data acquisition with the sensors, sample management in the library, and simple callbacks to route the data. These are components required to build gesture recognition applications often not provided by other systems. Together, these components enable a programmer to focus on application development instead of the gesture recognition system.

We have also designed the toolkit to be flexible and extensible. This aspect is most visible in the sensors. We have created several sensors that all have the same interface to an application and the rest of the toolkit. A developer can swap mouse sensors (which provide different types of post–processing) by changing only a few lines of code. Changing to a dramatically different type of sensor requires minimal modifications. In building the Virtual Hopscotch game, our developer started with a mouse sensor and used mouse based gestures to understand the issues with data segmentation and to facilitate application development. After creating the basics of the game, he then switched to the accelerometer sensor. While we currently have only one implementation of a machine learning back-end (the CU-HTK), our interface would remain the same if we had different underlying algorithms.

While we have abstracted away many of the underlying machine learning concepts, there are still some issues the developer needs to consider. Two such issues are data segmentation and sensor selection. Data segmentation involves denoting the start and stop of a gesture. This process can occur as an internal function of the sensor or as a result of signals from the application. Application signals can be from either user actions such as a button press or from the application structure itself. The MouseDragSensor uses internal functions to segment its data. The mouse pressed event starts the collection of a sample, and the mouse released function completes the sample and sends it to its listeners. Our camera sensor uses a signal generated by a button press in the application to segment its data. In Virtual Hopscotch, the application uses timing events corresponding to when the proper user interface elements are displayed on-screen to segment the accelerometer data.

In addition to segmentation, a key component in designing a gesture-based application is choosing the appropriate data to sense. This process includes selecting a physical sensor that can sense the intended activities as well as selecting the right post–processing to turn the raw data into samples. The data from one sensor can be interpreted in many ways. Cameras, for example, have a myriad of algorithms devoted to the classification of image content. For an application that uses mouse gestures, change in location $(\Delta x, \Delta y)$ is likely a more appropriate feature vector than absolute position (x, y). By using relative position, the same gesture can be composed in different locations.

We have designed GART to be extensible and much of our future work will be expanding the toolkit in various ways. We are interested in building an example "sensor fusion" module to provide infrastructure for easily combining multiple sensors of different types (i.e. cameras and accelerometers). We would also like to abstract out the data post–processing to allow greater code reuse between similar sensors. As previously mentioned, the machine learning back end is designed to be modular and to allow different algorithms to "plug in". Finally, we are interested in extending the toolkit to make use of continuous gesture recognition. Right now each gesture must be segmented by the user, the application, or using some knowledge about the sensor itself. While quite powerful, other applications would be enabled by adding a continuous recognition capability.

6 Conclusions

Our goal in creating GART was to provide a toolkit to simplify the development process involved in creating gesture-based applications. We have created a high-level abstraction of the machine learning process whereby the application developer selects a sensor and collects example gestures to use for training models. To use the gestures in an application, the programmer connects the same sensor to the recognition portion of our toolkit which in turn sends back classified gestures. The machine learning algorithms, associated configuration parameters and data management mechanisms are provided by the toolkit.

By using such a design, we allow a developer the ability to create gesture recognition systems without first needing to become experts in machine learning techniques. Furthermore, by encapsulating the gesture recognition, we reduce the burden of managing all of the associated data and models to build a gesture recognition system. Our intention is that GART will provide a platform to allow further exploration of gesture recognition as an interaction technique.

Acknowledgments

We want to give special thanks to Nirmal Patel for building the Virtual Hopscotch game. This material is supported, in part, by the Electronics and Telecommunications Research Institute (ETRI).

References

1. Frank, E., Hall, M.A., Holmes, G., Kirkby, R., Pfahringer, B., Witten, I.H., Trigg, L.: Weka - a machine learning workbench for data mining. In: Maimon, O., Rokach, L. (eds.): The Data Mining and Knowledge Discovery Handbook, pp. 1305–1314. Springer, Heidelberg (2005)
2. Grossman, T., Wigdor, D., Balakrishnan, R.: Multi-finger gestural interaction with 3d volumetric displays. In: UIST '04: Proceedings of the 17th annual ACM symposium on User interface software and technology, pp. 61–70. ACM Press, New York (2004)
3. Hinckley, K., Pierce, J., Sinclair, M., Horvitz, E.: Sensing techniques for mobile interaction. In: UIST '00: Proceedings of the 13th annual ACM symposium on User interface software and technology, pp. 91–100. ACM Press, New York (2000)
4. Kristensson, P.O., Zhai, S.: Shark2: a large vocabulary shorthand writing system for pen-based computers. In: UIST '04: Proceedings of the 17th annual ACM symposium on User interface software and technology, pp. 43–52. ACM Press, New York (2004)
5. Malik, S., Ranjan, A., Balakrishnan, R.: Interacting with large displays from a distance with vision-tracked multi-finger gestural input. In: UIST '05: Proceedings of the 18th annual ACM symposium on User interface software and technology, pp. 43–52. ACM Press, New York (2005)
6. Starner, T., Weaver, J., Pentland, A.: Real-time American Sign Language recognition using desk and wearable computer-based video. IEEE Transactions Pattern Analysis and Machine Intelligence, 20(12) (December 1998)
7. Vogler, C., Metaxas, D.: ASL recognition based on a coupling between HMMs and 3D motion analysis. In: ICCV, Bombay (1998)
8. Want, R., Schilit, B.N., Adams, N.I., Gold, R., Petersen, K., Goldberg, D., Ellis, J.R., Weiser, M.: An overview of the PARCTAB ubiquitous computing experiment. IEEE Personal Communications 2(6), 28–33 (1995)
9. Westeyn, T., Brashear, H., Atrash, A., Starner, T.: Georgia tech gesture toolkit: supporting experiments in gesture recognition. In: Proceedings of the 5th International Conference on Multimodal Interfaces (ICMI 2003), pp. 85–92. ACM (November 5-7, 2003)
10. Westeyn, T., Vadas, K., Bian, X., Starner, T., Abowd, G.D.: Recognizing mimicked autistic self-stimulatory behaviors using hmms. In: ISWC 2005, pp. 164–169. IEEE Computer Society, Washington (2005)
11. Wobbrock, J.O., Myers, B.A., Kembel, J.A.: Edgewrite: a stylus-based text entry method designed for high accuracy and stability of motion. In: UIST '03: Proceedings of the 16th annual ACM symposium on User interface software and technology, pp. 61–70. ACM Press, New York (2003)
12. Wu, M., Balakrishnan, R.: Multi-finger and whole hand gestural interaction techniques for multi-user tabletop displays. In: UIST '03: Proceedings of the 16th annual ACM symposium on User interface software and technology, pp. 193–202. ACM Press, New York (2003)
13. Young, S., Evermann, G., Gales, M., Hain, T., Kershaw, D., Moore, G., Odell, J., Ollason, D., Povey, D., Valtchev, V., Woodland, P.: The HTK Book (for HTK Version 3.3) Cambridge University Engineering Department (2005)

Static and Dynamic Hand-Gesture Recognition for Augmented Reality Applications

Stefan Reifinger, Frank Wallhoff, Markus Ablassmeier, Tony Poitschke, and Gerhard Rigoll

Technische Universität München, Institute for Man Machine Communication, Theresienstraße 90, 80333 Munich, Germany
{reifinger,wallhoff,ablassmeier,poitschke,rigoll}@mmk.ei.tum.de

Abstract. This contribution presents our approach for an instrumented automatic gesture recognition system for use in Augmented Reality, which is able to differentiate static and dynamic gestures. Basing on an infrared tracking system, infrared targets mounted at the users thumbs and index fingers are used to retrieve information about position and orientation of each finger. Our system receives this information and extracts static gestures by distance classifiers and dynamic gestures by statistical models. The concluded gesture is provided to any connected application. We introduce a small demonstration as basis for a short evaluation. In this we compare interaction in a real environment, Augmented Reality with a mouse/keyboard, and our gesture recognition system concerning properties, such as task execution time or intuitiveness of interaction. The results show that tasks executed by interaction with our gesture recognition system are faster than using the mouse/keyboard. However, this enhancement entails a slightly lowered wearing comfort.

Keywords: Augmented Reality, Gesture Recognition, Human Computer Interaction.

1 Introduction

Augmented Reality (AR) aims at a combination of reality and virtuality in a coordinated way. Major goal is the integration of virtual content embedded into the user's real environment as realistic as possible. Commonly, interaction between user and AR application occurs by use of non-natural interaction techniques (e.g. mice or keyboards). To achieve a fully immersive AR application, the system's output (e.g. visualization) as well as system's input has to adapt to the user's reality. Thus, AR applications have to comprehend the human's natural interaction techniques, e.g. speech or gestures. For this reason, our contribution focuses on the integration of a static and dynamic gesture recognition system for the use within AR applications.

2 Motivation and Previous Work

The most common way, which humans use for interaction in reality, is using speech or gestures. For the manipulation of a real object (e.g. translation) the user employs

J. Jacko (Ed.): Human-Computer Interaction, Part III, HCII 2007, LNCS 4552, pp. 728–737, 2007.

one or two hands. This natural technique directly associates user's action and object's reaction. Manipulation of virtual objects in commonly used AR systems is accomplished by non natural interaction techniques (using mice or keyboards). However, this artificial technique does not directly associate user's action and object's reaction. Thus the user has to transfer abstract paradigms to actions (e.g. predefined mouse and keyboard input combinations resulting to a specific interaction). For eliminating this abstract interaction, AR systems should be able to offer natural interaction techniques, such as interaction by hand reducing the user's cognitive load and increasing the immersive character of AR. Therefore, our contribution focuses the integration of an automatic hand gesture recognition system in Augmented Reality.

In general, there are two major approaches to implement automatic gesture recognition systems. Non-instrumented systems work with computer vision based algorithms, which extract information about the user's hand gestures from a visually captured stream (camera). This technique does not need additional hardware mounted at the user's hands, which have to be divided from the scene's background robustly. In a second step, the position of the hand and its fingers are calculated and used for recognizing predefined gestures by use of statistical methods. Instrumented systems on the other side need additional hardware mounted at the user's hand. This hardware as part of a tracking system provides information about the hand position and orientation from which gestures are calculated.

In [3], a non-instrumented gesture recognition interface, which differentiates pointing, clicking and five static gestures, has been developed. Advantage of this approach is the non-intrusive nature of recognition, as there is no need for the user to wear any hardware. On the negative side, the hand has to be permanently visible inside the user's personal field of view (FOV) for recognition. An instrumented gesture recognition system using optical markers mounted at the user's hand, as developed by [1] implies the same disadvantage. Instrumented systems basing on non-optical tracking systems, such as those used in [4], eliminate the necessity of visible hands, but entail that additional hardware has to be worn by the user.

As the non-instrumented approach does not depend on additional hardware, worn by the user, the interaction with the AR system is not limited. But this approach leads to the necessity of the visibility of the user's hand during interaction. When the user's hand within the camera's view is lost, no gesture information is available, which disables the user to interact with the AR system. This disadvantage entails big computational efforts and a limited radius of action for the user. Additionally, such systems are sensitive for changing environmental parameters such as lighting conditions or objects similar to a human hand.

An instrumented approach limits the user by the necessity of wearing additional hardware. But this hardware increases the recognition rate of the user's hand, because tracking systems are optimized to track this hardware and gather information about their position and orientation. Those systems are more resistant for changing environmental parameters. Instrumented approaches, using non vision based tracking systems offer the advantage that the hand has not to be visible for a camera permanently. Such non vision based systems come with larger hardware cutting down the radius of interaction and wearing comfort of the user.

3 Implementation

To avoid occlusions endangering the continuous visibility of user's hands, our approach bases on an instrumented infrared (IR) tracking system (ITS) containing a six camera array [2]. Originally, this tracking system has been implemented for measuring the user's position and orientation for AR applications. Now this ITS setup enables additional tracking of the user's hands at the same time. To keep down the intrusive character of instrumented systems, we use two light-weighted IR-tracking targets (IRTTs). These IRTTs are mounted at the user's finger to receive the position and orientation. Our ITS delivers tracking data in temporally and spationally high resolution. For a more flexible interaction, both hands are used for gesture recognition. Due to the human's way of gesturing, static (e.g. pointing) as well as dynamic gestures (e.g. clapping) will be recognized.

For our gesture recognition system, we differentiate static and dynamic gestures. Static and dynamic gestures differ in the angle between the user's fingers. Static gestures are defined by the angle between the fingers and do not vary in time, e.g. pointing or grasping. Dynamic gestures are marked by changing angles between fingers during elapsed time, e.g. waving or drawing letters in the air. The position of the hand can vary both in static and dynamic gestures during the time.

Our gesture recognition system is able to differentiate static and dynamic gestures. In our demonstration application, the user is able to point, grasp and scale by using static gestures. Pointing and grasping is performed by using one hand (either right or left), scaling by using both hands. Pointing implies a right angle between user's thumb and index finger (index finger points on the object), while other fingers are angled. Thumb and index finger are formed to an "O" (tips of both fingers are touching) for grasping an object, other fingers are angled again. For scaling, the user grasps the object with both hands in a defined minimum distance and pulls them apart.

Currently our demonstration application only recognizes two dynamic gestures, which are performed by either right or left hand drawing a symbol "X" or "O" in the air.

The subsequent gesture recognition systems bases on a master-client architecture and consists of three main parts (see Fig. 1.).

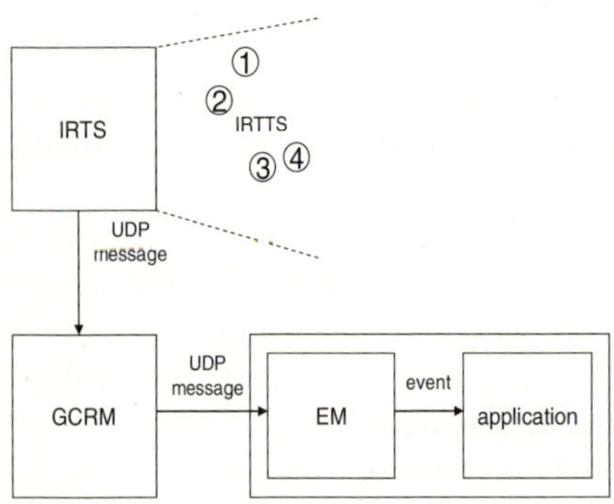

Fig. 1. Schematic Overview

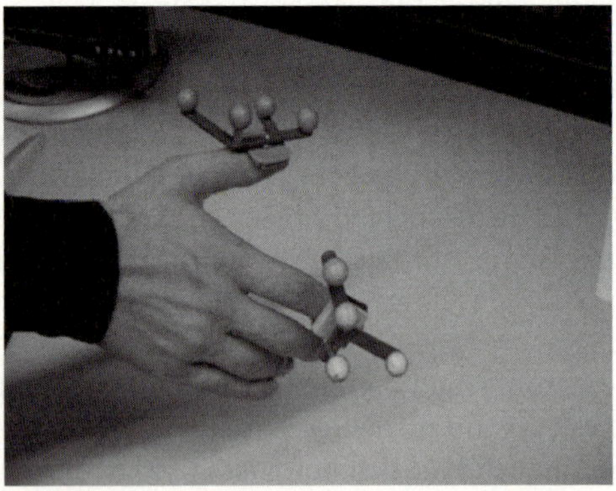

Fig. 2. IRTTs mounted at user's fingers

The ITS delivers information (position and orientation) about IRTTs worn by the user via UDP messages to the client. These IRTTs consist of four reflecting spheres fixed at a flexible tape. This tape ensures wearing comfort for the user. The first IRTT is worn at the thumb and the second at the index finger of the right hand (see Fig. 2.). The third and fourth is worn at the left hand arranged in the same way.

The Gesture Caption and Recognition Module (GCRM) acting as client receives this information and classifies observed data into static and dynamic gestures. Static gestures, such as pointing, can efficiently be classified by applying an Euclidean Distance measure. If the absolute mean difference of at least two position vectors is above a certain threshold, the recording of a dynamic observation is started. It is stopped if this difference is under the threshold again. In order to smooth the observation with variable length, a spline interpolation is applied. Hereafter an unknown gesture can be identified by finding the Hidden Markov Model (HMM) with the highest likelihood [5].

For the training phase of the above mentioned reference vectors and HMMs, a set of several samples from ten people has been gathered. Thus, the resulting gesture recognition system can be considered as person independent. Due to its low dimensionality and marginal preprocessing the entire recognition is running in real-time and has a very low latency so that it can be used on-line within the demonstrator. Any recognized gesture is sent as an UDP message to the Event Manager (EM) acting as master, implemented as a C# class. Depending on to recognized gesture, the EM raises an event, not only containing information about the gesture but also its confidence. This event can be processed by any connected application.

3.1 Gesture Caption and Recognition Module

The GCRM is the core recognition module receiving its data from the ITS tracking system and sending the decoded gestures to the EM via network (see Fig. 1).

As a consequence of the obeyed IRTT system, the fingers' positions and angles can be observed directly, i.e. the x-, y- and z coordinate as well as the three angles roll, azimuth and elevation. Thus no feature extraction technique has to be applied enabling a fast preprocessing. However, aiming at robust features including position and velocity, a Hermitian Spline Interpolation (HSI) is performed on the measured tracking data.

Besides a feature smoothing, this step is motivated in order to fill an invalid or missing tracking feature $P_{\text{interp.}}$ mainly caused by occluded infrared markers. These faulty observations arise when not both fingers' targets are visible in more than one camera. Otherwise these faulty observations would harm the confidence of the subsequent recognizers.

Aiming at filling a hole by reconstructing a valid gesture trajectory, a curve between the ends of the last visible observations is computed on the basis of the two points (P_1, P_2) and their tangents (T_1, T_2).

The velocity can also be reconstructed correctly, since a distance change is represented by the lengths of the tangents.

The HSI bases on a linear combination of four cubical elemental functions with start and end points and can be expressed in the following matrix expression, where s ranges from 0 in P_1 to 1 in P_2 :

$$P_{\text{interp.}} = \begin{pmatrix} s^3 \\ s^2 \\ s \\ 1 \end{pmatrix} \bullet \begin{pmatrix} 2 & -2 & 1 & 1 \\ -3 & 3 & -2 & -1 \\ 0 & 0 & 1 & 0 \\ 1 & 0 & 0 & 0 \end{pmatrix} \bullet \begin{pmatrix} P_1 \\ P_2 \\ T_1 \\ T_2 \end{pmatrix} \text{ with } s \in [0.0 - 1.0]$$

Since gestures are represented by their dynamic properties, the absolute position or rotation of the finger or hand is not significant and carries no further information. Therefore the feature vector has to be normalized by transforming it into the global origin. This can be achieved by deriving the relative position and angle change of all further samples with respect to the first sample.

In a next step this improved feature stream has to be segmented and classified into static and dynamic gestures. In order to decide if a relevant dynamic gesture starts, respectively ends, a threshold based decision is derived from the continuous data stream. If the magnitude of the difference of two previous positions is above the speed threshold $T_{\text{speed}} = 18$ cm/s at least the next $T_{\text{duration}} = 350$ ms are considered to be a separate feature. When the gesture velocity is below the threshold T_{speed} the segment is assumed to have ended.

3.1.1 Dynamic Gestures

Continuous classical left to right Hidden Markov Models (HMMs) with their excellent dynamical time warping capabilities and recognition performance are utilized to handle dynamic gestures [6]. With this paradigm the robust recognition of gestures is guaranteed no matter how fast or slow they are expressed.

An arbitrary HMM λ representing one certain gesture class is completely described by its number J of internal emitting states q_j, a state transition matrix (a_{ij}) including the non emitting start and end state (q_0 and q_{J+1}):, and the (continuous) production probability vector $b = [b_1 ... b_J]^T$.

The elements of the matrix A, $a_{qjq_{(j+1)}}$ represent the probabilities of being in state $q_{(j+1)}$ after having been in state q_j (1st order Markov Model).

The elements b_j in a certain state j for a D-dimensional observation $\vec{x}_j$ are given by a multivariate Gaussian distribution consisting of a mean value vector $\vec{\mu}_j$ and a covariance matrix $\sum_j$: $b_j(\vec{x}_j, \vec{\mu}_j \sum_j) = \frac{1}{\sqrt{(2\pi)^D |\sum_j|}} e^{-\frac{1}{2}(\vec{x}_j - \vec{\mu}_j)^T \sum_j^{-1} (\vec{x}_j - \vec{\mu}_j)}$, describing the probability of a given observation or feature $\vec{x}$ being in a certain state q_j.

In our case, a dynamic gesture is represented by an observation sequence X. This feature sequence X has to be at least a piecewise stationary signal and consists of the single observations or feature elements $X = [\vec{x}_1 ... \vec{x}_T]$.

The unknown parameters in A and $\vec{b}$ have to be estimated prior to the recognition process. For this purpose the well-known Baum-Welch-Estimation procedure [6] can be applied together with an appropriate amount of positive examples, here 30 from 10 different subjects for each class.

An unknown gesture can be classified by the following maximum-likelihood decision using all previously trained models λ: $\lambda^* = \underset{\lambda \in \text{GESTURES}}{\arg\max}\ P(X|\lambda)$.

Herein X represents the unknown gesture, λ one class out of the set of all prior trained gestures and λ^* the best matching model out of this set, which is the winner.

3.1.2 Static Gestures

Static gestures, such as pointing or grasping, are represented by the distance and the angle between the thumb and the index finger. They can efficiently be classified by applying the Euclidean Distance measure.

In order to train the prior defined set of classes, the static finger positions of several subjects are captured. The class is then represented by the mean of these reference examples. Unknown vectors can be classified by finding the class with the minimal distance to it.

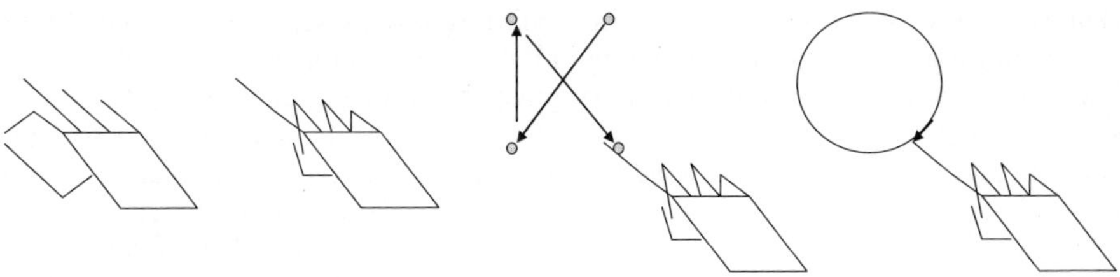

Fig. 3. Gestures used in our recognition system (grasp, point, dynamic X, dynamic O)

3.2 Event Manager

The EM is implemented in form of a C# class, which can be integrated in any application. The EM provides an event driven architecture as well as general functions and properties concerning the gesture recognition. High level functions, such as connecting to the GCRM, are provided for easy use of any developer. If a UDP connection between EM and GCRM is established, any information of the GCRM is sent by a UDP message to the EM.

Thus, the application is able to connect to events raised by the EM, if any gesture is recognized by the GCRM. Any gesture of the left or right hand (static and dynamic) as well as any position and orientation of any finger can be retrieved by the application in real-time.

Basing on this data the subsequent application logic can be controlled by our gesture recognition system.

4 Evaluation

Aiming at evaluating our system we performed a short system evaluation, which focused on the comparison of three interaction paradigms: interacting in the real world, AR with a mouse/keyboard, and AR with our gesture recognition system. Our main attention was to compare the execution time of similar tasks, the intuitiveness of the underlying system and the interaction comfort. In order to keep the evaluation straightforward, we decided, to only examine interaction by using the grasping gesture.

4.1 Evaluation Setup and Procedure

For testing our developed recognition system we designed a demonstration application, which integrates the system capabilities and acts as an evaluation procedure.

This demonstration application offers virtual building blocks integrated in AR (similar to kid's toys, see Fig. 4.). As in a real kit our virtual kit offers different building blocks, which can be used to compose a complex figure.

Manipulation of real building blocks is done by using hands, thus our system can be used in a reasonable way. All virtual building blocks can be manipulated by using the real hand simulating manipulation of a real kit in a realistic way.

This virtual kit consists of eight virtual building blocks separated in four different kinds of building blocks. At the beginning of the demonstration application these blocks are arranged side by side. All blocks can be grasped and displaced by using the grasping gesture of our system. At the moment of grasping a block is bound to the hand adopting movement and orientation of the hand. After releasing, the block is bound again to the world coordinate system. In that way, manipulation of each building block is possible. As the real kit, our virtual kit offers the opportunity to create complex models by using the hands only. All building blocks can be reset by use of the dynamic gesture "O", in case of deleting all blocks, gesture "X" can be used. For a better depth perception the fingers are covered with occlusion models. In that way, the user is able to differentiate hand position before and behind the virtual object (see fig. 5.).

Fig. 4. Virtual building blocks composing a complex model

Fig. 5. Grasped virtual building block with occluding thumb

For our evaluation, the demonstration application was limited to grasping only, since there is no possibility for resizing the real building blocks or the manipulation by dynamic gestures (e.g. deletion).

For a comparison of the three interaction paradigms we have chosen the virtual building blocks application. Basing on a real kit with building blocks, used for the part of interaction in reality, virtual models of these blocks were created (see fig. 4.). These models were loaded into the AR application. The subject sat in front of a desk on which the real respectively the virtual blocks were arranged. During the start the position of the real and virtual blocks was the same in order to assure the same conditions for every test run. The first tested system was the interaction in reality, thus, no additional hardware had to be worn by the user. The second system was AR using a mouse/keyboard for interaction. This system offered grasping by clicking a button and translating by moving the mouse. For differentiation of the three axes, the mouse input was combined with keyboard input in order to distinguish all three axes. Visualization was done by a Head-Mounted Display (HMD) worn by the test person. The third system was our gesture system demanding additional targets, which have been placed on the thumb and index finger of the user. Visualization was also done using a HMD.

At the beginning of the test, a short general introduction to AR was given to each subject. The users had five minutes to experience the functionality of each system and get comfortable with wearing a HMD and the targets mounted at their fingers.

The second part was the core evaluation task, which consisted of arranging the building blocks to a predefined model. This task had to be performed consecutively with all three different systems by the user while the needed execution time was recorded. After each part, a short questionnaire concerning a rating of intuitiveness and comfort had to be filled out by the subject.

4.2 Results

15 subjects, with 10 males among them, participated in our study. The average age was 25 years. The mean values of their ratings and task execution times are summarized in Tab. 1.

Table 1. Subjects' mean rating and task execution time

	Reality	Mouse/Keyboard	Gesture Recognition
Task Execution time in [s]	9	89	57
Intuitivness	5	1,8	4
Comfort	5	1,9	1,5

The results show that the fastest way to solve the given task is the interaction in reality. The average task duration time was 9 seconds. Interaction by mouse/keyboard turned out to be slower than interaction with our gesture recognition system. Average time using our system was 57 seconds, whereas mouse/keyboard required 89 seconds.

The test persons rated the interaction in reality as the most intuitive way to solve this task with a score of 5. Our gesture recognition system was rated with a score of 4, which states that gestures are more intuitive than using the mouse and keyboard.

Furthermore, reality turned out to be the most comfortable way of interaction. Interacting with mouse/keyboard and our gesture recognition system was rated rather low with 1.9 and 1.5 points.

These results show that using our gesture recognition system lowers the average task duration time by a third for this given task compared to the mouse/keyboard. However, this enhancement comes along with a lack of comfort, caused by additional hardware, which has to be worn by the user (IRTTs and HMD). As expected, the interaction in reality is still by factor six much faster than interaction in an augmented environment. Additionally it has turned out that the interaction in reality is the most intuitive and comfortable way of solving the given task.

5 Conclusion and Future Directions

In this contribution we presented an automatic gesture recognition system. This system is able to recognize static gestures (e.g. pointing or grasping) as well as dynamic gestures (e.g. drawing letters in the air). Basing on a master-client structure the gesture caption and recognition module receives tracking data of a connected infrared tracking system originated from Augmented Reality applications. This combination enables an easy integration into Augmented Reality. The user wears two light weighted infrared tracking targets at his thumb and index finger. Based on these captured data, which include the position and orientation of the targets, a feature vector is gained by a subsequent hermitian spline interpolation. The recognition module classifies unknown static gestures by calculating the nearest neighbors or Hidden Markov Models for the classification of predefined dynamic gestures.

Our presented system was benchmarked by a short evaluation procedure based on a construction task focusing on a comparison of the following three interaction paradigms: reality, Augmented Reality using a mouse/keyboard, and our developed system. The valuated parameters were average task execution time, intuitiveness, and comfort of interaction. As expected the results of this study proved that interaction in reality is the fastest, the most intuitive, and the most comfortable way of interaction. Using our gesture recognition system the average task duration time was lowered by a third compared to interaction by mouse/keyboard. It further increases the intuitiveness of the construction task. However, this enhancement comes with a slightly lowered wearing comfort, caused by additional hardware that has to be worn by the user. Therefore our presented way of human-machine interaction is the most preferable way to be used within AR applications.

References

1. Buchmann, V., Violich, S., Billinghurst, M., Cockburn, A.: FingARtips: gesture based direct manipulation in Augmented Reality. In: GRAPHITE '04: Proceedings of the 2nd international conference on Computer graphics and interactive techniques in Australasia and South East Asia (2004)
2. Advanced Realtime Tracking GmbH: ARTtrack1 (2005) http://www.ar-tracking.de

3. Stoerring, M., Moeslund, T.B., Liu, Y., Granum, E.: Computer Vision-Based Gesture Recognition for an Augmented Reality Interface. In: 4th IASTED International Conference on VISUALIZATION, IMAGING, AND IMAGE PROCESSING (2004)
4. Kaiser, E., Olwal, A., McGee, D., Benko, H., Corradini, A., Li, X., Cohen, P., Feiner, S.: Mutual disambiguation of 3D multimodal interaction in augmented and virtual reality. In: ICMI '03: Proceedings of the 5th international conference on Multimodal interfaces (2003)
5. Wallhoff, F., Zobl, M., Rigoll, G.: Action Segmentation And Recognition in Meeting Room Scenarios. In: Proceedings on IEEE International Conference on Image Processing (2004)
6. Rabiner, L.R.: A Tutorial on Hidden Markov Models and Selected Applications in Speech Recognition. In: Proceedings of the IEEE, vol. 77(2) (1989)

Multiple People Labeling and Tracking Using Stereo for Human Computer Interaction

Nurul Arif Setiawan, Seok-Ju Hong, and Chil-Woo Lee

Intelligent Image Media and Interface Lab, Department of Computer Engineering, Chonnam National University, Gwangju, Korea
arif@image.chonnam.ac.kr, seokju@image.chonnam.ac.kr, leecw@chonnam.ac.kr

Abstract. In this paper, we propose a system for multiple people tracking using fragment based histogram matching. Appearance model is based on Improved HLS color histogram which can be calculated efficiently using integral histogram representation. Since the histograms will loss all spatial information, we define a fragment based region representation which retains spatial information, robust against occlusion and scale issue by using disparity information. Multiple people labeling is maintained by creating an online appearance representation for each person detected in the scene and calculating fragment vote map. Initialization is performed automatically from the background segmentation step.

Keywords: Integral Histogram, Fragment Based Tracking, Multiple People, Stereo Vision.

1 Introduction

Detection and tracking of people in a dynamic scene is one of the important modules for many vision application systems including surveillance, activity analysis, robot vision and human computer interaction. For such systems, the challenge is to determine people trajectory and maintain a correct association of the tracked objects in a natural situation which poses several problems such as occlusion, feature similarity and dynamic environment.

Visual tracker utilized targets representation such as color distribution model as blobs [1,2], region pixels as the template [3,4], or region pixels modeled by its histogram [5,6]. In histogram based methods [7], a target is identified by an image region with the state of the region usually its center position and the scale. Object defined in a region is modeled by information contained in the region such as color, intensity or the gradient. Density of the chosen features within the region is estimated by its histogram. The tracking process itself can be defined as a simple histogram matching process by sliding model's template over the image in each frame hence called exhaustive search, or by optimization problem solved by a deterministic techniques such as the mean-shift algorithm [5] or a probabilistic model by means of particle filter [6,8].

J. Jacko (Ed.): Human-Computer Interaction, Part III, HCII 2007, LNCS 4552, pp. 738–746, 2007.

Color histogram representation is chosen because of its robustness to the view changes, noise and partial occlusion. However, histogram by itself suffers from illumination changes, color similarity with background objects and mainly the loss of spatial information. To handle histogram limitation, [8] adds Edge Orientation Histogram feature for their particle filter implementation. Several improvements on kernel and histogram definition for mean-shift tracker have also been proposed to maintain spatial information [9,10].

Multiple fragments to represent the object's template are proposed in [11]. Tracking is performed by comparing histogram of patches from the objects template to a new hypothesis of position and scale in the each frame. All patches vote for a template are combined using robust statistic estimator. The authors have shown that this method is robust to partial occlusion and preserve spatial information. The main tool for this method is the integral histogram structure proposed in [12] which enables us to extract histograms of multiple rectangular regions in efficient way. In [12], exhaustive search by histogram matching over image region can be performed efficiently for object localization and with better tracking result than a local minimization search performed by the mean-shift algorithm.

In this paper, we propose some improvement for fragment based tracking mainly by adding disparity information from stereo camera and multiple people tracking framework. As noted in [11] one issue in intensity only tracker is scale space search. To match over different range scale hypotheses, they enlarge and shrink the template by 10\% and evaluate new position in that scale. This exhaustive search over scale space can be reduced by using disparity. Inclusion of the disparity information to add robustness of the tracker has been proposed by [13,14]. Plan view construction is used in [14] to track people with stereo camera placement above head level. In [13], the authors use the disparity information to segment background and the foreground and to provide scale space estimation for template matching.

In the next section, we will describe our algorithm for initialization and building appearance model steps including adding of depth information to add trackers robustness against occlusion and to provide estimation of scale space search. In section 3, fragment based tracking and multiple people tracking framework will be outlined. Some experimental results will be discussed in section 4, and finally section 5 concludes this paper and discusses some future works.

2 Segmentation and Appearance Model

2.1 System Overview

Our system is built on Improved HLS color space [15]. First, we convert RGB color from right stereo view to Improved HLS (IHLS) color and extract foreground region using Gaussian Mixture Model [16]. This will provide us simple initialization for creating people appearance model. From the foreground regions bounding box, we create appearance model of people in scene by calculating the template's patches histograms from integral histogram structure. Instead of just using color information, we add depth information to the appearance model. Tracking is performed by associating a model with detected track and fragment based matching process as proposed in [11]. Our system architecture is shown in Fig. 1.

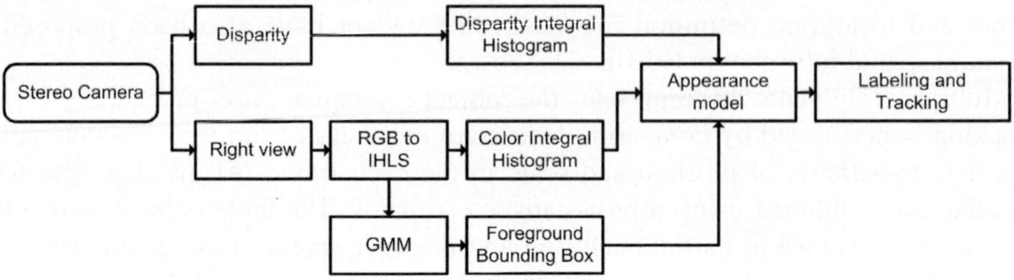

Fig. 1. System architecture

2.2 Background Segmentation

For automatic initialization, a background segmentation provide simple and quite reliable way to segment moving objects assuming that every moving object in a scene ia actually human. A more reliable and advanced method can be incorporated such as a face or people detector. We use Gaussian Mixture Model using Improved HLS color space [16] to segment the foreground objects from a fixed stereo camera. Segmentation gives a clue of the moving objects and can be utilized to limit search process only on foreground region instead of performing exhaustive search. Since we are using fragment based approach, people appearances will be modeled by its' bounding box region extracted from foreground mask.

2.3 Integral Histogram

The Integral histogram structure is first formalized by [12] as an extension to the integral image. The integral image structure holds at the point *(x,y)*, the sum of rectangular region defined by top left corner of the image and the point *(x,y)*. This structure allows computation of pixels sum in any rectangular region by using four integral image values at the four corners of the region.

Extending this idea into histogram representation is basically building integral image for each bin of the histogram. That is by counting the cumulative numbers of pixels falling into each bin. Thus complexity and speed up of the integral histogram compared to standard histogram structure depends on how many bins have been used. Computational requirement for several scenarios of data dimension is given in [12].

After integral histogram is computed, histogram extraction over any rectangular region of any size has similar computational cost. So in evaluating the hypotheses of a rectangular object's template in several positions and scales, as used in [11], is equal to the cost of the histogram comparison. And given disparity information from stereo camera, search over scale can be reduced by estimating scale directly with a linear equation.

2.4 Disparity Layer

Disparity can add more information to build a robust appearance model. This takes advantages of stereo's system ability to segment objects at different depth level. We build the integral histogram structure for disparity image. Let $v_{v:v=1..k}$ and v_M be the normalized histogram representation of a template and its maximum probability. If we assume that the bounding box encloses tightly the foreground object, then the disparity pixels which falls into maximum probability bin M, are the most likely to represent the depth of the object.

We segment disparity image into layers to represent scale variation and to find corresponding depth of objects given merging or partial occlusion. One can find scale of objects by using following linear equation [13]

$$s = dK \tag{1}$$

where s is the scale, d is the disparity value and K is a linear constants which can be estimated in a simple calibration step. If an object template is initialized with a scale $s = 1$ and has disparity value d corresponding to the maximum bin M as explained above, then when its observed that disparity value changes to d', the objects scale can be assumed to have changes to a new scale s' by a linear equation (1) above.

2.5 Fragment Based Appearance Model

Color histogram provides a good model to represent objects because it is rather invariant to object or camera motion or shape change assuming that objects have constant appearances throughout the scene. Although histogram itself has several issues mainly the loss of spatial information and color histogram by itself is not robust to illumination changes, fragment based template as proposed in [11] can overcome this limitation.

From IHLS color, we compute saturation-weighted hue histogram expressed by the following equation [15]:

$$W_\theta = \sum_x S_x \delta_{\theta H_x} \tag{2}$$

where H_x and S_x are the hue and saturation value at point x and δ_{ij} is Kronecker delta function. In this way, we have color information of objects in one dimensional histogram, thus reducing computational time to create integral histograms and to evaluate the metric between patches histograms. We also use histogram from disparity image as additional information to color model.

Color appearance of objects is more stable and relatively constant then depth since if people move forward or backward than depth information will change drastically. However, color information will also change slowly by illumination changes and new color appearance in the bounding box. Thus histogram representation of the color and the depth will be updated as in the following equation:

$$H^t(k) = (1-\alpha)H^{t-1}(k) + \alpha H^{new}(k) \tag{3}$$

A Parameter α is an update rate and k is the bin of the histogram. Depth and color histograms have different α since each will change at a different rate. Updating the template has an issue that occluded objects maybe introduced into the template. To reduce those possibilities, we choose to update the patches which have high similarity to the current template states. Figure 2 below shows the processes from background segmentation to a fragment based appearance model.

Fig. 2. Segmentation result and fragment based appearance model

3 Multiple People Tracking

In this section we will describe a box based tracking and the fragment based tracking. We will also extend the initial concept in [2] to use disparity information, foreground segmentation results, and tracking multiple people in a scene. Box based tracking is a direct method to utilize foreground segmentation results by associating each initialized model with detected tracks on each frame. If each track corresponds to only one model then the process is simple. When detecting merging and splits of tracks, we need to utilize appearance models to maintain labeling and tracking of people in scene consistently.

3.1 Box Tracking

Let $P_T = (c_x, c_y, h, w, s)$ be a state of the box where c_x and c_y make the center of the box, h and w are half height and half width and s is the scale of the box. We then associate model's boxes with detected tracks extracted from foreground region in each frame. The distance between the two boxes A and B is computed by the following equation [17]

$$D_{box} = \max(0, d_x) + \max(0, d_y) \tag{4}$$

where

$$d_x = \begin{cases} c_{xA} - w_A - c_{xB} - w_B, & \text{when } c_{xA} \geq c_{xB} \\ c_{xB} - w_B - c_{xA} - w_A, & \text{when } c_{xA} < c_{xB} \end{cases} \tag{5}$$

and similar for d_y.

We merge the small boxes less than $T_{minperson}$ to the closest large boxes. If the box's area is bigger than $T_{maxperson}$, we will assume that the box is a merging result from several people and proceed accordingly. By creating correspondence distance matrix between objects and detected tracks, we determine to: (a) update the track for existing object; (b) create a track for a new object; and (c) handle detected merge and split.

3.2 Fragment Based Tracking

In frontal view, such as from humanoid robot camera, it is rare that each track will always be separated compared to a higher mounted camera for surveillance system. Thus, merging boxes will always be observed. In this situation, an appearance model using color and disparity information from stereo camera will be utilized to understand the scene. Fragment based association and tracking utilize fast calculation of integral histogram to compute multiple histogram of sub region in one rectangular template [11]. In this method, tracking can be categorized as target representation and localization, where target representation is patches based template and localization is performed by histogram matching in the patch's neighboring region.

Given an object O represented by template image T which contains a patch P_T, in tracking process we wish to find the position and the scale of a region in current frame I which has high similarity to patch T. Tracking is performed by exhaustive search in the neighboring region by calculating the similarity of the histograms. Given image patch $P_{T;(x,y)}$ where (x,y) is the hypothesis of objects position in current frame and patch P_T, if $d(Q,P)$ is some measure of similarity between patch Q and patch P, then

$$V_{PT}(x,y) = d(P_{I;(x,y)}, P_T) \tag{6}$$

is the vote map corresponding to template patch P_T which gives a scalar score of every possible position of the patch in the current frame I [11]. In practice, any similarity metric can be used to obtain the vote map. In our experiment we use Bhattacharya distance as the metric.

After all template patches is evaluated and we obtain several vote maps, next is to combine this information to constitute new tracked object's position. One intuitive way to combine all vote maps is proposed in [11] by using robust statistics with LMedS-type estimator expressed as

$$C(x,y) = Q'th \text{ value in sorted set of } \{V_P(x,y) \mid \text{patches P}\} \tag{7}$$

$\{V_P(x,y) \mid \text{patches P}\}$ is the sorted set of obtained vote map and $Q'th$ is Q smallest score (they measure dissimilarity of patches by EMD distance). Q shows the expected inliers measurement which can be interpreted as the percentage of template's target visible. One desirable property of such robust estimator is that the outliers which will be rejected automatically can be assumed as occluded patches or partial pose change [11].

3.3 Multiple Templates Tracking

When we detect merging boxes, then there are two possibilities that all objects in the box have (a) same disparity or (b) different disparity level. By dividing this merging box histogram into layers of dominant disparity we can decide if one object is closer to the camera than the other objects. This is shown in Fig. 3.

When all objects have the same disparity level, the current position of each possible object in the merging box will be determined by using fragment based approach as previously explained in Sect. 3.2. If there is more than one dominant disparity layer then first we analyze the closest layer to the camera and do fragment

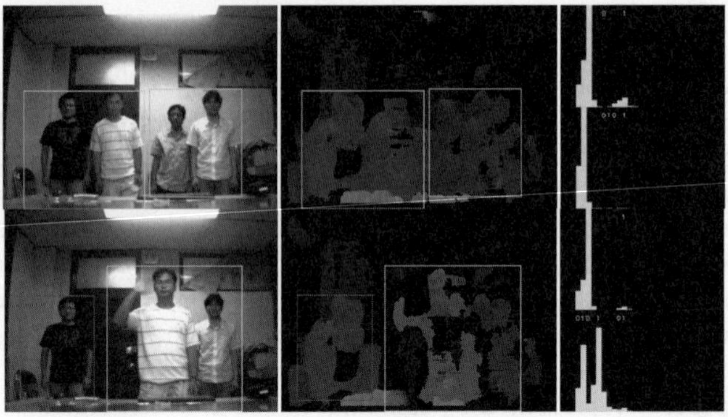

Fig. 3. Disparity histogram in bounding boxes. Top: same disparity level. Bottom: different disparity level, one object is closer to camera.

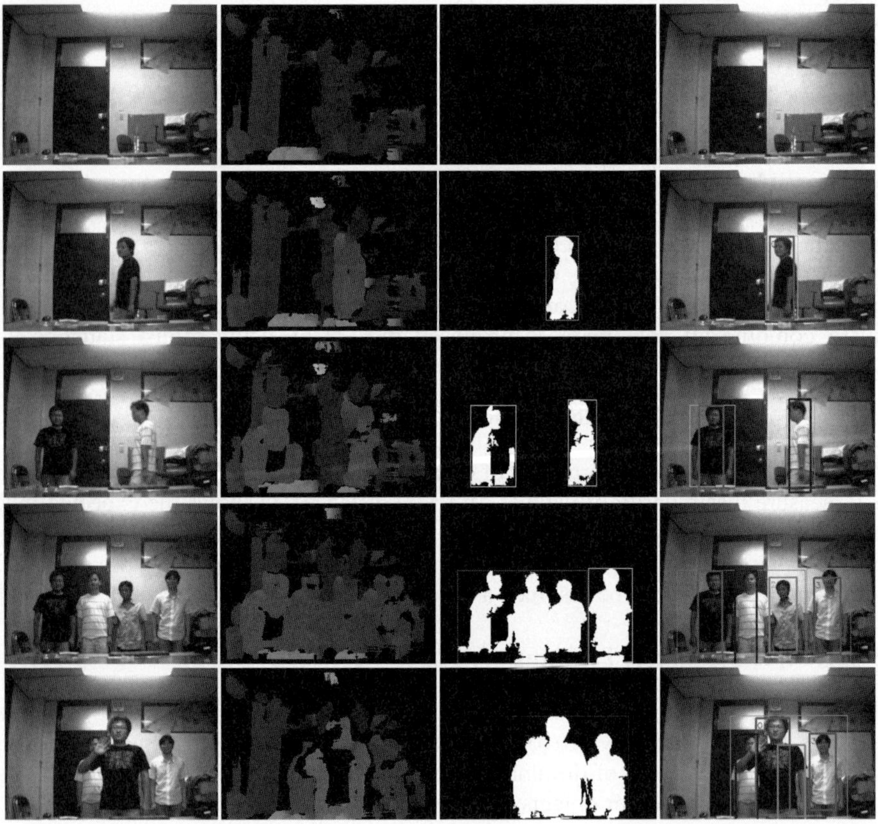

Fig. 4. Result of tracking using our sequences

based matching step after estimating the new object's scale accordingly. Thus, the implementation of fragment based appearance model to multiple people tracking is actually straightforward.

4 Experimental Results

We evaluate our algorithm in a challenging situation where color similarity of foreground and background objects still posing problem in foreground segmentation step, and similarity of people appearance model. In this sequence, one person entering the scene one by one giving initial time for initialization of appearance model. Then one by one each person is moving forward causing merging of foreground segment and partial or full occlusion of other persons. Results of our algorithm can be seen in Fig. 4.

Since all of these steps relied heavily on background segmentation module, there are possibilities that segmentation failed to generate correct foreground mask. This situation can occur if the foreground has similar color with the background. This can be handled by including disparity in segmentation step since most objects will have different disparity. This will be a part of our future works to improve the current system.

5 Conclusion and Future Works

We have proposed a novel method for multiple people tracking utilizing fragments based template modeled by IHLS histogram representation which are computed rapidly using integral histogram. A fragment based region representation is shown to be robust against occlusion and scale issue by using color and disparity information. Multiple people labeling is maintained by creating online appearance representation for each people detected in a scene and calculating fragment vote map.

In future works, we will investigate better methods to obtain disparity image and modeling relation between patches to resolve update problem and to select representative patches to model people in the scene. As this system will be implemented for robot vision, we will also need to add motion model to background segmentation process.

Acknowledgement. This research has been supported in part by MIC and IITA through IT Leading R\&D Support Project and Culture Technology Research Institute through MCT, Chonnam National University, Korea.

References

1. Wren, C.R., Azarbayejani, A., Darrell, T., Pentland, A.: Pfinder: Real-time tracking of the human body. IEEE Transactions on Pattern Analysis and Machine Intelligence 19(7), 780–785 (1997)
2. Isard, M., MacCormick, J.: Bramble: a bayesian multiple-blob tracker. In: Proceedings of the 2001 IEEE International Conference on Computer Vision (ICCV 2001) vol. 2, pp. 34–41 (2001)

3. Hager, G.D., Belhumeur, P.N.: Efficient region tracking with parametric models of geometry and illumination. IEEE Transactions on Pattern Analysis and Machine Intelligence 20(10), 1025–1039 (1998)
4. Jurie, F., Dhome, M.: Hyperplane approximation for template matching. IEEE Transactions on Pattern Analysis and Machine Intelligence 24(7), 996–1000 (2002)
5. Comaniciu, D., Ramesh, V., Meer, P.: Kernel-based object tracking. IEEE Transactions on Pattern Analysis and Machine Intelligence 25(5), 564–575 (2003)
6. P'erez, P., Hue, C., Vermaak, J., Gangnet, M.: Color-based probabilistic tracking. In: Proceedings of the 7th European Conference on Computer Vision vol. 1, pp. 661–675 (2002)
7. Deutsch, B., Gräßl, C., Bajramovic, F., Denzler, J.: A Comparative Evaluation of Template and Histogram Based 2D Tracking Algorithms. In: Kropatsch, W., Sablatnig, R., Hanbury, A. (eds.): Pattern Recognition, 27th DAGM Symposium, pp. 269–276 (2005)
8. Yang, C., Duraiswami, R., Davis, L.: Fast multiple object tracking via a hierarchical particle filter. In: Proceedings of the Tenth IEEE International Conference on Computer Vision (ICCV'05). vol. 1, pp. 212–219 (2005)
9. Birchfield, S.T., Rangarajan, S.: Spatiograms versus histograms for region-based tracking. In: Proceedings of the 2005 IEEE Computer Society Conference on Computer Vision and Pattern Recognition (CVPR'05). vol. 2, pp. 1158–1163 (2005)
10. Zhao, Q., Tao, H.: Object tracking using color correlogram. In: IEEE Workshop on Visual Surveillance and Performance Evaluation of Tracking and Surveillance (VS-PETS'05) in conjunction with ICCV 2005, pp. 263–270 (2005)
11. Adam, A., Rivlin, E., Shimshoni, I.: Robust fragments-based tracking using the integral histogram. In: Proceedings of the 2006 IEEE Computer Society Conference on Computer Vision and Pattern Recognition, pp. 798–805 (2006)
12. Porikli, F.M.: Integral histogram: A fast way to extract histograms in Cartesian spaces. In: Proceedings of the 2005 IEEE Computer Society Conference on Computer Vision and Pattern Recognition (CVPR'05). vol. 1, pp. 829–836 (2005)
13. Beymer, D., Konolige, K.: Real-time tracking of multiple people using stereo. In: Proceedings IEEE Frame Rate Workshop, 1999 (1999)
14. Bahadori, S., Grisetti, G., Iocchi, L., Leone, G., Nardi, D.: Real-time tracking of multiple people through stereo vision. In: Proceedings of the IEEE International Workshop on Intelligent Environments (2005), pp. 252–259 (2005)
15. Hanburry, A.: Circular statistics applied to colour images. In: Proceedings of The 8th Computer Vision Winter Workshop (2003)
16. Setiawan, N.A., Hong, S., Kim, J., Lee, C.: Gaussian mixture model in improved hls color space for human silhouette extraction. In: Pan, Z., Cheok, A., Haller, M., Lau, R.W.H., Saito, H., Liang, R. (eds.) ICAT 2006. LNCS, vol. 4282, pp. 732–741. Springer, Heidelberg (2006)
17. Wang, H., Sutter, D.: Tracking and segmenting people with occlusions by a sample consensus based method. In: Proceedings of The. IEEE International Conference on Image Processing (ICIP 2005) vol. 2, pp. 410–413 (2005)

A Study of Human Vision Inspection for Mura

Pei-Chia Wang[1,*], Sheue-Ling Hwang[2], and Chao-Hua Wen[3]

[1] TSMC,Hsin-Chu Taiwan
[2] Dept of IEEM, National Tsing-Hua Univ. Hsin-Chu, Taiwan
[3] Taiwan TFT LCD Association, Chutung, Hsinchu, Taiwan
slhwang@ie.nthu.edu.tw

Abstract. In the present study, some factors were considered such as the various types and sizes of real Mura, and Mura inspection experience. The steps of data collection and experiments were conducted systematically from the viewpoint of human factors. From the experimental results, Mura size was the most important factor on visual contrast threshold. The purpose of this research was to objectively describe the relationships between the Mura characteristics and visual contrast thresholds. Furthermore, a domestic JND model of LCD industry was constructed. This model could be an inspection criterion for LCD industry.

Keywords: Mura, JND, vision, LCD.

1 Introduction

Liquid crystal displays have become more and more popular in visual display units. For instance, Menozzi et al [1] compared cathode ray tube to liquid crystal display for their suitability in visual tasks and discovered that LCD gives better viewing conditions in comparison to CRT display.

Consequently, there are many manufacturers and users who try to build a common criterion for Mura in the numerous panel marketing. The present study is about the relationship between human eyes and Mura, and the concern among the region and the contrast of Mura.

1.1 The Definition of Mura

One class of defects includes a variety of blemishes is so called Mura, which sometimes occurs during the manufacturing of the flat panel liquid crystal displays. They appear as low contrast and non-uniform brightness regions, typically larger than single pixels, which caused by a variety of physical factors such as non-uniformity distributed liquid crystal material and foreign particles within the liquid crystal [4].

The acceptance level of Mura highly depends on the luminance contrast between the Mura region and its background [3][8].

1.2 The Classification of Mura Defects

Mura defects may be classified depending on the shapes and sizes. Comparison among spot-Mura, line Mura, and region-Mura defect is relatively difficult due to its low

[*] Corresponding author.

J. Jacko (Ed.): Human-Computer Interaction, Part III, HCII 2007, LNCS 4552, pp. 747–754, 2007.

contrast and irregular pattern of shape[4]. To separate different types of Mura may affect the classification of the panel products. For example, we can classify the shape of Mura by manufacturing process into three types, which are point, line and uniformity Mura.

There are several companies which developed or are developing standards of testing method and evaluation guideline. These standards focused on the average defect in the automatic detect system and was so called FPD Mura detection. The ultimate objective is to determine the practical detection method to complete or replace human eye detection method for quality control and quality proof.

1.3 Psychometric Method

Watson [6] demonstrated Bayesian adaptive psychometric method, QUEST. It is a psychometric function, which describes the relation between some physical measure of a stimulus and the probability of a particular psychophysical response. The psychometric function has the same shape under all conditions when express as a function of log intensity. From condition to condition, it differs only in position along the log intensity axis. The position is set by a parameter, T, the threshold, also expressed in units of log intensity.

SEMI[2] set up a new Mura standard to define the value of Mura, called SEMU. It is the first concept of relationship between Mura region and intensity. Moreover, the regression formula has been derived from experiment data to quantify the relationship between Mura region and intensity. The other concept is contrast, called Cx .

Definition: under specific conditions, regressive relationship between area and contrast for Human Mura JND is shown as follows.

$$C\,jnd = F(S\,jnd) = 1.97/S\,jnd^{0.33}+0.72$$

C jnd = Contrast of Mura at JND (units: % relative to background = 100%)

S jnd = Area of Mura at above contrast (units: mm^2)

$$Semu = |Cx| / Cjnd = |Cx| / F(Sx) = |Cx| / (1.97 / Sx^{0.33} + 0.72)$$

Cx: Average contrast of Mura being measured

(Unite: % relative to background = 100%)

Sx: Surface area of Mura being measured (Units: mm^2)

According to the data from IBM Japan, the relation between size of Mura and contrast JND threshold has the same trend with past experience as we check the formula of region of Mura and the linear regression of JND contrast. When the horizontal axis is $1/S^{0.33}$ (S is the size of Mura, unit is mm^2), the vertical axis is contrast. It expresses a strong relative coefficient for $1/S^{0.33}$ and JND contrast [7].

Comparative measurement method involves a panel and software which can stimulate Semu level. People compare a Mura on a real panel to make adjustments. Direct measurement method captures the real panel with a CCD camera and determines the Semu from the area and contrast of the Mura section.

2 Method

In order to understand the model of human vision, the direct way is to find the relation between vision efficiency and Mura in the experiment. It is expected that the human vision model can be applied on automatic Mura detection.

2.1 Experimental Environment and Equipment

The experimental environment simulated the real inspection station of LCD industry as follows,

1) Luminance is about 110 lux.
2) Illuminant is standard illuminant tube CIE D65.
3) The temperature is about 23~25℃.
4) Humidity is about 40~60%.
5) Distance between display and human eyes is about 30cm.

The experimental equipments included the following apparatus.

1) A 22 inch, 3840 × 2400 pixel TFT-LCD, and it was masked by the frame of black cardboard to simulate 17" size of TFT-LCD in the experiment. In order to display low contrast luminance Mura, the LCD was re-worked to display 1024 gradations in a 0.72cd/m^2 ~248cd/m^2 range.
2) One computer, a mouse and a keyboard.
3) A chin rest to fix the distance from display to human eyes.
4) A CSV-1000 Contrast Sensitivity to test human visual sensitivity.

2.2 Experimental Design

Experiments were modified based on SEMI and experiment of Mori [9]. In this study, JNDs of human eyes were measured by psychophysics method, carrying on 2AFC (two alternatives forced-choice) to prevent the large judging difference among subjects, and using QUEST [6] to shorten experimental time effectively. The visual contrast threshold of each pattern would be obtained depending on subject's response of changed pattern contrast.

2.2.1 Independent Variables

In this experiment, the types of real Mura which were captured from the TFT-LCD panels by CCD were simulated. They were similar to the defects of TFT-LCD panels. The inspection background was gray scale L368, and background luminance is about 23.86cd/m^2. The experimenter measured the gray scale of Mura and background, and which was converted into luminance levels to adjust the range of parameter. The program judged different percentage of identification of each subject and turned up different gray scale of Mura.

There were two variables in this experiment.

1) Mura type: 15 real Mura was shown in Fig. 1. They include,

- 03-spacer, stripe, rubbing, curtain, and light-leakage, each type had one pattern.

- There were five sizes of h-band and v-band, such as 10, 50, 100, 200,400 pixels. For the consistency, all units transferred from pixels to visual angles in this study. Therefore, the band size were 0.48°, 2.38°, 4.75°, 9.49° and 18.85° respectively.

2) The inspection experience

There were fifteen subjects who had normal sight participating in this experiment after wearing glasses and passing the eye sensitivity test. Eleven graduate students were novices who never had the experience to detect the Mura. Four operators were experts who had inspected the Mura for at least three years.

2.2.2 Dependent Variable

The dependent variable was Visual Contrast Threshold (VCT (%)) with the correction rate of identification as 82% under the 2AFC situation.

$$VCT(\%) = \frac{|L_{Mura} - L_b|}{L_b} \times 100\%$$

where L_{Mura} is luminance of Mura, L_b is luminance of background.

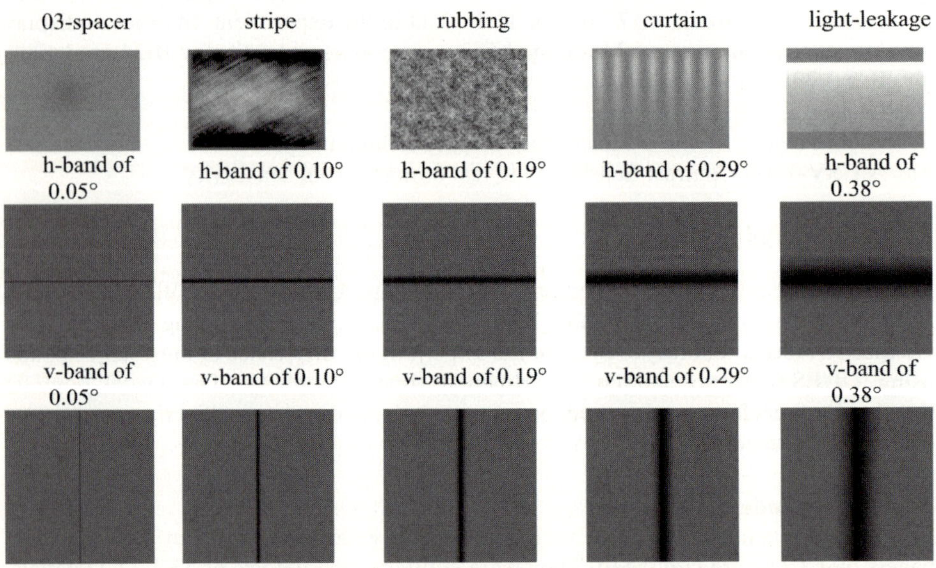

Fig. 1. The pattern of 15 Real Mura types

3 Results

The experimental data were analyzed by using Statistical methods and software (SPSS). For increasing R-squared and fitting the hypotheses of ANOVA, several outliers were removed depending on large residuals in the experiment.

The results of the experiment indicated that Mura types and experience affected visual contrast threshold significantly.

3.1 The Influence of VCT–Mura Types and Experience

There were two independent variables in this experiment. One was TYPE, which included 15 types of Mura as shown in Fig. 1. The other one was EXP (experience), which included novices and experts. The dependent variable was visual contrast threshold (VCT). Fig. 2 indicated that all the VCT of novices are higher than that of experts. Also, the average of VCT of novices was 0.026 greater than of experts.

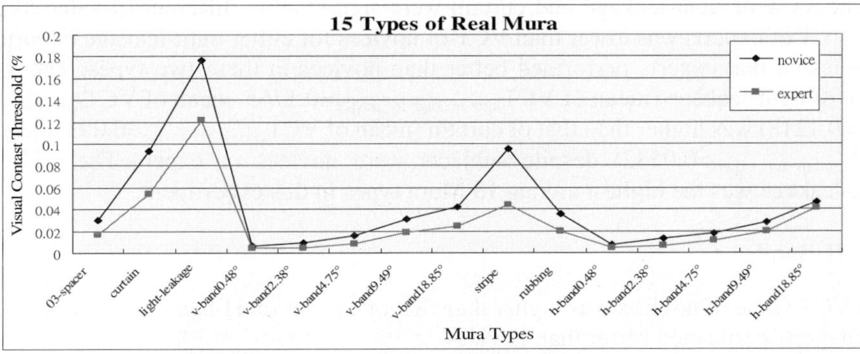

Fig. 2. The mean VCT of each Mura type of subjects

EXP ($F(1,858)=52.221$, p-value<0.05) and TYPE ($F(14,858)=109.770$, p-value<0.05) significantly affected VCT. Also, there was significant interaction ($F(14,858)=3.791$, p-value<0.05) between TYPE and EXP on VCT value.

As to the 15 Mura types, the VCT between novices and experts on h-band of 18.85°were not significantly different ($t_{55.891}=1.585$, p-value=0.119>0.05). On other 14 Mura types, the VCT of novices were significantly higher than that of experts. Experts performed better than novices. The h-band of 18.85° occupied more than half of the screen, and it was the largest area among 15 Mura types. Therefore, both novices and experts were hard to distinguish too large Mura.

To test the effect of Mura type on VCT for either novice or expert, there were significant difference among 15 Mura types for novices ($F(14,633)=78.538$, p-value<0.05) and experts ($F(14,225)=49.514$, p-value<0.05).

In the following sections, the similar shape among 15 real Mura types would be compared and discussed.

3.2 Stripe Versus Rubbing

The surface of stripe is slight oblique, and the appearance of rubbing is obvious slanted line. Stripe and rubbing appeared in the center of the screen and both of them are big size among the 15 Mura types.

The VCT of stripe was significantly different from VCT of rubbing (p-value<0.05). The VCT of experts was always lower than that of novices. It revealed that experts performed better than novices in these two types. The VCT (%) of stripe (mean of $VCT_{stripe\ for\ novice}=0.0952$, mean of $VCT_{stripe\ for\ expert}=0.0358$) was higher than VCT of rubbing (mean of $VCT_{rubbing\ for\ novice}=0.0441$, mean of $VCT_{stripe\ for\ expert}=0.0192$).

3.3 Light-Leakage Versus Curtain

Light-leakage and rubbing appeared in the upper edge were the longer ones among 15 types in the Mura experiment. Light-leakage is bright on the upper edge of the pattern, and curtain is a quasi-curtain which has eight shapes.

The VCT of light-leakage and curtain were significantly different (p-value<0.05). The VCT of experts was lower than VCT of novices for either light-leakage or curtain. It indicated that experts performed better than novices in these two types. The VCT value of light-leakage (mean of $VCT_{light\text{-}leakage\ for\ novice}=0.1765$, mean of $VCT_{light\text{-}leakage\ for\ expert}=0.1218$) was higher than that of curtain (mean of $VCT_{curtain\ for\ novice}=0.093$, mean of $VCT_{curtain\ for\ expert}=0.0542$) despite subjects were novices or experts.The VCT on light-leakage was the highest among 15 Mura types in this experiment.

3.4 H-Band

The VCT value of novices was higher than that of experts on H-band mura. It indicated that experts performed better than novices.

For novices, there were significant differences among Mura size, but VCT of 2.38° was not significantly different from the VCT of 0.48° and 4.75°. For experts, there were significant differences among Mura size, but VCT of 2.38° was not significantly different from the VCT of 0.48°.

3.5 V-Band

The VCT value of novices was greater than that of experts on V-band Mura. It indicated experts had better performance.

For novices, the multiple comparisons showed that VCT of 2.38° was significantly different from VCT of 0.48° and 4.75° at the significant level of 0.05. For experts, the multiple comparisons illustrated that VCT of 2.38° was not significantly different from VCT of 0.48°. The result was the same as h-band for experts.

3.6 The Masking Effect—Light-Leakage

In the previous experiment [5], light-leakage appeared in the center of the screen with a black edge above this pattern to simulate masking effect. The proposed method in this study was that light-leakage turned up in the upper center of the panel, and the appearance of pattern would fit to the real phenomenon. The result illustrated that different location significantly affected VCT ($t_{43.811}= -11.258$, p-value<0.05).

The VCT of light-leakage appeared in the center ($VCT_{center}=0.0312$) was lower than that appeared in the upper ($VCT_{upper}=0.1765$). The location of light-leakage affected VCTs. The VCT of subjects for light-leakage appeared in the upper center of real panel were higher than light-leakage appeared in the center with a simulated edge.

4 Conclusion

From the results of the experiment, new findings of this research were summarized as follows.

1) The effects of experience on visual contrast threshold were significant for 15 types of Real Mura. The visual contrast thresholds of experts were lower than those of novices. In other words, the performance of experts was better.
2) The effects of Mura size on visual contrast threshold were significant. The visual contrast threshold decreased with increasing size of Mura. From the equation of h-band, v-band and one shape of curtain, visual contrast thresholds can be predicted when Mura sizes were given.
3) Locations of Mura caused the masking effect. The visual contrast threshold of light-leakage in the upper edge was greater than light-leakage in the center of screen. The variation of one shape of curtain location affected visual contrast threshold. From the equation of distance from Mura and edge of panel, visual contrast thresholds could be obtained when the distances were known.

Mura is the critical factor of the quality of TFT-LCD. The industry of flat panel display invests a considerable amount of money in human vision inspection for Mura. However, visual inspection of LCDs usually takes a lot of time, people and costs. Recently, the manufacturing technology of LCDs has been improved and led to automated mass production. The findings of this study could be the reference of designing automatic inspection machines, and let the machine vision to be correspondent to human vision.

Acknowledgements. The authors would like to thanks the financial supporting from TTLA (Taiwan TFT LCD Association).

References

1. Menozzi, M., Napflin, U., Krueger, H.: CRT versus LCD: A pilot study on visual performance and suitability of two display technologies for use in office work. Displays 20, 3–10 (1999)
2. SEMI technical report, Definition of Measurement Index (SEMU) for luminance Mura in FPD image quality inspection, SEMI D31-1102 (2002)
3. Tamura, T., Tanaka, K., Baba, M., Suzuki, M., Furuhata, T.: Just noticeable difference (JND) contrast of Mura in LCDs on the five background luminance levels, IDW pp. 1623–1626 (2004)
4. Lee, J.Y., Yoo, S.I.: Automatic detection of region-mura defect in TFT-LCD, IEICE Trans (2004)
5. Hwang, S.-L., Chen, J.-C., Chang, J.-J., Hsu, Y.-H., Wang, P.-C.: Human vision database for LCD, TTLA project report, p. 16 (2005)
6. Watson, A.B., Quest, A.: Bayesian adaptive psychometric method, Perception and Psychophysics (1983)

7. Jiang, X., Gramopadhye, A.K., Melloy, B.J., Grimes, L.W: Evaluation of best system performance: human, automated, and hybrid inspection systems. Human Factors and Ergonomic in Manufacturing 13(2), 125–137 (2003)
8. Tamura, T., Tanaka, K., Satoh, T., Furuhata, T.: Relation between Just noticeable difference (JND) contrast of Mura in LCDs and its background luminance, IDW pp. 1843–1846 (2005)
9. Mori, Y., Yoshitake, R., Tamura, T.: Evaluation and discrimination method of mura in liquid crystal displays by just noticeable difference observation. In: Proceedings of SPIE, vol. 4902, pp. 715–720 (2002)

Tracing Users' Behaviors in a Multimodal Instructional Material: An Eye-Tracking Study

Esra Yecan, Evren Sumuer, Bahar Baran, and Kursat Cagiltay

Computer Education and Instructional Technology,
Middle East Technical University, 06531 Ankara Turkey
{yecan,sumuer,boztekin,kursat}@metu.edu.tr

Abstract. This study aims to explore user behaviors in instructional environments combining multimodal presentation of information. Cognitive load theory and dual coding theory were taken as the theoretical perspectives for the analyses. For this purpose, user behaviors were analyzed by recording participants' eye movements while they were using an instructional material with synchronized video and PowerPoint slides. 15 participants' eye fixation counts and durations for specific parts of the material were collected. Findings of the study revealed that the participants used the slide and video presentations in a complementary way.

Keywords: Producer, PowerPoint, video, eye tracking, cognitive load, dual coding, multiple channels.

1 Introduction

Instructional materials containing various media - like text, image, audio, video etc- allow learners receive information through multiple channels. The use of multiple representations has been regarded as powerful way of facilitating understanding for many years [1]. According to Mayer [2], learners learn better in well-designed multimedia environments which integrate different media types than in traditional learning environments. Multiple representations can make presentation of an application domain more complete than a single traditional source of information because they can complement each other [3]. On the other hand, multimodal approach requires learners to additional cognitive demand since they have to give attention simultaneously to different representations [4]. Therefore, these cognitive demands cause learners to experience cognitive overload, result is less learning.

In the use of multimodal representation, it is important to take cognitive processing theories into account. Two important cognitive processing theories are important in the scope of this study; namely cognitive load theory and dual coding theory [4], [5]. Cognitive load theory predicts that learner can hold few elements in the working memory because of limited amount of information that can be processed in visual and verbal channels at one time. Sweller and Chandler [6] presented two concerns for cognitive load theory; split attention and redundancy effect. Split attention effect occurs when learners are required to split their attention and combine multiple representations of information mentally [6]. Redundancy effect occurs when

J. Jacko (Ed.): Human-Computer Interaction, Part III, HCII 2007, LNCS 4552, pp. 755–762, 2007.

additional information are presented with two or more different media since organizing redundant information with essential information increases cognitive load [7]. On the other hand, dual coding theory suggests that the capacity of working memory is stretched by using both visual and verbal storage systems simultaneously [8]. When both visual and verbal elements are processed at the same time, the available amount of working memory is maximized, thereby promoting learning.

In the design of multimodal instructional materials, these issues are needed to be considered. Today, many universities and corporations provide multimodal instructional materials which may enhance learning by supporting the use of presentation slide sequences integrated with video lectures [9], [10]. Learners gain information from such materials through two sensory memory; eyes and ears. This information is processed in both visual and verbal processing areas simultaneously in the working memory.

In this study, user behaviors were explored by eye-tracking method while using an instructional material with synchronized video and PowerPoint slides. The aim is to explore learners' behavior patterns while using the instructional material. For this purpose, eye fixation counts and durations for specific parts of the material were collected. Based on cognitive load theory and dual coding theory, results are expected to be helpful in providing evidence related to the design of environments combining multimodal presentation of information.

2 Methodology

2.1 Participants

The participants were 15 first year undergraduate students from a major university in the central region of Turkey. The participants were students in the department of Computer Education and Instructional Technology. There were 6 females and 9 males, ranging from 18 to 21 years old. All students voluntarily participated to this study.

2.2 Material

An instructional material was developed in Microsoft Producer, a Microsoft PowerPoint add-in that makes it easy to produce engaging rich media presentation by capturing and synchronizing audio, video, slides and images [5]. The selected presentation topic was "Introduction to Instructional Technology (IT)". The content covered the definition and goals of IT, and a very brief summary of three main learning theories. The material consisted of three parts which were a video of the presenter, PowerPoint slides explaining the content in text format, and a navigation menu part presenting the links to the content (Fig. 1). PowerPoint slides were synchronized with video on computer as the lecture. Therefore, the material requires students to use visual and auditory sensory channels in parallel. Total length of the material is 8 minutes and 33 seconds consisting of 8 slides.

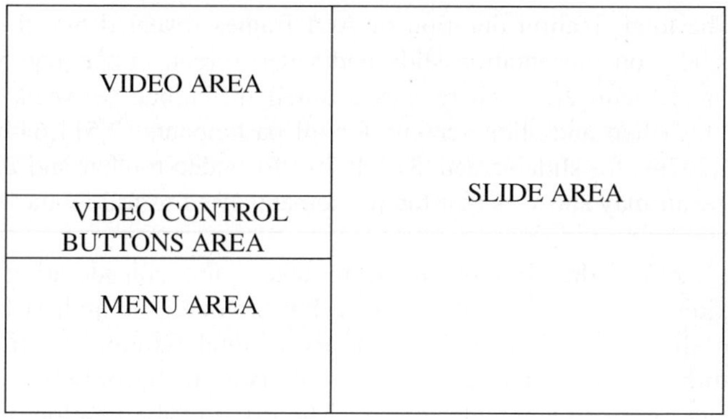

Fig. 1. Areas of interest (AOI)

2.3 Data Collection

The sessions were conducted in the Human-Computer Interaction laboratory. Data were collected through an eye-tracker device (The Tobii 1750 Eye Tracker, Tobii Technology). The device has an eye tracker that discretely integrated into a monitor without any visible "tracking devices" so this non-intrusiveness enables user to behave in a natural manner. It can collect the records of eye gaze location at 50 Hz. Data on fixation places and durations of the users were generated by the help of eye-tracking data analysis software. Eye tracking provides both qualitative and quantitative data.

2.4 Data Analysis

Before the analysis, areas of interests (AOI) on the screen were determined. The video area, video control buttons area, PowerPoint slides area, and menu area were determined as the main areas of the material, and each were defined as an area of interest (Fig. 1). This enables to analyze participants' fixation counts and durations on each AOI.

Descriptive and inferential statistics were applied to analyze the data of fixation counts and durations on the AOIs. In order to understand participants' behavior patterns in detail while using the instructional material, slide-based analyses were conducted. In addition, qualitative analyses of hotspot and gaze replay data were used.

3 Results

3.1 Total Eye-Fixation Durations and Fixation Counts for the Material

All participants' total fixation durations and fixation counts on defined areas of interests were examined, namely slide area, video area, video control buttons area and menu area. The total fixation duration of AOI frames revealed that the participants focused especially on presentation slide and video screen rather than video control buttons area and menu area. There was a small difference between total fixation durations of the video and slide screens for all participants (2,511,644ms for video screen, 2,424,797ms for slide screen, 318,497ms for video toolbar and 227,146ms for menu). This result may show us that the participants tried to follow these two screens together.

When the fixation duration means were taken into consideration, the highest fixation duration mean was for video screen. Furthermore, the highest fixation count comes out in slide screen (Table 1). Contrary to total fixation duration, means of fixation duration of the AOI and the counts of fixations according to the AOI has different results for video and slide screens. The mean of the fixation duration of the video screen ($\overline{X}$=618.4) is significantly higher than the slide screen ($\overline{X}$=238.8). However, the slide screen had more fixation count than video screen. These results show that the participants stared at the video while they were watching the video although they more fixated while they read the text on the slide screen.

Table 1. Eye-fixation durations and counts for fifteen participants based on AOIs

AOIs	Fixation count	Fixation Duration Means	Std. Deviation	Minimum fixation duration	Maximum fixation duration
Out of topic	168	247.1	178.0	100	937
video	4061	618.4	871.4	100	15730
video toolbar	846	376.4	355.0	100	3708
menu	884	256.9	189.1	100	2532
slide	10153	238.8	184.0	100	6200
Total	16112	342.8	498.1	100	15730

* Durations are given as 'seconds'.

3.2 Eye-Fixation Durations Based on Slide Presentation Styles

To analyze participants' eye fixations on different slide presentation types, hotspot data were collected from a sentence-based slide, a bulleted slide, and a table-based slide. Analysis results of hotspot data indicated that participants' eye-fixations were similar for these three types of slides, except less fixation counts on the slide part in sentence-based presentation (Fig. 2, 3, and 4). Therefore, we may claim that sentences are not likely to be read by participants as compared to bulleted and table-based presentation styles.

Data on fixation counts for each slide were used for further analysis (Table 2). The quantitative data indicated that there is a similarity in regards to fixation counts for bulleted and table-based presentation styles including slides 2,3,5,6, and 7 (Fig. 5). On the other hand, there is a similarity between slides 1, 4, and 8. The difference between these two groups of slides is the extra information given on video for slides

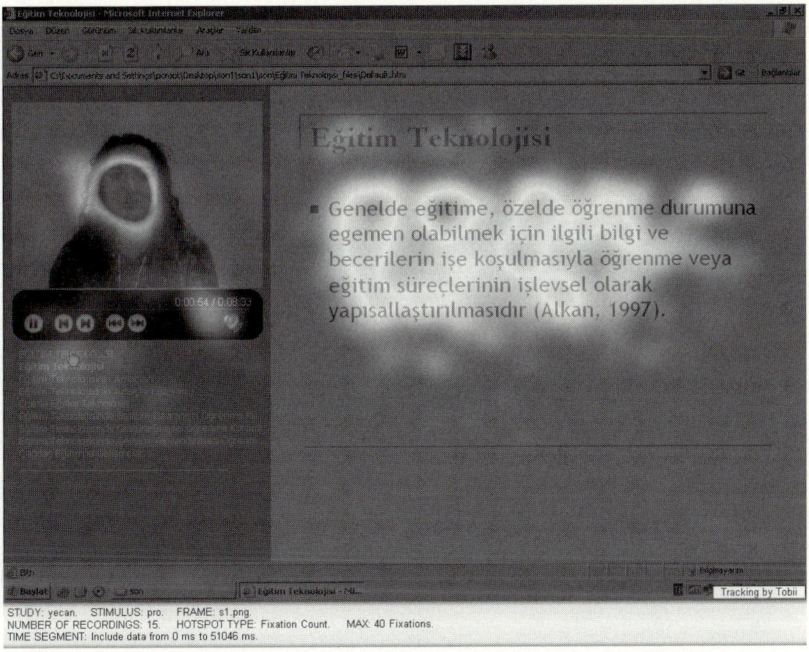

Fig. 2. Hotspot data for a sentence-based slide presentation (Slide 1)

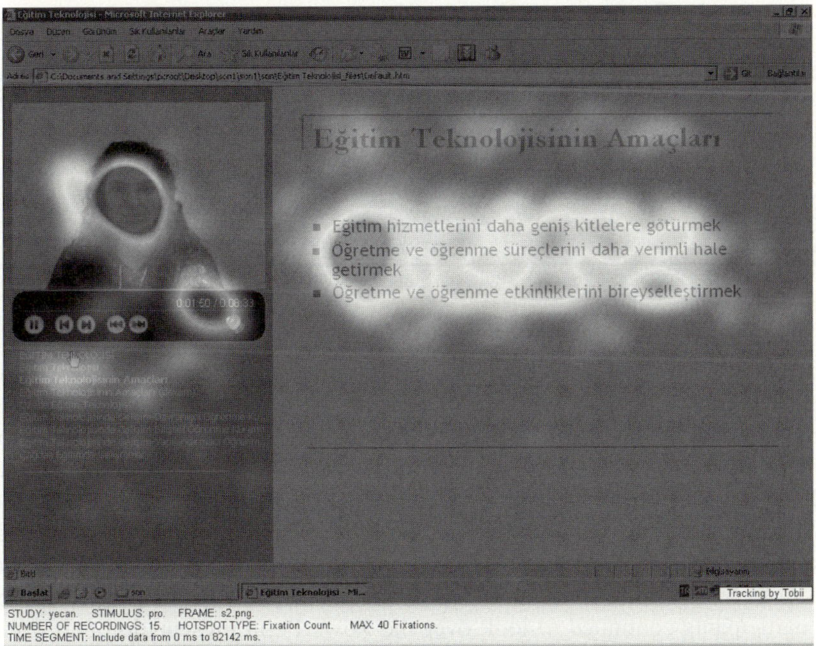

Fig. 3. Hotspot data for a bulleted slide presentation (Slide 2)

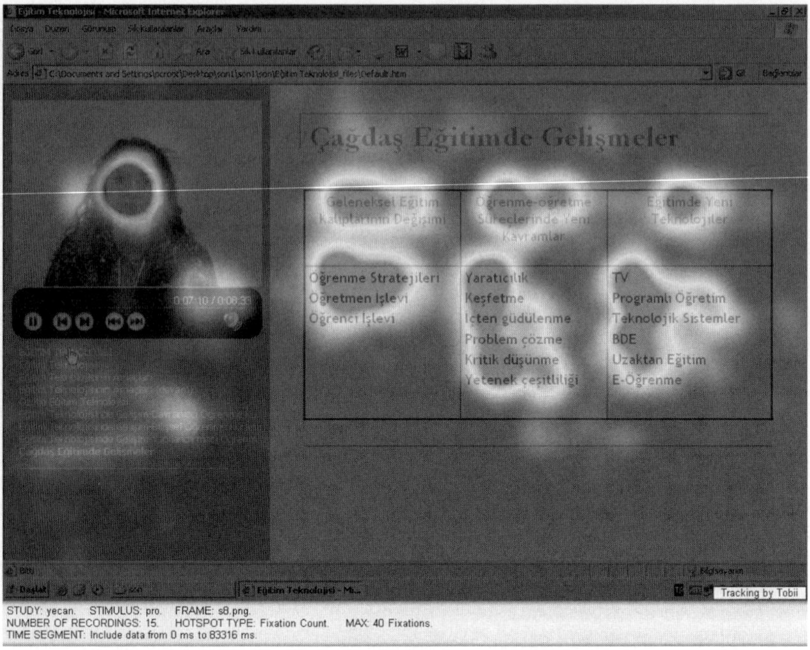

Fig. 4. Hotspot data for a table-based slide presentation with large amount of text (Slide 8)

Table 2. Fixation counts based on slides and AOIs.

	Slide 1	Slide 2	Slide 3	Slide 4	Slide 5	Slide 6	Slide 7	Slide 8
Video	370	730	714	76	841	491	334	314
Video toolbar	61	137	147	9	148	71	59	74
Menu	37	97	132	34	191	100	92	117
Slides	1184	1387	1373	419	1722	902	656	2356

* Slide1: Sentence based. Slides 2&3: Bulleted. Slide 4: Sentence-based. Slides 5,6 & 7: Table-based. Slide 8: Table-based with large amount of text.

2,3,5,6, and 7. While the content of the slide presentation and video are almost the same for slides 1, 4, and 8, for the rest there are some additional information and examples given by the instructor in the video, which are not presented in text format.

For further analysis, users' gaze replay records were analyzed by qualitative methods. It was observed that most of the participants first looked at the slide presentation after each slide transition. Then, they looked at the video after taking a look at the text-based material. Almost all of the participants showed continuous transitions between the slide presentation and video parts. Moreover, it was observed that participants continued to look over the PowerPoint presentation part even while the information given on the video was not available on slides. So, it could be suggested that the information given through video is searched by users in slides.

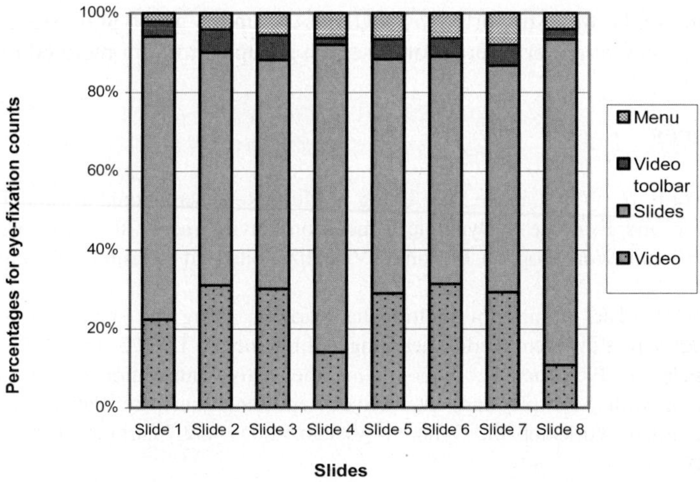

Fig. 5. Percentages of eye-fixation counts for AOIs of each slide

4 Conclusion

Multiple channel presentation of information integrating different media types may facilitate learning [1], [2]. The important point is to provide well-designed multimodal instructional environment. In this study, the researchers aimed to examine an instructional material with synchronized video and PowerPoint slides.

Findings of the study revealed that users use the slide and video presentations in a complementary way. Overall analysis of the data indicated that eye-fixation duration means are higher for video screen compared to slide presentation screen. On the other hand, fixation counts are higher for slide screen compared to video. This result indicates that participants stared at the video, while they were focusing on different places in text-based presentation.

Further analyses were conducted to explore the user behaviors based on each slide. Findings showed that participants firstly preferred to read the text at the beginning of each slide. Eye-fixation counts for video become higher if there is some additional information on video. Otherwise, the text-based material gains importance. It could be suggested that designers should put visual/verbal information as much as possible.

Moreover, the qualitative analysis of data revealed that the explanations on the video are searched by users in written material. So, there would not be missing information either in slide presentation or video. The text-based material might include all of the information or just some clues related to the information presented on the video. Dual coding theory also suggests that the available amount of working memory is maximized, when both visual and verbal elements are processed at the same time [8]. In order to propose principles for effective design for synchronized PowerPoint and video materials, different video and slide combinations should be examined in further studies.

Note: This study was supported by TUBITAK under grant SOBAG 104K098 and METU Human Computer Interaction research group (http://hci.metu.edu.tr).

References

1. Ainsworth, S., Van Labeke, N.: Using a Multi-Representational Design Framework to Develop and Evaluate a Dynamic Simulation Environment. In: Paper presented at the International Workshop on Dynamic Visualizations and Learning, Tubingen, Germany (2002)
2. Mayer, R.: The promise of multimedia learning: using the same instructional design methods across different media. Learning and Instruction 13, 125–139 (2003)
3. Bodemer, D., Ploetzner, R.: Encouraging the Active Integration of Information during Learning with Multiple and Interactive Representations. In: Paper presented at the International Workshop on Dynamic Visualizations and Learning, Tubingen, Germany (2002)
4. Sankey, M., Smith, A.: Multimodal Design Considerations for Developing Hybrid Course Materials: An Issue of Literacy. In: Paper presented at the Third Pan-Commonwealth Forum on Open Learning, Dunedin, New Zealand (2004)
5. Mark, G., Hans, V.D.M., Ton, D.J., Jules, P.: Multimodal versus unimodal instruction in a complex learning context. The Journal of Experimental Education 70(3), 215–239 (2002)
6. Sweller, J., Chandler, P.: Why Some Metarial is Difficult to Learn. Cognition and Instruction 12(3), 185–233 (1994)
7. Sweller, J.: The redundancy principle. In: Mayer, R. (ed.) Cambridge Handbook of Multimedia Learning, pp. 159–168. Cambridge University Press, New York (2005)
8. Clark, R.:Six Principles of Effective e-Learning: What Works and Why. The eLearning Developers Journal, 1–8 (2002)
9. Hartle, M., Bär, H., Trompler, C., Rößling, G.: Perspectives for Lecture Videos. In: Cunha, J.C., Medeiros, P.D. (eds.) Euro-Par 2005. LNCS, vol. 3648, pp. 901–908. Springer, Heidelberg (2005)
10. Rui, Y., Gupta, A., Grudin, J.: Videography for Telepresentations. In: Proceedings of the SIGCHI conference on Human factors in computing systems, Florida, USA (2003)
11. Microsoft Producer for Microsoft Office PowerPoint. Retrieved, from (December 2007) http://www.microsoft.com/windows/windowsmedia/technologies/producer.mspx

A Study on Interactive Artwork as an Aesthetic Object Using Computer Vision System

Joonsung Yoon and Jaehwa Kim

Dept. of Digital Media, Soongsil Univ., 511 Sangdo-dong,
Dongjak-gu, 156-743 Seoul, Korea
{jsy,art801}@ssu.ac.kr

Abstract. With the recent rapid rise of Human-Computer Interaction and surveillance system, various application systems are a matter of primary concern. However, the application systems mostly deal with the technologies of recognition facial characteristics, analyzing facial expression and automatic face recognition. By applying this kind of various technologies and methods of face recognition, I made an interactive artwork after computing the range of hands. This study is about the artwork application theory and using computer vision system method. The approach of this study makes possible to create artworks application in real-time. Now, I'd like to propose how to utilize analyze and make interactions, of created artworks. And also I'll explain the immersion of the viewers. The viewers can express their imagination freely and artists provide viewers an opportunity not to only enjoy visual experience, but also interact and be immersed in the works via interface. This interactive art makes viewers to actually take part in the works.

Keywords: aesthetic object, artistic desire, interactive art, art and science.

1 Introduction

In the interactive art using vision system, the core is a computer. The most common tools for interface between human and computer are keyboard, mouse, and joystick. However, in order to use these tools, users need to learn how to operate them. This paper uses PC camera that does not need specific skills. Interactive art that are made by computers mainly focuses on how to deal with huge capacity of image data that needs to be processed simultaneously. In order to process data input to camera smoothly, it would be better to set separate process function part. Camera captures moves of people who come into specific set area and distorts them. And viewer come to be involved with the work and that completes the interactive art.[1]

The creation unit in this study is a computer and the image projected to the screen is animation of 24 frames per second in consideration of viewer movement, confliction against interface and plot, in order to give audiences immersion to the process. The system used in this study is a Pentium IV PC and the program is Visual C++ programming in Windows, and the artworks made by the system are not influenced by changeable surroundings of the hands and brightness of the image.

J. Jacko (Ed.): Human-Computer Interaction, Part III, HCII 2007, LNCS 4552, pp. 763–768, 2007.

2 Discourse

In order to compute the range of hands, I gather of surrounding hands images from the input-image and extracted the range of hands. And I applied gradient operators such operator to the extracted range of hands, and detected the edge. And after transforming the edge map that contains the detected edge into binary image, I removed nose in the binary image, using a noise-removing method. And I detected a flag spot that is the center of the image of hands computed by pixel countering in the noise-removed image. And after that, images gather around the flag spot.[2]

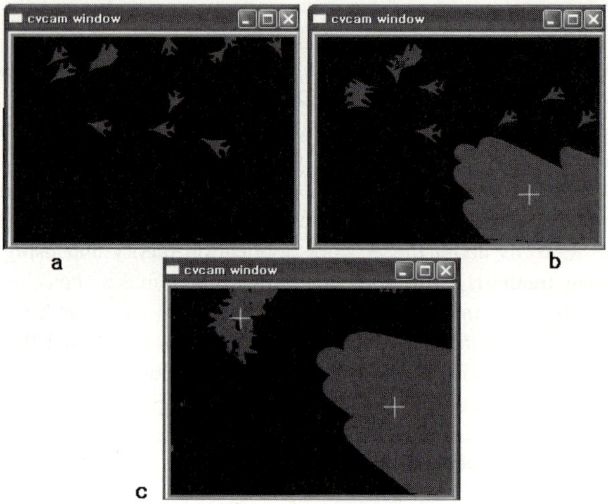

Fig. 1. The image course which finds the center after the conversion to the binary image

Fig. 1 shows the moment that camera is set to the screen and the process of finding out the center of the set area after making the objects' movement turn into binary image. The set area's image size is less than 30 pixels and when other object that has more than 1000 pixel size come into the area, then the system finds out the center. In other words, to distinguish both images, different image sizes were given.

The method of created artworks is enables to make images by sensing movement of a viewer and the viewer can create images that he wants. The method is analyzing images from the PC camera captures and projection the images that are created by sensing viewer's movement to the screen. Place a screen that is at same high as a desk and capture the range of hands with a camera and compute the range. And in the center of the computed range of hands, floating images will be gathered. These images come out in the form of fighter plane and during the images are gathered in the range of hands, and will transform into the shapes of rose and fly away. And the images will be drawn by means of animation.

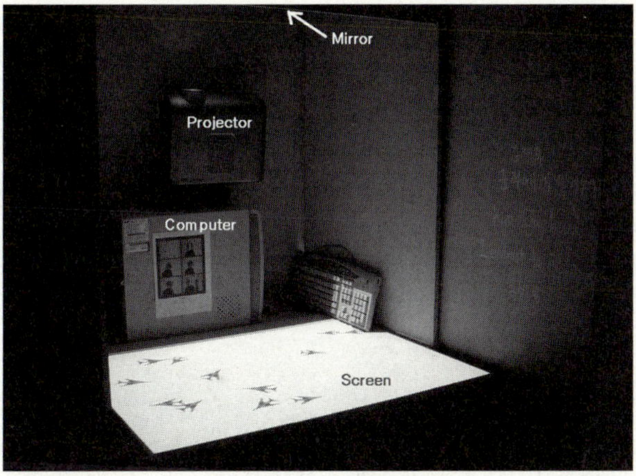

Fig. 2. The installation

Fig. 2 shows the case for narrow space. The interior space is bright. Therefore I needed a way to deal with this problem and used projections. Projection were settled upward and mirror was fixed in the ceiling which made the projection went downward. In this way, it was possible to use the screen in a wider scale in short distance and camera were manipulated to get input that were sent from upside. Computer became the main medium for showing and capturing. The author chose all command sources for input and output, and audiences find interest on the process of image change rather than on the computer processing, while interacting with the work.

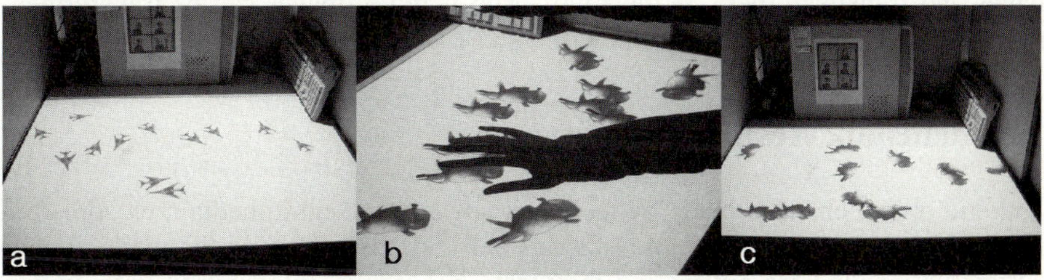

Fig. 3. The course to be functioned

Fig 3 shows two different images that are changing. Image of (a) and a image changes by audience's interaction (b) and the result is (c). Camera captures images on the screen and the captured images are transforming. In order to make this work, I used open source of openCV and the camera were made with the resolution of 640*480. Considering the computing process speed, I optimized the camera to work with resolution 320*240 and made the camera process automatically by move of audiences. And I optimized it to work real-time and minimized hardware limitations.

This artwork helps images on the screen move together with the images that are separated from the surroundings by means of computer pattern system. The methods are to capture the image of hands with a camera and find out the center of the captured image. And when projected images tend to gather to the center of the image, viewers can experience virtual reality of images, following their hands moving.

In order to induce natural interactions between images, it is necessary to make coordinates of physical space coincide with those of virtual space. The image of hands that are captured by a camera will be input into virtual space. And the variables of the input image will be created after calibration process. By conforming the variables to graphics object that is able to make interactions, virtual interactions will be realized in real-time.

3 A Next Subject

Still, there are several problems to solve, such as different flag spot position. The flag spot position changes depending on the size of the hands and also it's hard to get exact flag spot position when the movement of hand is wide.

I would say that this interactive art would ultimately change the art itself. Through various methods, viewers and artworks interaction each other and that leads people to a contemporary of advanced art. Interactive art will introduce viewers a contemporary art that virtual reality viewers' sense.

Interactive art system needs to be made of visually interesting contents. Because the system can be utilized in advertising, game, information providing, and exhibitions due to its appeal to entice people's attention.

And the solutions for some problems such as changing center point depending on the number of shadows and the method for finding center point of shadows in the wilder movement will be sought.

I hope the next work to become more interesting, if audiences can choose certain images and transform them by their will. And if more images can be transformed in the set of two images, the audiences will enjoy it better.

4 Conclusion: Aesthetic Object

Aesthetic object changes made by technical advances of multimedia now spread into the art. And that made us rethink relations between audience and the work, audience and the author, and the author and the work. Nowadays, interactivity with audience made the work coincides with audience and that let us think about the concept of art again. Interactive art will ultimately change the art itself. Through various ways, art now can interact with audience and that completes the work as a whole. Interactive art can be an alternative for art form that used to be a one-way presentation, by using various methods for processing images real live and this will ultimately be born as a prosperous new art form that stimulates audiences.

The system of interactive art should be made with easy contents that bring audiences interests and easy access. And if easy contents can be developed using interactive art works, then those can be used in advertisement, games, information providing, exhibition, performances that need to draw people's attention. In the directive communication between audience and the work, now it is possible to reorganize people's response and interaction between audience and works. And this means that now we can enjoy a new way of creation.

Interactive art has been experimented for some decades and nowadays computer makes the virtual space and real space to interact each other. In other words, real space can be recognized via virtual space and virtual space can be read through the relation with real world. The element of both 'the virtual' and 'the real' are mixed together. And there is a mid-space that is the interface. In the interface, reality is reorganized by computer. In the interface, we can experience reality of neither the virtual nor the real, or both worlds at the same time. If interactive media tools are used in the process, the experience will vary further.[9]

Using new media will give more possibility of interaction between the author and audiences in the interactive art. Because, the media give audience chances to enjoy visual presence of multiple time and space value and multi dimensions and time. Interactive art integrates exhibition space to provide new tools for understanding themselves for the author and audiences. It is different from conventional art object; interactive art is an active event that is created by physical presence and psychological response of audience. The physical movement of audience changes image consistently and physical intervention of audience determines or changes the form of image.

Audience's way of contemplation in the era of conventional art changed to active intervention of audience to the work in the electro era. This will help pursue communication between audience and works and interactive communication between multiple remote places, performance of audience in the cyber space in the comprehensive way. The understanding for new media will help set theoretical and critical essence for the future works and it has something to do with author's self conscious toward time and space and finding meaning of an art form that is a part of human and environment. From chosen works that are based upon these characteristics of interactive art, we can sort out forms to manipulate space and experience created environment. Interactive art works are a new way of expressing 'the real' that interacts with audience and the works are the environment that surrounded audience.[4]

These art works have something to do with technological advances and its territory is expanding. The creation of artwork is the result of the author's artistic desire interaction with aspiration of the author. The author's psychological activity is assumed in every process of creating artwork. Interactive art does not mean the creation of image based on conventional way of drawing and making picture, but means creating new narratives through random input of sensible data. The artworks made by the advance of technology not only expand our life's horizon, but also provide new frame for perceiving aesthetic object.

Artworks made by technology have technological advantage of media and convenience and the importance of media is quite evident, considering notion and development of art. However, in order to produce contents in the interactive art, it is important to make it with artistic approach as well as the perception toward technological artworks, and it needs to be discussed on the subject of finding new artistic objective.

The relation between each media and author and audience and the work depends on determining the subject and after that process, people can experience 'virtual reality' and contemporary art form. With various evolution and discussions, interactive art has taken its root firmly as a new aesthetic object. Interactivity that makes audience to intervene to the work and bring changes to the work is getting more popular nowadays. In order to give messages more effectively in the communication process between authors, audience and works, interactive art should be more dynamically engaged in making relationship with authors, audience and works via various media.

Acknowledgments. This work was supported by Soongsil University Research Fund.

References

1. Kim, J., Yoon, J.: An Interdisciplinary Research on Media Art and Information Science Technology focusing on the Computer-based interactive Art, KSBDA, 7(3) (2006)
2. Yoon, J., Kim, J.: The Interactive Artwork as the Aesthetic Object: Aesthetic Technology Converging Technological Applications and Aesthetic Discourses, TIDSE06 (2006)
3. Won-Kon, Y.I.: A Study on the INTERSPACE' of Video Installation. KSBDA, 40229 (2003)
4. Kim, K.: The Plastic elements in Media Art, KSBDA, 060304 (2005)
5. Azuma, R., Billinghurst, M., Hölerer, T., Kato, H., Poupyrev, I., Schmalstieg, D.: Augmented Reality- The interface is everywhere. SIGGRAPH course note, 27, Los Angeles (2001)
6. Miranda, E.R., Brouse, A.: Interfacing the Brain Directly with Musical Systems- On Developing System for Making Music with Brain Signal, LEONARDO, 38(4) (2005)
7. Fishwick, P.A. (ed.): Aesthetic Computing. MIT P, Cambridge (2006)
8. Krueger, M.: Artificial Reality II. Addison Wesley Publishing, Reading, MA (1991)
9. Miller, J-L., Sheridan, A.: The Seminar of Jacqes Lacan, W.W.Norton Company. London (translated) (1978)

Human-Computer Interaction System Based on Nose Tracking

Lumin Zhang, Fuqiang Zhou, Weixian Li, and Xiaoke Yang

Beihang University, 37 Xueyuan Road, Beijing, China
lumin.zhang@gmail.com, zfq@buaa.edu.cn, liweixian1985@163.com,
yxkmlstar@gmail.com

Abstract. This paper presents a novel Human-Computer Interaction (HCI) system with calibrated mono-camera which integrates active computer vision technology and embedded speech command recognition technology. Mainly by tracking the nose tip motion robustly as the mouse trace, this system completes mouse mission with recognition rate more than 85% at the speed 15 frame per second. To achieve the goal, we adopt a novel approach based on the symmetry of the nose plane feature to localize and track invariantly to the varied environment. Comparing to other kinds of pointing device, this hand-free HCI system is hands-free, cheap, real-time, convenient and unpolluted, which can be used in the field of disabled aid, entertainment and remote control.

Keywords: HCI, Nose Tracking, Calibration.

1 Introduction and Application

Recent years, with the increase of the microprocessor's powerful computational ability, multi-channel user interface plays more and more important part in Human-Computer Interaction (HCI). Among kinds of multi-channel user interfaces, active vision technology is one of the most efficient non-tactile alternatives to strengthen the traditional input device of the computer, which can bring convenient service for HCI. This paper presents a novel perceptual user interface based on face feature tracking and speech recognition technology, which responses according to the nose tip trace and voice command to accomplish the mouse control mission with hands-free operation.

Current HCI pointing system based on face feature tracking can be divided into wearable and non-wearable, structured (e.g. markings on the user's face)[1] and unstructured or tangible and virtual (such as laser pen)[3], which are somewhat limited. Meanwhile, scientists put more attention on active face feature tracking technology (i.e. non-tactile), which automatically recognizes the feature from the video stream.

The computerized process of localizing human facial features such as the eyes, nose, and mouth in the front view face image sequences is very important and essential technology. As one of the hot research topics in the computer vision and pattern recognition fields, many researchers focused on pursuing the precise location of the pupil, iris and mouth feature. Nevertheless the deformable contour and open-close data interrupt decrease the robustness of tracking. However, unlike the other

J. Jacko (Ed.): Human-Computer Interaction, Part III, HCII 2007, LNCS 4552, pp. 769–778, 2007.

facial features, the nose has some unique features that nose can be seen at all times during the interaction with the computer screen regardless of the orientation of the head and the camera and has rigid shape related to the face pose, hence the nose tip can be used as the main feature of the human face rigid motion which results from the global face pose translation.

To be operational, HCI interfaces require nose tracking to be real-time, affordable and, most importantly, precise and robust. Gorodnichy and Gerhard Roth[1] proposed that the convex-shape feature of the nose in the 3-dimention space can be used to localize and track the nose tip and the result is robust, but this method relies on the two-camera stereo vision which results in the narrow field-of-view, complex calibration and time-consuming computing. At the same time they used blink as the click event trigger which is not robust, because human may often blink without intention. So we adopt a new approach based on the symmetry of the nose plane feature and Lucas-Kanade Optical Flow[11] to localize and track with calibrated mono camera and used voice commands to take the click response.

We have developed a real-time robust nose tracking system with mono-camera integrating the embedded audio recognition and image processing technology, which shows hot prospect in many fields. Comparing to other kinds of mouse, this hand-free system is cheap, real-time, convenient and unpolluted. For instance, disabled people could control the computer by using the nose as the mouse, and even the normal individuals who are tired of using the ordinary mouse could operate the computer hands-free to have a net meeting or play a game. We add this system to the reader and browser software such as IE, MS Word and Acrobat Reader. By analyzing the nose trace and set the recovering time, this system can assist people to read the webpage and document without hands. When the reader's head move in special direction over threshold distance, the active software window which shows the document or webpage will scroll according to the motion.

This hand-free system can be healthily used in public. For instance, nowadays, as one of the city infrastructure, many electronic-map workstations have been set up at the side of the main avenue. Most of them use touch-screen as the interaction ways. But one obvious shortcoming is that the infectious disease could be spread by the hand touch of various people. Hence this hand-free in-distance interaction system can be used as the mouse in a clean way.

As well, robotics is another application aspect. Robotic furnished with this system can track the face and response to human's activity, as well, this system can be applied to hands-free remote control. With the help of the Robot Soccer Group of Beihang University, we try to use this system to control the robot motion. Successfully, we establish the reflection of the real robot coordinate system and the screen coordinate system and realized the robot slow motion according to the face motion with PID control[2].

The rest of the paper is organized as follows: the Section 2 introduces entire system constitution including nose tip localization and tracking, calibration and embedded speech command recognition system. Section 3 and 4 give the experiment results and conclusions of this HCI system respectively.

2 System Architecture

As the Fig.1 illustrates, the computer vision part of the system is based on PC and the voice detect module is based on SUNPLUS 61 Embedded system. Logitech QuickCam Pro5000 is adopted as the source camera. The computer vision part consists of the mono-camera calibration, nose tip location by symmetry transform and SVM, nose tracking with LK optical flow method. And SUNPLUS 61 embedded system is connected to PC by 9-point serial port, which can distinguish four instructions. Through the Win32API, the system can control the mouse and run in background of OS, which merely spend less than 25M Byte memory.

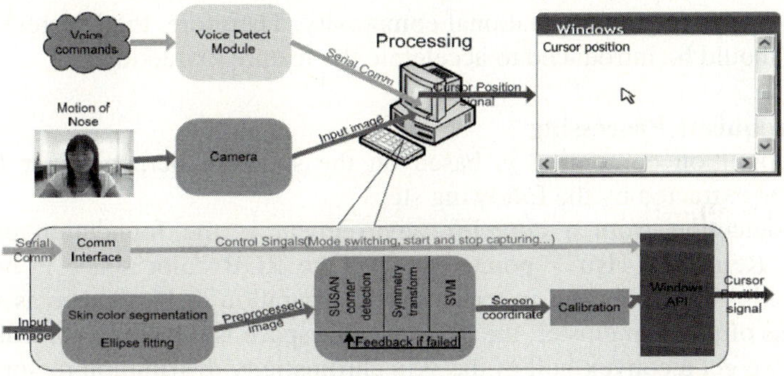

Fig. 1. The sketch of the HCI system based on nose tracking

Before the first time usage, user should calibrate the camera to work out the transform matrix and train the voice recognition system, which can be done lonely. Then the system launches and operates in three steps as follows. First of all, the nose tip is localized from the video frame, next, in terms of the transform matrix, the image's coordinates could be reflected to the screen coordinates and the third step is realizing the click or double-clicks event response by recognizing the voice command. The entire processing is real-time.

2.1 Nose Localization and Tracking

Several automatic methods have been proposed to detect the face organ from 2D front-view face image, for instance, deformable templates, Eigen-organ, adaptive thresholding, Generalized Symmetry Transform and so on. Yuille[4] used deformable templates to search for the facial features around the peaks and valleys of the intensity image, but this method depends on the starting location and parameters of the template and is sensitive to noise and initialization position. Gu Hua[5] applied the edge extracting to the face picture and then analyzes it to search the nostril, but the nostril feature is not always visible. Sankaran[6] used an adaptive thresholding and x-projection to get the coordinate of the nose, but it is often affected by the noise and the environment. While the initial aim of Eigen-organ method and organ-based statistical modeling method is to detect the existence of special organ, so their resulting map is similar to that of template matching methods directly made on gray image. The common problem of these methods mentioned above is the difficulty in post-processing, i.e. bad localization.

Classifiers such as Neural Network, Support Vector Machine[7] and Adaboost[8] are also performed into organ localization as the means of template matching. But the complexity of traversing all the sub-regions of the image is too high, so they should be combined with other feature extraction methods to simplify the input data. But nose lacks of the abundant texture feature. So symmetry computing is introduced as the way of feature extraction. The Generalized Symmetry Transform (GST)[9][10] method made use of the intrinsic local symmetry property instead of the special knowledge of human face, so it is robust and insensitive to the rotation, tilt and expression. But this method is noise sensitive and not suitable for real-time application due to huge computational complexity. Therefore, the Discrete Symmetry Transform should be introduced to accelerate the feature extraction.

2.1.1 Prerequisite Processing

All the recognition computing is based on the standard perpendicular face image which can be extracted by the following steps.

Face detection from a complex environment is the foundation of the later processing. Rein-Lien Hsu[12] points out that the RGB color space is not good to detect the skin-tone color and in terms of the separation of luminance as well as the compactness of the skin cluster, the YCbCr color space is adopted. According to prior clustering, we get a convex hull of the skin chromaticity distribution region in the Cb, Cr coordinates system. Given a point, whether it is a skin point or not can be determined by testing whether its CrCb coordinate of the point belongs to the convex hull or not. Therefore, the face region can be filtered out by the area constrain.

To process the symmetry transform more easily, the perpendicular face picture should be obtained. To get the face pose skew angle, ellipse fitting [13] is used. We suppose the angle between horizontal axis and first ellipse axis is the skew angle according which the image is rotated.

Finally, the perpendicular face rectangle shown in Fig.2 should be interpolated to the size 100×100 uniformly and converted to gray image.

Fig. 2. From left to right, source image, face region binary image, face region binary image after revising, color image after revising and standard scaled face image in order

2.1.2 Discrete Symmetry Transform in Corner Image

Due to the diversity of the lights, the nose tip point does not always appear as the strong corner in the face image or sometimes there exist more than one corner near the nose tip. And also the bridge of the nose doesn't always appear as a straight line so that it is hard to extract. Admittedly, the nose's two corner and the side edges along it are great self-symmetric objects and always visible. And the corner distribution of the nose will still keep this symmetry feature, so an appropriate corner extraction operator is needed. We choose SUSAN[14] method which has anti-noise ability. But the corner extraction is affected by the different image scales.

Choosing optimal scale factor t is a key problem in the linear scale space research[15]. If the scale chosen is too small, the probability of mistaken extracting the corner will be increased. Otherwise, the too big scale will result in increasing the error of the location coordinate. In the different scale, SUSAN operator will extract different number of corner and express different details with different noise. Because the area $n(r_0)$ determined by threshold T_h is the key foundation of the SUSAN operator, the relationship between t and T_h should be established. In terms of our experimental results, T_h is relevant to the scale factor t uniformly ($T_h = 2t/3$). As Fig.2 shows, the symmetry of the nose feature is clearer in the last corner image with $T_h = 6$ and $t = 9$.

Symmetry, like the other properties described in the Gestalt principles of perceptual grouping, represents information redundancy which may be used to overcome noise and occlusion [16]. The past methods based on this nature of shape feature can be classified into two aspects, namely global versus local. But both of them should consider the affine invariant or the gradients of the picture which costs a lot of time and is hard to use in the real-time system. With the prior knowledge on the shape of nose, a new local operator has been developed. This symmetry transform, based on discrete operation is more quick and appropriate for the real-time application.

The symmetricity values represent estimation of the likelihood for pairs of points to be local symmetries, and provide some robustness when noise is introduced.

Then we define the transform operator as following:

$$M_2(p) = \sum_{(i\,j)\in\Psi(p)} F(i,j)S(r_i,r_j) \quad (1)$$

Where $\Psi(p) = \{(i,j)|(p_i + p_j)/2 = p, |p_i - p_j| < 2\sigma\}$,

$$F(i,j) = \frac{1}{\sqrt{2\pi\sigma}} exp\left(-\frac{\left|\|p_i - p_j\|_2 - \mu\right|}{2\sigma}\right),$$

$$S(r_i,r_j) = \begin{cases} 1, \exists p \in R(p_i), r_p = 1 \wedge \exists q \in R(p_j), r_q = 1 \\ 0, \forall p \in R(p_i), r_p = 0 \wedge \forall q \in R(p_j), r_q = 0 \end{cases}$$ and $R(p) = \{(x,y)|\,|y - y\,| < l, |x - x\,| < l - 1\}$

$M_2(p)$ is called as the symmetry strength; p is any point of the image $u(x)$; $\Psi(p)$ is the point set of all the couple points whose mid-point of the joining line segment centers at the point p; is the log mapping of gradient magnitude of the point p_i; $F(i,j)$ is the Gaussian distance weight function with the variance σ; $R(p)$ is adjunct field of the point p; l is the number of direction considered in operator, generally less than 6 which can get the robust result.

From that, a corner based fast algorithm can be drawn. Because only the corner considered in operator S contribute to the symmetricity accumulator in LSSF, by merely traversing the linked list of the corner the symmetricity distribution of the whole face image can be got. And also the corner can be cut half off for the symmetry of the local search mask.

In fact, this binary Discrete Symmetry Transform in LSSF is a nonlinear filter, which provides a continuous measurement of the symmetry. Because every pixel's symmetry strength is determined independently by the neighborhood, this algorithm is suitable for the parallel computing. Comparing with GST's $O(n\sigma^2)$, the time complexity of this algorithm is improved to only $O(\sigma lc + n)$, in which n is the total pixel number of the image, σ is the width scale of the local search mask, c is the finally considered number of corner in the face image and l is the number of directions considered in operator S. n is scores of times as much as c and σ is only less than 50 generally. So the speed up factor is approximately $n\sigma/lc$ which is more than 20 generally.

2.1.3 Support Vector Machine (SVM) and Tracking

Given the candidate points which can also be reduced with some border constraints, the SVM[17] can distinguish whether it is the nose tip or not, and the Discrete Symmetry Transform reduce the input-point quantity much. The input vector is a vector of certain sub image region unfolded in the row-first order, which centered at the candidate point with the special size 45×17. And the point's coordinates in the front view image could be obtained by inverse interpolation and rotation. Then the Lucas-Kanada Optical Flow method is used to track the nose feature. The whole procedure is illustrated in the Fig.3

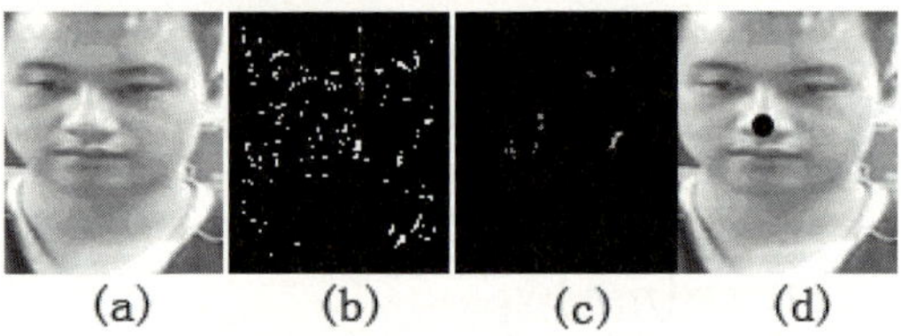

Fig. 3. Procedure for extracting the nose tip. (a)Standard scaled source face image, (b) image after SUSAN operation, (c) image of candidate points (d) SVM recognized nose tip point

2.2 Calibration

The camera parameters can be obtained using the calibration method described in reference[19]. In order to keep the user's ability to control his motion in virtual world just like in real world, the screen coordinates corresponding to the nose tip must be known. It is not easy to obtain the screen coordinates of the nose tip directly because the screen plane can't be seen by the camera in the observation position.

We proposed a novel calibration method for the pointing system based on one real planar target and one virtual planar target displayed on the screen plane. The virtual planar target is generated by the computer. The ray equation corresponding to the nose tip can be calculated by the optical center of the camera and the image coordinates according to the camera model. If the screen plane equation in the camera coordinate frame is known, the screen coordinates corresponding to the nose tip can be calculated by the intersection point between the ray and the screen plane in the camera coordinate frame.

As shown in Fig. 4, $o_{c1}x_{c1}y_{c1}z_{c1}$ is the camera coordinate frame in the observation position, $o_{c2}x_{c2}y_{c2}z_{c2}$ is the camera coordinate frame in the reference position, $o_{wt}x_{wt}y_{wt}z_{wt}$ is the world coordinate frame and $o_{ws}x_{ws}y_{ws}z_{ws}$ is the screen coordinate frame. The transformation $\mathbf{R}$ from $o_{ws}x_{ws}y_{ws}z_{ws}$ to $o_{c1}x_{c1}y_{c1}z_{c1}$ is as following:

$$\begin{cases} \mathbf{X}_{c1} = \mathbf{R}\mathbf{X}_{ws} \\ \mathbf{X}_{c1} = \mathbf{R}_1\mathbf{X}_{ws} \\ \mathbf{X}_{c2} = \mathbf{R}_2\mathbf{X}_{wt} \\ \mathbf{X}_{c1} = \mathbf{R}_3\mathbf{X}_{wt} \end{cases} \Rightarrow \mathbf{R} = \mathbf{R}_3\mathbf{R}_2^{-1}\mathbf{R}_1 \tag{2}$$

Where $\mathbf{X}_{c1}, \mathbf{X}_{c2}, \mathbf{X}_{wt}$ and $\mathbf{X}_{ws}$ are three dimensional coordinates of the feature point in $o_{c1}x_{c1}y_{c1}z_{c1}$, $o_{c2}x_{c2}y_{c2}z_{c2}$, $o_{wt}x_{wt}y_{wt}z_{wt}$ and $o_{ws}x_{ws}y_{ws}z_{ws}$ respectively. is the transformation from $o_{ws}x_{ws}y_{ws}z_{ws}$ to $o_{c1}x_{c1}y_{c1}z_{c1}$, is the transformation from $o_{wt}x_{wt}y_{wt}z_{wt}$ to $o_{c2}x_{c2}y_{c2}z_{c2}$, is the transformation from $o_{wt}x_{wt}y_{wt}z_{wt}$ to $o_{c1}x_{c1}y_{c1}z_{c1}$.

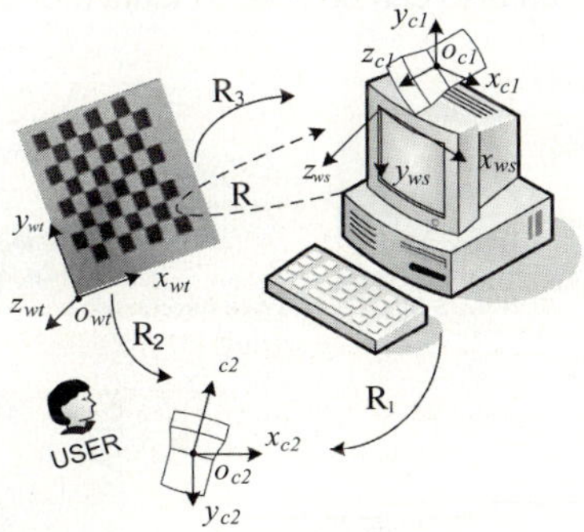

Fig. 4.. The sketch of transformation from the camera coordinate frame in the observation position to the screen coordinate frame

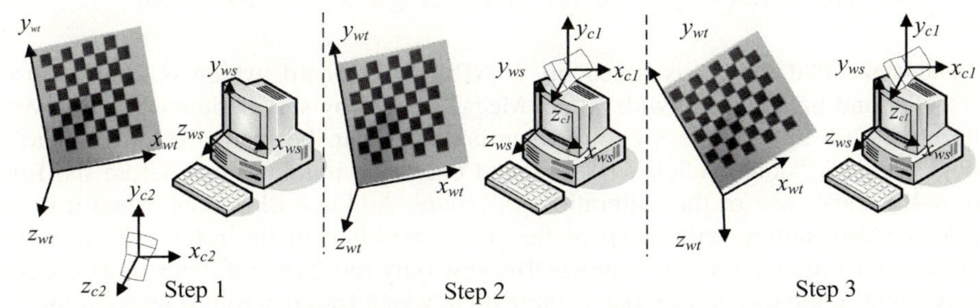

Fig. 5. The calibration procedure including three steps is shown. Step 1, capturing one image of containing the real target and the virtual target on the screen from the reference position. Step 2, capturing one image only containing the real target from the observation position. Step 3, capturing at least three images only containing the real target from the observation position when moving the real target freely.

The calibration procedure is shown in Fig. 5. The ray equation corresponding to the nose tip can be easily obtained with the optical center of the camera and the image coordinates of the nose tip according to the camera model. If three nonlinear points in the screen plane are known, the screen plane equation in the camera coordinate frame can be obtained.

$$ax_{c1} + by_{c1} + cz_{c1} + d = 0 \quad (3)$$

Then the intersection point between the ray and the screen plane in the camera coordinate frame can be calculated and used as the mouse position corresponding to the nose tip point.

2.3 Embedded Speech Recognition System

The old way to realize the click event is by the means of blink detection. But human being often blinks without intension, which results in the difficulty to make the right response. As well, it's hard to distinguish the click and double-click events. Nevertheless voice command recognition can provide an easy-going communication channel to simulate the click event, which also can be used to launch or shut down this system.

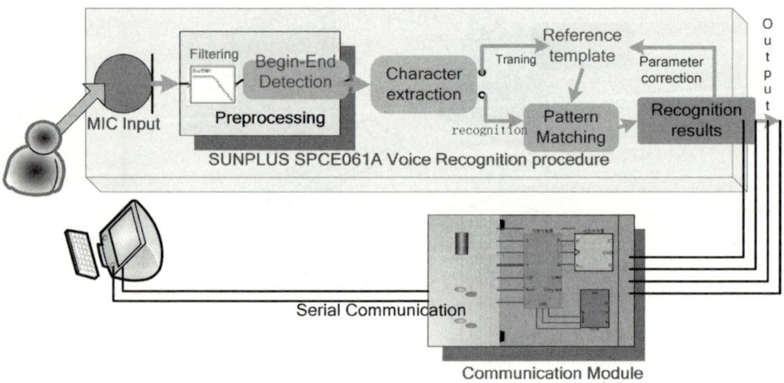

Fig. 6. Processing procedure of speech recognition embedded system

The embedded system is based on SUNPLUS 61 board, which is 16bit micro-controller and linked to PC with Atmel Mega32 board by serial communication with the rate 19200 bps[18]. We set four voice commands to be recognized, i.e. "start", "stop", "click", "double-click". User should only take training once before the first use at the same time of the calibration procedure. As Fig.6 illustrates, when it runs, the embedded system will compare the input speech with the reference character template got from the training samples. Because only four kinds of commands need to be recognized, the recognition rate is quite high, which lead to a robust application.

3 Experimental Results

We establish a database as the test input which contains up to 30 videos from 5 different people which could realize the mouse and its extended operation. To get accurate result, we also establish a image database including 1000 copies of photos. We use a PC furnished with Intel P4 2.4GHZ and 512 Mbytes memory to measure the system parameters, which are record in the following Table.1. The speed of the system can be enhanced in the dual-core CPU platform due to the hardware-based code optimization.

Table 1. System Test Result

System Speed	15 frames per second
Nose Tip Recognition Rate	more than 85%
Voice Command Recognition Rate	90%
Calibration RMS Error (pixels)	$\lvert\Delta x\rvert = 0.292; \lvert\Delta y\rvert = 0.181$
Total Memory Used	25 MByte

It can be found from the data that this real-time is very robust and accurate.

And 15 test users including 2 hand-disabled people give us the feedbacks. Our system can successfully realize the hands-free mouse operation. The average time that user can bear to continuous usage is 1 hour, because their necks need to relax.

4 Conclusion

This paper presented a nose tracking system integrating the computer vision and embedded vocal recognition technology which allows one to use such system designing perceptual user interfaces. This system has fast speed at 15 fps so that it can be used in real-time application and the recognition rate can reach more than 85%. This system shows hot prospect in many applications, which can be used as a novel hands-free pointing device.

Acknowledgments. This work is supported by Beihang University Student Research Training Plan (SRTP).

References

1. Gorodnichy, D.O., Roth, G.: Nouse use your nose as a mouse Perceptual Vision Technology for Hands-free Games and Interfaces. Image and Vision Computing 22, 931–942 (2004)
2. Zhang, X., Yang, Y., Li, Y.: Design of Intelligent Soccer Robot with DSP. Journal of Guangdong University of Technology 20(2), 1–4,25 (2003)
3. Tsang, W-W.M., Pun, K-P.: A Finger-Tracking Virtual Mouse Realized in an Embedded System. In: Proceedings of 2005 International Symposium on Intelligent Signal Processing and Communication Systems, pp. 781–784 (December 2005)
4. Yuille, A.L.: Deformable Templates for Face Recognition. J. Cognitive Neurosci 3, 59–70 (1991)

5. Hua, G., Guangda, S., Cheng, D.: Automatic Localization of the Corner of Eyes on Human Face. Infrared and Laser Engineering, 376–380 (2004)
6. Sankaran, P., Gundimada, S., Tompkins, R.C., Asari, V.K.: Pose Angle Determination by Face, Eyes and Nose Localization. In: Proceedings of the 2005 IEEE Computer Society Conference on Computer Vision and Pattern Recognition (CVPR'05) (2005)
7. Li, D., Podolak, I.T., Lee, S.W.: Facial Component Extraction And Face Recognition with Support Vector Machines. In: Proceedings of Automatic Face and Gesture Recognition, Washington, DCUSA, pp. 76–81 (2002)
8. Freund, Y., Schapire, R.E.: A decision-theoretic generalization of online learning and an application to boosting. Computational Learning Theory: Eurocolt '95, Springer-Verlag, pp. 23–37 (1995)
9. Reisfeld, D., Wolfson, H., Yeshurun, Y.: Context-Free Attentional Operators:The Generalized Symmetry Transform. Inter. J.Computer Vision 14, 119–130 (1995)
10. Jie, Z., Chunyu, L., Changshui, Z., Yanda, L.: Human Face Location Based on Directional Symmetry Transform. ACTA ELECTRONICA SINICA 27, 12–15 (1999)
11. Lucas, B., Kanade, T.: An Iterative Image Registration Technique with an Application to Stereo Vision. In: Proc. of 7th International Joint Conference on Artificial Intelligence (IJCAI) pp. 674–679
12. Hsu, R-L., Abdel-Mottaleb, M., Jain, A.K.: Face Detection in Color Image. IEEE Transactions on Pattern Analysis and Machine Intelligence, 696–706 (MAY 2002)
13. Bookstein, F.L: Fitting conic sections to scattered data. Computer Graphics and Image Processing 9, 56–71 (1979)
14. Smith, S.M., Brady, J.M.: Susan-a new approach to low level image processing, International Journal of Computer Vision, 45–78 (1997)
15. Witkin, A.P: Scale Space Filtering. In: Int. Joint Conf. Artificial Intelligence, 1019-1021 (1983)
16. Tat-Jen., Cipolla, C.R.: A Local Approach to Recovering Global Skewed Symmetry, Pattern Recognition 1 , Conference A: Computer Vision and Image Processing. In: Proceedings of the 12th IAPR International Conference on, pp. 222–226 (1994)
17. Vapnik, V.N.: Statistical Learning Theory. John Wiley and Sons, New York (1998)
18. Gen, D.: AVR high speed microcontroller theory and application [M].Beihang University Press (2000)
19. Zhang, Z.: A Flexible New Technique for Camera Calibration. IEEE Transactions on Pattern Analysis and Machine Intelligence, 22(11) (November 2000)

Appendix

The video demo of this approach can be downloaded from the following URL:

http://www.mediamax.com/nosetrack2/Hosted/TheRealTimeAutomaticNoseTrackingSystemLongVersion.avi

Evaluating Eye Tracking with ISO 9241 - Part 9

Xuan Zhang and I. Scott MacKenzie

Department of Computer Science and Engineering
York University
Toronto, Ontario, Canada M3J 1P3
{xuan,mack}@cse.yorku.ca

Abstract. The ISO 9241-9 standard for computer pointing devices proposes an evaluation of performance and comfort [4]. This paper is the first eye tracking evaluation conforming to ISO 9241-9. We evaluated three techniques and compared them with a standard mouse. The evaluation used throughput (in bits/s) as a measurement of user performance in a multi-directional point-select task. The "Eye Tracking Long" technique required participants to look at an on-screen target and dwell on it for 750 ms for selection. Results revealed a lower throughput than for the "Eye Tracking Short" technique with a 500 ms dwell time. The "Eye+Spacebar" technique allowed participants to "point" with the eye and "select" by pressing the spacebar upon fixation. This eliminated the need to wait for selection. It was the best among the three eye tracking techniques with a throughput of 3.78 bits/s, which was close to the 4.68 bits/s for the mouse.

Keywords: Pointing devices, ISO 9241, Fitts' law, performance evaluation, eye movement, eye tracking.

1 Introduction

ISO 9241 - Part 9

Beginning with the Apple *Macintosh* in 1984, graphical user interfaces (GUIs) have evolved and matured. The key feature of modern GUIs is the ability for users to interact with simple point-and-select operations. The most common pointing device in desktop systems is the mouse. To select an on-screen target with a mouse, a user manipulates the mouse to maneuver the cursor to a target, then selects the target by pressing and releasing a button. Simple as this seems, the interaction is even simpler with an eye tracker. The user locates the target by looking at it and follows immediately with selection [10].

Although considerable research exists in eye tracking [3], [6], [9], [10], none has evaluated eye tracking with the *ISO 9241 Ergonomic requirements for office work with visual display terminals (VDTs) - Part 9: Requirements for non-keyboard input devices*. ISO 9241-9 establishes uniform guidelines and testing procedures for evaluating computer pointing devices. The metric for comparison is *Throughput*, in bits per second (bits/s), which includes both the speed and accuracy of users'

J. Jacko (Ed.): Human-Computer Interaction, Part III, HCII 2007, LNCS 4552, pp. 779–788, 2007.

performance. The equation for throughput is Fitts' Index of Performance except using an *effective* index of difficulty (ID_e). Specifically,

$$Throughput = ID_e / MT . \qquad (1)$$

where MT is the mean movement time, in seconds, for all trials within the same condition, and

$$ID_e = log_2(D / W_e + 1) . \qquad (2)$$

ID_e, in bits, is calculated from D, the distance to the target, and W_e, the effective width of the target. W_e is calculated as

$$W_e = 4.133 \times SD . \qquad (3)$$

where SD is the standard deviation in the selection coordinates measured along the line from the center of the home square to the center of a target. Using effective width allows throughput to incorporate the spatial variability in human performance. It includes both speed and accuracy [5].

Prior Evaluations

ISO 9241-9 was in Draft International Standard form in 1998 and became an International Standard in 2000. If one considers mouse evaluations in research not following the standard, throughput ranged from about 2.6 bits/s to 12.5 bits/s. On the contrary, studies conforming to the standard reported throughput from about 3.7 bits/s to 4.9 bits/s [8]. The data appear much more uniform and consistent. In short, ISO 9241-9 improves the quality and comparability of device evaluations.

Although several papers follow ISO 9241-9 and dozens of others use Fitts' law to evaluate non-keyboard input devices, Ware and Mikaelian published in 1987 what remains the only Fitts' law evaluation of an eye tracking system [10]. They used a serial Fitts' law task to test three eye tracking techniques. Task completion time was the only performance measure used. They compared eye tracking with the mouse but did not calculate or report on throughput as a performance measure. No eye tracking evaluation paper has ever been published since then using Fitts' law (or ISO 9241-9).

By following the standard and comparing throughput for eye tracking with a baseline technique (i.e., a mouse), we can determine how good an eye tracking system is. This paper is the first eye tracking evaluation conforming to ISO 9241-9.

The rest of this paper is organized as follows. In section 2, we described the methodology of our experiment. In section 3, the results are presented and discussed. Finally, we present our conclusions in section 4.

2 Methodology

An experiment was designed to implement the performance and comfort elements of ISO 9241-9. Effort was not tested since we do not have the sophisticated equipment necessary for measuring biomechanical load.

Performance testing was limited to pointing and selecting using multi-directional point-and-select tasks following ISO 9241-9 [2]. The testing environment was modeled on Annex B in the ISO standard [4]. Comfort was evaluated using the ISO

"Independent Rating Scale". The design followed, as reasonably as possible, the description in Annex C [4].

Participants
Sixteen paid volunteer participants (11 male, 5 female) were recruited from the local university campus. Participants ranged from 22 to 33 years (*mean* = 25). All were daily users of computers, reporting 4 to 12 hours usage per day (*mean* = 7). None had prior experience with eye tracking. All participants had normal vision, except one who wore contact lenses. Nine participants were right-eye dominant, seven left-eye dominant, as determined using the eye dominance test described by Collins and Blackwell [1].

Apparatus
A head-fixed eye tracking system, *ViewPoint*™ from ArringtonResearch, served as the input device (Fig. 1). The measurement method was Pupil and Corneal Reflection for greater tolerance to head movements. The infrared camera was set to focus on a participant's dominant eye. The monitor was a 19-inch 1280 x 1024 pixel LCD. Participants sat at a viewing distance of approximately 60 cm. The eye tracker sampled at 30 Hz with an accuracy of 0.25° - 1.0° visual arc, or about 10 – 40 pixels with our configuration. Calibration was performed before the first technique involved with the eye, with re-calibration as needed. Raw eye data and event data were collected and calculated using experimental software developed in our laboratory.

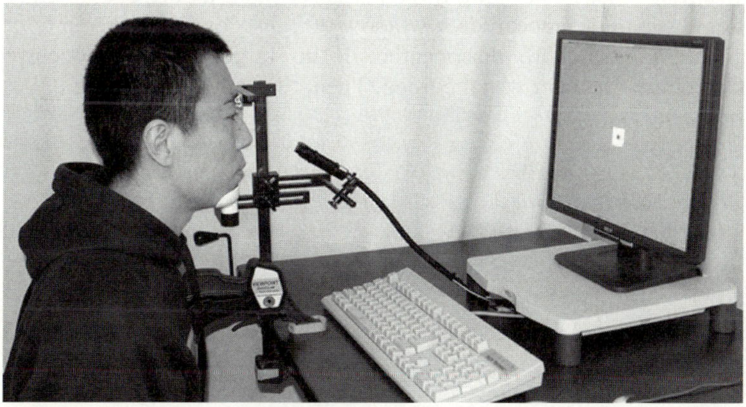

Fig. 1. Eye Tracking System

Procedure
The main independent variable was Interaction Technique with four levels:

- ETL - Eye Tracking Long
- ETS - Eye Tracking Short
- ESK - Eye+Spacebar
- M - Mouse

The ETL technique required participants to look at an on-screen target and dwell on it for 750 ms for selection. The dwell time was 500 ms for the ETS technique. The ESK technique allowed participants to "point" with the eye and "select" by pressing the spacebar upon fixation. To minimize asymmetric learning effects, the four interaction techniques were counterbalanced using a 4 × 4 balanced Latin square [7].

There were three additional independent variables. These were included to ensure that the trials covered a reasonable range of difficulties and to collect multiple sample points for each condition:

- Target Width: 75 pixels, 100 pixels
- Distance: 275 pixels, 350 pixels
- Trial: 1 to 16

Target width was the diameter of the circle target. Distance was the radius of the big circle, which was the distance from the center of the home square to the center of the circle target. These four conditions and the desired target were randomized. For each of the four conditions, the task involved 16 circle targets (Fig. 2). The total number of trials was 4096 (16 participants × 4 interaction techniques × 2 distances × 2 widths × 16 trials).

At the onset of each trial, a home square appeared on the screen. The home square allowed the distance of eye movement for each trial to be approximately the same. The home square disappeared after participants dwelled on it, pressed the spacebar, or clicked the left mouse button depending on the interaction technique. To exclude physical reaction time, positioning time started as soon as the eye or mouse moved after the home square disappeared. A window of 2.5 seconds was given to complete a trial after the home square disappeared. If no target selection occurred within 2.5 seconds, a time-out error was recorded. Then, the next trial followed.

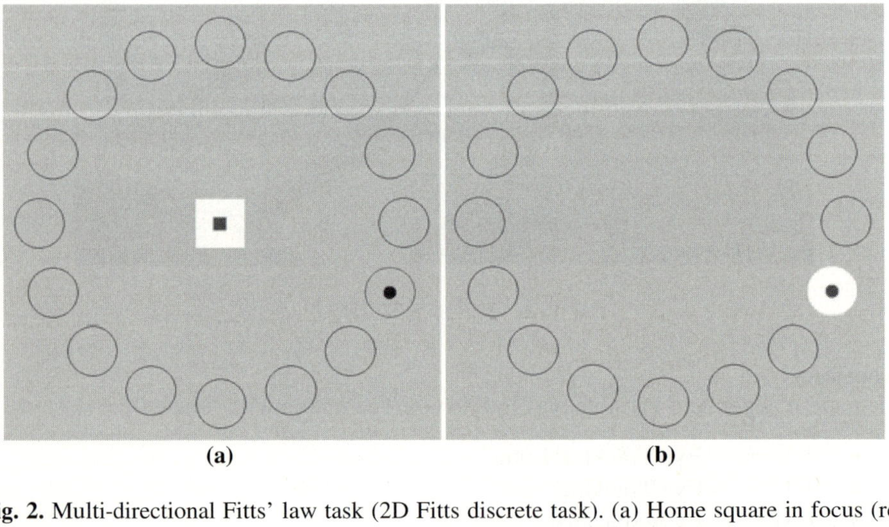

(a) (b)

Fig. 2. Multi-directional Fitts' law task (2D Fitts discrete task). (a) Home square in focus (red dot with white background). Current target not in focus (blue dot with blue outline). (b) Home square disappeared (time started). Current target in focus (red dot with white background).

To minimize visual reaction time, the desired target was highlighted as soon as the participant fixated on the home square (Fig. 2a). The current target showed a blue dot when not in focus and a red dot when in focus (Fig. 2b). The dot helped participants fixate at the center of the target. The gray background was designed to reduce the eye stress caused by a bright color, such as a white background. For all three eye techniques, the mouse pointer was hidden to reduce visual distraction.

Participants were instructed to point to the target as quickly as possible (look at the target or move the mouse depending on the interaction technique), and select the target as quickly as possible (dwell on the target, press spacebar, or click the left mouse button depending on the interaction technique). After finishing the trials, we interviewed each user and gave a questionnaire.

3 Results and Discussion

Throughput

As evident in Fig. 3, there was a significant effect of interaction technique on throughput ($F_{3,45}$ = 47.46, p < .0001). The 500 ms dwell time of the ETS technique seemed just right. Too short and participants accidentally selected the wrong target; too long and participants became impatient while waiting for selection. ETL had a lower throughput than ETS due to this. ESK was the best among the three eye tracking techniques. We attribute this to participants effectively pressing the spacebar immediately upon fixation on the target. This eliminated the need to wait for selection. The throughput of the ESK technique was 3.78 bits/s, which was close to the 4.68 bits/s for the Mouse. Considering the mouse has the best performance among non-keyboard input devices [8], the ESK technique is very promising. As the user

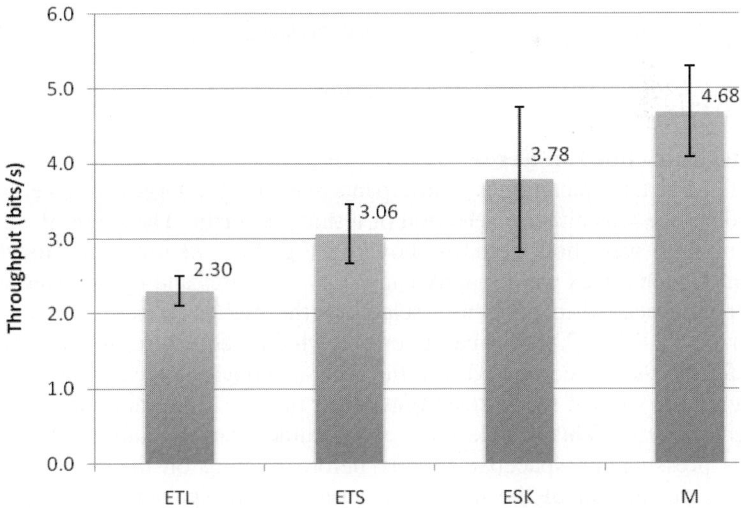

Fig. 3. Throughput as a function of interaction technique

must press the spacebar (or other key), this observation is qualified by noting that the ESK technique is only appropriate where an additional key press is possible and practical.

Point-select Time

Point-select time is the sum of the positioning time and the selection time. As shown in Fig. 4, the point-select time of the ESK technique was significantly lower than for the other interaction techniques ($F_{3,45}$ = 60.82, p < .0001). A post hoc multiple comparisons test was performed using the Student-Newman-Keuls method. This revealed significance at the p = .05 level for all six comparisons except ETS vs. Mouse.

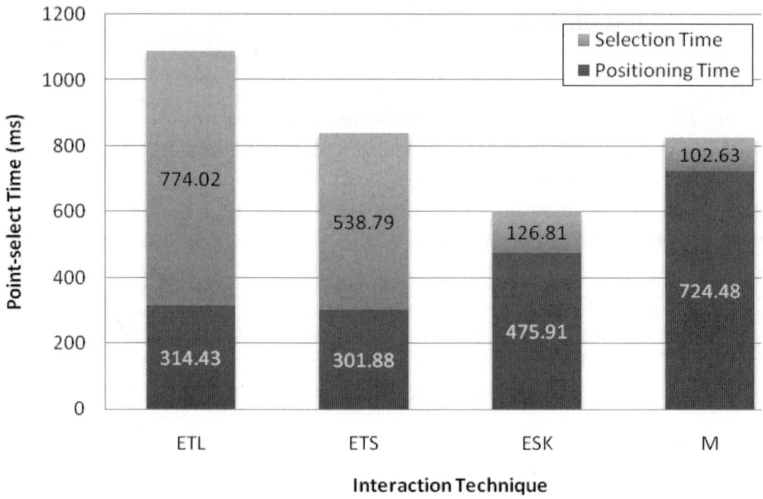

Fig. 4. Point-select Time as a function of interaction technique

Error Rates and Time-out Error

For the ETL and ETS techniques, participants selected the target by dwelling on it. Thus, the outcome was either a selection or a time-out error. Therefore, the error rate for ETL and ETS were both zero, as shown in Fig. 5. Time-out errors for the ETL, ETS and ESK techniques were mainly caused by eye jitter and eye tracker accuracy. The longer time needed to perform a selection, the higher chance there would be a time-out error. ESK had 2.89% time-out errors, which much closer to the 1.07% time-out errors for the mouse, compared with the other eye tracking techniques.

Although ESK yielded the fastest point-select time, as aforementioned, it suffered from a high error rate. This is a classic speed-accuracy tradeoff and we attributed it to participants pressing the spacebar slightly before fixating on the target, or slightly after the eye moved out of the target. Because no participant had prior experience with eye tracking, few could do the coordinated work of eye pointing and hand pressing of the spacebar very well. The error rate for the ESK technique varied a lot across participants (*standard deviation* = 11.43, *max* = 35.59, *minimum* = 3.13). We

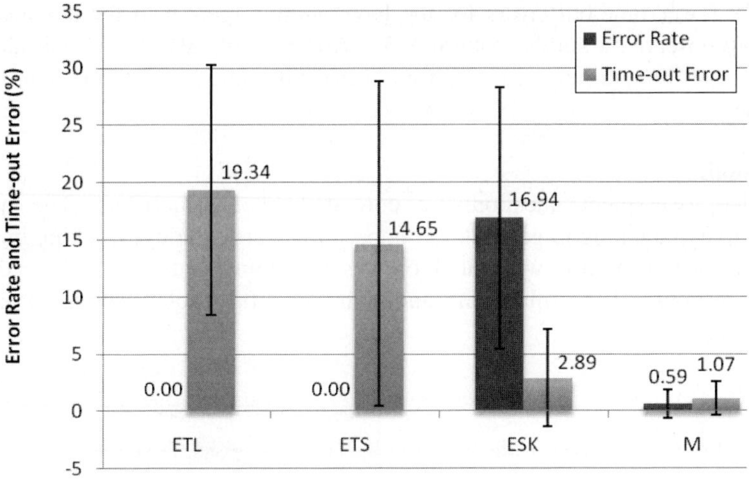

Fig. 5. Error Rate and Time-out Error as a function of interaction technique

believe participants could have much lower error rates if further training was provided and improved feedback mechanisms were considered and tested.

Target Width

As we analyzed all data, an interesting finding surfaced. The width of a target can affect the error rate and time-out error. For the ETL, ETS and ESK techniques shown in Fig. 6, the time-out error of the large-width target was generally better than for the small-width target. For the ETS and ESK techniques, the difference was substantial, with

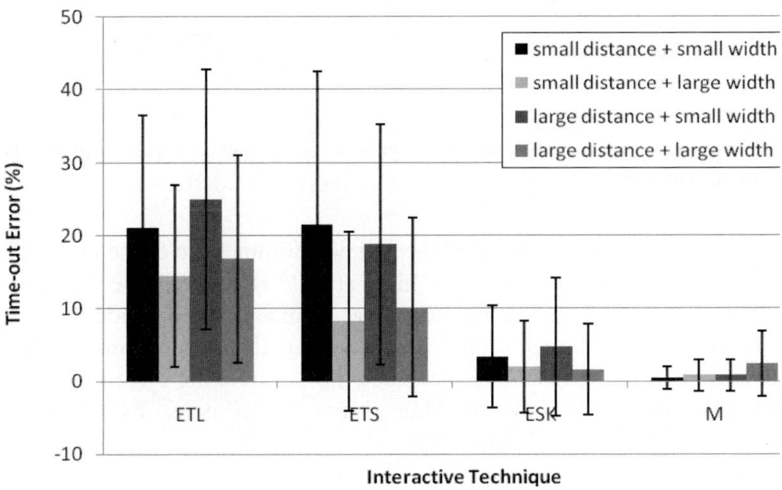

Fig. 6. Time-out Error as a function of interaction technique, target width, and distance

about 50% fewer time-out errors for the large-width targets than for the small-width targets. We observed a similar pattern as in error rate. We also found that although a larger target width can help reduce errors, it had little impact on throughput or point-select time.

Questionnaire

The device assessment questionnaire consisted of 12 questions. The questions pertained to eye tracking in general, as opposed to a particular eye tracking interaction technique. Each response was rated on a seven-point scale, with 7 as the most favorable response, 4 the mid-point, and 1 the least favorable response. Results are shown in Fig. 7.

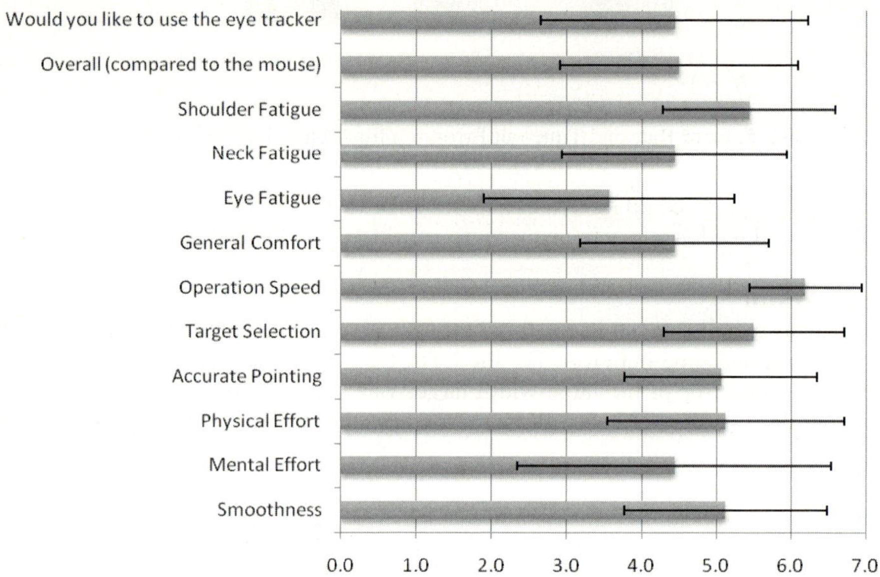

Fig. 7. Eye tracker device assessment questionnaire. Response 7 was the most favorable, response 1 the least favorable.

As seen, participants generally liked the fast positioning time of the eye tracker. On Operation Speed, the mean score was high at 6.2. However, Eye Fatigue was a concern. Participants complained that staring at so many targets made their eyes dry and uncomfortable. Eye Fatigue scored lowest among all the questions. Neck Fatigue and Shoulder Fatigue were also an issue, since the eye tracking system we tested was head-fixed. Participants gave eye tracking a favorable response overall of 4.5, just slightly higher than the mid-point (see top two entries in Fig. 7). Discussions following the experiment revealed that participants liked to use eye tracking and believed it could perform similar to the mouse. Of the three eye tracking techniques, participants expressed a preference for the Eye+Spacebar technique. Concerns were voiced, however, on the likely expense of eye tracking system, the troublesome calibration procedure, and uncomfortable need to maintain a fixed head position.

4 Conclusion

This paper is the first eye tracking evaluation conforming to ISO 9241-9. Four point-select interaction techniques were evaluated, three involving eye tracking and one using a standard mouse. The Eye Tracking Long technique yielded a lower throughput than the Eye Tracking Short technique. The Eye+Spacebar technique was the best among the three eye tracking interaction techniques. It had a throughput of 3.78 bits/s, which was close to the 4.68 bits/s for the Mouse. Participants generally liked the Eye+Spacebar technique.

More work is planned to determine the best settings for eye tracking, for example, the optimal target size and color highlighting. In the future, we intend to evaluate eye tracking in a longitudinal study and in text entry applications.

Acknowledgments. We would like to acknowledge Prof. John Tsotsos and others at the Center for Vision Research for allowing us generous access to the lab and eye tracking apparatus. This research was sponsored by the Natural Sciences and Engineering Research Council of Canada. This support is gratefully acknowledged.

References

1. Collins, J.F., Blackwell, L.K.: Effects of eye dominance and retinal distance on binocular rivalry. Perceptual and Motor Skills 39, 747–754 (1974)
2. Douglas, S.A., Kirkpatrick, A.E., MacKenzie, I.S.: Testing pointing device performance and user assessment with the ISO 9241, Part 9 standard. In: Proceedings of the ACM Conference on Human Factors in Computing Systems - CHI '99, New York, ACM, pp. 215–222 (1999)
3. Hennessey, C., Noureddin, B., Lawrence, P.A: single camera eye-gaze tracking system with free head motion. In: Proceedings of the Symposium on Eye Tracking Research and Applications – ETRA 2006 New York, ACM, pp. 87–94 (2006)
4. Ergonomic requirements for office work with visual display terminals (VDTs) - Part 9: Requirements for non-keyboard input devices. International Standard, International Organization for Standardization (2000) ISO. ISO/DIS 9241-9
5. MacKenzie, I.S.: Fitts' law as a research and design tool in human-computer interaction. Human-Computer Interaction 7, 91–139 (1992)
6. Majaranta, P., MacKenzie, I.S., Aula, A., Räihä, K.-J.: Effects of feedback and dwell time on eye typing speed and accuracy. Universal Access in the Information Society (UAIS) 5, 199–208 (2006)
7. Martin, D.W.: Doing psychology experiments, 6th edn. Wadsworth Publishing, Belmont, CA (2004)
8. Soukoreff, R.W., MacKenzie, I.S.: Towards a standard for pointing device evaluation: Perspectives on 27 years of Fitts' law research in HCI. International Journal of Human-Computer Studies 61, 751–789 (2004)

9. Wagner, P., Bartl, K., Günthner, W., Schneider, E., Brandt, T., Ulbrich, H.: A pivotable head mounted camera system that is aligned by three-dimensional eye movements. In: Proceedings of the Symposium on Eye Tracking Research and Applications – ETRA 2006, New York, ACM, pp. 117–124 (2006)
10. Ware, C., Mikaelian, H.H.: An evaluation of an eye tracker as a device for computer input. In: Proceedings of the ACM Conference on Human Factors in Computing Systems – CHI+GI '87 New York, ACM, pp. 183–188 (1987)

Impact of Mental Rotation Strategy on Absolute Direction Judgments: Supplementing Conventional Measures with Eye Movement Data

Ronggang Zhou[1] and Kan Zhang[2]

[1] Department of Industrial Engineering, Tsinghua University, Beijing 100084, China
[2] State Key Laboratory of Brain and Cognitive Science, Institute of Psychology, Chinese Academy of Sciences, Beijing 100101, China
zhourg@tsinghua.edu.cn, zhangk@psych.ac.cn

Abstract. By training participants to use map-first mental rotation as their primary strategy on absolute navigational task, this study focused on how integration of heading information (from the exocentric reference frame) with target position information (from the egocentric reference frame) affects absolute direction judgments. Comparing with previous studies, the results in this study showed (1) response was not better for north than for south, (2) response was the slowest for back position in canonical position condition, and (3) the cardinal direction advantage of right-back position was not impaired. Eye movement data supported these conclusions partially, and should be cautious to use for similar goals. These findings can be applied to navigational training and interfaces design such as electric space.

Keywords: absolute direction judgments, mental rotation strategy, eye movement, reference frame.

1 Introduction

People can not specify spatial location and orientation of objects relative to other objects without using, at least basically, a frame of reference. The distinction between egocentric, or body-reference frame and exocentric, or world-reference frame is used most frequently to classify spatial reference frames for the purposes of understanding human spatial navigation [1] [2] [3]. The egocentric reference frame presents spatial knowledge with respect to navigator's view using words such as front, back, left, right, up, and down; the exocentric frame defines navigational relations with respect to bird's-eye perspective in the word using environmental elements such as the landmarks, cardinal direction (e.g. north, south, east, and west), and compass coordinates [1] [2] [3]. Relative and absolute spatial relation can be presented with using a single required corresponding reference frame. However most people are familiar with using a map to make navigation decision on way finding in an unfamiliar crossing road, and in this situation direction judgments should be based on integrating information from the exocentric reference frame (the map) with egocentric frame (the navigator's forward view). In this study, we focused on navigational tasks

J. Jacko (Ed.): Human-Computer Interaction, Part III, HCII 2007, LNCS 4552, pp. 789–798, 2007.

like the decision of "turn to south" in the situation, and participants were trained with using mental rotation strategy and provided egocentric and exocentric reference frames to identify direction using terminology of north (N), north-east (NE), east (E), south-east (SE), south (S), south-west (SW), west (W), and north-west (NW)-we called this absolute direction judgments. Among theses points, the point of N, E, S, and W are four main points, direction judgments using these four concepts are call cardinal direction judgments.

1.1 Previous Studies Review

Absolute Direction Judgments Studies. Recently absolute direction judgments have been more investigated with starting of cardinal direction judgments studies. The representative task used in these absolute direction judgments studies can be shown in Fig. 1. Participants saw a north-up map indicating the location and heading of observer, and a ground target ahead of the observer (right part of Fig.1), and the heading can be selected from N to NW in 45° or 30° increments. In particular heading, the ground target was provided with corresponding forward view, which showed a central building surrounded symmetrically with four lots (left part of Fig.1). When read the 3D display, participants would be deictic to the central building, so the target lot would be located in canonical position (e.g. front (F), back (B), left (L), or right (R)) or noncanonical position (e.g. front-left (FL), front-right (FR), back-left (BL), or back-right (BR)) relative to the reference building. The task was to determine whether the target object was N, NE, E, SE, S, SW, W, and NW of the central building.

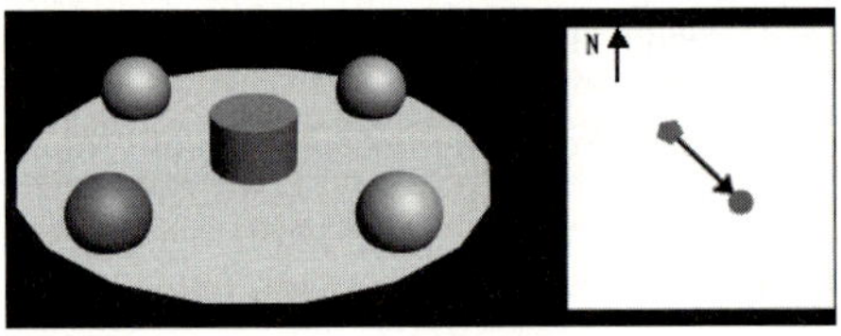

Fig. 1. Map display (exocentric reference frame) and three-dimensional display (egocentric reference frame) used in the typical absolute direction task. In the map, the heading was southeast, so the red target lot in the 3D display was north of the building. The actual displays were in color, and objects can be discriminated clearly.

The results of cardinal direction judgments studies indicated that (1) reference frame misalignment was found to slow judgment performance (slow response time and decrease accuracy), and the advantage effect of cardinal direction follow N < S < E = W < NE = NW< SE = SW pattern completely or partly [2] [5] [7] [8], and the advantage effect of canonical position was in accordance with the pattern of F < B < L = R < BL = BR < FL = FR [7] [8], and (2) mental rotation strategy and analytical inference strategy were used for cardinal direction judgments [2] [5] [9].

However, the advantage effect of right and left position may be dependent of heading. With absolute direction judgments tasks, Zhou et al found that when viewer faced to the cardinal direction, the judgment performance on left or right position was better than that on noncanonical positions, while the result was reverse for noncardinal direction [3] [10]. Fig. 2 showed illustratively the result of theses studies.

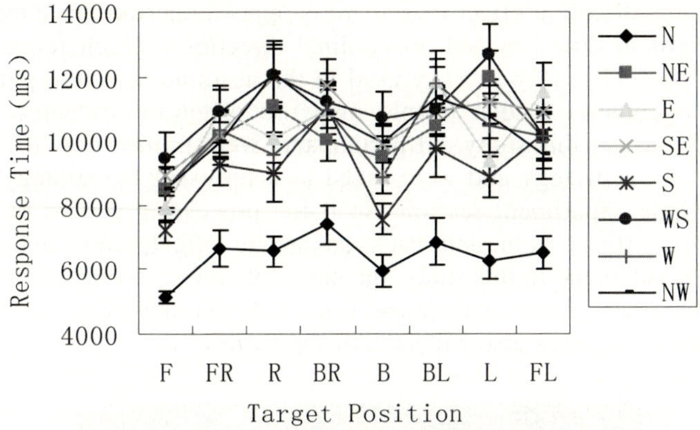

Fig. 2. Response time in absolute direction judgments was plotted as a function of target position and camera heading in one of our pervious experiments [3]

Strategies Used in Judgments. Zhou suggested that the canonical-cardinal reference advantage effect could be related to the use of different strategies in the absolute direction task [3]. With absolute direction problem shown in Fig.1, the main strategies were described as follows [2] [3] [9].

Mental rotation strategy. For the problem, the *map-first mental rotation strategy* can be stated as "from the map display, the current heading was rotated by 135 degree clockwise from the north, so the target lot in the 3D display should also be rotated in the same way, then the target will reach the front of the reference building, that is to say it is the north of the central object". With using this strategy, the 3D display will be looked potentially as a north-up map. In *3D-first mental rotation strategy*, the statement will be described as "in order to solve the problem, the 3D display will be imagined and coordinated into the map display until the top of the 3D display reached the ground point in the southeast, and the target lot will be the top in the map after rotation, so it is the north of the central object".

Analytical inference strategy. This strategy does not involve mental rotation, "from the map, the heading faced to southeast, so the forward view of the 3D display is southeast, which is equal to say that the top or the front position in the 3D display is the southeast of the central object. So the object positioned in the bottom of the 3D display is the northwest, while the target object is near to the bottom, and the absolute direction of the target lot relative to the central object could be inferred as north." This strategy involves using the exocentric frame heading as a direction inferred cue within the egocentric frame.

In absolute direction judgments, the difference of strategies using is associated with individual and group difference [2] [4] [5] [8].

1.2 Overview of the Study

The purpose of this study was to investigate how strategies used in absolute direction judgments affect judgment performance, especially to test whether the advantage of canonical-cardinal direction effect (e.g. there is opposite performance on left or right position for cardinal direction and noncardinal direction), which found in previous studies, could be changed by strategy used in the absolute direction judgments. The basic related hypothesis is that people may use different strategies for different problem conditions. In this study, all participants were trained how to use the map-first mental rotation strategy and were asked to keep using the strategy to complete tasks in the whole experiment session. So if the processing pattern (e.g. north and south advantage effect, front and back advantage effect, and canonical-cardinal advantage effect) changed in this study, the basic hypothesis would be supported. The conventional measures (such as response time and accuracy) were analyzed mainly and eye movement data was also collected to supply to it.

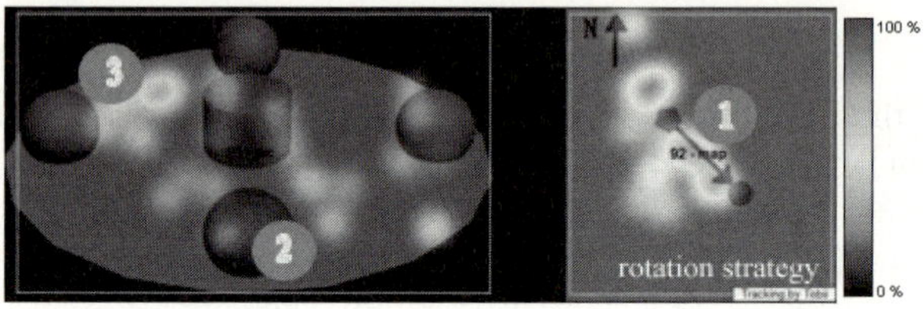

Fig. 3. Sample pattern of eyes' fixation when used map-first mental strategy to make absolute direction judgments. Areas of fixation and its duration were marked with color.

In this study we defined two areas of interest (AOI) (AOI-map display and AOI-3D display) to analyze eye movement variables including durations of fixation and numbers of fixation. When using map-first mental rotation strategy, the typical pattern of eye fixation can be shown as Fig. 3. Labeled 1, 2, and 3 were used to illustrate fixation with using map-first mental rotation strategy: firstly the north was rotated 135 degree clockwise to the current heading in the map, then target object was found in the area of label 2, thirdly rotated target object 135 degree clockwise in imagination and eye fixation was transferred to the area of label 3, so the target lot was the northwest of the reference building. In the figure, the map and 3D display was defined as AOI respectively.

2 Methods

2.1 Participants

The 20 undergraduates (10 men; 10 women) from China Agricultural University, ranging in age from 18 to 22 years (M = 19.50, SD = 1.10), participated in return for monetary compensation.

2.2 Materials, Tasks, and Apparatus

The tasks used in this study were similar with navigational task showed in Fig. 1. On each trial, participants first saw a test message "press the blank key to continue". When the key was pressed, the map and the 3D display were shown as Fig. 4.

Participants were asked to identify which direction of target relative to the reference building using absolute concepts. And response was determined using the number pad on the right of the keyboard, pressing 8 for N, 9 for NE, 6 for E, 3 for SE, 2 for S, 1 for SW, 7 for W, and 7 for NW. After responding, RIGHT message with responding time (e.g., "2.567 seconds") or WRONG message without RT message was provided, and this feedback remained visible for 1.0 s, then next trial began. A total of 8 camera headings were used, from N to NW, in 45° clockwise increments. For each heading, there were 8 problems with the direction of target object relative to the central object (N, NE, E, SE, S, SW, W, and NW). For each heading, the target lot would be located in canonical position (e.g. F, B, L, or R, as part a shown in Fig. 4) or noncanonical position (e.g. FL, FR, BL, or BR, as part b shown in Fig. 4) relative to the reference building from the participants' deictic view.

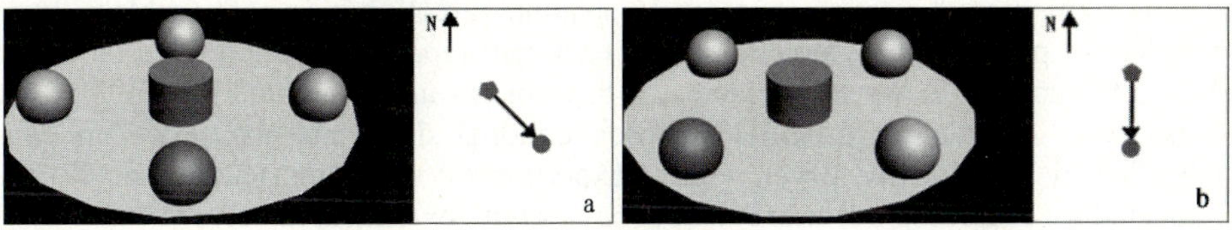

Fig. 4. Map display (exocentric reference frame) and Camera display (egocentric reference frame) used in this study. "Part a" and "part b" were designed for canonical and noncanonical position respectively. Other key information in the two parts was in accordance. In part a, the target lot was the northwest of the central building, and the target lot in part b was the northeast of the reference object.

Combined the way of computer, the instructions were presented clearly to participants by the same experimenter. Participants were instructed how to read key information on the map and camera (3D) display, and they were explained that the 3D display show the forward view from a particular camera heading and especially were trained well on how to use map-first mental rotation strategy to make response using keyboard. During the session of collecting eye movement data, participants were asked to keep appropriate posture for recording eye movement behavior. For all experiment sessions, participants were asked to answer the problems as quickly as possible without making mistakes.

The absolute direction tasks were presented on 17'' monitor interfaced with personal computers. The screen resolution was set to 1024 × 768 pixels. Eye movements behavior were collected with a Tobii 1750 binocular remote eye tracker with 75 Hz temporal resolution and a 0.5o spatial resolution.

2.3 Design

In the north-up map, NE and NW can be rotated to N with the same degree, and based on the process pattern indicated in previous studies, combination of NE and NW was considered as a level of headings in this study. E-W and SE-SW were also combined as corresponding level with the same way. Similarly, the levels of target position were presented as F, FL-FR, L-R, BL-BR, and B. Since interaction effect was intended to be considered for canonical and noncanonical position respectively, response time and accuracy were tested with two with-in subject designs: canonical position, 5 (camera heading: N, NE-NW, E-W, and SE-SW) × 3 (target position: F, R-L, and B); noncanonical position, 5 (camera heading: N, NE-NW, E-W, and SE-SW) × 2 (target position: FL-FR, and BL-BR).

For eye movement data, numbers of fixation and durations of fixation were tested for camera (3D) display and map separately: for AOI-3D, target position were provided with 5 levels as F, R-L, B, FL-FR, and BL-BR; for AOI-map, 5 levels of N, NE-NW, E-W, and SE-SW were selected for camera heading.

2.4 Procedures

Before absolute direction judgment, participants completed 32 times practice for response using corresponding keyboard. After presenting instructions of how to respond using mental rotation strategy, 16 absolute direction judgment problems were provided for participants to practice. Then each participant completed three blocks of trials, and each block were provided 8 × 8 problems and presented randomly. Two blocks were completed for collecting conventional data, and the procedure was controlled by the E-prime psychological experimental software. The last block was conducted for recording eye movement behavior with eye tracker.

3 Results

3.1 Conventional Behavior Measures

Accuracy Data. Mean accuracy on absolute direction judgment is plotted as a function of heading and position in Table 1. As shown in the table: (1) the overall accuracy was the highest for S, and response was more accurate for N than for other headings, and (2) response was more accurate for position of FL-FR than BL-BR. A repeated measure analysis of variance showed that the main effect of heading was significant: for canonical position, F (4, 76) = 7.4, MSE = 76.7, $p < 0.01$; for noncanonical position, F (4, 76) = 7.0, MSE = 73.9, $p < 0.01$. Pairwise comparisons supported N (98.1) = S (99.2) > E-W (94.4) = NE-NW (91.5) = SE-SW (94.7) for canonical position, and S (96.3) = N (98.8) > E-W (91.5) = NE-NW (90.4) = SE-SW (91.7) for noncanonical position. The main effect of target position was significant for noncanonical position condition, F (1, 76) = 7.6, MSE = 65.9, $p < 0.5$, pairwise

Table 1. Accuracy (Percent Correct) with Standard Deviation

Variables	Canonical Position			Non-Canonical Position	
	F	L-R	B	FL-FR	BL-BR
N	98.8 ± 5.6	96.9 ± 6.9	98.8 ± 5.6	98.1 ± 6.1	94.4 ± 10.3
S	100 ± 0.0	100 ± 0.0	97.5 ± 11.2	98.7 ± 5.6	98.8 ± 5.6
NE-NW	93.3 ± 13.7	95.8 ± 5.7	94.7 ± 9.8	93.3 ± 7.9	89.6 ± 12.4
E-W	92.5 ± 11.4	90.4 ± 15.1	91.7 ± 12.7	92.5 ± 8.5	88.3 ± 10.6
SE-SW	96.7 ± 6.8	93.3 ± 6.4	94.7 ± 11.2	93.8 ± 8.9	89.6 ± 11.1

comparisons showed FL-FR (95.3) > BL-BR (92.1). The difference between F (96.3), L-R (95.3), and B (95.3) wasn't significant. No other main effect and interaction effect was reliable.

Response Time. Average response time for canonical position and noncanonical position is plotted of heading and position in Fig. 5. As shown in the figure, (1) as position changes from F to B, the overall response time increased markedly, and response was slower for FR-FL than for BR-BL; and (2) the heading process pattern of S < N < E-W < NE-NW < SE-SW was obvious.

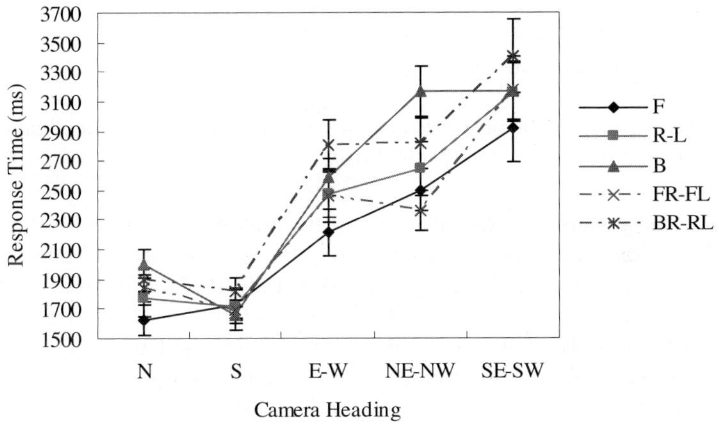

Fig. 5. Average response time for absolute direction judgments was plotted as a function of camera heading and target position, with standard error

A repeated measure analysis of variance showed the main effect of heading was significant: for canonical position, F (4, 76) = 61.0, MSE = 354548.1, $p < 0.01$; for noncanonical position, F (4, 76) = 55.8, MSE = 284531.2, $p < 0.01$. Pairwise comparisons supported N (1800.6) = S (1701.4) < E-W (2428.7) < NE-NW (2768.5) < SE-SW (3084.0) for canonical position, and S (1752.4) < N (1868.5) < E-W (2630.9) = NE-NW (2585.1) < SE-SW (3295.1) for noncanonical position. The main effect of position was significant: for canonical position, F (2, 38) = 12.0, MSE = 214188.4, $p < 0.01$; for noncanonical position, F (1, 19) = 11.3, MSE = 250039.7, $p < 0.01$. Pairwise comparisons supported the statistical ordering of F (2197.3) < R-L (2354.6) < B (2518.0) for canonical position, and FL-FR (2307.3) < 135-225 (2545.4) for noncanonical position. Interaction effect existed in canonical position, F (8, 152) = 3.0, MSE = 149345.9, $p < 0.01$.

3.2 Eye Movement Data

The fixations were eliminated if the duration was less than 100 ms. Durations and numbers of fixation are plotted of heading in AOI1 (map) and position in AOI2 (3D) in Fig. 6.

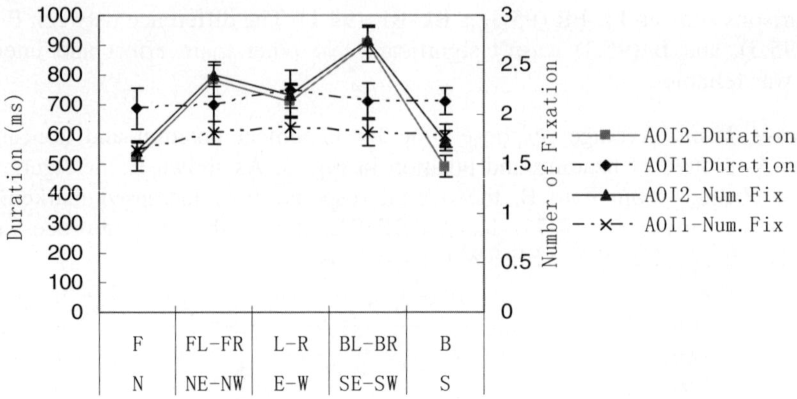

Fig. 6. Average duration and numbers of fixation were plotted as a function of camera heading and target position respectively, with standard error

For AOI1, the differences for headings were not obvious on both durations and numbers of fixation. The effect of headings was not significant with repeated measure analysis of variance: for duration, F (4, 76) = 0.7, MSE = 16730.5, $p > 0.5$; for number of fixation, F (4, 76) = 2.7, MSE = 0.08, $p > 0.5$. For AOI2, the pattern of F = B < L-R < FL-FR < BL-BR was evident for duration and number of duration. A repeated measures analysis of variance show that the position was significant: for duration, F (4, 76) = 43.3, MSE = 13283.9, $p < 0.001$; for number of duration, F (4, 76) = 39.27, MSE = 0.11, $p < 0.001$. The overall pattern of F = B < L-R < FL-FR < BL-BR was supported by pairwise comparison. And the comparison of AOI1 to AOI2 wasn't significant: for duration, F (1, 19) = 0.001, MSE = 34733.5, $p < 0.001$; for number of duration, F (1, 19) = 13.2, MSE = 0.14, $p < 0.001$.

4 Discussion

Absolute direction judgment is close related to human spatial cognitive ability, and is used in a variety of navigation related jobs such as air traffic control, driving, piloting, tracking, and police work [2] [3] [5] [9]. Previous studies were conducted to investigate how people coordinate egocentric reference frame with exocentric reference frame to make absolute direction judgments. Integrating with cardinal direction judgments, effective factors contributed to the absolute direction tasks are summarized as: (1) north and south advantage effect may be presented for headings, (2) front and back advantage effect may be formed with position of target object relative to reference object, and (3) canonical-cardinal direction advantage effect is derived from coordinating of the heading information with position information. This study was conducted to investigate how these effects varied with using map-first mental rotation strategy. No trade-off between accuracy and response time was found, so only the results of response time were discussed.

For the effect of heading, the process ordering pattern of S = N < E-W < NE-NW < SE-SW (slow response time) was supported, and it was evident that the response was quicker for south than for north, and the difference was even significant in canonical position condition. Previous studies suggested that north has better performance than other headings, so in some degree the process pattern changed with the rotation strategy using. This conclusion can be supported by eye movement: it is easier to know how much degree need be rotated from north to current heading, so there was no evident difference on the durations and numbers of fixation for headings. For the effect of target position, the average response was slowest for back position in the canonical position condition. The result indicated that the back-advantage effect, which was found in previous studies [3] [5] [6] [7] [8] [10], was associated with strategies using in absolute direction judgments. However back and front positions were fixed the same duration and numbers of fixation in statistics. For interaction effect, as an example, Fig. 2 showed the advantage of L-R position for cardinal direction, and the response was detached mostly in L-R position between cardinal and noncardinal directions. The tendency wasn't affected with rotation strategy using. However, response was more centralized in back position than in other positions. The result of this study suggested that the mental rotation strategy may impact the process pattern of the headings and positions, and transformation and diversity of strategies using in absolute was proved further. But this study can not provide more details for explaining why the pattern changed with mental rotation strategy, even supplied with eye movement data (which should be used cautiously for similar navigation tasks). This can be considered in the future.

One of potential applications of these findings is the interface design of electric space. How to organize and visualize effectively information on computers has been a key issue in user interface design such as World-Wide Web and virtual environments. In order to solver the problem, spatial metaphor (e.g. data mountain, data wall, and cone tree) is well entrenched well in this field. And indeed there is need to provide both a local, egocentric reference frame and a more global, exocentric reference frame in navigational multidimensional space [1]. Based on the results of studies on cardinal direction judgments, the position of target object relative to reference object, user's forward view, and reference alignments should be considered when use spatial metaphor to improve navigation performance in electric space. However the process pattern of these factors may present difference among specific spatial presentations. This needs more investigations in future researches.

Acknowledgments. This research project was funded by a grant from the National Natural Science Foundation of China (#30270465), and was partially supported by a grant from the China Air Force Office of Pilot Recruit.

References

1. Wickens, C.D., Hollands, J.G.: Engineering psychology and human performance (3rd). Prentice Hall, New Jersey (2000)
2. Gugerty, L., Brooks, J.: Seeing where you are heading: Integrating Environmental and egocentric reference frames in cardinal direction judgments. Journal of experimental psychology: Applied 7, 251–266 (2001)

3. Zhou, R.: Absolute Direction Judgments Based on Integrating Egocentric and Environmental Reference Frames. Doctoral dissertation, Institute of Psychology, Chinese Academy of Sciences. Bejing (2005)
4. Gugerty, L., Brooks, J.: Reference-frame misalignment and cardinal direction judgments: Group differences and strategies. Journal of experimental psychology: Applied 10, 68–75 (2004)
5. Zhou, R., Zhang, K.: The Cardinal Direction Judgments in Integrating Environmental and Egocentric Reference Frames. Acta Psychologica Sinica 37, 298–307 (2005)
6. Zhou, R., Zhang, K.: The Direction of Integrating Reference Frames and Gender-related Difference in Cardinal Direction Judgments. Ergonomics (In Chinese) 10, 10–13 (2004)
7. Zhou, R., Yang, J., Zhang, K.: Training-related difference in Cardinal Direction Judgments Based on Integrating Reference Frames. In: Proceedings of IEA-the XVth Triennial Congress of the International Ergonomics Association, Seoul, Korea, vol. 1, pp. 1189–1192 (2003)
8. Yang, J., Zhou, R., Zhang, K.: The Training Effect and Direction Effect on Spatially Cardinal Direction Judgment. Psychological Sciences (In Chinese) 27, 1322–1325 (2004)
9. Gugerty, L., Brooks, J., Treadaway, C.: Individual differences in situation awareness for transportation tasks. In: Banbury, S., Tremblay, S. (eds.) A Cognitive Approach to Situation Awareness: Theory, Measures and Application, pp. 193–212. Ashgate Publishers, London (2004)
10. Zhou, R., Zhang, K.: Direction Judgments Based on Integrating Reference Frames in Imagination. Ergonomics (In Chinese) 11, 7–10 (2005)

Part IV

Interactive TV and Media

Beyond Mobile TV: Understanding How Mobile Interactive Systems Enable Users to Become Digital Producers

Anxo Cereijo Roibás[1] and Riccardo Sala[2]

[1] SCMIS, University of Brighton, Watts Building, Moulsecoomb,
BN2 4GJ Brighton, UK
a.c.roibas@brighton.ac.uk
[2] Dare, 13-14 Margaret Street
W1W 8RN London, UK
riccardosala@gmail.com

Abstract. This paper aims to explore the quality of the user experience with mobile and pervasive interactive multimedia systems that enable the creation and sharing of digital content through mobile phones. It also looks at discussing the use and validity of different experimental in-situ and other data gathering and evaluation techniques for the assessment of how the physical and social contexts might influence the use of these systems. This scenario represents an important shift away from professionally produced digital content for the mass-market. It addresses methodologies and techniques that are suitable to design co-creative applications for non-professional users in different contexts of use at home or in public spaces. Special focus is be given to understand how user participation and motivation in small themed communities can be encouraged, and how social interaction can be enabled through mobile interfaces. An enhancement of users creativity, self-authored content sharing, sociability and co-experience can be evidence for how creative people can benefit from Information and Communication Technologies.

Keywords: users' generated content, pervasive multimedia, mobileTV.

1 Introduction

Users' adoption of powerful handhelds with multimedia features is resulting not only in expanding the iTV consumption beyond the domestic context (See Fig. 1). However, There are several reasons to believe that the future of pervasive TV won't consist of merely broadcast of traditional TV content on mobile devices. The first one is related to the intrinsic physical diversity between both interfaces (TV and handhelds) making them unsuitable for the same way of delivering of content. The second regards the context of use: TV is traditionally used in a domestic private environment [18] and usually involves a social sharing [11] while mobile phones are mainly used in public environments, entail an individual experience [13] and generally the viewing time is much shorter. Moreover, unlike TV, handhelds are regularly used in different situations and with different purposes and they are likely to

J. Jacko (Ed.): Human-Computer Interaction, Part III, HCII 2007, LNCS 4552, pp. 801–810, 2007.

be used as an auxiliary tool to assist users' in a main activity (in this sense, mobile content could be related to the specific context of the user - context awareness) [6]. Finally, there are also operability differences: TV (including interactive TV) is considered a passive or low interactive medium while handhelds entail a high interactivity and connectivity. Therefore, broadcasting of TV programs on handhelds is likely to be as deluding as interactive TV was. In other words, pervasive iTV will be something else and will have to do with issues such as socialibility, context awareness, creativity, interactivity, convergence (iTV, mobile phones, in-car-navigators & Internet) and connectivity (one to one and one to many).

Fig. 1. TV broadcasting on a handheld

Websites such as YouTube, AOL and Yahoo providing access to personal videos that have been taken using webcams, video cameras or mobile phones, evidence an emerging trend where users become authors of multimedia content. This self-authored content production is finding application in different areas: information (travel, finance, mortgages, cooking, culture, health, etc), entertainment (sports, gossips, performance, etc), government, commerce, etc. For example, BeenThere and TheWorldisnotFlat are user generated travel sites where people can share tips about places to go on holiday. Moreover, some major newspapers like The Guardian, use this content in their Travel section. Furthermore, other more structured websites link the videos to specific places – using, for example, Google maps - enabling users to locate the videos in a map, relating the self-authored content to a specific context. Another interesting example of self-authored content is http://www.wefeelfine.org, which is an 'exploration of human emotion on a global scale', or in other words, a navigation among different people's feelings (self-authored texts, sounds, pictures or videos) and emotions in the past few hours. These feelings are organized by the users into six formal movements titled: Madness, Murmurs, Montage, Mobs, Metrics, and Mounds.

User centered design methodologies that take effectively into account peripatetic users interacting in their real contexts are crucial in order to identify realistic scenarios and applications for pervasive interactive multimedia systems that provide positive user experiences. This article supports the statement that handhelds due to intrinsic attributes such as friendly multimedia production tools (video, pictures and text mainly), ubiquitous presence, communication capabilities and nimbleness to dialog with surrounding platforms such as iTV, PCs, PDAs, in-car-navigators and smart-house deployments, are highly plausible tools to support users' creation and distribution of self-authored multimedia content in pervasive communication scenarios.

2 Understanding the Context

Designing user interfaces for pervasive systems implies that the consideration of all other objects in the domain need to follow. Somehow designing such interactive systems can be compared to producing a play in theatre. It needs to know and take into account holistically the whole environment in the stage (light, acoustic, furniture, etc.) [8]. In fact, three elements need to be taken into consideration in order to design appropriate ubiquitous systems: the characteristics of the users, the attributes of the interfaces and the properties of the context. Cognitive psychology and human factors research is not enough to provide adequate solutions to pervasive communication systems. In fact, focusing on users and their human information-processing abilities disregards an important aspect of the user experience, which is the physical and social context. Ethnographic studies and the activity theory aiming to analyze the use of systems in the users' real environments have been successfully applied in industrial design [16].

The level of usability and accessibility are important factors when evaluating the quality of mobile and pervasive interactive systems with older users. However, due to the fragile relationship between this user group and technology, it is also crucial to assess their overall experience with the system. This includes getting information about their emotions and feelings.

McCarthy and Wright argue that the user experience must take into consideration the emotional, intellectual, and sensual aspects of our interactions with technology. "Today we don't just use technology, we live with it. Much more deeply then ever before we are aware that interacting with technology involves us emotionally, intellectually and sensually. So people who design, use, and evaluate interactive systems need to be able to understand and analyze people's felt experience with technology.". According to them, the felt experience of technology can be understood according to a framework of four threads of experience: sensual, emotional, compositional and spatio-temporal. With the notion of threads, the authors try to capture the multi-facetted, interweaved nature of the different aspects of human experience, which are continually "active" in parallel and more or less perceived as a "unity". As a tool for analyzing experience, the authors address the following six processes: anticipating, connecting, interpreting, reflecting, appropriating and recounting [10].

Mobile and pervasive communications occur in physical and social spaces. When we think to the user experience we move from the concept of space to the concept of place. In fact, spaces are characterized by physical properties, while places are also characterized by social properties [3]. A place implies a sense of personal and cultural meaning and this meaning needs to be caught by designers as having a strong influence on the use of a system (for example during this research it has been acknowledged how some older users felt embarrassed to use a camera-phone when traveling by train).

In-situ evaluation techniques have been used in several projects regarding the design of interactive systems in public or semi-public environments such as the evaluation of ambient displays at work and in the University, to evaluate ambient displays for the deaf that visualizes peripheral sound in the office, to evaluate a sound system to provide awareness to office staff about events taking place at their desks and to evaluate a system of interactive office door displays that had the function of electronic post-it notes to leave messages to the office occupant then they are not there.

Simulations and enactments are very useful when the usage contexts make particularly difficult the mediated data collection due to highly privacy, technical or legal issues (e.g. military environments) or when the system is at a very experimental level. Simulations using proof of concept mockups or explorative prototypes in labs have been largely used to evaluate the usability and accessibility of interactive systems. Although they might provide valuable information about the user experience with a certain interface, they tend to disregard the contextual and emotional aspect of the interaction. Moreover, they can only be used when the conceptual model of the system reaches an adequate level of maturity as they presume the use of a sort of prototype.

3 Description of Methods

The work presented here integrates a variety of methods such as time studies of user panels, observation, mapping of movements and other ethnographic techniques in order to answer the factual questions about the user experience in future scenarios of mobile multimedia systems such as mobile iTV, interpret the meaning of the findings and describe the relations between more levels of empirical experience and analytical outcome. In fact, such a research needs to combine experience, data, analysis and evaluations from more perspectives in order to achieve a multi-disciplinarily built platform for understanding how and why specific concrete needs, the demand for specific services and technological and aesthetic solutions are integrated in users' social, cultural and aesthetic practices; in short how these shifting trends among commuters evolve and shape. The work has been divided into three main stages:

The first one is devoted to the analysis of the user experience in future scenarios of mobile and ubiquitous i-TV. It consisted of two initial focus group sessions with each of the target group. Each workshop involved twelve participants and aimed to get the users view about trends on multimedia mobile applications, TV at home and on the move, new forms of content for mobile TV, advanced interaction possibilities and finally, possible interconnections between handhelds and other devices. This activity has been combined with a theoretical investigation of existing technologies and successful interactive user experiences in other areas (e.g. games, HCI in the Space, etc.). This phase also included ethnographic research using Cultural Probes –used initially by Gaver applied to conceptual design [4], questionnaires and naturalistic observation (photo/video recording in-the-field and data analysis). While focus groups and analysis of study-cases were good sources of functional and data requirements; Cultural Probes and questionnaires provided good information about users' requirements and finally in-the-field observation has been a very valuable technique to identify environmental and usability requirements (see Fig. 2). Moreover, the information collected here provided the basis for the scripts for the scenarios that have been evaluated in the following stage.

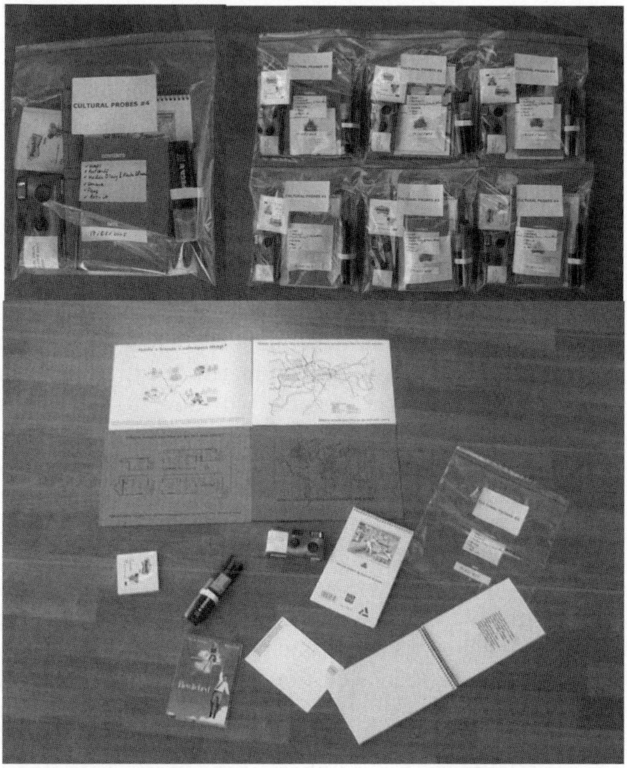

Fig. 2. Cultural Probes packs

The second and the third phase availed of enactments and simulations instead of mediated data collection. Creation of usage scenarios is a diffused ethnographic technique used to identify requirements and concept assessment, often combined with laboratory evaluation. Activity scenarios (e.g. based on experiential narratives) are useful during preparatory fieldwork early in the design process; mock-up scenarios aim to understand how the designed system suits users' activities; prototype evaluation scenarios that aim to evaluate the interface models of the system; integration scenarios that simulate the effect of the finished design.

The second phase aimed to validate some significant usage scenarios and subsequently to identify and classify innovative related applications exploring, at the same time, radically new forms of 'smart' and 'malleable' content. This process consisted in two workshops that used the technique of pretending (theatre) as a collaborative design approach. It involved twelve representatives of both target groups of users directly who were asked to represent and discuss the scripts of the scenarios (that have been elaborated in the previous phase) in order to guarantee the legitimacy of the scenarios and experience models proposed in terms of relevance, effectiveness and soundness.

The third phase consisted in the creation of proof of concept mock-ups and development of user experiments in order to bring to light the feasibility and usability of the scenarios, applications and forms of content previously identified. In this phase there have been developed (and empirically evaluated in-the field) some experimental Low-Fi prototypes of applications that operate in an integrated system of interfaces that connote pervasive iTV (typically mobile phones, PCs and iTV). Thirty users aged between eighteen and sixty years old, with a peripatetic lifestyle and with mixed cultural and professional backgrounds have taken part in this evaluation.

4 Review of Results

Unsurprisingly, this research uncovered a scarce users' appeal in having broadcasting of traditional TV (or iTV) formats on their mobile phones (except some exceptions such as brief life updates of a decisive football match or extraordinary news). Mobile and pervasive interactive multimedia systems will have to do with issues such as socialibility [9], context awareness, creativity, interactivity [12], convergence (iTV, mobile phones, in-car-navigators & Internet) and connectivity (one to one and one to many). Therefore the concept of mobile and pervasive multimedia systems will likely have more to do with the emerging of mobile communities that are a sort of 'DIY producers' of multimedia content: they will create multimedia content in specific contexts and with precise purposes and share it with others. Moreover, the questionnaires, observations and focus groups revealed two main categories of users in terms of sending multimedia messages (photo/video with or without text & sound).

The first one regards the spontaneous or impulsive user (e.g. when traveling, during an exciting night out, when sighting an interesting thing, place or performance, or just to update on domestic issues such as children, new partner, etc). The addressees of these messages are the members of the user's restricted social personal circle: family, friends & colleagues. The second one – much less frequent in older users – is about the reiterative or structured user (e.g. mob blogs). Here the addressees belong to a broader social circle such as enlarged communities.

Also identified were users' preferences when receiving multimedia content on their handset from people, places or things: 'If on the move, better if related to my context'. Context awareness provides customized information that can be defined as the right information in the right place and in the right time. The cultural probes showed clearly the desire of users to access to multimedia content on their handhelds with two main purposes: as an enhanced democratic tool (e.g. voting on public issues or having '5 minutes of fame') and to leave their 'signature' along the way (e.g. by putting down personal digital content on public digital boards).

Therefore the definition of mobile or pervasive multimedia content will likely have more to do with the emerging of mobile communities that are a sort of 'DIY producers' (they will create content in multimedia formats and share it with others) rather than a sort of mobile TV.

5 Users' Generated Content

It is quite obvious how mobile devices are limited as broadcasting interfaces. As testing with users aged 18-25 in Milan have proven, their small size makes difficult for the user to follow a long video even with the newest multimedia mobile phones [2].

However, recent technological developments in handsets have converted them into tools for creation, editing and diffusion of multimedia content. The last mobile phones are endowed with large screen, colour display, photo and video camera, and with functionalities as MMS, video call, image, sound and video editing software.

As an intrinsic characteristic to these interfaces, all these operations can be done in any place, time and environment. This freedom of action for the user can be interpreted as a scenario of ubiquitous multimedia interaction. Since the earliest days of cinema, artists and technologists have dreamt of a future in which everyone could create and share their vision of the world. With the evolution of ubiquitous mobile networks and the enhanced mobile handset as creative device, we are on the cusp of realizing improvisational media fabrics as an active expression in our daily lives.

At the same time, the new nomad generation will benefit from interactive TV systems not only playing an active role in interacting with TV programs. The most challenging aspect of iTV is found in the one-to-one connectivity that the media will enable. This attribute will allow users to become a sort of 'home-made producers' of multimedia content. They will be able to create and share their own contents (mainly in multimedia format) and share them with other users. The diffusion of fast wireless data networks raises interesting possibilities for the use of video. Media firms, with their countless hours of programming content, clearly sense opportunities for "Ubiquitous TV," and yet future demand for traditional mass-media content over personal wireless devices is far from predictable. Even with powerful user profiling and customized programming, there are reasons to believe that "personal video" exchanged between friends, colleagues, and family will be a bigger driver of the technology than "TV" content.

Other strong evidence for personal video exchange in informal groups to occur is regarding the retention of intellectual property and media regulation, where users groups (such as friends and family) operate in more informal systems and fall outside public jurisdiction.

Handhelds will play a crucial role in scenarios of ubiquitous broad and narrowcasting, or better 'ubiquitous interactive broad and narrowcasting'. Multimedia mobile-phones can be used to create and to receive reality TV programs. Moblogging is a new phenomenon where users can use their mobile phones to send their own multimedia content in form of MMS (e.g. regarding their travels, cooking recipes, etc.) to a broadcaster who will moderate and edit them into a certain program and then deliver it across iTV, mobile phones or Internet. Another feasible scenario is that the user itself can edit the content and narrowcast to specific users of an informal small community like friends and family or common interest communities e.g. amateur photography group. In a third possible scenario users can store their multimedia files in shared repositories and interested users can upload the wanted files from time to time.

At the other end, receivers will be able to reply to the senders with a SMS, Email or messenger across the iTV, Internet of a mobile phone. It will be also possible for viewers to save or send a received video to other users.

In these new scenarios, users are not passive viewers but actors, or better, producers. According to them it is easy to imagine formats for games within the ambit of 'reality TV', where users will be able to produce the contents by themselves. Considering Gibson's concept of cyberspace, as a real non-space world, characterized by the ability for virtual presence of, and interaction between people through 'icons, waypoints and artificial realities'. This conception of cyberspace is a peculiar urban space [7], where real experiences and socio-economic conflicts take place [5]. In this new ubiquitous gaming scenario, users will design the elements of the cyberspace [1] where the game takes place, being designers and actors at the same time. This passage from passive viewers to actors, and finally to authors (producers) characterizes the iTV social revolution.

5.1 Evolution of Digital Content

Digital content will undergo dramatic change in the next ten years. It will evolve from simple authoring, editing, displaying and proofing environments to "smart" content that is interactive, clustered, predictive, contextual and proximity sensitive, and accessible on the move. Using speech, surround sound and seamless real and synthetic images, it will enable a highly interactive and visual user experience. Today, the interactivity with systems like digital TV and radio or with mobile devices is more about handling files or streaming media, not going much beyond smart menus. In the future, based on digital cross-media platforms, interactivity should be more about the user-control of objects and sequences within the file or content stream.

In the next decade, we could envisage an interactive infrastructure where digital content flows from multiple sources, over different pipelines, is created and stored in many formats and data types, is processed, purposed and enriched for different contexts and different audiences and is displayable on a wide range of devices.

Each interface (PC, iTV, mobile phone, PDA, car navigator, etc.) has its own characteristics from both the interactive (screen size, resolution, etc.) and the technical viewpoints (memory, transfer. info speed, processing capability, etc) and its own business systems. HCI designers, thus, need to know the most suitable service formats and the distinctive interaction patterns for each interface [17], towards optimizing its usability. They are also compelled to preserve the unity of the service they design (e.g. in terms of recognisability by communicating one coherent identity) and, enhance the interoperability of all its features. This will represent new challenges to current business models ranging from innovative collaborative work to competition in the business market and new systems of media production.

Therefore, to be able to express all the potentiality of the new interactive system in this prospected new scenario of ubiquitous communication, and, more specifically in the case of ubiquitous gaming, content will need to evolve towards new forms including virtual objects, multi-user environments and immersive, animated content.

It will need to be smart, automated, multi-channel and multi-format content, flexible, affective [19] cost-effective and device-independent digital content, context dependent content.

6 Conclusions

Recent technological developments in handsets transform them into tools for creation, editing and diffusion of personalized and personal multimedia content on a ubiquitous network. It is not difficult to imagine how when these mobile devices intersect with i-TV will contribute to create a scenario of ubiquitous gaming. This new scenario requires change in production processes, creating adequate design to new technological as well as social contexts.

In order to address complex issues such as understanding, emotion, security, trust and privacy, the data gathering techniques presented in this paper focus on users rather than on their tasks or objectives with the analyzed interfaces. This research shows how the physical and social contexts have a strong impact in the users' attitudes towards mobile interactive multimedia applications: the context influences in a positive or negative way the users' emotions and feelings towards the interaction process, persuading or discouraging its use.

Surprisingly, this research uncovered a scarce users' appeal in having broadcasting of traditional TV formats on their mobile phones (except some exceptions such as brief life updates of a decisive football match or extraordinary news). Therefore the definition of mobile or pervasive iTV will likely have more to do with the emerging of mobile communities that are a sort of 'DIY producers' of multimedia content: they will create content in multimedia formats and share it with others. Therefore the concept of mobile and pervasive multimedia systems will likely have more to do with the emerging of mobile communities that are a sort of 'DIY producers' of multimedia content: they will create multimedia content in specific contexts and with precise purposes and share it with others.

References

1. Benedikt, M.: Cyberspace. First step. MIT Press, MA (1991)
2. Cereijo Roibás, A. et al.: How will mobile devices contribute to an accessible ubiquitous iTV scenario. In: Proceedings of the 2nd International Conference on Universal Access in Human - Computer Interaction (ICUAHCI), Crete (2003)
3. Dourish, P.: Where the Action Is: The Foundations of Embodied Interaction. MIT Press, Cambridge, MA, USA (2001)
4. Gaver, W., Martin, H.: Alternatives: exploring information appliances through conceptual design proposals. CHI 2000, pp. 209–216 (2000)
5. Gibson, W.: Neuromancer, Ace Books New York, NY (1984)
6. Harper, R.: People versus Information: The Evolution of Mobile Technology. In: Chittaro, L. (ed.) Mobile HCI 2003. LNCS, vol. 2795, pp. 1–15. Springer, Heidelberg (2003)
7. Kneale, J.: The Virtual Realities of Technology and Fiction: Reading William Gibson's Cyberspace. In: Crang, M., et al. (eds.) Virtual Geographies: Bodies, Space and Relations, pp. 205–221. Routledge, London (1999)

8. Laurel, B.: Computers as Theatre. Addison-Wesley Publishing Company, Reading, MA (1991)
9. Lull, J.: The social uses of television. In: Human Communication Research, 6(3) (1980)
10. McCarthy, J., Wright, P.: Technology as experience. MIT Press, Cambridge (2004)
11. Morley, D.: Family Television. Cultural Power and Domestic Leisure. Comedia, London (1986)
12. Palen, L., Salzman, M., Youngs, E.: Going Wireless: Behavior of Practices of New Mobile Phone Users. In: proc CSCW 2000, pp. 201–210 (2000)
13. Perry, M., O'Hara, K., Sellen, A., Harper, R., Brown, B.A.T.: Dealing with mobility: understanding access anytime, anywhere. ACM Transactions on Computer-Human Interaction (ToCHI) 4(8), 1–25 (2001)
14. Picard, R.: Affective Computing. MIT Press, Boston, MA (2000)
15. Spigel, L.: Make Room for TV: Television and the Family Ideal in Postwar America. Chicago, U Chicago P (1992)
16. Wasson, C.: Collaborative work: integrating the roles of ethnographers and designers. In: Squires, S., Byrne, B. (eds.): Creating breakthrough ideas: the collaboration of anthropologists and designers in the product development industry, Westport: Bergin Garvey (2002)
17. Weiss, S.: Handheld Usability. Wiley, New York (2002)

Media Convergence, an Introduction

Sepideh Chakaveh and Manfred Bogen

Fraunhofer Institute IAIS
Schloss Birlinghoven, Sankt Augustin, Germany

Abstract. Media convergence is a theory in communications where every mass medium eventually merges to the point where they become one medium due to the advent of new communication technologies. The Media Convergence research theme normally refers to entire production, distribution, and use process of future digital media services from contents production to service delivery through various channels such as mobile terminals, digital TV, or the Internet.

1 Introduction

According to the theory of media convergence, very soon, there will be no more need for having a television and a computer separate from each other, since both would be able to do the job of the other, ultimately making both extinct and creating a new medium from the synthesis.

From technical point of view the core research topics include content management (contents production, archival, indexing, structuring, semantics), service management, and content delivery (content adaptation, XML technologies). Moreover special research focus is on machine-process able semantics, i.e., representing data and knowledge in such a way that machines can "understand" its meaning, and developing algorithmic methods for creating intelligent applications based on such representations.

The unique thing about television is that television is both a medium and a transmission system. That is to say that television is used to refer to the screen that you watch, as well as what you see on that screen. The Internet on the other hand is a system for transmitting bits, and is different from the device which receives those bits, the computer. For this debate we will consider the content of the Internet to be primarily World Wide Web style content and an extension thereof. In other words, multimedia pages with dynamic content including audio and video clips as well as 3D scene rendering.

Another special focus is on user-created content that often is created, managed, and distributed by a community of users.

2 Strategies Behind Media Convergence

Next to technical concepts postulated which should eventually be implemented, media convergence is an economic strategy in which communications companies seek

J. Jacko (Ed.): Human-Computer Interaction, Part III, HCII 2007, LNCS 4552, pp. 811–814, 2007.

financial benefit by making the various media properties they own work together. The strategy is a product of three elements:

1. corporate concentration, whereby fewer large companies own more and more media properties;
2. digitization, whereby media content produced in a universal computer language can be easily adapted for use in any medium; and
3. government deregulation, which has increasingly allowed media conglomerates to own different kinds of media (e.g., television and radio stations and newspapers) in the same markets, and which has permitted content carriage companies (e.g., cable TV suppliers) to own content producers (e.g., specialty TV channels). The strategy allows companies to reduce labour, administrative and material costs, to use the same media content across several media outlets, to attract increased advertising by providing advertisers with package deals and one-stop shopping for a number of media platforms, and to increase brand recognition and brand loyalty among audiences through cross-promotion and cross-selling. At the same time, it raises significantly the barriers to newcomers seeking to enter media markets, thus limiting competition for converged companies.

Historically, communications companies have formed newspaper chains and networks of radio and TV stations to realize many of these same advantages, and convergence can be seen as the expansion and intensification of this same logic.

AOL Time Warner in the United States is seen as a model for media convergence. Time Inc. and Warner Brothers first merged in 1989, creating the world's largest media and entertainment company with its complementary properties in magazine publishing, music recording, film production and distribution. AOL subsequently bought Time Warner in January 2001 in an attempt to expand the Time Warner synergies to the global computer network called the Internet.

A number of Canadian media companies have moved in the same direction since 2000. The telephone company BCE Inc., for example, has expanded into television, with the purchase of the national CTV network; newspaper publishing, with the acquisition of *The Globe and Mail*; and new media, with a family of World Wide Web sites. CanWest Global Communications Corp. has added to its national Global television network by acquiring television stations in Australia, New Zealand, Ireland and Northern Ireland, daily and weekly newspapers across Canada, film and television production and distribution properties in Canada, the U.S. and Great Britain, radio stations in Canada and New Zealand, and a national Internet portal. Quebecor Inc. has newspapers, magazines and book publishing companies, the cable TV and Internet service provider Videotron, six of ten stations in the TVA French-language television network, the Radiomedia radio network and the CANOE Internet portal. Besides being Canada's largest cable television provider, Rogers Communications Inc. is involved in television broadcasting, wireless telephone service, magazine publishing and video sales and rentals.

While most of the promised financial benefits of convergence have yet to be realized by media owners, some of the social costs are already apparent. Media content is increasingly treated as a product like any other, and notions of public service take a back seat to private enterprise. The substantial costs of corporate mergers have led converged companies to seek profits through cost-cutting rather than increased investment in communication services. The market power exerted by corporate giants such as BCE, CanWest Global, Quebecor and Rogers makes it increasingly difficult for new corporate players to compete and reduces the number of choices media consumers face in deciding among information and entertainment sources. In the news media particularly, newsroom staffs have been substantially reduced and journalists are being asked to produce more stories each day, stories which can be used by more than one news medium. This trend has the potential to reduce the quantity, the quality and the diversity of news coverage.

Convergent technology, which can provide one with text, still pictures, moving pictures, sound, search - in fact, anything till very recently one needed multiple devices to receive - has been a possibility for some time. But it is only now becoming a reality. In this case for instant one can upload and search videos via the all-powerful search engine.

Recent research activities at Fraunhofer Institute has considered several interesting possibilities. This include voice-activating and artificial intelligent activated content. In the future, it will be possible for instance for a television set or PC to audio-recognise what the viewer is watching (as it will "listen in") while interacting with the content and informing the viewer with similar types of content, using emails or mms. In addition a special focus is given to apply mixed reality (virtual & real) events in media convergence.

Moreover not in a very distance, one reaches a point of consolidation when the pace of technological change slows and the audience catches up, but at the moment most companies with both offline and online enterprises still see the vast majority of their revenues and costs lying with their traditional, offline businesses. Yet they are increasingly aware that this will tip in the opposite direction in the middle distance.

An attempt to address how to overcome this challenge has been considered by many media companies for some time now. Their part assumptions about the dominant medium, be it print or TV, is that they will both be transferred to some newly converged online world without adequate and relevance to recognise that the two are completely different entities.

3 Content Is Key

Content has emerged as king in the fierce battle of television channels. The success of channel is dependent on the quality of content, which attracts the attention of an audience. The content would drive the success of the channel.

Content has high recyclable value, no storage cost and can be exported. A successful and good quality content has high recyclable value and can also be delivered through various delivery mechanisms such as Compact Disc, and Web Casting.

Current original programming is 5 hour per day per channel and with the competition intensifying it could be increased to seven hours/day/channel. This would translate into substantial opportunity of the content providers. As the industry experience suggests, the average production by a content producer is six to eight hour a week. this translates into an opportunity for 35 producers in the current demand scenario and more to join the fray.

The content is shown either on terrestrial or C&S Network . the popularity of content depends upon the understanding of the audience and making the right genre of program for the target audience. The availability of intellect and low manpower cost has made the Indian content popular world over and exports of content has opened a new revenue stream for the content provider.

A good quality content has a recyclable value, can be exported and can add to the revenue stream of the IPR holder. The content producers working with DD have built up a substantial library (IPR) of content and are exploring the same.

The merger between telecommunications, computer and broadcasting is going to change the way people will work, play and live.

The 'convergence' of these technologies has given birth to the prospect of multimedia services which will offer interactive compute based applications that will combine text, graphics, audio and animation features into a media experience for users.

4 Conclusion

The increasingly competitive environment in the multimedia industry promises tremendous user benefits through increased savings in time, greater choice, and an explosion of innovative services and products. This is the promise, to date, truly interactive services allowing the viewer to descend through a series of levels of information are still at the experimental stage.

The development of multimedia services will not replace judgment value that is provided by the traditional media. Hence, the traditional media will still have a large role to play in the new multimedia world.

Multimedia has the potential to vastly increase the range of services available, and offer its users a larger choice of applications but new technology alone will not ensure success; it is the people who use it who will decide the future of multimedia. The users' wants and needs; how they will manage the flood of options; and, above all, whether or not they will pay for the freedom of choice are what counts.

An Improved H.264 Error Concealment Algorithm with User Feedback Design

Xiaoming Chen and Yuk Ying Chung

School of Information Technologies, University of Sydney
NSW 2006, Australia
{xche2902,vchung}@it.usyd.edu.au

Abstract. This paper proposes a new Error Concealment (EC) method for the H.264/AVC [1] video coding standard using both spatial and temporal information for intra-frame concealment. Five error concealing modes are offered by this method. The proposed EC method also allows feedback from users. It allows users to define and change the thresholds for switching between five different modes during the error concealing procedure. As a result, the concealing result for a video sequence can be optimized by taking advantage of relevant user feedback. The concealed video quality has been measured by a group of users and compared with the H.264 EC method which is without user feedback. The experimental results show that the proposed new EC algorithm with the user feedback performs better (3 dB gains) than the H.264 EC without user feedback.

Keywords: H.264, Error Concealment, User Feedback, Video Compression.

1 Introduction

Human eyes are highly sensitive to picture (video frame) distortions. For instance, noises introduced into video frame when transmitted through the error-prone channel; spatial information missing caused by the package loss during video transmission; edge distortions (including both impairments on existing edges and the creation of false edges)[2] caused by failed motion compensation and etc. These problems are especially more difficult to be solved for real-time applications while the retransmission of the video is not applicable. As a result, reliable real-time transmission of compressed video data in error-prone wireless networks is a challenging task. In video communications over error-prone environments, compressed video is extremely fragile to transmission errors which may results in the video quality being seriously degraded. On one hand, the wireless networks introduce vast amounts of random and burst bit errors due to fading, signal attenuations, and co-channel interference[3]. On the other hand, the compressed video utilizes the Variable Length Coding (VLC) technique therefore is extremely susceptible to channel noises. Error Concealment (EC) is an alternative way to solve these problems. Error concealment makes use of the redundancies that remain in temporal or spatial domain and tries to recover the lost data based on the received data.

J. Jacko (Ed.): Human-Computer Interaction, Part III, HCII 2007, LNCS 4552, pp. 815–820, 2007.

Typically there are two types of error concealment algorithms: spatial error concealment and temporal error concealment. Spatial error concealment exploits the spatially correlated information around the missing part of the video while the temporal error concealment utilize the similarity exists between the successive frames. As a non-normative feature in the H.264 test model, the EC at decoder side is one of the error-resilient tools that implemented in the H.264 standard. The advantage of EC is that it can be independent to the encoding process and it does not require any modification to the H.264 standard.

However, the standard EC methods do not provide user-feedback mechanism. This paper will study the feasibility of incorporating user feedback into EC procedure to achieve better objective and subjective video quality. The H.264/AVC is chosen as the video coding tool for testing. A group of users were involved into the evaluation of the proposed EC method.

2 H.264 Coding Standard

H.264 is the denomination of ITU-T's most recent video codec recommendation. It is also known as MPEG-4 Advanced Video Codec (AVC) [1]. In 2001, the Joint Video Team (JVT) formed by the ITU-T Video Coding Experts Group (VCEG) and the ISO/IEC Moving Picture Experts Group (MPEG) started to develop the new H.264 video coding standard with higher coding efficiency and better network adaptation (channel error resilient) capability. The final draft of H.264/AVC was completed in 2003. So far the H.264 is the video coding standard that outperforms all other standards in terms of compression ratio and network friendliness. With the same video quality, the coding efficiency of the H.264 can be double when compared with MPEG4 and four times when compared with MPEG2 [4].

3 Proposed EC Algorithm

In the H.264 reference EC implementation has several disadvantages. Firstly the user feedback is not allowed. Secondly, only spatial information is used to conceal intra-frames. Thirdly, the concealment in the reference implementation is applied on 16x16 macroblocks which is not accurate enough for EC in small-size pictures. The proposed new EC method for intra-frame allows user feedback, and uses both of the temporal and spatial information. The macroblock is divided into small subblocks so that one part of a macroblock can be concealed using temporal information and other part of this macroblock can be spatially concealed using the temporally concealed part.

In the proposed EC algorithm, there will be a user-defined threshold for each EC mode. These thresholds are depending on the smoothness of the recovered area, which is measured by Average Border Error (ABE). If the error concealment result of a segment of video exceeds the threshold of the current mode, the decoder will ignore the current mode and go to the next mode to do the error concealment.

Based on the degree of satisfaction for the error-concealed video, the users are allowed to change these thresholds in order to obtain the best recovered video quality. Since the threshold values depend on spatial smoothness of the error-concealed region, it indicates that the higher threshold value will have more temporal information and less spatial information used for EC and vice versa. If temporal information is used in EC, when the video contains frequent scene cuts, the lower threshold value will have higher chance to achieve better concealment results.

When a corrupted macroblock(MB) is detected, the proposed algorithm will select one or more concealment modes from the followings based on the user feedback:

(a) TRP: Temporal RePlacement from the spatially corresponding position in the previous frame. If the Average Border Error (ABE) between the corrupted MB and the subsitute MB is less than the user defined threshold, the TRP will be adopted, otherwise proceed to (b). The ABE is defined as:

$$ABE = \frac{1}{N}\sum_{i=1}^{N}\left|P_i^{IN} - P_i^{OUT}\right|$$

While N is the total number of the calculated boundary pixels; P_i^{IN} is the ith inner boundary pixel of the replacing MB; and P_i^{OUT} is the ith outer boundary pixel of the surrounding MBs of the corrupted MB.

(b) 16BM: 16x16 Boundary Matching concealment from previous frame. The 4 outer-borders of the corrupted MB are used to search within a small range (typical values are 32x32 pixels) in the previous frame in order to match a substitute MB to replace the corrupted MB. The substitute MB is the MB that minimizes the sum of squared border errors between the corrupted MB and the substitute MB in the previous frame. If the substitute MB cannot be found (that means ABE exceeds user defined threshold), proceed to (c).

(c) 8BM: 8x8 Boundary Matching concealment from previous frame. The corrupted MB is divided into four 8x8 subblocks. The decoder then will try to find substitutes for each subblock. If the substitute for a subblock can not be found, this subblock will be passed to (d) or (e).

(d) 16DI: 16x16 DIrectional spatial error concealment within the same frame. The edge tendency of the corrupted MB is estimated and quantized into 8 directions. Directional pixel interpolation is applied to the corrupted MB using the borders of the neighboring MBs of the corrupted MB.

(e) 8DI: 8x8x Directional Spatial error concealment. The directional trend of the 8x8 subblock is estimated from its neighbouring MBs. And directional interpolation is applied to the subblock using outer borders of its neighboring MBs and virtual inner borders constructed by 8BM if any.

The cooperation of the provided EC modes can be further explained in Fig.1.

The central region is a corrupted MB, SB0-SB3 is the 4 8x8 subblocks of the corrupted MB; and MB0-MB7 are its neighbouring MBs. 0-7 (as shown in the Fig.1) are the outer borders and 8-11 are the perceptual inner borders for the missing MB.

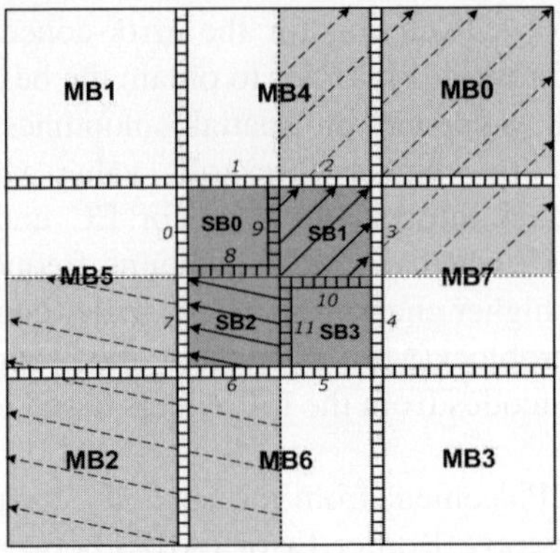

Fig. 1. The proposed new EC modes

The decoder will use TRP by default. If the TRP could not apply (that means it exceeds user-defined threshold) the 16BM will then be tried. After that, the decoder will apply 8BM. In Fig.1, the decoder successfully finds the substitutions for SB0 and SB3 in the previous frame, so SB0 and SB3 will be temporally concealed. After concealing SB0 and SB3, the "virtual" inner borders 8, 9, 10 and 11 can be constructed. As the corrupted MB is subdivided into smaller blocks, the 16DI will be ignored. The last step is applying 8DI, the edge directions of SB1 and SB2 will be estimated (e.g. direction of SB1 will be estimated using MB0, right half of MB4 and top half of MB7), then the SB1 will be concealed using it's outer boundary 2, 3 in the current frame and the virtually constructed inner boundary 9, 10 with respect to its estimated direction trend. Similarly, the SB2 is concealed using borders 6, 7, 8 and 11.

4 Experimental Results

The standard video testing sequences: foreman, carphone and stefan are chosen to conduct the evaluation. They are all in QCIF format containing 400, 372 and 300 frames respectively. These videos are encoded using JM8 of the H.264/AVC release. To simulate the error-prone network conditions, the proposed EC algorithm has been evaluated when the MB loss rates are 5%, 10%, 15% and 20%. Both subjective and objective evaluations have been conducted. The Peak Signal Noise Ratio (PSNR) was used for subjective evaluation, the subjective results are presented in Table 1. The objective evaluation was conducted as follows: A group of users were invited to evaluate the video quality. The group will consist of both experts in image processing and people have little knowledge in image or video processing. When viewing the concealed videos, each user is allowed to change the threshold values until they are satisfied or admitted with the best possible video quality. The Degree Of Satisfactory (DOS) of the video quality is classified into 5 levels: Excellent, Good, Acceptable, Bad and Very Bad. The DOSs are then recorded and compared with the default concealment method without user feedbacks. The objective results (average results obtained from the group of users) are shown in Table 2.

Table 1. Subjective Results: PSNR calculated

Test Seq.	Original PSNR (in dB)	Loss Rate	PSNRJM (in dB)	PSNRPRO (in dB)
Foreman	35.88	5%	31.19	34.93
		10%	29.13	33.74
		15%	28.21	33.04
		20%	27.41	32.63
Trevor	37.17	5%	34.32	36.06
		10%	31.59	34.43
		15%	30.94	34.14
		20%	29.60	32.61
Carphone	37.17	5%	33.17	35.44
		10%	31.28	34.40
		15%	29.67	32.32
		20%	29.01	33.45
Stefan	34.97	5%	32.30	33.46
		10%	30.20	32.65
		15%	29.18	30.86
		20%	28.60	30.26

PSNRJM – PSNR obtained by the original H.264 algorithm without user feedback
PSNRPRO – PSNR obtained by the proposed algorithm

Table 2. Object Results: DOS by a group of users

Noise Ratio	EC Algorithms	DOS				
		Excellent	Good	Acceptable	Bad	Very Bad
5%	DOSJM		✓			
	DOSPRO	✓				
10%	DOSJM			✓		
	DOSPRO	✓				
15%	DOSJM				✓	
	DOSPRO		✓			
20%	DOSJM				✓	
	DOSPRO			✓		

DOSJM - DOS obtained by the original H.264 algorithm without user feedback
DOSPRO - DOS obtained by the original H.264 algorithm without user feedback

5 Summary and Conclusion

This paper proposes an Error Concealment (EC) method for the H.264/AVC video coding standard. The proposed EC method utilizes available spatial information and temporal information to conceal the corrupted regions in 8x8 subblock level instead of MB level. Several concealing methods are provided by the EC method. Subjective and objective experiments are conducted to evaluate the proposed algorithm. The experimental results show that by using these different modes provided and taking the user feedback into accounts, the proposed EC method can perform better and have 3 dB gains compared with the H.264 EC without user feedback.

References

1. Wiegand, T., Sullivan, G.J., Bjntegaard, G., Luthra, A.: Overview of the H.264/AVC video coding standard. IEEE Trans. on Circuits Syst. Video Technol 13(7), 560–576 (2003)
2. Ong, E., Lin, W., Lu, Z., Yao, S., Etoh, M.: Visual distortion assessment with emphasis on spatially transitional regions. IEEE Trans. on Circuits Syst. Video Technol. 14(e 4), 559–566 (2004)
3. Sklar, B.: Rayleigh fading channels in mobile digital communication systems.I. Characterization. IEEE Commun. Mag. 35(7), 90–100 (1997)
4. Ostermann, J., et al.: Video Coding with H.264/AVC: Tools, Performance and Complexity. IEEE Circuits And Systems Magazine 4(1), 7–28 (2004)
5. Varsa, V., Hannuksela, M.M., Wang, Y.K.: Nonnormative error concealment algorithms, ITU-T VCEC-N62 (2001)

Classification of a Person Picture and Scenery Picture Using Structured Simplicity

Myoung-Bum Chung and Il-Ju Ko

Department of Media, Soongsil University,
SangDo-Dong Dongjak-Gu Seoul Korea
{nzin,andy}@ssu.ac.kr

Abstract. We can classify various images as either people pictures, if they contain one or more persons, or scenery pictures, if they lack people, by using face region detection. However, the precision of a picture's classification is low if it uses existing face region detection technique. This paper proposes the algorithm about structured simplicity of the picture to do classification with higher accuracy. To verify the usefulness of an offer method, we did a classification experiment which uses 500 people pictures and scenery pictures. The experiment to use only face region detection in Open CV showed an accuracy of 79% detection rate. While the experiment to use face region detection in structured simplicity with Open CV showed an accuracy of 86.4%. Therefore by using structured simplicity with face region detection, we can do an efficient picture classification of a person picture and scenery picture.

Keywords: Face region detection, Picture classification, Structured simplicity.

1 Introduction

Recently, there has been concern about content processing technique as various multimedia techniques advanced. A lot of research has been focused on image processing techniques over living body recognition (face recognition, iris recognition, fingerprint identification, etc) and content manufacturing (image composition, movie manufacture, etc). Living body recognition technique can be useful for identification by classifying a person in a suspect retrieval system and an identity authentication of entrance and exit control system: [1-3].

Existing face recognition technology is divided into face region detection and face recognition. Face region detection method uses a color analysis to compare skin color reference map which is made beforehand in a color space. Face region detection method uses the following these: YCbCr, Hue/Red, and Log-opponent: [4-7]. Intel company offered Open CV (Open Source Computer Vision: A real-time computer image program whose library is open source) as various techniques advanced. Open CV can recognize object, face, and behavior, and is useful for face region recognition: [8].

Face region detection can be used for identity authentication, face recognition, as well as automatic picture classification. The picture is divided into two classes: a people picture and a scenery picture. We can classify a people picture when there are

J. Jacko (Ed.): Human-Computer Interaction, Part III, HCII 2007, LNCS 4552, pp. 821–828, 2007.

people in the picture and a scenery picture when there are no people in the picture. Existing face region detection tries to find a face region when there are people in the picture. However, face region detection also tries to find a face region in a scenery picture which there is no people in the picture. This causes errors in identification when similar colors or forms emerge.

This paper proposes the algorithm about structured simplicity of the picture for picture classification. This can classify as a people picture and scenery picture. When we take a people picture, we don't pay attention to the place or structure. In contrast, when we take a scenery picture, we think about the color, structure, and place. The probability which a scenery picture has the feature point of a picture structure is high. We can rescue structured simplicity from such a feature point. Structured simplicity means the simplicity rate of a color structure in the picture and can be used to distinguish a people picture and scenery picture. At the same time we check whether there are the people in the picture using face region detection in Open CV. Therefore if we use structured simplicity with Open CV, we can do efficient picture classification.

The rest of the paper is organized as follows: Section 2 reviews the related work on face region detection. Section 3 explains a proposal way for the structured simplicity. Section 4 does the reference about a combination rate of Open CV and structured simplicity. Section 5 analyzes with experiment about the structured simplicity that is proposed. Finally, Section 6 provides our conclusions.

2 Paper Preparation

The method of the face region detection is the trend to be becoming variety such as color, terrain characteristic, statistic, template conformer. The one method is use color analysis. This is to compare color in the picture with color map to be made in the color space. This shows the performance to be good for the size and direction of the face. However, this has the defect to take big influence at the lighting. The other method is the method to base at a terrain feature of the face. This extracts a main component of the face such as eye, nose and mouth. And this extracts a face region from main component's interrelations through the study. This can extract a face region although the face comes to hide partially or slants. But, this is difficult that the interrelation among face elements is determined to the rule and made the algorithm.

In this paper we describe simply about log-opponent detection, Hue/Red detection, and face detection method of Open CV.

Log-opponent method is the method to use a skin filter of Fleck from an input image. This converts R, G and B of the images into I, R_g and B_y of log-opponent color representation (1), (2).

$$L(x) = 105 \times \log_{10}(x + 1 + n) \tag{1}$$

$$I = L(G),\ R_g = L(R) - L(G),$$
$$B_y = L(B) - \frac{L(G) + L(R)}{2} \tag{2}$$

At this time the n value expresses the random noise to exist between 0 and 1. The color value (H) and chroma value (S) comes to get from (3).

$$H = \tan^{-1}(R_g / B_y),\ S = \sqrt{R_g^2 + B_y^2} \tag{3}$$

We compare H, S value with the color value to correspond to the skin color of the people. And we detect a face region of an input image from marking all pixels value. The skin color of people is color=[110, 150], chroma=[20, 60] or color= [130,170], chroma=[30, 130].

Hue/Red method is the method to use R to a skin color detection factor. To use R is because the skin color is bigger the relation of R than G and B. Fig 1 is to express RGB distribution of the skin color in RGB space.

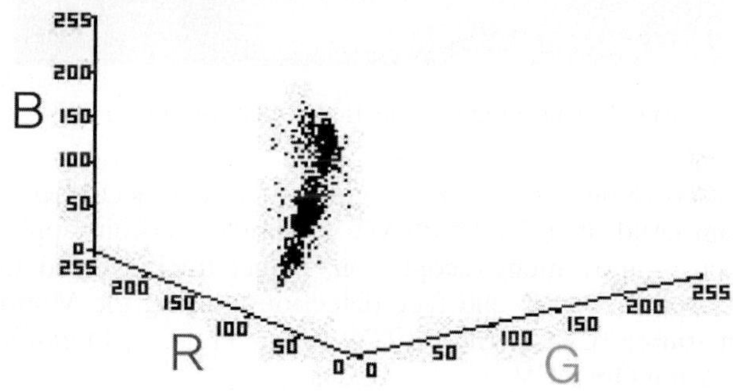

Fig. 1. A skin color distribution of the RGB space

RGB image can separate intensity easily in color information to reduce the influence of a lighting change in a skin color processing. And RGB image converts to HSI color space to detect various skin colors efficiently. So, we exclude I that is sensitive to the change of the lighting in HIS color space and S that is to detect various skin color in a skin color detection element.

$$H = \cos^{-1}\left[\frac{\frac{1}{2}[(R-G)+(R-B)]}{\sqrt{(R-G)^2+(R-B)(G-B)}}\right] \tag{4}$$

Equation (4) is the expression to get H, when we convert RGB color space to HIS color space. Hue/Red method detects the skin color from the rate of H and R to get in (4).

Open CV is an abbreviation for Open Source Computer Vision Library which is made by Intel Corporation. It is provided to Standard Dynamic Link Library (DLL) or Static Library form which is a low function for the image processing. It is implemented basic functions as well as function algorithms of a high level for the image processing. The functions of Open CV are composed of the Intel Image Processing Library (IPL).

Fig. 2. A face region detection which uses Open CV

Open CV is used in an application program such as object, face, movement, and motion detection. And it is supported a computer vision application program development such as movement recognition, object tracking, and face recognition. Currently, it released to Beta-5 and face detection is using the Motion Analysis and Object Tracking source (CBCH file) at CV group. Fig. 2 is to extract a face region from the picture using Open CV.

3 Structured Simplicity of the Picture (SSP)

The picture is divided to people picture and scenery picture generally. We used SSP and face region detection for a picture classification in this paper. SSP is to classify the picture efficiently as algorithm which proposes in this paper. It is the method to think about that people pay attention the place, composition, color and etc when they take the scenery picture. It finds the feature of a picture structure and changes the feature into the numerical value. A people picture takes around the people without thinking about the color or composition. On the other hand, a scenery picture takes around the composition or disposition of the color. Especially, the difference about the top and bottom of a scenery picture appears greatly in the color. We can calculate the difference of the color to the numerical value. This is SSP and is calculated as follows.

First, we must get a color complexity to get SSP. A color complexity is calculated by dividing the picture into nine parts. Each area to be divided calculates a difference average about all pixels like (5).

$$\sum_{i=2}^{m-1}\sum_{j=2}^{n-1}\frac{1}{8}\Big(\left|p_{ij}-p_{(i-1)(j-1)}\right|+\left|p_{ij}-p_{(i-1)j}\right|+\left|p_{ij}-p_{(i-1)(j+1)}\right|+ \left|p_{ij}-p_{i(j-1)}\right|+\left|p_{ij}-p_{i(j+1)}\right|+\left|p_{ij}-p_{(i+1)(j-1)}\right|+ \left|p_{ij}-p_{(i+1)j}\right|+\left|p_{ij}-p_{(i+1)(j+1)}\right|\Big) \tag{5}$$

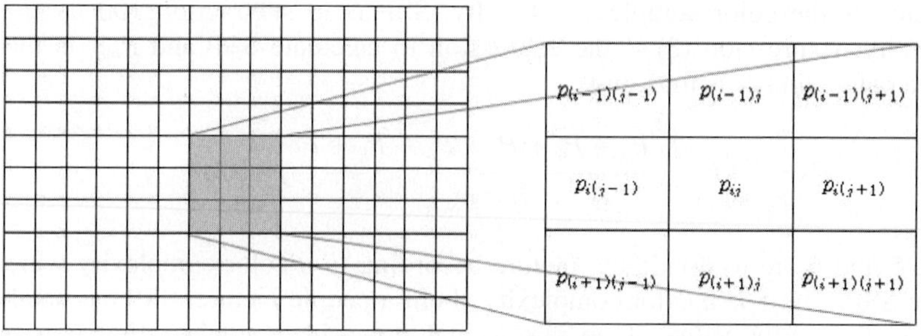

Fig. 3. The pixel expression to calculate color complexity

Fig. 3 is to express the pixel which is to calculate color complexity.

An each area to be divided calculates a complexity of the area. If a complexity is over the fixed value, we divide again into nine parts and calculate a complexity of the new area recursively. We can get the number of panes in each area which uses the complexity. A character *a*, *b*, *c*, *d*, *e*, *f*, *g*, *h* and *i* of Fig. 4 is the number of panes in each area.

We calculate the complexity about the area of the picture from each pane numbers at (6) and (7). Expression (6) is a complexity about the *d*, *e*, *f*, *g*, *h* and *i* of the *a* area. We calculate the complexity about *b* and *c* using (6). And we calculate the complexity about *g*, *h* and *i* using (7).

$$P_a = \left| a - \frac{d+g}{2} \right| + \left| a - \frac{e+h}{2} \right| + \left| a - \frac{f+i}{2} \right| \tag{6}$$

$$P_g = \left| g - \frac{a+d}{2} \right| + \left| g - \frac{b+e}{2} \right| + \left| g - \frac{c+f}{2} \right| \tag{7}$$

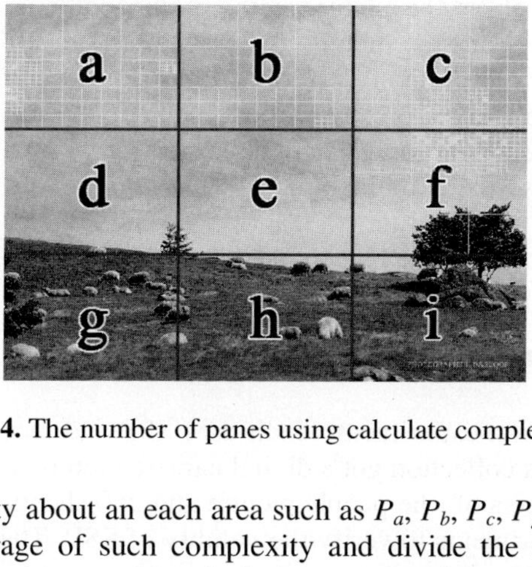

Fig. 4. The number of panes using calculate complexity

We get a complexity about an each area such as P_a, P_b, P_c, P_g, P_h and P_i. The next, we calculate the average of such complexity and divide the average by the value which a pane number is most big. And then, to multiply 100 at the value to be calculated is the color complexity. Finally, SSP is to subtraction 100 by the color complexity. Expression (8) is the expression to calculate SSP and P_{max} is the value which a pane number is most big.

$$Ps = 100 - \left\{ \left(\frac{P_a + P_b + P_c + P_g + P_h + P_i}{6 \times p_{\max}} \right) \times 100 \right\} \tag{8}$$

Fig. 5 and 6 are to divide the picture according to a color complexity which is to get t he SSP. Fig. 5 is a color complexity about a people picture. SSP has small value because all a color value of an upside and downside complex. Fig. 6 is a color complexity about a scenery picture. We can see an upside's color complex than the downside. Therefore, SSP of the scenery picture is big.

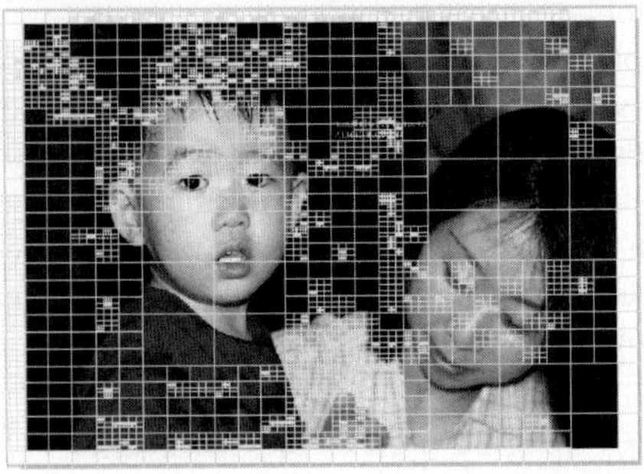

Fig. 5. Color complexity of people picture

Fig. 6. Color complexity of scenery picture

4 Combination of Face Region Detection and SSP

A picture classification uses SSP and face region detection. If we use only SSP, the error could happen such as the picture without skin color is a people picture. The reason is that SSP classifies the picture as a structure rate of the color. On the other hand, if we use only face region detection, the error could happen such as make efforts to find the people in the picture without the people. Consequently, we must use SSP and face region detection for efficient classification.

In this paper, we use the combination which is composed of SSP and face region detection. The rate of combination is 70% of SSP and 30% of face region detection. The reason is that it got most high precision, when it uses the rate.

5 Experiment and Analysis

The picture classification experiment which uses SSP and face region detection is as follows. A picture data collection got a digital camera picture at random from internet. This data uses 250 sheets of t he people picture and 250 sheets of the scenery picture. We did two kind experiments to verify the validity of SSP. The one experiment is the

Table 1. The result of the experiment about a picture classification

		Correct	Error	Total Correct	Total Error	Accuracy
Face region detection	People	192	58	395	105	79.0 %
	Scenery	219	31			
SSP + Face region detection	People	203	47	432	68	86.4 %
	Scenery	213	37			

experiment to use face region detection only. The other experiment is the experiment to use SSP and face region detection.

Table 1 is the result to classify the picture in the experiment. The experiment which uses face region detection only classified the 192 sheets of picture as a people picture among the 250 sheets of people picture (76.8%). And it classified the 203 sheets of picture as a scenery picture among the 250 sheets of scenery picture (81.2%). On the other hand, the experiment which use SSP and face region detection classified the 219 sheets of picture as a people picture among the 250 sheets of people picture (87.6%). And it classified the 213 sheets of picture as a scenery picture among the 250 sheets of scenery picture (85.2%). We can know that the experiment which uses SSP and face region detection is better than the experiment which uses face region detection only.

The reason why accuracy of people picture is lower than scenery picture is predicted to the error of face region detection. Face region detection tries to find similar color with skin color and face form such as eyes, nose, and lips. But people of people picture are not the front side. Sometimes, they are the left side or right side and covered with other object.

6 Conclusion

We proposed a picture automatic classification method which uses SSP and face region detection in this paper. We can know that face region detection method is used picture classification as well as a face retrieval of a crime suspect retrieval system or an identity authentication of entrance and exit control system. And we know that the method using SSP with face region detection is more efficient than using face region detection only.

Face region detection has the defect to try to find the face in the all picture. So, we supplement the defect using SSP which is proposed in this paper. But, this method must take the influence of result of the face region detection. Finally, we need more correct face region detection. If precision of face region detection is improved more, precision of the picture classification is improved too.

We use SSP and face region detection to classification pictures in this paper. The picture has the feature such as color, color temperature as well as SSP and face region detection. We expect that such features are more useful to classify the picture. Consequently, it is our next research subject to find efficient feature for a picture classification.

Acknowledgments

This work was supported by the Soongsil University Research Fund.

References

1. Moghaddam, B., Pentland, A.: Face Recognition using View-Based and Modular Eigenspaces. Automatic Systems for the Identification and Inspection of Humans, SPIE, 2277 (1994)
2. LAM, H.-K., AU, O.C., WONG, C.-W.: Automatic White Balance Using Luminance Component and Standard Deviation of RGB Components. ICASSP (2004)
3. Gasparini, F., Schettini, R.: Color Correction for Digital Photographs. In: Proceedings of the 12th ICIAP'03 (2003)
4. Chai, D., Ngan, K.N.: Locating facial region of a head-and-shoulders color image. IEEE Proc. Automatic Face and Gesture Recognition, 124–129 (1998)
5. Yang, M.-H., Ahuja, N.: Detecting Human Faces in Color Images. In: Proceedings of the 1998 IEEE International Conference on Image Processing(ICIP 98), Chicago, vol. 1, pp. 127–130 (1998)
6. Fleck, M., Forsyth, D., Bregler, C.: Finding naked people. In: Buxton, B.F., Cipolla, R. (eds.) ECCV 1996. LNCS, vol. 1065, pp. 593–602. Springer, Heidelberg (1996)
7. Forsyth, D., Fleck, M.: Automatic detection of human nudes. International Journal of Computer Vision 32, 63–77 (1999)
8. Ahn, H.S., Park, M.S., Na, J.H., Choi, J.Y.: Face feature processor on mobile service robot. In: Proceedings of SPIE, vol. 6042 (2006)

Designing Personalized Media Center with Focus on Ethical Issues of Privacy and Security

Alma Leora Culén[1] and Yonggong Ren[2]

[1] Institute of Informatics, Design of Information Systems,
Post Boks 1080,University of Oslo, 0316 Oslo, Norway
almira@ifi.uio.no

[2] School of Computer and Information Technology
Liaoning Normal University, China
renyonggong@gmail.com

Abstract. While considering the development of interactive television (iTV), we also need to consider new possibilities for personalization of its audio-video content as well as ethical issues related to such personalization. While offering immense possibilities for new ways of informing, communicating, gaming as well as watching selected and personalized broadcasted content, doors also open to misuse, manipulation and destructive behavior. Our goal is to propose and analyze a user-centered prototype for iTV, while keeping in mind ethical principles that we hope would lead to a positive experience of this forthcoming technology.

Keywords: interactive television, experience, ethics, privacy, multi-touch interface.

1 Introduction

We believe that the trend is for all of the technology that is embedded in our daily lives to support relationships and activities that enrich user's experience. Therefore, designers design products with interesting features, such as, for example, an electric water cooker with neon lights, added purely for the sake of aesthetics [16]. In their book, Technology as Experience [15], McCarthy and Wright claim that the "zestful integration" or transcendent nature of the aesthetic experience is a model of what human experience with technology might become. They also argue that user experience of the interaction with technology always has several components and they provide theoretical framework for analyzing user's experience by looking more closely into each of the components. We will use some of their work in Section 2 while looking into our conceptual model for interactive television.

This article is about TV, one of the technologies we have been living with for over 70 years and the one that has been in the process of transformation for the past decade. Interactive television has been on everyone's lips for a while, but the interactive experience for most of us has been limited to the remote control. Rather than talking about the state of the iTV industry, the historical context from which it emerged, or an overview of important technologies and platforms that have been

J. Jacko (Ed.): Human-Computer Interaction, Part III, HCII 2007, LNCS 4552, pp. 829–835, 2007.

developed and are in use today, we wish to give a conceptual design with some use scenarios for iTV based on multi-touch interface [7] and aimed at personalization of audio-visual content according to user preferences and needs at the moment.

Many papers have already appeared on personalization (such as [1], [12], [17], [19], [20] for example) and probably even more on fear of it [2], [5], [6]. For us, personalization becomes much simpler and more creative, due to Jeffrey Han's new multi-touch interactive interface [7], [8]. Seeing his demos have opened the door to what we believe is a suitable interface for iTV. It is in place to remark here that we have not yet had a chance to place our hands on a Perceptive Pixels screen. However, we have had an opportunity to test the Oslo produced, "Humanizing Technology Award" prize winning interface demonstrated in [10].

In the mean time, old analog TV seems to be all but forgotten. As Fortune 500 recently reports in [3]:

"Life After Television" was the title of George Gilder's 1992 book envisioning a not-distant future, and most people seemed to think he was right. Once the World Wide Web appeared in the mid-1990s, the future looked very clear. Boring old TV, the scheduled programs that come to you through a coaxial cable or satellite dish or antenna, would fade away.

Seen from this perspective, the latest announcements of new TV-related technology look simply like additional ways to put more TV in front of American consumers. The evidence suggests that it will cause us to watch even more. The supposed threat from the Internet was that we'd cut back on TV as we spent more time on MySpace or in Second Life. We may well spend more time on such new Net attractions, but we're unlikely to take that time away from video viewing. We're more likely to cut back on things we consider less important, like sleep.

Another article [11] from the current issue of Fortune shows another interesting trend:

Last November in Beijing, IBM gathered 2,000 employees, with 5,000 more watching on the web, to unveil a series of global initiatives on digital storage, branchless banking, and the like. During the presentation, CEO Sam Palmisano walked up to an onstage PC, logged onto the online three-dimensional virtual world called Second Life, and took command of the cartoon-like "avatar" that represents him there.

He then visited a version of Beijing's Forbidden City built on virtual real estate, dropping by an IBM (Charts) meeting where avatars controlled by employees in Australia, Florida, India, Ireland, and elsewhere were discussing supercomputing. Among the initiatives announced by Palmisano that day: a $10 million project to help build out the "3-D Internet" exemplified by Second Life.

By early January more than 3,000 IBM employees had acquired their own avatars, and about 300 were routinely conducting company business inside Second Life. "The 3-D Internet may at first appear to be eye candy," Palmisano writes in an e-mail interview, "but don't get hung up on how frivolous some of its initial uses may seem." He calls 3-D realms such as Second Life the "next phase of the Internet's evolution" and says they may have "the same level of impact" as the first Web explosion.

Television as a medium has established traditions for how it is used, which are not likely to change drastically in the near future, if the opinions and findings mentioned in the first Fortune article are true. We surely hope they are not, as interactive television is then just about going to eliminate our sleep. The potential it has is really starting to become apparent. Much research has been done on potential different usages of iTV, such as for example ieTV [14]. Putting those ideas together with a fun and creative interface, such as multi-touch screen, some of the 3D development in gaming and communication ([13], [18]), possibilities of multiple open streamlined channels and one is ready for the new experience.

In Section 3, the down-side of personalization is discussed with some guidelines as to how the fears can be tamed and iTV enjoyed fully.

2 Conceptual Model and Problem Space

We assume that our iTV is fully, seamlessly, integrated with PCs. Many issues we had involving interface design, as part of the design of the conceptual model for the use of iTV, have disappeared totally between the time this article was proposed and it's final appearance. Also, understanding the problem space (what it is that one would like to be doing with this interface and how it would support users in the intended manner) has become very natural with multi-touch screen. This, for us, is an indication of true value of the product. While it is transparent in its use, it offers possibilities we did not have before. For example, the streamlined audio and visual content could be available just like any other file on the desktop, with little new "live" icons for radio or TV. By touching the icon, a multitude of live icons representing channels or stations appear. As Jeff Han demonstrates [7] with NASA's Earth maps, in the same manner, little live TV icons can be stretched, enlarged, rotated, closed etc.

Demos [7] and [8] were shown in the HCI course one of the authors was teaching. The result was that the involved students really got inspired, spontaneously, to think about various other usages one could have for such interface; all kinds of things were envisioned, from making café table tops to installing them by the main entrance at home, as the first item one would wish to see and check: who is at home, what is in the fridge, is there news or email, start music etc. (smart house concept with multi-touch as the interface). One observation was made: until recently such things as making your own digital room were reserved for geeks and hackers, but this interface can make anyone desire to make not only Second Life, but First Life, too.

2.1 Organization

We envision three main usage areas for our iTV: 1) PC-like use including internet browsing, 2) media center with entertainment (radio and streamlined visual content) and 3) a user-created area consisting of locally stored digital content, such as music, video libraries, photos, documents, game collections etc. The last item would include many creative applications such as those demonstrated in [7] and [8], as well as offering room for creativity of various types, installations [9], digital art, viewing of museum artifacts, making your own games etc.

2.2 User Experience Framework

The user experience framework tries to capture the multi-faceted nature of the different aspects of human experience. These different aspects are active at the same time and are often perceived as one, as unity. However, McCarty and Write ([15],[18]) chose to split the experience into several components (called threads), most important ones being: emotional, sensory, compositional and spatio-temporal. We can use this framework to look into how iTV may relate to these main threads through which we humans have our experiences.

The Emotional Thread. It is concerned with an understanding or sense-making process. We humans tend to assign meaning to various actors in our life based on our own set of values, goals and desires. Our values, goals and desires are really the major driving force when it comes to determining what we are going to do with our new iTV. The emotional thread is then concerned with the sense-making process related to those three main drivers that are, more often than not, in conflict within us. What a user is in the mood for (her desires) may dramatically differ from what she needs to do (her goals) at any particular point in time. For example, she may feel like watching a film while really her article needs to be finished and she needs to work. This inner conflict may affect the experience with iTV. Understandings of these inner works and states may bring users to a meta-level of personalization. For example, if writing the article is winning, several "incentives" may be proposed for a combination of work, creativity and entertainment. One possibility is to simply turn the voice synthesizer on, reading the content of the article so far. This may be enough to tune the mind to work. Another possibility is to work on figures or photos for the article and try to be creative visually; this also may start the user on her road towards concentration and a productive writing time period. The user can herself design the incentives, and depending on the day some may work better than the others. But understanding her experience with situations like the one described can really bring about a new level of personalization: something highly individual, noncommercial and perhaps effective.

If our user has decided on entertainment, how can she choose entertainment content based on the emotions she is experiencing at the moment she turns towards the media part of iTV? Here the user may visually search large film databases and with a single sweep of a hand make selections of the following kind: these I like to watch when I need relaxation, these when I want to feel an adrenalin rush, these for scares, these for pure aesthetical experience and for the sake of art etc. User can create her own categories and classifications in an extremely simple and natural manner. Once the classification and categorization job is done, the procedure is simple: she may choose the category she feels for, start viewing several samples from the chosen category and making a final decision by simply touching the icon of her choice.

Her categories and classifications will continuously be refined and tuned with the aid of agents and herself. Depending on the category, experience enhancers can be added. Those can be haptic [haptic], olfactory or kinesthetic. Each one of us may really turn the whole iTV adventure into a science of how to get maximum satisfaction and enjoy the process of doing it too.

The Sensory Thread. It is concerned with our sensory engagement with actors participating in generation of the experience. Freed from its exclusively mechanical device framework, iTV can now be experienced through the tactile and kinesthetic senses as well. These can significantly contribute to a very different experience while viewing the television. A touch screen, combined with other sensory enhancers such as smells, air motion etc, used when needed and in accordance to selected program or activity can contribute to a much stronger impact of the audio-visual material that is presented. Installations such as [3], and others that make users an active part of presented material, are worth mentioning as another possible arena for play at home that could be using sensory threads even more.

Fig. 1. Jeff Han's Media Mirrors Installation from 2005

The Compositional Thread. Positive relationship between part and whole of the experience is strongly enforced by the interface itself.

The Spatio-Temporal Thread. Encompasses the spatio-temporal component of an experience, and how it relates to our past, future, and whether we experience life as emergent or as determined. Given the level of control the user has in her way of using iTV, even when limited to broadcasted material, the experience is likely to be on the emerging side. For example, the act of personalization may be perceived as an endless hunt for the ultimate match between the machine and the self.

3 Ethics and Privacy

Many are very skeptical of iTV because of ethical issues it raises: will we become subjects of large scale experiments in our own homes? Will there be someone out there with all the data about us: psychological, emotional, behavioral etc. that could be used for subtle, or not so subtle, manipulation through personally targeted advertising? Who could guarantee privacy and safety of the well of information that users could be giving out during an act of personalization of, and interaction with, their iTVs? Can these issues be avoided using careful, value based (where profit for someone is just one of the possible values [4]) design, resting firmly on intention of bringing maximum value and most pleasant experience of the iTV technology with minimum risk for misuse?

Public opinion on "smart appliances" ranges from awe to fear. Here is what Wired News reporter reports in [5]:

Some potential users are concerned over the prospect of being observed by their household appliances, and said they would not knowingly purchase a product that tracked their entertainment preferences.

"I don't want my TV taking notes on what I'm watching. I don't want my kid's game console tracking what he's playing. I don't want my CD player collecting data on my music collection," said Kelley Consco, who was shopping for holiday gifts at Radio Shack. "It's just too creepy."

However, if Kelley felt that it is not radio or game console or iTV collecting information on her, but that she is collecting information on herself and for a good purpose, the story she gives would certainly be different. Whether she would want to do it or not is not the main concern here, the feeling of creepiness is. The reason for this feeling, we are becoming familiar with. We have come to the point where we are to a larger and larger degree aware of manipulation through advertising, social pressure for using certain technologies etc. We would have much less serious problems with privacy if we believed in the security of data gathered by various devices in our homes. Our real concerns are about security of our children, security of our bank accounts, personal identity. Simply, security is about protecting ourselves, against unwanted third party who could get hold of our data. So we try to protect it rationally and irrationally, the best we can. We put our trust into manufacturers of various "smart products", into legislatures and likes. Because not all of us understand how different technologies really work, a certain amount of mysticism, insecurity and fear will keep us away until some other force wins over (such as for example convenience). It is perhaps true that interactive TV and privacy might not mix [6] as was reported on Geek.com, but we believe that if users can participate in personalization (as opposed to for example Predictive Networks) and feel in control and protected, experience of technology would be a much better one.

In the proposed version of iTV, user is responsible for defining her tastes and preferences. The user is empowered and is a creator of her personalized center she is enjoying (though she might choose to accept help from some "nice" intelligent agents). Relying on informed users and really good, natural interfaces might help to win over fears of breach of privacy and security.

References

1. Ardissono, L., Kobsa, A., Maybury, M.T. (eds.): Personalized Digital Television: Targeting Programs to Individual Viewers. In: Human-Computer Interaction Series, vol. 6 (2004)
2. Center for Digital Democracy, report: TV That Watches You, The Prying Eyes of Interactive Television (2001)
3. Colvin, G.: Fortune Magazine (January 23, 2007) (Accessed February 2007) http://money.cnn.com/magazines/fortune/fortune_archive/2007/02/05/8399123/index.htm

4. Culén, A.: Value Creation and it's Visualisation in E-Business, Information Visualization (2006)
5. Delio, M.: Wired News: MS TV: It'll be watching you (2001) (Accessed February 2007) http://www.wired.com/news/privacy/0,1848,49028,00.html
6. Geek.com Geek News: Interactive TV and Privacy May not Mix (2001) (Accessed February 2007) http://www.geek.com/news/geeknews/2001dec/gee20011212009268.htm
7. Han, J.: Accessed February 2007 URL: http://www.macrumors.com/2007/02/12/more-multitouch-from-jeff-han/
8. Han, J.: Accessed February 2007 URL: http:youtube.com/watch?v=watch?v=QKh1Rv0PlOQ
9. Han, J.: Accessed February 2007 URL: http://cs.nyu.edu/ jhan/mediamirror/index.html
10. Eikenes, J. O.: Accessed February 2007 http://jonolave.blogspot.com/2006/06/working-prototype-video.html
11. Kirkpatrick, D.: Fortune Magazine (January 23, 2007) (Accessed February 2007) http://money.cnn.com/2007/01/22/magazines/fortune/whatsnext_secondlife.fortune/index.htm
12. Kurapati, K.,Gutta S.: TV personalization through Stereotypes. In: Workshop on Personalization in future TV (2002)
13. Lankoski, P., Ekman, I.: Integrating a Multi-User Game with Dramatic Narrative for Interactive Television. In: Proceedings of the 1st European Conference on Interactive Television: from Viewers to Actors? (2003) (Accessed February 2007) http://www.brighton.ac.uk/interactive/euroitv/euroitv03/Papers/Paper9.pdf
14. Luckin, R., du Boulay, B.: Can stereotypes be used to profile content? In: Proceedings of the Future TV: Adaptive Instruction In Your Living Room (A workshop for ITS 2002) (Accessed February 2007) http://www.it.bton.ac.uk/staff/jfm5/FutureTV/Luckin.pdf
15. McCarty, J., Wright, P.: Technology as Experience. MIT press, Cambridge (2004)
16. Norman, D.A.: Attractive things work better. In: Emotional design: Why we love (or hate) everyday things, Basic Books, New York (2003)
17. Olivier Potonniee, O.: A decentralized privacy-enabling TV personalization framework. In: Proceedings of the 2nd European Conference on Interactive Television: Enhancing the Experience (2004) (Accessed February 2007) http://www.gemplus.com/smart/rd/publications/pdf/Pot04itv.pdf
18. O'Modhrain, S., Oakley, I.: Touch TV: Adding Feeling to Broadcast Media. In: Proceedings of the 1st European Conference on Interactive Television: from Viewers to Actors? (Accessed February 2007) http://www.brighton.ac.uk/interactive/euroitv/euroitv03/Papers/Paper5.pdf
19. Stroud, J.: TV personalization: a key component of interactive TV, a Carmel Group white paper (2001)
20. van Setten, M., Tokmakoff, A., van Vliet, H.: Designing Personalized Information Systems - A Personal Media Center. In: Workshop on Personalization in Future TV (2001) (Accessed February 2007) http://www.di.unito.it/ liliana/UM01/vanSetten.pdf
21. Wright, P., McCarthy, J.: Making Sense of Experience. In: Funology: from usability to user enjoyment, by Blythe, Monk, Overbeeke and Wright (2003)

Evaluation of VISTO: A New Vector Image Search TOol

Tania Di Mascio, Daniele Frigioni, and Laura Tarantino

Dipartimento di Ingegneria Elettrica e dell'Informazione
Università dell'Aquila, Monteluco di Roio, I-67040, L'Aquila, Italy
{tania,frigioni,laura}@ing.univaq.it

Abstract. We present en experimental evaluation of VISTO (Vector Image Search TOol), a new content-based image retrieval (CBIR) system that deals with vector images in SVG (Scalable Vector Graphics) format, differently to most of the CBIR tools available in the literature that deal with raster images. The experimental evaluation of retrieval systems is a critical part in the process of continuously improving the existing retrieval metrics. While researchers in text image retrieval have long been using a sophisticated set of tools for user-based evaluation, this does not yet apply to image retrieval. In this paper, we make a step forward toward this direction and present an experimental evaluation of VISTO in a framework for the production of 2D animation.

Keywords: Content Based Image Retrieval, vector images, SVG, evaluation.

1 Introduction

In computer graphics there are two types of data models: raster and vectorial. In the former model images are composed of pixels, in the latter an image is composed of drawing paths. For a comprehensive discussion about raster and vectorial data models we refer to [8]. Though unsuitable for photo-realistic imagery, vectorial data models are continually becoming more advanced and diffused. In fact, vector images are made up of individual, scalable objects defined by mathematical equations rather than pixels. This makes vector images fully scalable, resolution independent, not restricted to rectangular shape, allowing layering and editable/searchable text. Notwithstanding this increasing interest, the great majority of content-based image retrieval (CBIR) systems proposed in the literature deal with raster images. For a complete survey on these systems we refer to [13]. On the contrary, the research area concerning CBIR systems for images described by the vectorial model is quite new. In fact, as pointed out in [5] "*to the best of authors' knowledge, there are no proposals (neither theoretical, nor applicative) that try to solve CBIR when images are represented in a vectorial model*".

To our knowledge, the unique existing CBIR system dealing with vector images is our system, called VISTO (Vector Image Search TOol); a first prototype of VISTO has been introduced in [3, 4], the last prototype is described in [2]. VISTO has been designed for the retrieval of vector images in SVG (Scalable Vector Graphics) format and includes different engines, in order to support different application domains, and one common graphical interface providing query-by-sketch and query-by-example

J. Jacko (Ed.): Human-Computer Interaction, Part III, HCII 2007, LNCS 4552, pp. 836–845, 2007.

interaction with query results, and analysis of result's quality. Most notably, due to its modular architecture, the system allows users to add engines even at runtime. For retrieval purposes a vector image is discretized within VISTO to be viewed as an inertial system in which material points are associated with descriptors obtained by discretization. This leads to a representation of the vector image that is invariant to translation, rotation, and scaling. To support requirements of different application domains, the VISTO engine offers a variety of moment sets as well as different metrics for similarity computation (see Section 2.1). The interface is designed for two classes of users: application domain users and researchers in the field of multimedia (see Section 2.2). Application domain users can use both query-by-sketch and query-by-example to search collections. Researchers can test, tune, and compare engines, and they can design datasets to be used in batch mode. The interface helps in the selection of criteria and parameters necessary to tune the system to a specific application domain.

The experimental evaluation of retrieval systems is a critical part in the process of continuously improving the existing retrieval metrics. While researchers in text image retrieval have long been using a sophisticated set of tools for user-based evaluation, this does not yet apply to image retrieval [9]. In this paper, we make a step forward toward this direction and present an experimental evaluation of VISTO (see Section 3). We validate VISTO in a framework for the production of 2D animation, in particular within an advanced high quality 2D animation environment supporting cartoon episodes management [14]. In this case, cartoonists represent application domain users; it is very common that cartoonists reuse animation scenes and frames from previous episodes into new episodes. Possibilities for scene reuse usually stem from the memory of the animators, with little or no computational aid. Efficient archival and searching of animation material is hence appropriate. It is also appropriate considering the images of this application domain as images classified in the following categories: BacKground, PErson, FAces, and Not Classified, from now on denoted as BK, PE, FA, and NC respectively.

In this framework, we performed our experiments as follows. We consider the four mentioned image categories collected in a database of 400 images, 100 for each category. The result of the searching process is a ranking of database images based on a metric obtained as weighted combination of the first seven moments of the inertial system. For the present study we deploy the two measures, Precision and Recall, in order to evaluate the *effectiveness* and the *efficiency* of VISTO. The effectiveness of our system is demonstrated by the fact that the behaviour of Precision vs Recall curves is always descendent. Furthermore, we demonstrate that VISTO efficiency increases with the decrease of the recall degree. We have also studied the discriminating power of different metrics implemented in our system. The most important observation is that Euclidean metric and City Block metric produce the same results. Finally, we have highlighted that there is a functional dependence between the discriminating power of metrics and the image category.

2 Main Features of VISTO

In this section we summarize the main features of the search engine and the interface of VISTO as presented in [2, 3, 4].

2.1 The VISTO Engine

In Figure 1 the dataflow scheme of VISTO search engine is depicted. Given a query image, database images are ranked based on the similarity with the input image, so that more relevant images are returned first in the query result. The processing hence requires a Feature Process to associate images with descriptors representing visual features, and Comparison Process to evaluate distances between descriptors (the similarity between two images is computed as the similarity between the two corresponding descriptors).

It is worth remember that the purpose of image processing in image retrieval is to enhance aspects in the image data relevant to the query, and to reduce the remaining aspects. Without loss of generality, VISTO engine deals with shape extraction [6], since shape adequately identifies and classifies images typical of the application domains so far considered (treatment of other visual features is however a direct generalization of the shape case). Moreover, the shape representation is required to be invariant to translation, rotation, and scaling. These affine transformations are to be regarded as applied to a selected point belonging to the image and representative for the image. VISTO approach is to consider the image like an inertial system and to use the center of mass as selected point. The inertial system is obtained in the Feature Extraction Module discretizing the vectorial image, and associating material points with basic elements obtained by the discretization process. The origin of the inertial system is then moved to the center of mass.

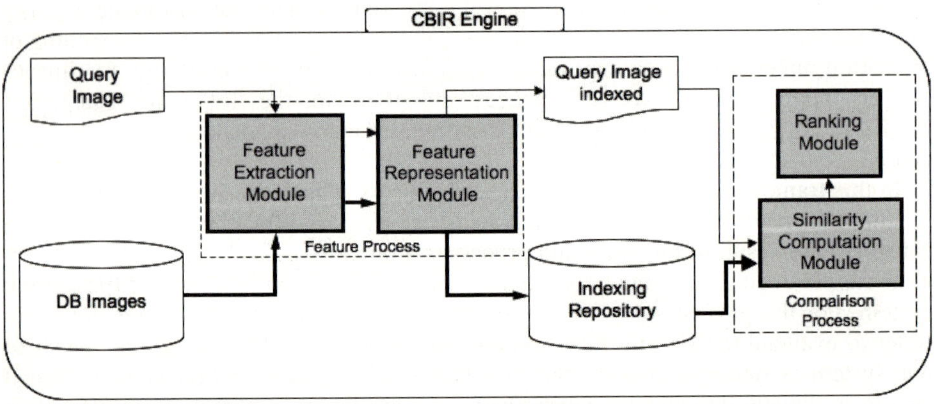

Fig. 1. The search engine architecture

Once images are transformed into inertial systems, the natural way to represent image's shape is to exploit the inertial systems characteristics, which provide useful information about the images. In our context, the inertial system average represents the dimension of image: low average means image poor in strokes, high average means image rich in strokes; the variance of the inertial system represents how the image center of mass area is composed: low variance means image center of mass area poor in strokes, high variance means image center of mass area rich in strokes; the skew of the inertial system represents the symmetry of images: high value of skew means low symmetry of image, low value of skew means high symmetry of image; finally, kurtosis of the inertial system represents how image is composed, high kurtosis means image poor in empty areas, low kurtosis means image rich in empty areas.

In conclusion, four invariant central moments and in general all invariant central moments representative for the inertial system have been considered; then feature descriptors have been created in the Feature Representation Module as vectors containing values of invariant central moments. In the literature, different invariant central moments sets have been proposed [12], differing in the way the moments are computed (see, e.g., [15, 16]). At the present implementation stage, VISTO engine includes the following Moments set: Bamieh's moments [15], Hu's moments [10], and Zernike's moments [1]. Concerning the similarity computation, different metrics have been proposed in the literature [7]. All metrics need a vector of coefficients to adequately weigh the individual values of descriptor vectors. Our CBIR engine can be tuned to the discrimination requirements of a selected application domain by choosing a moment set and a metric (along with a vector of weights) among those included in the system. The engine includes several metrics: Chebyschev distance (CH) [15], City Block distance (CY) [15], Cross Correlation distance (CC) [1], Discrimination Cost distance (DC) [1], and Euclidean distance (EU) [15].

2.2 The VISTO Interface

The VISTO interface was designed to help two different type of users well described in the introduction; the main task of the researchers in multimedia field is tuning the engine in an interactive way, based on system feedback; the main task of the application domain users is retrieving an image by providing a sketch of it, or retrieving images similar to an example one, or to retrieving images of given categories. Broadly speaking, the VISTO interface is a windows-like interface type; it supports both kind of query formulation, query by example and query by image; moreover, it supports a tool to draw images as query input. Result images may be selected providing as target image in a new search, in an incremental querying process. The VISTO interface provides a Basic Mode for application-domain users, and an Advanced Mode for researchers in the field of multimedia. As for the Basic Mode then for the Advanced Mode, the architecture of the VISTO includes a query-selection window and a query-result window. Designed to handle user's input actions, the query-selection window is composed of two tabbed panels (Basic Search Tab and Advanced Search Tab) to activate a query-selection window of the basic and advanced modes. The query-result window is invoked when the results of the query are ready to visualize. It shows results and additional system feedback to favor an in-depth tuning analysis. For further information we refer to [2].

3 Experiments and Discussion

The experimental evaluation of retrieval systems is a critical part in the process of continuously improving the existing retrieval metrics. For this experiment session, we deploy the two measures, here described, Precision and Recall in order to evaluate the effectiveness and the efficiency of VISTO and to examine the discriminating power of implemented metrics.

3.1 Experiments

To conduct a preliminary experiment in order to discover the effectiveness and the efficiency of our system and to examine the discriminating power of implemented metrics we fixed the Hu's set as moments set and we assigned to each moment of Hu's set the weight [1, 1, 1, 1, 1, 1, 1], to validate the effectiveness in the worst case. We tested our system on a 933MHz CPU Pentium III PC with 256MB RAM. We use images falling in four different categories: BacKground, PErson, FAces, and Not Classified, as mentioned in the introduction. We use a database, from now on denoted as DB, of 400 images (|DB| = 400), 100 for each category.

Table 1. List of query images

Query	*Images Name*	*Category*
1	BKTest5	BacKground
2	BKTest6	BacKground
3	PEdog1	PErson
4	PEpotato1	PErson
5	FAbye	FAce
6	FAface4	FAce
7	NCflower	Not Classified
8	NCrain	Not Classified
9	NCcircle	Not Classified

We performed experiments by submitting to VISTO a set of nine queries listed in Table 1 on images randomly selected from DB. We say that an image *j* of the database DB is relevant for a query *Q* on image *i*, denoted as Q(i), if and only if *j* and Q(i) belong to the same category. For instance, for the query 1 in Table 1 (Q(BKTest5)), the relevant images are all BK images in DB. Further, given a query Q(i), we denote as $R_{Q(i)}$ the set of images of DB relevant to Q(i). As a result to a query Q(i), the system produces a set, denoted as $A_{Q(i)}$, containing all images of DB ranked by similarity with respect to *i*; in other words, the first image of the set $A_{Q(i)}$ is the more relevant images for the query Q(i). The system shows the firsts images of this ranking $A_{Q(i)}$, starting from the top, but the system does not necessary show all images of $A_{Q(i)}$.

Given a query Q(i) and his set of results $A_{Q(i)}$, we define:

- $Sh_{Q(i)}$ the set of first elements of $A_{Q(i)}$, shown by the system;
- R_{deg} the recall degree that is the percentage of images of the set $A_{Q(i)}$ that the system shows; in formula:

$$R_{deg} = (|Sh_{Q(i)}| \,/\, |A_{Q(i)}|)\ .$$

For instance, if the system shows the firsts 200 elements of $A_{Q(i)}$, the recall degree is 50%. Furthermore, given a query Q(i), the notions of Precision and Recall of Q(i), are hence the following:

$$\text{Precision}_{Q(i),\,j,\,M} = |R_{Q(i)} \cap A_{Q(i)}| \,/\, |Sh_{Q(i)}|.$$

$$\text{Recall}_{Q(i),\,j,\,M} = |R_{Q(i)} \cap A_{Q(i)}| \,/\, |R_{Q(i)}|.$$

In other words, Precision is the fraction of the retrieved documents which is relevant and Recall is the fraction of the relevant images which has been retrieved. Obviously, the relevant images are images belonging to the same category. These formulas highlight that the Precision vs Recall depend from $|R_{Q(i)}|$ and $|Sh_{Q(i)}|$. In our experiments, while the value of $|R_{Q(i)}|$ is fixed (it is always equal to 100, because, as above mentioned, our DB is composed of 100 BK images, 100 PE image, 100 FA images, and 100 NC images), the value $|Sh_{Q(i)}|$ is not fixed; it depends from the recall degree. For our experiments, we depicted three sets of Precision vs Recall curves:

- *set I* : the Precision vs Recall curves for each query and for each metric, fixing R_{deg} = 100% ($|Sh_{Q(i)}|$ = 400);
- *set II* : the Precision vs Recall curves for each query and for each metric, fixing R_{deg} = 50% ($|Sh_{Q(i)}|$ = 200);
- *set III* : the Precision vs Recall curves for each query and for each metric, choosing $|Sh_{Q(i)}|$ = t, where t is the position in $A_{Q(i)}$ of the unique element of $A_{Q(i)}$ such that the $\text{Recall}_{Q(i),j,M}$ is 50%; in this case R_{deg} is variable.

Each of these sets is composed of 9*5 = 45 curves (5 metrics per 9 queries), where each curve is the representation of a sample of Precision vs Recall values, obtained by fixing the query Q(i) and the metric M; this sample is denoted as $S_{Q(i)}(M)$. Before conducting experiments on curves of sets I, II, and III, we have performed a preliminary ANOVA test (ANalysis Of VAriance test [11]) to statistically estimate the consistency of samples $S_{Q(i)}(M)$. Since these tests meet the expectation, we conducted the following several experiments:

- we evaluated the retrieval effectiveness of our system, studying the behaviour of the Precision vs Recall curves of set I; the results of these experiments are shown in Figures 2 and 3;
- we conducted a critical study of the retrieval efficiency of our system making an in depth analysis of the Precision vs Recall curves of sets II and III; the results of these experiments are shown in Figure 4;
- we studied the discriminating power of metrics using the values of Precision and Recall obtained in experiments. The resulting histograms are shown in Figure 5.

The same experiments have been performed also on a database of 2000 images, where each image has been assigned to one of the four above mentioned categories. The size of the categories varies from 220 to 1020. We have noticed that the results are basically the same of the previous set of experiments, and hence we do not report on them.

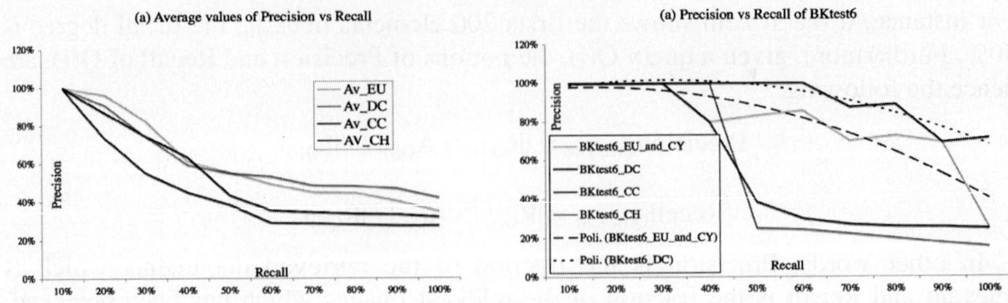

Fig. 2. (a) average values of Precision and Recall for each metric; (b) Precision vs Recall values of BKtest6 for each metric

3.2 Discussion

The results of the preliminary ANOVA test results, carrying out from the samples used, meet the expectation; in fact all $S_{Q(i)}(M)$ produce P values near to the zero and F values greater than Fcrit values; for instance, for the $S_{Q(BKtest6)}(EU)$: F = 7, 466454459, P = 0, 000336378, and Fcrit = 1, 578739184. These results allow us to study the effectiveness and the efficiency of our system and to conduct an in-depth study about the discriminating power of metrics. To verify the effectiveness of our system, we evaluated the retrieval performance of all metrics M over all queries Q(i) in Table 1

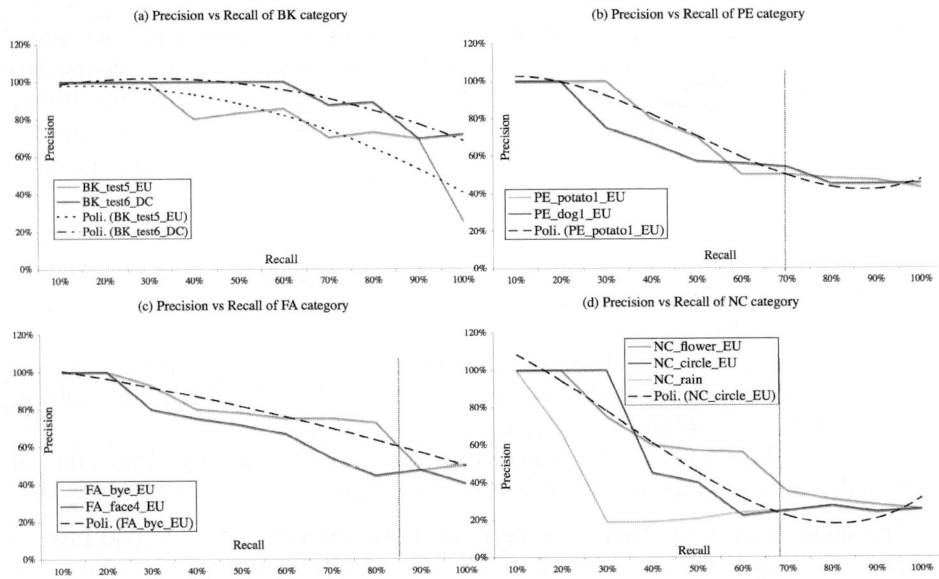

Fig. 3. Precision vs Recall for each category; (a) Precision vs Recall of Euclidean Distance for the Q1 and Discrimination Cost for Q2; (b) Precision vs Recall of Euclidean Distance for the Q3, Q4; (c) Precision vs Recall of Euclidean Distance for the Q5, Q6; (d) Precision vs Recall of Euclidean Distance for the Q7, Q8, Q9.

averaging the Precision of all metrics at hypothesis: the efficiency of our system depends from the recall degree. Therefore we can assume that our CBIR system increases in efficiency with the decrease of R_{deg}. Finally, consulting histograms in Figure 5 representing average values of Precision at different level of Recall for each category, we can study the discriminating power of different metrics implemented in our system. The first important observation is that: Euclidean metric and City Block metric produce the same results, furthermore:

- *BK category*: the Discrimination Cost offers a great performance in both the cases depicted in Figure 5; others metrics have appreciatively the same discriminating power;
- *PE category*: while the Euclidean metric and the City Block metric produce the better results, the lower discriminating power is performed by the Cross Correlation metric;
- *FA category*: the Euclidean and the City Block metrics, produce the better results;
- *NC category*: both in the case depicted in Figure 5, there are no significant differences in discriminating power of different metrics performed.

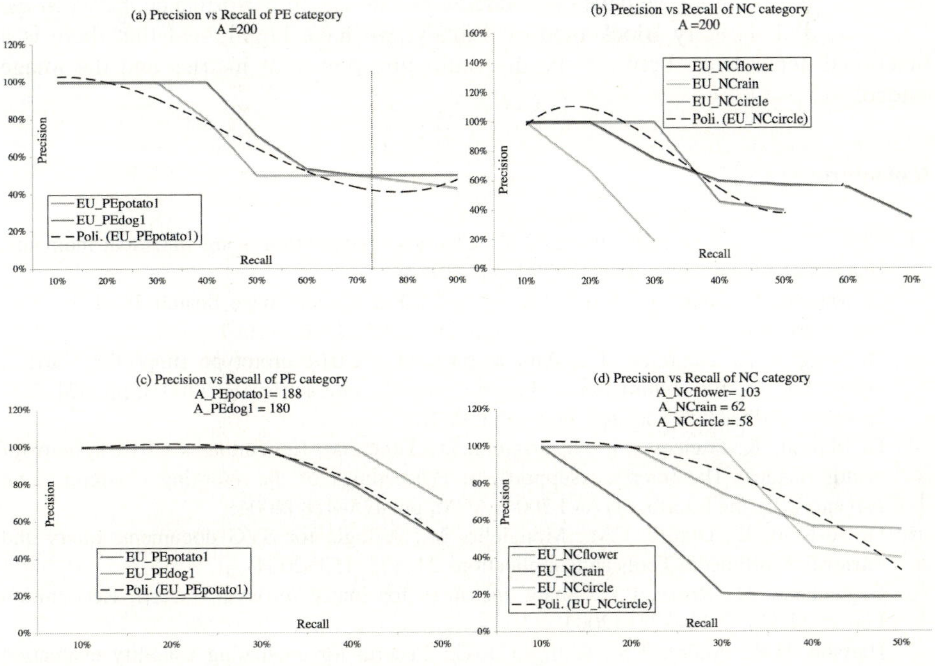

Fig. 4. Precision vs Recall for the PE and NC categories; (a) Precision vs Recall (set II) of Euclidean Distance for the Q3, Q4; Precision vs Recall (set II) of Euclidean Distance for the Q7, Q8, Q9; (c) Precision vs Recall (set III) of Euclidean Distance for the Q3, Q4; (d) Precision vs Recall (set III) of Euclidean Distance for the Q7, Q8, Q9. In these graphics we highlighted the $|Sh_{Q(i)}|$.

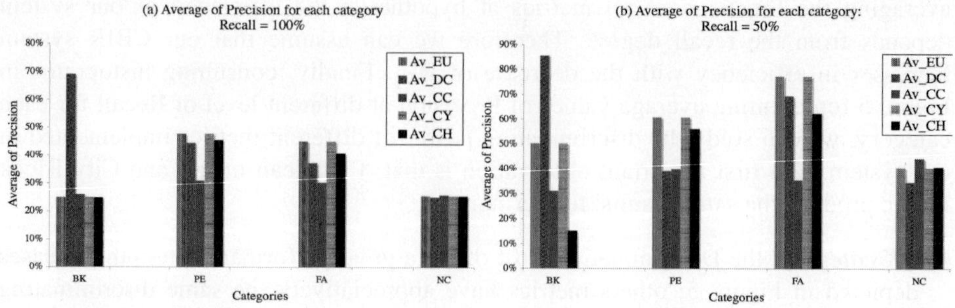

Fig. 5. Average of Precision for each category; (a) Recall 100%; (b) Recall 50%

4 Conclusions

The experiments demonstrated the effectiveness and the efficiency of our system, especially if the degree of recall is a value around the 50%, which increases if the R_{deg} decreases. Furthermore we have discovered equivalence, in performance, between the Euclidean and the City Block metrics. Finally, we have highlighted that there is a functional dependence between the discriminating power of metrics and the image category.

References

1. Chim, Y.C., Kassim, A.A., Ibrahim, Y.: Character recognition using statistical moments. Image and Vision Computing 17, 299–307 (1997)
2. Di Mascio, T., Laura, L., Mirabella, V.: VISTO, a Visual Image Search TOol. In: 12th International Human Computer Interaction (HCI2007). LNCS (2007)
3. Di Mascio, T., Tarantino, L.: Main features of a CBIR prototype supporting cartoon production. In: 10th International Human Computer Interaction (HCI2003), pp. 921–925. Lawrence Erlbaum Associates, Mahwah (2003)
4. Di Mascio, T., Francesconi, M., Frigioni, D., Tarantino, L.: Tuning a CBIR system for vector images: The interface support. In: Proceedings of the Working Conference on Advanced Visual Interfaces (AVI 2004) ACM, pp. 425–428 (2004)
5. Di Sciascio, E., Donini, F.M., Mongiello, M.: A logic for SVG documents query and retrieval. Multimedia Tools and Applications 24, 125–153 (2004)
6. Gagaudakis, G., Rosin, P.L.: Shape measures for image retrieval. Pattern Recognition Letters 24(15), 2711–2721 (2003)
7. Hartson, H.R., Andre, T.S., Williges, R.C.: Criteria for evaluating usability evaluation methods. International Jurnal of Human Computer Interaction 13(4), 373–410 (2001)
8. Hearns, D., Baker, M.P.: Computer graphics, 3rd edn. Pearson Prentice Hall, Englewood Cliffs (2004)
9. Heesch, D., Ruger, S.: Combining features for content-based sketch retrieval: a comparative evaluation of retrieval performance. In: Crestani, F., Girolami, M., van Rijsbergen, C.J.K. (eds.) Advances in Information Retrieval. LNCS, vol. 2291, Springer, Heidelberg (2002)

10. Hu, M.K.: Visual pattern recognition by moments invariants. IRE Transactions on Information Theory 8, 179–187 (1997)
11. Miller, R.G.: Beyond ANOVA. Chapman and Hall/CRC (1997)
12. Trier, O., Jain, A.K., Taxt, T.: Feature extraction methods for character recognition: a survey. Pattern Recognition 29(4), 641–662 (1996)
13. Veltkamp, R.C., Tanase, M.: A survey of content-based image retrieval systems. In: Content based image and video retrieval, pp. 47–101. Kluwer Academic Publishers, Dordrecht (2002)
14. Vennarini, V., Todesco, G.: Tools for paperless animation. Technical report, IST Project fact sheet (2001)
15. Yang, L., Algregtsen, F.: Fast computation of invariant geometric moments: a new method giving correct results. In: IEEE International Conference on Pattern Recognition. IEEE, pp. 201–204 (1994)
16. Yang, L., Albregtsen, F.: Fast and exact computation of cartesian geometric moments using discrete green's theorem. Pattern Recognition 29(7), 1061–1073 (1996)

G-Tunes – Physical Interaction Design of Playing Music

Jia Du and Ying Li

User System Interaction, Technische Universiteit Eindhoven,
P.O. Box 513, IPO Building 0.17
5600 MB Eindhoven
The Netherlands
{J.du,Y.li}@tm.tue.nl

Abstract. In this paper we present G-tunes, a music player that couples tangible interface with digital music. The design is done based on the research of tangible interface and interaction engineering. We offer an overview of design concept, explain the prototyping and discuss the result. One of the goals of this project is to create rich experiences for people to play music; another goal is to explore how external physical expressions relate to human's inner perception and emotion, and how we can couple this with the design of a tangible music player.

Keywords: Interaction design, Tangible interaction, Sensory perception, Music player, Scale, Weight.

1 Introduction

Human interact with world emotionally. We may slam the door heavily to express our anger, whereas we will carefully close it when seeing a sleeping baby. However, nowadays many products and systems are designed to work automatically, which doesn't provide a contextual environment for people to apply physical actions. Thus people lose the opportunities of expressing themselves by means of rich physical interactions [1].

Nowadays graphical user interfaces (GUIs) are commonly employed to design digital music players such as Windows Media Player and i-Tunes. However using mouse and keyboard limits the richness of interaction people could have with their favorite music. We believe that a tangible interface, which turns everyday objects into physical inputs of a computerized system [2], can expand the dimension and freedom for human machine interactions. Thus, enhancing the experience of listening to music becomes possible through various physical ways of controlling it.

To expand our views of design possibilities, we started exploring experiences of people interacting with everyday products. We took an example of using a professional digital camera as a starting point. Taking a good photo requires the setting of right angle, right explosion time, and the right moment of pressing the shutter. Serial delicate physical interactions such as holding, rotating, bending and coordinating between two hands combining with precise visual perception contribute to the creation of a great artwork. This example shows how sophisticated motor skills possessed by human can be employed to interaction design.

J. Jacko (Ed.): Human-Computer Interaction, Part III, HCII 2007, LNCS 4552, pp. 846–851, 2007.

2 Related Work

For many years, research regarding tangible musical instrument has been conducted aiming at mapping human physical interaction with musical output. As the examples, the Music Cube [3] and Embroidered Music Balls [4] will be discussed later in this session.

By looking at these examples, we found that the process of manipulating and creating music with a musical instrument can be designed more expressively through many innovative tangible interfaces.

2.1 Music Cube

Music Cube is a project that explores ways of adding physical experiences to digital music playing. With a cube interface, users can shake to shuffle music and place cube on its different side to select or stop music. A speaker like button can be rotated to scroll a list of music. Each side of the cube shows a different color to represent certain type of music because it is believed that color can show certain expressions. Music Cube uses many metaphors for designing interactions of playing and selecting music. However, it is noticed that interactions with Music cube are constrained by its physical shape.

2.2 Embroidered Music Balls

Another similar design that applies tangible object to manipulate music expressively is called Embroidered Music Balls. Through simple interactions with the Embroidered Music Balls users can easily compose artistic music. Unlike common musical instruments such as piano and violin that require years of practicing, it allows untrained people (children, novices or professionals) to use simple and natural hand gestures (such as squeezing and stretching) to perform music. Embroidered Music Balls provides more freedom in terms of interaction style. However, although interactions like squeezing and stretching offer more fun, it is rather limited when used to compose professional music.

2.3 Design Insight

Based on the previous research, we tried to explore free, direct and expressive interaction styles that not only offer fun experiences but also combine auditory sensation with physical interactions [5].

3 Concept of G-Tunes

As we know, music can be categorized as classical, jazz, pop, rock-and-roll, etc. Different types of music can create different atmosphere, which may also influence the way people interact with the environment. Interestingly, people call classical music as light music and associate rock-and-roll with heavy. The words "light" and "heavy" reflect that people tend to relate their sensory perception to physical object in a certain extent. The concept of G-tunes employs a metaphor of "musical scale", which does not represent a series of music note, but a weight measurement device for music since we assume each song has it's "weight". Furthermore, since gravity of physical objects drives music playing, the concept is called G-tunes.

3.1 Defining Music Weight

One of the essential issues of this design is how to define the "weight" of music, and map the physical interactions properly to music effect. In this paper, we tried to define the weight of music from two different perspectives: acoustic effect and cognitive perception.

From the acoustic effect perspective, volume of the music can be a criterion of music weight measurement. The louder the music is, the longer the distance it can be spread. We can also imagine that the more space it occupies, the heavier the music should be. Besides volume, frequency of the music is also one of the key factors for "weighing" music. Within the audible range of human beings, low frequency sound evokes "oppressive" & "intensive" feelings to people. It is also an indispensable part of heavy music like rock-and-roll; meanwhile, high frequency sound brings "euphoric" & "releasing" feeling to people, one example is classical music.

Regard to the cognitive perception, as we already discussed, people relate different types of music to physical objects by adding "light" or "heavy" into the music name. In fact, frequency is the reason why people have this kind of feeling. Each different instrument produces a certain range of frequency. Typical instruments for playing classical music are string instruments. Although its' frequency range is very broad, they are often used to generate high frequency pitch. However in rock-and-roll music, percussion instruments, which play important role to the band, can only locate at low frequency range [6]. Besides, some rock-and-roll music apply digital technology, such as a equalizer, to enhance the sound effect by adjusting frequency, which makes the music sounds heavier as well.

Viewing from these two perspectives, in this paper we define classical music as the lightest and rock-and-roll music as the heaviest. Jazz and pop songs are in between. These four types of music were used for prototyping.

3.2 Interaction with G-Tunes

Interaction with G-tunes can be described as selecting different styles of music by putting different weights on a scale. The metaphor is illustrated in Figure 1.

G-tunes provides two modes of playing music for people to experience. One is to change the weight of a selected music; the other is to switch among different type of music. In the first mode, depending on the weight people put to the scale, sound effects within different frequency ranges of that music will be enhanced or weakened accordingly, so that it sounds lighter or heavier. In another mode, putting different weight on G-tunes can result in the selection of different types of music. For instance, classical music is lighter than rock music, putting enough weights to G-tunes will switch the music being played from classical to rock music.

Moreover, any everyday objects can activate G-tunes as long as they can be put onto the scale. Throwing or gently placing weight to G-tunes will result in different effect of music.

Fig. 1. Concept of weighing music

4 Prototyping

A working prototype was developed as shown in Figure2. A standard mechanical scale was taken apart, and used as the core mechanical components of the prototype. A slider is used as scale to measure weight. These two parts are assembled on a base made of foam. A basket is connected with the slider and used as the weight container. Phiget tool kits [7] were used for hardware implementation. RFID tags were used as "music disks". Each of the tag is linked with one type of music which can be switched according to the weight put into the container. The slider is used together

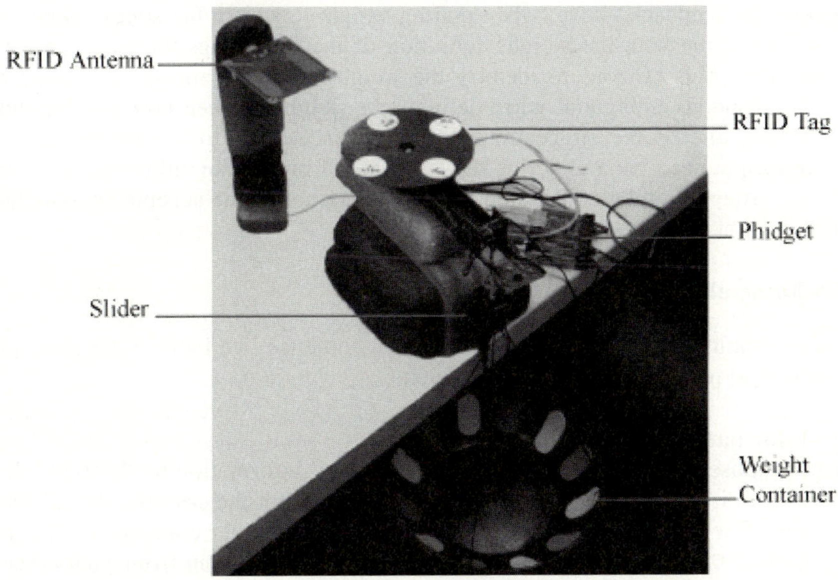

Fig. 2. G-tunes prototype

with a rubber band as a scale. Continuous changes in music can be experienced when the scale increases or decreases. MAX/MSP [8] was used for software implementation and processing music effects. Volume control and frequency control are the core parts of the code. The basic principle is to filter the frequency of music to change the effect between "heavy" and "light".

5 Discussion and Application

5.1 Feedback of G-Tunes

The concept of G-tunes was discussed in an internal demonstration at our design institute. We presented the concept and prototype to twenty audiences and four of them experienced playing music by G-tunes after the presentation.

The general feedback from audience is that G-tunes is an innovative way of playing music and gives lots of fun. Experiences of playing with G-tunes are very expressive and fun, especially when the tune changes synchronously while putting different amount of weight into the container.

Another important feedback is that people perceive the "weight" of music in different ways. This was revealed when the "weight" of a selected song was changed. Some people need to put more weight to perceive the changes of volume and frequency, some people can perceive the changes by a slighter adjustment. In general, it is easier to perceive the music going to be "heavier" than "lighter". One reason lies in the limitation of the prototype. The sensitivity of the slider needs to be improved for weight measurement. Another reason is that, unlike physical entity, it is impossible to give one standard sensory measurement of human beings since people own various cognitive perceptions.

Besides the feedback above, when putting weight to switch the songs, some people did not fully agree with the weight definition of the four songs that were chosen for demonstration. It is obvious to identify the weight of classic music and heavy metal music, but it sounds ambiguous when defining the weight between Jazz and Pop music.

Therefore, one of the suggestions from audiences was to further research how different people perceive and define the "weight" of music. An online survey within a large user group could be considered to obtain insights on the acceptable associations between weight and types of music.

5.2 Additional Application

By demonstrating and discussing G-tunes with audience, we believe the concept can be extended to use in other areas and contexts.

5.2.1 Information Visualization

G-tunes proposed a new method to categorize digital information by "weight". In this term, the definition of information "weight" can represent the size of a digital file and file folders. For example, the more and bigger files the folder contains, the heavier it is. Accordingly, the icon of the folder can look slightly different from each other. For example, heavy folders look more metal and bigger, while the texture of light folders can look more plastic. This could offer a more intuitive and direct way for people to check how much disc space the folder occupies than to find it out from the property menu of the folder.

5.2.2 Music Education of Children

A game could be designed based on the platform of G-tunes for education of music frequency and composition. We can create a simple music sample consists of several ranges of frequency, such as bass, treble or middle range frequency sound, which are produced by different instruments. With G-tunes, music can be decomposed into pieces that associate with different frequency sound, and each piece can be represented by a certain physical object such as a toy. By manipulating and rearranging physical objects, children can compose the same sample music or create their own music. In this way of playing they can learn about music frequency and composition. Moreover, as an advantage of using tangible interface, G-tunes provides a platform for social interactions as well [9]. Children can play together and learn from each other collaboratively.

6 Conclusion and Future Work

By presenting G-tunes concept, we proposed a new approach of playing music that adds physicality and fun for people when interacting with digital information. In the next step, a more delicate algorithm of how to compute weight of music needs to be developed. Thus, the issue of how to define the weight of music has to be more clear and concrete. The mapping between the weight of physical object and music requires not only interaction design techniques but also professional acoustic domain knowledge. In the end, extended applications can be further experimented and realized if feasible.

References

1. Zimmerman, J.: Exploring the role of emotion in the interaction design of digital music. In: POSTER SESSION, pp. 152–153. ACM Press, New York (2003)
2. Ishii, H., Ullmer, B.: Tangible bits: towards seamless interfaces between people, bits and atoms. ACM Press, New York, NY (1997)
3. Alonso, B.M., Keyson, V.: Music cube: a physical experience with digital music, vol. 10. Springer, London, UK (2006)
4. Weinberg, G., Orth, M., Russo, P.: The embroidered musical ball: a squeezable instrument for expressive performance. MIT Media Lab. ACM Press, New York (2000)
5. Verplank, B., Sspp, C., Mathews, M.: A course on controllers. In: Proceedings of the 2001 conference on New interfaces for musical expression. National University of Singapore, Singapore, pp. 1–4 (2001)
6. Audio Topic: http://www.tnt-audio.com/topics/frequency_e.html
7. Phidget Forum.: http://www.phidgets.com
8. MAX/MSP: http://www.cycling74.com
9. Mazalek, A., Davenport, G., Ishii, H.: Tangible viewpoints: A physical approach to multimedia stories. MIT Media Lab, pp. 153–160. ACM Press, New York (2002)

nan0sphere: Location-Driven Fiction for Groups of Users

Kevin Eustice, V. Ramakrishna, Alison Walker,
Matthew Schnaider, Nam Nguyen, and Peter Reiher

University of California, Los Angeles
kfe@cs.ucla.edu

Abstract. We developed a locative fiction application called *nan0sphere* and deployed it on the UCLA campus. This application presents an interactive narrative to users working in a group as they move around the campus. Based on each user's current location, previously visited locations, actions taken, and on the similar attributes of other users in the same group, the story will develop in different ways. Group members are encouraged by the story to move independently, with their individual actions and progress affecting the narrative and the overall group experience. Eight different locations on campus are involved in this story. Groups consist of four participants, and the complete story unfolds through the actions of all four group members. The supporting system could be used to create other similar types of locative literature, possibly augmented with multimedia, for other purposes and in other locations. We will discuss benefits and challenges of group interactions in locative fiction, infrastructure required to support such applications, issues of determining user locations, and our experiences using the application.

1 Introduction

Our work on ubiquitous computing has focused on group interactions among users and devices. One important element of this work has been to deliver useful and interesting content to users based on their physical locations, often modulated by the social groups to which they belong. We built a sample application based on applying these ideas to stories that are presented to users based on their location. This paper discusses the design of our system, important issues we addressed in building the application, and experiences in its use in a real environment, the UCLA campus.

We built a story called *nan0sphere* that would play out across several locations on the UCLA campus. Because of our interest in group interactions, we designed it as a story told to a small group of users.

Members of this group take on different story roles and move from place to place, either individually or together. The story unfolds as they visit different locations, and depending on the participation of other group members, the plot may vary. It can only reach its conclusion if all members participate and all locations are visited.

Though the text of the story itself is particular to a single narrative, the software infrastructure used to present it to the groups of users is general and would support many other pieces of literature or other forms of content with similar characteristics.

J. Jacko (Ed.): Human-Computer Interaction, Part III, HCII 2007, LNCS 4552, pp. 852–861, 2007.

Common infrastructural elements include methods of determining location, a parser to convert raw text and interaction logic into material to present to the readers, primitives to handle group formation and interactions, and networking and event communications support. We also addressed how caching and cooperation can be used to handle problems arising from poor or intermittent network connectivity.

We discuss not only the issues of the story we actually wrote and tested, but also the generality of the system and its usability for a wider variety of locative media. The experiences we present include discussions both of the difficulties in writing this kind of story and in debugging and experiencing it.

2 System Support for Location-Based Interactive Narratives

Our narrative framework allows authors to deploy content and dynamically provides services to individual mobile users and groups of users. Our Panoply middleware supports the creation and management of decentralized groups of computing entities called *spheres of influence*, which serve as an organizing principle for applications. In our target environment, story participants carry mobile devices that represent them in cyberspace. Panoply enables the formation of spheres and provides tools for application design and content authoring. These tools were designed to be useful for a wide variety of interactive experiences involving groups and locations.

2.1 Story-Telling Application

nan0sphere, was designed to be an interactive, location-and character-driven work of speculative fiction that involved a wide variety of different physical locations on our campus. *nan0sphere* is a non-linear, team-based narrative in which each member assumes the role of a story character. They each receive a customized experience, which includes pieces of the story and clues, based on their location, the location of other team members, and the overall progress of the narrative. Each user has the opportunity to manipulate virtual objects and perform virtual actions that change the state at the present location. No individual player is exposed to the whole narrative; only by combining the team's individual experiences does the entire narrative emerge.

nan0sphere requires the creation and management of groups of entities. These could be location-based groups, such as all the characters who happen to be in the library at a given time. Social relationships and shared tasks or experiences could also define a group. For our application, we created a virtual social group that maintained story state and was responsible for disseminating content. This social group is represented by a network server; mechanisms for on-demand communication of story events and delivery of locative media content are provided as core features. Discovery of peers and mediation of interactions between two participants, or a participant and a virtual location, were supported. These features are common to many applications, independent of the content or the nature of the participants.

Media Language and Parser: For the creation and interpretation of locative media content, we provided a media description language based on XML that consists of basic media elements such as location descriptions, conditional scenarios, and actions that users may take. Additionally, we provided social conditionals that let the media engine test various constraints such as the presence of another team member or the presence of someone exploring a different media piece. Figure 1 shows an example of a location description. This example shows a simple location and also illustrates a triggerable scenario that is activated when the participant is playing the "Rowan" character, and the "Renata" character is also present in the vicinity.

```
<LocationDesc name="Office" path="Narrative">
    <LocationText>Morrison's office had become a second home. Bookshelves covered one wall. Books, old journals,
sheaves of paper, and photos of family and friends covered the shelves. Mementos from travels to Thailand, Germany,
Australia dotted his walls. A box of blocks and stuffed animals lay in the back corner of the office, just in case Paulette,
his two year-old visited for the afternoon. He liked to surround himself with things and images that made him
comfortable, especially since he dedicated so much of his time to research.</LocationText>
    <Scenario>
            <Cond>
                    <And>
                    <ActorCondition var="name" val="Rowan"/>
                            <PresentCondition name="Renata"/>
                            <ValueCondition var="Office_Rowan" val="false"/>
                    </And>
            </Cond>
    <LocationText>A frazzled student answers the door. "Yes?"<p/>"I need to talk with Professor Morrison. Right now.
It can't wait!"<p/>"Professor Morrison, I'll
talk with you later. Call me if you need anything." The student opens the door and leaves. </LocationText>
    </Scenario>
</LocationDesc>
```

Fig. 1. Example Locative Media Description

User Interface: *nan0sphere* presents users with a Java-based interface (Figure 2). The interface presents a portion of the story to the participant on his mobile device; this content is relevant to his current position, and reflects the progress of the story based on actions performed by all the characters. In the figure, the user has assumed the role of William, one of the story characters, who has just arrived at the *Inverted Fountain.* The main panel, marked "Location Description," displays relevant story text, laying out the scene as it would appear at the virtual *Inverted Fountain*. The interface also indicates important events that provide the user with more information and also supplies contextual hints or prompts in an "Event Log" panel. The user can also influence the course of the story through actions; choices for these are provided in an "Available Actions" panel. As the user moves around campus and enters other locations, the interface automatically updates the scene description and the available options.

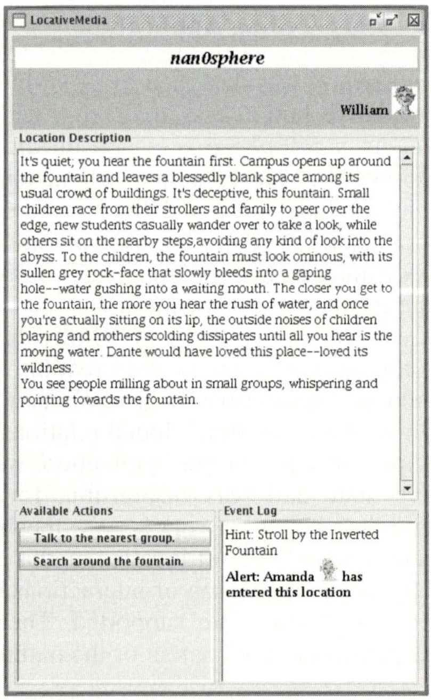

Fig. 2. nan0sphere's User Interface

2.2 The Panoply Middleware

Applications such as *nan0sphere* run on top of Panoply, our ubiquitous computing middleware, which handles location inference, networking and configuration, group context management, and communication with other devices and services.

Location Inference: In mobile story-telling applications, location is an important component in determining what part of the story is immediately relevant to the user. Panoply provides a localization module for sensing of *semantic locations*, which are regions that are meaningful to users or applications. Semantic locations are obtained by mapping low-level hardware observables to semantic identifiers. The framework is modular to allow the use of different low-level localization techniques [5,10]. Our current implementation uses a combination of 802.11 scene analysis [1] and attenuation monitoring. The semantic localization component reports when a user is inside or outside of a particular office or when a user is likely within visual proximity of a relevant campus landmark. These semantic regions can be defined over a wide range of sizes, and can be subdivided or aggregated into other related semantic zones.

Network Configuration: Devices participating in an interactive narrative application need to dynamically retrieve content and maintain relationships to peers and story groups. Administrative realities do not permit deployment of content servers at every location. As users explore the campus with their mobile device, Panoply monitors the wireless landscape to identify appropriate 802.11 networks. Based on configuration information provided by the *nan0sphere* application, Panoply manages network and media server connectivity. In practice, Internet connectivity is not always available. Where no connectivity is available, ad hoc 802.11 networks are used to discover and form connections to nearby peers in order to allow local coordination and interaction.

Groups-Based Infrastructure: In Panoply, groups and group connectivity are managed by *Spheres of Influence* [9], a device management and coordination system. These *spheres* are based on user and device characteristics such as social memberships, location, network presence, etc. Panoply provides low-level primitives, including group creation and discovery. Spheres maintain policy, state, memberships and relationships, provide contextual sensors, and securely mediate interactions.

A sphere represents a single device, or, recursively, a structured group of spheres. Most groups occurring in mobile story-telling applications will fit in one of the following classes: device spheres, location spheres, and social or attribute-based spheres. A *device sphere* represents a single mobile device. A *location sphere* is associated with describable physical regions, such as a room, building, or the area within range of a specific access point, and can include any device spheres currently in that space. *Social spheres* represent groupings of other spheres to achieve tasks or indicate common interests or goals, such as being members of a club. All spheres are maintained by one or more devices and have a network presence. An example in our application is an interactive narrative sphere, a type of social sphere. The participants' mobile devices have device spheres, and are transient and peripatetic members of the narrative sphere.

Event Communication: Panoply uses a publish-subscribe event model for communication, which is well suited to the loosely coupled mobile computing model we are building our applications on. Events can be used to deliver low-level context changes and notifications, as well as on-demand content. Sphere components and applications register with their local sphere for desired event types, and corresponding events are delivered to the interested component. System events include *discovery, membership, location, policy, cache, heartbeat,* and *management events*, etc. These events are generated by core Panoply components. Applications use these events to react to external changes and adapt their behavior. Application-defined events are specific to the creating application, e.g., *nan0sphere* uses media-update events from the media sphere to the mobile devices, and action events from mobile devices to the media sphere.

Media Caching: Various locations that are critical to developing the story may have poor or no connectivity, yet provide sufficient information to allow a mobile device to determine the identity of that location. Therefore, we enable predictive delivery of content from the social media sphere to individuals' devices during periods of connectivity. This content is then stored in a sphere *cache*. Then, if the media sphere is disconnected and our location subsystem indicates we have entered a new location, we can check to see if the cache contains appropriate media. If it does, the local infrastructure reveals the content to the application. Additionally, changes to virtual story state made by the local device are cached until connectivity is restored, or may be shared with locally discovered team members if any exist.

3 The *nan0sphere* Locative Media Experience

nan0sphere is an interactive and location-aware narrative, written by a UCLA graduate student in the English department and two undergraduates (one in English and one in Computer Science). The goal of this project was to showcase group interactivity and location-aware media, and at the same time, tell a story.

The story is a speculative, fictional narrative about nanotechnology on the UCLA campus. Four users each play a different character (a security guard, a graduate student, a campus information technology specialist, and a professor of sociology) and interact with the campus from that person's perspective. The narrative is goal-driven, and uses this concept as the impetus for each character to move from location to location.

The authors used the construction of a new biotechnology building on UCLA's campus as the main plot-device for the narrative. The story begins with the theft of an extremely dangerous prototype technology from a campus nanotechnology lab. Specifically, the story takes the four users through eight specific points on the campus. They are able to read descriptions of the surroundings as they stand in a location. As the character visits more locations, the true story behind the theft is revealed. Each character has a different reason for being involved in the story: for example, the graduate student might lose her funding, while the sociology professor is best friends with the head of the lab that was broken into.

The story has a definite plot arc, with each player entering at the "beginning" of his or her involvement in the story. Players gather clues at each location and can engage in virtual conversations with other characters. Multiple players in a single location or two players crossing paths can lead to more of the story being revealed or to the clues changing. Players are also encouraged to engage in actual conversation and discuss the narrative if they happen to cross paths.

In addition to the exploration of the central storyline of *nan0sphere*, the authors wanted to create more conceptual media experiences for users using the same story. Based on the same locations, the authors created three other alternative *paths* that users could take, allowing them to experience the same story from various, and often unexpected, points of view. The paths use different forms of narrative, ranging from poetry and song to drama and prose, freely quoting other authors in order to form complex layers of experience. The nanite path follows the stolen swarm of nano-scale robots as they gain sentience and awareness; the future path considers the UCLA campus in a post-nanite world; the Wesley path follows the thief who originally stole the technology, and his descent into madness. It is possible to switch back and forth between these three paths. The authors also wanted to create an "infectious" paradigm within the story. When any of the four players come close to being infected with the stolen nanites, they can "jump" to the nanite path for a moment as a way to suggest infection; the same would occur if any of the players accidentally came too close to Wesley: they can choose to enter his path and explore his mind.

4 Lessons from *nan0sphere*

Our experience with the deployment has yielded interesting insights into design issues for locative media and locative media infrastructure, as well as issues and questions for authors developing location-aware media. The relationship between software author and storyteller is significantly blurred as infrastructural limitations feed into the narrative, and narratives approach the level of software in their complexity.

Social Issues in *nan0sphere*: It became clear that the storyline's dependencies on coordinated actions taken by multiple characters could be problematic. The story could only progress when different characters took specific actions, pushing forward the story's progress. At a given moment, any given character might find that they had no options in any story location as the story was blocked, waiting for some other character to make progress. If a participant took a break from the story, he could effectively prevent other characters from accessing new content and completing the narrative. Depending on author intent, this might be not acceptable. One possible solution would be to implement narrative event timers that ensure the narrative advances at a reasonable rate by triggering unresolved game events necessary for active characters to progress. From a larger perspective, the infrastructure should not always be forcing narrative progress. A content author might in fact want to require one character to wait upon another's actions without any other narrative recourse.

Debugging Interactive Narratives: While refining our framework, we built a number of debugging tools. We found that it was desirable to exercise the application without actually moving about the campus, and thus we created a clickable map of the campus to simulate location transitions. Additionally, we built a version of our media interpreter that displayed and logged the conditional decisions affecting the current story. In our experience, it would be useful to have a comprehensive debugging framework so that developers and authors could easily isolate narrative components and test them under both real and simulated conditions.

For example, in the narrative description language, the authors were able to specify what text they wanted to associate with various locations. They were also able to specify various conditions that controlled when certain portions of the text were made available for display. During testing, it became evident that the authors did not, and with available tools could not, completely anticipate all possible paths that individual characters could take. On occasion an individual user's experience might include character introduction or plot development that seems to be "out of order," at least to the extent that text in interactive media can be so. Clearly, we need better support for authors to express high-level flow constraints on their stories, akin to software invariants. One role of a debugging framework could be constraint verification on the narrative content, to point out possible narrative flow problems to the author.

Localization Issues: The *nan0sphere* authors selected eight locations on campus to be semantic regions that play a part in the narrative, prior to the implementation of our localization code. Some of the referenced locations are highly specific, intending that the user be in one small area, such as an individual room, or a particular bench in a garden. Others are intended to be more broadly defined and aim to have the user in the general proximity of a landmark. In both cases, accurate localization is important. In the former case, we wanted to be somewhat forgiving how about how precisely a user had to be in a particular location. Users might be discouraged if they go to an area specified in the story, but are unable to situate themselves in the exact position the authors envisioned. By defining a slightly larger zone, users need only approach the general area to know that they are on the right track. Three of the locations chosen are particularly close to one another. Two of these are outdoor locations and one is indoor. Although these regions do not overlap, they are close enough that it can be difficult to absolutely differentiate one from another, clearly presenting difficulties for participants. This is a limitation of our localization technique; however, in general, some limitations will exist in many localization schemes. Content authors need to be aware of the limitations of the localization support and design accordingly.

When the device determines that it has moved to a new location, our prototype gives both auditory and visual cues. The auditory cue was added during debugging, and though it is configurable, we have typically left it enabled. We discovered that users tend to focus their attention on their devices when they changed location, possibly as a result of the tone. The change in location results in a corresponding change of text displayed to the user. Users tended to immediately read the new text and proceed with the story directly from that location. Thus, in the cases where the user was supposed to reach a specific point, they sometimes did not get to the authors' exact intended location before progressing with the story. It may be possible to modify the interface to inform users when they are getting "warmer" so as to lead them all the way to the intended location before allowing the story to progress.

Authorial Issues: From the authors' perspective, *nan0sphere* was difficult to write for two reasons: First, it is always hard for three individuals with different levels of expertise in creative writing, and especially creative writing within a new media framework, to come together with cohesive ideas and execute them in a manner that is fair to all involved. Second, two of the writers did not have much expertise in computer science, which made it hard to understand how to use and showcase the features of Panoply. An important and difficult question for future collaborations between technologists and artists is which should come first, the making of the software—in itself an artistic process—or the creative components of locative storytelling?

This question is not easily answered, other than to leave locative narratives to those who are adept at both technological and artistic pursuits. This answer is unsatisfactory to most people pursuing media projects, and overlooks the rich tradition of collaboration within new media and electronic literature. Electronic literature that uses innovative interfaces and novel means of communication is often a collaboration between artists and programmers. As Strickland and Lawson, the creators of Vniverse [17] suggest, their project "could not have existed as an individual project, and we find that we most enjoy performing it in collaboration as well." We agree with Lawson and Strickland: true collaboration between artists and technologists occurs when the project is conceived by both parties.

Another challenge was how to engage the reader to *want* to walk around campus. It is easy to keep the users' attentions when locative media is performed in a small space; how does an author capture the users' interest enough for them to trek through a mile-long campus? *nan0sphere*'s narrative "bounced" between physically distant locations on the UCLA campus. To fully explore the story, participants traveled back and forth between different story locations. Sometimes a character would arrive at a new location, only to be told to go back to the last location she visited. Unless the focus of a narrative is to encourage exercise, forcing user mobility can be tedious. If a narrative is to effectively influence a participant to change locations, the narrative must offer sufficient allure to overcome human inertia. A very compelling narrative, or some form of competition and reward may be sufficient.

The decision was made early to make *nan0sphere* a plot-driven mystery and use clues and cliffhangers that propel the narrative forward and encourage people to walk around the campus to try and find more clues. Experience with running users through the story suggested that this approach was not sufficient for the amount of user movement the story demanded. Perhaps a narrative designed to serve as a tour of an interesting area could solve this problem. One promising possibility to avoid too much user movement is to restructure the notion of locations in the locative media. Events in locative media may not be tied to a specific location, e.g. "Café Roma," but rather to a type of location, e.g. a café or restaurant, etc., or location *template*. Using this technique, a locative narrative might progress as the participant goes about their daily routine, only forcing particular movements for major story events.

The project's conceptual layers (the different "paths" one can take to reveal more of the story) were a response to the artistic constraints that such a plot-driven story implied. They enabled the authors to experiment with prose styles and use the software in novel ways with regards to location and user interaction. The authors needed to agree on what kind of story they should construct and who their intended audience was. The group vacillated between wanting to present their audience with a very abstract media experience that worked with the same concepts (nanotechnology, the body, the relationship between scholar and subject), but relied on users to draw their own connections as to how they would navigate through the project, and a straightforward narrative that presented a "real" story, one with reasons behind every action. Here is the fundamental divide that was encountered when creating *nan0sphere*: what constitutes a *real* and maybe more importantly *enjoyable* story? It proved difficult to create a narrative that was exciting conceptually, yet concrete enough so that users would feel they were really getting somewhere.

5 Related Work

Mobile Bristol [12] and InStory [2] take a toolkit-based approach towards supporting the authoring of locative media, similar to Panoply. Mobile Bristol focuses on enabling rapid authoring of locative media contents, or *mediascapes*, on Windows-based PCs and palmtops. InStory provides an authoring environment that supports mobile storytelling, gaming activities and access to relevant geo-referenced information through mobile devices such as PDAs and mobile phones. The infrastructure provides localization services, as well as relevant media encoded in XML, as does Panoply. InStory also enables explicit interactions among users through GUIs. Mobile Bristol and InStory primarily focus on enabling easy content development by authors who have limited programming skills, Similarly, the iCAP [7] toolkit allows users more control over how their designed applications behave without having to write code, though it provides no infrastructural features like localization. We add to the richness of the experiences that can be created by such toolkits by treating groups as first-class primitives in the Panoply infrastructure, and make group interactions implicit. Panoply also manages dynamic network selection and configuration, a hard problem that is crucial to the success of mobile applications.

The fields of social entertainment (Ghost Ship [11], Pirates! [3], SeamfulGame [4], CitiTag [15]) and museum tours [6][8][14][16] have done much to enhance user experience through locative media. Users can play games or gain knowledge about the objects in their immediate environment through interfaces on their mobile devices. But many of these systems do not provide the level of interactivity and freedom of movement that Panoply-based applications do. Even those applications that are more interactive than the others [6] are not cannot be generalized beyond their immediate application, do not support user-specific customization, and are not group-aware.

6 Conclusions

The success of *nan0sphere* is mixed. We learned much about the realities of building this kind of locative media application, and it helped improve the Panoply infrastructure. Some of tools built in conjunction with *nan0sphere* may be helpful in building other such applications, and the lessons that we learned will benefit other groups. On the other hand, *nan0sphere* did not become popular. Even members of our own group found working through the entire story somewhat tedious, and there was no enthusiasm for running through multiple story outcomes or exercising optional features, in large part because of the amount of physical movement required. Perhaps the single greatest lesson that this application offers is that peripatetic stories require strong motivations for the movements they require. A story must be extremely compelling to get its readers to walk up and down hills, go into and out of several buildings, and figure out exactly which locations need to be visited next.

An important lesson in regards to the group aspects of *nan0sphere* is that the group experience must be designed to involve the group, yet not require too stringently that all group members participate at once or experience the story at the same speed. This offers extra challenges in designing such stories.

From a technical point of view, fixing an exact location is often difficult. While technologies like GPS would handle some of our difficult situations well, those technologies have their own weaknesses and challenges. Storytellers using these technologies must keep these limitations and inaccuracies in mind, both when choosing locations and determining how to ensure that their stories make progress.

Designing and supporting a good peripatetic story is not easy. There are major challenges in conceiving the story, in providing technology that supports its needs, and with ensuring that the experience meets the desires of one's audience. Much work will be required to make this form of storytelling easy to create (or, at least, as easy as writing any good story can be) and enticing to its audience.

References

[1] Bahl, P., Padmanabhan, V.N.: Radar: An In-Building User Location and Tracking System. In: Proceedings of IEEE Conference on Computer Communication, vol. 2.

[2] Barrenho, F., Romao, T., Martins, T., Correia, N.: InAuthoring environment: interfaces for creating spatial stories and gaming activities. In: Proceedings of the, ACM SIGCHI Intl. conference on Advances in Computer Entertainment Technology, Hollywood, CA (2006)

[3] Bjork, S., Falk, J., Hansson, R., Ljungstrand, P.: Pirates! - Using the Physical World as a Game Board. In: Proceedings of Interact 2001. Tokyo, JAPAN (July 2001)

[4] Borriello, G., Chalmers, M., LaMarca, A., Nixon, P.: Delivering Real-World Ubiquitous Location Systems. Communications of ACM 48(3), 36–41 (2005)

[5] Capkun, S., Hamdi, M., Hubaux, J.: GPS-Free Positioning in Mobile Ad Hoc Networks. In: Proceedings of Hawaii Int. Conference on System Science (January 2001)

[6] Chou, S.-C., Hsieh, W.-T., Gandon, F., Sadeh, N.: Semantic Web Technologies for Context-Aware Museum Tour Guide Applications. In: Proc. WAMIS 2005 (March 2005)

[7] Dey, A.K., Sohn, T., Streng, S., Kodama, J.: iCAP: Interactive Prototyping of Context-Aware Applications. In: Proc. Fourth Intl. Conference on Pervasive Computing (2006)

[8] eDocent Website http://www.ammi.org/site/extrapages/edoctext.html

[9] Eustice, K., Kleinrock, L., Markstrum, S., Popek, G., Ramakrishna, V., Reiher, P.: Enabling Secure Ubiquitous Interactions. In: Proceedings of 1st International Workshop on Middleware for Pervasive and Ad Hoc Computing (co-located with Middleware 2003) (2003)

[10] Kaplan, E.: Understanding GPS, Artech House (1996)

[11] Hindmarsh, J., Heath, C.: vom Lehn, D., Cleverly, J.: Creating Assemblies: Aboard the Ghost Ship. In: Proc, ACM Conference on Computer Supported Cooperative Work (2002)

[12] Hull, R., Clayton, B., Melamed, T.: Rapid Authoring of Mediascapes. In: Proceedings of Ubicomp (2004)

[13] Kindberg, T., Barton, J., Morgan, J., Becker, G., Caswell, D., Debaty, P., Gopal, G., Frid, M., Krishnan, V., Morris, H., Schettino, J., Serra, B., Spasojevic, M.: People, Places, Things: Web Presence for the Real World. Mobile Networks and Applications, vol. 7(5)

[14] Kwak, S.Y.: Designing a Handheld Interactive Scavenger Hunt Game to Enhance Museum Experience. MA Thesis. Michigan State University (2004)

[15] Quick, K., Vogiazou, Y.: CitiTag Multiplayer Infrastructure, TR: KMI-04-7 (March 2004)

[16] Schmalstieg, D., Wagner, D.: A Handheld Augmented Reality Museum Guide. In: Proc. IADIS Intl Conf. on Mobile Learning (ML2005). Qawra, Malta (June 2005)

[17] Strickland, C., Lawson, C.: Making the Vniverse http://www.cynthialawson.com/vniverse/essay/index.html

How Panoramic Photography Changed Multimedia Presentations in Tourism

Nelson Gonçalves

Contacto Visual Lda – R 1 de Dezembro, 8 2 Dto,
4740-226 Esposende, Portugal
nelson.gonçalves@contactovisual.pt

Abstract. An overview of the use of panoramic photography, the panorama concept, and evolution of presentation and multimedia projects targeting tourism promotions The purpose is to stress the importance of panoramic pictures in the Portuguese design of the multimedia systems for the promotion of tourism. Through photography in the multimedia support on-line and off-line, the user can go back in time and watch what those landscapes were like in his/her childhood, for example. Consequently, one of the additional quality options in our productions is the diachronic view of the landscape.

Keywords: Design, Multimedia, CD-ROM, DVD, Web, Photography, Panorama, Tourism, Virtual Tour.

1 Introduction

Panoramic photography changed the static viewing of photographs to interactive participation. The viewer is no long a spectator, to become an explorer, just like in a real world. Looking around, up and down, getting closer, obtaining more information on a particular subject, seeing details, moving to another point a view, to another room or place in a virtual tour.

This sort of interactive images can only be used on digital media: CD-ROMs or DVD, websites, and other multimedia displays. Panoramic photography is a key element in the interface of the interactive system, which is geared to tourism promotion in Portugal and favours visualization of information, as Shneiderman claims [1].

One of the motives for this paper is our interest in maintaining the quality of multimedia systems in terms of the originality or innovative contents, principally for young, adult and senior users. An analysis of the multimedia content in the time or diacrhronics (from, Greek, *dia*, through, accross and *chrono*, time) is very positive for this end [2]. For example in appendix 1, when the user see in multimedia system a set of the pictures of oneself place (diacronics order in figures 6, 7, 8) [3].

The target of this work is to review what was done so far and its applications on tourism and cultural projects, the Contacto Visual Portuguese experience [3], [4] and to feel the progress for the upcoming technologies and digital transfer speeds [5], [6].

J. Jacko (Ed.): Human-Computer Interaction, Part III, HCII 2007, LNCS 4552, pp. 862–871, 2007.

2 Apple's QuicktimeVR

VR stands for Virtual Reality. Apple appended these letters to its multimedia container software Quicktime to emphasize the possibility of viewing a real environment inside a digital window, where the user can interact in a virtual world. In fact, Apple developed a concept and a software capable of assembling photos captured around an axis (panoramas), showing and manipulating the resulting image in a single file [7]. The result was a new way to look into a photograph, exploring interactively the full environment, rather than simple looking to the same limited area the traditional photo allows. In addition, the software can include hot spots, clickable areas in the image that can be linked to other panoramas creating a set a various point of views, and virtual tours on any place. This technology opened a new world for multimedia projects, where tourism and culture soon became one of the best targets. On tourism, to show on a computer virtual reality tours of distance places, anywhere in the world, like tourist and vacation destinations, hotels and resorts, while cultural projects could show monuments, exhibitions, allowing people to view them, even places where, for security or temporal reasons, could not be visited in real life.

QuicktimeVR also includes Object Movies. In opposite to panoramas, which are an environment viewed from a centered single point of view, quicktimeVR objects are a set of photos of an object captured from around a circle pointing to the object. It is possible to add rows of captured photos showing the object from different angles. The resulting file is an interactive image where an object can be rotated and even tilted using the mouse.

Mixing both panoramas and objects, and adding sounds, links to other media, web pages or other source of documents, is a set of resources where multimedia developers find themselves in a potential new virtual world of possibilities.

Fig. 1. Cylindrical panorama of Esposende, 46º of Field of View

At first, panoramas were obtained from a series of photos, taken from a fixed position and pointing in sequence around a 360 degrees circle. Laying the photos side by side, creates a cylindrical set of photos which in the end touches the first, creating a cylindrical photo.

Cylindrical panoramas have a limited vertical field of view, cutting the top and bottom of the real place. But then a new technology emerged with Quicktime version 5, the Apple's cubic engine or IPIX spherical version, which rendered a full environment, including the top and bottom. Moving from cylindrical to spherical means the ability to see the full surrounding space, instead of just a cylindrical photo. This was an astonishing progress. For indoor panoramas, with detailed ceilings such as churches, or places where space is extremely limited like inside cars or small rooms, spherical panoramas taken with fisheye or wide lens made these possible.

Tight streets also became an easy subject, with the façades visible no matter how high and close they are. And imagine the interior of a shop, with all the details of products and shelves. All that kind if imagery is possible with panoramic photography.

Fig. 2. Spherical panorama (equirectangular image) of Esposende, 360x180º of Field of View

Fig. 3. Quicktime Cubic version of the same full 360x180º panorama

Cylindrical panoramas have a limited vertical field of view, cutting the top and bottom of the real place. But then a new technology emerged with Quicktime version 5, the Apple's cubic engine or IPIX spherical version, which rendered a full environment, including the top and bottom. Moving from cylindrical to spherical means the ability to see the full surrounding space, instead of just a cylindrical photo. This was an astonishing progress. For indoor panoramas, with detailed ceilings such as churches, or places where space is extremely limited like inside cars or small rooms, spherical panoramas taken with fisheye or wide lens made these possible. Tight streets also became an easy subject, with the façades visible no matter how high and close they are. And imagine the interior of a shop, with all the details of products and shelves. All that kind if imagery is possible with panoramic photography.

But… is panoramic photography better than normal photos? By no means. It's a different perception of a place and time. A photo is a detail of time and light, a moment captured and frozen by a machine, an expression of nature, people, emotions, or whatever was photographed. A panorama captures the whole place. What is in front of you, but also what is behind, up, or at your feet. But there is no "first person". No feet. No body. The viewer is invisible. It mimics a movie, as it appears to have a timeline. But there is not a really moving through the time of narration. So it leaves us with an image of a place. Complete. It's up to the viewer to explore it.

The goal of using panoramic photography in cultural projects, is to carry into a media, to be seen in a computer, the places and surrounding elements, in a way a user can walk around, stop and see, zoom in, move to another location. It's more than a photo, it's an interactive experience. Just like a real visit, but at the distance of a computer mouse and screen.

3 The Virtual Experience

Panoramic photography can be used in virtual tours of museums, cultural institutions, endangered monuments, architectural and real estate marketing, nature parks and most of tourism places. Virtual reality allows participants to interactively explore and examine environments, three-dimensional virtual worlds, from any computer. Tours can be exhibited on the internet, as a CD-Rom insert in exhibition catalogs or stand-alone products, or used on a variety of media:

- CD/DVD-ROM –interactive virtual tours, along with text and photos, video and sound, either naturally captured sounds of each point of view, as narration or music.
- DVD, either DVD-ROM for larger interactive projects including video clips, or DVD for television viewing.
- Websites, with all its unlimited capacity for linking to other websites, pages, content, and different kind of media, and, most of all, its capacity for continuous updating of content.

Let's see for example, an exhibition of works of art. An exhibition is a time limited display of works of art or other special interest products. Public can attend it in that period of time at where the exhibition takes place. But if we do a Virtual Tour with panoramic photos of the exhibition, it can be viewed trough internet anywhere in the world. And if printed in a CD-ROM, it can be archived as an invaluable document, which would last for a long period of time, long after the real exhibition would end, and seen any time anywhere.

In such a Virtual Visit to the Exhibition, the photographer would capture the exhibition rooms, in strategic points where all works of art would be visible. Each of the them could be photographed separately in high definition, and additional information, such as author, title, date, history, and whatever more, could be stored. We could also record the audio of a narrator for a guided tour. If some of the pieces are sculptures or three-dimensional objects, it would be possible to capture each of them as QuicktimeVR objects. Assembling the photos and information would result in a set of panoramas corresponding to the tour in the exhibition. On the screen, the visitor could explore the room, zoom in the paintings and sculptures, moving to other points of view. Each work of art can have a layer with an icon of sound, which would switch the narration about the particular object [6]. Clicking on a painting, or other fixed display, could jump to the high resolution photo and additional information about that particular work of art. Can be a screen, a web page or other multimedia document, with no limitations. If the object is a sculpture, clicking on it would let rotate it. The advantages of such a virtual tour is obvious as a multimedia document and as tourism and cultural promotion.

4 Hardware Limitations

Technology depends on both hardware and software [5]. The most challenging on panoramic photography, is the image detail. The photos are captured with fish-eye or wide lens, and usually, in two or more takes. Some special photo equipments were created to capture the whole panorama in a single shot, like de Kaidan's "360 One VR", but most used are 2 to 6 shots, to achieve the best image quality. These are done with 8mm or less lens. These lens create distortions that have to be corrected. And the final image is an equirectangular flat sphere. For the viewer, this has to be re-adjusted, so the image becomes "natural". In addition, to retrieve a maximum of detail, the image has to be very large, or it will loose viewing quality. And if we want to allow zooming, it's even a bigger problem. The photographer will want to make it as big as possible. But computers and internet will not support the computing power needed for this effort. This is why most of the first multimedia projects with panoramas, used small windows and small files, a compacted version of the captured image. As PCs and internet are every day faster and faster, so panoramic photography can use more and more larger and better quality photos. It opens our minds and expectations on what we can do. Full-screen panoramas, detailed objects, sounds, integrated information, animated or video elements, and so on. The possibilities are endless. Or maybe a moving point of view — today's technology only let us do a fixed point of view —, something like panoramic video. But that's another challenge. Larger, also means jumping out of the computer screen, like the US Denver's Gates Planetarium, a sophisticated high technology planetarium where virtual reality panoramic images are at its maximum human experiencing. Here, panoramas are projected on the ceiling and around an audience at very high definition and realism. Instead of through one window people can see the whole panorama at once.For distributable media, like CDs, DVDs, or the Internet as a spreadable medium, it still has to be in a compact format.

5 The Portuguese Experience

Soon on 1997, in the earlier days of this technology, Contacto Visual embraced the concept, and started its own projects. At first, the equipment used to capture was roughly basic, with a video camera and a tripod. Taking photos was a challenge, as twelve photos were needed for each panorama. Panoramas were cylindrical and based on a set of normal photos taken around an axis. The results, were however outstanding for the time. Natural captured sounds, map locations, other photos and text information were added for completing the virtual tour. The CD-ROMs Alto Minho, Verde Minho, and Esposende, were rewarded in international contests in Portugal and Spain [8] [9]. These projects covered the northern region of Portugal, the province of Minho (see www.contactovisual.pt/altominho). Panoramas were captured in the most important tourist places, towns, castles, nature parks, rivers. The assemblage also included maps to locate each place, and text was added with the history of those places.

Fig. 4. Detail of a cylindrical panorama from de CD-ROM Verde Minho

On the CD Verde Minho, the house of an important 19th century Portuguese writer, Camilo Castelo Branco, was covered with a virtual tour. The concept explained above, was tested in the house gallery room where most of Camilo's original documents, paintings and sculptures, are public displayed. Here is an illustration of the virtual tour:

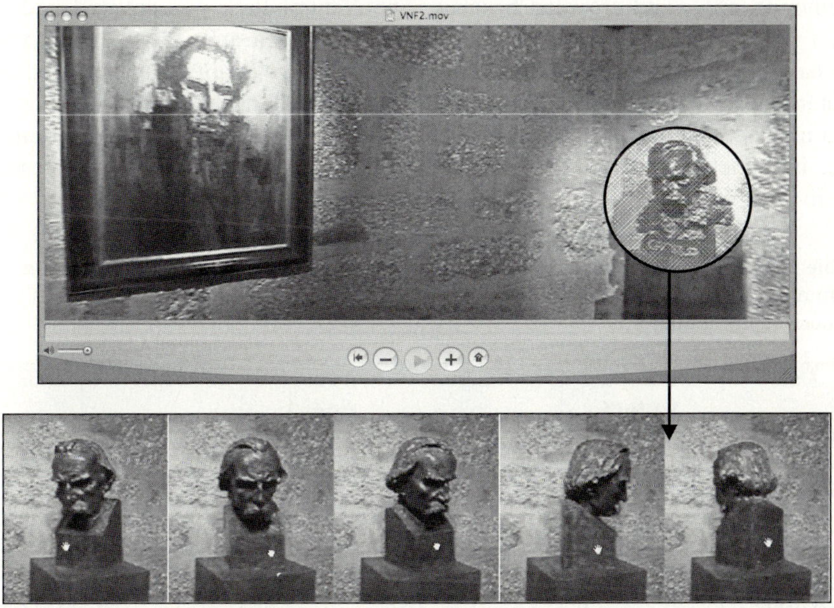

Fig. 5. Detail of the Virtual Tour at Camilo Castelo Branco Gallery

Clicking on Camilo's bust, it is possible to rotate it, without leaving the gallery environment. The virtual tour also includes links to different areas of the gallery, and the writer's house. The history of the writer, the house, and his biography can be read or printed. Selecting print, the resulting printing page includes the viewing of the panorama in the position the user selected and a plant or map locating where the virtual tour and the panorama was taken.

Esposende, 1999. Contacto Visual develops an interactive tour on this locality using panoramic photography. At first, the idea was to create a CD-ROM with just panoramic photography, natural sounds, and locating on the points of view in an interactive map. But than we understood it could be a lot more, explaining to the viewer what it was seeing. Text information and photos were added to show deeper contents. And for the virtual experience, we made a research on old photos and captured new ones on the same point of view. We made both photos merging one to the other, as a time traveling photo. For the virtual tour, more than 300 cylindrical panoramas were captured in the streets, main buildings, and nature.

The CD-ROM was distributed around the world in tourism promotion events, showing Esposende as a place to discover in the north of Portugal.

Esposende 2005. A new edition of the 1999 project was accomplished. Now with near 500 spherical panoramas covering most of the city, coast line, rivers and surroundings, mountain with landscape views, main cultural buildings such as the museum, the city hall, the city library, churches, historical houses and pre-historical villages, hotels and tourism locations, even social events such as the local street fair, swimming pools and crowded beaches. The Natural Park was covered with virtual tours showing details of flora and river mills, and sea and river sounds to include dramatic life feeling to the photographs. General image quality was increased, and the contents was reorganized to promote the tourist lodging at Esposende. Each Hotel also included panoramas along with conventional illustration and information. A fly-over introduction shows the river and the coast-line as a bird view of the estuary of the river Cavado and the sea at Esposende.

Table 1. From July 2005 to December 2006 near 20,000 people visited the website, most of them more than once, navigating through 245,252 pages. For a small town, that was a success in tourism promotion.

Date	Unique visitors	Visits	Pages viewed	Hits	Bandwidth
May 2005	9	28	304	1156	41.30 MB
Jun 2005	15	20	93	414	15.30 MB
Jul 2005	166	253	5158	17631	400.88 MB
Aug 2005	449	615	12058	43395	779.83 MB
Sep 2005	184	231	3698	9837	228.61 MB
Oct 2005	380	509	7973	23480	666.98 MB
Nov 2005	8	9	226	724	12.48 MB
Dec 2005	511	645	8952	31077	660.73 MB
Jan 2006	702	885	11570	43934	830.34 MB
Feb 2006	783	933	12023	41014	907.00 MB
Mar 2006	1139	1385	17807	65044	1.29 GB
Apr 2006	1204	1388	18336	64347	1.25 GB
May 2006	1283	1494	19383	68382	1.41 GB
Jun 2006	1359	1570	18898	69001	1.34 GB
Jul 2006	2176	2528	28749	106045	1.88 GB
Aug 2006	2366	2594	27589	97954	1.84 GB
Sep 2006	1401	1616	13007	45819	938.08 MB
Oct 2006	1756	2183	11784	46542	887.24 MB
Nov 2006	2048	2482	14540	53660	1.02 GB
Dec 2006	1666	2063	13104	45822	955.77 MB

Among the 36 virtual tours with hundreds of panoramas included, various techniques were pursued to explore the quicktimeVR technology. For example, the sound of the river on a river-mill wheel, the sound of the sea waves on the beach, are listened only when pointing the viewing window to where it is supposed to come from. And still photos of details were added on the vegetation of the beach dunes, to show some of the protected plants, and in the pre-historical village, on the buildings showing the interior.

It was also developed a website to extend the number of possible people interested in knowing Esposende. The website, a live project still under development, can be seen in two different ways: the virtual visual tour of Esposende, with the panoramas, and photo galleries, at esposende.com.pt, and another website for the cultural and tourist information at visitesposende.com.

After being published, on 2005, it is now possible to review its success on promoting the tourism of Esposende. A thousand CDs were distributed to tourism agents and the website saw a growing increase of visits, as it can be seen on this table.

6 Tourism and Cultural Multimedia Projects: Next Generation

Panoramic photography, virtual tours, and all the possibilities quicktime and other special software offers, along with the increasing on hardware and communications capabilities, make it possible to create even more sophisticated multimedia projects, where experiencing the visual contact with remote places will be the next level challenge.

According to a survey by the Pew Internet & American Life Project, done in 2004, 45% of online American adults have taken virtual tours of another location online [10]. That represents 54 million adults, just in United States of America, who have used the internet to venture somewhere else. The most popular virtual tours, are of famous places, such as the Taj Mahal in India, the White House in USA, or most Hotels around the world. On a typical day, more than two million people are using the internet to take a virtual tour.

And photographers, together with multimedia programmers, are exploring new concepts and techniques, like the amazing Chinese ChinaVR floating panoramas (www.chinavr.net) and the aerial panorama experiences, or cultural and tourism projects such as the World Heritage Tour (www.world-heritage-tour.org) which covers the full planet with virtual tours, with the collaboration of photographers from all over the world, or the Full-Screen Project from panoramas.dk, a ever growing community around panoramic photography [11].

7 Conclusions

Virtual panoramic tours has an increasing roll on multimedia tourism projects, either for internet or distributable media. This is a technology that reveals the true meaning of immersive interactive exploration of remote places. By increasing its capacities, and adding new multimedia features, virtual tours might become the skeleton of multimedia products and websites. The use of the current techniques in Portuguese photography is very wide spread in the on-line/off-line multimedia in our days, aimed at the tourism, real state and marketing sectors, etc. Besides, a diachronic and synchronic view of the passing of time in the pictures can help to a greater acceptance of the system by the elderly users, and so establish a communication link between the different generations in the home.

Acknowledgments

The author wish to acknowledge Francisco V. C. Ficarra for their contributions. Also a special thanks to the Council of the city of Esposende, Portugal.

References

1. Shneiderman, B.: Designing the User Interface, 3rd edn. Addison-Wesley, Massachusetts (1998)
2. Ficarra, F.: Diachronics for Original Contents in Multimedia Systems. In: World Multiconference on Systemics, Cybernetics and Informatics 2000, IIS, Florida, vol. 2, pp. 17–22 (2000)
3. Esposende CD-ROM: ContactoVisual, Esposende (1999)
4. Esposende: um privilégio da natureza CD-ROM: Contacto Visual Esposende (2005)
5. Fogg, B.: Persuasive Technology, Using Computers to Change What We Think and Do. Morgan Kaufmann Publishers, San Francisco (2003)
6. Meadows, M.: Pause & Effect. New Riders, Indianapolis (2002)
7. Apple Developers website - QuicktimeVR: http://developer.apple.com/documentation/QuickTime/InsideQT_QTVR
8. Alto Minho CD-ROM. Contacto Visual. Esposende (1998)
9. Verde Minho CD-ROM. Contacto Visual. Esposende (1999)
10. PEW Internet and American Life Project: http://www.pewinternet.org
11. Fullscreen QTVR Features: www.panoramas.dk

Appendix 1: Diachronic for Originality and Quality

Fig. 6. Esposende CD-ROM (photo 1920)

Fig. 7. Esposende CD-ROM (photo 1980)

Fig. 8. Esposende CD-ROM (photo 1999)

Frame Segmentation Used MLP-Based X-Y Recursive for Mobile Cartoon Content

Eunjung Han[1], Kirak Kim[1], HwangKyu Yang[2], and Keechul Jung[1]

[1] HCI Lab., School of Media, College of Information Technology,
Soongsil University, 156-743, Seoul, S. Korea
{hanej,raks,kcjung}@ssu.ac.kr
[2] Department of Multimedia Engineering, Dongseo University, 617-716, Busan, S. Korea
hayang88@hanmail.net

Abstract. With rapid growth of the mobile industry, the limitation of small screen mobile is attracting a lot of researchers attention for transforming on/off-line contents into mobile contents. Frame segmentation for limited mobile browsers is the key point of off-line contents tranformation. The X-Y recursive cut algorithm has been widely used for frame segmentation in document analysis. However, this algorithm has drawbacks for cartoon images which have various image types and image with noises, especially the online cartoon contents obtain during scanning. In this paper, we propose a method to segment on/off-line cartoon contents into fitted frames for the mobile screen. This makes the x-y recursive cut algorithm difficult to find the exact cutting point. Therefore we use a method by combining two concepts: an X-Y recursive cut algorithm to extract candidate segmenting positions which shows a good performance on noises free contents, and Multi-Layer Perceptrons (MLP) concept use on candidate for verification. These methods can increase the accuracy of the frame segmentation and feasible to apply on various off-line cartoon images with frames.

Keywords: MLP, X-Y recursive, frame segmentation, mobile cartoon contents.

1 Introduction

As mobile devices are widespread, the request for the use of mobile contents has recently increased and attracts attention in mobile and ubiquitous computing research. For the purpose of satisfying the request, not only producing various contents but transforming on/off-line contents into fitted size is being issue for the mobile devices with a small screen. The transformation of off-line contents has two general types: first is a passive method that person directly transforms the contents, and second is using auto transformation system from off-line to mobile contents. The automatic system can provide the most efficient and convenient method for manipulating and processing the contents. However, these automatic systems have some problems to apply on various contents. Especially to solve some problems of the auto transformation from off-line cartoon contents to mobile contents. The paper-based image of off-line cartoon should

J. Jacko (Ed.): Human-Computer Interaction, Part III, HCII 2007, LNCS 4552, pp. 872–881, 2007.

transform to limited size on various mobile browsers. In this case, the key point of transformation the cartoon contents is how to segment the frame of the image effectively in order to fit in small mobile screen.

A number of approaches to page segmentation or page decomposition have been proposed in the literature. Wang et al. [1] used such an approach to segment newspaper images into component regions and Li and Gray [2] used wavelet coefficient distributions to do top-down classification of complex document images. Etemad et al. [3] used fuzzy decision rules for bottom-up clustering of pixels using a neural network. An alternative approach is to use the white spaces available in document images to find the boundaries of text or image regions as proposed by Pavlidis [4]. Many approaches to page segmentation concentrate on processing background pixels or using the "white space" [5-8] in a page to identify homogeneous regions. These techniques include X-Y tree [9-10], pixel-based projection profile [11] and connected component-based projection profile [12], white space tracing and white space thinning [13]. They can be regarded as top-down approaches [14-16] which segment a page recursively by X-cut and Y-cut from large components, starting with the whole page to small components eventually reaching individual characters.

In our previous work [17], we implement frame segmentation[1] for cartoon images, which are one of the most popular ones, with frames, and used X-Y recursive cut algorithm to separate the cartoon contents with frames into frames to fix into small screen mobile device. However, the X-Y recursive cut algorithm has some problems. If the frame boundary has some noises, the algorithm can not segment the frame. The noise data of the image affects the value of the image by projection profile process therefore the method can not detect the frame. And if the frame line is not a straight line, the X-Y recursive algorithm can not make correct segmentation. It can not recognize the line as frame boundary. Due to this reason, the X-Y recursive method can apply to on a limited normal image.

In this paper, we propose an improved method to segment the off-line cartoon frame using the MLP-based X-Y recursive algorithm. The input of the neural network is a scanned image of the cartoon and the output is candidate cutting points of the input image. In this method, several candidate cutting points are first generated by

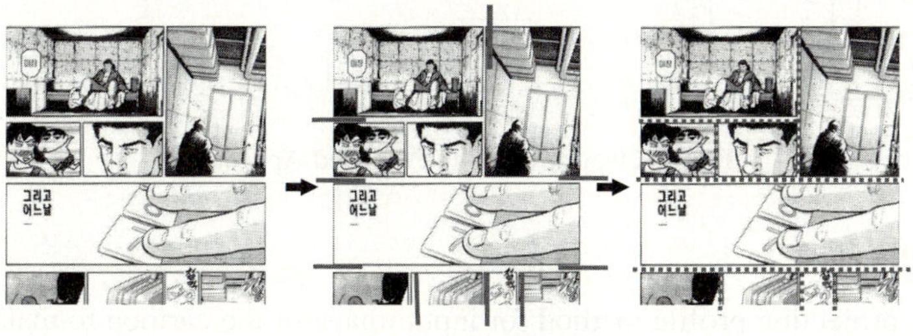

(a) (b) (c)

Fig. 1. Outline of the proposed method: (a) an input image [19], (b) a result (the gray line denotes boundary) of the forward process, (c) a segmented result

[1] It is a prerequisite stage for extracting important information (salient regions).

X-Y recursive cut algorithm, and we can identify whether the point indicates the right position using the MLP-based segmentation process on only candidate cutting points per each step (Fig.1).

2 Frame Segmentation

We use the input data from the scanned image of off-line cartoon, and change it the binary image (Fig.2). In the binary image of the input data, the black and white pixels are recognized values in the MLP-based frame segmentation process. The input data makes the cutting point by MLP-based segmentation process. In this process, the MLP use the weight which is calculated by training process of some input images. The MLP finds the position of frame segmentation for the cartoon image. Then we can use the cutting-point for the segmenting position and segment the frame using X-Y recursive concept. If the results have two or more candidate points, we could choose the right point by the verification process using projection profile method. In chapter 3, it will be explained the MLP structure and the cutting-point marking process.

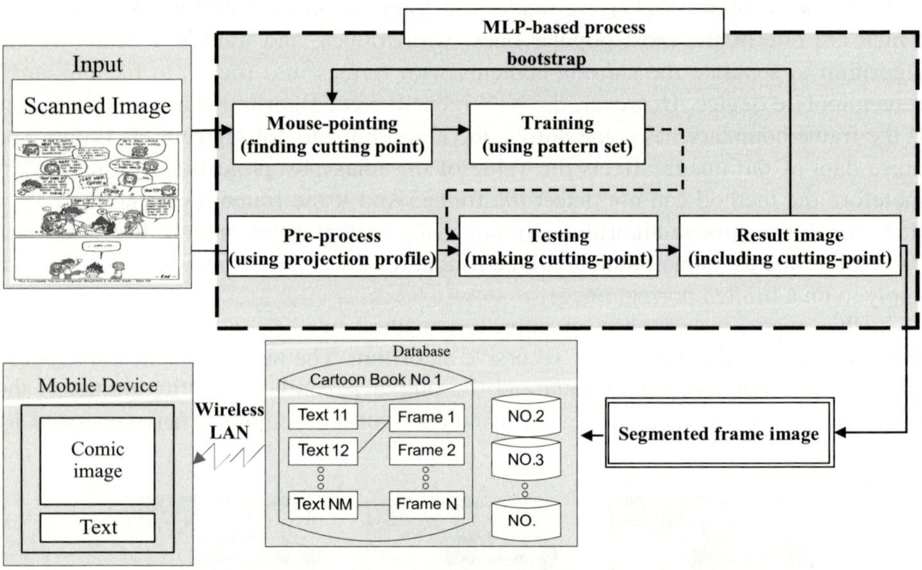

Fig. 2. Overview of the Proposed Approach

2.1 Pre-process

We use the projection profile method for input image of the cartoon to make the input of the Testing process. As shown in Fig. 3, the histogram of the image is used to find the candidate cutting-point area using loose threshold value. Then, the position from the x-y projection profile indicates the input to the Testing process. It has less input value than whole input from the image that can be more efficient processing time.

Fig. 3. The input area of Testing process (dotted line indicates the input area)

2.2 Structure of MLP

The structure of the MLP of our proposed design consists of 48 input nodes, 40 hidden nodes, and 1 output node. Fig. 4 shows the structure of two-layer neural network.

It has a fully-connected structure and uses a back-propagation learning algorithm. The MLP inputs a 48-order mesh vector to the network, which is extracted from a 30×40 normalized binary image. The 48 integer values are obtained by counting the number of pixels in each 5×5 local window in the normalized binary image. The resulting 25 intensities are normalized to the range of [0.0 .. 1.0]. Forty-eight floating point numbers are then input into the network in column major order. If the position of the cartoon image is clicked by the mouse, the MLP recognize it frame boundary to

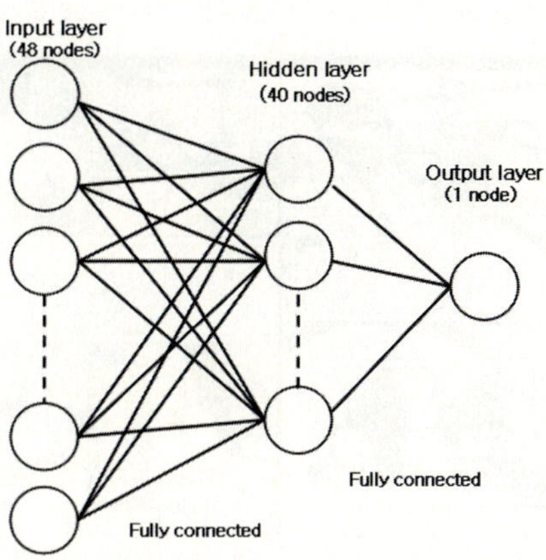

Fig. 4. Structure of two-layer neural network

Fig. 5. The MLP input data of the cartoon image and zoomed in images

segment the image. A desired cutting point is determined manually and saved behind the 48-order mesh vector. Fig. 5 shows the process of obtaining neural input values.

The input values from the image are obtained to the boundary area of the images as a quadrangle from left to right and from top to bottom. The output value of the MLP is 1 or 0. In the forward process, the input image which is analyzed into 30×40 input pixels that made by 48-nodes would have the MLP results. The true value indicates the frame boundary. If the area of the 30×40 input has true value, the process can marking the cutting point. The position of the cutting-point takes a role of segmenting point. If the result is false the process can recognize that the area of the 30×40 input is not the frame boundary.

2.3 Cutting-Point Marking

The MLP can find the frame boundary and segment the frame. Fig. 6 shows the cutting-point area.

The line of the frame boundary indicates the cutting-point. The process can recognize the segmentation area with the MLP results. As you can see in the Fig. 6, it is

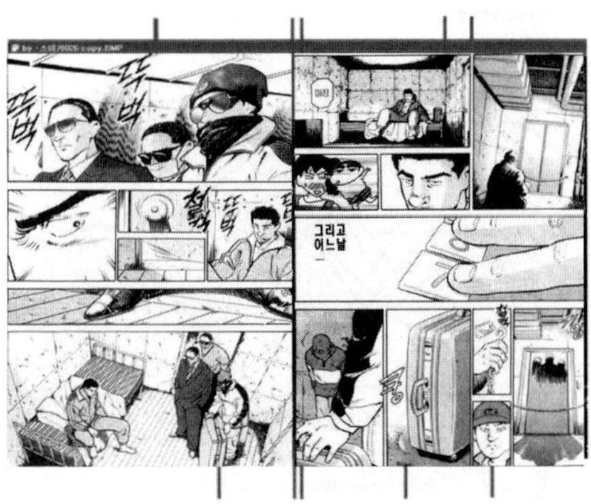

Fig. 6. The result of finding cutting-points

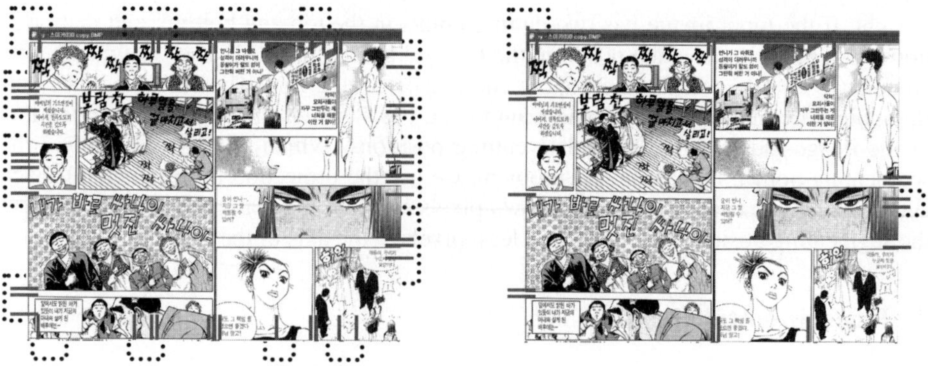

(a) (b)

Fig. 7. Errors on frame segmentation result. (a) the first forward image, (b) a result of bootstrap method (The box of the image boundary is errors.).

possible to segment artificially for off-line cartoon images by training images. Although the frame has some noises, the MLP can recognize the frame boundary. Then we can mark the cutting-point in the boundary and make the cutting-line. However, the result of the MLP is not complete.

As shown in Fig. 7, if the object is near the frame boundary, or the feature of the object in the frame is like a frame boundary, the MLP process can not recognize completely. To handle this problem we use the bootstrap method recommended by Sung and Poggio [18], which was initially developed to train neural networks for face detection. Some non-frame samples are collected and used for training. Plus, the partially trained MLP is repeatedly applied to images for more complete segmentation, and then patterns with a positive output are added to the training set as non-frame samples. This process iterates until no more patterns are added to the training set.

2.4 Verification

The output of MLP can have incorrect cutting-points. In the forward process, the cutting-line in the frame boundary shifts the position from top to bottom and from left

Fig. 8. One or more candidate cutting points

to right. If the input image has two cutting-points in the top and bottom, and that position is projected to the same position, the forward process in MLP also would make the cumulative cutting-point in the bottom and makes cutting-line. Then the candidate cutting-points are more than we would want to get. Fig. 8 shows this result. The dotted line of the image indicates the candidate cutting positions. Which one should we find the segmenting point? To handle this problem, we use the projection profile method. Each cutting-point, we can check the top-down pixels and find the real cutting-point which is the segmenting position that there is at least pixels in the axis of the position.

3 Experimental Results

This method is implemented in C++ language on an IBM-PC. 30 images of off-line cartoon were used to train MLP for the frame segmentation. The remaining 30 images were used for testing. Fig. 9 shows the frame segmentation results.

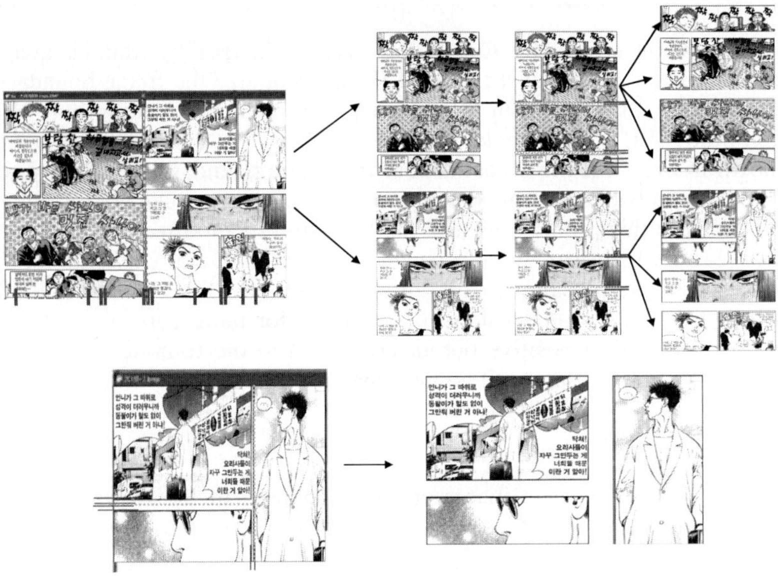

Fig. 9. One of the frame segmentation result for cartoon A images

The segmentation rates were evaluated using two metrics: precision and recall rate (Table 1). Equation (1) and (2) are the formula to compute the precision and recall rate. As shown in table 1, our method produced higher precision and recall rate than X-Y recursive cut algorithm without a MLP process, yet lower recall rates, as lack of training data for cartoons A, B and C.

$$precision\ (\%) = \frac{\#\,of\ \text{correctly detected cutting points}}{\#\,of\ \text{detected cutting points}} \times 100 \quad (1)$$

$$recall\ (\%) = \frac{\#\,of\ \text{correctly detected cutting points}}{\#\,of\ \text{desired cutting points}} \times 100 \quad (2)$$

Table 1. Comparison of precision rates

Cartoon Book Type	Category	without MLP process		with MLP process	
		Precision	Recall	Precision	Recall
Cartoon A	Training set	83.5%	78%	91.3%	96.5%
	Test set	-	-	87.7%	92.6%
Cartoon B	Training set	81.5%	76%	90.3%	92.5%
	Test set	-	-	87.3%	95.5%
Cartoon C	Training set	83.5%	78%	93.6%	98.5%
	Test set	-	-	87.2%	92.5%

Table 2. Comparison of execution time

Measurement	with pre-process	without pre-process
Time (sec)	**2.8**	**10**

The execution time with pre-process is more efficient than without pre-process, because the size of input data from the cartoon is different (table 2). When we execute pre-process, we can reduce the input size.

The segmentation errors in this experiment may classify into MLP-based segmentation step. This problem is mainly the result of a shortage of training data. An existing method for frame segmentation, X-Y recursive, has some problems because the noise and non-straight frame line affect the frame segmentation. The X-Y recursive method to compare the frame segmentation result is a sample data that the threshold value finding for the frame segmenting position is coordinated by our experimental environment. The results of this algorithm are not exact that show in Fig. 9 (a). Our new method using MLP-based X-Y recursive improves frame segmentation accuracy and variety of scanned images for transforming from off-line to mobile that Fig. 10 (b) shows this result.

Fig. 11 shows frame segmentation proposed result of mobile cartoon content that fit well on the mobile screen. The propose method has advantage to resize the cartoon content depends on the mobile device screen [17].

(a) (b)

Fig. 10. Comparing two methods. (a) a X-Y recursive result, (b) a MLP-based segmentation result.

(a) (b) (c)

Fig. 11. Frame Segmentation Proposes Result. (a) original image, (b) a MLP-based segmentation result, (c) mobile cartoon content.

4 Conclusion

Users generally access the cartoon content through mobile devices. This paper proposed a method for frame segmentation from a scanned image of paper-based cartoon image to the small screen mobile device**.** In this method, the segmentation process was implemented by a Multi-Layer Perceptron (MLP) trained by a back-propagation algorithm. The MLP-based frame segmentation process generates several candidate cutting points and the verification process using projection profile method recognizes these cutting-points in order to select the correct cutting point among candidates. Through experiments with various kinds of scanned images, it has been shown that the proposed method is very effective for the segmentation. However, various scanned images of off-line cartoon have a lot of frame features which are not a quadrangle. In this case, we can find the boundary point of segmenting frame, but our process can not segment inside the frame of the scanned images because of the non-quadrangle frame. As well, we are trying to segment the non-quadrangle frame and plan to extend our works to the frame that includes objects.

Acknowledgements. This work was supported by the Soongsil University Research Fund.

References

1. Wang, D., Srihari, S.N.: Classification of newspaper image blocks using texture analysis. Computer Vision Graphics, and Image Processing 47, 327–352 (1989)
2. Li, J., gray, R.M.: Text and picture segmentation by distribution analysis of wavelet coefficients. In: Proceedings of the 5th International conference on Image Processing Chicago, Illinois, pp. 790–794 (October 1998)
3. etemad, K., Doermann, D.S., Chellappa, R.: Multiscale segmentation of unstructured document pages using soft decision integration. IEEE Transactions on Pattern Analysis and Machine Intelligence 19, 92–96 (1997)
4. Pavlidis, T., Zhou, J.: Page segmentation by white streams. In: Proceedings of the First International Conference on Document Analysis and Recognition, St, Malo, France, pp. 945–953 (September 1991)

5. Akindele, O., Belaid, A.: Page Segmentation by Segment Tracing. In: proceedings of Second Int'l Conf. Document Analysis and Recognition, pp. 341–344 (1993)
6. Amamoto, N., Torigoe, S., Hirogaki, Y.: Block Segmentation and Text Area Extraction of Vertically/Horizontally Written Document. In: Proceedings of Second Int'l Conf. Document Analysis and Recognition, pp. 739–742 (1993)
7. Ittner, D., Baird, H.: Language-Free Layout Analysis. In: Proceedings of Second Int'l Conf. Document Analysis and Recognition, Tsukuba, Japan, pp. 336–340 (1993)
8. Antonacopoulos, A., Ritchings, R.: Flexible Page Segmentation Using the Background. In: Proceedings of 12 th Int'l Conf. Pattern Recognition, pp. 339–344 (1994)
9. Nagy, G., Seth, S.: Hierarchical Representation of Optically Scanned Documents. In: Proceedings of Seventh Int'l Conf. Pattern Recognition, pp. 347–349 (1984)
10. Krishnamoorthy, M., Nagy, G., Seth, S., Viswanathan, M.: Syntactic Segmentation and Labeling of Digitized Pages From Technical Journals. IEEE Trans. Pattern Analysis and Machine Intelligence 15, 743–747 (1993)
11. Pavlidis, T., Zhou, J.: Page Segmentation by White Streams. In: Proceedings of First Int'l Conf. Document Analysis and Recognition, pp. 945–953 (1991)
12. Ha, J., Haralick, R., Phillips, I.: Document Page Decomposition by the Bounding-Box Projection Technique. In: Proceedings of Third Int'l Conf. Document Analysis and Recognition, pp. 1119–1122 (1995)
13. Kise, K., Yanagida, O., Takamatsu, S.: Page Segmentation Based on Thinning of Background. In: Proceedings of 13th Int'l Conf. Pattern Recognition, pp. 788–792 (1996)
14. Fujisawa, H., Nakano, Y.: A Top-Down Approach for the Analysis of Documents. In: Proceedings of 10th Int'l Conf. Pattern Recognition, pp. 113–122 (1990)
15. Chenevoy, Y., Belaid, A.: Hypothesis Management for Structured Document Recognition. In: Proceedings of First Int'l Conf. Document Analysis and Recognition, pp. 121–129 (1991)
16. Ingold, R., Armangil, D.: A Top-Down Document Analysis Method for Logical Structure Recognition. In: Proceedings of First Int'l Conf. Document Analysis and Recognition, pp. 41–49 (1991)
17. Eunjung, H., Sungkuk, J., Anjin, P., Keechul, J.: Automatic Conversion System for Mobile Cartoon Contents. In: Proceedings of International Conference on Asian Digital Libraries, vol. 3815, pp. 416–423 (2005)
18. Sung, K.K., Poggio, T.: Example-based Learning for View-based Human Face Detection. IEEE Transactions on Pattern Analysis and Machine Intelligence 20(1), 39–51 (1998)
19. Takehiko Inoue: SLAMDUNK. All rights reserved First published in Japan in, by Shueisha Inc., Tokyo Korean translation rights arranged with through Shueisha Inc. and Dai-Won Publishing Co., Ltd (1990)
20. Yim, J.O. : ZZANG. All rights reserved First published in Korea by DaiWon Inc.

Browsing and Sorting Digital Pictures Using Automatic Image Classification and Quality Analysis

Otmar Hilliges, Peter Kunath, Alexey Pryakhin,
Andreas Butz, and Hans-Peter Kriegel

Institute for Informatics,
Ludwig-Maximilians-Universität,
Munich, Germany
otmar.hilliges@ifi.lmu.de, kunath@dbs.ifi.lmu.de,
prykhin@dbs.ifi.lmu.de, butz@ifi.lmu.de,
kriegel@dbs.ifi.lmu.de

Abstract. In this paper we describe a new interface for browsing and sorting of digital pictures. Our approach is two-fold. First we present a new method to automatically identify similar images and rate them based on sharpness and exposure quality of the images. Second we present a zoomable user interface based on the details-on-demand paradigm enabling users to browse large collections of digital images and select only the best images for further processing or sharing.

Keywords: Photoware, digital photography, image analysis, similarity measurement, informed browsing, zoomable user interfaces, content based image retrieval.

1 Introduction

In recent years analog photography has practically been replaced by digital cameras and pictures, which led to an ever increasing amount of images taken in both professional and private contexts. In response to this, a variety of software for browsing, organizing and searching of digital pictures has been created as commercial products, in research [1,10,17,20] and for online services (e.g., Flickr.com, Zoomr.com, Photobucket.com).

With the rise of digital photography the costs of film and paper no longer apply and the storage and duplication costs have become negligible. Hence, not only the pure number of photos that are being taken has changed but also are people taking more pictures of similar or identical motives such as series of a scenery or person from just slightly different perspectives [9].

In consequence these changes in consumer behavior require more flexibility from digital photo software than support for pure browsing or finding a specific image. In this paper we present a software that supports basic browsing of image libraries namely the grouping of images into collections and the inspections thereof. In addition, the presented approach does specifically support users in

J. Jacko (Ed.): Human-Computer Interaction, Part III, HCII 2007, LNCS 4552, pp. 882–891, 2007.

selecting good (or bad) pictures from a series of similar pictures by the means of automatic image quality analysis.

1.1 Browsing, Organizing and Sorting Photos

An extensive body of HCI literature deals with the activities users engage with when dealing with image collections (digital or physical) [4,6,11]. For digital photos the whole life cycle – from taking the pictures, through downloading, selecting, and often sharing the photos as an ultimate goal – has been researched extensively.

All studies confirm that users share a strong preference for browsing through their collections as opposed to explicit searching. This might be due to the difficulty of accurately describing content as a search query versus the ease of recognizing an image once we see it. But even more important might be the fact that the goal for a search is, at best, unclear (e.g., "find a good winter landscape picture") even if the task (e.g., "create a X-mas album") is not.

Two strategies to support the browsing task can be identified. First, maximization of screen real-estate and fast access to detailed information through zooming interfaces [1,8] is a common strategy. Second, search tools and engines help users to find pictures in a more goal-oriented way. Since images are mostly perceived semantically (i.e., the content shown), effective searching relies on textual annotation or so-called tagging of pictures with meta-data [10,13,20,22]. However, users are reluctant to make widespread use of annotation techniques [19]. Hence, textual annotation of image collections is mostly found in the public and shared context (i.e., web communities or commercial image databases). In some commercial products (e.g., Adobe Photoshop), a content-based image retrieval (CBIR) mechanism is available, but its results are hard to understand for humans who apply semantic measurements for the similarity of images [18].

In addition to the browsing and searching activities users often and repeatedly sort, file and select their images. These activities sometimes serve archiving purposes so that only the best pictures are kept and are additionally organized in a systematic fashion. Users also sort and select subsets of images for short term purposes such as sharing and storytelling. For example, selecting just a small number of vacation pictures to present them at a dinner party with friends and family.

Current photoware does not account for this wider flexibility in users' behavior. Especially the sorting and selecting activities are seldom explicitly supported. Hence the common approach to assess the qualities of new photo software is to construct a browsing or searching task and then measuring the retrieval times [8,17]. However, the time users spend with selecting and sorting is significant especially because these activities occur repeatedly (e.g., at capture time, before and after downloading, upon revising the collection). This suggests that supporting these processes may be central for photoware.

We think that automatic image analysis can help supporting users in the sorting and selecting tasks especially when these technologies are carefully instrumented to support the users' semantical understanding of images instead of stubbornly collecting as much data as possible to be used in a search-by-similarity approach – an attempt whose results might in the end be hard to understand for users.

2 Combining CBIR and Zoomable Interfaces

In our work we present a new approach to browsing and selecting of images based on a combination of CBIR and the zooming interface paradigm. The presented solution provides two mechanisms to help users in gaining overview of their collection in a first step. Furthermore the tool specifically supports selecting of images to decide which images "to keep" and which "to delete" in a second step.

In previous work similarity based approaches often pursued a search-by-similarity approach, for example returning similar images in response to specifying a certain image as query item. The problem with this approach is, that one has to find the search query item in the first place. Current photo collections easily extend the amount of several thousand images. Hence, without special treatment it is easy to get lost and as a consequence frustrated in this process.

We propose to utilize a pre-clustering algorithm to help users in narrowing down the search space so that users are supported in a more focused way of browsing. This makes it possible to deal with only a limited set of image groups (of similar content) instead of several thousand individual images. Ultimately this approach eases the process of finding pictures without explicit support for query based searching.

In addition to browsing we wanted to support the selection of "good" and "bad" pictures. After grouping similar pictures together our software does an automated quality labeling on the members of each cluster. The criteria for the

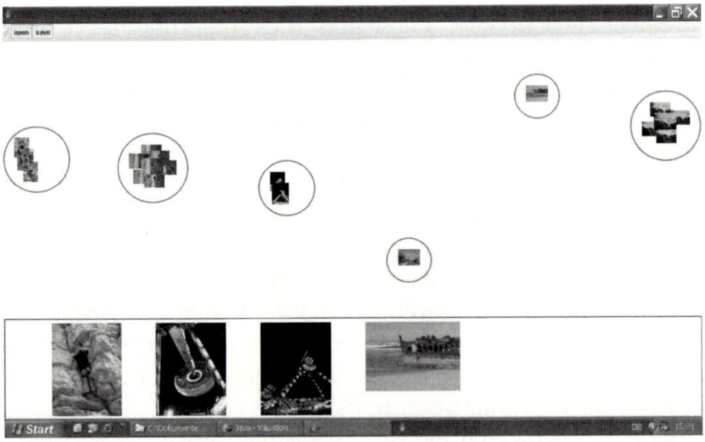

Fig. 1. Similar pictures are grouped into clusters. A temporary tray holds selected pictures from different clusters.

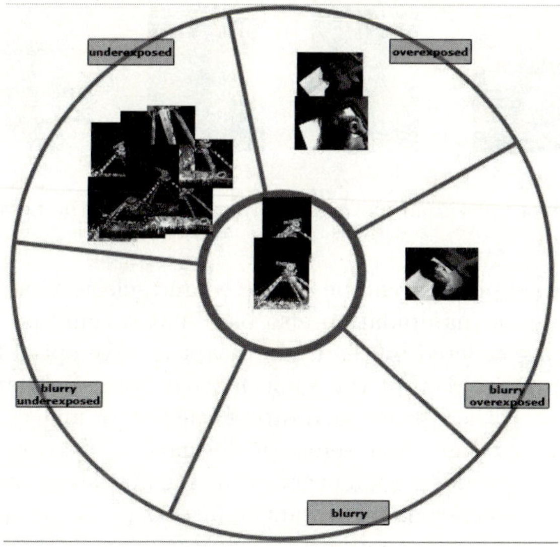

Fig. 2. Quality-based presentation of a cluster. The best pictures are in the center. Out of focus or too dark/bright pictures are grouped around the centroid.

quality assessment are exposure and sharpness of images. Again, this step is meant to support users in isolating unwanted images or otherwise identifying wanted images while still maintaining an overview of all images in the respective cluster to facilitate the selecting process.

2.1 Selection Support Through Semantic Zooming

In order to present a space-efficient view onto image collections we opted for an zoomable user interface which allows salient transitions between overview, filtered and finally detailed views of the collection and individual images respectively.

Upon startup the system is in the overview mode where pictures are matched according to a set of low level features. While this is not a real semantic analysis, it reliably finds groups of pictures of the same situation, which very often have similar content (See Figure 1). A few representatives are selected for each cluster (shown as thumbnails). The number of thumbnails in this view gives an approximation of the ratio of "good" pictures in the group versus the "bad" pictures. A cluster with many representatives has many pictures in the best quality group. The overall size of the cluster is depicted by the groups diameter - so spatially larg clusters contain many pictures.

Through fully zooming into one cluster users begin the selection of images. In this stage of the process clusters are broken down into six quality regions. The best rated pictures are shown in the center region while the five other regions serve as containers for the combinations of "blurry" and "under-" or "overexposed" images (See Figure 2).

Fig. 3. Detail view of individual pictures in order to identify the best available picture

Finally, individual pictures can be inspected and selected for further use, such as printing, sharing or manipulation also bad images could be deleted. On this last level images are ordered by the time of capture. We opted for this ordering to ensure that images taken of the same motive from slightly different angles appear next to each other, hence facilitating triaging of images (See Figure 3).

Users can zoom through these semantically motivated layers in a continuous way. The interface provides a good overview at the first levels by hiding unnecessary details. Whenever users need or want to inspect particular pictures they can retrieve these by simply zooming into the cluster or quality group respectively. At the lowest level, single pictures can also be zoomed and panned.

3 Image Analysis

In this section, we describe our approach to analyze a given collection of images. The analysis is based on a set of low-level features which are extracted from the images. In the first step, we identify series of images automatically by applying a clustering algorithm. The second step operates on each single series and matches the images contained in this series to different quality categories.

3.1 Extracting Meaningful Features

In order to describe the content of a given set of images, color and texture features are commonly used. Thus, for all pictures in a given collection, we calculate several low-level features which are needed later for grouping picture series and organizing each group by quality. The extracted features are color histograms, textural features, and roughness.

For the color histograms, we use the YUV color space which is defined by one luminance (Y) and two chrominance components (U and V). Each pixel in an image is converted from the original RGB color space to the YUV color space.

Similar to the Corel image features [14], we partition the U and V chrominance components into 6 sections each, resulting in a 36 dimensional histogram. Although the HSV color space models the human perception more closely than the YUV color space, and is therefore more commonly used, we have shown in our experiments (cf. Section 4) that the YUV color space is most effective for our purposes.

The textural features are generated from 32 gray-scale conversions of the images. We compute the Haralick textural feature number 11 using the co-occurrence matrix [7], where N is the number of gray levels in the co-occurrence matrix $C = p(i,j), 1 \leq i,j \leq N$:

$$f_{11} = -\sum_{i=0}^{N-1} p_{x-y}(i) \cdot log(p_{x-y}(i)) \text{ , where } p_{x-y}(k) = \sum_{i=1}^{N}\sum_{j=1}^{N} p(i,j), |i-j| = k$$

Finally, we also compute the first 4 roughness moments of the images [2]. The roughness basically measures some small-scale variations of a gray-scale image which correspond to local properties of a surface profile.

3.2 Identifying Series of Images

Our next goal is to detect image series. Pictures which belong to the same series have a very similar content, but it is possible that the quality of the pictures differs. So it seems reasonable to use UV histograms as the basis for this task. We ignore the luminance component (Y) because we are only interested in similar colors at this stage, but not in the brightness of the pictures.

In general, the detection of image series is an unsupervised task because there is usually no general valid training set for all kinds of pictures. Moreover, the number of image series in an image collection is usually unknown. As a consequence of these two observations, the method for image series detection should be unsupervised and has to determine the number of groups automatically.

We propose to apply an clustering algorithm for the image series detection. In order to distinguish series of images and to determine the number of image series automatically, we employ a clustering algorithm using X-Means [15]. X-Means is a variant of K-Means [12] which performs model selection. It incorporates various algorithmic enhancements over K-Means and uses statistically-based criteria which helps to compute a better fitting clustering model.

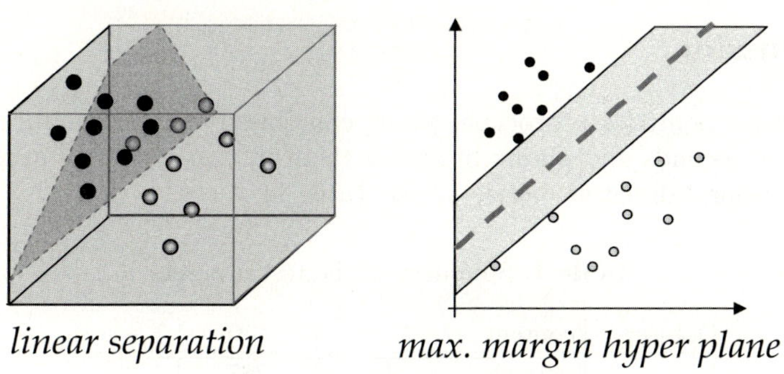

Fig. 4. Basic idea of a Support Vector Machine (SVM)

3.3 Labeling Images by Quality

The quality of a picture is a rather subjective impression and can be described by so called high-level features such as "underexposed", "blurry", "overexposed". We propose to use classifiers in order to derive high-level features from low-level features.

Support vector machines (SVM) [3] have received much attention for offering superior performance in various applications. Basic SVMs use the idea of linear separation of two classes in feature space and distinguish between two classes by calculating the maximum margin hyperplane between the training examples of both given classes as illustrated in Figure 4. Several approaches have been proposed in order to distinguish more than two classes by using a set of SVMs.

A common method for adapting a two-class SVM to support N different classes is to train N single SVMs. Each SVM distinguishes objects of one class versus objects of the remaining classes, this is also known as the "one-versus-rest" approach [21]. Another commonly used technique is to calculate a single SVM for each pair of classes. This results in $N * (N-1)/2$ binary classifiers. Finally, the classification results have to be combined by an AND-operation. This approach is also called "one-versus-one" [16]. The author of [5] proposes to improve the latter approach by calculating so-called confidence vectors. A confidence vector consists of N entries which correspond to the N classes. The entries are computed by collecting voting scores from each SVM. Thus, $N * (N-1)/2$ votings are summarized in one vector. The resulting class corresponds to the position of the maximum value in the confidence vector.

A SVM-based classifier maps low-level features, such as texture and roughness to group labels, which correspond to semantic groups such as "blurry" or "underexposed". We propose to apply an "one-versus-one" approach which is enhanced by confidence vectors because the "one-versus-rest" method tends to overfit, as shown in [16]. Users can either use an already trained classifier which comes with the installation archive of our tool, or provide training data to define their own quality classes.

4 Discussion

We have implemented a prototype, which can classify several hundred pictures within a few seconds and allows browsing them in real time. We evaluated our prototype using 3 different datasets (See Table 1).

Table 1. Summary of the test datasets

Dataset	content	# pictures	# series
DS1	animals	287	26
DS2	flowers & landscapes	328	35
DS3	flowers & people	233	18

In a first experiment, we turned our attention to finding a suitable feature representation for the automatic detection of image series. For each dataset, we investigated 3 different color models HSL, HSV and YUV. As discussed in Section 3, the luminance was ignored (i.e., we used only two of the three color dimensions for the histogram generation). Figure 5 depicts the quality of the clustering result for our datasets, which reflects the percentage of correctly clustered instances. We observed that the YUV feature achieves the best quality of the clustering-based image series detection for our datasets. Therefore the YUV feature was implemented in our prototype.

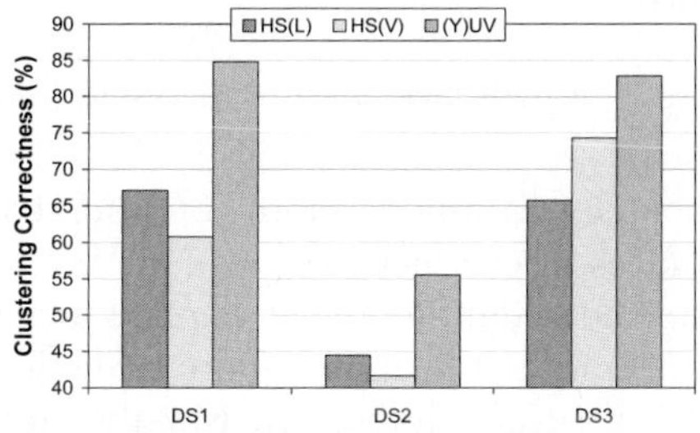

Fig. 5. Quality of clustering-based image series detection

In a second experiment, various features were tested in order to find representations for the high-level feature mapping. We compared the suitability of different features which measure local structures of an image. Since the Haralick texture features and the roughness feature are based on a grayscale version of an image, we also included grayscale histograms in our evaluation. Figure 6 illustrates the results of our experiments. We observed that roughness performs well when distinguishing the classes 'underexposed/normal/overexposed'. For labeling the pictures according to 'sharp/blurry', the Haralick feature 11 seems to be the best choice.

To sum up, the performance of our prototype is encouraging and the classification according to high-level features matches human perception surprisingly well.

To this end we have not formally evaluated our prototype in a user study. The results from experience sessions with few users (who brought their own pictures with them) are encouraging. The things they liked most were the support for selecting images. One user said "this tool makes it easier to get rid of bad pictures and keep those I want". Also the possibility to quickly compare a series of similar images was appreciated. Others were surprised how good the similarity analysis worked.

However, there were also things that our test candidates did not like. Foremost the lack of alternative sorting options. While most users found the grouping by similarity helped on narrowing down the search space some pointed out that a chronological ordering would make more sense in some situations. In future versions we plan to add support for different clustering criteria – basic ones –

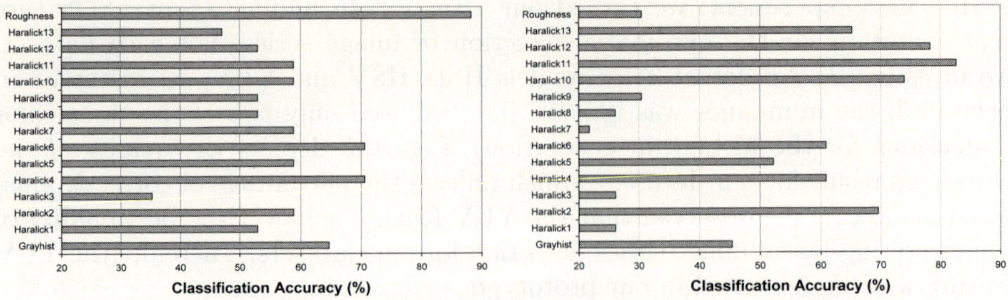

(a) Accuracy w.r.t. underexposed/normal/overexposed.

(b) Accuracy w.r.t. sharp/blurry.

Fig. 6. Accuracy of high-level feature mapping (dataset DS1)

such as time or file properties as well as more complicated ones like identifying similar objects or even faces in the pictures.

We also plan to extend the scalability of the applied image analysis mechanism as well as the interface techniques to support more realistic amounts of data (i.e., several thousand instead of several hundred). Finally we plan to run extended user tests to further assess the quality of the similarity and quality measurements as well as the usability of interface.

References

1. Bederson, B.B.: Photomesa: a zoomable image browser using quantum treemaps and bubblemaps. In: UIST '01: Proceedings of the 14th annual ACM Symposium on User interface Software and Technology, pp. 71–80. ACM Press, New York, USA (2001)
2. Chinga, G., Gregersen, O., Dougherty, B.: Paper Surface Characterisation by Laser Profilometry and Image Analysis. MICROSCOPY AND ANALYSIS 96, 21–24 (2003)
3. Cortes, C., Vapnik, V.: Support-vector networks. Machine Learning 20(3), 273–297 (1995)
4. Crabtree, A., Rodden, T., Mariani, J.: Collaborating around collections: informing the continued development of photoware. In: CSCW '04: Proceedings of the 2004 ACM conference on Computer supported cooperative work, pp. 396–405. ACM Press, New York, USA (2004)
5. Friedman, J.: Another approach to polychotomous classification. Technical report, Statistics Department, Stanford University (1996)
6. Frohlich, D., Kuchinsky, A., Pering, C., Don, A., Ariss, S.: Requirements for photoware. In: CSCW '02: Proceedings of the 2002 ACM conference on Computer supported cooperative work, pp. 166–175. ACM Press, New York, USA (2002)
7. Haralick, R.M., Dinstein, I., Shanmugam, K.: Textural features for image classification. IEEE Transactions on Systems, Man, and Cybernetics 3, 610–621 (1973)
8. Huynh, D.F., Drucker, S.M., Baudisch, P., Wong, C.: Time quilt: scaling up zoomable photo browsers for large, unstructured photo collections. In: CHI '05: extended abstracts on Human factors in computing systems, pages, pp. 1937–1940. ACM Press, New York, USA (2005)

9. Jaimes, A., Chang, S.-F., Loui, A.C.: Detection of non-identical duplicate consumer photographs. Information, Communications and Signal Processing 1, 16–20 (2003)
10. Kang, H., Shneiderman, B.: Visualization methods for personal photo collections: Browsing and searching in the photofinder. In: IEEE International Conference on Multimedia and Expo (III), pp. 1539–1542 (2000)
11. Kirk, D., Sellen, A., Rother, C., Wood, K.: Understanding photowork. In: CHI '06: Proceedings of the SIGCHI conference on Human Factors in computing systems, pp. 761–770. ACM Press, New York, USA (2006)
12. McQueen, J.: Some methods for classification and analysis of multivariate observations. In: 5th Berkeley Symposium on Mathematics, Statistics, and Probabilistics, vol. 1, pp. 281–297 (1967)
13. Naaman, M., Harada, S., Wang, Q.Y., Garcia-Molina, H., Paepcke, A.: Context data in geo-referenced digital photo collections. In: MULTIMEDIA '04: Proceedings of the 12th annual ACM international conference on Multimedia, pp. 196–203. ACM Press, New York, USA (2004)
14. Ortega, M., Rui, Y., Chakrabarti, K., Porkaew, K., Mehrotra, S., Huang, T.S.: Supporting ranked boolean similarity queries in MARS. IEEE Transactions on Knowledge and Data Engineering 10(6), 905–925 (1998)
15. Pelleg, D., Moore, A.W.: X-means: Extending k-means with efficient estimation of the number of clusters. In: ICML '00: Proceedings of the Seventeenth International Conference on Machine Learning, pp. 727–734. Morgan Kaufmann Publishers, San Francisco, CA, USA (2000)
16. Platt, J., Cristianini, N., Shawe-Taylor, J.: Large margin dags for multiclass classification. In: Solla, S.A., Leen, T.K., Mueller, K.-R., (eds.), Advances in Neural Information Processing Systems, vol. 12, pp. 547–553 (2000)
17. Platt, J.C., Czerwinski, M., Field, B.A.: Phototoc: Automatic clustering for browsing personal photographs (2002)
18. Rodden, K., Basalaj, W., Sinclair, D., Wood, K.R.: Does organisation by similarity assist image browsing. In: CHI, pp. 190–197 (2001)
19. Rodden, K., Wood, K.R.: How do people manage their digital photographs? In: CHI '03: Proceedings of the SIGCHI conference on Human factors in computing systems, pp. 409–416. ACM Press, New York, USA (2003)
20. Shneiderman, B., Kang, H.: Direct annotation: A drag-and-drop strategy for labeling photos. In: Fourth International Conference on Information Visualisation (IV'00), pp. 88 (2000)
21. Vapnik, V.N.: Statistical Learning Theory. Wiley-Interscience, Chichester (1998)
22. von Ahn, L., Dabbish, L.: Labeling images with a computer game. In: Proceedings of the SIGCHI conference on Human Factors in Computing Systems (2004)

A Usability Study on Personalized EPG (pEPG) UI of Digital TV

Myo Ha Kim[1], Sang Min Ko[2], Jae Seung Mun[2], Yong Gu Ji[2,*], and Moon Ryul Jung[3]

[1] Cognitive Science Program, The Graduate School, Yonsei University
[2] Department of Information and Industrial Engineering, Yonsei University
[3] Department of Media Technology, Sogang University
[1,2]{myohakim,sangminko,msj,yongguji}@yonsei.ac.kr
moon@sogang.ac.kr

Abstract. As the use of digital television (D-TV) has spread across the globe, usability problems on D-TV have become an important issue. However, so far, very little has been done in the usability studies on D-TV. The aim of this study is developing evaluation methods for the user interface (UI) of a personalized electronic program guide (pEPG) of D-TV, and evaluating the UI of a working prototype of pEPG using this method. To do this, first, the structure of the UI system and navigation for a working prototype of pEPG was designed considering the expanded channel. Secondly, the evaluation principles as the usability method for a working prototype of pEPG were developed. Third, lab-based usability testing for a working prototype of pEPG was conducted with these evaluation principles. The usability problems founded by usability testing were reflected to improve the UI of a working prototype of pEPG.

Keywords: Usability, User Interface (UI), Evaluation Principles, Personalized EPG (pEPG), Digital Television (D-TV).

1 Introduction

As recent years have changed the TV transmission system, multi-channels have become popular to many viewers through the use of D-TV in the U.S.A., Europe, and Japan [1]. Digital TV offers the consumer hugely expanded channel choices with interactive services offering hundreds of channels in a day as a standard. Therefore, the problem with selection of channels and programs is unavoidable in using the Personalized Electronic Program Guide (pEPG). A working prototype was developed that provided suitable programs for users by analyzing the user's viewing history of TV in addition to channel and program information. However, so far, very little has been done in the usability studies on pEPG of D-TV.

The aim of this study is developing evaluation methods for user interface (UI) of personalized electronic program guide (PEPG) of D-TV and evaluating the UI of a working prototype of PEPG using this method. To do this, first, the structure of the UI system and navigation for a working prototype of PEPG was designed considering the

* Corresponding author.

J. Jacko (Ed.): Human-Computer Interaction, Part III, HCII 2007, LNCS 4552, pp. 892–901, 2007.

expanded channel. Secondly, the evaluation principles as the usability method for a working prototype of PEPG were developed. Third, lab-based usability testing for a working prototype of PEPG was conducted with these evaluation principles and the result of testing was reflected to the UI design as feedback.

2 A Review of the Literature

The approach of previous studies on EPG has focused on the implementation of pEPG and the development of interactive EPG, like voice recognition or agent technology [1]. However, relatively little has been done about the usability study on EPG. In the usability study on EPG, the two types of navigation prototypes were tested with real users using "think aloud" and video camera recording in order to compare them [2]. EPG prototype and some interactive TV applications were also tested using typical user tasks, a short questionnaire, and a brief interview about global opinion under the similar circumstance of watching TV. In [3], Tadashi I, et al. conducts a test in which users select programs among approximately 100 actual satellite channels after implementing a TV reception navigation system that helps to choose channels according to mood and interest with subjective evaluation. In [4], Konstantionos, C proposes the 7 design principles focusing on entertainment and leisure activity of watching TV. In [5], Sabina address a design model for an EPG interface as a step-by-step guide [6]. As evidenced, previous usability testing of EPG seems to use very simple tasks or questionnaires and has focused on the technical implementation of D-TV. To address this limitation, we intend to develop the organized evaluation methods that can be applied to D-TV generally, reflecting and complementing the limitation of previous studies.

3 Methods

The entire process of this study can be divided into five stages: (1) Designing the structure and navigation of UI for a prototype pEPG. (2) Conducting a focus group interview (FGI) for real users to roughly understand the problem with EPG and pEPG. (3) Developing the structure of usability principle on D-TV as the evaluation method. (4) Usability Testing through observation, questionnaires and interview. (5) The Improvement of the UI of PEPG prototype.

3.1 Designing the Structure and Navigation of UI for a Prototype pEPG

Based on the benchmarked three current EPG systems, the main menus were selected: "User selection," "User register," "All TV program list," "Recommended program list" and "Search program." The selected UI of a working prototype of pEPG is shown in Figure 1.

3.2 Focus Group Interview (FGI)

To understand the usability problem with EPG and a prototype of PEPG, FGI was conducted involving nine EPG users aged 20-29. As a result, the clear meaning of icon, diverse color, easy manipulation, fast speed to search programs and simple menu structure were required for EPG. At the same time, the usefulness of recommendation information, the appreciated amount of information, the reliability of recommendation information, and controllability were required for a prototype of PEPG.

3.3 The Development of Structure Usability Principles

We systematically classified usability principles for a prototype of PEPG. For this, we collected a total of 108 usability principles from previous literature, including Nielson (1994)'s checklist [7-12]. Those principles were screened in terms of selection, unification and elimination through FGI with 8 HCI experts. As a result, the final 21 principles were selected and redefined considering the features of a prototype of PEPG and D-TV. After that, by Factor Analysis, those 21 principles were categorized into "interaction support," "cognition support," "performance support" and "design principle" through statistical analyzing shown in Table 1.

Table 1. The structure of usability principles

Usability Principles				
The First Step	**The Second Step**	**The Third Step**	**Definitions**	**No.**
Interaction Support	Controllability	User Control	The users should be able to control the system by their own decisions.	1
		controllability	The system should allow user to make a decision with clear information considering the current situation of the system. on their own	2
	Feedback	Responsiveness	The system should be respond in an appropriate time.	3
		Feedback	The system should constantly provide user with current action or the state of change with the familiar word or clear meaning.	4
	Error	Prevention	The system should prevent user from an error caused by incorrect action.	5
		Tolerance Principle	The system should be flexible and generous by decreasing an error and incorrect usage with the function of cancel and back. The system should permit various input and sequence by interpreting every action flexibly.	6
		Error Indication	The meaning and expression in an error message is should be clear.	7
Cognition Support	Predictability	Predictability	The user interface should response as the same way to be expected for user.	8
	Learnability	Learnability	The user interface should be designed for user to learn easily the way to use.	9
		Memorability	The user interface should be designed to remember easily to learn.	10
	Consistency	Consistency	The user interface should be designed consistently. (Likeness in input-output behavior arising from similar situations or similar task objectives) (consistency in the naming and organization of command)	11
	Familiarity	Familiarity	The user interface should be designed in a familiar way.	12
		Generalizability	The user should be able to generalize and learn the interaction way without manual extending knowledge of specific interaction within and across applications to other similar situations.	13

Table 1. (*contitued*)

Usability Principles				
The First Step	**The Second Step**	**The Third Step**	**Definitions**	**No.**
Performance Support	Efficiency	Ratio of Task Completion Time and Error-Free-Time	The ratio of task completion by non-expert error-free-time by expert	14
		Success Ratio (SR)	The ratio of successful tasks and entire tasks	15
		Number of Command (NOC)	The number of command or interface component with task performance	16
	Effectiveness	Search and Delay Time (SDT)	The amount of time spent to explore for finding the exact key or manipulation of button.	17
		Task Completion Time (TCT)	The given task completion time	18
		Task Standard Time (TST)	Standard task completion time	19
		System Response Delay Time	The delayed time to be responded from system.	20
	Accuracy	Frequency of Errors (FOE)	The frequency of errors by user's mistake or incorrect action	21
		Percentage of Errors (POE)	The percentage of errors by user's mistake or incorrect action	22
		Help Frequency	The frequency to request the help or information	23
Design Principle	Physical component	Icon	The meaning of user interface icon should be clear.	24
		Text	The text of user interface should be designed easy to be recognized.	25
		Color	The color of user interface should be designed easy to be recognized.	26
	Visibility	Visibility	The information of user interface should be conspicuous and enough to be recognized	27
		Observability	The user interface should allow user to understand the internal state of the system and how to react from its perceivable representation	28

Lastly, the means of measuring each principle was selected. The interaction support, cognitive support and design principle were measured by subjective satisfaction evaluation. Performance support was measured by observation of task performance.

3.4 The Development of the Questionnaire for the Subjective Satisfaction Evaluation

The questionnaire items to measure the subjective satisfaction evaluation for usability testing were developed based on the structure of usability principles in previous satisfaction questionnaires, including QUIS (1988) [13-14], and were modified to be made suitable for a working prototype of pEPG. A total of 55 items were produced on a 7-point Likert scale shown in Table 2.

Table 2. The questionnaire for subjective satisfaction evaluation

Usability Principles				
The First Step	**The Second Step**	**The Third Step**	**Questionnaire Items**	**No.**
Interaction Support	Controllability	User Control	Does it provide UNDO option at every action ?	1
		controllability	Is cancel option available without any problem?	2
			Does it provide an appropriate way back to previous screen or menu?	3
			Does it provide clear completion of process on every menu?	4
			Does it provide various ways to explore?	5
	Feedback	Responsiveness	Is the response time in moving between menus appropriate?	6
			Is the time appropriate in response to the remote control?	7
			Is the response time appropriate in the search program?	8
		Feedback	Does it provide indication to available items visually?	9
			Is visual indication to select items clear?	10
			Does it indicate task completion visually?	11
			Is indication to what being operated on clear and appropriate?	12
	Error	Prevention	Does it prevent unavailable movement or selection from being activated in advance?	13
			Does it indicate the amount of information at data entry field?	14
			Does it provide default value?	15
		Tolerance Principle	Is data entry flexible?	16
		Error Indication	Is error message clear and easy to understand?	17
			Does error message provide the cause to error?	18
			Does error message provide further action for error?	19
Cognition Support	Predictability	Predictability	Is it expected how to move on the menu and program list without any help?	20
			Is the amount of information expected through a scroll bar?	21
	Learnability	Learnability	Does wording for a menu and function clear?	22
			Does it provide the feedback for the process to use the function?	23
			Does it provide a process to use menu function logically?	24
			Is the wording familiar and easy to remember?	25
		Memorability	Do the key between in the screen and remote control face each other?	26
			Are items organized logically?	27
	Consistency	Consistency	Is the way to use and to scroll a menu consistent?	28
			Is the remote control key located consistent on the screen?	29
			Is the usage of remote control key consistent for every menu??	30
			Is the shape and location of title consistent?	31
			Is the wording for function consistent?	32
			Is the wording for menu consistent?	33
	Familiarity	Familiarity	Is the meaning of Icon familiar?	34
			Is the location of title familiar?	35
			Is the location for menu and function familiar?	36
		Generalizability	Does the color code accord with expectation?	37
			Is the sequential of menu selection natural?	38
Design Principle	Physical component	Icon	Does icon deliver a clear meaning visually?	39
			Is the icon label appropriate?	40
			Does icon indicate the current state clearly?	41
		Text	Is the test clear?	42
			Is the test easy to read?	43
		Color	Are the colors distinctive?	44
			Does it use same color to related item?	45
			Is the color consistent?	46

Table 2. (*continued*)

Usability Principles				
The First Step	**The Second Step**	**The Third Step**	**Questionnaire Items**	**No.**
	Visibility	Visibility	Is the item indicative between selective and non-selective items?	47
			Are the title area and list area distinguished from?	48
			Is the text and color distinctive at title area?	49
			Is the content area distinguished from other area?	50
			Is the title for item distinctive?	51
			Is the current location is clear at text data entry field?	52
		Observability	Does it provide the current location clearly?	53
			Does it provide what is operated on the system?	54
			Is the selected item clear on the menu?	55

3.5 A Usability Evaluation

The usability testing of pEPG on D-TV was conducted for the purpose of diagnosis of the UI. Usability issues in the interaction between a working prototype and user were revealed. The result can be utilized to improve and complement the UI of a working prototype pEPG. The testing setup included a set-top box, a TV set, a remote control, a PC, an infrared signal receiver, and a video camera. We recruited twenty-nine subjects, fifteen men and fourteen women, ranging in age from 20 to 29. They were all moderate to heavy viewers who watch TV more than 2 hours in a day. Six were experienced users of D-TV, and thirteen were inexperienced users.

Table 3. Selected Use Scenario

The First Level	The Second Level	The Third Level	No.
A. Register a User	Register a new user		1
	Input a user ID		2
	Input user information		3
	Select preferred genres		4
	Select preferred channel		5
	Complete to register a user		6
	Select the user ID to delete		7
	Complete to delete the user		8
B. Select a watching program	All TV Program List	Select the user	9
		The Screen of TV program	10
		Select a program in all TV program list	11
		The Screen of TV program	12
	Recommended Program List	Select the user	13
		The Screen of TV program	14
		Select a program in recommended program list	15
		The Screen of TV program	16
	Search Program	Select the user	17
		The Screen of TV program	18
		Select a program in search program	19
		The Screen of TV program	20
C. Use program alarming	Setting use program alarming		21
	Check the message of alarming on the screen of TV program		22
	Modify the input data on program alarming		23

Task and Use Scenarios. The tasks are composed of three parts like Table 3.

The Procedure of Usability Testing. The subjects were first given clear instructions about the general nature of the experiment and how to use a remote control and the process of usability testing. Next, the actual task performance session commenced without a break time. The task performance was recorded by video camera and subjects were interviewed briefly at the end of each main task. After completing an entire task, we asked the subjects to answer qualitative and quantitative questions on a 7-point Likert scale for satisfaction assessment.

3.6 Results

Task Performance. Among the performance support usability principles, we measured 4 types of task performances. Task completion time (TCT) was drawn from the mean of a total of 19 subjects according to each task. In addition, for the ratio of task completion time and error-free-time, we measured the task completion time without error by 4 HCI experts. The Number of Command refers to the mean value of the interface component used for each task by a total of 19 subjects.

Table 4. The result of task performance

Usability Principle	Tasks	Measurement	
Task Completion Time (TCT)		Average elapsed time (Min.: Sec.)	
		Novice	Expert
	Task A	8:21	7:09
	Task B	5:36	4:05
	Task C	0:86	0:31
Ratio of Task Completion Time and Error-Free-Time		Average elapsed time (Min.: Sec.)	
	Task A	1.16	
	Task B	1.32	
	Task C	2.77	
Number of Command (NOC)		Mean of NOC	
	Task A	209	
	Task B	62	
	Task C	10	
Frequency of Errors (FOE)		Total FOE	
	Task A	5	
	Task B	19	
	Task C	1	
Help Frequency		Total Help Frequency	
	Task A	27	
	Task B	34	
	Task C	2	

Subjective satisfaction evaluation (SSE). The usability principles for interaction support, cognition support, and usability principles were measured by a subjective satisfaction evaluation with a questionnaire. Table 5 and Figure 1 refer to the mean of subjective satisfaction evaluations for each usability principle. As a result, Responsiveness (2.74), Prevention (3.88), and Predictability (3.74) measured less than 4 points and need to be improved in UI design. The result of the subjective satisfaction evaluation was utilized to produce the usability issue.

Table 5. The mean of subjective satisfaction evaluation

No.	1	2	3	4	5	6	7	8	9	10
Mean	4.48	4.53	2.74	4.5	3.88	5	4.48	3.74	4.88	5.48
No.	**11**	**12**	**13**	**24**	**25**	**26**	**27**	**28**		
Mean	5.51	5.22	4.69	4.87	4.98	4.96	4.92	5.15		

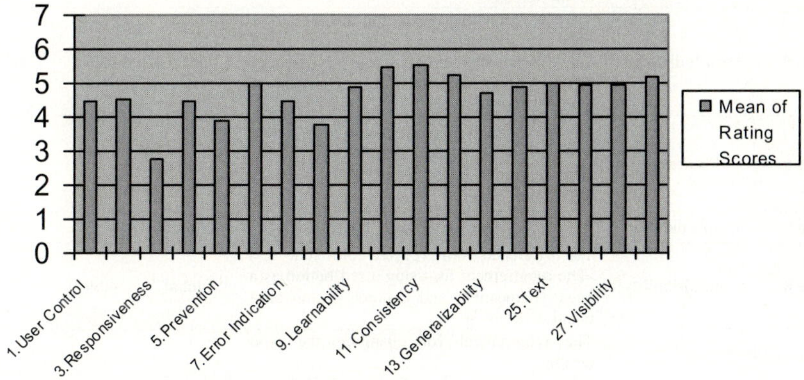

Fig. 1. The mean of subjective satisfaction evaluation

Usability Issues. We identified a total of 14 usability issues according to usability principles based on the result of usability testing like Table 6. The usability issues are ranked by the mean of subjective satisfaction evaluations. The scope defines how widely a usability problem is distributed throughout a product. Local usability issues represent problems that occur only within a limited range of a system. Global issues in usability represent overall design flaws. This usability issues are reflected as feedback to a working prototype pEPG.

Table 6. The usability issues

No.	Usability Principle	Usability Issues	Scope	Mean of SSE	Users Affected
Issue 1	Responsiveness	Too slow the button response time and screen shift speed with remote control	Global	2.74	22/29
Issue 2	Predictability	No indication to the amount of information - The requirement for scroll bar or the number of current page. / the number of entire pages The difficulty in usage of button -The requirement for a separate cancel key	Global	3.74	14/29
Issue 3	Prevention	No indication to the available amount of letters when input a user ID -The requirement for using star mark or blank	Local	3.88	9/29

Table 6. (*continued*)

No.	Usability Principle	Usability Issues	Scope	Mean of SSE	Users Affected
Issue 4	User Control	The difficulty in intuitive recognition of UNDO or cancel function -The requirement for visually clear indication on the screen.	Local	4.48	13/29
Issue 5	Error Indication	The low readability on error message -The requirement for distinctive color between the letter and text for error message -The requirement for reducing the amount of words for error message	Local	4.48	12/29
Issue 6	Feedback	More indication for action completion and what is operated on the system. -The requirement for a pop-up or auditory feedback	Global	4.5	7/29
Issue 7	Controllability	The requirement for separate UNDO key	Global	4.53	8/29
Issue 8	Generalizability	The difference from expected color code -The requirement for using a red button as a negative meaning and a green button as a positive meaning	Global	4.69	6/29
Issue 9	Icon	The requirement for changing the icon design -The requirement for esthetic or 3-D design and enlargement. -The requirement for indication for focusing on selected user ID	Local-	4.87	9/29
Issue 10	Learnability	The requirement for appropriate word labeling The difficulty in reminding EPG button of back function The requirement for shorter wording	Local-	4.88	2/29
Issue 11	Visibility	The requirement for enlargement for the letter size	Global	4.92	8/29
Issue 12	Color	The requirement for distinctive color between the letter and text	Global	4.96	10/29
Issue 13	Text	The requirement for reducing amount of wording and enlargement for spacing	Global	4.98	4/29
Issue 14	Observability	No current location indication for inputting user information -The requirement of cursor blink for user age registering	Local	5.15	6/29

3.7 Conclusion and Discussion

This study evaluates usability on a prototype of PEPG through usability testing. To do this, we developed the structure of usability principles, and then divided the usability principles by means of evaluation measurement. As the result, a total of 14 usability issues were produced through the mean of subjective satisfaction evaluations, task performance observations and interviews. Lastly, these usability issues were reflected to improve the UI of PEPG prototype.

The developed structure of usability principles and the results of the usability testing are expected to be utilized as a design guideline for PEPG of D-TV. However, further studies with subjects of more various ages under real broadcasting settings seem to be needed.

Acknowledgments. This work was supported by grant No. (R01-2005-000-10764-0) from the Basic Research Program of the Korea Science & Engineering Foundation.

References

1. Park, J.S., Lee, W.H., Ru, D.S.: Deriving Required Functions and Developing a Working Prototype of EPG on Digital TV. J. Ergonomics Society of Korea 23(2), 55–80 (2004)
2. Leena, E., Petri, V.: User Interface for Digital Television: a Navigator Case Study. In: Proceedings of the Conference on Advanced Visual Interface, pp. 276–279 (2000)
3. Pedro, C., Santiago, G., Rocio, R., Jose, A., Miguel, A.C.: Usability testing of an Electronic Programme Guide and Interactive TV applications, In: Proceedings of the Conference on Human Factors in Telecommunications (1999)
4. Tadashi, I., Fujiwara, M., Kaneta, H., Morita, T., Uratan, N.: Development of a TV Reception Navigation System Personalized with Viewing Habits. Proceedings of IEEE Trans. on Consumer Electronics 51(2), 665–674 (2005)
5. Konstantionos, C.: User Interface Design Principles for Interactive Television Applications The HERMES Newsletter by ELTRUN 32 (2005)
6. Sabina, B.: What Channel is That On; A Design Model for Electronic Programme Guides, In: Proceedings of the Conference on the 1st European Conference on Interactive Television: from Viewers to Actors? (2003)
7. Nieson, J.: Enhancing the explanatory power of usability heuristics. In: Proceedings of CHI '04, pp. 152–158 (1994)
8. Dix, A., Finlay, J., Abowd, G., Beale, R.: Human-Computer Interaction. Prentice Hall, Upper Saddle River, NJ, USA (1998)
9. Constantine, L. L.: Collaborative Usability Inspections for Software. In: Proceedings of the Conference on Software Development '94, San Francisco (1994)
10. Preece, J., Rogers, Y., Sharp, H.: Interaction Design. Wiley, UK (2002)
11. Treu, S.: User Interface Evaluation: A Structured Approach. Plenum Press, NY (1994)
12. Ravden, S.J., Graham, J.: Evaluating Usability of Human-Computer Interface: A Practical Approach. E Horwood, West Sussex, UK (1989)
13. Han, X.L., Choong, Y.Y, Gavriel, S.: A Proposed index of Usability: a Method for Comparing the Relative Usability of Different Software System. Int. J. Behavior and Information Technology 16(4), 267–278 (1997)
14. John, P.C, Virgina, A., Diehl, K.L.N.: Development of an Instrument Measuring User Satisfaction of Human-Computer Interaction. In: Proceedings of CHI '88, pp. 213–218 (1998)
15. Park, J.H., Yun, M.H.: Development of a Usability Checklist for Mobile Phone User Interface Developers. J. Korean Institute of Industrial Engineers 32(2), 111–119 (2006)

Recognizing Cultural Diversity in Digital Television User Interface Design

Joonhwan Kim and Sanghee Lee

Samsung Electronics Co., Ltd
416 Maetan3, Yeongtong, Suwon, Gyeonggi 443-742 Republic of Korea
{joonhwan.kim,sanghee21.lee}@samusung.com

Abstract. Research trends in user interface design and human-computer interaction have been shifting toward the consideration of use context. The reflection of differences in users' cultural diversity is an important topic in the consumer electronics design process, particularly for widely internationally sold products. In the present study, the authors compared users' responses to preference and performance to investigate the effect of different cultural backgrounds. A high-definition display product with digital functions was selected as a major digital product domain. Four user interface design concepts were suggested, and user studies were conducted internationally with 57 participants in three major market countries. The tests included users' subjective preferences on the suggested graphical designs, performances of the on-screen display navigation, and feedback on newly suggested TV features. For reliable analysis, both qualitative and quantitative data were measured. The results reveal that responses to design preference were affected by participants' cultural background. On the other hand, universal conflicts between preference and performance were witnessed regardless of cultural differences. This study indicates the necessity of user studies of cultural differences and suggests an optimized level of localization in the example of digital consumer electronics design.

Keywords: User Interface Design, Cultural Diversity, Consumer Electronics, Digital Television, Usability, Preference, Performance, International User Studies.

1 Introduction

Research trends in user interface design and human-computer interaction have been shifting toward consideration of use context [1], [3], [5]. Providing a high quality use experience to customers is one of the most important goals in the consumer electronics product. Reflecting differences caused by users' cultural diversity is an interesting topic in the user interface design process, particularly for widely internationally sold products.

One common example of an internationally selling consumer electronics product is the television. Broadcasting format change, shifting from analog to digital, leads the users to new experiences. The main differences in comparing the high-definition digital television to the analog television are more channels and higher quality picture and

J. Jacko (Ed.): Human-Computer Interaction, Part III, HCII 2007, LNCS 4552, pp. 902–908, 2007.

sound. Technically, hundreds of high-definition broadcasting channels are receivable and multiple sound channels and languages are available. On the other hand, functionalities of playing and managing multimedia files, such as photo and music, and the networking between the multimedia playable products in a home become important parts of the user experience design due to a digital convergence trend. In addition, the use of a flat panel screen such as LCD (Liquid Crystal Display) or PDP (Plasma Display Panel) and the tendency toward larger-sized screens are both resulting in the TV as a high-end consumer electronics product in consumer's home. Given these changes, the importance of user interface using On Screen Display (OSD) and its usability becomes greater than before [2]. From this point of view, it is important to investigate whether the user interface in digital television is affected by users' different cultural background, and to discuss what causes such differences if they do exist.

In the present paper, authors compared users' responses to subjective preference and task performance of the suggested user interface designs to investigate the effect of different cultural backgrounds. A large-sized, high-definition digital television was selected as a major digital product in consumer electronics domain.

2 Methods

2.1 Initial Designs

Through consideration of various context of use and analysis of currently collected usability problems in the previous user interface design at the time, four initial user interface design concepts of OSD menus were suggested (*Type A, B, C, & D)* based on outcomes of a previous review of usability issues in a similar interface, and the proposed contexts of use. Each type was designed to fulfill requirements and presented a unique design concept. Figure 1 provides an illustration of the four design concepts.

- *Type A* used full graphics on the screen with real, photo-like graphic elements. The graphic illustrated a building and houses in a street, each representing selectable items. This type was designed to maximize the designer's creativity and adopt a differentiated design concept in TV OSD.
- *Type B* applied an opposite version of the drop-down menu OSD at the bottom of the screen, though usually displayed at the top of the screen in PC software. This type was designed to minimize the size of the OSD and to allow users not to be disturbed when watching TV programs.
- *Type C* used full graphics on the screen, as in Type A, and maximized the introduction to and help offered by each functionality as a highlighter rolled over each item on OSD.
- *Type D* used two axes, X and Y, with a fixed highlight zone in the middle. This type moved vertically and horizontally with the highlight position. This type was designed to maximize the highlight navigation efficiency with less OSD space.

A Traditional TV menu was added for the subjective preference measure to compare whether the newly suggested four types of concept designs had benefited as planned. Basic interactions were used as the input method for all OSD menus. All five

OSD user interfaces were designed to be manipulated with four-directional buttons, an ENTER button, and a button that functions to go back to the previous level, such as BACK, which is the most common input method in TV surroundings. In addition, ideas to improve functionalities and increase usefulness of TV were suggested. The ideas focused on minimizing basic setup steps and providing personalized TV viewing surroundings.

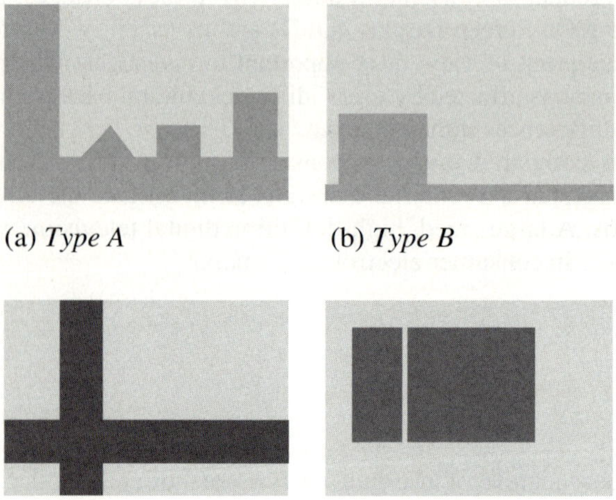

(a) *Type A* (b) *Type B* (c) *Type C*

(d) *Type D* (e) *Traditional*

Fig. 1. Draft samples of design concept (*Type A, B, C, D, & Traditional*)

2.2 Participants

User studies were conducted internationally with a total of 57 participants in three major market countries: 19 participants in the Republic of Korea, 20 participants in China, and 18 participants in US. The participants were required to have the motivation to purchase a digital TV in the near future or current digital TV owners. No specific technical knowledge or skills were required. Their ages ranged from 21 to 60, and the female-male ratio was about 50:50. Participants were divided into three age groups in each country (21-35, 36-55, 55 and above). Each group consisted of 6 to 8 people.

2.3 Procedure

The studies consisted of three parts: users' subjective preference on the suggested graphical designs; task performance of the on-screen display menu navigation and control; and feedback on suggested new features to enhance usefulness of TV. In each part, both qualitative and quantitative data were collected.

1. In the subjective design preference, relative comparisons using AHP (Analytic Hierarchy Process) [4] were conducted between the five user interface designs. Participants were shown a pair of concept designs one by one and asked to choose

which one they preferred between the two. Then, they were asked of thoughts and impressions of each design one by one.

2. In the task performance, the suggested concept designs were built into PC-based interactive prototypes using Flash. The numeric keyboard replaced the remote control buttons, and the prototype was displayed in a 40 inch LCD TV or projector. The tasks were selected to investigate the ease of menu navigation and control under the same condition in the five concept designs. The tasks were given in random order. Error rate, task completion, and task time was measured. The measured three quantitative data were calculated on a 7-point scale for analysis convenience. An error was counted as minus 0.5 point; task completion failure was counted as minus 2 point; and task time over than given maximum time in each task was counted as minus 1 point. After each task, participants were questioned about the difficulties they experienced as well as ideas for improvement.
3. In feedback on the newly suggested digital TV features, participants were given visualized simulation and verbal explanation of user scenarios which utilize the seven newly suggested features and ideas. Participants' expected use frequency and acceptance rate of the features were collected given the condition that their digital TV has those new features. In addition, a moderator elicited participants' detailed opinion of each feature.

This study employed a within-subject experimental design. Prior to task performance, participants were given an introduction and allowed to use prototype for a brief familiarization period. The average test time was 100 minutes per person and regular breaks were given between the sessions.

3 Results

3.1 Subjective Preference on the Suggested Graphical Designs

The analysis of AHP result showed differences between the three countries. *Type A* was considered most preferred by Chinese participants (27%), while it was least preferred by both Korean and American participants (12%). *Type D* (23.6%) and *Type B* (22.9%) were preferred overall in all three countries.

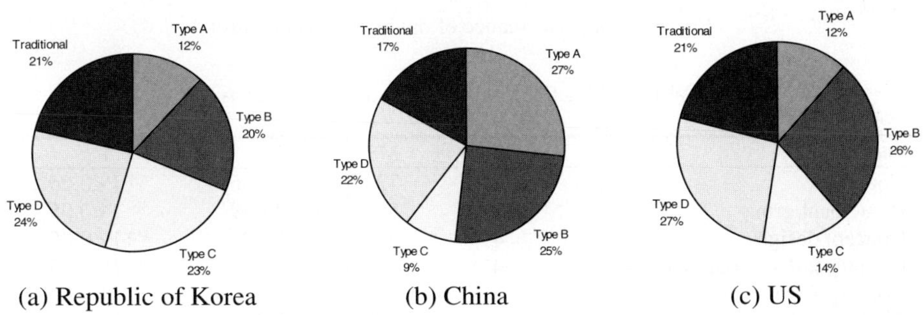

(a) Republic of Korea (b) China (c) US

Fig. 2. Subjective preference of graphical designs

3.2 Task Performance of the On-Screen Display Menu Navigation and Control

Task performance ratings in American participants were highest overall, (average: 5.57, standard deviation: 1.20), Korean participants were second (average: 4.36, standard deviation: 0.95), and Chinese participants were lowest (average: 3.51, average: 2.25). Unlike in subjective design preference, similar patterns were found between three countries. The calculated point revealed that *Type A*, which was closest to the traditional TV menu in navigation, showed the higher performance in all three countries (4.86 in Republic of Korea, 3.50 in China, and 5.82 in US). *Type B* showed the higher performance rating in Republic of Korea (5.07) and US (5.43), but lower for Chinese participants (3.54). *Type D* showed the lowest performance in Republic of Korea (3.00) and US (5.10), while Chinese participants showed slightly higher performance (3.71). However, interviews after the tasks revealed that participants in all countries were confused about what item was currently selected in the OSD and had difficulty with the basic highlighting movement in *Type D*.

In 3 Factor within-subject ANOVA, it was found that all factors (country, participant group, and concept design) showed significant differences (Table 1). In Korea, Type A and Type C showed higher performance, and no significant difference between participant age groups. In China, no significant difference was found between both concept designs and participant age groups. In US, Type A and Type C showed higher performance than Type D, which is similar to Republic of Korea, and age group of 36 to 55 showed significantly lower performance.

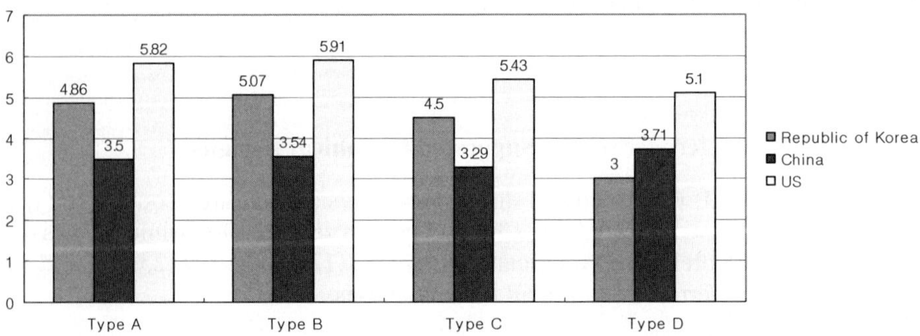

Fig. 3. Task performance of navigation and control

Table 1. 3 Factor within-subject design ANOVA

Factor	DF	MS	F	P < F
Country	2	72.09	23.66	** P<0.05
Participant group	2	55.83	17.69	** P<0.05
Concept design	4	9.80	22.20	** P<0.05
Country x Participant Group	4	23.70	5.68	** P<0.05
Country x Concept design	8	6.67	19.60	** P<0.05
Concept design x Participant Group	8	2.29	7.62	** P<0.05

3.3 Feedback on Suggested New Features to Enhance Usefulness of TV

The suggested features rated higher in expected use frequency also rated higher in overall acceptance. Participants tended to give slightly lower ratings in expected use frequency than overall acceptance (4.63 in Expected use frequency average and 5.06 in overall acceptance average). Chinese participants showed somewhat higher overage ratings in both expected use frequency (5.29) and overall acceptance rate (5.85) compared to American (4.05 and 4.33) and Korean participants (4.56 and 5.01). In the qualitative verbal data, it was found that participants had negative thoughts in all three countries to the additional features in TV comparing to the one they currently owned.

Table 2. Rating average of suggested new features

Country / Category	Republic of Korea	China	US
Expected use frequency	4.56	5.29	4.05
Overall acceptance	5.01	5.85	4.33

4 Conclusion and Discussion

There are more elements which consist of user interface design of a complete TV than those discussed in the present paper. This paper focused on three main elements, which were design preference, task performance, and new functionalities.

Difference in subjective design preference between the three countries was found, indicating that preference could be influenced by cultural differences. *Type A*, which showed the most significant differences between countries, was considered new and unique by Chinese participants, while American participants viewed it as dull and obsolete. It was interesting that the two Asian countries showed different results. This may imply a weakness in the small number of samples in this study or possible differences in the countries from a similar region. On the other hand, similar patterns were found in task performance analysis in the three countries, indicating no significant influence by country differences. Participants in all three countries outperformed with *Type A* and *Type C*, which is closest to a traditional TV menu. People still feel comfortable and perform better with a familiar interface.

The results also revealed conflicts between preference and task performance regardless of participants' cultural differences. *Type D* was ranked high in the design preference, but showed lowest performance in the tasks. This indicates that visually preferred design does not always guarantee best usability and user performance, and vice versa.

Participants generally showed negative responses to newly suggested features of TV because of the anxiety of increased complexity in everyday use. The lower point in expected use frequency than overall acceptance indicates that possibility of the new features usage in the real use surroundings may be lower than expected. This implies the importance of deep considerations before accepting a new feature. It is interesting that Chinese participants gave slightly higher ratings than the other two countries, while people in all three countries showed negative feedback in verbal. The numeric rating did not always match the participants' qualitative feedback.

In the later part of process of the present study, the concept designs which showed significant differences between countries were eliminated. The navigational rules were made according to the way that participants performed better regardless of countries in the final outcomes. Based on findings in the present study, the authors completed a new interface design for the large-sized high-definition television that has been commercialized in the major TV markets. This study indicates the necessity of user studies of cultural differences, and suggests an optimized level of localization in the example of the product user interface design of digital consumer electronics.

Acknowledgements. We would like to thank task force team members in Visual Display Division in the company for their support and collaboration.

References

1. Beyer, H., Holtzblatt, K.: Contextual Design: Defining Customer-Centered System. Morgan Kaufmann, San Francisco (1998)
2. Jeffres, L.W., Atkin, D.J., Neuendorf, K.A., Lin, C.A.: The influence of expanding media menus on audience content selection. Telematics and Informatics 21, 317–334 (2004)
3. Lindholm, C., Keinonen, T., Kiljander, H.: Mobile Usability: How NOKIA Changed the Face of the Mobile Phone. McGraw-Hill, New York (2003)
4. Saaty, T.L.: The Analytic Hierarchy Process. McGraw-Hill, New York (1980)
5. Verdenburg, V., Isensee, S., Righi, C.: USER-CENTERED DESIGN: An Integrated Apprach. Prentice Hall PTR, New Jersey (2002)

A Study on User Satisfaction Evaluation About the Recommendation Techniques of a Personalized EPG System on Digital TV

Sang Min Ko[1], Yeon Jung Lee[2], Myo Ha Kim[1], Yong Gu Ji[1], and Soo Won Lee[2]

[1] Department of Information and Industrial Engineering, Yonsei University.,
134 Sinchon-Dong, Seodaemun-gu, Seoul, Korea
{sangminko, myohakim, yongguji}@yonsei.ac.kr
[2] Department of Computer Science, Soongsil Univ.,
Sangdo 5(o)-dong, Dongjak-gu, Seoul, Korea
zzeong81@mining.ssu.ac.kr, swlee@computing.ssu.ac.kr

Abstract. With the growing popularity of digital broadcasting, viewers the have chance to watch various programs. However, they may have trouble choosing just one among many programs. To solve this problem, various studies about EPG and Personalized EPG have been performed. In this study, we reviewed previous studies about EPG, Personalized EPG and the results of recommendation evaluations, and evaluated PEPG system's recommendation, which was implemented as working prototype. We collected preference information about categorys and channels with 30 subjects and executed evaluation through e-mail. Recall and Precision were calculated by analyzing recommended programs from an E-mail questionnaire, and an evaluation of subjective satisfaction was conducted. As a result, we determined how much the result of an evaluation reflects viewer satisfaction by comparing the variation of subjects' satisfaction and the variation of objective evaluation criteria.

Keywords: EPG, PEPG, Satisfaction, Digital TV, DTV.

1 Introduction

With the beginning of digital broadcast services, increased television channels are being provided to TV viewers through terrestrial, satellite and cable broadcasting. Multi-channel television supplies viewers with hundreds of programs in various categories, but viewers often have trouble obtaining a preferred program's information. To solve this problem, personalized EPG (electronic program guide), which supports selecting programs, is offered from a Set-top box. However, previous EPG's offered only program information, such as channel and time, with a simple program table. Also, EPG users had to browse a whole list of programs or change channels one by one. So, the previous EPG is not enough to support a multi-channel environment. Considering this limitation of the previous EPG, a personalized TV program recommendation system that recommends suitable programs to users automatically based on viewer preference has become necessary [10]. Recently, many

J. Jacko (Ed.): Human-Computer Interaction, Part III, HCII 2007, LNCS 4552, pp. 909–917, 2007.

studies about personalized TV program recommendation systems have been conducted in the USA, Asia (China, Japan) and Europe (Ireland, Italy) [5], [8], [11]. So, in this study, we reviewed previous studies about EPG, Personalized EPG and recommendation engine's performance. We calculated Recall and Precision by e-mail questionnaire and evaluated subjective satisfaction.

2 Background Literature

2.1 Electronic Program Guide

EPG is a system that helps viewers select a channel they want in a multi-channel broadcasting environment. EPG is similar to the TV program guide in the newspaper and provides program data for each channel with a simple program table through a Set-Top box using EPG information from a broadcasting station. Now, EPG is serviced to viewers though domestic and foreign cable broadcasting.

TiVo in the US provides EPG, which allows users to search programs by program category or title, and it gives user program recommendations based on the user's WishList, which consists of Actor, Director, Category, Keyword, or Title. TiVo has various functions of recording and channel reservation like Personal Video Recorder, or PVR [13]. Also, it provides an Internet program scheduling function so controlling program recording under the Internet-connected environments without direct control of the Set-Top box is possible. SkyLife, the Korean Digital Satellite Broadcast service, has EPG that shows all channel information and offers program searching by category and time [12]. Viewers can obtain information about programs that are broadcasted at the same time based on user preference of channels.

Until now, commercial EPG mainly provided a program searching service by category, time, actor name, and preferred channel information. Even when EPG is provided, it is still difficult for the viewer to find programs that they want to watch among a large number of programs [10]. So, advanced EPG is needed to overcome the current EPG's limitations. It will help viewers select programs they want to watch in a multi-channel environment.

2.2 Personalized EPG

The personalized recommendation service uses information-filtering technology to decrease the scope of selection, and provides program information that is proper for viewers. In other words, PEPG is a Personalized TV program recommendation system using a personalized recommendation service. Studies about personalized TV program recommendation systems can be divided into: algorithm of recommendation system, building engine, performance evaluation and constructing, and evaluating user interface aimed to raise ease of system use [3], [4], [5], etc. Recommendation technologies in Personalized EPG to raise a recommendation's accuracy are classified into Content-Based, Collaborative Filtering and recommendation based on Stereo Type [6], [9]. Each recommendation method has pros and cons. Recently, a hybrid system that mixes two or more recommendation technologies was studied to improve recommendation's performance.

Table 1. Personalized EPG system's major recommendation method

Recommendation Method	*Description*
Content-Based	Calculate programs' contents information and similarity between viewer's preference and watching history and reflect that to recommendation.
Collaborative Filtering	Exploit recommendation for other user who has similar preference.
Stereo Type	Generate initial user's model using Stereo type from viewer's demographic profile information

Smith & Cotter developed a PTV that has ClixSmart Personalization Engine, which mixes Content-Based recommendations and Collaborative Filtering recommendations [10]. PTV provides suitable programs by automatically learning viewer's TV-watching preference information. After viewing the input program list or category and times preferred and not preferred, PTV recommends programs using the inputted data. Viewer preference is automatically revised by feedback of the recommended program's correctness through the Internet. PTV recommends not only programs which are related to the viewer's preference, but also programs which are related to other viewers who have similar preference. However, it cannot be used while watching TV due to its Web-based methods and has a problem of being unable to catch a viewer's preference directly from the viewer's watch history, so users have to input their own preferences or the recommended program's correctness through the Internet.

Th Personalized TV Program Recommendation System is called Personalized EPG (PEPG), Personalized Program Guide (PPG) and Adaptive Content Guide (ACG). Recently, it has been actively studied in many countries; US (CMU, Philips), Europe (Ireland, Italy) and Asia (China, Japan) [5], [8], [10], etc.

2.3 Research on Evaluation of Recommendation Engine

Generally, to evaluate a recommendation engine's performance, precision and recall is used [1], [2], [5]. Recall is the ratio of watched programs among recommended programs to whole watched programs. It can be described as (1).

$$\text{Recall} = \frac{\text{N(Watched Program} \cap \text{Recommended Program)}}{\text{N(Watched Program)}} \tag{1}$$

Precision is the ratio of watched programs among recommended programs to whole recommended programs. It can be described as (2).

$$\text{Precision} = \frac{\text{N(Watched Program} \cap \text{Recommended Program)}}{\text{N(Recommended Program)}} \tag{2}$$

Recall and Precision are in inverse proportion so that the proper adjustment is needed. To solve this problem, Lewis et al. proposed F-measure combining recall and precision, shown as (3) [2].

$$F_\beta = \frac{(\beta^2+1)\times \text{Precision}\times \text{Recall}}{\beta^2\times(\text{Precision}+\text{Recall})} = \frac{2(\text{Precision}\times \text{Recall})}{\text{Precision}+\text{Recall}} \quad (3)$$

β means weight based on recall and precision value. In many studies, the same weight(β =1) is used for both recall and precision to evaluate recommendation performance. These factors measure only the view ratio of a broadcasting program, so they cannot evaluate a viewer's subjective satisfaction. To improve this, the reliability of the recommendation engine's evaluation should be raised by measuring each viewer's satisfaction about the recommendation. So in this paper, we calculated recall and precision of the recommendation program list given by the recommendation engine, and compared the results with each viewer's subjective satisfaction.

3 Research Outline

In this study, we built a working prototype of Personalized EPG (PEPG) system and. Using 30 subjects (15 males and 15 females), an evaluation of usability and user satisfaction about the recommendation engine was conducted.

3.1 Process of Research

To provide a multi channel environment to subjects, there was a limitation: preparing all the equipment that is used in a broadcast station. To solve the problem, the usability test was conducted in two ways: usability evaluation of a working prototype and satisfaction evaluation of the recommendation result, shown as Figure 1.

Before the subjective satisfaction evaluation was conducted, data for the program recommendation was collected from the subjects by pre-questionnaire. We collected not only personal information and TV-watching pattern, but also preferences about

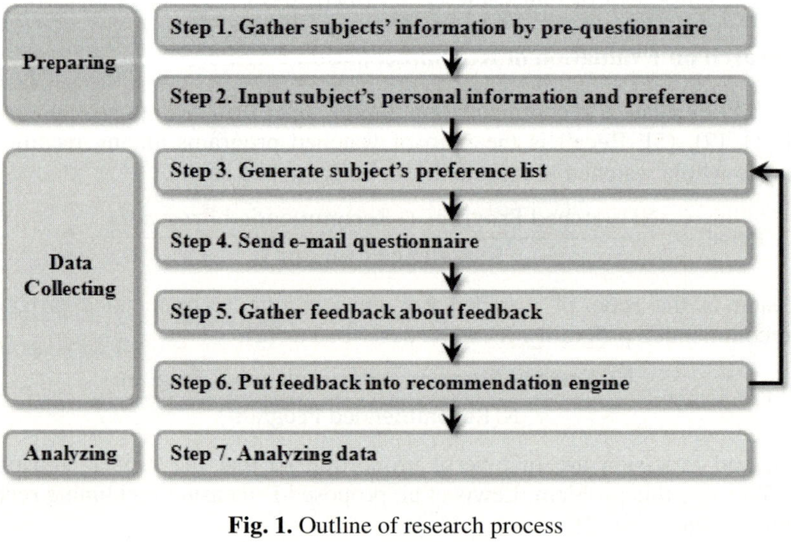

Fig. 1. Outline of research process

category and channel. Based on the pre-questionnaire, the top 5 recommended programs which were given by the recommendation engine were selected in accordance with each subject's viewing time and e-mail questionnaire. Subjects evaluated satisfaction score, intention of watching recommended programs, and subjective order of priority for each program in the recommendation list on a scale of 1-10. In next step, data from the results of the questionnaires was inputted to the recommendation engine and each subject's information about preference was revised and used to generate the next recommendation list. Through the data analysis of the recommendation program by e-mail questionnaire, recall and precision of the recommendation engine's performance and subject satisfaction were evaluated. By comparing the objective value in the result of the evaluation, we determined how much program recommendations reflect a viewer's satisfaction as time goes by.

3.2 Experiment Data

Raw data for the study was data of broadcasted programs in 3 months: June-August 2006. In the research of preference information about categories and channels, 13 main categories of information, 183 sub-categories of information, and 126 channels of information were collected from EPG, Inc., which provides EPG services in Korea. Subjects marked their preference about each category and channel as 5 steps—0.2, 0.4, 0.6, 0.8 and 1. Namely, 0.2 is the most negative mark about recommended programs and 1 is the most positive mark about recommended programs.

3.3 Subjects

In this study, the subjects were 15 males and 15 females, totaling 30, whose age is 21 to 37 (Average age: 26.9), and consisted of undergraduates, graduate students and office workers. On the average, they watched TV for 2 hours and 56 minutes per day. Also, they usually watch TV from 7 p.m. to 1 a.m. on weekdays and from 9 a.m. to 3 p.m. and 6 p.m. to 1 a.m. on weekends. Table 2 shows the preference information about categories. Subjects preferred drama and entertainment programs. Moreover, male subjects liked games in the hobby/leisure category and female subjects liked drama and entertainment programs.

Table 2. Subjects' preference about category

Category	*Total*	*Men*	*Women*
Drama	**21**	**7**	**14**
Entertainment	**18**	**8**	**10**
Hobby/Leisure	8	**8**	0
Movie	7	4	3
Sports	6	4	2
News	5	4	1
Documentary	4	2	2
Music	1	1	0
Culture/Information	1	0	1
Comics, education, shopping and satellite TV	0	0	0

4 Experiment Result

Evaluation tests about the recommendation list were conducted in 3 months: June-August, 2006. The recommendation engine was content-based. Programs of each subject's main view time were recommended based on preference information about category and channel. Table 3 shows Precision, Recall, and F of recommendation engine, which was used in the working prototype in this study.

Table 3. Precision, Recall and F-measure of a recommendation system

	1	*2*	*3*	*4*	*5*	*6*	*7*	*8*	*9*	*10*	*11*	*12*	*13*	*14*	*15*	*16*	*17*	*18*	*19*	*20*	*21*
Precision	0.157	0.180	0.187	0.187	0.187	0.180	0.193	0.193	0.193	0.193	0.187	0.193	0.193	0.186	0.193	0.193	0.200	0.193	0.193	0.200	0.200
Recall	0.933	0.900	0.933	0.933	0.933	0.900	0.967	0.967	0.967	0.967	0.933	0.966	0.966	0.931	0.966	0.966	1.000	0.964	0.964	1.000	1.000
F	0.268	0.300	0.311	0.311	0.311	0.300	0.322	0.322	0.322	0.322	0.311	0.322	0.322	0.310	0.322	0.322	0.333	0.321	0.321	0.333	0.333

In the first study, 5 programs on the top of the recommendation list were shown to subjects 2 times per day, and in other studies, 5 programs on the top of the recommendation list were shown to subjects 1time per day. Subjects filled in a score

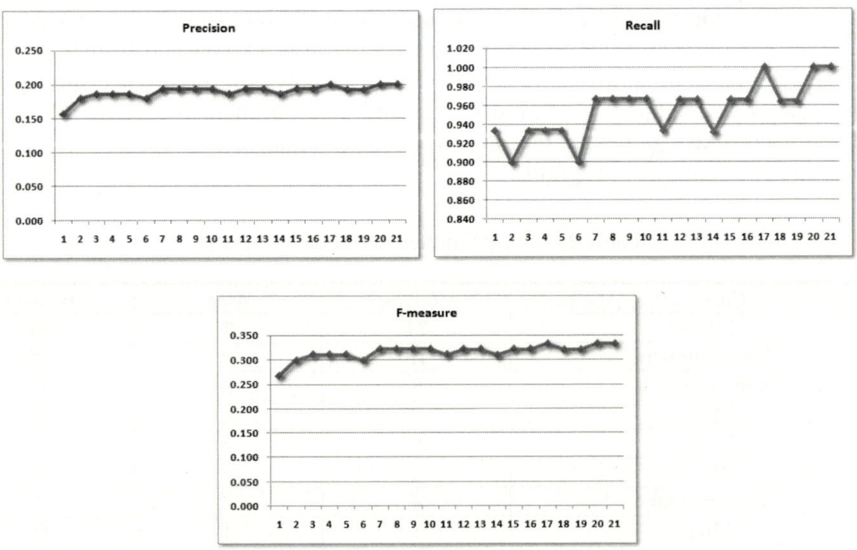

Fig. 2. Precision, Recall and F-measure of a recommendation system

about satisfaction and intention of watching recommended programs. Precision and Recall were calculated from the result of subjects' feedback. Figure 2 shows change of Precision, Recall and F. x axis in tests' iteration.

The first research study shows a high value by using preference information about category and channel from the pre-questionnaire. (Precision: 0.157/0.200, Recall: 0.933/1.000) The experiment period can be reduced by offering, in advance, subjects' preference information that has been accumulated for a long time. However, in this research, we are assuming that 'intention of watching recommended program' means 'programs that subjects watch actually' so, it is possible that Precision and Recall were calculated incorrectly. Table 4 shows the values of Recall, which was used in the working prototype of PEPG system, and the average of subjects' satisfaction score of the recommendation list.

Table 4. Recall and Satisfaction of a recommendation system

	1	*2*	*3*	*4*	*5*	*6*	*7*	*8*	*9*	*10*
Recall	0.933	0.900	0.933	0.933	0.933	0.900	0.967	0.967	0.967	0.967
Satisfaction	6.117	6.340	6.453	6.447	6.507	6.513	6.680	6.627	6.720	6.707

11	*12*	*13*	*14*	*15*	*16*	*17*	*18*	*19*	*20*	*21*
0.933	0.966	0.966	0.931	0.966	0.966	1.000	0.964	0.964	1.000	1.000
6.747	6.710	6.752	6.676	6.724	6.752	6.786	6.743	6.786	6.764	6.821

The satisfaction score was the result of calculating the average satisfaction. The range of satisfaction scores was 1-10. Figure 3 shows change of Recall and Satisfaction. X axis is the tests' iteration.

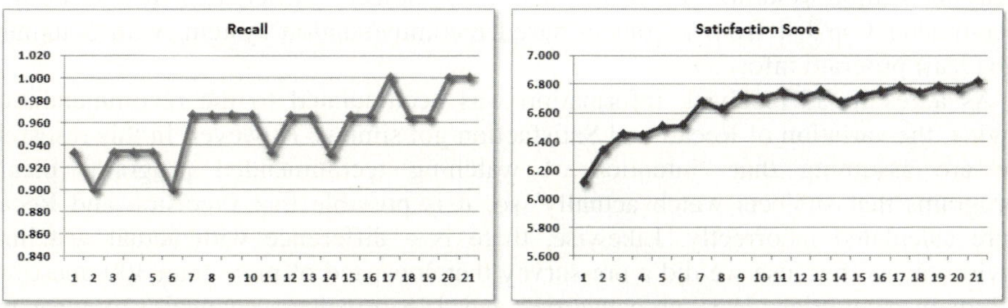

Fig. 3. Recall and Satisfaction of a recommendation system

Figure 4 shows the standardization of Recall and Satisfaction to compare their changes directly. Even though it is hard to compare quantitative data (Recall) and qualitative data (Satisfaction) directly, it is possible to check Recall and Satisfaction's variation in this figure.

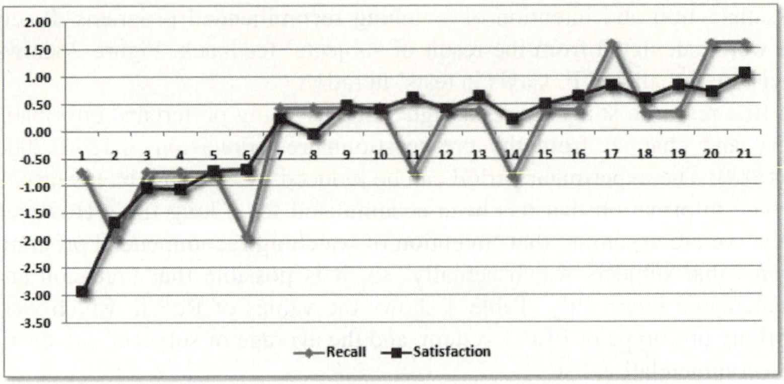

Fig. 4. Standardized comparison of Recall and Satisfaction

As feedback from subjects was accumulated in the recommendation engine, the variation of Recall and Satisfaction got similar. This means that as the recommendation engines performance was getting better, users satisfaction was getting higher.

5 Conclusion

As the digital broadcasting market grows rapidly, developing an efficient recommendation system is more and more important. So, there are many studies about personalized EPG. In previous studies, a calculation of the values of Precision and Recall based on data from EachMovie and MovieLens about hardware or software recommendation systems was performed. However, these previous studies did not involve actual subjects so they were not practical studies of the performance of recommendation systems. So in this study, 30 subjects participated in evaluating a recommendation list from a content-based recommendation system, with 3 months broadcast program information.

As a result, as feedback information was accumulated to the recommendation engine, the variation of Recall and Satisfaction got similar. However, in this research, we are assuming that 'intention of watching recommended program' means 'programs that subjects watch actually' so, it is possible that Precision and Recall were calculated incorrectly. Likewise, there is a difference with actual watching environments, because we did a pre-survey that consisted of more than 300 questions (13 main categories, 183 sub-categories and 126 broadcast channels) to raise the accuracy of recommendation.

In further studies, we expect to make viewer input information as small as possible by applying a stereotype recommendation technique. Construction on viewers' homes by applying the result of this study in user interfaces and evaluating recommendation results will produce a more accurate result.

Acknowledgments. This work was supported by grant No. (R01-2005-000-10764-0) from the Basic Research Program of the Korea Science & Engineering Foundation.

References

1. Basu, C., Hirsh, H., Cohen, W.: Recommendation as classification: Using social and content-based information in recommendation. In: Recommender Systems. Papers from 1998 Workshop. Technical Report WS-98-08. AAAI Press, California (1998)
2. Billsus, D., Pazzani, M.: Learning collaborative information filters. In: International Conference on Machine Learning, Morgan Kaufmann Publishers, San Francisco (1998)
3. Peng, C., Lugmayr, A., Vuorimaa, P.: A Digital Television Navigator. Multimedia Tools and Applications 17(1), 429–431 (2002)
4. Westerink, J., Bakker, C., De Ridder, H., Siepe, H.: Human factors in the design of a personalizable EPG: preference-indication strategies, habit watching and trust. Behaviour and Information Technology 21(4), 249–258 (2002)
5. Xu, J.A., Araki, K.: A Personalized Recommendation System for Electronic Program Guide. In: Zhang, S., Jarvis, R. (eds.) AI 2005. LNCS (LNAI), vol. 3809, pp. 1146–1149. Springer, Heidelberg (2005)
6. Konstan, J.A., Miller, B.N., Maltz, D., Herlocker, J.L., Gordon, L.R., Ried, J.: GroupLens: applying collaborative filtering to Usenet news. Communications of the ACM 40(3), 77–87 (1997)
7. Eronen, L., Vuorimaa, P.: User interfaces for digital television: a navigator case study. In: Proceedings of the working conference on Advanced visual interfaces, Palermo Italy, pp. 276–279 (2000)
8. Ardissono, L., Gena, C., Torasso, P., Bellifemine, F., Difino, A., Negro, B.: User Modeling and Recommendation Techniques for Personalized Electronic Program Guides. Human-Computer Interaction Series. Personalized Digital Television, vol. 6, pp. 3–26 (2004)
9. Pazzani, M.J.: A Framework for Collaborative, Content-Based and Demographic Filtering. Artificial Intelligence Review, 13(5-6) (December 1999)
10. Smyth, B., Cotter, P.: A Personalized Television Listing Service. Communications of the ACM 43(8), 107–111 (2000)
11. Zimmerman, J., Kurapati, K., Buczak, A.L., Schaffer, D., Gutta, S., Martino, J.: TV Personalization System. Human-Computer Interaction Series. Personalized Digital Television, vol. 6, pp. 27–51 (2004)
12. SkyLife.: http://www.skylife.co.kr
13. TiVo.: http://www.tivo.com

Usability of Hybridmedia Services – PC and Mobile Applications Compared

Jari Laarni[1], Liisa Lähteenmäki[1], Johanna Kuosmanen[2], and Niklas Ravaja[3]

[1] VTT Technical Research Centre of Finland, P.O. Box 1000, FI-02044 VTT, Finland
{Jari.Laarni,Liisa Lähteenmäki}@vtt.fi
[2] Taloustutkimus Oy, Lemuntie 9, FIN-00510 Helsinki, Finland
{Johanna,Kuosmanen}@taloustutkimus.fi
[3] Helsinki School of Economics, P.O. Box 1210, FIN-00101 Helsinki, Finland
{Niklas,Ravaja}@hse.fi

Abstract. The aim is to present results of a usability test of a prototype of a context-based personalized hybridmedia service for delivering product-specific information to consumers. We recorded participants' eye movements when they used the service either with a camera phone or with the web browser of a PC. The participants' task was to search for product-specific information from the food product database and test calculators by using both a PC and mobile user interface. Eye movements were measured by a head-mounted eye tracking system. Even though the completion of the tasks took longer when the participants used the mobile phone than when they used the PC, they could complete the tasks successfully with both interfaces. Provided that the barcode tag was not very small, taking pictures from the barcodes with a mobile phone was quite easy. Overall, the use of the service via the mobile phone provides a quite good alternative for the PC.

Keywords: Hybridmedia, usability, eye tracking, barcode reading.

1 Introduction

Two trends in computer technology can be identified: On the one hand, devices become smaller and more mobile; on the other hand, their interfaces become more complex. For example, mobile phones are more than just telephones: they have developed into multifunctional tools of everyday life. From the end user's point of view this means that the use of computers is more and more demanding.

Even though mobile devices may provide wireless access to the Internet with its potentially useful information and services it is quite clear that mobile phones do not suit very well for the presentation of web-based information. Most of these problems are caused by the small screen size.

Several approaches have been developed to transform web pages to small screens. For example, it has developed methods to summarize parts of web pages on small-screen devices [1]. Several ways to improve reading and information search have also been suggested and designed [2].

J. Jacko (Ed.): Human-Computer Interaction, Part III, HCII 2007, LNCS 4552, pp. 918–925, 2007.

1.1 Reading of Barcodes by a Camera Phone

Mobile cameras can be exploited in barcode reading. Barcode tags of packages are first read with a camera phone, and after that product-related information is delivered to the mobile phone. Barcode reading by mobile cameras provide, in principal, immediate access to relevant information - search phase can be totally skipped. Since there are good reasons to assume that making pictures of barcodes is quite easy after a short period of practice, the mobile application generally provides a good alternative for the PC version of a hybridmedia service.

1.2 Eye Tracking in the Usability Evaluation

There are a growing number of studies on the usability of human-computer interfaces in which eye tracking is used. Eye tracking can supplement behavioural studies by providing more specific information, e.g., about the specific areas of the stimuli that cause problems and cognitive processes that are involved in a particular task [3].

Our previous results suggest that eye tracking is a useful method, but it is only applicable for solving certain kinds of usability problems [3]. We still need more studies on which kinds of problems can be successfully solved by eye-tracking methodology.

1.3 Present Study

The present study is a part of the Finnish project called "A context-based personalized information system for delivering product information to the consumer (TIVIK)". In this project, a hybridmedia service was developed to deliver product-specific information to consumers about foods. The system can be accessed both with a PC web browser or a camera phone, which was used to read barcode tags of food packages.

Our first aim here was to compare the usability of mobile phone and PC-versions of the TIVIK service. The second aim was to study barcode reading by means of a camera mobile phone, and the third aim was to assess the usefulness of eye tracking in the study of usability of mobile phones. An experiment was carried out to test the pilot version of the system in the laboratory while users' eye movements were recorded.

2 Method

2.1 Participants

Eight volunteers participated in the experiment (four men, four women). The mean age of the participants was 31. They were all unaware of the purpose of the experiment. None of them had used the service earlier. Participants were paid for their participation. All of them had experience using PCs and were regular Internet users. One participant did not own a mobile phone, and she had only little practice on its use.

2.2 Apparatus and Stimuli

The PC-version was displayed on a normal PC computer monitor. Display resolution was 1024 x 768 pixels. The mobile device was a mobile phone with a camera (model Nokia 3660). Viewing distance was 70 cm when using the PC service and 50 cm when using the mobile phone.

A pilot service was developed to deliver health-related information to consumers about the nutritional quality of food products. In the prototype the user could obtain product-specific information by reading barcodes of food packages with the camera phone. After reading the barcode, product information is shown on the XHTML browser. The same information could also be accessed with a web browser on a PC. The mobile phone provided basic information about the product. On PC a larger amount of nutrition related information could be examined, and products could be compared.

2.3 Procedure

Eight information search tasks were carried out with the PC and five tasks with the mobile phone. Five of the tasks were common for the two applications. When using PC participants had to search for a particular product, and after that they had to find product-specific information and/or put the product into different calculators that calculated, e.g., the energy content of the consumed food. When using the mobile service the product was displayed on the screen immediately after barcode reading, and the participant's task was to search for product-specific information or put the product into the calculators. Half of the participants carried out the tasks first with the PC application and half with the mobile device.

There were two products for each task. One of the products was used when using the PC, the other one when using the mobile phone.

Participants did not practice the search tasks beforehand. They were provided basic information about the content of the application, and they were asked to read the introductory text that was presented on the portal page of the service. They also read the instructions of the mobile service. After the product search task, reading of barcodes of the packages was examined. Reading of barcodes was practised for about five minutes. The time to accomplish the task was measured and the search performance was measured and video-recorded.

2.4 Eye Movement Recordings

Participants' eye movements were recorded using a head-mounted gaze tracking system (SMI iView^{TM}). A participant's right eye was monitored with a miniature infra-red camera while one infra-red LED illuminated the eye. The scene camera video-recorded the scene the reader was viewing. The eye tracking system was controlled by a PC computer. It computes the centres of the pupil and corneal reflection, from which it can compute the point of regard.

Video images of the pupil and corneal reflections were captured at 50 Hz by the eye tracker. The resolution of the system is better than one degree. The eye movement system was calibrated using a set of 5 screen locations. The participant had to stay immobile during the calibration process. After calibration the participant was asked not to move. However, since the tracker is head-mounted, small movements of a participant's head do not spoil the measurement (SensoriMotoric Instruments, 1999). iView software was used to detect fixations and calculate their durations. Fixation points were identified using a dispersion-based algorithm [4]. To be considered a fixation, a gaze point had to fall within a spatial area between about 30pt x 30pt deg, and had to have a minimum duration of 100 msec. Gaze position in iView is related to the calibration area settings. This area was in the present study 692pt x 278pt.

The eye movement data included the x and y coordinates of eye position and the processed fixations. The data collected were saved for subsequent analysis. The recorded video displayed the current field of view and the superimposed gaze cursor.

We also used an observational method to analyze the eye-movement data. Observer Video-Pro™ application was used in the analysis. The analyses were based on the location of the cursor which was superimposed over the scene. Here we were interested in by which way the user's gaze moves around the device.

3 Results and Discussion

3.1 Basic Findings

Except for the first task, the search for the target product seems to last for 20-40 sec. Because of occasional problems with connection speed, the length of time the product page took to upload was subtracted from the search times.

The completion of the first search task took over six times longer than the second one. One reason for the difficulties is that the titles of the product categories did not provide enough information of where a particular product can be found.

A two-dimensional ANOVA with service type and task as factors was carried out for the study of the completion of a task after the subtraction of search time. The effect of service type (PC application vs. mobile phone application) was significant, $F(1,61) = 12.69$, $p < 0.001$. The completion of a task lasted significantly longer when using the mobile phone. Also, the effect of task was significant, $F(4,61) = 3.06$, $p < 0.05$, and the interaction between service type and task was marginally significant, $F(4,61) = 2.39$, $0.05 < p < 0.1$. For example, the fifth task was the easiest one for the PC application, but it was the second slowest for the mobile application. The comparison of execution times for all tasks when using the PC showed that all tasks requiring the searching for products from product category lists were time-consuming.

We compared search with the PC application to that of the mobile phone for three products. With the mobile application, in order to estimate the total time required, we added the mean barcode reading time to the duration of time required for the completion of the task. According to a two-way ANOVA, the effect of service type and task were not statistically significant, $p > 0.1$, whereas the interaction between service type and task was, $F(2,40) = 5.8$, $p < 0.01$. For the first task, the mobile application performed better than the PC version, that is, the search was faster when using the mobile phone. For the second and third tasks, the search with PC was somewhat faster than search with a mobile phone.

3.2 Evaluation of the Hybridmedia Service

All the participants thought that the information was comprehensible and satisfactory. Product-specific information was quite easily found, even though many of the product names were not familiar to them. Many of the participants also thought that both services were quite easy to use. Many of them, however, blamed the slowness of both applications. There were many reasons for this slowness, for example, the uploading of the service lasted in some cases a long time. For many participants the terms and the product names were quite unfamiliar, and the mobile-phone interface was somewhat confusing.

Four of the eight participants thought that the product information could be better visualized, for example by using images and graphics. Moreover, two participants thought that the width of the PC screen should be better utilized. Since the names of the product categories are not very familiar to people, it might be useful if the same product could be found under several categories. Another possibility is to provide more information of the products. Illustrative pictures of the products could also be used.

Overall, the service was considered to be quite useful. Especially, the exercise counter was considered to be an interesting and useful feature. Most of the participants thought that they might use the service at least on some occasions.

The mean usability score for the mobile service was 6.5, the scores ranging from the minimum of 4 to the maximum of 7; the mean score of the PC service was 7.8, the scores ranging from the minimum of 6 to the maximum of 9. It must be specially emphasized that the participants used the service for the first time, and their evaluations were based on one usage occasion.

3.3 Eye Movement Recordings

According to a two-way ANOVA, the service type had a marginally significant effect on fixation duration, $F(1,61) = 3.3$, $0.05 < p < 0.1$. However, the effect of task was not significant, $p > 0.1$, neither was the interaction between task and service type, $p > 0.1$.

Since the fourth and the fifth task were identical for the PC- and mobile-phone application, we could compare them in respect of the number of fixations they required. A two-way ANOVA showed that the task had a significant effect on fixation number, $F(4,24) = 9.4$, $p < 0.001$, and the service type also had a marginally significant effect, $F(1,24) = 3.94$, $0.05 < p < 0.1$. The number of fixations was somewhat higher when using the mobile phone, partly because the participants had problems in closing the mobile application.

3.4 Qualitative Analysis of Eye Movements

PC-based service. When using PC the participants' gaze moved from the top of the page to the bottom along the product lists. The gaze typically moved from one product name highlighted with a bold typeface to another one and passed by product information that was marked by a normal typeface. Yet, the participants typically did not pass by a target product if its name was visible on the screen. Many participants, however, selected first the wrong item from the product category list. A central problem seemed, thus, to be how to find the right product category.

When searching for a product name from a list, the participants moved their gaze from the top to the bottom and back again. Quite often the wrong category was selected, and the users had to return to the previous page and select another product category. The participants easily failed to notice that the list continued from one page to another. One participant searched for a particular product over six minutes. After that the experimenter interrupted the execution of the task.

When the right page was in view, the product was quite easily found. However, when the list included many products that have a quite similar name, the user typically had to read the list from the beginning until the target was found.

In general, after the product has been found, the participants had no problems to find the searched-for information. In the beginning, the participants had some problems to find the buttons linking to relevant calculators. When using the exercise calculator the gaze easily wandered around the screen before the right button was found. Five of the eight participants did not notice the Compare products -button and thus, they were not able to compare the products by having the text side-by side on two columns.

Mobile service. When using the mobile application the participants typically had no problems to find the buttons of the calculators. However, it was somewhat confusing to them that they first had to select the favourites or food calculator from the list, and after the upload of the product information they had to press a specific button. The participants, thus, had to make two choices in order to add the product to the calculators and favourites.

One participant accidentally logged out from the service, and another one searched for the asked for information over four minutes. Participants did not immediately notice that the information was located under a specific link. Most of the participants had some problems to find the right link from the list of product information. Additionally, some participants had a lot of problems in leaving the service.

3.5 Reading of Barcodes by a Mobile Phone

The duration of time that was needed for barcode reading somewhat differ between food packages. According to a one-way ANOVA the effect of package type was significant, $F(1,7) = 4.5$, $p < 0.001$. The slowest reading time was over 20 seconds longer than the fastest one. The size of the barcode tag can in part explain the differences in reading time. For example, the barcode which was read at the slowest speed was much smaller than the barcode which was read at the fastest speed. The correlation between the size of the barcode and the reading time was not linear, however. The reading of a small barcode was difficult, but when the size of the barcode was above a threshold value its size had no effect on reading time.

The curvedness or the evenness of the surface did not seem to have any effect: the reading of a barcode was quite successful even when the surface was curved or crumbled. However, the level of lightness seems to play some role: If the surface does not receive enough light, the reading of the barcode was quite difficult. During the session, the participants learned to turn the package in such way that its surface was sufficiently lit.

The participants were sitting at the table. Four of the eight participants supported the product against the table or against the knee, rest of them held the package in the air during barcode reading.

The participants tried to keep the package immobile during the barcode reading and move instead the mobile phone as was needed. Seven of the eight participants kept the package in an upright position during the barcode reading, and they turn the package in a horizontal position when the barcode was in an upright position. One participant, however, held the package in a horizontal position during the barcode reading.

4 Conclusions

The main problem with the usability of the PC application was the slowness of the product search. Some products were extremely difficult to find. After the searched-for product had been found, the participants could typically complete the task quite fast.

Reading of barcodes was quite fast and easy. When using the mobile service and when the product is selected by reading the barcode from the package, the product search is nearly an instant process. Therefore, the use of the mobile service is nearly as efficient as the use of the PC-based service.

Despite of this, the mobile service was evaluated much worse than the PC-based service. The problems with the mobile service are more related to the properties of the device than to the properties of the mobile-phone version of the service. Because of small screen size, the product information has to be more densely packed, e.g., the fonts have to be smaller, and the spacing between lines has to be narrower. Input methods are also more cumbersome when using the mobile phone keyboard than using the mouse.

Difficulties with product search were the most serious problem with the PC-based service. The search could be made more efficient by different ways. For example, the product could be found from different product categories; there could be additional information with the category names; and the content of the categories could be illustrated by pictures. If the number of products in a category is large, the search based on product names is the easiest and most convenient way to find the searched-for product. It is important that the search based on product names often led to a successful result even when the participant did not know the exact name of the product.

Since most of the information is presented on PC as vertical lists, the user has to scroll the content. Since the list often continues from one page to another, the reading of this kind of list is often cumbersome. The user may also fail to notice that the list continues from one page to another. One possibility is to better utilize the width of the page when using the PC-based service.

In sum, our findings suggest that even though the PC-based service was thought to be more usable than the mobile service, the completion of the tasks was comparable to that of the phone camera-based service. Overall, mobile service is thus a considerable alternative, and reading of barcodes is not a serious problem. Additionally, our results suggest that eye tracking and eye movement analysis can support traditional usability evaluation methods. For example, eye movement data could provide quite specific information of the users' behavior during task execution.

Acknowledgments

This work was produced with the financial support of the National Technology Agency of Finland. We wish to thank all the colleagues, especially Caj Södergård, Timo Järvinen, Paula Järvinen, Sari Vainikainen and Anne-Mari Ottelin, whose work has provided the basis for this study.

References

[1] Buyukkokten, O., Garcia-Molina, H., Paepcke, P.: Seeing The Whole in Parts: Text Summarization for Web Browsing on Handheld Devices. In: Proceedings of the 10th InternationalWorld Wide Web Conference, May 2001, pp. 652–662. ACM Press, New York, NY (2001)

[2] Jones, M., Marsden, G., Mohd-Nasir, N., Boone, K., Buchanan, G.: Improving Web Interaction on Small Displays. In: Proceedings of the 8th International World Wide Web Conference (WWW8), Toronto, pp. 51–60 (1999)

[3] Pölönen, M., Häkkinen, J., Laarni, J.: Does Eye Tracking Provide a Window to the Soul of Mobile Phone Users? In: Proceedings of the 11th International Display Workshops (IDW04) (2004)

[4] Salvucci, D.D., Goldberg, J.H.: Identifying Fixations and Saccades in Eye-Tracking Protocols. In: Proceedings of the Eye Tracking Research and Applications Symposium, pp. 71–78. ACM Press, New York (2000)

m-YouTube Mobile UI: Video Selection Based on Social Influence

Aaron Marcus and Angel Perez

Aaron Marcus and Associates, Inc., 1196 Euclid Avenue, Suite 1F, Berkeley, CA, 94708 USA
{Aaron.Marcus,Angel.Perez}@AMandA.com
www.AMandA.com

Abstract. The ease-of-use of Web-based video-publishing services provided by applications like YouTube has encouraged a new means of asynchronous communication, in which users can post videos not only to make them public for review and criticism, but also as a way to express moods, feelings, or intentions to an ever-growing network of friends. Following the current trend of porting Web applications onto mobile platforms, the authors sought to explore user-interface design issues of a mobile-device-based YouTube, which they call m-YouTube. They first analyzed the elements of success of the current YouTube Web site and observed its functionality. Then, they looked for unsolved issues that could give benefit through information-visualization design for small screens on mobile phones to explore a mobile version of such a product/service. The biggest challenge was to reduce the number of functions and amount information to fit into a mobile phone screen, but still be usable, useful, and appealing within the YouTube context of use and user experience. Borrowing ideas from social research in the area of social influence processes, they made design decisions aiming to help YouTube users to make the decision of what video content to watch and to increase the chances of YouTube authors being evaluated and observed by peers. The paper proposes a means to visualize large amounts of video relevant to YouTube users by using their friendship network as a relevance indicator to help in the decision-making process.

Keywords: design, interface, mobile, network, social, user, YouTube, video.

1 Introduction

The popularization of the World-Wide Web among early technology adopters and younger generations, in addition to the new technologies giving faster and more reliable Internet connections, paved the way for new products and services that addressed, among others, one of the most basic human needs: social networking. In this way, a product/service that seems to make it easier to meet people, to keep in touch with friends and loved ones, and to share interests and opinions becomes the most successful one. The product/service success is not only given by its acceptance, but also by how effectively it opens new business opportunities. In fact, YouTube is

J. Jacko (Ed.): Human-Computer Interaction, Part III, HCII 2007, LNCS 4552, pp. 926–932, 2007.

arguably the most successful of the aforementioned "social network" products/services. The ease-of-use of the Web video publishing service provided by YouTube, encouraged a new way of asynchronous communication in which users can post videos not only to make them public for critique, but also as a way to express moods, feelings or intentions to an always growing network of friends. According to *Wired* magazine, YouTube went from 10,000 daily video uploads in December 2005, to about 65,000 in September 2006. Furthermore, Google, which acquired YouTube for $1.6b dollars is betting on the reallocation of the money being currently invested in TV advertising (about $67 billion dollars) [1].

Nowadays, the Web is becoming mobile, meaning that mobile devices such as PDAs, mobile phones, and smart phones have ever-improving Web-browsing capabilities. However, the current trend of porting Web applications onto mobile platforms has focused primarily on mirroring desktop applications in mobile devices. Moreover, the nature of the mobile platform elements, such as screen size and interaction styles, has led to design efforts that purely reduce the functionality of the Web-desktop application to fit the constraints of the mobile platform [2][4][5]. Although necessary, functionality reduction is not sufficient to render a usable, useful, and appealing mobile user-experience version of a Web-desktop application. The lack of usability is due (1) to the basic unsolved problems and limitations initially inherited by the new platform from the desktop user interface and its WIMP paradigm and (2) to the further challenging and inherent constraints of the mobile platform. Within this context, the authors explored porting a Web-desktop application such as YouTube to a mobile platform, specifically, improving and extending the functionality reduction by using clues provided by human-to-human social interaction. In this way, the authors propose a mobile UI to visualize large amounts of video relevant to the YouTube users, and support quick video selection by using their friendship networks as a relevance indicator to help in the decision-making process [3].

After observation of the practices of the YouTube community the authors borrowed ideas from social psychology research in the area of "social influence processes" and proposed a user-interface design solution that accomplishes the following:

- First, reduces the amount of functions and the load of information to fit in a mobile phone, but seems to remain usable, useful, and appealing within an application context like that of YouTube.
- Second, helps the YouTube users to make a fast decision about what video content to watch.

Third, increases the chances of YouTube authors to be evaluated and observed by peers.

2 Design Approach

YouTube Anatomy: Key success aspects
A one-and-a-half week observation of YouTube use by typical users and personal use revealed key concepts that contribute to the success of YouTube as a Web-desktop application.

First, the Web-based ubiquitous access to video, allows easy sharing of viral video hits (video that gains widespread popularity through Internet sharing) not only by simply sending the link to the video by e-mail, but also by allowing groups of friends to conglomerate around a screen in the same way they would do around a TV set. Furthermore, the interactivity given by the Web application (search, selection, rate, *etc*), supports social dynamics by involving in the process groups of friends who are either next to each other or connected through a remote communication service such as a messenger or a chat room (e.g. iChat, MSM, ICQ, AIM, *etc*).

Second, YouTube shows a very easy-to-use publication environment. After registration, uploading a video takes only two steps. The simplicity of the uploading process allows users to focus on their final goal (the social interaction, *e.g.*, making a friend laugh) rather than on a potentially cumbersome frustrating process (uploading the video).

Third, because the YouTube service is free, no exchange of money is involved at any part of the process (*e.g.*, AOL video charges for some videos). Finally, there is little control of the video content to be posted, which is done by the YouTube self-organized community: if some video content is believed to be inappropriate, it will be flagged by the YouTube community and soon removed from the Website by the service provider. This flexible means of control directly affects the user experience (UX) by giving immediate gratification to the YouTube user, because there are no major delays associated with posting a video.

YouTube Anatomy: YouTube community practices

First, YouTube users watch posted videos from either random sources, friends, contacts, or special interests lists. In turn, the URL of the videos can be copied and pasted by the users to be shared with others.

Second, any YouTube user can upload a video for Web publishing: virtually any kind of video can be uploaded, and for improved quality the YouTube Websites gives recommendations on the format of the video. In this way, the video repository is always growing and has a very large range of topics.

Third, YouTube users can add videos and authors to favored lists. Among others, quick lists, groups' lists, play lists, and favorites lists. Furthermore, YouTube users can subscribe to channels, groups, and other users, and have videos delivered to them.

Fourth, YouTube users can post video responses, personal and copyrighted videos, text comments on videos watched. Also, they can rate and/or flag other YouTube members' videos.

YouTube Anatomy: New design opportunities

The variety in the user population, taking into account elements such as age, nationality, genre, occupation, *etc.,* opens new design opportunities in many different directions, among others:

Corporate partners: establish new business relationships for content creation and distribution as currently explored with Warner to avoid copyright infringement.

Functionality: identify possible new applications on top of the current ones. As an example, some online providers give tools that allow easy, quick editing of video.

Incorporate Web 2.0: creation of products and services that make extensive use of APIs provided by YouTube to development communities.

Information design: taking into account the complexity of the information displayed to improve the UX.

Make it mobile: port YouTube to phones and PDAs freeing YouTube from the desktop usage and address the YouTube population on the go.

Markets: address both wide user population and different interests of each population sector.

New strategies: new strategies for traditional businesses such as advertisement, which is currently being explored by Google.

Personalization of functionality: direct functions to particular users' communities, as currently done by My Space with music artists.

Reinforce functionality: to improve self-expression with personal video by giving some extra functionality that reinforces the concept of easy Web publishing for regular users who see YouTube as a new space for art and media.

v-Mail: Although there is a widely variety of "kind of users," each one with different motivations to post video, the YouTube functionality represents a *de facto* tool for asynchronous communication for which video is the media of preference.

2.1 Design Concept: m-YouTube

Considering the design opportunities previously described, the authors focused on the YouTube community always-on-the-go for a conceptual design. For users, the authors identified the most relevant functions in the YouTube application that potentially complement the YouTube easy video publishing, viewing, and sharing service when ported to mobile platform. Furthermore, in the proposal for **m-YouTube**, the authors generated added value in the form of information visualization that simplifies the video selection. In this way, they attempt to propose a design that takes full advantage of the mobile platform while supporting and extending some of the key elements of the YouTube UX.

In practice, with m-YouTube one wants to save "on the go" users from selecting irrelevant content by helping them choose videos that match their preferences. Additionally, one also aims to increase the chances for video authors to be reviewed by peers making it easier to be spotted and selected from large amount of videos.

The concept design is based on social psychology theories that suggest decision-making is influenced by friendship networks. According to author Martin Kilduff [3], social network as a decision-making resource may be as much an expression of personality as it is a constraint on individual choice. In this way, Kilduff proposes that two personality variables, self-monitoring and social uniqueness moderate social influence on choices and the values of these variables differentiate between people on the basis of susceptibility to social comparisons. Furthermore, Kilduff suggests that self-monitoring and social uniqueness personality types differ in their preferences in relation to how much their decision patterns resembled those of their friends and with respect to the criteria they used in the decision making process. Kilduff continues by stating that high self-monitoring actions relative to lows, are more likely to shape people's behavior in accordance with cues supplied by the social circles to which they belong. Finally, Kilduff also states that social comparison theories imply that one's susceptibility to social influence depends on the availability of others who are perceived to be especially similar to one's self.

2.2 Context Approach to Video Recording

In m-YouTube, the results are grouped per page. In Figure1, assuming either a hypothetical outcome of a search (*e.g.*, after searching YouTube for a video) or after having a default-state for the application (*e.g.*, the very large list of featured videos on the YouTube main page), each page will show nine results in a 3x3 matrix. This arrangement not only allows five-way jog-pad navigation through the page, but also nine results can be quickly accessed (with just one click) via the numeric keys [4]. Additionally, the design proposes a visual reinforcement given by a highlighted column. The column width varies per page hinting at the total amount of pages: a dramatic change in the page width when jumping from two consecutive pages suggests little content.

The presence of a thumbnail of the video content has a twofold intention: first, as shown in Figure 1-a, the thumbnail image could contain a face that can be recognized, hence selected (*e.g.*, my best friend), or, as shown in Figures 1-a and 1-b, the thumbnail has something that might interest the users (*e.g.*, funny couples video or funny animals). Furthermore, within the YouTube community the posting user is as important as the video posted (*e.g.*, the "famous" lonelygirl15). Consequently, the author's name is coupled with the video thumbnail.

In m-YouTube, the results are pre-filtered and sorted based on the number of times the video was seen, discussed, or linked by the rest of the YouTube community. Only the most watched, linked and discussed are shown with the corresponding amount of hits. The intention of this design concept is to use the evidence that high self-monitors choose on the base of socially defined realities (*e.g.*, image projected: the most discussed, must be good) whereas low self-monitors choose on the basis of intrinsic quality (*e.g.*, most linked, must be good) [3].

As previously mentioned, the susceptibility of a user to be socially influenced depends on the availability of other users who are perceived as similar. In this way, in Figure 2, visual cues are shown intended to link some of the video results with the users' affiliations. Assuming users subscribe to certain groups because they have similar interests, taste, humor, *etc.*, the visual cues in the base design should not only speed the decision making, but also the chances of picking an enjoyable video to watch. Aditionally, when the affiliations are present, the opinion of similar users is the best way to estimate the quality of a given video. The design, in consequence, includes a rating given by the members of the users' affiliations and reduces the hue of the numbers of hits emphasize the users peers' (similar users) opinion.

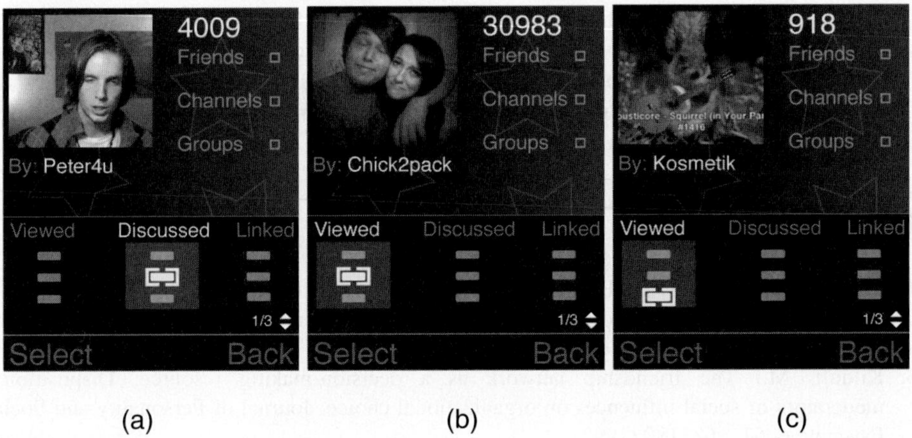

Fig. 1. m-YouTube user interface (UI) shows three pages, nine results per page, social affiliations, and number of hits. (a) Video thumbnail showing author's face. (b) Video thumbnail showing possible interesting content image. (c) Changed cursor position.

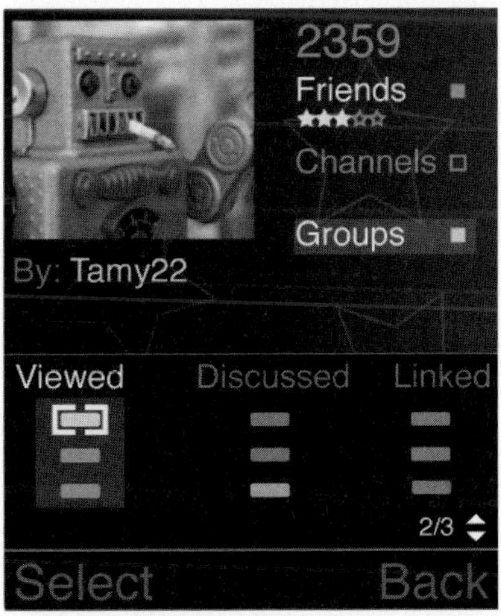

Fig. 2. The video in green has been rated three stars out of five by the friends of the user

3 Conclusion

This conceptual design successfully explores information-visualization and social psychology in a UI to make decision making faster and more effective in a mobile platform. The proposed base design should simplify and speed the decision making with the several visual cues that address two users types: high self-reflective and low self-reflective users. Additionally, the designs are sufficiently complete to take them to users for testing to fine tune the UI elements that will render the best user experience. Finally, the design analysis was successful in that it showed a very diverse set of possibilities that can be further explored from the UX-design point of view and may illustrate how social psychology theory can be used as a catalyst for UX design. Design of a mobile user-interface for YouTube is taking place worldwide (see for example [6].) The authors hope this work done in November 2006 contributes to the exploration of practical and effective possibilities.

References

1. Garfield, B.: The YouTube Effect. Wired Magazine, p. 222 (December 2006)
2. Jones, M., Marsden, G.: Mobile Interaction Design. John Wiley and Sons, Chichester (2006)
3. Kilduff, M.: The friendship network as a decision-making resource: Dispositional moderators of social influences on organizational choice. Journal of Personality and Social Psychology 61, 168–180 (1992)
4. Lindholm, C., et al.: Mobile Usability. McGraw-Hill, New York (2003)
5. Studio 7.5. Designing for Small Screens, AVA Publishing, Lausanne (2005)
6. Paul, M.: Nokia's YouTube features in action. Engadget.com (2007) http://www.engadget.com/2007/02/13/nokias-youtube-features-in-action/ (last visited: February 15th 2007)

Can Video Support City-Based Communities?

Raquel Navarro-Prieto and Nidia Berbegal

Barcelona Media – Innovation Center, Barcelona, Spain
Raquel.Navarro@barcelonamedia.org,
Nidia.Berbegal@upf.edu

Abstract. The goal of our research has been to investigate the different ways in with using new communication technologies, especially mobile multimedia communications, could support the city-based communities. In this paper we review the research done about the effect of mobile technology, specially mobile video, into communities' communication patterns, and highlight the new challenges and gaps still not covered in this area. Finally, we will describe how we have tried to respond to these challenges by using User Centered Design in two very different types of communities: women associations, and elderly people.

1 Introduction

The goal of our research was to understand the role of mobile multimedia applications, with special emphasis on video, in the communities that already exist in cities. While a lot of research have focus on virtual communities, less attention have been paid to physical communities what would benefit from the use of new mobile technologies.

Our research has been conducted as part of the EC funded IST project ICING (Innovative Cities of the Next Generation), which goal is to reach a model of a city more responsive to the citizen through the usage of multi-access and multi-modal infrastructures to explore new ways of communication and interaction.

Indeed, although in the last years, there has been several papers about different applications of mobile video and TV [1] most of the research have been focus on either a passive consumption of videos and TV content; or on peer to peer exchange of videos (without studying the impact into a group). Several applications and services have been build recently trying to help communities based in a particular city or an area (like an university campus), so far they are including chat, voice conversations, emails and SMS [2,3,4] but only now video is starting to emerge as an complementary way to communicate.

In our paper we will review the exiting literature in the areas mentioned above starting with defining the scope of our definition of community. Regarding the usage of video first, we will look at the usage of video on remote groups and virtual communities. Second, we will explore the challenges introduce by the new emerging technologies that facilitate mobile social networks. After that, we will see how the existing literature does not answer the question about how these technologies have an

J. Jacko (Ed.): Human-Computer Interaction, Part III, HCII 2007, LNCS 4552, pp. 933–942, 2007.

effect in the communication needs of physically based communities. In order to understand the effect of mobile multimedia applications on these special types of communities we will describe our work in the ICING project, using User Centered Design approach with several already existing communities of citizens.

2 Towards a Definition of Community

The term "community" has not a unique definition, but covers a wide range of social links. One of the broadest definitions of community considers that a community is a collection of livings that form a social group characterized by a territorial or demographical link or that share common interests, hobbies or ideological convictions that establish personal relationships between them through physical and/or virtual environments. According to [5] we have several ways to classify the nature of a community Demographic, Geographical and Topical Communities. In Figure 1, we illustrate the cross of these categories with the way its members communicate to each other, which is the focus of our study:

If defining the term "community" was not simple, trying to define "virtual communities" is, indeed, an even harder difficult task. Several definitions have been written by different authors, focusing on different aspects of these communities. As a consequence sometimes they not seem to be defining the same term.

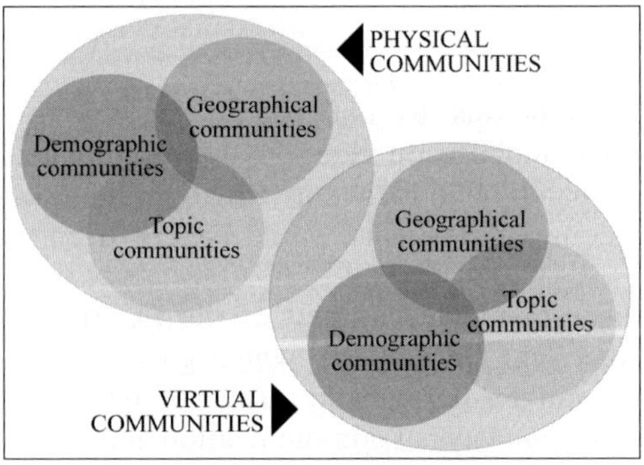

Fig. 1. Communities' classification

Several definitions from well-known e-community specialists have been found in [6]. For instance, according to Amy Jo Kim, a virtual community "is a group of people who gather together around a shared purpose, activity, or interest". Because of the lack of a common physical location as a factor of their identity, this definition implies that its members have to use some kind of virtual tools to communicate to each other and to be able to establish personal relations. There is a debate among sociologists about how cyberspace communities' behaviours relate to physical communities theories. In the essence, virtual and physical communities do not differ so much, both involve personal relationships among the different people that share same interests, so a virtual community is, in a sense, "a community that happens to exist online rather than in the physical word" [7]. Online communities have many characteristics borrowed from real-world communities [8], [9]. It is outside the scope of this paper to review all the characteristics of these communities.

3 Usage of Video on Remote Groups and Virtual Communities

The usages of video to enhance people collaborating in teams which members are remotely located have been investigated since the early times of HCI. During the 90s a several researchers investigated the advantages and when would it be more effective to use video-mediated communication among groups collaborating remotely. The hypothesis that they were trying to test was whether video could substitute face-to-face communication effectively [10, 11, 12]. Therefore, the research questions were focus on comparing users interacting with video versus face-to-face situations. For instance, the work from Credé and Sniezek [13] compared 94 groups of size three while completing a estimation task interacting either by video-conferencing or face-to face collocated in the same room. Their results show that the video-conferencing groups scored lower than the face-to-face in several metrics as level of confidence (being lower and more accurate in the video-conferencing groups). On the other hand "there were no significant differences between the two interaction media on the following outcome dimensions: accuracy; overconfidence; commitment to the group decision; size of credible intervals; improvement over average initial individual estimates; and the number of beliefs discussed or learned".

Other studies found different advantages of one type of communication depending on several variables [14]. It seems that Video-mediated communication, as well as other forms of remote interpersonal communication are distinctive by the nature of the medium from which they are constituted. We agree with Fels and Weiss [15] that "each form of communication has particular strengths and weaknesses". Therefore, the goal should be to define the interactions needed to complete a particular task and to select the most efficient way to provide then. Although most of the research in the area of video mediated communication has been done in with remote groups that it is not equivalent to the definition of community that we show bellow, we think that their findings are interesting for our work.

Focusing now on research about communities (as they have been defined in the previous section) people have been communicating using online spaces since the beginning of the Internet, "including prior to the World Wide Web, when BBS or electronic bulletin boards and email loops connected folks across time and space" [16]. Nowadays, online communities are web-based communities, mostly held by chats, discussion forums, online salons, mailing lists, bulletin boards, MUDs (multi-user dimension), MOOS (Multi-user objected oriented), listservs, etc. or combinations of these software programs along with web pages; in addition video communications between virtual community members are shyly increasing. Nevertheless, most of the research on virtual communities has not contemplated the usage of video. We believe that one explanation for that is that in a lot of the virtual communities users have a fake identity using an avatar that does not correspond to their image.

In contrast with the lack of research on the impact of video exchange on the life of online communities, the exchange of videos is an well know recent phenomenon growing every day. According to the Timothy Tuttle the VP of AOL Video [17] the numbers are "10 billion videos streamed every month, 60 billion dollar market opportunity, internet video doubling every 6 months". It is clear that people like to share the videos, most of the time user generated videos, inside small and wide communities. A great example is the popularity of the site YouTube [18], that allow not only sharing but making links to the videos in blog and personal webs.

4 New Research Challenges of Mobile Multimedia Applicatiosns

In addition the research challenges of the use of video in online communities, recently the possibility of exchanging multimedia files and information while mobile has introduced even more questions that will need to be studied. At present, there are already several studies on the way people use the camera phones and which type of message do people create and send. For instance, Kindberg, Spasojevic, Fleck, and Sellen [19], conducted an in-depth research using interviews and discussions about a sample of real user's photos. They created a 6-part taxonomy to describe the way images are use "both for sharing and personal use, and for affective and functional use". According to the authors, the main usages could be Social or Individual. The social usages cold be classified as Affective (to share mutual experiences or to link with an absent friend or family) or Functional (for mutual tasks or for remote tasks). The Individual usages were found to be mainly for Personal Reflection or for Personal Tasks. Other example is [20], where the authors described emerging practices with camera phones in Japan illustrating these practices with ethnographic material. This research is still in early stages (as the adoption of these technologies) and we still not do know if these exchange on information has any effect on the use of multimedia in the communication's pattern of these communities.

In addition to all these challenges, very recently we have seen the launch of new applications that will allow us to connect to some of the features of the social networks from the mobile. For instance, from early this year we can receive alerts whenever a new comment is added to your MySpace page, or you can upload images from your mobile to Flickr. These new developments have brought some business analyst: "Could mobile social networks be the next big thing?" [21]. A new term of mobile social networks have emerged, which according to [22] is "a network of interpersonal ties that provides sociability, support, information, a sense of belonging, social identity, and which always connects its members regardless of where they go." Indeed, it already exist some exclusively mobile-based mobile social networks as the one operated buy AirG [23], Jumbuck [24], and Trilibis Mobile [25].

As social software has increases its usage in the last years, some researchers are staring to research questions, coming directions and relevant technologies surrounding the adoption of this type of software. The main example of this emerging research area is the workshop that was hold during CHI 2006 about "Mobile Social Software. In their conclusions, the workshop organisers stated that the primary discussion topics that will need to be investigated are [26]: "Antisocial Mobile Software; Supporting special communities; Mobile social awareness and presence; Mobile support for multiple cultures (i.e. Mobile support for "cultural translation" on the fly); Personal projectors (co-located, multi-user applications); Supporting epidemiology (i.e. combating spreading of disease); and Barriers (critical mass, interoperability)". Most of these challenges lied in the software development site. We did not find information about mixed presence and virtual communities.

5 Physical Communities with Technological Support

We have found a research gap while searching for data about the relationships that may exist between physical communities with technological support and their communication patterns (or any other characteristic) of these communities in the real world. In recent years a number of applications of mobile technologies tried to explore the relationship between location-based communities and virtual means of communication. For instance, a group of finish young people, led by Jyri Engestrom, started a club in Helsinki where they combined the physical location, virtual community and SMS. The "Aula" [3] allows the contact face to faces with groups of people that meet physically at the club, but it also allows the contact among the members of the group not physically present in the club through mobile communications. Other examples are, "ImaHima" (are you free now?) [4], which allow I-mode users in Tokio to send a message to their friends that are physically close at a particular time. COSMOS [2] is project with the stated goal of offering the mobile support of communities. Their activities were based on the development of generic services and technologies for operating mobile communities. They established two pilot communities in the domains Lifestyle and Healthcare. The main focus of the application domain "Lifestyle" was mobility-driven recreation behaviour.

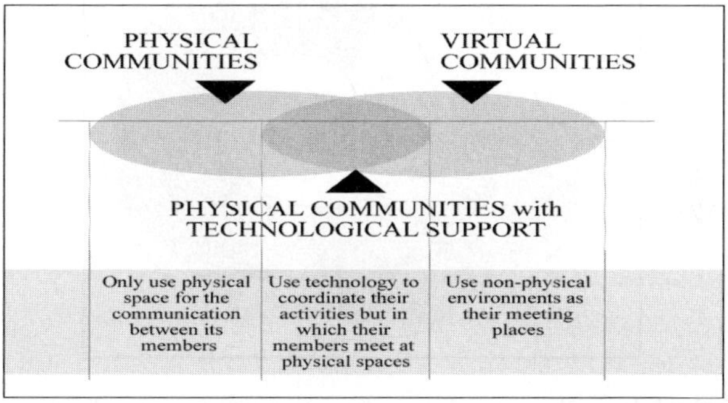

Fig. 2. Types of communities according to the ways of communication of their members

In fact, there are not many studies about how electronic support can help physical communities' communications. It is known that mobile phones, email, forums, chats, etc. help people to plan community activities, meetings and etc; but we have not found empirical data to scientifically prove the impact of the usage of these technologies in their communication patterns or any other intrinsic characteristic of the community.

One example of the studies that claim that the usage of IT could help the performance of physical communities is the work by Sproull and Patterson [27]

regarding Boy Scouts groups. The assumption behind is that if the members can begin to participate electronically in local groups, they may become more motivated to do so in the physical world. Nevertheless, we have not been able to find data that prove this well extended claim.

Therefore, we conclude that further research would bee needed to understand with empirical data from the live of location based (what we called physical) communities the impact of the use of innovative technologies. Only after accumulative research in this area we would be able to understand if the impact of technology in the physical communities is related to body of knowledge that we have about virtual communities.

6 Our UCD Approach

After the review of the literature in the area that we have summarise in the previous sections, our hypothesis is that in order to understand how technology could help and the impact that technology, and in particular mobile multimedia technologies, have in the communication patterns and life of a physical community we need to follow a complete User Centred Design Cycle. Our research in ICING has been centred in investigating the impact of social and human factors on ways of establishing communication among the members of communities with technological support in Barcelona. We followed a UCD approach our research in ICING which will involve 3 phases: (1) User requirements and creation of scenarios for new services; (2) Prototyping the services; and (3) User trials.

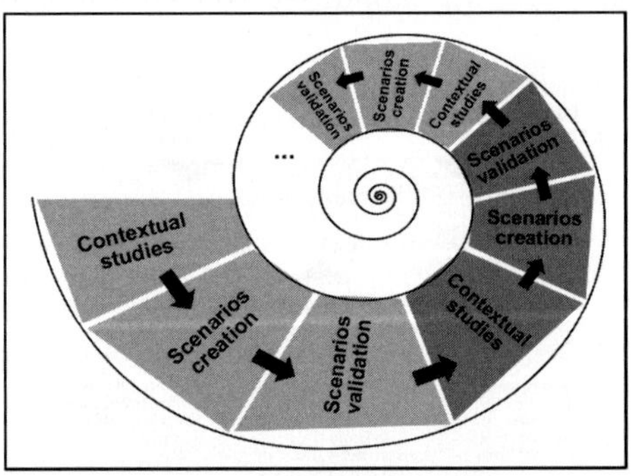

Fig. 3. Methodological approach for scenario creation and validation in ICING

We will present here the work done during phase (1); as we are currently starting phase (2). For this first phase the methodology involved observing people in their own environments, where people behave more naturally and where we can explore surroundings and artefacts to add validity to the collected data. Through field research we will gain a deeper understanding of people needs and expectances. In our research we have gathered data from real prospective users in real urban spaces and different social networks: we conducted observational studies to obtain user requirements to improve mobile services between community members to enhance their cohesion and relationship. This task had a specific focus on disadvantaged social groups (women associations and elderly people) with the aim of identifying broader support measures needed to ensure services acceptance by all citizens.

In this section we will briefly describe the process followed. The identification of the communities in the Barcelona city was done thanks to the studies carried on by municipal and public entities, that have direct contact with the communities and that know their contact people and processes. Once communities were identified we interviewed and observed the members of these two selected communities groups. The aim of having this two steps approach was that the community responsible would provide us information about community's members and dynamics, allowing us to discover preliminary user cases and scenarios that were them validated and enlarged s we approached the community members, as we illustrate in Figure 3.

7 Data from City-Based Communities

We will describe the research with two communities of people based on Barcelona.

7.1 Women Associations

We have visited 9 women associations and an approximate total of 50 associate. The typical profile of the women associated to most Women associations is: married housewives and older than 50 years. Younger women do not use to participate at this associative level. The main aim of women organizations is to help each other to grow and confront common problems and concerns in their lives, typically from one are of the neighbourhood. These associations are also very active in the social life of the community, giving support to most of the special events that occur in the neighbourhood and a lot of initiatives from the city council.

- **Actual patterns of communication:** Although the communication among the members of the association is very intense (p.e. to announce a talk, to invite them to attend a meeting, etc), most of these exchanges are done over the phone. At present, they use "telephone chains" (i.e. person A calls person B, person B calls person C, etc.) to communicate urgent notices among them, creating recursive communication problems. They do not use email and their usage of PCs is very low. They have problems exchanging multimedia material.
- **Detected problem:** (1) Women need an effective way of communication between them for two main types of communication: communication with all the associates to share information related to their association life and activities; and for communicating with the association because they need to find a person that have do a particular job. (2) They will like a way to share multimedia information.
- **Solution:** Create a mobile service for women to (1) keep in touch anytime and anywhere in case of one of them needs something and (2) enable them to exchange multimedia content (p.e. send video of their activities live to the members of the community wherever they are and being able to archive these information). During our interviews we also gather information about the need to

expand this service so that it could also be used to find the nearest person of a concrete community.

7.2 Elderly People

We contacted two Day Centre for retired people ("*Casal*") as they organize most of the activities targeted for elderly people. One of the "*Casal*" has more tham 500 elderly people associated to it, which represents almost 90% of the elderly population in this part of town. We interviewed 25 elders. Most of the associates are widow and they life alone or married couple living together. Most of the women and men go to the Day Centre to play table-games, to talk, etc. In addition, the "*Casal*" organises day out excursions, courses (paining, singing, internet, etc.), concerts, parties, etc.

- **Social communication needs:** Elderly whose family lives far away from their home would like to see their relatives more often, but due to distance and mobility problems it is quite difficult to meet them frequently. They use fix and mobile phones to stay in regular contact, but they miss seeing them. A similar thing happens when the family is on holiday, because despite they communicate by phone, they would like to receive images and videos from where they are spending their holidays to see the landscapes and place they visit, and to see their beloved ones there. In addition, quite often they cannot go to the "*Casal*" and they miss meeting with their friends, and having contact with them.
- **Detected problem:** We have detected several problems: (1) Be in touch with their family and the community at the "*Casal*". They reported that the problem is that their family are not usually at home and they can not always go to the "*Casal*". (2) Be aware if some of the activities to which they are inscribed is cancelled at last minute and to remind them the activities they want to attend
- **Solution:** (1) ICING system will allow them to receive video and images from their loved ones. They would have the possibility of saving them and classify them, and revisit this multimedia material. The key factor here is that they would not want to send images or videos themselves, just to have the possibility to passively receive them. (2) ICING services will present travel information in their mobile phones, new ways or interaction are being researched.

Because of the scope of this paper we will not be able to present here the scenarios that explain in detail how the ICING system works in each case.

8 Conclusions

As we stated previously our goal is understand how technology, especially mobile multimedia technology, can enhance the communication and other aspects among physical communities. We have found a research gap regarding empirical data about the impact of mixing virtual and physical communities through mobile multimedia (images and video) communication technologies. We claim that in order to generate accumulative knowledge to address this gap more research is needed following an UCD approach to the implementation of new technologies. The focus of our work was on women associations and elders. In a later stage, we will broader our communities' sample to ensure that the proposed services will be acceptance by all citizens. In brief, after performing detailed contextual research in the selected communities, we found that both of these communities have a need for informal communications while they are not together and they are "on the move". These informal communications depend on the characteristics of e and required different type of services for each community:

- Services that help community members to strength cohesion between them, as a whole (inner services). More useful for Women associations.
- Services that are intended for individuals of a concrete community. These services do not relate the members of the community with other members of the community, but with people outside of the community (in-to-out services). More wanted by Elderly people.

In the light of these data, our claim is that the need for this informal communication while they are mobile could be fulfilled by video communication. We are, at present, investigating multimodal interfaces and technological architectures that would allow us to gather evidence in support of this claim. We are now in phase 2 of the project, which includes two main tasks:

- Research on user interfaces that would allow this information to be presented in an intuitive and easy to interact way.
- Development of the test beds that will allow us to test the acceptance and efficiency of the proposed services in solving the real problems that we found.

Acknowledgement. We are grateful for the EU support in the frame of the ICiNG project, IST-200424 26665, and to all the partners in ICiNG. We also want to thank the communities and associations that gently have collaborated with our research.

References

[1] Workshop CHI2006. Investigating new user experience challenges in iTV: mobility and sociability (2006) http://soc.kuleuven.be/com/mediac/chi2006workshop/papers.htm

[2] Koch, M., Groh, G., Hillebrand, C., Fremund, N.: COSMOS (Community Online Services and MObile Solutions) Mobile Support Lifestyle Communities. Arbeitsberichte des Lehstuhls für Allegemeine und Industrielle Betriebswirschaftslehre an der Technischen Universität München (2002)

[3] Aula (n.d.).: Retrieved September 7th, 2006 from http://www.aula.cc

[4] ImaHima (n.d.).: Retrieved September 7th, 2006 from http://www.imahima.com

[5] Community types (n.d.).: Retrieved September 7th, 2006 from http://virtual-communities.com

[6] Defining Communities (n.d.).: Retrieved September 7th, 2006 from http://virtual-communities.com

[7] Kim, A.J. (n.d.).: Calling all community builders (2006). Retrieved September 7th, 2006 from http://www.naima.com

[8] Bishop, J. (n.d.).: Online communities are often real communities. (2006) Retrieved September 7th, 2006 from http://www.jonathanbishop.com/Web/Weblog/Default.asp?MID=1&NID=59

[9] Kim, A.J. (n.d.).: Community building on the web. Roles: from newcomer to oldtimer (2006) Retrieved September 7th, 2006 from http://www.naima.com

[10] Boetcher, S., Duggan, H., White, N. (n.d.).: (2006) What is a Virtual Community and Why Would you Ever Need One??. Retrieved September 7th, 2006 from http://www.fullcirc.com/community/communitywhatwhy.htm

[11] Fish, R.S., Kraut, R.E., Root, R.W., Ronald E.: Rice Evaluating Video as a Technology for Informal Communication Studies of Media Supported Collaboration. In: Proceedings of ACM CHI'92 Conference on Human Factors in Computing Systems pp. 37–48 (1992)

[12] Veinott, E.S., Olson, J.S., Olson, G.M., Fu, X.: Video Matters! When communication is stressed video Helps. In: Abstracts of CHI '97, Atlanta GA, pp. 315–316. ACM Press, Newyork (April 1997)

[13] Finn, K., Sellen, A., Wilbur, S. (eds): Video Mediated Communication,Hillsdale, NJ (1997)

[14] Marcus Credé Janet, A.: Sniezek Group judgment processes and outcomes in video-conferencing versus face-to-face groups. International Journal of Human-Computer Studies 59(6), 875–897 (2003)

[15] Olson, J.S., Olson, G.M.: Face-to-face group work compared to remote group work with and without video. In: Finn, K., Sellen, A., Wilbur, S. (eds.) Video Mediated Communication, Lawrence Erlbaum Associates, Hillsdale, NJ (1997)

[16] Toward determining an attention getting device for improving interaction during video-mediated communication Fels, D.I.1 and Weiss, P.L.2 1 Ryerson Polytechnic University, Toronto, Canada 2 Hadassah-Hebrew University, Jerusalem, Israel http://www.telbotics.com/research_5.htm

[17] Castillo, J.: (2007) Power, wifi and ideas. Retrieved February 13th, 2007 from http://www.thinkjose.com/2006/10/

[18] YouTube: http://www.youtube.com/

[19] Kindberg, T., Spasojevic, M., Fleck, R., Sellen, A.: The Ubiquitous Camera: An In-depth Study of Camera Phone Use. IEEE Pervasive Computing, special issue on The Smart Phone (April-June, 2005)

[20] Okabe, D., Itto, M.: (I print) Everyday Contexts of Camera Phone Use: Steps Toward Technosocial Ethnographic Frameworks. In: Höflich, Joachim and Hartmann, Maren Eds. Mobile Communication in Everyday Life: An Ethnographic View. Berlin: Frank and Timme

[21] blog, B.B.: Could mobile social networks be the next big thing? Retrieved September 7th, 2006 http://www.mobileactive.org/node/2357

[22] Mobile Design Communities.: Retrieved January 12t 2007 from http://www.mobilecommunitydesign.com/pages/faq.html#1

[23] AirG: http://www.airg.com/, [24] Jumbuck: http://www.jumbuck.com, [25] Tribilis Mobile: http://www.trilibis.com/

[24] Counts, S., ter Hofte, H., Smith, I.: Retrieved May 20th, 2006 from http://chi2006mososo.telin.nl/index.html

[25] Sproull, L., Patterson, J.F.: Making information cities livable. Communications of the ACM 47(2), 3337 (2004)

Watch, Press, and Catch – Impact of Divided Attention on Requirements of Audiovisual Quality

Ulrich Reiter[1] and Satu Jumisko-Pyykkö[2]

[1] Institute of Media Technology, Technische Universität Ilmenau, Helmholtzplatz 2, 98693 Ilmenau, Germany
ulrich.reiter@tu-ilmenau.de

[2] Institute of Human-Centered Technology, Tampere University of Technology, P.O. BOX 553, 33101 Tampere, Finland
satu.jumisko-pyykko@tut.fi

Abstract. Many of today's audiovisual application systems offer some kind of interactivity. Yet, quality assessments of these systems are often performed without taking into account the possible effects of divided attention caused by interaction or user task. We present a subjective assessment performed among 40 test subjects to investigate the impact of divided attention on the perception of audiovisual quality in interactive application systems. Test subjects were asked to rate the overall perceived audiovisual quality in an interactive 3D scene with varying degrees of interactive tasks to be performed by the subjects. As a result we found that the experienced overall quality did not vary with the degree of interaction. The results of our study make clear that in the case where interactivity is offered in an audiovisual application, it is not generally possible to technically lower the signal quality without perceptual effects.

Keywords: audiovisual quality, subjective assessment, divided attention, interactivity, task.

1 Introduction

Several multimedia applications offer interactivity between the system and the user. In these applications, the technical constraints such as computing power available or error sensitivity of data transmission require some form of quality optimization. To adapt the quality under these circumstances, subjective quality evaluation tests are conducted to assess the signal or system performance. A typical example for such a quality optimization is the optimum distribution of computing power between auditory and visual rendering processes. However, final applications like games typically demand interaction with users. This interactivity or the user's actual task is usually not taken into account in the subjective quality evaluation studies done for quality optimization purposes. This paper investigates whether the requirements of perceived audiovisual quality varies when the evaluation of quality is performed in parallel with interactive tasks of different complexity.

J. Jacko (Ed.): Human-Computer Interaction, Part III, HCII 2007, LNCS 4552, pp. 943–952, 2007.

2 Audiovisual Perception, Quality and Attention

Audiovisual perception is more complex than the sum of the two sensory channels, and its processes are not known in depth [2]. However, the goal of many audiovisual application systems is to provide unified perception, like in complex every day life perception [5]. The multimodal perception requires proper synthesis of stimuli, which can be violated by asynchrony of auditory and visual material. Audiovisual perception is also dependent on content, for example human talking heads' cross-modal interaction is very high compared to other content types [18]. Experiments of audiovisual quality in different contexts (from multimodal data compression to virtual environments) have also shown that one modality can enhance and modify the experience derived from another modality. The perceived quality in one modality affects the perceived quality in another modality, especially if the qualities clearly differ [1,18,19]. Stimuli presented in accordance in two modalities also improve the feeling of enjoyment and presence compared to one modality in virtual environments. In these environments, presence as "a feeling of being there in space and time" is assumed to be a goal for multimodality and is reached when auditory and visual information merges [12].

Most of the experiments assessing the audiovisual quality have been studied under passive stimuli viewing by focusing all attention on quality evaluation task. On the other hand, many of these evaluations are conducted for systems with active human-computer interaction. In these systems, user's attention is expected to be focused on tasks relevant to user's goals (gaming as entertainment, watch the story of content) rather than quality. To improve the ecological validity of the experiments some previous studies have tackled effects of focused and divided attention on quality evaluations. The main question in these experiments is do we perceive the quality similarly if we pay attention only on quality than if we divided it to some other task simultaneously to quality evaluation task.

To clarify the concepts, attention as information selection process is characterized by limited information processing recourses (overviews e.g. in [14,21]). Studies of focused attention give several inputs for participants and ask them to follow one. Typically the nature of unfocused stimuli is examined. In the divided attention tasks, also called dual task experiments, several input are given and participant is asked to pay attention several of them at the same time which describes the individuals processing limitations. The similarity, difficulty and training of tasks affect to the ability of processing. Taken together, it could be assumed that in the real use of system the focused attention is on the relevant task and not very detailed information is not extracted from unfocused input of quality. This would give an option to provide the technically lower quality without perceptual effects in the relevant use.

Rimell & Owen [20] have studied the impact of focused attention on audiovisual quality with talking head material. In their experiment, participants paid attention on either auditory or visual stimuli. After the presentation they were asked to rate either audio or video quality. The results showed that the modality to which attention is paid dominates over the perceived quality of the other modality. This phenomenon is symmetrical between the auditory and visual senses. On the other hand, when attention is focused on one modality, the ability to detect errors in another modality is greatly impaired. This study would support the idea to lower level of produced quality in unattended modality without perceptual costs.

Hands [6] has studied multimodal quality perception when dividing attention also to content simultaneously to quality evaluation task. Overall quality of transmitted audiovisual sequences with severe impairments was evaluated. The experiment was conducted with two samples: One sample was asked to evaluate the quality. The other sample was asked to recall the audiovisual content in parallel to performing the quality evaluation. The results showed no difference between the samples, thus indicating that quality ratings are independent of content recall. Practically, these results would mean that the produced quality cannot be lowered eventhough participants would pay attention on content.

Zielinski et al. [22] studied multi-channel audio quality in a computer game. In their study, six participants assessed the audio quality, firstly with gaming as a parallel task and secondly with simultaneously watching static screen shots of the game, by using the single stimulus method with reference. The audio stimuli presented instrumental jazz music with static changes (low pass filtering). Their study concluded some listener specific, but not any global effects. Later on, Kassier et al. [13] have conducted a similar experiment for time variant audio degradations with seven participants. To involve participants even more in the gaming task ("Tetris") they added a more advanced scoring system suitable for short time playing. The study summarized that involvement in the task decreased the consistency of audio quality grading and therefore may impacted in evaluation of audio impairments.

All these previous studies illustrating inconsistent results show a clear need to further study the effect of divided attention on requirements of perceived multimodal quality.

3 Audiovisual Rendering

Most of today's audio visual application systems aim at simulating an accurate representation of the real world by focusing on the (arguably) most important human sense, vision. Auditory stimuli are used in these systems to enhance the overall impression of realism. Still, the stimuli of the two modalities are rendered and presented mostly independently from the other modality. The level of detail in the respective (visual or auditory) simulation is kept as high as possible with regard to computing power available, independently from the level of detail in the other modality.

In contrast, the MPEG-4 standard ISO/IEC 14496 provides a so-called object oriented approach where objects may have both auditory and visual characteristics [7]. These characteristics are attached to the object at the description level, so that they form an integral part of the object itself. A sound source object may have shape and color attributes and at the same time a certain directional pattern for the sound radiation. An obstructing object may have shape, color and (visual) transparency and at the same time acoustic properties like frequency-dependent reflection and transmission characteristics.

Unfortunately, real time acoustic simulation processes are computationally very expensive. Only recently have we seen personal computers capable of handling the necessary calculations based on the physical and geometrical characteristics of the virtual room to be rendered audible. Still, a significant number of compromises in the accuracy of the simulation have to be accepted for real time performance.

In geometry-based room acoustic simulations that use the so-called mirror-source method, the main factor for computational load is the maximum order of mirror sources that are rendered audible. The order of mirror sources correlates exponentially to the number of mirror sources computed. Each mirror source represents a single early reflection coming from one of the walls of the (virtual) room. In the simulation algorithm used for this experiment, the number of early reflections (and therefore the order of mirror sources) also influences the total amount of reverberation, its strength and its length. Reverberation is increased with increasing order of mirror sources.

In the work described here we have used an MPEG-4 player (I3D) as a platform for subjective assessments of overall perceived quality. The I3D was developed over the last four years at the Institute for Media Technology (IMT) at Technische Universität Ilmenau / Germany. It can render three-dimensional virtual scenes, it allows users to navigate freely inside of these scenes, and it provides real time rendering of auditory simulation via its modular TANGA audio engine [15].

4 Research Method

The tests were conducted at Technische Universität Ilmenau between May and June 2006. Three pilot tests were done prior to finalizing the test set-up. The average duration of the test was 65 minutes including an interview.

Participants - The experiment was conducted with 40 participants, mostly university students, aged from 23 to 39 years (M: 26, SD: 3.6). Ten participants were female and 30 males. All participants reported to have normal hearing. 30% of the participants could be regarded as experienced assessors.

Test procedure - The experiment consisted of three different parts. In the beginning, demo-/psychographic data (age, gender, professionalism in video and audio handling, attendance to earlier listening experiments, playing computer games and instruments and listening experience with surround sound systems) was collected with a pre-questionnaire.

The actual test contained a quality anchoring and three evaluation tasks including a training prior to each of them, see fig. 1. The anchoring introduced the quality extremes of the test materials with different contents. The quality evaluation included three different parallel tasks: *listen and watch* task, *listen and press the button* task and *listen and catch the ball* task. All tasks had the same evaluation instructions and the order of the tasks was randomized between the experiments.

The Single stimulus method, also known as Absolute Category Rating, is suitable for multimedia performance and system evaluation (e.g. ITU-T BT.500 [8], ITU-R P.910 [10]). The stimuli were viewed one by one, overall quality was rated independently and retrospectively (e.g. ITU-R BT.500-11 [8]) on a continuous and unlabelled scale from 0 to 100 in the randomized presentation order. Even though

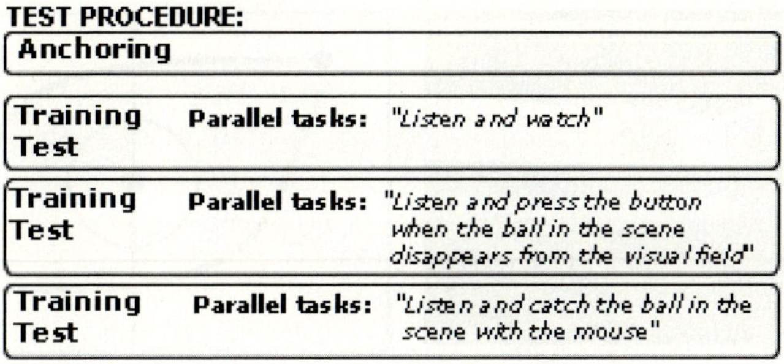

Fig. 1. The actual test procedure was divided into quality anchoring and three different tasks

double and multi stimulus methods are powerful for high quality discrimination, they would have made the quality evaluation with parallel task becoming very complicated for the participants.

The final part of the test session focused on the quality evaluation criteria and the impressions of the evaluation tasks. A semi-structured interview gathered data about the overall quality evaluation criteria with and without parallel task (detailed description in [11]). A post-questionnaire about the experienced easiness of the evaluation tasks and the presented quality in the tasks ended the test session.

Stimulus materials - All test materials were 30 seconds long audio visual contents. Two different audio contents, music (acoustic guitar) and speech (male voice), were presented with three different reverberation strengths: the lowest amount of reverberation was produced by a mirror source algorithm of order one, the highest by an algorithm of order three. Two different audio contents were selected because of the different spectral distribution, familiarity and the preference of reverberation amount [17]. The visual content, a sports gym (see fig. 2, left), was presented with two different motion paths representing a spatial movement within a virtual space (fig. 2, right). These were selected to have an equal number of items with main direction of sound incidence from the left as from the right hand side and they were made as equal as possible between the parallel tasks.

Experimental environment – The experiment was conducted in a laboratory environment in accordance to ITU-R BS.1116 [9] and EBU 3276 [4], suitable for listening tests with wide screen and 8-channel loudspeaker setup. The loudspeaker setup consisted of eight active full-range monitor speakers located in a circular array, with four speakers in the frontal area to increase the precision of localization, and four speakers to the sides and to the back (fig. 3). This particular setup is not standardized, but orientated on the human directional hearing capabilities. The test subject was positioned at the center of the circular loudspeaker array and visual content was displayed on a projecting screen (width 2.7m, viewing distance 2.8m). The sound pressure level within each scene varied depending on the virtual distance between the loudspeaker in the center of the gym and the position of the test subject in the scene (max. SPL 78dB(A)).

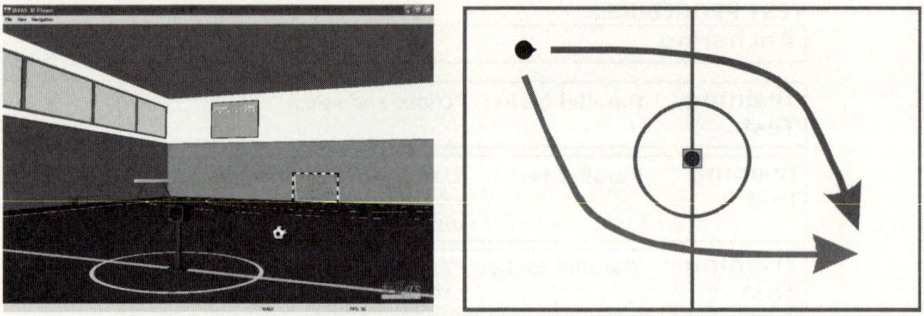

Fig. 2. (left) Visualization of the virtual room (sports gym) as used in the stimulus material. **(right)** Motion paths one and two inside the sports gym.

Data-collection and analysis - During the experiment the data collection was done with the help of an electronic input device especially built for the purpose of audio visual subjective assessments, see [16].

The results were analyzed using SPSS for Windows version 13.0. Non-parametric methods of analysis were applied because the data did not reach the preconditions of normality for parametric methods. Friedman's and Wilcoxon's tests were used to compare the differences between ordinal independent variables in the related design [3]. In the analysis of the questionnaire data, Kuskall-Wallis' and Mann-Whitney U tests were used to compare differences between two groups in the unrelated design [3].

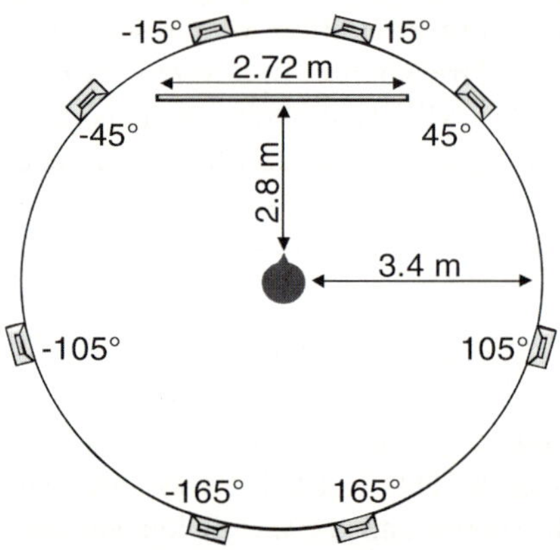

Fig. 3. Loudspeaker and projecting screen setup used in the subjective assessments

5 Results

5.1 Experiment – Tasks, Reverberation Orders, Auditory Content and Visual motion Paths

Tasks did not have effect on the quality evaluation (Friedman: $\chi^2 = 3.3$, df = 2, p>.05, p=.190, ns) when the values were averaged across the reverberation orders, contents and motion paths.

Reverberation strength impacted on the quality evaluation (Friedman: $\chi^2 = 106.6$, df = 2, p>.001). The material presented with the lowest reverberation order was the most pleasant, followed by second order and then third reverberation order. The differences were significant between all reverberation orders when results were averaged over other factors. (Wilcoxon: Order 1 vs. Order 2: Z=-8.16, p<0.001; Order 1 vs. Order 3: Z=-9.87, p<0.001; Order 2 vs. Order 3: Z=-2.43, p<0.05). The results remained the same within task examination, with the exception that there were not significant differences between the second and third reverberation order in any of the parallel tasks (watch: p>.08, press: p>.190, catch: p>.224).

Quality evaluations were not affected by the audio content types or visual motion paths. The music and speech contents were mostly rated into the same level within each task (p>0.05). The exception that the music content was preferred over the speech content appeared with the presentation of the first reverberation order (*watch* task: Wilcoxon Z=-3.01, p>0.01; *press the button* task: Wilcoxon Z=-2.92, p>0.01). When the contents were averaged over the other factors the music content was rated as more pleasant than speech content (Wilcoxon: Z=-2.88, p<0.01).

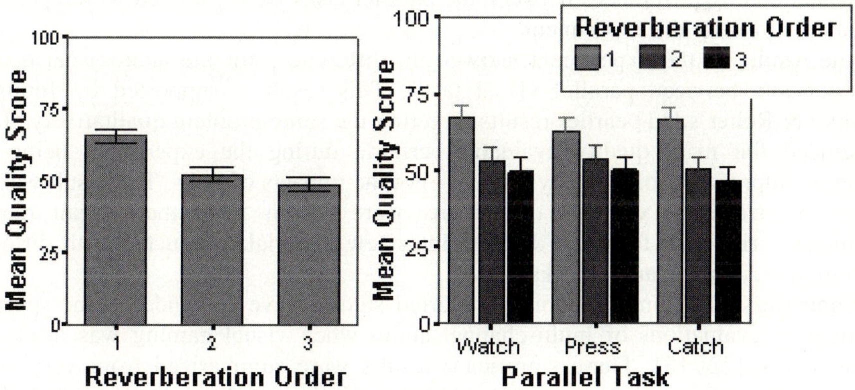

Fig. 3. Error bars show 95% CI of mean

Two different motion paths were equally rated in each task (p>0.05). The only exception appeared in the *listen and press the button* task with music content presented with the second reverberation order (Wilcoxon: Z= -2.2 p>.03).

5.2 Effect of Task and Content Experiences on Quality Evaluation

Evaluation easiness between the tasks: A difference of the evaluation easiness between the tasks was reported by 90% of the participants. The *watch* task was experienced as the easiest, followed by *press the button*, and the hardest *catch the ball* task with significant differences between them (p<0.05). However, the reported evaluation easiness did not impact on the evaluations between the tasks (Krusskal-Wallis: Chi=1.41, df=2, p>0.05).

Quality differences between the tasks: The majority of the participants (62.5%) experienced the presented quality as being the same between the parallel tasks. Within the group that experienced differences (37.5%), the *watch* task had shown higher quality compared to other tasks ($p<0.001$) which were evaluated being in the same level (Wilcoxon $p>0.05$). There were no differences in the ratings with respect to the level of experienced quality between the tasks (Krusskal-Wallis: Chi= 2.05, df=2, $p>0.05$).

6 Discussion

This study investigated the effects of interaction tasks with different complexity on the requirements of perceived audiovisual quality. Ideally, the goal was to see if the produced quality could be lowered due to interaction without perceptual impact. In the experiment, simultaneously to the overall audiovisual quality evaluation task, participants had to perform three different types of parallel tasks: passive *listen and watch* presentation, *listen and press* the button in the case a visual object appeared, and *listen and catch* the ball tasks. Different reverberation orders, audio and visual contents were varied in the virtual room presentation. Easiness and impressions of presented quality differences between the parallel tasks were gathered with a post-test questionnaire after the experiment.

The results of the experiment showed no differences for the audiovisual quality requirements between parallel visual tasks. This result is supported by Jumisko-Pyykkö & Reiter's [11] earlier results targeting the same problem qualitatively. They concluded the main quality evaluation criteria during the experiment being the different impressions of auditory quality – not the impacts of tasks. The result was the same independently whether the results were drawn from the overall quality evaluation criteria or from the detailed interview material, conducted with different stimuli material and parallel tasks.

Controversially, some previously reported studies have concluded some sporadic changes in evaluations of multi-channel audio when visual gaming was used as a parallel task [22, 13]. These significant results were summarized from very small sample sizes (<7) and with a possibly more involving parallel task than in our study.

Even though in our study participants reported that some evaluation tasks were experienced as being more complicated than others, neither our study nor others' have been able to conclude any real trend in changes of audiovisual quality requirements. Difficulty, similarity and training of tasks are the basic factors affecting dual-task performance [21]. It is possible that the levels of dual-tasks in our experiment were so easy and separate from each other that people were able to divide the attention between the tasks without assumed processing difficulties. In addition, it is possible that these dual-tasks do not distract so much the relatively experienced assessors which we had compared to naïve assessors. Hands' [6] study of quality evaluation and content recall also gives some support for separate processing of content and quality. He concluded that simultaneous content recall did not affect the requirements of multimodal quality in television contents. These results might indicate that the signal quality cannot be technically lowered without perceptual effects in the case where interactivity is involved with the application. Further research conducted with a variety of more complicated and involving tasks, still relevant to user's goals, is needed to confirm this finding.

Acknowledgments

This work is supported by the EC within FP6 under Grant 511568 with the acronym '3DTV'. Satu Jumisko-Pyykkö's work is supported by the Graduate School in User-Centered Information Technology (UCIT) and this publication preparation work by Ulla Tuominen Foundation.

References

1. Beerends, J.G., de Caluwe, F.E.: The influence of video quality on perceived audio quality and vice versa. Journal of the Audio Engineering Society 47(5), 355–362 (1999)
2. Coen, M.: Multimodal Integration - A Biological View. In: Proceedings of IJCAI'01, Seattla, WA (2001)
3. Coolican, H.: Research methods and statistics in psychology, 4th edn. J. W. Arrowsmith Ltd, London (2004)
4. EBU Tech. 3276-E-2nd edn., Listening conditions for the assessment of sound programme material, Geneva (1998)
5. Gibson, J.J.: The Ecological Approach to Visual Perception. Lawrence Eribaum, Houghton Mifflin, Boston (1979)
6. Hands, D.: Multimodal Quality Perception: The Effects of Attending to Content on Subjective Quality Ratings. In: Proceedings of IEEE 3rd Workshop on Multimedia Signal Processing, 1999, Copenhagen, Denmark, pp. 503–508 (1999)
7. ISO/IEC 14496:2001, Coding of audio-visual objects (MPEG-4) (2001)
8. ITU-R BT.500-11 Methodology for the subjective assessment of the quality of television pictures, International Telecommunications Union – Radiocommunication sector (2002)
9. ITU-R BS.1116-1, Methods for the subjective assessment of small impairments in audio systems including multichannel sound systems, International Telecommunication Union, Geneva (1997)
10. ITU-T P.910 Recommendation P.910, Subjective audiovisual quality assessment methods for multimedia application, International Telecommunication Union – Telecommunication sector (1998)
11. Jumisko-Pyykkö, S., Reiter, U.: Produced quality is not the perceived quality – A Qualitative Approach to Overall Audiovisual Quality. In: Proceedings of 3DTV Conference, IEEE (May 2007)
12. Larsson, P., Vastfjall, D., Kleiner, M.: Ecological Acoustics and the Multimodal Perception of Rooms: Real and Unreal Experiences of Auditory-Visual Virtual Environments. In: Proc. 2001 International Conference on Auditory Display, Espoo, Finland (July 29 - August 1, 2001)
13. Kassier, R., Zielinski, S.K., Rumsey, F.: Computer Games And Multichannel Audio Quality Part 2- Evaluation Of Time-Variant Audio Degradations Under Divided and Undivided Attention. In: Proceedings of the AES 115th International Conference, New York, USA (October 10-13, 2003)
14. Pashler, H.E.: The psychology of attention. MIT Press, Cambridge, MA (1999)
15. Reiter, U., Schwark, M.: A plug-in based audio rendering concept for an MPEG-4 Audio subset. In: Proc. IEEE/ISCE'04 International Symposium on Consumer Electronics, Reading/UK (September 2004)

16. Reiter, U., Holzhäuser, S.: An Input Device for Subjective Assessments of Bimodal Audio visual Perception. In: IEEE/ISCE'05, International Symposium on Consumer Electronics, Macau SAR/China (June 2005) ISBN 0-7803-8920-4
17. Reiter, U., Großmann, S., Strohmeier, D., Exner, M.: Observations on Bimodal Audio visual Subjective Assessments. In: Proceedings of the 120th AES Convention, Paris, France, Convention Paper 6852 (May 20-23, 2006)
18. Rimell, A.N., Hollier, M.P., Voelcker, R.M.: The influence of cross-modal interaction on audio-visual speech quality perception. In: Presented at the AES Convention, San Francisco, Audio Engineering Society Preprint 4791 (September 26-29, 1998)
19. Rimell, A.N., Hollier, M.P.: The Significance of Cross-Modal Interaction in Audio-Visual Quality Perception. In: e-proceedings of Workshop on Multimedia Signal Processing, September 13-15, 1999, Copenhagen, Denmark. IEEE Signal Processing Society (1999)
20. Rimell, A., Owen, A.: The effect of focused attention on audio-visual quality perception with applications in multi-modal codec design. In: Proceedings of International Conference on Acoustics, Speech, and Signal Processing, 2000. ICASSP '00, 5-9 June 2000, vol. 6, pp. 2377–2380, vol.4. IEEE (2000)
21. Styles, E.A.: The psychology of attention. Psychology Press, Hove, England (1997)
22. Zielinski, S.K., Rumsey, F., Bech, S., Bruyn, B., Kassier, R.: Computer Games And Multichannel Audio Quality - The Effect Of Division Of Attention Between Auditory And Visual Modalities. In: presented at the AES 24th International Conference on Multichannel Audio, Banff, Canada (June 26-28, 2003)

Media Service Mediation Supporting Resident's Collaboration in ubiTV*

Choonsung Shin, Hyoseok Yoon, and Woontack Woo

GIST U-VR Lab.
Gwangju 500-712, S. Korea
{cshin,hyoon,wwoo}@gist.ac.kr

Abstract. A smart home is an intelligent and shared space, where various services coexist and multiple residents with different preferences and habits share these services most of the time. Due to the sharing of space and time, service conflicts may occur when multiple users try to access media services. In this paper, we propose a context-based mediation method, consisting of service mediators and mobile mediators, to resolve the service conflicts in a smart home. The service mediators detect service conflicts among the residents and recommend their preferred media contents on a shared screen and their own mobile devices by exploiting users' preferences and service profiles. The mobile mediators collect the recommendation information and give the users personal recommendation. With combination of the service and mobile mediator, the residents are allowed to negotiate the media contents in the conflict situation. Based on experiments in the ubiHome, we observed that mediation is useful to encourage discussion and helps to choose a proper service in a conflict situation. Therefore, we expect the proposed mediation method to play a vital role in resolving conflicts and providing multiple residents with harmonized services in a smart home environment.

1 Introduction

With an increasing number of researches on smart homes and offices, the interest for context-aware applications, aimed at multiple users, is growing as well. Unlike applications intended for a single user, applications for multiple users have to deal with different preferences of users. Therefore, those applications have related mechanism for service provision such as priority assignment and policy management [1].

Most researches, aimed at resolving conflicts, have been done on smart homes and intelligent offices. MusicFX, a music arbiter, selects music stations based on the group preferences to reflect multiple users' preferences in a fitness center [3]. The reactive behavioral system (ReBa) resolves conflicts among devices in an office environment by applying a layered architecture of activity bundles consisting of

* This works was supported by the UCN Project, the MIC 21C Frontier R&D Program in Korea, under CTRC at GIST.

J. Jacko (Ed.): Human-Computer Interaction, Part III, HCII 2007, LNCS 4552, pp. 953–962, 2007.

users' activities and reactions of the environment [4]. Finally, Dynamo system supports media content sharing and data exchange between multiple users, based on social protocols [5]. However, the previous researches have following limitations when they are applied to a smart home. Firstly, autonomous selection as a resolution can also cause other conflicts since the selection may take a service away from another user who owned the service before, without his consent. Furthermore, conflicts are only temporarily resolved because users can not recognize and exchange their contrary opinions. Even though social protocols can manage the use of media content among them, the problem with unexpected resident's behaviors still exists.

In order to overcome the above mentioned limitations, we propose a context-based mediation method exploiting mobile devices for residents. The proposed method detects service conflict among users by exploiting service profiles as well as the individual user preferences. It then generates a list of common interest services from all conflicting users and displays this list to notify the conflict and the different preferences. Finally, the method mediates the selection of the recommedation list by gathering the users' inputs and highlighting the users' choices. Therefore, the proposed mediation method enables residents to negotiate on media services by recommending their interested media contents. Furthermore, it allows users to exchange their preferences and experiences related to media contents with the recommendation during mediation. Therefore, the proposed method resolves conflicts among users under their agreements while it supports sharing of their preference and experiences even though they have different preferences and habits.

The remaining part of this paper is organized as follows. In chapter 2, we describe conflicts and their mediation method considering ubiTV. We discuss how to mediate multiple users' requests in ubiTV in chapter 3. In chapter 4, we show implementation of the proposed mediation method. Experiments and related analysis are presented in chapter 5 and we conclude in chapter 6.

2 Resident's Collaboration in ubiTV

The ubiTV is a context-based media service for providing users with various media content by exploiting various kinds of context obtained form users and their environments [7]. In the ubiTV, conflicts among multiple users who want to access the same media service occur as follows. Firstly, service conflicts occur when multiple users try to access the same media service. In this situation, the media service recognizes the users' personalized services by exploiting his context. Furthermore, service conflicts often occur when multiple users access different media services which share the same space. In this situation, the media service can react on the user's context. However, the users cannot enjoy their media content due to interference of different media service such as sound and visual contents in a limited space.

In order to reflect the characteristics of a smart home and its residents, the proposed mediation approach handles service conflicts by exploiting the context such as the users' preferences and media service profiles. First of all, it detects a service conflict by utilizing the user`s context as a triggering information of the deployed media services. The user context includes not only the profile such as identity,

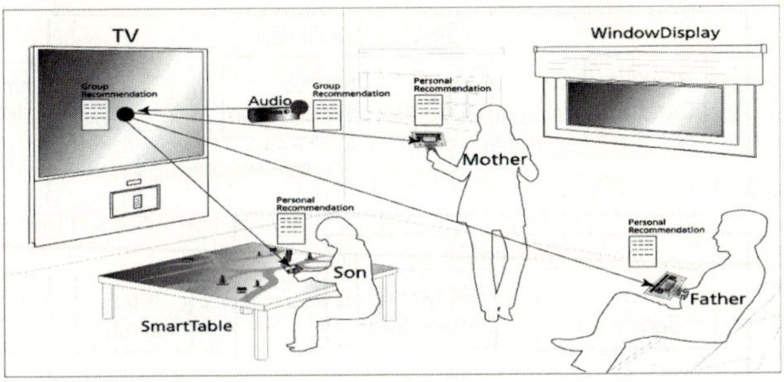

Fig. 1. Media Service Mediation

individual preferences and so on, but also media service profiles such as media service identity or required resources. The method displays (recommends) the users' commonly interested media contents on a shared screen and personal interested media contents on the user's own mobile device. With the commonly interested media content, the user can recognize other persons' interests while he can select an item out of the personally interested media contents. When the recommendation is given to the users, they can choose their preferred item among the recommended list. In order to provide a consented service, the method arbitrates the user inputs. Figure 1 shows a conflict resolution of the previous service conflict based on the proposed mediation method.

As can be seen in Figure 1, a recommendation list of TV content is displayed on a shared screen and the user's mobile devices when a service conflict is detected. According to family member's preferences, the recommendation list consisting of {drama, news, animation} reflects the preferences of father and son. The recommendation is given to the users and is reordered individually by each user's preferences based on user's profile manager. Therefore, the father can see the recommendation consisting of news, sitcom and animation, and the son can see the recommendation consisting of animation, sitcom and news. If they choose an item of the recommended content, the selection is highlighted on the TV screen. Therefore, they can recognize each others preferences and opinions. They can also discuss about proper contents among the recommendation. Furthermore, if the mother, the third user, wants to access the audio service, her media service is similarly managed by the proposed mediation method due to a service conflict with the TV service. Consequently a recommendation list, reflecting the mother's preferences is given to all conflicting users. Therefore, the users can choose an item of the media content to harmonize their preference and to solve the conflict in the shared space.

3 Media Service Mediation

In order to detect possible service conflicts among users who share media services and resolve them harmoniously afterward, the proposed mediation method exploits personal companions equipped with mobile mediators. In conflict detection, the proposed method utilizes unified context to reflect rich information about users. It then recommends commonly interested media contents of users to resolve the detected

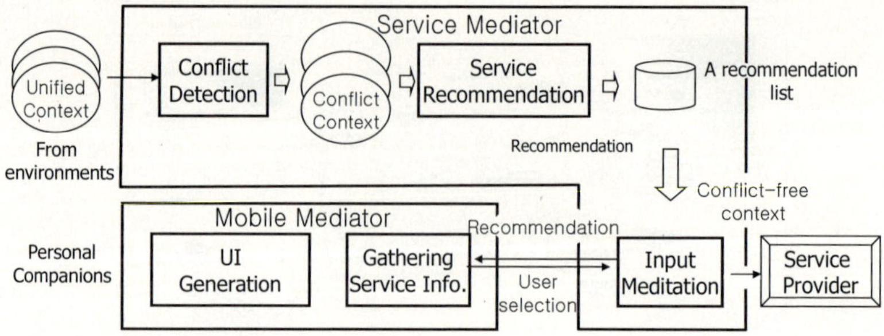

Fig. 2. Media Service Mediation Framework

conflicts by exploiting personal companions as well as a shared screen. Figure 2 shows the overall procedure of the proposed mediation framework.

As shown in Figure 2, the proposed method gathers two types of unified contexts to detect possible service conflicts: unified contexts describing users who are using the same media service and unified contexts describing users who want to access different media services. In the conflict detection component, service conflicts among users accessing the shared screen to visualize the users' choices, until the users consent on an item the same media service are detected by exploiting those unified contexts. In the conflict resolution component, the recommendation information is generated for user centered conflict resolution by exploiting the context of the conflicting users. As a result, a recommendation list is displayed for the service mediation after the conflict management process. In the last step, the mediator highlights user inputs on of recommended contents. During the mediation between two users, the recommendation list can be updated with different preferences of new users who try to use the same service. Finally, the conflict-free context as a result of the service mediation, containing user's consented service is delivered to a service provider.

3.1 Context for Media Service Mediation

The proposed mediation method requires context information in order to manage service conflicts. The method utilizes unified context describing two kinds of information: the user profile and the media service profile. The following Table 1 describes part of the unified context consisting of user profile and service profile used for media service mediation. The user profile includes the users' dynamic and static information when they access a media service. The media service profile contains dynamic and static information of the media service.

3.2 Service Mediator

First of all, the proposed method detects service conflicts by utilizing unified contexts. As mentioned before, the unified context includes the user's contextual information and the media service profile. Let *ACS* be the set of currently active

Table 1. Unified context for media services

Context Elements	Description
User	A unique identifier indicating a user giving a command to the media service implicitly or explicitly.
MediaService	A unique identifier indicating a media service that generated this unified context as a consequence of a user issuing a command to it
ContentItems	A set of identifiers for contents the *MediaService* provides
UserPreference (UP)	A function mapping the *ContentItems* to preference values for the user. It is represented as an M: 1 relation. The values range from 0 to 10, 10 being the highest preference.
Resource	Resources that the *MediaService* needs to provide its media services. It is represented as a set of resources. According to *MediaService*, more than one resource can be included.
The Number of Users (NU)	The number of users associated with *UP*. It is generally 1; otherwise it has higher value to indicate multiple users for group preference.

contexts in a space and *MCS* be the subset of *ACS* for a specific media service kept locally by the media service. Service conflicts are detected by Eq. (1) with a set of collected unified contexts *MCS* in the specific media service.

$$\begin{aligned} Service\_Conflict(C_A, C_S) \Leftrightarrow\ & User(C_A), \neq User(C_B) \wedge \neg\exists x : (PreferredItem(C_A, x) \\ & \wedge (PreferredItem(C_{S,} x)) \vee (MediaService(C_A) \neq (MediaService(C_S) \\ & \wedge Resources(C_A) \cap Resources(C_S) \neq \phi)) \end{aligned} \tag{1}$$

where C_A is a unified context of a user accessing a media service and C_S is the unified context of currently active service state which was the result of another action. *PreferredItem*, obtained from Eq. (2), is an item having the highest preference among the set of media contents.

$$PreferredItem(C, x) \Leftrightarrow \exists x \forall y : UP(C, x) \geq UP(C, y) \tag{2}$$

where x and y are elements of *ContentItems* of a particular media service.

The mediator then generates recommendation information containing commonly interested media contents of all conflicting users by utilizing user profile and media service profiles. For the purpose, the method obtains a recommendation list from the unified contexts describing all users who access the same media service by ordering media contents. Therefore, we rearrange the items of media contents by applying group preference and utility errors. The group preference (GP) is a function mapping

ContentItems to degree of preference in [0, 10]. It is obtained by summing and normalizing the *UPs* as shown in Eq. (3).

$$GP(Item) = \frac{1}{|MCS|} \sum_{C \in MCS}^{N} UP(C, Item) \quad (3)$$

The utility error is a mean square error (MSE) of individual user's preferences. Especially, the media content having the smallest MSE has a higher priority than other media contents. It means that the items which have a lower preference distribution have a higher priority than other items even though they have the same group preferences. Eq. (4) shows UtilityMSE of group preferences.

$$Utiltiy_{MSE}(Item) = \frac{1}{|MCS|} \sum_{C \in MCS}^{N} (UP(C, Item) - GP(Item))^2 \quad (4)$$

Finally, the proposed method obtains new *UP* consisting of $\{(Item, Preference)_{(0)}, (Item, Preference)_{(1)}, \ldots, (Item, Preference)_{(K)}\}$ ordered by the *GP* and utility errors.

Finally, the proposed method mediates the user inputs in order to allow the media service to only react on items all conflicting users agree with and to remain consistency when dealing with multiple individual input devices. The proposed technical augmented social mediation handles potentially conflicting explicit user input from multiple input devices. Especially, it utilizes three parameters to make a final decision among multiple inputs because the media service cannot guarantee that all users give inputs corresponding to the recommendation. The parameters include individual *weight*, *decision_ threshold* and *decision_timeout*. *Individul_weight* is a weight on an individual user input. The individual weight is assigned when mediation starts with recommendation. The weight is also assigned differently according to users and policy since user's selection is not always the same. *Decision_threshold* is a threshold weight when a final decision is made. We assume that all users agreed on one selection if the sum of individual weights is greater than this value. *Decision_timeout* is a waiting time until a final decision is made automatically. The timeout is used to finish mediation ahead of time, because no more user input is expected. Users need to some time limitation to decide their choices with others although they easily select their preferred contents among recommended media content.

3.3 Mobile Mediator

When a conflict occurs, users involved in the conflicting situation need to be notified. As an interface between the media service and users, we introduce a user interface called personal companion. Each user has his or her own personal companion to interact with services. The mobile mediator receives group recommendation information whenever its user causes or encounters a service conflict with other users. It also generates a personalized recommendation list onto a user interface by exploiting user

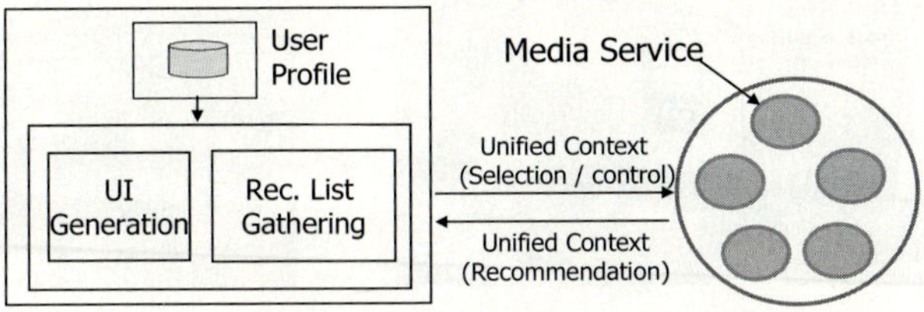

Fig. 4. Mobile Mediator

profile from the obtained group recommendation information. Figure 4 shows the overall architecture of the mobile mediator.

As shown in Figure 4, the mobile mediator gathers recommendation information as unified context from a conflicting media service. The obtained group recommendation list is refined and tailored into a personalized recommendation list by utilizing user profile on the conflicting media service. A personalized recommendation list is constructed by including items of a user's interest and excluding any irrelevant items from group recommendation list. The items on the personalized recommendation list are sorted based on a user's preferences, so a highly preferred item is placed on top for easy access. After constructing the personalized recommendation, UI generation uses this information to build a proper user interface for selecting items from the recommendation list. The recommendation list is graphically represented and each item is mapped with corresponding command and content. Whenever a selection is made in the conflicting situation, the unified context is transferred to the conflicting media service to notify the selection.

4 Implementation

In order to implement the proposed mediation method, we utilized the ubi-UCAM 2.0. The ubi-UCAM 2.0 is a unified context-aware application model for ubiquitous computing environments, supporting the independence between sensors and services [6]. The proposed method was implemented as a part of the context manager of the ubiService in the ubi-UCAM 2.0. We then applied the ubiService to the ubiTV application [7]. Furthermore, in order to control these services, users can utilize personal companion with a remote controller, implemented with Personal Java. Based on the media services and sensors, the ubiTV application is able to mediate multiple residents with media services according to users and their context. For example, the ubiTV application starts to mediate while displaying the available contents ordered by their preferences on the screen as shown in Figure 5(a). In addition, each user' mobile personal companion shows his/her preferred items as shown in Figure 5(b).

Based on the mediation, they are able to share their preferences through the recommended information. After their discussion about media contents with the recommended contents, they decide their proper program in this conflict situation.

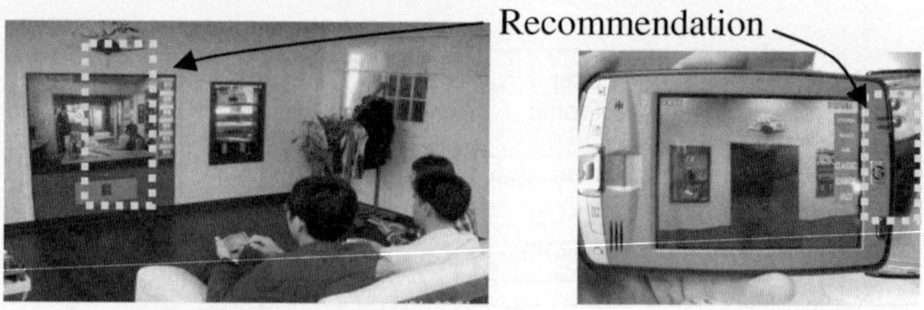

(a)TV screen (b) User's Personal Companion

Fig. 5. Media Service Mediation in ubiTV

5 Experiments

In the following experiment we wanted to get a first impression on how users react on recommendation and mediation. In order to do that, we carried out the experiment in two different scenarios with 16 people aged from 20 to 35. The users were divided into groups of two persons and experienced both scenarios to form an opinion about the TV service. In the first scenario (ordinary TV watching) we tried to create a relaxed atmosphere like a home environment. The participants were told to make themselves comfortable in the ubiHome and to do everything like on a normal day, when they come home from work or school. No service recommendation and only an ordinary remote control were provided. The second scenario was designed exactly like the first one, with the difference in a recommendation list which was displayed on the TV and on the users own personal companion, which were the new input device to mediate the input for the TV application.

We also designed two different questionnaires for each scenario which the participants were asked to answer after each experiment. In the first questionnaire we were only interested in the user's normal behavior about the TV usage with their families. Additionally we were interested if family members verbally fight over the TV program and how satisfied they are with the decisions about the TV content home. Table 2 shows those questions for participants over the scenario 1.

Table 2. Questions for scenario 1

	Questions	A	B	C
1	*Do you think the personal companion mediation can prevent one person from making all the decisions over the program?*	60	20	20
2	*What do you think about the personal companion mediation?*	60	10	30

A: Positive answer, B: Don't Know, C: Negative answer

As shown Table 2, Question 1 clearly shows that the main opinion of the asked users is that the personal companion-based mediation provides an equitable input device (60 %). This result hardens the idea that a technology augmented mediation can prevent family members from feeling passed over in the TV content decision making process. In this question we wanted to find out the general opinion of the users about the personal companion-based mediation (an instance of the technical augmented social mediation). Our concern was that most people find it boring and disturbing to use multiple personal companions as input devices for a context aware TV service. The evaluation showed that most people like the personal companion-based mediation (60%) and will accept this new equitable input device. Only 20% answered that it is too laborious to use. This result indicates that the personal companion-based mediation is a acceptable approach to provide equitable input but we also should consider the fact that some users felt disturbed by this new mediated input technique.

After the observation of the users in the second scenario we could investigate that the recommendation list encouraged people to discuss about each others interests. As soon as the recommendation list was displayed on the TV screen and the personal companion, most participants immediately started to talk about the recommended content. Additionally we asked the participants directly what they think about this new technique.

Table 3. Questions for scenario 2

	Questions	A	B	C
3	*Did the recommendation help you to discuss?*	70	10	20
4	*Did the recommendation help you to make a decision?*	60	30	10
5	*Can the recommendation list prevent fights?*	60	40	0

A: Positive answer, B: Don't know, C: Negative answer

Table 3 shows the result from the questions from the participants. According to the Question 3, 70 % of the users answered that they are supported by the recommendation list in the discussion process. This indicated that the visualization of other people's interests supports verbal discussion. Besides the support of the discussion about the TV content we were additionally interested if the recommendation technique can help the users to make a decision. That comes because the discussion is the first part of a convenient TV content decision for families. The goal of the recommendation list is besides supporting a discussion to help the users to make a fast and convenient decision. The whole process should be supported by visualizing each family member's preferences. The analysis of the results show that 60% of the experiment participants felt that the recommendation list had supported the decision making process, as shown in Question 4. This indicates that the recommendation list seems to be a proper technique to support the whole process of harmoniously choosing the TV contents for a family.

In the last question we asked the participants directly if they think that the recommendation list can prevent fights. This would be an important factor to harmonize the TV content decision from multiple family members. Question 5 clearly shows that most users think that verbal fights can be prevented (60%). More interesting observation is that no participants disagreed with this assertion. Accordingly it seems that recommendation and mediation can be used to harmoniously resolve conflicts caused by multiple users.

6 Conclusion

In this paper we proposed a mediation method to support collaboration among multiple residents for sharing media services in a smart home. In order to support the collaboration, the proposed method detected service conflicts and recommended harmonized service contents by utilizing users' preferences and service profiles. We applied the mediation method to the ubiTV in a smart home. According to the result, more than half of the participants thought that the ubiTV was useful to share the media services by helping them to negotiate their preferences. Furthermore, we found out that discussion and mediation among residents are meaningful to resolve conflicts in the aspect of user's view and that the proposed method can support finding a harmonious decision. Therefore, the proposed method can play an important role to resolve service conflicts among multiple residents by regarding the preferences of all users.

References

1. Edwards, W.K.: Policies and roles in collaborative applications. In: Proc. ACM 1996 Conference on Computer Supported Cooperative Work (CSCW'96), Cambridge, USA, pp. 11–20 (November 1996)
2. Hughes, J., O'Brien, J., Rodden, T.: Understanding Technology in Domestic Environments: Lessons for Cooperative builds. In: Streitz, N.A., Konomi, S., Burkhardt, H.-J. (eds.) CoBuild 1998. LNCS, vol. 1370, pp. 248–262. Springer, Heidelberg (1998)
3. McCarthy, J.F., Anagnost, T.D.: Music FX: An arbiter of group preferences for computer supported collaborative workouts. In: Proceedings of CSCW '98, Settle, WA, ACM Press, New York (1998)
4. Hanssens, N., Kulkarni, A., Tuchinda, R., Horton, T.: Building Agent-Based Intelligent Workspaces. In: ABA Conference Proceedings (June 2002)
5. Izadi, S., Brignull, H., Rodden, T., Rogers, Y., Underwood, M.: Dynamo: A public interactive surface supporting the cooperative sharing and exchange of media. In: Proceedings of UIST 2003, Vancouver, Nov'03, pp. 159–168. ACM Press, New York (2003)
6. Oh, Y., Shin, C., Jang, S., Woo, W.: ubi-UCAM 2.0: Unified Context-aware Application Model for ubiquitous computing environments. In: the 1st Korea/ Japan Joint workshop on Ubiquitous Computing and Network Systems (2005)
7. Oh, Y., Shin, C., Jung, W., Woo, W.: The ubiTV application for a Family in ubiHome, 2nd Ubiquitous Home workshop, pp. 23–32 (2005)

Implementation of a New H.264 Video Watermarking Algorithm with Usability Test

Mohd Afizi Mohd Shukran, Yuk Ying Chung, and Xiaoming Chen

School of Information Technologies, University of Sydney, NSW 2006 Australia
{afizi,vchung,xche2902}@it.usyd.edu.au

Abstract. With the proliferation of digital multimedia content, issues of copyright protection have become more important because the copying of digital video does not result in the decrease in quality that occurs when analog video is copied. One method of copyright protection is to embed a digital code, "watermark", into the video sequence. The watermark can then unambiguously identify the copyright holder of the video sequence. In this paper, we propose a new video watermarking algorithm for the H.264 coded video with considering usability factors. The usability testings based on the concept of Human Computer Interface (HCI) have been performed on the proposed approach. The usability testing has been considered representative for most image manipulations and attacks. The proposed algorithm has passed all the attack testings. Therefore, the watermarking mechanisms in this paper have been proved to be robust and efficient to protect the copyright of H.264 coded video.

Keywords: Video watermarking, H.264, Human Computer Interface (HCI).

1 Introduction

In today's video delivery and broadcast networks, issues of copyright protection have become more urgent than in analog times due to increased analog video technology. One method of copyright protection is to use information hiding technique in video sequences. The common approaches used video watermarking approaches can be categorised as two main kinds, namely embedding watermark in the compressed domain [1-3] and in the uncompressed domain [5-7]. For the compressed domain approach, the typical information hiding method in [1] embeds the watermark data into Video Length Coding (VLC). Some other methods embed the watermark data in the residual of the motion vectors [2], and Lagendijk [3] proposed XDEW algorithm to embed the watermark data in both I-frame and P-frame. These methods in compressed domain can gain low computational complexity, but they are not robust against some common attacks such as image manipulations and collusion attacks.

In order to improve the robustness of video watermarking algorithm, the uncompressed domain approach using 3D-DFT [4], 3-D DWT [5] and 3-D DCT [6] are proposed. These methods take temporal redundancy into account, but they require too high computational complexity to meet the real-time requirement. Besides that, both information hiding techniques in uncompressed and compressed domain have

J. Jacko (Ed.): Human-Computer Interaction, Part III, HCII 2007, LNCS 4552, pp. 963–970, 2007.

failed to provide user feedback mechanism that would provide higher objective video quality. In order to solve these problems, this paper has proposed a new information hiding technique that can clearly identify the copyright holder of the video sequence without sacrificing the robustness of watermarking and alleviating the computational complexities. The proposed new algorithm using the usability testing based on HCI evaluation methods. These evaluation methods are known as cognitive walkthrough and heuristics evaluation.

This paper is structured as follows: Section 2 presents the concept of H.264 video standard. Section 3 presents the concept of HCI in relation to the proposed approach. Section 4 describes the proposed new video watermarking approach for H.264 video sequence. Section 5 presents the analytical usability evaluation based on two HCI evaluation methods (cognitive walkthrough and heuristics evaluation) for H.264 video sequence. Section 6 gives the summary and conclusion.

2 H.264 Video Standard

The H.264 standard (also known as MPEG4 AVC) offers a significant improvement over the previous video compression standards (i.e. the video sequences get better bit rate/distortion ratios). Section 2.1 to 2.3 describes the important parts of the H.264 video standard used in the proposed video watermarking system.

2.1 Sub Blocks

A sub block is the basic part of a H.264 video stream. There are two types of sub blocks: luminance sub blocks and chroma sub blocks. Luminance sub blocks consist of 4x4 pixels whereas chroma sub blocks consist of 2x2 pixels. The blocks are transform, prediction and entropy coded. There are several different ways for a sub block used in the prediction code. The simplest way is that the first transform coefficient of each sub block use the first transform coefficient of neighbouring sub blocks and the other transform coefficients do not use prediction coding at all. Entropy coding can be done using two different algorithms, named CAVLC (Context Adaptive Variable Length Coding) and CABAC (Context Adaptive Binary Arithmetic Coding) [7].

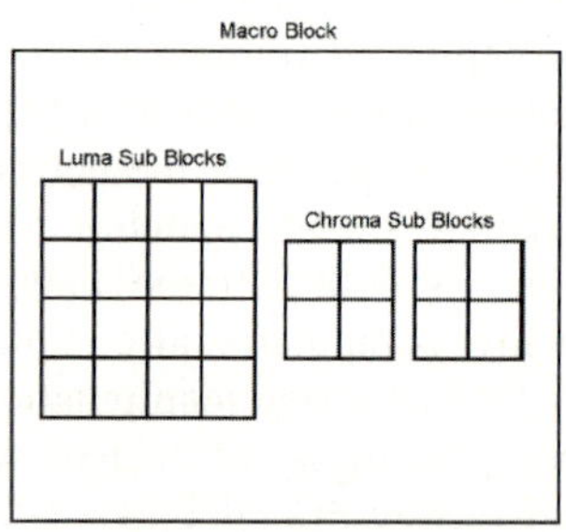

Fig. 1. Example of macro block

2.2 Macro Blocks

A macro block consists of 4x4 luminance sub blocks and 2x2x2 chroma sub blocks. A macro block contains information on what kind of prediction coding is used in sub blocks. Fig. 1 shows an example of macro blocks.

2.3 Picture/Slice Management

H.264 has efficient methods in handling each picture or slice. In its standard, it has a picture that consist three types of slices. These slices are I slices, P slices and B slices. A slice can be parsed and decoded independently without using the data from other slices.

2.4 Network Abstraction Layer

A network abstraction layer unit contains a header and either a slice or a parameter set. The NAL units are placed after each other in H.264 file as shown in Fig. 2.

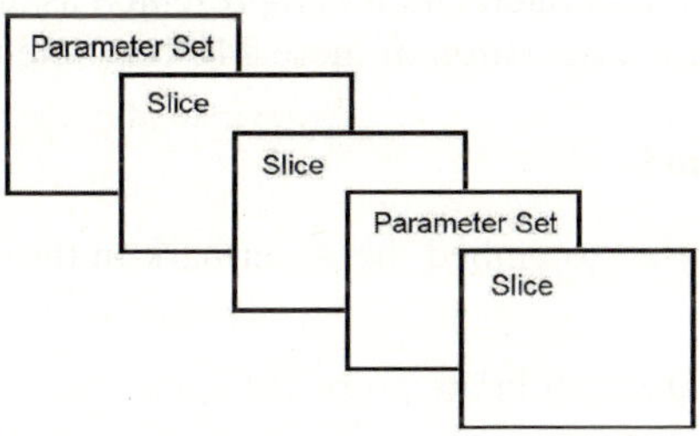

Fig. 2. Example of NAL unit

3 Human Computer Interface

Human-Computer Interaction (HCI) is the study of how people design, implement, and use interactive computer systems and how computers affect individuals, organizations, and society [8]. Moreover, the proposed approach has used two evaluation methods in HCI which are cognitive walkthrough and heuristics evaluation. Cognitive walkthrough method tries to model the thoughts and actions of test users when they are using H.264 video for the first time. The goal is to simulate how a test user or a user population would perform certain tasks [8]. As for heuristics evaluation, a small set of evaluators (people with usability expertise) judge how well a system complies with recognized usability principles (the 'heuristics') [8]. First, each evaluator independently examines the interface. Next, the results of the individual evaluators are combined. Many sets of heuristics exist, varying in detail and specificity for a certain platform. The proposed video watermarking system can have a better visual quality by using these two usability tests.

4 Proposed Approach

The proposed approach contains four components:

- *Generate watermark* – This will generate a random watermark.
- *Insert watermark* – This will insert a watermark into a video sequence and save the resulting watermark video sequence.
- *Generate threshold* – This will generate a threshold. If the squared difference generated by a comparison is higher than the threshold, there is a match.
- *Compare watermark* – This will, given a watermark, a watermarked video sequence and the original non-watermarked video sequence, insert the watermark to the original video sequence and calculate the square difference.

4.1 Generate Watermark

In the proposed approach, the generated watermark data contains 240 coefficients. This is the same as the number of non-prediction coded luminance coefficients in a H.264 macro block that uses the simplest prediction coding scheme [8]. These coefficients are randomly generated and it is represented as amplitude. In this context, the amplitude is the standard deviation of these 240 coefficients.

4.2 Inserting Watermark

The algorithm that was used to embed the watermark in the video sequence is shown below:

The following formulas are used in the proposed approach:

$$v_i^* = v_i (1 + \alpha w_i) \qquad (1)$$

Where v is the host video sequence to watermark, and v_i is its i:th transform coefficient. Moreover, v^* is the output watermarked video sequence, and v_i^* is its i:th coefficient. w is the watermark and w_i is its i:th number. Parameter α is a constant.

4.3 Comparing a Watermark

When the owners of a video sequence v finds an illegal copy of it, v^*, they might want to find out if it contains a certain watermark. There are two basic ways for them to do that:

- Extract w_i^* from v_i^* for every i by using the inverse insertion formula and calculate the total squared difference d as:

$$d = \Sigma(w_i^* - w_i)^2 \qquad (2)$$

- Insert w into v to get v^{**} and calculate the total squared difference d as:

$$d = \Sigma(v_i^{**} - v_i^*)^2 \qquad (3)$$

If the squared difference d is less than the threshold t, the comparison is defined as a match. A way to generate a threshold is described in section 4.4.

4.4 Generating Threshold

After calculating the squared difference d in step (**2**) of section 4.3, the next step is to generate the threshold t and determine whether the value of d is low enough to be considered as a match. This can be done as follows:

1. Assume that the given watermark w is not the watermark in the watermarked video sequence v^*, but some other random watermark. This means that each coefficient w_i is a stochastic variable.
2. Since the squared difference d is a sum of many stochastic variables, it is likely using roughly a normal distribution. Steps 3 to 5 are used to calculate its mean m and standard deviation σ.
3. Generate M (where M is large) random watermarks, w^1 to w^M, with the same amplitude as w.
4. Insert each w^i into v and calculate each squared difference d^i.
5. If M was chosen large enough, the sample mean of the values of d^i is roughly equal to m and the sample standard deviation is roughly equal to σ.
6. We now have that d is a stochastic variable with a normal distribution with a known mean m and standard deviation σ. This means that we can find a t such that

$$P(d \leq t) = e \tag{4}$$

where e is the accepted error probability, and should be chosen to something very small.
7. The desired threshold is t. For $e = 0.01$,

$$t = m - 2.33\sigma \tag{5}$$

5 Analytical Usability Evaluation

This section describes the usability testing that was performed. The video sequence used was stored in a file called video0.264.This video sequence is 352x288 pixels and contains 300 frames. In this analysis, group of users were asked to perform the analytical usability evaluation with different categories of users. Based on the users' knowledge and experience in H.264 video, the users are divided into three different categories, which are ***novice users***, ***occasional users*** and ***expert users***. Novice users are users who have never or very rarely played H.264 video. As for occasional users, they can be regular users of H.264 video but only occasionally use it to perform a specified task. Finally, expert users are users who have a great knowledge in using H.264 video.

For this analysis, the video sequence with the watermarked information would have different amplitudes of 800, 1600 and 3200. Fig. 3 to 6 show the worst frame of the video sequences watermarked with amplitudes of 800, 1600 and 3200 respectively. The corresponding frame of the original non-watermarked video sequence is provided for comparison.

Furthermore, all the users evaluated the video sequence based on the heuristics evaluation technique. In a heuristic evaluation, a small set of evaluators judge the quality of the video sequence complies with recognized usability principles (the 'heuristics'). The heuristics principles used in this analysis is the level of the users' recognition in the quality of the video sequence [8]. The users would compare the non-watermarked video sequence with other video sequences that have different amplitudes. Then, each user will decide the degree of the quality of the video frames based on the amplitude. This will eventually determine the optimum level of amplitude in generating watermarked frames without sacrificing the robustness and quality of the video. As a result, we found that all the video sequences have visible differences. However, the differences are only severe for the watermark with amplitude 3200.

Another usability testing was to determine the robustness of the proposed approach. This test uses cognitive walkthrough approach where all the users pretend to be a novice user, someone who encounters the H.264 video for the first time [8]. To be more precise, all the users need to perform a detailed correct action sequence on how to perform with the proposed approach. For example, the users will perform four

Fig. 3. Non-watermarked

Fig. 4 800 Amplitude

Fig. 5. 1600 Amplitude

Fig. 6. 3200 Amplitude

basic functions which are generating, inserting, comparing and threshold calculation. The detailed correct actions that need to be performed by the users are shown below:

1. Two thousands watermarks with amplitude of 100 were generated, by executing the following command for each *i* in 1 to 2000:
   watermark generate 100 i.txt
2. The first of these watermarks was inserted into video0.264 by executing:
   watermark insert 1.txt video0.264 video1.264
3. A threshold was calculated by executing:
   watermark threshold 1.txt video0.264 video1.264
   Threshold: 6.2107
4. The following command was executed for each *i* in 1 to 2000:
   watermark compare i.txt video0.264 video1.264

An example of the results of basic insertion and comparison is shown in the Fig. 7:

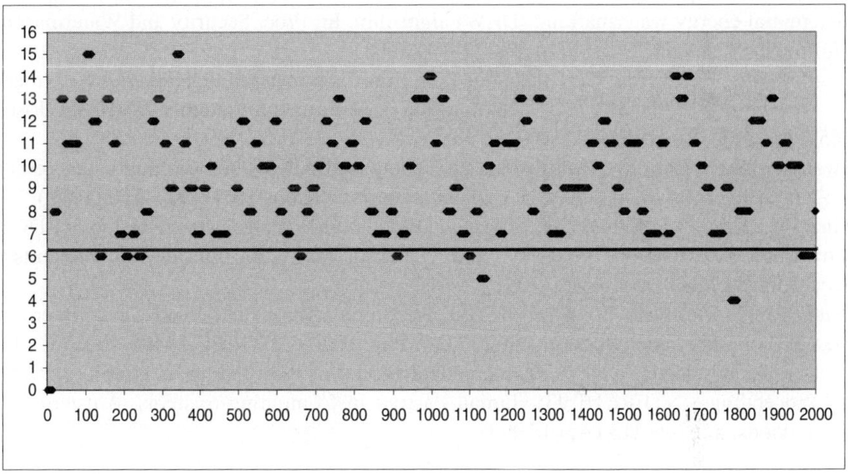

Fig. 7. Diagram of results of basic insertion and comparison

According to Fig. 7, a dot at location (*x, y*) means that the *x*:th watermark got a squared difference of *y*. The line represents the threshold which has the value of 6.2107. Here, there are only a few false positives. The first watermark, which is the one that was put into the video sequence, got a very small squared difference (*d*) value than the other watermarks.

6 Conclusion

In this paper, a new video watermarking technique for H.264 video sequences has been proposed and developed. The hidden information is inserted by altering the transform coefficients. In the usability testing, two heuristics evaluations have been performed in order to determine the best video sequence. We found that the increase of the amplitude factor would decrease the quality of the video sequence. There is no reduction in the video quality for the watermarked H.264 video sequence. For the robustness of the proposed approach, a test was performed using usability testing. The testing results show that there was only a minor false positive values produced by the proposed approach. Therefore, the proposed new video watermarking approach with user evaluation is proved to be efficient and robust to the signal processing attack. It can be used for the copyright protection for the H.264 coded video.

References

1. Cross, D., Mobasseri, B.G.: watermarking for self-authentication of compressed video. IEEE ICIP, vol. 2, pp. 913–916 (2002)
2. Dai, Y., Zhang, L., Yang, Y.: A new method of MPEG video watermarking technology. IEEE ICCT, pp. 1845–1847 (2003)
3. Setyawan, I., Lagendijk, R. L.: Low bit rate video watermarking using temporally extended differential energy watermarking (DEW) algorithm. In: Proc. Security and Watermarking of Multimedia Contents ? vol. 4314, pp. 73–44 (2001)
4. Deguillaume, F., Csurka, G., Ruanaidh, J.O., Pun, T.: Robust 3D DFT video watermarking. In: Proceedings of Security and Watermarking of Multimedia Contents, SPIE, San Jose, vol. 3657, pp. 113–124 (1999)
5. Swanson, M.D., Zhu, B.: Multiresolution scene-based video watermarking using perceptual models. IEEE Journal on Selected Areas in Communications 16(4), 540–550 (1998)
6. Lim, J.H., Kim, D.J., Kim, H.T., Won, C.: Digital Video Watermarking Using 3D-DCT and Intra-Cubic Correlation, Security and Watermarking of Multimedia Contents? In: Proceedings of SPIE vol. 4314 (2001)
7. Wiegand, T., Sullivan, G.: Draft ITU-T Recommendation and Final Draft International Standard of Joint Video Specification, ITU-T Rec. H.264 | ISO/IEC 14496-10 AVC (2003)
8. Nielsen, J., Landauer, T.K.: A Mathematical Model of the Finding of Usability Problems. In: Proceedings INTERCHI'93: Human Factors in Computing Systems, Amsterdam, The Netherlands, pp. 206-213 (April 1993)

Innovative TV: From an Old Standard to a New Concept of Interactive TV – An Italian Job

Rossana Simeoni[1], Linnea Etzler[2], Elena Guercio[1], Monica Perrero[1], Amon Rapp[1], Roberto Montanari[2], and Francesco Tesauri[2]

[1] Telecom Italia, Technology, Research and Trends department
Via G. Reiss Romoli, 274, 10148 Turin, Italy
{Rossana.Simeoni,Elena.Guercio}@telecomitalia.com,
{Amon.Rapp,Monica.Perrero}@guest.telecomitalia.com
[2] University of Modena and Reggio Emilia, Department of Science and Methods of Engineering, Via Amendola 2, Padiglione Tamburini, 42100 Reggio Emilia, Italy
{Etzler.Linnea,Montanari.Roberto,Tesauri.Francesco}@unimore.it

Abstract. The current market of television services adopts several broadcast technologies (e.g. IPTV, DVBH, DTT), delivering different ranges of contents. These services may be extremely heterogeneous, but they're all affected by the continuous increase in quantity of contents and this trend is becoming more and more complicated to manage. Hence, future television services must respond to an emerging question: in what way could the navigation among this increasing volume of multimedia contents be facilitated? To answer this question, a research study was conducted, resulting in a set of guidelines for Interactive TV development. At first, the current scenario was portrayed through a functional analysis of existing TV systems and a survey of actual and potential users. Subsequently, interaction models which could possibly be applied to Interactive TV (e.g.: peer-to-peer programs) were assessed. Guidelines were eventually defined as a synthesis of current best practices and new interactive features.

Keywords: Interactive TV, IPTV, enhanced TV, media consumers, peer-to-peer; focus group; heuristic evaluation.

1 Introduction

The current market of television services offers several broadcast technologies (e.g. IPTV, DVBH, DTT), delivering different ranges of contents. The direct effect of the introduction of these technologies is the increase of available information in combination with the possibility for future developments and additional content amplification. Previously unrelated communication principles are today merging and giving life to two main types of television interaction namely *information search* (web-like) and *media fruition* (TV-like). The traditional television is moving towards interactivity, although there is a long way to go. To start the journey of designing a new Interactive TV of the future, it's vital to answer the following questions:

- How should the future Interactive TV allow the user to relax and at the same time to interact?

J. Jacko (Ed.): Human-Computer Interaction, Part III, HCII 2007, LNCS 4552, pp. 971–980, 2007.

- Is there a communication model to connect the interaction experience (continuous dialogue between user and technology) and the fruition experience (start and stop in user control)?
- In which way may the user be helped in navigating and selecting among the increasing quantity of available information?
- How can the quantity and diversification of contents be combined with good accessibility and usability?
- Who are the potential users of the "new" TV?

As an evolution of previous studies principally focused on technical aspects [1], this paper presents a methodology conceived for the design of a future *Innovative Interactive Television Service* to be offered on the Italian market. As a *first step*, a brief theoretical review was conducted on previous works attempting to define the basic features of "Interactive TV". The *second step* focused on TV, videogames (VG) and peer-to-peer (P2P) consumption in Italy, in order to draw and compare prototypical users' profiles for each of these media. It is here hypothesized that the lack of interactivity may be a relevant reason why traditional TV is unsatisfactory to several users; especially to users of Videogames and P2P. The *third step* was to analyze four of the most significant digital TV services currently available on the Italian market, in order to detect *de facto* standards and best practices for design of Interactive TV systems and in general to outline the "as-is" in Italy concerning Interactive TV. To do that, some specific grids to describe functionalities, main usability aspects and offered services were "built" and used. The *fourth step* took into consideration the growing field of P2P applications, which was investigated in order to define the main characteristics of these systems (communication protocol, file sharing, server access, archiving method and so on) and the typical habits of their users. Two sessions of focus groups were conducted, aiming to isolate the interactive aspects of P2P experts' behaviour and their expectations. Some examples of realistic behaviours were also analysed during the focus groups. Then a heuristic analysis was carried out on the most popular P2P programmes to highlight the main features and their positive and negative aspects from the usability point of view. The aim was to apply the best practics and to avoid the worst ones in designing the future TV system. Following on the results of the four steps, basic guidelines for designing an innovative TV system could be outlined and a new navigation metaphor could be "created".

2 Interactive TV: User Needs and Technologies in Literature

There are several available definitions of interactive television (iTV) in literature. According to a work by Jensen and Toscan [2] the interactive television may be seen as a "two-way TV", in which the user produces inputs that will have a remarkable effect on the content which turns the "viewer" into a "user". According to this definition, what today is sometimes referred to as "interactive television" doesn't actually show all the features of "interactivity". As suggested by [3], it would be more appropriate to use the term "enhanced television" (eTV) for the range of television offer that we know today, such as satellite TV, digital TV and cable TV. The information flow in today's eTV is still linear and unidirectional, from the broadcaster to the receiver but it offers a less passive use compared to the traditional television.

Van Dijk et al. [3] suggest four factors defining the level of interactivity, namely: *multi-lateralness* (bilateral information flow); *synchronicity* (real time outputs); *control* (opportunity to intervene and decide on the contents) and *understanding* (understanding of the completed actions). Livaditi [4] suggests a dissimilarity between the television users' *Needs* and *Patterns of use*. In particular, she makes a distinction between *Rational Need* with informative or economic reasons (e.g. shopping, use of programme guides) and *Emotional Needs* driven by entertainment and communication reasons (e.g. videogames, interactive shows). The use models are divided into active and passive; in the active models, the interaction is driven by active user decisions (e.g. use of bank services) whilst the passive models require a guidance for the interaction (e.g. video on demand, personalized news).

In another work by Van Dijk et al. [5] there are some interesting data regarding the level of interactivity of a set-top-box that may be defined as *enhanced TV*. Although the study was performed only on the Dutch market, many of the results and the theoretic models may be used also in other countries. The study examined the need for interactivity expressed by TV-users. Most of the users consider that the offered interactivity level is still too low in comparison with their expectations although the majority is satisfied by the user experience. The authors comment that the interactivity in television services is mainly based on actions such as reaction and selection and the concluding proposal is to give more chances for the users to intervene during the programmes.

In a study on interactive television by Bernoff and Herigstad [6] the users were asked what kind of additional features they would like to see in their everyday TV-systems. It was seen that the most commonly mentioned features can be found in Personal Video Recorders (PVRs). Several other features requested by the users could be connected to the functions of an on-demand system.

3 Interactive TV: What the Market Offers

Several technologies and services developed so far has aimed at or has proclaied itself as iTV systems: in the following, a prospect of the known interactive (TV) systems.

Hybrid TV is defined as a detached technology that is being used together with the TV set in order to enhance its normal function and increase the interactivity. User participation in shows, live surveys and pay-per-view programs are some examples. The interaction technologies are commonly cell phone texts, telephone calls, web-vote or e-mail messages. Presumably, most of these Hybrid functions will soon be embraced by interactive function integrated into the TV-service.

Internet TV could be described as audio-video streaming on the Internet. It can be used from a broadband PC and the service isn't guaranteed: in fact all data are carried on IP network in a "best effort" way. Since Internet TV cannot be used through a TV-set but only through PC it will not be taken into account specifically in our research.

IPTV, on the other hand, supplies regular programmes, both live or "on-demand", that can be seen on a TV-set. Hence, IPTV is an out-and-out service to transmit TV on IP-infrastructure. The infrastructure is managed by the telco operator that guarantees the service quality and provides the customer with the set top box.

In general, the interactivity level of these systems is quite low and similar to the generic TV, even if the usage and the technology approach are very different. According to a recent study by "Screen Digest" (www.screendigest.com) the use of IPTV is foreseen to reach nine million users in Europe by 2009. This means almost 10% of the entire market (including cable TV and satellite TV). The study also predicts that the TV operators that don't want to loose market shares will have to adapt and offer own internet platforms.

Mobile TV, finally, is defined as the use of television programmes on portable devices originally designed for other purposes (e.g. PDAs or cell phones). The present spread of these systems is limited, but according to a research completed by Global Information [7] by 2007 there will be at least 270 million subscribers to mobile TV services in the world. The diffusion of Mobile TV implies some important problems for the development of interactive television applications. Primarily, the use in mobility commonly implies a double task situation where the most common example is driving whilst using a cell phone but the "hands-free" solution would not be applicable to this scenario. Additionally, two different functional areas have to coexist in the interface, namely the navigation of the menu system (of a cell phone or PDA) and the visualization of moving images on a very limited screen. Seeing the increasing quantity of available information, the mobile systems have to be developed with the aim to help the user in managing the complexity of the information.

We are hence witnessing a simultaneous development of several different interaction technologies. The challenge for the future TV is to give those interaction technologies the chance to coexist and to include all possible devices in the design of the TV-experience. The well-known media convergence should therefore go along with the convergence of the interaction devices.

Most of the presented television services have the same limitations as the traditional TV (linear channel contents as opposed to on-demand non-linear content; different EPGs for different channels, generic remote controls not allowing free interaction with the TV etc.) although the quantity of offered contents has increased. Today we therefore prefer to talk about *enhanced TV* and not *Interactive TV*.

A qualitative change in the interaction between user and system is necessary for the future TV: this will involve an interface redesign and a completely new paradigm to access, to navigate and to explore contents. First and foremost, this transformation will need a completely new navigation paradigm. It would be clearly unfeasible to adapt the current interface style to an Interactive TV since it was designed for a limited range of information and without interactivity. Moreover, the average television user has low acquaintance with computer-like devices and it would therefore be unwise to use web navigation models for the new Interactive TV.

The development of new television technologies has interested several researchers to study and to prototype alternative ways of interaction with the medium exploiting these new opportunities. Most of the studies are focused on the user interface and the improvement of the traditional EPGs that don't appear suitable for large numbers of contents. Video Scout [8] for example, shows contents in a graphical way, as raindrops that fall down the screen depending on their scheduling hour; Time Pillars [9] introduces the concept of 3D environment where TV channels are symbolized by pillars and the contents are placed on their surface. Other studies try to introduce very innovative form of interaction. Zimmerman et al. [10] propose touch screen devices in which users can act directly on the medium with their hands; Diederiks [11] underlines the importance of introducing animated characters in the television interface because they can help user in the interaction with the medium (giving him or her information and suggestions). The characters can be controlled both by the traditional remote control or by vocal commands (e.g. Bello). Joly [12] introduces "Toupee", a prototype of an interactive application developed for children, where a virtual pet helps in navigating and interacting with games and applications. The suitability of animated characters for iTV applications is confirmed also in Chorianopoulos [13] that analyzes MTvBoX, an interactive application where an animated character presents video-clip information. In [14] usability evaluations sustain the theory that animated characters in Interactive TV interfaces could enhance the user entertainment.

These studies refer in particular to the problem of choosing among a large number of contents; in fact they present innovative interfaces (possibly linked to recommendation systems) and they don't examine all the aspects related to the Interactive TV. Anyway they contain interesting innovative ideas and their study represents an important step in order to design a new Interactive TV.

4 Consumer Analysis

To have a general picture of the context in which new Interactive TV systems find its place, a consumer analysis on the Italian television users was carried out. Particular attention was paid to analyse the characteristics of the consumer and especially the needs or requirements of the so-called "unsatisfied consumers". As a large share of "unsatisfied" TV-users was found, further consumer analyses were conducted on other domestic entertainment. In particular videogames (VG) and peer-to-peer systems (P2P) were analyzed to understand if some of the unsatisfied users are going towards other more interactive systems. At the end of the analysis some astonishing similarities between the unsatisfied TV-users and the latter two groups could be outlined, suggesting that traditional Italian TV lacks of interactive features which may be of interest for VG-and P2P-users.

Firstly, television users were analyzed. A Censis[1] survey [15] completed in 2005 shows that 95.4% of the Italian population regularly watches television, which is an increase of 1% since the 2001 survey. In spite of TV is the most used media in Italy, a survey by Livolsi [16] exposes great differences between user groups. In particular two main groups were identified, namely the *quantity-consumers* (poorly selective consumers) representing 60% of the Italian population and the *quality-consumers* (highly selective consumers) corresponding to 35%. The *quantity-consumers* are generally women, elderly with a low educational background and limited economic means. These consumers commonly follow their deep-rooted habits when selecting TV-programs and are poorly selective which may be seen by the low zapping frequency. These users watch a lot of TV (up to three hours per day) but they are

[1] Censis is an important socio-economical research institute in Italy.

found to be scarcely selective and critic to what they watch. The *quality-consumer* group, on the other hand, is mainly composed of persons between 20 and 45 years old, mainly men, with higher education (high school or university) and with greater economic means than the average *quantity-consumer*. In general, this group is highly selective and critic to what is broadcasted and a decrease in the TV consumption has been seen in the group during recent years. A high percentage of the *quality-consumers* are found to search for news and entertainment from alternative sources.

The features of the videogame[2] (VG) users turned out to be of particular interest since this group has some astonishing similarities with the group of quality-consumers of TV. According to the annual report of the Italian Videogame Industry [17] 43% of the Italians over 4 years of age regularly use videogames. Apart from the big group of underage users, the majority of the VG-users have a high educational level. Above 60% are men and most users are between 18 and 44 years old. Hence, a significant part of the VG-users may presumably be found in the group of quality-consumers of television. This would show that an important part of the Italian population is poorly satisfied with what the traditional TV has to offer. This group is used to interact with more complex systems like videogames and might be more attracted by an Interactive TV than by the traditional TV-services.

In the end, also users of P2P systems were analysed: the phenomenon of file sharing via Internet, also referred as P2P, doesn't seem to decrease. There are few data on the Italian market and a comparison with the TV and videogame consumption is hence unfeasible. Anyhow, according to the 2005 a Cachelogic survey [18], P2P represented 60 % of the world Internet traffic. Italy is the eighth country in the world in using P2P systems. The same survey shows that an average of eight million Europeans are logged on to a P2P network in any given moment sharing 10 Petabytes (1015 bytes). Over 60% of these files are video. The P2P systems may consequently been seen as a concurrent to the television services when it comes to audio-video files. It is presumable to think that part of the quality-consumers of TV may be found in the P2P users. It is possible that unsatisfied people by the TV broadcast coincide with users who are looking for alternative ways to get audio-video material in a more critical and interactive way, like P2P users do.

5 Current eTV-Services: Comparative Analysis

Four enhanced TV services (Alice Home TV, Fastweb TV, DTT, Sky) currently available on the Italian market were analyzed in order to detect *de facto* standards [19] best and worst practices in the design of TV systems. It was carried out a comparative analysis of the four systems from the main usability aspects, functionalities and services point of view. Particular attention was paid to *de facto* standards, which are the most consolidated and widely accepted design features in a given domain. As *de facto* standards are closely related to users' expectations, they can be considered as "cornerstones" in designing new systems' interfaces.

[2] The data on videogame use was collected through interviews conducted between 18th-26th of May 2006. The sample was 2240 people, representative of the Italian population over 4 years of age (about 53.5 million people).

By means of specific grids for analysing and picking up data of the different interfaces, different design solutions were highlighted to access and navigate the system and all offered services: the solutions were classified into three main levels of standardization as below:

- *Established design solutions or standard de facto:* have to be taken into account in future design.
- *Partially established design solutions:* basic traits of the specific solution are found in the main service suppliers. These solutions may well become base lines for future design.
- *Non-established solutions:* there isn't an unidirectional design line although every interface shows the same functionalities. They concern principally the recent introduced functions.

It is important to underline that this classification is neither definitive nor permanent. A current solution adapted by only one system may be "standardized" with the launch of new services and an established solution may vice versa be transformed by future innovations. It is also possible that future enrichment of the available functions increases the number of standardization levels depicted here. The figure below (Fig. 1) shows a "Stratigraphy" of the three described standardization levels. A geographical metaphor of sand, stone and rock was used to illustrate the degree of sedimentation of the specific design solution we analysed.

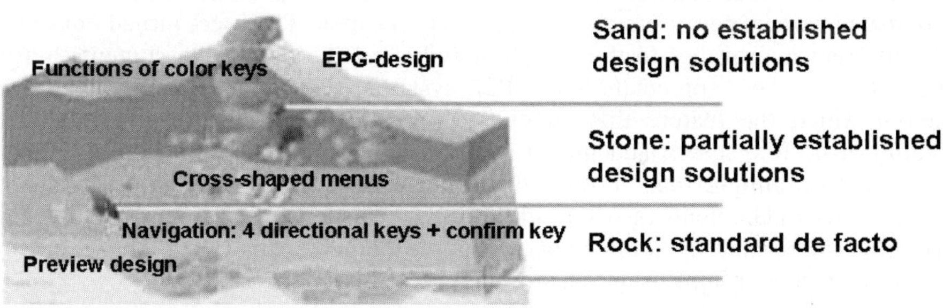

Fig. 1. Stratigraphy of Interactive TV designs

The functions where there are fewer similarities and more frequent changes are shown *close to the surface*. For instance, every system uses color key to activate specific functionalities but every system does it in a different way. Another example of not universally recognised standard in designing is EPG. In fact it can be present or not in the analysed systems and if there's, it is organized in different ways (i.e. integrated in the main menu or in a specific separate area of the interface). The changeability of these solutions is illustrated by the instability of the sand. Meanwhile there is also a tendency of design practices without any evident standard; these solutions are shown in the *middle of the figure*. For example the "cross shaped menu" is going to be a standard (in fact every new interactive interface has this kind of conformation) but it isn't universally recognised. These kinds of solutions are in a partially stable environment as found in the stone area. At the end the well-established solutions are presented at the *bottom of the figure*. These areas present stable design practices, called standard de facto. The navigation system is one example since they are almost always based on movements in four directions (up, down, left, right) and a confirm command on the input device. Then also the preview of the contents were resulted a standard de facto adopted by all systems. These are clear example of a functionality that's stable as the rock: it can be found in every examined interface.

6 P2P: Behavioural and Heuristic Analysis

The P2P applications are in several ways the opposite of the television services: they are founded spontaneously, purely interactive and offer an unlimited quantity of information. Another fundamental aspect that was analyzed is the different research criteria used for searching a content on TV and searching it using P2P. In the first case the user can choose only between a program list or an on demand content, in the second case the user can also access niche and not precoinceved contents. As seen from the number of P2P-users there is a call for this kind of systems and data about this group was therefore considered crucial in the perspective of television experiences which will depend on the user's decisions, instead of *ex-ante* programming. In order to understand and to analyse the user's behaviour in using P2P systems and in particular in looking for the most commons searching, archiving and sharing methods of the P2P users, two focus groups with "experienced" users of P2P systems were carried out; one with students and one with gainfully employed. All 18 participants were expert users and the majority was men. The users turned out to have very different approaches to the search activity and the use of the contents but one aspect that all users appreciate about P2P systems is the vast quantity of available material whilst the feature that annoys the most is when there are limits in the freedom of access, search and use in addition to the "fakes", e.g. corrupt files. It's important to highlight that "fakes" is the negative side of serendipity: in fact the possibility to find contents the user didn't look for has a double value: if the user finds something more that is interesting it is "serendipity", but when the user finds something boring or unpleasant but still unexpected it is "fakes".

Additionally, initiatives that offers hints on what to download, that directs the user toward the material to download or that proposes ways to catalogue the material are not popular among the experienced users. The P2P users generally prefer to search without constraints although they appreciate the change to followed search paths they didn't expect. "To find what you weren't searching for" pronounces the richness of the P2P world. Consequently, in order to satisfy this user group, the "serendipity" or the phenomenon of finding something whilst searching for something else should be a key-concept in the design of future TV-services. To design for the serendipity means to overturn the traditional perspective of the TV paradigm which is based on the predictability of the TV use.

Since the P2P systems have several characteristics that may be positively implemented in the design of future Interactive TV services, a heuristic analysis was conducted on three different systems that according to the results of the focus groups are the most widely used in Italy namely eMule, BitTorrent and Direct Connect. The dissimilarities were wound in different approaches for file sharing, downloading and archiving digital material. Some of the most important issues that came out from the focus group and heuristic analysis were "transformed" in input for new navigation model of a more interactive future TV.

7 Conclusions: Guidelines to Design a New Interactive TV Interface and Future Steps

According to the results of the enhanced TV analysis and the focus groups and heuristic analysis on P2P systems, some issues and drivers for designing new future TV interface were found out. Firstly, the interface design should *encourage the "serendipity",* which means that the user has to find more than he or she is looking for, avoiding the risk of "fakes", i.e. non-wanted contents. It's important that user doesn't "receive" or "see" non-wanted contents. Hence, the system has to limit the frustration arising from unexpected contents: a content preview or an online community could help the user in finding only wanted contents. Another requirement is that the system should be perceived as *non intrusive*: the user should get the chance to choose whether he or she wants to be profiled when accessing the system. Additionally the interface has to be *adjustable to different kind of users* so as to respond to different requests and profiles (e.g. expert or non expert but also "P2P like" or TV like). Moreover, the remote control of the traditional TV is not suitable for an interactive interface and therefore the *input device has to be reconceived* to allow a straightforward interaction with the content (e.g. joystick, mobile phone, avatar, etc.).

Some more general issues in designing the new user TV interface are given in the following. *Active navigation* implies that the user should get the chance to freely explore the contents (as on the web), without being obliged to select contents from a list. The *time-dependency* should be loosen up and the attention has to be moved towards the user-requests to obtain a change from "when and where" to "what and why". This implies a change of the traditional organization of the TV where the programmes are ordered according to start time and channel (EPG). *Multiple TV design* means that the same content has to be usable on several different devices. This requires a major flexibility of the contents (e.g. small displays).

Starting from these drivers and guidelines, our research is now focused on the definition of new concepts for a new iTV experience. We are working to find out more effective metaphors for the interaction process and the graphical TV interface giving "feeling" to the interaction, with the aim of leading the passive user to an active experience. The definition of alternative ways of navigation, different from EPG, is our first step to offer a growing interactivity that could merge the TV viewer and the prosumer in today's era of social media.

References

1. Belli, A., Geymonat, M., Perrero, M., Simeoni, R., Badella, M.: Dynamic TV: the long tail applied to a broadband-broadcast integration. In: Proceedings of the 4th European Interactive TV conference: Beyond Usability, Broadcast, and TV (2006)
2. Jensen, J.F., Toscan, C.: Interactive Television. TV of the Future or the Future of TV? Aalborg University Press, Denmark (1999)

3. van Dijk, J., Heuvelman, A., Peters, O.: Interactive Television or Enhanced Television? The Dutch users interest in applications of ITV via set-top boxes, 2003. In: Annual Conference Of the International Communication Association in San Diego USA (2003)
4. Livaditi, J.: A Media Consumption Analysis of Digital TV Applications (2002) http://itv.eltrun.aueb.gr/articles/2002/09livaditi
5. van Dijk, J., de Vos, L.: Searching for the holy grail – Images of interactive television, in New Media and Society, vol.3, SAGE (2001)
6. Bernoff, J., Herigstad, D.: seminar on interactive television http://web.mit.edu/comm-forum/forums/interactive_television.html (2004)
7. Global Information: Report: Mobile TV and Video Content Strategies (2006) http://www.gii.co.jp
8. Zimmerman, J., Marmaropoulos, G., Van Heerden, C.: Interface Design of Video Scout: A Selection, Recording, and Segmentation System for TVs. In: Proceedings of Human Computer Interaction International, pp. 277–281, Lawrence Erlbaum Associates, Mahwah (2001)
9. Pittarello, F.: Wandering through Time-pillars: a Serendipitous 3D Approach for the TV Information Domain. Rapporto di Ricerca CS-2002-14, Ottobre (2002)
10. Zimmerman, J., Kurapati, K., Buczak, A.L., Schaffer, D., Martino, J., Gutta, S.: TV Personalization System: Design of a TV Show Recommender Engine and Interface. In: Ardissono, L., Kobsa, A., Maybury, M. (eds.) (2004)
11. Diederiks, E.: Buddies in a box - animated characters in consumer electronics, in Intelligent User Interfaces. In: Johnson, W.L., Andre, E., Domingue, J. (eds.): ACM Press, Miami, pp. 34–38 (2003)
12. Joly, A.V.: Toupee – a prototype. An interactive television application developed for children. In: Proceedings of the 4th European Interactive TV conference: Beyond Usability, Broadcast, and TV (2006)
13. Chorianopoulos, K.: MtvBoX: Interactive Music Television Programming with the Virtual Channel API. In: Adjunct Proceedings of the 10th HCI International 2003 conference pp.279–280 (2003)
14. Chorianopoulos, K.: Animated Characters in Interactive TV. In: Proceedings of the 4th European Interactive TV conference: Beyond Usability, Broadcast, and TV (2006)
15. Censis: Quinto Rapporto Censis-Ucsi sulla comunicazione in Italia 2005: 2001-2005 cinque anni di evoluzione e rivoluzione nell'uso dei media, Roma (2005)
16. Livolsi, M.: Dietro il telecomando. Profili dello spettatore televisivo, Franco Angeli, Italy (2003)
17. AEVSI: Secondo Rapporto Annuale sull'Industria Videoludica in Italia (2006)
18. Cachelogic: Peer-to-peer in 2005 http://www.cachelogic.com/home/pages/research/p2p2005.php
19. Bernard, M.: Examining User Expectations for the Location of Common E-Commerce Web Objects, Usability News 4.1 (2002)

Evaluating the Effectiveness of Digital Storytelling with Panoramic Images to Facilitate Experience Sharing

Zuraidah Sulaiman[1], Nor Laila Md Noor[2], Narinderjit Singh[1], and Suet Peng Yong[1]

[1] Universiti Teknologi PETRONAS, Perak, Malaysia
{zuraidahs,narinderjit,yongsuetpeng}@petronas.com.my
[2] Universiti Teknologi MARA, Selangor, Malaysia
norlaila@tmsk.uitm.edu.my

Abstract. Technology advancement has now enabled experience sharing to happen in a digital storytelling environment that is facilitated through different delivery technologies such as panoramic images and virtual reality. However, panoramic images have not being fully explored and formally studied especially to assist experience sharing in digital storytelling setting. This research aims to study the effectiveness of an interactive digital storytelling to facilitate the sharing of experience. The interactive digital storytelling artifact was developed to convey the look and feel of Universiti Teknologi PETRONAS through the panoramic images. The effectiveness of digital storytelling through panoramic images was empirically tested based on the adapted Delone and McLean IS success model. The experiment was conducted on participants who have never visited the university. Six hypotheses were derived and experiment showed that there are correlations between user satisfaction of digital storytelling with panoramic images and user's individual impact of the application to assist experience sharing among users. Hence, this research concludes a model on the production of an effective digital storytelling with panoramic images for specific experience sharing to bloom among users.

Keyword: Digital storytelling, interactivity, panoramic images, experience sharing, effective system, effectiveness study, human computer interaction.

1 Introduction

In the digital storytelling realm, many types of digital technology and media have long being the enabler for narrative entertainment to reach its audience. Traditional narrative form of storytelling is transformed into a more dynamic and powerful system of communication with sound, music, visuals, interactivity navigation and user-control mechanism [1], [2]. Digital storytelling can act as glue that holds things together when developers are about to offer users with all different kinds of information, media, types of images and ideas [3].

Indicators of effectiveness of a system or application include quality of solution and error rates. In this study, the quality of solution is used as a primary indicator of effectiveness to measure the outcome when users (students) interact with the digital

J. Jacko (Ed.): Human-Computer Interaction, Part III, HCII 2007, LNCS 4552, pp. 981–989, 2007.

storytelling with panoramic images application [4]. Our research, UTP-PanoView, is a system with an attempt of sharing information about the Universiti Teknologi PETRONAS using digital storytelling as the medium that utilizes Information Technology in views of multimedia and virtual reality. A systematic measure to study the effectiveness of a digital storytelling must start somewhere and this study aims to fulfill that call.

2 Literature Review

Panoramic (from the Greek *pan* means all and *horama* meaning see) are orientation-independent images that contain all the information needed to look around in 360 degrees. A number of these images can be connected or stitched together to form a walkthrough sequence. These orientation-independent images allow a greater degree of freedom in interactive viewing and navigation [5]. Experience refers to the nature of events that has been undergone by someone or something [6]. Humans have countless and unique ways that consist of expressions, behaviors, language and emotions to characterize and convey their moment-to-moment experiences. Hence, experience also is as an act that produces, create, and invent knowledge for effects upon the future. Interactive image sharing application nowadays [7], [8], enable users to feel like they are sharing experiences rather than just looking at pictures or sending and receiving messages with the images. With the availability of mechanisms such as MMS, online albums and moblogs, the experience sharing aspect remains problematic than the capture aspect. More fundamentally, experience sharing is highly relationship-specific.

Several measures have been examined by different prominent literatures to define the effectiveness of Information System applications. The diversity of the various measures from the previous research and empirical study on IS effectiveness was initially a cause for concern that lead DeLone and McLean to synthesize the measures into a unified model [9], [10], [11]. The DeLone and McLean's (henceforth "D&M") Model of IS Success has been regarded by many authors as a major contribution [12]. Realizing the fact that this model has been a great influence and inspiration to the succeeding research, D&M Model is adapted to suit digital storytelling application in our research. D&M Model is believed to be significant in evaluating the effectiveness of digital storytelling; which can also be considered as an Information System. The D&M model basically incorporated several of the already accepted and tested dimensions or constructs of IS Success into a single model.

3 Research Methodology

3.1 Research Model and Hypotheses

Although claims on the effectiveness of digital storytelling are often made, the current literature does not reflect work on the evaluation of the effectiveness digital storytelling [13]. In addition to that, there is a lack of formal guidelines or standard model on how to produce an effective digital storytelling for the purpose of facilitating the experience sharing to bloom among users. Our work was driven by the following research questions:

- Do system quality, information quality and interactivity have any significant relationship with user satisfaction of digital storytelling with panoramic images?
- Will user satisfaction of digital storytelling with panoramic images lead to any individual impact to the user?
- Will user satisfaction and individual impact of digital storytelling with panoramic images encourage the sharing of experience to bloom in user?

The hypotheses formulated are as follows:

H1: Perceived System Quality positively relates to User Satisfaction
H2: Perceived Information Quality positively relates to User Satisfaction
H3: Interactivity positively relates to User Satisfaction
H4: User Satisfaction positively relates to Individual Impact
H5: User Satisfaction positively relates to Experience Sharing
H6: Individual Impact positively relates to Experience Sharing

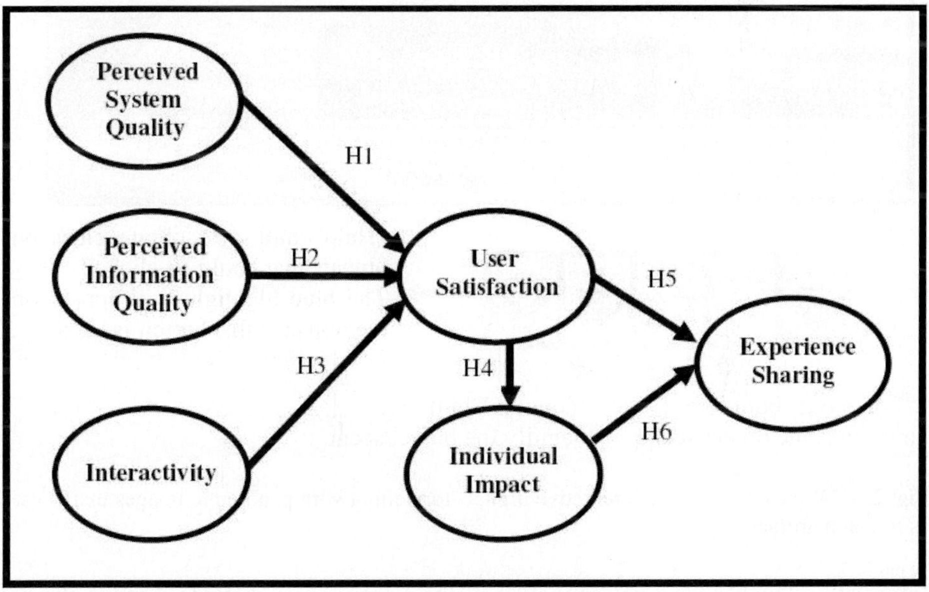

Fig. 1. Research model for evaluating the effectiveness of digital storytelling with panoramic images to facilitate experience sharing

To determine the effectiveness of panoramic digital storytelling for experience sharing, we adapted the well-established DeLone and McLean's (1992) Information System Success model that has been validated empirically in several settings. We thus produced our effectiveness research model as shown in Fig. 1. We eliminated existing constructs of Use and Organizational Impact in the existing model and incorporated constructs of Interactivity together with existing constructs on Systems Quality and

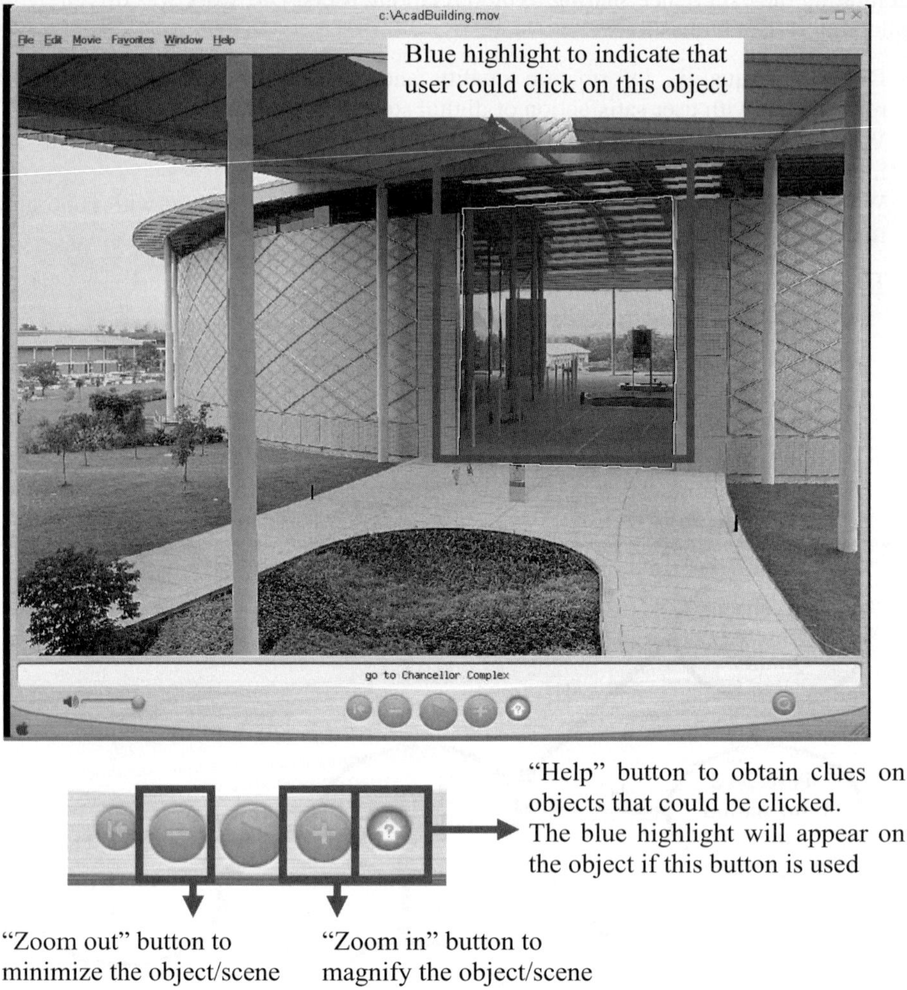

Fig. 2. UTP-PanoView - The interactive digital storytelling with panoramic images that is used as research artifact

Information Quality. The determination of the effectiveness is made through the use of constructs of User's Satisfaction, Individual Impact and perception of Experience Sharing. The relationship of Systems Quality, Information Quality and Interactivity towards User Satisfaction [14], [15], will be determined and the relation of User Satisfaction towards Individual impact and the perception on Experience Sharing will also be determined in this adapted model.

3.2 The UTP-PanoView Digital Storytelling

We created a digital storytelling artefact to foster experience sharing among users to encourage or persuade them to experience the real thing. The panoramic digital storytelling artefact, UTP-PanoView, as shown in Fig. 2 is categorized as "place-based storytelling". It was produced in QuickTime Virtual Reality (QTVR) which is able to display spherical panoramas format in cubic or cylindrical panoramas projection, in a viewer where the user can move around, zooming in and out the or rotate the object using the mouse and keyboard.

UTP-PanoView is an interactive digital story that also allows varying degrees of choice and control from the user's part. It aims to facilitate audiences in connecting to locations through self-discovery where experience is revealed in context via rich visualizations of places and buildings. The experience sharing offered by UTP-PanoView allow users to experience the same thing as in the real world such as walking, stopping, running or changing direction. In other words, it is like an online expedition that is close to real campus walking tour. The panoramic images used in the study illustrated the buildings and scenes of a local Malaysian university, Universiti Teknologi Petronas (UTP) and its surroundings. Virtual campus tour could be a useful reference in the future for architects, urban planners, and government entities. In this artefact development, elements of the experience sharing consideration is fulfilled from the paradigm of experience sharing via the Systems Quality, Information Quality and Interactivity that based on user interaction and user-control mechanism such as navigation properties.

An experiment was conducted on 128 participants consisting of students selected from a secondary school. The participants were given 20 minutes to view and interact with UTP-PanoView in the school computer laboratory. At the end of the session, 5-point Likert scale survey questions were distributed for the participants to answer.

4 Results and Discussion

The results and discussions are organized as follows: Section 4.1 discuss on data analysis and results for Instrument Reliability, Descriptive Analysis and Normality Test while this is followed by the data analysis and results for Correlation Coefficients in Section 4.2.

4.1 Data Analysis on Instrument Reliability, Descriptive Analysis and Normality Test

To validate the data, the Cronbach's Alpha coefficient is conducted to test the consistency for all variables involved in this study. Shapiro-Wilk test of normality is then conducted to further determine the data distribution.

With reference to Table 1, the Cronbach's Alpha values for all variables are more than 0.6. This indicates all variables scale have high reliability and internal consistency [16]. The values for skewness/standard error for all variables are out of range, which is between -2 and +2. This indicates that the data for all variables are not normally distributed. To support this analysis, Shapiro-Wilk test has been further conducted and it is noticed that the significance values for all variables are 0.00 which is less than 0.05. This testifies that the data for all variables are not normally distributed and hence, nonparametric test has to be conducted for any hypotheses testing purpose.

Table 1. Reliability (Cronbach's Alpha), Descriptive and Shapiro-Wilk Statistics

Variables	Cron-bach's Alpha	Mean	Std. Dev.	Std. Error	Skew-ness	Skew-ness/ Std. Error	Shapiro – Wilk Test Stat.	Sig.
Perceived System Quality	0.749	3.965	0.485	0.214	-1.169	-5.462	0.911	0.00
Perceived Information Quality	0.642	4.002	0.620	0.214	-0.493	-2.304	0.955	0.00
Interactivity	0.795	4.109	0.532	0.214	-1.525	-7.126	0.873	0.00
User Satisfaction	0.663	4.159	0.707	0.214	-0.918	-4.290	0.910	0.00
Individual Impact	0.755	3.966	0.520	0.214	-0.774	-3.617	0.935	0.00
Experience Sharing	0.752	3.845	0.555	0.214	-0.644	-3.009	0.938	0.00

4.2 Data Analysis on Correlation Coefficients

Since the data for all variables are not normally distributed, nonparametric test (Bivariate Spearman correlation coefficients) is conducted in this research to independently measure the linear association between two scale variables for all variables towards digital storytelling with panoramic images. The Rowntree correlation classification [17] by was adopted in this study to indicate the strength of the relationship.

With reference to Table 2 above, the significance level or p-value for all relationships is 0.000, which is less than 0.05. This indicates that all variables in study are positively correlated to each other. Results from the Spearman test also indicates that the correlation coefficient value between Perceived System Quality and User Satisfactory is 0.368 which is considered as weak correlation; whereas the value of correlation coefficient between Perceived Information Quality and Interactivity towards User Satisfaction is 0.611 and 0.409 respectively, which both are considered as moderate relationship. These positive relationships suggest that developers or designers of digital storytelling with panoramic images should consider and focus their efforts on maintaining the overall System Quality, Information Quality and Interactivity of digital storytelling application because there is an appreciable effect of those factors on User Satisfaction level towards the application. From a more practical viewpoint, the power of System Quality, Information Quality and Interactivity as positive factors of User Satisfaction suggests that they provide an effective diagnostic framework in which to analyze system features, which may cause user satisfaction and dissatisfaction. Among these three factors, digital storytelling developers and designers should invest more resources and put high emphasis on maintaining the quality of the information or story as the core element of digital storytelling. They must ensure that the information or story quality is suitable, accurate, understandable,

Table 2. Summary of Correlation based on Bivariate Spearman

		Perceived System Quality	Perceived Information Quality	Interactivity	User Satisfaction	Individual Impact
User Satisfaction	Correlation Coefficient	0.368 (positive weak)	0.611 (positive moderate)	0.409 (positive moderate)		
	Sig.	0.000	0.000	0.000		
Individual Impact	Correlation Coefficient				0.471 (positive moderate)	
	Sig.				0.000	
Experience Sharing	Correlation Coefficient				0.287 (positive weak)	0.604 (positive moderate)
	Sig.				0.001	0.000

and bring meaning to their target audience. This is followed by the considerable importance should be given to the interactivity element of the digital storytelling design, which emphasize on user's involvement into the storyline, users ability to control the environment as well as the user-friendliness of the application.

These two aspects of Information Quality and Interactivity should be given higher priority than the overall System Quality in order to generate high user's satisfaction towards the digital storytelling. These relationships are clearly delineated in Table 2 where Perceived Information Quality and Interactivity are of moderate correlations to User Satisfaction as compared to Perceived System Quality with weak correlation. Better still, all the relationships are with positive values showing that all the three elements are vital to support an effective digital storytelling to achieve User's Satisfaction.

Besides that, Table 2 also signifies the correlation coefficient value between User Satisfaction and Individual Impact is 0.471 which is also positively moderate correlated. The positive association between User Satisfaction and Individual Impact also suggests that User Satisfaction towards the digital storytelling may serve as a valid factor that encourages the overall personal impact of that application to the users for instance the ability for users to appreciate and enjoy the application. User's individual impact of digital storytelling with panoramic images is also reflected via user's memory retain of the story and user's decision making ability while the application simultaneously manage to ignite user's deeper curiosity and inspiration towards the story.

Nevertheless, the correlation coefficient value between User Satisfaction and Experience Sharing is only 0.287 which indicates they are positively correlated but with weak relationship. The result differs with the value of correlation coefficient between Individual Impact and Experience Sharing which is 0.604 that are positively correlated with moderate correlation. As such, it can be inferred that User Satisfaction does not highly influence the sharing of experience that users obtained compared to the effect of Individual Impact. The level of overall User Satisfaction towards digital storytelling with panoramic images may be low but as long as the application has given adequate Individual Impact to the users, the Experience Sharing could still bloom in users.

5 Conclusion

This section concludes the paper by describing the specific outcomes of the study and describes their importance. This research has creatively explored and formally studied panoramic images especially to assist experience sharing in digital storytelling setting. The results of this research yields evidence that UTP-PanoView is a proof of concept that panoramic images could express the experience of a place to the user thus later on encouraging the users to share that experience. Since the challenge with digital storytelling today is the determination on the best possible way to tell a story via the objects that the place or event happen to have, telling a story could be done by putting forward the objects such as buildings and places into a narrative or storylines. Due to its wide-view characteristic, panoramic images is a wise choice in order to weave together objects that tell stories and sharing of experience. This study postulates that digital storytelling with panoramic images is worth to be experimented in other field and setting such as a classroom teaching aid, electronic museums and historical purposes, marketing and promotional arm in tourism setting and the list is endless.

This study is significant to the field as currently the area of digital storytelling is lacking a systematic approach to determine the effectiveness of such application. As such, a model for an effective digital storytelling is proposed in the end as the primary contribution of the study. This model should encourage the examination of System Quality, Information Quality, Interactivity, User Satisfaction, Individual Impact and Experience Sharing factors that impact the effectiveness of a digital storytelling. Researchers, designers, developers or other interested parties of digital storytelling could then utilize this effectiveness model produced by this study as a benchmark or preliminary checklist to construct a much better and effectiveness digital storytelling that meets the user's need.

This research also notably contributes as another empirical evidence on the effectiveness study of an Information System especially in the area of digital storytelling. This study has discussed and modified DeLone and McLean's Success Model in which it has greatly inspired and influenced the researcher to develop an effectiveness model to fill the gaps in the body of knowledge of an Information System Success Model. In addition, this study also contribute indirectly as an empirical evidence to the theory set forth [18] on the taxonomy of important elements to be considered in digital storytelling.

References

1. Miller, C.H.: Digital Storytelling: A Creator's Guide to Interactive Entertainment. Focal Press Elsevier, Burlington, MA (2004)
2. Kannan, S.: Online Documentary. In Interactive Storytelling. In: Paper presented at the Proceedings of Web Designs for Interactive Learning Conference 2005, New York (2005)
3. Johnson, B.: The Second Story in Interactive Storytelling. In: Paper presented at the Proceedings of Web Designs for Interactive Learning Conference 2005, New York (2005)
4. Frokjaer, E., Herzum, M., Hornbaek, K.: Measuring Usability: Are Effectiveness, Efficiency, and Satisfaction Really Correlated? In: Paper presented at the Conference on Human Factors in Computing Systems, Hague, Netherlands (2000)
5. Chen, S.E.: QuickTime VR: An Image-Based Approach to Virtual Environment Navigation. In: Paper presented at the SIGGRAPH 1995, Los Angeles, CA (1995)
6. Neill, J.: What is Experience? (2006) Retrieved July 23, 2006, from http://wilderdom.com/experiential/ExperienceWhatIs.html
7. Aoki, P.M., Szymanski, M.H., Woodruff, A.: Turning From Image Sharing to Experience Sharing. In: Paper presented at the Ubicomp 2005 Workshop on Pervasive Image Capture and Sharing: New Social Practices and Implications for Technology, Tokyo (2005)
8. Balabanovic, M., Chu, L.L., Wolff, G.J.: Storytelling with Digital Photographs. In: Proc. CHI 2000, ACM, pp. 564–571 (2000)
9. DeLone, W.H., McLean, E.R.: Information System Success: The Quest for the Dependent Variable. Information Systems Research 3(1), 60–95 (1992)
10. DeLone, W.H., McLean, E.R.: Information Systems Success Revisited. In: Paper presented at the Proceedings of the 35th Hawaii International Conference on System Sciences (HICSS-35'02), Hawaii (2002)
11. DeLone, W.H., McLean, E.R.: The DeLone and McLean Model of Information Systems Success: A Ten-Year Update. Journal of Management Information Systems 19(4), 9–30 (2003)
12. Molla, A., Licker, P.S.: E-Commerce Systems Success: An Attempt to Extend and Respecify the Delone and MaClean Model of IS Success. Journal of Electronic Commerce Research 2(4), 131–141 (2001)
13. Davenport, G., Murtaugh, M.: Automatist Storyteller Systems and The Shifting Sands of Story. IBM Systems Journal 36(3), 446–456 (1999)
14. Baroudi, J.J., Olson, M.H., Ives, B.: An Empirical Study of the Impact of User Involvement on System Usage and Information Satisfaction. Communication of the ACM 29(3), 232–238 (1986)
15. Ives, B., Olson, M.H., Baroudi, J.J.: The Measurement of User Information Satisfaction Communications of the ACM, 26(10), 785–793 (1983)
16. Sekaran, U.: Research Methods for Business: A Skill Building Approach, 2nd edn. Wiley, New York (1992)
17. Rowntree, D.: Statistics Without Tears: A Primer for Non-Mathematicians. Charles Scribner's Sons, New York (1981)
18. Paul, N., Fiebich, C.: The Elements of Digital Storytelling. A project of the University of Minnesota School of Journalism and Mass Communication's Institute for New Media Studies and New Directions for News (2002) Retrieved April 25, 2006, from http://www.inms.umn.edu/elements/

User-Centered Design and Evaluation of a Concurrent Voice Communication and Media Sharing Application

David J. Wheatley

Motorola Labs, Social Media Research Lab,
1295 E. Algonquin Road, Schaumburg,
Illinois, 60196, USA
David.j.Wheatley@motorola.com

Abstract. This paper describes two user-centered studies undertaken in the development of a concurrent group voice and media sharing application. The first used paper prototyping to identify the user values relating to a number of functional capabilities. These results informed the development of a prototype application, which was ported to a 3G handset and evaluated in the second study using a conjoint analysis approach. Results indicated that concurrent photo sharing was of high user value, while the value of video sharing was limited by established mental models of file sharing. Overall higher ratings were found among female subjects and among less technologically aware subjects and most media sharing would be with those who are close and trusted. This, and other results suggest that the reinforcement of social connections, spontaneity and emotional communications would be important user objectives of such a media sharing application.

Keywords: User centered design, wireless communications, concurrent media sharing, cell-phone applications.

1 Introduction

The rapid and widespread acceptance of camera enabled cell phones has introduced new opportunities for the immediate and spontaneous sharing of still visual images using the cellular network and such capabilities are now almost ubiquitous. In fact, in 2004, camera phones outsold digital cameras by nearly 4 to 1 [11], with an estimated 60 million photos taken daily. There is also an increasing trend towards public photojournalism. The latter was well illustrated in the context of the London Underground bombings where still and video images captured by personal cell phones were, for the first time, extensively used by the broadcast media [3]. In fact, approximately 1000 photos and 20 pieces of video were sent in to the BBC News website [13]. This capability for the spontaneous creation and immediate sharing of visual images via wireless networks is changing the landscape of picture usage, both in terms of the content of images as well as the motivations for sharing [5, 12]. A next step would be to enable this real-time sharing of visual media (photos and video clips) to take place concurrently with a one to one or multi-point (group) conversation.

J. Jacko (Ed.): Human-Computer Interaction, Part III, HCII 2007, LNCS 4552, pp. 990–999, 2007.

Since these studies were completed, a number of concurrent media sharing applications have been, or will be introduced in 2007, such as Ericsson IMS "weShare" [1] and Motorola's European 3G Video-sharing solution. This paper describes how user centered design methods were applied to design, develop and evaluate an integrated application such as these, through a process of use case definition, paper prototyping, user interface design and finally, user evaluation of a handset based prototype.

2 Related Research

Evidence suggests that the rapid uptake and use of camera-enabled cell phones might have been driven by quite different motivations than was the case with traditional film or digital cameras. Image quality and careful photo composition appear to be of relatively low value while the fleeting capture of serendipitous and everyday events seem to be a fundamental user value created by the ubiquitous nature of the device. In a survey by IPSe Marketing in Dec 2002, the majority of camera phone users (42.4%) reported that they took photos of *"things that they happened upon that were interesting"*, this was followed by family members (39.5%), friends (36.6%), self (26.4%), pets (23.7%) and travel photos (21.5%) [4]. This same survey of 2007 Japanese respondents also concluded that *"nearly half"* had taken a photo in place of jotting a memo or sketching something on paper. The value of the photo and video enabled cell phone in capturing unexpected events has also not gone unnoticed by the news media, NBC News *"believes in it so much that they've begun equipping reporters and other staff members with video enabled cell phones..... [since] you never know where or when news is going to happen"* [4]. The BBC has also been formally evaluating such mobile imaging technologies [13].

In addition to the immediate and pragmatic usefulness of camera phones, sharing pictures with other people also frequently has a significant personal and emotional component [1, 9]. However, in a study by Kurvinen of four groups of 5 subjects sharing digital images, *"practically all of the messages sent ... contained both images and text"* in order to fulfil these emotional needs and to assist the recipient in interpreting the visual image [6]. Kurvinen also found that the capability to fulfil this emotional need produced much of the value derived from sharing sequences of pictures in a turn-by-turn process of group communication. A number of papers have concluded that social/emotional communication is a key objective of mobile media sharing [4, 6, 9, 10]. One of the aims of these studies was to develop a prototype media sharing application and to evaluate how this user objective might be facilitated.

3 Methods

3.1 Phase 1 – Paper Prototyping

This process of user centered development, consisted of two phases. In the first phase, carried out in partnership with Purdue University, use case scenarios were developed to communicate the hypothesised functionality of a concurrent voice and media sharing application and were decomposed into seven, sequentially dependent user tasks. Paper prototypes, representing the operations and screen flows required to complete each of these tasks, were designed based on the Motorola "Tactium" touch screen interface (see Fig. 1). Paper prototypes were specifically chosen in this phase so that they would be perceived as being very early in the development process such that subjects would be more willing to provide both positive and negative feedback to influence the development. If the prototype were perceived as being more finished then they might consider the qualitative feedback to be less influential in the development and would consequently be more reluctant to be critical.

Individual interview sessions were held in which these seven task scenarios were presented visually on a laptop PC, then carried out by subjects using the paper prototypes. These scenarios probed user values associated with the following functions;

- *Initiating a group voice call*
- *Availability of presence information*
- *Sharing still images concurrent with a group voice call*
- *Sharing live video concurrent with a group voice call*

After completing each task, subjects were asked a series of open-ended questions relating to each task and the functional capabilities represented. They also completed a short questionnaire (TAQ) to assess their level of technological awareness. This consisted of 12 alternative choice questions relating to the ownership and frequency of use of a number of representative portable media devices and services. Within this, subjects also self-reported levels of interest and capability in acquiring and learning about new electronic devices. The questionnaire was numerically scored, the highest score being 42. The mean score was 20.9, with values ranging from 1 to 42.

In order to reduce the qualitative data (from the open-ended questions) to a more readily analyzable quantitative form, a set of questions were generated from the response data, and the dichotomised answers to these questions coded. In this process 84 unique codes were generated, reflecting the 84 most frequently raised issues. The content of each paragraph unit of transcribed text was then coded, based on consensus by three or more of the experimental team, in order to facilitate quantitative analysis within a relational database, which reduced the qualitative data to a total of 1371 codes. The coded data was analysed using the Eztext/Answer qualitative analysis software suite, produced and widely used by the CDC (Centers for Disease Control) for analysis in medical projects [2].

Subject sampling was intentionally biased towards younger subjects, for whom using a cell phone and other communications and media rendering devices would be a familiar and integral part of their everyday lives. They also represented the early adopters for whom such an application would likely have relatively high value. The sample of 23 subjects consisted of 12 female and 11 male, (mean 20.7 yrs). The age range was from 18 to 28 yrs.

3.2 Phase 2 – Application Prototyping

The phase 1 findings were used to specify the functional capabilities of a handset based concurrent voice and media sharing application, the objective of this study

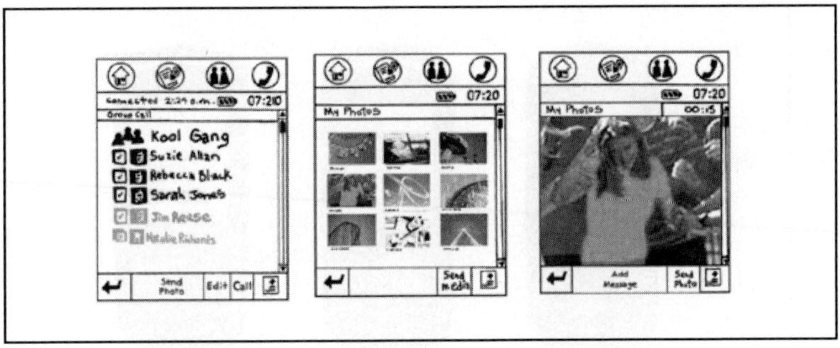

Fig. 1. Examples of touch-screen interface simulated in paper prototype

being to assess the relative impact of a number of functions and price, on subjective ratings of the application. This prototype was developed using J2ME on a Motorola E1000 3G handset and operated over a 3G test network. The application prototype represented the following functionality:

• *Separate individual and group contacts listings*
• *Presence/availability information presented within the contacts lists*
• *The ability to select and send a still image concurrent with a one-to one-voice call and with no voice call (similar to MMS)*

Where possible, existing screens and menus were used in the design of the prototype while new screens were designed to have a similar look and feel (Fig. 2). Specific task flows were developed to be as intuitive as possible in order that subject responses would be focused primarily on the overall functional capability and value of the application rather than the specific UI implementation. Subjects were presented with scenario storyboards to set the context for each task and to illustrate the functions and capabilities of the prototype. They then carried out each of six tasks using the prototype. Each task demonstrated a different permutation of the key functions within a conjoint analysis experimental structure. In order to control for order effects, two sequences of presentation of the task scenarios were defined and used with alternate subjects. After completing each task, subjects were asked how much they would rate that version of the service if it was free, and also what their rating would be if it added $10 to the monthly cost of their cell phone bill. In each case, they gave their rating on a 7-point Likert scale. After each of the two task groups (sending and receiving media), subjects were asked a series of open-ended questions to qualitatively explore the expected contexts of use. The task completion and open-ended question responses were recorded on both video and audio for later analysis.

Each task consisted of a combination of attributes on three dimensions. These dimensions were:

Contact List: Calling using Group phonebook ("G") vs. individual phonebook ("Ind")
Presence Information: Available before calling ("PI") vs. not available ("No PI")
Media Sharing: Concurrent media sharing with a call ("CMS") vs. media sharing only outside a call ("No CMS")

Fig. 2. Examples of prototype application screens

Subjects were first presented with the highest and lowest versions of the service, with the highest including all three attributes (G, PI and CMS), and the lowest including none of these attributes. These initial versions were intended to convey to the subjects the extreme ranges of the service, so that they would initially use the high and low ends of the response scale. Then four other versions were presented that combined the attributes in a partial factorial design. The sample of 12 subjects was selected using similar criteria to phase 1 and consisted of 6 males and 6 females. Two of these subjects did not report their ages, but the reported average age of the remaining 10 was 23.4 (s.d. 2.1), and their median age was 23. The youngest subject in this sample was 19 and the oldest was 26.

4 Results and Discussion

Results from Phase 1 indicated that concurrent media sharing was very positively regarded by subjects: with 91% positively evaluating photo sharing and 87% positively evaluated video sharing. In addition, 26% ranked media sharing as their favorite function of those presented in the study; interestingly, all of these were low and medium technology awareness users – a trend which was to be repeated in the second phase of the study. The positive evaluation was relatively equal across genders, and slightly correlated with technology awareness.

In terms of the intention to share photos concurrent with a call, 78% stated that they would actually do it but here there were clear differences between genders and technology awareness levels. 92% of the females (compared to 64% of the males) and 100% of the highly sophisticated users (compared to 66% of the low and medium users, combined) indicated that they would actively use (in addition to value) photo sharing. Nonetheless, technologically sophisticated subjects did not support the concept without qualification. One of them felt that although photo and video sharing was *"a good idea. . . basically [it] depends on technology at the moment, transfer speeds, wireless connections, processing power and battery life."*

As well as technical limitations, image quality was a recurring theme for technologically sophisticated subjects. Many were concerned about the resolution needed to provide acceptable image quality. Many also indicated that they would use media sharing for reasons of convenience, particularly that this would enable the sharing of daily and unexpected moments with friends or family. One subject concluded, however, that despite technical drawbacks, *"It would be cool. It would be an interesting way to share random things with your friends, attach some text, 'Oh, something cool happened.' "* This seems to confirm the value of spontaneity in mobile media sharing predicted by previous research.

When sending and receiving media, subjects were generally trusting in the honesty and discretion of their content recipients, an overwhelming majority (91%) believing that the media recipients should be able to forward and/or save that media. Interestingly, males were, relatively speaking, slightly less trusting. Only 82% of the males, compared to 100% of the females, indicated that they would have no objection to the media being forwarded by the recipient. In the end, 35% expressed an interest in having some kind of media "locking" function, which would enable control over whether it could be further forwarded. These results suggested that the application prototype should focus on enabling still image sharing concurrently with a group voice call, the ability to initiate a call from either an individual or group contacts list and presence information.

In phase 2, subjects showed high agreement on the top-rated scenarios, but less agreement on lower-rated ones. When the service was free, the highest rated scenario included all three attributes—G, PI, and CMS—with an average of 6.6 (median 7.0, s.d. 0.79) in fact 11 of the 12 subjects gave this their top rating. The scenario that excluded all attributes had the lowest average rating (ave. 5.5, median 5.0, s.d. 1.5). When there was a monthly charge of $10 for the service, the highest-rated scenario included PI and CMS, but excluded G. It had an average rating of 4.5 (median 4.5, s.d. 1.4).

The impact of the service attributes on the conjoint ratings was assessed using ANOVA, the Attribute factor having 3 levels: type of contact list (G vs Ind), Presence information (PI), and Concurrent Media Sharing (CMS). The results showed significant main effects of Price ($F(1,11) = 34.7$, $MSe = 0.95$, $p < .001$, $\eta^2 = 0.76$) and a trend toward a significant effect of Attribute Present ($F(1,11) = 8.94$, $MSe = 0.17$, $p < .05$, $\eta^2 = 0.45$). Ratings were significantly higher when the service was free than when it cost $10/mo (5.96 vs. 3.87), and were higher when the attributes were present than when they were absent (5.13 vs. 4.69). A series of *t*-tests did show some significant or near-significant effects of the individual attributes. When the service was free, there were marginally significantly higher ratings for CMS than for no CMS ($t(11) = 1.91$, $p < .05$; Fig. 3). When the service cost $10 per month, there were significant preferences for CMS ($t(11) = 3.28$, $p < .01$) and marginally significantly higher ratings for PI ($t(11) = 2.25$, $p < .05$).

In order to assess the impact of the grouping variables on ratings of the functional permutations, a stepwise regression was performed on the transformed conjoint data. The overall ANOVA for the regression was statistically significant ($F(13, 77) = 82.3$, $p < .001$, $MSe = 0.021$, $R^2 = 0.93$). There was a significant effect of Cost ($t(77) = 15.7$), with the free versions of the service being given higher ratings than the $10 versions. The following were some of the significant 2-way interactions:

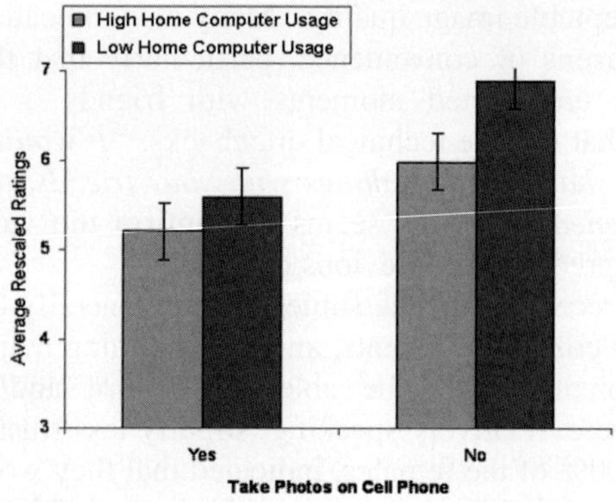

Fig. 3. Average Rescaled Ratings for each Attribute and Price

Gender X Technology Awareness. There was no significant difference between males and females who were high in technical awareness, however, of those who scored low on this scale, females gave significantly higher average ratings than males ($t(11) = 3.67, p < .01$).

Home Computer Usage X Cell Phone Photos. Subjects who did not take photos on their cell phones and were low on the computing usage variable gave significantly higher ratings than users who did take photos on their cell phones and were high on computing usage ($t(11) = 5.26, p < .001$; Fig. 4).

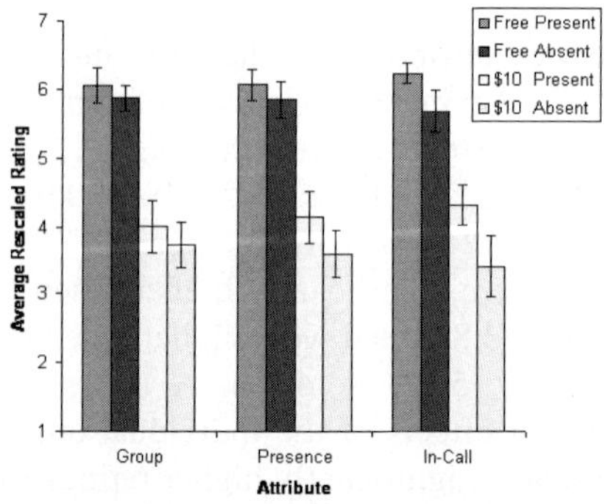

Fig. 4. Average Rescaled Ratings for each level of Home Computer Technology Usage and use of Cell Phone for taking Photos

Technology Awareness X Cost. Among subjects who were low in technical awareness, the ratings were significantly higher when the service was free than when it cost $10/mo ($t(11) = 2.73, p < .01$).

Gender X Cost. For males, ratings were significantly higher when the service was free than when it cost $10/mo ($t(11) = 2.86, p < .01$). Females gave significantly higher ratings when the service was free than males did when the service cost $10/mo ($t(11)$

= 3.22, $p < .01$). However, there was no significant difference in ratings between females with the $10/mo service compared to males with the free service.

5 Conclusions

Phase 1 demonstrated that the concept of concurrent media sharing was of significant user value and that photos were slightly more valued than video. It was found that many subjects did not fully grasp that the video sharing was "live"; but defaulted to a file sharing mental model with the expectation that a video clip would be captured, saved and then shared as a video file, possibly contributing to the lower score. The more technologically aware subjects were also conscious of potential technical limitations of such media sharing, which may also have been a factor in this group rating the function somewhat lower than the less technologically aware subjects. Gender differences were also found in that female subjects generally rated photo sharing higher than males; suggesting a social element also found in phase 2. The group calling capability also revealed concerns about the accuracy of presence information and the unambiguous knowledge of who was in the group call. The latter was found to be most important when sharing visual media.

On the whole, subjects were willing for recipients to be able to save and/or forward media, but there was also an interesting process of self-censoring, in that they would simply not share media which was sensitive or private and/or they would not share media with those whom they did not trust. Despite this, there was also interest in the concept of 'locking" media to control or limit whether it could be saved or forwarded. There was also mixed reaction to adding text messages to shared media, particularly within a concurrent voice call, which contrasts with that found in [6]. This negative reaction seemed to be based on two factors; the difficulties inherent in text entry using a mobile device and the redundancy of a text message during a concurrent voice call. As one subject described it; *"adding text would take too long, it would be such a hassle, especially if I could tell them on the 'phone what the caption would be"*. For the same reasons, the ability to personalize or modify the media (with borders, word balloons etc.) was also felt to be somewhat irrelevant. There were also concerns about the physical operation of the handset, arising from a necessity to hold the device in the hand to look at the screen and/or operate the touch screen (to select and share media) while simultaneously involved in a voice call (with an expectation of holding the device to the ear).

Results from phase 2 further confirmed that incorporating concurrent media sharing was likely to add significant value to wireless communications services. While there was a trend suggesting that adding *any* of the attributes tested would increase the value for users, concurrent voice and media sharing were the only individual attributes that significantly increased subjects' ratings. The other attributes, Presence and Group Calling, did not significantly increase subjects' value judgments. A second finding was that value for the service was inversely related to subjects' technology usage and awareness. As in phase 1, there were higher value judgments among low technology aware users. This also appeared to play a role in the results, interacting with gender. While females gave higher value judgments than did males (as found in phase 1), this effect was limited to subjects who were low in technology awareness, as measured by the TAQ.

These results could arise because individuals who do not use technology as much may consider more of the social implications of in-call media sharing than its value as a new technology. The interaction with gender also fits in with this hypothesis. This interaction may be influenced by males basing their judgments on the perceived usefulness of the technology for job performance [14]. Low technology-aware females, on the other hand, may primarily consider the social possibilities that would be afforded by the technology [14]. If this is the case, then the capability of enhancing social contacts could contribute positively to the value that these females place in the application. These conclusions about gender differences may also account for an interaction between gender and price. While females' average ratings for the free service were significantly higher than the males' ratings for the $10 service, their ratings for the $10 service did not significantly differ from the males' ratings for the free service. One possible conclusion from this result is that females are more willing than males to pay to receive the social benefits of this technology.

Overall, these results suggest that providing the capability of sharing media concurrently with a group voice call does enhance the value of mobile phone services for some users. However, this increased value may depend on those users' goals and it seems to provide added benefit mainly for users who are interested in using media content to supplement the social aspects of their communications. The results also suggest that more technologically sophisticated subjects may have been less impressed by the functional capabilities and that this led them to assign lower ratings.

Acknowledgments. Thanks are due to Prof. Sorin Matei and Wendy Zeitz-Anderson of Purdue University, IN, for undertaking the phase 1 data collection and analysis, and to Lynne Ferguson and Jim Wolf of Motorola Labs and the staff of Motorola Networks, Arlington Heights, IL, for permitting the use of the 3G test network for phase 2.

References

1. Bjorling, M.E, Carlsten, J., Kessler, P., Kruse, E., Stille, M.: Sharing Everyday Experiences. Ericsson Review No 1 (2006)
2. CDC EZ-Text; CDC Home: www.cdc.gov/hiv/software/ez-text.htm
3. Gough, P.J, Marlowe, C.: Cell Phone Video first from London Bombing Scene, Hollywood Reporter.com (8 July 2005) http://www.hollywoodreporter.com/thr/new_media/article_display.jsp?vnu_content_id=1000975698
4. IPSe Marketing Inc.: The Mobile Phone Morphs into Camera-equipped email Terminal, Online Report (Feb 21 2003) http://www.ipse-m.com/company/release/release_02_e.htm
5. Ito, M., Okabe, D.: Camera phones changing the definition of picture-worthy. Japan media Review, (29 August 2003) http://www.ojr.org/japan/wireless/1062208524.php
6. Kurvinen E.: Emotions in Action: A Case in Mobile Visual Communication. In: Proceedings of the Design + Emotion Conference, Loughborough, UK (1-3 July, 2002)
7. Lehtonen, T-K., Koskinen, I., Kurvinen, E.: Mobile Digital Pictures – The Future of the Postcard? Findings from an Experimental Field Study. In: Laakso, V., Östman J. Postcard in the Social Context. Korttien talo. Hämeenlinna (2002)

8. Matei, S., Zeitz-Anderson, W., Wheatley, D., Ferguson, L.: CEC/Ensembles User Requirements Study – Final Report, Motorola Internal Report (October 4, 2004)
9. Pering, T., Nguyen, D.H, Light, J., Want, R.: Face-to-Face Media Sharing Using Wireless Mobile Devices. In: Proc. Of 7th IEEE Int'l Symposium on Multimedia (ISM '05) (2005)
10. Sarvas, R., Viikari, M., Pesonen, J., Nevanlinna, H.: MobShare: Controlled and Immediate Sharing of Mobile Images. ACM Multimedia, New York (October 10-16, 2004)
11. Strategy Analytics, Camera Phone Sales Surge to 257 Million Units Worldwide in 2004 (April 14, 2005)
12. The Pitch: The Cameraphone could be the Next Little Big Thing, The Pitch: Special cameraphone Supplement, Issue 9.1 (December 2003) www.the-pitch.com
13. Twist, J.: Mobiles Capture Blast Aftermath. BBC News World Edition (8 July, 2005)
14. http://news.bbc.co.uk/2/hi/technology/4663561.stm
15. Venkatesh, V., Morris, M.G.: Why Don't Men Ever Stop to Ask for Directions?, Gender, Social Influence and their role in technology acceptance and usage behavior. MIS Quarterly 24(1), 115–139 (2000)

Customer-Dependent Storytelling Tool with Authoring and Viewing Functions

Sunhee Won[1], Miyoung Choi[2], Gyeyoung Kim[1], and Hyungil Choi[2]

[1] Department of Computer, Graduate school of Soongsil Univ. , Korea
[2] Department of Media, Graduate school of Soongsil Univ. , Korea
{nifty12,utopialove,gykim11,hic}@ssu.ac.kr

Abstract. The animation is the main content of the digital storytelling. It usually has the fixed number of characters. We want a customer to appear in the animation as a main character. For this purpose, we have developed the tool that helps to automatically implants facial shapes of a customer into the existing animation images. Our tool first takes an image of a customer and extracts out a face region and some valuable features that depicts the shape and facial expression of the customer. Our tool has the module that changes the existing character's face with that of the customer. This module employs the facial expression recognition and warping functions so that the customer's face fits into the confined region with the similar facial expression. Our tool also has the module that shows the sequence of images in the form of animation. This module employs the data compression function and produces the AVI format files and throws them into the graphic board.

Keywords: facial expression recognition, warping functions.

1 Introduction

Generally we divide to face recognition, facial feature extraction, face expression recognition work with human face. Facial feature extraction consists of face region extraction and face components (eyes, nose and mouth) extraction, facial feature extraction is earlier step of face recognition and face expression recognition, and facial feature extraction is very important part of research for human face. Human face is very sensitive to morphological changes as direction of human face (degree of frontal, either side), size of face image according to distance between camera and human face, and external changes as differences of face region's intensity for illumination, complex background or occlusion for other object. So research of face extraction has many difficulties and problems, and last until these days continuously make research in this field.

Method of analysis projection to extract the facial feature[4] that one way of the basic facial feature extraction divide into region using analysis of each element feature for x, y coordinate. This method has constraints as simple background and sensitive to rotation, so these constraints must be satisfied to get fine results. Second, method using deformable templates that make a template of become a target face and

J. Jacko (Ed.): Human-Computer Interaction, Part III, HCII 2007, LNCS 4552, pp. 1000–1009, 2007.

detect face as compare with input image. This method is robust for illumination change and background, but it has a weak point that sensitive to gradient, rotation angle in the change size of face or face direction along to distance and difficult to produce average templates include information of each person. Third, a method used in this paper that estimate energy of image, it defines that contour is minimum energy and energy function is spline curves. This measure is active contour model (snake) converged on contour of object through process of minimizing the energy from initial position of contour. It has merit that detect with activity for deformable object but it must be given initial function to detect a minimize direction and it is heavily influenced by object around noise. But background is very simple and initial position of snake point is previously given in our system, so we use active contour model (snake) that optimal algorithm to detect contour of human face and character face in animation.

After procedure of facial feature extraction, there is another very important step of image processing that warping for face expression. We can expression of character reflect in human face through control eyes and mouth, therefore apply warping function to eyes and mouth extracted from user image. Client can directly extract source line of eyes and mouth to execute the line warping used in our system using MER region of eyes and mouth. We use control points on source line to apply more accurate warping, each point is corresponding to point of destination line.

The system in this paper is implemented that extracted user face to apply warping function proper for character's expression using expression parameter, and then, automatically implants animation for multiple user's face through equal procedure.

The rest of the paper is organized as follows. In section 2, the system architecture is produced. In section 3, the algorithm used in this system (Snake and Line warping) is explained. The experiment results are analyzed in section 4. Finally, section 5 concludes the paper and points out the next research aspects.

2 System Architecture

This system is edit tool that helps to automatically implants facial shapes of a customer into the existing animation images. It is consists of total three modules as FaceExtracter, AniMaker, AviMaker. In next section, define that these modules.

2.1 FaceExtracter Module

This module consists of two modes that extract mode and edit mode follows by figure 2. First step, extract the face, eyes, and mouth components from input user image in extract mode. In our system, we use snake algorithm that contour detection algorithm for extract user face, and it defined at section 3.1. User directly select the snake initial point by click for extract face contour, maximally close to user face contour cause a defect of snake that it react sensitively by object around noise. Second step, the snake algorithm search for user face contour use this position of initial snake point, we make second mode that edit mode for case that search for unacceptable face contour. Customer can select the edit mode for color image or binary image, this mode consists of three functions as Move, Erase, Draw. Move function used in binary image, in case of snake point go astray cause snake energy function is influenced by noise, it function is moving that point by mouse controlled for right direction. We can obtained clearly and completely face contour by this function use. Erase function is a function that removes the unnecessary edges cause that if user image has too many edges in binary image, searching for inside or outside of actuality contour. Draw function is function that draw new edge for case of edge of actuality contour is weak. We can obtain more clearly face contour by these three functions, and can extract user face to use this contour.

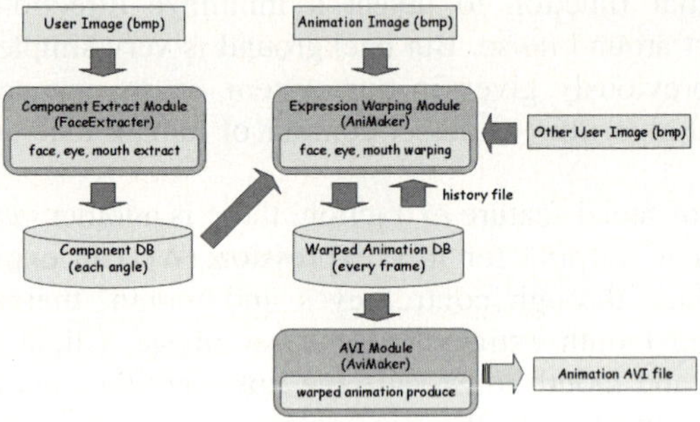

Fig. 1. System architecture – this system consist of total 3 modules as FaceExtracter, AniMaker, and AviMaker

After extract to user face, extract eyes and mouth components by use MER. Customer should draw MER maximally close to eyes and mouse for obtain natural warping result. And then, specify the angle of user face for tilt and panning. Next step for saving, saved that four components image files (.bmp) of extracted face, two eyes and mouth, information file of direction (.inf) and project file (.prj) at once. These files are important data for warping of user image in AniMaker.

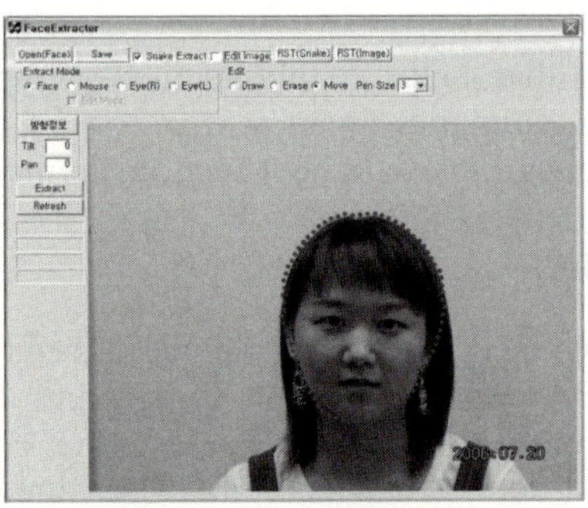

Fig. 2. FaceExtracter

2.2 AniMaker Module

This module is user face image extracted from FaceExtracter overlapping with each frame from animation. First, extract character's face using snake algorithm. But, at this time we need rather position of character's face than completely contour of character's face, so estimate a center of gravity from information of contour using snake algorithm. And then, user project file (.prj) accesses from user database and load user face model adjust to character's face angle. When customer want to change that user facial expression adjust to character's facial expression, customer can select to expression type of eyes and mouth. Eyes type can selected from five general expression type – "open", "close", "smile", "cry", "anger" , and mouth type can selected from four type – "Um", "A", "E", "U".

Fig. 3. AniMaker

User facial expression can make using these types and apply warp to extracted face, eyes, and mouth component image from FaceExtracter module, details of warping is explained in section 3.2.

After overlapping face and making facial expression, customer can control user face image adjust to size and angle of character's face for three functions – Move, Angle, Scale. First, customer can move user face using Move functions when use face out of line with position of character's face. Second, angle can controlled using Angle function when need to adjust the angle of user face. Third, customer can control the scale of user face using Scale function.

After apply warping with all steps, saved that transformed animation file (.bmp) and history file (.hist) for automate produce function at once in saving step. Apply warping with each frame go through previous all steps, if customer want that apply other user face image to same animation, then we make a skill that transformed animation is automatically produce function using user's history file without repetition of same stage. A history file for this skill has the information of snake point conclude to angle, size, and position, the information of type for expression of eyes and mouth, the information of user image file. Using this information can produce transformed animation for other user face image equal to previous user face image. If user face image is not fitted to animation image, customer can modify to position, size, angle in total animation with input the gap value in Move, Angle, Scale.

2.3 AviMaker Module

It is a module that make to actuality animation format of transformed animation image using AniMaker and general animation format is AVI using OpenCV library.

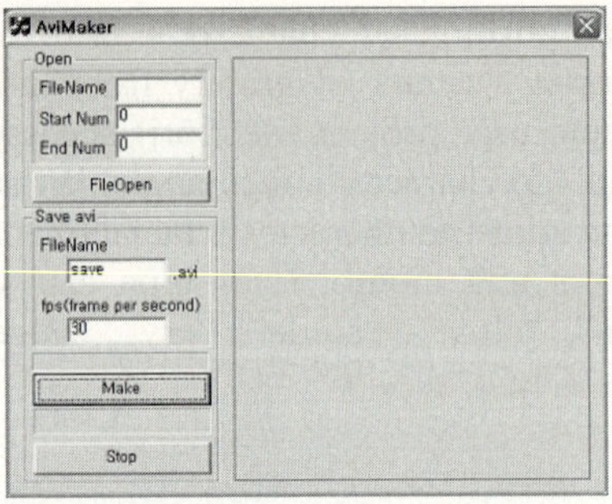

Fig. 3. AviMaker – input Last frame number, FileName, fps

This module produce to transformed animation file of AVI format with information of last frame number, filename, fps(frame per second). Follows figure 4. is a screen captured of AniMaker.

3 The Algorithm

In this section, explain implemented algorithm for our system. First, snake algorithm for extract to face contour explained in section 3.1 and warping algorithm for facial expression explained in section 3.2.

3.1 Active Contour Model (Snake) Algorithm

The active contour model algorithm, first introduced by Kass et al., deforms a contour to lock onto features of interest within in an image [3]. Usually the features are lines, edges, and/or object boundaries. Kass et al. named their algorithm, ``Snakes'' because the deformable contours resemble snakes as they move. A snake is defined as an energy function. To find the best fit between a snake and an object's shape, we minimize the energy follows by equation (1).

$$E^*_{snake} = \int_0^1 E_{snake}(v(s))ds = \int_0^1 \left[E_{\text{int}}(v(s)) + E_{image}(v(s)) + E_{con}(v(s))\right]ds \ . \tag{1}$$

Where the snake is parametrically defined as $v(s) = (x(s), y(s))$. $E_{\text{int}\,ernal}$ is a internal spline energy caused by stretching and bending, E_{image} measure of the attraction of image features such as contours, and E_{con} measure of external constraints either from higher level shape information or user applied energy. First, the internal energy provides a smoothness constraint. This can be further defined as equation (2).

$$E_{\text{int}} = \alpha(s)\left|\frac{dv}{ds}\right|^2 + \beta(s)\left|\frac{dv^2}{ds^2}\right|^2 \ . \tag{2}$$

$\alpha(s)$ is a measure of the elasticity and $\beta(s)$ is a measure of stiffness of the snake. The first order term makes the snake act like a membrane; the constant $\alpha(s)$ controls the tension along the spine (stretching a balloon or elastic band). The second order term makes the snake act like a thin plate; the constant β controls the rigidity of the spine (bending a thin plate or wire). If $\beta(s)=0$ then the function is discontinuous in its tangent, i.e. it may develop a corner at that point. If $\alpha(s)=\beta(s)=0$ then this also allows a break in the contour, a positional discontinuity.

The image energy is derived from the image data follows by equation (3). Considering a two dimensional image, the snake may be attracted to lines, edges or terminations.

$$E_{image} = \omega_{line} E_{line} + \omega_{edge} E_{edge} + \omega_{term} E_{term} \ . \tag{3}$$

ω_i is an appropriate weighting function. Commonly, the line functional is defined simply by the image function follows equation (4).

$$E_{line} = f(x, y) \ . \tag{4}$$

So that if ω_{line} is large positive the spline is attracted to light lines (or areas) and if large negative then it is attracted to dark lines (or areas). The use of the terminology ``line" is probably misleading.

The edge functional is defined by equation (5).

$$E_{edge} = \left|\nabla f(x, y)\right|^2 \ . \tag{5}$$

Hence, the spline is attracted to large image gradients. i.e. parts of the image with strong edges. Finally, the termination functional allows terminations (i.e. free ends of lines) or corners to attract the snake. The constraint energy is determined by external constraints. This energy my come in the form of a spring attached by the user. Or, the constraint energy may come from higher knowledge about the images in question.

3.2 Line Warping

In this section, explain the execution of warping using control line. First, estimate vertical crossing point between pixel and control line, use displacement information of between pixel and vertical crossing point and position of vertical crossing point on control line, and then execute warping using reverse mapping. Figure 4, control line PQ in destination image is corresponding to control line P'Q', and pixel V in destination image copy to pixel V' in source image. For estimate the position of pixel V' by reverse mapping, search for position of C' in P'Q and search for pixel V' far from C' as displacement of between C and V.

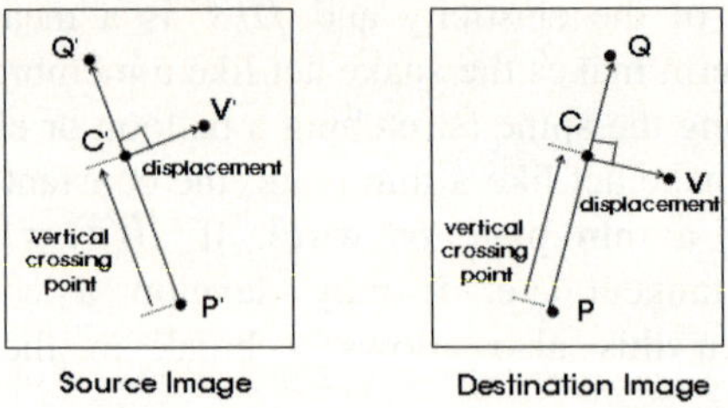

Fig. 4. Information for execute warping using control line

In case of multiple control line, follows algorithm of warping function to estimate each pixel in destination image corresponding to pixel in source image.

```
warping(){
        each pixel v(x, y) of output image,{
            tx = 0          // sum of x coordinate displacement is initialized.
            ty = 0          // sum of y coordinate displacement is initialized.
            each control line L_i ,{
              estimate the vertical crossing point u of V and L_i .
              estimate the vertical displacement of V and L_i .
              get a corresponding position v'(x', y') of input image using u and h .
              estimate the distance d of V and L_i .
                Error! Objects cannot be created from editing field codes.
                Error! Objects cannot be created from editing field codes.
              }
              Error! Objects cannot be created from editing field codes.
            make a copy of pixel v'(x', y') to pixel v(x, y) .
        }
}
```

First step in warping function, estimate the position of vertical crossing point with each control line L_i for each pixel $v(x, y)$ in destination image. Suppose to u is distance of vertical crossing point $C(x_c, y_c)$ from end point $P(x_i, y_i)$ of L_i , value of u can estimated by equation (6).

$$u = \frac{(x - x_i)(x_{i+1} - x_i) + (y - y_i)(y_{i+1} - y_i)}{(x_{i+1} - x_i)^2 + (y_{i+1} - y_i)^2} \ . \tag{6}$$

Second step, estimate the vertical displacement h from each control line L_i for pixel $v(x, y)$ in destination image. Formulation of displacement h follows by equation (7).

$$h = \frac{(y - y_i)(x_{i+1} - x_i) - (x - x_i)(y_{i+1} - y_i)}{\sqrt{(x_{i+1} - x_i)^2 + (y_{i+1} - y_i)^2}} \ . \tag{7}$$

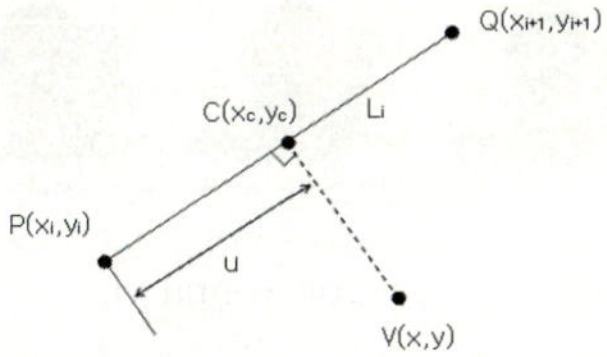

Fig. 5. Vertical crossing point between pixel *V* and control line *Li*

Third step, search for pixel $v'(x',y')$ in source image corresponding to $v(x,y)$ in destination image using u and h. Suppose to either side end point of control line L_i' in source image corresponding to control line L_i in destination image is (x_i',y_i') and (x_{i+1}',y_{i+1}'), $v'(x',y')$ can estimated by equation (8).

$$x' = x_i' + u\times(x_{i+1}'-x_i') - \frac{h\times(y_{i+1}'-y_i')}{\sqrt{(x_{i+1}'-x_i')^2+(y_{i+1}'-y_i')^2}} \; . \qquad (8)$$
$$y' = y_i' + u\times(y_{i+1}'-y_i') + \frac{h\times(x_{i+1}'-x_i')}{\sqrt{(x_{i+1}'-x_i')^2+(y_{i+1}'-y_i')^2}}$$

Final step, distance d between pixel and control line can estimated follows by equation (9).

$$d = \begin{cases} \sqrt{(x-x_i)^2+(y-y_i)^2} \\ \sqrt{(x-x_{i+1})^2+(y-y_{i+1})^2} \\ h \end{cases} . \qquad (9)$$

4 Experiment Result

In this paper, extract user's face, eyes, and mouth of facial feature from animation image and transform user's facial expression adjust to character's facial expression. We use animation that has simply character face and no great change of expression. Also, we experiment with the style of user's hair is very simple, background is not complex and filmed at various direction. User's face direction is left, right, up, and down in the range of $\pm$45 degrees of an angle, and all images are opened eyes and closed mouth.

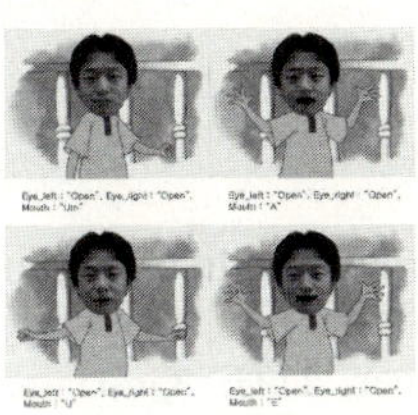

Fig. 6. Change of mouth for frontal view – "Um", "A", "U", "E"

Fig. 7. Change of eyes for frontal view – close, open

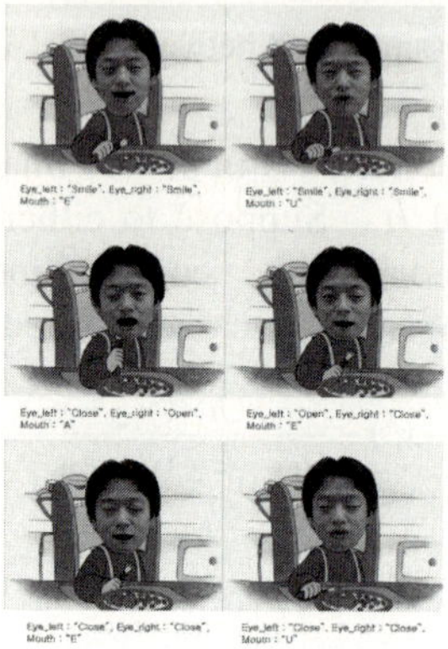

Fig. 8. Change of eyes and mouth for frontal view – various facial expressions

Figure 6 is experiment result that selected opened eyes and changed mouth. Mouth expression type is "Um", "A", "U", "E" as Korean pronunciation, we can see that facial expression is presented only use changing shape of mouth. On the contrary, figure 7 is experiment result that presented only use changing shape of eyes and also figure 8 is presented by changing shape of eyes and mouth.

5 Conclusion

In this paper basically extract to user's face and character's face using snake algorithm and automatically produce transformed user facial expression adjust to character's facial expression in animation. We read up on completely extract of facial feature for more natural facial expression and robust about facial warping at various direction.

Acknowledgments. This work was supported by the Korea Science and Engineering Foundation (KOSEF) through the Advanced Information Technology Research Centerm (AItrc).

References

1. Cootes, T.F., Taylor, C.J.: Active Shape Models - Smart Snakes. In: Proc. British Machine Vision Conference, pp. 266–275 (1992)
2. Cootes, T.F., Taylor, C.J., Cooper, D.H., GraHam, J.: Active Shape Models - Theirs Training and Application. Computer Vision and Image Understanding 61(1), 38–59 (1995)
3. Kass, M., Witkin, A., Terzopoulus, D.: Snakes: Active Contour Models. Internation Journal of Computer Vision 1(4), 321–331 (1987)

4. Garcia, G., Vicente, C.: Face Detection on Still Images Using HIT Maps. In: Bigun, J., Smeraldi, F. (eds.) AVBPA 2001. LNCS, vol. 2091, pp. 102–107. Springer, Heidelberg (2001)
5. Sun, D., Wu, L.: Face Boundary Extraction by Statistical Constraint Active Contour Model. In: IEEE Int. Conf. Neural Networks and Signal Processing, China (December 14-17, 2003)
6. Wan, K-W.: An accurate active shape model for facial feature extraction. Pattern Recognition Letters 26, 2409–2423 (2005)
7. Du, Y., Lin, X.: Emotional facial expression model building. Pattern Recognition Letters 24, 2923–2934 (2003)
8. Mukaigawa, Y., Nakamura, Y., Ohta, Y.: Face synthesis with arbitrary pose and expression from several images – an integration of image-based and model-based approaches. In: Proc. of Asian Conference on Computer Vision, pp. 680–687 (1998)

Reliable Partner System Always Providing Users with Companionship Through Video Streaming

Takumi Yamaguchi[1], Kazunori Shimamura[2], and Haruya Shiba[1]

[1] Kochi National College of Technology, 200-1 Monobe, Nankoku, Kochi 783-8508, Japan
yama@ee.kochi-ct.ac.jp, shiba@ee.kochi-ct.ac.jp
[2] Kochi University of Technology, 185 Miyanokuchi, Tosayamada, Kami-gun, Kochi 782-8502, Japan
shimamura.kazunori@kochi-tech.ac.jp

Abstract. This paper presents a basic configuration of a system that provides dynamic delivery of full-motion video while following target users in ubiquitous computing environments. The proposed system is composed of multiple computer displays with radio frequency identification (RFID) tag readers, which are automatically connected to a network via IP, and RFID tags worn by users and some network servers. We adopted a passive tag RFID system. The delivery of full-motion video uses adaptive broadcasting. The system can continuously deliver streaming data, such as full-motion video, to the display, through the database and the streaming server on the network, moving from one display to the next as the user moves through the network. Because it maintains the information about the user's location in real time, it supports the user wherever he or she is, without requiring a conscious request to obtain their information. This paper describes a prototype implementation of this framework and a practical application.

Keywords: Ubiquitous, Partner system, Video streaming, Awareness.

1 Introduction

As information technology (IT) developed, it provided attractive new uses of information resources, making them available in all areas of people's lives. Its application is expanding to all of our daily lives through information appliances, such as mobile computing environments and home electric appliances. As computers and networked environment have become popular in homes, various home appliances need to be organically connected through a network. Consequently, information appliances will offer high performance, and more functions.

As Mark Weiser [1] envisioned, the goal of ubiquitous computing is to provide various services by making multiple computers available throughout the physical environment, but, in effect, making them invisible to the user.

Perceptual technologies have made it possible to detect the presence or positions of people, as well as any other object we care to think about. Context-awareness, particularly user- and location-awareness, is becoming an essential feature of services that assist our everyday lives in ubiquitous computing environments.

J. Jacko (Ed.): Human-Computer Interaction, Part III, HCII 2007, LNCS 4552, pp. 1010–1018, 2007.

Several researchers have explored location-aware services [2][3]. The existing services can be classified into two approaches. The first type uses computing devices that move with the user. This approach often assumes that such devices are attached to positioning systems, such as global positioning system (GPS) receivers, which enable them to determine their own location. For example, in Hewlett-Packard's Cooltown project [4], mobile computing devices, such as personal digital assistants (PDAs) and smart phones, are attached to GPSs to provide location-awareness for web-based applications running on the devices.

The second approach assumes that the physical space is equipped with tracking systems which establish the location of physical entities, including people and objects, within the space. This allows the system to provide application-specific services to appropriate computers. A typical example is the follow-me application, developed by Cambridge University's Sentient Computing project [5], to support ubiquitous and personalized services on computers located near users.

In related work, a general infrastructure and framework was proposed to seamlessly integrate the assembly and management of the application in ubiquitous computing by applying an agent in mobile computing [3][6]. They presented several typical location-based services developed using this infrastructure. For instance, they implemented "personalized services anywhere," which is an agent system that provides a desktop teleporting system using a radio frequency identification (RFID) system. In addition, they developed a mobile window manager, which is a mobile agent that can carry complete desktop applications to another computer and controls the size, position, and overlap of the application windows.

In this paper, we focus on the delivery of full-motion video to a user moving through an environment.

Existing systems deliver full-motion video to a computer display, by recognizing a RFID tag that is registered beforehand with the system. However, no system exists that can seamlessly deliver full-motion video to multiple computer displays within a network, while following user's movement. This paper presents a basic configuration and implementation of such a system. The proposed system is composed of a computer display with an attached RFID-tag reader, which automatically connects to the network via an IP, and RFID tags on the users, and also on some network servers. We adopted a passive-tag RFID system.

The delivery of full-motion video uses adaptive broadcasting. Using a database server and a streaming server, the system continuously delivers streaming data as full-motion video to the display nearest to the user as he or she moves past displays on the network. We also discuss a system that delivers each video to several users simultaneously. We investigate how to display multiple data streams at the same time on a single system without confusing the user. In addition, we implement an application that allows multiple users to get desired information, including videos, on demand.

This makes it possible to support the user automatically, regardless of where he or she moves throughout the network. We would like to study the configuration of a new interaction.

We would like to describe the configuration of a new interaction system by adding entities like honey, family pet and angel, etc. This system is an ambient human interface system, which becomes friendly advisers and gives users naturally awareness, through making real images via a network to follow users. We will expect to propose a human interface system of a user-oriented ubiquitous computing through implementing this system.

2 Approach

This section describes a realistic scenario for providing dynamic delivery of full-motion video in ubiquitous computing environments. Our goal is room- and building-wide deployment of our system. It is almost impossible to deploy and administer a system in a scalable way when the control and management functions are centralized. Thus, our software system consists of multiple servers, which are connected to individual servers in a peer-to-peer manner. At least one streaming and one database server are necessary for implementing the system. The database server maintains up-to-date layer information on the tag identifiers [7].

2.1 Delivery Procedure for Reliable Partner System

In this section, the procedure involved in delivering a streaming digital media to the target host is described. Fig. 1 shows our system, which allocates RFID-tagged users, and a number of target hosts with attached RFID tag readers. When an RFID-tagged user enters a reader's coverage area, the unique RFID identification tag is authenticated through the database server, and the streaming digital media is delivered to the display of the target host in the area of the RFID tag reader. If the RFID-tagged user moves, the streaming delivery migrates to the appropriate target host within the same coverage area to offer services to the same user.

The streaming server is notified of the IP address of the target host by the RFID tag and the database server. If the target ID is already registered in the database, the registered address is returned to the target host.

When the target host receives the address, it demands the data stream from the streaming server. This begins the broadcast delivery from the streaming server. The broadcast streams in real time to the appropriate target host.

Broadcast delivery is different from unicast delivery in that it is transmitted like the terrestrial television. Consequently, there is no time lag in the animation reproduction time even if the streaming data migrates from one target host to another. Thus, it is possible to deliver animation seamlessly.

2.2 Network Composition

To consider the dynamic delivery of full-motion videos, it is necessary to analyze the network composition to ensure that the load is distributed. This section reviews a computing system and a network topology for implementing our proposed delivery system.

To avoid concentrating the load on the server, this system is configured as a decentralized P2P computing system. The composition of the overall topology is pure P2P, however, when other peer (client) is retrieved, pure P2P wastes time to discover the target peer. Adding an index-server, creates a hybrid P2P system, which solves this problem and greatly decreases the retrieval time.

The peer that provides this function is called the "entrusted host". This host allocates and manages a unique ID on the P2P network that is different from its IP address. Here, we would like to consider when the host comes off the P2P network. Although only the client peer is excluded from the network, it causes the P2P network to collapse. This system entrusts the function of the host to another peer when the host comes off the P2P network, and conveys the new host's IP address to all other peers. The peer that received new host's address creates a new P2P network.

Next, the network topology of our proposed delivery system is considered.

Servers and peer hosts may be dynamically deployed and may frequently shut down. To make the network extensible, we apply the network design clarified by Tanizawa [8] that optimizes network robustness.

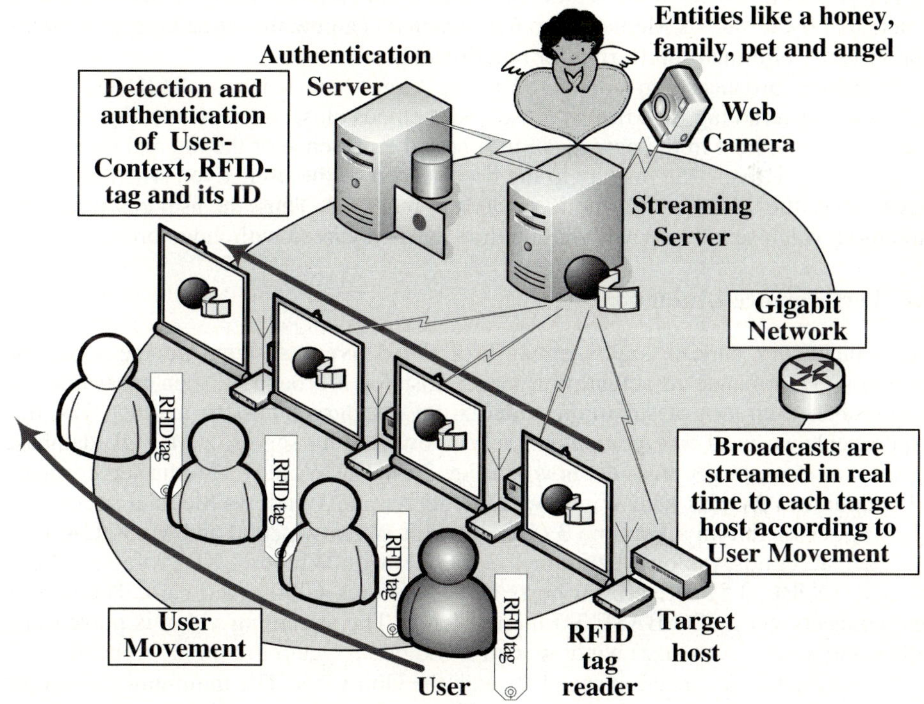

Fig. 1. Basic configuration of Reliable Partner System providing users with companionship through dynamic delivery of full-motion video

3 Implementation

The system presented in this paper was implemented in Microsoft Visual Basic .NET framework version 1.1 or later versions, including Phidget SDK, in particular, the Phidget [9] software components. This section discusses some features of the current implementation.

3.1 Prototype

The current implementation uses the Phidget RFID tag reader and its tags: 125 kHz RFID-tag system, using the universal serial bus (USB). Phidgets are an easy-to-use set of building blocks for low-cost sensing and can be controlled from a PC. Using the USB as the basis for all Phidgets, allows management with a simple and robust application programming interface (API). Applications can be developed quickly in Visual Basic.

Additionally the database realizing the user's authentication and the address reference of the streaming server used MySQL database.

After completing user authentication, the target host requests for the delivery of animation from the streaming server.

The streaming server used Windows Server 2003 and Windows Media 9 Series. It is actuated by Windows Media streaming, which has a new fast-streaming technology that virtually eliminates buffering for broadband hosts.

Therefore, broadcasts are delivered to the target host when its RFID tag reader senses a registered tag ID worn by a user, who comes close, as shown in Fig. 2. If the user moves, the host in the new location senses the presence of the tag and the system continuously delivers the display to the host nearest to the user. Even when changing target hosts, the user sees full-motion videos in real time. Thus, the user can watch the streaming video seamlessly without the time lags associated with video broadcasting.

3.2 Performance Evaluation

To evaluate our current implementation of the delivery system, we measured the system's performance in actuating a target host for a broadcast, then measured the response in migrating a streaming video from one target host to another. For this experiment, we used five computers: a Windows Media server, a MySQL database server, and three target hosts as shown in Fig. 2(a). The Windows Media server ran on a Pentium 4 (2.8 GHz) with Windows 2003 Server and Windows Media 9 series. The MySQL server ran on a Pentium 3 (1 GHz) with Windows 2000 and MySQL 4.0.21-nt. Each target host ran on a Pentium 4 (2.8 GHz) with Windows XP Professional and MySQL ODBC 3.51 Driver. All hosts had a GeForce 6200 video card. The system interconnects via a 1000BASE-T Ethernet LAN. The streaming video is played in a 640 × 480-pixel (VGA size) window with a "Logicool Qcam Pro 4000" webcam.

We verified the connection speed through the Gbit LAN. The minimum throughput speed between the server and a host was 170 megabit per second (Mbps).

We measured the time lag before a target host's actuation. The latency from reading a RFID tag to passing a streaming server's IP address to a target host was 20 to 30 ms and the latency of the Windows Media Player's connection between a streaming server and a target host over a TCP connection was 180 ms. Thus, the total time for system actuation and migration is 210 ms. This latency corresponds to a normal human walking speed.

3.3 Subjective Evaluation

As shown in Fig. 2(b), we have also implemented more practical prototype system of the same specification as Fig. 2(a). We carried out a questionnaire survey to

(a) Configuration of prototype model

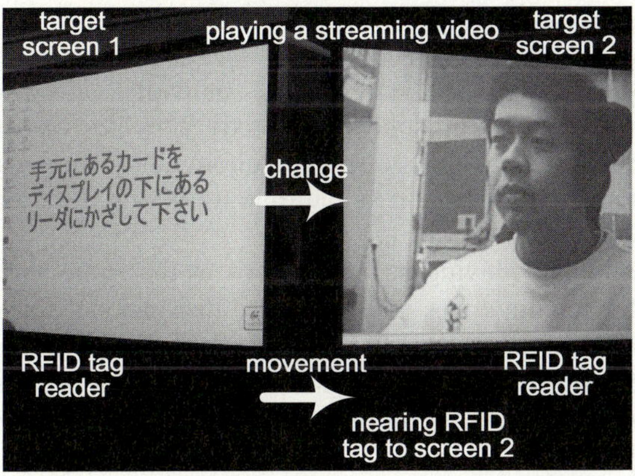

(b) Experimental model using 60-inch screen

Fig. 2. Overview of prototype system and its image that we see through display units, namely, Fig. 2(a) shows the prototype system consisted of three PC displays, Fig. 2(b) shows the experimental prototype system consisted of two 60-inch screens

investigate the subjective impression of the prototype system. Test subjects are 10 students of the department of electrical engineering in their twenties. The subjects in their twenties are experienced in the PC operations in their daily life.

The experiment was conducted on two PC-class desktop computers laying side-by-side with a 60-inch screen as shown in Fig. 2(b). We explained and demonstrated how to use the prototype system for the subjects before they filled out the questionnaire. After that, questionnaires on the subjective impression were evaluated in a five category rating scale where: Better=5, Slightly better=4, Fair=3, Slightly worse=2, Worse=1.

Table 1 indicates the results of the questionnaire. The category judgments in Table 1 calculated as a mean score shown on a scale of 1 to 5 and its standard deviation (SD).

Subjects' rating of the visual clarity of objects, the realism as user following and the system response was quite high with 4.2 points or more. On the other hand, subjects' rating of the presence as entities and their interest level of this system was not so high about 3 points or less. So the evaluated value of the prototype system for these users might prove greater with more familiarity and experience with this system.

Table 1. Results of questionnaire

Items	Mean score	SD
Visual clarity of objects	4.2	0.98
Realism as user following	4.4	1.0
System response	4.2	0.69
Presence as entities	2.9	0.94
Interest level of this system	3.3	1.1

3.4 Delivering for Several Users

In this section, we discuss a system that delivers video for several users simultaneously on a common display. We study how to simultaneously display multiple data streams on a single display without confusing users. We are also implementing an application that allows multiple users to request and receive desired information, including videos.

The current method of playing several videos at the same time is to divide the screen into multiple viewing areas, and uses three-dimensional space. However, there is no system capable of providing each video to each user on the same display. Moreover, the interaction between each user and the videos becomes unnatural. If a video corresponding to each user can play without the need for dividing the display, we would have an effective tool to interactively share one display space. We look at flip books (i.e. a cut-off animation) as a way of obtaining this interaction.

In general, you can make a flipbook with a pad of paper. Rendering a still image on a screen, at regular time intervals, works the same way, which creates a flipbook that works similar to GIF animation. In this way, we can consider the possibilities of playing several videos at the same time on the same display. Alternately, rendering several still images at regular time intervals is similar to time-division multiplexing. Through time-sharing, one still image of each video can alternate with others, each using the whole display. Although a frame rate of animations decreases only a number of multiplexed images, different animations can be looked like overlapping each animation. It appears that a frame rate of 15 fps or more could work.

4 Conclusions and Further Work

In this paper, we have proposed a system configuration for providing dynamic delivery of full-motion video to mobile users, by using RFID-based tracking systems. The system detects the user location and delivers a streaming video.

With an RFID tracking system and RFID tag-layer architecture, the system can track the location and environment of target hosts or the devices. In addition, this system responds adaptively to the environment for various user supports.

The implementation and experimental results indicate that it is possible to continuously deliver streaming data as full-motion video over the network, through the database server and the streaming server. Further experiments to validate system performance determined a lag time (response time) that corresponds to a person's normal walking speed.

Also, we investigated users' impression about the prototype system through the subjective evaluation experiment. While the subjects evaluated the prototype system as more effective, they feel that the presence of the displayed image as entities is not enough.

We need to implement a more actual and effective application system, and propose a more simple and adaptable support-model as a service for context-awareness applications. As a related application, there is a system that projects an advertisement onto a full window of a running subway car. It uses a special display on the subway tunnel's wall [10]. Although it is quite different from the approach presented in this paper, it might give us some pointers.

We would like to further study the configuration of a new interaction system by adding entities. This system is an ambient human interface system, which becomes friendly advisers and gives users naturally awareness, through making real images via a network to follow users. We would like to expect to realize ambient human interface system of a user-oriented ubiquitous computing through implementing this system.

This study is supported by the Telecommunications Advancement Foundation. In addition, this work was partially supported by the Shikoku JGN2 research center of National Institute of Information and Communications Technology (NICT). This work investigates a scheme of User Interfaces in ubiquitous environments.

We thank T.Yanahiro, R.Taniwaki for their helpful discussions and experiments and Shimamura, Lab staff, and Dr. T.Tanizawa of Kochi National College of Technology for their support.

References

1. Weiser, M.: The Computer for the 21st Century, Scientific American, pp. 94–104 (1991)
2. Yamada, S., Kamioka, E.: An Overview of Researches on Ubiquitous Computing Networks. NII Journal (in Japanese) 5, 41–47 (2003)
3. Satoh, I.: Linking Physical Worlds to Logical Worlds with Mobile Agents. In: Proceedings of International Conference on Mobile Data Management (MDM 2004), IEEE Computer Society, pp. 332–343 (2004)
4. Kindberg, T., et al.: People, Places, Things: Web Presence for the Real World, Technical report hpl-2000-16, HP Laboratories (2000)
5. Harter, A., Hopper, A., Steggeles, P., Ward, A., Webster, P.: The Anatomy of a Context-Aware Application. In: Proceedings of Conference on Mobile Computing and Networking (MOBICOM'99), pp. 59–68. ACM Press, New York (1999)
6. Satoh, I.: Physical Mobility and Logical Mobility in Ubiquitous Computing Environments. In: Suri, N. (ed.) MA 2002. LNCS, vol. 2535, pp. 186–202. Springer, Heidelberg (2002)

7. Takahashi, S., Akamatsu, J., Yamaguchi, T., Shimamura, K.: An AV file repeated delivery using plural cooperable passive RFIDs based on a layered data architecture. In: Proceedings of the IEICE General Conference (in Japanese), p. 305 (2004)
8. Tanizawa, T., Paul, G., Havlin, S., Stanley, H.E.: Optimization of the Robustness of Multimodal Networks. Phys. Rev. E 74, 020608 (2006)
9. Phidgets, INC.: http://www.phidgetsusa.com/
10. Submedia, LLC.: http://www.sub-media.com/

Modeling of Places Based on Feature Distribution

Yi Hu[1], Chang Woo Lee[1], Jong Yeol Yang[2], and Bum Joo Shin[3,*]

[1] Dept. of Computer Information Science,
Kunsan National University, S. Korea
{sharpoo7,leecw}@kunsan.ac.kr
[2] Dept. of Media, Soongsil University, S. Korea
jryang@atsolution.co.kr
[3] Dept. of Bio-Systems, Pusan National University, S. Korea
bjshin@pusan.ac.kr

Abstract. In this paper, a place model based on a feature distribution is proposed for place recognition. In many previous proposed methods, places are modeled as images or a set of extracted features. In those methods, a database of images or feature sets should be built. The cost of search time will grow exponentially when the database goes large. The proposed feature distribution method uses global information of each place and the search space grows linearly according to the number of places. In the experiments, we evaluate the performance using different number of frames and features for the recognition each time. Additionally, we have shown that the proposed method is applicable to many real-time applications such as robot navigation, wearable computing systems, and so on.

1 Introduction

We have a dream that all the housework can be done by a robot. Then the most basic ability that the robot should have is to recognize a where it is. A lot of work has been done in this area. Some author use color information [1] and artificial landmarks [2] to achieve the task. The drawback of these methods is that the color information is not distinguishable and the artificial landmarks need to be pinned in the place by people. More popular method is based on the natural features exploited in the scene and recognizing the place by image retrieval methods [3], [4], [5], [6]. These methods create a database of images or feature sets represent places and use feature match methods to recognize a place. In additional, some authors combine voting or statistical method to achieve higher accuracy [3], [4], [5], [6], [17], [18]. These methods need a database to store the labeled features for matching, the drawback is that the size of database will go large with the number of places, and the matching time will be longer.

In this paper, we propose a method to model a place using the distribution of the interest features. There are a mass of features in each place, and each place contains different distribution of features, for example, place A contains more white points than place B but contains less black lines. So if we observe several white points, the

[*] Corresponding author.

J. Jacko (Ed.): Human-Computer Interaction, Part III, HCII 2007, LNCS 4552, pp. 1019–1027, 2007.

probability that we are in place A is higher. Based on this idea, good interest features are important in modeling the place. Among the interest feature detectors, Harris interest point detector [7] is shown to be high repeatability and stable but is not invariant to scale and affine transformations [8]. To achieve scale invariant, scale-space theory is deeply studied in [9] and several detectors [10], [11], [12], 13] is proposed based on scale-space. Among the invariant features, evaluations [7], [14], [15], [16] have shown that the Harris-Laplacian detector attains best performance and SIFT [13] descriptor is the best descriptor. So Harris-Laplacian detector and SIFT descriptor is adopt in our approach.

The distribution of interest features are built by using a histogram method and later a Bayesian method [22] is applied for recognition. The paper is organized as follow: Our proposed approach will be introduced in section 2, in section 3, the experimental result is presented and the conclusion is in section 4.

2 Our Proposed Method

We consider the distribution of interest features to model a place. The idea is motivated from the text classification [23] where the distribution of the words in a category of documents is estimated. In practice, this is done by creating a histogram of features. The features are detected and extracted from the images which are captured from the places. To get the size of the histogram, the features are divided into limited types, k, for instance. Here we call a feature type as a "key feature". In other words, we build a dictionary containing k words with each word represents a "key feature". For each place, a histogram is generated by learning from the training data. In recognition, a Bayesian method is used to calculate the probabilities that a set of observed features fit to the models.

2.1 Interest Features

The interest features are salient regions in the image that contain several important characteristics such as high repeatability and contain rich information, for instance, corners. Interest features have been proved useful in matching and recognition tasks as they are robust to several image transformations such as scaling, rotation and partially illumination changes and 3D projection [16], [19], [20]. The features used in our model is first detected using Harris-Laplacian detector and then descriptors are generated from the small region centered in the corners' position in the same manner of the SIFT [13].

The Harris-Laplacian detector contains three main steps:

1. *A scale-space is built by smoothing the input image with different Gaussian kernels,* $\sigma_n = s^n * \sigma_0$ *, where* σ_0 *is the initial sigma of the Gaussian kernels to smooth the first level image and s is a scale factor between successive levels of the scale-space (suggested be 1.4) [21].*
2. *For each image in the scale-space, detect candidate points using Harris detector [7]. In experiment, we use a function cvGoodFeatureToTrack in the OpenCV library[24] to detect the Harris corners.*

3. *Accept the candidate points as feature point that the response of the normalized Laplacian of Gaussian (LoG) is local maxima between neighbor scales*:

$$LoG_{norm}(x, y, \sigma_n) = \sigma_n^{\;2} \cdot \left| I_{xx}(x, y, \sigma_n) + I_{yy}(x, y, \sigma_n) \right| \tag{1}$$

In Eq. 1, LoG_{norm} is the normalized Laplacian of Gaussian function, I_{xx} and I_{yy} denote the second derivatives of the image intensity and σ_n is the sigma corresponds to the image in scale space.

After detection step, the features should be extracted for measurement. This is done by using the same method of generating SIFT descriptors [13], witch is evaluated to be much better than other descriptors, such as gray grid [15], [18]. Finally, all the patches are converted to 128 dimensional vectors.

2.2 Build Feature Dictionary

To make the feature distribution histogram to model the places, we should select a limited number of "key features" to act as the index of the histogram. Then all the features will be labeled as one of the "key feature" and we can count the number of each "key feature" to make the feature distribution histogram.

To build dictionary, a clustering method, k-means, is employed. The distance measurement is squared Euclidian distance. This method first chooses k initial cluster centers randomly and then iterates two steps till a terminate condition is satisfied: 1) Assignments all the points to their nearest center. 2) Compute the clusters centers again.

One problem of using k-means is that k is difficult to choose. Here we test different k to find a proper value. We had tested k as 100, 500 and 1000 and found that when k is 1000 the system gets a very good performance. So k is set to 1000.

Another problem is that it's not easy to define the terminate condition of the k-means. In experiment, we ran the k-means by 200 iterations and got the performance that satisfy us.

The data for clustering is a large set of features which are collected from large number images from the places. The aim is to cover the feature space as more as possible. After building the feature dictionary, 1000 "key features" is obtained and we denote them as $C = \{c_1, c_2, \ldots, c_{1000}\}$.

2.3 Model the Places

We model a place as a feature distribution histogram which contains k bins corresponding to the k "key features" obtained in the section above. To model a place, ω, for instance, a set of training data should be collected. The training data is a set of features extracted from the images belonging to the place to be modeled. We denote the training data as *D*.

The first step is feature labeling. All the features $d \in D$ is labeled as one of the "key features". The labeling is done by comparing a feature in *D* with all the "key features" and labeling the feature as the nearest "key feature".

Then we can make the histogram. Suppose there are h_j features in D are labeled as c_j, then the j'th bin of the histogram is:

$$P(c_j \mid \omega) = \frac{h_j}{|D|}, \tag{2}$$

where $|D|$ denotes the total number of features in D.

In order to avoid the value $p(c_j|\omega)$ of zero, A simple Laplacian smoothing is used:

$$P(c_j \mid \omega) = \frac{h_j + 1}{|D| + k} \tag{3}$$

Thus, for the place ω we generate a feature distribution histogram with k bins and k is 1000 from above section. Fig.1. shows the example of the histogram from one of the places in our experiment. For all the places, make the histograms.

Further more, each value of the histogram bins are thresholded to be no large than 0.02. For example, $P(c_j| \omega = \omega_m) >> P(c_j| \omega = \omega_n)$, then a feature labeled with c_j appeared in place ω_n may be recognized as from place ω_m.

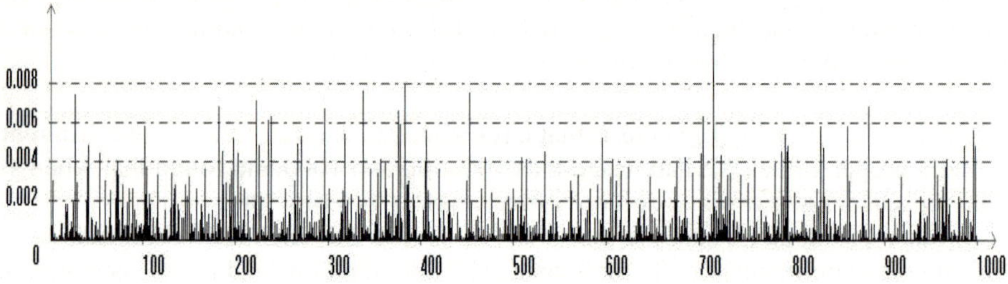

Fig. 1. Example of the feature distribution histogram

2.4 Place Recognition Using the Feature Distribution Model

In recognition step, images are captured from a testing place using PC camera. We want to recognize the place by analyzing the images. First, features detected and extract from the images using the method in section 2.1. We denote the features as X. Then the features are labeled to "key features" in the same manner as described in section 2.3. For example, there are $N(j)$ features which is labeled as c_j in key feature dictionary. Then, Naive Bayesian classifier [22] is adopted. From the Bayesian rule:

$$P(\omega \mid X) = \frac{P(X \mid \omega) \cdot P(\omega)}{P(X)} \tag{4}$$

We can omit $P(X)$ which acts as a normalizing constant. $P(\omega)$ is a prior probability which means the probability that each place will appear, it does not take into account any information about X and in our system all places will be appeared with same probability. So we can focus on the $P(X|\omega)$ and rewrite term (4) as:

$$P(\omega \mid X) = \alpha \cdot P(X \mid \omega), \tag{5}$$

where α is normalizing constant.

From the Naive Bayesian classifier "naive" assumption that the observed data are conditionally independent, so the term (5) can be rewritten as:

$$P(\omega \mid X) = \alpha \cdot \prod_{j=1}^{|X|} P(x_j \mid \omega), \tag{6}$$

where $|X|$ denotes the size of the feature set X.

Since the features X is labeled with "key features", and the histogram approximately represents the probability distribution of the features. We replace the feature X by the "key features" C, then term (6) can to rewritten as:

$$P(\omega \mid X) = \alpha \cdot \prod_{j=1}^{k} P(c_j | \omega)^{N(j)} \tag{7}$$

To avoid the value of $P(\omega|X)$ be too small, We take the logarithmic measurement of the $P(\omega|X)$:

$$\log P(\omega \mid X) = \log \alpha + \sum_{j=1}^{k} N_j \cdot \log P(c_j \mid \omega) \tag{8}$$

For all the places, calculate the probability $P(\omega=\omega_i \mid X)$. Then we recognize the place as its posterior probability takes maxima among all the places.

$$Classify(X) = \arg\max_i \{\log P(\omega = \omega_i \mid X)\} \tag{9}$$

3 Experimental Results

The dataset for the training was a set of frames captured over 6 places. Each frame has the size of 320x240. In the recognition step, we took a laptop shipped with a PC camera walking around the places. The application system analyzes the captured images and output the recognition result.

From Bayesian rule, we know that the size of the observed data affects the posterior probability. If more data can be used as observed data, generally more trustable result can be obtained. The limitation is that the data should be from one place. As shown in Fig. 2, the data is from lab 3407 and the x-axis means frame number and the y-axis means the posterior probability which the value was scaled up for visualization, but dose not affect the result. When there are more frames as observed data, the posterior probability of the places will be separated more which means the result is more confident.

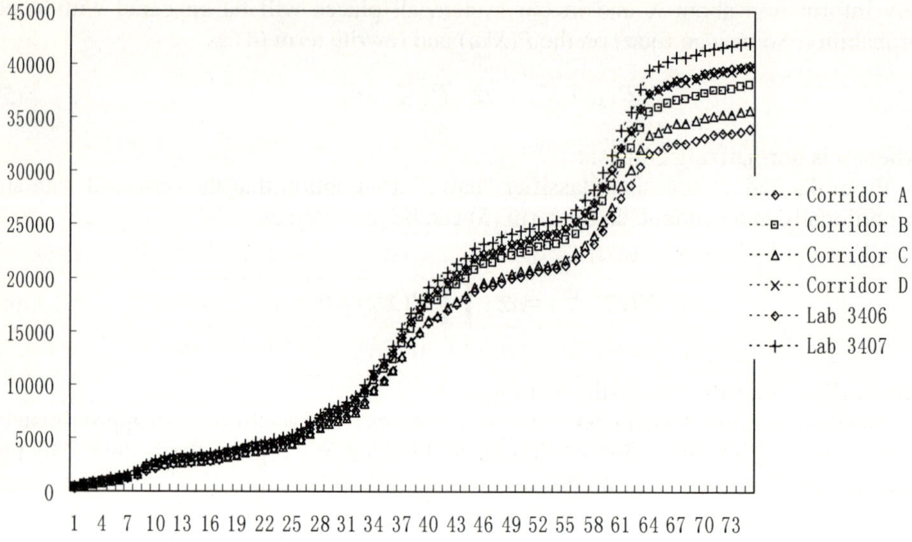

Fig. 2. Posterior probability in different frames

Then, we evaluate the recognition performance using different number of frames for recognition each time. As shown in Table 1, we test the performance in separated places. If we recognize the place by every frame, the correct rate will be a little bit low. When we use 15 frames for recognition, the correct rate goes much better.

We found that the correct rate in some places (e.g. corridor2) is still not high even cost 15 frames for recognition. This is mainly because that some places contain the areas that produce few features (e.g. plane wall). So from these frames, few observed data can be obtained and the Bayesian result will not be confident. Then we evaluate the performance when observe different number of features for recognition.

Table 1. Correct rate when using different frames for recognition

frames	1 frame	5 frames	10 frames	15 frames
corridor1	97.4%	99.3%	99.3%	100.0%
corridor2	58.3%	67.2%	85.0%	85.0%
corridor3	99.0%	95.3%	100.0%	100.0%
corridor4	75.0%	87.7%	100.0%	100.0%
lab 3406	71.2%	84.8%	100.0%	100.0%
lab 3407	67.2%	78.7%	86.5%	95.8%
average rate	78.0%	85.5%	95.1%	96.8%

As shown in table 2, we get best performance when using 300 features as observed data each time. To obtain 300 features, 1 to 20 frames will be used. Our method achieves better performance comparing to others such as [17] [18].

Table 2. Correct rate when using different number of features for recognition

features	50	100	150	200	250	300	350
corridor1	99.1%	100.0%	100.0%	100.0%	100.0%	100.0%	100.0%
corridor2	78.2%	86.7%	90.5%	93.8%	95.4%	100.0%	100.0%
corridor3	98.3%	100.0%	100.0%	100.0%	100.0%	100.0%	100.0%
corridor4	95.1%	90.9%	93.3%	100.0%	100.0%	100.0%	100.0%
lab 3406	85.3%	93.2%	94.9%	96.8%	99.3%	99.6%	99.6%
lab 3407	80.7%	85.3%	88.1%	88.7%	93.0%	97.2%	97.2%
average rate	89.5%	92.7%	94.5%	96.6%	98.0%	99.5%	99.5%

One problem of using a sequence of frames for recognition is that more frames need more time to recognize. As illustrated in Fig. 3, if we use 350 features for recognition, the time cost will be more than 2 seconds. Another problem will be occurred in the transition period. For example, when the robot goes from place A to place B, several frames are from place A and other frames frame B, so the recognition result will be unexpected. So we should take a tradeoff to select a proper number of features as observed data.

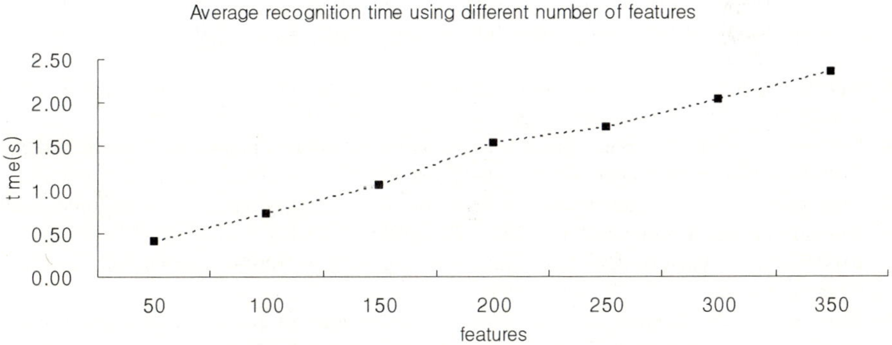

Fig. 3. Average recognition time using different number of features

4 Conclusions and Further Works

In this paper, we proposed the place model based on a feature distribution for place recognition. Although we used only 6 places for the test, the two labs in the dataset were closely similar and the 4 corridors were difficult to classify. In the experiments, we have shown that the proposed method achieved good performance enough to apply the real-time applications. For the future work, we will test more places to evaluate the efficiency of our approach. Further more, the topological information will be considered to make the system more robust.

Acknowledgement

This work was supported by the Korea Research Foundation Grant funded by the Korean Government(MOEHRD)" (KRF-2005-041-D00725).

References

1. Ulrich, I., Nourbakhsh, I.: Appearance-based place recognition for topological localization. In: IEEE International Conference on Robotics and Automation. vol. 2, pp. 1023–1029 (2000)
2. Briggs, A., Scharsctein, D., Abbott, S.: Reliable mobile robot navigation from unreliable visual cues. In: Fourth International Workshop on Algorithmic Foundations of Robatics, WAFR 2000 (2000)
3. Wolf, J., Burgard, W., Burkhardt, H.: Robust Vision-based Localization for Mobile Robots using an Image Retrieval System Based on Invariant Features. In: Proceedings of the IEEE International Conference on Robotics and Automation (ICRA) (2002)
4. Dudek, G., Jugessur, D.: Robust place recognition using local appearance based methods. In: IEEE International Conference on Robotics and Automation, San Francisco, CA, USA, pp. 1030–1035 (April 2000)
5. Kosecka, J., Li, L.: Vision based topological markov localization. In: IEEE International Conference on Robotics and Automation (2004)
6. Se, S., Lowe, D., Little, J.: Mobile robot localization and mapping with uncertainty using scale-invariant visual landmarks. International Journal of Robotics Research 21(8), 735–758 (2002)
7. Harris, C., Stephens, M.: A combined corner and edge detector. In: Proceedings of the Fourth Alvey Vision Conference, pp. 147–151 (1988)
8. Schmid, C., Mohr, R., Bauckhage, C.: Evaluation of interest point detectors. International Journal of Computer Vision 37(2), 151–172 (2000)
9. Lindeberg, T.: Scale-space theory: A basic tool for analysing structures at different scales. Journal of applied statistics 21(2), 225–270 (1994)
10. Lindeberg, T.: Feature detection with automatic scale selection. International Journal of Computer Vision 30(2), 77–116 (1998)
11. Mikolajczyk, K. Schmid, C.: An affine invariant interest point detector. In: European Conference on Computer Vision, Copenhagen, pp. 128–142 (2002)
12. Mikolajczyk, K. Schmid, C.: Indexing based on scale invariant interest points. In: Proceedings of the International Conference on Computer Vision, Vancouver, Canada, pp. 525–531 (2001)
13. Lowe, D.: Distinctive Image Features from Scale-Invariant Keypoints. International Journal of Computer Vision 60(2), 91–110 (2004)
14. Schmid, C., Mohr, R., Bauckhage, C.: Evaluation of interest point detectors. International Journal of Computer Vision 37(2), 151–172 (2000)

15. Mikolajczyk, K., Schmid, C.: A performance evaluation of local descriptors. In: International Conference on Computer Vision and Pattern Recognition (CVPR) vol. 2, pp. 257–263 (2003)
16. Lowe, D.: Object Recognition from Local Scale-Invariant Features. In: Proceedings of the International Conference on Computer Vision, Corfu, Greece, pp. 1150–1157 (1999)
17. Ledwich, L., Williams, S.: Reduced SIFT features for image retrieval and indoor localization. In: Australian Conference on Robotics and Automation (ACRA) (2004)
18. Andreasson, H., Duckett, T.: Topological localization for mobile robots using omni-directional vision and local features. In: Proceedings of the 5th IFAC Symposium on Intelligent Autonomous Vehicles, Lisbon, Portugal (2004)
19. Lowe, D.: Local feature view clustering for 3D object recognition. In: International Conference on Computer Vision and Pattern Recognition (CVPR), pp. 682–688. Springer, Heidelberg (2001)
20. Lowe, D., Little, J.: Vision-based Mapping with Backward Correction. In: Proceedings of the IEEE/RSJ International Conference on Intelligent Robots and Systems (IROS) (2002)
21. Lindeberg, T.: Feature detection with automatic scale selection. International Journal of Computer Vision 30(2), 77–116 (1998)
22. Lewis, D.D.: Naive (Bayes) at forty: The independence assumption in information retrieval. In: Proceedings of the 10th European Conference on Machine Learning. Chemnitz, Germany, pp. 4–15 (1998)
23. McCallum, A., Nigam, K.: A comparison of event models for naive bayes text classification. In: Proceedings of AAAI-98 Workshop on Learning for Text Categorization, Madison, Wisconsin, pp. 137–142 (1998)
24. Intel Corporation, OpenCV Library Reference Manual (2001) http://developer.intel.com

Knowledge Transfer in Semi-automatic Image Interpretation

Jun Zhou[1], Li Cheng[2], Terry Caelli[2,3], and Walter F. Bischof[1]

[1] Department of Computing Science,
University of Alberta,
Edmonton, Alberta, Canada T6G 2E8
{jzhou,wfb}@cs.ualberta.ca

[2] Canberra Laboratory, National ICT Australia,
Locked Bag 8001, Canberra ACT 2601, Australia
{li.cheng,terry.caelli}@nicta.com.au

[3] School of Information Science and Engineering,
Australian National University,
Bldg.115, Canberra ACT 0200, Australia

Abstract. Semi-automatic image interpretation systems utilize interactions between users and computers to adapt and update interpretation algorithms. We have studied the influence of human inputs on image interpretation by examining several knowledge transfer models. Experimental results show that the quality of the system performance depended not only on the knowledge transfer patterns but also on the user input, indicating how important it is to develop user-adapted image interpretation systems.

Keywords: knowledge transfer, image interpretation, road tracking, human influence, performance evaluation.

1 Introduction

It is widely accepted that semi-automatic methods are necessary for robust image interpretation [1]. For this reason, we are interested in modelling the influence of human input on the quality of image interpretation. Such modelling is important because users have different working patterns that may affect the behavior of computational algorithms [2]. This involves three components: first, how to represent human inputs in a way that computers can understand; second, how to process the inputs in computational algorithms; and third, how to evaluate the quality of human inputs. In this paper, we propose a framework that deals with these three aspects and focus on a real world application of updating road maps using aerial images.

2 Road Annotation in Aerial Images

Updating of road data is important in map revision and for ensuring that spatial data in GIS databases remain up to date. This requires normally an interpretation of maps

J. Jacko (Ed.): Human-Computer Interaction, Part III, HCII 2007, LNCS 4552, pp. 1028–1034, 2007.

where aerial images are used as the source of update. In real-world map revision environments, for example the software environment used at the United State Geological Survey, manual road annotation is mouse- or command-driven. A simple road drawing operation can be implemented by either clicking a tool icon on the tool bar followed by clicking on maps using a mouse, or by entering a key-in command. The tool icons correspond to road classes and view-change operations, and the mouse clicks correspond to the road axis points, view change locations, or a reset that ends a road annotation. These inputs represent two stages of human image interpretation, the detection of linear features and the digitizing of these features.

We have developed an interface to track such user inputs. A parser is used to segment the human inputs into action sequences and to extract the time and locations of road axis point inputs. These time-stamped points are used as input to a semi-automatic system for road tracking. During the tracking, the computer interacts with the user, keeping the human at the center of control. A summary of the system is described in the next section.

3 Semi-automatic Road Tracking System

The purpose of semi-automatic road tracking is to relieve the user from some of the image interpretation tasks. The computer is trained to perform road feature tracking as consistent with experts as possible. Road tracking starts from an initially human provided road segment indicating the road axis position. The computer learns relevant road information, such as range of location, direction, road profiles, and step size for the segment. On request, the computer continues with tracking using a road axis predictor, such as a particle filter or a novelty detector [3], [4]. Observations are extracted at each tracked location and are compared with the knowledge learned from the human operator. During tracking, the computer continuously updates road knowledge from observing human tracking while, at the same time, evaluating the tracking results. When it detects a possible problem or a tracking failure, it gives control back to human, who then enters another road segment to guide the tracker.

Human input affects the tracker in three ways. First, the input affects the parameters of the road tracker. When the tracker is implemented as a road axis predictor, the parameters define the initial state of the system that corresponds to the location of road axis, the direction of road and the curvature change. Second, the input represents the user's interpretation of a road situation, including dynamic properties of the road such as radiometric changes caused by different road materials, and changes in road appearance caused by background objects such as cars, shadows, and trees. The accumulation of these interpretations in a database constitutes a human-to-computer knowledge transfer. Third, human input keeps the human at the center of the control. When the computer fails tracking, new input can be used to set the correct the tracking direction. The new input also permits prompt and reliable correction of the tracker's state model.

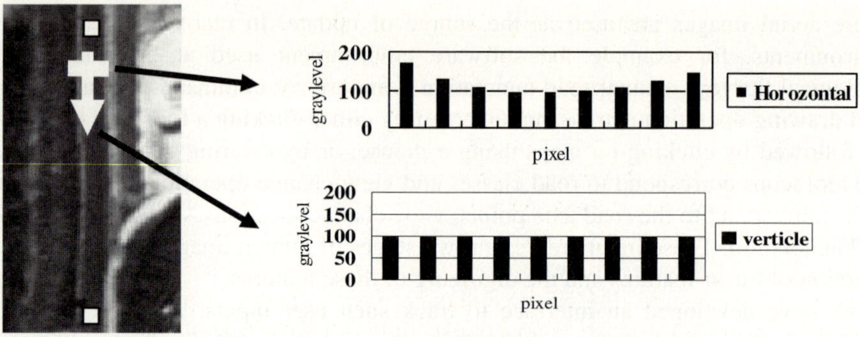

Fig. 1. Profiles of a road segment. In the left image, two white dots indicate the starting and ending points of road segment input by human. The right graphs shows the road profiles perpendicular to (upper) and along (lower) the road direction.

4 Human Input Processing

The representation and processing of human input determines how the input is used and how it affects the behavior of image interpreter.

4.1 Knowledge Representation

Typically, a road is long, smooth, homogenous, and it has parallel edges. However, the situation is far more complex and ambiguous in real images, and this is why computer vision systems often fail. In contrast, humans have a superb ability to interpret these complexities and ambiguities. Human input to the system embeds such interpretation and knowledge on road dynamics.

The road profile is one way to quantize such interpretation in the feature extraction step [5]. The profile is normally defined as a vector that characterizes the image greylevel in certain directions. For road tracking applications, the road profile perpendicular to the road direction is important: Image greylevel values change dramatically at the road edges and the distance between these edges is normally constant. Thus, the road axis can be calculated as the mid-points between the road edges. The profile along the road is also useful because the greylevel value varies very little along the road direction, whereas this is not the case in off-road areas.

Whenever we obtain a road segment entered by the user, the road profile is extracted at each road axis point. The profile is extracted in both directions and combined into a vector (shown in Fig. 1). Both the individual vector at each road axis point and an average vector for the whole input road segment are calculated and stored in a knowledge base. They characterize a road situation that human has recognized. These vectors form the template profiles that the computer uses when observation profile is extracted during road tracking.

4.2 Knowledge Transfer

Depending on whether machine learning is involved in creating a road axis point predictor, there are two methods to implement the human-to-computer knowledge transfer using the created knowledge base. The first method is to select a set of road profiles from the knowledge base so that a road tracker can compare to during the automatic tracking. An example is the Bayesian filtering model for road tracking [4]. At each predicted axis point, the tracker extracts an observation vector that contains two directional profiles. This observation is compared to template profiles in knowledge base for a matching. Successful matching means that the prediction is correct, and tracking continues. Otherwise, the user gets involved and provides new input. The second method is to learn a road profile predictor from stored road profiles in the knowledge base, for example, to construct profile predictors as one-class support vector machines [6]. Each predictor is represented as a weighted combination of training profiles obtained from human inputs in the Reproducing Kernel Hilbert space, where past training samples in the learning session are associated with different weights with proper time decay.

Both knowledge transfer models are highly dependent on the knowledge obtained from the human. Direct utilizing of human inputs is risky because low quality inputs lower the performance of the system. This is especially the case when profile selection model without machine learning is used. We propose that human inputs can be processed in two ways. First, similar template profiles may be obtained from different human inputs. The knowledge base then expands quickly with redundant information, making profile matching inefficient. Thus, new inputs should be evaluated before being added into the knowledge base, and only profiles that are quite different should be accepted. Second, the human input may contain points of occlusions, for example when a car is in a scene. This generates noisy template profile. On the one hand, such profiles deviate from the dominant road situation. Other the other hand, they expand the knowledge based with barely useful profiles. To solve this problem, we remove those points whose profile has a low correlation with the average profile of the road segment.

5 Human Input Analysis

5.1 Data Collection

Eight participants were required to annotate roads by mouse in an software environment that displays the aerial photos on the screen. None of the users was experienced in using the software and the road annotation task. The annotation was performed by selecting road drawing tools, followed by mouse clicks on the perceived road axis points in the image. Before performing the data collection, each user was given 20 to 30 minutes to become familiar with the software environment and to learn the operations for file input/output, road annotation, viewing change, and error correction. They did so by working on an aerial image for the Lake Jackson area in Florida. When they felt confident in using the tools, they were assigned 28 tasks to annotate roads for the Marietta area in Florida. The users were told that road plotting should be as accurate as possible, i.e. the mouse clicks should be on the true road axis points. Thus, the user had to decide how close the image should be zoomed in to identify the true road axis. Furthermore, the road had to be smooth, i.e. abrupt changes in directions should be avoided and no zigzags should occur.

The plotting tasks included a variety of scenes in the aerial photo of Marietta area, such as trans-national highways, intra-state highways and roads for local transportation. These tasks contained different road types such as straight roads, curves, ramps, crossings, and bridges. They also included various road conditions including occlusions by vehicles, trees, or shadows.

5.2 Data Analysis

We obtained eight data sets, each containing 28 sequences of road axis coordinates tracked by users. Such data was used to initialize the particle filters, to regain control when road tracker had failed, and to correct tracking errors. It was also used to compare performance between the road tracker and manual annotation.

Table 1. Statistics on users and inputs

	User1	User2	User3	User4	User5	User6	User7	User8
Gender	F	F	M	M	F	M	M	M
Total number of inputs	510	415	419	849	419	583	492	484
Total time cost (in seconds)	2765	2784	1050	2481	1558	1966	1576	1552
Average time per input (in seconds)	5.4	6.6	2.5	2.9	3.7	3.4	3.2	3.2

Table 2. Performance of semi-automatic road tracker. The meaning of n_h, t_t, and t_c is described in the text.

	User1	User2	User3	User4	User5	User6	User7	User8
n_h	125	142	156	135	108	145	145	135
t_t (in seconds)	154.2	199.2	212.2	184.3	131.5	196.2	199.7	168.3
t_c (in seconds)	833.5	1131.3	627.2	578.3	531.9	686.2	663.8	599.6
Time saving (%)	69.9	59.4	40.3	76.7	65.9	65.1	57.8	61.4

Table 1 shows some statistics on users and data. The statistics include the total number of inputs, the total time for road annotation, and average time per input. The number of inputs reflects how close the user zoomed in the image. When the image is zoomed in, mouse clicks traverse the same distance on the screen but correspond to shorter distances in the image. Thus, the user needed to input more road segments. The average time per input reflects the time that users required to detect one road axis and annotate it.

From the statistics, it is obvious that the users had performed the tasks in different patterns, which influenced the quality of the input. For example, more inputs were recorded for user 4. This was because user 4 zoomed the image into more detail than the other users. This made it possible to detect road axis locations more accurately in the detailed image. Another example is that of user 3, who spent much less time per input than the others. This was either because he was faster at detection than the others, or because he performed the annotation with less care.

6 Experiments and Evaluations

We implemented the semi-automatic road tracker using profile selection and particle filtering. The road tracker interacted with the recorded human data and used the human data as a virtual user. We counted the number of times that the tracker referred to the human data for help, which is considered as the number of human inputs to the semi-automatic system. In evaluating the efficiency of the system, we computed the savings in human inputs and savings in annotation time. The number of human inputs and plotting time are related and so reducing the number of human inputs also decreases plotting time. Given an average time for a human input, we obtained an empirical function for calculating the time cost of the road tracker:

$$t_c = t_t + \lambda n_h \ . \quad (1)$$

where t_c is the total time cost, t_t is the tracking time used by road tracker, n_h is the number of human inputs required during the tracking, and λ is an user-specific variable, which is calculated as the average time for an input

$$\lambda_i = \frac{total\ time\ for\ user\ i}{total\ number\ of\ inputs\ for\ user\ i} \ . \quad (2)$$

The performance of semi-automatic system is shown in Table 2. We observe a large improvement in efficiency compared to a human doing the tasks manually. Further analysis showed that the majority of the total time cost came from the time used to simulate the human inputs. This suggests that reducing the number of human input can further improve the efficiency of the system. This can be achieved by improving the robustness of the road tracker.

The performance of the system also reflects the quality of human input. Input quality determines how well the template road profiles can be extracted. When an input road axis deviates from the true road axis, the corresponding template profile may include off-road content perpendicular to the road direction. Moreover, the profile along the road direction may no more be constant. Thus, the road tracker may not find a match between observations and template profiles, which in turn requires more human inputs, reducing the system efficiency.

Fig. 2 shows a comparison of system with and without processing of human input during road template profile extraction. When human input processing is skipped, noisy template profiles enter the knowledge base. This increases the time for profile matching during the observation step of the Bayesian filter, which, in turn, causes the system efficiency to drop dramatically.

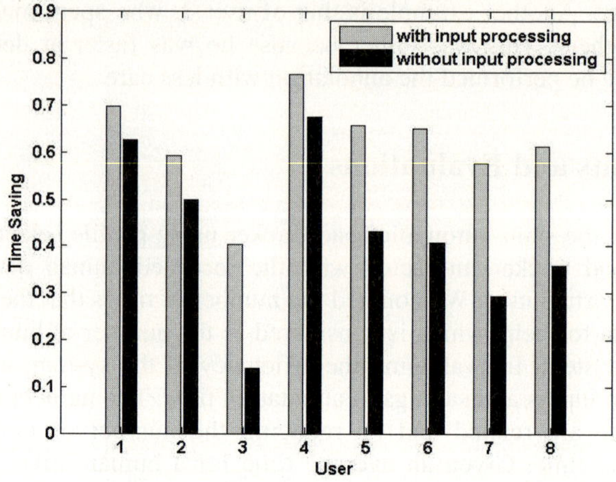

Fig. 2. Efficiency comparison of semi-automatic road tracking

7 Conclusion

Studying the influence of human input to the semi-automatic image interpretation system is important, not only because human input affects the performance of the system, but also because it is a necessary step to develop user-adapted systems. We have introduced a way to model these influences in an image annotation application. The user inputs were transferred into knowledge that computer vision algorithm can process and accumulate. Then they were processed to optimize the road tracker in profile matching. We analyzed the human input patterns and pointed out how the quality of the human input affected the efficiency of the system.

References

1. Myers, B., Hudson, S., Pausch, R.: Past, present, and future of user interface software tools. ACM Transactions on Computer-Human Interaction 7, 3–28 (2000)
2. Chin, D.: Empirical evaluation of user models and user-adapted systems. User Modeling and User-Adapted Interaction 11, 181–194 (2001)
3. Isard, M., Blake, A.: CONDENSATION-conditional density propagation for visual tracking. International Journal of Computer Vision 29, 5–28 (1998)
4. Zhou, J., Bischof, W., Caelli, T.: Road tracking in aerial image based on human-computer interaction and bayesian fltering. ISPRS Journal of Photogrammetry and Remote Sensing 61, 108–124 (2006)
5. Baumgartner, A., Hinz, S., Wiedemann, C.: E±cient methods and interfaces for road tracking. International Archives of Photogrammetry and Remote Sensing 34, 28–31 (2002)
6. Zhou, J., Cheng, L., Bischof, W.: A novel learning approach for semi-automatic road tracking. In: Proceedings of the 4th International Workshop on Pattern Recognition in Remote Sensing, Hongkong, China, pp. 61–64 (2006)

Author Index

Ablassmeier, Markus 728
Ahlenius, Mark 232
Ahn, Sang-Ho 659, 669
Al Hashimi, Sama'a 3
Alexandris, Christina 13
Alsuraihi, Mohammad 196
Argüello, Xiomara 527

Bae, Changseok 331
Banbury, Simon 313
Baran, Bahar 555, 755
Basapur, Santosh 232
Behringer, Reinhold 564
Berbegal, Nidia 933
Bischof, Walter F. 1028
Bogen, Manfred 811
Botherel, Valérie 60
Brashear, Helene 718
Butz, Andreas 882

Caelli, Terry 1028
Cagiltay, Kursat 555, 755
Catrambone, Richard 459
Cereijo Roibás, Anxo 801
Chakaveh, Sepideh 811
Chan, Li-wei 573
Chang, Jae Sik 583
Chen, Fang 23, 206
Chen, Nan 243
Chen, Wenguang 308
Chen, Xiaoming 815, 963
Chen, Yingna 535
Cheng, Li 1028
Chevrin, Vincent 265
Chi, Ed H. 589
Chia, Yi-wei 573
Chignell, Mark 225
Cho, Heeryon 31
Cho, Hyunchul 94
Choi, Eric H.C. 23
Choi, HyungIl 634, 1000
Choi, Miyoung 1000
Chu, Min 40
Chuang, Yi-fan 573
Chung, Myoung-Bum 821
Chung, Vera 206
Chung, Yuk Ying 815, 963
Churchill, Richard 76
Corradini, Andrea 154
Couturier, Olivier 265
Cox, Stephen 76
Culén, Alma Leora 829

Daimoto, Hiroshi 599
Dardala, Marian 486
Di Mascio, Tania 836
Dogusoy, Berrin 555
Dong, Yifei 605
Du, Jia 846

Edwards, Pete 176
Elzouki, Salima Y. Awad 275
Eom, Jae-Seong 659, 669
Etzler, Linnea 971
Eustice, Kevin 852

Fabri, Marc 275
Feizi Derakhshi, Mohammad Reza 50
Foursa, Maxim 615
Fréard, Dominique 60
Frigioni, Daniele 836
Fujimoto, Kiyoshi 599
Fukuzumi, Shin'ichi 440
Furtuna, Felix 486

Gauthier, Michelle S. 313
Göcke, Roland 411, 465
Gonçalves, Nelson 862
Gopal, T.V. 475
Gratch, Jonathan 286
Guercio, Elena 971
Gumbrecht, Michelle 589

Hahn, Minsoo 84
Han, Eunjung 298, 872
Han, Manchul 94
Han, Seung Ho 84
Han, Shuang 308
Hariri, Anas 134

Hempel, Thomas 216
Hilliges, Otmar 882
Hirota, Koichi 70
Hong, Lichan 589
Hong, Seok-Ju 625, 738
Hou, Ming 313
Hsu, Jane 573
Hu, Yi 1019
Hua, Lesheng 605
Hung, Yi-ping 573
Hwang, Jung-Hoon 321
Hwang, Sheue-Ling 747

Ikegami, Teruya 440
Ikei, Yasushi 70
Inaba, Rieko 31
Inoue, Makoto 449
Ishida, Toru 31
Ishizuka, Mitsuru 225

Jamet, Eric 60
Jang, Hyeju 331
Jang, HyoJong 634
Janik, Hubert 465
Jenkins, Marie-Claire 76
Ji, Yong Gu 892, 909
Jia, Yunde 710
Jiao, Zhen 243
Ju, Jinsun 642
Jumisko-Pyykkö, Satu 943
Jung, Do Joon 649
Jung, Keechul 298, 872
Jung, Moon Ryul 892
Jung, Ralf 340

Kang, Byoung-Doo 659, 669
Kangavari, Mohammad Reza 50
Khan, Javed I. 679
Kim, Chul-Soo 659, 669
Kim, Chulwoo 358
Kim, Eun Yi 349, 583, 642, 690
Kim, GyeYoung 634, 1000
Kim, Hang Joon 649, 690
Kim, Jaehwa 763
Kim, Jinsul 84
Kim, Jong-Ho 659, 669
Kim, Joonhwan 902
Kim, Jung Soo 718
Kim, Kiduck 366
Kim, Kirak 872
Kim, Laehyun 94
Kim, Myo Ha 892, 909
Kim, Na Yeon 349
Kim, Sang-Kyoon 659, 669
Kim, Seungyong 366
Kim, Tae-Hyung 366
Kirakowski, Jurek 376
Ko, Il-Ju 821
Ko, Sang Min 892, 909
Kolski, Christophe 134
Komogortsev, Oleg V. 679
Kopparapu, Sunil 104
Kraft, Karin 465
Kriegel, Hans-Peter 882
Kunath, Peter 882
Kuosmanen, Johanna 918
Kurosu, Masaaki 599
Kwon, Dong-Soo 321
Kwon, Kyung Su 649, 690
Kwon, Soonil 385

Laarni, Jari 918
Lähteenmäki, Liisa 918
Lamothe, Francois 286
Le Bohec, Olivier 60
Lee, Chang Woo 1019
Lee, Chil-Woo 625, 738
Lee, Eui Chul 700
Lee, Ho-Joon 114
Lee, Hyun-Woo 84
Lee, Jim Jiunde 393
Lee, Jong-Hoon 401
Lee, Kang-Woo 321
Lee, Keunyong 124
Lee, Sanghee 902
Lee, Soo Won 909
Lee, Yeon Jung 909
Lee, Yong-Seok 124
Lehto, Mark R. 358
Lepreux, Sophie 134
Li, Shanqing 710
Li, Weixian 769
Li, Ying 846
Li, Yusheng 40
Ling, Chen 605
Lisetti, Christine L. 421
Liu, Jia 535
Luo, Qi 544
Lv, Jingjun 710
Lyons, Kent 718

MacKenzie, I. Scott 779
Marcus, Aaron 144, 926
Masthoff, Judith 176
Matteo, Deborah 232
McIntyre, Gordon 411
Md Noor, Nor Laila 981
Mehta, Manish 154
Moldovan, Grigoreta Sofia 508
Montanari, Roberto 971
Moore, David 275
Morales, Mathieu 286
Morency, Louis-Philippe 286
Mori, Yumiko 31
Mun, Jae Seung 892

Nair, S. Arun 165
Nam, Tek-Jin 401
Nanavati, Amit Anil 165
Nasoz, Fatma 421
Navarro-Prieto, Raquel 933
Nguyen, Hien 176
Nguyen, Nam 852
Nishimoto, Kazushi 186
Noda, Hisashi 440
Nowack, Nadine 465

O'Donnell, Patrick 376
Ogura, Kanayo 186
Okada, Hidehiko 449
Okhmatovskaia, Anna 286
Otto, Birgit 216

Park, Jin-Yung 401
Park, Jong C. 114
Park, Junseok 700
Park, Kang Ryoung 700
Park, Ki-Soen 124
Park, Se Hyun 583, 690
Park, Sehyung 94
Park, Sung 459
Perez, Angel 926
Perrero, Monica 971
Peter, Christian 465
Poitschke, Tony 728
Ponnusamy, R. 475
Poulain, Gérard 60
Pryakhin, Alexey 882

Rajput, Nitendra 165
Ramakrishna, V. 852
Rao, P.V.S. 104
Rapp, Amon 971
Ravaja, Niklas 918
Reifinger, Stefan 728
Reiher, Peter 852
Reiter, Ulrich 943
Ren, Yonggong 829
Reveiu, Adriana 486
Rigas, Dimitrios 196
Rigoll, Gerhard 728
Rouillard, José 134
Ryu, Won 84

Sala, Riccardo 801
Sarter, Nadine 493
Schnaider, Matthew 852
Schultz, Randolf 465
Schwartz, Tim 340
Seifert, Inessa 499
Şerban, Gabriela 508
Setiawan, Nurul Arif 625, 738
Shi, Yu 206
Shiba, Haruya 1010
Shimamura, Kazunori 1010
Shin, Bum-Joo 659, 669, 1019
Shin, Choonsung 953
Shin, Yunhee 349, 642
Shirehjini, Ali A. Nazari 431
Shukran, Mohd Afizi Mohd 963
Simeoni, Rossana 971
Singh, Narinderjit 981
Smith, Dan 76
Soong, Frank 40
Srivastava, Akhlesh 104
Starner, Thad 718
Sugiyama, Kozo 186
Sulaiman, Zuraidah 981
Sumuer, Evren 755
Sun, Yong 206

Tabary, Dimitri 134
Takahashi, Hideaki 599
Takahashi, Tsutomu 599
Takasaki, Toshiyuki 31
Takashima, Akio 518
Tanaka, Yuzuru 518
Tarţa, Adriana 508
Tarantino, Laura 836
Tarby, Jean-Claude 134
Tatsumi, Yushin 440
Tesauri, Francesco 971

Urban, Bodo 465

van der Werf, R.J. 286
Vélez-Langs, Oswaldo 527
Vilimek, Roman 216
Voskamp, Jörg 465

Walker, Alison 852
Wallhoff, Frank 728
Wang, Heng 308
Wang, Hua 225
Wang, Ning 23, 286
Wang, Pei-Chia 747
Watanabe, Yosuke 70
Wen, Chao-Hua 747
Wesche, Gerold 615
Westeyn, Tracy 718
Whang, Min Cheol 700
Wheatley, David J. 990
Won, Jongho 331
Won, Sunhee 1000
Woo, Woontack 953

Xu, Shuang 232
Xu, Yihua 710

Yagi, Akihiro 599
Yamaguchi, Takumi 1010
Yan, Yonghong 253
Yang, Chen 243
Yang, HwangKyu 298, 872
Yang, Jie 225
Yang, Jong Yeol 1019
Yang, Jonyeol 298
Yang, Xiaoke 769
Yecan, Esra 755
Yiu, Anthony 376
Yong, Suet Peng 981
Yoon, Hyoseok 953
Yoon, Joonsung 763

Zhang, Kan 789
Zhang, Lumin 769
Zhang, Peng-fei 243
Zhang, Pengyuan 253
Zhang, Xuan 779
Zhao, Qingwei 253
Zhong, Shan 535
Zhou, Fuqiang 769
Zhou, Jun 1028
Zhou, Ronggang 789
Zhu, Aiqin 544
Zhu, Chunyi 535
Zou, Xin 40

Printing: Mercedes-Druck, Berlin
Binding: Stein+Lehmann, Berlin

Vol. 4559: N. Aykin (Ed.), Usability and Internationalization, Part I. XVIII, 661 pages. 2007.

Vol. 4553: J.A. Jacko (Ed.), Human-Computer Interaction, Part IV. XXIV, 1225 pages. 2007.

Vol. 4552: J.A. Jacko (Ed.), Human-Computer Interaction, Part III. XXI, 1038 pages. 2007.

Vol. 4551: J.A. Jacko (Ed.), Human-Computer Interaction, Part II. XXIII, 1253 pages. 2007.

Vol. 4550: J.A. Jacko (Ed.), Human-Computer Interaction, Part I. XXIII, 1240 pages. 2007.

Vol. 4549: J. Aspnes, C. Scheideler, A. Arora, S. Madden (Eds.), Distributed Computing in Sensor Systems. XIII, 417 pages. 2007.

Vol. 4548: N. Olivetti (Ed.), Automated Reasoning with Analytic Tableaux and Related Methods. X, 245 pages. 2007. (Sublibrary LNAI).

Vol. 4547: C. Carlet, B. Sunar (Eds.), Arithmetic of Finite Fields. XI, 355 pages. 2007.

Vol. 4546: J. Kleijn, A. Yakovlev (Eds.), Petri Nets and Other Models of Concurrency – ICATPN 2007. XI, 515 pages. 2007.

Vol. 4545: H. Anai, K. Horimoto, T. Kutsia (Eds.), Algebraic Biology. XIII, 379 pages. 2007.

Vol. 4544: S. Cohen-Boulakia, V. Tannen (Eds.), Data Integration in the Life Sciences. XI, 282 pages. 2007. (Sublibrary LNBI).

Vol. 4543: A.K. Bandara, M. Burgess (Eds.), Inter-Domain Management. XII, 237 pages. 2007.

Vol. 4542: P. Sawyer, B. Paech, P. Heymans (Eds.), Requirements Engineering: Foundation for Software Quality. IX, 384 pages. 2007.

Vol. 4541: T. Okadome, T. Yamazaki, M. Makhtari (Eds.), Pervasive Computing for Quality of Life Enhancement. IX, 248 pages. 2007.

Vol. 4539: N.H. Bshouty, C. Gentile (Eds.), Learning Theory. XII, 634 pages. 2007. (Sublibrary LNAI).

Vol. 4538: F. Escolano, M. Vento (Eds.), Graph-Based Representations in Pattern Recognition. XII, 416 pages. 2007.

Vol. 4537: K.C.-C. Chang, W. Wang, L. Chen, C.A. Ellis, C.-H. Hsu, A.C. Tsoi, H. Wang (Eds.), Advances in Web and Network Technologies, and Information Management. XXIII, 707 pages. 2007.

Vol. 4536: G. Concas, E. Damiani, M. Scotto, G. Succi (Eds.), Agile Processes in Software Engineering and Extreme Programming. XV, 276 pages. 2007.

Vol. 4534: I. Tomkos, F. Neri, J. Solé Pareta, X. Masip Bruin, S. Sánchez Lopez (Eds.), Optical Network Design and Modeling. XI, 460 pages. 2007.

Vol. 4533: F. Baader (Ed.), Term Rewriting and Applications. XII, 419 pages. 2007.

Vol. 4531: J. Indulska, K. Raymond (Eds.), Distributed Applications and Interoperable Systems. XI, 337 pages. 2007.

Vol. 4530: D.H. Akehurst, R. Vogel, R.F. Paige (Eds.), Model Driven Architecture- Foundations and Applications. X, 219 pages. 2007.

Vol. 4529: P. Melin, O. Castillo, L.T. Aguilar, J. Kacprzyk, W. Pedrycz (Eds.), Foundations of Fuzzy Logic and Soft Computing. XIX, 830 pages. 2007. (Sublibrary LNAI).

Vol. 4528: J. Mira, J.R. Álvarez (Eds.), Nature Inspired Problem-Solving Methods in Knowledge Engineering, Part II. XXII, 650 pages. 2007.

Vol. 4527: J. Mira, J.R. Álvarez (Eds.), Bio-inspired Modeling of Cognitive Tasks, Part I. XXII, 630 pages. 2007.

Vol. 4526: M. Malek, M. Reitenspieß, A. van Moorsel (Eds.), Service Availability. X, 155 pages. 2007.

Vol. 4525: C. Demetrescu (Ed.), Experimental Algorithms. XIII, 448 pages. 2007.

Vol. 4524: M. Marchiori, J.Z. Pan, C.d.S. Marie (Eds.), Web Reasoning and Rule Systems. XI, 382 pages. 2007.

Vol. 4523: Y.-H. Lee, H.-N. Kim, J. Kim, Y. Park, L.T. Yang, S.W. Kim (Eds.), Embedded Software and Systems. XIX, 829 pages. 2007.

Vol. 4522: B.K. Ersbøll, K.S. Pedersen (Eds.), Image Analysis. XVIII, 989 pages. 2007.

Vol. 4521: J. Katz, M. Yung (Eds.), Applied Cryptography and Network Security. XIII, 498 pages. 2007.

Vol. 4519: E. Franconi, M. Kifer, W. May (Eds.), The Semantic Web: Research and Applications. XVIII, 830 pages. 2007.

Vol. 4517: F. Boavida, E. Monteiro, S. Mascolo, Y. Koucheryavy (Eds.), Wired/Wireless Internet Communications. XIV, 382 pages. 2007.

Vol. 4516: L. Mason, T. Drwiega, J. Yan (Eds.), Managing Traffic Performance in Converged Networks. XXIII, 1191 pages. 2007.

Vol. 4515: M. Naor (Ed.), Advances in Cryptology - EUROCRYPT 2007. XIII, 591 pages. 2007.

Vol. 4514: S.N. Artemov, A. Nerode (Eds.), Logical Foundations of Computer Science. XI, 513 pages. 2007.

Vol. 4513: M. Fischetti, D.P. Williamson (Eds.), Integer Programming and Combinatorial Optimization. IX, 500 pages. 2007.

Vol. 4511: C. Conati, K. McCoy, G. Paliouras (Eds.), User Modeling 2007. XVI, 487 pages. 2007. (Sublibrary LNAI).

Vol. 4510: P. Van Hentenryck, L. Wolsey (Eds.), Integration of AI and OR Techniques in Constraint Programming for Combinatorial Optimization Problems. X, 391 pages. 2007.

Vol. 4509: Z. Kobti, D. Wu (Eds.), Advances in Artificial Intelligence. XII, 552 pages. 2007. (Sublibrary LNAI).

Vol. 4508: M.-Y. Kao, X.-Y. Li (Eds.), Algorithmic Aspects in Information and Management. VIII, 428 pages. 2007.

Vol. 4507: F. Sandoval, A. Prieto, J. Cabestany, M. Graña (Eds.), Computational and Ambient Intelligence. XXVI, 1167 pages. 2007.

Vol. 4506: D. Zeng, I. Gotham, K. Komatsu, C. Lynch, M. Thurmond, D. Madigan, B. Lober, J. Kvach, H. Chen (Eds.), Intelligence and Security Informatics: Biosurveillance. XI, 234 pages. 2007.

Lecture Notes in Computer Science

For information about Vols. 1–4505

please contact your bookseller or Springer

Vol. 4611: J. Indulska, J. Ma, L.T. Yang, T. Ungerer, J. Cao (Eds.), Ubiquitous Intelligence and Computing. XXIII, 1257 pages. 2007.

Vol. 4610: B. Xiao, L.T. Yang, J. Ma, C. Muller-Schloer, Y. Hua (Eds.), Autonomic and Trusted Computing. XVIII, 571 pages. 2007.

Vol. 4605: D. Papadias, D. Zhang, G. Kollios (Eds.), Advances in Spatial and Temporal Databases. X, 479 pages. 2007.

Vol. 4602: S. Barker, G.-J. Ahn (Eds.), Data and Applications Security XXI. X, 291 pages. 2007.

Vol. 4600: H. Comon-Lundh, C. Kirchner, H. Kirchner, Rewriting, Computation and Proof. XVI, 273 pages. 2007.

Vol. 4598: G. Lin (Ed.), Computing and Combinatorics. XII, 570 pages. 2007.

Vol. 4597: P. Perner (Ed.), Advances in Data Mining. XI, 353 pages. 2007. (Sublibrary LNAI).

Vol. 4596: L. Arge, C. Cachin, T. Jurdzinski, A. Tarlecki (Eds.), Automata, Languages and Programming. XVII, 953 pages. 2007.

Vol. 4595: D. Bošnački, S. Edelkamp (Eds.), Model Checking Software. X, 285 pages. 2007.

Vol. 4592: Z. Kedad, N. Lammari, E. Métais, F. Meziane, Y. Rezgui (Eds.), Natural Language Processing and Information Systems. XIV, 442 pages. 2007.

Vol. 4591: J. Davies, J. Gibbons (Eds.), Integrated Formal Methods. IX, 660 pages. 2007.

Vol. 4590: W. Damm, H. Hermanns (Eds.), Computer Aided Verification. XV, 562 pages. 2007.

Vol. 4589: J. Münch, P. Abrahamsson (Eds.), Product-Focused Software Process Improvement. XII, 414 pages. 2007.

Vol. 4588: T. Harju, J. Karhumäki, A. Lepistö (Eds.), Developments in Language Theory. XI, 423 pages. 2007.

Vol. 4587: R. Cooper, J. Kennedy (Eds.), Data Management. XIII, 259 pages. 2007.

Vol. 4586: J. Pieprzyk, H. Ghodosi, E. Dawson (Eds.), Information Security and Privacy. XIV, 476 pages. 2007.

Vol. 4585: M. Kryszkiewicz, J.F. Peters, H. Rybinski, A. Skowron (Eds.), Rough Sets and Intelligent Systems Paradigms. XIX, 836 pages. 2007. (Sublibrary LNAI).

Vol. 4584: N. Karssemeijer, B. Lelieveldt (Eds.), Information Processing in Medical Imaging. XX, 777 pages. 2007.

Vol. 4583: S.R. Della Rocca (Ed.), Typed Lambda Calculi and Applications. X, 397 pages. 2007.

Vol. 4582: J. Lopez, P. Samarati, J.L. Ferrer (Eds.), Public Key Infrastructure. XI, 375 pages. 2007.

Vol. 4581: A. Petrenko, M. Veanes, J. Tretmans, W. Grieskamp (Eds.), Testing of Software and Communicating Systems. XII, 379 pages. 2007.

Vol. 4580: B. Ma, K. Zhang (Eds.), Combinatorial Pattern Matching. XII, 366 pages. 2007.

Vol. 4578: F. Masulli, S. Mitra, G. Pasi (Eds.), Applications of Fuzzy Sets Theory. XVIII, 693 pages. 2007. (Sublibrary LNAI).

Vol. 4577: N. Sebe, Y. Liu, Y. Zhuang (Eds.), Multimedia Content Analysis and Mining. XIII, 513 pages. 2007.

Vol. 4576: D. Leivant, R. de Queiroz (Eds.), Logic, Language, Information, and Computation. X, 363 pages. 2007.

Vol. 4575: T. Takagi, T. Okamoto, E. Okamoto, T. Okamoto (Eds.), Pairing-Based Cryptography. XI, 408 pages. 2007.

Vol. 4574: J. Derrick, J. Vain (Eds.), Formal Techniques for Networked and Distributed Systems – FORTE 2007. XI, 375 pages. 2007.

Vol. 4573: M. Kauers, M. Kerber, R. Miner, W. Windsteiger (Eds.), Towards Mechanized Mathematical Assistants. XIII, 407 pages. 2007. (Sublibrary LNAI).

Vol. 4572: F. Stajano, C. Meadows, S. Capkun, T. Moore (Eds.), Security and Privacy in Ad-hoc and Sensor Networks. X, 247 pages. 2007.

Vol. 4570: H.G. Okuno, M. Ali (Eds.), New Trends in Applied Artificial Intelligence. XXI, 1194 pages. 2007. (Sublibrary LNAI).

Vol. 4569: A. Butz, B. Fisher, A. Krüger, P. Olivier, S. Owada (Eds.), Smart Graphics. IX, 237 pages. 2007.

Vol. 4566: M.J. Dainoff (Ed.), Ergonomics and Health Aspects of Work with Computers. XVIII, 390 pages. 2007.

Vol. 4565: D.D. Schmorrow, L.M. Reeves (Eds.), Foundations of Augmented Cognition. XIX, 450 pages. 2007. (Sublibrary LNAI).

Vol. 4564: D. Schuler (Ed.), Online Communities and Social Computing. XVII, 520 pages. 2007.

Vol. 4563: R. Shumaker (Ed.), Virtual Reality. XXII, 762 pages. 2007.

Vol. 4562: D. Harris (Ed.), Engineering Psychology and Cognitive Ergonomics. XXIII, 879 pages. 2007. (Sublibrary LNAI).

Vol. 4561: V.G. Duffy (Ed.), Digital Human Modeling. XXIII, 1068 pages. 2007.

Vol. 4560: N. Aykin (Ed.), Usability and Internationalization, Part II. XVIII, 576 pages. 2007.